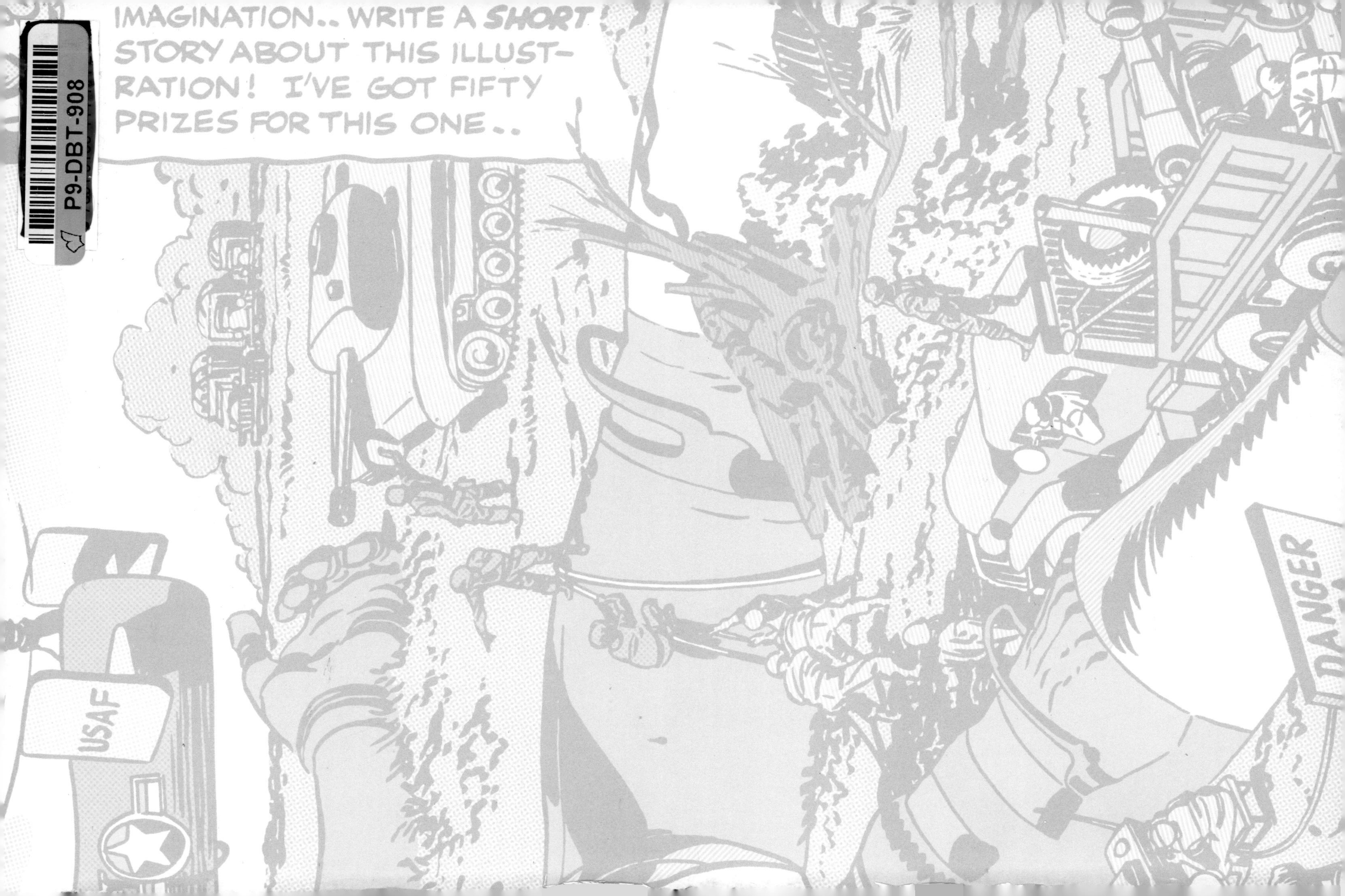
IMAGINATION.. WRITE A SHORT
STORY ABOUT THIS ILLUST-
RATION! I'VE GOT FIFTY
PRIZES FOR THIS ONE..
USAF
DANGER

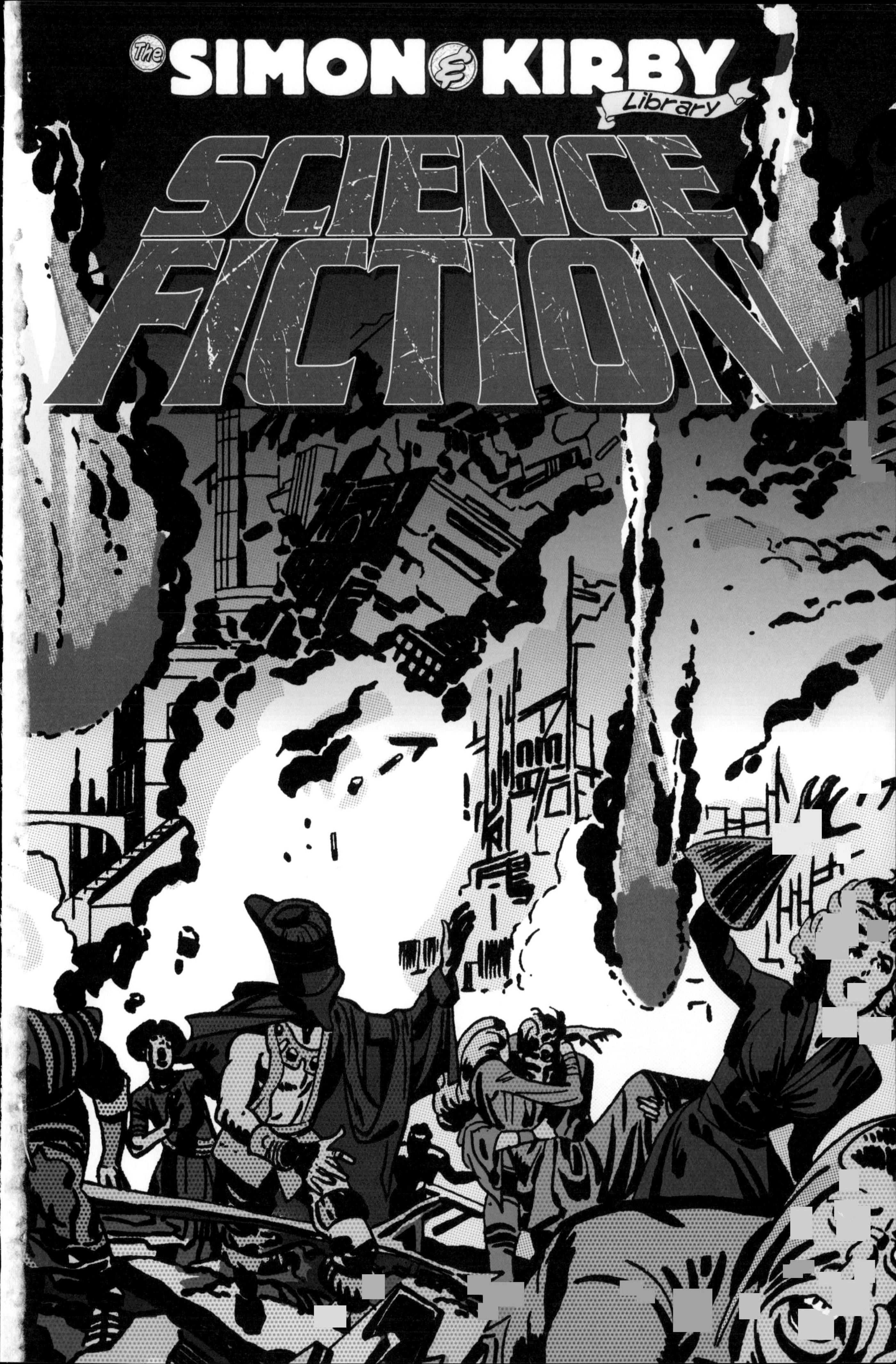
The SIMON & KIRBY Library
SCIENCE FICTION

ACKNOWLEDGEMENTS:

As always, thanks to Harry Mendryk and Tedd Kessler for their invaluable assistance.
Thanks to the Simon family and the Kirby family, John Morrow, and the team at Titan
Books—Nick Landau, Vivian Cheung, Katy Wild, JP Rutter, and Tim Scrivens.

Dedicated to Joe Simon. One of a kind.

THE SIMON AND KIRBY LIBRARY: SCIENCE FICTION

ISBN: 9781848569614

Published by Titan Books
A division of Titan Publishing Group Ltd.
144 Southwark Street
London
SE1 0UP

First edition: March 2013
1 3 5 7 9 10 8 6 4 2

What did you think of this book? We love to hear from our readers.
Please email us at: readerfeedback@titanemail.com, or write to us at the above address.

To receive advance information, news, competitions, and exclusive offers online,
please sign up for the Titan newsletter on our website: www.titanbooks.com

A CIP catalogue record for this title is available from the British Library.

Printed and bound in China.

ALSO AVAILABLE

The Best of Simon and Kirby (ISBN: 9781845769314)
The Simon and Kirby Library: Superheroes (ISBN: 9781848563650)
The Simon and Kirby Library: Crime (ISBN: 9781848569607)
Fighting American (ISBN: 9780857681157)
Joe Simon: My Life in Comics (ISBN: 9781845769307)

The Simon & Kirby Library

Science Fiction

TITAN BOOKS

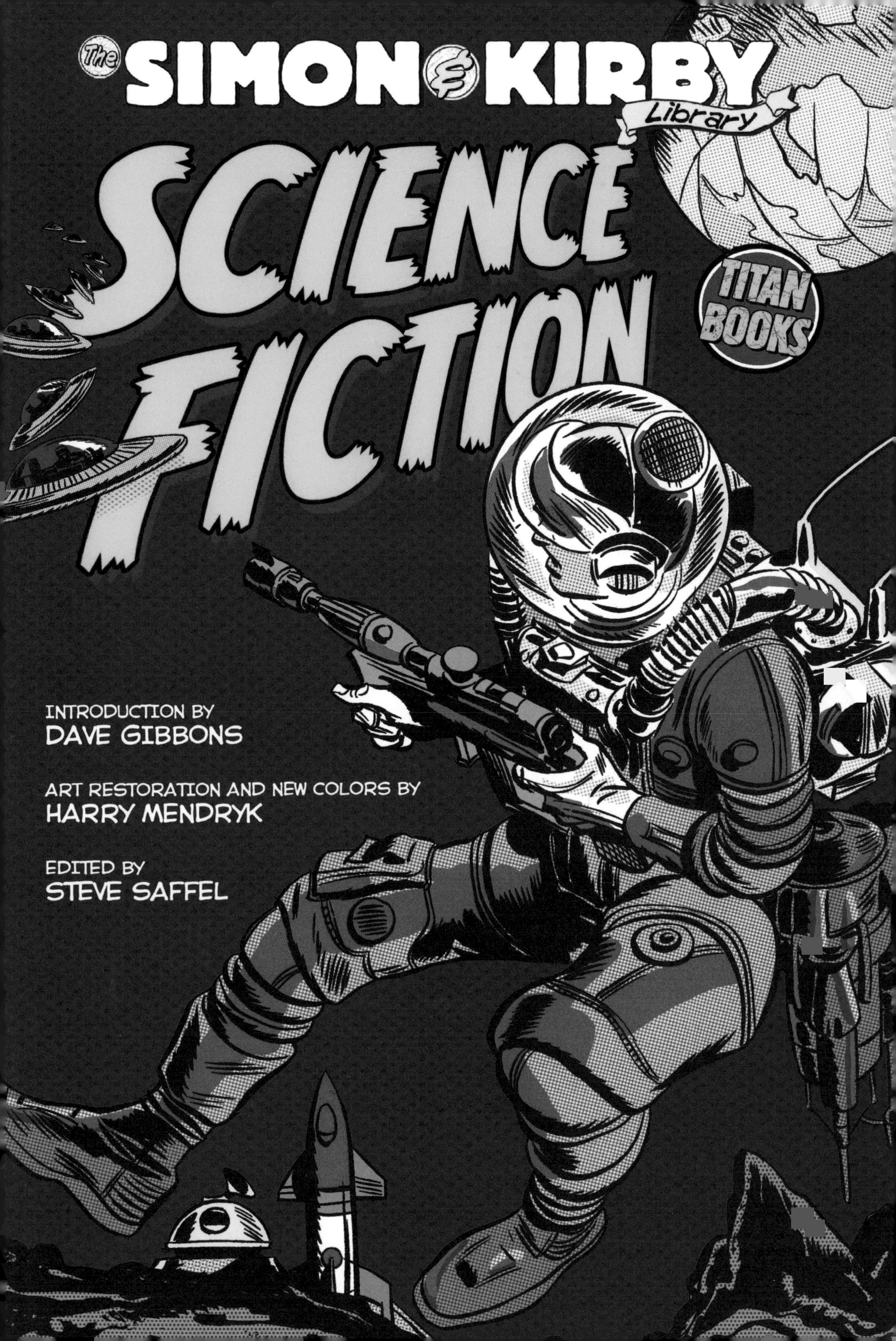

INTRODUCTION BY
DAVE GIBBONS

ART RESTORATION AND NEW COLORS BY
HARRY MENDRYK

EDITED BY
STEVE SAFFEL

Unless otherwise noted, all stories are credited to Simon & Kirby. While the best effort has gone into identifying all contributors to this volume, we regret any missing or erroneous attributions.

OF FUTURE CONVICTS & GRUBBY SPACEMEN

BY DAVE GIBBONS

I've loved comic books since my granddad bought me my first one, a *Superman* reprint, when I was seven years old. From the very start I was fascinated by the artwork and, for a kid, had a remarkably forensic attitude towards it. My investigations were aided by the fact that, until the very end of the 1950s, I usually saw American comics in reprint form, in crisp black and white.

However, for the young art sleuth, the almost total lack–or worse, the ambiguity–of creator credits in the comics of the time was a source of tremendous confusion and frustration.

For instance, there was the question of the *Batman* artists. Every Bat-story was signed by Bob Kane, but it seemed that either there were two Bob Kanes, or just one Bob Kane who had good days and bad days at the drawing board. Years later I discovered that there was only one Bob Kane and he, unfortunately, was the less good Bat-artist.

Okay, I'll be honest, he was the bad Bat-artist.

The good Bat-artist–I later discovered–was actually named Dick Sprang. Bob Kane had nothing to do with those stories other than the legal right to have his name put on them.

But the Bat-artist mystery was nothing compared to the bewildering case of Jack Kirby.

I didn't even know his name then, but his style was so strong that I could spot his work anywhere. Unlike the Bat-artists, though, whose work was either very good or very bad, Kirby (as it is easiest to call him in hindsight) *always* drew well. It was just that the lines he drew had a variable feel. Sometimes of a constant thickness, sometimes heavy, sometimes scratchy, sometimes "swooshy".

Maybe he just had different pens or something.

Little did I know I was halfway to the truth, although it was years before I realized that more than one artist could work on a single story. In drawing my own comics–which I did, starting the same week I got that *Superman* comic–I always sketched things out in pencil, then drew over them carefully with a ballpoint or a dip pen. I had the advantage of watching my dad draw house plans, and that was the way he worked. But I still didn't make the leap to figuring out that one artist could make the pencil drawing, and another ink over it.

Until I made that breakthrough, Kirby really bugged me. For instance, I had a hoard of British reprints of *Challengers of the Unknown*. A few of the stories looked a bit like my favorite artist from old *MAD* reprints. His name, I *knew*, was Wood– he signed his *MAD* work in Old English script. But his *MAD* art lacked the power of Kirby. So maybe Kirby was Wood, and just very versatile, able to draw detailed and funny or dramatic and straight?

Even more difficult to square was *Sky Masters of the Space Force*. This American newspaper strip appeared weekly in the centre spread of a native British comic called *Rocket*. The artwork would sometimes be signed Kirby & Wood–this was the first time I saw the "Kirby" name–so seemed to prove my theory. Wood must be the artist and this "Kirby" perhaps the writer. But sometimes it looked like the *Challengers* work and sometimes– to my eyes–completely different.

I was, of course, 180 degrees out. Kirby was the pencil artist and this Wood was Dave Wood, the writer. The other Wood, Wallace Wood,

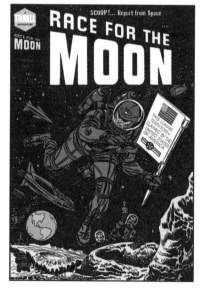

sometimes inked Kirby's pencils on *Challengers* and *Sky Masters*, but not always. Dave Wood also had a brother, Dick, who himself wrote for Kirby.

I told you it was confusing.

And then there was my favorite Kirby comic book. No, scratch that, my favorite comic book, period: *Race for the Moon*.

Here again was the unmistakable drama and excitement of *Challengers* and *Sky Masters*, but this time with the absolute best drawing style Kirby had ever exhibited. Lines were sharp and clear, ranging from bold to delicate, with areas of black exquisitely balanced; there were small areas of texture, other areas left dramatically empty. This was something beyond pulp thrills; this was visual poetry. This was true inspiration, a glimpse of something sublime.

SCOOP!... Report from Space
THRILL ADVENTURE
RACE FOR THE MOON
RACE FOR THE MOON
THIS LUNAR TERRITORY CLAIMED BY THE UNITED STATES OF AMERICA

This was, in fact, another EC artist, Al Williamson, inking over Kirby's pencils. Learning of Al's involvement years later, I became aware that his artistic peers–Angelo Torres and Reed Crandall–had also contributed to the inking. However, these were piecemeal contributions that evaded the expertise of a young art sleuth.

Not only did *Race for the Moon* have the best artwork I'd ever seen in a comic book, it had the best stories. As you'll have gathered, I loved science fiction, but was often bored by the repetition of smooth detective or strongman heroes, and also by the plots, which were usually about endless monster invasions or creepy scientists with death rays. In stark contrast, *Race for the Moon* had tales of future convicts, grubby space-miners, hard-bitten military officers and aliens with nobility and pathos.

Many of these stories were written by Joe Simon, whose science fiction collaborations with Kirby stretched right back to their earliest teaming on *Blue Bolt*. At least in the early days a reader could tell who was responsible for the work, since those 1940s tales were among the first to carry the byline "Joe Simon and Jack Kirby".

Simon was the architect behind *Race for the Moon*, pulling together the creative teams on behalf of Harvey Comics. Other writers included long-time comic book scripter Eddie Herron and the Wood brothers mentioned above. At the time they were more of a mystery to me than the artists. Decrypting illustrative styles was enough of a challenge. Analysis of verbal patterns was far beyond my expertise (and interest). All I knew was that the stories were as good as the art. In every respect, *Race for the Moon* was a revelation.

It was also very short-lived. Search as I might, I discovered that there were only three issues of this masterpiece to be found. The title continued long beyond that in British reprints, though, featuring lesser works–often DC or ACG stories.

The absence of top-quality material was periodically assuaged by randomly scattered Simon and Kirby stories reprinted from the original American *Alarming Tales* and *Black Cat* comics. In themselves, they were truly wonderful examples of quirky, engaging science fiction. But it was really *Race for the Moon* that was Ground Zero for my aspirations to be a comic artist.

In the several decades since then, I've got hold of all the original American issues, along with the other titles mentioned above and the mid-sixties *Blast-Off* issue. I managed to meet Jack Kirby, I spoke to Joe Simon briefly on the phone, and I've held and studied the original art for many of the pages here. And you can bet that I'll sit down and read all these stories over again and again in this exhaustive collection you're now holding.

But I still wish–in some bizarre Simon and Kirby science fiction way–that I could send a message of explanation back to the school teacher to whom I was assigned when I first read *Race for the Moon*. When I was first truly inspired.

And here's why.

I always loved art at school, so I was always first with my big sheet of grainy paper clipped to a wobbly easel for the latest lesson. One day, rather than tell us what we should paint, Miss Patrick said we could do whatever we wanted. Elsewhere, pencils scratched and thick poster paint spattered

around the room. Crude depictions of ponies, footballers, fairies, and racing cars took shape. But my thoughts were on other things.

Towards the end of the time, Miss Patrick paused before my work, smiling thinly.

"That's, er, nice, David. What is it?"

"It's a spaceman, miss."

"A spaceman. I see. And what's he doing?"

"Nothing, miss. He's been manacled to an asteroid and left to die."

Thank you, Jack, Thank you, Joe. Thank you, Al. Sorry, Miss Patrick.

Dave Gibbons
April 2012

DAVE GIBBONS has worked in comics since 1973. Cutting his teeth on undergrounds and fanzines, he became a frequent contributor to Britain's *2000 AD*, illustrating *Harlem Heroes*, *Dan Dare* and co-creating *Rogue Trooper*. Since then, he has drawn and written for comic publishers on both sides of the Atlantic. His work includes *Doctor Who*, *Superman*, *Batman*, *Green Lantern*, *Captain America*, *Predator*, *Aliens*, the Hugo Award-winning *Watchmen* with writer Alan Moore, and *Give Me Liberty* with Frank Miller. His semi-autobiographical *The Originals* won an Eisner Award in 2005. He is currently consulting on digital storytelling techniques and illustrating *The Secret Service*, written by Mark Millar.

THE 1940s

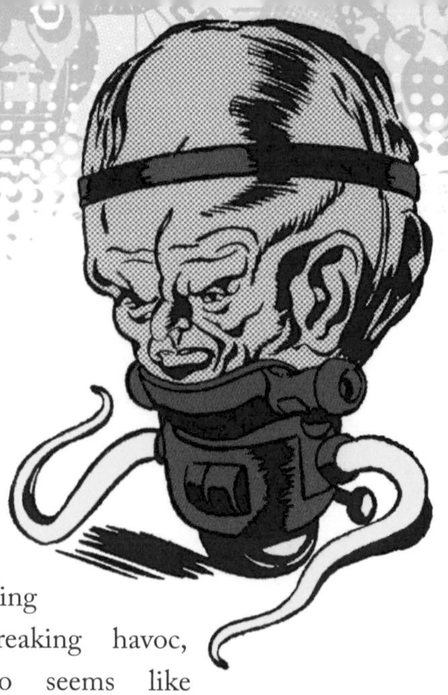

The first American comic book appeared in 1933, yet it was the debut of Superman in *Action Comics* #1 (1938) that turned this new medium into a publishing success. But while superheroes dominated the Golden Age in the late 1930s and 1940s, comics invaded many other genres, as well.

Among them was science fiction, which had grown popular through pulp magazines such as Hugo Gernsback's *Amazing Stories*, in which Philip Nolan's creation Buck Rogers debuted in 1928. Buck's adventures exemplified the subgenre known as "space opera," and he quickly moved into newspaper comic strips, radio, and film. Another such hero, Flash Gordon, debuted in 1934 in a comic strip illustrated by the great Alex Raymond, and famously starred in movie serials featuring Buster Crabbe.

Jack Kirby's "Solar Legion" series in Tem Publishing's *Crash Comics* is a powerful example of space opera. Its hero–Adam Starr–organized a police force to combat space pirates who ruthlessly slaughtered entire populations of colonists. Since this series appeared in 1940, as Germany was invading Denmark, Norway, and France, Kirby may have based his pirates on the Nazis. If so, Adam Starr represented the need to take action, thus making him the ideological forerunner of Captain America.

Joe Simon ventured into space opera with his Solar Patrol (a.k.a. Planet Patrol) in Lev Gleason's *Silver Streak Comics*. One of Simon and Kirby's earliest collaborations was the science fiction tale "Daring Disk," unpublished until the 2003 edition of Simon's memoir *The Comic Book Makers*. Hurtling through the air, wreaking havoc, the flying disc also seems like a sinister forerunner–this time of Captain America's shield.

It was Simon who created the Blue Bolt, for Novelty Press's *Blue Bolt Comics* #1 (Jun. 1940). In his origin story, Fred Parrish was an all-American athlete who was struck by lightning. A scientist named Dr. Bertoff used "radium deposits" to harness the "power of the lightning" within Parrish's body, granting him super-strength and the ability to fly. This anticipated Captain America's super-soldier serum, and the use of radiation as the source of super-powers for 1960s characters such as Spider-Man.

Like Flash Gordon, Simon's Blue Bolt adventures fused the superhero genre with science fiction. The hero led the legions of Bertoff's underground realm Deltos against the seductive Green Sorceress, who intended to conquer the world. As of issue #2 (Jul. 1940), Jack Kirby began collaborating with Simon on the series, and the story in issue #5 (Oct. 1940) was a major landmark.

It was the first to bear the credit "by Joe Simon and Jack Kirby".

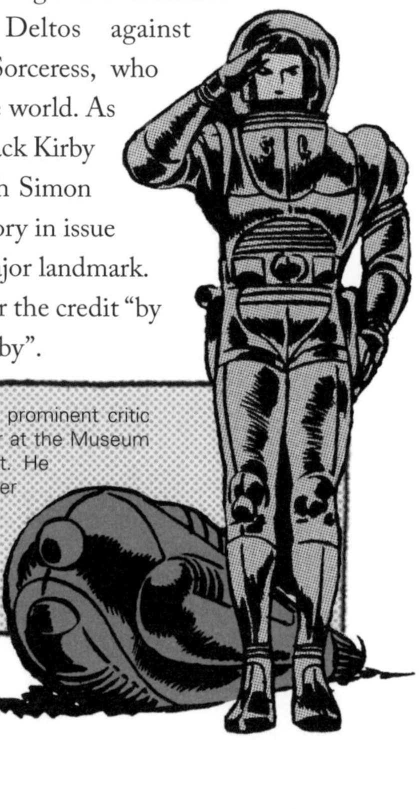

PETER SANDERSON is a prominent critic and historian, and a curator at the Museum of Comic and Cartoon Art. He has been a writer/researcher for Marvel and DC Comics, a reviewer for Publishers Weekly, and writer of numerous books on the subject of comics.

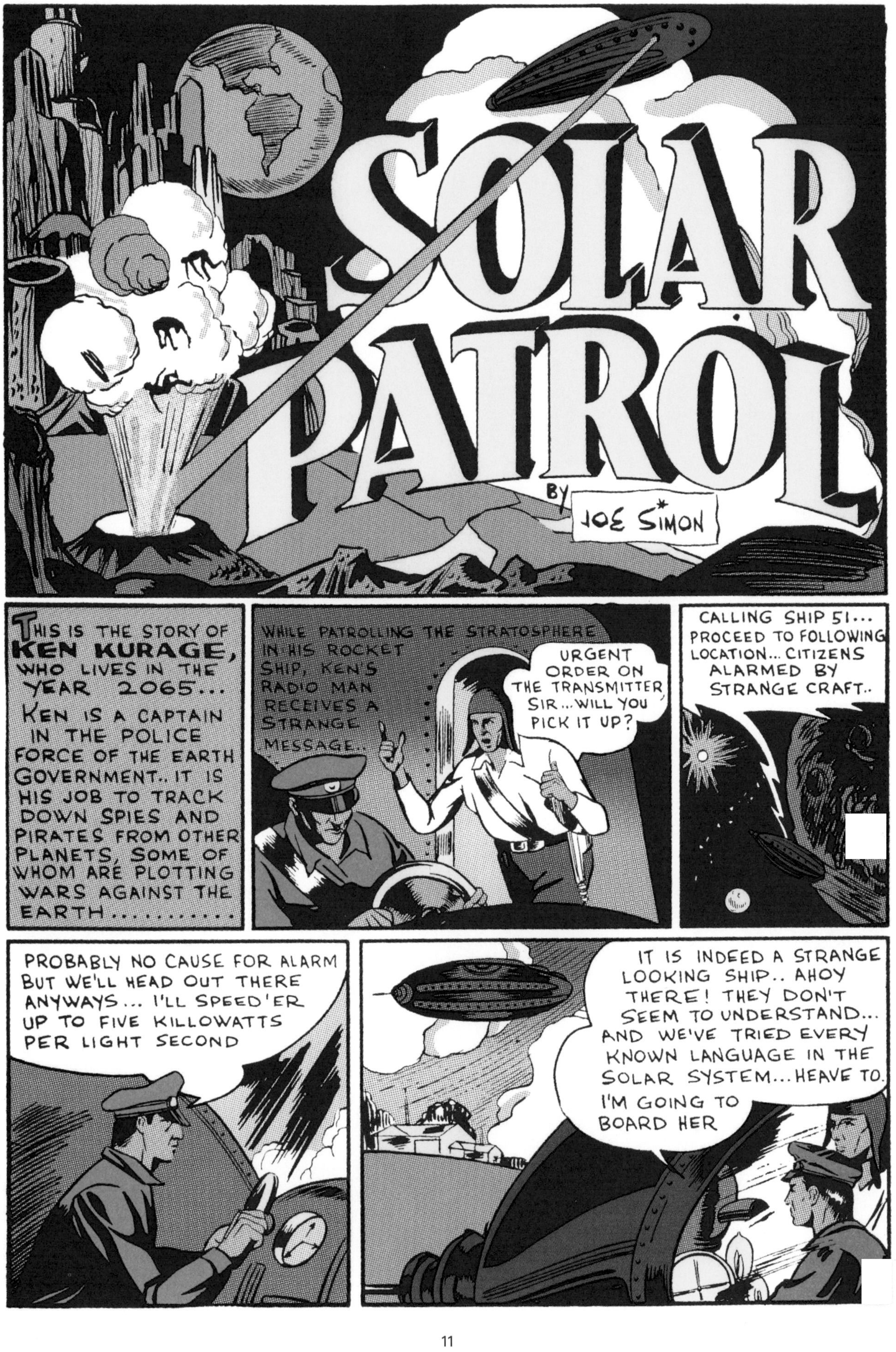
SOLAR PATROL
BY JOE SIMON
THIS IS THE STORY OF KEN KURAGE, WHO LIVES IN THE YEAR 2065... KEN IS A CAPTAIN IN THE POLICE FORCE OF THE EARTH GOVERNMENT.. IT IS HIS JOB TO TRACK DOWN SPIES AND PIRATES FROM OTHER PLANETS, SOME OF WHOM ARE PLOTTING WARS AGAINST THE EARTH..........
WHILE PATROLLING THE STRATOSPHERE IN HIS ROCKET SHIP, KEN'S RADIO MAN RECEIVES A STRANGE MESSAGE..
URGENT ORDER ON THE TRANSMITTER SIR...WILL YOU PICK IT UP?
CALLING SHIP 51... PROCEED TO FOLLOWING LOCATION... CITIZENS ALARMED BY STRANGE CRAFT..
PROBABLY NO CAUSE FOR ALARM BUT WE'LL HEAD OUT THERE ANYWAYS... I'LL SPEED'ER UP TO FIVE KILLOWATTS PER LIGHT SECOND
IT IS INDEED A STRANGE LOOKING SHIP.. AHOY THERE! THEY DON'T SEEM TO UNDERSTAND... AND WE'VE TRIED EVERY KNOWN LANGUAGE IN THE SOLAR SYSTEM... HEAVE TO. I'M GOING TO BOARD HER

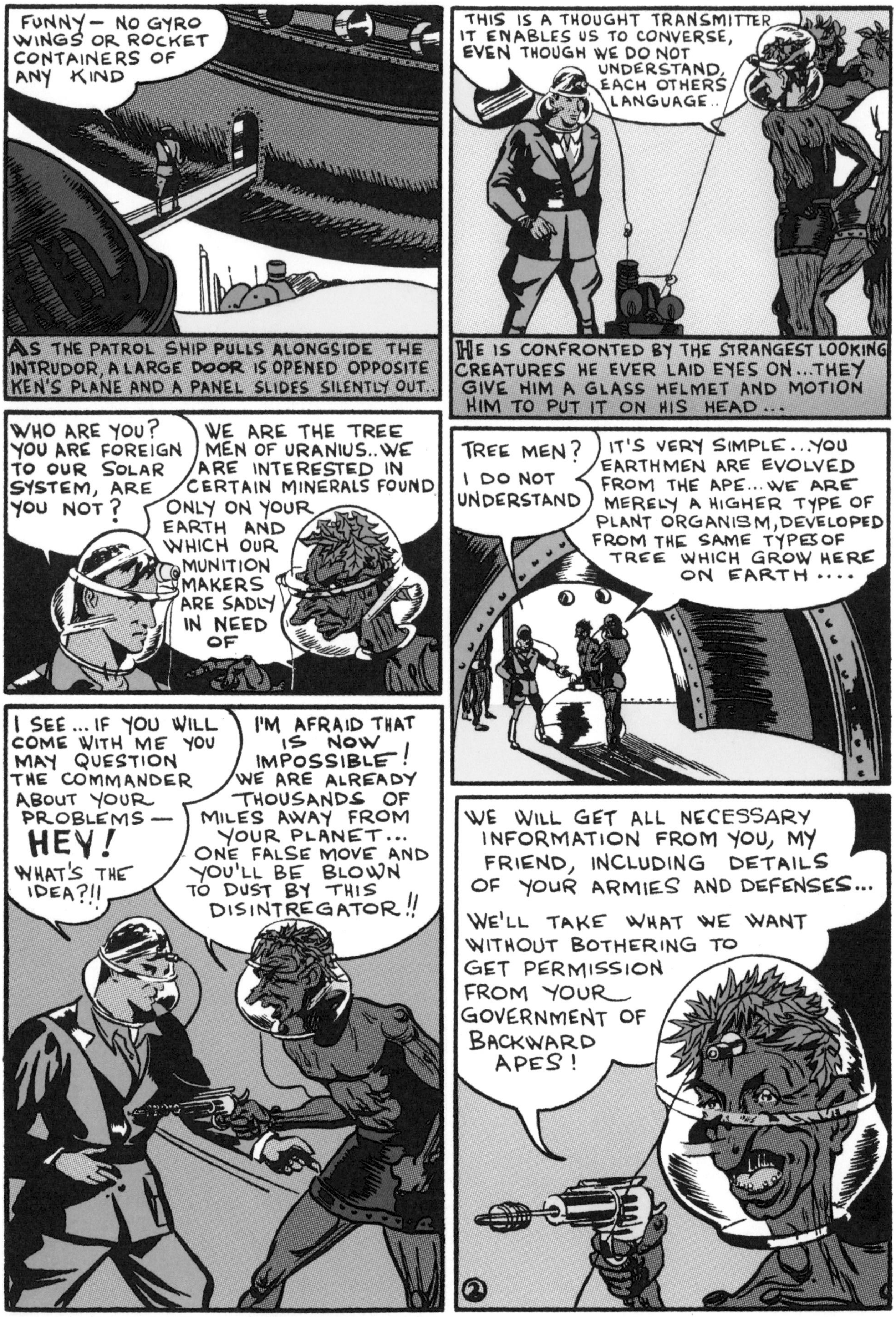
FUNNY— NO GYRO WINGS OR ROCKET CONTAINERS OF ANY KIND
AS THE PATROL SHIP PULLS ALONGSIDE THE INTRUDOR, A LARGE DOOR IS OPENED OPPOSITE KEN'S PLANE AND A PANEL SLIDES SILENTLY OUT..
THIS IS A THOUGHT TRANSMITTER IT ENABLES US TO CONVERSE, EVEN THOUGH WE DO NOT UNDERSTAND EACH OTHERS LANGUAGE..
HE IS CONFRONTED BY THE STRANGEST LOOKING CREATURES HE EVER LAID EYES ON...THEY GIVE HIM A GLASS HELMET AND MOTION HIM TO PUT IT ON HIS HEAD...
WHO ARE YOU? YOU ARE FOREIGN TO OUR SOLAR SYSTEM, ARE YOU NOT?
WE ARE THE TREE MEN OF URANIUS..WE ARE INTERESTED IN CERTAIN MINERALS FOUND ONLY ON YOUR EARTH AND WHICH OUR MUNITION MAKERS ARE SADLY IN NEED OF
TREE MEN? I DO NOT UNDERSTAND
IT'S VERY SIMPLE...YOU EARTHMEN ARE EVOLVED FROM THE APE...WE ARE MERELY A HIGHER TYPE OF PLANT ORGANISM, DEVELOPED FROM THE SAME TYPES OF TREE WHICH GROW HERE ON EARTH....
I SEE...IF YOU WILL COME WITH ME YOU MAY QUESTION THE COMMANDER ABOUT YOUR PROBLEMS— HEY! WHAT'S THE IDEA?!!
I'M AFRAID THAT IS NOW IMPOSSIBLE! WE ARE ALREADY THOUSANDS OF MILES AWAY FROM YOUR PLANET... ONE FALSE MOVE AND YOU'LL BE BLOWN TO DUST BY THIS DISINTREGATOR!!
WE WILL GET ALL NECESSARY INFORMATION FROM YOU, MY FRIEND, INCLUDING DETAILS OF YOUR ARMIES AND DEFENSES...
WE'LL TAKE WHAT WE WANT WITHOUT BOTHERING TO GET PERMISSION FROM YOUR GOVERNMENT OF BACKWARD APES!
2

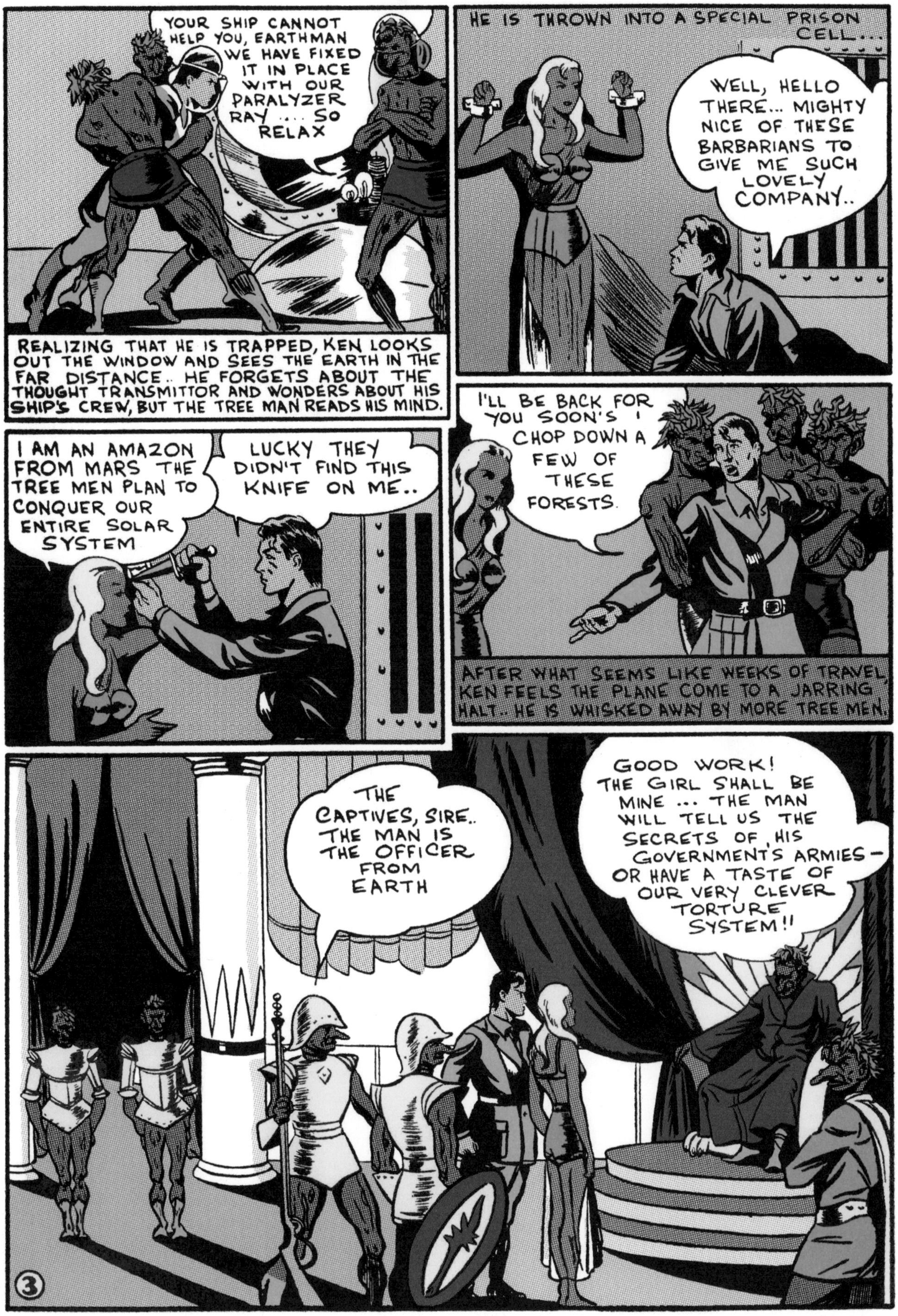
YOUR SHIP CANNOT HELP YOU, EARTHMAN WE HAVE FIXED IT IN PLACE WITH OUR PARALYZER RAY ... SO RELAX
REALIZING THAT HE IS TRAPPED, KEN LOOKS OUT THE WINDOW AND SEES THE EARTH IN THE FAR DISTANCE.. HE FORGETS ABOUT THE THOUGHT TRANSMITTOR AND WONDERS ABOUT HIS SHIP'S CREW, BUT THE TREE MAN READS HIS MIND.
HE IS THROWN INTO A SPECIAL PRISON CELL...
WELL, HELLO THERE... MIGHTY NICE OF THESE BARBARIANS TO GIVE ME SUCH LOVELY COMPANY..
I AM AN AMAZON FROM MARS THE TREE MEN PLAN TO CONQUER OUR ENTIRE SOLAR SYSTEM
LUCKY THEY DIDN'T FIND THIS KNIFE ON ME..
I'LL BE BACK FOR YOU SOON'S I CHOP DOWN A FEW OF THESE FORESTS.
AFTER WHAT SEEMS LIKE WEEKS OF TRAVEL, KEN FEELS THE PLANE COME TO A JARRING HALT.. HE IS WHISKED AWAY BY MORE TREE MEN.
THE CAPTIVES, SIRE.. THE MAN IS THE OFFICER FROM EARTH
GOOD WORK! THE GIRL SHALL BE MINE ... THE MAN WILL TELL US THE SECRETS OF HIS GOVERNMENT'S ARMIES — OR HAVE A TASTE OF OUR VERY CLEVER TORTURE SYSTEM!!
3

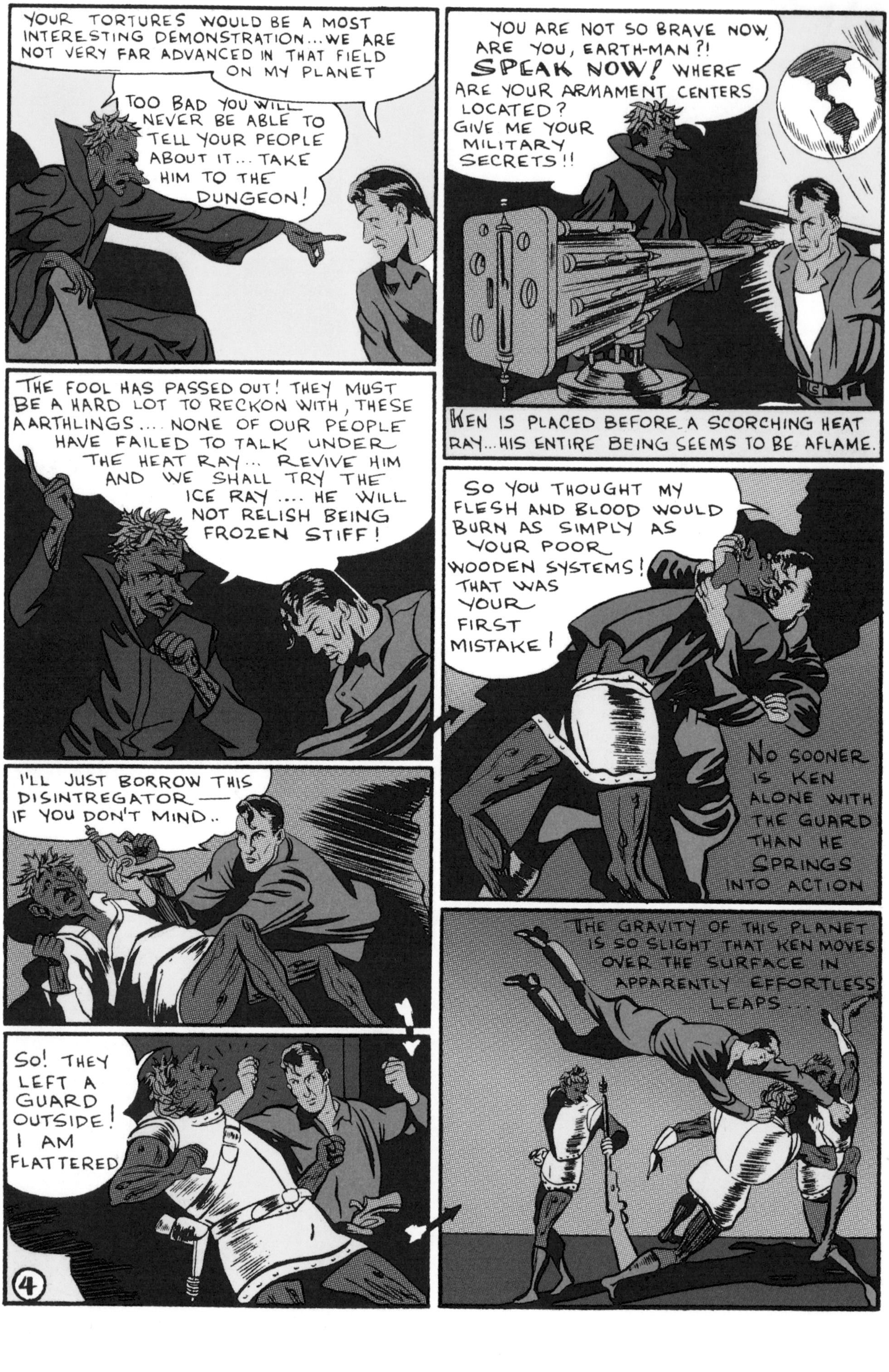
YOUR TORTURES WOULD BE A MOST INTERESTING DEMONSTRATION... WE ARE NOT VERY FAR ADVANCED IN THAT FIELD ON MY PLANET
TOO BAD YOU WILL NEVER BE ABLE TO TELL YOUR PEOPLE ABOUT IT... TAKE HIM TO THE DUNGEON!
YOU ARE NOT SO BRAVE NOW, ARE YOU, EARTH-MAN?! SPEAK NOW! WHERE ARE YOUR ARMAMENT CENTERS LOCATED? GIVE ME YOUR MILITARY SECRETS!!
KEN IS PLACED BEFORE A SCORCHING HEAT RAY... HIS ENTIRE BEING SEEMS TO BE AFLAME.
THE FOOL HAS PASSED OUT! THEY MUST BE A HARD LOT TO RECKON WITH, THESE AARTHLINGS.... NONE OF OUR PEOPLE HAVE FAILED TO TALK UNDER THE HEAT RAY... REVIVE HIM AND WE SHALL TRY THE ICE RAY.... HE WILL NOT RELISH BEING FROZEN STIFF!
SO YOU THOUGHT MY FLESH AND BLOOD WOULD BURN AS SIMPLY AS YOUR POOR WOODEN SYSTEMS! THAT WAS YOUR FIRST MISTAKE!
NO SOONER IS KEN ALONE WITH THE GUARD THAN HE SPRINGS INTO ACTION
I'LL JUST BORROW THIS DISINTREGATOR — IF YOU DON'T MIND..
SO! THEY LEFT A GUARD OUTSIDE! I AM FLATTERED
THE GRAVITY OF THIS PLANET IS SO SLIGHT THAT KEN MOVES OVER THE SURFACE IN APPARENTLY EFFORTLESS LEAPS....
4

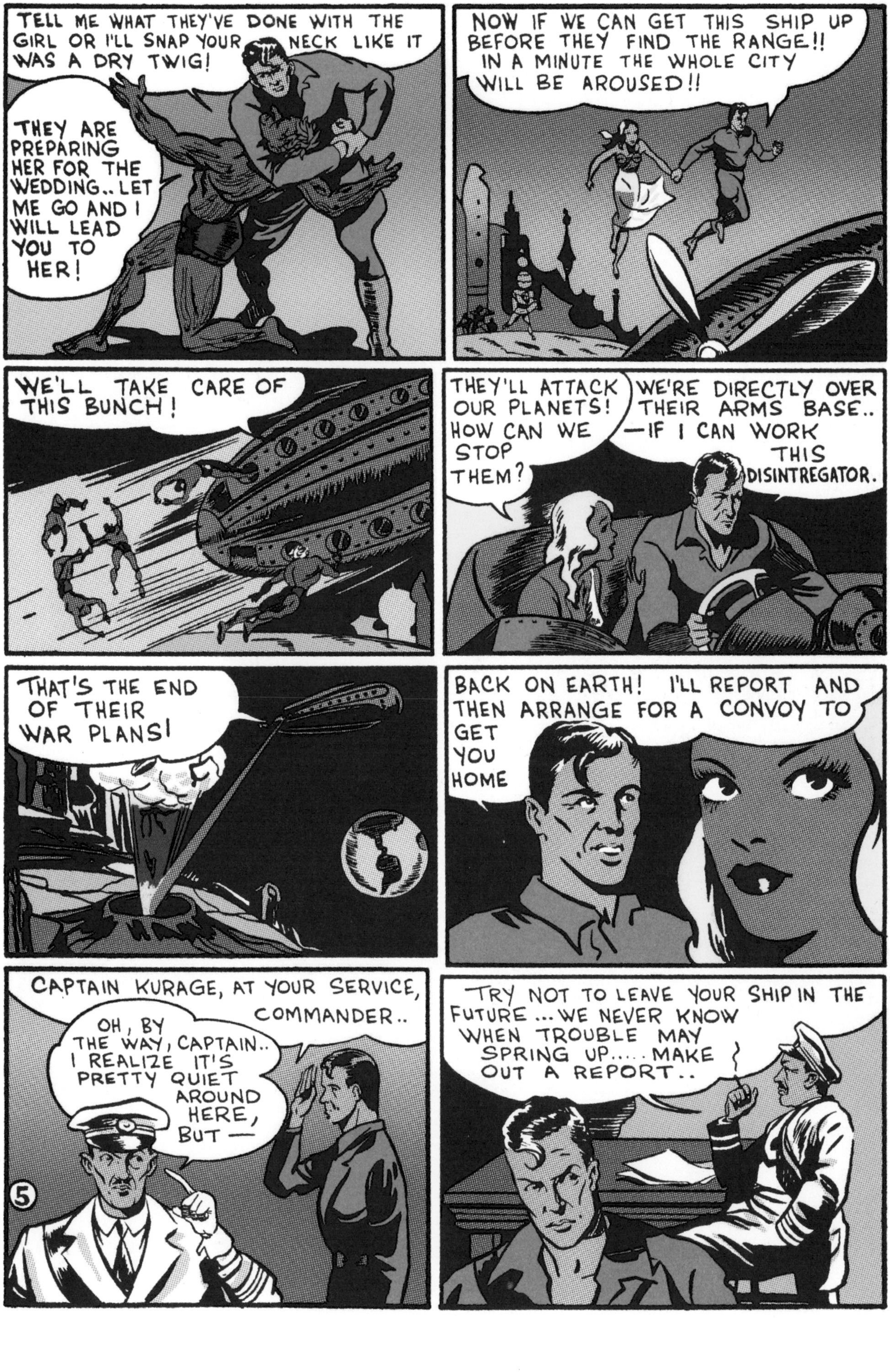
TELL ME WHAT THEY'VE DONE WITH THE GIRL OR I'LL SNAP YOUR NECK LIKE IT WAS A DRY TWIG!
THEY ARE PREPARING HER FOR THE WEDDING.. LET ME GO AND I WILL LEAD YOU TO HER!
NOW IF WE CAN GET THIS SHIP UP BEFORE THEY FIND THE RANGE!! IN A MINUTE THE WHOLE CITY WILL BE AROUSED!!
WE'LL TAKE CARE OF THIS BUNCH!
THEY'LL ATTACK OUR PLANETS! HOW CAN WE STOP THEM?
WE'RE DIRECTLY OVER THEIR ARMS BASE.. —IF I CAN WORK THIS DISINTREGATOR.
THAT'S THE END OF THEIR WAR PLANS!
BACK ON EARTH! I'LL REPORT AND THEN ARRANGE FOR A CONVOY TO GET YOU HOME
CAPTAIN KURAGE, AT YOUR SERVICE, COMMANDER..
OH, BY THE WAY, CAPTAIN.. I REALIZE IT'S PRETTY QUIET AROUND HERE, BUT —
5
TRY NOT TO LEAVE YOUR SHIP IN THE FUTURE ... WE NEVER KNOW WHEN TROUBLE MAY SPRING UP..... MAKE OUT A REPORT..

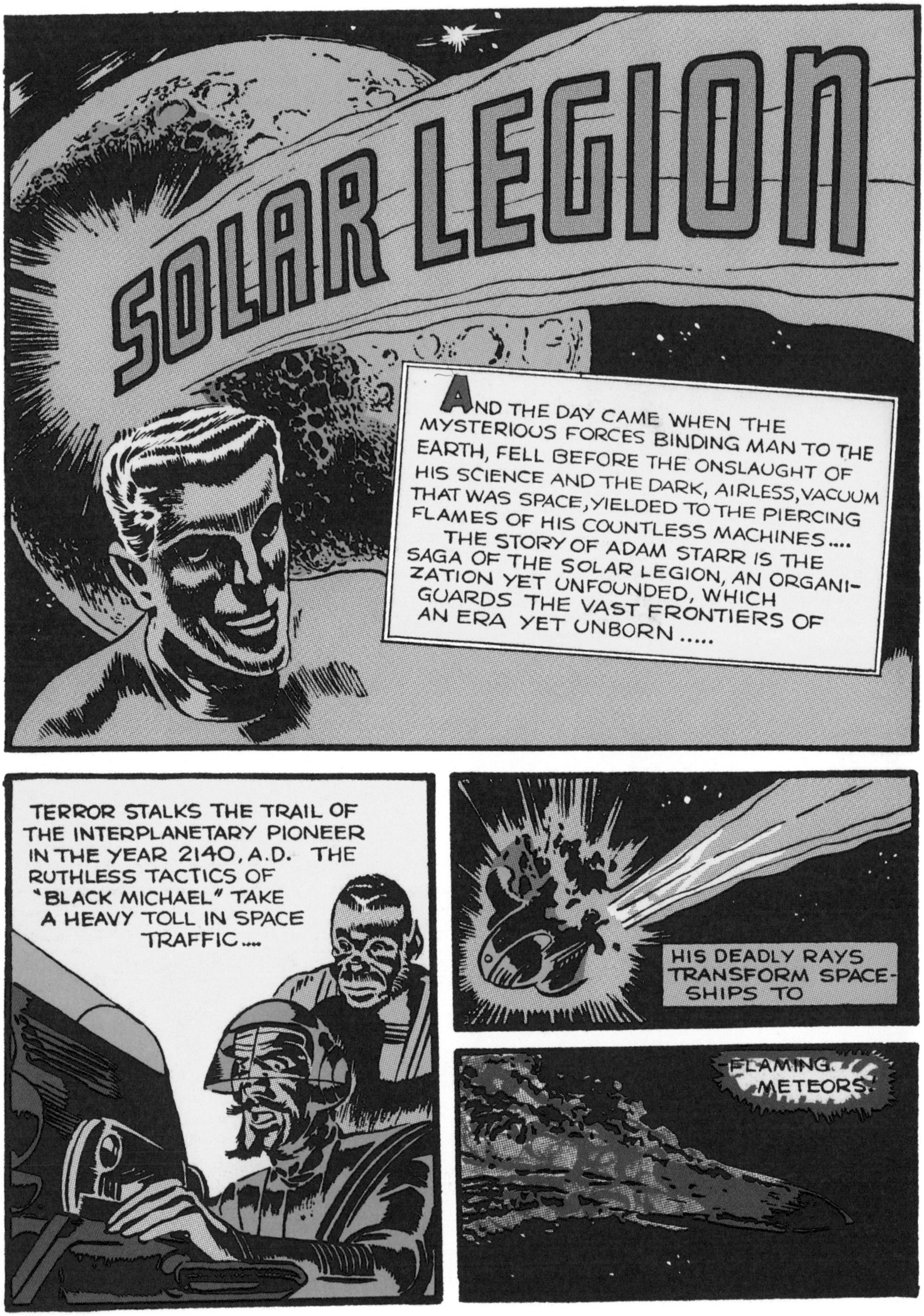
SOLAR LEGION
AND THE DAY CAME WHEN THE MYSTERIOUS FORCES BINDING MAN TO THE EARTH, FELL BEFORE THE ONSLAUGHT OF HIS SCIENCE AND THE DARK, AIRLESS, VACUUM THAT WAS SPACE, YIELDED TO THE PIERCING FLAMES OF HIS COUNTLESS MACHINES.... THE STORY OF ADAM STARR IS THE SAGA OF THE SOLAR LEGION, AN ORGANIZATION YET UNFOUNDED, WHICH GUARDS THE VAST FRONTIERS OF AN ERA YET UNBORN.....
TERROR STALKS THE TRAIL OF THE INTERPLANETARY PIONEER IN THE YEAR 2140, A.D. THE RUTHLESS TACTICS OF "BLACK MICHAEL" TAKE A HEAVY TOLL IN SPACE TRAFFIC....
HIS DEADLY RAYS TRANSFORM SPACE-SHIPS TO
-FLAMING METEORS!

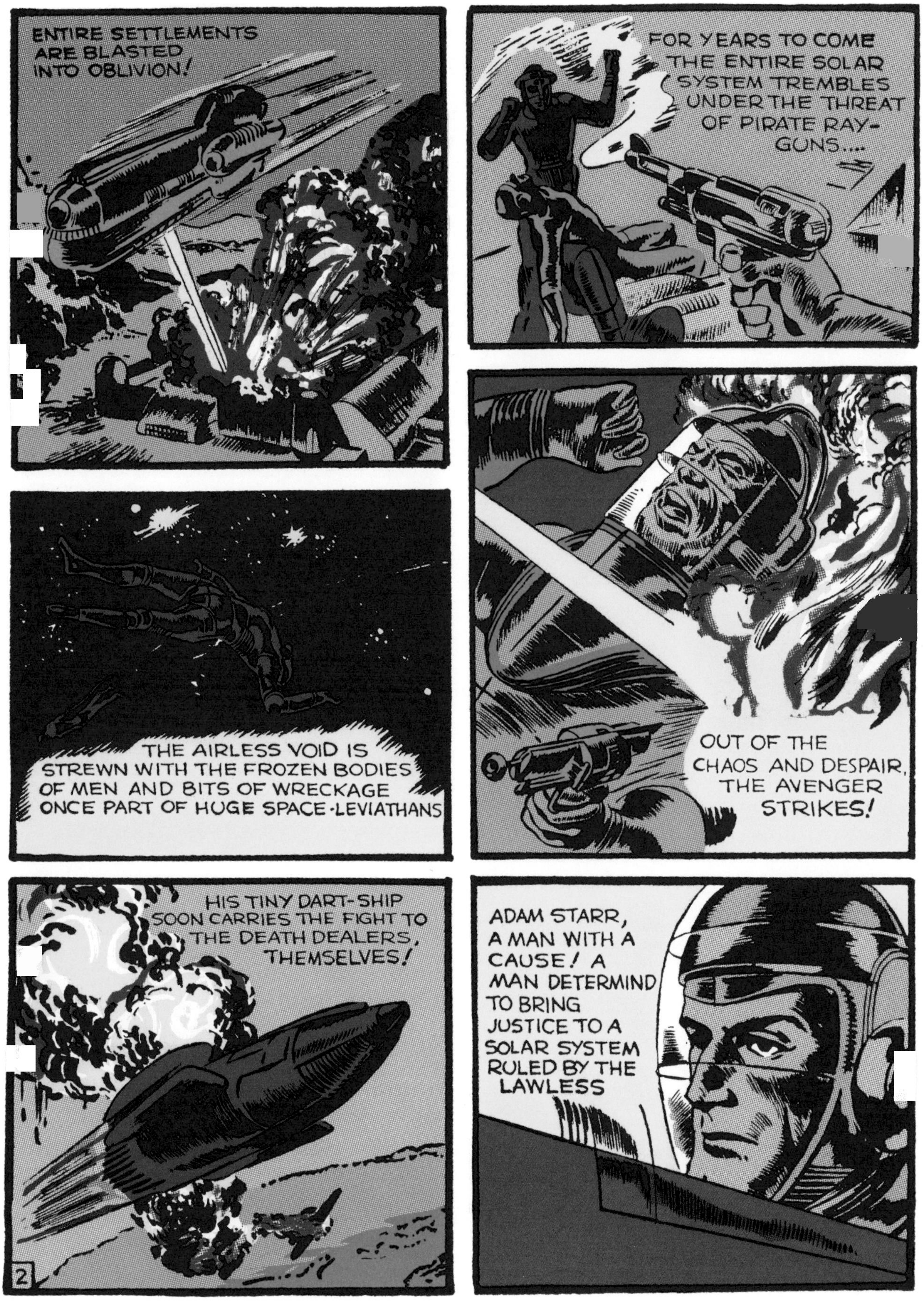
ENTIRE SETTLEMENTS ARE BLASTED INTO OBLIVION!
FOR YEARS TO COME THE ENTIRE SOLAR SYSTEM TREMBLES UNDER THE THREAT OF PIRATE RAY-GUNS....
THE AIRLESS VOID IS STREWN WITH THE FROZEN BODIES OF MEN AND BITS OF WRECKAGE ONCE PART OF HUGE SPACE-LEVIATHANS
OUT OF THE CHAOS AND DESPAIR, THE AVENGER STRIKES!
HIS TINY DART-SHIP SOON CARRIES THE FIGHT TO THE DEATH DEALERS, THEMSELVES!
2
ADAM STARR, A MAN WITH A CAUSE! A MAN DETERMIND TO BRING JUSTICE TO A SOLAR SYSTEM RULED BY THE LAWLESS

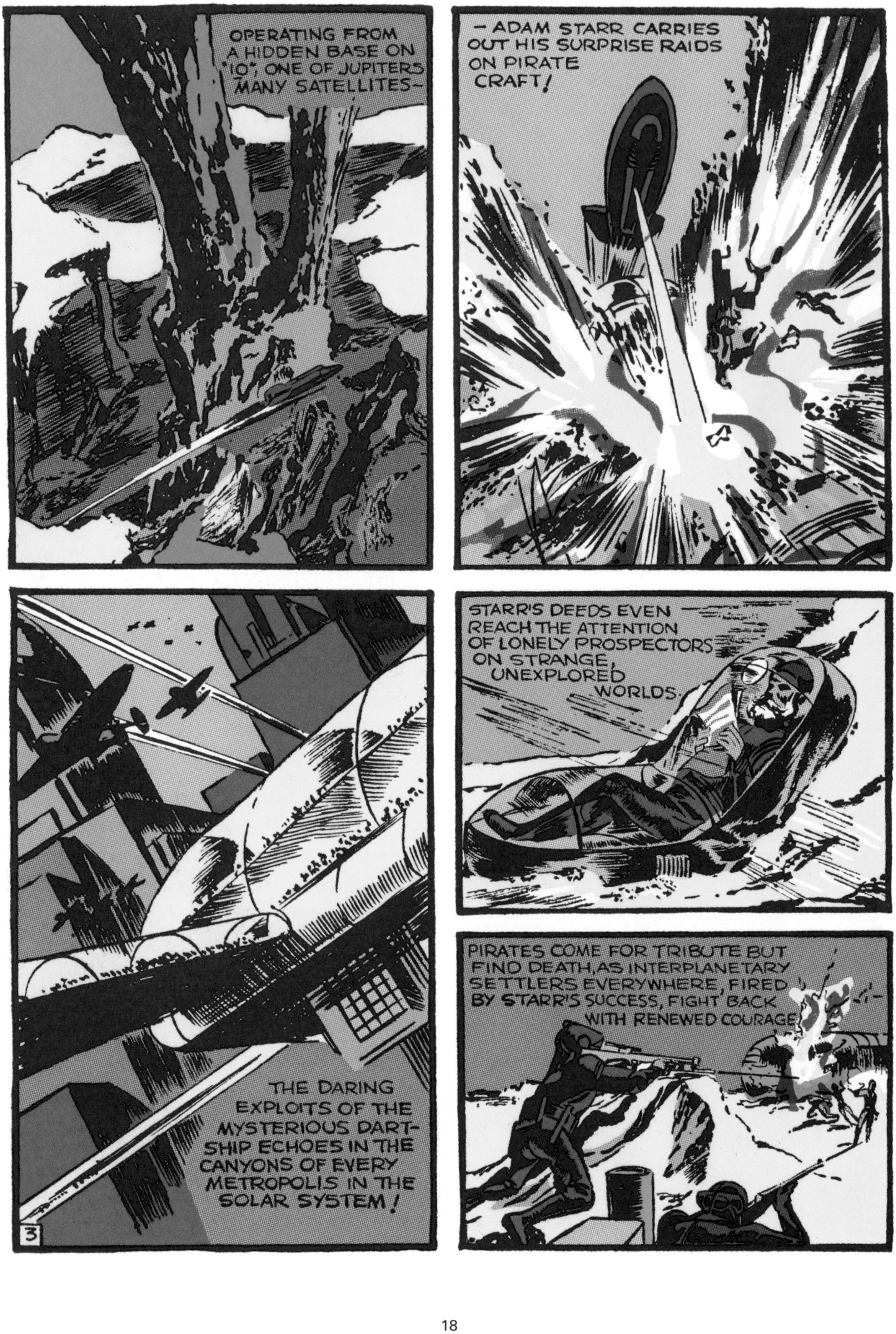
OPERATING FROM A HIDDEN BASE ON "IO", ONE OF JUPITERS MANY SATELLITES-
- ADAM STARR CARRIES OUT HIS SURPRISE RAIDS ON PIRATE CRAFT!
THE DARING EXPLOITS OF THE MYSTERIOUS DART-SHIP ECHOES IN THE CANYONS OF EVERY METROPOLIS IN THE SOLAR SYSTEM!
3
STARR'S DEEDS EVEN REACH THE ATTENTION OF LONELY PROSPECTORS ON STRANGE, UNEXPLORED WORLDS-
PIRATES COME FOR TRIBUTE BUT FIND DEATH, AS INTERPLANETARY SETTLERS EVERYWHERE, FIRED BY STARR'S SUCCESS, FIGHT BACK WITH RENEWED COURAGE!

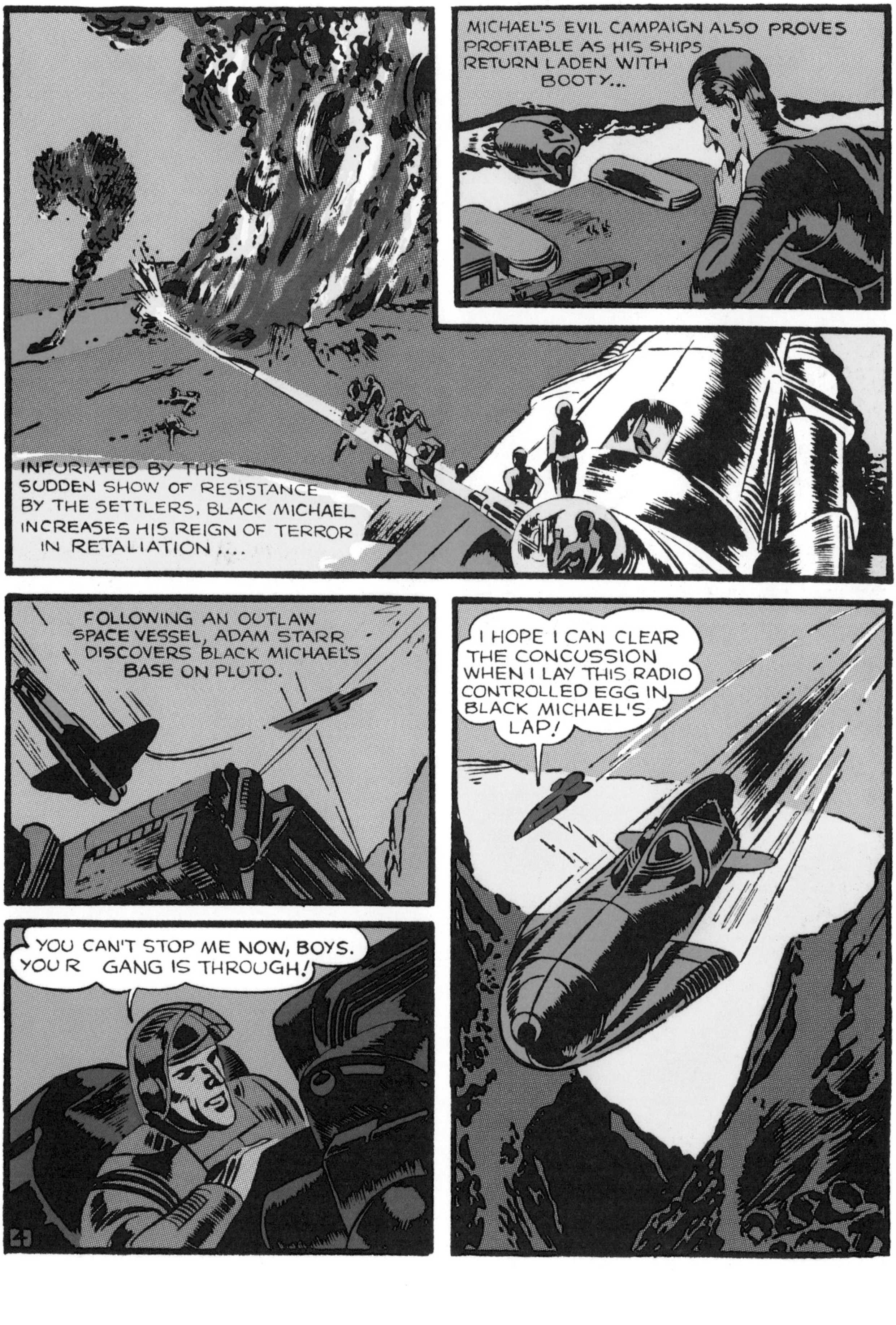
INFURIATED BY THIS SUDDEN SHOW OF RESISTANCE BY THE SETTLERS, BLACK MICHAEL INCREASES HIS REIGN OF TERROR IN RETALIATION....
MICHAEL'S EVIL CAMPAIGN ALSO PROVES PROFITABLE AS HIS SHIPS RETURN LADEN WITH BOOTY...
FOLLOWING AN OUTLAW SPACE VESSEL, ADAM STARR DISCOVERS BLACK MICHAEL'S BASE ON PLUTO.
I HOPE I CAN CLEAR THE CONCUSSION WHEN I LAY THIS RADIO CONTROLLED EGG IN BLACK MICHAEL'S LAP!
YOU CAN'T STOP ME NOW, BOYS. YOU R GANG IS THROUGH!

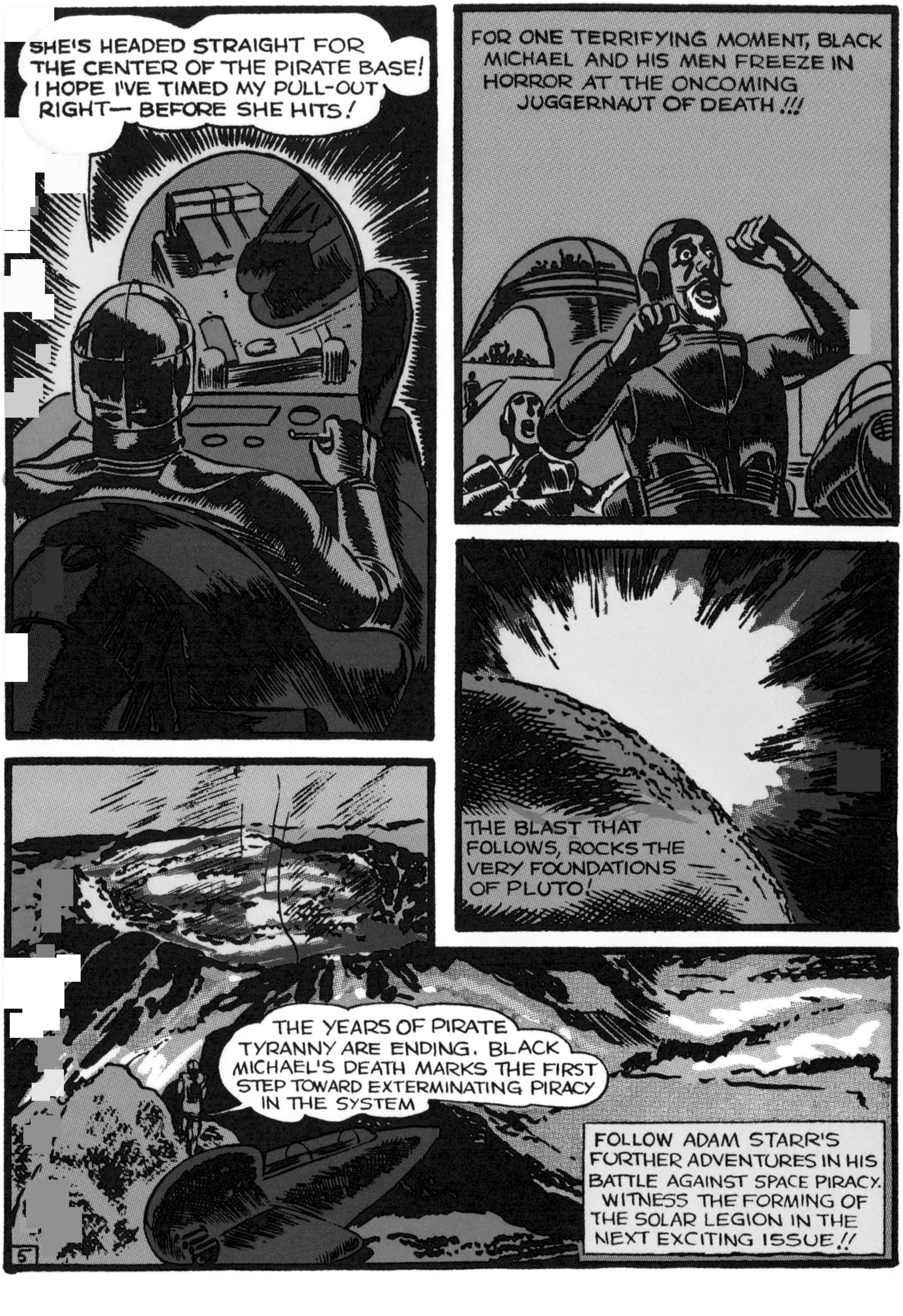
SHE'S HEADED STRAIGHT FOR THE CENTER OF THE PIRATE BASE! I HOPE I'VE TIMED MY PULL-OUT RIGHT— BEFORE SHE HITS!
FOR ONE TERRIFYING MOMENT, BLACK MICHAEL AND HIS MEN FREEZE IN HORROR AT THE ONCOMING JUGGERNAUT OF DEATH!!!
THE BLAST THAT FOLLOWS, ROCKS THE VERY FOUNDATIONS OF PLUTO!
THE YEARS OF PIRATE TYRANNY ARE ENDING. BLACK MICHAEL'S DEATH MARKS THE FIRST STEP TOWARD EXTERMINATING PIRACY IN THE SYSTEM
FOLLOW ADAM STARR'S FURTHER ADVENTURES IN HIS BATTLE AGAINST SPACE PIRACY. WITNESS THE FORMING OF THE SOLAR LEGION IN THE NEXT EXCITING ISSUE!!
5

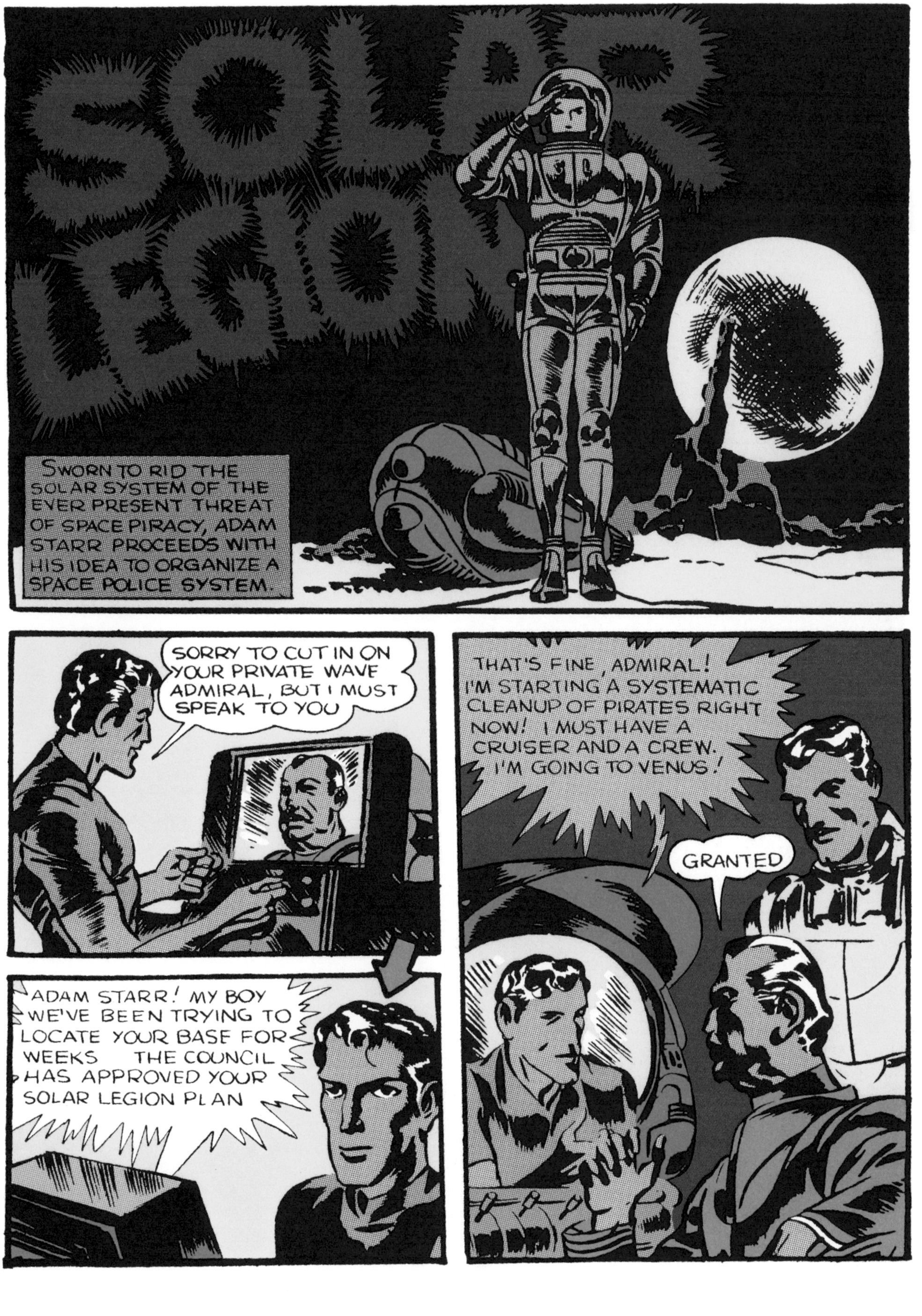
SOLAR LEGION
SWORN TO RID THE SOLAR SYSTEM OF THE EVER PRESENT THREAT OF SPACE PIRACY, ADAM STARR PROCEEDS WITH HIS IDEA TO ORGANIZE A SPACE POLICE SYSTEM.
SORRY TO CUT IN ON YOUR PRIVATE WAVE ADMIRAL, BUT I MUST SPEAK TO YOU
ADAM STARR! MY BOY WE'VE BEEN TRYING TO LOCATE YOUR BASE FOR WEEKS THE COUNCIL HAS APPROVED YOUR SOLAR LEGION PLAN
THAT'S FINE, ADMIRAL! I'M STARTING A SYSTEMATIC CLEANUP OF PIRATES RIGHT NOW! I MUST HAVE A CRUISER AND A CREW. I'M GOING TO VENUS!
GRANTED

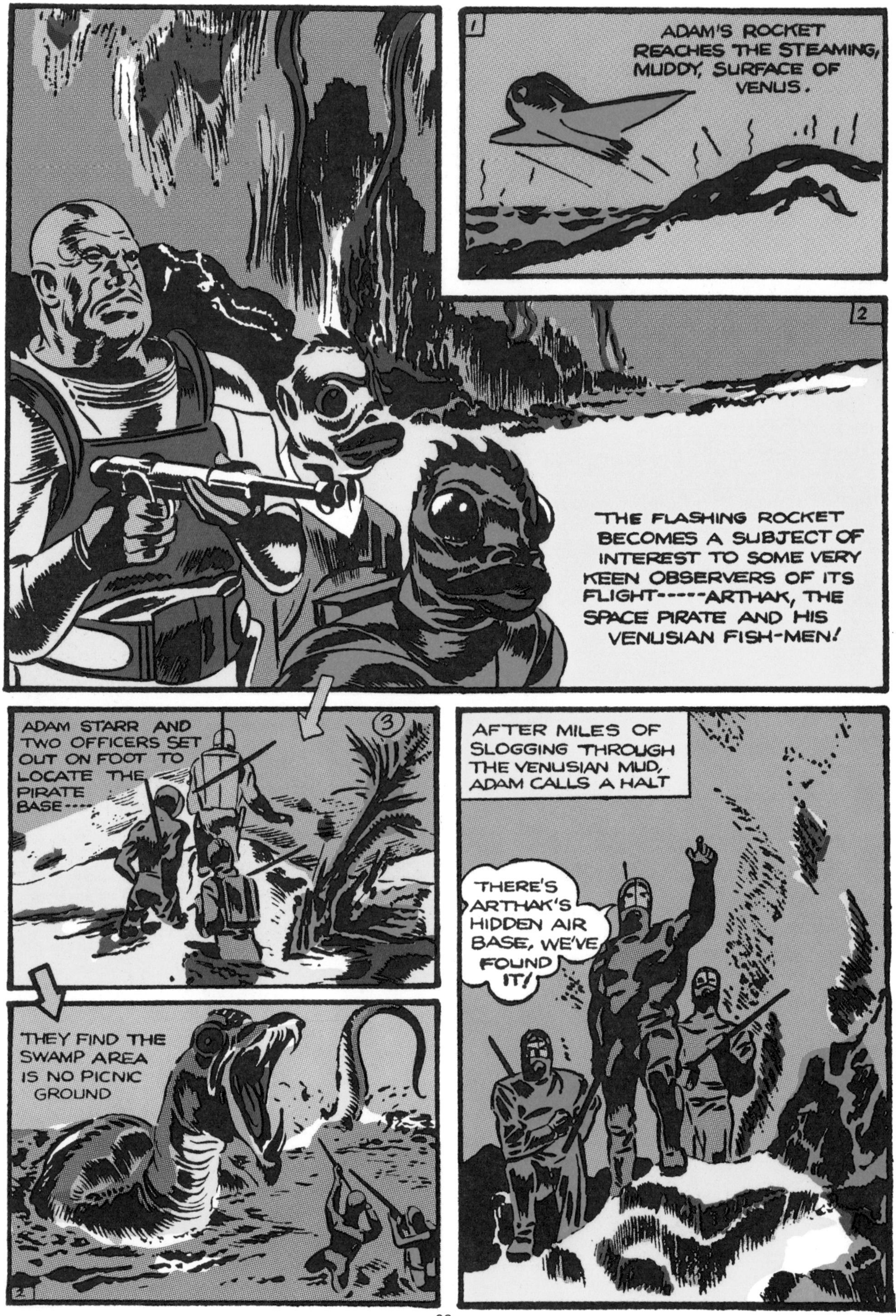
1
ADAM'S ROCKET REACHES THE STEAMING, MUDDY, SURFACE OF VENUS.
2
THE FLASHING ROCKET BECOMES A SUBJECT OF INTEREST TO SOME VERY KEEN OBSERVERS OF ITS FLIGHT-----ARTHAK, THE SPACE PIRATE AND HIS VENUSIAN FISH-MEN!
3
ADAM STARR AND TWO OFFICERS SET OUT ON FOOT TO LOCATE THE PIRATE BASE----
THEY FIND THE SWAMP AREA IS NO PICNIC GROUND
AFTER MILES OF SLOGGING THROUGH THE VENUSIAN MUD, ADAM CALLS A HALT
THERE'S ARTHAK'S HIDDEN AIR BASE, WE'VE FOUND IT!

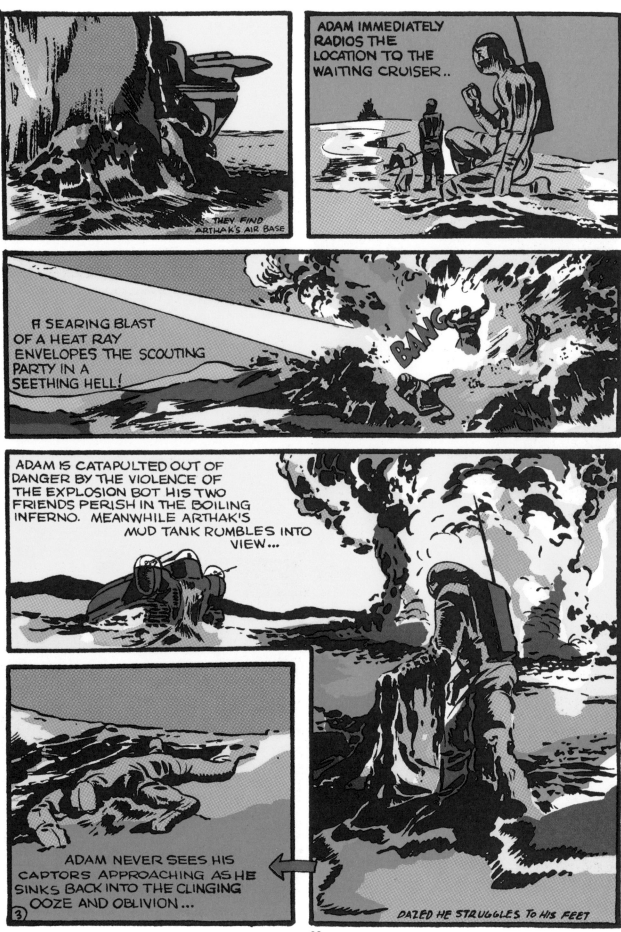

THEY FIND ARTHAK'S AIR BASE

ADAM IMMEDIATELY RADIOS THE LOCATION TO THE WAITING CRUISER...

A SEARING BLAST OF A HEAT RAY ENVELOPES THE SCOUTING PARTY IN A SEETHING HELL!

BANG

ADAM IS CATAPULTED OUT OF DANGER BY THE VIOLENCE OF THE EXPLOSION BOT HIS TWO FRIENDS PERISH IN THE BOILING INFERNO. MEANWHILE ARTHAK'S MUD TANK RUMBLES INTO VIEW...

ADAM NEVER SEES HIS CAPTORS APPROACHING AS HE SINKS BACK INTO THE CLINGING OOZE AND OBLIVION...

3

DAZED HE STRUGGLES TO HIS FEET

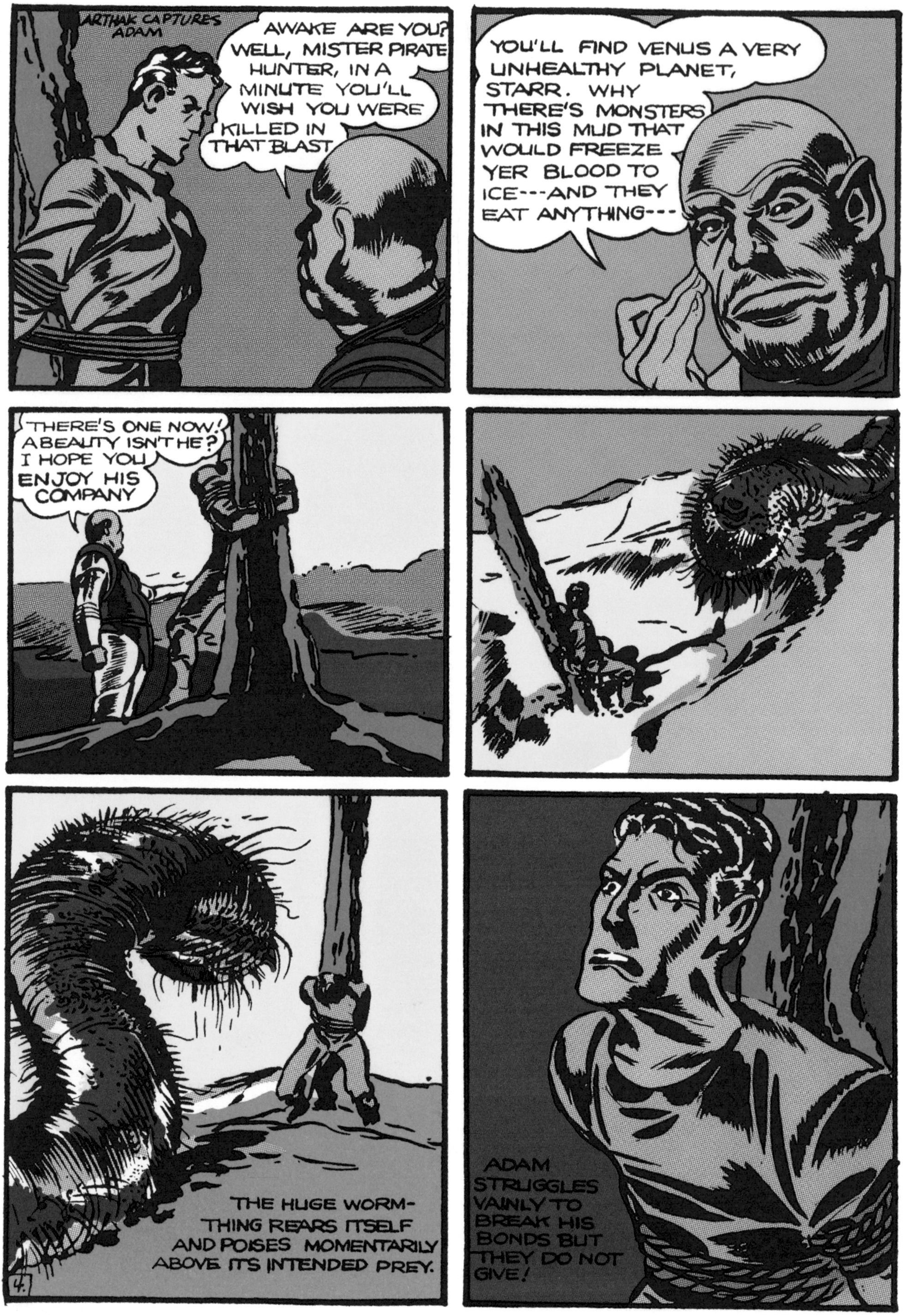
ARTHAK CAPTURES ADAM
AWAKE ARE YOU? WELL, MISTER PIRATE HUNTER, IN A MINUTE YOU'LL WISH YOU WERE KILLED IN THAT BLAST
YOU'LL FIND VENUS A VERY UNHEALTHY PLANET, STARR. WHY THERE'S MONSTERS IN THIS MUD THAT WOULD FREEZE YER BLOOD TO ICE---AND THEY EAT ANYTHING---
THERE'S ONE NOW! A BEAUTY ISN'T HE? I HOPE YOU ENJOY HIS COMPANY
THE HUGE WORM-THING REARS ITSELF AND POISES MOMENTARILY ABOVE ITS INTENDED PREY.
4.
ADAM STRUGGLES VAINLY TO BREAK HIS BONDS BUT THEY DO NOT GIVE!

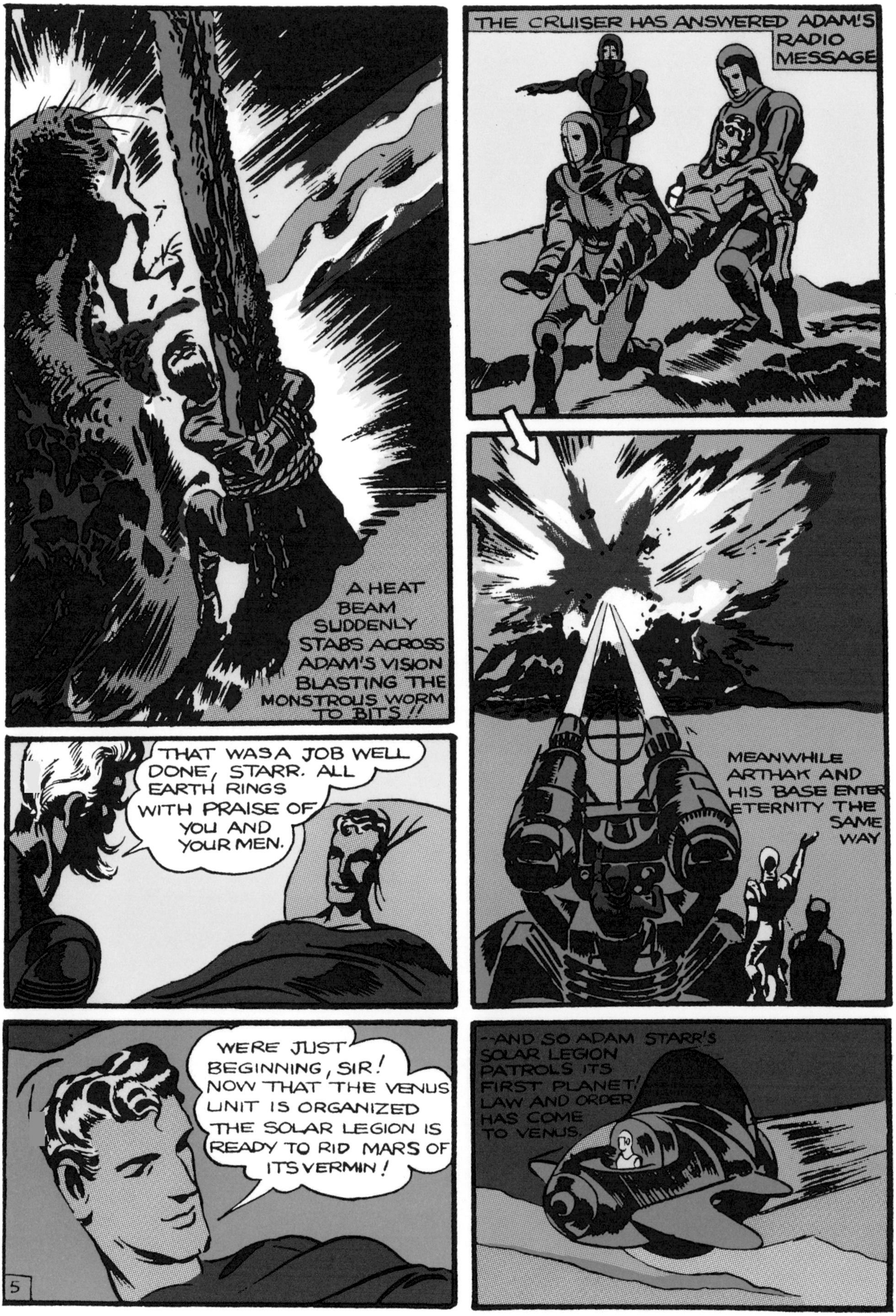
A HEAT BEAM SUDDENLY STABS ACROSS ADAM'S VISION BLASTING THE MONSTROUS WORM TO BITS!!
THE CRUISER HAS ANSWERED ADAM'S RADIO MESSAGE
MEANWHILE ARTHAK AND HIS BASE ENTER ETERNITY THE SAME WAY
THAT WAS A JOB WELL DONE, STARR. ALL EARTH RINGS WITH PRAISE OF YOU AND YOUR MEN.
WERE JUST BEGINNING, SIR! NOW THAT THE VENUS UNIT IS ORGANIZED THE SOLAR LEGION IS READY TO RID MARS OF ITS VERMIN!
5
--AND SO ADAM STARR'S SOLAR LEGION PATROLS ITS FIRST PLANET! LAW AND ORDER HAS COME TO VENUS.

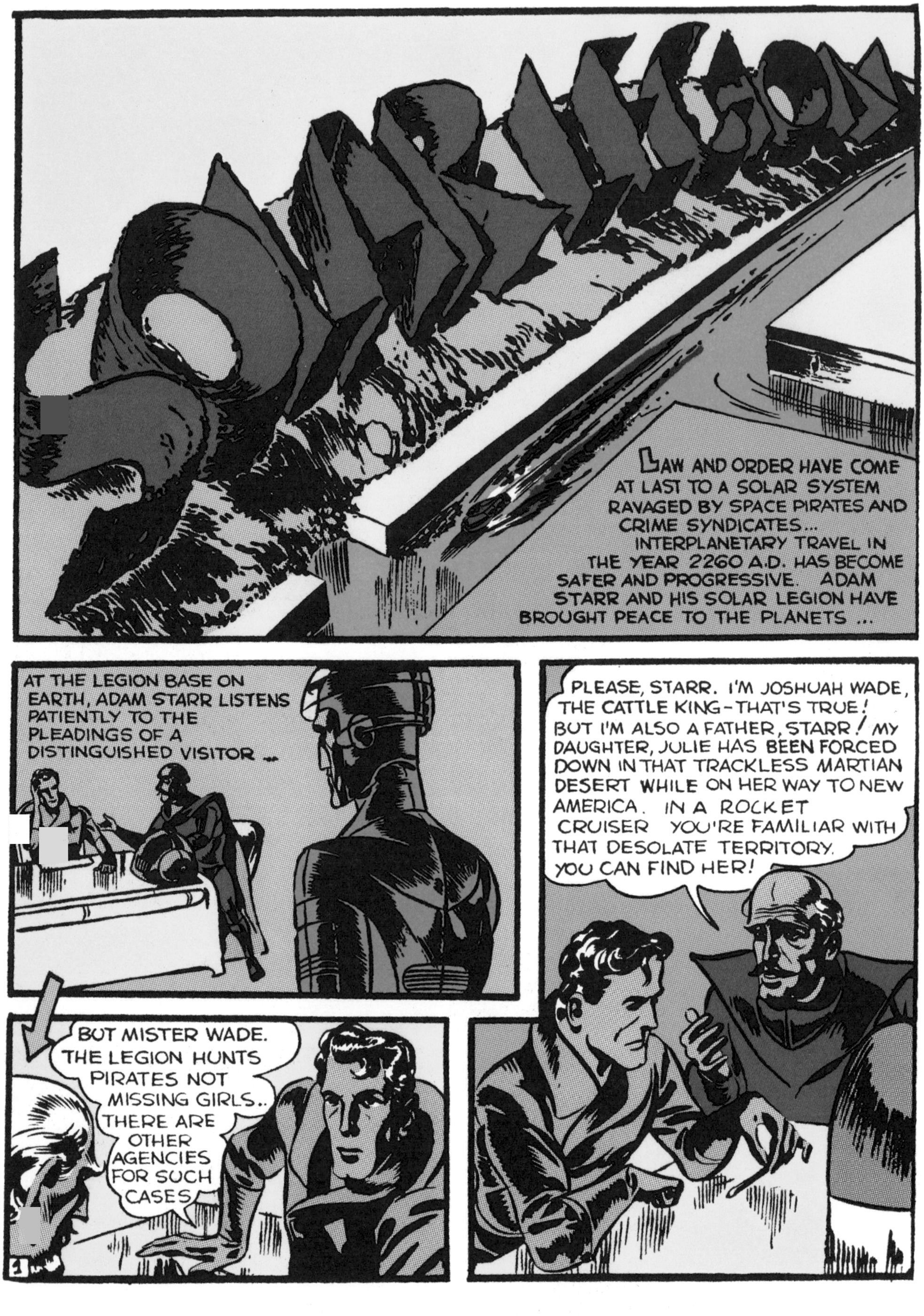

LAW AND ORDER HAVE COME AT LAST TO A SOLAR SYSTEM RAVAGED BY SPACE PIRATES AND CRIME SYNDICATES... INTERPLANETARY TRAVEL IN THE YEAR 2260 A.D. HAS BECOME SAFER AND PROGRESSIVE. ADAM STARR AND HIS SOLAR LEGION HAVE BROUGHT PEACE TO THE PLANETS ...
AT THE LEGION BASE ON EARTH, ADAM STARR LISTENS PATIENTLY TO THE PLEADINGS OF A DISTINGUISHED VISITOR ...
PLEASE, STARR. I'M JOSHUAH WADE, THE CATTLE KING - THAT'S TRUE! BUT I'M ALSO A FATHER, STARR! MY DAUGHTER, JULIE HAS BEEN FORCED DOWN IN THAT TRACKLESS MARTIAN DESERT WHILE ON HER WAY TO NEW AMERICA. IN A ROCKET CRUISER YOU'RE FAMILIAR WITH THAT DESOLATE TERRITORY. YOU CAN FIND HER!
BUT MISTER WADE. THE LEGION HUNTS PIRATES NOT MISSING GIRLS.. THERE ARE OTHER AGENCIES FOR SUCH CASES.
1

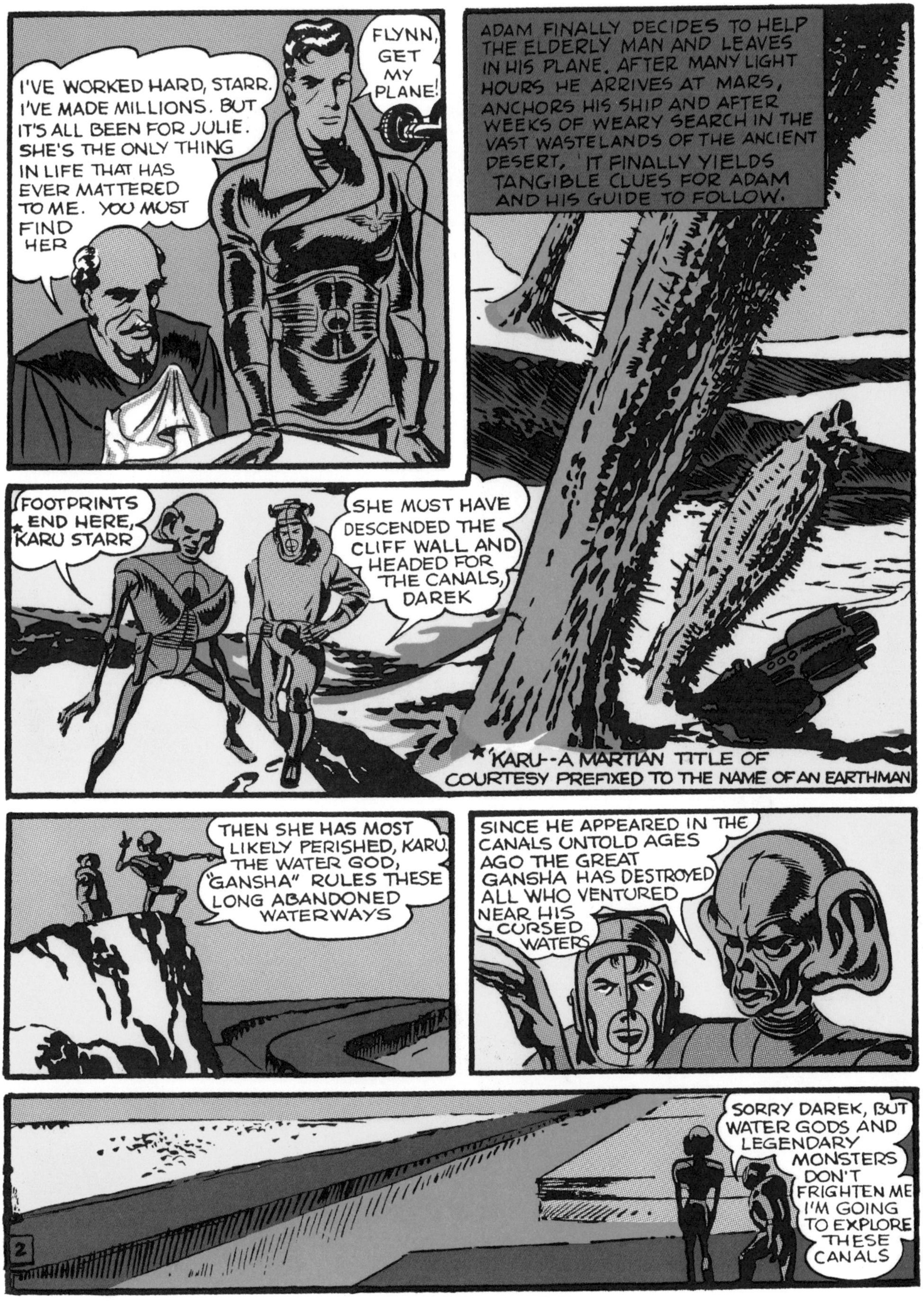
I'VE WORKED HARD, STARR. I'VE MADE MILLIONS. BUT IT'S ALL BEEN FOR JULIE. SHE'S THE ONLY THING IN LIFE THAT HAS EVER MATTERED TO ME. YOU MUST FIND HER
FLYNN, GET MY PLANE!
ADAM FINALLY DECIDES TO HELP THE ELDERLY MAN AND LEAVES IN HIS PLANE. AFTER MANY LIGHT HOURS HE ARRIVES AT MARS, ANCHORS HIS SHIP AND AFTER WEEKS OF WEARY SEARCH IN THE VAST WASTELANDS OF THE ANCIENT DESERT, IT FINALLY YIELDS TANGIBLE CLUES FOR ADAM AND HIS GUIDE TO FOLLOW.
FOOTPRINTS END HERE, ★KARU STARR
SHE MUST HAVE DESCENDED THE CLIFF WALL AND HEADED FOR THE CANALS, DAREK
★KARU--A MARTIAN TITLE OF COURTESY PREFIXED TO THE NAME OF AN EARTHMAN
THEN SHE HAS MOST LIKELY PERISHED, KARU. THE WATER GOD, "GANSHA" RULES THESE LONG ABANDONED WATERWAYS
SINCE HE APPEARED IN THE CANALS UNTOLD AGES AGO THE GREAT GANSHA HAS DESTROYED ALL WHO VENTURED NEAR HIS CURSED WATERS
SORRY DAREK, BUT WATER GODS AND LEGENDARY MONSTERS DON'T FRIGHTEN ME I'M GOING TO EXPLORE THESE CANALS
2

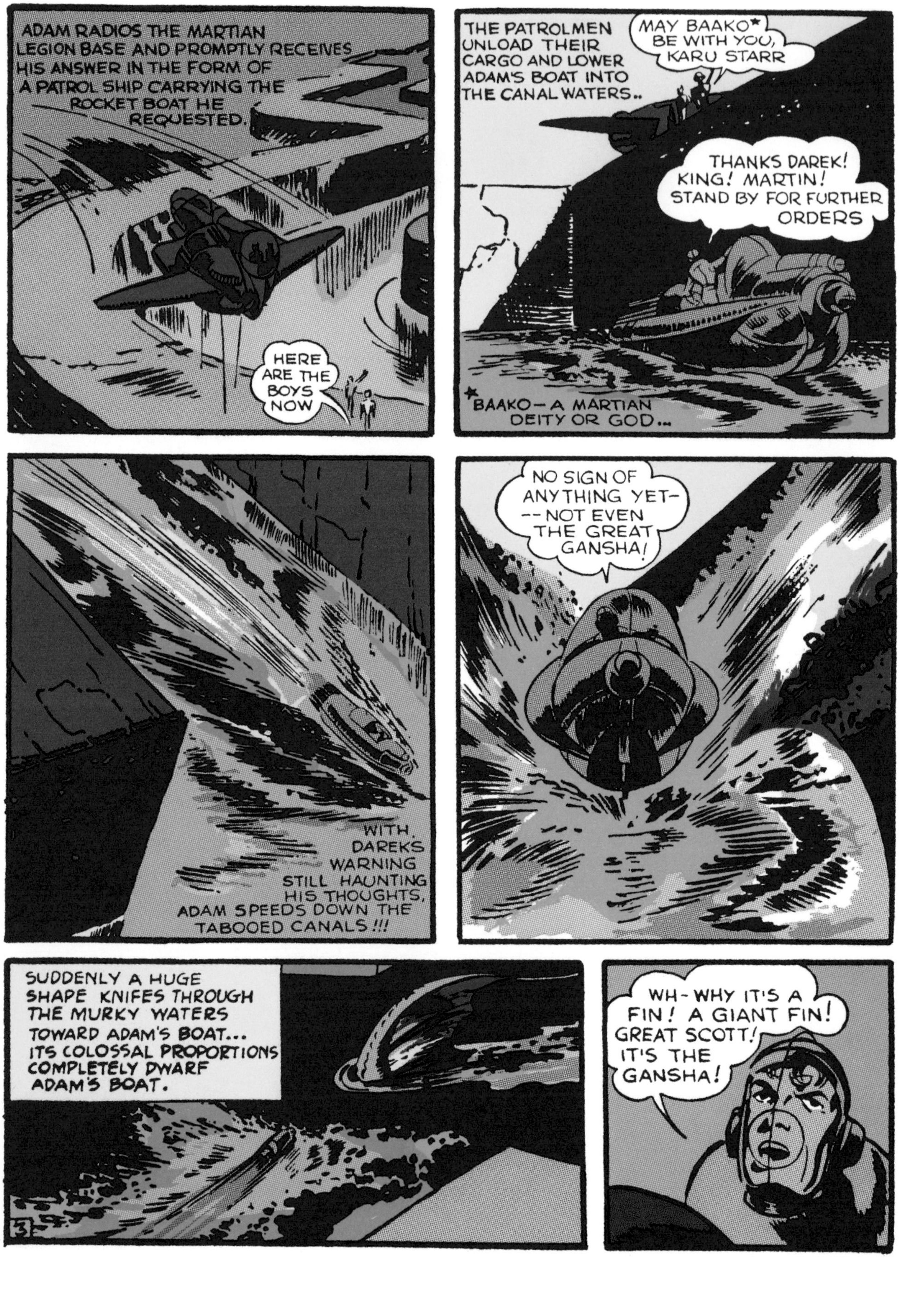
ADAM RADIOS THE MARTIAN LEGION BASE AND PROMPTLY RECEIVES HIS ANSWER IN THE FORM OF A PATROL SHIP CARRYING THE ROCKET BOAT HE REQUESTED.
HERE ARE THE BOYS NOW
THE PATROLMEN UNLOAD THEIR CARGO AND LOWER ADAM'S BOAT INTO THE CANAL WATERS..
MAY BAAKO* BE WITH YOU, KARU STARR
THANKS DAREK! KING! MARTIN! STAND BY FOR FURTHER ORDERS
*BAAKO—A MARTIAN DEITY OR GOD...
WITH DAREKS WARNING STILL HAUNTING HIS THOUGHTS, ADAM SPEEDS DOWN THE TABOOED CANALS!!!
NO SIGN OF ANYTHING YET--NOT EVEN THE GREAT GANSHA!
SUDDENLY A HUGE SHAPE KNIFES THROUGH THE MURKY WATERS TOWARD ADAM'S BOAT... ITS COLOSSAL PROPORTIONS COMPLETELY DWARF ADAM'S BOAT.
3
WH-WHY IT'S A FIN! A GIANT FIN! GREAT SCOTT! IT'S THE GANSHA!

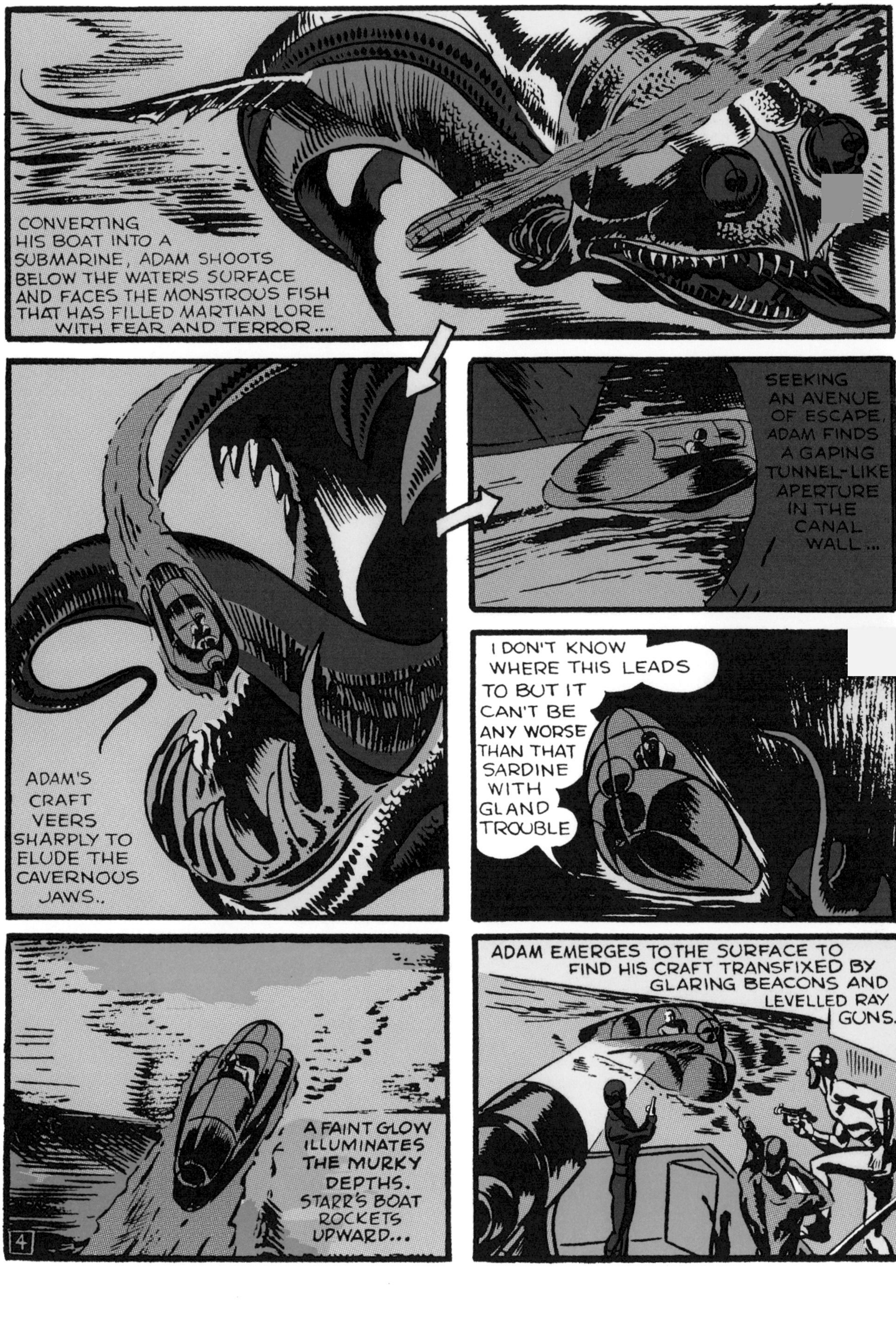
CONVERTING HIS BOAT INTO A SUBMARINE, ADAM SHOOTS BELOW THE WATER'S SURFACE AND FACES THE MONSTROUS FISH THAT HAS FILLED MARTIAN LORE WITH FEAR AND TERROR....
ADAM'S CRAFT VEERS SHARPLY TO ELUDE THE CAVERNOUS JAWS..
SEEKING AN AVENUE OF ESCAPE, ADAM FINDS A GAPING TUNNEL-LIKE APERTURE IN THE CANAL WALL...
I DON'T KNOW WHERE THIS LEADS TO BUT IT CAN'T BE ANY WORSE THAN THAT SARDINE WITH GLAND TROUBLE
A FAINT GLOW ILLUMINATES THE MURKY DEPTHS. STARR'S BOAT ROCKETS UPWARD...
4
ADAM EMERGES TO THE SURFACE TO FIND HIS CRAFT TRANSFIXED BY GLARING BEACONS AND LEVELLED RAY GUNS.

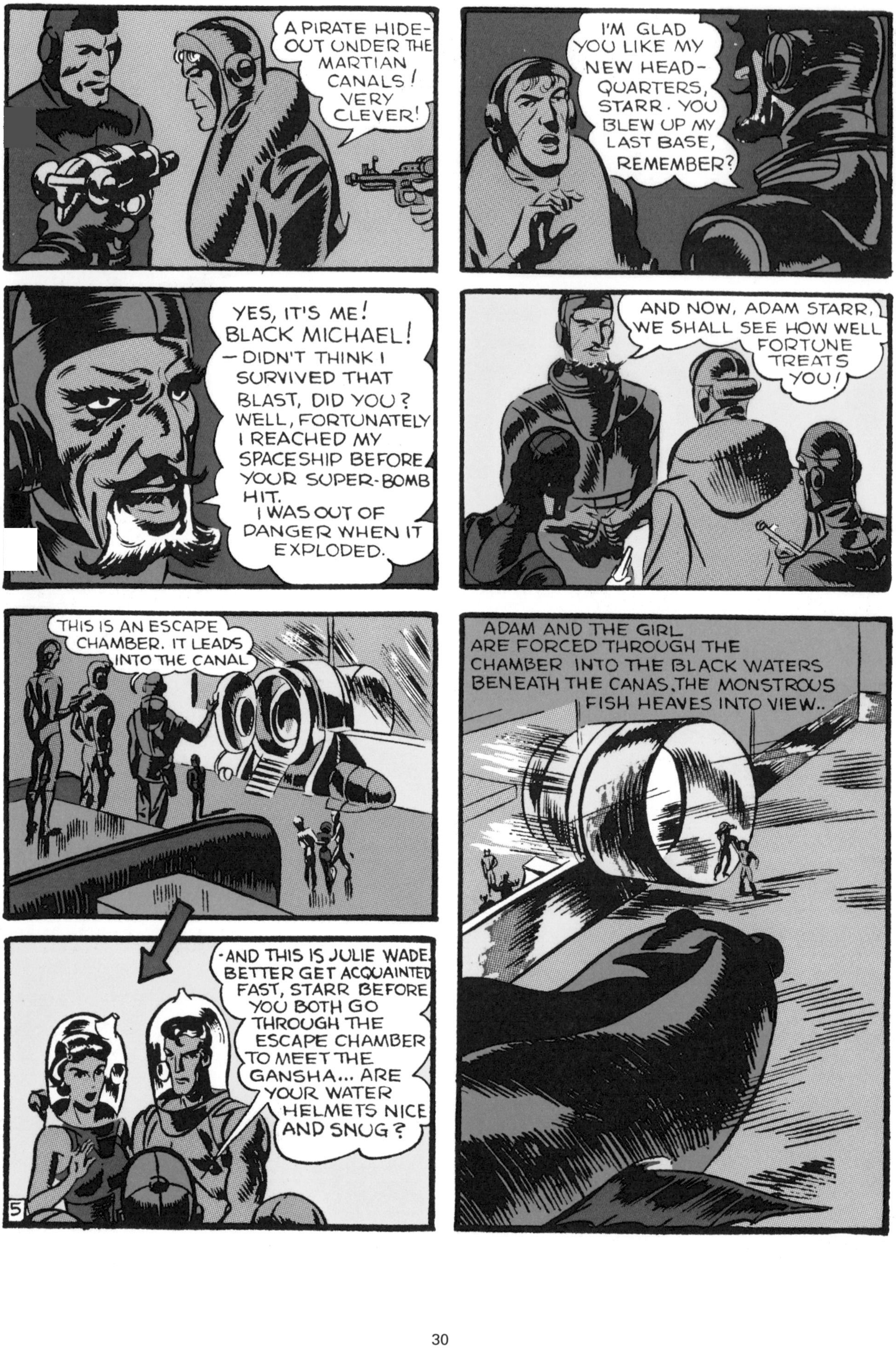
A PIRATE HIDE-OUT UNDER THE MARTIAN CANALS! VERY CLEVER!
I'M GLAD YOU LIKE MY NEW HEAD-QUARTERS, STARR. YOU BLEW UP MY LAST BASE, REMEMBER?
YES, IT'S ME! BLACK MICHAEL! — DIDN'T THINK I SURVIVED THAT BLAST, DID YOU? WELL, FORTUNATELY I REACHED MY SPACESHIP BEFORE YOUR SUPER-BOMB HIT. I WAS OUT OF DANGER WHEN IT EXPLODED.
AND NOW, ADAM STARR, WE SHALL SEE HOW WELL FORTUNE TREATS YOU!
THIS IS AN ESCAPE CHAMBER. IT LEADS INTO THE CANAL
-AND THIS IS JULIE WADE. BETTER GET ACQUAINTED FAST, STARR BEFORE YOU BOTH GO THROUGH THE ESCAPE CHAMBER TO MEET THE GANSHA... ARE YOUR WATER HELMETS NICE AND SNUG?
5
ADAM AND THE GIRL ARE FORCED THROUGH THE CHAMBER INTO THE BLACK WATERS BENEATH THE CANAS, THE MONSTROUS FISH HEAVES INTO VIEW..

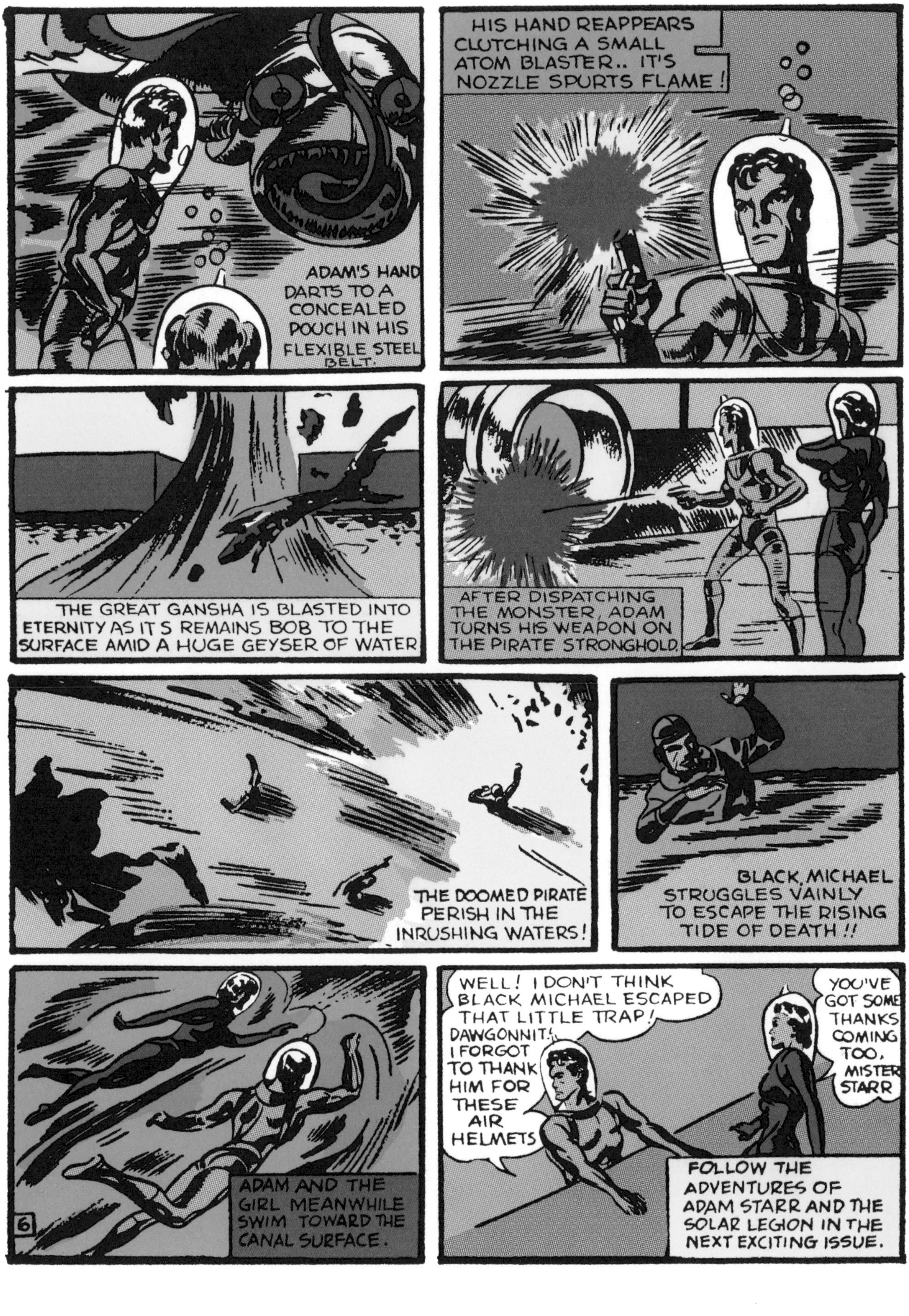
ADAM'S HAND DARTS TO A CONCEALED POUCH IN HIS FLEXIBLE STEEL BELT.
HIS HAND REAPPEARS CLUTCHING A SMALL ATOM BLASTER.. IT'S NOZZLE SPURTS FLAME!
THE GREAT GANSHA IS BLASTED INTO ETERNITY AS ITS REMAINS BOB TO THE SURFACE AMID A HUGE GEYSER OF WATER
AFTER DISPATCHING THE MONSTER, ADAM TURNS HIS WEAPON ON THE PIRATE STRONGHOLD.
THE DOOMED PIRATE PERISH IN THE INRUSHING WATERS!
BLACK MICHAEL STRUGGLES VAINLY TO ESCAPE THE RISING TIDE OF DEATH!!
6
ADAM AND THE GIRL MEANWHILE SWIM TOWARD THE CANAL SURFACE.
WELL! I DON'T THINK BLACK MICHAEL ESCAPED THAT LITTLE TRAP!
DAWGONNIT! I FORGOT TO THANK HIM FOR THESE AIR HELMETS
YOU'VE GOT SOME THANKS COMING TOO, MISTER STARR
FOLLOW THE ADVENTURES OF ADAM STARR AND THE SOLAR LEGION IN THE NEXT EXCITING ISSUE.

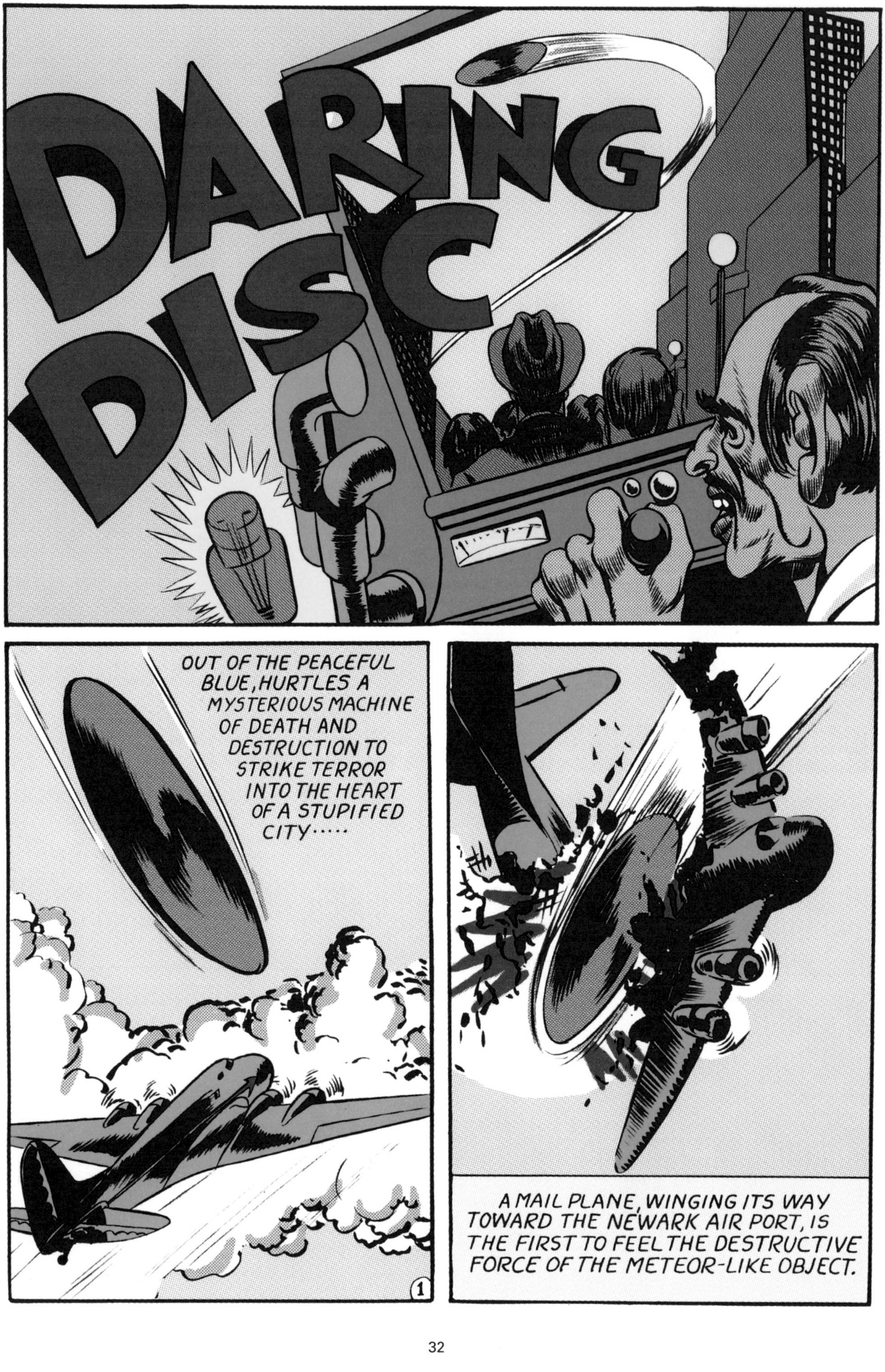
DARING DISC
OUT OF THE PEACEFUL BLUE, HURTLES A MYSTERIOUS MACHINE OF DEATH AND DESTRUCTION TO STRIKE TERROR INTO THE HEART OF A STUPIFIED CITY.....
1
A MAIL PLANE, WINGING ITS WAY TOWARD THE NEWARK AIR PORT, IS THE FIRST TO FEEL THE DESTRUCTIVE FORCE OF THE METEOR-LIKE OBJECT.

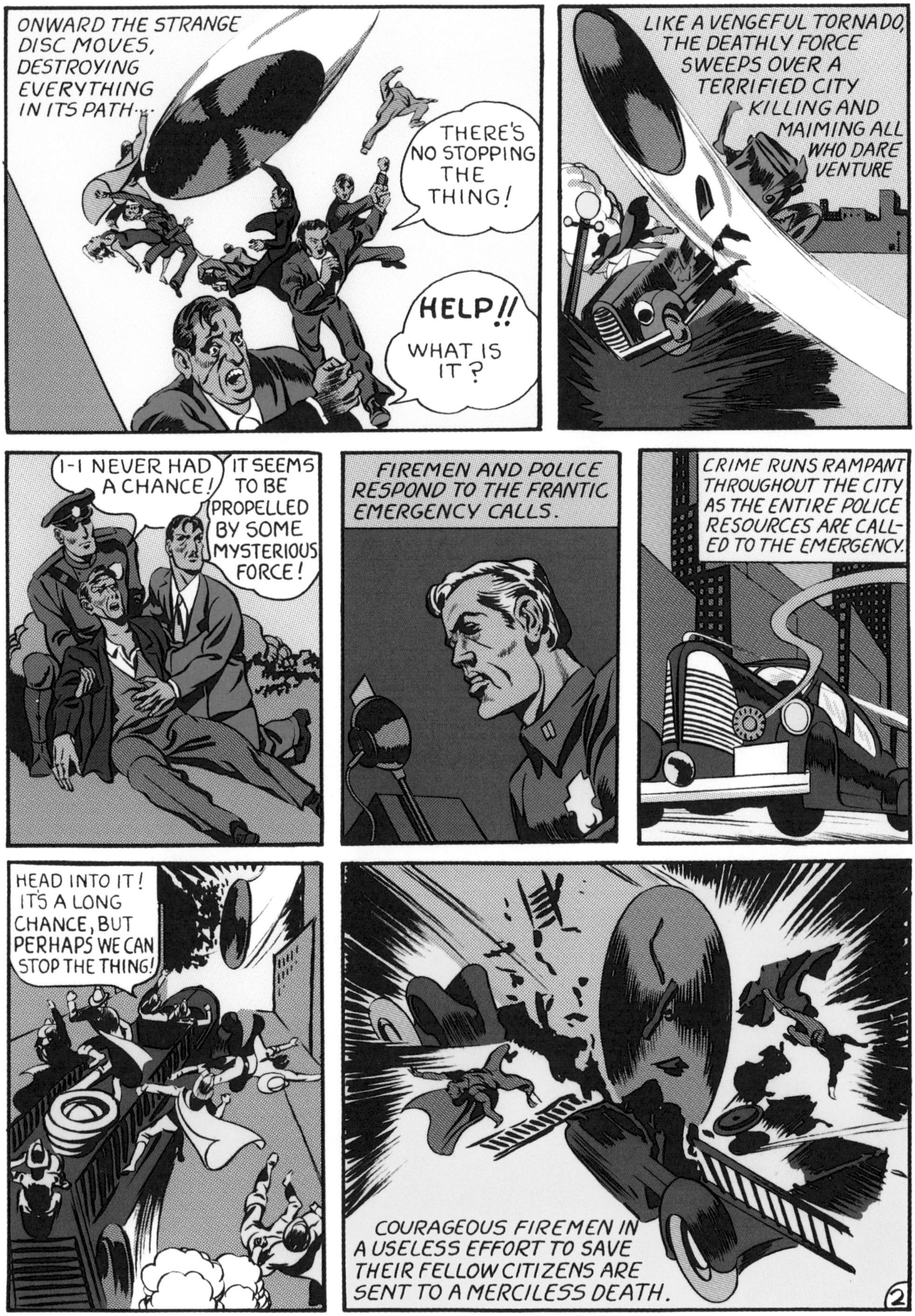

ONWARD THE STRANGE DISC MOVES, DESTROYING EVERYTHING IN ITS PATH...
THERE'S NO STOPPING THE THING!
HELP!! WHAT IS IT?
LIKE A VENGEFUL TORNADO, THE DEATHLY FORCE SWEEPS OVER A TERRIFIED CITY KILLING AND MAIMING ALL WHO DARE VENTURE
I-I NEVER HAD A CHANCE!
IT SEEMS TO BE PROPELLED BY SOME MYSTERIOUS FORCE!
FIREMEN AND POLICE RESPOND TO THE FRANTIC EMERGENCY CALLS.
CRIME RUNS RAMPANT THROUGHOUT THE CITY AS THE ENTIRE POLICE RESOURCES ARE CALL-ED TO THE EMERGENCY.
HEAD INTO IT! IT'S A LONG CHANCE, BUT PERHAPS WE CAN STOP THE THING!
COURAGEOUS FIREMEN IN A USELESS EFFORT TO SAVE THEIR FELLOW CITIZENS ARE SENT TO A MERCILESS DEATH.
2

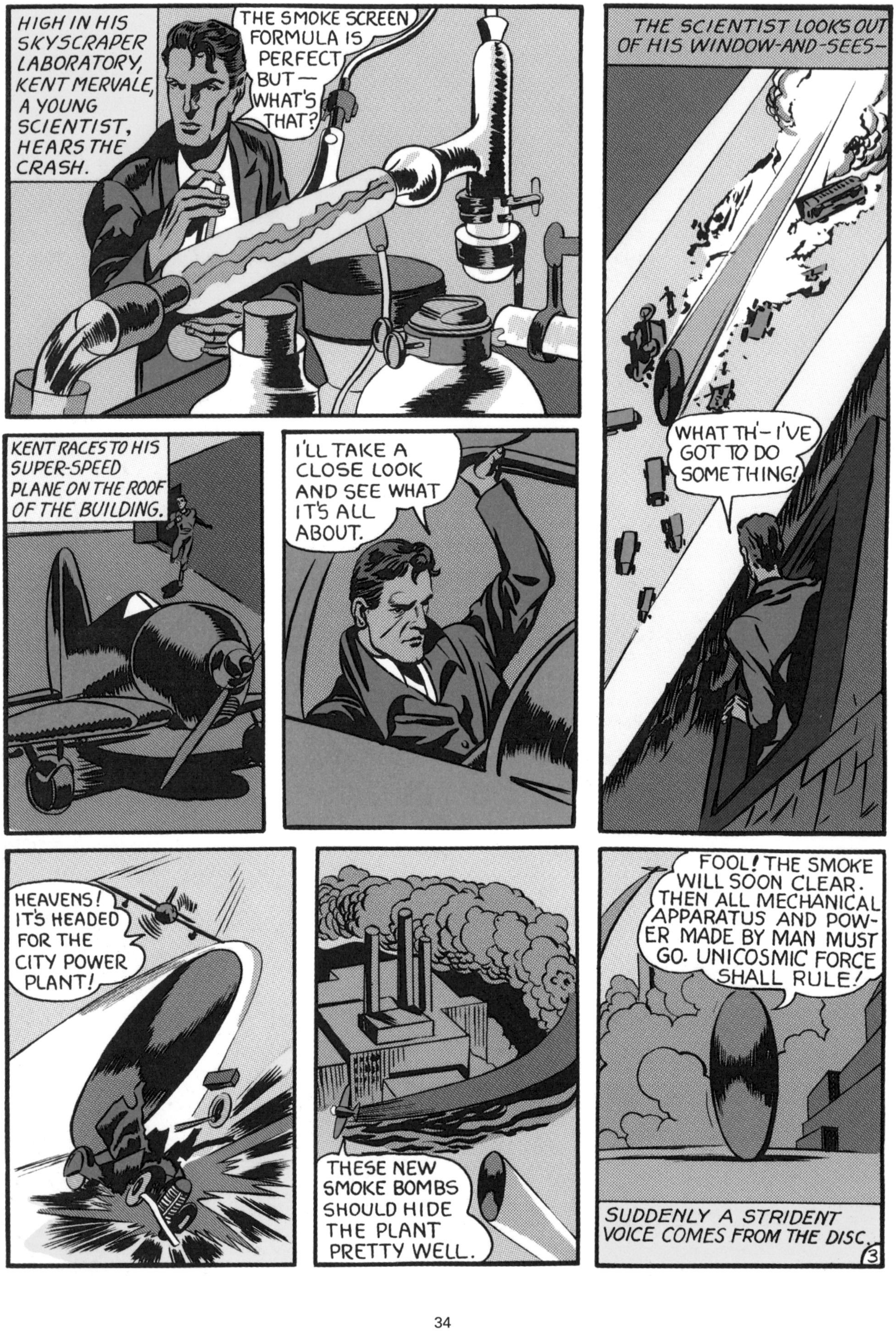
HIGH IN HIS SKYSCRAPER LABORATORY, KENT MERVALE, A YOUNG SCIENTIST, HEARS THE CRASH.
THE SMOKE SCREEN FORMULA IS PERFECT BUT — WHAT'S THAT?
THE SCIENTIST LOOKS OUT OF HIS WINDOW-AND-SEES-
WHAT TH'- I'VE GOT TO DO SOMETHING!
KENT RACES TO HIS SUPER-SPEED PLANE ON THE ROOF OF THE BUILDING.
I'LL TAKE A CLOSE LOOK AND SEE WHAT IT'S ALL ABOUT.
HEAVENS! IT'S HEADED FOR THE CITY POWER PLANT!
THESE NEW SMOKE BOMBS SHOULD HIDE THE PLANT PRETTY WELL.
FOOL! THE SMOKE WILL SOON CLEAR. THEN ALL MECHANICAL APPARATUS AND POWER MADE BY MAN MUST GO. UNICOSMIC FORCE SHALL RULE!
SUDDENLY A STRIDENT VOICE COMES FROM THE DISC.
3

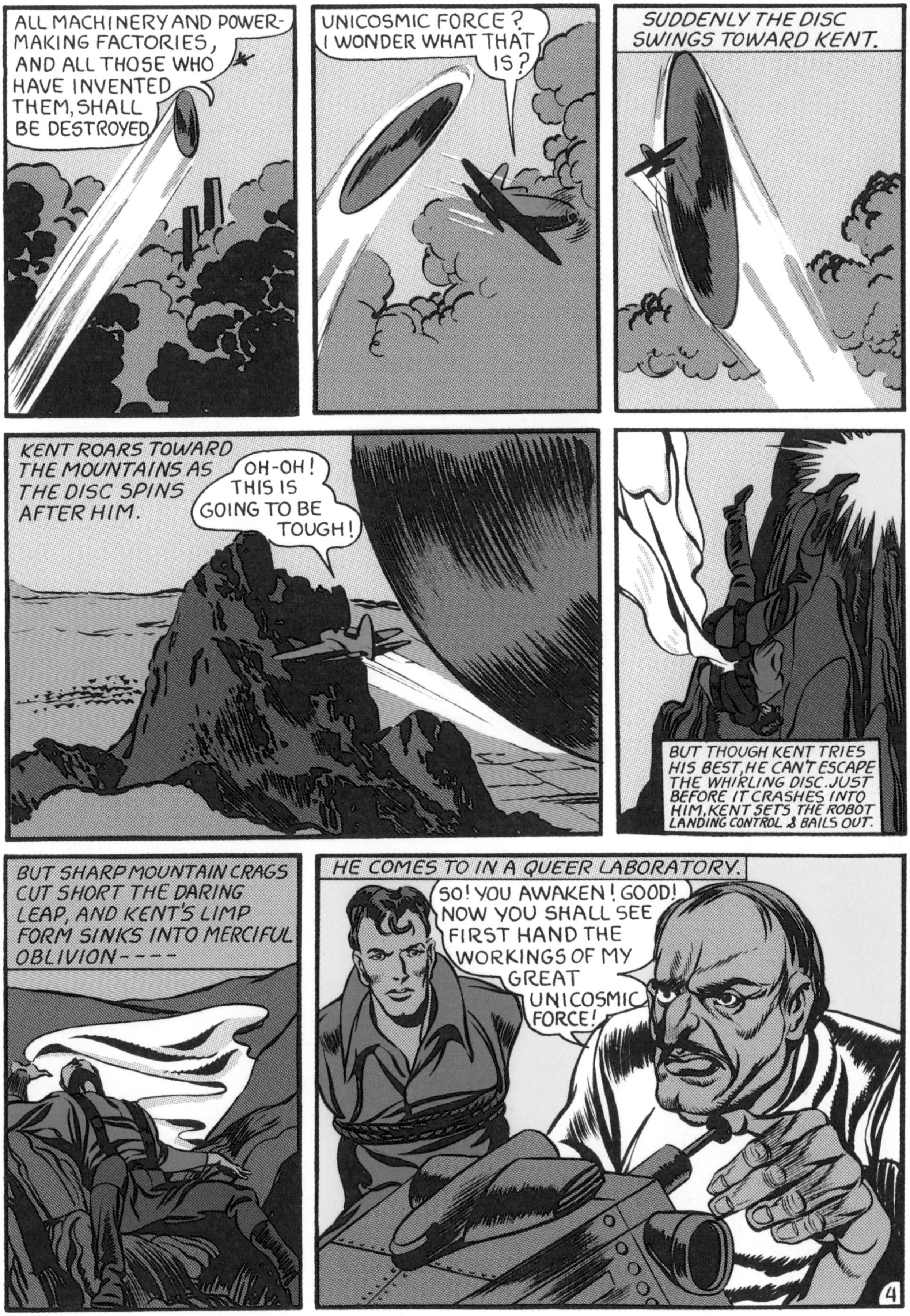
ALL MACHINERY AND POWER-MAKING FACTORIES, AND ALL THOSE WHO HAVE INVENTED THEM, SHALL BE DESTROYED
UNICOSMIC FORCE? I WONDER WHAT THAT IS?
SUDDENLY THE DISC SWINGS TOWARD KENT.
KENT ROARS TOWARD THE MOUNTAINS AS THE DISC SPINS AFTER HIM.
OH-OH! THIS IS GOING TO BE TOUGH!
BUT THOUGH KENT TRIES HIS BEST, HE CAN'T ESCAPE THE WHIRLING DISC. JUST BEFORE IT CRASHES INTO HIM, KENT SETS THE ROBOT LANDING CONTROL & BAILS OUT.
BUT SHARP MOUNTAIN CRAGS CUT SHORT THE DARING LEAP, AND KENT'S LIMP FORM SINKS INTO MERCIFUL OBLIVION----
HE COMES TO IN A QUEER LABORATORY.
SO! YOU AWAKEN! GOOD! NOW YOU SHALL SEE FIRST HAND THE WORKINGS OF MY GREAT UNICOSMIC FORCE!
4

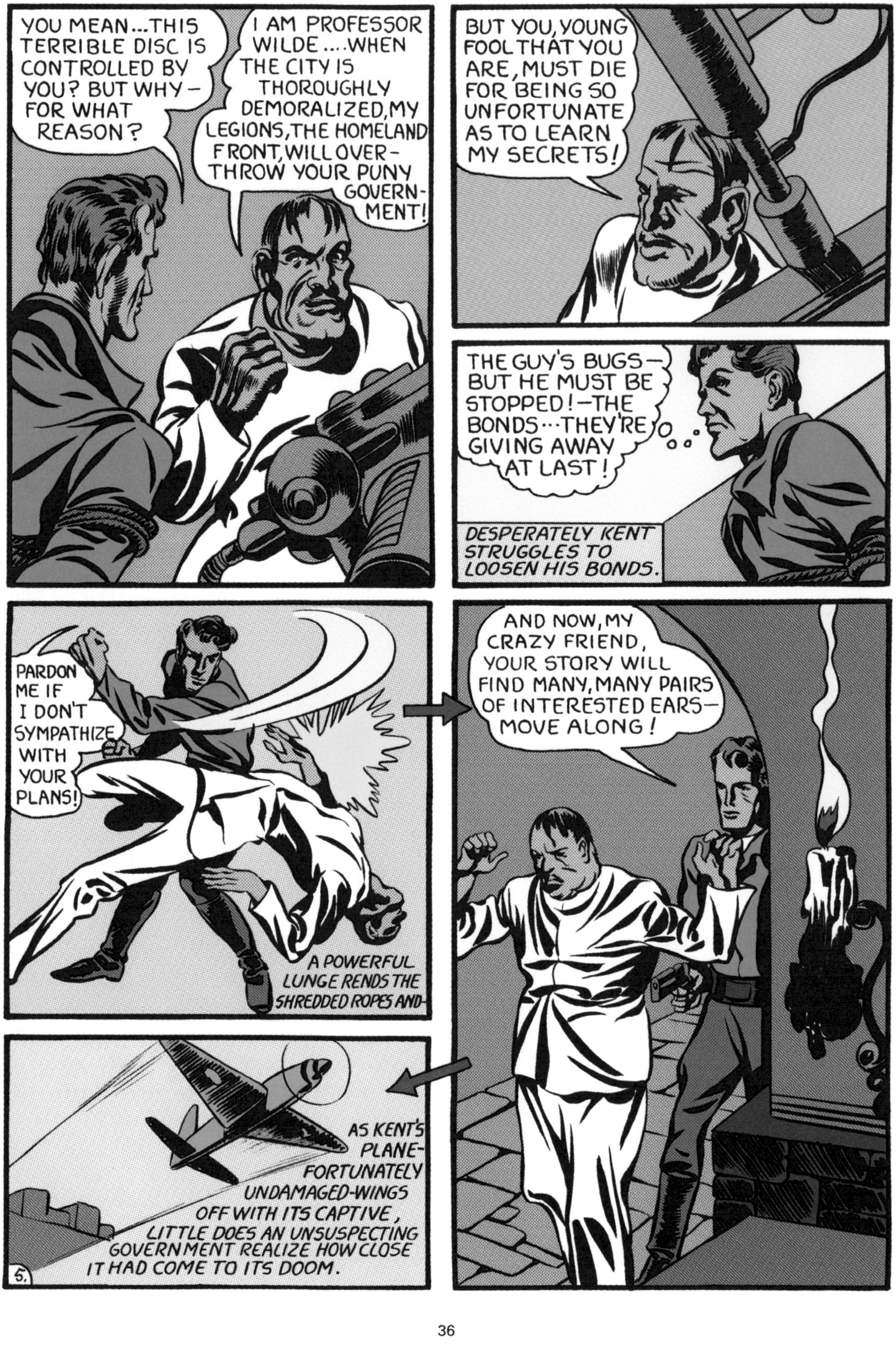
YOU MEAN...THIS TERRIBLE DISC IS CONTROLLED BY YOU? BUT WHY– FOR WHAT REASON?
I AM PROFESSOR WILDE....WHEN THE CITY IS THOROUGHLY DEMORALIZED, MY LEGIONS, THE HOMELAND FRONT, WILL OVER-THROW YOUR PUNY GOVERN-MENT!
BUT YOU, YOUNG FOOL THAT YOU ARE, MUST DIE FOR BEING SO UNFORTUNATE AS TO LEARN MY SECRETS!
THE GUY'S BUGS– BUT HE MUST BE STOPPED!–THE BONDS···THEY'RE GIVING AWAY AT LAST!
DESPERATELY KENT STRUGGLES TO LOOSEN HIS BONDS.
PARDON ME IF I DON'T SYMPATHIZE WITH YOUR PLANS!
A POWERFUL LUNGE RENDS THE SHREDDED ROPES AND–
AND NOW, MY CRAZY FRIEND, YOUR STORY WILL FIND MANY, MANY PAIRS OF INTERESTED EARS– MOVE ALONG!
AS KENT'S PLANE– FORTUNATELY UNDAMAGED–WINGS OFF WITH ITS CAPTIVE, LITTLE DOES AN UNSUSPECTING GOVERNMENT REALIZE HOW CLOSE IT HAD COME TO ITS DOOM.
5.

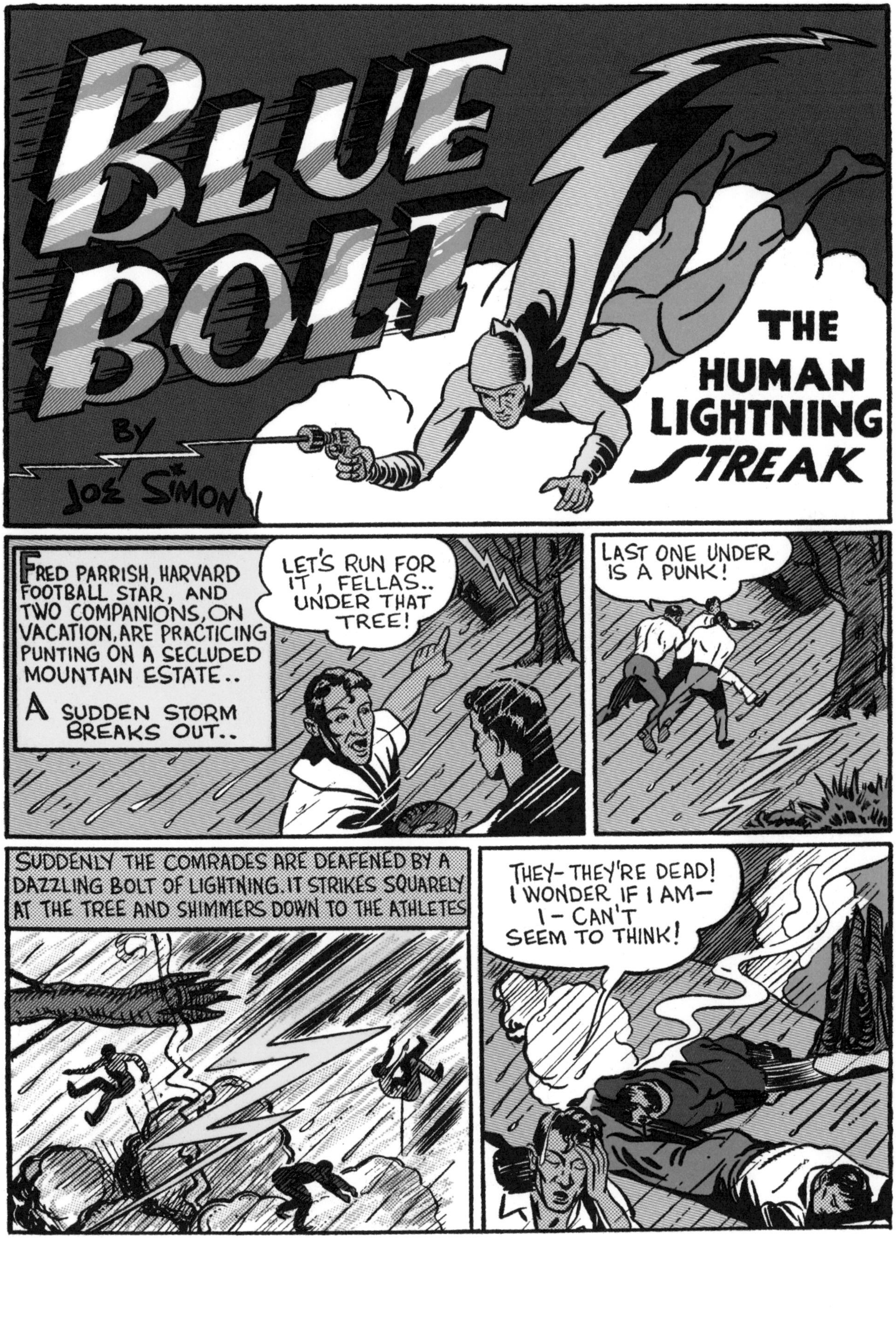
BLUE BOLT
BY JOE SIMON
THE HUMAN LIGHTNING STREAK
FRED PARRISH, HARVARD FOOTBALL STAR, AND TWO COMPANIONS, ON VACATION, ARE PRACTICING PUNTING ON A SECLUDED MOUNTAIN ESTATE.. A SUDDEN STORM BREAKS OUT..
LET'S RUN FOR IT, FELLAS.. UNDER THAT TREE!
LAST ONE UNDER IS A PUNK!
SUDDENLY THE COMRADES ARE DEAFENED BY A DAZZLING BOLT OF LIGHTNING. IT STRIKES SQUARELY AT THE TREE AND SHIMMERS DOWN TO THE ATHLETES
THEY- THEY'RE DEAD! I WONDER IF I AM- I- CAN'T SEEM TO THINK!

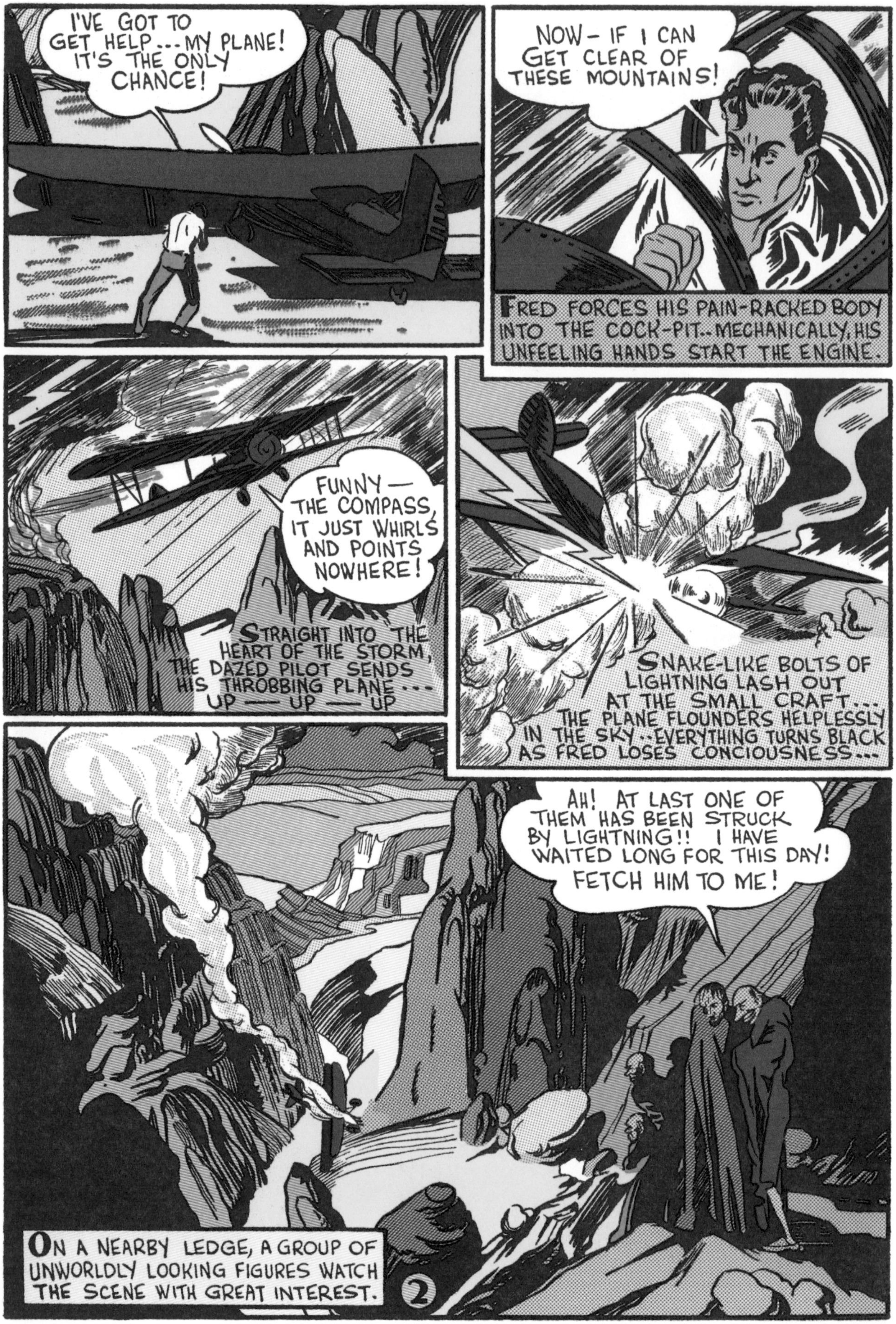
I'VE GOT TO GET HELP---MY PLANE! IT'S THE ONLY CHANCE!
NOW- IF I CAN GET CLEAR OF THESE MOUNTAINS!
FRED FORCES HIS PAIN-RACKED BODY INTO THE COCK-PIT..MECHANICALLY, HIS UNFEELING HANDS START THE ENGINE.
FUNNY— THE COMPASS, IT JUST WHIRLS AND POINTS NOWHERE!
STRAIGHT INTO THE HEART OF THE STORM, THE DAZED PILOT SENDS HIS THROBBING PLANE--- UP — UP — UP
SNAKE-LIKE BOLTS OF LIGHTNING LASH OUT AT THE SMALL CRAFT... THE PLANE FLOUNDERS HELPLESSLY IN THE SKY..EVERYTHING TURNS BLACK AS FRED LOSES CONCIOUSNESS---
AH! AT LAST ONE OF THEM HAS BEEN STRUCK BY LIGHTNING!! I HAVE WAITED LONG FOR THIS DAY! FETCH HIM TO ME!
ON A NEARBY LEDGE, A GROUP OF UNWORLDLY LOOKING FIGURES WATCH THE SCENE WITH GREAT INTEREST.
2

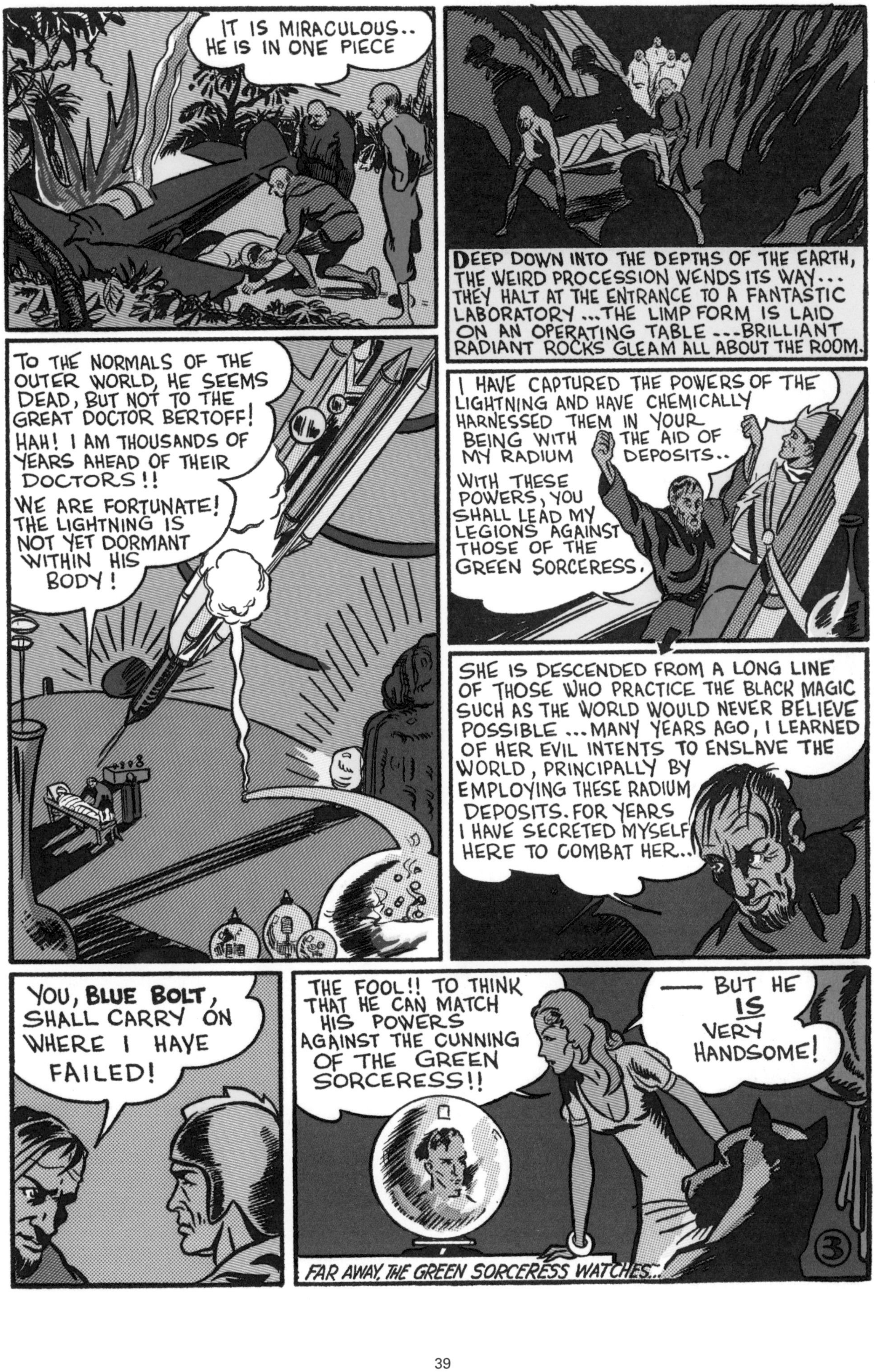
IT IS MIRACULOUS.. HE IS IN ONE PIECE
DEEP DOWN INTO THE DEPTHS OF THE EARTH, THE WEIRD PROCESSION WENDS ITS WAY... THEY HALT AT THE ENTRANCE TO A FANTASTIC LABORATORY ...THE LIMP FORM IS LAID ON AN OPERATING TABLE ---BRILLIANT RADIANT ROCKS GLEAM ALL ABOUT THE ROOM.
TO THE NORMALS OF THE OUTER WORLD, HE SEEMS DEAD, BUT NOT TO THE GREAT DOCTOR BERTOFF! HAH! I AM THOUSANDS OF YEARS AHEAD OF THEIR DOCTORS!! WE ARE FORTUNATE! THE LIGHTNING IS NOT YET DORMANT WITHIN HIS BODY!
I HAVE CAPTURED THE POWERS OF THE LIGHTNING AND HAVE CHEMICALLY HARNESSED THEM IN YOUR BEING WITH THE AID OF MY RADIUM DEPOSITS.. WITH THESE POWERS, YOU SHALL LEAD MY LEGIONS AGAINST THOSE OF THE GREEN SORCERESS.
SHE IS DESCENDED FROM A LONG LINE OF THOSE WHO PRACTICE THE BLACK MAGIC SUCH AS THE WORLD WOULD NEVER BELIEVE POSSIBLE ...MANY YEARS AGO, I LEARNED OF HER EVIL INTENTS TO ENSLAVE THE WORLD, PRINCIPALLY BY EMPLOYING THESE RADIUM DEPOSITS. FOR YEARS I HAVE SECRETED MYSELF HERE TO COMBAT HER..
YOU, BLUE BOLT, SHALL CARRY ON WHERE I HAVE FAILED!
THE FOOL!! TO THINK THAT HE CAN MATCH HIS POWERS AGAINST THE CUNNING OF THE GREEN SORCERESS!!
— BUT HE IS VERY HANDSOME!
3
FAR AWAY, THE GREEN SORCERESS WATCHES..

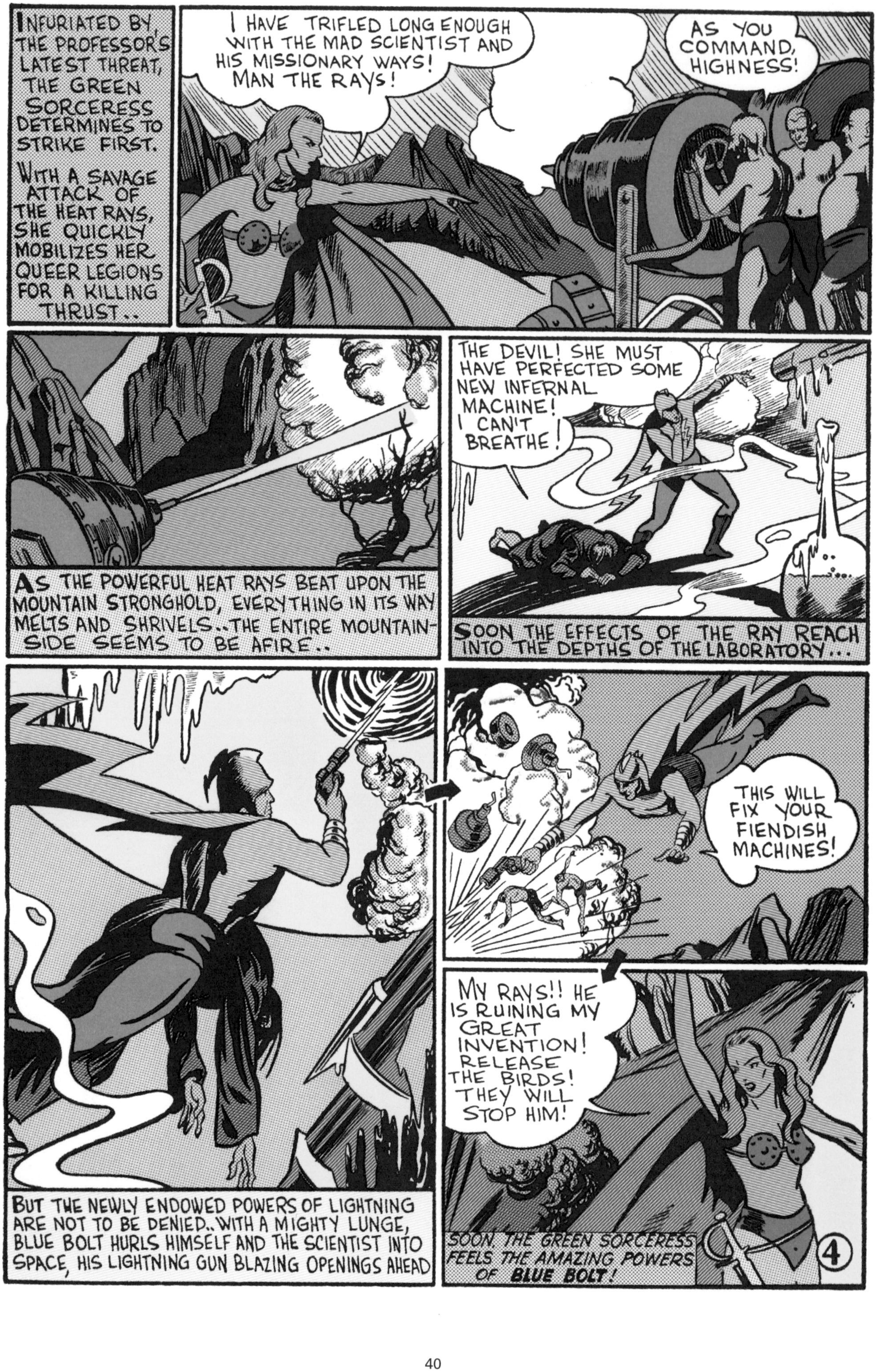
INFURIATED BY THE PROFESSOR'S LATEST THREAT, THE GREEN SORCERESS DETERMINES TO STRIKE FIRST.
WITH A SAVAGE ATTACK OF THE HEAT RAYS, SHE QUICKLY MOBILIZES HER QUEER LEGIONS FOR A KILLING THRUST..
I HAVE TRIFLED LONG ENOUGH WITH THE MAD SCIENTIST AND HIS MISSIONARY WAYS! MAN THE RAYS!
AS YOU COMMAND, HIGHNESS!
AS THE POWERFUL HEAT RAYS BEAT UPON THE MOUNTAIN STRONGHOLD, EVERYTHING IN ITS WAY MELTS AND SHRIVELS..THE ENTIRE MOUNTAIN-SIDE SEEMS TO BE AFIRE..
THE DEVIL! SHE MUST HAVE PERFECTED SOME NEW INFERNAL MACHINE! I CAN'T BREATHE!
SOON THE EFFECTS OF THE RAY REACH INTO THE DEPTHS OF THE LABORATORY...
BUT THE NEWLY ENDOWED POWERS OF LIGHTNING ARE NOT TO BE DENIED.. WITH A MIGHTY LUNGE, BLUE BOLT HURLS HIMSELF AND THE SCIENTIST INTO SPACE, HIS LIGHTNING GUN BLAZING OPENINGS AHEAD
THIS WILL FIX YOUR FIENDISH MACHINES!
MY RAYS!! HE IS RUINING MY GREAT INVENTION! RELEASE THE BIRDS! THEY WILL STOP HIM!
SOON, THE GREEN SORCERESS FEELS THE AMAZING POWERS OF BLUE BOLT!
4

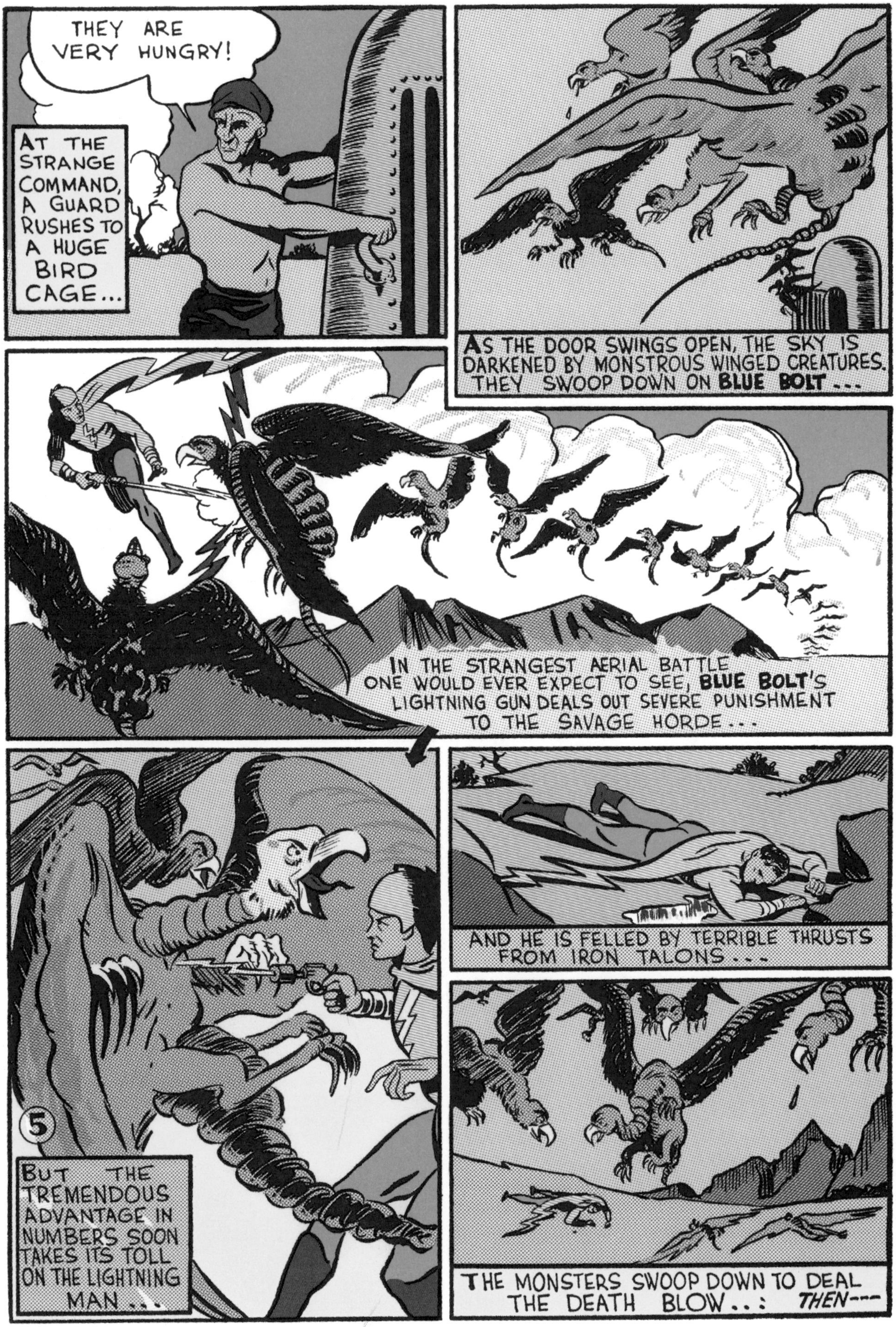
THEY ARE VERY HUNGRY!
AT THE STRANGE COMMAND, A GUARD RUSHES TO A HUGE BIRD CAGE...
AS THE DOOR SWINGS OPEN, THE SKY IS DARKENED BY MONSTROUS WINGED CREATURES. THEY SWOOP DOWN ON BLUE BOLT...
IN THE STRANGEST AERIAL BATTLE ONE WOULD EVER EXPECT TO SEE, BLUE BOLT'S LIGHTNING GUN DEALS OUT SEVERE PUNISHMENT TO THE SAVAGE HORDE...
5
BUT THE TREMENDOUS ADVANTAGE IN NUMBERS SOON TAKES ITS TOLL ON THE LIGHTNING MAN...
AND HE IS FELLED BY TERRIBLE THRUSTS FROM IRON TALONS...
THE MONSTERS SWOOP DOWN TO DEAL THE DEATH BLOW..: THEN---

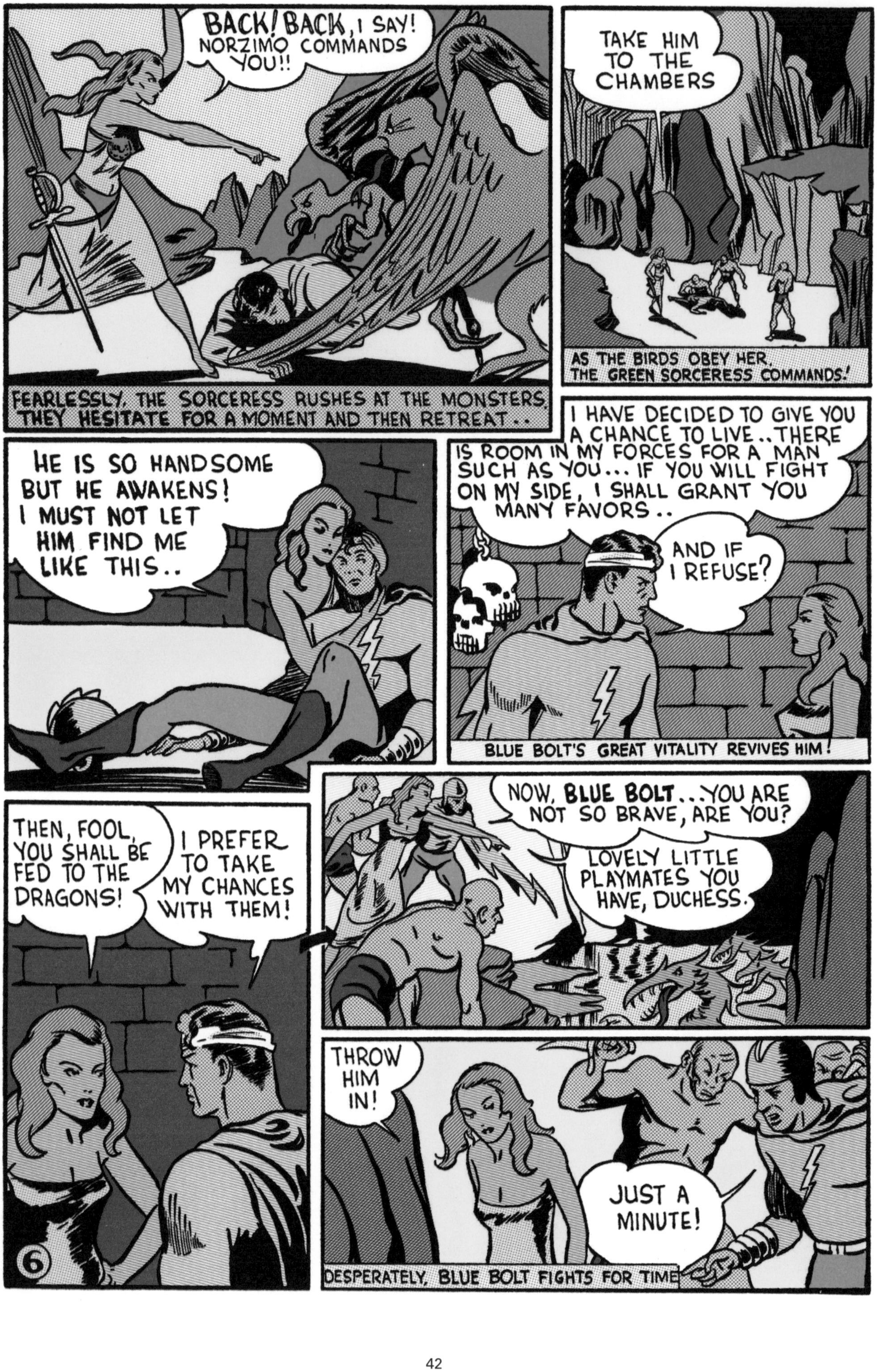
BACK! BACK, I SAY! NORZIMO COMMANDS YOU!!
FEARLESSLY, THE SORCERESS RUSHES AT THE MONSTERS, THEY HESITATE FOR A MOMENT AND THEN RETREAT..
TAKE HIM TO THE CHAMBERS
AS THE BIRDS OBEY HER, THE GREEN SORCERESS COMMANDS!
HE IS SO HANDSOME BUT HE AWAKENS! I MUST NOT LET HIM FIND ME LIKE THIS..
I HAVE DECIDED TO GIVE YOU A CHANCE TO LIVE.. THERE IS ROOM IN MY FORCES FOR A MAN SUCH AS YOU... IF YOU WILL FIGHT ON MY SIDE, I SHALL GRANT YOU MANY FAVORS..
AND IF I REFUSE?
BLUE BOLT'S GREAT VITALITY REVIVES HIM!
THEN, FOOL, YOU SHALL BE FED TO THE DRAGONS!
I PREFER TO TAKE MY CHANCES WITH THEM!
6
NOW, BLUE BOLT... YOU ARE NOT SO BRAVE, ARE YOU?
LOVELY LITTLE PLAYMATES YOU HAVE, DUCHESS.
THROW HIM IN!
JUST A MINUTE!
DESPERATELY, BLUE BOLT FIGHTS FOR TIME

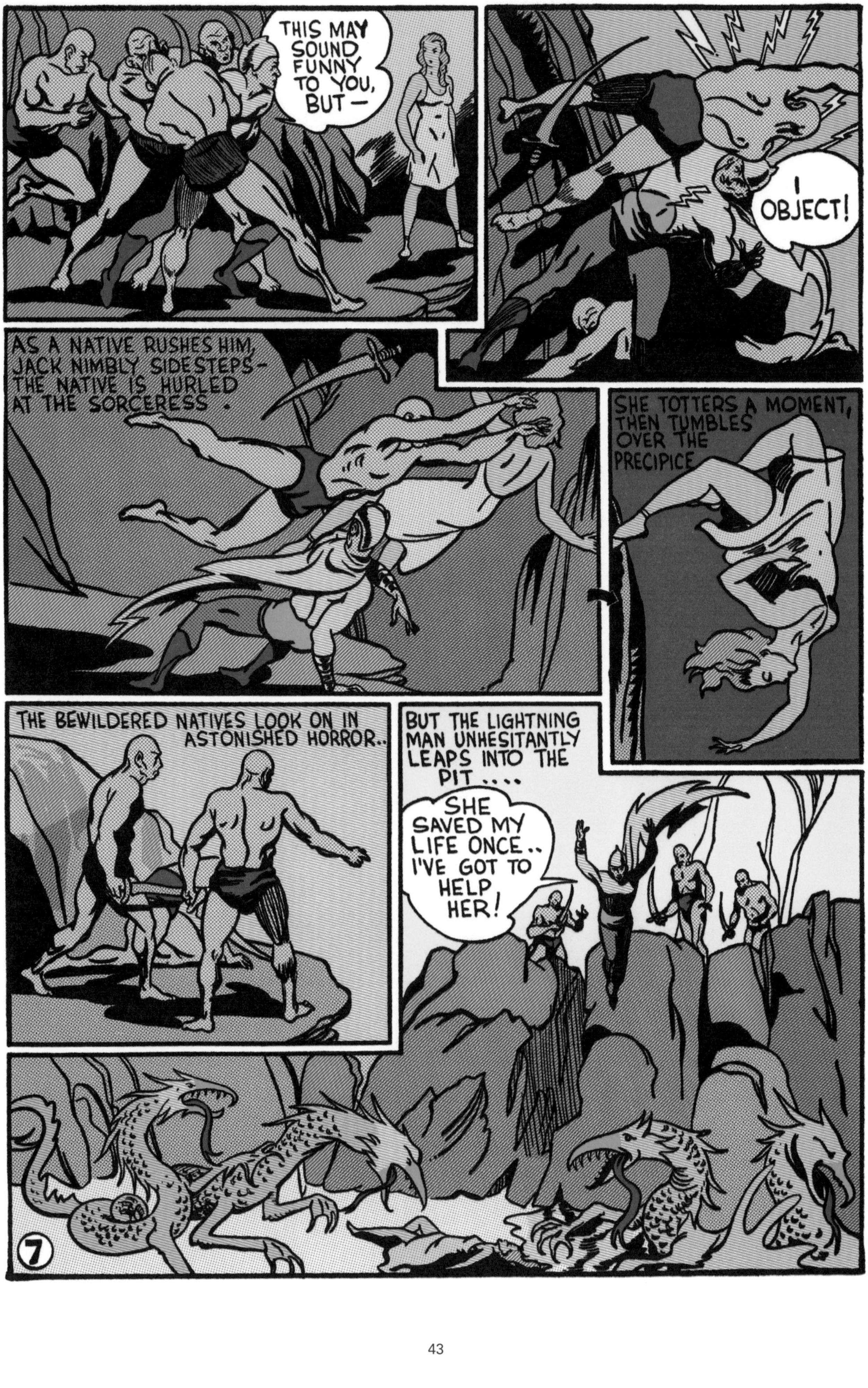
THIS MAY SOUND FUNNY TO YOU, BUT—
I OBJECT!
AS A NATIVE RUSHES HIM, JACK NIMBLY SIDESTEPS- THE NATIVE IS HURLED AT THE SORCERESS.
SHE TOTTERS A MOMENT, THEN TUMBLES OVER THE PRECIPICE
THE BEWILDERED NATIVES LOOK ON IN ASTONISHED HORROR..
BUT THE LIGHTNING MAN UNHESITANTLY LEAPS INTO THE PIT....
SHE SAVED MY LIFE ONCE.. I'VE GOT TO HELP HER!
7

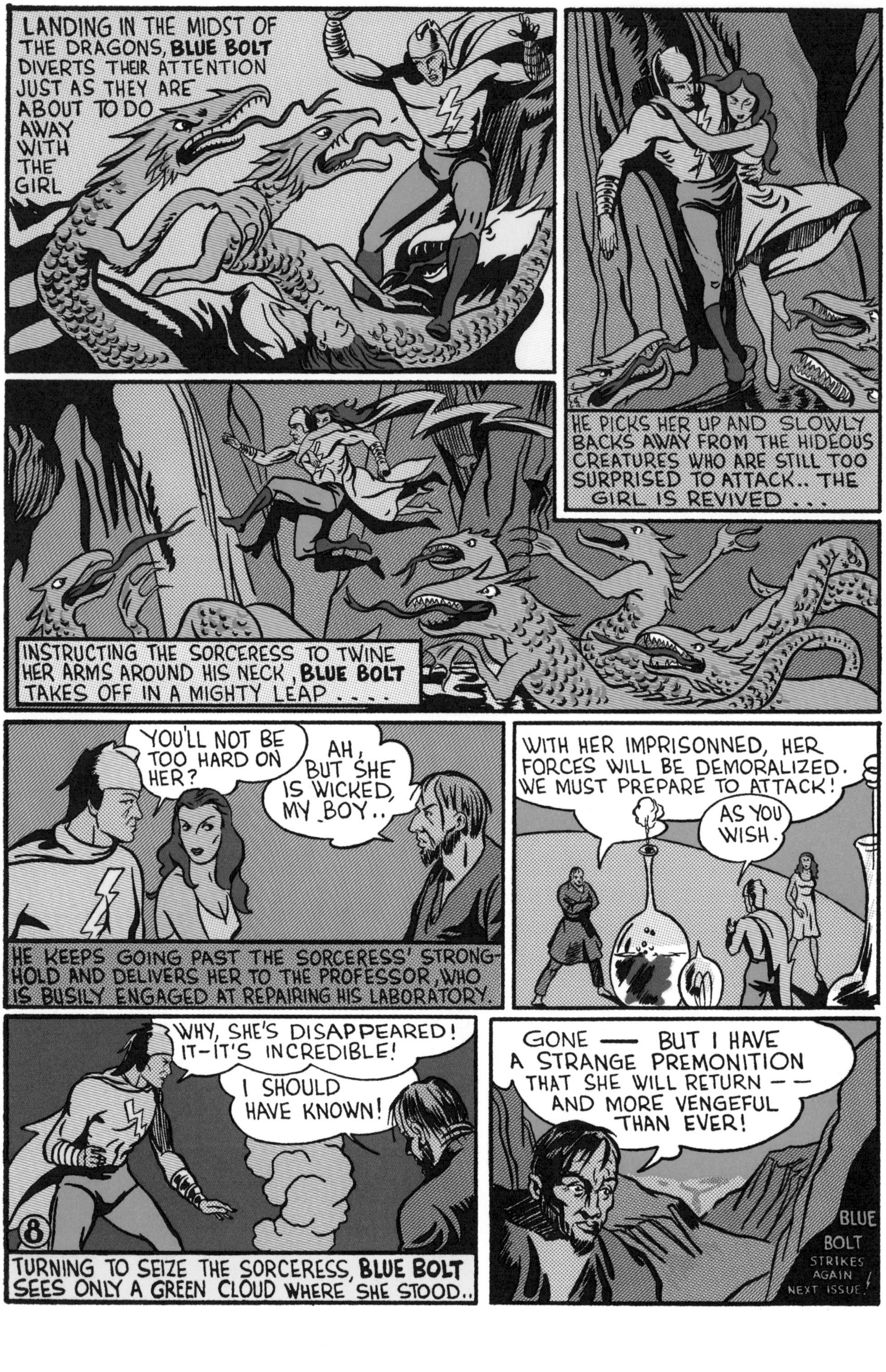
LANDING IN THE MIDST OF THE DRAGONS, BLUE BOLT DIVERTS THEIR ATTENTION JUST AS THEY ARE ABOUT TO DO AWAY WITH THE GIRL
HE PICKS HER UP AND SLOWLY BACKS AWAY FROM THE HIDEOUS CREATURES WHO ARE STILL TOO SURPRISED TO ATTACK.. THE GIRL IS REVIVED . . .
INSTRUCTING THE SORCERESS TO TWINE HER ARMS AROUND HIS NECK, BLUE BOLT TAKES OFF IN A MIGHTY LEAP . . . .
YOU'LL NOT BE TOO HARD ON HER?
AH, BUT SHE IS WICKED, MY BOY..
HE KEEPS GOING PAST THE SORCERESS' STRONGHOLD AND DELIVERS HER TO THE PROFESSOR, WHO IS BUSILY ENGAGED AT REPAIRING HIS LABORATORY.
WITH HER IMPRISONNED, HER FORCES WILL BE DEMORALIZED. WE MUST PREPARE TO ATTACK!
AS YOU WISH.
8
WHY, SHE'S DISAPPEARED! IT-IT'S INCREDIBLE!
I SHOULD HAVE KNOWN!
TURNING TO SEIZE THE SORCERESS, BLUE BOLT SEES ONLY A GREEN CLOUD WHERE SHE STOOD..
GONE — BUT I HAVE A STRANGE PREMONITION THAT SHE WILL RETURN — — AND MORE VENGEFUL THAN EVER!
BLUE BOLT STRIKES AGAIN NEXT ISSUE!

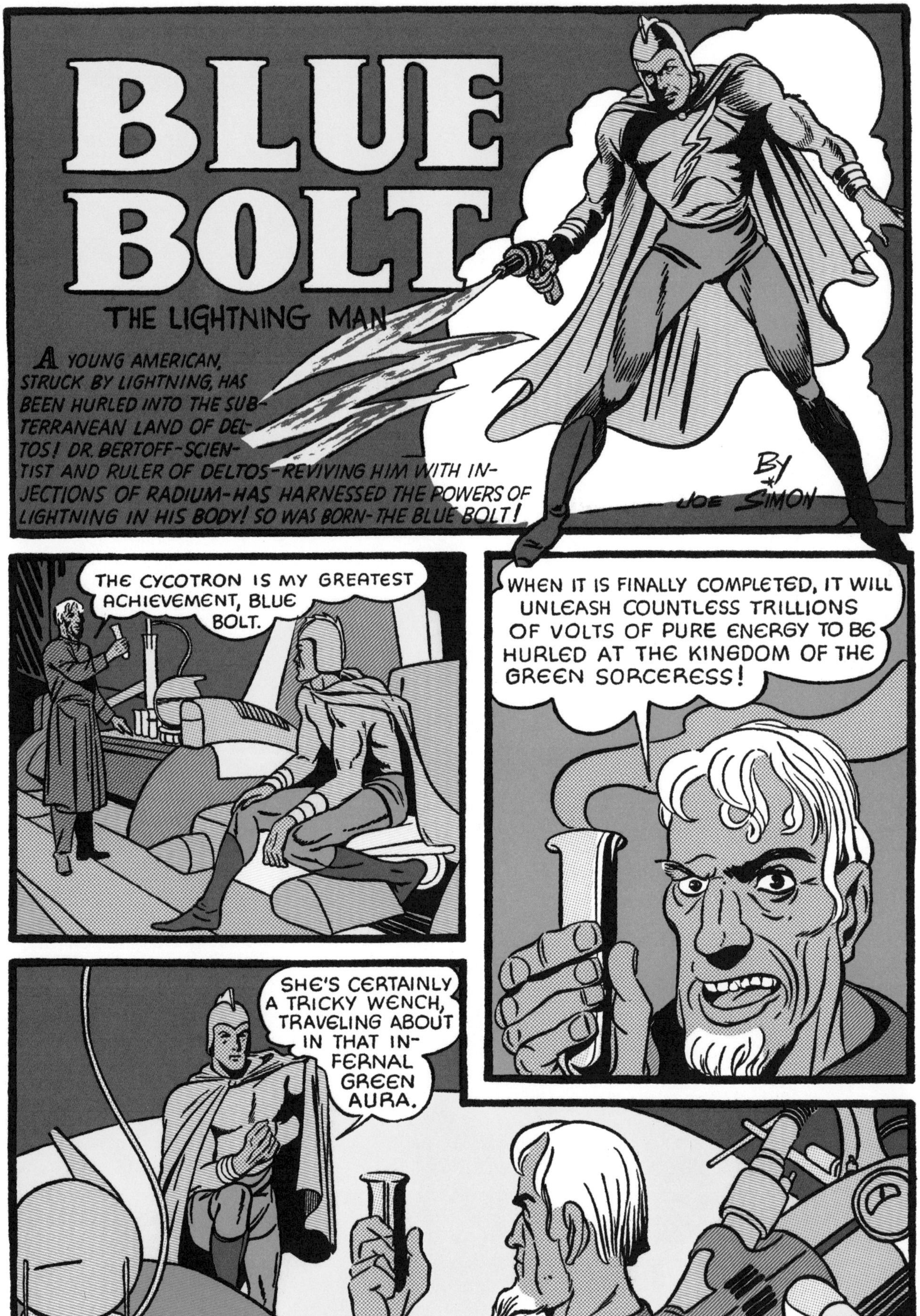
BLUE BOLT
THE LIGHTNING MAN
A YOUNG AMERICAN, STRUCK BY LIGHTNING, HAS BEEN HURLED INTO THE SUBTERRANEAN LAND OF DELTOS! DR. BERTOFF-SCIENTIST AND RULER OF DELTOS-REVIVING HIM WITH INJECTIONS OF RADIUM-HAS HARNESSED THE POWERS OF LIGHTNING IN HIS BODY! SO WAS BORN-THE BLUE BOLT!
BY JOE SIMON
THE CYCOTRON IS MY GREATEST ACHIEVEMENT, BLUE BOLT.
WHEN IT IS FINALLY COMPLETED, IT WILL UNLEASH COUNTLESS TRILLIONS OF VOLTS OF PURE ENERGY TO BE HURLED AT THE KINGDOM OF THE GREEN SORCERESS!
SHE'S CERTAINLY A TRICKY WENCH, TRAVELING ABOUT IN THAT INFERNAL GREEN AURA.

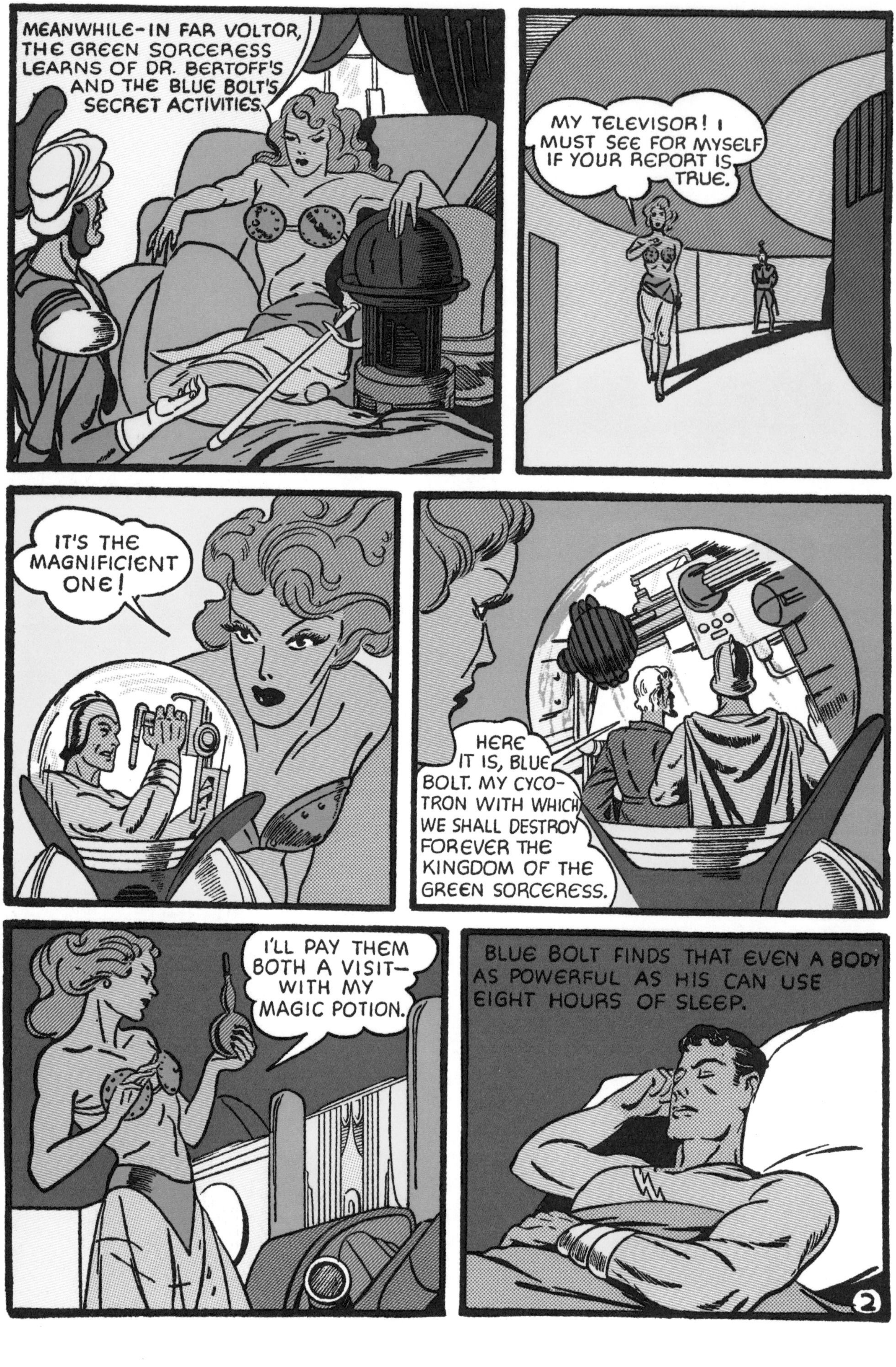
MEANWHILE-IN FAR VOLTOR, THE GREEN SORCERESS LEARNS OF DR. BERTOFF'S AND THE BLUE BOLT'S SECRET ACTIVITIES.
MY TELEVISOR! I MUST SEE FOR MYSELF IF YOUR REPORT IS TRUE.
IT'S THE MAGNIFICIENT ONE!
HERE IT IS, BLUE BOLT. MY CYCO-TRON WITH WHICH WE SHALL DESTROY FOREVER THE KINGDOM OF THE GREEN SORCERESS.
I'LL PAY THEM BOTH A VISIT- WITH MY MAGIC POTION.
BLUE BOLT FINDS THAT EVEN A BODY AS POWERFUL AS HIS CAN USE EIGHT HOURS OF SLEEP.
2

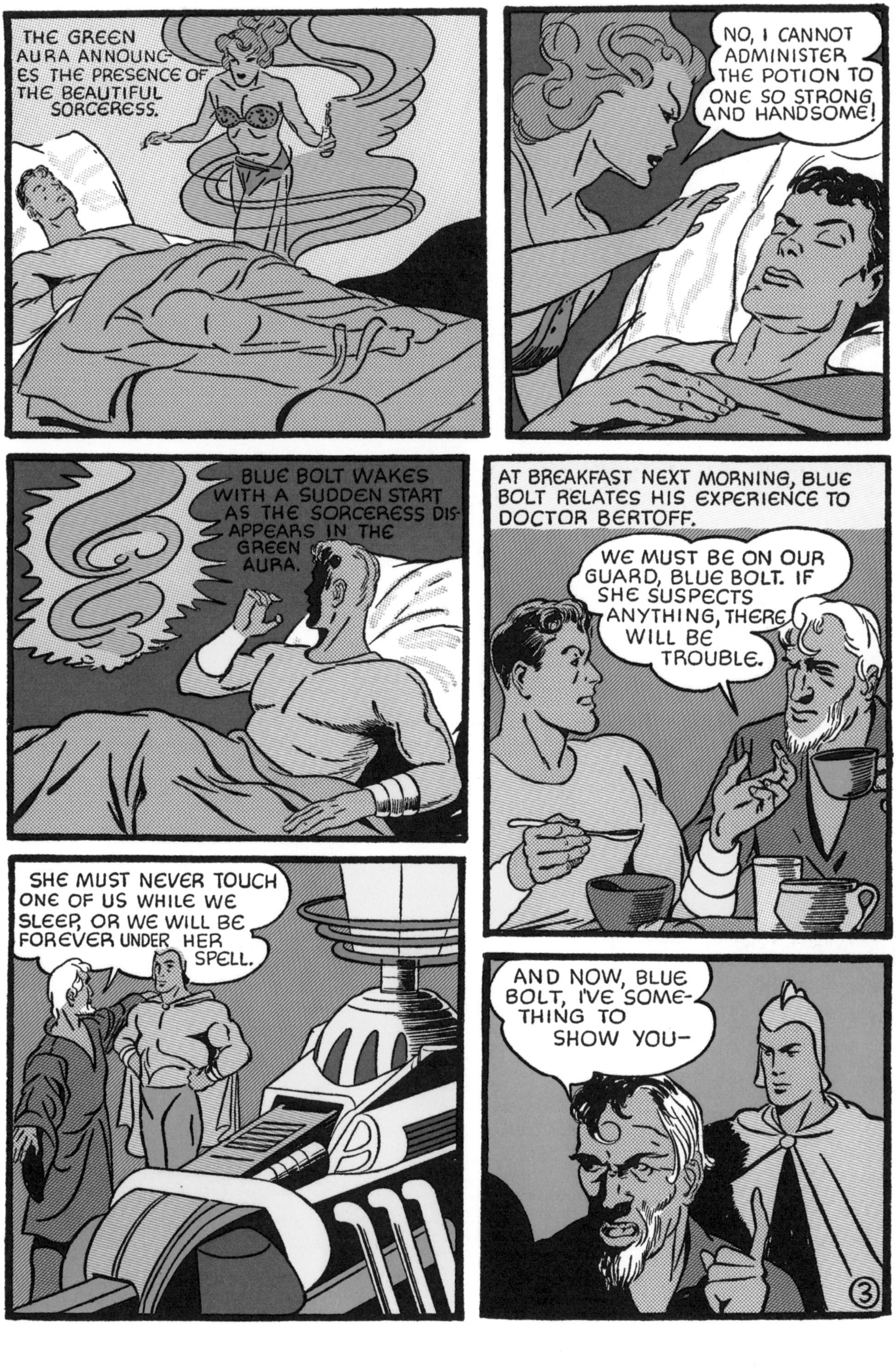
THE GREEN AURA ANNOUNCES THE PRESENCE OF THE BEAUTIFUL SORCERESS.
NO, I CANNOT ADMINISTER THE POTION TO ONE SO STRONG AND HANDSOME!
BLUE BOLT WAKES WITH A SUDDEN START AS THE SORCERESS DISAPPEARS IN THE GREEN AURA.
AT BREAKFAST NEXT MORNING, BLUE BOLT RELATES HIS EXPERIENCE TO DOCTOR BERTOFF.
WE MUST BE ON OUR GUARD, BLUE BOLT. IF SHE SUSPECTS ANYTHING, THERE WILL BE TROUBLE.
SHE MUST NEVER TOUCH ONE OF US WHILE WE SLEEP, OR WE WILL BE FOREVER UNDER HER SPELL.
AND NOW, BLUE BOLT, I'VE SOMETHING TO SHOW YOU—
3

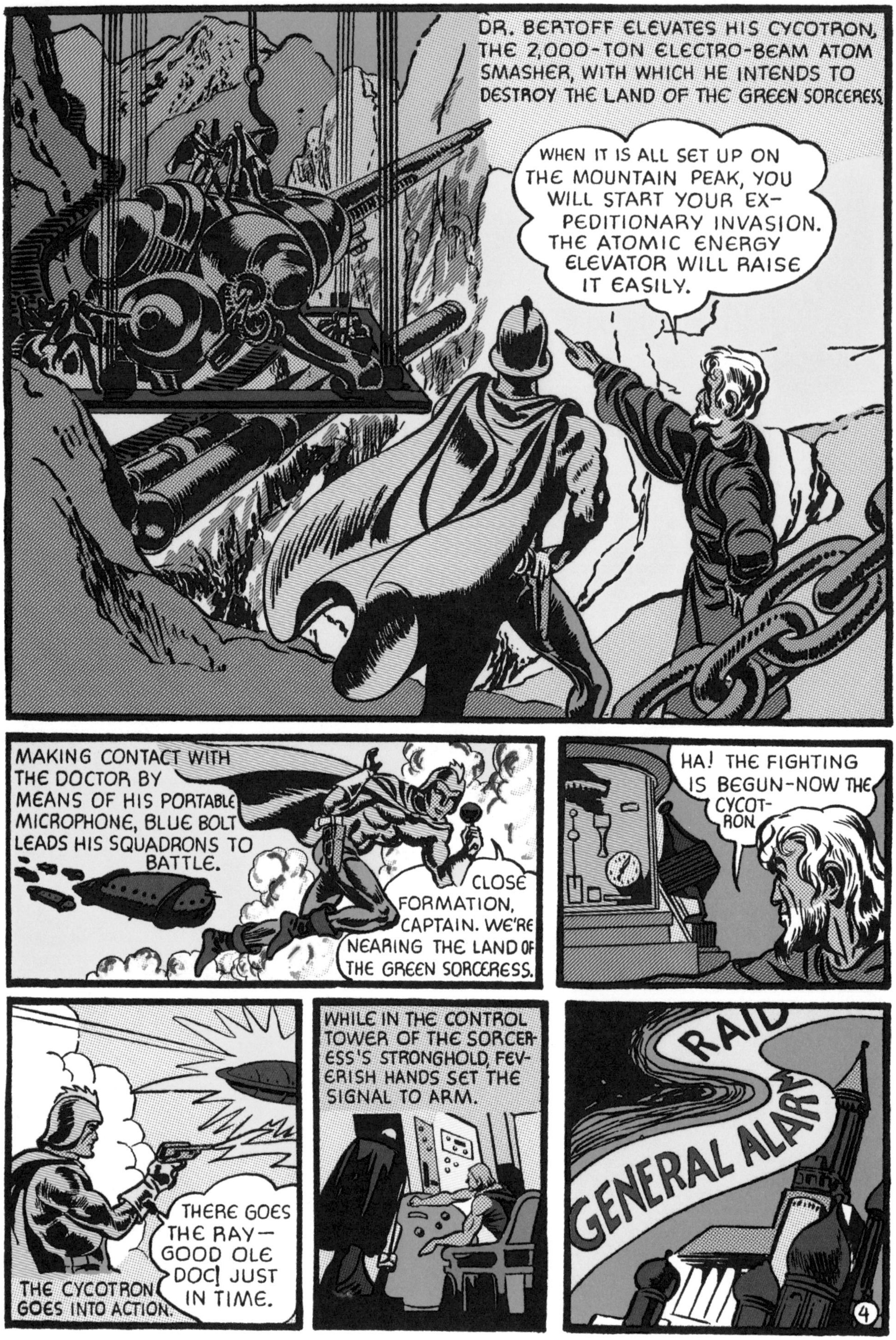
DR. BERTOFF ELEVATES HIS CYCOTRON, THE 2,000-TON ELECTRO-BEAM ATOM SMASHER, WITH WHICH HE INTENDS TO DESTROY THE LAND OF THE GREEN SORCERESS.
WHEN IT IS ALL SET UP ON THE MOUNTAIN PEAK, YOU WILL START YOUR EX-PEDITIONARY INVASION. THE ATOMIC ENERGY ELEVATOR WILL RAISE IT EASILY.
MAKING CONTACT WITH THE DOCTOR BY MEANS OF HIS PORTABLE MICROPHONE, BLUE BOLT LEADS HIS SQUADRONS TO BATTLE.
CLOSE FORMATION, CAPTAIN. WE'RE NEARING THE LAND OF THE GREEN SORCERESS.
HA! THE FIGHTING IS BEGUN-NOW THE CYCOT-RON.
THE CYCOTRON GOES INTO ACTION.
THERE GOES THE RAY— GOOD OLE DOC! JUST IN TIME.
WHILE IN THE CONTROL TOWER OF THE SORCER-ESS'S STRONGHOLD, FEV-ERISH HANDS SET THE SIGNAL TO ARM.
RAID
GENERAL ALARM
4

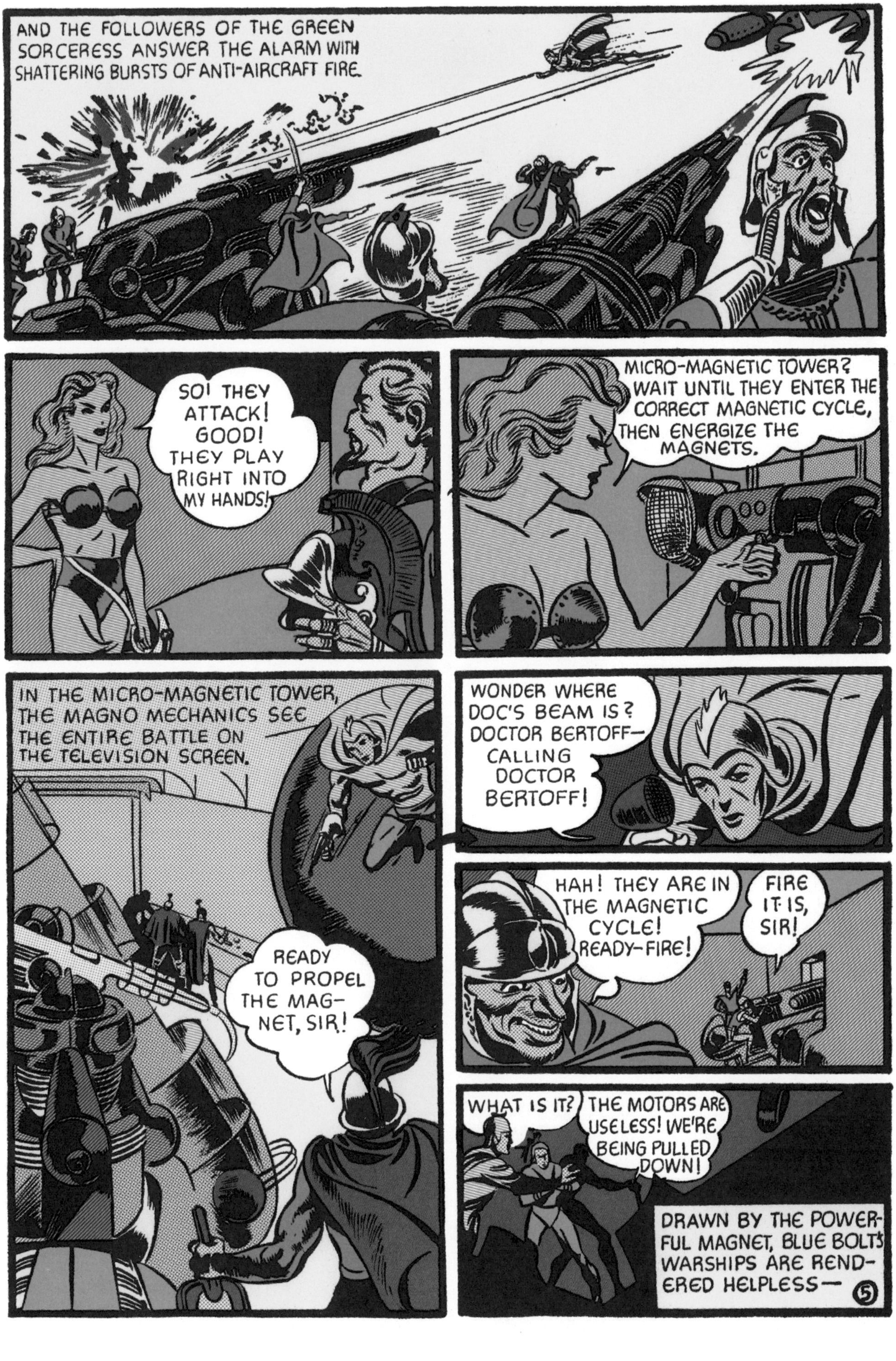
AND THE FOLLOWERS OF THE GREEN SORCERESS ANSWER THE ALARM WITH SHATTERING BURSTS OF ANTI-AIRCRAFT FIRE.
SO! THEY ATTACK! GOOD! THEY PLAY RIGHT INTO MY HANDS!
MICRO-MAGNETIC TOWER? WAIT UNTIL THEY ENTER THE CORRECT MAGNETIC CYCLE, THEN ENERGIZE THE MAGNETS.
IN THE MICRO-MAGNETIC TOWER, THE MAGNO MECHANICS SEE THE ENTIRE BATTLE ON THE TELEVISION SCREEN.
READY TO PROPEL THE MAG-NET, SIR!
WONDER WHERE DOC'S BEAM IS? DOCTOR BERTOFF— CALLING DOCTOR BERTOFF!
HAH! THEY ARE IN THE MAGNETIC CYCLE! READY—FIRE!
FIRE IT IS, SIR!
WHAT IS IT?
THE MOTORS ARE USELESS! WE'RE BEING PULLED DOWN!
DRAWN BY THE POWER-FUL MAGNET, BLUE BOLT'S WARSHIPS ARE REND-ERED HELPLESS—
5

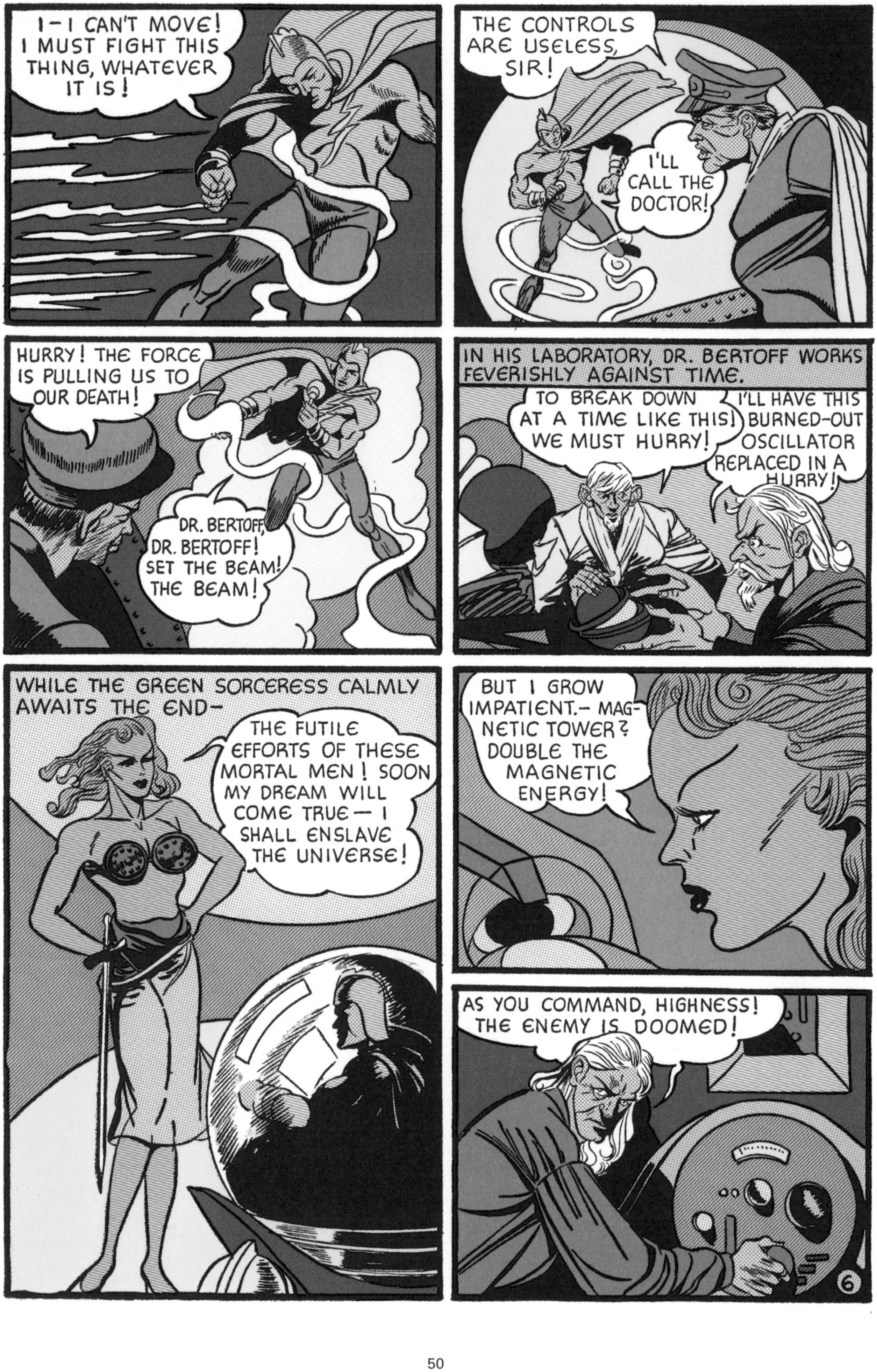
I-I CAN'T MOVE! I MUST FIGHT THIS THING, WHATEVER IT IS!
THE CONTROLS ARE USELESS, SIR!
I'LL CALL THE DOCTOR!
HURRY! THE FORCE IS PULLING US TO OUR DEATH!
DR. BERTOFF, DR. BERTOFF! SET THE BEAM! THE BEAM!
IN HIS LABORATORY, DR. BERTOFF WORKS FEVERISHLY AGAINST TIME.
TO BREAK DOWN AT A TIME LIKE THIS! WE MUST HURRY!
I'LL HAVE THIS BURNED-OUT OSCILLATOR REPLACED IN A HURRY!
WHILE THE GREEN SORCERESS CALMLY AWAITS THE END-
THE FUTILE EFFORTS OF THESE MORTAL MEN! SOON MY DREAM WILL COME TRUE — I SHALL ENSLAVE THE UNIVERSE!
BUT I GROW IMPATIENT.- MAGNETIC TOWER? DOUBLE THE MAGNETIC ENERGY!
AS YOU COMMAND, HIGHNESS! THE ENEMY IS DOOMED!
6

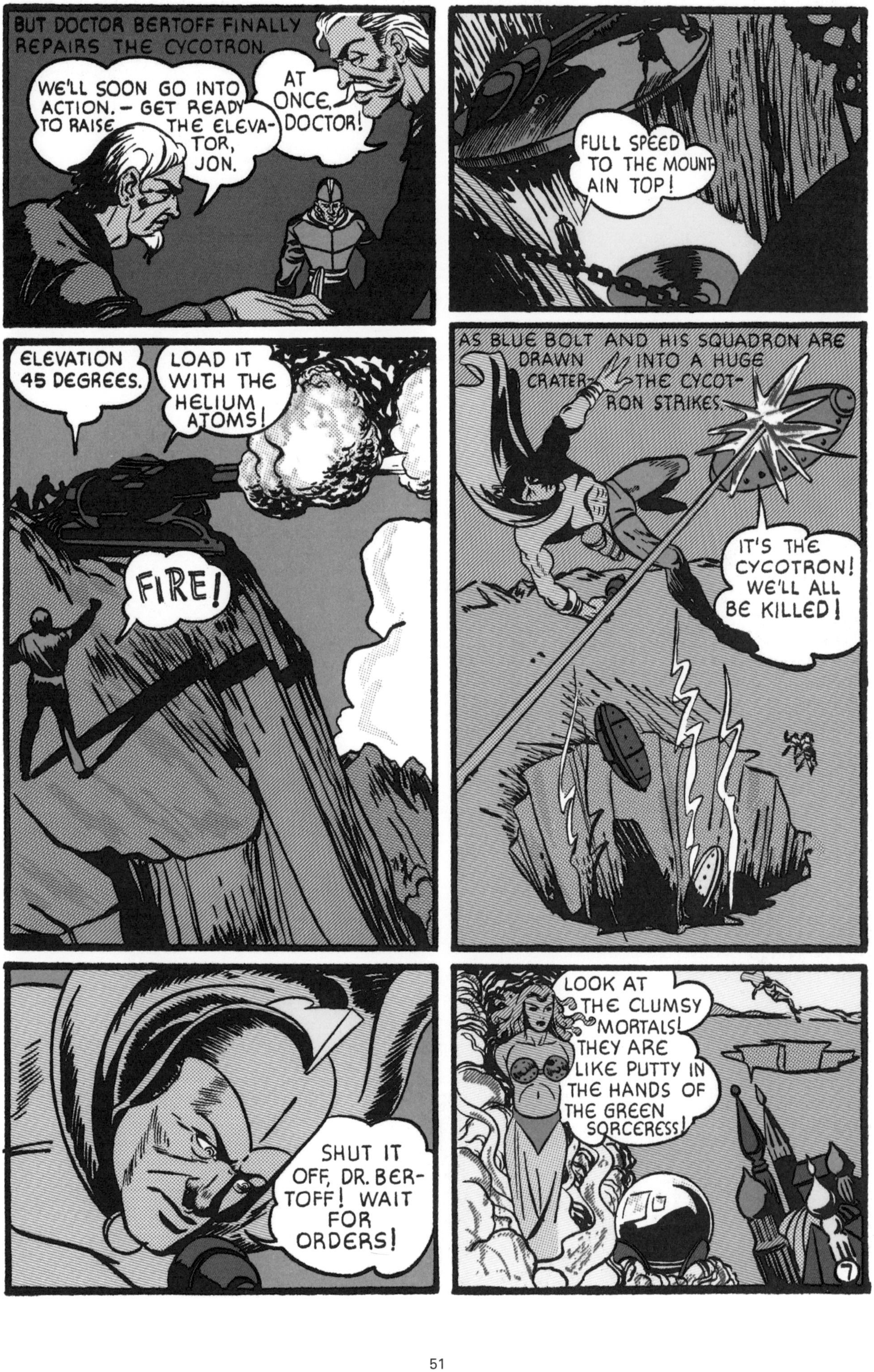
BUT DOCTOR BERTOFF FINALLY REPAIRS THE CYCOTRON.
WE'LL SOON GO INTO ACTION. – GET READY TO RAISE THE ELEVATOR, JON.
AT ONCE, DOCTOR!
FULL SPEED TO THE MOUNTAIN TOP!
ELEVATION 45 DEGREES.
LOAD IT WITH THE HELIUM ATOMS!
FIRE!
AS BLUE BOLT AND HIS SQUADRON ARE DRAWN INTO A HUGE CRATER– THE CYCOTRON STRIKES.
IT'S THE CYCOTRON! WE'LL ALL BE KILLED!
SHUT IT OFF, DR. BERTOFF! WAIT FOR ORDERS!
LOOK AT THE CLUMSY MORTALS! THEY ARE LIKE PUTTY IN THE HANDS OF THE GREEN SORCERESS!
7

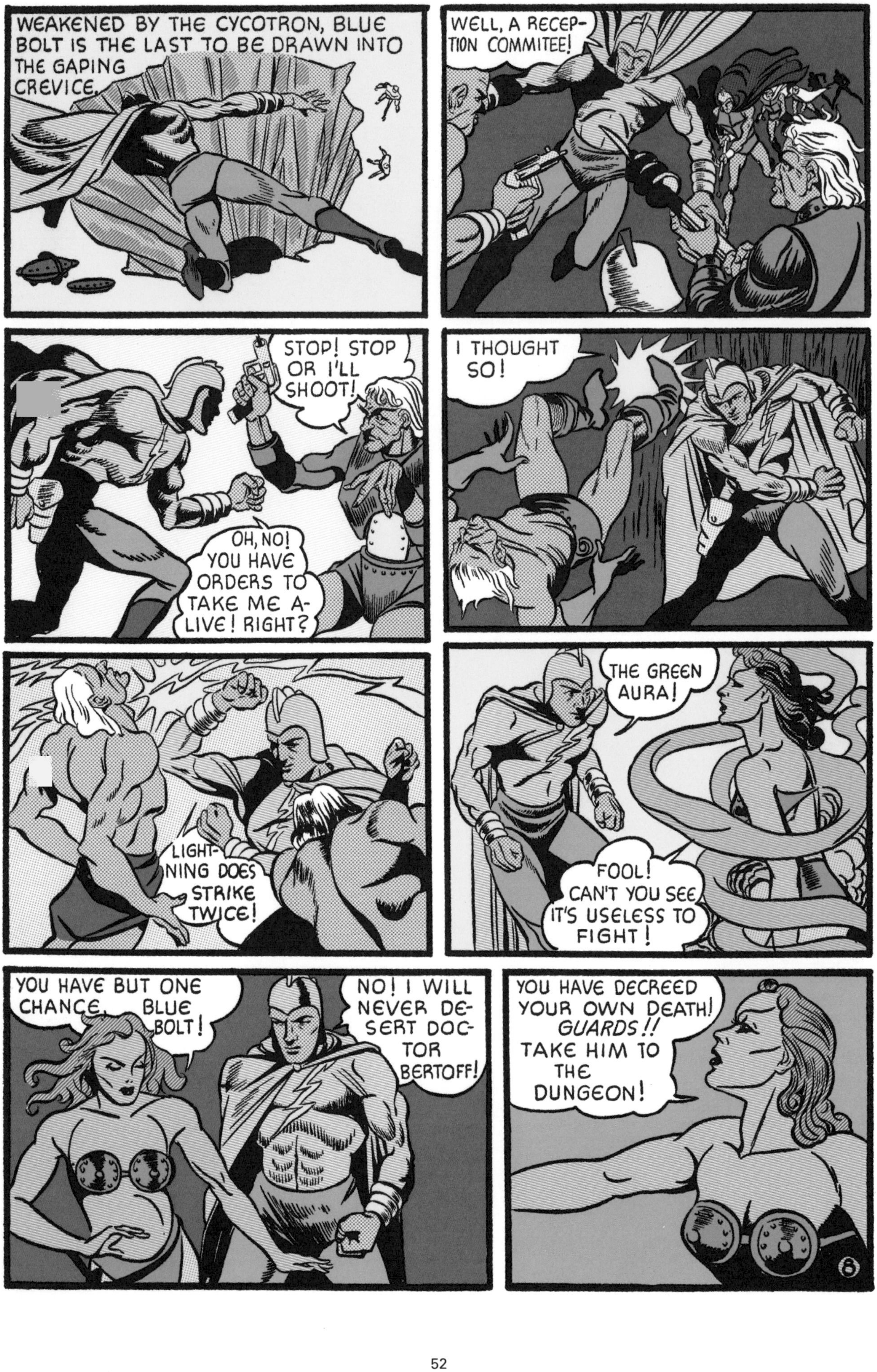
WEAKENED BY THE CYCOTRON, BLUE BOLT IS THE LAST TO BE DRAWN INTO THE GAPING CREVICE.
WELL, A RECEPTION COMMITEE!
STOP! STOP OR I'LL SHOOT!
OH, NO! YOU HAVE ORDERS TO TAKE ME ALIVE! RIGHT?
I THOUGHT SO!
LIGHTNING DOES STRIKE TWICE!
THE GREEN AURA!
FOOL! CAN'T YOU SEE IT'S USELESS TO FIGHT!
YOU HAVE BUT ONE CHANCE, BLUE BOLT!
NO! I WILL NEVER DESERT DOCTOR BERTOFF!
YOU HAVE DECREED YOUR OWN DEATH! GUARDS!! TAKE HIM TO THE DUNGEON!
8

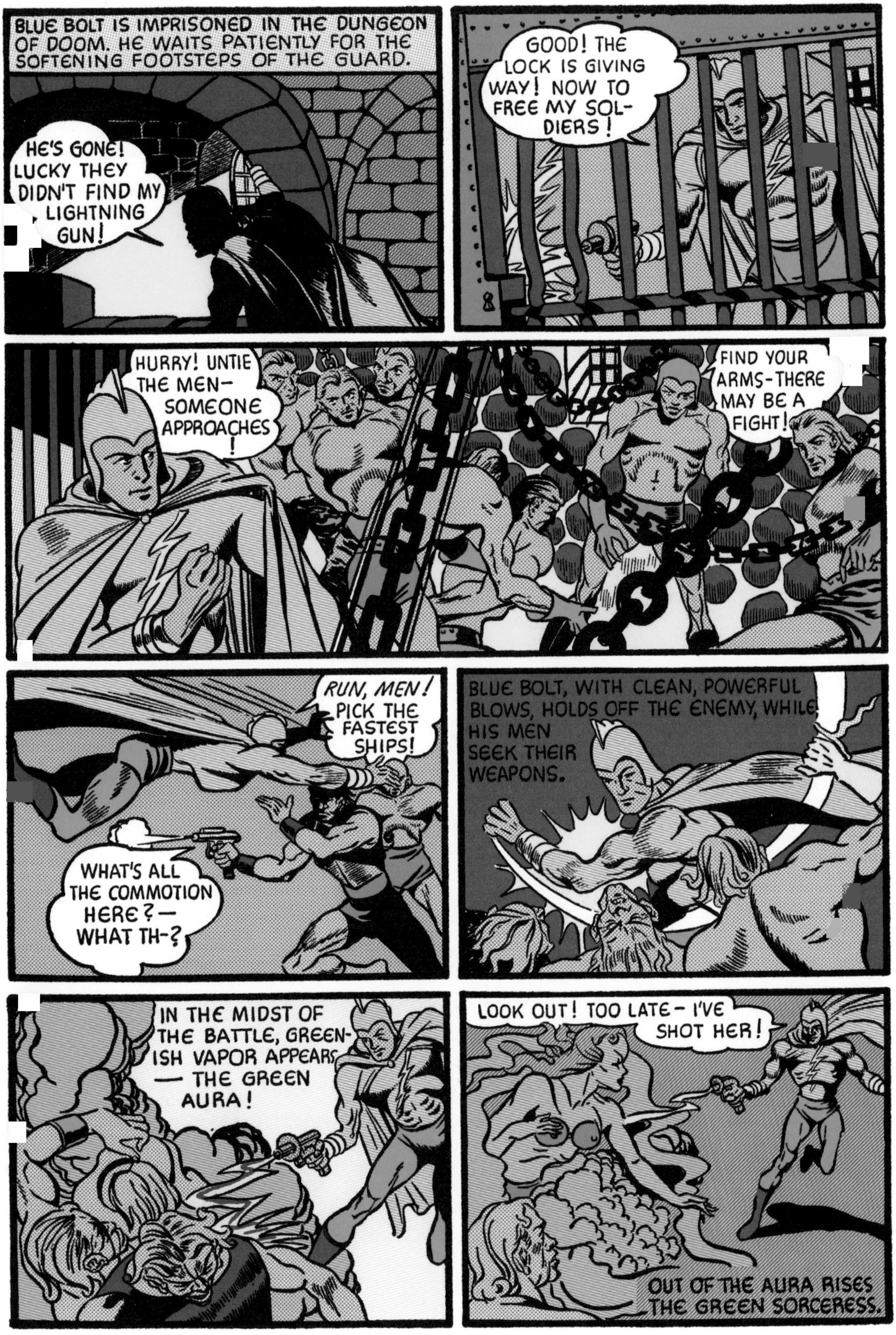
BLUE BOLT IS IMPRISONED IN THE DUNGEON OF DOOM. HE WAITS PATIENTLY FOR THE SOFTENING FOOTSTEPS OF THE GUARD.
HE'S GONE! LUCKY THEY DIDN'T FIND MY LIGHTNING GUN!
GOOD! THE LOCK IS GIVING WAY! NOW TO FREE MY SOL-DIERS!
HURRY! UNTIE THE MEN— SOMEONE APPROACHES!
FIND YOUR ARMS-THERE MAY BE A FIGHT!
RUN, MEN! PICK THE FASTEST SHIPS!
WHAT'S ALL THE COMMOTION HERE?— WHAT TH-?
BLUE BOLT, WITH CLEAN, POWERFUL BLOWS, HOLDS OFF THE ENEMY, WHILE HIS MEN SEEK THEIR WEAPONS.
IN THE MIDST OF THE BATTLE, GREEN-ISH VAPOR APPEARS — THE GREEN AURA!
LOOK OUT! TOO LATE- I'VE SHOT HER!
OUT OF THE AURA RISES THE GREEN SORCERESS.

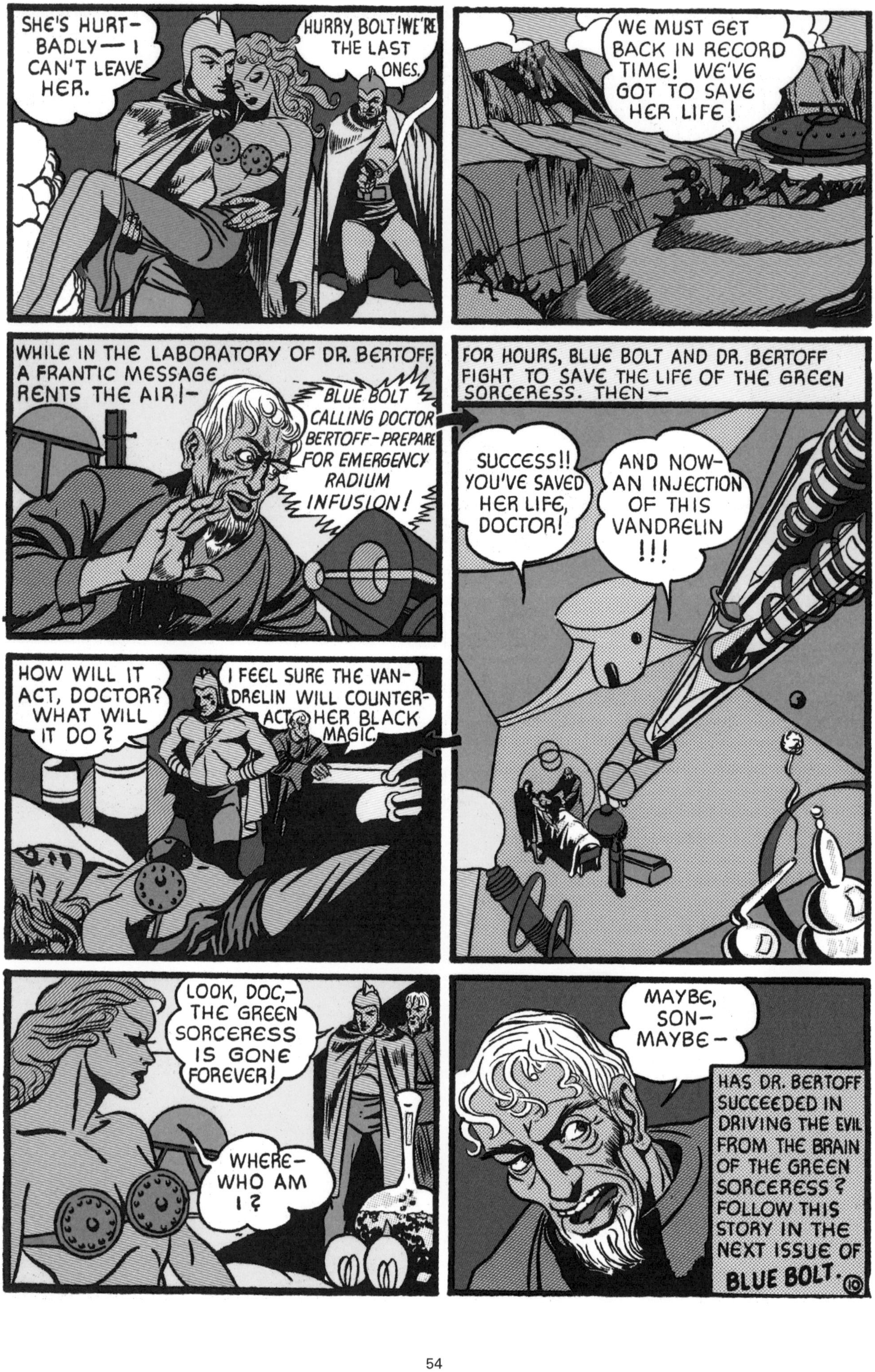
SHE'S HURT-BADLY— I CAN'T LEAVE HER.
HURRY, BOLT! WE'RE THE LAST ONES.
WE MUST GET BACK IN RECORD TIME! WE'VE GOT TO SAVE HER LIFE!
WHILE IN THE LABORATORY OF DR. BERTOFF, A FRANTIC MESSAGE RENTS THE AIR!—
BLUE BOLT CALLING DOCTOR BERTOFF-PREPARE FOR EMERGENCY RADIUM INFUSION!
HOW WILL IT ACT, DOCTOR? WHAT WILL IT DO?
I FEEL SURE THE VAN-DRELIN WILL COUNTER-ACT HER BLACK MAGIC.
FOR HOURS, BLUE BOLT AND DR. BERTOFF FIGHT TO SAVE THE LIFE OF THE GREEN SORCERESS. THEN—
SUCCESS!! YOU'VE SAVED HER LIFE, DOCTOR!
AND NOW- AN INJECTION OF THIS VANDRELIN !!!
LOOK, DOC,– THE GREEN SORCERESS IS GONE FOREVER!
WHERE- WHO AM I?
MAYBE, SON- MAYBE-
HAS DR. BERTOFF SUCCEEDED IN DRIVING THE EVIL FROM THE BRAIN OF THE GREEN SORCERESS? FOLLOW THIS STORY IN THE NEXT ISSUE OF BLUE BOLT.
10

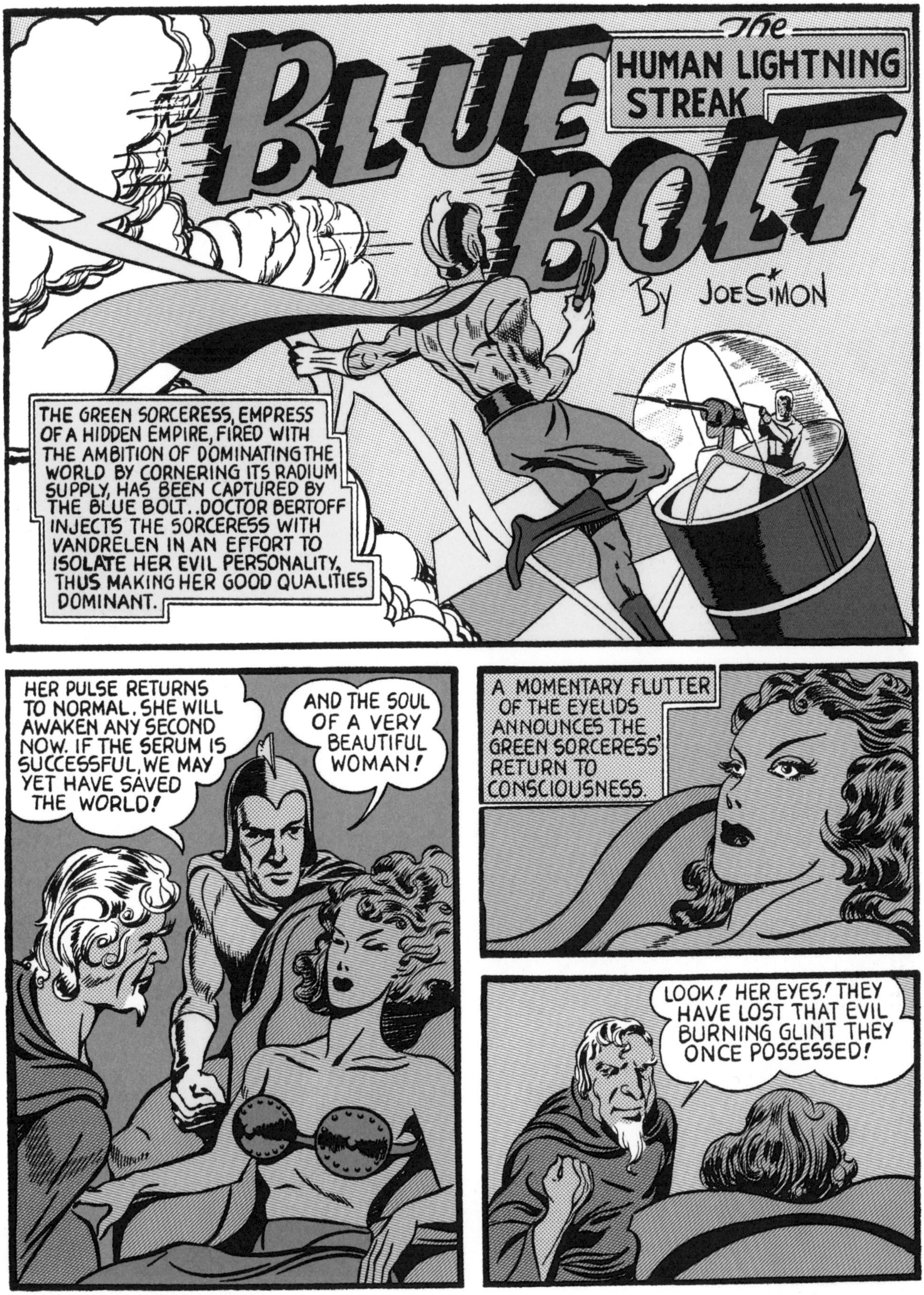
The
BLUE BOLT
HUMAN LIGHTNING STREAK
By JOE SIMON
THE GREEN SORCERESS, EMPRESS OF A HIDDEN EMPIRE, FIRED WITH THE AMBITION OF DOMINATING THE WORLD BY CORNERING ITS RADIUM SUPPLY, HAS BEEN CAPTURED BY THE BLUE BOLT..DOCTOR BERTOFF INJECTS THE SORCERESS WITH VANDRELEN IN AN EFFORT TO ISOLATE HER EVIL PERSONALITY, THUS MAKING HER GOOD QUALITIES DOMINANT.
HER PULSE RETURNS TO NORMAL. SHE WILL AWAKEN ANY SECOND NOW. IF THE SERUM IS SUCCESSFUL, WE MAY YET HAVE SAVED THE WORLD!
AND THE SOUL OF A VERY BEAUTIFUL WOMAN!
A MOMENTARY FLUTTER OF THE EYELIDS ANNOUNCES THE GREEN SORCERESS' RETURN TO CONSCIOUSNESS.
LOOK! HER EYES! THEY HAVE LOST THAT EVIL BURNING GLINT THEY ONCE POSSESSED!

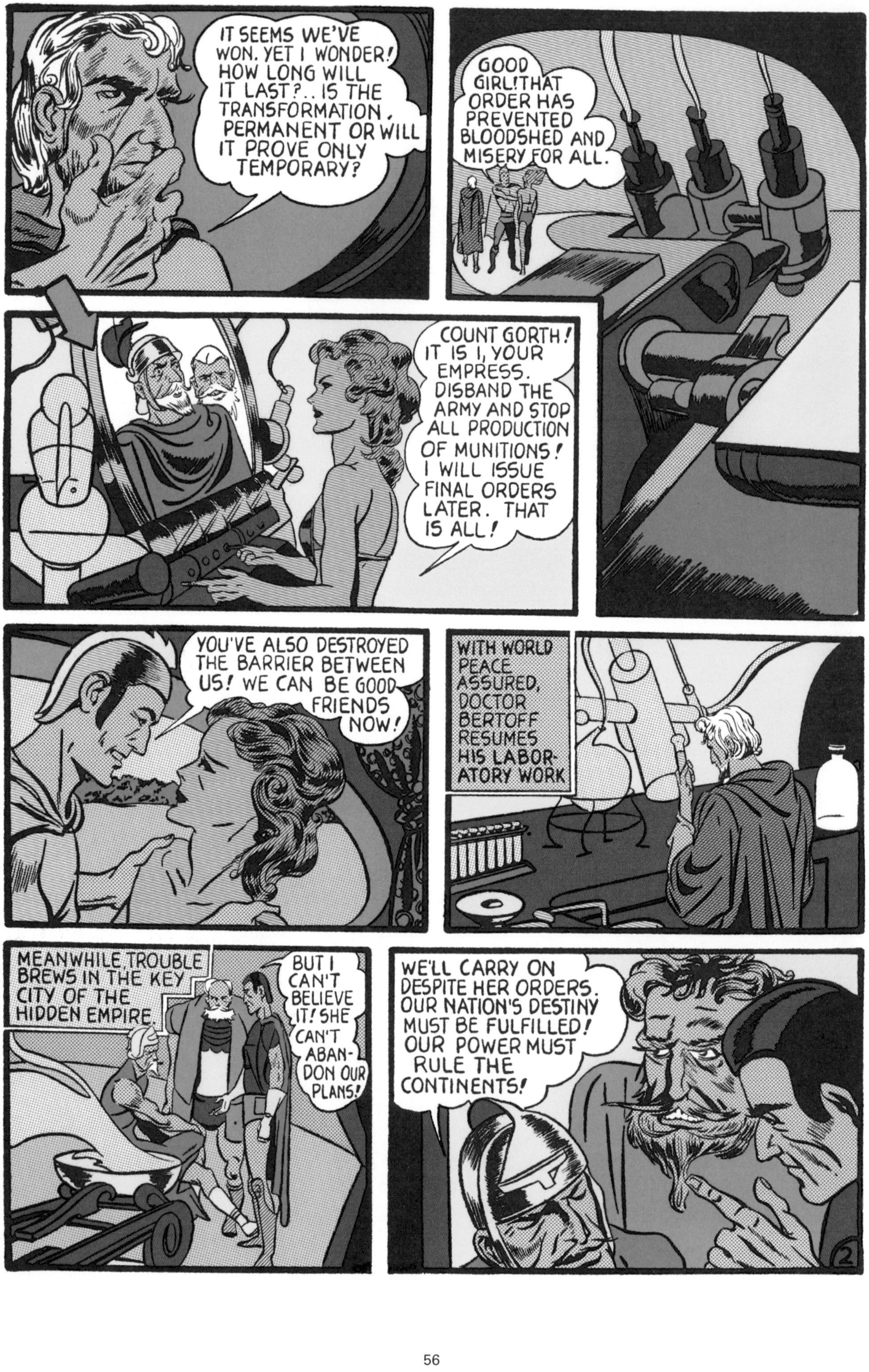
IT SEEMS WE'VE WON. YET I WONDER! HOW LONG WILL IT LAST?.. IS THE TRANSFORMATION, PERMANENT OR WILL IT PROVE ONLY TEMPORARY?
GOOD GIRL! THAT ORDER HAS PREVENTED BLOODSHED AND MISERY FOR ALL.
COUNT GORTH! IT IS I, YOUR EMPRESS. DISBAND THE ARMY AND STOP ALL PRODUCTION OF MUNITIONS! I WILL ISSUE FINAL ORDERS LATER. THAT IS ALL!
YOU'VE ALSO DESTROYED THE BARRIER BETWEEN US! WE CAN BE GOOD FRIENDS NOW!
WITH WORLD PEACE ASSURED, DOCTOR BERTOFF RESUMES HIS LABORATORY WORK
MEANWHILE TROUBLE BREWS IN THE KEY CITY OF THE HIDDEN EMPIRE
BUT I CAN'T BELIEVE IT! SHE CAN'T ABANDON OUR PLANS!
WE'LL CARRY ON DESPITE HER ORDERS. OUR NATION'S DESTINY MUST BE FULFILLED! OUR POWER MUST RULE THE CONTINENTS!
2

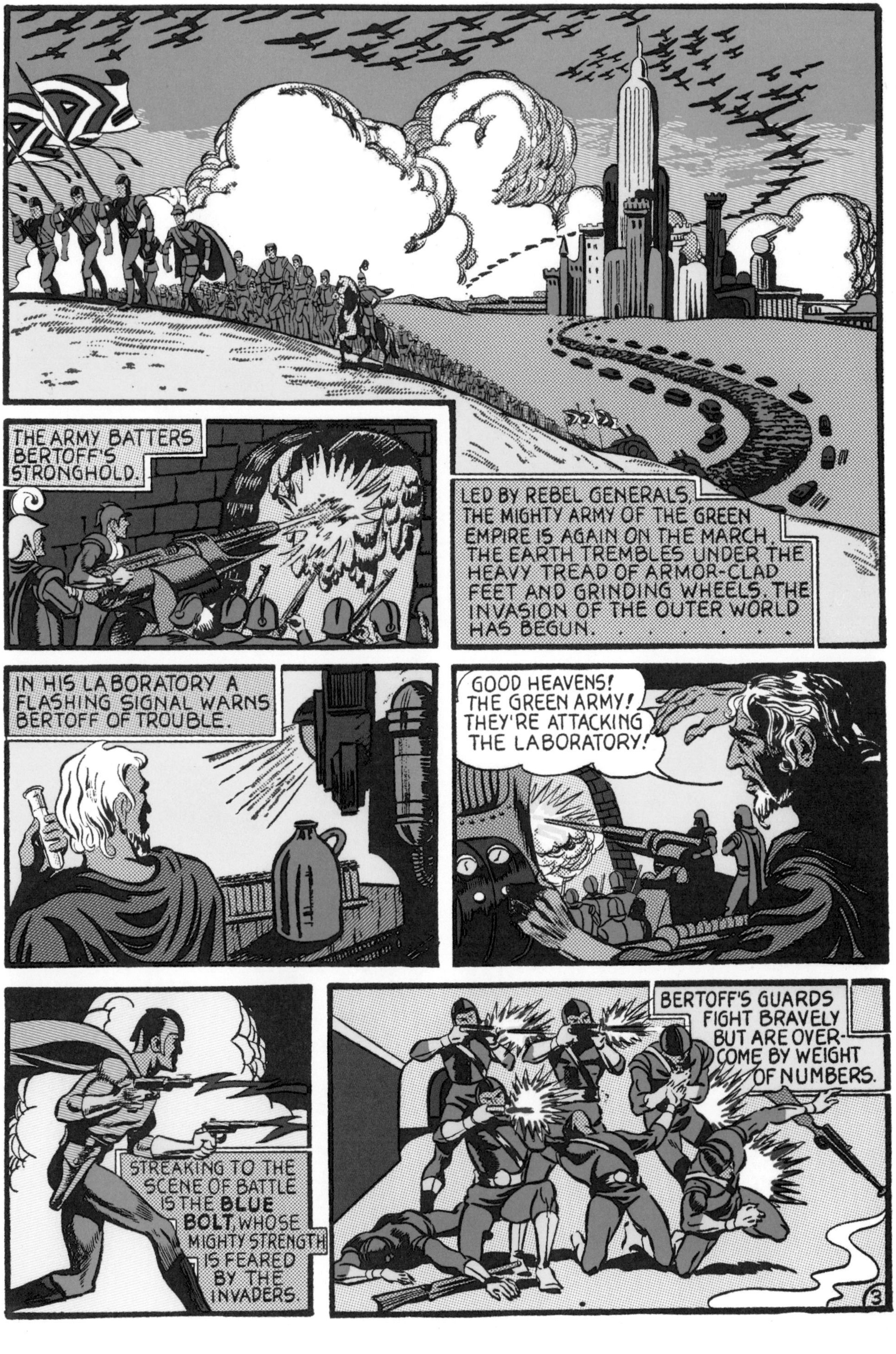
LED BY REBEL GENERALS, THE MIGHTY ARMY OF THE GREEN EMPIRE IS AGAIN ON THE MARCH. THE EARTH TREMBLES UNDER THE HEAVY TREAD OF ARMOR-CLAD FEET AND GRINDING WHEELS. THE INVASION OF THE OUTER WORLD HAS BEGUN. . . . . .
THE ARMY BATTERS BERTOFF'S STRONGHOLD.
IN HIS LABORATORY A FLASHING SIGNAL WARNS BERTOFF OF TROUBLE.
GOOD HEAVENS! THE GREEN ARMY! THEY'RE ATTACKING THE LABORATORY!
STREAKING TO THE SCENE OF BATTLE IS THE BLUE BOLT, WHOSE MIGHTY STRENGTH IS FEARED BY THE INVADERS.
BERTOFF'S GUARDS FIGHT BRAVELY BUT ARE OVERCOME BY WEIGHT OF NUMBERS.
3

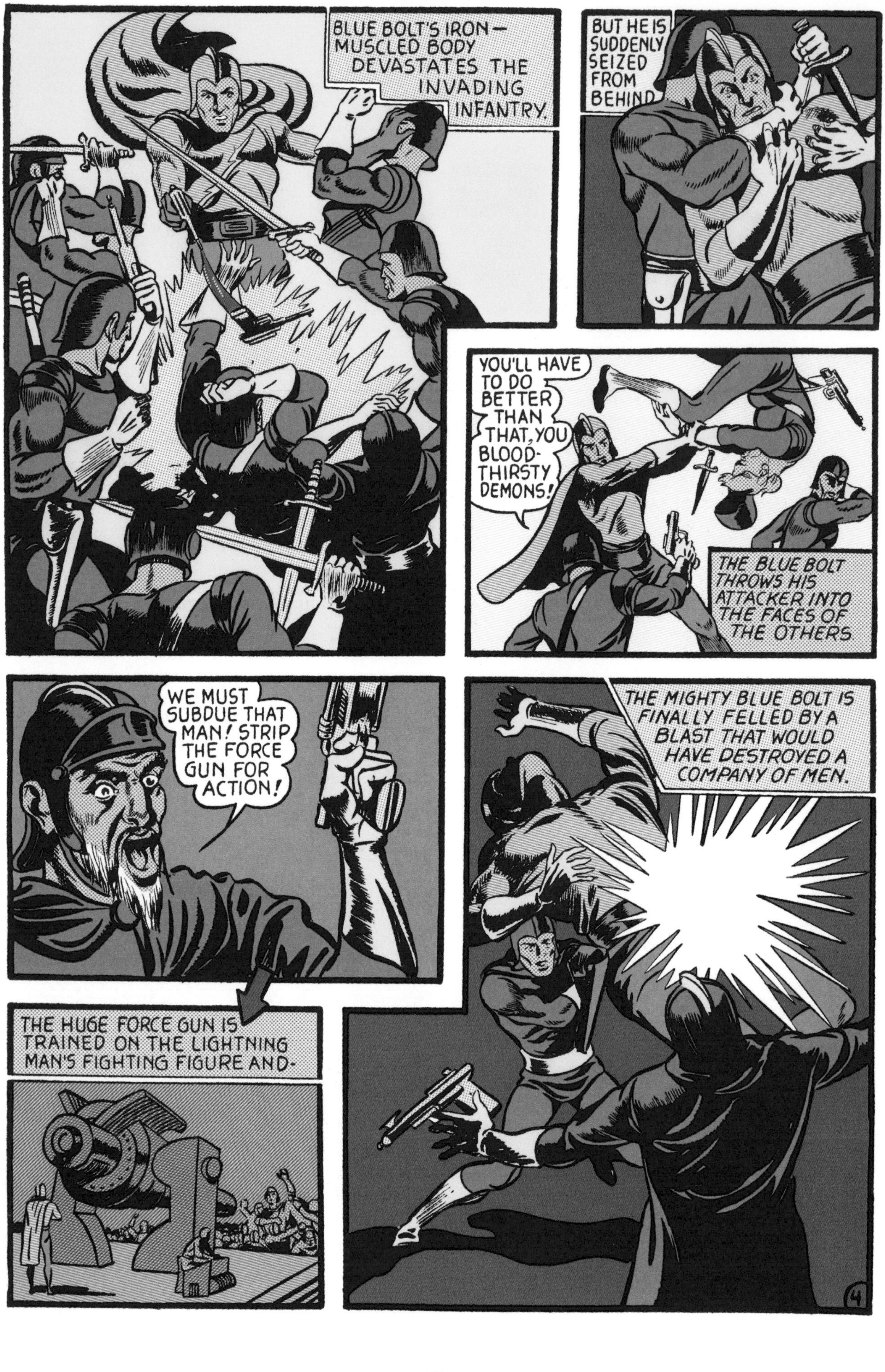
BLUE BOLT'S IRON-MUSCLED BODY DEVASTATES THE INVADING INFANTRY.
BUT HE IS SUDDENLY SEIZED FROM BEHIND
YOU'LL HAVE TO DO BETTER THAN THAT, YOU BLOOD-THIRSTY DEMONS!
THE BLUE BOLT THROWS HIS ATTACKER INTO THE FACES OF THE OTHERS
WE MUST SUBDUE THAT MAN! STRIP THE FORCE GUN FOR ACTION!
THE HUGE FORCE GUN IS TRAINED ON THE LIGHTNING MAN'S FIGHTING FIGURE AND-
THE MIGHTY BLUE BOLT IS FINALLY FELLED BY A BLAST THAT WOULD HAVE DESTROYED A COMPANY OF MEN.
4

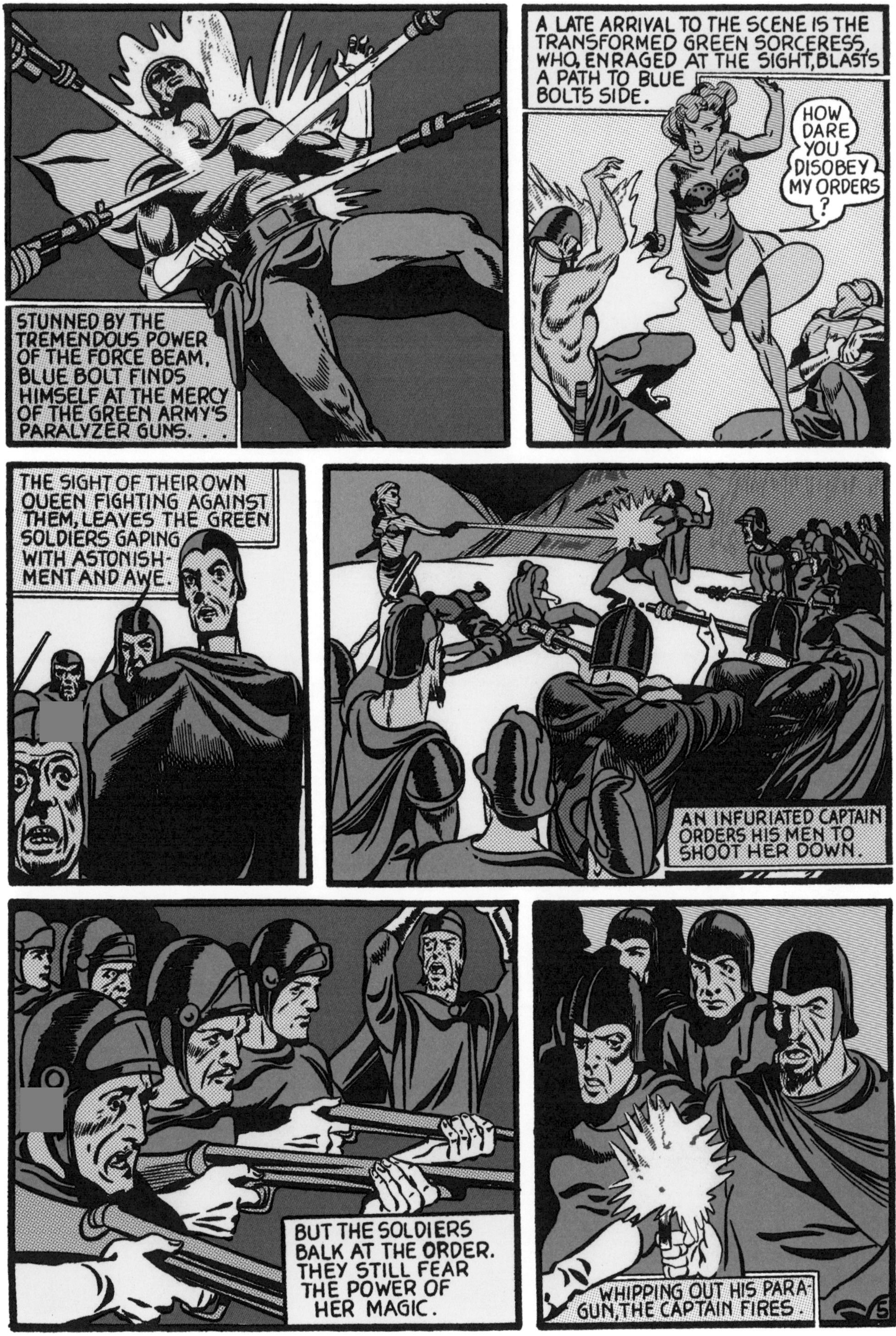
STUNNED BY THE TREMENDOUS POWER OF THE FORCE BEAM, BLUE BOLT FINDS HIMSELF AT THE MERCY OF THE GREEN ARMY'S PARALYZER GUNS. . .
A LATE ARRIVAL TO THE SCENE IS THE TRANSFORMED GREEN SORCERESS, WHO, ENRAGED AT THE SIGHT, BLASTS A PATH TO BLUE BOLT'S SIDE.
HOW DARE YOU DISOBEY MY ORDERS ?
THE SIGHT OF THEIR OWN QUEEN FIGHTING AGAINST THEM, LEAVES THE GREEN SOLDIERS GAPING WITH ASTONISH-MENT AND AWE.
AN INFURIATED CAPTAIN ORDERS HIS MEN TO SHOOT HER DOWN.
BUT THE SOLDIERS BALK AT THE ORDER. THEY STILL FEAR THE POWER OF HER MAGIC.
WHIPPING OUT HIS PARA-GUN, THE CAPTAIN FIRES.
5

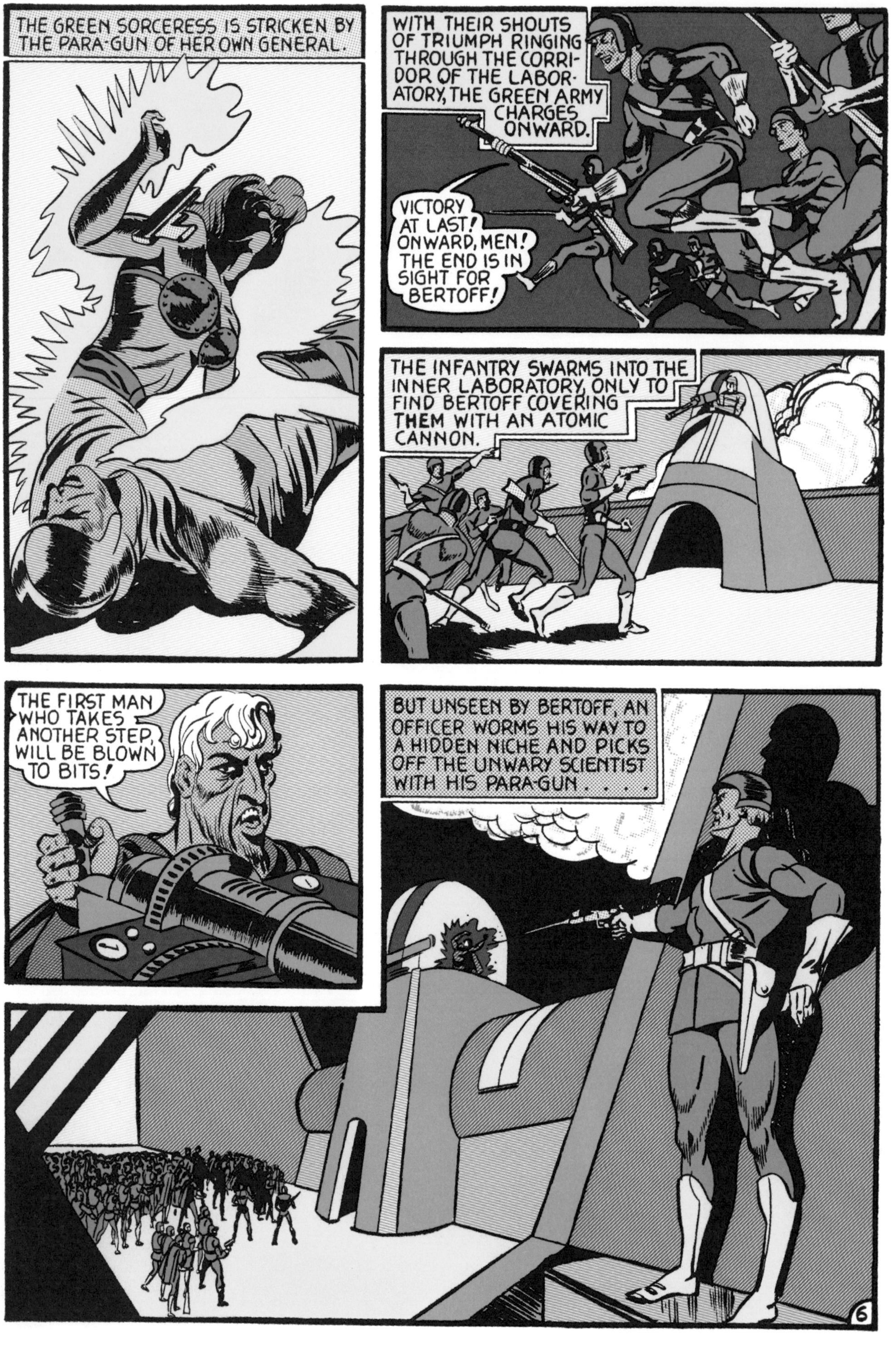
THE GREEN SORCERESS IS STRICKEN BY THE PARA-GUN OF HER OWN GENERAL.
WITH THEIR SHOUTS OF TRIUMPH RINGING THROUGH THE CORRIDOR OF THE LABORATORY, THE GREEN ARMY CHARGES ONWARD.
VICTORY AT LAST! ONWARD, MEN! THE END IS IN SIGHT FOR BERTOFF!
THE INFANTRY SWARMS INTO THE INNER LABORATORY, ONLY TO FIND BERTOFF COVERING THEM WITH AN ATOMIC CANNON.
THE FIRST MAN WHO TAKES ANOTHER STEP, WILL BE BLOWN TO BITS!
BUT UNSEEN BY BERTOFF, AN OFFICER WORMS HIS WAY TO A HIDDEN NICHE AND PICKS OFF THE UNWARY SCIENTIST WITH HIS PARA-GUN . . . .
6

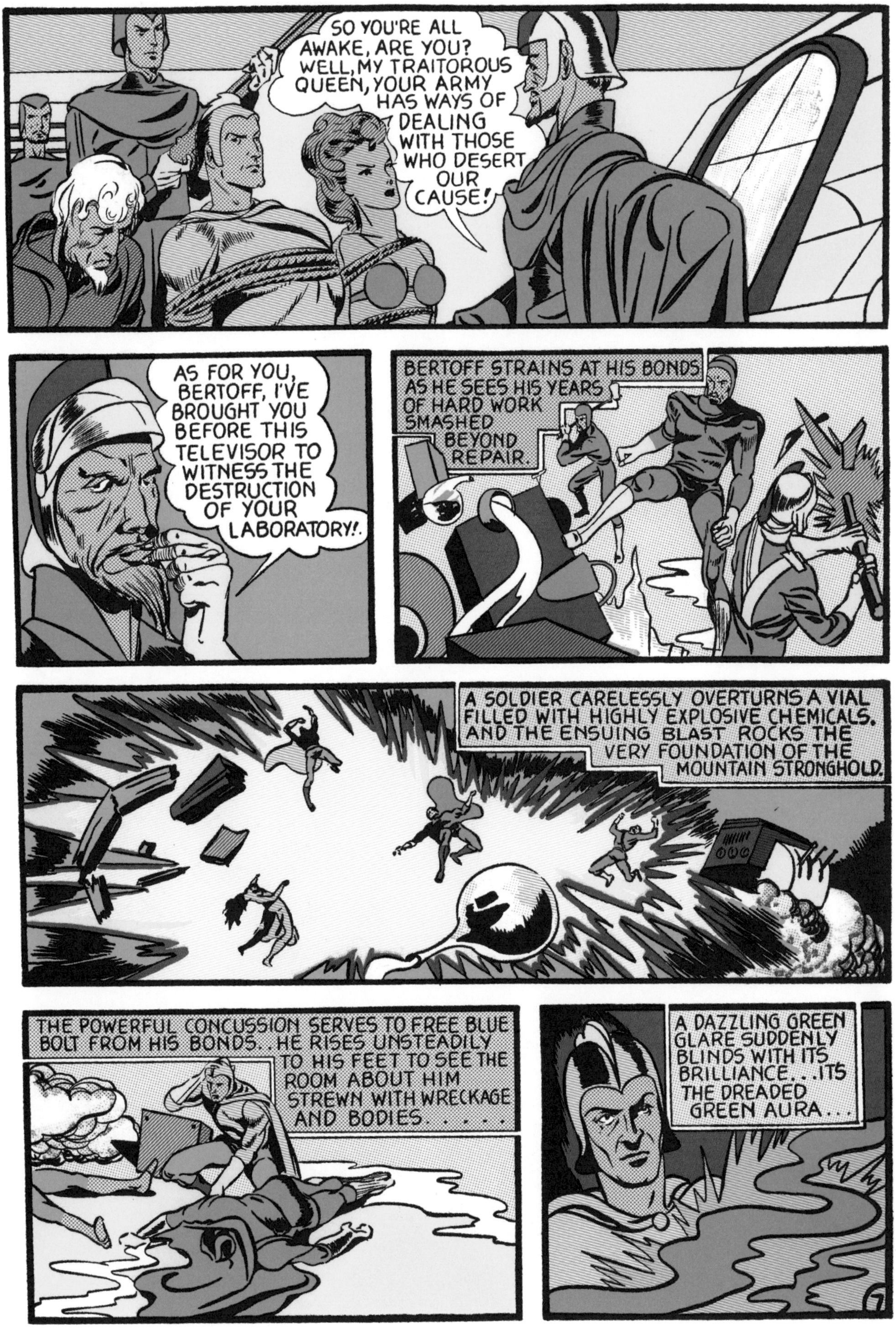

SO YOU'RE ALL AWAKE, ARE YOU? WELL, MY TRAITOROUS QUEEN, YOUR ARMY HAS WAYS OF DEALING WITH THOSE WHO DESERT OUR CAUSE!
AS FOR YOU, BERTOFF, I'VE BROUGHT YOU BEFORE THIS TELEVISOR TO WITNESS THE DESTRUCTION OF YOUR LABORATORY!.
BERTOFF STRAINS AT HIS BONDS AS HE SEES HIS YEARS OF HARD WORK SMASHED BEYOND REPAIR.
A SOLDIER CARELESSLY OVERTURNS A VIAL FILLED WITH HIGHLY EXPLOSIVE CHEMICALS. AND THE ENSUING BLAST ROCKS THE VERY FOUNDATION OF THE MOUNTAIN STRONGHOLD.
THE POWERFUL CONCUSSION SERVES TO FREE BLUE BOLT FROM HIS BONDS. . HE RISES UNSTEADILY TO HIS FEET TO SEE THE ROOM ABOUT HIM STREWN WITH WRECKAGE AND BODIES. . . . .
A DAZZLING GREEN GLARE SUDDENLY BLINDS WITH ITS BRILLIANCE. . .ITS THE DREADED GREEN AURA. . .
7

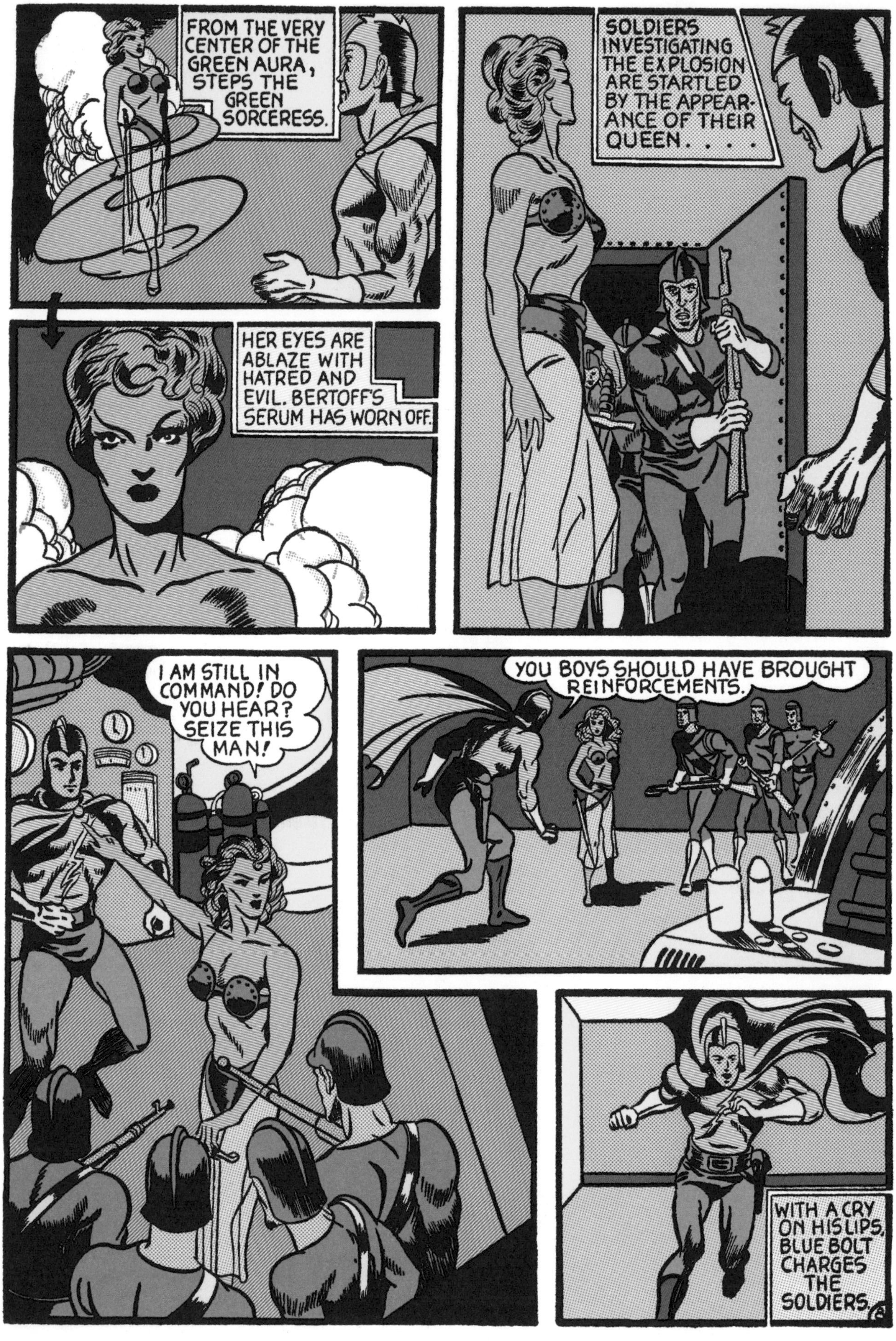
FROM THE VERY CENTER OF THE GREEN AURA, STEPS THE GREEN SORCERESS.
SOLDIERS INVESTIGATING THE EXPLOSION ARE STARTLED BY THE APPEARANCE OF THEIR QUEEN . . . .
HER EYES ARE ABLAZE WITH HATRED AND EVIL. BERTOFF'S SERUM HAS WORN OFF.
I AM STILL IN COMMAND! DO YOU HEAR? SEIZE THIS MAN!
YOU BOYS SHOULD HAVE BROUGHT REINFORCEMENTS.
WITH A CRY ON HIS LIPS, BLUE BOLT CHARGES THE SOLDIERS.

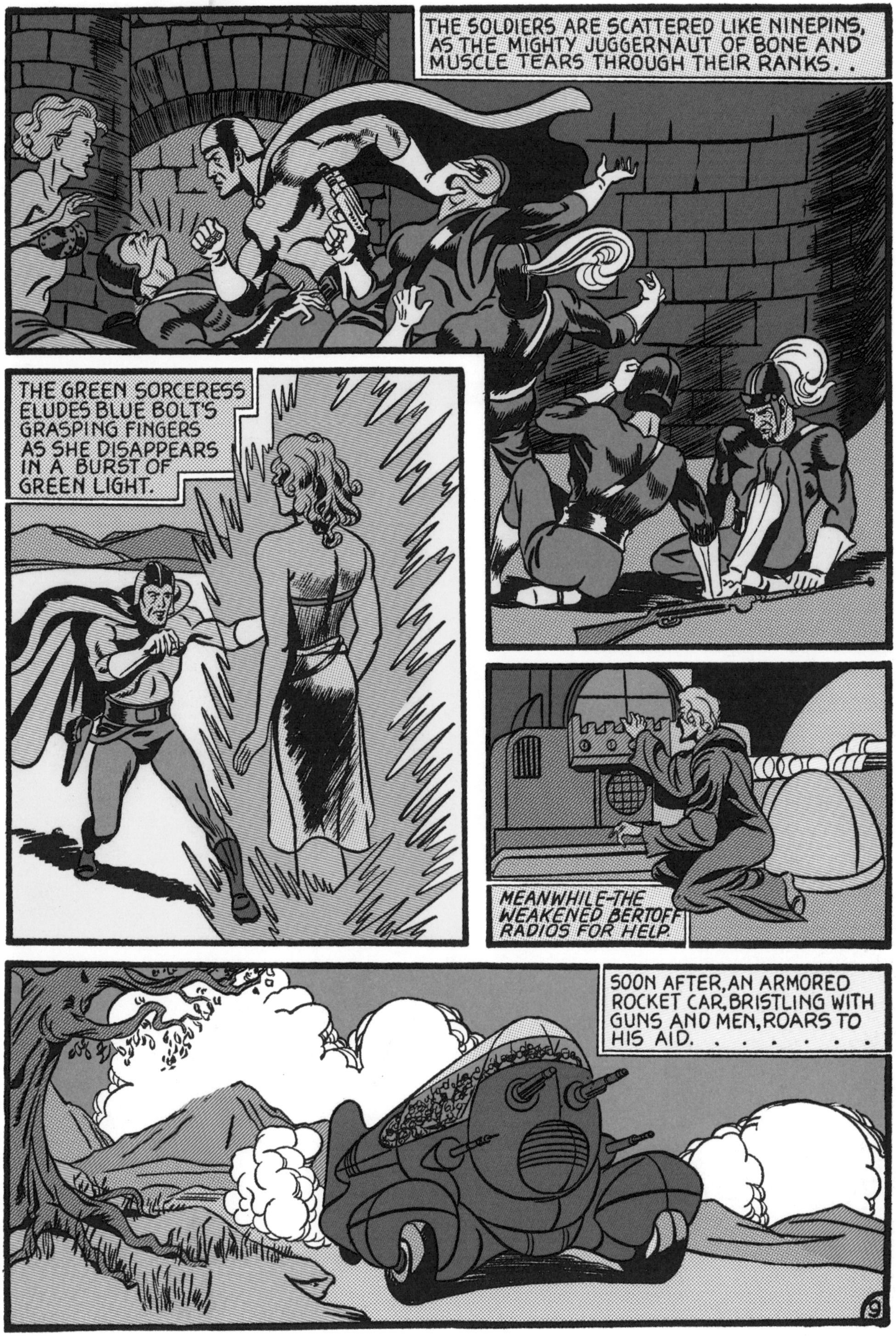
THE SOLDIERS ARE SCATTERED LIKE NINEPINS, AS THE MIGHTY JUGGERNAUT OF BONE AND MUSCLE TEARS THROUGH THEIR RANKS. .
THE GREEN SORCERESS ELUDES BLUE BOLT'S GRASPING FINGERS AS SHE DISAPPEARS IN A BURST OF GREEN LIGHT.
MEANWHILE-THE WEAKENED BERTOFF RADIOS FOR HELP.
SOON AFTER, AN ARMORED ROCKET CAR, BRISTLING WITH GUNS AND MEN, ROARS TO HIS AID. . . . . .
9

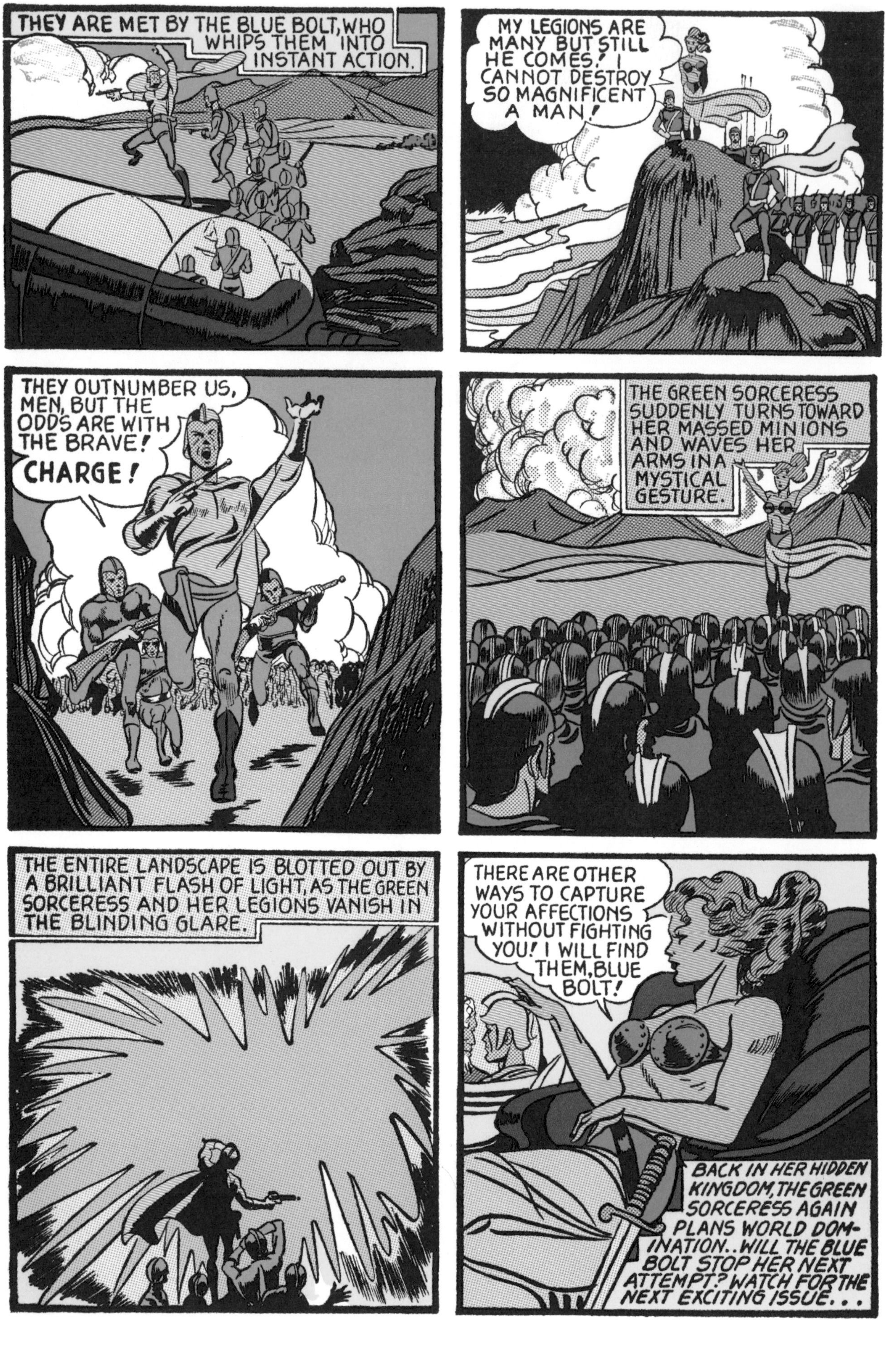
THEY ARE MET BY THE BLUE BOLT, WHO WHIPS THEM INTO INSTANT ACTION.
MY LEGIONS ARE MANY BUT STILL HE COMES! I CANNOT DESTROY SO MAGNIFICENT A MAN!
THEY OUTNUMBER US, MEN, BUT THE ODDS ARE WITH THE BRAVE! CHARGE!
THE GREEN SORCERESS SUDDENLY TURNS TOWARD HER MASSED MINIONS AND WAVES HER ARMS IN A MYSTICAL GESTURE.
THE ENTIRE LANDSCAPE IS BLOTTED OUT BY A BRILLIANT FLASH OF LIGHT, AS THE GREEN SORCERESS AND HER LEGIONS VANISH IN THE BLINDING GLARE.
THERE ARE OTHER WAYS TO CAPTURE YOUR AFFECTIONS WITHOUT FIGHTING YOU! I WILL FIND THEM, BLUE BOLT!
BACK IN HER HIDDEN KINGDOM, THE GREEN SORCERESS AGAIN PLANS WORLD DOMINATION.. WILL THE BLUE BOLT STOP HER NEXT ATTEMPT? WATCH FOR THE NEXT EXCITING ISSUE. . .

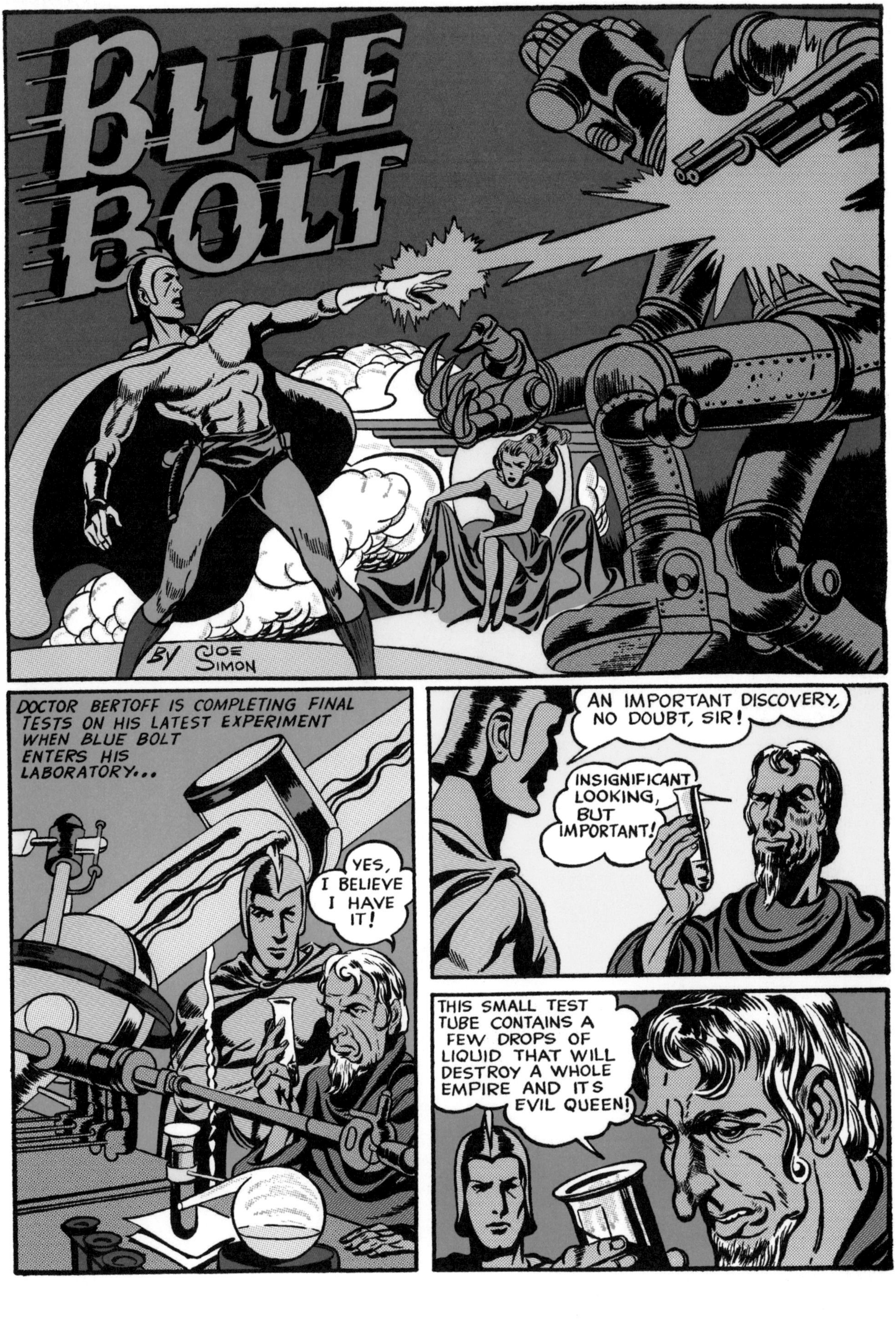
BLUE BOLT
BY JOE SIMON
DOCTOR BERTOFF IS COMPLETING FINAL TESTS ON HIS LATEST EXPERIMENT WHEN BLUE BOLT ENTERS HIS LABORATORY...
YES, I BELIEVE I HAVE IT!
AN IMPORTANT DISCOVERY, NO DOUBT, SIR!
INSIGNIFICANT LOOKING, BUT IMPORTANT!
THIS SMALL TEST TUBE CONTAINS A FEW DROPS OF LIQUID THAT WILL DESTROY A WHOLE EMPIRE AND ITS EVIL QUEEN!

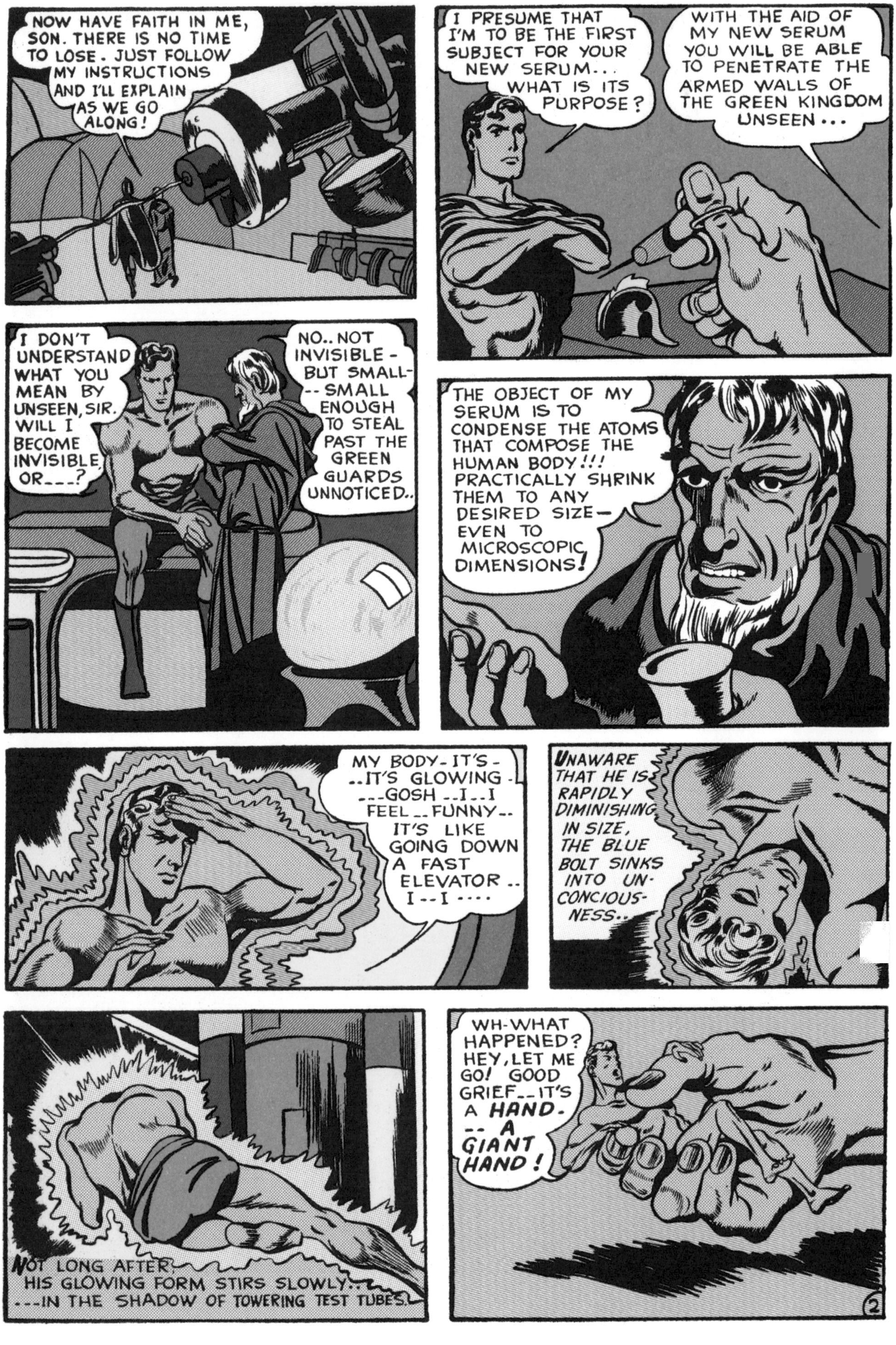
NOW HAVE FAITH IN ME, SON. THERE IS NO TIME TO LOSE. JUST FOLLOW MY INSTRUCTIONS AND I'LL EXPLAIN AS WE GO ALONG!
I PRESUME THAT I'M TO BE THE FIRST SUBJECT FOR YOUR NEW SERUM... WHAT IS ITS PURPOSE?
WITH THE AID OF MY NEW SERUM YOU WILL BE ABLE TO PENETRATE THE ARMED WALLS OF THE GREEN KINGDOM UNSEEN...
I DON'T UNDERSTAND WHAT YOU MEAN BY UNSEEN, SIR. WILL I BECOME INVISIBLE, OR---?
NO.. NOT INVISIBLE - BUT SMALL- -- SMALL ENOUGH TO STEAL PAST THE GREEN GUARDS UNNOTICED..
THE OBJECT OF MY SERUM IS TO CONDENSE THE ATOMS THAT COMPOSE THE HUMAN BODY!!! PRACTICALLY SHRINK THEM TO ANY DESIRED SIZE— EVEN TO MICROSCOPIC DIMENSIONS!
MY BODY- IT'S- ..IT'S GLOWING- ---GOSH --I--I FEEL--FUNNY-- IT'S LIKE GOING DOWN A FAST ELEVATOR.. I--I ....
UNAWARE THAT HE IS RAPIDLY DIMINISHING IN SIZE, THE BLUE BOLT SINKS INTO UN- CONCIOUS- NESS..
NOT LONG AFTER- HIS GLOWING FORM STIRS SLOWLY.. ---IN THE SHADOW OF TOWERING TEST TUBES.
WH-WHAT HAPPENED? HEY, LET ME GO! GOOD GRIEF--IT'S A HAND- -- A GIANT HAND!
2

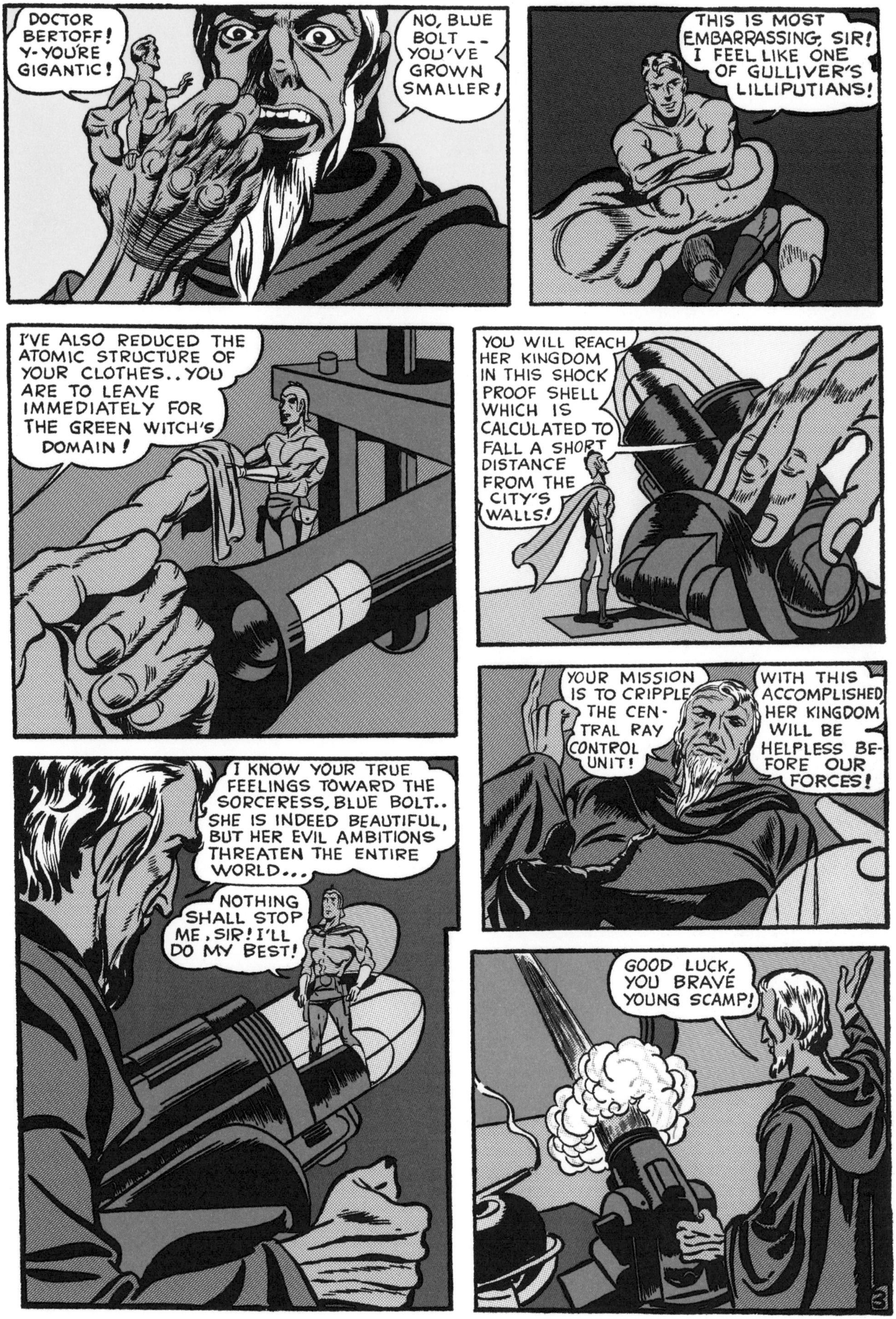
DOCTOR BERTOFF! Y-YOU'RE GIGANTIC!
NO, BLUE BOLT -- YOU'VE GROWN SMALLER!
THIS IS MOST EMBARRASSING, SIR! I FEEL LIKE ONE OF GULLIVER'S LILLIPUTIANS!
I'VE ALSO REDUCED THE ATOMIC STRUCTURE OF YOUR CLOTHES.. YOU ARE TO LEAVE IMMEDIATELY FOR THE GREEN WITCH'S DOMAIN!
YOU WILL REACH HER KINGDOM IN THIS SHOCK PROOF SHELL WHICH IS CALCULATED TO FALL A SHORT DISTANCE FROM THE CITY'S WALLS!
YOUR MISSION IS TO CRIPPLE THE CENTRAL RAY CONTROL UNIT!
WITH THIS ACCOMPLISHED HER KINGDOM WILL BE HELPLESS BEFORE OUR FORCES!
I KNOW YOUR TRUE FEELINGS TOWARD THE SORCERESS, BLUE BOLT.. SHE IS INDEED BEAUTIFUL, BUT HER EVIL AMBITIONS THREATEN THE ENTIRE WORLD...
NOTHING SHALL STOP ME, SIR! I'LL DO MY BEST!
GOOD LUCK, YOU BRAVE YOUNG SCAMP!
3

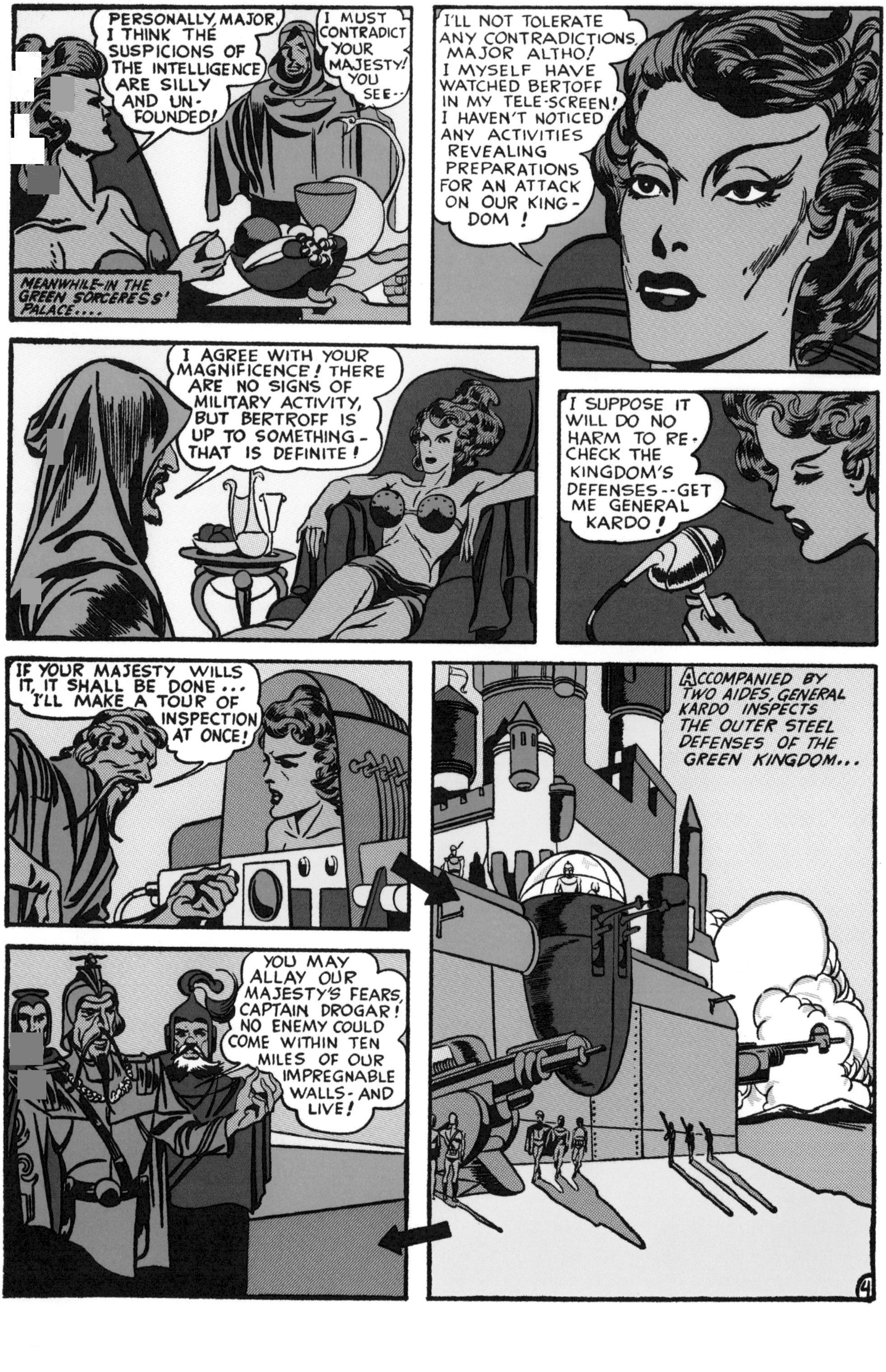
MEANWHILE-IN THE GREEN SORCERESS'S PALACE....
PERSONALLY, MAJOR, I THINK THE SUSPICIONS OF THE INTELLIGENCE ARE SILLY AND UN-FOUNDED!
I MUST CONTRADICT YOUR MAJESTY! YOU SEE--
I'LL NOT TOLERATE ANY CONTRADICTIONS, MAJOR ALTHO! I MYSELF HAVE WATCHED BERTOFF IN MY TELE-SCREEN! I HAVEN'T NOTICED ANY ACTIVITIES REVEALING PREPARATIONS FOR AN ATTACK ON OUR KING-DOM!
I AGREE WITH YOUR MAGNIFICENCE! THERE ARE NO SIGNS OF MILITARY ACTIVITY, BUT BERTROFF IS UP TO SOMETHING - THAT IS DEFINITE!
I SUPPOSE IT WILL DO NO HARM TO RE-CHECK THE KINGDOM'S DEFENSES--GET ME GENERAL KARDO!
IF YOUR MAJESTY WILLS IT, IT SHALL BE DONE... I'LL MAKE A TOUR OF INSPECTION AT ONCE!
YOU MAY ALLAY OUR MAJESTY'S FEARS, CAPTAIN DROGAR! NO ENEMY COULD COME WITHIN TEN MILES OF OUR IMPREGNABLE WALLS- AND LIVE!
ACCOMPANIED BY TWO AIDES, GENERAL KARDO INSPECTS THE OUTER STEEL DEFENSES OF THE GREEN KINGDOM...
4

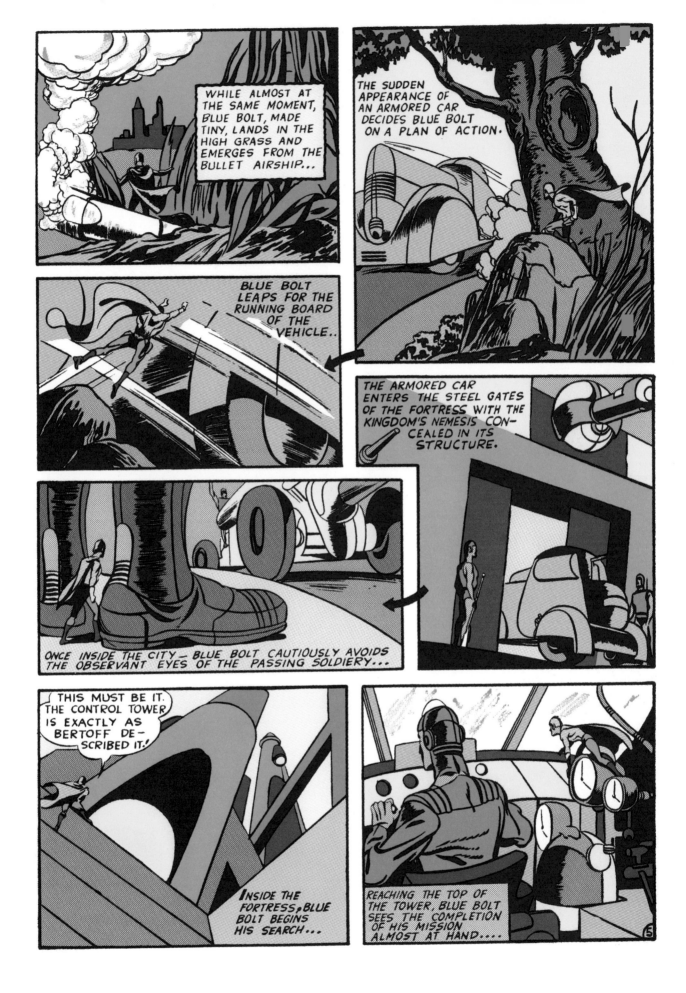

WHILE ALMOST AT THE SAME MOMENT, BLUE BOLT, MADE TINY, LANDS IN THE HIGH GRASS AND EMERGES FROM THE BULLET AIRSHIP...

THE SUDDEN APPEARANCE OF AN ARMORED CAR DECIDES BLUE BOLT ON A PLAN OF ACTION.

BLUE BOLT LEAPS FOR THE RUNNING BOARD OF THE VEHICLE..

THE ARMORED CAR ENTERS THE STEEL GATES OF THE FORTRESS WITH THE KINGDOM'S NEMESIS CONCEALED IN ITS STRUCTURE.

ONCE INSIDE THE CITY – BLUE BOLT CAUTIOUSLY AVOIDS THE OBSERVANT EYES OF THE PASSING SOLDIERY...

THIS MUST BE IT. THE CONTROL TOWER IS EXACTLY AS BERTOFF DESCRIBED IT.'

INSIDE THE FORTRESS, BLUE BOLT BEGINS HIS SEARCH...

REACHING THE TOP OF THE TOWER, BLUE BOLT SEES THE COMPLETION OF HIS MISSION ALMOST AT HAND....

5

69

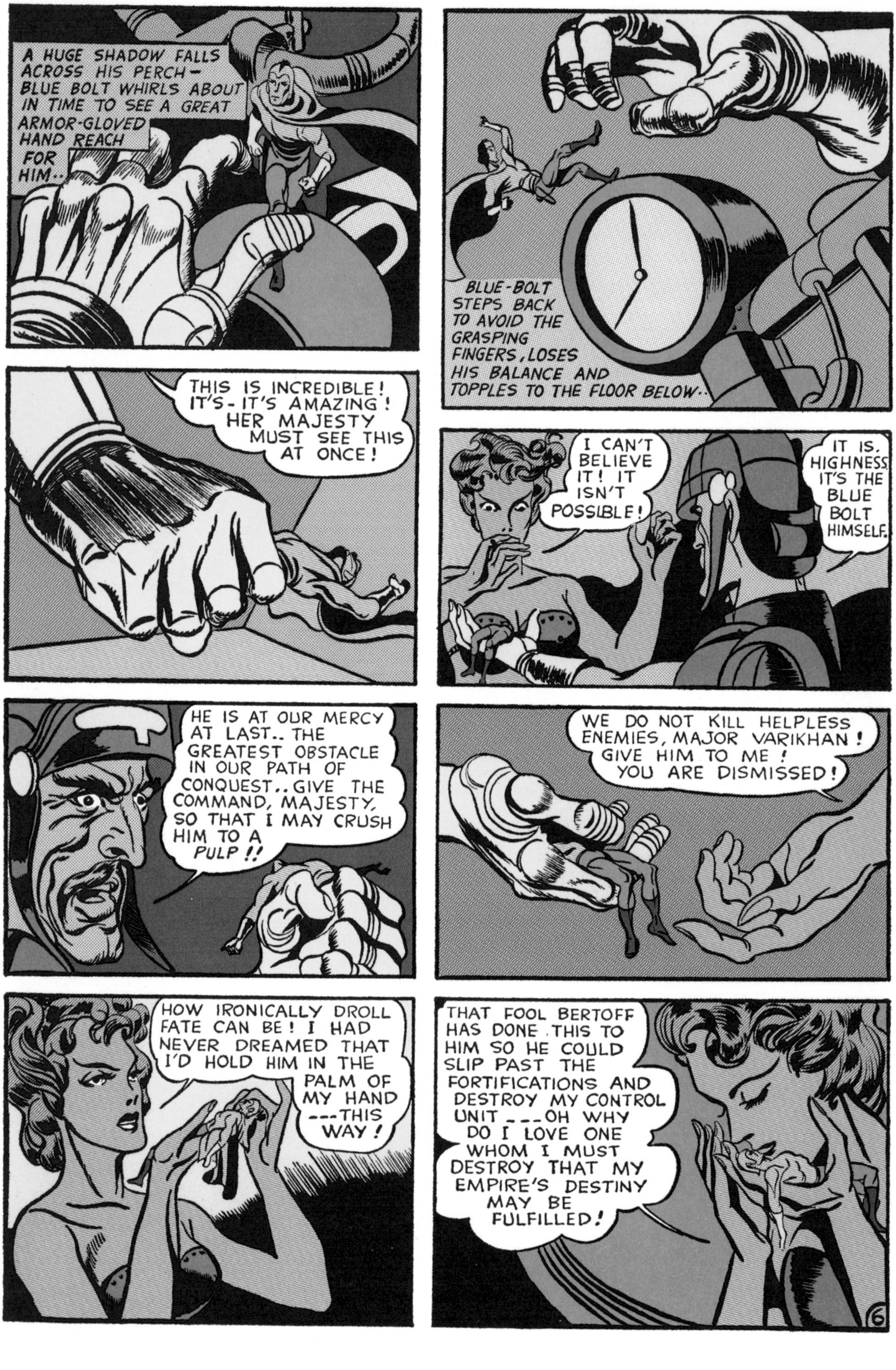

A HUGE SHADOW FALLS ACROSS HIS PERCH— BLUE BOLT WHIRLS ABOUT IN TIME TO SEE A GREAT ARMOR-GLOVED HAND REACH FOR HIM..
BLUE-BOLT STEPS BACK TO AVOID THE GRASPING FINGERS, LOSES HIS BALANCE AND TOPPLES TO THE FLOOR BELOW..
THIS IS INCREDIBLE! IT'S- IT'S AMAZING! HER MAJESTY MUST SEE THIS AT ONCE!
I CAN'T BELIEVE IT! IT ISN'T POSSIBLE!
IT IS, HIGHNESS, IT'S THE BLUE BOLT HIMSELF.
HE IS AT OUR MERCY AT LAST.. THE GREATEST OBSTACLE IN OUR PATH OF CONQUEST.. GIVE THE COMMAND, MAJESTY, SO THAT I MAY CRUSH HIM TO A PULP!!
WE DO NOT KILL HELPLESS ENEMIES, MAJOR VARIKHAN! GIVE HIM TO ME! YOU ARE DISMISSED!
HOW IRONICALLY DROLL FATE CAN BE! I HAD NEVER DREAMED THAT I'D HOLD HIM IN THE PALM OF MY HAND ---THIS WAY!
THAT FOOL BERTOFF HAS DONE THIS TO HIM SO HE COULD SLIP PAST THE FORTIFICATIONS AND DESTROY MY CONTROL UNIT ---OH WHY DO I LOVE ONE WHOM I MUST DESTROY THAT MY EMPIRE'S DESTINY MAY BE FULFILLED!
6

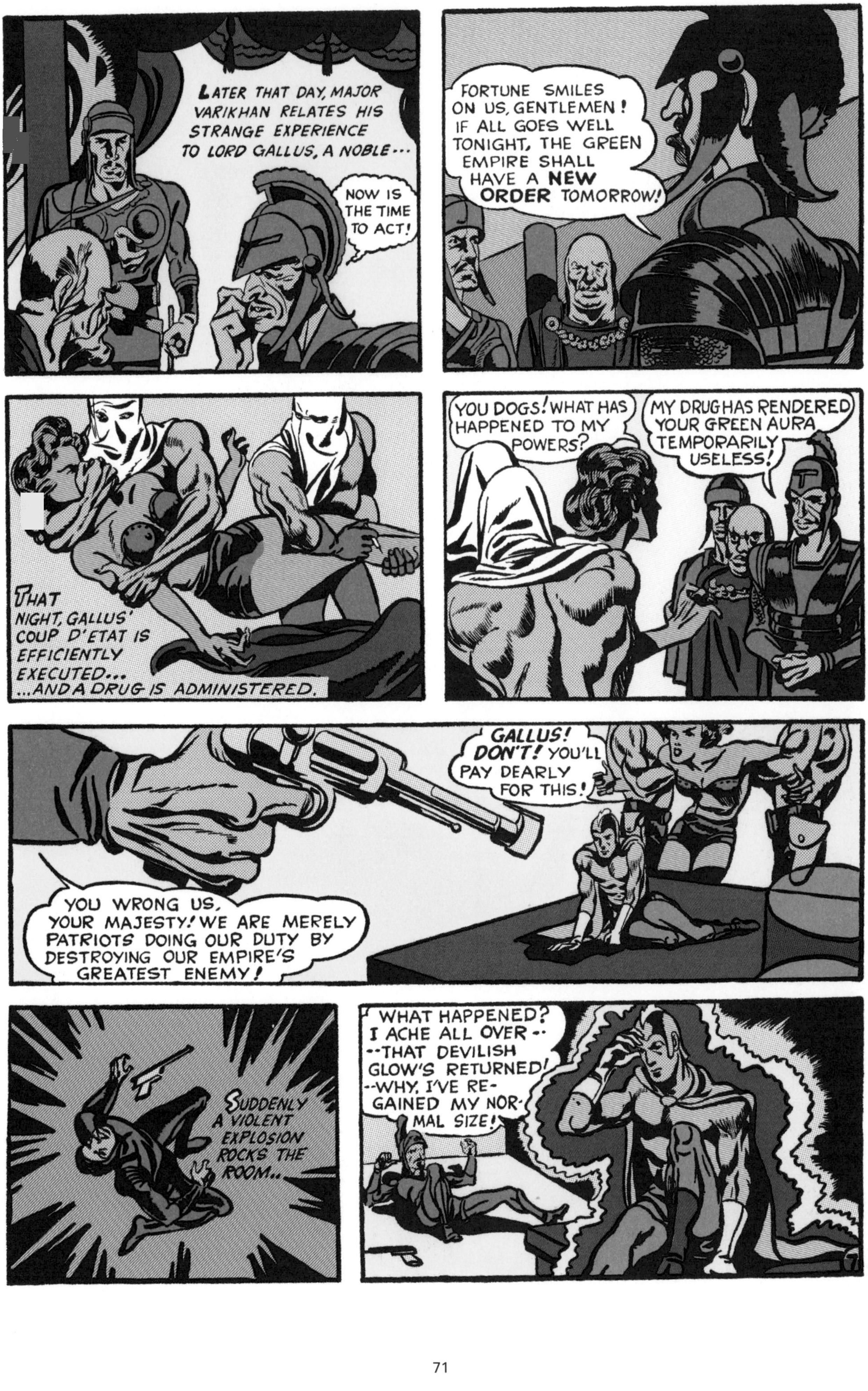
LATER THAT DAY, MAJOR VARIKHAN RELATES HIS STRANGE EXPERIENCE TO LORD GALLUS, A NOBLE...
NOW IS THE TIME TO ACT!
FORTUNE SMILES ON US, GENTLEMEN! IF ALL GOES WELL TONIGHT, THE GREEN EMPIRE SHALL HAVE A NEW ORDER TOMORROW!
THAT NIGHT, GALLUS' COUP D'ETAT IS EFFICIENTLY EXECUTED... ...AND A DRUG IS ADMINISTERED.
YOU DOGS! WHAT HAS HAPPENED TO MY POWERS?
MY DRUG HAS RENDERED YOUR GREEN AURA TEMPORARILY USELESS!
GALLUS! DON'T! YOU'LL PAY DEARLY FOR THIS!
YOU WRONG US, YOUR MAJESTY! WE ARE MERELY PATRIOTS DOING OUR DUTY BY DESTROYING OUR EMPIRE'S GREATEST ENEMY!
SUDDENLY A VIOLENT EXPLOSION ROCKS THE ROOM..
WHAT HAPPENED? I ACHE ALL OVER -- --THAT DEVILISH GLOW'S RETURNED! --WHY, I'VE RE-GAINED MY NOR-MAL SIZE!
7

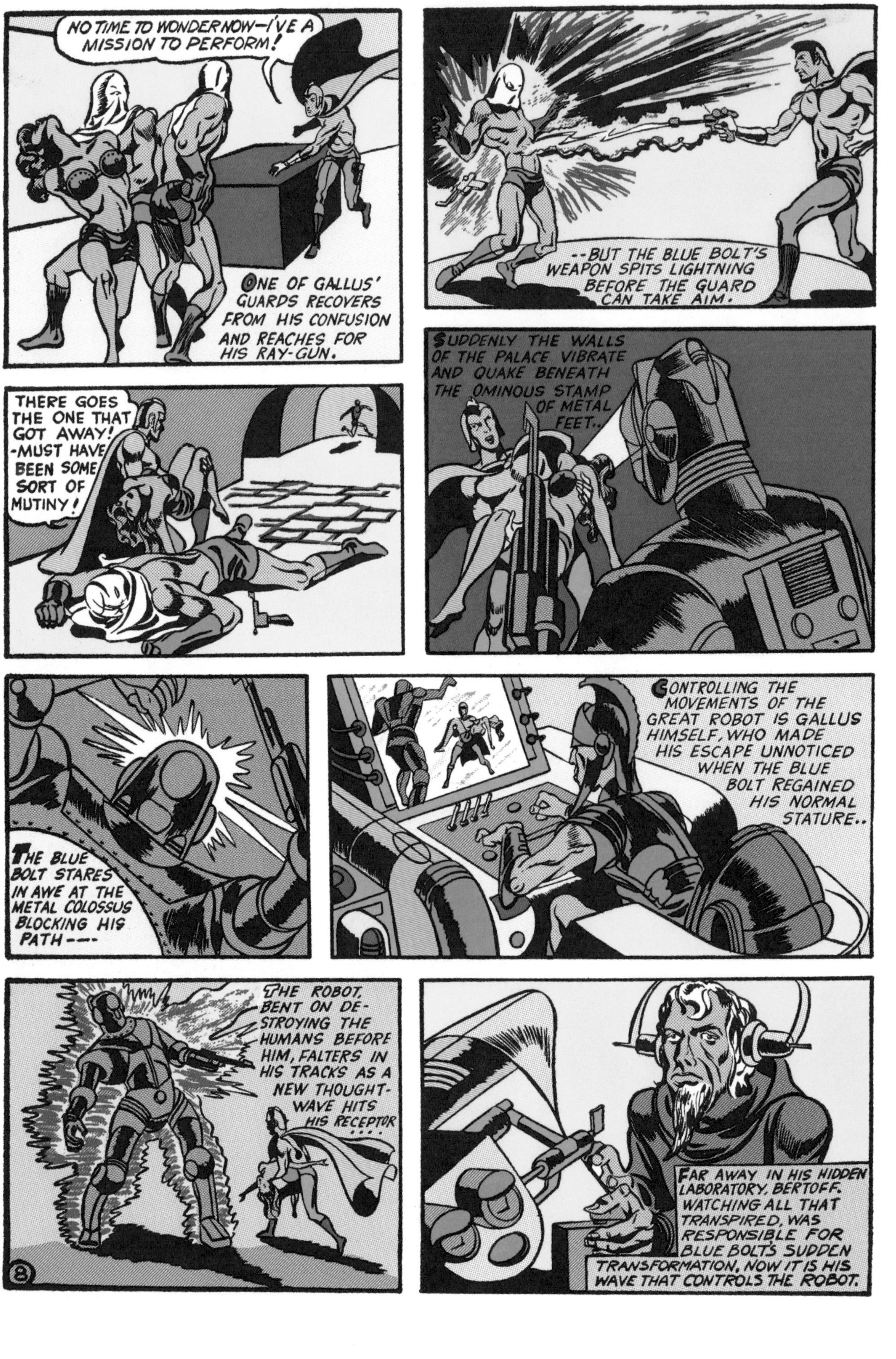
NO TIME TO WONDER NOW—I'VE A MISSION TO PERFORM!
ONE OF GALLUS' GUARDS RECOVERS FROM HIS CONFUSION AND REACHES FOR HIS RAY-GUN.
--BUT THE BLUE BOLT'S WEAPON SPITS LIGHTNING BEFORE THE GUARD CAN TAKE AIM.
THERE GOES THE ONE THAT GOT AWAY! -MUST HAVE BEEN SOME SORT OF MUTINY!
SUDDENLY THE WALLS OF THE PALACE VIBRATE AND QUAKE BENEATH THE OMINOUS STAMP OF METAL FEET..
THE BLUE BOLT STARES IN AWE AT THE METAL COLOSSUS BLOCKING HIS PATH---
CONTROLLING THE MOVEMENTS OF THE GREAT ROBOT IS GALLUS HIMSELF, WHO MADE HIS ESCAPE UNNOTICED WHEN THE BLUE BOLT REGAINED HIS NORMAL STATURE..
THE ROBOT, BENT ON DESTROYING THE HUMANS BEFORE HIM, FALTERS IN HIS TRACKS AS A NEW THOUGHT-WAVE HITS HIS RECEPTOR...
8
FAR AWAY IN HIS HIDDEN LABORATORY, BERTOFF, WATCHING ALL THAT TRANSPIRED, WAS RESPONSIBLE FOR BLUE BOLT'S SUDDEN TRANSFORMATION, NOW IT IS HIS WAVE THAT CONTROLS THE ROBOT.

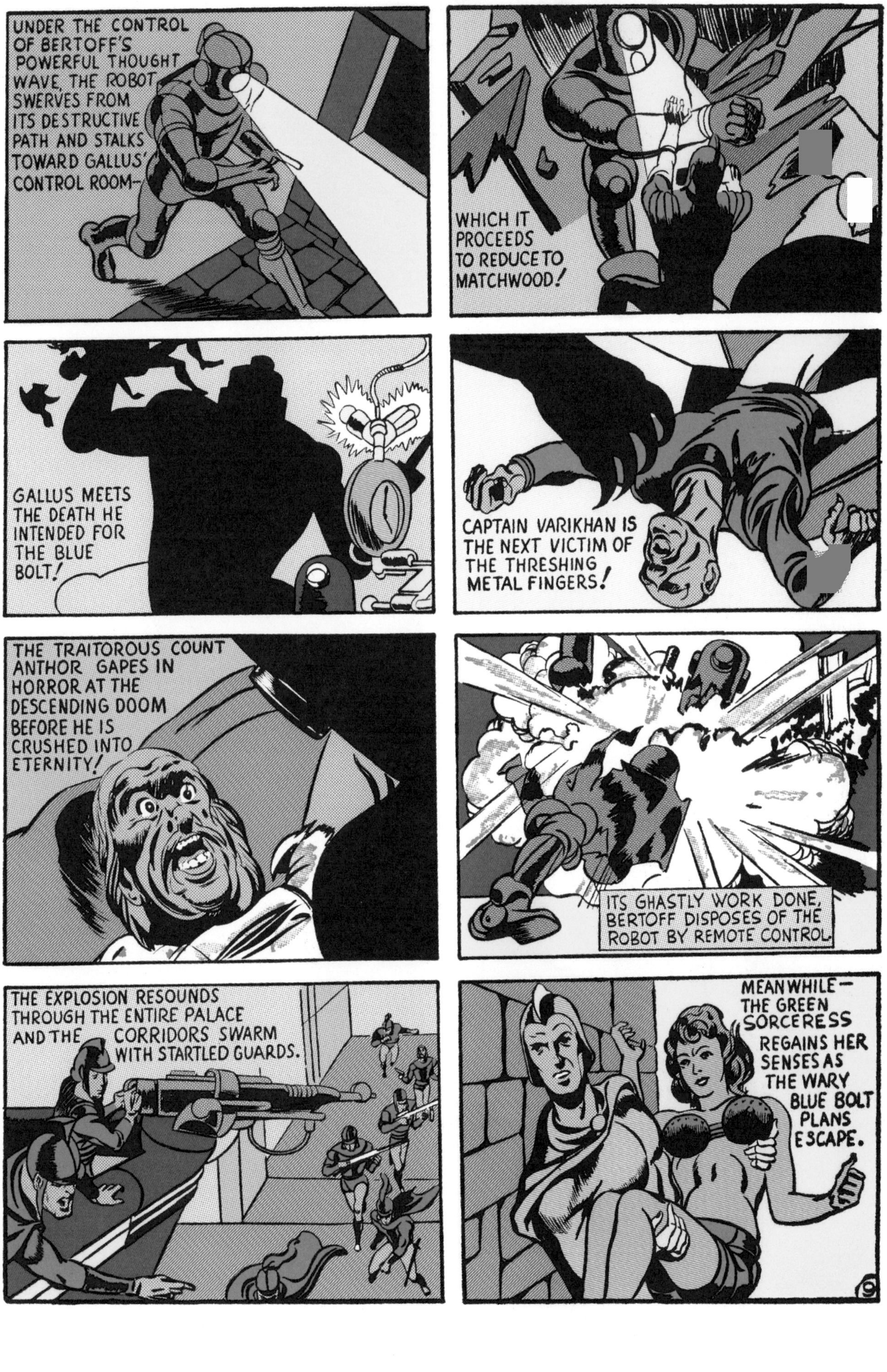
UNDER THE CONTROL OF BERTOFF'S POWERFUL THOUGHT WAVE, THE ROBOT SWERVES FROM ITS DESTRUCTIVE PATH AND STALKS TOWARD GALLUS' CONTROL ROOM—
WHICH IT PROCEEDS TO REDUCE TO MATCHWOOD!
GALLUS MEETS THE DEATH HE INTENDED FOR THE BLUE BOLT!
CAPTAIN VARIKHAN IS THE NEXT VICTIM OF THE THRESHING METAL FINGERS!
THE TRAITOROUS COUNT ANTHOR GAPES IN HORROR AT THE DESCENDING DOOM BEFORE HE IS CRUSHED INTO ETERNITY!
ITS GHASTLY WORK DONE, BERTOFF DISPOSES OF THE ROBOT BY REMOTE CONTROL.
THE EXPLOSION RESOUNDS THROUGH THE ENTIRE PALACE AND THE CORRIDORS SWARM WITH STARTLED GUARDS.
MEANWHILE— THE GREEN SORCERESS REGAINS HER SENSES AS THE WARY BLUE BOLT PLANS ESCAPE.
9

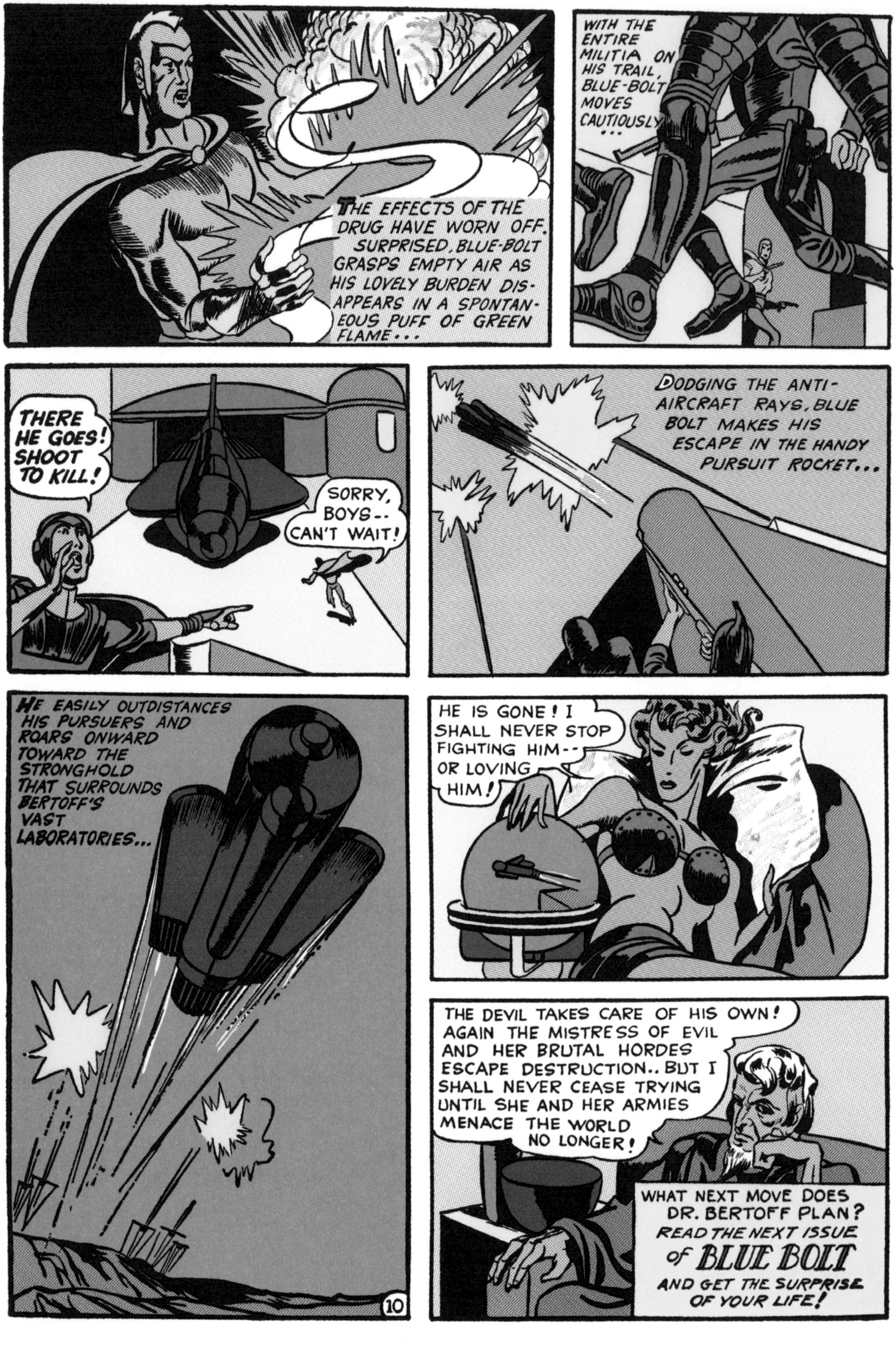
THE EFFECTS OF THE DRUG HAVE WORN OFF. SURPRISED, BLUE-BOLT GRASPS EMPTY AIR AS HIS LOVELY BURDEN DISAPPEARS IN A SPONTANEOUS PUFF OF GREEN FLAME...
WITH THE ENTIRE MILITIA ON HIS TRAIL, BLUE-BOLT MOVES CAUTIOUSLY...
THERE HE GOES! SHOOT TO KILL!
SORRY, BOYS-- CAN'T WAIT!
DODGING THE ANTI-AIRCRAFT RAYS, BLUE BOLT MAKES HIS ESCAPE IN THE HANDY PURSUIT ROCKET...
HE EASILY OUTDISTANCES HIS PURSUERS AND ROARS ONWARD TOWARD THE STRONGHOLD THAT SURROUNDS BERTOFF'S VAST LABORATORIES...
10
HE IS GONE! I SHALL NEVER STOP FIGHTING HIM-- OR LOVING HIM!
THE DEVIL TAKES CARE OF HIS OWN! AGAIN THE MISTRESS OF EVIL AND HER BRUTAL HORDES ESCAPE DESTRUCTION.. BUT I SHALL NEVER CEASE TRYING UNTIL SHE AND HER ARMIES MENACE THE WORLD NO LONGER!
WHAT NEXT MOVE DOES DR. BERTOFF PLAN? READ THE NEXT ISSUE OF BLUE BOLT AND GET THE SURPRISE OF YOUR LIFE!

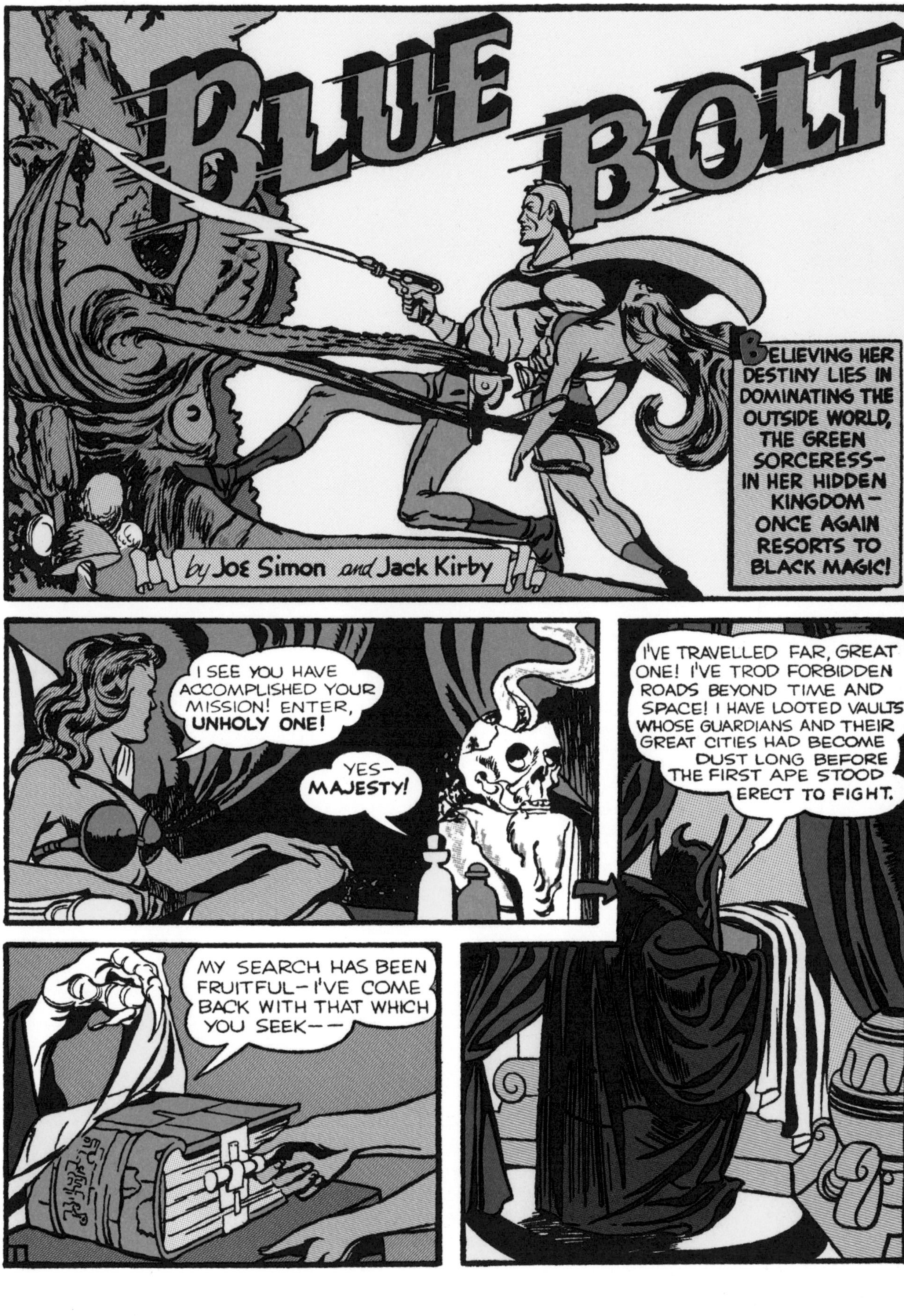
BLUE BOLT
BELIEVING HER DESTINY LIES IN DOMINATING THE OUTSIDE WORLD, THE GREEN SORCERESS— IN HER HIDDEN KINGDOM— ONCE AGAIN RESORTS TO BLACK MAGIC!
by Joe Simon and Jack Kirby
I SEE YOU HAVE ACCOMPLISHED YOUR MISSION! ENTER, UNHOLY ONE!
YES— MAJESTY!
I'VE TRAVELLED FAR, GREAT ONE! I'VE TROD FORBIDDEN ROADS BEYOND TIME AND SPACE! I HAVE LOOTED VAULTS WHOSE GUARDIANS AND THEIR GREAT CITIES HAD BECOME DUST LONG BEFORE THE FIRST APE STOOD ERECT TO FIGHT.
MY SEARCH HAS BEEN FRUITFUL— I'VE COME BACK WITH THAT WHICH YOU SEEK——

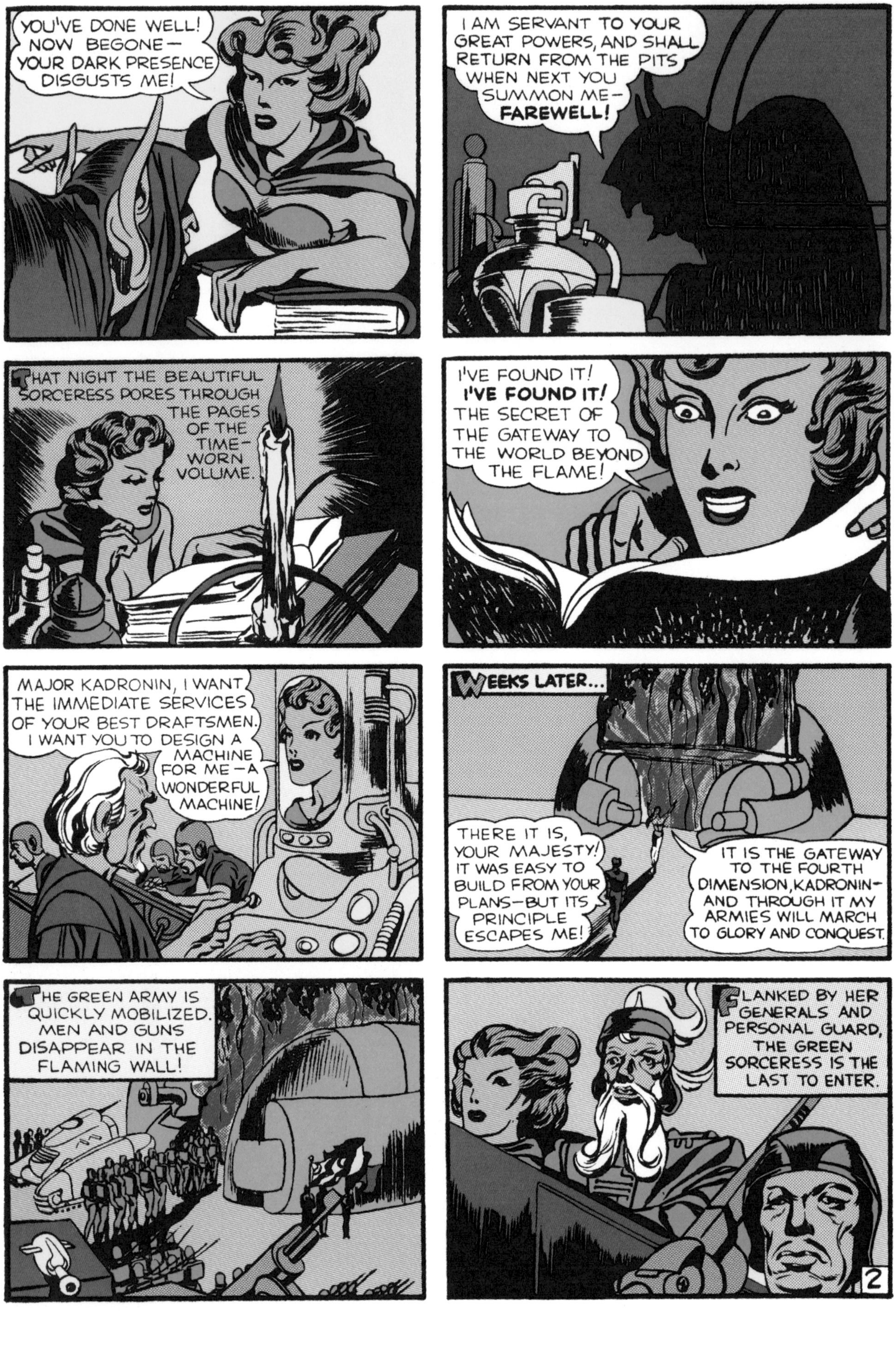
YOU'VE DONE WELL! NOW BEGONE— YOUR DARK PRESENCE DISGUSTS ME!
I AM SERVANT TO YOUR GREAT POWERS, AND SHALL RETURN FROM THE PITS WHEN NEXT YOU SUMMON ME— FAREWELL!
THAT NIGHT THE BEAUTIFUL SORCERESS PORES THROUGH THE PAGES OF THE TIME-WORN VOLUME.
I'VE FOUND IT! I'VE FOUND IT! THE SECRET OF THE GATEWAY TO THE WORLD BEYOND THE FLAME!
MAJOR KADRONIN, I WANT THE IMMEDIATE SERVICES OF YOUR BEST DRAFTSMEN. I WANT YOU TO DESIGN A MACHINE FOR ME—A WONDERFUL MACHINE!
WEEKS LATER...
THERE IT IS, YOUR MAJESTY! IT WAS EASY TO BUILD FROM YOUR PLANS—BUT ITS PRINCIPLE ESCAPES ME!
IT IS THE GATEWAY TO THE FOURTH DIMENSION, KADRONIN— AND THROUGH IT MY ARMIES WILL MARCH TO GLORY AND CONQUEST.
THE GREEN ARMY IS QUICKLY MOBILIZED. MEN AND GUNS DISAPPEAR IN THE FLAMING WALL!
FLANKED BY HER GENERALS AND PERSONAL GUARD, THE GREEN SORCERESS IS THE LAST TO ENTER.
2

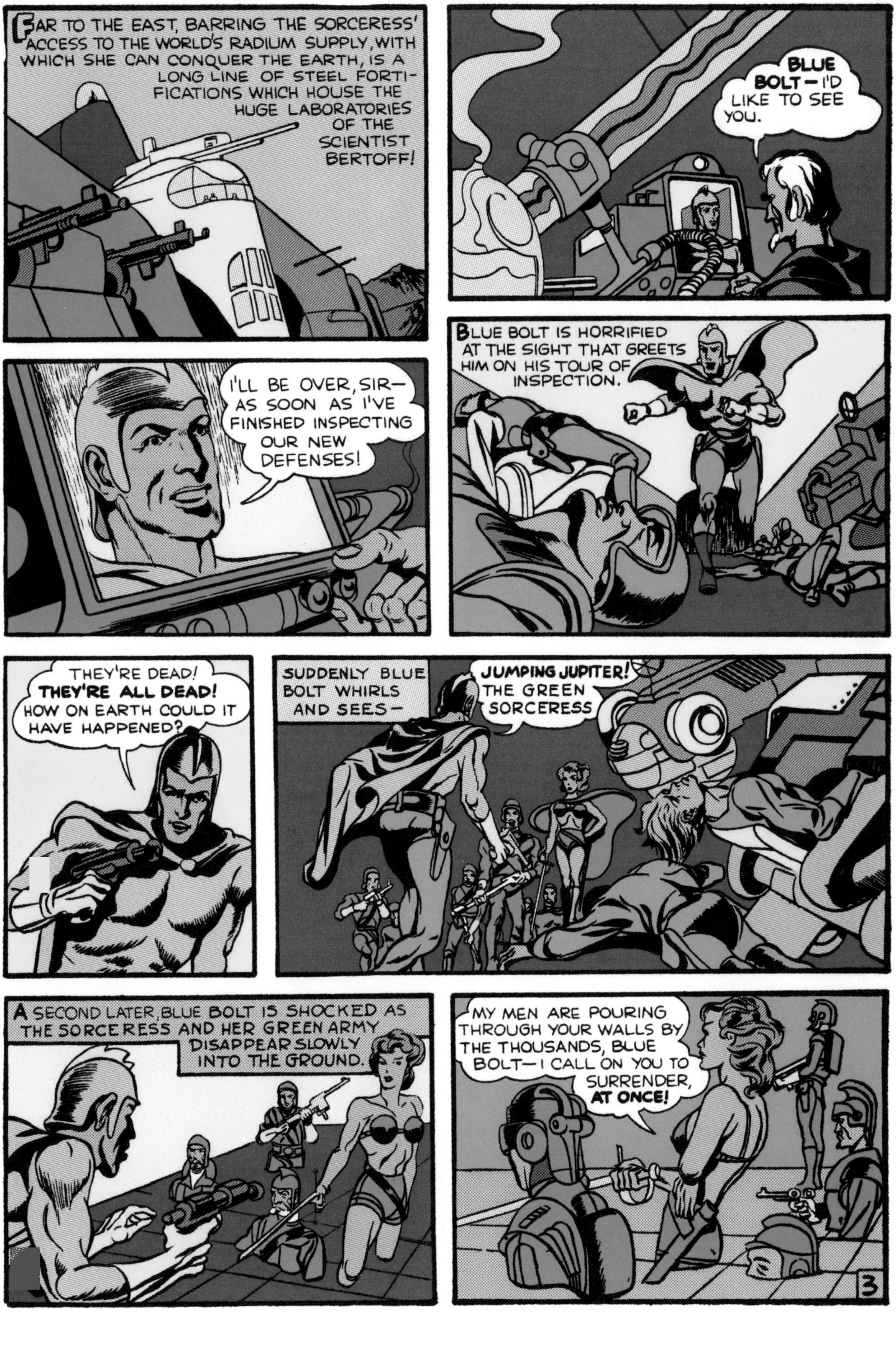
FAR TO THE EAST, BARRING THE SORCERESS' ACCESS TO THE WORLD'S RADIUM SUPPLY, WITH WHICH SHE CAN CONQUER THE EARTH, IS A LONG LINE OF STEEL FORTIFICATIONS WHICH HOUSE THE HUGE LABORATORIES OF THE SCIENTIST BERTOFF!
BLUE BOLT—I'D LIKE TO SEE YOU.
I'LL BE OVER, SIR—AS SOON AS I'VE FINISHED INSPECTING OUR NEW DEFENSES!
BLUE BOLT IS HORRIFIED AT THE SIGHT THAT GREETS HIM ON HIS TOUR OF INSPECTION.
THEY'RE DEAD! THEY'RE ALL DEAD! HOW ON EARTH COULD IT HAVE HAPPENED?
SUDDENLY BLUE BOLT WHIRLS AND SEES—
JUMPING JUPITER! THE GREEN SORCERESS
A SECOND LATER, BLUE BOLT IS SHOCKED AS THE SORCERESS AND HER GREEN ARMY DISAPPEAR SLOWLY INTO THE GROUND.
MY MEN ARE POURING THROUGH YOUR WALLS BY THE THOUSANDS, BLUE BOLT—I CALL ON YOU TO SURRENDER, AT ONCE!
3

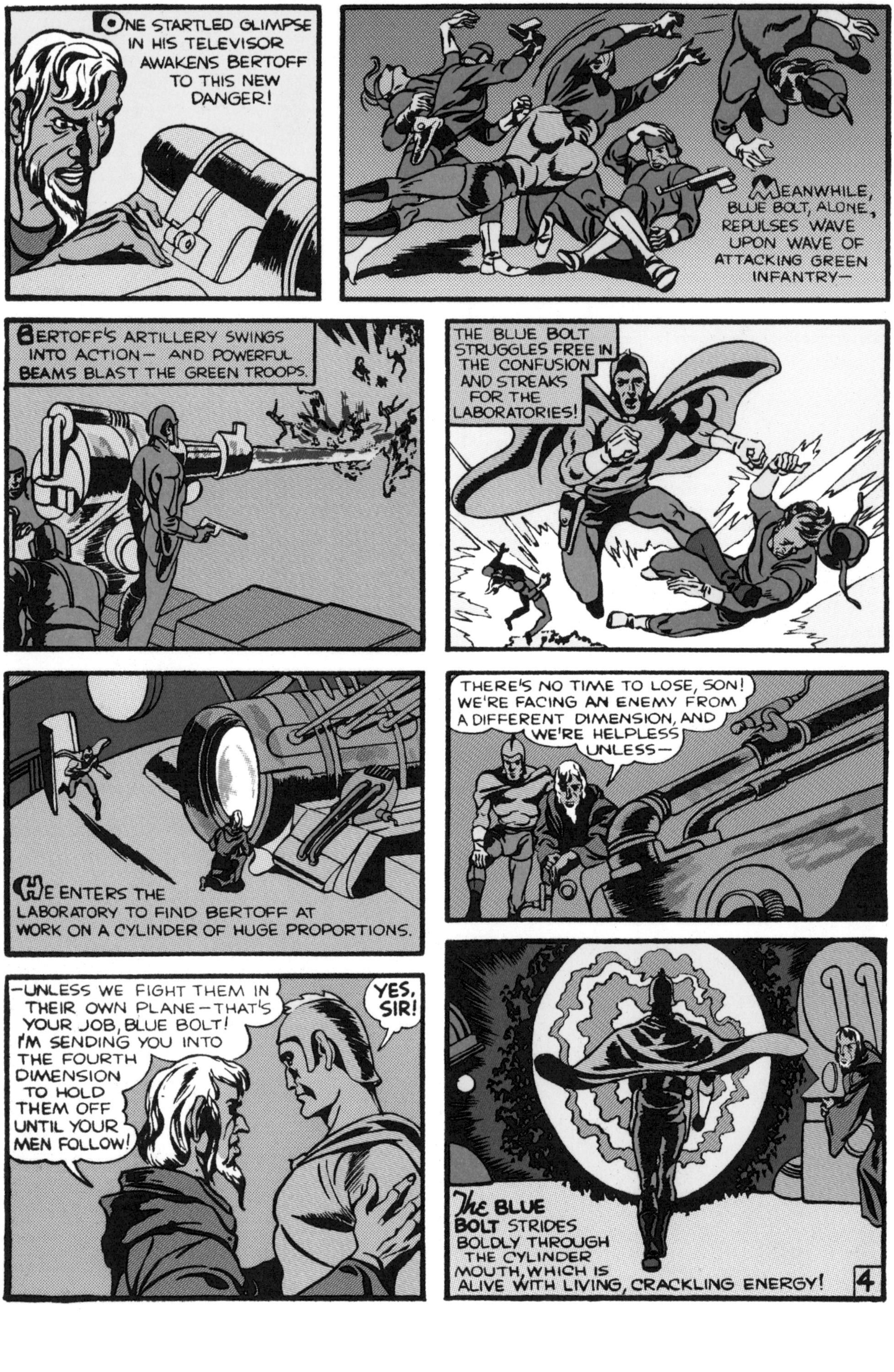
ONE STARTLED GLIMPSE IN HIS TELEVISOR AWAKENS BERTOFF TO THIS NEW DANGER!
MEANWHILE, BLUE BOLT, ALONE, REPULSES WAVE UPON WAVE OF ATTACKING GREEN INFANTRY—
BERTOFF'S ARTILLERY SWINGS INTO ACTION— AND POWERFUL BEAMS BLAST THE GREEN TROOPS.
THE BLUE BOLT STRUGGLES FREE IN THE CONFUSION AND STREAKS FOR THE LABORATORIES!
HE ENTERS THE LABORATORY TO FIND BERTOFF AT WORK ON A CYLINDER OF HUGE PROPORTIONS.
THERE'S NO TIME TO LOSE, SON! WE'RE FACING AN ENEMY FROM A DIFFERENT DIMENSION, AND WE'RE HELPLESS UNLESS—
—UNLESS WE FIGHT THEM IN THEIR OWN PLANE—THAT'S YOUR JOB, BLUE BOLT! I'M SENDING YOU INTO THE FOURTH DIMENSION TO HOLD THEM OFF UNTIL YOUR MEN FOLLOW!
YES, SIR!
THE BLUE BOLT STRIDES BOLDLY THROUGH THE CYLINDER MOUTH, WHICH IS ALIVE WITH LIVING, CRACKLING ENERGY!
4

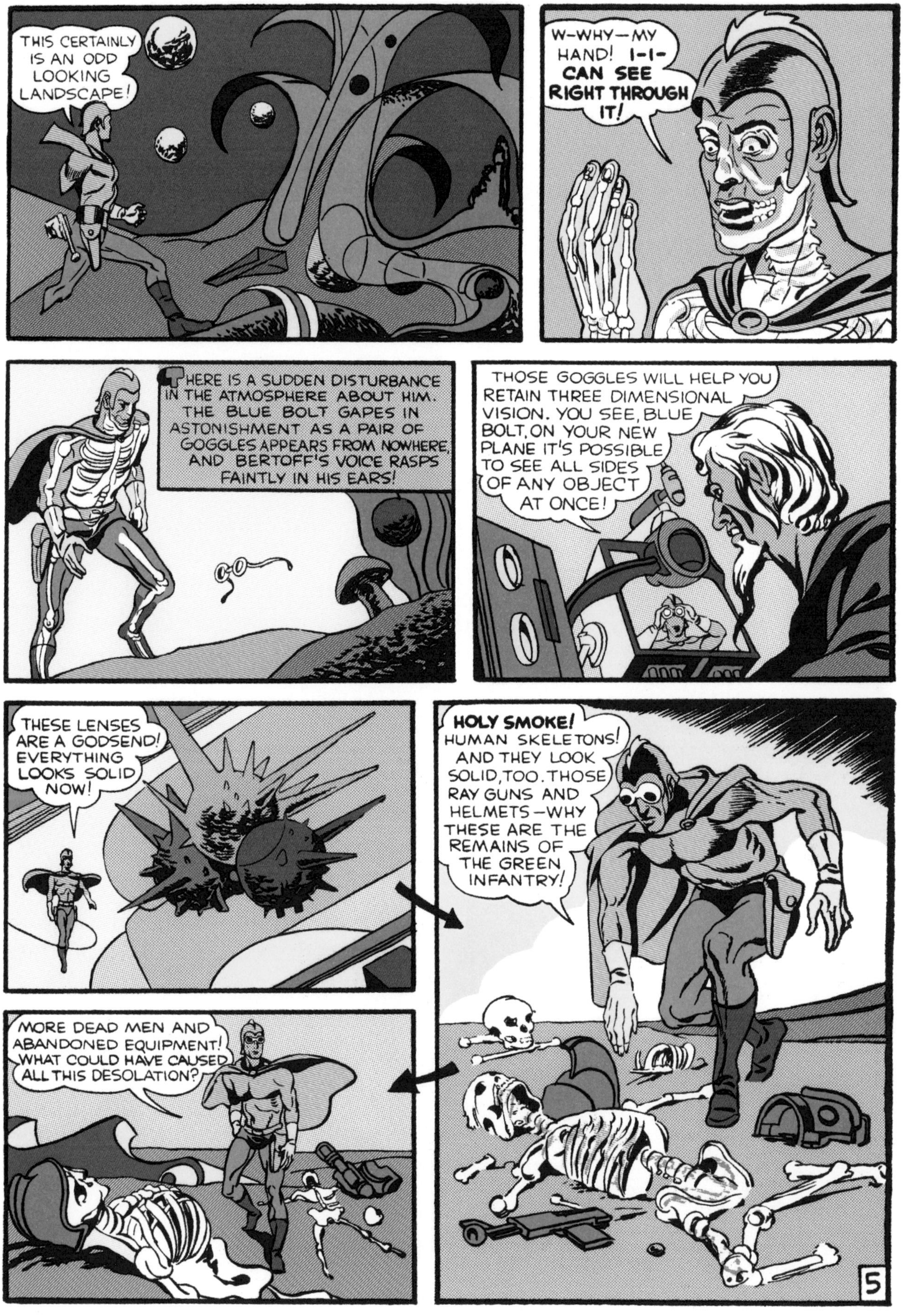

THIS CERTAINLY IS AN ODD LOOKING LANDSCAPE!
W-WHY—MY HAND! I-I- CAN SEE RIGHT THROUGH IT!
THERE IS A SUDDEN DISTURBANCE IN THE ATMOSPHERE ABOUT HIM. THE BLUE BOLT GAPES IN ASTONISHMENT AS A PAIR OF GOGGLES APPEARS FROM NOWHERE, AND BERTOFF'S VOICE RASPS FAINTLY IN HIS EARS!
THOSE GOGGLES WILL HELP YOU RETAIN THREE DIMENSIONAL VISION. YOU SEE, BLUE BOLT, ON YOUR NEW PLANE IT'S POSSIBLE TO SEE ALL SIDES OF ANY OBJECT AT ONCE!
THESE LENSES ARE A GODSEND! EVERYTHING LOOKS SOLID NOW!
HOLY SMOKE! HUMAN SKELETONS! AND THEY LOOK SOLID, TOO. THOSE RAY GUNS AND HELMETS—WHY THESE ARE THE REMAINS OF THE GREEN INFANTRY!
MORE DEAD MEN AND ABANDONED EQUIPMENT! WHAT COULD HAVE CAUSED ALL THIS DESOLATION?
5

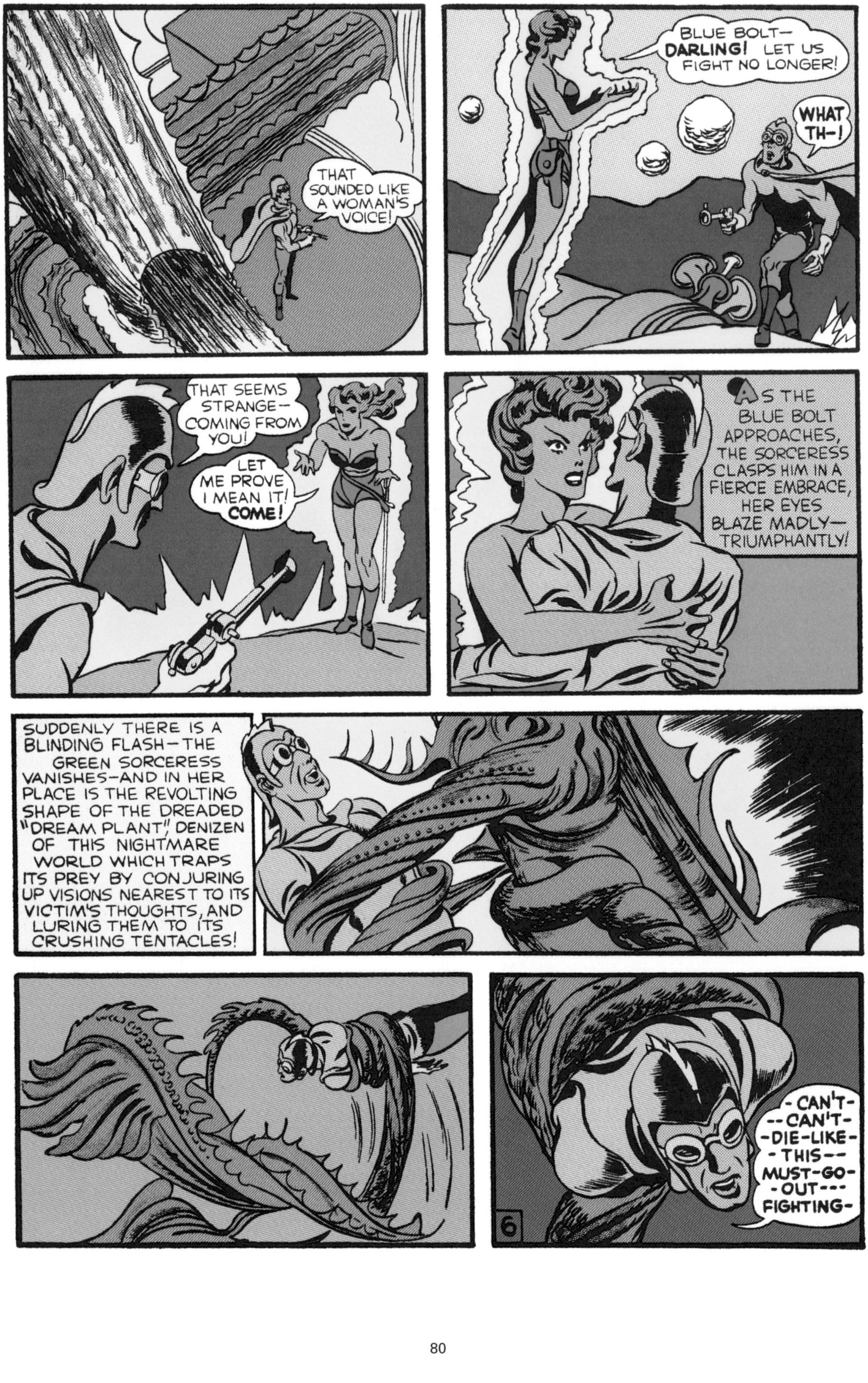
THAT SOUNDED LIKE A WOMAN'S VOICE!
BLUE BOLT— **DARLING!** LET US FIGHT NO LONGER!
WHAT TH—!
THAT SEEMS STRANGE— COMING FROM YOU!
LET ME PROVE I MEAN IT! **COME!**
AS THE BLUE BOLT APPROACHES, THE SORCERESS CLASPS HIM IN A FIERCE EMBRACE, HER EYES BLAZE MADLY— TRIUMPHANTLY!
SUDDENLY THERE IS A BLINDING FLASH— THE GREEN SORCERESS VANISHES—AND IN HER PLACE IS THE REVOLTING SHAPE OF THE DREADED "DREAM PLANT," DENIZEN OF THIS NIGHTMARE WORLD WHICH TRAPS ITS PREY BY CONJURING UP VISIONS NEAREST TO ITS VICTIM'S THOUGHTS, AND LURING THEM TO ITS CRUSHING TENTACLES!
-CAN'T--CAN'T-DIE-LIKE-THIS--MUST-GO-OUT---FIGHTING-
6

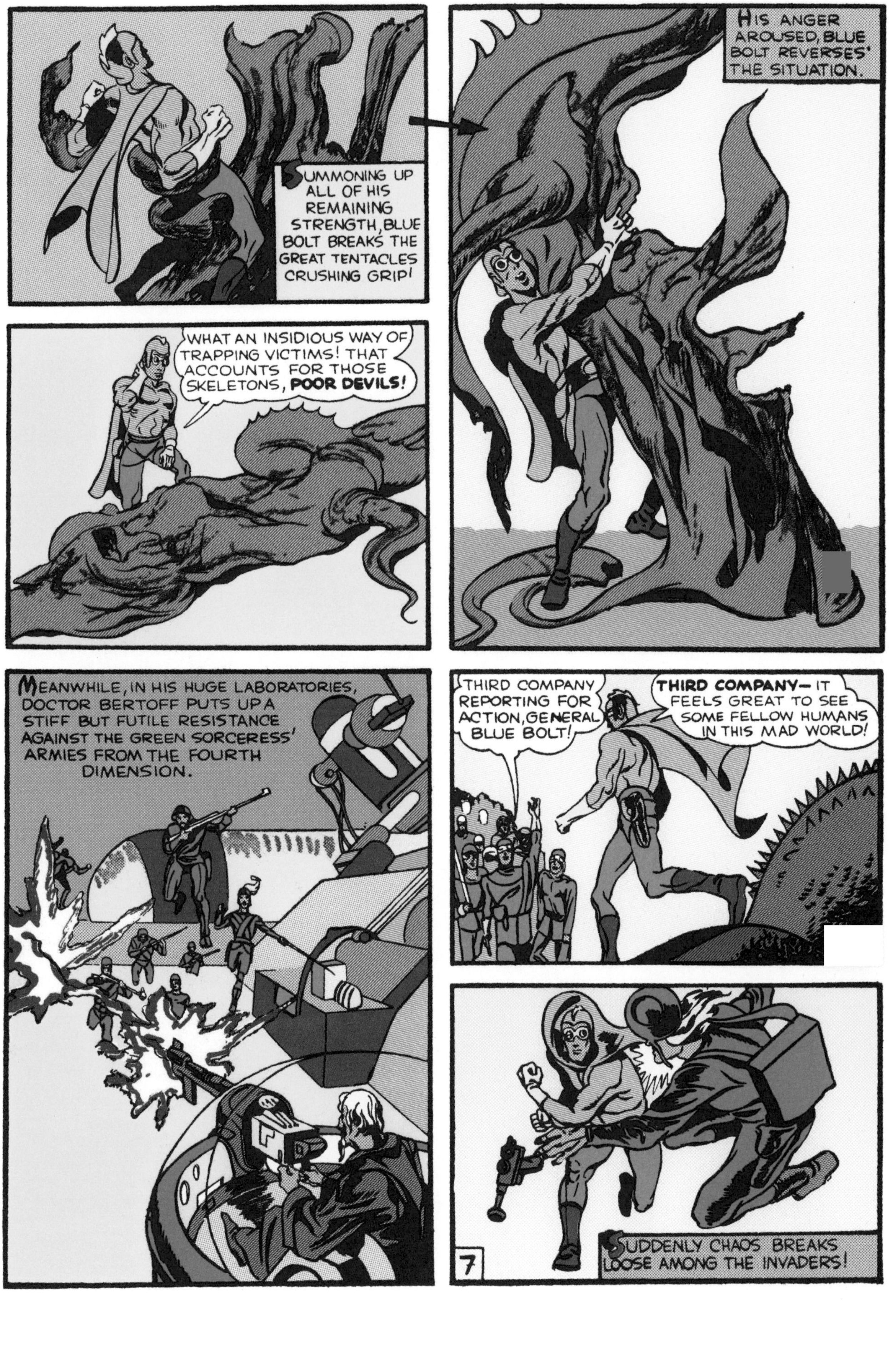
SUMMONING UP ALL OF HIS REMAINING STRENGTH, BLUE BOLT BREAKS THE GREAT TENTACLES CRUSHING GRIP!
HIS ANGER AROUSED, BLUE BOLT REVERSES' THE SITUATION.
WHAT AN INSIDIOUS WAY OF TRAPPING VICTIMS! THAT ACCOUNTS FOR THOSE SKELETONS, POOR DEVILS!
MEANWHILE, IN HIS HUGE LABORATORIES, DOCTOR BERTOFF PUTS UP A STIFF BUT FUTILE RESISTANCE AGAINST THE GREEN SORCERESS' ARMIES FROM THE FOURTH DIMENSION.
THIRD COMPANY REPORTING FOR ACTION, GENERAL BLUE BOLT!
THIRD COMPANY— IT FEELS GREAT TO SEE SOME FELLOW HUMANS IN THIS MAD WORLD!
7
SUDDENLY CHAOS BREAKS LOOSE AMONG THE INVADERS!

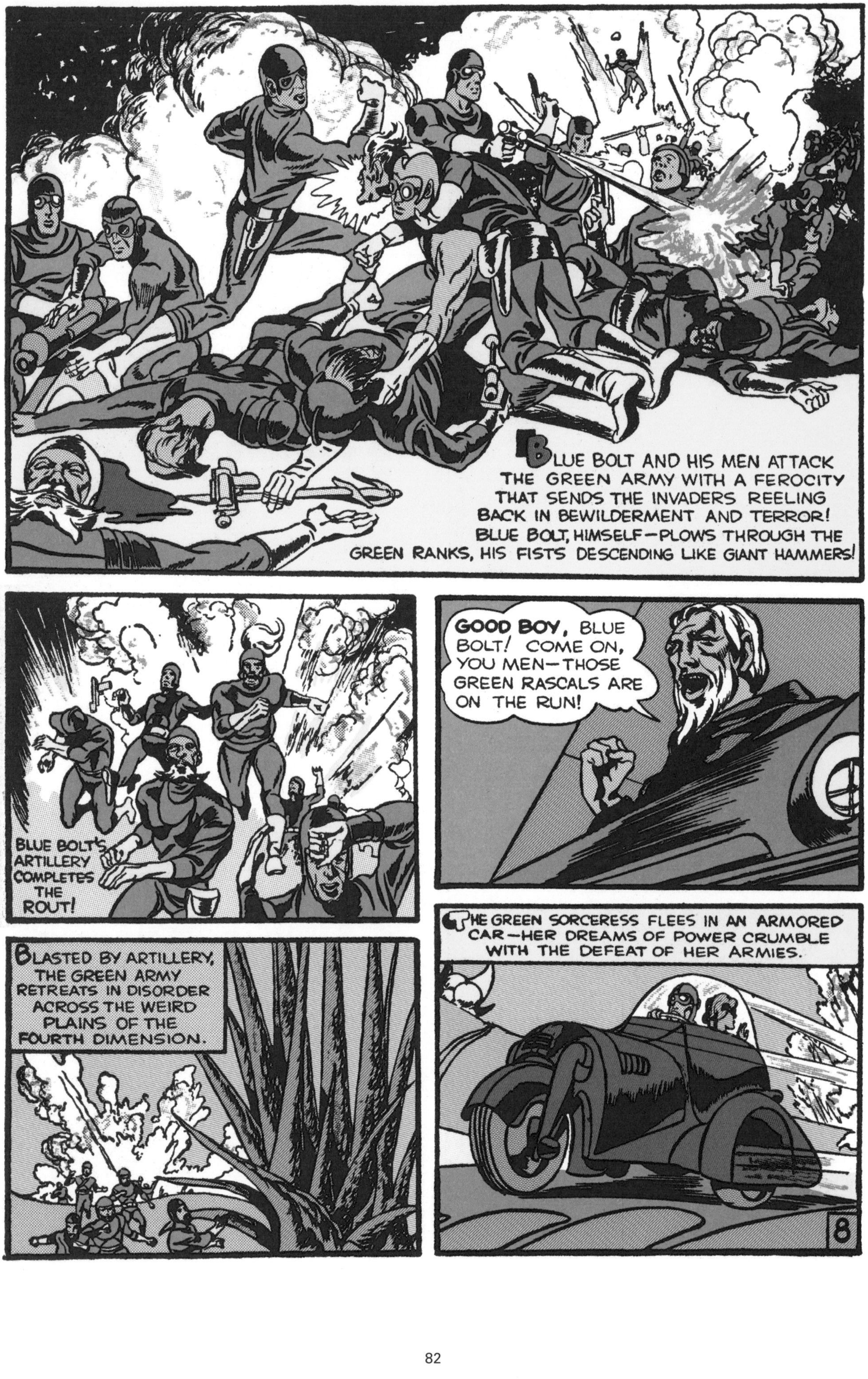
BLUE BOLT AND HIS MEN ATTACK THE GREEN ARMY WITH A FEROCITY THAT SENDS THE INVADERS REELING BACK IN BEWILDERMENT AND TERROR! BLUE BOLT, HIMSELF—PLOWS THROUGH THE GREEN RANKS, HIS FISTS DESCENDING LIKE GIANT HAMMERS!
BLUE BOLT'S ARTILLERY COMPLETES THE ROUT!
GOOD BOY, BLUE BOLT! COME ON, YOU MEN—THOSE GREEN RASCALS ARE ON THE RUN!
BLASTED BY ARTILLERY, THE GREEN ARMY RETREATS IN DISORDER ACROSS THE WEIRD PLAINS OF THE FOURTH DIMENSION.
THE GREEN SORCERESS FLEES IN AN ARMORED CAR—HER DREAMS OF POWER CRUMBLE WITH THE DEFEAT OF HER ARMIES.
8

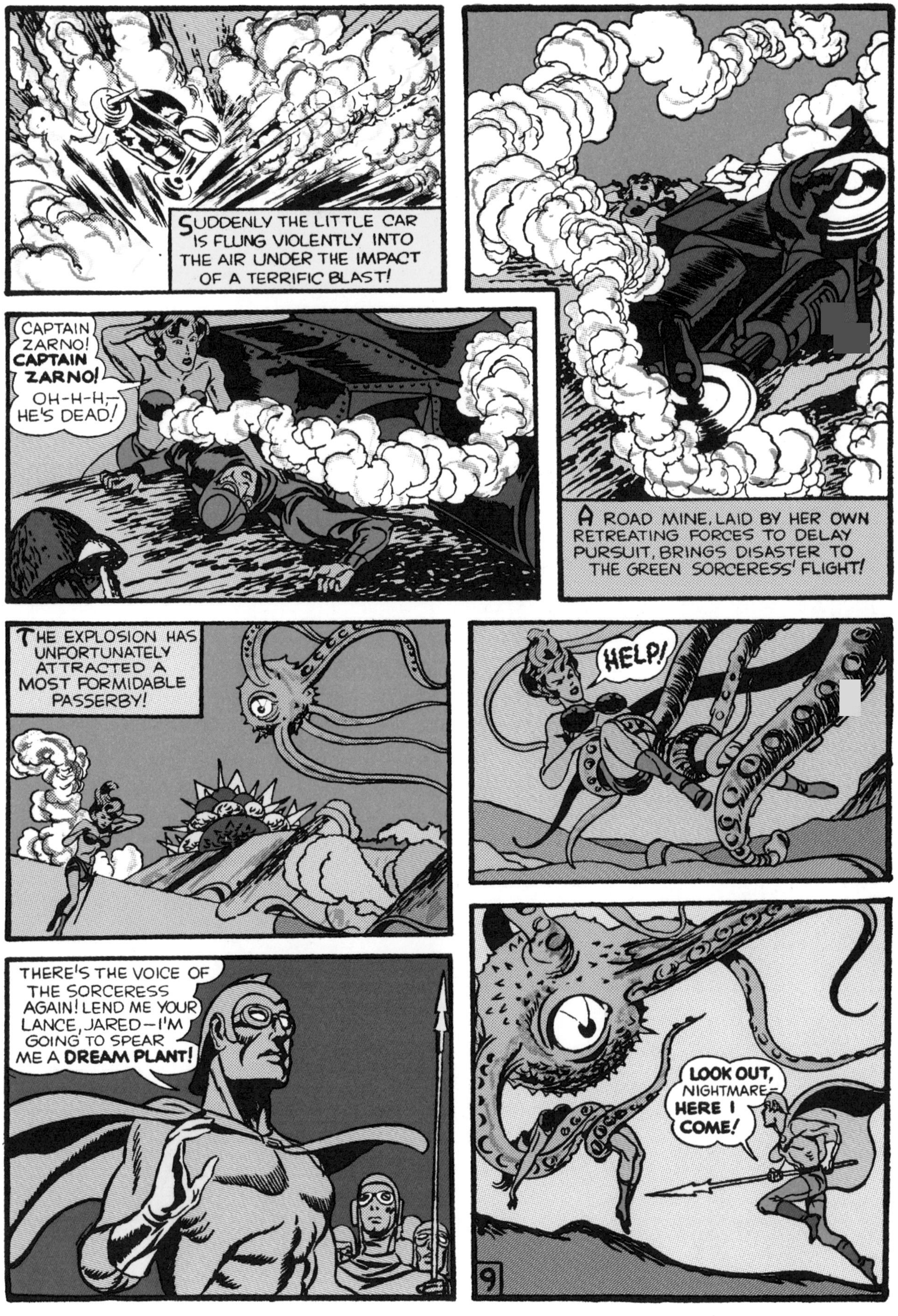

SUDDENLY THE LITTLE CAR IS FLUNG VIOLENTLY INTO THE AIR UNDER THE IMPACT OF A TERRIFIC BLAST!
A ROAD MINE, LAID BY HER OWN RETREATING FORCES TO DELAY PURSUIT, BRINGS DISASTER TO THE GREEN SORCERESS' FLIGHT!
CAPTAIN ZARNO! CAPTAIN ZARNO! OH-H-H,— HE'S DEAD!
THE EXPLOSION HAS UNFORTUNATELY ATTRACTED A MOST FORMIDABLE PASSERBY!
HELP!
THERE'S THE VOICE OF THE SORCERESS AGAIN! LEND ME YOUR LANCE, JARED—I'M GOING TO SPEAR ME A DREAM PLANT!
LOOK OUT, NIGHTMARE— HERE I COME!
9

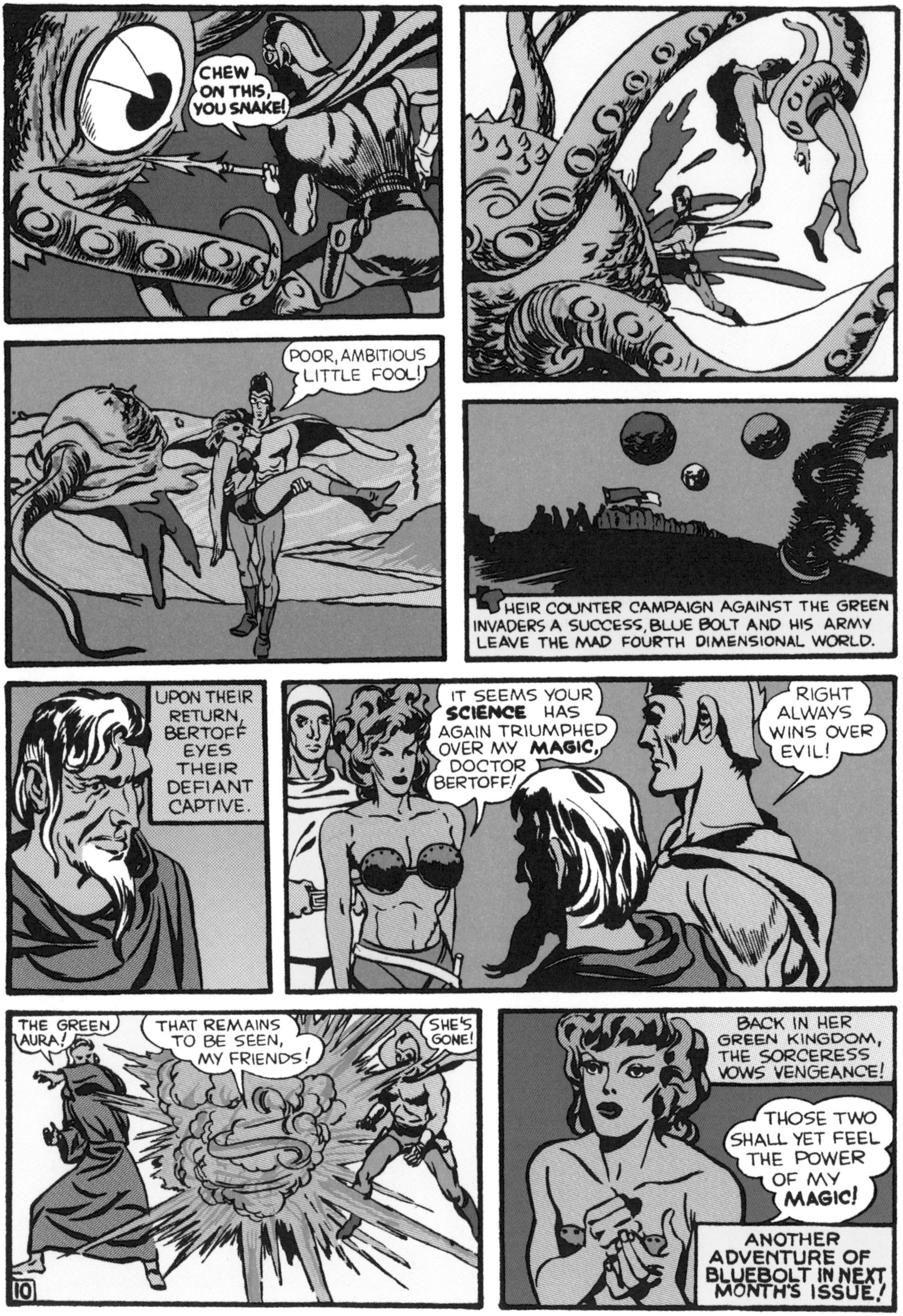
CHEW ON THIS, YOU SNAKE!
POOR, AMBITIOUS LITTLE FOOL!
THEIR COUNTER CAMPAIGN AGAINST THE GREEN INVADERS A SUCCESS, BLUE BOLT AND HIS ARMY LEAVE THE MAD FOURTH DIMENSIONAL WORLD.
UPON THEIR RETURN, BERTOFF EYES THEIR DEFIANT CAPTIVE.
IT SEEMS YOUR SCIENCE HAS AGAIN TRIUMPHED OVER MY MAGIC, DOCTOR BERTOFF!
RIGHT ALWAYS WINS OVER EVIL!
THE GREEN AURA!
THAT REMAINS TO BE SEEN, MY FRIENDS!
SHE'S GONE!
10
BACK IN HER GREEN KINGDOM, THE SORCERESS VOWS VENGEANCE!
THOSE TWO SHALL YET FEEL THE POWER OF MY MAGIC!
ANOTHER ADVENTURE OF BLUEBOLT IN NEXT MONTH'S ISSUE!

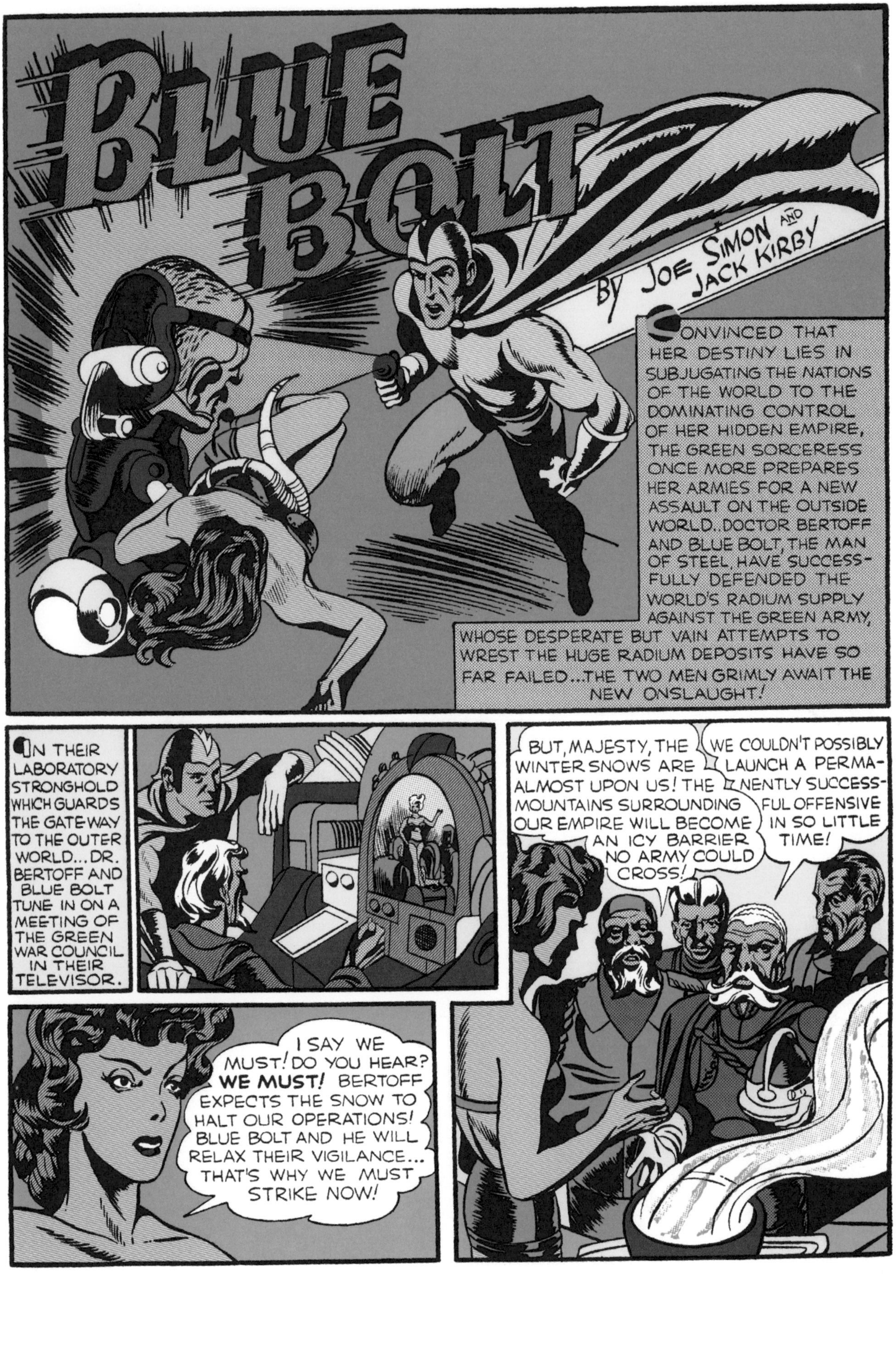
BLUE BOLT
BY JOE SIMON AND JACK KIRBY
CONVINCED THAT HER DESTINY LIES IN SUBJUGATING THE NATIONS OF THE WORLD TO THE DOMINATING CONTROL OF HER HIDDEN EMPIRE, THE GREEN SORCERESS ONCE MORE PREPARES HER ARMIES FOR A NEW ASSAULT ON THE OUTSIDE WORLD..DOCTOR BERTOFF AND BLUE BOLT, THE MAN OF STEEL, HAVE SUCCESSFULLY DEFENDED THE WORLD'S RADIUM SUPPLY AGAINST THE GREEN ARMY, WHOSE DESPERATE BUT VAIN ATTEMPTS TO WREST THE HUGE RADIUM DEPOSITS HAVE SO FAR FAILED...THE TWO MEN GRIMLY AWAIT THE NEW ONSLAUGHT!
IN THEIR LABORATORY STRONGHOLD WHICH GUARDS THE GATEWAY TO THE OUTER WORLD... DR. BERTOFF AND BLUE BOLT TUNE IN ON A MEETING OF THE GREEN WAR COUNCIL IN THEIR TELEVISOR.
BUT, MAJESTY, THE WINTER SNOWS ARE ALMOST UPON US! THE MOUNTAINS SURROUNDING OUR EMPIRE WILL BECOME AN ICY BARRIER NO ARMY COULD CROSS!
WE COULDN'T POSSIBLY LAUNCH A PERMANENTLY SUCCESSFUL OFFENSIVE IN SO LITTLE TIME!
I SAY WE MUST! DO YOU HEAR? WE MUST! BERTOFF EXPECTS THE SNOW TO HALT OUR OPERATIONS! BLUE BOLT AND HE WILL RELAX THEIR VIGILANCE... THAT'S WHY WE MUST STRIKE NOW!

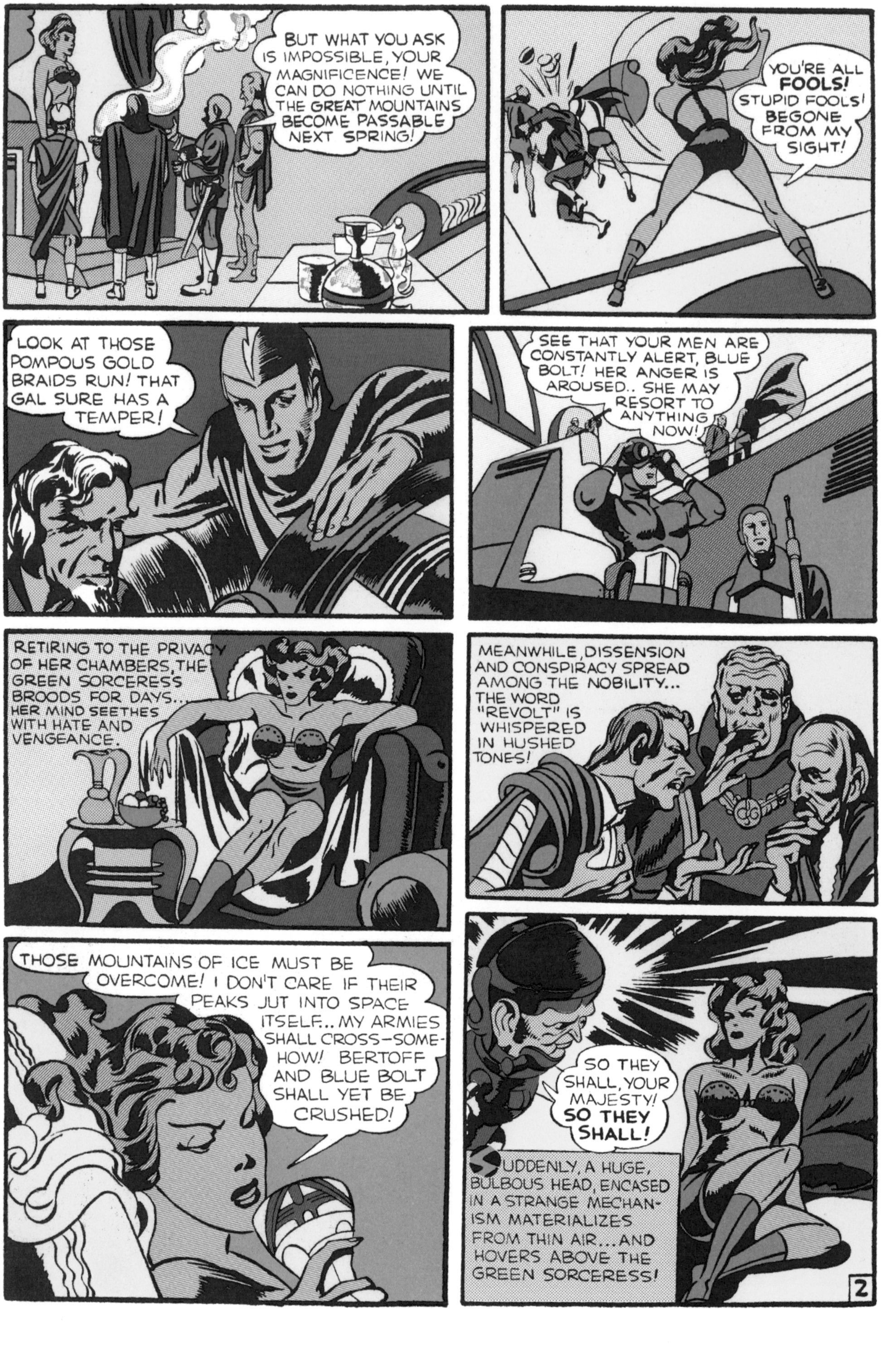

BUT WHAT YOU ASK IS IMPOSSIBLE, YOUR MAGNIFICENCE! WE CAN DO NOTHING UNTIL THE GREAT MOUNTAINS BECOME PASSABLE NEXT SPRING!
YOU'RE ALL FOOLS! STUPID FOOLS! BEGONE FROM MY SIGHT!
LOOK AT THOSE POMPOUS GOLD BRAIDS RUN! THAT GAL SURE HAS A TEMPER!
SEE THAT YOUR MEN ARE CONSTANTLY ALERT, BLUE BOLT! HER ANGER IS AROUSED.. SHE MAY RESORT TO ANYTHING NOW!
RETIRING TO THE PRIVACY OF HER CHAMBERS, THE GREEN SORCERESS'S BROODS FOR DAYS... HER MIND SEETHES WITH HATE AND VENGEANCE.
MEANWHILE, DISSENSION AND CONSPIRACY SPREAD AMONG THE NOBILITY... THE WORD "REVOLT" IS WHISPERED IN HUSHED TONES!
THOSE MOUNTAINS OF ICE MUST BE OVERCOME! I DON'T CARE IF THEIR PEAKS JUT INTO SPACE ITSELF... MY ARMIES SHALL CROSS—SOMEHOW! BERTOFF AND BLUE BOLT SHALL YET BE CRUSHED!
SO THEY SHALL, YOUR MAJESTY! SO THEY SHALL!
SUDDENLY, A HUGE, BULBOUS HEAD, ENCASED IN A STRANGE MECHANISM MATERIALIZES FROM THIN AIR... AND HOVERS ABOVE THE GREEN SORCERESS!
2

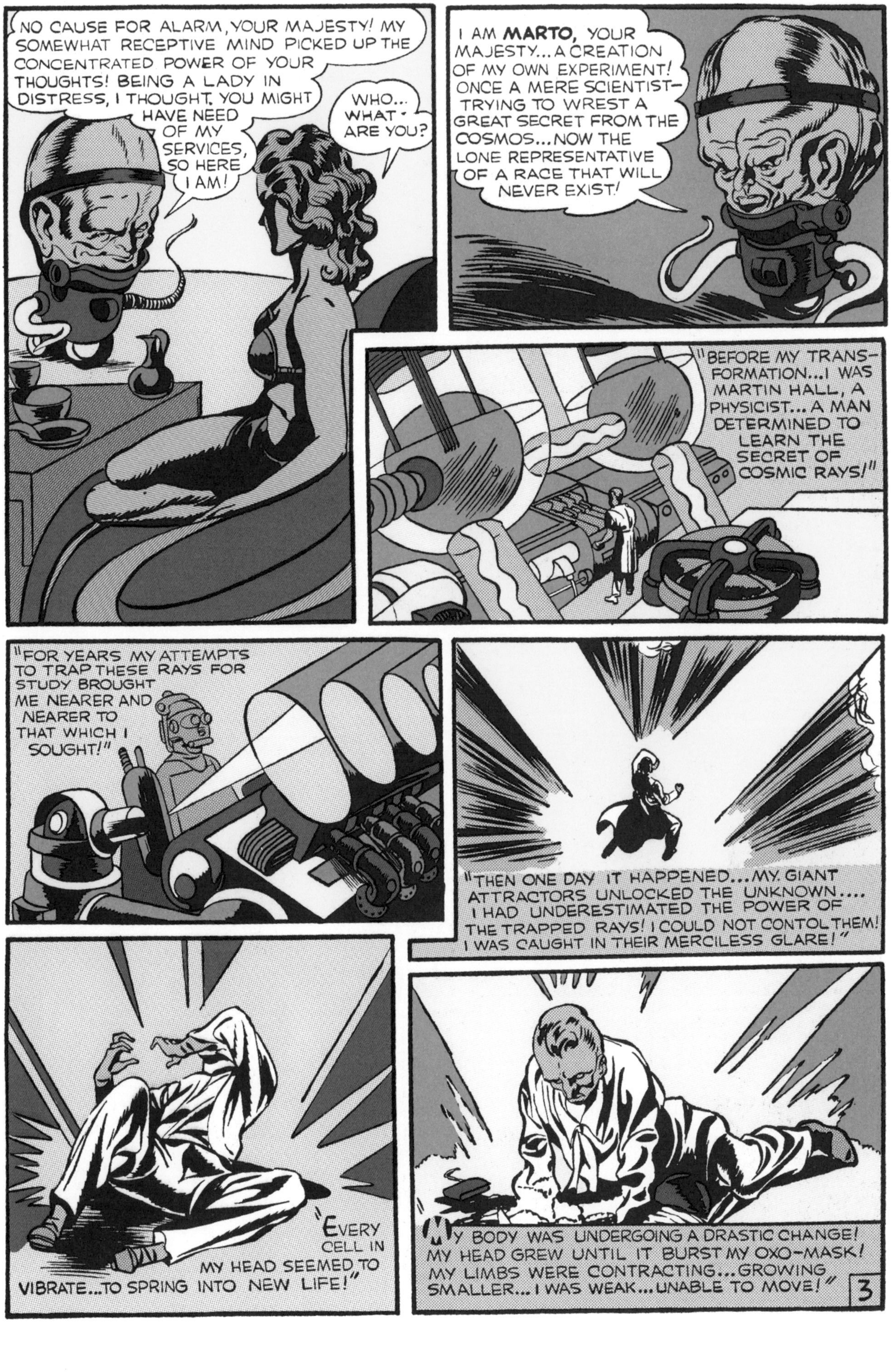
NO CAUSE FOR ALARM, YOUR MAJESTY! MY SOMEWHAT RECEPTIVE MIND PICKED UP THE CONCENTRATED POWER OF YOUR THOUGHTS! BEING A LADY IN DISTRESS, I THOUGHT YOU MIGHT HAVE NEED OF MY SERVICES, SO HERE I AM!
WHO... WHAT - ARE YOU?
I AM MARTO, YOUR MAJESTY... A CREATION OF MY OWN EXPERIMENT! ONCE A MERE SCIENTIST-TRYING TO WREST A GREAT SECRET FROM THE COSMOS... NOW THE LONE REPRESENTATIVE OF A RACE THAT WILL NEVER EXIST!
"BEFORE MY TRANSFORMATION... I WAS MARTIN HALL, A PHYSICIST... A MAN DETERMINED TO LEARN THE SECRET OF COSMIC RAYS!"
"FOR YEARS MY ATTEMPTS TO TRAP THESE RAYS FOR STUDY BROUGHT ME NEARER AND NEARER TO THAT WHICH I SOUGHT!"
"THEN ONE DAY IT HAPPENED... MY GIANT ATTRACTORS UNLOCKED THE UNKNOWN.... I HAD UNDERESTIMATED THE POWER OF THE TRAPPED RAYS! I COULD NOT CONTOL THEM! I WAS CAUGHT IN THEIR MERCILESS GLARE!"
"EVERY CELL IN MY HEAD SEEMED TO VIBRATE... TO SPRING INTO NEW LIFE!"
"MY BODY WAS UNDERGOING A DRASTIC CHANGE! MY HEAD GREW UNTIL IT BURST MY OXO-MASK! MY LIMBS WERE CONTRACTING... GROWING SMALLER... I WAS WEAK... UNABLE TO MOVE!"
3

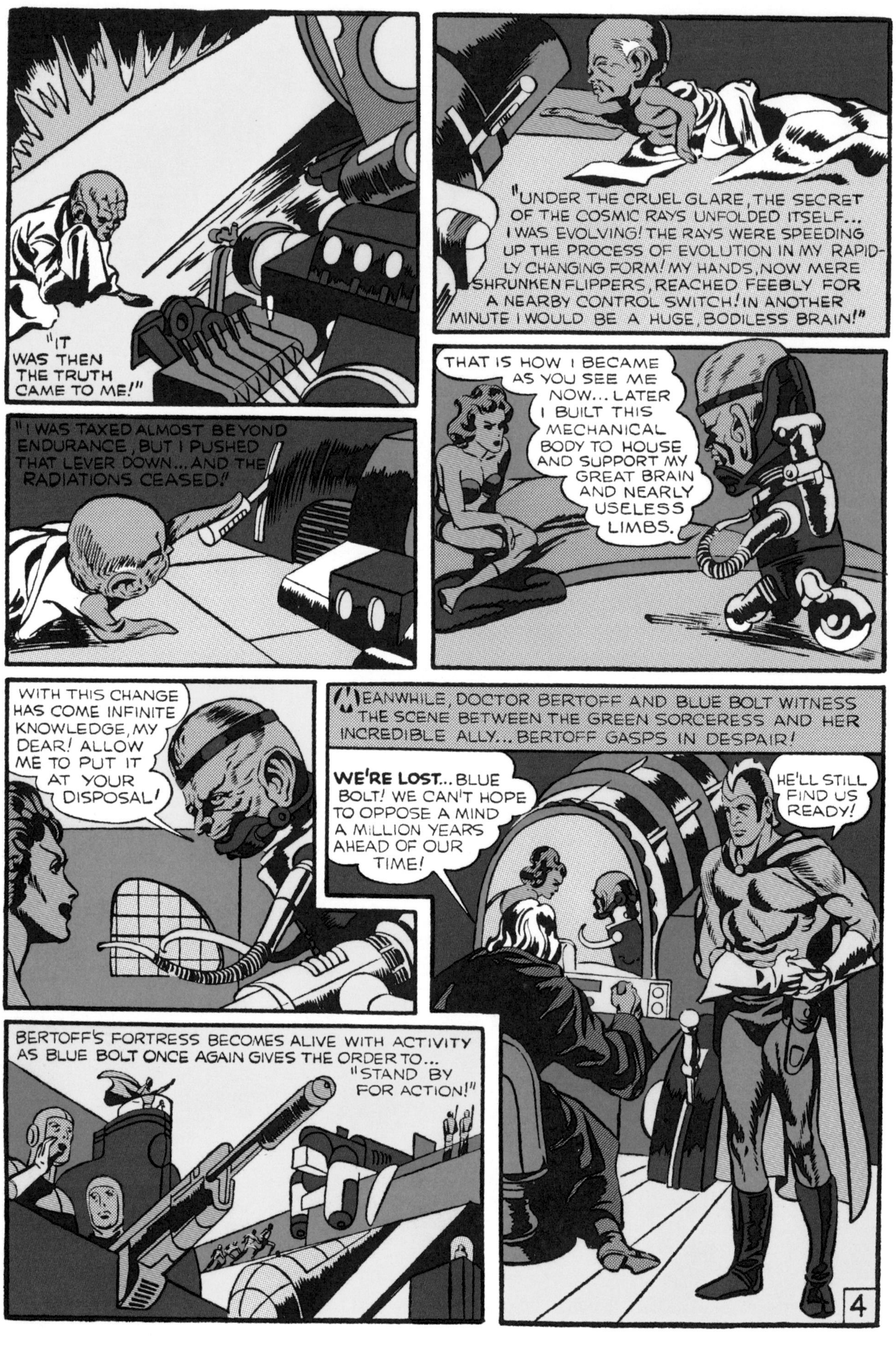

"IT WAS THEN THE TRUTH CAME TO ME!"
"UNDER THE CRUEL GLARE, THE SECRET OF THE COSMIC RAYS UNFOLDED ITSELF... I WAS EVOLVING! THE RAYS WERE SPEEDING UP THE PROCESS OF EVOLUTION IN MY RAPIDLY CHANGING FORM! MY HANDS, NOW MERE SHRUNKEN FLIPPERS, REACHED FEEBLY FOR A NEARBY CONTROL SWITCH! IN ANOTHER MINUTE I WOULD BE A HUGE, BODILESS BRAIN!"
"I WAS TAXED ALMOST BEYOND ENDURANCE, BUT I PUSHED THAT LEVER DOWN... AND THE RADIATIONS CEASED!"
THAT IS HOW I BECAME AS YOU SEE ME NOW... LATER I BUILT THIS MECHANICAL BODY TO HOUSE AND SUPPORT MY GREAT BRAIN AND NEARLY USELESS LIMBS.
WITH THIS CHANGE HAS COME INFINITE KNOWLEDGE, MY DEAR! ALLOW ME TO PUT IT AT YOUR DISPOSAL!
MEANWHILE, DOCTOR BERTOFF AND BLUE BOLT WITNESS THE SCENE BETWEEN THE GREEN SORCERESS AND HER INCREDIBLE ALLY... BERTOFF GASPS IN DESPAIR!
WE'RE LOST... BLUE BOLT! WE CAN'T HOPE TO OPPOSE A MIND A MILLION YEARS AHEAD OF OUR TIME!
HE'LL STILL FIND US READY!
BERTOFF'S FORTRESS BECOMES ALIVE WITH ACTIVITY AS BLUE BOLT ONCE AGAIN GIVES THE ORDER TO... "STAND BY FOR ACTION!"
4

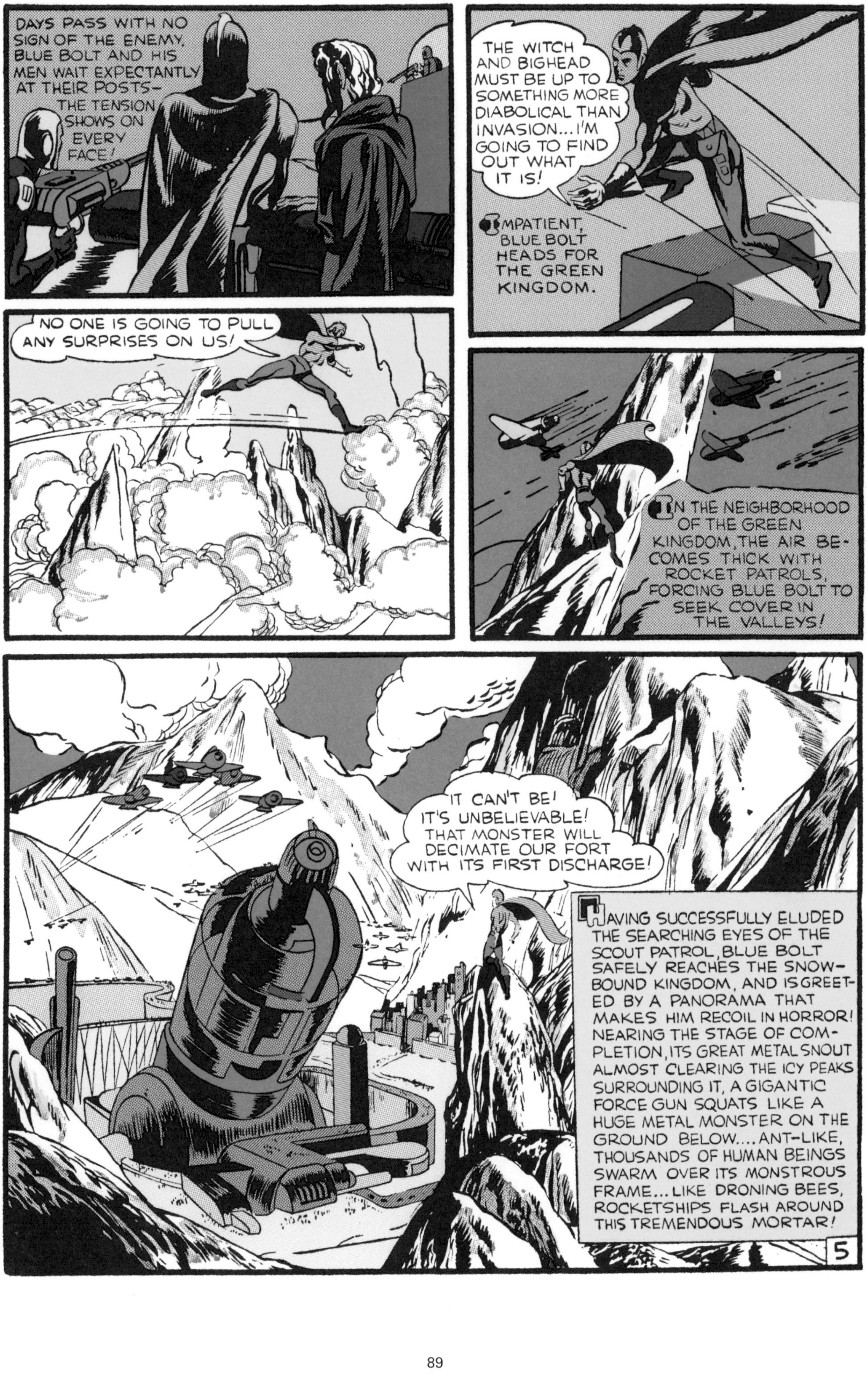
DAYS PASS WITH NO SIGN OF THE ENEMY. BLUE BOLT AND HIS MEN WAIT EXPECTANTLY AT THEIR POSTS— THE TENSION SHOWS ON EVERY FACE!
THE WITCH AND BIGHEAD MUST BE UP TO SOMETHING MORE DIABOLICAL THAN INVASION... I'M GOING TO FIND OUT WHAT IT IS!
IMPATIENT, BLUE BOLT HEADS FOR THE GREEN KINGDOM.
NO ONE IS GOING TO PULL ANY SURPRISES ON US!
IN THE NEIGHBORHOOD OF THE GREEN KINGDOM, THE AIR BECOMES THICK WITH ROCKET PATROLS, FORCING BLUE BOLT TO SEEK COVER IN THE VALLEYS!
IT CAN'T BE! IT'S UNBELIEVABLE! THAT MONSTER WILL DECIMATE OUR FORT WITH ITS FIRST DISCHARGE!
HAVING SUCCESSFULLY ELUDED THE SEARCHING EYES OF THE SCOUT PATROL, BLUE BOLT SAFELY REACHES THE SNOW-BOUND KINGDOM, AND IS GREETED BY A PANORAMA THAT MAKES HIM RECOIL IN HORROR! NEARING THE STAGE OF COMPLETION, ITS GREAT METAL SNOUT ALMOST CLEARING THE ICY PEAKS SURROUNDING IT, A GIGANTIC FORCE GUN SQUATS LIKE A HUGE METAL MONSTER ON THE GROUND BELOW.... ANT-LIKE, THOUSANDS OF HUMAN BEINGS SWARM OVER ITS MONSTROUS FRAME... LIKE DRONING BEES, ROCKETSHIPS FLASH AROUND THIS TREMENDOUS MORTAR!
5

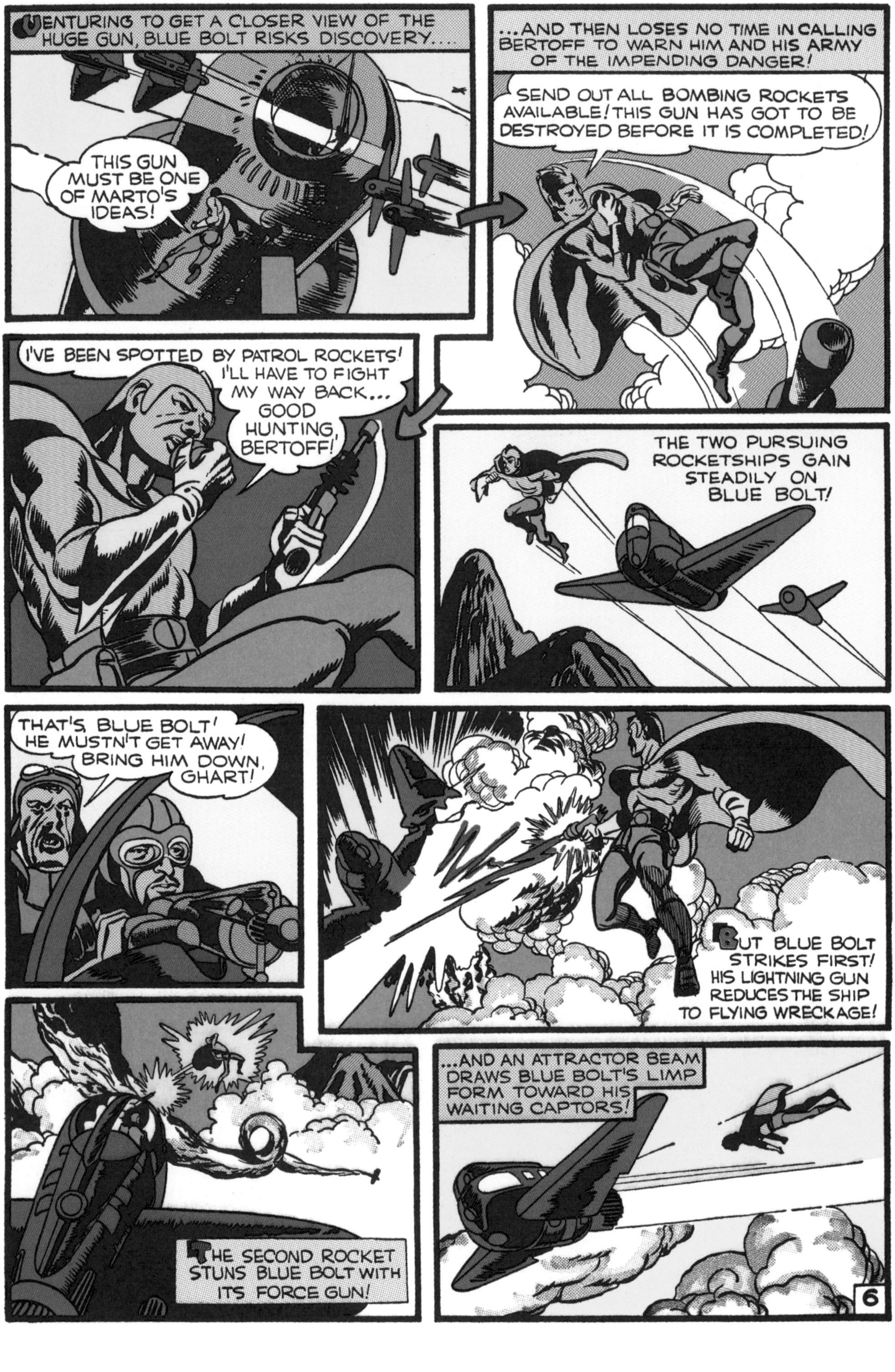
VENTURING TO GET A CLOSER VIEW OF THE HUGE GUN, BLUE BOLT RISKS DISCOVERY...
THIS GUN MUST BE ONE OF MARTO'S IDEAS!
...AND THEN LOSES NO TIME IN CALLING BERTOFF TO WARN HIM AND HIS ARMY OF THE IMPENDING DANGER!
SEND OUT ALL BOMBING ROCKETS AVAILABLE! THIS GUN HAS GOT TO BE DESTROYED BEFORE IT IS COMPLETED!
I'VE BEEN SPOTTED BY PATROL ROCKETS! I'LL HAVE TO FIGHT MY WAY BACK... GOOD HUNTING, BERTOFF!
THE TWO PURSUING ROCKETSHIPS GAIN STEADILY ON BLUE BOLT!
THAT'S BLUE BOLT! HE MUSTN'T GET AWAY! BRING HIM DOWN, GHART!
BUT BLUE BOLT STRIKES FIRST! HIS LIGHTNING GUN REDUCES THE SHIP TO FLYING WRECKAGE!
THE SECOND ROCKET STUNS BLUE BOLT WITH ITS FORCE GUN!
...AND AN ATTRACTOR BEAM DRAWS BLUE BOLT'S LIMP FORM TOWARD HIS WAITING CAPTORS!
6

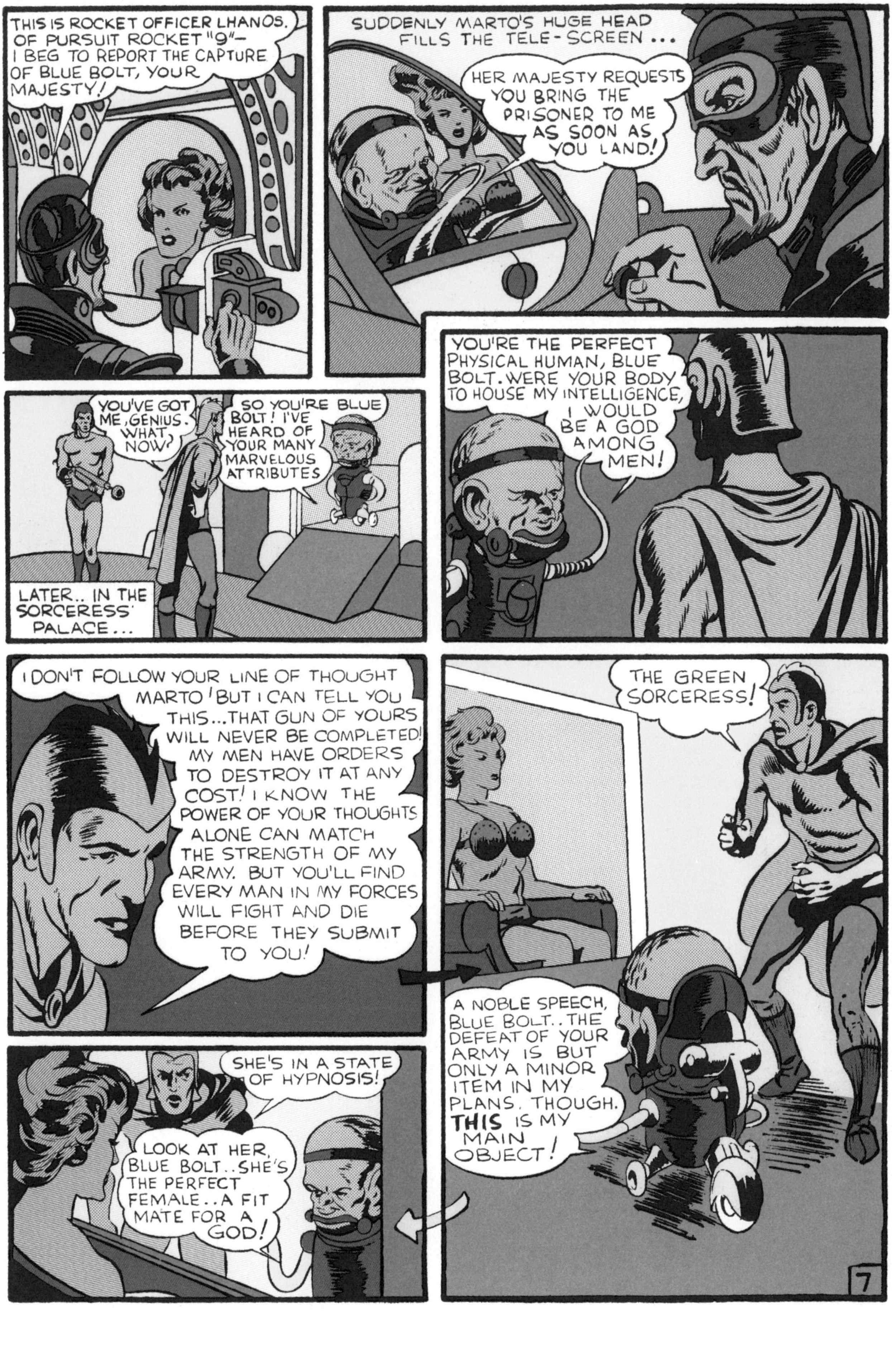

THIS IS ROCKET OFFICER LHANOS. OF PURSUIT ROCKET "9"— I BEG TO REPORT THE CAPTURE OF BLUE BOLT, YOUR MAJESTY!
SUDDENLY MARTO'S HUGE HEAD FILLS THE TELE-SCREEN...
HER MAJESTY REQUESTS YOU BRING THE PRISONER TO ME AS SOON AS YOU LAND!
LATER.. IN THE SORCERESS' PALACE...
YOU'VE GOT ME, GENIUS. WHAT NOW?
SO YOU'RE BLUE BOLT! I'VE HEARD OF YOUR MANY MARVELOUS ATTRIBUTES
YOU'RE THE PERFECT PHYSICAL HUMAN, BLUE BOLT. WERE YOUR BODY TO HOUSE MY INTELLIGENCE, I WOULD BE A GOD AMONG MEN!
I DON'T FOLLOW YOUR LINE OF THOUGHT MARTO! BUT I CAN TELL YOU THIS...THAT GUN OF YOURS WILL NEVER BE COMPLETED! MY MEN HAVE ORDERS TO DESTROY IT AT ANY COST! I KNOW THE POWER OF YOUR THOUGHTS ALONE CAN MATCH THE STRENGTH OF MY ARMY. BUT YOU'LL FIND EVERY MAN IN MY FORCES WILL FIGHT AND DIE BEFORE THEY SUBMIT TO YOU!
THE GREEN SORCERESS!
A NOBLE SPEECH, BLUE BOLT.. THE DEFEAT OF YOUR ARMY IS BUT ONLY A MINOR ITEM IN MY PLANS. THOUGH. THIS IS MY MAIN OBJECT!
SHE'S IN A STATE OF HYPNOSIS!
LOOK AT HER, BLUE BOLT.. SHE'S THE PERFECT FEMALE.. A FIT MATE FOR A GOD!
7

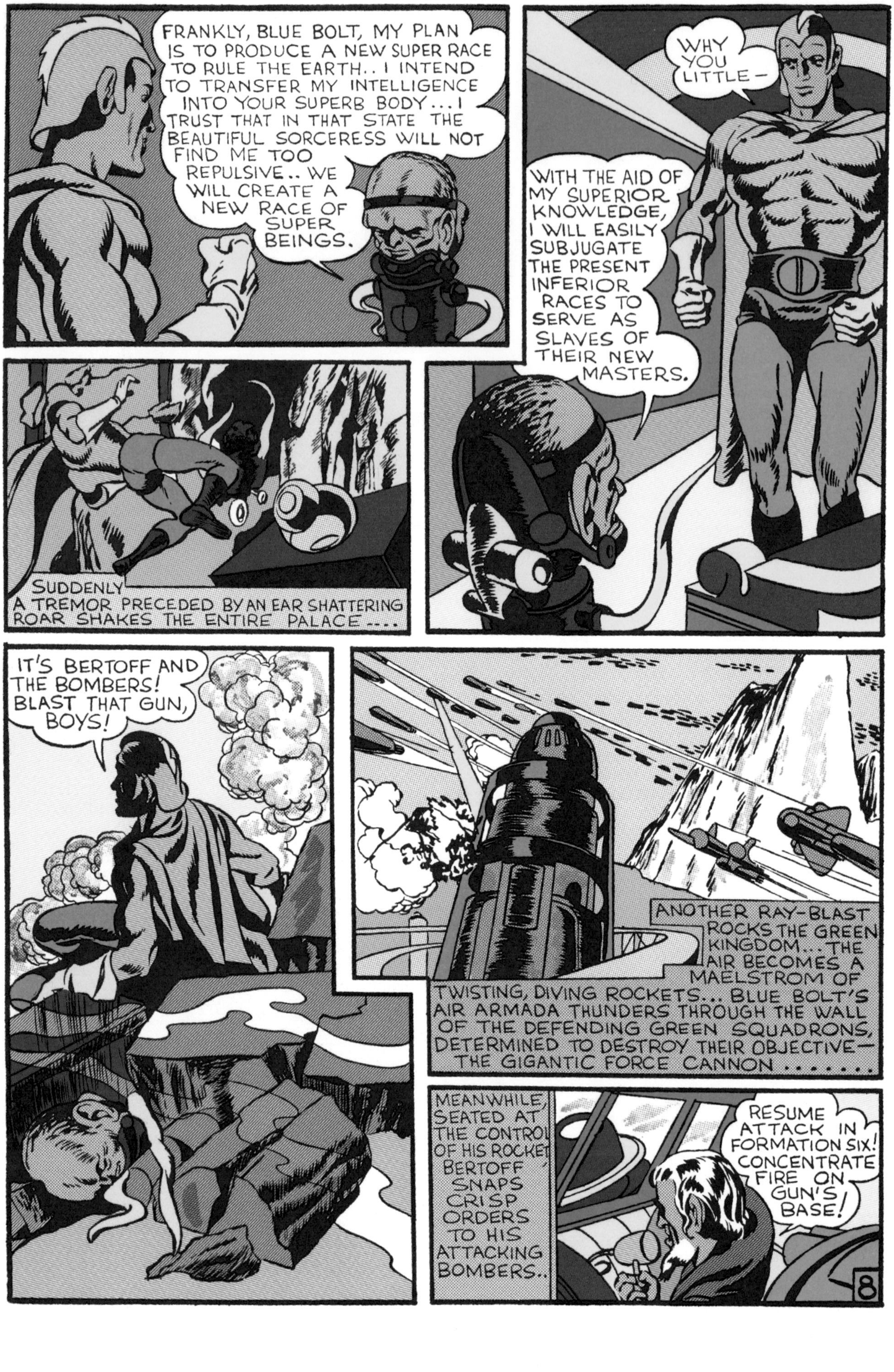

FRANKLY, BLUE BOLT, MY PLAN IS TO PRODUCE A NEW SUPER RACE TO RULE THE EARTH.. I INTEND TO TRANSFER MY INTELLIGENCE INTO YOUR SUPERB BODY... I TRUST THAT IN THAT STATE THE BEAUTIFUL SORCERESS WILL NOT FIND ME TOO REPULSIVE.. WE WILL CREATE A NEW RACE OF SUPER BEINGS.
WHY YOU LITTLE—
WITH THE AID OF MY SUPERIOR KNOWLEDGE, I WILL EASILY SUBJUGATE THE PRESENT INFERIOR RACES TO SERVE AS SLAVES OF THEIR NEW MASTERS.
SUDDENLY A TREMOR PRECEDED BY AN EAR SHATTERING ROAR SHAKES THE ENTIRE PALACE....
IT'S BERTOFF AND THE BOMBERS! BLAST THAT GUN, BOYS!
ANOTHER RAY-BLAST ROCKS THE GREEN KINGDOM... THE AIR BECOMES A MAELSTROM OF TWISTING, DIVING ROCKETS... BLUE BOLT'S AIR ARMADA THUNDERS THROUGH THE WALL OF THE DEFENDING GREEN SQUADRONS, DETERMINED TO DESTROY THEIR OBJECTIVE— THE GIGANTIC FORCE CANNON......
MEANWHILE, SEATED AT THE CONTROL OF HIS ROCKET BERTOFF SNAPS CRISP ORDERS TO HIS ATTACKING BOMBERS..
RESUME ATTACK IN FORMATION SIX! CONCENTRATE FIRE ON GUN'S BASE!
8

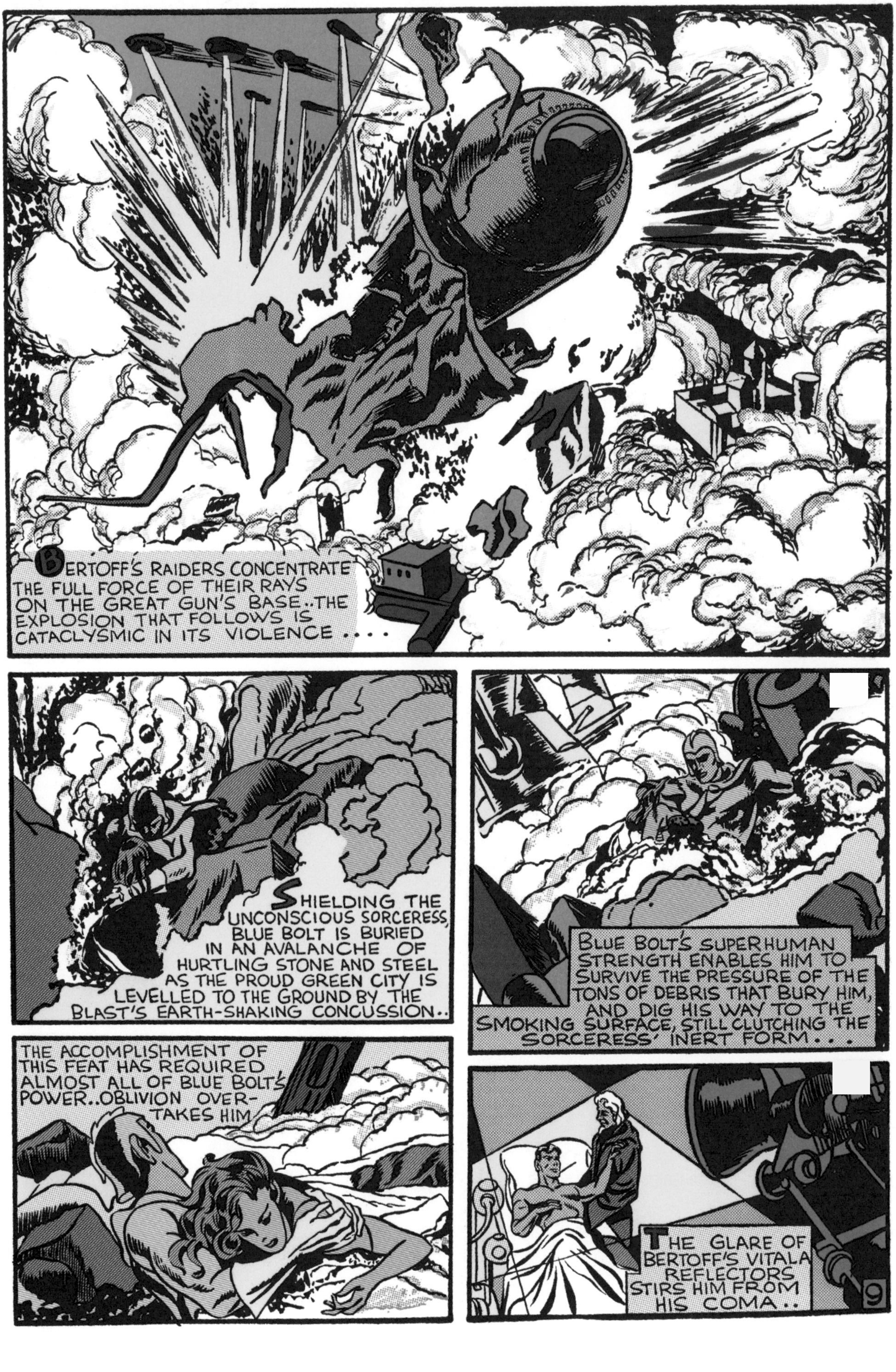
BERTOFF'S RAIDERS CONCENTRATE THE FULL FORCE OF THEIR RAYS ON THE GREAT GUN'S BASE..THE EXPLOSION THAT FOLLOWS IS CATACLYSMIC IN ITS VIOLENCE....
SHIELDING THE UNCONSCIOUS SORCERESS, BLUE BOLT IS BURIED IN AN AVALANCHE OF HURTLING STONE AND STEEL AS THE PROUD GREEN CITY IS LEVELLED TO THE GROUND BY THE BLAST'S EARTH-SHAKING CONCUSSION..
BLUE BOLT'S SUPERHUMAN STRENGTH ENABLES HIM TO SURVIVE THE PRESSURE OF THE TONS OF DEBRIS THAT BURY HIM, AND DIG HIS WAY TO THE SMOKING SURFACE, STILL CLUTCHING THE SORCERESS' INERT FORM...
THE ACCOMPLISHMENT OF THIS FEAT HAS REQUIRED ALMOST ALL OF BLUE BOLT'S POWER..OBLIVION OVER-TAKES HIM
THE GLARE OF BERTOFF'S VITALA REFLECTORS STIRS HIM FROM HIS COMA..
9

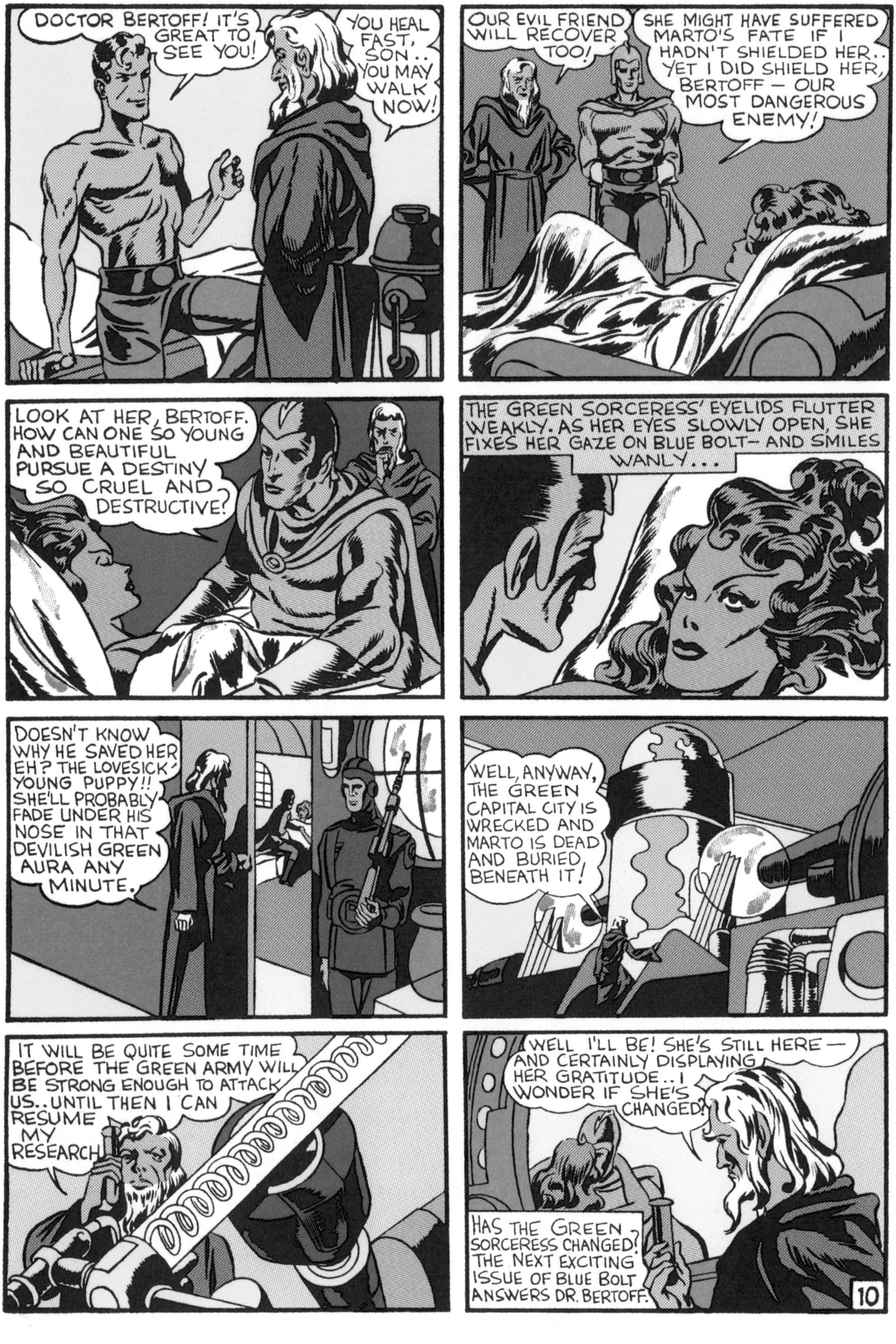
DOCTOR BERTOFF! IT'S GREAT TO SEE YOU!
YOU HEAL FAST, SON.. YOU MAY WALK NOW!
OUR EVIL FRIEND WILL RECOVER TOO!
SHE MIGHT HAVE SUFFERED MARTO'S FATE IF I HADN'T SHIELDED HER.. YET I DID SHIELD HER, BERTOFF — OUR MOST DANGEROUS ENEMY!
LOOK AT HER, BERTOFF. HOW CAN ONE SO YOUNG AND BEAUTIFUL PURSUE A DESTINY SO CRUEL AND DESTRUCTIVE?
THE GREEN SORCERESS' EYELIDS FLUTTER WEAKLY. AS HER EYES SLOWLY OPEN, SHE FIXES HER GAZE ON BLUE BOLT— AND SMILES WANLY...
DOESN'T KNOW WHY HE SAVED HER EH? THE LOVESICK YOUNG PUPPY!! SHE'LL PROBABLY FADE UNDER HIS NOSE IN THAT DEVILISH GREEN AURA ANY MINUTE.
WELL, ANYWAY, THE GREEN CAPITAL CITY IS WRECKED AND MARTO IS DEAD AND BURIED BENEATH IT!
IT WILL BE QUITE SOME TIME BEFORE THE GREEN ARMY WILL BE STRONG ENOUGH TO ATTACK US.. UNTIL THEN I CAN RESUME MY RESEARCH.
WELL I'LL BE! SHE'S STILL HERE — AND CERTAINLY DISPLAYING HER GRATITUDE.. I WONDER IF SHE'S CHANGED?
HAS THE GREEN SORCERESS CHANGED? THE NEXT EXCITING ISSUE OF BLUE BOLT ANSWERS DR. BERTOFF.
10

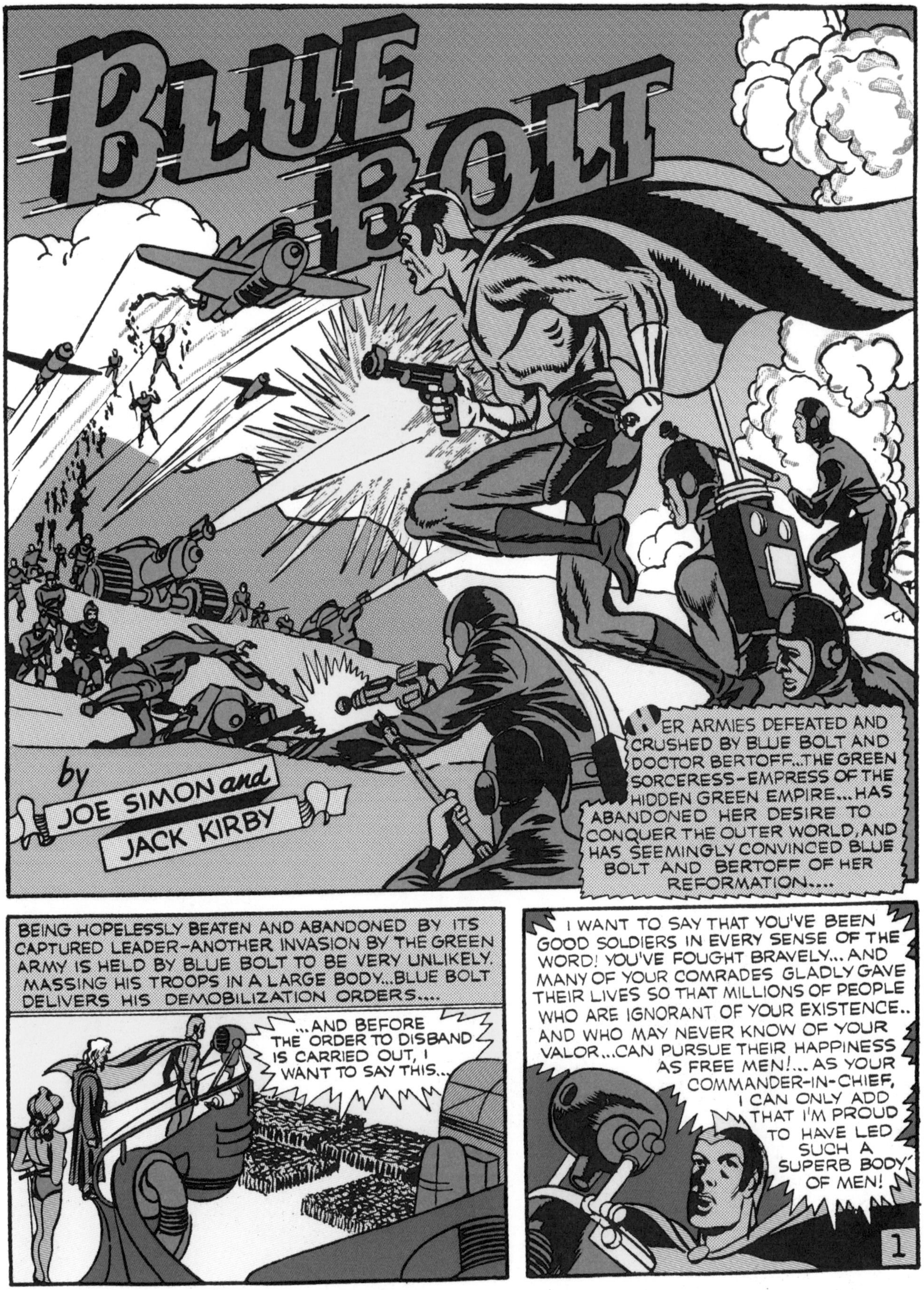
BLUE BOLT
by
JOE SIMON and
JACK KIRBY
HER ARMIES DEFEATED AND CRUSHED BY BLUE BOLT AND DOCTOR BERTOFF..THE GREEN SORCERESS-EMPRESS OF THE HIDDEN GREEN EMPIRE...HAS ABANDONED HER DESIRE TO CONQUER THE OUTER WORLD, AND HAS SEEMINGLY CONVINCED BLUE BOLT AND BERTOFF OF HER REFORMATION....
BEING HOPELESSLY BEATEN AND ABANDONED BY ITS CAPTURED LEADER-ANOTHER INVASION BY THE GREEN ARMY IS HELD BY BLUE BOLT TO BE VERY UNLIKELY. MASSING HIS TROOPS IN A LARGE BODY...BLUE BOLT DELIVERS HIS DEMOBILIZATION ORDERS....
...AND BEFORE THE ORDER TO DISBAND IS CARRIED OUT, I WANT TO SAY THIS...
I WANT TO SAY THAT YOU'VE BEEN GOOD SOLDIERS IN EVERY SENSE OF THE WORD! YOU'VE FOUGHT BRAVELY... AND MANY OF YOUR COMRADES GLADLY GAVE THEIR LIVES SO THAT MILLIONS OF PEOPLE WHO ARE IGNORANT OF YOUR EXISTENCE.. AND WHO MAY NEVER KNOW OF YOUR VALOR...CAN PURSUE THEIR HAPPINESS AS FREE MEN!... AS YOUR COMMANDER-IN-CHIEF, I CAN ONLY ADD THAT I'M PROUD TO HAVE LED SUCH A SUPERB BODY OF MEN!
1

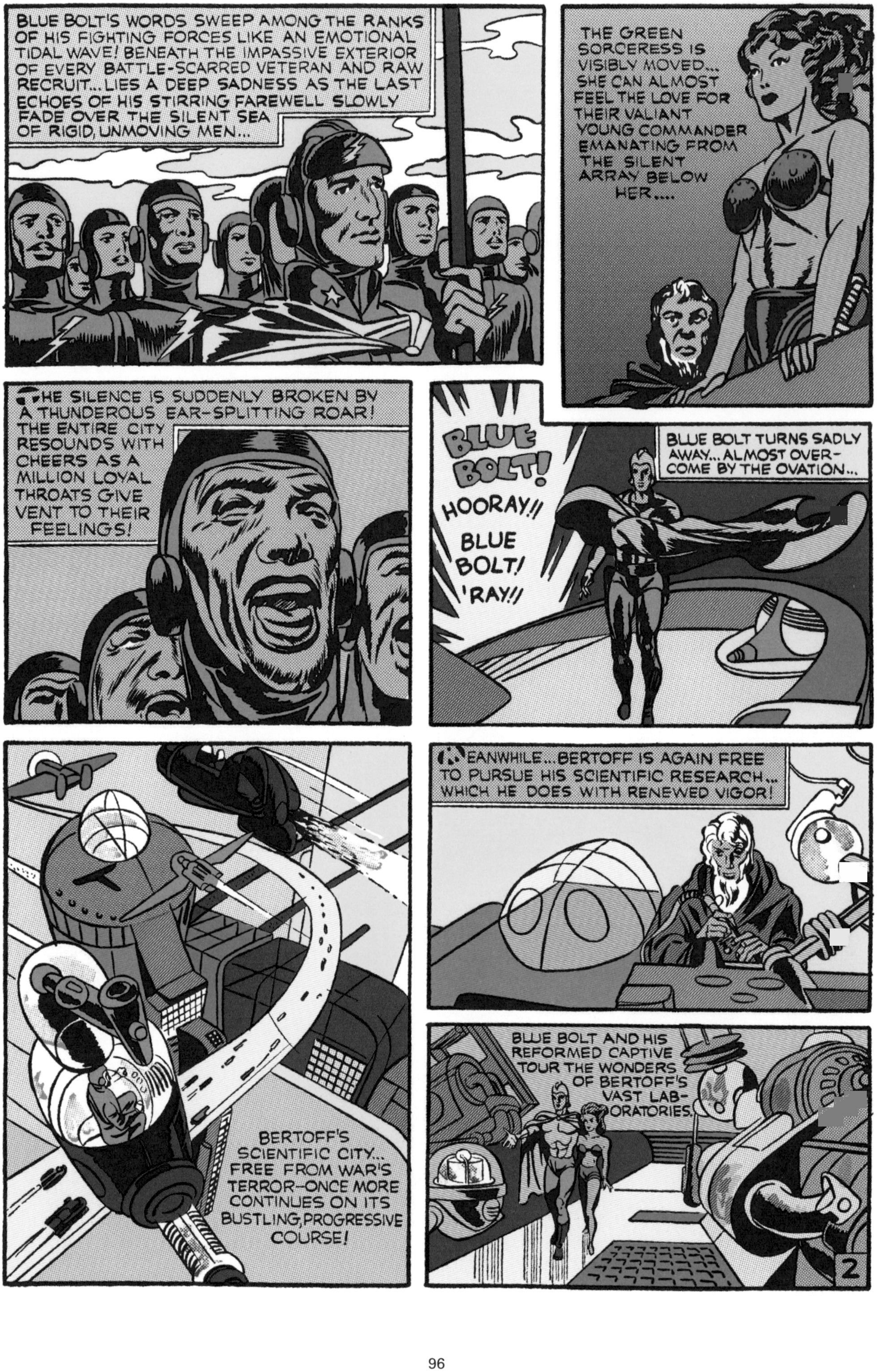
BLUE BOLT'S WORDS SWEEP AMONG THE RANKS OF HIS FIGHTING FORCES LIKE AN EMOTIONAL TIDAL WAVE! BENEATH THE IMPASSIVE EXTERIOR OF EVERY BATTLE-SCARRED VETERAN AND RAW RECRUIT...LIES A DEEP SADNESS AS THE LAST ECHOES OF HIS STIRRING FAREWELL SLOWLY FADE OVER THE SILENT SEA OF RIGID, UNMOVING MEN...
THE GREEN SORCERESS IS VISIBLY MOVED... SHE CAN ALMOST FEEL THE LOVE FOR THEIR VALIANT YOUNG COMMANDER EMANATING FROM THE SILENT ARRAY BELOW HER....
THE SILENCE IS SUDDENLY BROKEN BY A THUNDEROUS EAR-SPLITTING ROAR! THE ENTIRE CITY RESOUNDS WITH CHEERS AS A MILLION LOYAL THROATS GIVE VENT TO THEIR FEELINGS!
BLUE BOLT!
HOORAY!!
BLUE BOLT!
'RAY!!
BLUE BOLT TURNS SADLY AWAY... ALMOST OVER-COME BY THE OVATION...
BERTOFF'S SCIENTIFIC CITY... FREE FROM WAR'S TERROR-ONCE MORE CONTINUES ON ITS BUSTLING, PROGRESSIVE COURSE!
MEANWHILE...BERTOFF IS AGAIN FREE TO PURSUE HIS SCIENTIFIC RESEARCH... WHICH HE DOES WITH RENEWED VIGOR!
BLUE BOLT AND HIS REFORMED CAPTIVE TOUR THE WONDERS OF BERTOFF'S VAST LAB-ORATORIES.
2

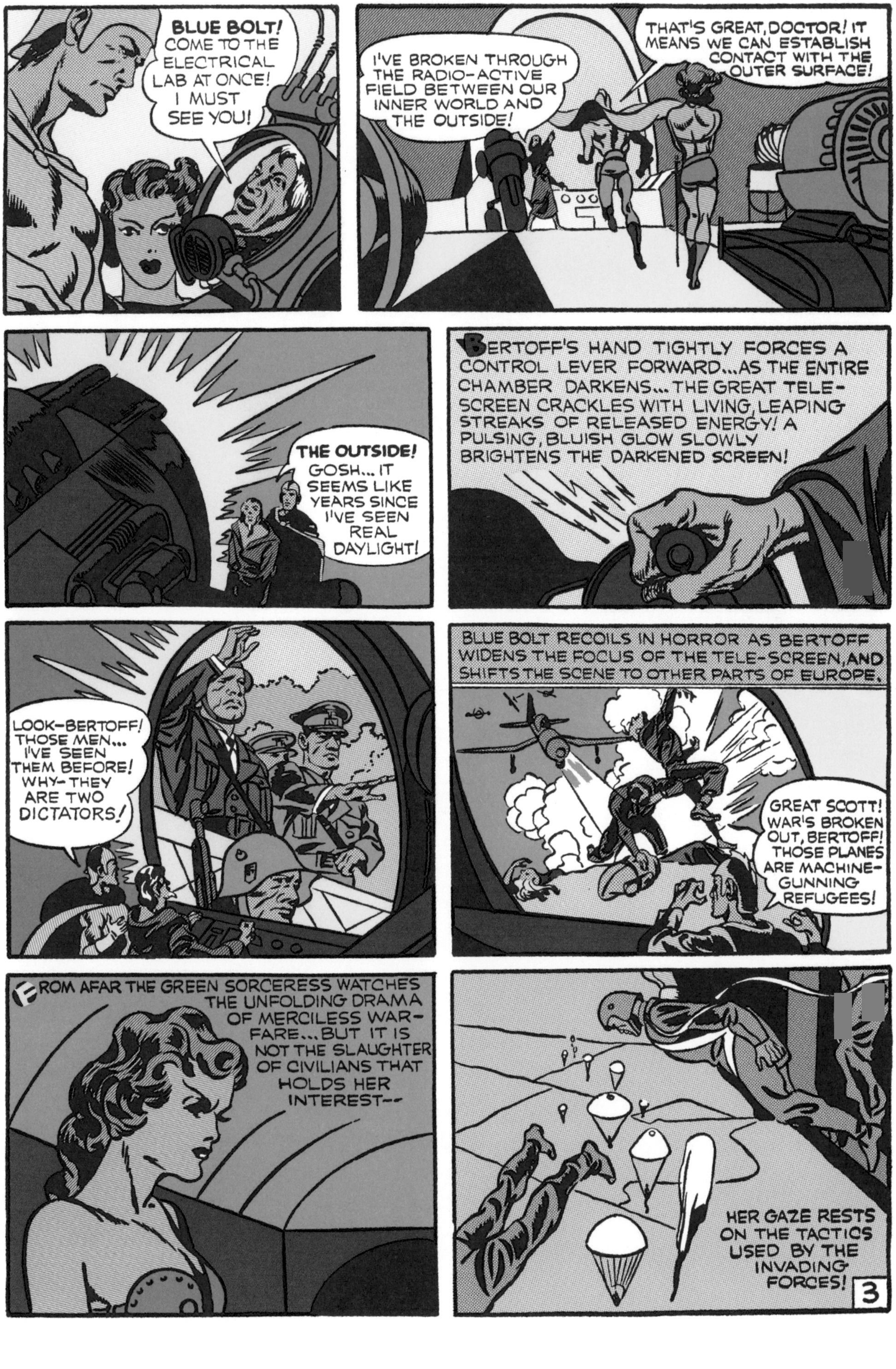
BLUE BOLT! COME TO THE ELECTRICAL LAB AT ONCE! I MUST SEE YOU!
I'VE BROKEN THROUGH THE RADIO-ACTIVE FIELD BETWEEN OUR INNER WORLD AND THE OUTSIDE!
THAT'S GREAT, DOCTOR! IT MEANS WE CAN ESTABLISH CONTACT WITH THE OUTER SURFACE!
THE OUTSIDE! GOSH... IT SEEMS LIKE YEARS SINCE I'VE SEEN REAL DAYLIGHT!
BERTOFF'S HAND TIGHTLY FORCES A CONTROL LEVER FORWARD...AS THE ENTIRE CHAMBER DARKENS...THE GREAT TELE-SCREEN CRACKLES WITH LIVING, LEAPING STREAKS OF RELEASED ENERGY! A PULSING, BLUISH GLOW SLOWLY BRIGHTENS THE DARKENED SCREEN!
LOOK-BERTOFF! THOSE MEN... I'VE SEEN THEM BEFORE! WHY- THEY ARE TWO DICTATORS!
BLUE BOLT RECOILS IN HORROR AS BERTOFF WIDENS THE FOCUS OF THE TELE-SCREEN, AND SHIFTS THE SCENE TO OTHER PARTS OF EUROPE.
GREAT SCOTT! WAR'S BROKEN OUT, BERTOFF! THOSE PLANES ARE MACHINE-GUNNING REFUGEES!
FROM AFAR THE GREEN SORCERESS WATCHES THE UNFOLDING DRAMA OF MERCILESS WAR-FARE...BUT IT IS NOT THE SLAUGHTER OF CIVILIANS THAT HOLDS HER INTEREST--
HER GAZE RESTS ON THE TACTICS USED BY THE INVADING FORCES!
3

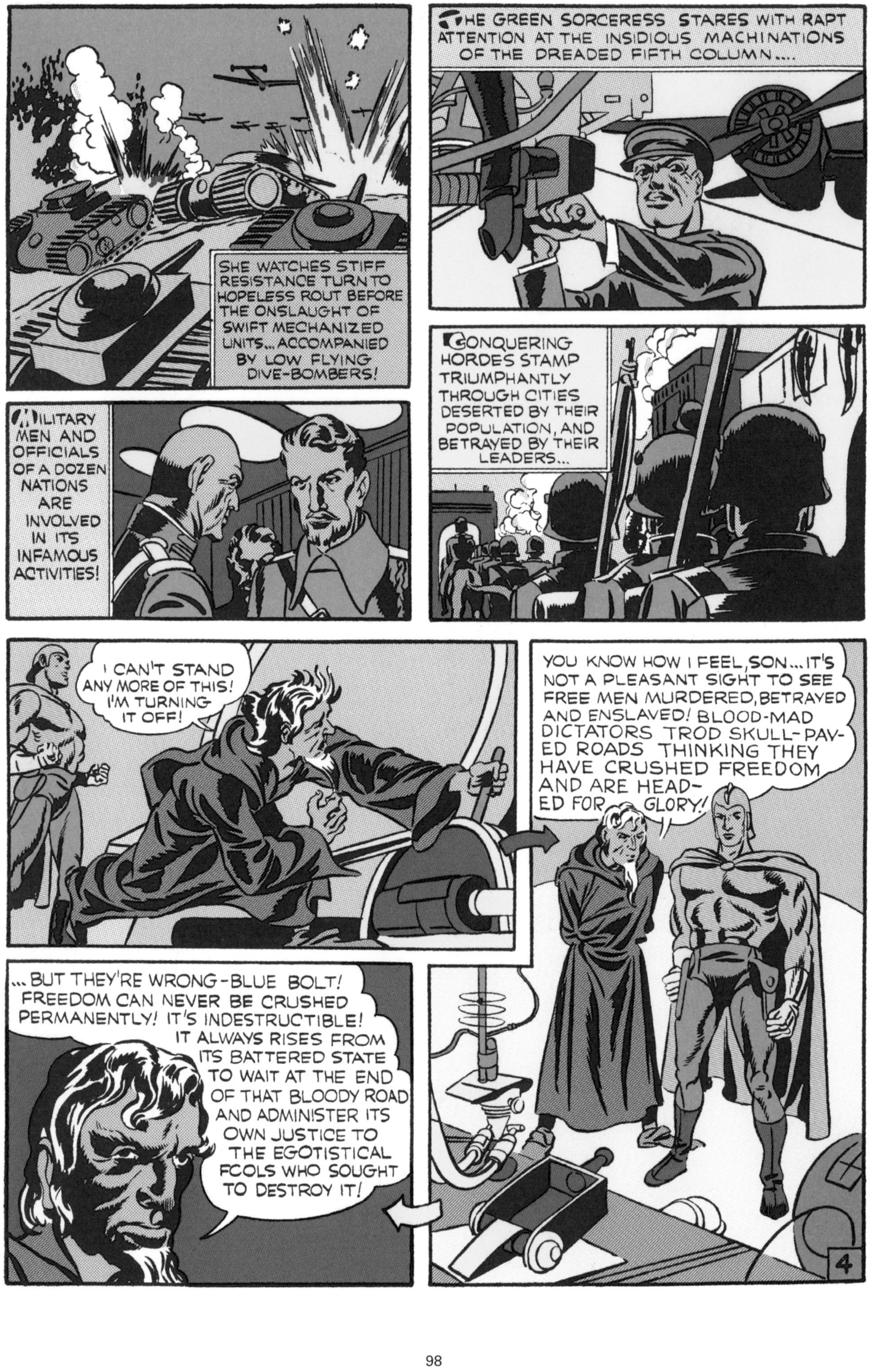
THE GREEN SORCERESS STARES WITH RAPT ATTENTION AT THE INSIDIOUS MACHINATIONS OF THE DREADED FIFTH COLUMN....
SHE WATCHES STIFF RESISTANCE TURN TO HOPELESS ROUT BEFORE THE ONSLAUGHT OF SWIFT MECHANIZED UNITS...ACCOMPANIED BY LOW FLYING DIVE-BOMBERS!
MILITARY MEN AND OFFICIALS OF A DOZEN NATIONS ARE INVOLVED IN ITS INFAMOUS ACTIVITIES!
CONQUERING HORDES STAMP TRIUMPHANTLY THROUGH CITIES DESERTED BY THEIR POPULATION, AND BETRAYED BY THEIR LEADERS...
I CAN'T STAND ANY MORE OF THIS! I'M TURNING IT OFF!
YOU KNOW HOW I FEEL, SON...IT'S NOT A PLEASANT SIGHT TO SEE FREE MEN MURDERED, BETRAYED AND ENSLAVED! BLOOD-MAD DICTATORS TROD SKULL-PAVED ROADS THINKING THEY HAVE CRUSHED FREEDOM AND ARE HEADED FOR GLORY!
...BUT THEY'RE WRONG-BLUE BOLT! FREEDOM CAN NEVER BE CRUSHED PERMANENTLY! IT'S INDESTRUCTIBLE! IT ALWAYS RISES FROM ITS BATTERED STATE TO WAIT AT THE END OF THAT BLOODY ROAD AND ADMINISTER ITS OWN JUSTICE TO THE EGOTISTICAL FOOLS WHO SOUGHT TO DESTROY IT!
4

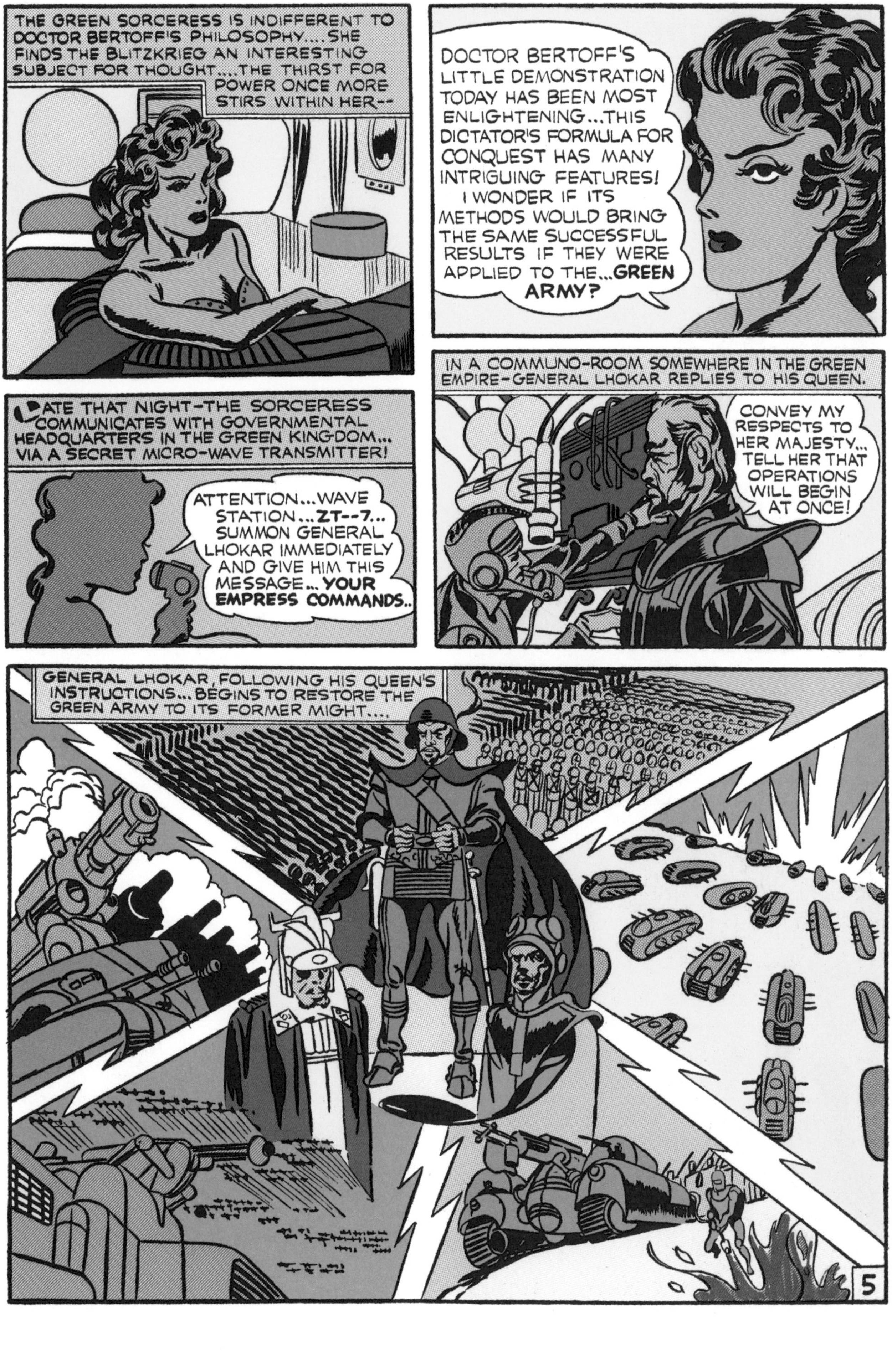
THE GREEN SORCERESS IS INDIFFERENT TO DOCTOR BERTOFF'S PHILOSOPHY.... SHE FINDS THE BLITZKRIEG AN INTERESTING SUBJECT FOR THOUGHT.... THE THIRST FOR POWER ONCE MORE STIRS WITHIN HER--
DOCTOR BERTOFF'S LITTLE DEMONSTRATION TODAY HAS BEEN MOST ENLIGHTENING...THIS DICTATOR'S FORMULA FOR CONQUEST HAS MANY INTRIGUING FEATURES! I WONDER IF ITS METHODS WOULD BRING THE SAME SUCCESSFUL RESULTS IF THEY WERE APPLIED TO THE...GREEN ARMY?
LATE THAT NIGHT-THE SORCERESS COMMUNICATES WITH GOVERNMENTAL HEADQUARTERS IN THE GREEN KINGDOM... VIA A SECRET MICRO-WAVE TRANSMITTER!
ATTENTION...WAVE STATION...ZT--7... SUMMON GENERAL LHOKAR IMMEDIATELY AND GIVE HIM THIS MESSAGE... YOUR EMPRESS COMMANDS..
IN A COMMUNO-ROOM SOMEWHERE IN THE GREEN EMPIRE-GENERAL LHOKAR REPLIES TO HIS QUEEN.
CONVEY MY RESPECTS TO HER MAJESTY... TELL HER THAT OPERATIONS WILL BEGIN AT ONCE!
GENERAL LHOKAR, FOLLOWING HIS QUEEN'S INSTRUCTIONS... BEGINS TO RESTORE THE GREEN ARMY TO ITS FORMER MIGHT....
5

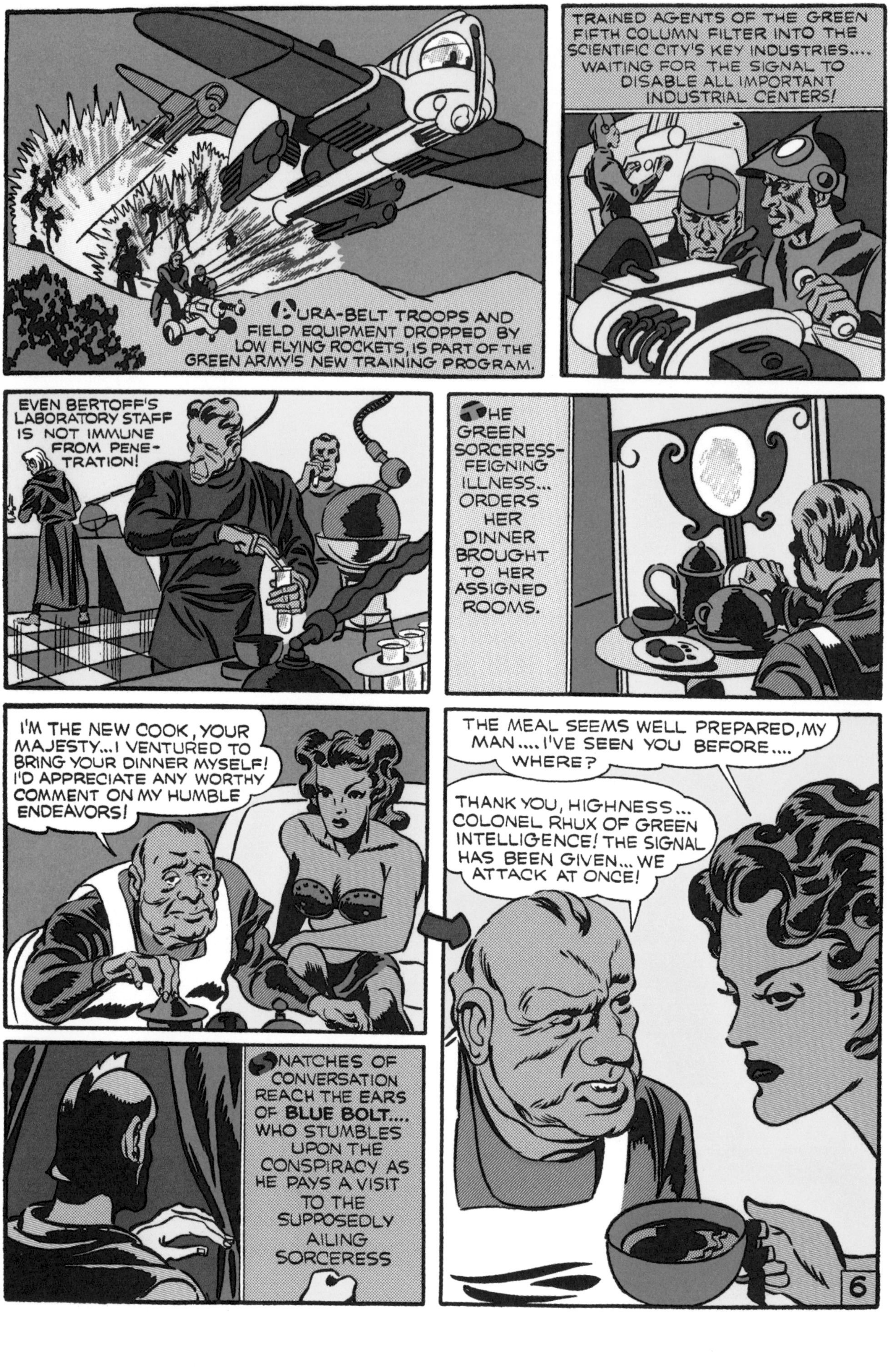
AURA-BELT TROOPS AND FIELD EQUIPMENT DROPPED BY LOW FLYING ROCKETS, IS PART OF THE GREEN ARMY'S NEW TRAINING PROGRAM.
TRAINED AGENTS OF THE GREEN FIFTH COLUMN FILTER INTO THE SCIENTIFIC CITY'S KEY INDUSTRIES.... WAITING FOR THE SIGNAL TO DISABLE ALL IMPORTANT INDUSTRIAL CENTERS!
EVEN BERTOFF'S LABORATORY STAFF IS NOT IMMUNE FROM PENE-TRATION!
THE GREEN SORCERESS- FEIGNING ILLNESS... ORDERS HER DINNER BROUGHT TO HER ASSIGNED ROOMS.
I'M THE NEW COOK, YOUR MAJESTY...I VENTURED TO BRING YOUR DINNER MYSELF! I'D APPRECIATE ANY WORTHY COMMENT ON MY HUMBLE ENDEAVORS!
THE MEAL SEEMS WELL PREPARED, MY MAN.... I'VE SEEN YOU BEFORE.... WHERE?
THANK YOU, HIGHNESS... COLONEL RHUX OF GREEN INTELLIGENCE! THE SIGNAL HAS BEEN GIVEN... WE ATTACK AT ONCE!
SNATCHES OF CONVERSATION REACH THE EARS OF BLUE BOLT.... WHO STUMBLES UPON THE CONSPIRACY AS HE PAYS A VISIT TO THE SUPPOSEDLY AILING SORCERESS
6

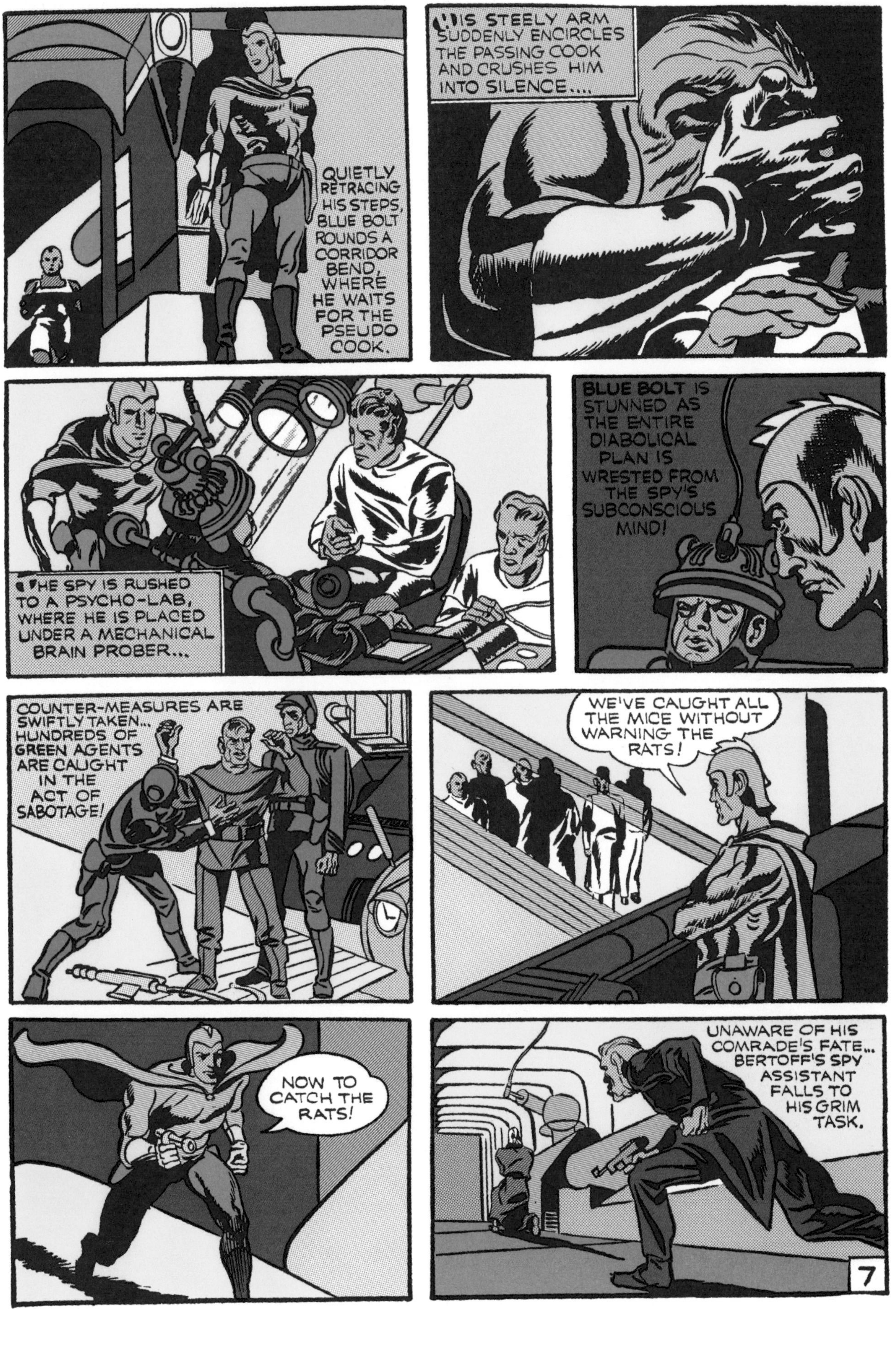
QUIETLY RETRACING HIS STEPS, BLUE BOLT ROUNDS A CORRIDOR BEND, WHERE HE WAITS FOR THE PSEUDO COOK.
HIS STEELY ARM SUDDENLY ENCIRCLES THE PASSING COOK AND CRUSHES HIM INTO SILENCE....
THE SPY IS RUSHED TO A PSYCHO-LAB, WHERE HE IS PLACED UNDER A MECHANICAL BRAIN PROBER...
BLUE BOLT IS STUNNED AS THE ENTIRE DIABOLICAL PLAN IS WRESTED FROM THE SPY'S SUBCONSCIOUS MIND!
COUNTER-MEASURES ARE SWIFTLY TAKEN... HUNDREDS OF GREEN AGENTS ARE CAUGHT IN THE ACT OF SABOTAGE!
WE'VE CAUGHT ALL THE MICE WITHOUT WARNING THE RATS!
NOW TO CATCH THE RATS!
UNAWARE OF HIS COMRADE'S FATE... BERTOFF'S SPY ASSISTANT FALLS TO HIS GRIM TASK.
7

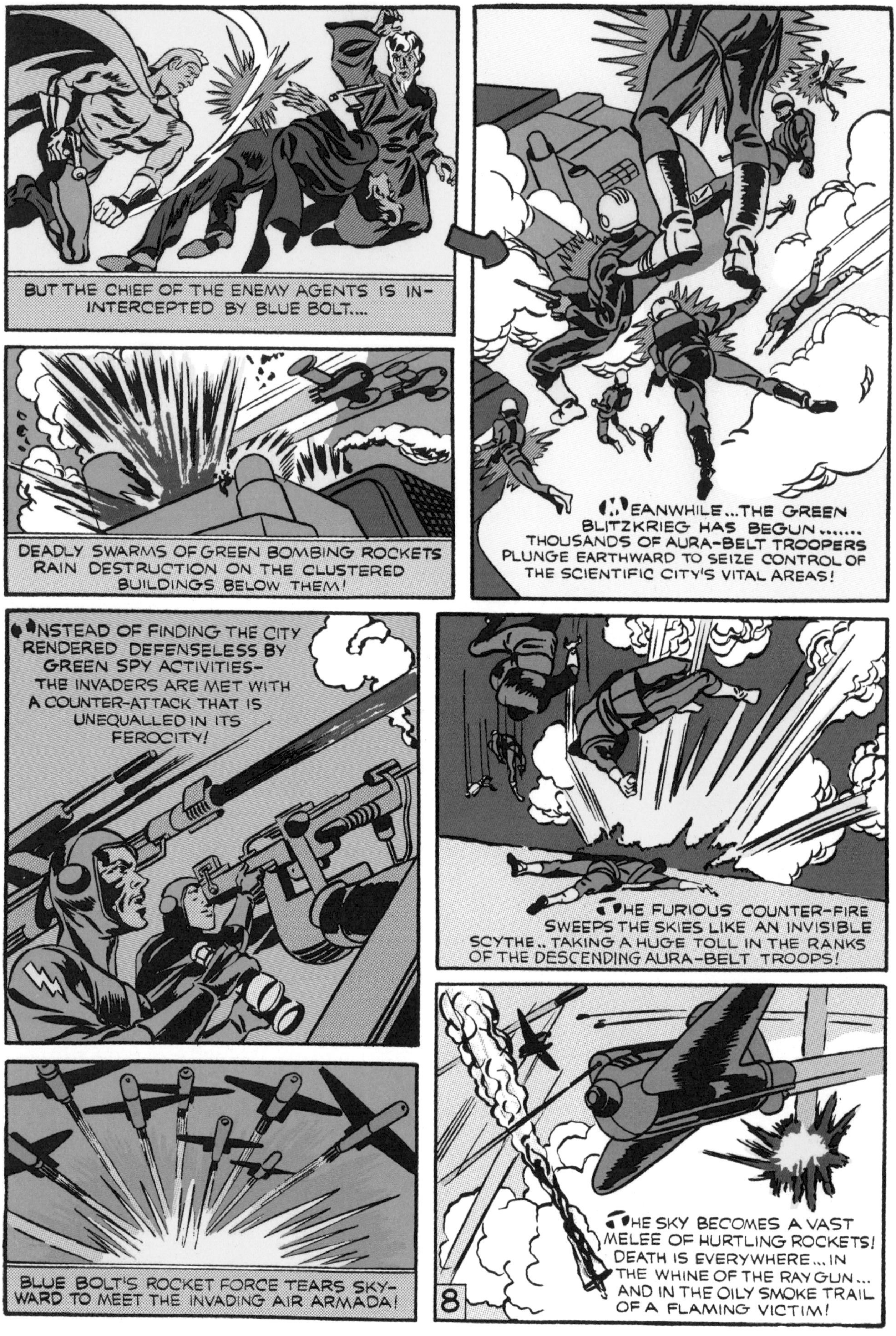
BUT THE CHIEF OF THE ENEMY AGENTS IS IN-INTERCEPTED BY BLUE BOLT....
MEANWHILE...THE GREEN BLITZKRIEG HAS BEGUN....... THOUSANDS OF AURA-BELT TROOPERS PLUNGE EARTHWARD TO SEIZE CONTROL OF THE SCIENTIFIC CITY'S VITAL AREAS!
DEADLY SWARMS OF GREEN BOMBING ROCKETS RAIN DESTRUCTION ON THE CLUSTERED BUILDINGS BELOW THEM!
INSTEAD OF FINDING THE CITY RENDERED DEFENSELESS BY GREEN SPY ACTIVITIES- THE INVADERS ARE MET WITH A COUNTER-ATTACK THAT IS UNEQUALLED IN ITS FEROCITY!
THE FURIOUS COUNTER-FIRE SWEEPS THE SKIES LIKE AN INVISIBLE SCYTHE.. TAKING A HUGE TOLL IN THE RANKS OF THE DESCENDING AURA-BELT TROOPS!
BLUE BOLT'S ROCKET FORCE TEARS SKY-WARD TO MEET THE INVADING AIR ARMADA!
THE SKY BECOMES A VAST MELEE OF HURTLING ROCKETS! DEATH IS EVERYWHERE... IN THE WHINE OF THE RAY GUN... AND IN THE OILY SMOKE TRAIL OF A FLAMING VICTIM!
8

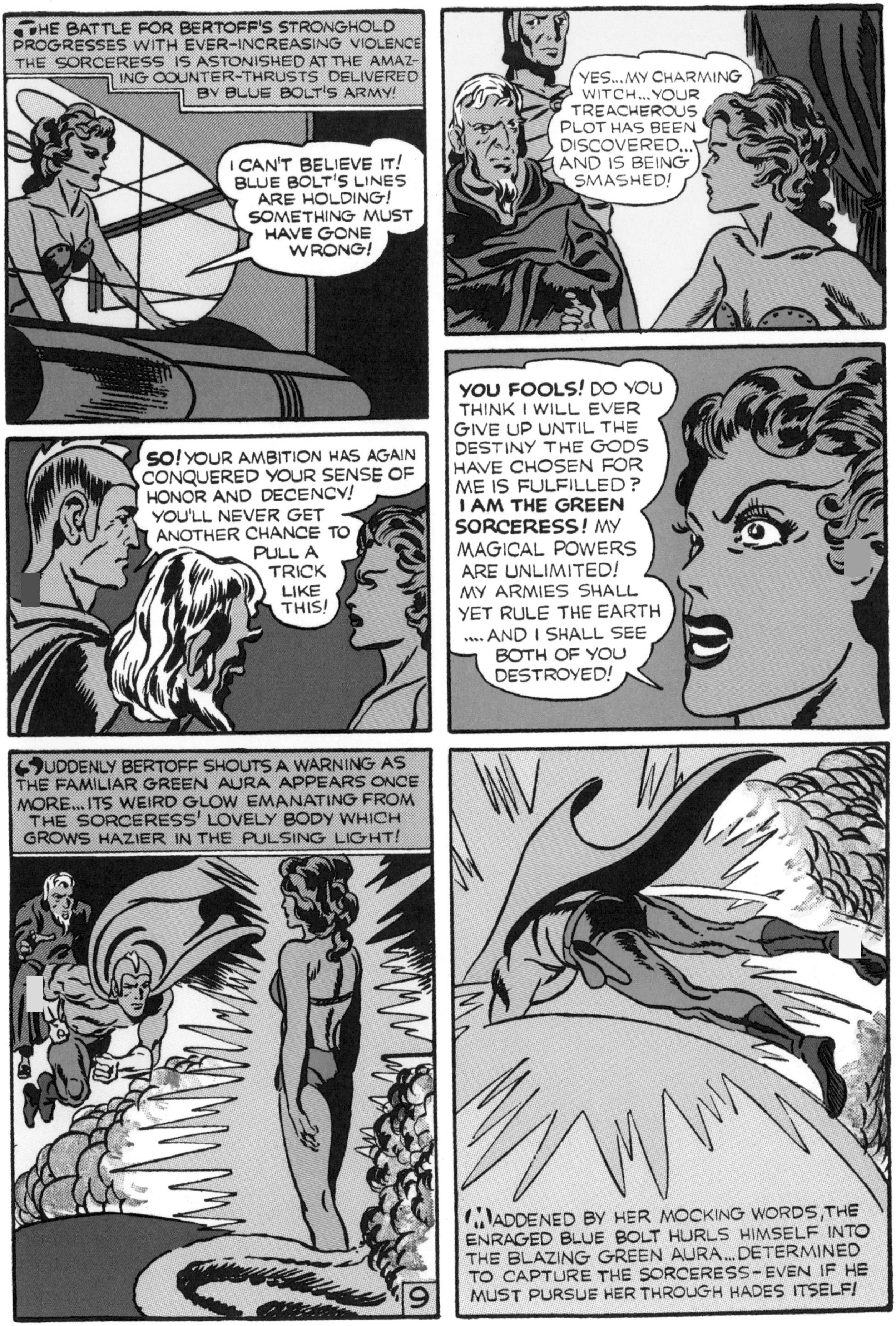
THE BATTLE FOR BERTOFF'S STRONGHOLD PROGRESSES WITH EVER-INCREASING VIOLENCE. THE SORCERESS IS ASTONISHED AT THE AMAZING COUNTER-THRUSTS DELIVERED BY BLUE BOLT'S ARMY!
I CAN'T BELIEVE IT! BLUE BOLT'S LINES ARE HOLDING! SOMETHING MUST HAVE GONE WRONG!
YES...MY CHARMING WITCH...YOUR TREACHEROUS PLOT HAS BEEN DISCOVERED... AND IS BEING SMASHED!
SO! YOUR AMBITION HAS AGAIN CONQUERED YOUR SENSE OF HONOR AND DECENCY! YOU'LL NEVER GET ANOTHER CHANCE TO PULL A TRICK LIKE THIS!
YOU FOOLS! DO YOU THINK I WILL EVER GIVE UP UNTIL THE DESTINY THE GODS HAVE CHOSEN FOR ME IS FULFILLED? I AM THE GREEN SORCERESS! MY MAGICAL POWERS ARE UNLIMITED! MY ARMIES SHALL YET RULE THE EARTH ....AND I SHALL SEE BOTH OF YOU DESTROYED!
SUDDENLY BERTOFF SHOUTS A WARNING AS THE FAMILIAR GREEN AURA APPEARS ONCE MORE...ITS WEIRD GLOW EMANATING FROM THE SORCERESS' LOVELY BODY WHICH GROWS HAZIER IN THE PULSING LIGHT!
9
MADDENED BY HER MOCKING WORDS, THE ENRAGED BLUE BOLT HURLS HIMSELF INTO THE BLAZING GREEN AURA...DETERMINED TO CAPTURE THE SORCERESS-EVEN IF HE MUST PURSUE HER THROUGH HADES ITSELF!

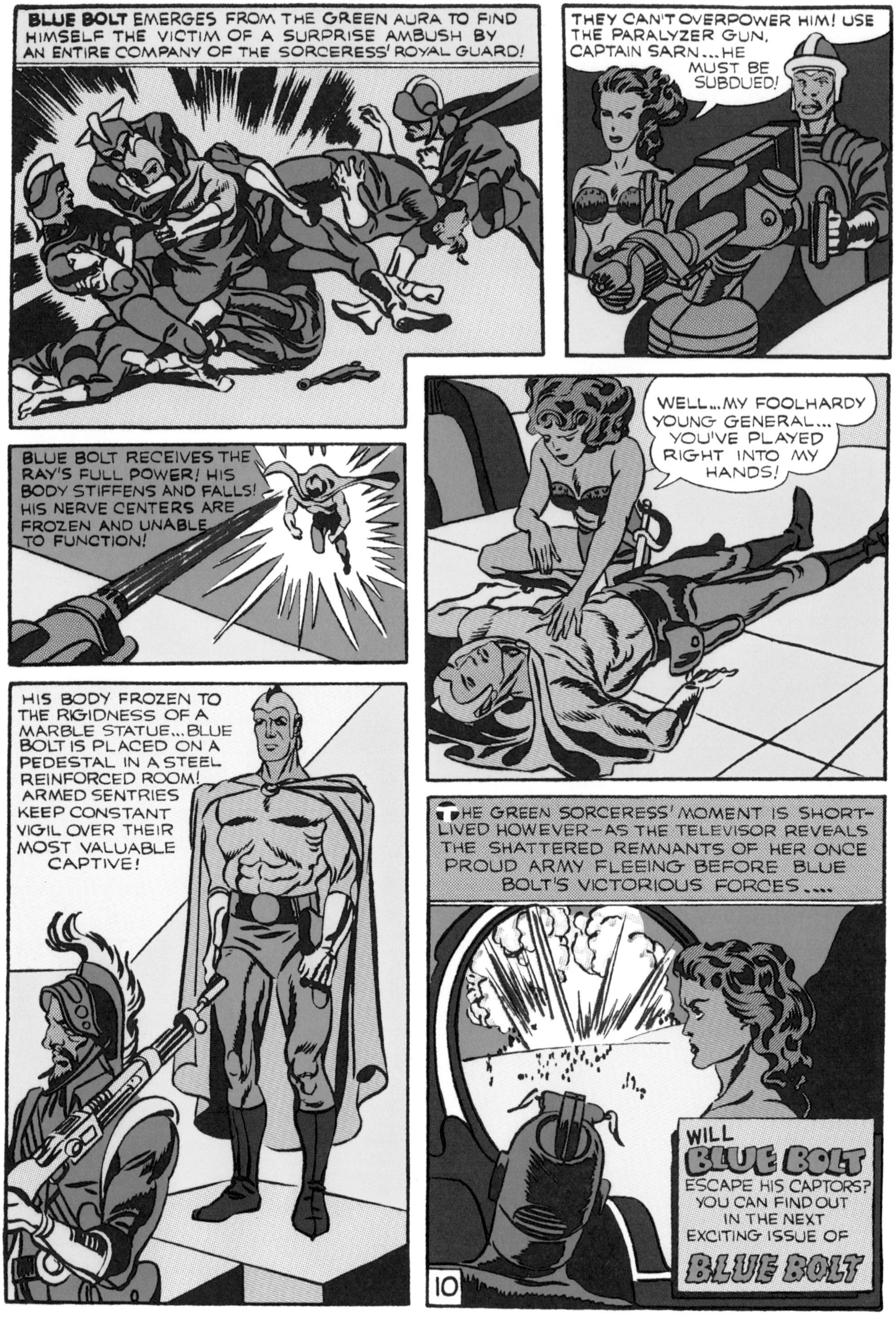

BLUE BOLT EMERGES FROM THE GREEN AURA TO FIND HIMSELF THE VICTIM OF A SURPRISE AMBUSH BY AN ENTIRE COMPANY OF THE SORCERESS' ROYAL GUARD!
THEY CAN'T OVERPOWER HIM! USE THE PARALYZER GUN, CAPTAIN SARN...HE MUST BE SUBDUED!
BLUE BOLT RECEIVES THE RAY'S FULL POWER! HIS BODY STIFFENS AND FALLS! HIS NERVE CENTERS ARE FROZEN AND UNABLE TO FUNCTION!
WELL...MY FOOLHARDY YOUNG GENERAL... YOU'VE PLAYED RIGHT INTO MY HANDS!
HIS BODY FROZEN TO THE RIGIDNESS OF A MARBLE STATUE...BLUE BOLT IS PLACED ON A PEDESTAL IN A STEEL REINFORCED ROOM! ARMED SENTRIES KEEP CONSTANT VIGIL OVER THEIR MOST VALUABLE CAPTIVE!
THE GREEN SORCERESS' MOMENT IS SHORT-LIVED HOWEVER—AS THE TELEVISOR REVEALS THE SHATTERED REMNANTS OF HER ONCE PROUD ARMY FLEEING BEFORE BLUE BOLT'S VICTORIOUS FORCES....
WILL BLUE BOLT ESCAPE HIS CAPTORS? YOU CAN FIND OUT IN THE NEXT EXCITING ISSUE OF BLUE BOLT
10

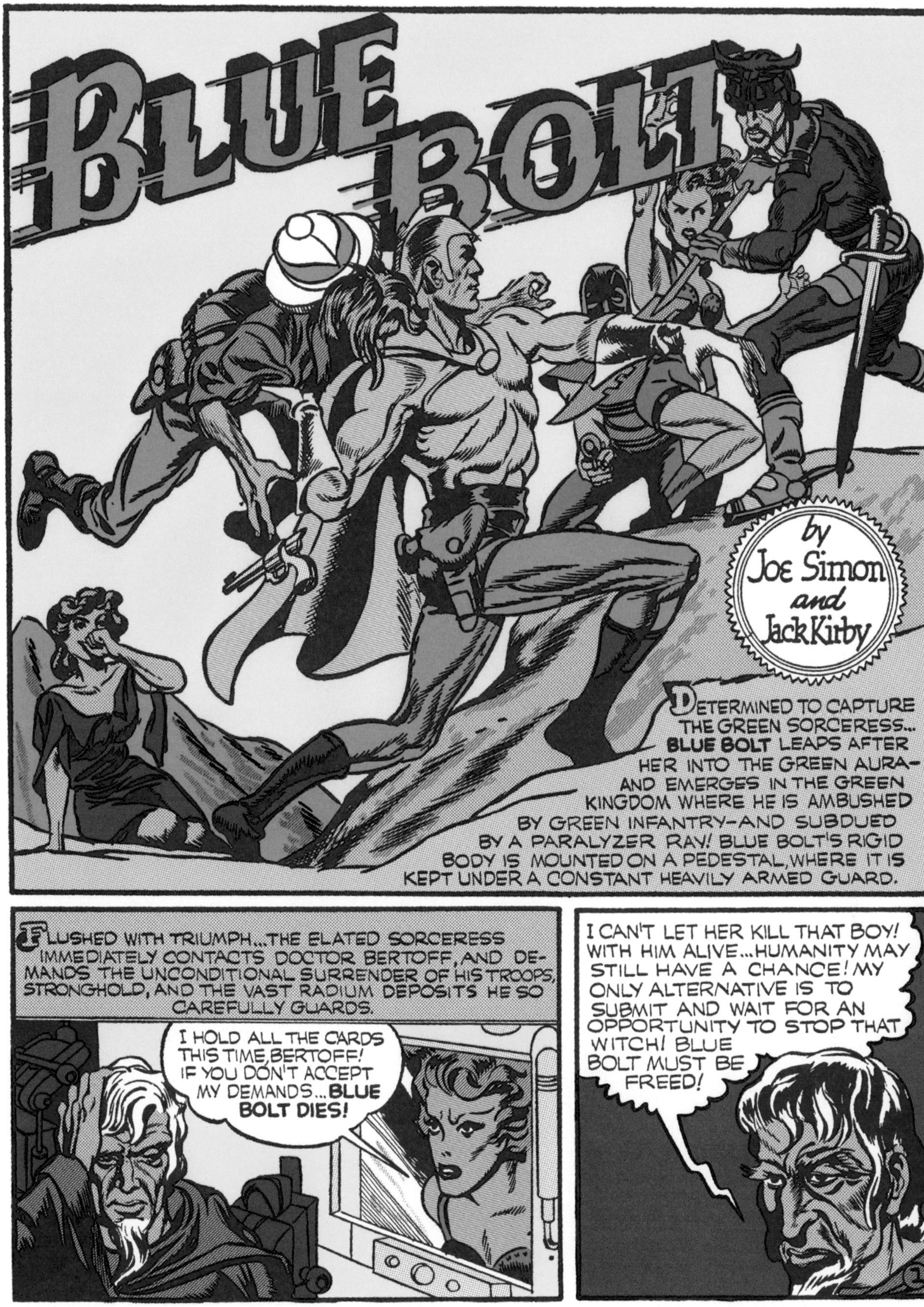
BLUE BOLT
by Joe Simon and Jack Kirby
DETERMINED TO CAPTURE THE GREEN SORCERESS... BLUE BOLT LEAPS AFTER HER INTO THE GREEN AURA-AND EMERGES IN THE GREEN KINGDOM WHERE HE IS AMBUSHED BY GREEN INFANTRY-AND SUBDUED BY A PARALYZER RAY! BLUE BOLT'S RIGID BODY IS MOUNTED ON A PEDESTAL, WHERE IT IS KEPT UNDER A CONSTANT HEAVILY ARMED GUARD.
FLUSHED WITH TRIUMPH... THE ELATED SORCERESS IMMEDIATELY CONTACTS DOCTOR BERTOFF, AND DEMANDS THE UNCONDITIONAL SURRENDER OF HIS TROOPS, STRONGHOLD, AND THE VAST RADIUM DEPOSITS HE SO CAREFULLY GUARDS.
I HOLD ALL THE CARDS THIS TIME, BERTOFF! IF YOU DON'T ACCEPT MY DEMANDS... BLUE BOLT DIES!
I CAN'T LET HER KILL THAT BOY! WITH HIM ALIVE... HUMANITY MAY STILL HAVE A CHANCE! MY ONLY ALTERNATIVE IS TO SUBMIT AND WAIT FOR AN OPPORTUNITY TO STOP THAT WITCH! BLUE BOLT MUST BE FREED!
1

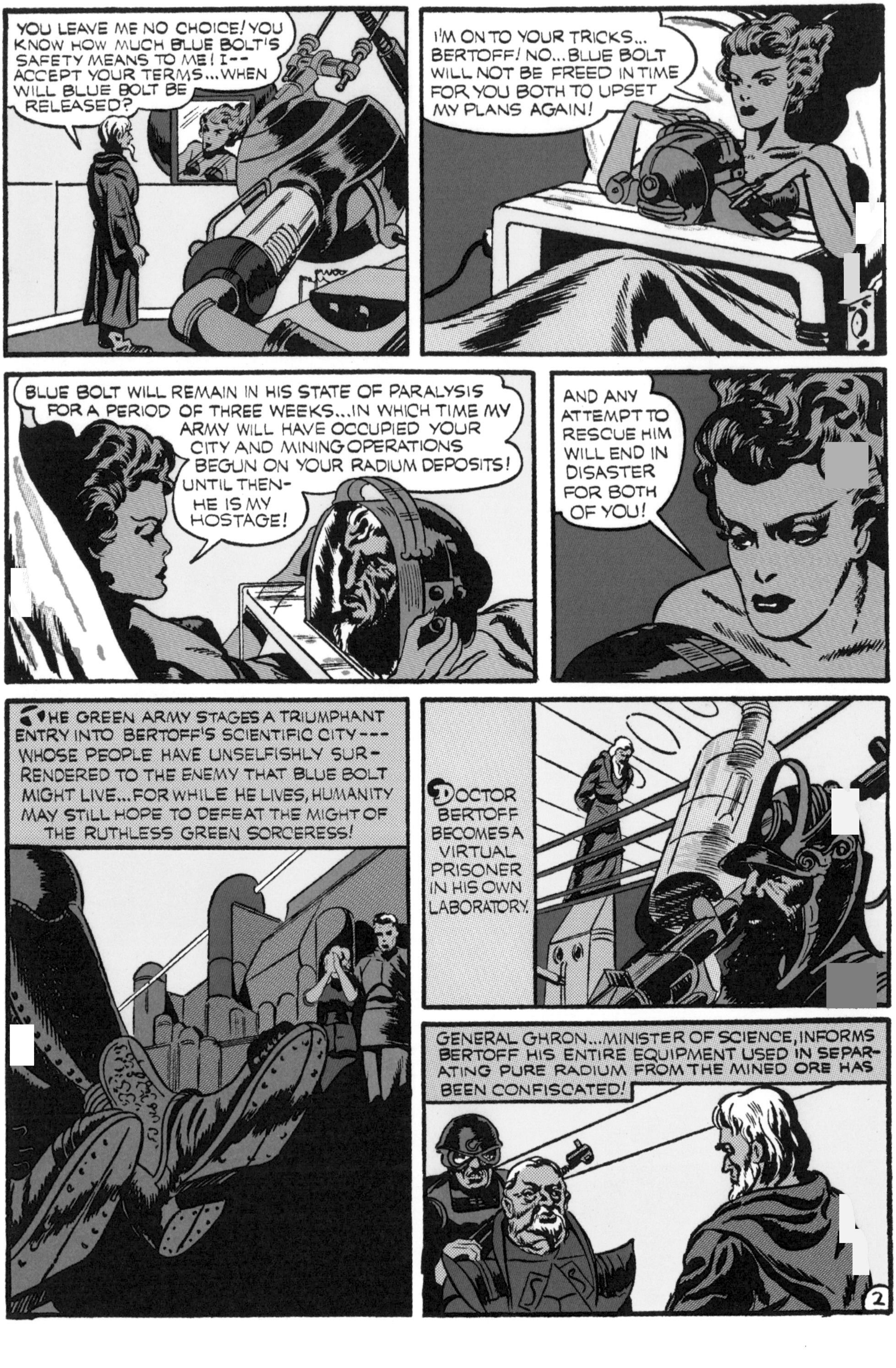
YOU LEAVE ME NO CHOICE! YOU KNOW HOW MUCH BLUE BOLT'S SAFETY MEANS TO ME! I-- ACCEPT YOUR TERMS...WHEN WILL BLUE BOLT BE RELEASED?
I'M ON TO YOUR TRICKS... BERTOFF! NO...BLUE BOLT WILL NOT BE FREED IN TIME FOR YOU BOTH TO UPSET MY PLANS AGAIN!
BLUE BOLT WILL REMAIN IN HIS STATE OF PARALYSIS FOR A PERIOD OF THREE WEEKS...IN WHICH TIME MY ARMY WILL HAVE OCCUPIED YOUR CITY AND MINING OPERATIONS BEGUN ON YOUR RADIUM DEPOSITS! UNTIL THEN- HE IS MY HOSTAGE!
AND ANY ATTEMPT TO RESCUE HIM WILL END IN DISASTER FOR BOTH OF YOU!
THE GREEN ARMY STAGES A TRIUMPHANT ENTRY INTO BERTOFF'S SCIENTIFIC CITY--- WHOSE PEOPLE HAVE UNSELFISHLY SURRENDERED TO THE ENEMY THAT BLUE BOLT MIGHT LIVE...FOR WHILE HE LIVES, HUMANITY MAY STILL HOPE TO DEFEAT THE MIGHT OF THE RUTHLESS GREEN SORCERESS!
DOCTOR BERTOFF BECOMES A VIRTUAL PRISONER IN HIS OWN LABORATORY.
GENERAL GHRON...MINISTER OF SCIENCE, INFORMS BERTOFF HIS ENTIRE EQUIPMENT USED IN SEPARATING PURE RADIUM FROM THE MINED ORE HAS BEEN CONFISCATED!
2

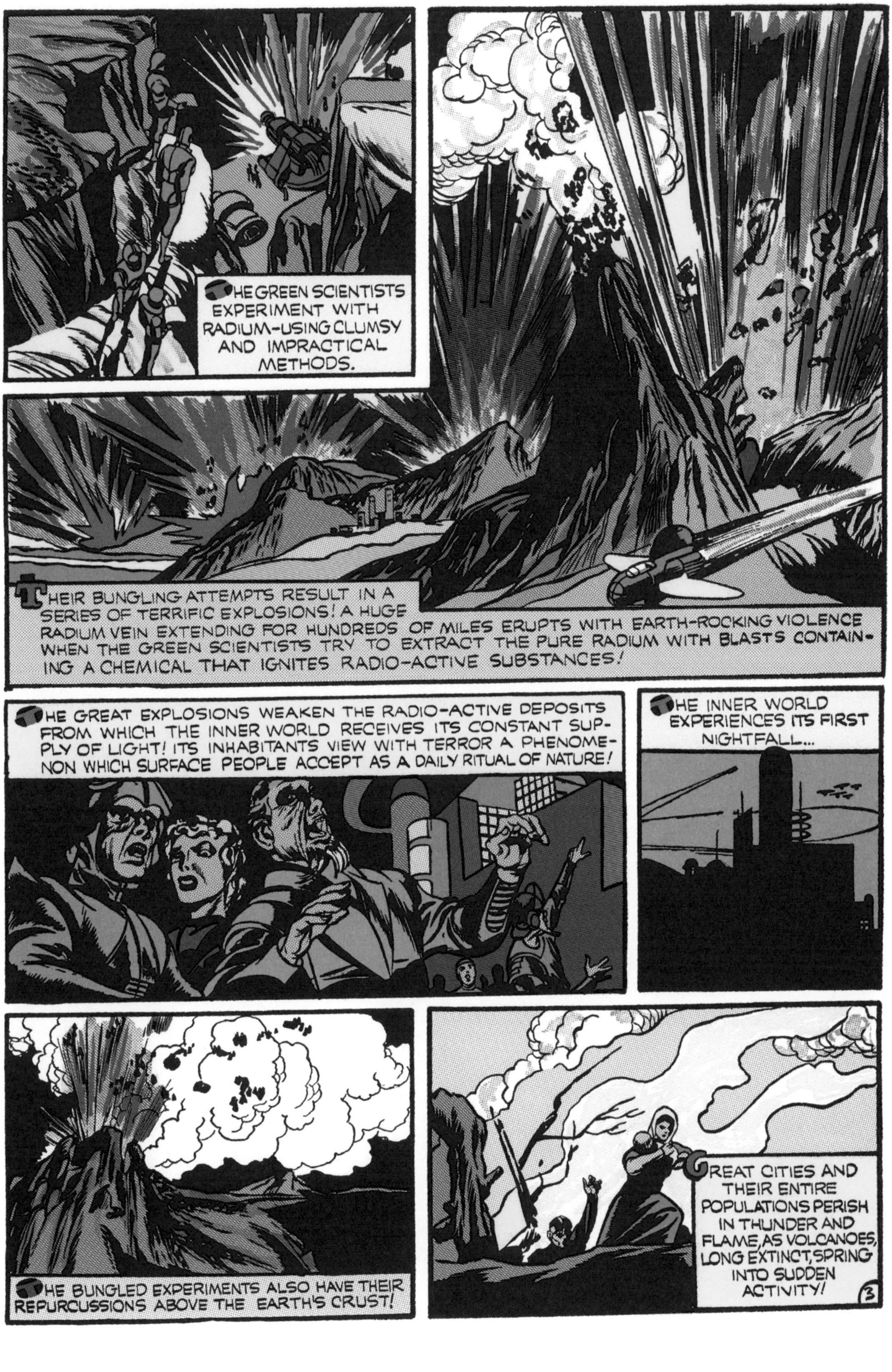
THE GREEN SCIENTISTS EXPERIMENT WITH RADIUM-USING CLUMSY AND IMPRACTICAL METHODS.
THEIR BUNGLING ATTEMPTS RESULT IN A SERIES OF TERRIFIC EXPLOSIONS! A HUGE RADIUM VEIN EXTENDING FOR HUNDREDS OF MILES ERUPTS WITH EARTH-ROCKING VIOLENCE WHEN THE GREEN SCIENTISTS TRY TO EXTRACT THE PURE RADIUM WITH BLASTS CONTAINING A CHEMICAL THAT IGNITES RADIO-ACTIVE SUBSTANCES!
THE GREAT EXPLOSIONS WEAKEN THE RADIO-ACTIVE DEPOSITS FROM WHICH THE INNER WORLD RECEIVES ITS CONSTANT SUPPLY OF LIGHT! ITS INHABITANTS VIEW WITH TERROR A PHENOMENON WHICH SURFACE PEOPLE ACCEPT AS A DAILY RITUAL OF NATURE!
THE INNER WORLD EXPERIENCES ITS FIRST NIGHTFALL...
THE BUNGLED EXPERIMENTS ALSO HAVE THEIR REPURCUSSIONS ABOVE THE EARTH'S CRUST!
GREAT CITIES AND THEIR ENTIRE POPULATIONS PERISH IN THUNDER AND FLAME, AS VOLCANOES, LONG EXTINCT, SPRING INTO SUDDEN ACTIVITY!
3

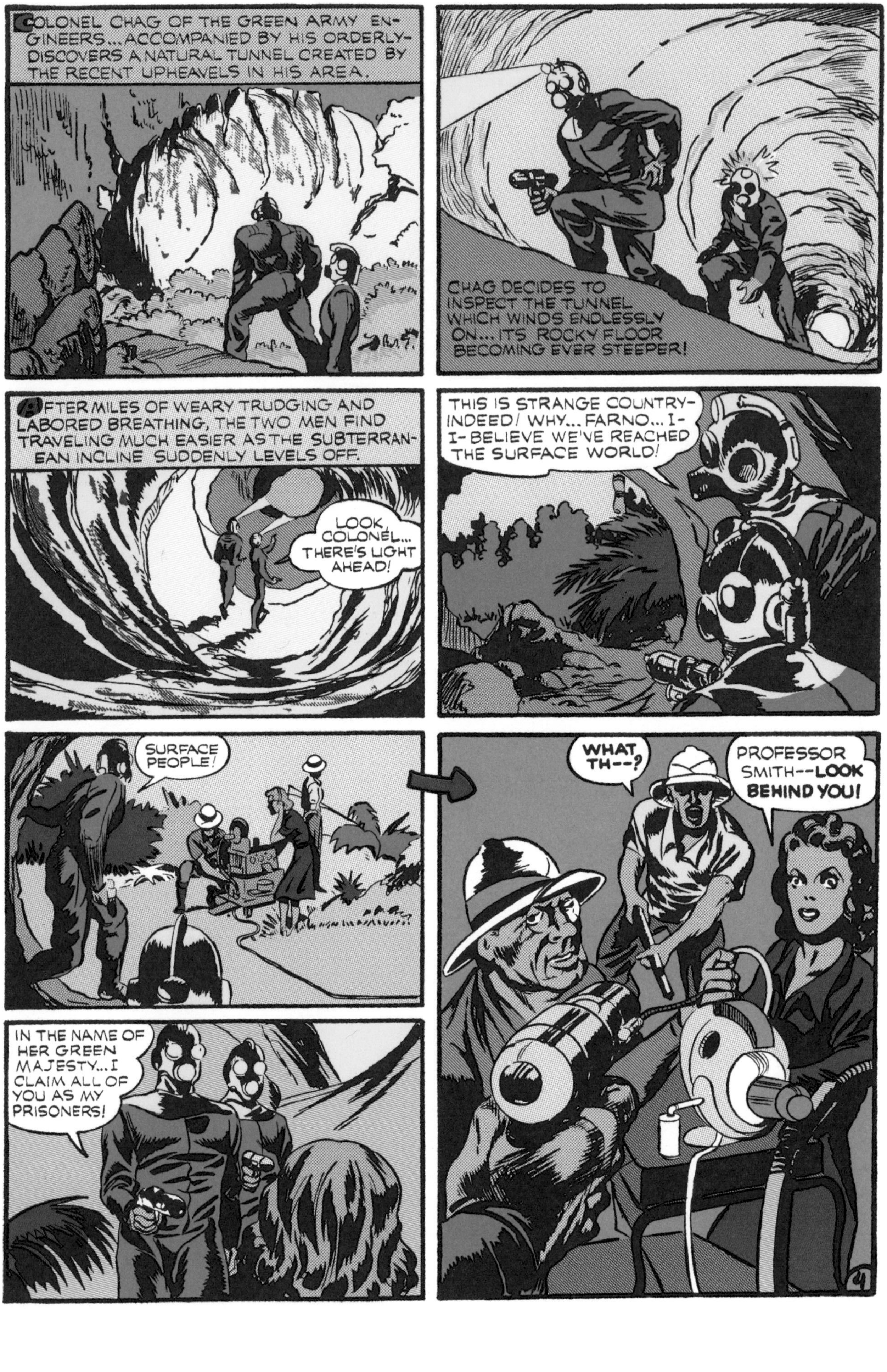
COLONEL CHAG OF THE GREEN ARMY ENGINEERS...ACCOMPANIED BY HIS ORDERLY-DISCOVERS A NATURAL TUNNEL CREATED BY THE RECENT UPHEAVELS IN HIS AREA.
CHAG DECIDES TO INSPECT THE TUNNEL WHICH WINDS ENDLESSLY ON...ITS ROCKY FLOOR BECOMING EVER STEEPER!
AFTER MILES OF WEARY TRUDGING AND LABORED BREATHING, THE TWO MEN FIND TRAVELING MUCH EASIER AS THE SUBTERRANEAN INCLINE SUDDENLY LEVELS OFF.
LOOK, COLONEL... THERE'S LIGHT AHEAD!
THIS IS STRANGE COUNTRY-INDEED! WHY... FARNO... I-I-BELIEVE WE'VE REACHED THE SURFACE WORLD!
SURFACE PEOPLE!
IN THE NAME OF HER GREEN MAJESTY...I CLAIM ALL OF YOU AS MY PRISONERS!
WHAT TH--?
PROFESSOR SMITH--LOOK BEHIND YOU!
4

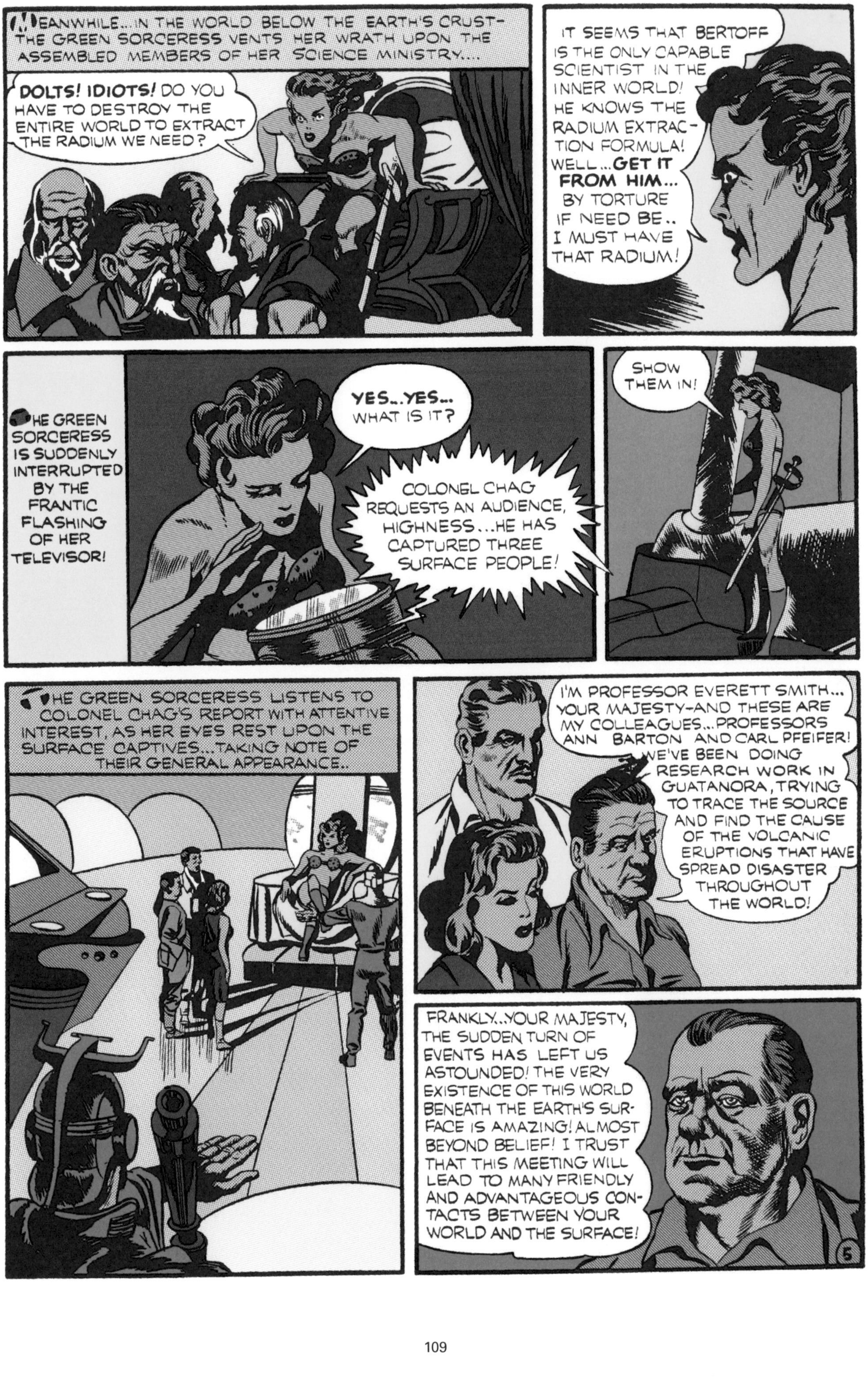
MEANWHILE... IN THE WORLD BELOW THE EARTH'S CRUST-THE GREEN SORCERESS VENTS HER WRATH UPON THE ASSEMBLED MEMBERS OF HER SCIENCE MINISTRY...
DOLTS! IDIOTS! DO YOU HAVE TO DESTROY THE ENTIRE WORLD TO EXTRACT THE RADIUM WE NEED?
IT SEEMS THAT BERTOFF IS THE ONLY CAPABLE SCIENTIST IN THE INNER WORLD! HE KNOWS THE RADIUM EXTRACTION FORMULA! WELL... GET IT FROM HIM... BY TORTURE IF NEED BE.. I MUST HAVE THAT RADIUM!
THE GREEN SORCERESS IS SUDDENLY INTERRUPTED BY THE FRANTIC FLASHING OF HER TELEVISOR!
YES...YES... WHAT IS IT?
COLONEL CHAG REQUESTS AN AUDIENCE, HIGHNESS... HE HAS CAPTURED THREE SURFACE PEOPLE!
SHOW THEM IN!
THE GREEN SORCERESS LISTENS TO COLONEL CHAG'S REPORT WITH ATTENTIVE INTEREST, AS HER EYES REST UPON THE SURFACE CAPTIVES... TAKING NOTE OF THEIR GENERAL APPEARANCE..
I'M PROFESSOR EVERETT SMITH... YOUR MAJESTY-AND THESE ARE MY COLLEAGUES... PROFESSORS ANN BARTON AND CARL PFEIFER! WE'VE BEEN DOING RESEARCH WORK IN GUATANORA, TRYING TO TRACE THE SOURCE AND FIND THE CAUSE OF THE VOLCANIC ERUPTIONS THAT HAVE SPREAD DISASTER THROUGHOUT THE WORLD!
FRANKLY... YOUR MAJESTY, THE SUDDEN TURN OF EVENTS HAS LEFT US ASTOUNDED! THE VERY EXISTENCE OF THIS WORLD BENEATH THE EARTH'S SURFACE IS AMAZING! ALMOST BEYOND BELIEF! I TRUST THAT THIS MEETING WILL LEAD TO MANY FRIENDLY AND ADVANTAGEOUS CONTACTS BETWEEN YOUR WORLD AND THE SURFACE!
5

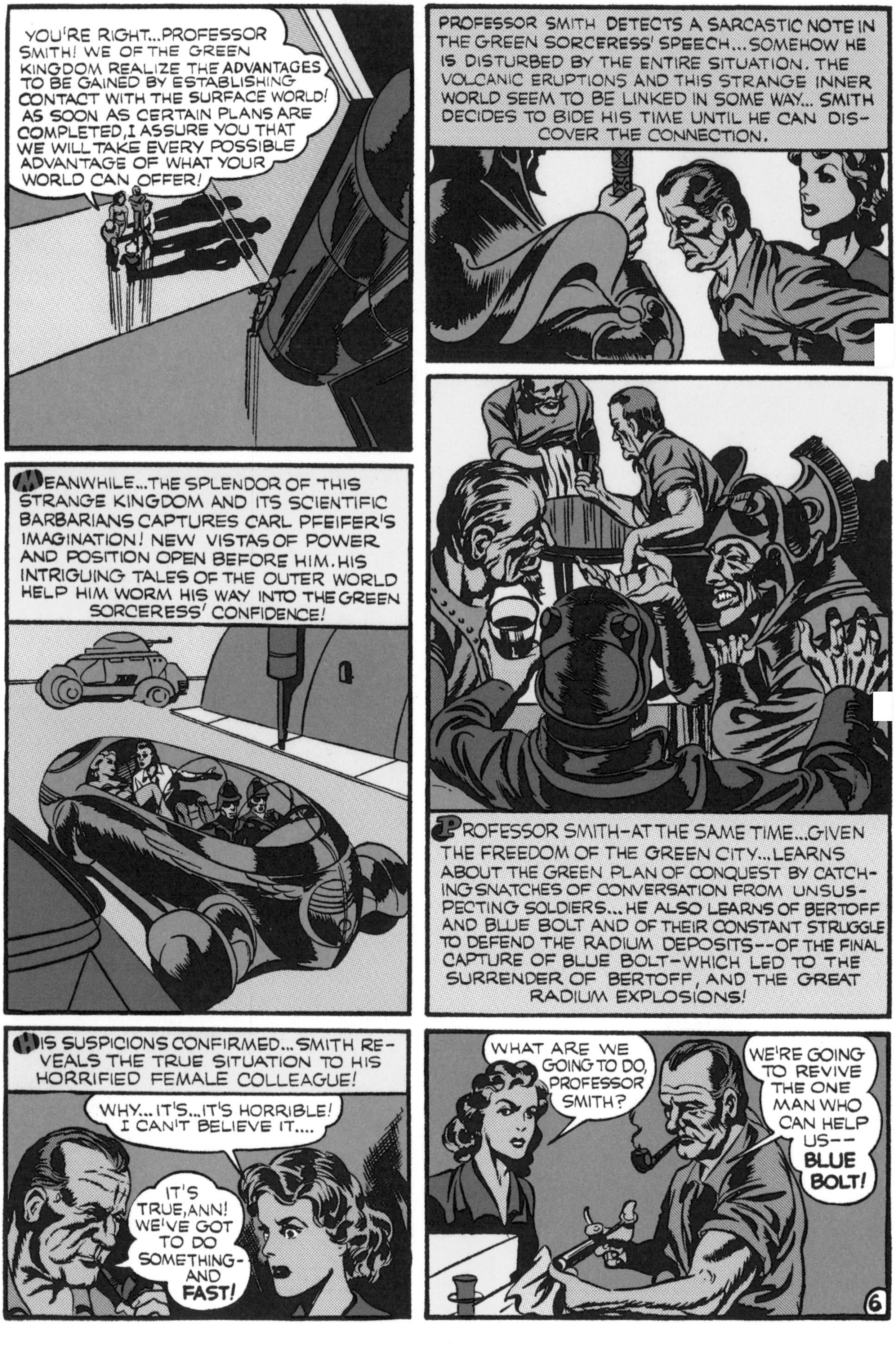
YOU'RE RIGHT...PROFESSOR SMITH! WE OF THE GREEN KINGDOM REALIZE THE ADVANTAGES TO BE GAINED BY ESTABLISHING CONTACT WITH THE SURFACE WORLD! AS SOON AS CERTAIN PLANS ARE COMPLETED, I ASSURE YOU THAT WE WILL TAKE EVERY POSSIBLE ADVANTAGE OF WHAT YOUR WORLD CAN OFFER!
PROFESSOR SMITH DETECTS A SARCASTIC NOTE IN THE GREEN SORCERESS' SPEECH... SOMEHOW HE IS DISTURBED BY THE ENTIRE SITUATION. THE VOLCANIC ERUPTIONS AND THIS STRANGE INNER WORLD SEEM TO BE LINKED IN SOME WAY... SMITH DECIDES TO BIDE HIS TIME UNTIL HE CAN DISCOVER THE CONNECTION.
MEANWHILE...THE SPLENDOR OF THIS STRANGE KINGDOM AND ITS SCIENTIFIC BARBARIANS CAPTURES CARL PFEIFER'S IMAGINATION! NEW VISTAS OF POWER AND POSITION OPEN BEFORE HIM. HIS INTRIGUING TALES OF THE OUTER WORLD HELP HIM WORM HIS WAY INTO THE GREEN SORCERESS' CONFIDENCE!
PROFESSOR SMITH—AT THE SAME TIME...GIVEN THE FREEDOM OF THE GREEN CITY...LEARNS ABOUT THE GREEN PLAN OF CONQUEST BY CATCHING SNATCHES OF CONVERSATION FROM UNSUSPECTING SOLDIERS... HE ALSO LEARNS OF BERTOFF AND BLUE BOLT AND OF THEIR CONSTANT STRUGGLE TO DEFEND THE RADIUM DEPOSITS--OF THE FINAL CAPTURE OF BLUE BOLT—WHICH LED TO THE SURRENDER OF BERTOFF, AND THE GREAT RADIUM EXPLOSIONS!
HIS SUSPICIONS CONFIRMED...SMITH REVEALS THE TRUE SITUATION TO HIS HORRIFIED FEMALE COLLEAGUE!
WHY...IT'S...IT'S HORRIBLE! I CAN'T BELIEVE IT....
IT'S TRUE, ANN! WE'VE GOT TO DO SOMETHING- AND FAST!
WHAT ARE WE GOING TO DO, PROFESSOR SMITH?
WE'RE GOING TO REVIVE THE ONE MAN WHO CAN HELP US-- BLUE BOLT!
6

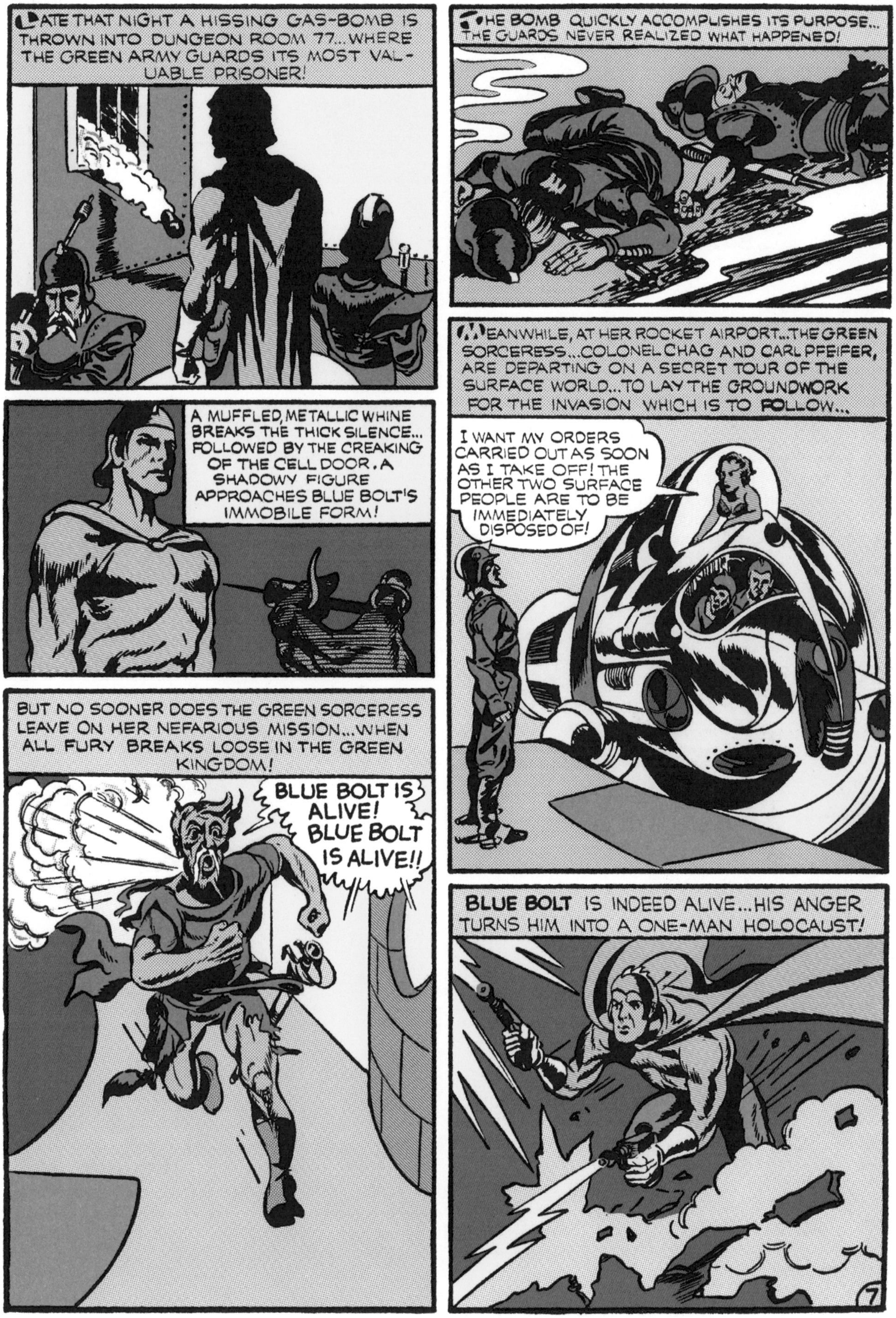
LATE THAT NIGHT A HISSING GAS-BOMB IS THROWN INTO DUNGEON ROOM 77...WHERE THE GREEN ARMY GUARDS ITS MOST VAL-UABLE PRISONER!
THE BOMB QUICKLY ACCOMPLISHES ITS PURPOSE.. THE GUARDS NEVER REALIZED WHAT HAPPENED!
A MUFFLED, METALLIC WHINE BREAKS THE THICK SILENCE... FOLLOWED BY THE CREAKING OF THE CELL DOOR. A SHADOWY FIGURE APPROACHES BLUE BOLT'S IMMOBILE FORM!
MEANWHILE, AT HER ROCKET AIRPORT...THE GREEN SORCERESS...COLONEL CHAG AND CARL PFEIFER, ARE DEPARTING ON A SECRET TOUR OF THE SURFACE WORLD...TO LAY THE GROUNDWORK FOR THE INVASION WHICH IS TO FOLLOW...
I WANT MY ORDERS CARRIED OUT AS SOON AS I TAKE OFF! THE OTHER TWO SURFACE PEOPLE ARE TO BE IMMEDIATELY DISPOSED OF!
BUT NO SOONER DOES THE GREEN SORCERESS LEAVE ON HER NEFARIOUS MISSION...WHEN ALL FURY BREAKS LOOSE IN THE GREEN KINGDOM!
BLUE BOLT IS ALIVE! BLUE BOLT IS ALIVE!!
BLUE BOLT IS INDEED ALIVE...HIS ANGER TURNS HIM INTO A ONE-MAN HOLOCAUST!
7

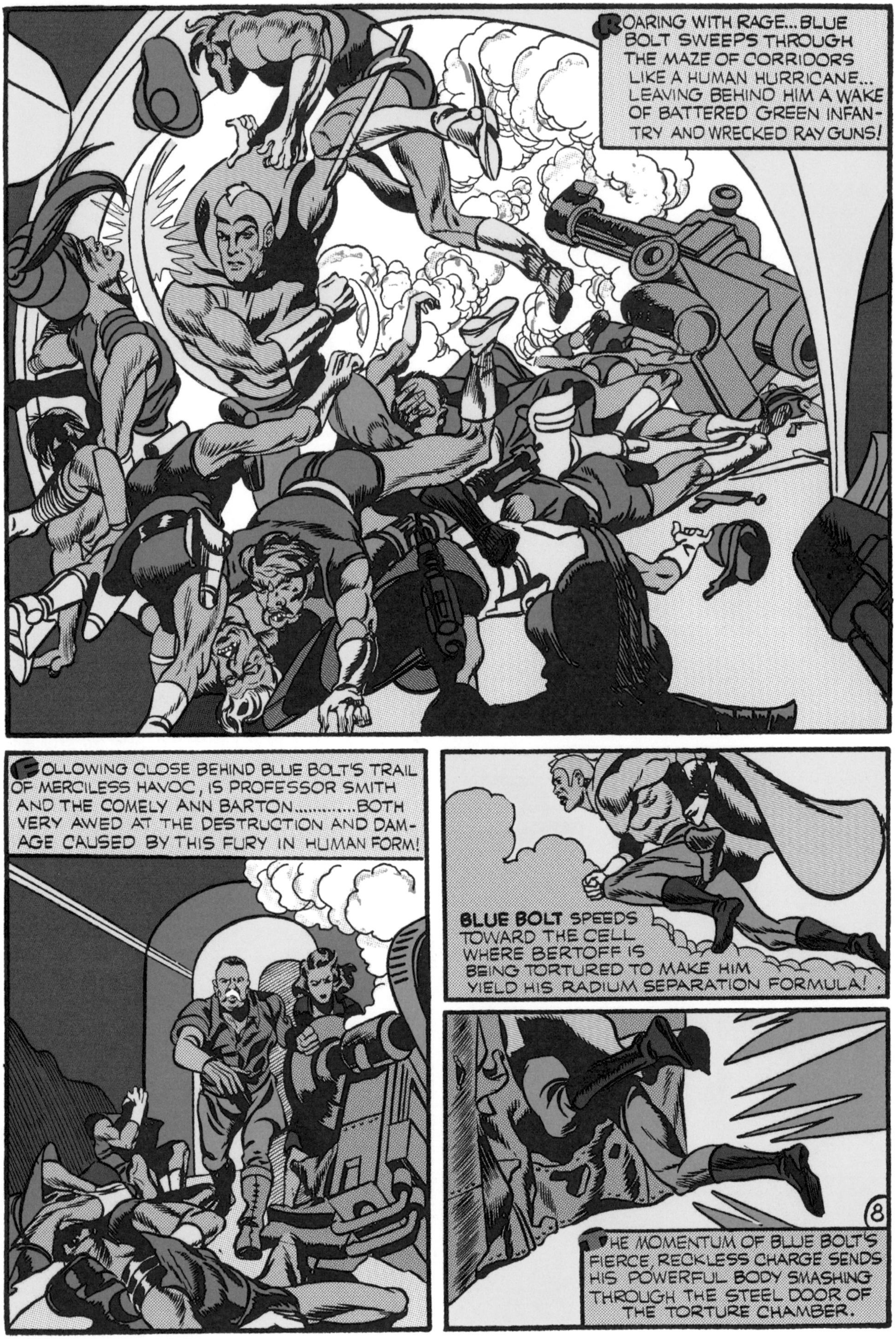
ROARING WITH RAGE...BLUE BOLT SWEEPS THROUGH THE MAZE OF CORRIDORS LIKE A HUMAN HURRICANE... LEAVING BEHIND HIM A WAKE OF BATTERED GREEN INFAN-TRY AND WRECKED RAY GUNS!
FOLLOWING CLOSE BEHIND BLUE BOLT'S TRAIL OF MERCILESS HAVOC, IS PROFESSOR SMITH AND THE COMELY ANN BARTON............BOTH VERY AWED AT THE DESTRUCTION AND DAM-AGE CAUSED BY THIS FURY IN HUMAN FORM!
BLUE BOLT SPEEDS TOWARD THE CELL WHERE BERTOFF IS BEING TORTURED TO MAKE HIM YIELD HIS RADIUM SEPARATION FORMULA!
8
THE MOMENTUM OF BLUE BOLT'S FIERCE, RECKLESS CHARGE SENDS HIS POWERFUL BODY SMASHING THROUGH THE STEEL DOOR OF THE TORTURE CHAMBER.

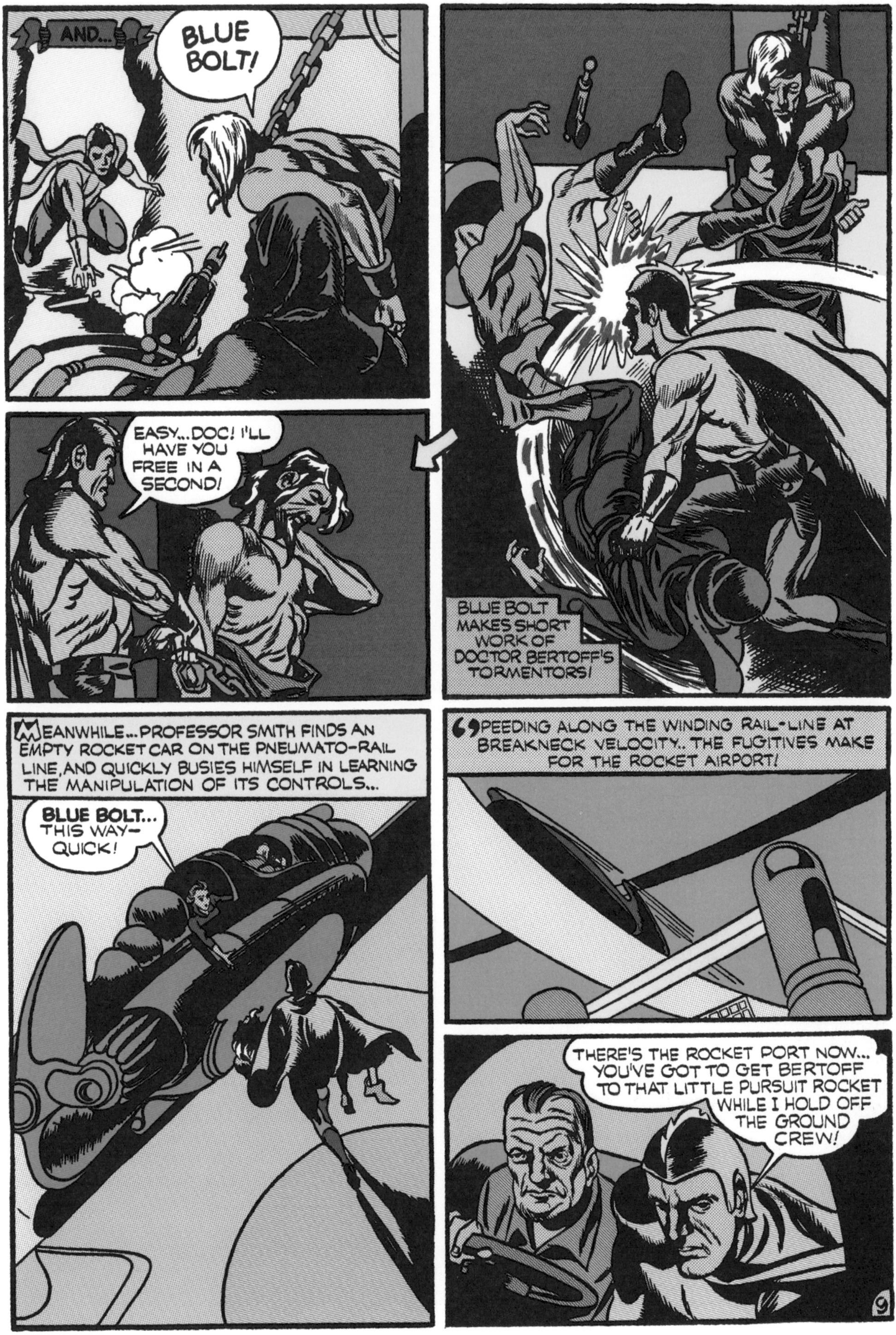
AND...
BLUE BOLT!
EASY...DOC! I'LL HAVE YOU FREE IN A SECOND!
BLUE BOLT MAKES SHORT WORK OF DOCTOR BERTOFF'S TORMENTORS!
MEANWHILE...PROFESSOR SMITH FINDS AN EMPTY ROCKET CAR ON THE PNEUMATO-RAIL LINE, AND QUICKLY BUSIES HIMSELF IN LEARNING THE MANIPULATION OF ITS CONTROLS...
BLUE BOLT... THIS WAY-QUICK!
SPEEDING ALONG THE WINDING RAIL-LINE AT BREAKNECK VELOCITY.. THE FUGITIVES MAKE FOR THE ROCKET AIRPORT!
THERE'S THE ROCKET PORT NOW... YOU'VE GOT TO GET BERTOFF TO THAT LITTLE PURSUIT ROCKET WHILE I HOLD OFF THE GROUND CREW!
9

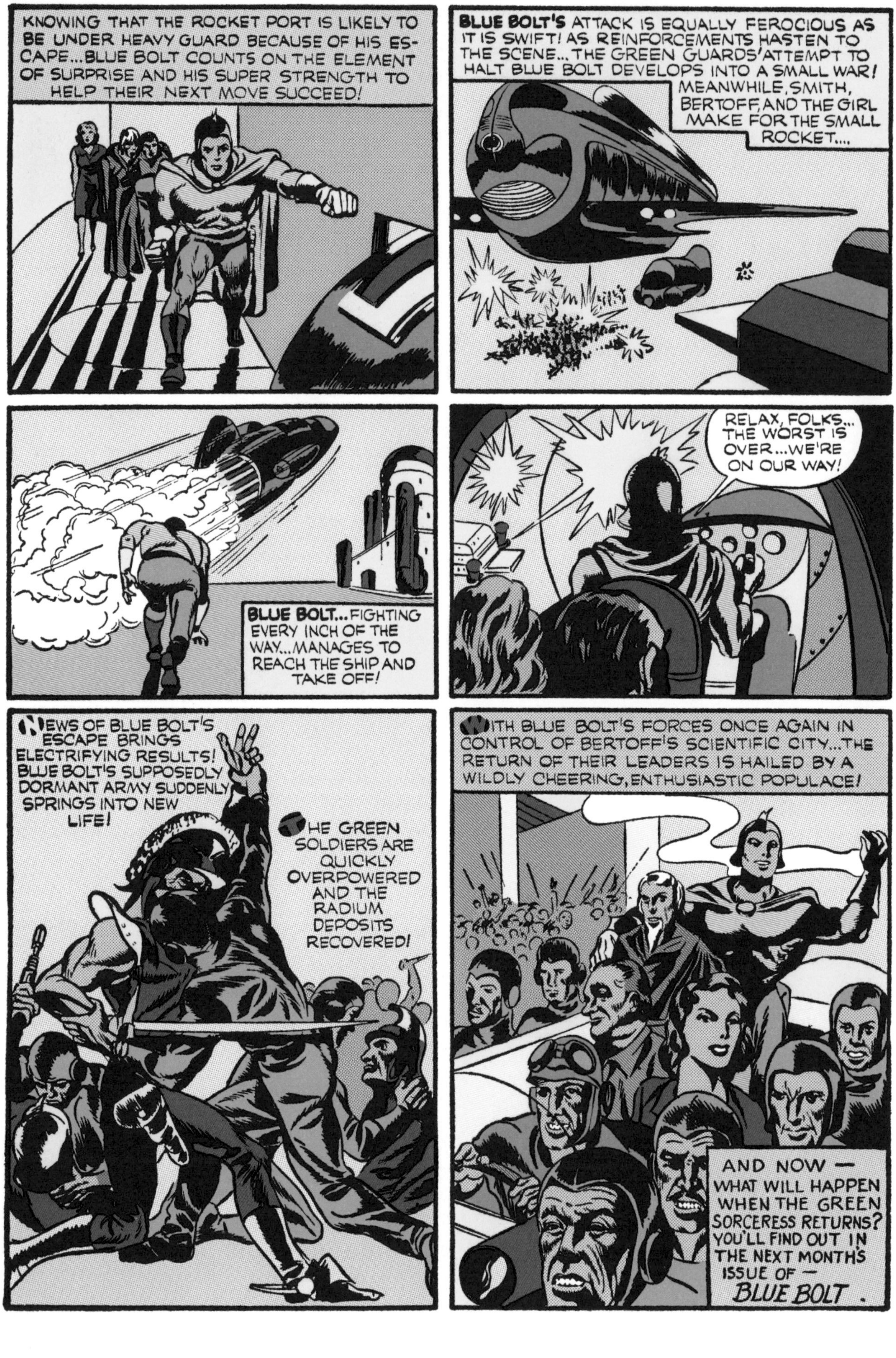
KNOWING THAT THE ROCKET PORT IS LIKELY TO BE UNDER HEAVY GUARD BECAUSE OF HIS ESCAPE... BLUE BOLT COUNTS ON THE ELEMENT OF SURPRISE AND HIS SUPER STRENGTH TO HELP THEIR NEXT MOVE SUCCEED!
BLUE BOLT'S ATTACK IS EQUALLY FEROCIOUS AS IT IS SWIFT! AS REINFORCEMENTS HASTEN TO THE SCENE... THE GREEN GUARDS' ATTEMPT TO HALT BLUE BOLT DEVELOPS INTO A SMALL WAR!
MEANWHILE, SMITH, BERTOFF, AND THE GIRL MAKE FOR THE SMALL ROCKET....
BLUE BOLT... FIGHTING EVERY INCH OF THE WAY... MANAGES TO REACH THE SHIP AND TAKE OFF!
RELAX, FOLKS... THE WORST IS OVER... WE'RE ON OUR WAY!
NEWS OF BLUE BOLT'S ESCAPE BRINGS ELECTRIFYING RESULTS! BLUE BOLT'S SUPPOSEDLY DORMANT ARMY SUDDENLY SPRINGS INTO NEW LIFE!
THE GREEN SOLDIERS ARE QUICKLY OVERPOWERED AND THE RADIUM DEPOSITS RECOVERED!
WITH BLUE BOLT'S FORCES ONCE AGAIN IN CONTROL OF BERTOFF'S SCIENTIFIC CITY... THE RETURN OF THEIR LEADERS IS HAILED BY A WILDLY CHEERING, ENTHUSIASTIC POPULACE!
AND NOW — WHAT WILL HAPPEN WHEN THE GREEN SORCERESS RETURNS? YOU'LL FIND OUT IN THE NEXT MONTH'S ISSUE OF — BLUE BOLT.

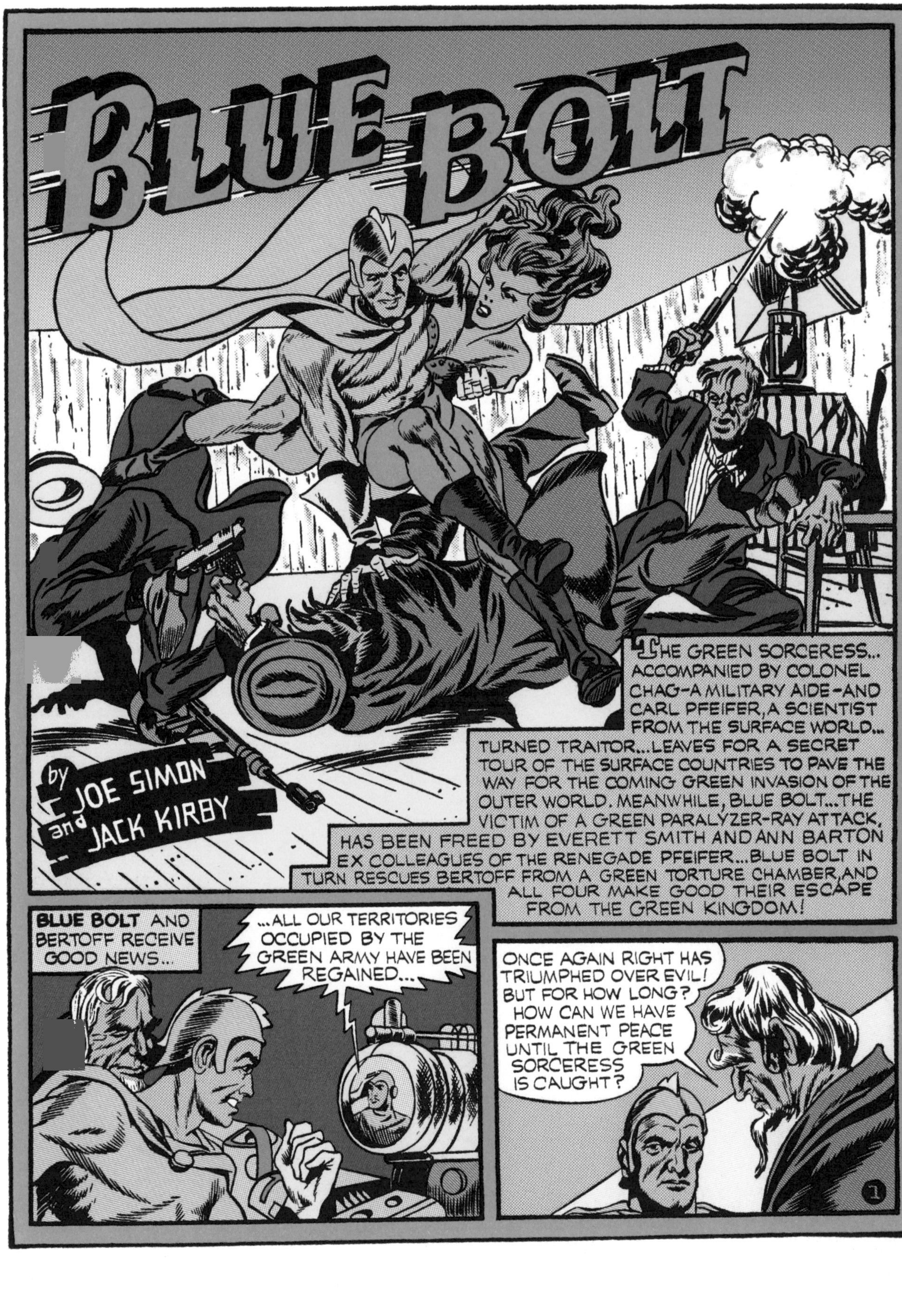
BLUE BOLT
by JOE SIMON and JACK KIRBY
THE GREEN SORCERESS... ACCOMPANIED BY COLONEL CHAG-A MILITARY AIDE-AND CARL PFEIFER, A SCIENTIST FROM THE SURFACE WORLD... TURNED TRAITOR...LEAVES FOR A SECRET TOUR OF THE SURFACE COUNTRIES TO PAVE THE WAY FOR THE COMING GREEN INVASION OF THE OUTER WORLD. MEANWHILE, BLUE BOLT...THE VICTIM OF A GREEN PARALYZER-RAY ATTACK, HAS BEEN FREED BY EVERETT SMITH AND ANN BARTON EX COLLEAGUES OF THE RENEGADE PFEIFER...BLUE BOLT IN TURN RESCUES BERTOFF FROM A GREEN TORTURE CHAMBER, AND ALL FOUR MAKE GOOD THEIR ESCAPE FROM THE GREEN KINGDOM!
BLUE BOLT AND BERTOFF RECEIVE GOOD NEWS...
...ALL OUR TERRITORIES OCCUPIED BY THE GREEN ARMY HAVE BEEN REGAINED...
ONCE AGAIN RIGHT HAS TRIUMPHED OVER EVIL! BUT FOR HOW LONG? HOW CAN WE HAVE PERMANENT PEACE UNTIL THE GREEN SORCERESS IS CAUGHT?
1

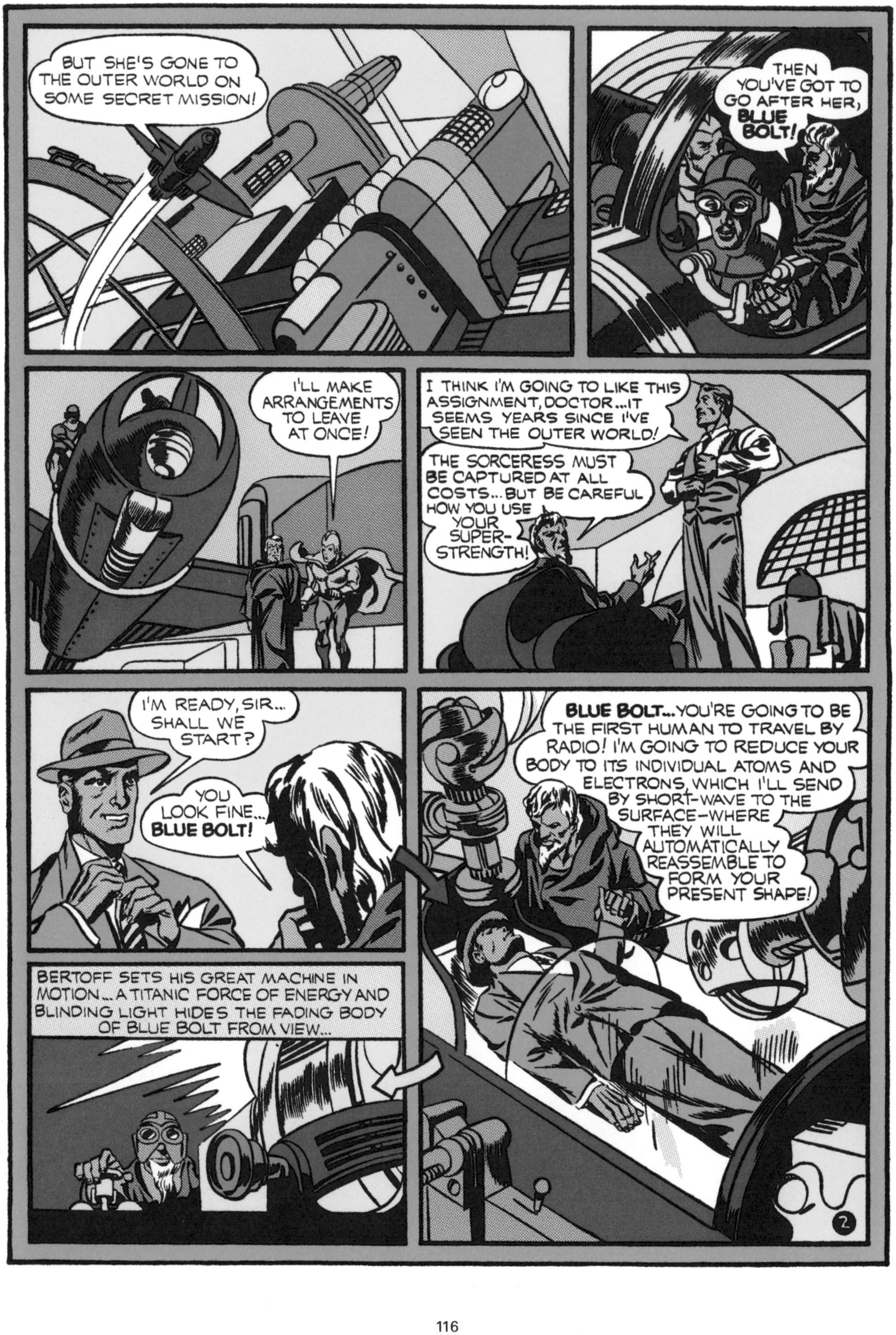
BUT SHE'S GONE TO THE OUTER WORLD ON SOME SECRET MISSION!
THEN YOU'VE GOT TO GO AFTER HER, BLUE BOLT!
I'LL MAKE ARRANGEMENTS TO LEAVE AT ONCE!
I THINK I'M GOING TO LIKE THIS ASSIGNMENT, DOCTOR...IT SEEMS YEARS SINCE I'VE SEEN THE OUTER WORLD!
THE SORCERESS MUST BE CAPTURED AT ALL COSTS...BUT BE CAREFUL HOW YOU USE YOUR SUPER-STRENGTH!
I'M READY, SIR... SHALL WE START?
YOU LOOK FINE... BLUE BOLT!
BLUE BOLT...YOU'RE GOING TO BE THE FIRST HUMAN TO TRAVEL BY RADIO! I'M GOING TO REDUCE YOUR BODY TO ITS INDIVIDUAL ATOMS AND ELECTRONS, WHICH I'LL SEND BY SHORT-WAVE TO THE SURFACE—WHERE THEY WILL AUTOMATICALLY REASSEMBLE TO FORM YOUR PRESENT SHAPE!
BERTOFF SETS HIS GREAT MACHINE IN MOTION...A TITANIC FORCE OF ENERGY AND BLINDING LIGHT HIDES THE FADING BODY OF BLUE BOLT FROM VIEW...
2

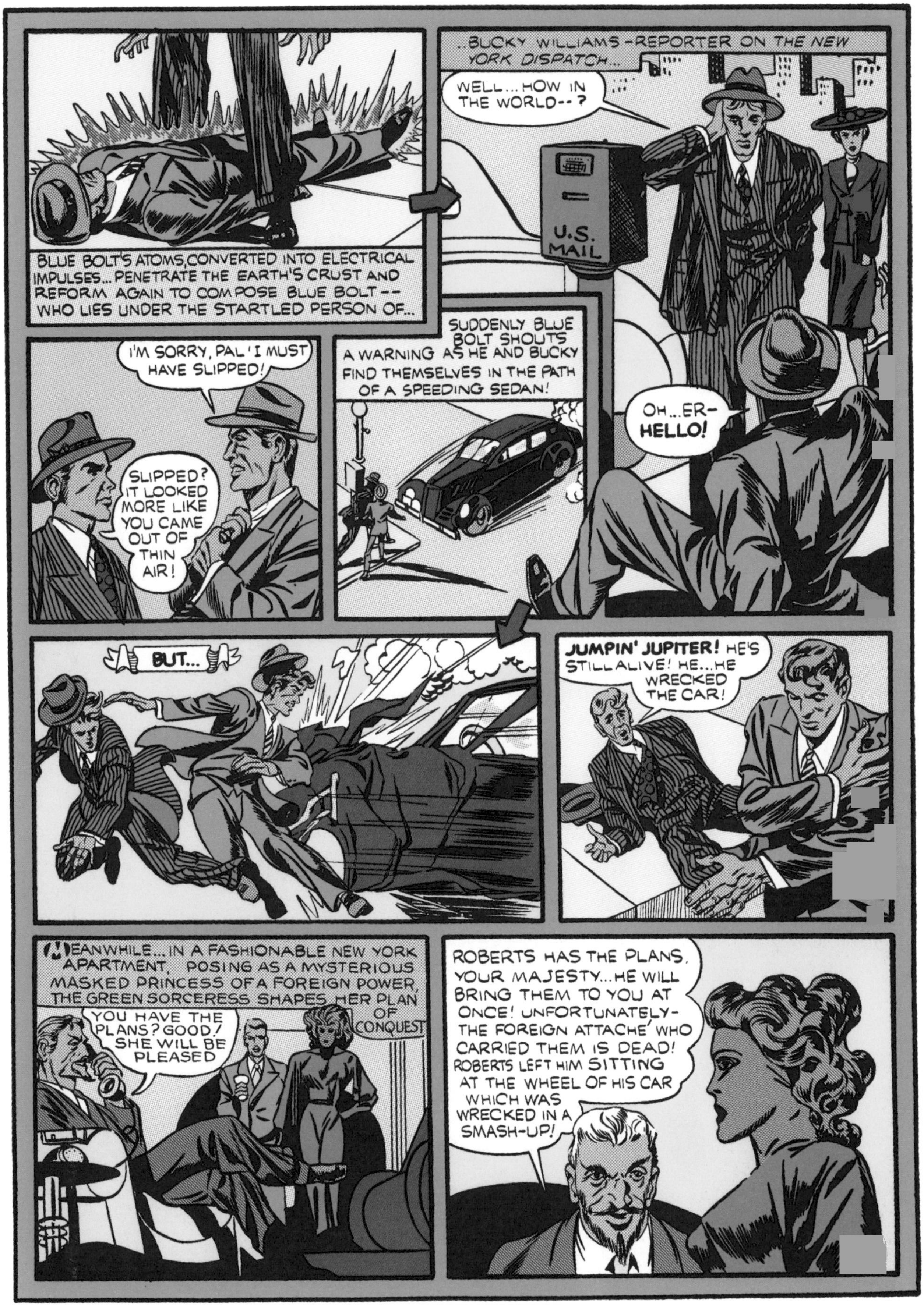
BLUE BOLT'S ATOMS, CONVERTED INTO ELECTRICAL IMPULSES... PENETRATE THE EARTH'S CRUST AND REFORM AGAIN TO COMPOSE BLUE BOLT -- WHO LIES UNDER THE STARTLED PERSON OF..
..BUCKY WILLIAMS - REPORTER ON THE NEW YORK DISPATCH..
WELL... HOW IN THE WORLD -- ?
U.S. MAIL
OH...ER- HELLO!
I'M SORRY, PAL' I MUST HAVE SLIPPED!
SLIPPED? IT LOOKED MORE LIKE YOU CAME OUT OF THIN AIR!
SUDDENLY BLUE BOLT SHOUTS A WARNING AS HE AND BUCKY FIND THEMSELVES IN THE PATH OF A SPEEDING SEDAN!
BUT...
JUMPIN' JUPITER! HE'S STILL ALIVE! HE...HE WRECKED THE CAR!
MEANWHILE... IN A FASHIONABLE NEW YORK APARTMENT, POSING AS A MYSTERIOUS MASKED PRINCESS OF A FOREIGN POWER, THE GREEN SORCERESS SHAPES HER PLAN OF CONQUEST
YOU HAVE THE PLANS? GOOD! SHE WILL BE PLEASED
ROBERTS HAS THE PLANS, YOUR MAJESTY...HE WILL BRING THEM TO YOU AT ONCE! UNFORTUNATELY- THE FOREIGN ATTACHE' WHO CARRIED THEM IS DEAD! ROBERTS LEFT HIM SITTING AT THE WHEEL OF HIS CAR WHICH WAS WRECKED IN A SMASH-UP!

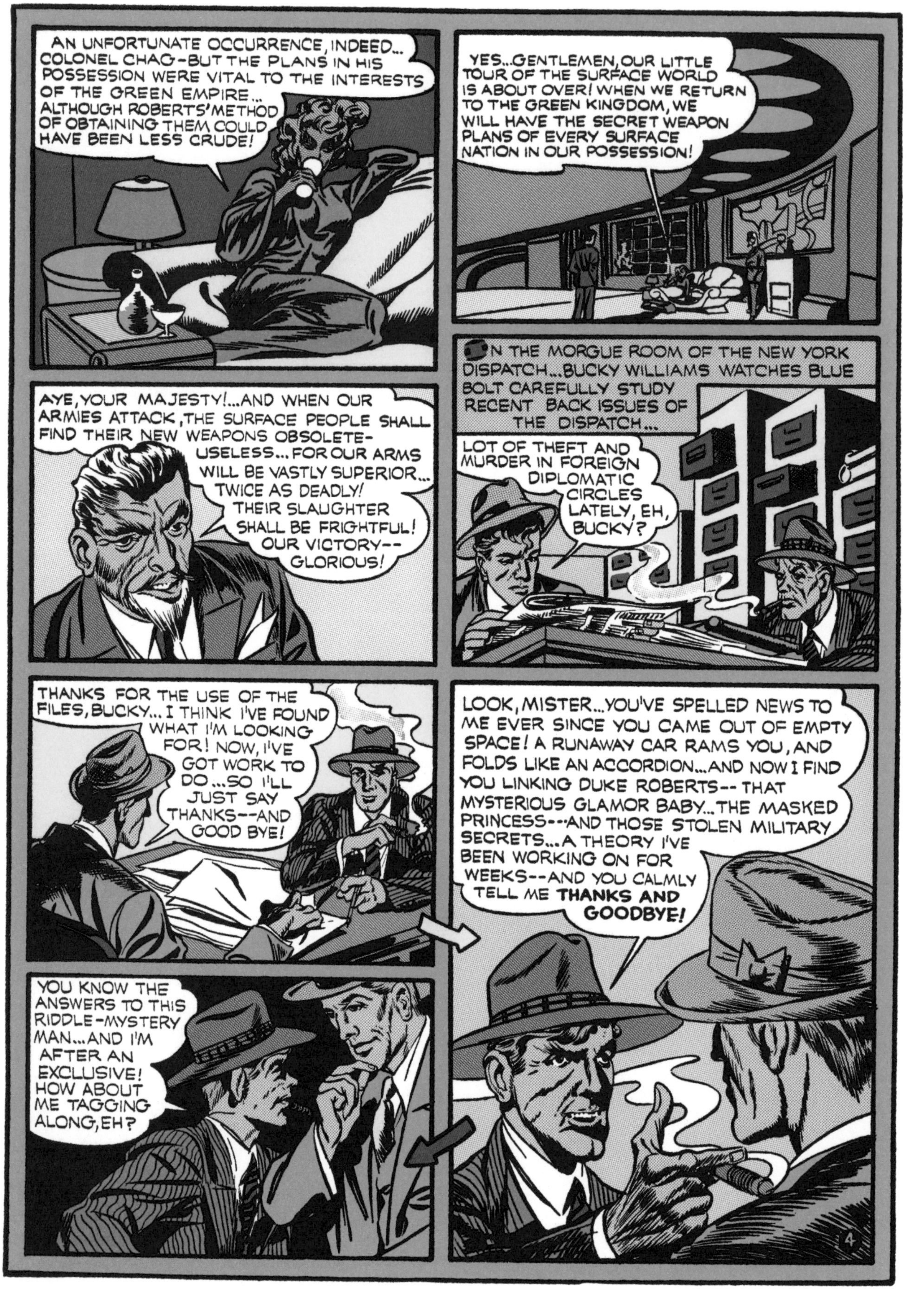
AN UNFORTUNATE OCCURRENCE, INDEED... COLONEL CHAG-BUT THE PLANS IN HIS POSSESSION WERE VITAL TO THE INTERESTS OF THE GREEN EMPIRE... ALTHOUGH ROBERTS' METHOD OF OBTAINING THEM COULD HAVE BEEN LESS CRUDE!
YES...GENTLEMEN, OUR LITTLE TOUR OF THE SURFACE WORLD IS ABOUT OVER! WHEN WE RETURN TO THE GREEN KINGDOM, WE WILL HAVE THE SECRET WEAPON PLANS OF EVERY SURFACE NATION IN OUR POSSESSION!
AYE, YOUR MAJESTY!...AND WHEN OUR ARMIES ATTACK, THE SURFACE PEOPLE SHALL FIND THEIR NEW WEAPONS OBSOLETE-USELESS... FOR OUR ARMS WILL BE VASTLY SUPERIOR... TWICE AS DEADLY! THEIR SLAUGHTER SHALL BE FRIGHTFUL! OUR VICTORY--GLORIOUS!
IN THE MORGUE ROOM OF THE NEW YORK DISPATCH...BUCKY WILLIAMS WATCHES BLUE BOLT CAREFULLY STUDY RECENT BACK ISSUES OF THE DISPATCH...
LOT OF THEFT AND MURDER IN FOREIGN DIPLOMATIC CIRCLES LATELY, EH, BUCKY?
THANKS FOR THE USE OF THE FILES, BUCKY... I THINK I'VE FOUND WHAT I'M LOOKING FOR! NOW, I'VE GOT WORK TO DO...SO I'LL JUST SAY THANKS--AND GOOD BYE!
LOOK, MISTER...YOU'VE SPELLED NEWS TO ME EVER SINCE YOU CAME OUT OF EMPTY SPACE! A RUNAWAY CAR RAMS YOU, AND FOLDS LIKE AN ACCORDION...AND NOW I FIND YOU LINKING DUKE ROBERTS-- THAT MYSTERIOUS GLAMOR BABY...THE MASKED PRINCESS---AND THOSE STOLEN MILITARY SECRETS...A THEORY I'VE BEEN WORKING ON FOR WEEKS--AND YOU CALMLY TELL ME THANKS AND GOODBYE!
YOU KNOW THE ANSWERS TO THIS RIDDLE-MYSTERY MAN...AND I'M AFTER AN EXCLUSIVE! HOW ABOUT ME TAGGING ALONG, EH?
4

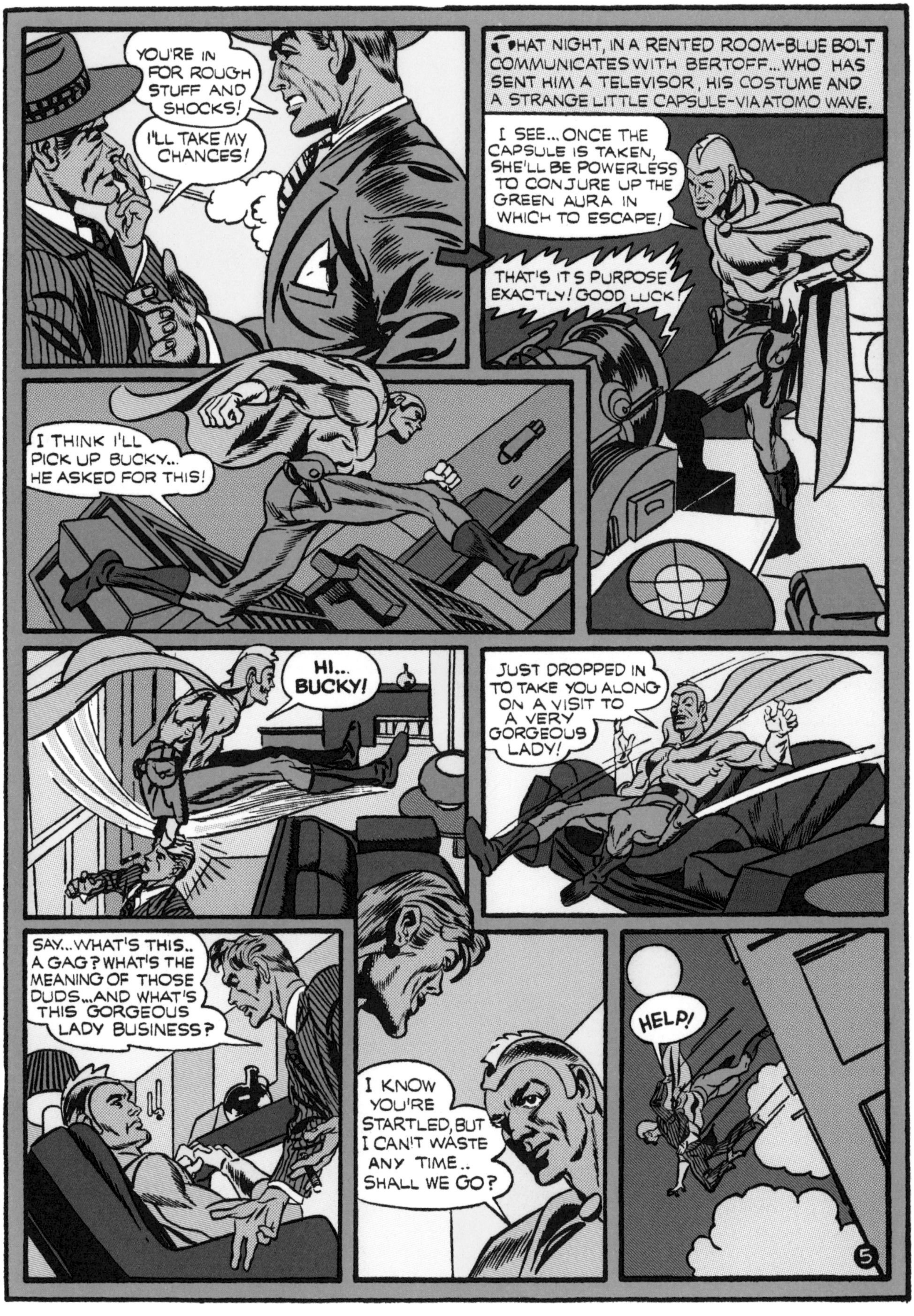

YOU'RE IN FOR ROUGH STUFF AND SHOCKS!
I'LL TAKE MY CHANCES!
THAT NIGHT, IN A RENTED ROOM-BLUE BOLT COMMUNICATES WITH BERTOFF...WHO HAS SENT HIM A TELEVISOR, HIS COSTUME AND A STRANGE LITTLE CAPSULE-VIA ATOMO WAVE.
I SEE...ONCE THE CAPSULE IS TAKEN, SHE'LL BE POWERLESS TO CONJURE UP THE GREEN AURA IN WHICH TO ESCAPE!
THAT'S ITS PURPOSE EXACTLY! GOOD LUCK!
I THINK I'LL PICK UP BUCKY... HE ASKED FOR THIS!
HI... BUCKY!
JUST DROPPED IN TO TAKE YOU ALONG ON A VISIT TO A VERY GORGEOUS LADY!
SAY...WHAT'S THIS.. A GAG? WHAT'S THE MEANING OF THOSE DUDS...AND WHAT'S THIS GORGEOUS LADY BUSINESS?
I KNOW YOU'RE STARTLED, BUT I CAN'T WASTE ANY TIME.. SHALL WE GO?
HELP!
5

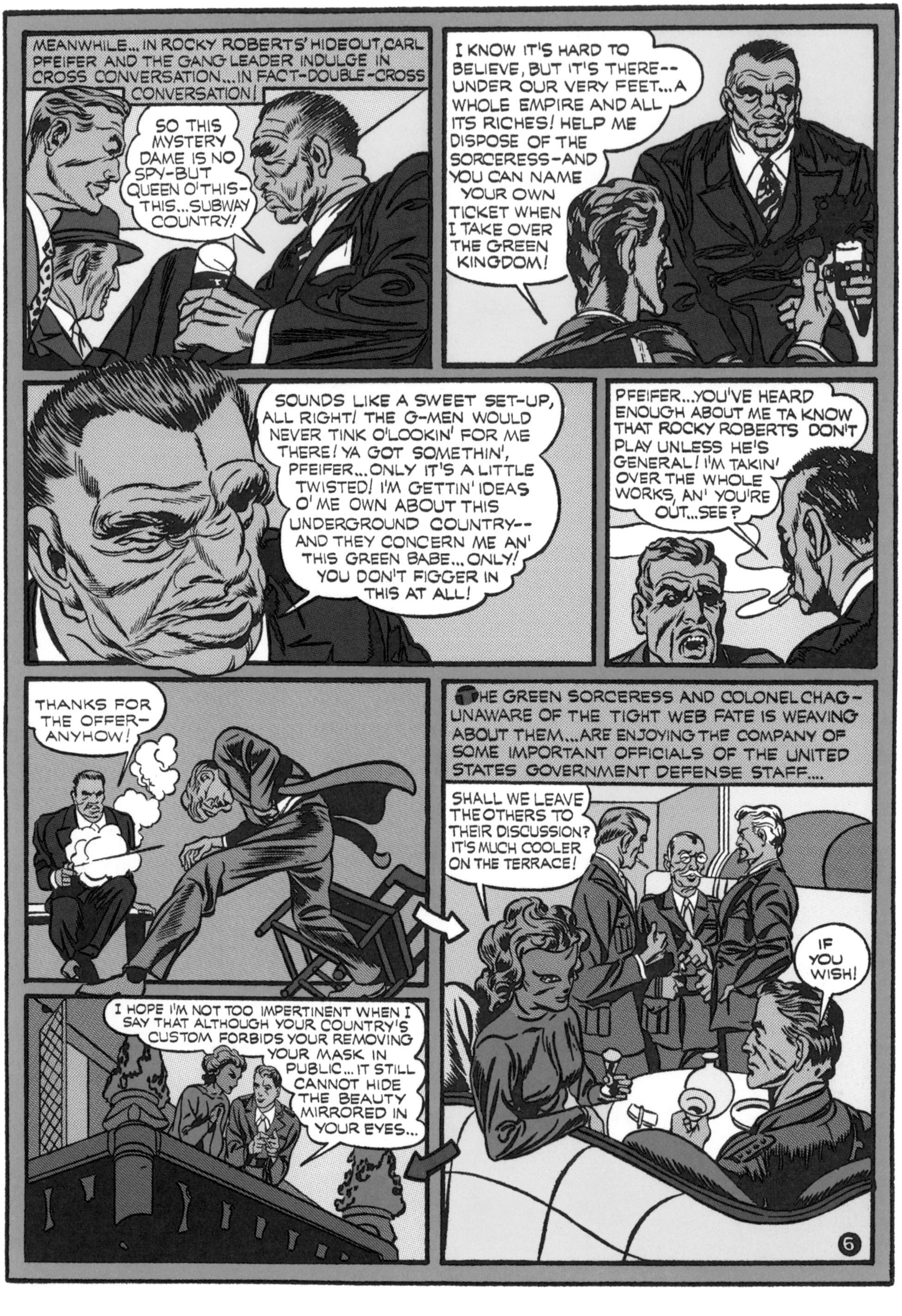

MEANWHILE... IN ROCKY ROBERTS' HIDEOUT, CARL PFEIFER AND THE GANG LEADER INDULGE IN CROSS CONVERSATION... IN FACT-DOUBLE-CROSS CONVERSATION!
SO THIS MYSTERY DAME IS NO SPY-BUT QUEEN O'THIS-THIS... SUBWAY COUNTRY!
I KNOW IT'S HARD TO BELIEVE, BUT IT'S THERE-- UNDER OUR VERY FEET... A WHOLE EMPIRE AND ALL ITS RICHES! HELP ME DISPOSE OF THE SORCERESS-AND YOU CAN NAME YOUR OWN TICKET WHEN I TAKE OVER THE GREEN KINGDOM!
SOUNDS LIKE A SWEET SET-UP, ALL RIGHT! THE G-MEN WOULD NEVER TINK O'LOOKIN' FOR ME THERE! YA GOT SOMETHIN', PFEIFER... ONLY IT'S A LITTLE TWISTED! I'M GETTIN' IDEAS O' ME OWN ABOUT THIS UNDERGROUND COUNTRY-- AND THEY CONCERN ME AN' THIS GREEN BABE... ONLY! YOU DON'T FIGGER IN THIS AT ALL!
PFEIFER... YOU'VE HEARD ENOUGH ABOUT ME TA KNOW THAT ROCKY ROBERTS DON'T PLAY UNLESS HE'S GENERAL! I'M TAKIN' OVER THE WHOLE WORKS, AN' YOU'RE OUT... SEE?
THANKS FOR THE OFFER- ANYHOW!
THE GREEN SORCERESS AND COLONEL CHAG- UNAWARE OF THE TIGHT WEB FATE IS WEAVING ABOUT THEM... ARE ENJOYING THE COMPANY OF SOME IMPORTANT OFFICIALS OF THE UNITED STATES GOVERNMENT DEFENSE STAFF...
SHALL WE LEAVE THE OTHERS TO THEIR DISCUSSION? IT'S MUCH COOLER ON THE TERRACE!
IF YOU WISH!
I HOPE I'M NOT TOO IMPERTINENT WHEN I SAY THAT ALTHOUGH YOUR COUNTRY'S CUSTOM FORBIDS YOUR REMOVING YOUR MASK IN PUBLIC... IT STILL CANNOT HIDE THE BEAUTY MIRRORED IN YOUR EYES...
6

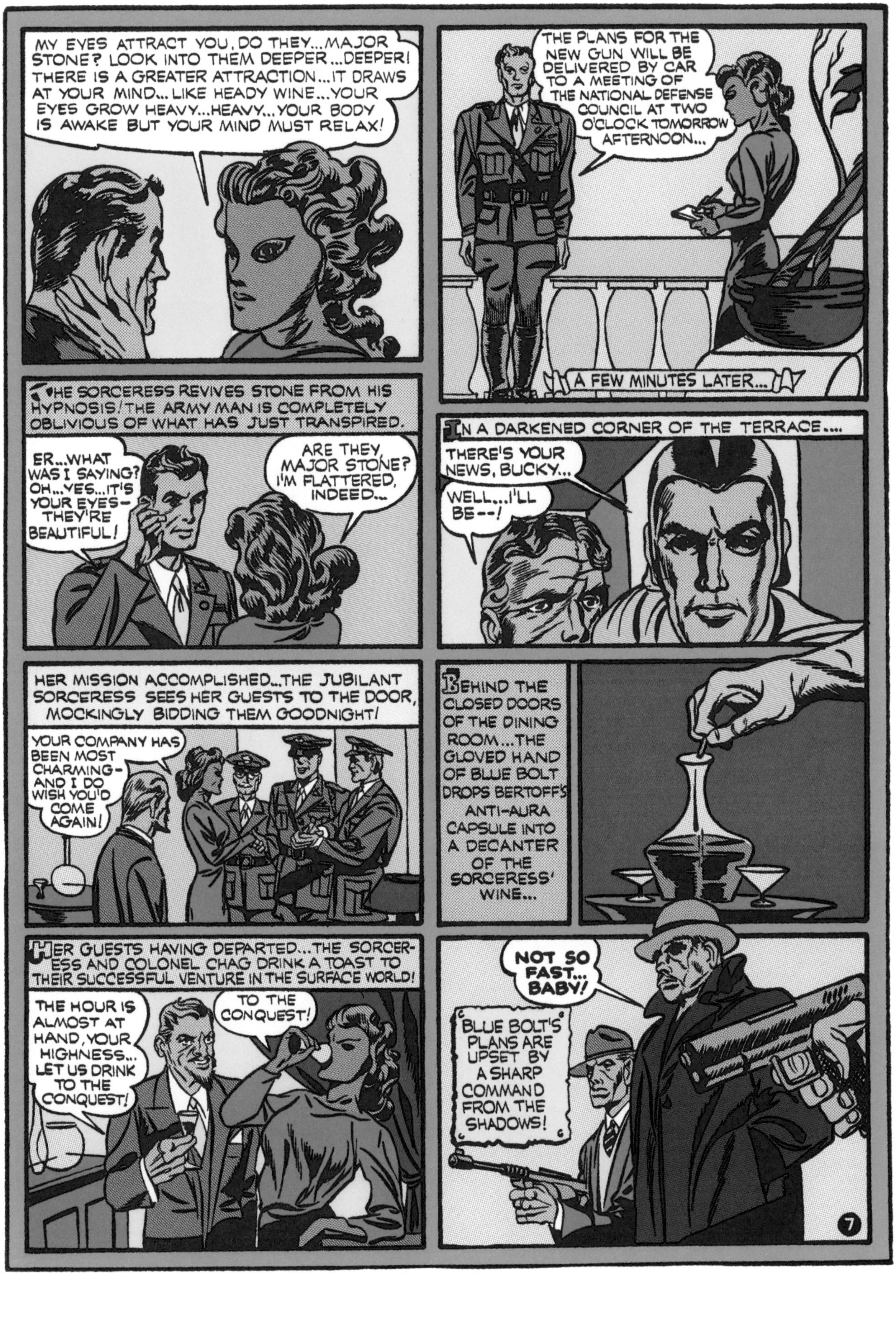
MY EYES ATTRACT YOU, DO THEY...MAJOR STONE? LOOK INTO THEM DEEPER ...DEEPER! THERE IS A GREATER ATTRACTION...IT DRAWS AT YOUR MIND... LIKE HEADY WINE...YOUR EYES GROW HEAVY...HEAVY...YOUR BODY IS AWAKE BUT YOUR MIND MUST RELAX!
THE PLANS FOR THE NEW GUN WILL BE DELIVERED BY CAR TO A MEETING OF THE NATIONAL DEFENSE COUNCIL AT TWO O'CLOCK TOMORROW AFTERNOON...
A FEW MINUTES LATER...
THE SORCERESS REVIVES STONE FROM HIS HYPNOSIS! THE ARMY MAN IS COMPLETELY OBLIVIOUS OF WHAT HAS JUST TRANSPIRED.
ER...WHAT WAS I SAYING? OH...YES...IT'S YOUR EYES- THEY'RE BEAUTIFUL!
ARE THEY, MAJOR STONE? I'M FLATTERED, INDEED...
IN A DARKENED CORNER OF THE TERRACE....
THERE'S YOUR NEWS, BUCKY...
WELL...I'LL BE--!
HER MISSION ACCOMPLISHED...THE JUBILANT SORCERESS SEES HER GUESTS TO THE DOOR, MOCKINGLY BIDDING THEM GOODNIGHT!
YOUR COMPANY HAS BEEN MOST CHARMING- AND I DO WISH YOU'D COME AGAIN!
BEHIND THE CLOSED DOORS OF THE DINING ROOM...THE GLOVED HAND OF BLUE BOLT DROPS BERTOFF'S ANTI-AURA CAPSULE INTO A DECANTER OF THE SORCERESS' WINE...
HER GUESTS HAVING DEPARTED...THE SORCERESS AND COLONEL CHAG DRINK A TOAST TO THEIR SUCCESSFUL VENTURE IN THE SURFACE WORLD!
THE HOUR IS ALMOST AT HAND, YOUR HIGHNESS... LET US DRINK TO THE CONQUEST!
TO THE CONQUEST!
NOT SO FAST... BABY!
BLUE BOLT'S PLANS ARE UPSET BY A SHARP COMMAND FROM THE SHADOWS!
7

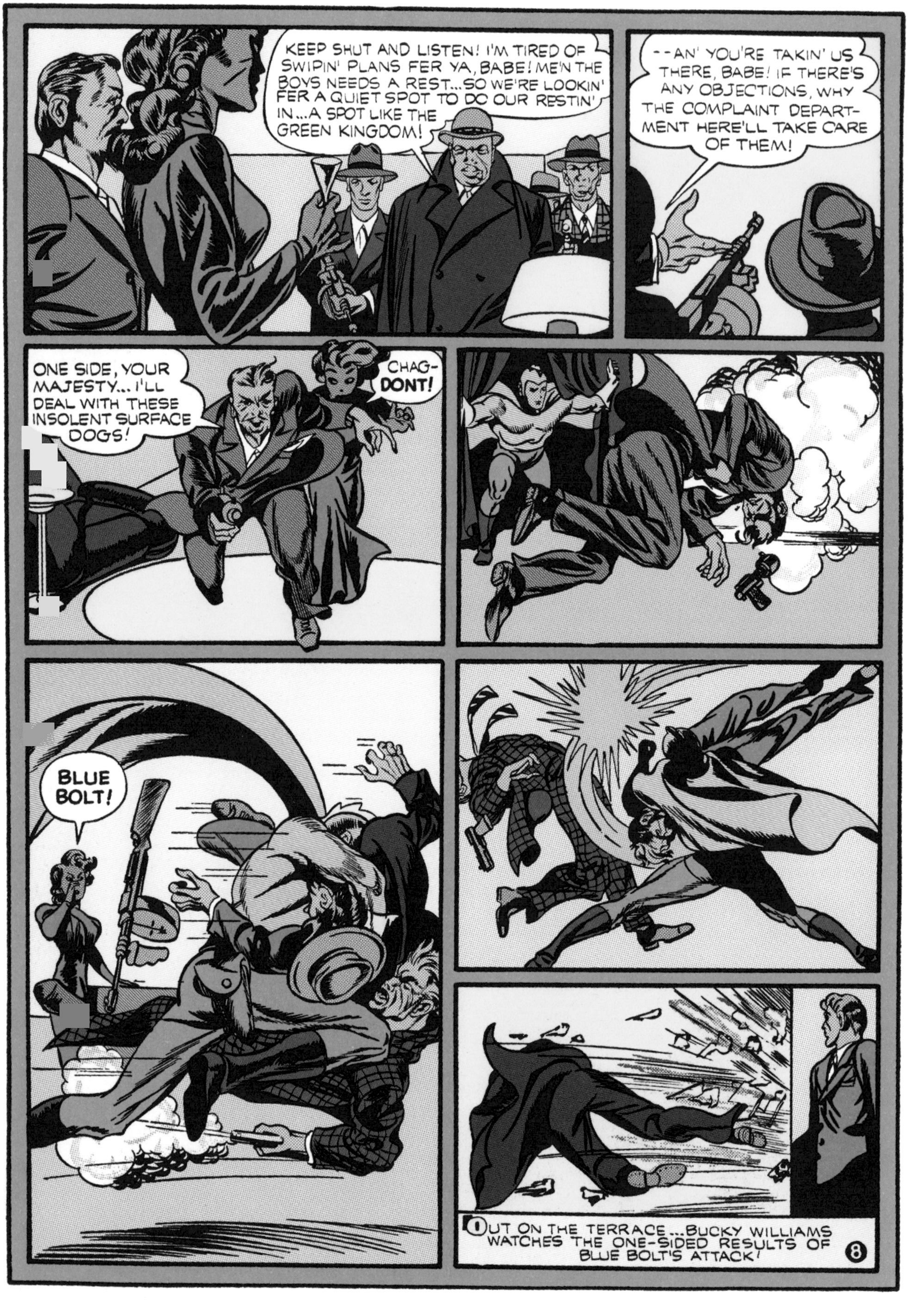
KEEP SHUT AND LISTEN! I'M TIRED OF SWIPIN' PLANS FER YA, BABE! ME'N THE BOYS NEEDS A REST...SO WE'RE LOOKIN' FER A QUIET SPOT TO DO OUR RESTIN' IN...A SPOT LIKE THE GREEN KINGDOM!
--AN' YOU'RE TAKIN' US THERE, BABE! IF THERE'S ANY OBJECTIONS, WHY THE COMPLAINT DEPARTMENT HERE'LL TAKE CARE OF THEM!
ONE SIDE, YOUR MAJESTY... I'LL DEAL WITH THESE INSOLENT SURFACE DOGS!
CHAG-DONT!
BLUE BOLT!
OUT ON THE TERRACE...BUCKY WILLIAMS WATCHES THE ONE-SIDED RESULTS OF BLUE BOLT'S ATTACK!
8

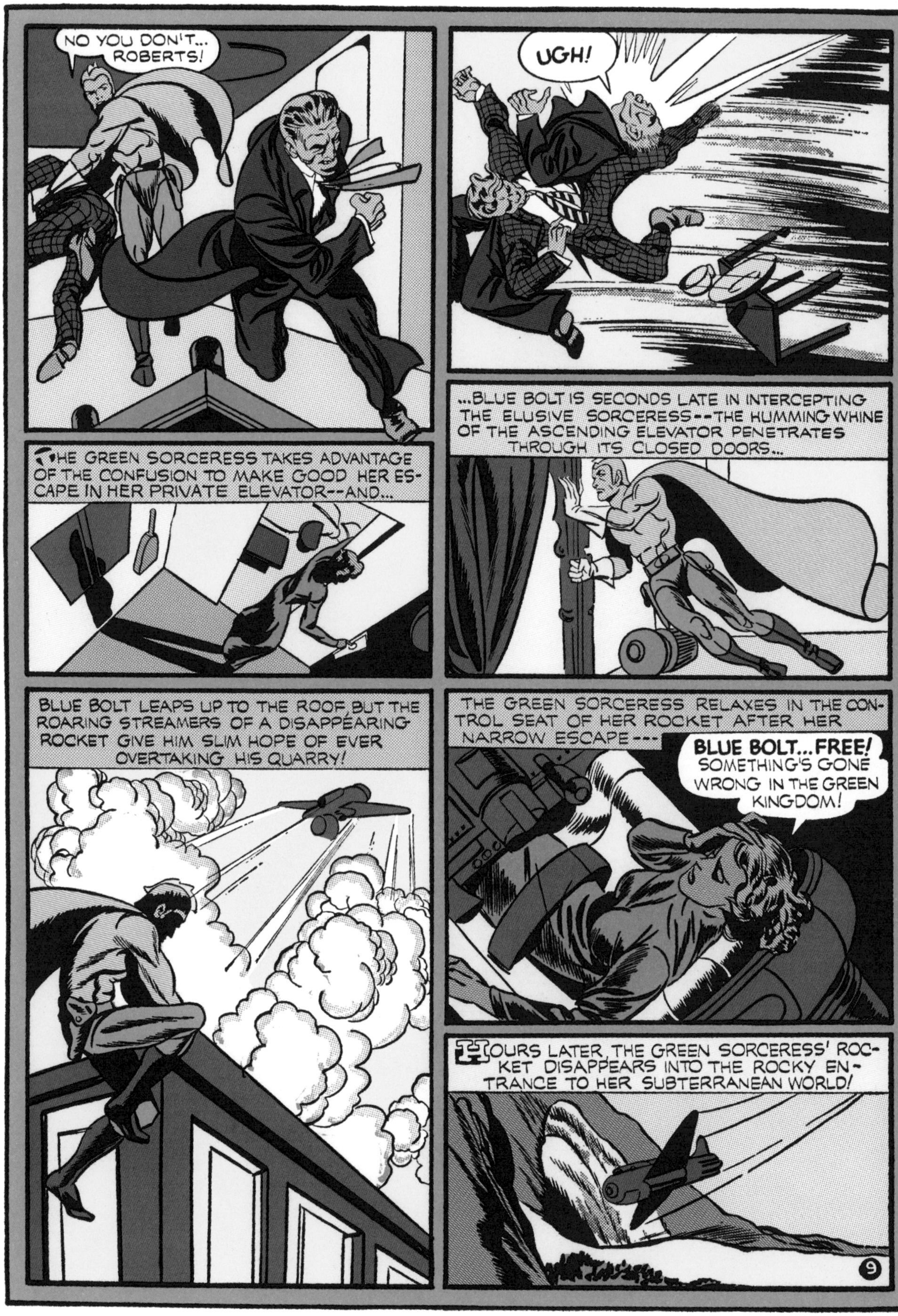
NO YOU DON'T... ROBERTS!
UGH!
...BLUE BOLT IS SECONDS LATE IN INTERCEPTING THE ELUSIVE SORCERESS--THE HUMMING WHINE OF THE ASCENDING ELEVATOR PENETRATES THROUGH ITS CLOSED DOORS...
THE GREEN SORCERESS TAKES ADVANTAGE OF THE CONFUSION TO MAKE GOOD HER ES-CAPE IN HER PRIVATE ELEVATOR--AND...
BLUE BOLT LEAPS UP TO THE ROOF, BUT THE ROARING STREAMERS OF A DISAPPEARING ROCKET GIVE HIM SLIM HOPE OF EVER OVERTAKING HIS QUARRY!
THE GREEN SORCERESS RELAXES IN THE CON-TROL SEAT OF HER ROCKET AFTER HER NARROW ESCAPE---
BLUE BOLT...FREE! SOMETHING'S GONE WRONG IN THE GREEN KINGDOM!
HOURS LATER THE GREEN SORCERESS' ROC-KET DISAPPEARS INTO THE ROCKY EN-TRANCE TO HER SUBTERRANEAN WORLD!
9

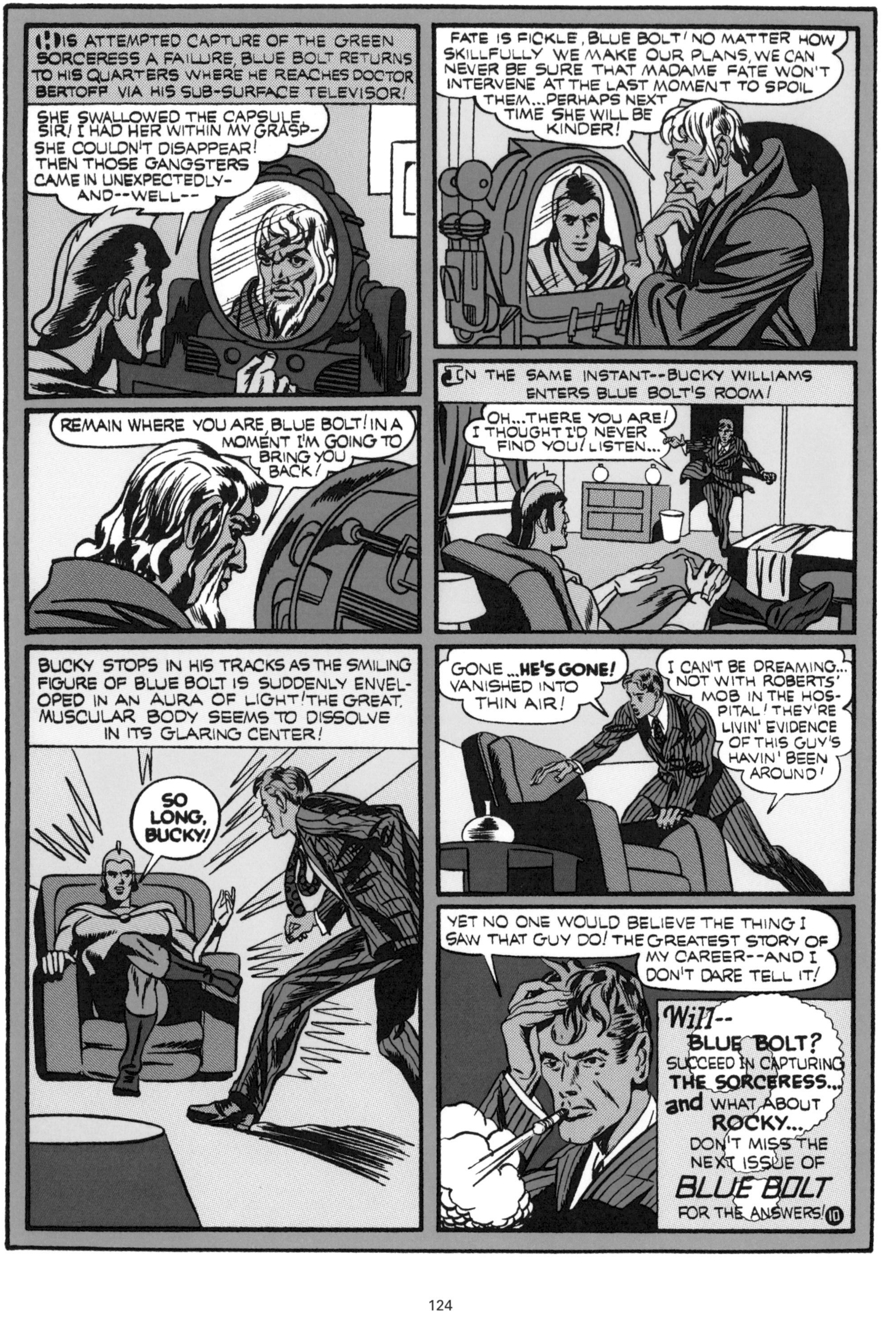
HIS ATTEMPTED CAPTURE OF THE GREEN SORCERESS A FAILURE, BLUE BOLT RETURNS TO HIS QUARTERS WHERE HE REACHES DOCTOR BERTOFF VIA HIS SUB-SURFACE TELEVISOR!
SHE SWALLOWED THE CAPSULE, SIR! I HAD HER WITHIN MY GRASP-SHE COULDN'T DISAPPEAR! THEN THOSE GANGSTERS CAME IN UNEXPECTEDLY-AND--WELL--
FATE IS FICKLE, BLUE BOLT! NO MATTER HOW SKILLFULLY WE MAKE OUR PLANS, WE CAN NEVER BE SURE THAT MADAME FATE WON'T INTERVENE AT THE LAST MOMENT TO SPOIL THEM...PERHAPS NEXT TIME SHE WILL BE KINDER!
REMAIN WHERE YOU ARE, BLUE BOLT! IN A MOMENT I'M GOING TO BRING YOU BACK!
IN THE SAME INSTANT--BUCKY WILLIAMS ENTERS BLUE BOLT'S ROOM!
OH...THERE YOU ARE! I THOUGHT I'D NEVER FIND YOU! LISTEN...
BUCKY STOPS IN HIS TRACKS AS THE SMILING FIGURE OF BLUE BOLT IS SUDDENLY ENVELOPED IN AN AURA OF LIGHT! THE GREAT, MUSCULAR BODY SEEMS TO DISSOLVE IN ITS GLARING CENTER!
SO LONG, BUCKY!
GONE...HE'S GONE! VANISHED INTO THIN AIR!
I CAN'T BE DREAMING... NOT WITH ROBERTS' MOB IN THE HOSPITAL! THEY'RE LIVIN' EVIDENCE OF THIS GUY'S HAVIN' BEEN AROUND!
YET NO ONE WOULD BELIEVE THE THING I SAW THAT GUY DO! THE GREATEST STORY OF MY CAREER--AND I DON'T DARE TELL IT!
Will-- BLUE BOLT? SUCCEED IN CAPTURING THE SORCERESS... and WHAT ABOUT ROCKY... DON'T MISS THE NEXT ISSUE OF BLUE BOLT FOR THE ANSWERS!
10

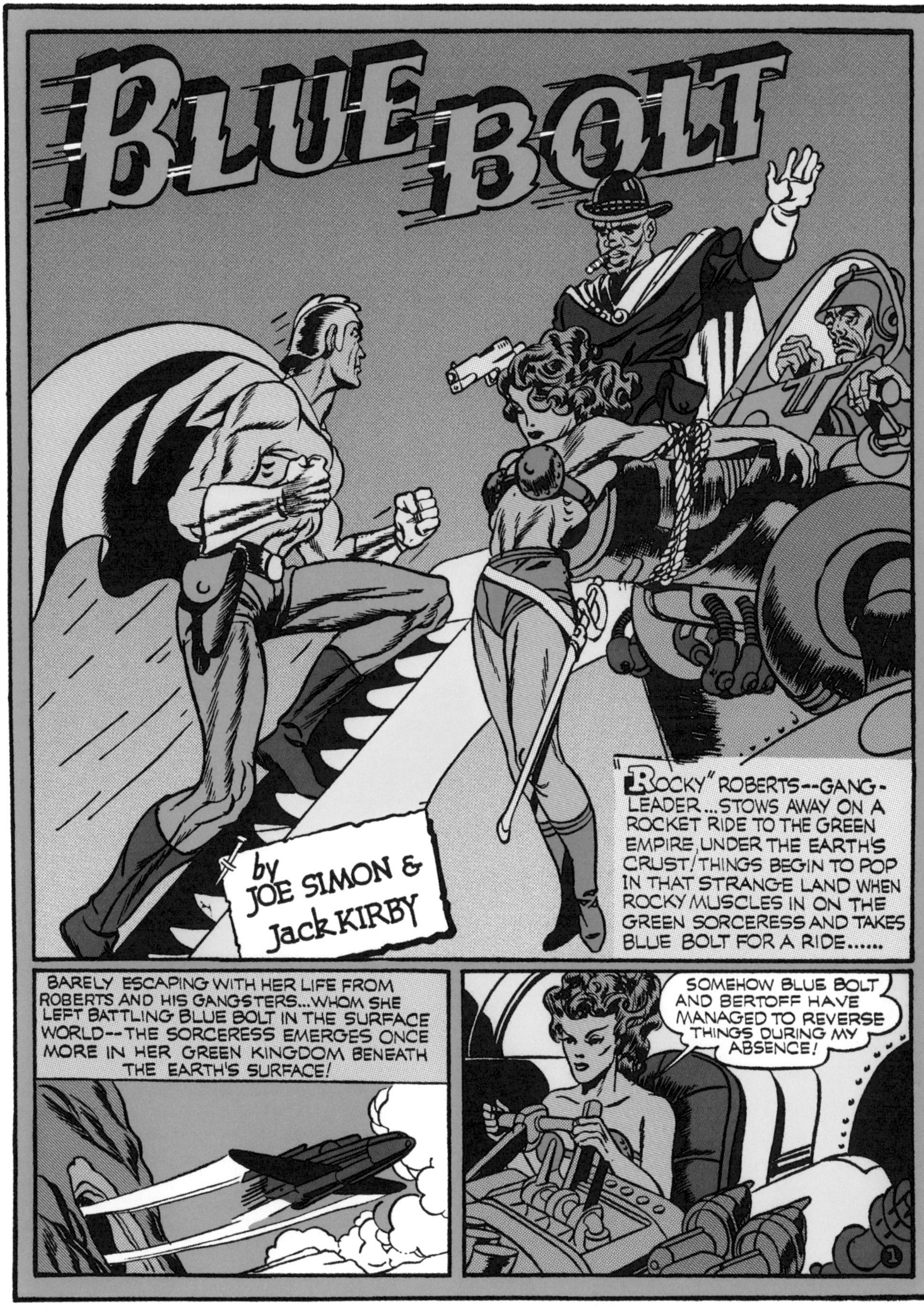
BLUE BOLT
by JOE SIMON & Jack KIRBY
"ROCKY" ROBERTS--GANG-LEADER...STOWS AWAY ON A ROCKET RIDE TO THE GREEN EMPIRE, UNDER THE EARTH'S CRUST! THINGS BEGIN TO POP IN THAT STRANGE LAND WHEN ROCKY MUSCLES IN ON THE GREEN SORCERESS AND TAKES BLUE BOLT FOR A RIDE......
BARELY ESCAPING WITH HER LIFE FROM ROBERTS AND HIS GANGSTERS...WHOM SHE LEFT BATTLING BLUE BOLT IN THE SURFACE WORLD--THE SORCERESS EMERGES ONCE MORE IN HER GREEN KINGDOM BENEATH THE EARTH'S SURFACE!
SOMEHOW BLUE BOLT AND BERTOFF HAVE MANAGED TO REVERSE THINGS DURING MY ABSENCE!
1

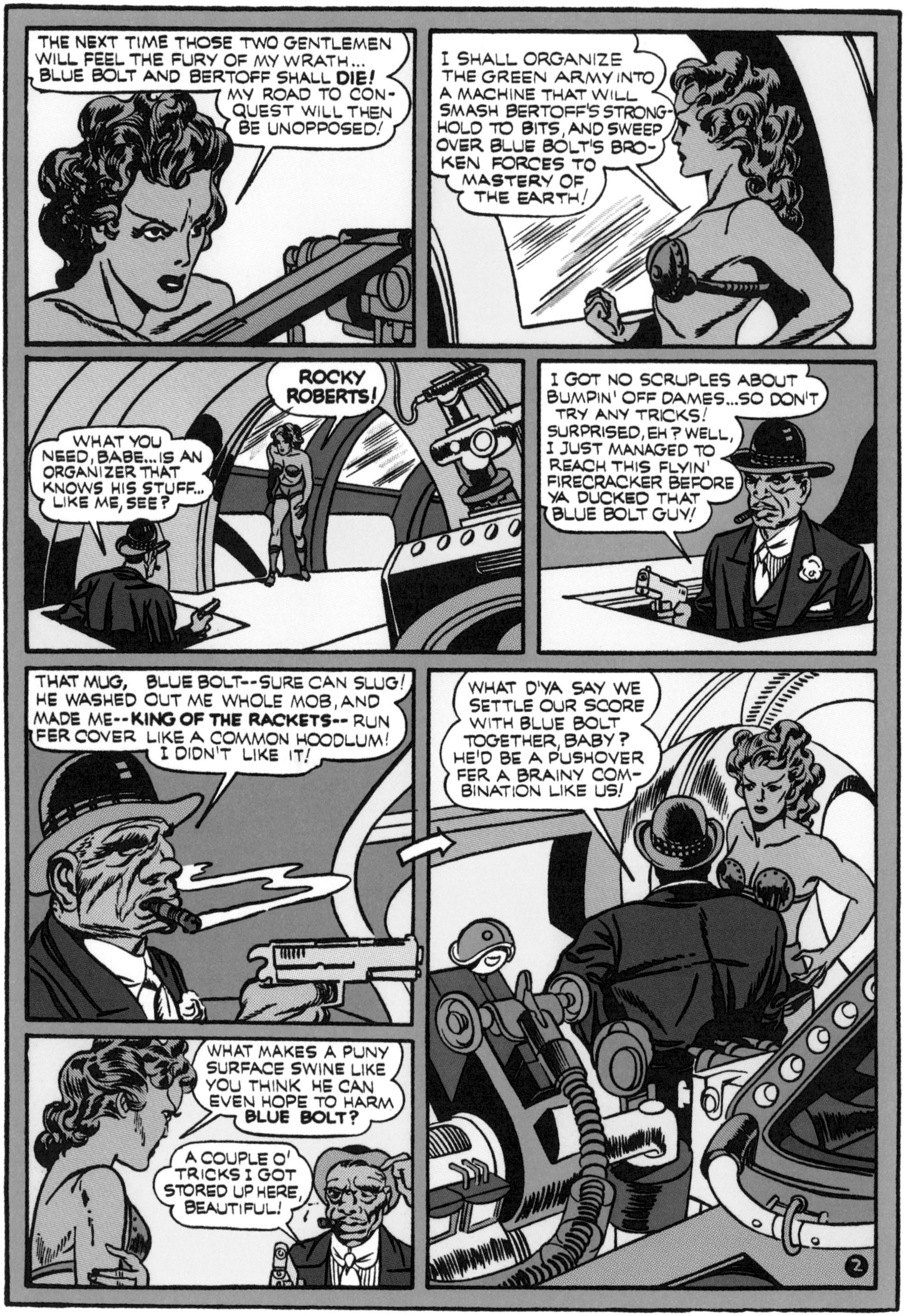
THE NEXT TIME THOSE TWO GENTLEMEN WILL FEEL THE FURY OF MY WRATH... BLUE BOLT AND BERTOFF SHALL DIE!
MY ROAD TO CONQUEST WILL THEN BE UNOPPOSED!
I SHALL ORGANIZE THE GREEN ARMY INTO A MACHINE THAT WILL SMASH BERTOFF'S STRONGHOLD TO BITS, AND SWEEP OVER BLUE BOLT'S BROKEN FORCES TO MASTERY OF THE EARTH!
WHAT YOU NEED, BABE...IS AN ORGANIZER THAT KNOWS HIS STUFF.. LIKE ME, SEE?
ROCKY ROBERTS!
I GOT NO SCRUPLES ABOUT BUMPIN' OFF DAMES...SO DON'T TRY ANY TRICKS!
SURPRISED, EH? WELL, I JUST MANAGED TO REACH THIS FLYIN' FIRECRACKER BEFORE YA DUCKED THAT BLUE BOLT GUY!
THAT MUG, BLUE BOLT--SURE CAN SLUG! HE WASHED OUT ME WHOLE MOB, AND MADE ME--KING OF THE RACKETS--RUN FER COVER LIKE A COMMON HOODLUM! I DIDN'T LIKE IT!
WHAT D'YA SAY WE SETTLE OUR SCORE WITH BLUE BOLT TOGETHER, BABY? HE'D BE A PUSHOVER FER A BRAINY COMBINATION LIKE US!
WHAT MAKES A PUNY SURFACE SWINE LIKE YOU THINK HE CAN EVEN HOPE TO HARM BLUE BOLT?
A COUPLE O' TRICKS I GOT STORED UP HERE, BEAUTIFUL!
2

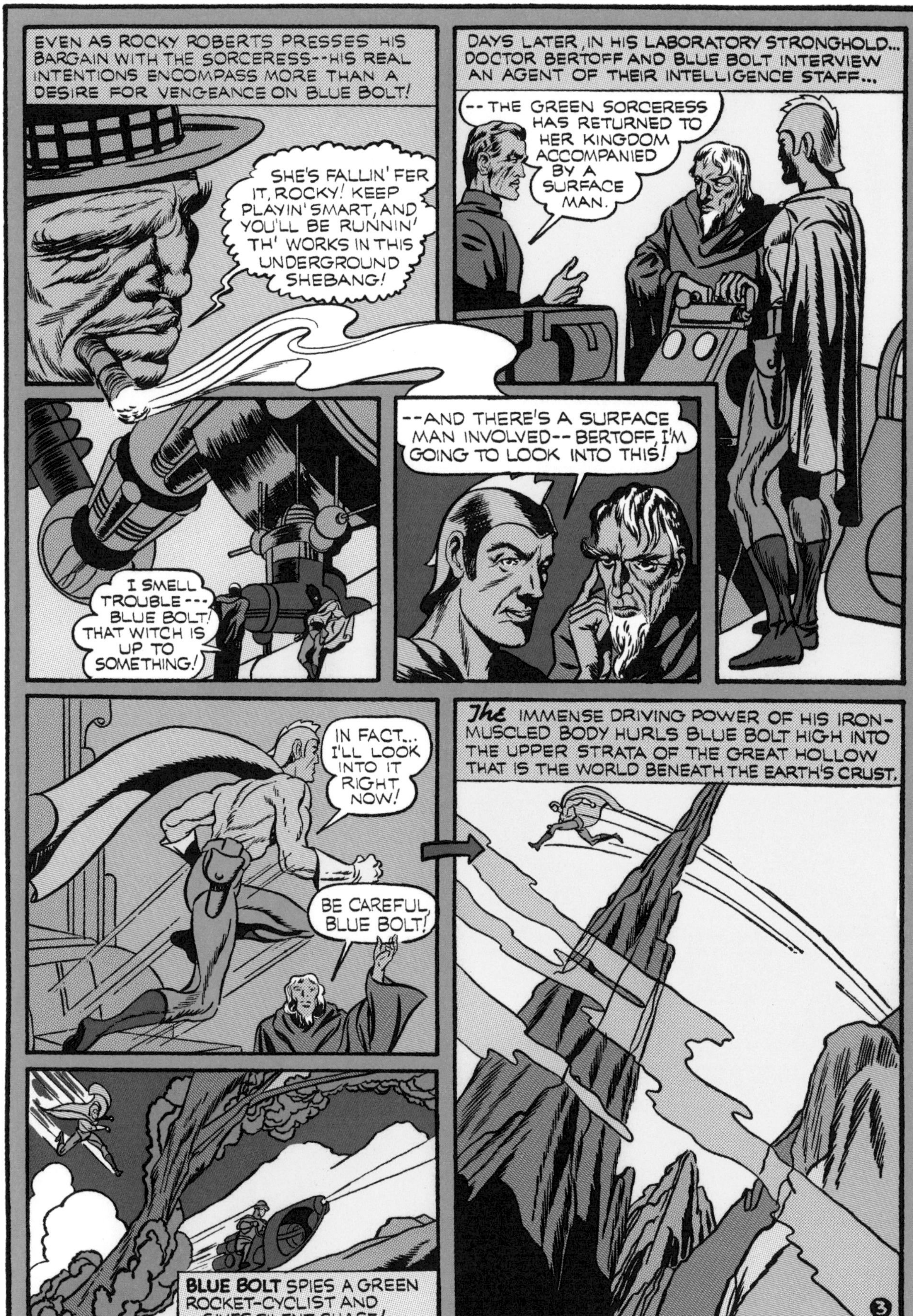
EVEN AS ROCKY ROBERTS PRESSES HIS BARGAIN WITH THE SORCERESS--HIS REAL INTENTIONS ENCOMPASS MORE THAN A DESIRE FOR VENGEANCE ON BLUE BOLT!
SHE'S FALLIN' FER IT, ROCKY! KEEP PLAYIN' SMART, AND YOU'LL BE RUNNIN' TH' WORKS IN THIS UNDERGROUND SHEBANG!
DAYS LATER, IN HIS LABORATORY STRONGHOLD... DOCTOR BERTOFF AND BLUE BOLT INTERVIEW AN AGENT OF THEIR INTELLIGENCE STAFF...
--THE GREEN SORCERESS HAS RETURNED TO HER KINGDOM ACCOMPANIED BY A SURFACE MAN.
I SMELL TROUBLE--- BLUE BOLT! THAT WITCH IS UP TO SOMETHING!
--AND THERE'S A SURFACE MAN INVOLVED-- BERTOFF, I'M GOING TO LOOK INTO THIS!
IN FACT... I'LL LOOK INTO IT RIGHT NOW!
BE CAREFUL, BLUE BOLT!
THE IMMENSE DRIVING POWER OF HIS IRON-MUSCLED BODY HURLS BLUE BOLT HIGH INTO THE UPPER STRATA OF THE GREAT HOLLOW THAT IS THE WORLD BENEATH THE EARTH'S CRUST.
BLUE BOLT SPIES A GREEN ROCKET-CYCLIST AND GIVES SILENT CHASE!
3

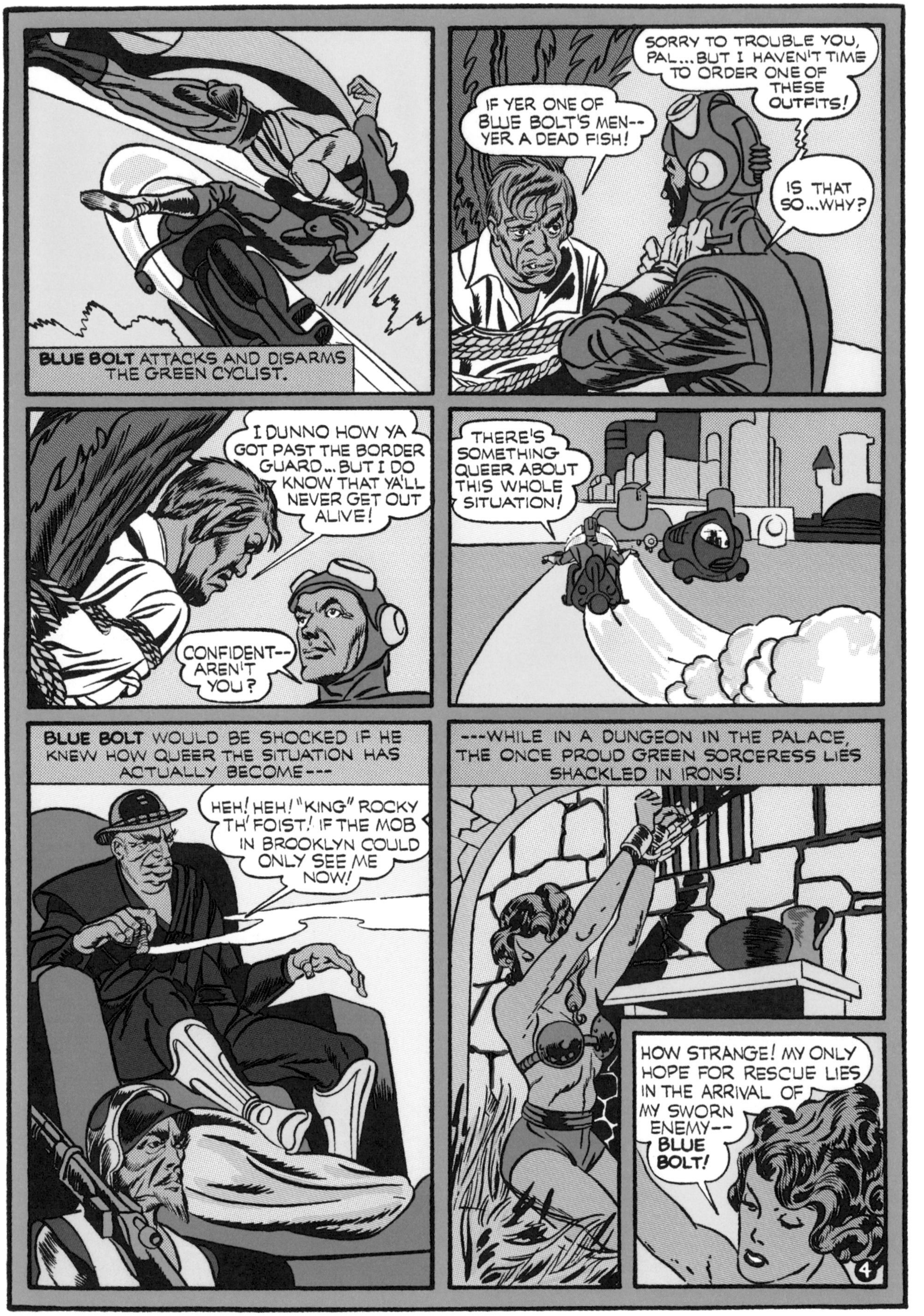
BLUE BOLT ATTACKS AND DISARMS THE GREEN CYCLIST.
IF YER ONE OF BLUE BOLT'S MEN-- YER A DEAD FISH!
SORRY TO TROUBLE YOU, PAL... BUT I HAVEN'T TIME TO ORDER ONE OF THESE OUTFITS!
IS THAT SO...WHY?
I DUNNO HOW YA GOT PAST THE BORDER GUARD... BUT I DO KNOW THAT YA'LL NEVER GET OUT ALIVE!
CONFIDENT-- AREN'T YOU?
THERE'S SOMETHING QUEER ABOUT THIS WHOLE SITUATION!
BLUE BOLT WOULD BE SHOCKED IF HE KNEW HOW QUEER THE SITUATION HAS ACTUALLY BECOME---
HEH! HEH! "KING" ROCKY TH' FOIST! IF THE MOB IN BROOKLYN COULD ONLY SEE ME NOW!
---WHILE IN A DUNGEON IN THE PALACE, THE ONCE PROUD GREEN SORCERESS LIES SHACKLED IN IRONS!
HOW STRANGE! MY ONLY HOPE FOR RESCUE LIES IN THE ARRIVAL OF MY SWORN ENEMY-- BLUE BOLT!
4

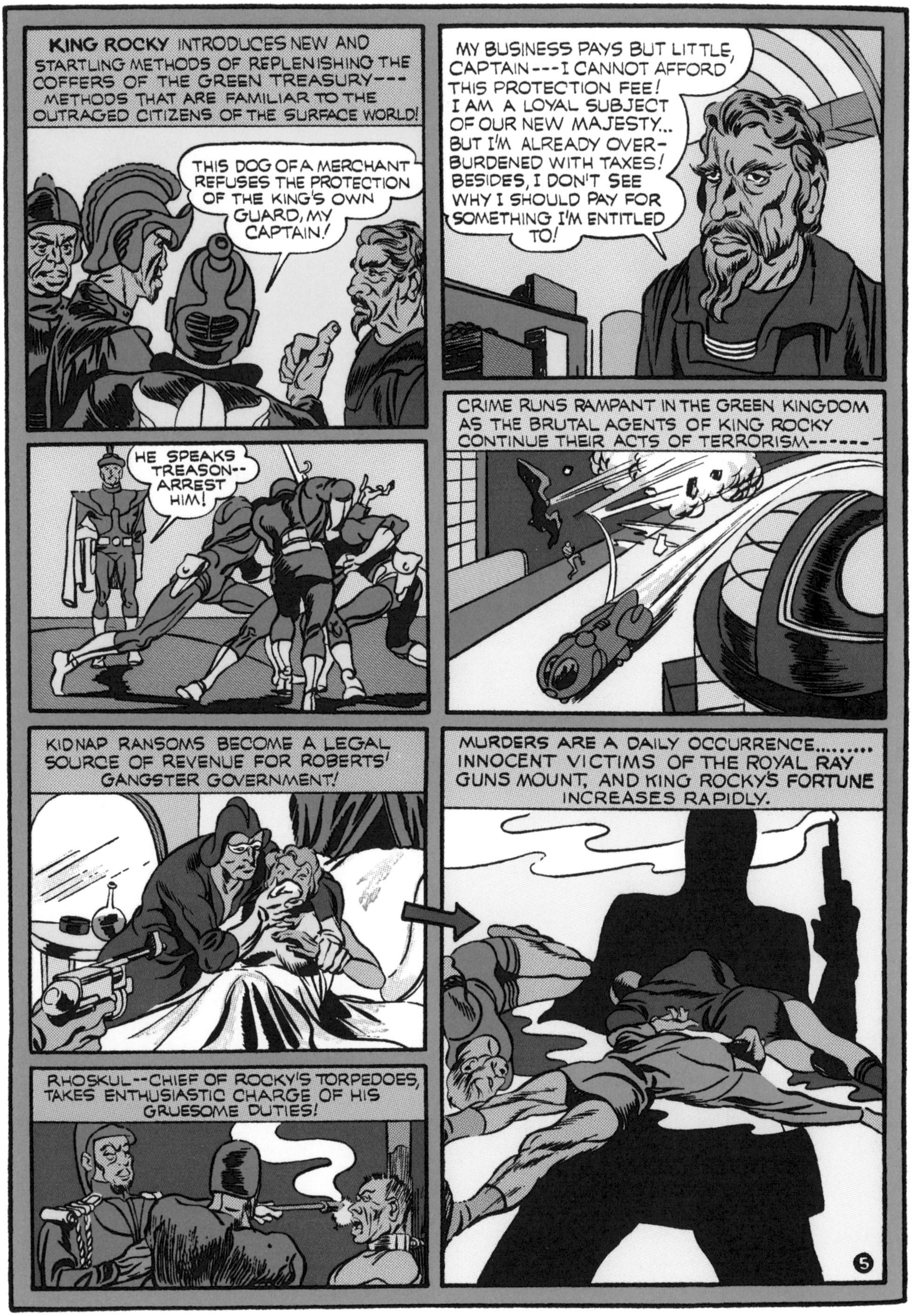
KING ROCKY INTRODUCES NEW AND STARTLING METHODS OF REPLENISHING THE COFFERS OF THE GREEN TREASURY--- METHODS THAT ARE FAMILIAR TO THE OUTRAGED CITIZENS OF THE SURFACE WORLD!
THIS DOG OF A MERCHANT REFUSES THE PROTECTION OF THE KING'S OWN GUARD, MY CAPTAIN!
MY BUSINESS PAYS BUT LITTLE, CAPTAIN---I CANNOT AFFORD THIS PROTECTION FEE! I AM A LOYAL SUBJECT OF OUR NEW MAJESTY... BUT I'M ALREADY OVER-BURDENED WITH TAXES! BESIDES, I DON'T SEE WHY I SHOULD PAY FOR SOMETHING I'M ENTITLED TO!
HE SPEAKS TREASON--ARREST HIM!
CRIME RUNS RAMPANT IN THE GREEN KINGDOM AS THE BRUTAL AGENTS OF KING ROCKY CONTINUE THEIR ACTS OF TERRORISM------
KIDNAP RANSOMS BECOME A LEGAL SOURCE OF REVENUE FOR ROBERTS' GANGSTER GOVERNMENT!
MURDERS ARE A DAILY OCCURRENCE........ INNOCENT VICTIMS OF THE ROYAL RAY GUNS MOUNT, AND KING ROCKY'S FORTUNE INCREASES RAPIDLY.
RHOSKUL--CHIEF OF ROCKY'S TORPEDOES, TAKES ENTHUSIASTIC CHARGE OF HIS GRUESOME DUTIES!
5

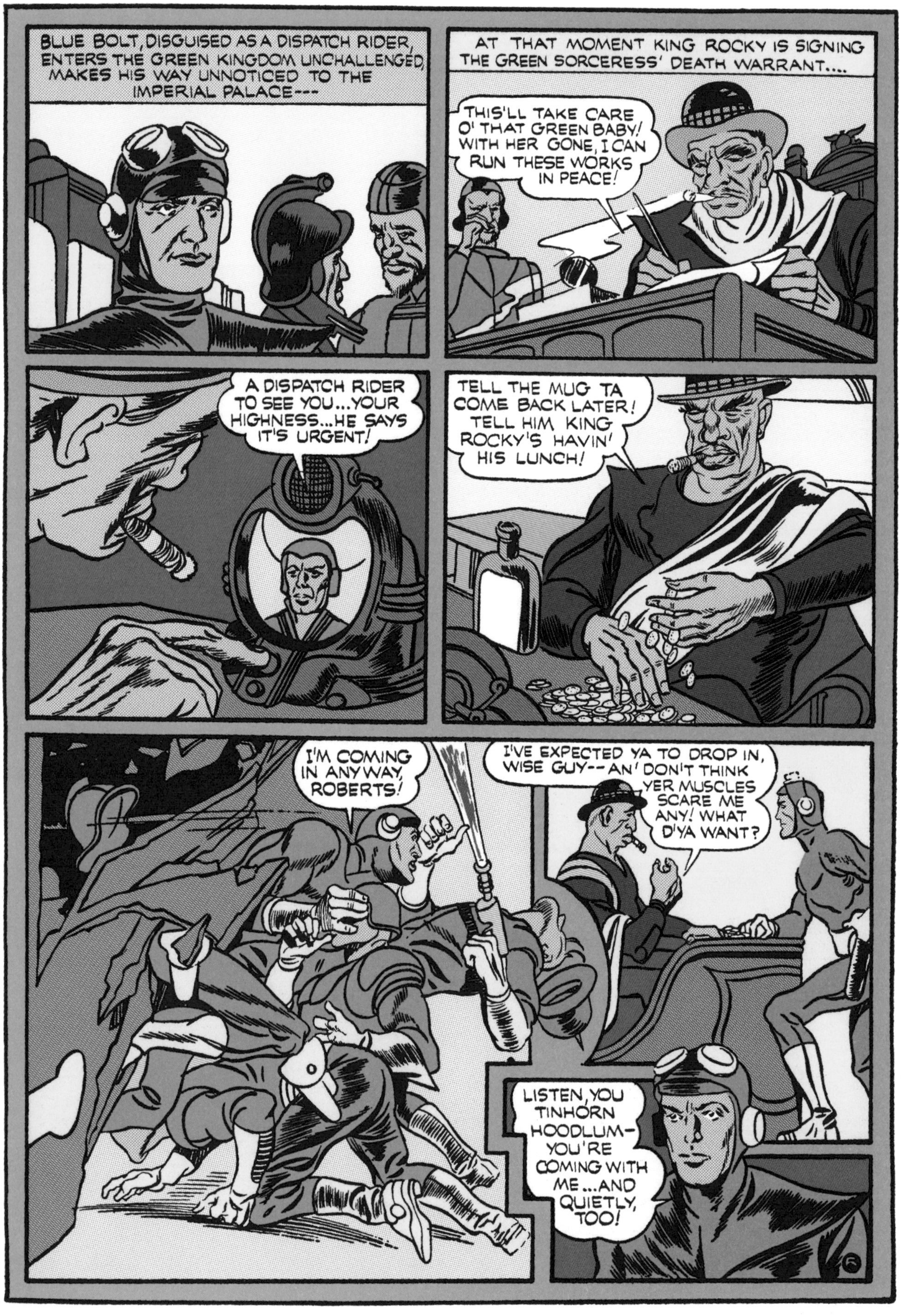

BLUE BOLT, DISGUISED AS A DISPATCH RIDER, ENTERS THE GREEN KINGDOM UNCHALLENGED, MAKES HIS WAY UNNOTICED TO THE IMPERIAL PALACE---
AT THAT MOMENT KING ROCKY IS SIGNING THE GREEN SORCERESS' DEATH WARRANT....
THIS'LL TAKE CARE O' THAT GREEN BABY! WITH HER GONE, I CAN RUN THESE WORKS IN PEACE!
A DISPATCH RIDER TO SEE YOU...YOUR HIGHNESS...HE SAYS IT'S URGENT!
TELL THE MUG TA COME BACK LATER! TELL HIM KING ROCKY'S HAVIN' HIS LUNCH!
I'M COMING IN ANYWAY, ROBERTS!
I'VE EXPECTED YA TO DROP IN, WISE GUY-- AN' DON'T THINK YER MUSCLES SCARE ME ANY! WHAT D'YA WANT?
LISTEN, YOU TINHORN HOODLUM- YOU'RE COMING WITH ME...AND QUIETLY, TOO!
6

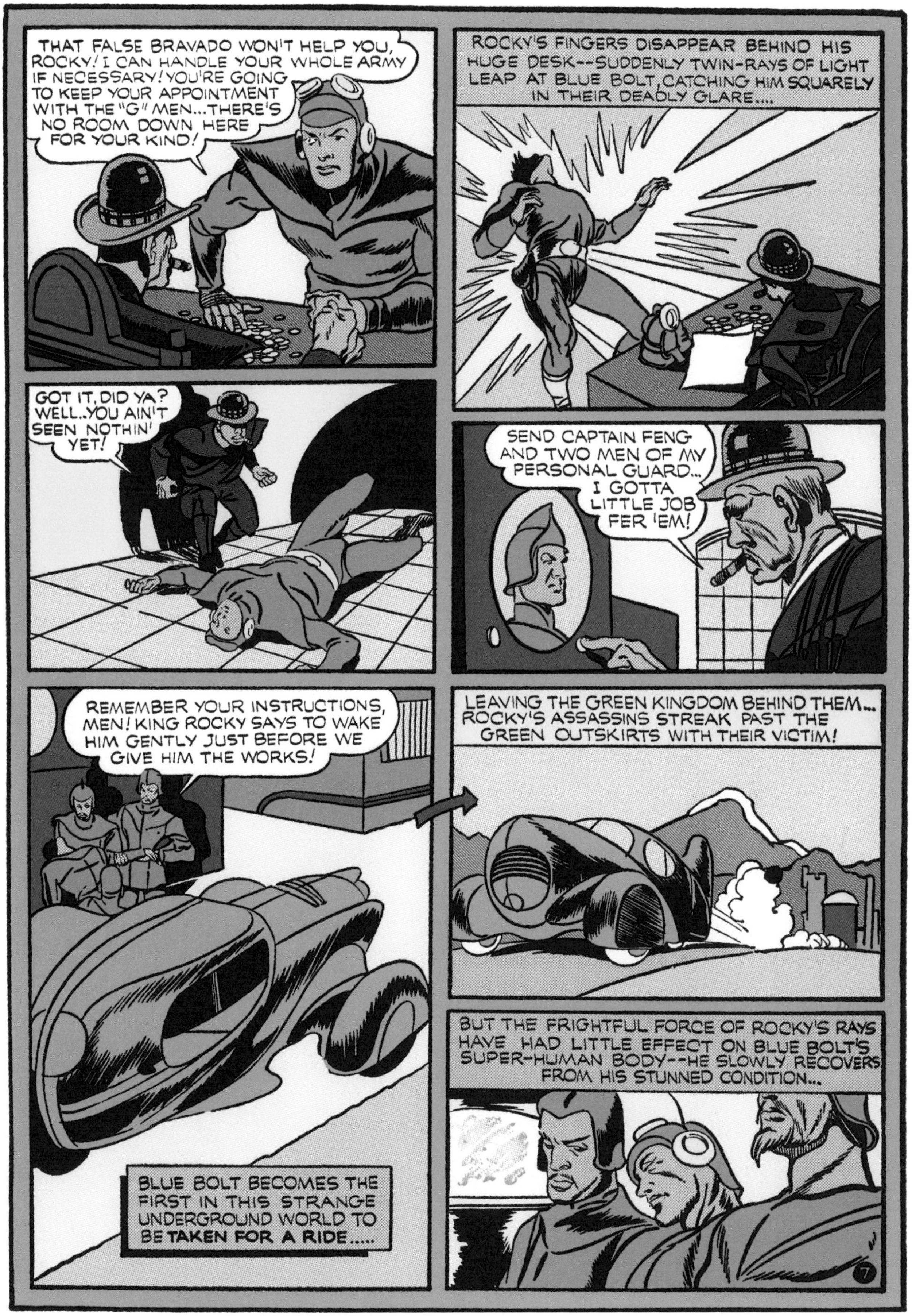
THAT FALSE BRAVADO WON'T HELP YOU, ROCKY! I CAN HANDLE YOUR WHOLE ARMY IF NECESSARY! YOU'RE GOING TO KEEP YOUR APPOINTMENT WITH THE "G" MEN...THERE'S NO ROOM DOWN HERE FOR YOUR KIND!
ROCKY'S FINGERS DISAPPEAR BEHIND HIS HUGE DESK--SUDDENLY TWIN-RAYS OF LIGHT LEAP AT BLUE BOLT, CATCHING HIM SQUARELY IN THEIR DEADLY GLARE....
GOT IT, DID YA? WELL..YOU AIN'T SEEN NOTHIN' YET!
SEND CAPTAIN FENG AND TWO MEN OF MY PERSONAL GUARD... I GOTTA LITTLE JOB FER 'EM!
REMEMBER YOUR INSTRUCTIONS, MEN! KING ROCKY SAYS TO WAKE HIM GENTLY JUST BEFORE WE GIVE HIM THE WORKS!
BLUE BOLT BECOMES THE FIRST IN THIS STRANGE UNDERGROUND WORLD TO BE TAKEN FOR A RIDE.....
LEAVING THE GREEN KINGDOM BEHIND THEM... ROCKY'S ASSASSINS STREAK PAST THE GREEN OUTSKIRTS WITH THEIR VICTIM!
BUT THE FRIGHTFUL FORCE OF ROCKY'S RAYS HAVE HAD LITTLE EFFECT ON BLUE BOLT'S SUPER-HUMAN BODY--HE SLOWLY RECOVERS FROM HIS STUNNED CONDITION...
7

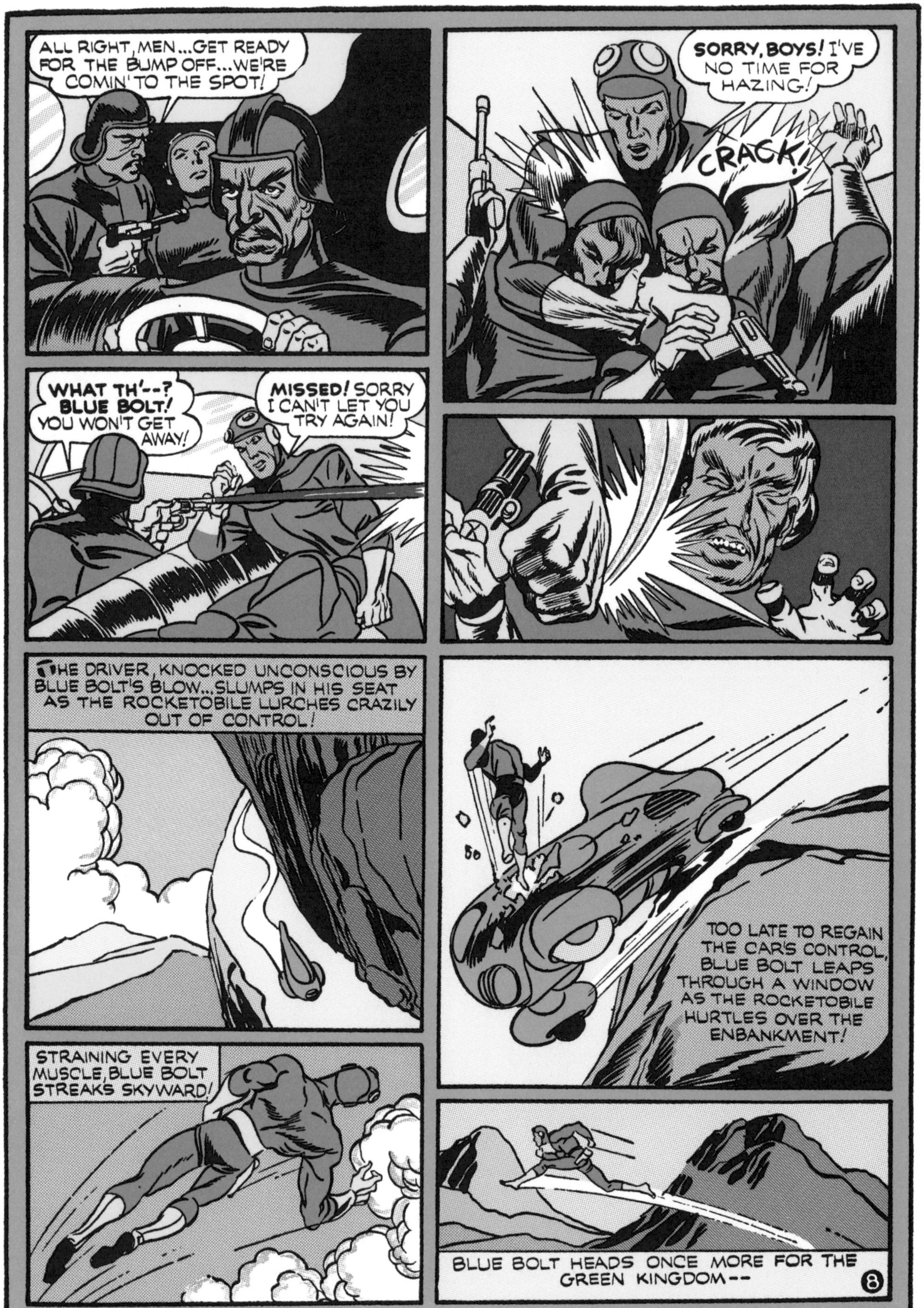
ALL RIGHT, MEN...GET READY FOR THE BUMP OFF...WE'RE COMIN' TO THE SPOT!
SORRY, BOYS! I'VE NO TIME FOR HAZING!
CRACK!
WHAT TH'--? BLUE BOLT! YOU WON'T GET AWAY!
MISSED! SORRY I CAN'T LET YOU TRY AGAIN!
THE DRIVER, KNOCKED UNCONSCIOUS BY BLUE BOLT'S BLOW...SLUMPS IN HIS SEAT AS THE ROCKETOBILE LURCHES CRAZILY OUT OF CONTROL!
TOO LATE TO REGAIN THE CAR'S CONTROL, BLUE BOLT LEAPS THROUGH A WINDOW AS THE ROCKETOBILE HURTLES OVER THE ENBANKMENT!
STRAINING EVERY MUSCLE, BLUE BOLT STREAKS SKYWARD!
BLUE BOLT HEADS ONCE MORE FOR THE GREEN KINGDOM--
8

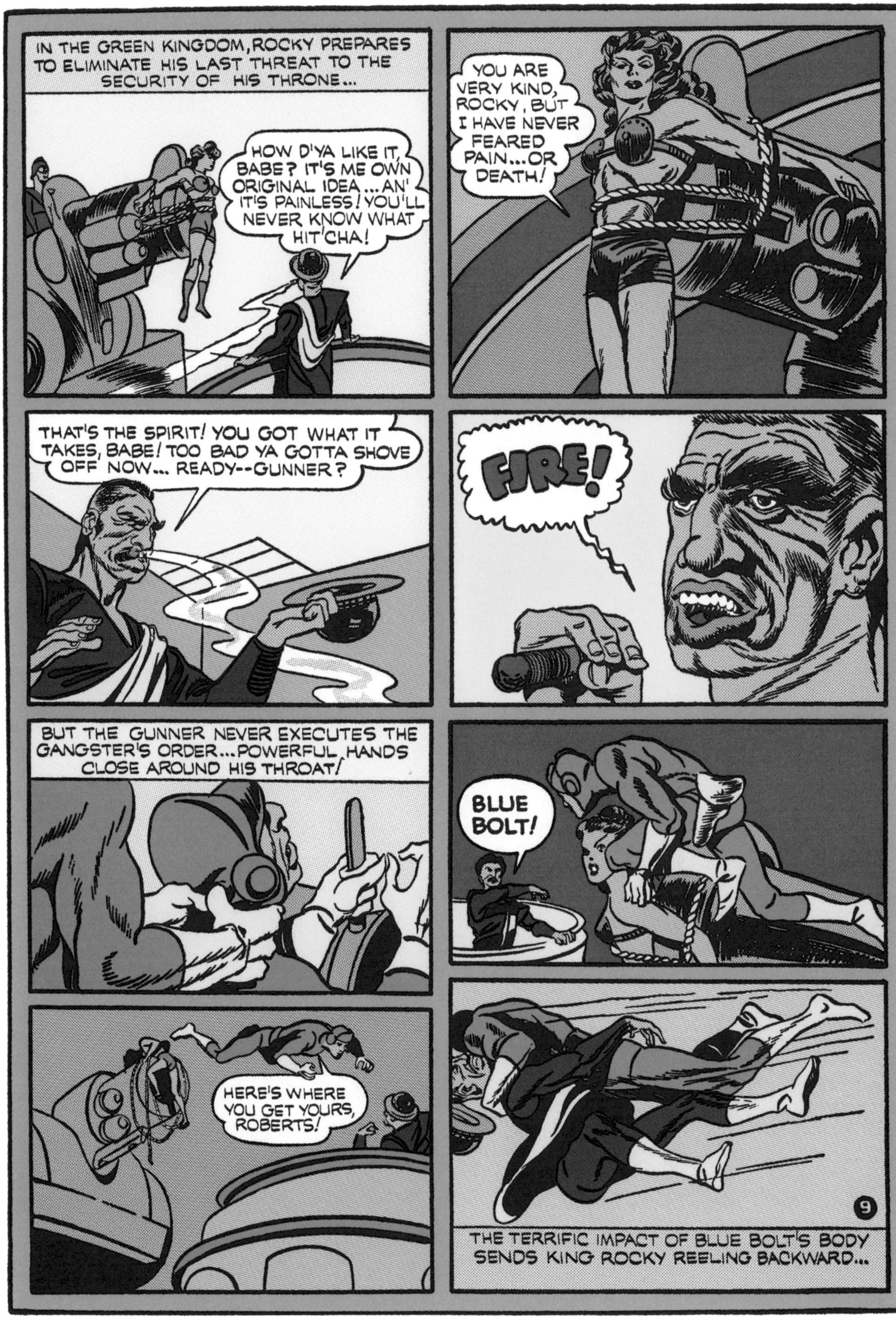

IN THE GREEN KINGDOM, ROCKY PREPARES TO ELIMINATE HIS LAST THREAT TO THE SECURITY OF HIS THRONE...
HOW D'YA LIKE IT, BABE? IT'S ME OWN ORIGINAL IDEA...AN' IT'S PAINLESS! YOU'LL NEVER KNOW WHAT HIT'CHA!
YOU ARE VERY KIND, ROCKY, BUT I HAVE NEVER FEARED PAIN...OR DEATH!
THAT'S THE SPIRIT! YOU GOT WHAT IT TAKES, BABE! TOO BAD YA GOTTA SHOVE OFF NOW... READY--GUNNER?
FIRE!
BUT THE GUNNER NEVER EXECUTES THE GANGSTER'S ORDER...POWERFUL HANDS CLOSE AROUND HIS THROAT!
BLUE BOLT!
HERE'S WHERE YOU GET YOURS, ROBERTS!
9
THE TERRIFIC IMPACT OF BLUE BOLT'S BODY SENDS KING ROCKY REELING BACKWARD...

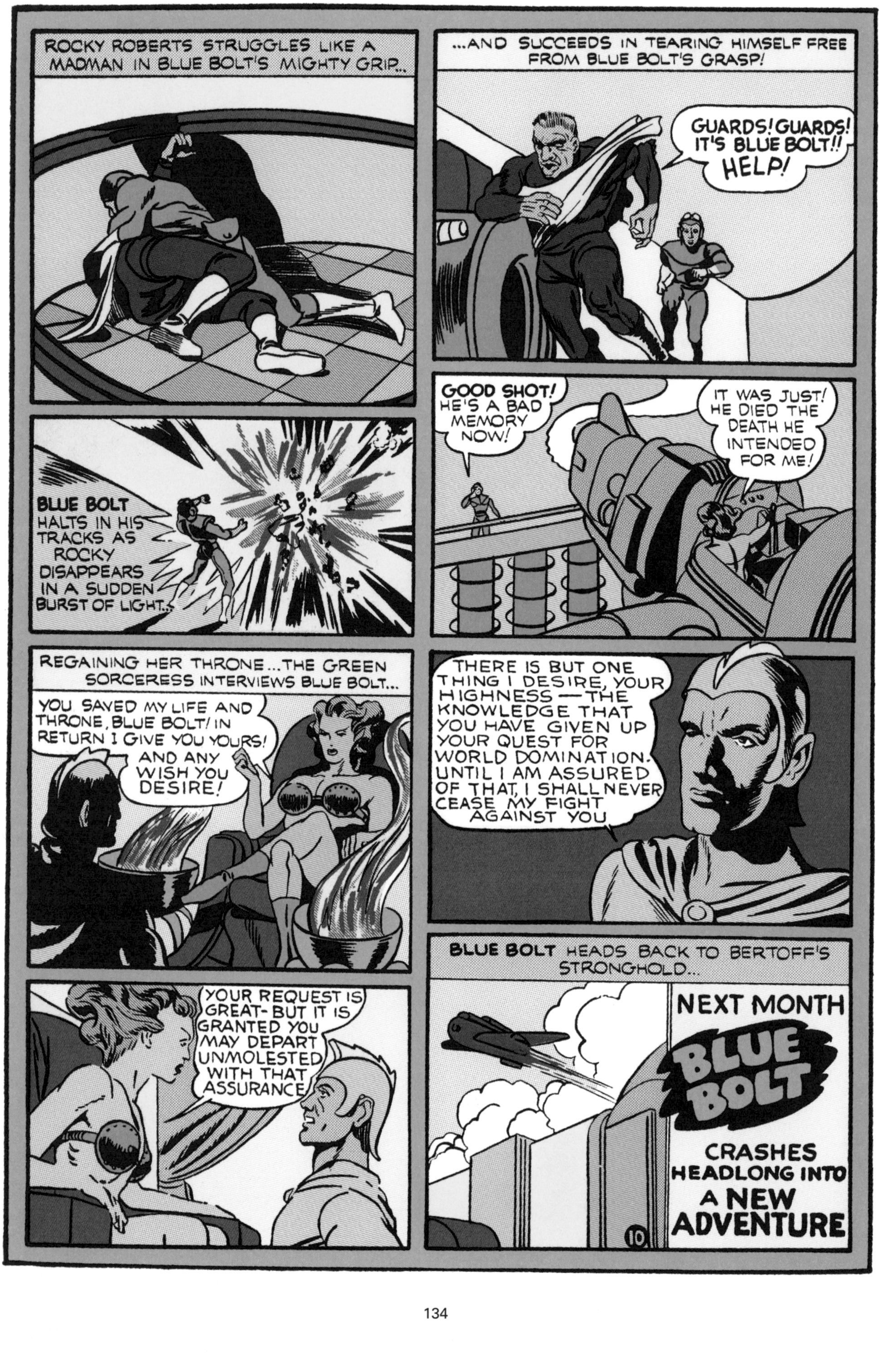
ROCKY ROBERTS STRUGGLES LIKE A MADMAN IN BLUE BOLT'S MIGHTY GRIP...
...AND SUCCEEDS IN TEARING HIMSELF FREE FROM BLUE BOLT'S GRASP!
GUARDS! GUARDS! IT'S BLUE BOLT!! HELP!
BLUE BOLT HALTS IN HIS TRACKS AS ROCKY DISAPPEARS IN A SUDDEN BURST OF LIGHT...
GOOD SHOT! HE'S A BAD MEMORY NOW!
IT WAS JUST! HE DIED THE DEATH HE INTENDED FOR ME!
REGAINING HER THRONE...THE GREEN SORCERESS INTERVIEWS BLUE BOLT...
YOU SAVED MY LIFE AND THRONE, BLUE BOLT! IN RETURN I GIVE YOU YOURS!
AND ANY WISH YOU DESIRE!
THERE IS BUT ONE THING I DESIRE, YOUR HIGHNESS — THE KNOWLEDGE THAT YOU HAVE GIVEN UP YOUR QUEST FOR WORLD DOMINATION. UNTIL I AM ASSURED OF THAT, I SHALL NEVER CEASE MY FIGHT AGAINST YOU
YOUR REQUEST IS GREAT- BUT IT IS GRANTED YOU MAY DEPART UNMOLESTED WITH THAT ASSURANCE
BLUE BOLT HEADS BACK TO BERTOFF'S STRONGHOLD...
NEXT MONTH
BLUE BOLT
CRASHES HEADLONG INTO A NEW ADVENTURE
10

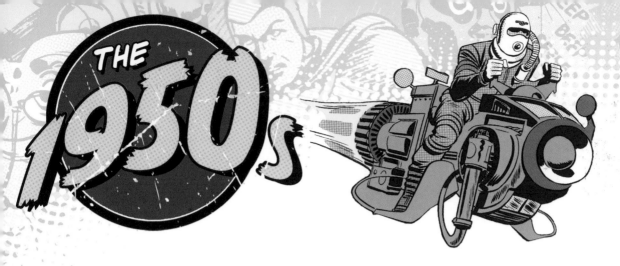

THE 1950s

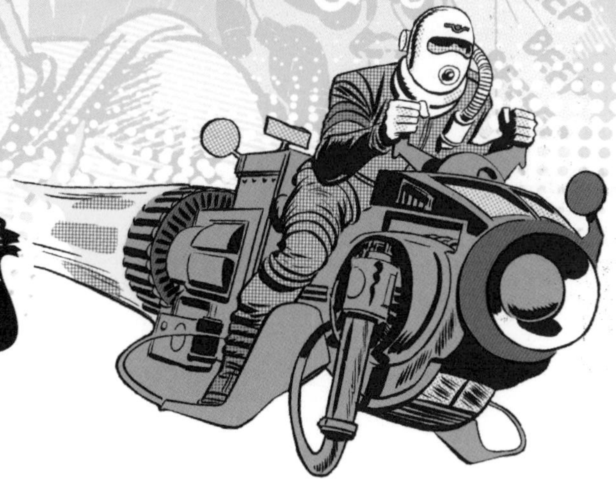

By the start of the 1950s, the popularity of superheroes had collapsed, and Simon and Kirby turned again to other genres, including westerns, crime, and science fiction.

In movie theaters, science fiction experienced a renaissance with films ranging from major releases like George Pal's *Destination Moon* (1950) and MGM's *Forbidden Planet* (1956), to scores of low budget "B-movies." Science fiction also conquered the new medium of television, starting with children's shows like *Captain Video and His Video Rangers* (beginning in 1949) and *Tom Corbett, Space Cadet* (1950).

Although the influence of space opera persisted in children's programs, science fiction as a genre grew more sophisticated. Much of the credit goes to John W. Campbell, the editor of *Astounding Science Fiction*, who emphasized scientific plausibility and multidimensional characterizations, and to authors such as Arthur C. Clarke, Robert Heinlein, and Ray Bradbury. This inspired better science fiction in other media, including the television series *Tales of Tomorrow* (beginning in 1951) and Rod Serling's classic *The Twilight Zone*, which premiered in 1959.

Comics likewise embraced the genre, most notably in EC Comics' *Weird Science* and *Weird Fantasy*, with art by Wally Wood and Frank Frazetta, among others. Then in 1957 Joe Simon launched a science fiction anthology series for Harvey Comics, *Alarming Tales*, enlisting great artists like: Jack Kirby, Al Williamson, John Severin, and Doug Wildey. The first issue included "The Cadmus Seed," drawn by Kirby, in which tiny "seeds" resembling human infants were genetically engineered. This anticipated the "DNA Project" in Kirby's Jimmy Olsen stories of the early 1970s.

In another Kirby story, "The Last Enemy," a time traveler fled to the future after a nuclear war had wiped out humanity, only to find the Earth populated by talking animals. This tale was published six years before Pierre Boulle's 1963 novel *Planet of the Apes*, which inspired the famous film series. It's also the first version of a concept Kirby later

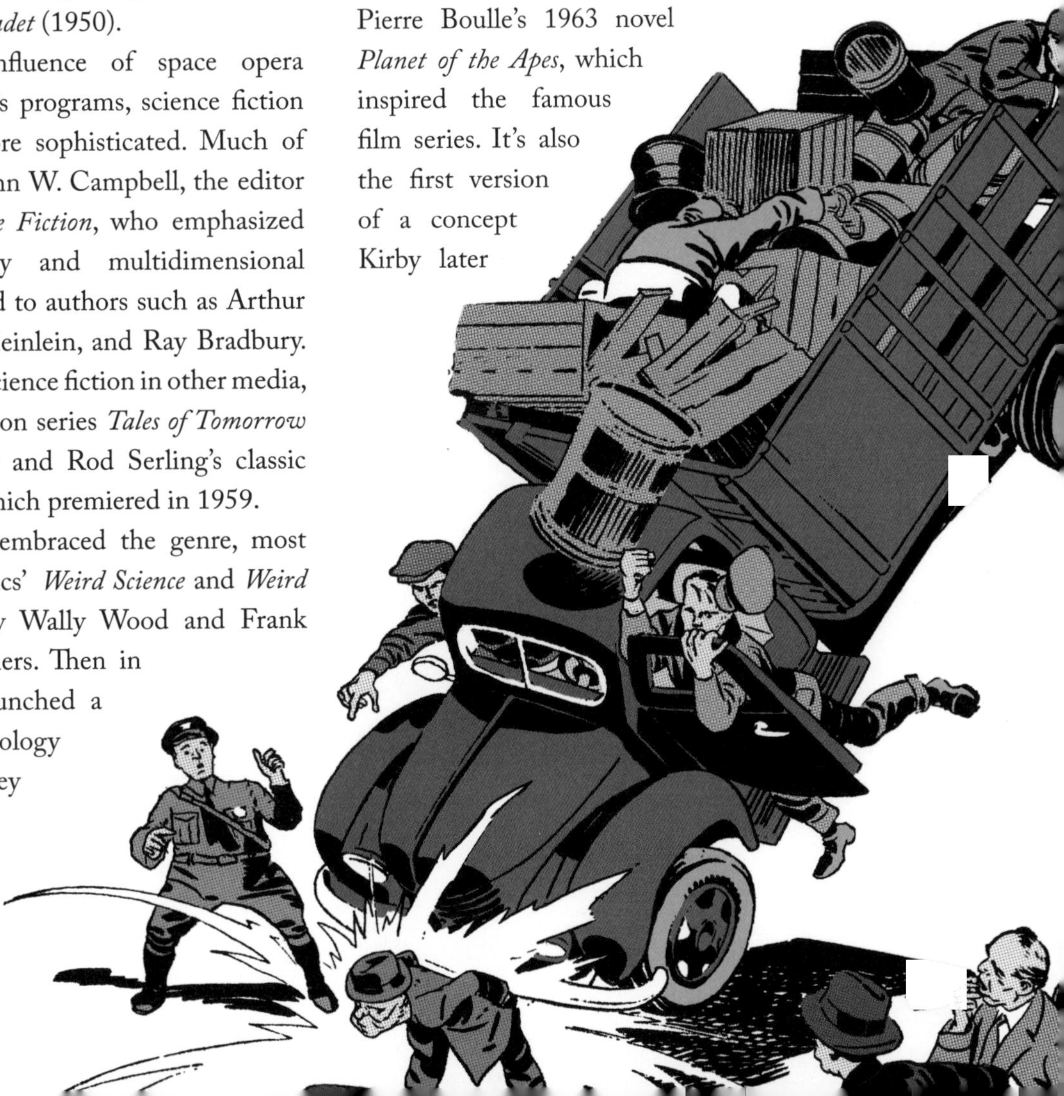

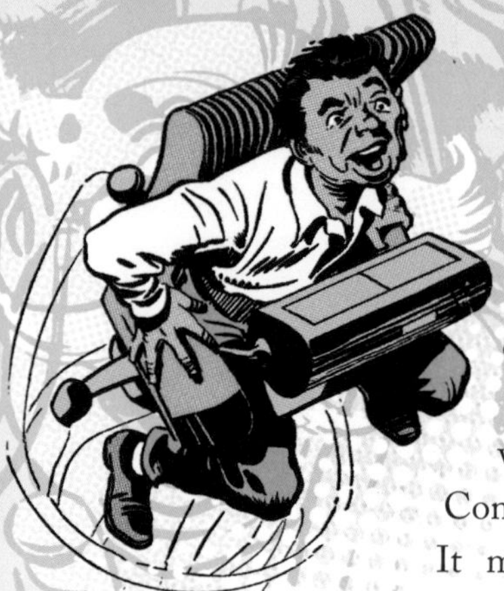

developed into *Kamandi: The Last Boy on Earth*, which debuted as a DC Comics series in 1972.

It may be that the flying furniture from "Donnegan's Daffy Chair" was the forerunner of Metron's Mobius Chair from *The New Gods*. And in *Alarming Tales* #2 Kirby illustrated "I Want to Be a Man!"–depicting the plight of a computer that thinks of itself as human, a precursor of Kirby's *Machine Man* at Marvel.

Al Williamson and Angelo Torres provided art for "King of the Ants" in *Alarming Tales* #6, yet the story–about a scientist who shrinks and becomes leader of an ant colony–will remind readers of Marvel's Dr. Henry Pym, alias Ant-Man.

In the 1950s, space exploration moved from fantasy into reality with the launch of Sputnik. In his memoir *Joe Simon: My Life in Comics*, Simon recalled, "when the Soviets put the first satellite in space in 1957, America was surprised, and so was I." It also inspired him, and the result was *Race for the Moon*, published by Harvey Comics in 1958. Simon was the primary writer, with artwork by Jack Kirby, Reed Crandall, Angelo Torres, Al Williamson, and others. (Though Williamson is generally credited with inking the Kirby stories, Simon recalled that the task was shared by Crandall and Torres.)

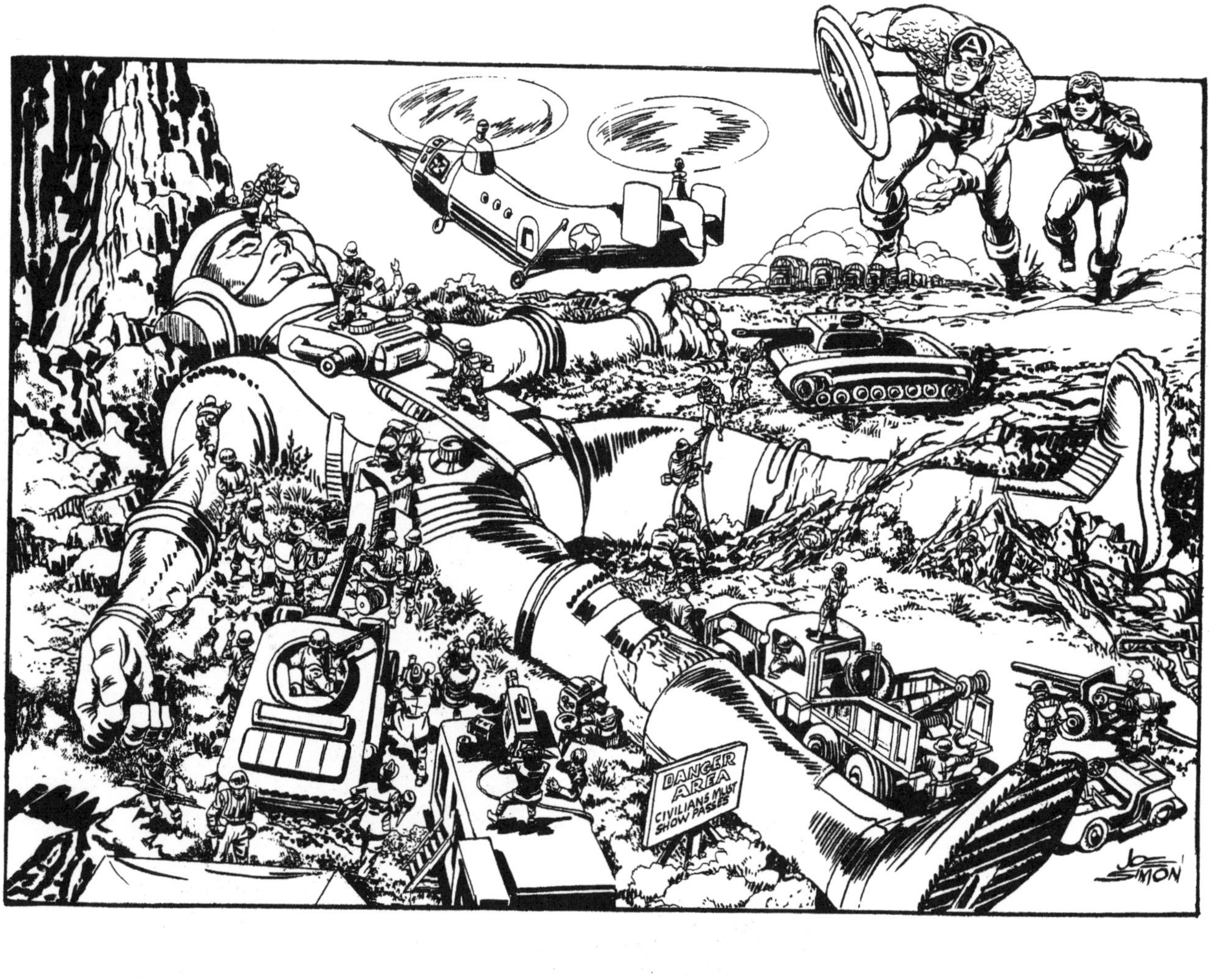
DANGER AREA
CIVILIANS MUST SHOW PASSES
JOE SIMON

Here again, Kirby and Williamson's story "Garden of Eden" foreshadowed Lee and Kirby's "Ego, the Living Planet" in *The Mighty Thor*. And in the final issue, Simon and Kirby introduced their team of space explorers, the Three Rocketeers. Other Harvey titles, including *Black Cat Mystery*, featured Simon and Kirby tales such as "Gismo," which anticipated Lee and Kirby's "Infant Terrible" from *Fantastic Four* #24. But Charlton's *Win-a-Prize* #1 (1955) boasted one of the strangest artifacts of the era, as Simon and Kirby reworked an unpublished double-page spread they had done in 1941 for *Captain America Comics* #11, converting it into a picture of an astronaut surrounded by Lilliputians.

As a bonus to the readers, many of the 1950s and 1960s stories offered here have been reproduced directly from original art kept in the Joe Simon archives. Modern printing processes–far better than those of the comics of the time–make them look sharper and clearer than they ever have before.

Peter Sanderson

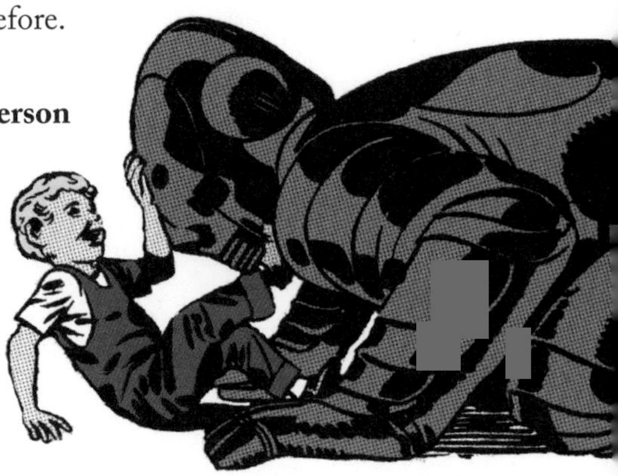

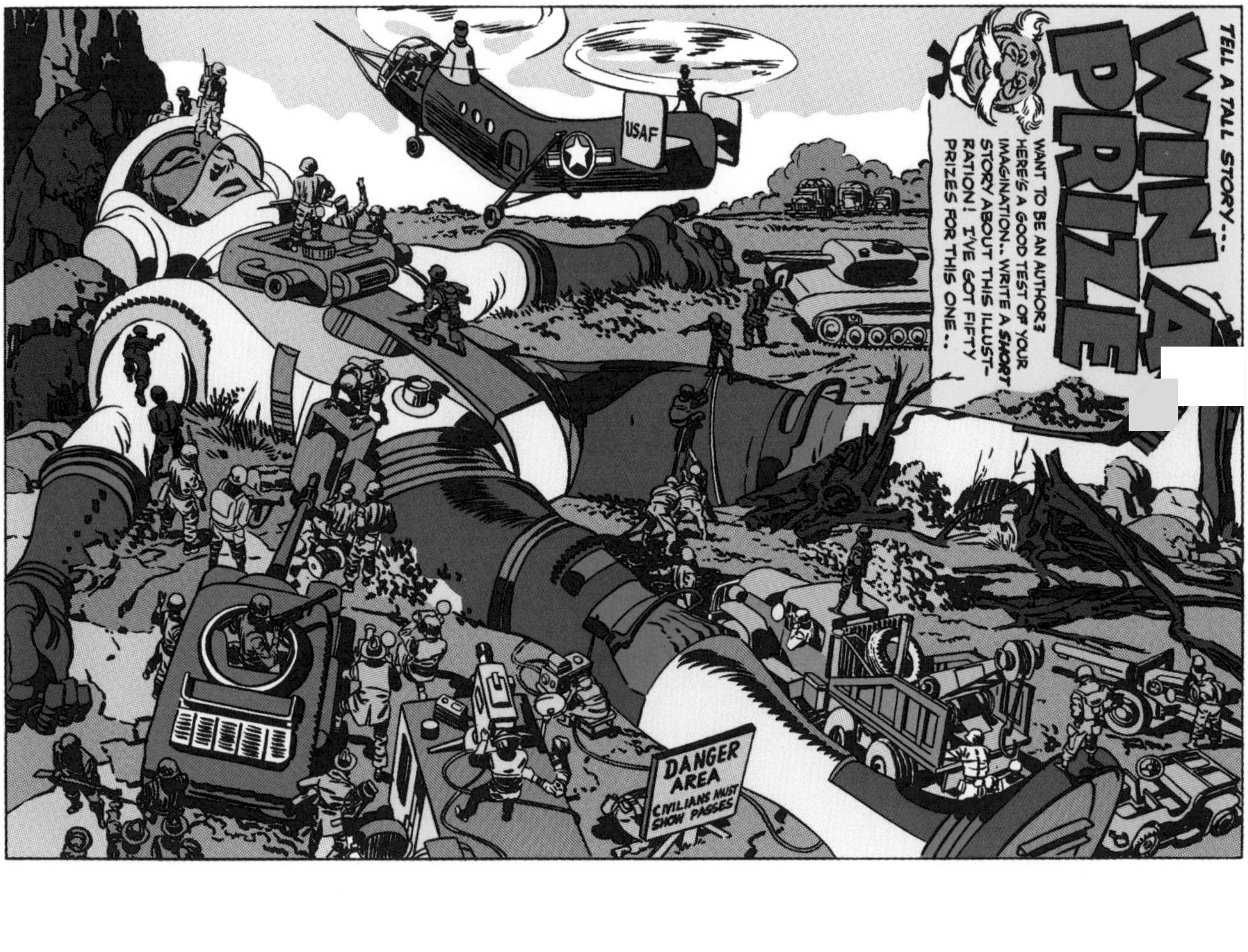
TELL A TALL STORY...
WIN A
PRIZE
WANT TO BE AN AUTHOR? HERE'S A GOOD TEST OF YOUR IMAGINATION... WRITE A SHORT STORY ABOUT THIS ILLUST-RATION! I'VE GOT FIFTY PRIZES FOR THIS ONE..
USAF
DANGER AREA
CIVILIANS MUST SHOW PASSES

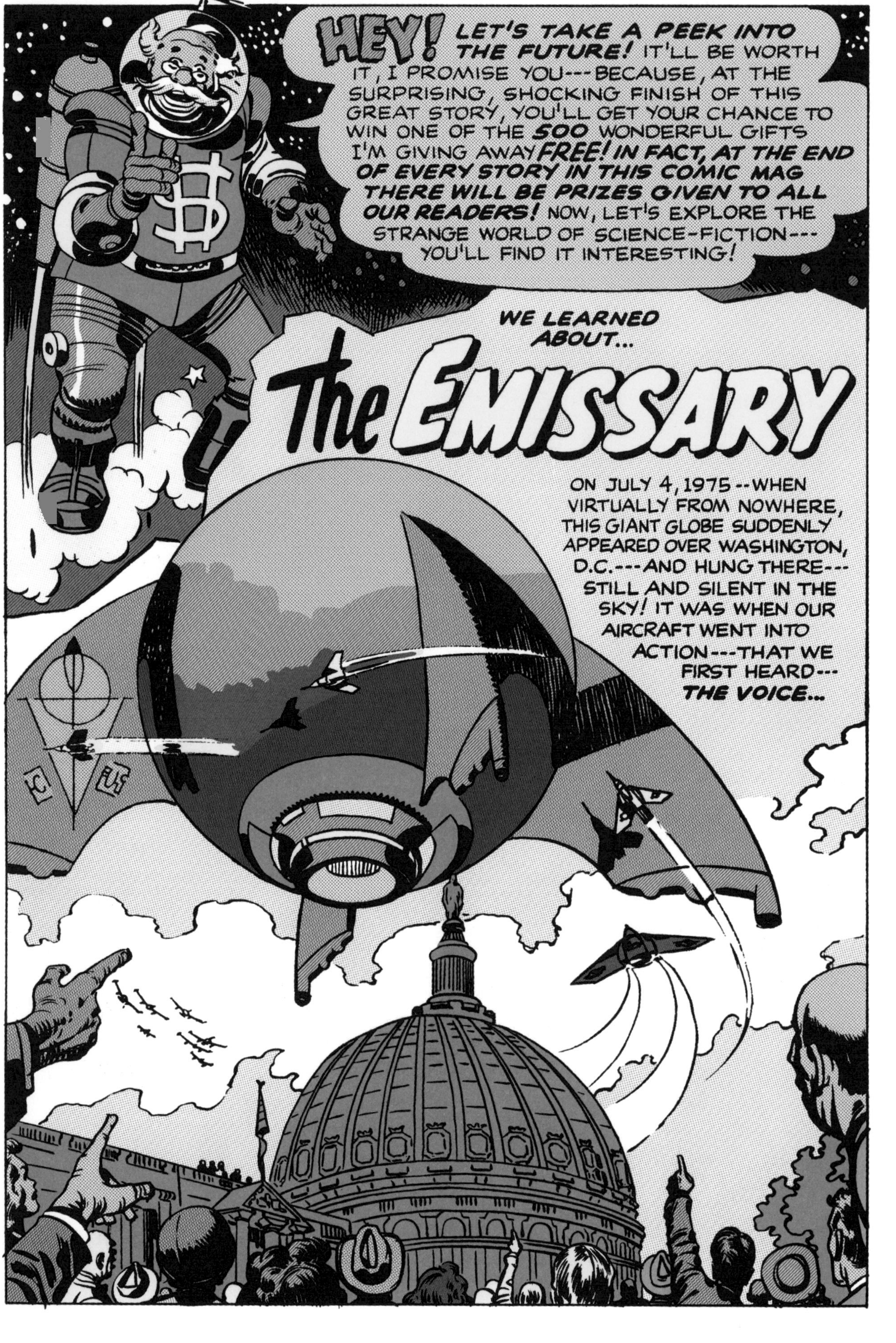
HEY! LET'S TAKE A PEEK INTO THE FUTURE! IT'LL BE WORTH IT, I PROMISE YOU---BECAUSE, AT THE SURPRISING, SHOCKING FINISH OF THIS GREAT STORY, YOU'LL GET YOUR CHANCE TO WIN ONE OF THE 500 WONDERFUL GIFTS I'M GIVING AWAY FREE! IN FACT, AT THE END OF EVERY STORY IN THIS COMIC MAG THERE WILL BE PRIZES GIVEN TO ALL OUR READERS! NOW, LET'S EXPLORE THE STRANGE WORLD OF SCIENCE-FICTION--- YOU'LL FIND IT INTERESTING!
WE LEARNED ABOUT...
The EMISSARY
ON JULY 4, 1975 --WHEN VIRTUALLY FROM NOWHERE, THIS GIANT GLOBE SUDDENLY APPEARED OVER WASHINGTON, D.C.---AND HUNG THERE--- STILL AND SILENT IN THE SKY! IT WAS WHEN OUR AIRCRAFT WENT INTO ACTION---THAT WE FIRST HEARD--- THE VOICE...

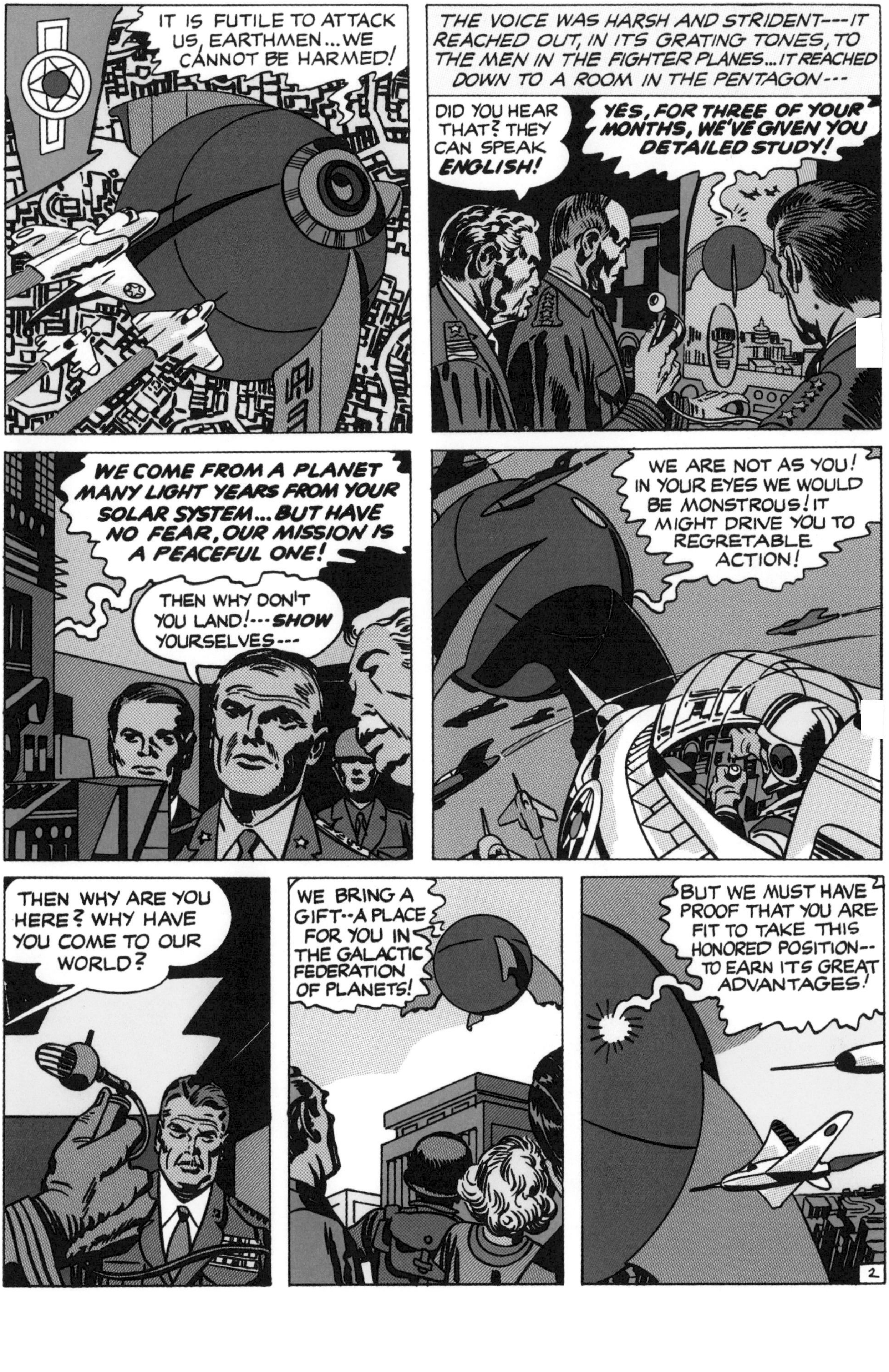

IT IS FUTILE TO ATTACK US, EARTHMEN... WE CANNOT BE HARMED!
THE VOICE WAS HARSH AND STRIDENT---IT REACHED OUT, IN ITS GRATING TONES, TO THE MEN IN THE FIGHTER PLANES...IT REACHED DOWN TO A ROOM IN THE PENTAGON---
DID YOU HEAR THAT? THEY CAN SPEAK ENGLISH!
YES, FOR THREE OF YOUR MONTHS, WE'VE GIVEN YOU DETAILED STUDY!
WE COME FROM A PLANET MANY LIGHT YEARS FROM YOUR SOLAR SYSTEM...BUT HAVE NO FEAR, OUR MISSION IS A PEACEFUL ONE!
THEN WHY DON'T YOU LAND!---SHOW YOURSELVES---
WE ARE NOT AS YOU! IN YOUR EYES WE WOULD BE MONSTROUS! IT MIGHT DRIVE YOU TO REGRETABLE ACTION!
THEN WHY ARE YOU HERE? WHY HAVE YOU COME TO OUR WORLD?
WE BRING A GIFT--A PLACE FOR YOU IN THE GALACTIC FEDERATION OF PLANETS!
BUT WE MUST HAVE PROOF THAT YOU ARE FIT TO TAKE THIS HONORED POSITION--TO EARN ITS GREAT ADVANTAGES!
2

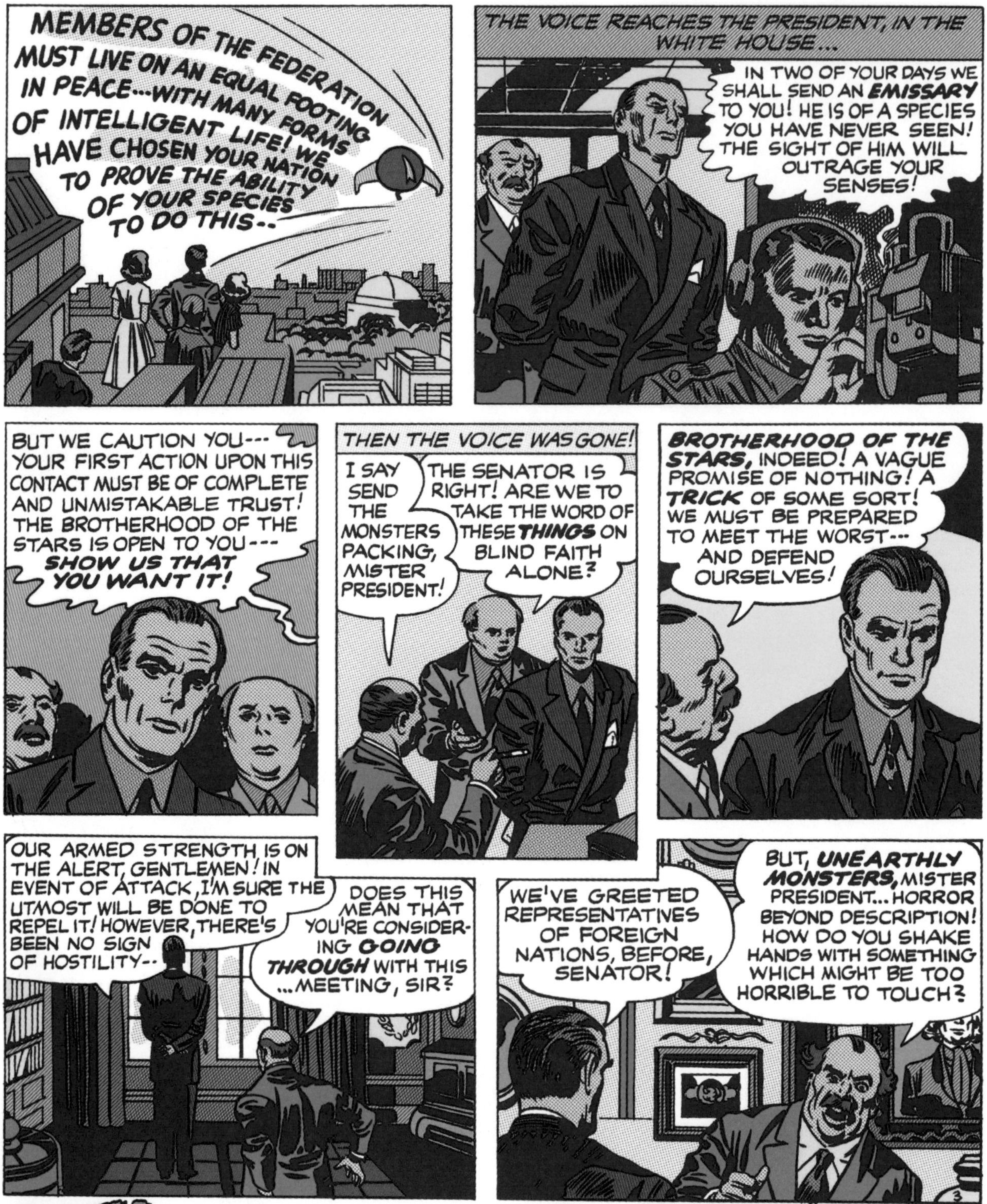
MEMBERS OF THE FEDERATION MUST LIVE ON AN EQUAL FOOTING IN PEACE...WITH MANY FORMS OF INTELLIGENT LIFE! WE HAVE CHOSEN YOUR NATION TO PROVE THE ABILITY OF YOUR SPECIES TO DO THIS--
THE VOICE REACHES THE PRESIDENT, IN THE WHITE HOUSE...
IN TWO OF YOUR DAYS WE SHALL SEND AN EMISSARY TO YOU! HE IS OF A SPECIES YOU HAVE NEVER SEEN! THE SIGHT OF HIM WILL OUTRAGE YOUR SENSES!
BUT WE CAUTION YOU--- YOUR FIRST ACTION UPON THIS CONTACT MUST BE OF COMPLETE AND UNMISTAKABLE TRUST! THE BROTHERHOOD OF THE STARS IS OPEN TO YOU--- SHOW US THAT YOU WANT IT!
THEN THE VOICE WAS GONE!
I SAY SEND THE MONSTERS PACKING, MISTER PRESIDENT!
THE SENATOR IS RIGHT! ARE WE TO TAKE THE WORD OF THESE THINGS ON BLIND FAITH ALONE?
BROTHERHOOD OF THE STARS, INDEED! A VAGUE PROMISE OF NOTHING! A TRICK OF SOME SORT! WE MUST BE PREPARED TO MEET THE WORST--- AND DEFEND OURSELVES!
OUR ARMED STRENGTH IS ON THE ALERT, GENTLEMEN! IN EVENT OF ATTACK, I'M SURE THE UTMOST WILL BE DONE TO REPEL IT! HOWEVER, THERE'S BEEN NO SIGN OF HOSTILITY--
DOES THIS MEAN THAT YOU'RE CONSIDERING GOING THROUGH WITH THIS ...MEETING, SIR?
WE'VE GREETED REPRESENTATIVES OF FOREIGN NATIONS, BEFORE, SENATOR!
BUT, UNEARTHLY MONSTERS, MISTER PRESIDENT...HORROR BEYOND DESCRIPTION! HOW DO YOU SHAKE HANDS WITH SOMETHING WHICH MIGHT BE TOO HORRIBLE TO TOUCH?
3

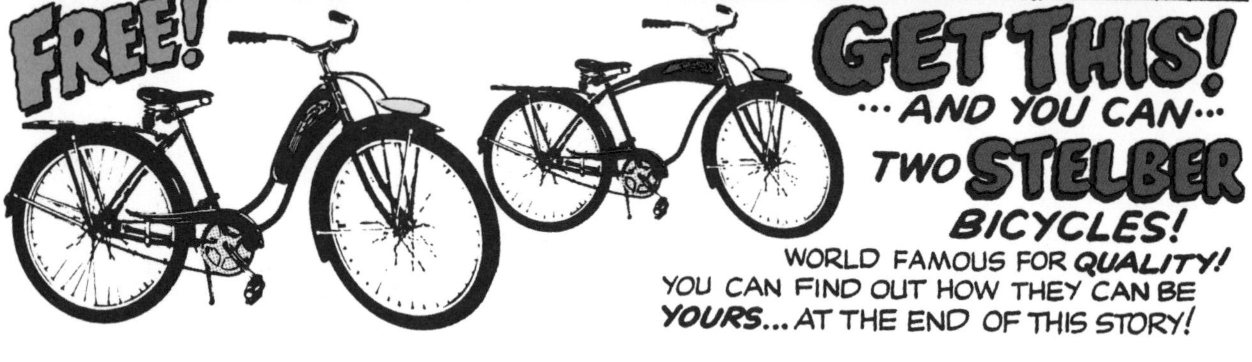
FREE!
GET THIS!
...AND YOU CAN...
TWO STELBER BICYCLES!
WORLD FAMOUS FOR QUALITY!
YOU CAN FIND OUT HOW THEY CAN BE YOURS... AT THE END OF THIS STORY!

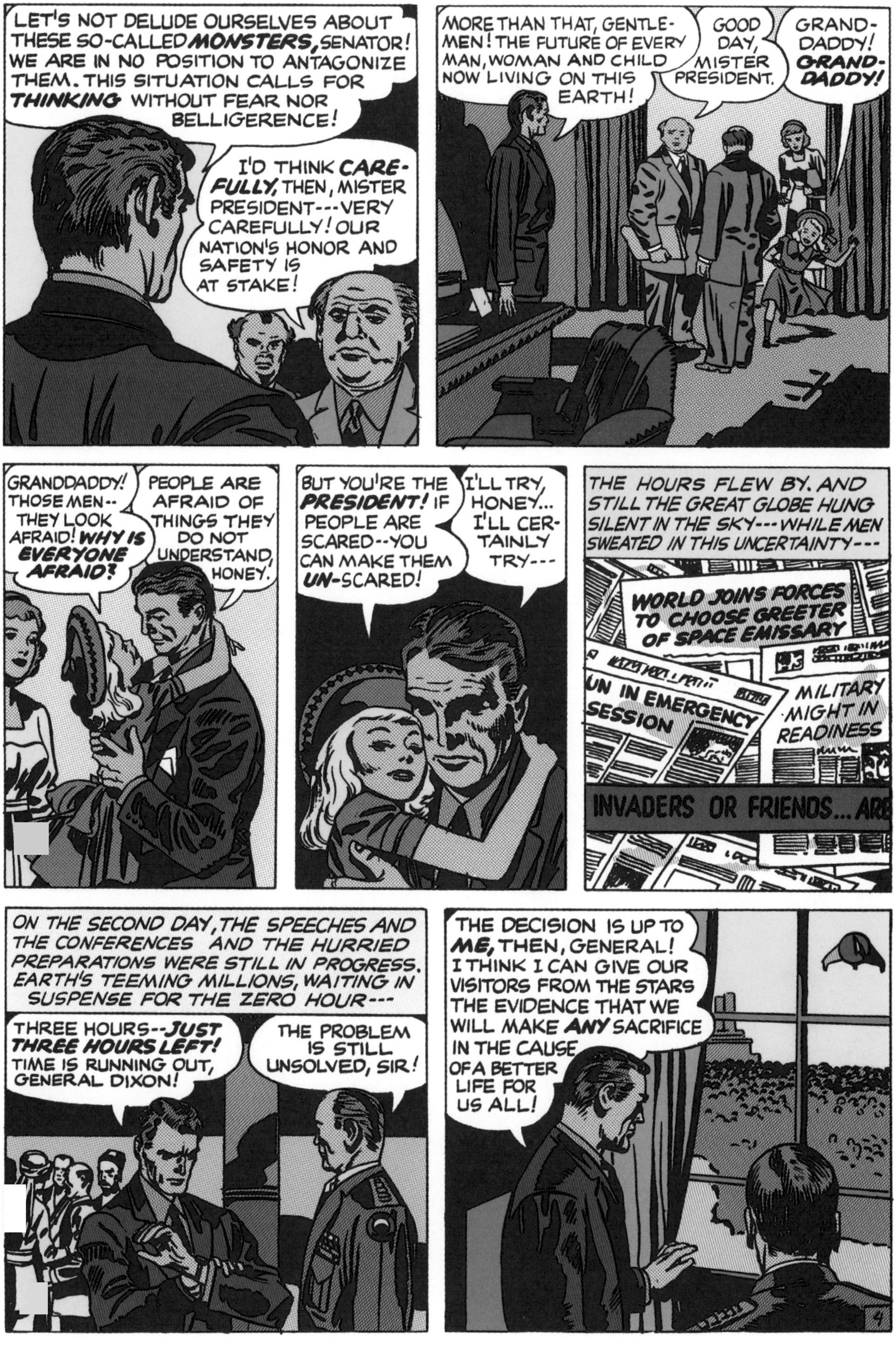

LET'S NOT DELUDE OURSELVES ABOUT THESE SO-CALLED MONSTERS, SENATOR! WE ARE IN NO POSITION TO ANTAGONIZE THEM. THIS SITUATION CALLS FOR THINKING WITHOUT FEAR NOR BELLIGERENCE!
I'D THINK CAREFULLY, THEN, MISTER PRESIDENT---VERY CAREFULLY! OUR NATION'S HONOR AND SAFETY IS AT STAKE!
MORE THAN THAT, GENTLEMEN! THE FUTURE OF EVERY MAN, WOMAN AND CHILD NOW LIVING ON THIS EARTH!
GOOD DAY, MISTER PRESIDENT.
GRAND-DADDY! GRAND-DADDY!
GRANDDADDY! THOSE MEN-- THEY LOOK AFRAID! WHY IS EVERYONE AFRAID?
PEOPLE ARE AFRAID OF THINGS THEY DO NOT UNDERSTAND, HONEY.
BUT YOU'RE THE PRESIDENT! IF PEOPLE ARE SCARED--YOU CAN MAKE THEM UN-SCARED!
I'LL TRY, HONEY... I'LL CERTAINLY TRY---
THE HOURS FLEW BY. AND STILL THE GREAT GLOBE HUNG SILENT IN THE SKY---WHILE MEN SWEATED IN THIS UNCERTAINTY---
WORLD JOINS FORCES TO CHOOSE GREETER OF SPACE EMISSARY
UN IN EMERGENCY SESSION
MILITARY MIGHT IN READINESS
INVADERS OR FRIENDS... ARE
ON THE SECOND DAY, THE SPEECHES AND THE CONFERENCES AND THE HURRIED PREPARATIONS WERE STILL IN PROGRESS. EARTH'S TEEMING MILLIONS, WAITING IN SUSPENSE FOR THE ZERO HOUR---
THREE HOURS--JUST THREE HOURS LEFT! TIME IS RUNNING OUT, GENERAL DIXON!
THE PROBLEM IS STILL UNSOLVED, SIR!
THE DECISION IS UP TO ME, THEN, GENERAL! I THINK I CAN GIVE OUR VISITORS FROM THE STARS THE EVIDENCE THAT WE WILL MAKE ANY SACRIFICE IN THE CAUSE OF A BETTER LIFE FOR US ALL!
4

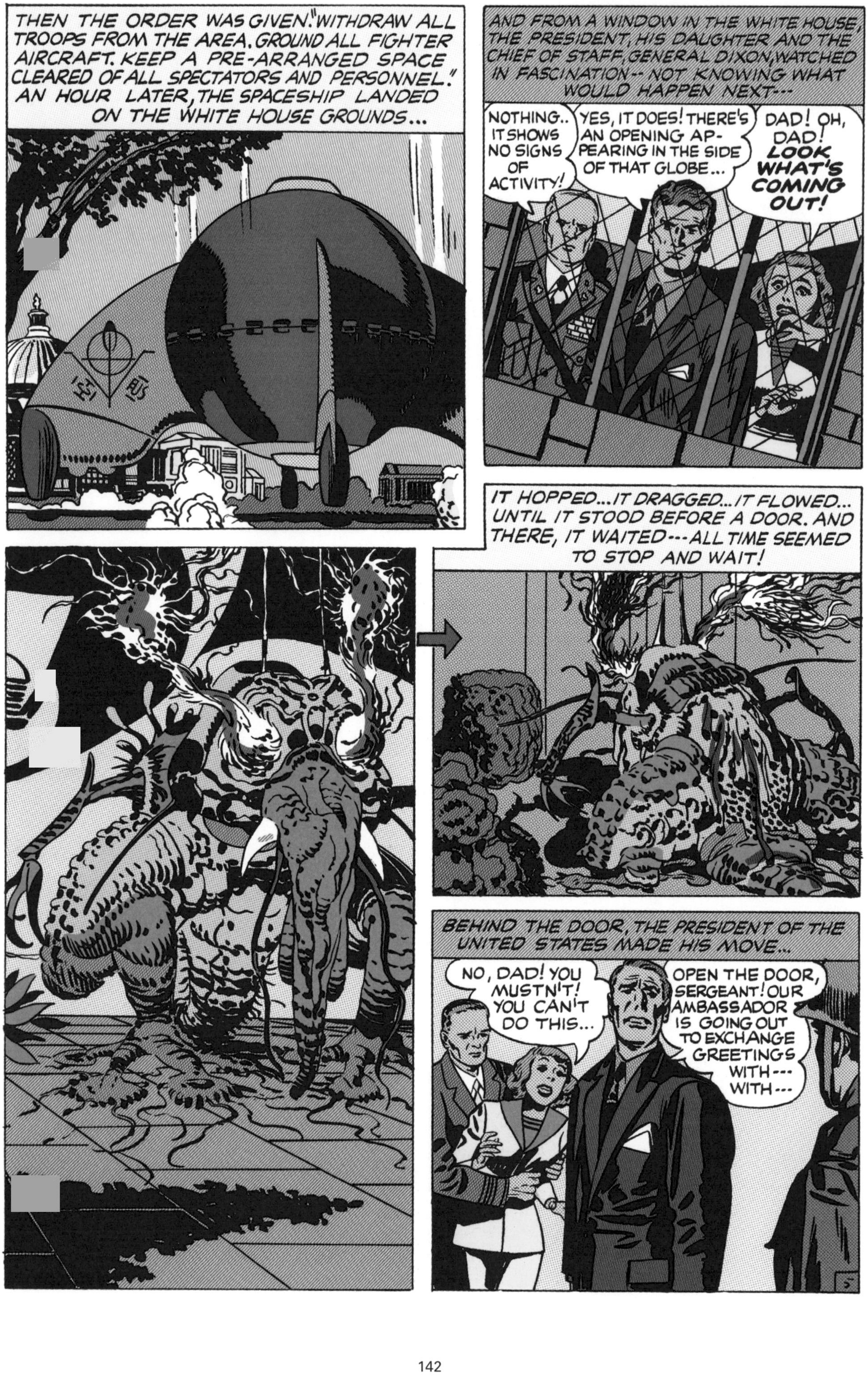

THEN THE ORDER WAS GIVEN! "WITHDRAW ALL TROOPS FROM THE AREA. GROUND ALL FIGHTER AIRCRAFT. KEEP A PRE-ARRANGED SPACE CLEARED OF ALL SPECTATORS AND PERSONNEL." AN HOUR LATER, THE SPACESHIP LANDED ON THE WHITE HOUSE GROUNDS...
AND FROM A WINDOW IN THE WHITE HOUSE, THE PRESIDENT, HIS DAUGHTER AND THE CHIEF OF STAFF, GENERAL DIXON, WATCHED IN FASCINATION -- NOT KNOWING WHAT WOULD HAPPEN NEXT---
NOTHING.. IT SHOWS NO SIGNS OF ACTIVITY!
YES, IT DOES! THERE'S AN OPENING AP-PEARING IN THE SIDE OF THAT GLOBE...
DAD! OH, DAD! LOOK WHAT'S COMING OUT!
IT HOPPED...IT DRAGGED...IT FLOWED... UNTIL IT STOOD BEFORE A DOOR. AND THERE, IT WAITED---ALL TIME SEEMED TO STOP AND WAIT!
BEHIND THE DOOR, THE PRESIDENT OF THE UNITED STATES MADE HIS MOVE...
NO, DAD! YOU MUSTN'T! YOU CAN'T DO THIS...
OPEN THE DOOR, SERGEANT! OUR AMBASSADOR IS GOING OUT TO EXCHANGE GREETINGS WITH--- WITH---

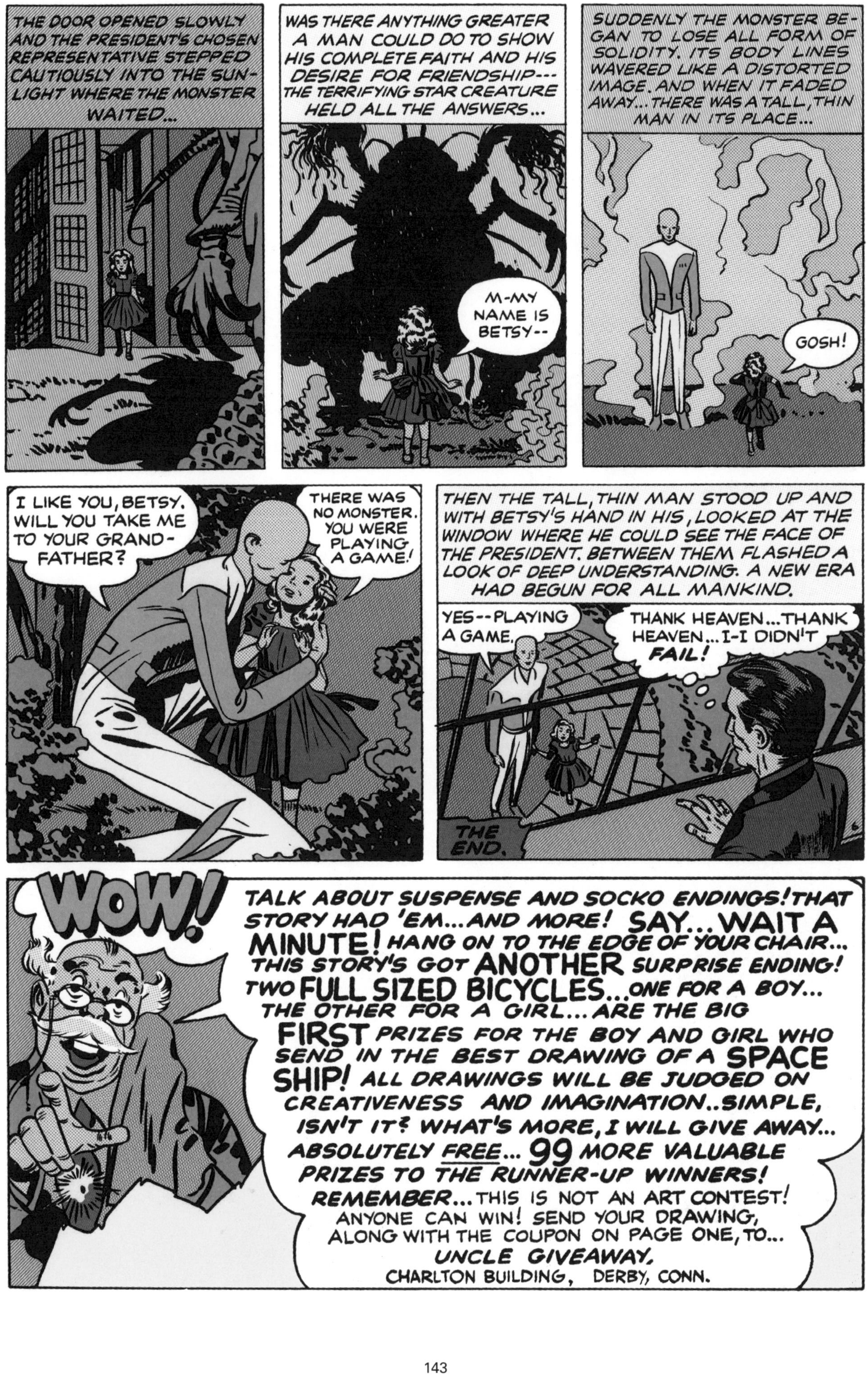
THE DOOR OPENED SLOWLY AND THE PRESIDENT'S CHOSEN REPRESENTATIVE STEPPED CAUTIOUSLY INTO THE SUN-LIGHT WHERE THE MONSTER WAITED...
WAS THERE ANYTHING GREATER A MAN COULD DO TO SHOW HIS COMPLETE FAITH AND HIS DESIRE FOR FRIENDSHIP--- THE TERRIFYING STAR CREATURE HELD ALL THE ANSWERS...
M-MY NAME IS BETSY--
SUDDENLY THE MONSTER BE-GAN TO LOSE ALL FORM OF SOLIDITY. ITS BODY LINES WAVERED LIKE A DISTORTED IMAGE. AND WHEN IT FADED AWAY... THERE WAS A TALL, THIN MAN IN ITS PLACE...
GOSH!
I LIKE YOU, BETSY. WILL YOU TAKE ME TO YOUR GRAND-FATHER?
THERE WAS NO MONSTER. YOU WERE PLAYING A GAME!
THEN THE TALL, THIN MAN STOOD UP AND WITH BETSY'S HAND IN HIS, LOOKED AT THE WINDOW WHERE HE COULD SEE THE FACE OF THE PRESIDENT. BETWEEN THEM FLASHED A LOOK OF DEEP UNDERSTANDING. A NEW ERA HAD BEGUN FOR ALL MANKIND.
YES--PLAYING A GAME.
THANK HEAVEN...THANK HEAVEN...I-I DIDN'T FAIL!
THE END.
WOW!
TALK ABOUT SUSPENSE AND SOCKO ENDINGS! THAT STORY HAD 'EM...AND MORE! SAY...WAIT A MINUTE! HANG ON TO THE EDGE OF YOUR CHAIR... THIS STORY'S GOT ANOTHER SURPRISE ENDING! TWO FULL SIZED BICYCLES...ONE FOR A BOY... THE OTHER FOR A GIRL... ARE THE BIG FIRST PRIZES FOR THE BOY AND GIRL WHO SEND IN THE BEST DRAWING OF A SPACE SHIP! ALL DRAWINGS WILL BE JUDGED ON CREATIVENESS AND IMAGINATION..SIMPLE, ISN'T IT? WHAT'S MORE, I WILL GIVE AWAY... ABSOLUTELY FREE... 99 MORE VALUABLE PRIZES TO THE RUNNER-UP WINNERS! REMEMBER... THIS IS NOT AN ART CONTEST! ANYONE CAN WIN! SEND YOUR DRAWING, ALONG WITH THE COUPON ON PAGE ONE, TO... UNCLE GIVEAWAY, CHARLTON BUILDING, DERBY, CONN.

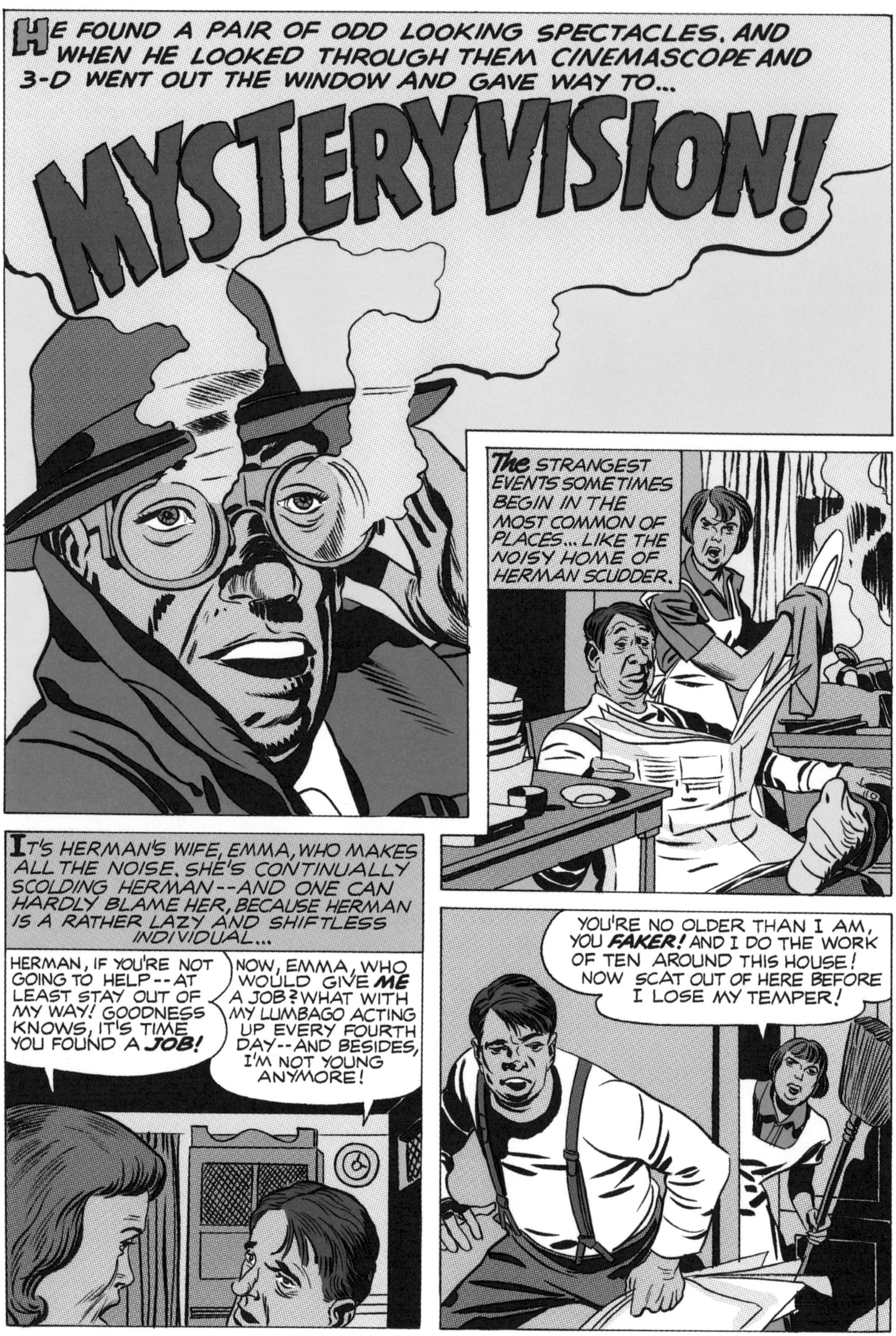
HE FOUND A PAIR OF ODD LOOKING SPECTACLES. AND WHEN HE LOOKED THROUGH THEM CINEMASCOPE AND 3-D WENT OUT THE WINDOW AND GAVE WAY TO...
MYSTERYVISION!
THE STRANGEST EVENTS SOMETIMES BEGIN IN THE MOST COMMON OF PLACES... LIKE THE NOISY HOME OF HERMAN SCUDDER.
IT'S HERMAN'S WIFE, EMMA, WHO MAKES ALL THE NOISE. SHE'S CONTINUALLY SCOLDING HERMAN--AND ONE CAN HARDLY BLAME HER, BECAUSE HERMAN IS A RATHER LAZY AND SHIFTLESS INDIVIDUAL...
HERMAN, IF YOU'RE NOT GOING TO HELP--AT LEAST STAY OUT OF MY WAY! GOODNESS KNOWS, IT'S TIME YOU FOUND A JOB!
NOW, EMMA, WHO WOULD GIVE ME A JOB? WHAT WITH MY LUMBAGO ACTING UP EVERY FOURTH DAY--AND BESIDES, I'M NOT YOUNG ANYMORE!
YOU'RE NO OLDER THAN I AM, YOU FAKER! AND I DO THE WORK OF TEN AROUND THIS HOUSE! NOW SCAT OUT OF HERE BEFORE I LOSE MY TEMPER!

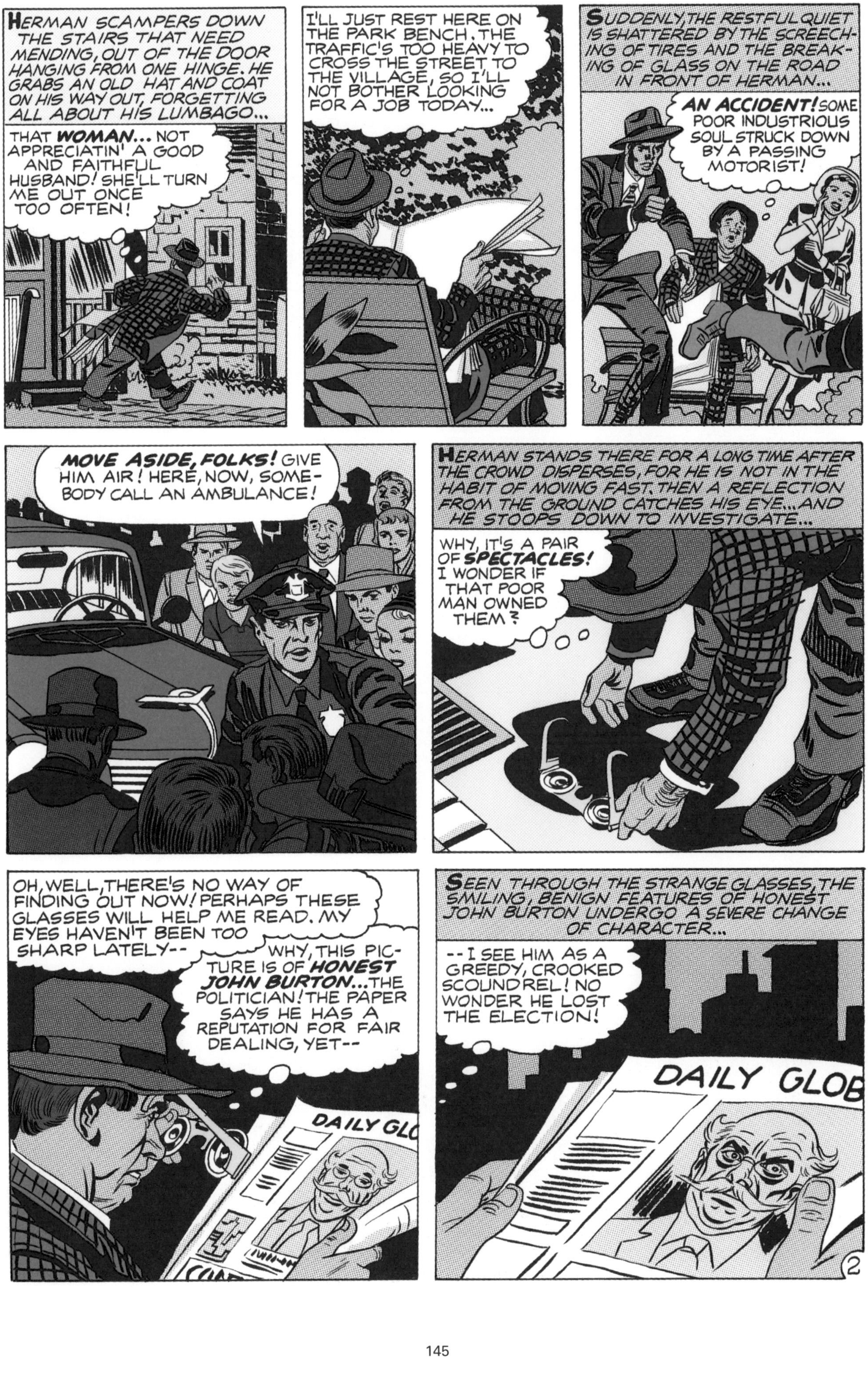
HERMAN SCAMPERS DOWN THE STAIRS THAT NEED MENDING, OUT OF THE DOOR HANGING FROM ONE HINGE. HE GRABS AN OLD HAT AND COAT ON HIS WAY OUT, FORGETTING ALL ABOUT HIS LUMBAGO...
THAT WOMAN... NOT APPRECIATIN' A GOOD AND FAITHFUL HUSBAND! SHE'LL TURN ME OUT ONCE TOO OFTEN!
I'LL JUST REST HERE ON THE PARK BENCH. THE TRAFFIC'S TOO HEAVY TO CROSS THE STREET TO THE VILLAGE, SO I'LL NOT BOTHER LOOKING FOR A JOB TODAY...
SUDDENLY, THE RESTFUL QUIET IS SHATTERED BY THE SCREECHING OF TIRES AND THE BREAKING OF GLASS ON THE ROAD IN FRONT OF HERMAN...
AN ACCIDENT! SOME POOR INDUSTRIOUS SOUL STRUCK DOWN BY A PASSING MOTORIST!
MOVE ASIDE, FOLKS! GIVE HIM AIR! HERE, NOW, SOMEBODY CALL AN AMBULANCE!
HERMAN STANDS THERE FOR A LONG TIME AFTER THE CROWD DISPERSES, FOR HE IS NOT IN THE HABIT OF MOVING FAST. THEN A REFLECTION FROM THE GROUND CATCHES HIS EYE... AND HE STOOPS DOWN TO INVESTIGATE...
WHY, IT'S A PAIR OF SPECTACLES! I WONDER IF THAT POOR MAN OWNED THEM?
OH, WELL, THERE'S NO WAY OF FINDING OUT NOW! PERHAPS THESE GLASSES WILL HELP ME READ. MY EYES HAVEN'T BEEN TOO SHARP LATELY--
WHY, THIS PICTURE IS OF HONEST JOHN BURTON... THE POLITICIAN! THE PAPER SAYS HE HAS A REPUTATION FOR FAIR DEALING, YET--
DAILY GL
SEEN THROUGH THE STRANGE GLASSES, THE SMILING, BENIGN FEATURES OF HONEST JOHN BURTON UNDERGO A SEVERE CHANGE OF CHARACTER...
--I SEE HIM AS A GREEDY, CROOKED SCOUNDREL! NO WONDER HE LOST THE ELECTION!
DAILY GLOB
2

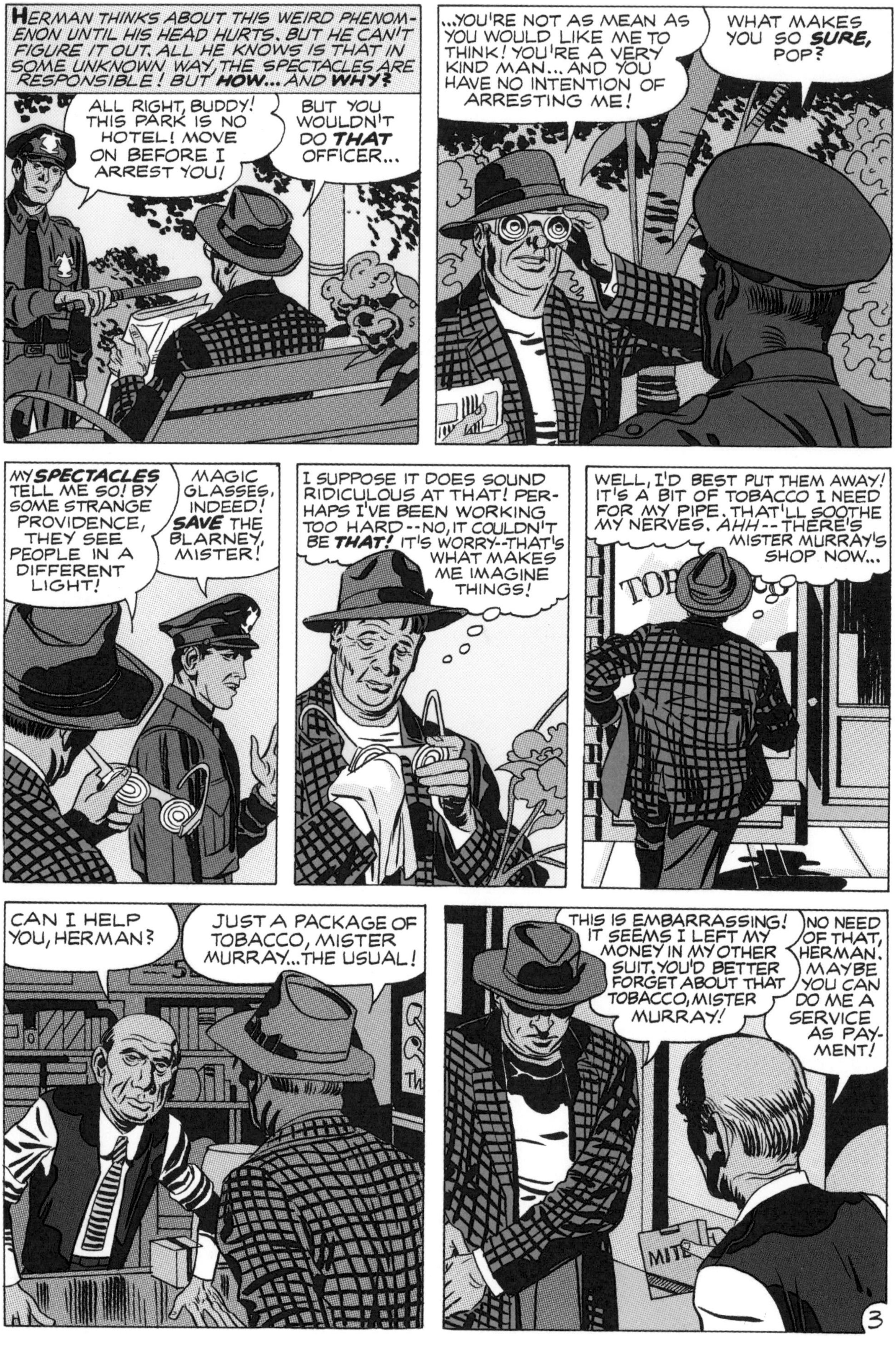
HERMAN THINKS ABOUT THIS WEIRD PHENOMENON UNTIL HIS HEAD HURTS. BUT HE CAN'T FIGURE IT OUT. ALL HE KNOWS IS THAT IN SOME UNKNOWN WAY, THE SPECTACLES ARE RESPONSIBLE! BUT HOW... AND WHY?
ALL RIGHT, BUDDY! THIS PARK IS NO HOTEL! MOVE ON BEFORE I ARREST YOU!
BUT YOU WOULDN'T DO THAT OFFICER...
...YOU'RE NOT AS MEAN AS YOU WOULD LIKE ME TO THINK! YOU'RE A VERY KIND MAN... AND YOU HAVE NO INTENTION OF ARRESTING ME!
WHAT MAKES YOU SO SURE, POP?
MY SPECTACLES TELL ME SO! BY SOME STRANGE PROVIDENCE, THEY SEE PEOPLE IN A DIFFERENT LIGHT!
MAGIC GLASSES, INDEED! SAVE THE BLARNEY, MISTER!
I SUPPOSE IT DOES SOUND RIDICULOUS AT THAT! PERHAPS I'VE BEEN WORKING TOO HARD--NO, IT COULDN'T BE THAT! IT'S WORRY--THAT'S WHAT MAKES ME IMAGINE THINGS!
WELL, I'D BEST PUT THEM AWAY! IT'S A BIT OF TOBACCO I NEED FOR MY PIPE. THAT'LL SOOTHE MY NERVES. AHH--THERE'S MISTER MURRAY'S SHOP NOW...
CAN I HELP YOU, HERMAN?
JUST A PACKAGE OF TOBACCO, MISTER MURRAY...THE USUAL!
THIS IS EMBARRASSING! IT SEEMS I LEFT MY MONEY IN MY OTHER SUIT. YOU'D BETTER FORGET ABOUT THAT TOBACCO, MISTER MURRAY!
NO NEED OF THAT, HERMAN. MAYBE YOU CAN DO ME A SERVICE AS PAYMENT!
3

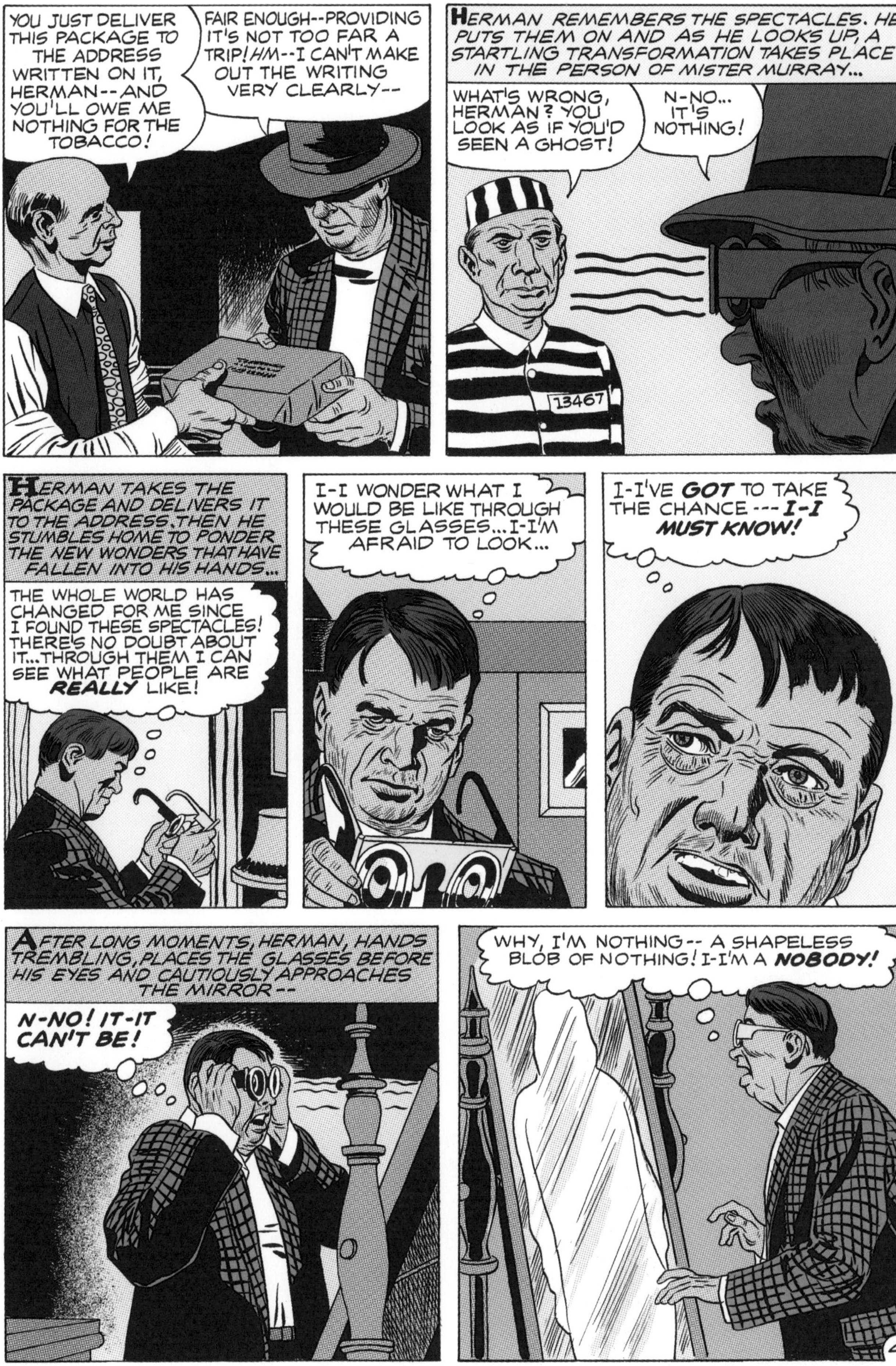
YOU JUST DELIVER THIS PACKAGE TO THE ADDRESS WRITTEN ON IT, HERMAN--AND YOU'LL OWE ME NOTHING FOR THE TOBACCO!
FAIR ENOUGH--PROVIDING IT'S NOT TOO FAR A TRIP! HM--I CAN'T MAKE OUT THE WRITING VERY CLEARLY--
HERMAN REMEMBERS THE SPECTACLES. HE PUTS THEM ON AND AS HE LOOKS UP, A STARTLING TRANSFORMATION TAKES PLACE IN THE PERSON OF MISTER MURRAY...
WHAT'S WRONG, HERMAN? YOU LOOK AS IF YOU'D SEEN A GHOST!
N-NO... IT'S NOTHING!
13467
HERMAN TAKES THE PACKAGE AND DELIVERS IT TO THE ADDRESS. THEN HE STUMBLES HOME TO PONDER THE NEW WONDERS THAT HAVE FALLEN INTO HIS HANDS...
THE WHOLE WORLD HAS CHANGED FOR ME SINCE I FOUND THESE SPECTACLES! THERE'S NO DOUBT ABOUT IT...THROUGH THEM I CAN SEE WHAT PEOPLE ARE REALLY LIKE!
I-I WONDER WHAT I WOULD BE LIKE THROUGH THESE GLASSES...I-I'M AFRAID TO LOOK...
I-I'VE GOT TO TAKE THE CHANCE---I-I MUST KNOW!
AFTER LONG MOMENTS, HERMAN, HANDS TREMBLING, PLACES THE GLASSES BEFORE HIS EYES AND CAUTIOUSLY APPROACHES THE MIRROR--
N-NO! IT-IT CAN'T BE!
WHY, I'M NOTHING-- A SHAPELESS BLOB OF NOTHING! I-I'M A NOBODY!
4

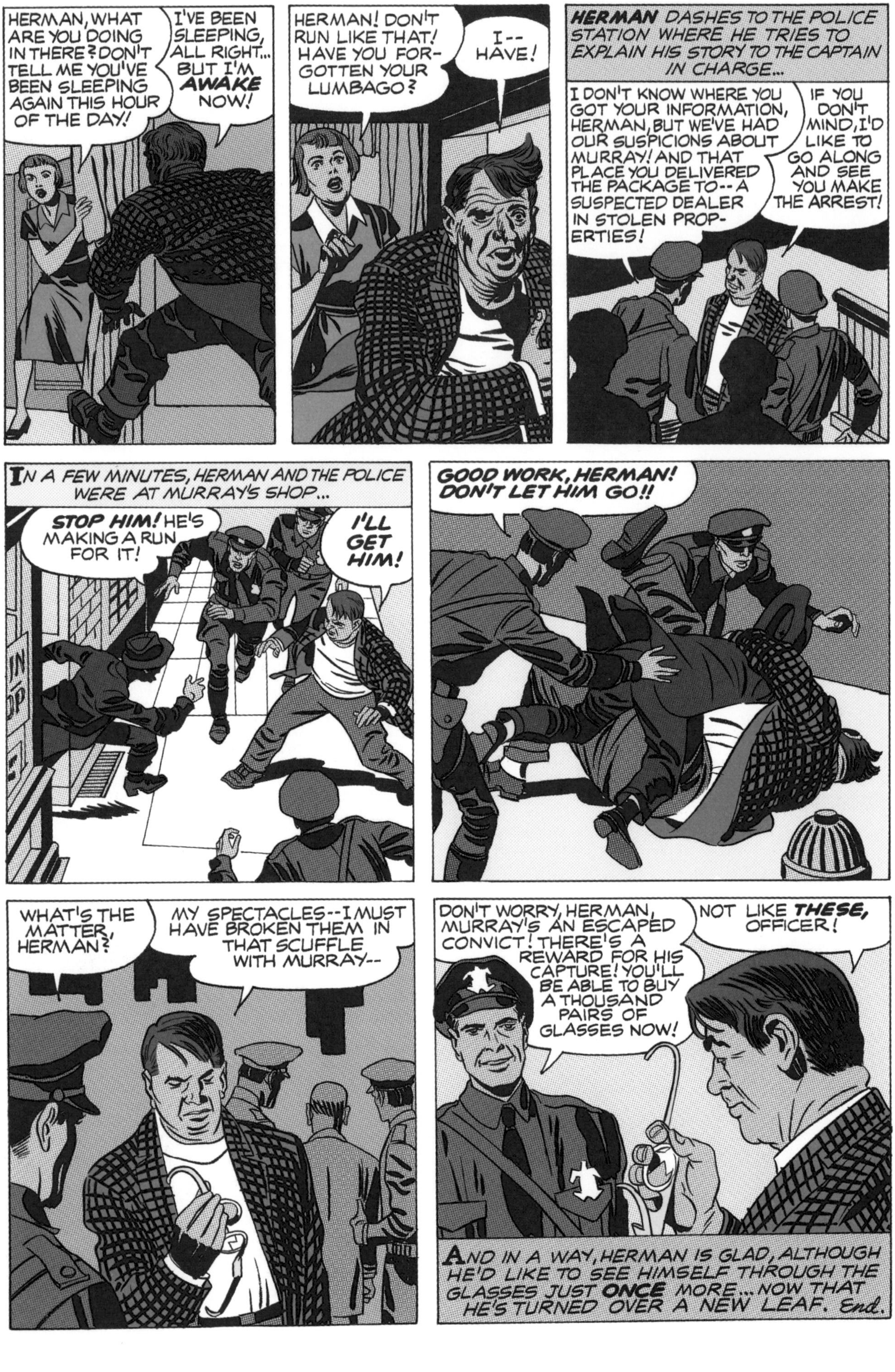
HERMAN, WHAT ARE YOU DOING IN THERE? DON'T TELL ME YOU'VE BEEN SLEEPING AGAIN THIS HOUR OF THE DAY!
I'VE BEEN SLEEPING, ALL RIGHT... BUT I'M **AWAKE** NOW!
HERMAN! DON'T RUN LIKE THAT! HAVE YOU FORGOTTEN YOUR LUMBAGO?
I-- HAVE!
HERMAN DASHES TO THE POLICE STATION WHERE HE TRIES TO EXPLAIN HIS STORY TO THE CAPTAIN IN CHARGE...
I DON'T KNOW WHERE YOU GOT YOUR INFORMATION, HERMAN, BUT WE'VE HAD OUR SUSPICIONS ABOUT MURRAY! AND THAT PLACE YOU DELIVERED THE PACKAGE TO-- A SUSPECTED DEALER IN STOLEN PROPERTIES!
IF YOU DON'T MIND, I'D LIKE TO GO ALONG AND SEE YOU MAKE THE ARREST!
IN A FEW MINUTES, HERMAN AND THE POLICE WERE AT MURRAY'S SHOP...
STOP HIM! HE'S MAKING A RUN FOR IT!
I'LL GET HIM!
GOOD WORK, HERMAN! DON'T LET HIM GO!!
WHAT'S THE MATTER, HERMAN?
MY SPECTACLES--I MUST HAVE BROKEN THEM IN THAT SCUFFLE WITH MURRAY--
DON'T WORRY, HERMAN, MURRAY'S AN ESCAPED CONVICT! THERE'S A REWARD FOR HIS CAPTURE! YOU'LL BE ABLE TO BUY A THOUSAND PAIRS OF GLASSES NOW!
NOT LIKE **THESE,** OFFICER!
AND IN A WAY, HERMAN IS GLAD, ALTHOUGH HE'D LIKE TO SEE HIMSELF THROUGH THE GLASSES JUST **ONCE** MORE... NOW THAT HE'S TURNED OVER A NEW LEAF. End.

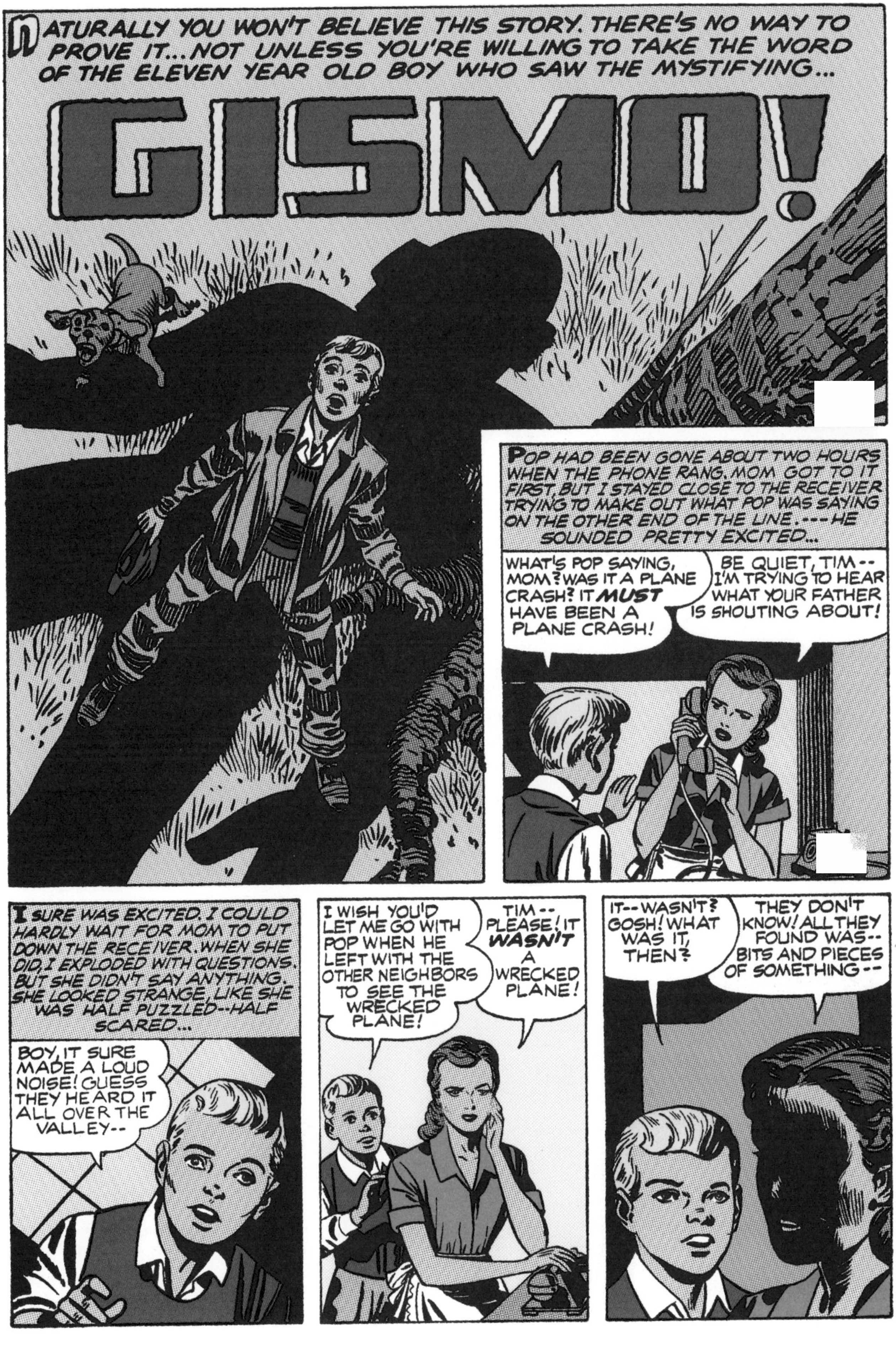
NATURALLY YOU WON'T BELIEVE THIS STORY. THERE'S NO WAY TO PROVE IT... NOT UNLESS YOU'RE WILLING TO TAKE THE WORD OF THE ELEVEN YEAR OLD BOY WHO SAW THE MYSTIFYING...
GISMO!
POP HAD BEEN GONE ABOUT TWO HOURS WHEN THE PHONE RANG. MOM GOT TO IT FIRST, BUT I STAYED CLOSE TO THE RECEIVER TRYING TO MAKE OUT WHAT POP WAS SAYING ON THE OTHER END OF THE LINE.---HE SOUNDED PRETTY EXCITED...
WHAT'S POP SAYING, MOM? WAS IT A PLANE CRASH? IT MUST HAVE BEEN A PLANE CRASH!
BE QUIET, TIM-- I'M TRYING TO HEAR WHAT YOUR FATHER IS SHOUTING ABOUT!
I SURE WAS EXCITED. I COULD HARDLY WAIT FOR MOM TO PUT DOWN THE RECEIVER. WHEN SHE DID, I EXPLODED WITH QUESTIONS. BUT SHE DIDN'T SAY ANYTHING. SHE LOOKED STRANGE, LIKE SHE WAS HALF PUZZLED--HALF SCARED...
BOY, IT SURE MADE A LOUD NOISE! GUESS THEY HEARD IT ALL OVER THE VALLEY--
I WISH YOU'D LET ME GO WITH POP WHEN HE LEFT WITH THE OTHER NEIGHBORS TO SEE THE WRECKED PLANE!
TIM-- PLEASE! IT WASN'T A WRECKED PLANE!
IT--WASN'T? GOSH! WHAT WAS IT, THEN?
THEY DON'T KNOW! ALL THEY FOUND WAS-- BITS AND PIECES OF SOMETHING--

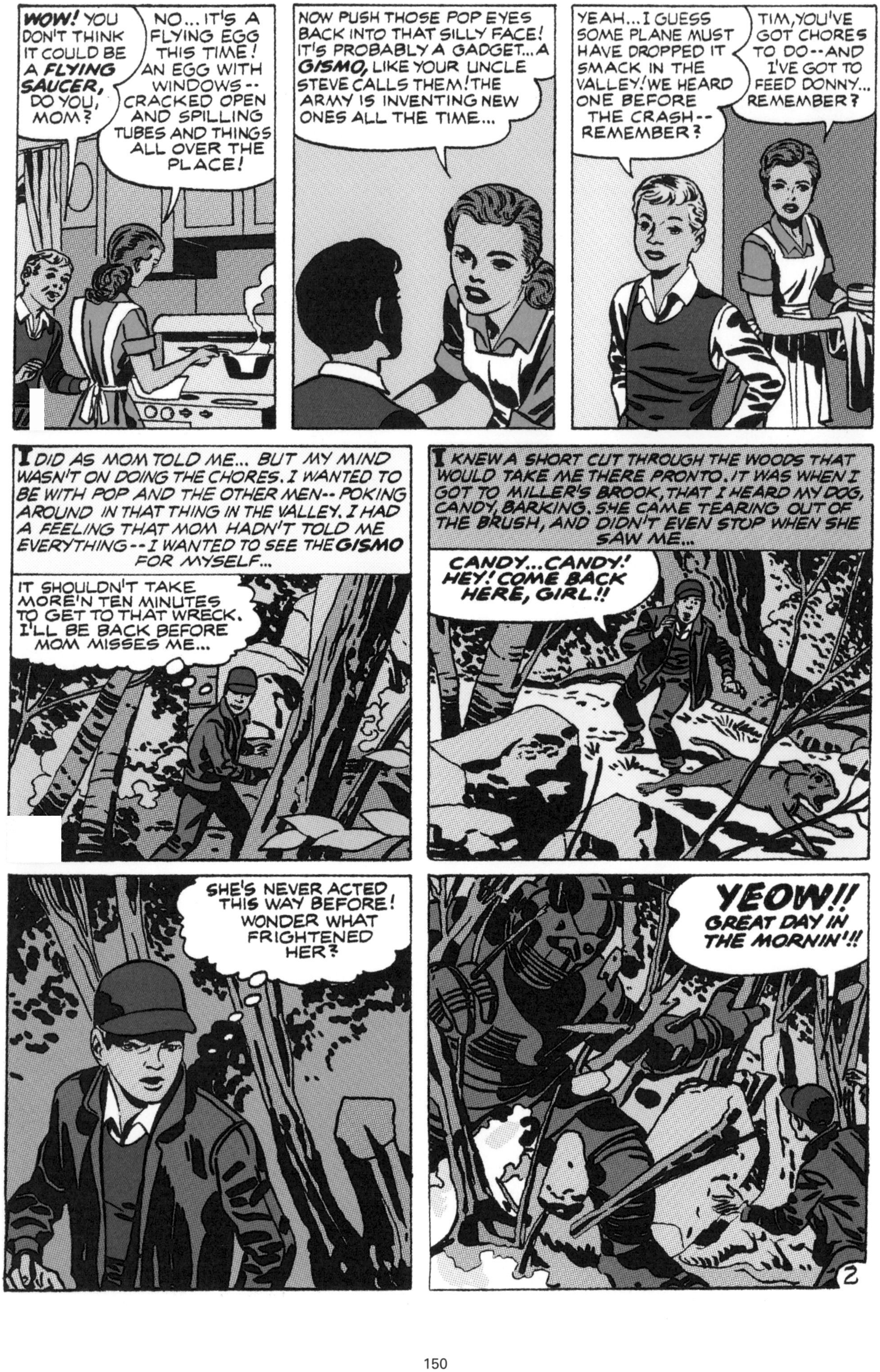
WOW! YOU DON'T THINK IT COULD BE A FLYING SAUCER, DO YOU, MOM?
NO... IT'S A FLYING EGG THIS TIME! AN EGG WITH WINDOWS -- CRACKED OPEN AND SPILLING TUBES AND THINGS ALL OVER THE PLACE!
NOW PUSH THOSE POP EYES BACK INTO THAT SILLY FACE! IT'S PROBABLY A GADGET... A GISMO, LIKE YOUR UNCLE STEVE CALLS THEM! THE ARMY IS INVENTING NEW ONES ALL THE TIME...
YEAH... I GUESS SOME PLANE MUST HAVE DROPPED IT SMACK IN THE VALLEY! WE HEARD ONE BEFORE THE CRASH -- REMEMBER?
TIM, YOU'VE GOT CHORES TO DO -- AND I'VE GOT TO FEED DONNY... REMEMBER?
I DID AS MOM TOLD ME... BUT MY MIND WASN'T ON DOING THE CHORES. I WANTED TO BE WITH POP AND THE OTHER MEN -- POKING AROUND IN THAT THING IN THE VALLEY. I HAD A FEELING THAT MOM HADN'T TOLD ME EVERYTHING -- I WANTED TO SEE THE GISMO FOR MYSELF...
IT SHOULDN'T TAKE MORE'N TEN MINUTES TO GET TO THAT WRECK. I'LL BE BACK BEFORE MOM MISSES ME...
I KNEW A SHORT CUT THROUGH THE WOODS THAT WOULD TAKE ME THERE PRONTO. IT WAS WHEN I GOT TO MILLER'S BROOK, THAT I HEARD MY DOG, CANDY, BARKING. SHE CAME TEARING OUT OF THE BRUSH, AND DIDN'T EVEN STOP WHEN SHE SAW ME...
CANDY...CANDY! HEY! COME BACK HERE, GIRL!!
SHE'S NEVER ACTED THIS WAY BEFORE! WONDER WHAT FRIGHTENED HER?
YEOW!! GREAT DAY IN THE MORNIN'!!
2

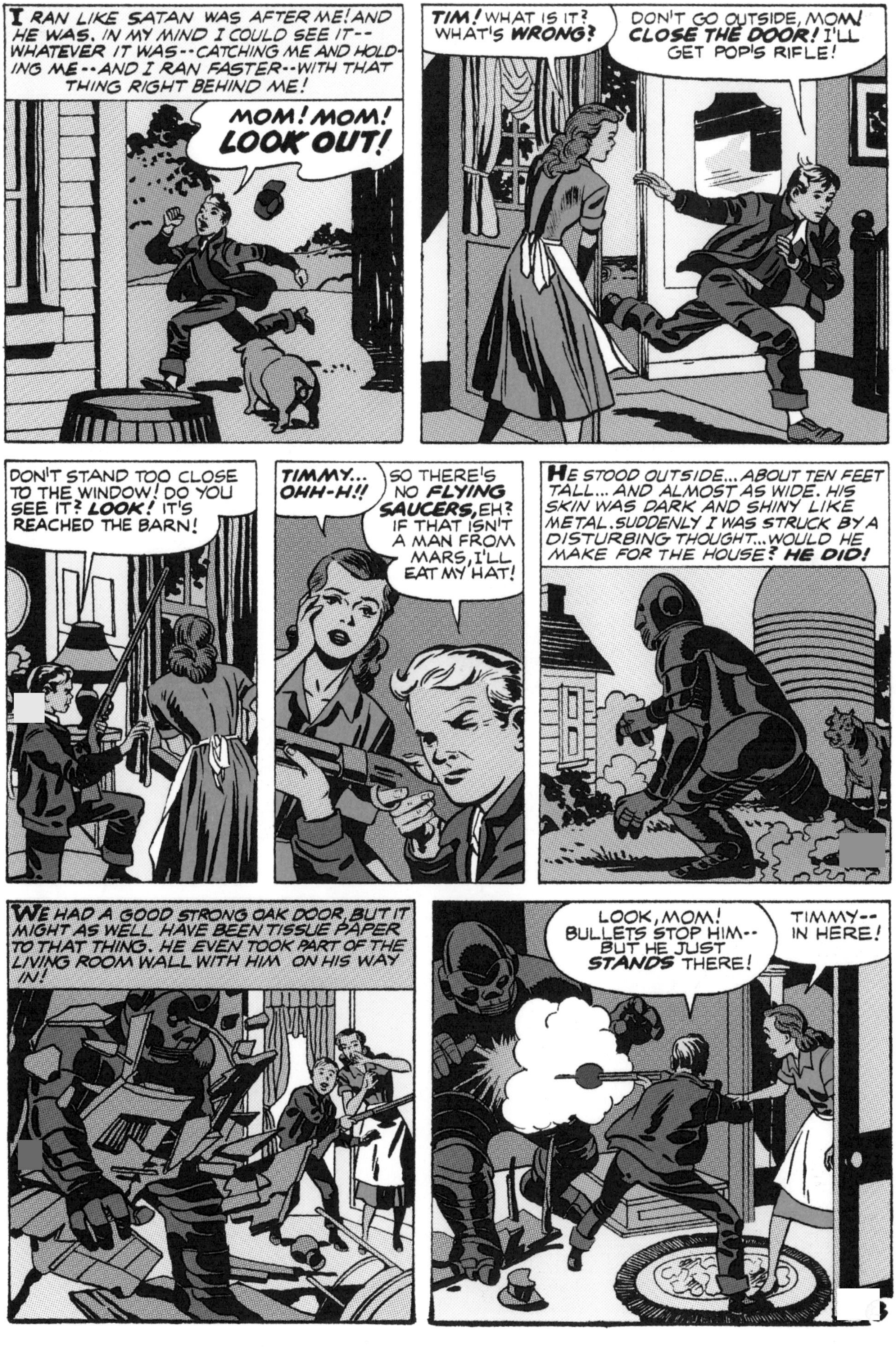
I RAN LIKE SATAN WAS AFTER ME! AND HE WAS. IN MY MIND I COULD SEE IT--WHATEVER IT WAS--CATCHING ME AND HOLDING ME--AND I RAN FASTER--WITH THAT THING RIGHT BEHIND ME!
MOM! MOM! LOOK OUT!
TIM! WHAT IS IT? WHAT'S WRONG?
DON'T GO OUTSIDE, MOM! CLOSE THE DOOR! I'LL GET POP'S RIFLE!
DON'T STAND TOO CLOSE TO THE WINDOW! DO YOU SEE IT? LOOK! IT'S REACHED THE BARN!
TIMMY... OHH-H!!
SO THERE'S NO FLYING SAUCERS, EH? IF THAT ISN'T A MAN FROM MARS, I'LL EAT MY HAT!
HE STOOD OUTSIDE... ABOUT TEN FEET TALL... AND ALMOST AS WIDE. HIS SKIN WAS DARK AND SHINY LIKE METAL. SUDDENLY I WAS STRUCK BY A DISTURBING THOUGHT... WOULD HE MAKE FOR THE HOUSE? HE DID!
WE HAD A GOOD STRONG OAK DOOR, BUT IT MIGHT AS WELL HAVE BEEN TISSUE PAPER TO THAT THING. HE EVEN TOOK PART OF THE LIVING ROOM WALL WITH HIM ON HIS WAY IN!
LOOK, MOM! BULLETS STOP HIM-- BUT HE JUST STANDS THERE!
TIMMY-- IN HERE!

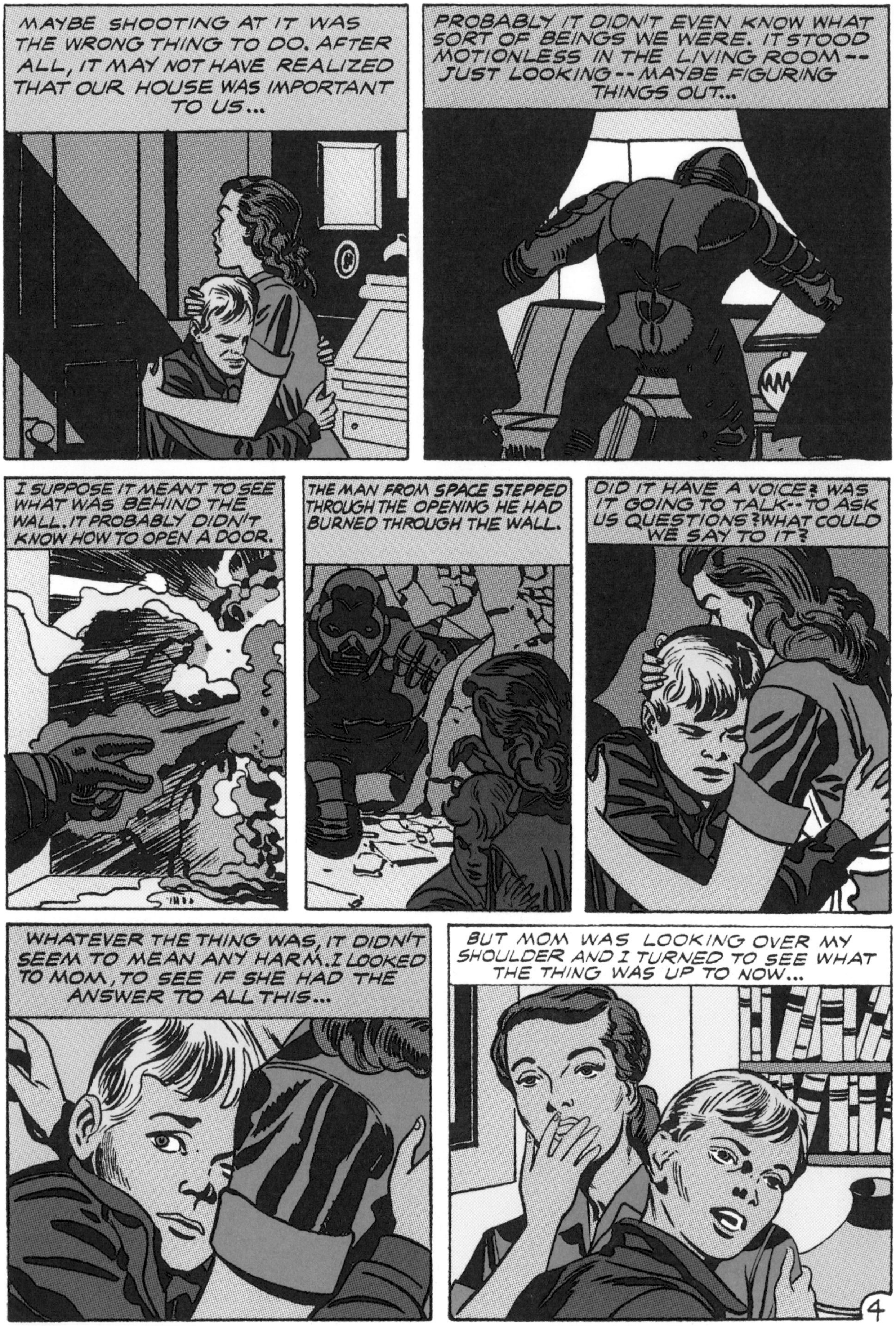
MAYBE SHOOTING AT IT WAS THE WRONG THING TO DO. AFTER ALL, IT MAY NOT HAVE REALIZED THAT OUR HOUSE WAS IMPORTANT TO US...
PROBABLY IT DIDN'T EVEN KNOW WHAT SORT OF BEINGS WE WERE. IT STOOD MOTIONLESS IN THE LIVING ROOM-- JUST LOOKING--MAYBE FIGURING THINGS OUT...
I SUPPOSE IT MEANT TO SEE WHAT WAS BEHIND THE WALL. IT PROBABLY DIDN'T KNOW HOW TO OPEN A DOOR.
THE MAN FROM SPACE STEPPED THROUGH THE OPENING HE HAD BURNED THROUGH THE WALL.
DID IT HAVE A VOICE? WAS IT GOING TO TALK--TO ASK US QUESTIONS? WHAT COULD WE SAY TO IT?
WHATEVER THE THING WAS, IT DIDN'T SEEM TO MEAN ANY HARM. I LOOKED TO MOM, TO SEE IF SHE HAD THE ANSWER TO ALL THIS...
BUT MOM WAS LOOKING OVER MY SHOULDER AND I TURNED TO SEE WHAT THE THING WAS UP TO NOW...
4

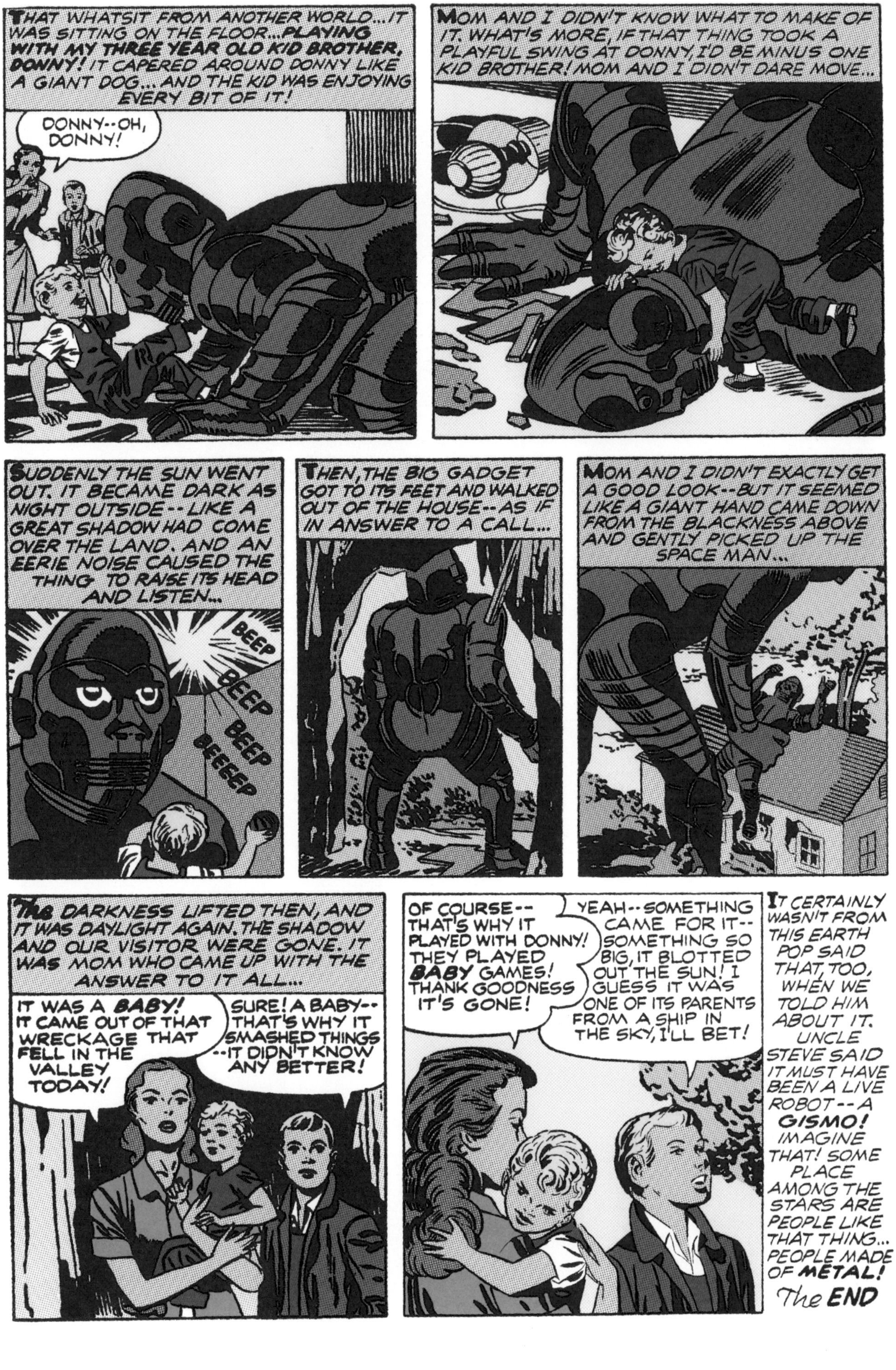
THAT WHATSIT FROM ANOTHER WORLD... IT WAS SITTING ON THE FLOOR... PLAYING WITH MY THREE YEAR OLD KID BROTHER, DONNY! IT CAPERED AROUND DONNY LIKE A GIANT DOG... AND THE KID WAS ENJOYING EVERY BIT OF IT!
DONNY--OH, DONNY!
MOM AND I DIDN'T KNOW WHAT TO MAKE OF IT. WHAT'S MORE, IF THAT THING TOOK A PLAYFUL SWING AT DONNY, I'D BE MINUS ONE KID BROTHER! MOM AND I DIDN'T DARE MOVE...
SUDDENLY THE SUN WENT OUT. IT BECAME DARK AS NIGHT OUTSIDE--LIKE A GREAT SHADOW HAD COME OVER THE LAND. AND AN EERIE NOISE CAUSED THE THING TO RAISE ITS HEAD AND LISTEN...
BEEP
BEEP
BEEP
BEEEEEP
THEN, THE BIG GADGET GOT TO ITS FEET AND WALKED OUT OF THE HOUSE--AS IF IN ANSWER TO A CALL...
MOM AND I DIDN'T EXACTLY GET A GOOD LOOK--BUT IT SEEMED LIKE A GIANT HAND CAME DOWN FROM THE BLACKNESS ABOVE AND GENTLY PICKED UP THE SPACE MAN...
THE DARKNESS LIFTED THEN, AND IT WAS DAYLIGHT AGAIN. THE SHADOW AND OUR VISITOR WERE GONE. IT WAS MOM WHO CAME UP WITH THE ANSWER TO IT ALL...
IT WAS A BABY! IT CAME OUT OF THAT WRECKAGE THAT FELL IN THE VALLEY TODAY!
SURE! A BABY--THAT'S WHY IT SMASHED THINGS--IT DIDN'T KNOW ANY BETTER!
OF COURSE--THAT'S WHY IT PLAYED WITH DONNY! THEY PLAYED BABY GAMES! THANK GOODNESS IT'S GONE!
YEAH--SOMETHING CAME FOR IT--SOMETHING SO BIG, IT BLOTTED OUT THE SUN! I GUESS IT WAS ONE OF ITS PARENTS FROM A SHIP IN THE SKY, I'LL BET!
IT CERTAINLY WASN'T FROM THIS EARTH POP SAID THAT, TOO, WHEN WE TOLD HIM ABOUT IT. UNCLE STEVE SAID IT MUST HAVE BEEN A LIVE ROBOT--A GISMO! IMAGINE THAT! SOME PLACE AMONG THE STARS ARE PEOPLE LIKE THAT THING... PEOPLE MADE OF METAL!
The END

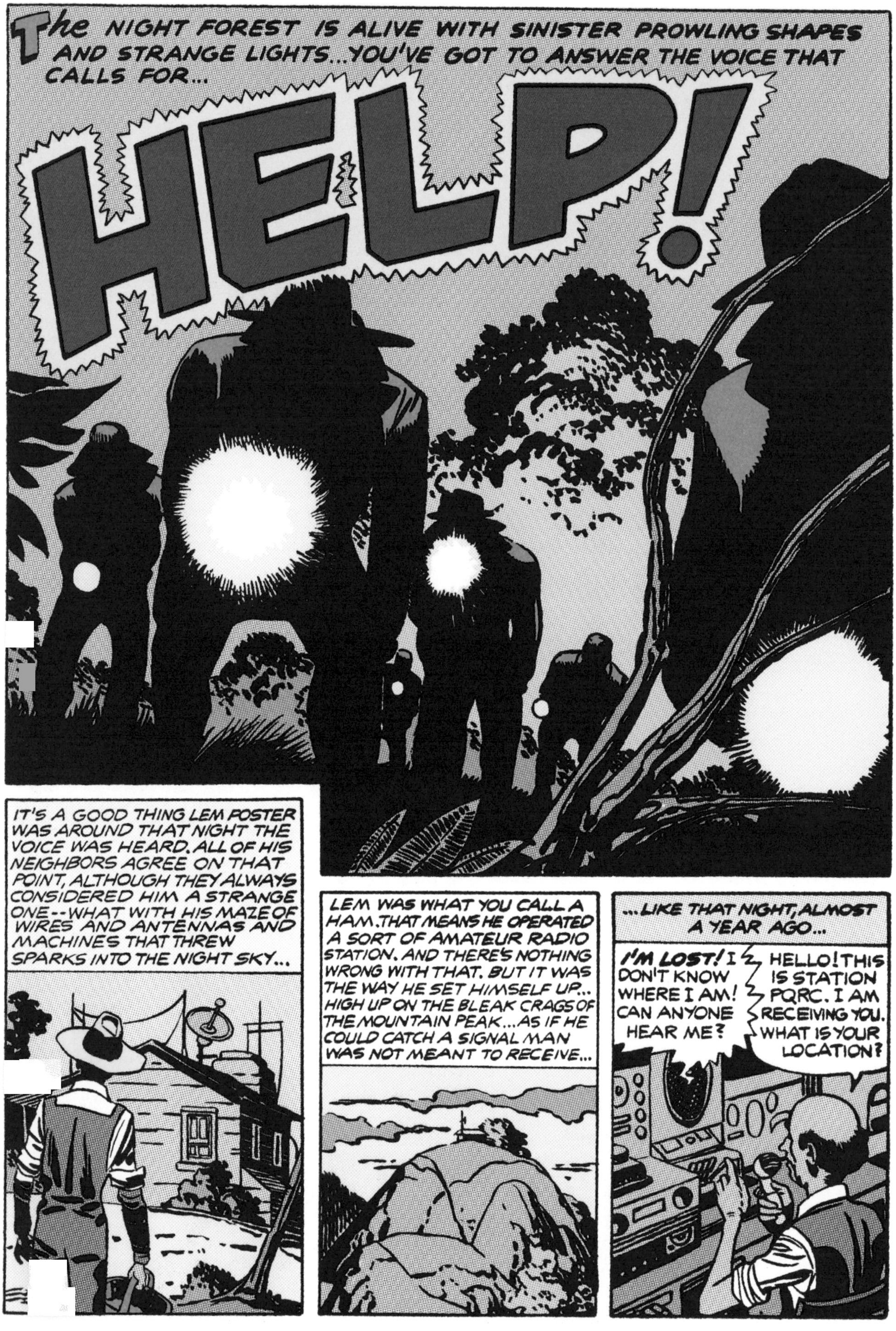
The NIGHT FOREST IS ALIVE WITH SINISTER PROWLING SHAPES AND STRANGE LIGHTS...YOU'VE GOT TO ANSWER THE VOICE THAT CALLS FOR...
HELP!
IT'S A GOOD THING LEM FOSTER WAS AROUND THAT NIGHT THE VOICE WAS HEARD. ALL OF HIS NEIGHBORS AGREE ON THAT POINT, ALTHOUGH THEY ALWAYS CONSIDERED HIM A STRANGE ONE--WHAT WITH HIS MAZE OF WIRES AND ANTENNAS AND MACHINES THAT THREW SPARKS INTO THE NIGHT SKY...
LEM WAS WHAT YOU CALL A HAM. THAT MEANS HE OPERATED A SORT OF AMATEUR RADIO STATION. AND THERE'S NOTHING WRONG WITH THAT. BUT IT WAS THE WAY HE SET HIMSELF UP... HIGH UP ON THE BLEAK CRAGS OF THE MOUNTAIN PEAK...AS IF HE COULD CATCH A SIGNAL MAN WAS NOT MEANT TO RECEIVE...
...LIKE THAT NIGHT, ALMOST A YEAR AGO...
I'M LOST! I DON'T KNOW WHERE I AM! CAN ANYONE HEAR ME?
HELLO! THIS IS STATION PQRC. I AM RECEIVING YOU. WHAT IS YOUR LOCATION?

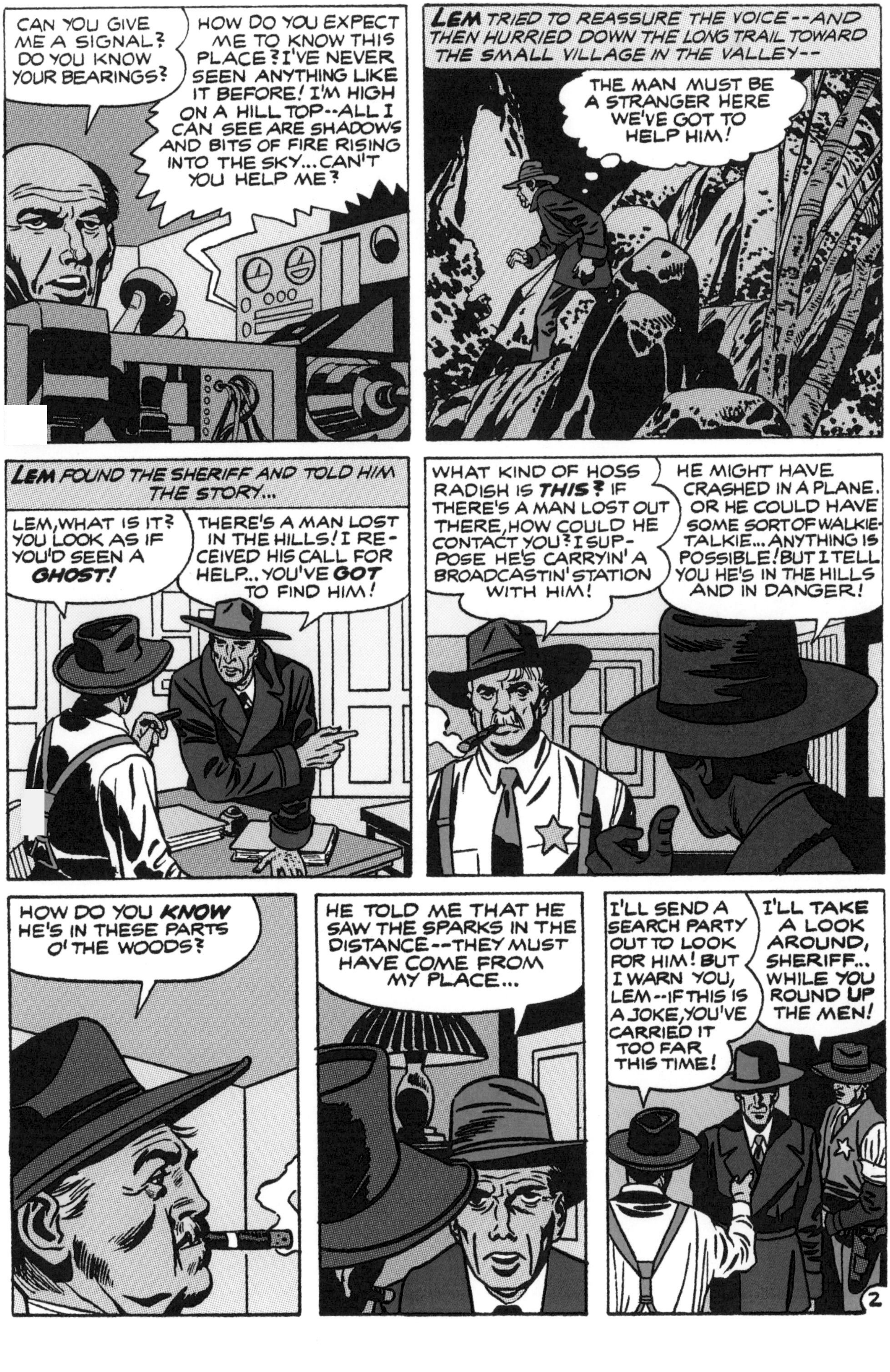
CAN YOU GIVE ME A SIGNAL? DO YOU KNOW YOUR BEARINGS?
HOW DO YOU EXPECT ME TO KNOW THIS PLACE? I'VE NEVER SEEN ANYTHING LIKE IT BEFORE! I'M HIGH ON A HILL TOP--ALL I CAN SEE ARE SHADOWS AND BITS OF FIRE RISING INTO THE SKY...CAN'T YOU HELP ME?
LEM TRIED TO REASSURE THE VOICE--AND THEN HURRIED DOWN THE LONG TRAIL TOWARD THE SMALL VILLAGE IN THE VALLEY--
THE MAN MUST BE A STRANGER HERE WE'VE GOT TO HELP HIM!
LEM FOUND THE SHERIFF AND TOLD HIM THE STORY...
LEM, WHAT IS IT? YOU LOOK AS IF YOU'D SEEN A GHOST!
THERE'S A MAN LOST IN THE HILLS! I RECEIVED HIS CALL FOR HELP...YOU'VE GOT TO FIND HIM!
WHAT KIND OF HOSS RADISH IS THIS? IF THERE'S A MAN LOST OUT THERE, HOW COULD HE CONTACT YOU? I SUPPOSE HE'S CARRYIN' A BROADCASTIN' STATION WITH HIM!
HE MIGHT HAVE CRASHED IN A PLANE. OR HE COULD HAVE SOME SORT OF WALKIE-TALKIE...ANYTHING IS POSSIBLE! BUT I TELL YOU HE'S IN THE HILLS AND IN DANGER!
HOW DO YOU KNOW HE'S IN THESE PARTS O' THE WOODS?
HE TOLD ME THAT HE SAW THE SPARKS IN THE DISTANCE--THEY MUST HAVE COME FROM MY PLACE...
I'LL SEND A SEARCH PARTY OUT TO LOOK FOR HIM! BUT I WARN YOU, LEM--IF THIS IS A JOKE, YOU'VE CARRIED IT TOO FAR THIS TIME!
I'LL TAKE A LOOK AROUND, SHERIFF... WHILE YOU ROUND UP THE MEN!
2

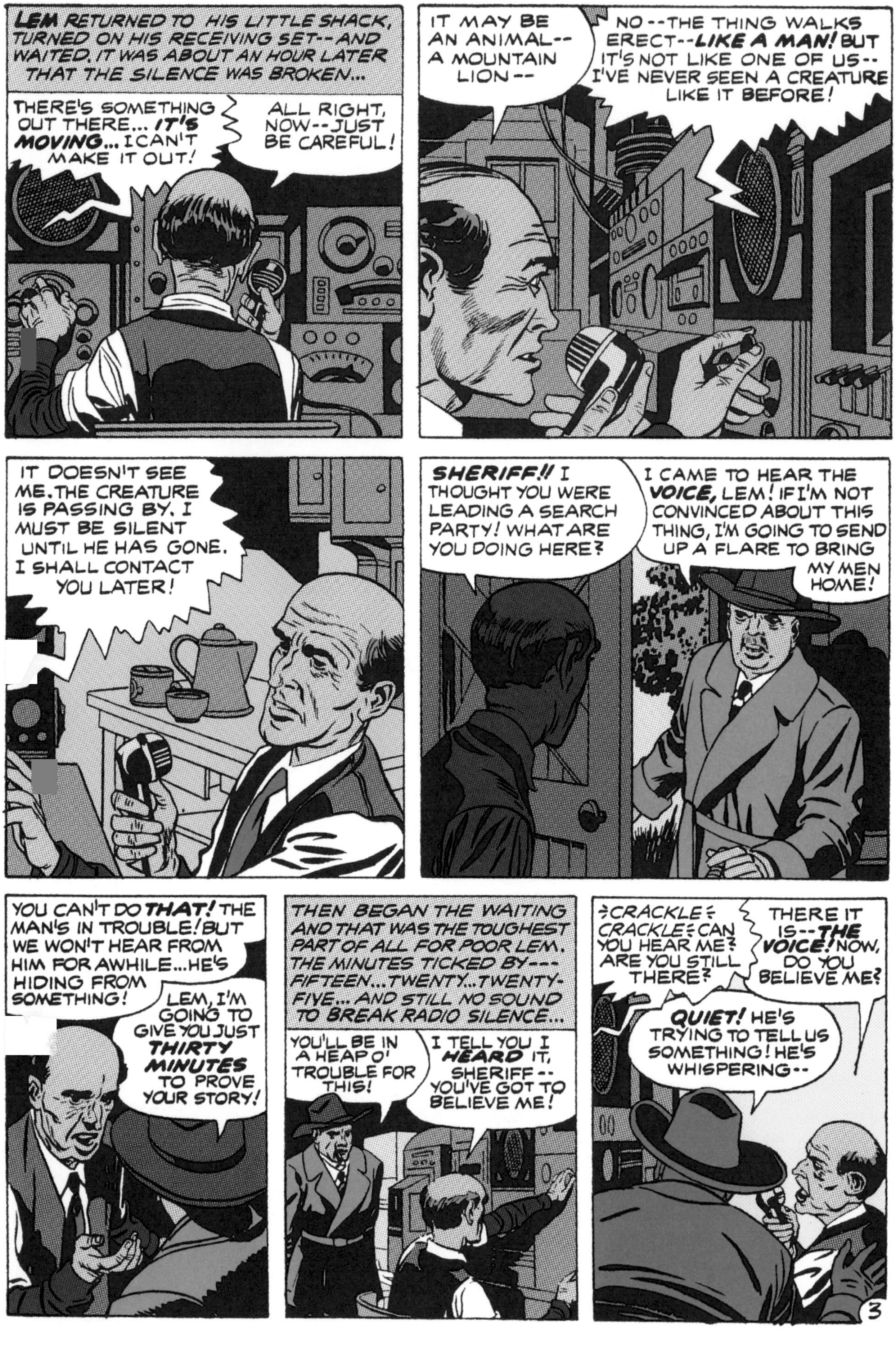
LEM RETURNED TO HIS LITTLE SHACK, TURNED ON HIS RECEIVING SET--AND WAITED. IT WAS ABOUT AN HOUR LATER THAT THE SILENCE WAS BROKEN...
THERE'S SOMETHING OUT THERE... IT'S MOVING... I CAN'T MAKE IT OUT!
ALL RIGHT, NOW--JUST BE CAREFUL!
IT MAY BE AN ANIMAL-- A MOUNTAIN LION--
NO--THE THING WALKS ERECT--LIKE A MAN! BUT IT'S NOT LIKE ONE OF US-- I'VE NEVER SEEN A CREATURE LIKE IT BEFORE!
IT DOESN'T SEE ME. THE CREATURE IS PASSING BY. I MUST BE SILENT UNTIL HE HAS GONE. I SHALL CONTACT YOU LATER!
SHERIFF!! I THOUGHT YOU WERE LEADING A SEARCH PARTY! WHAT ARE YOU DOING HERE?
I CAME TO HEAR THE VOICE, LEM! IF I'M NOT CONVINCED ABOUT THIS THING, I'M GOING TO SEND UP A FLARE TO BRING MY MEN HOME!
YOU CAN'T DO THAT! THE MAN'S IN TROUBLE! BUT WE WON'T HEAR FROM HIM FOR AWHILE...HE'S HIDING FROM SOMETHING!
LEM, I'M GOING TO GIVE YOU JUST THIRTY MINUTES TO PROVE YOUR STORY!
THEN BEGAN THE WAITING AND THAT WAS THE TOUGHEST PART OF ALL FOR POOR LEM. THE MINUTES TICKED BY--- FIFTEEN...TWENTY...TWENTY-FIVE... AND STILL NO SOUND TO BREAK RADIO SILENCE...
YOU'LL BE IN A HEAP O' TROUBLE FOR THIS!
I TELL YOU I HEARD IT, SHERIFF-- YOU'VE GOT TO BELIEVE ME!
CRACKLE CRACKLE CAN YOU HEAR ME? ARE YOU STILL THERE?
THERE IT IS--THE VOICE! NOW, DO YOU BELIEVE ME?
QUIET! HE'S TRYING TO TELL US SOMETHING! HE'S WHISPERING--
3

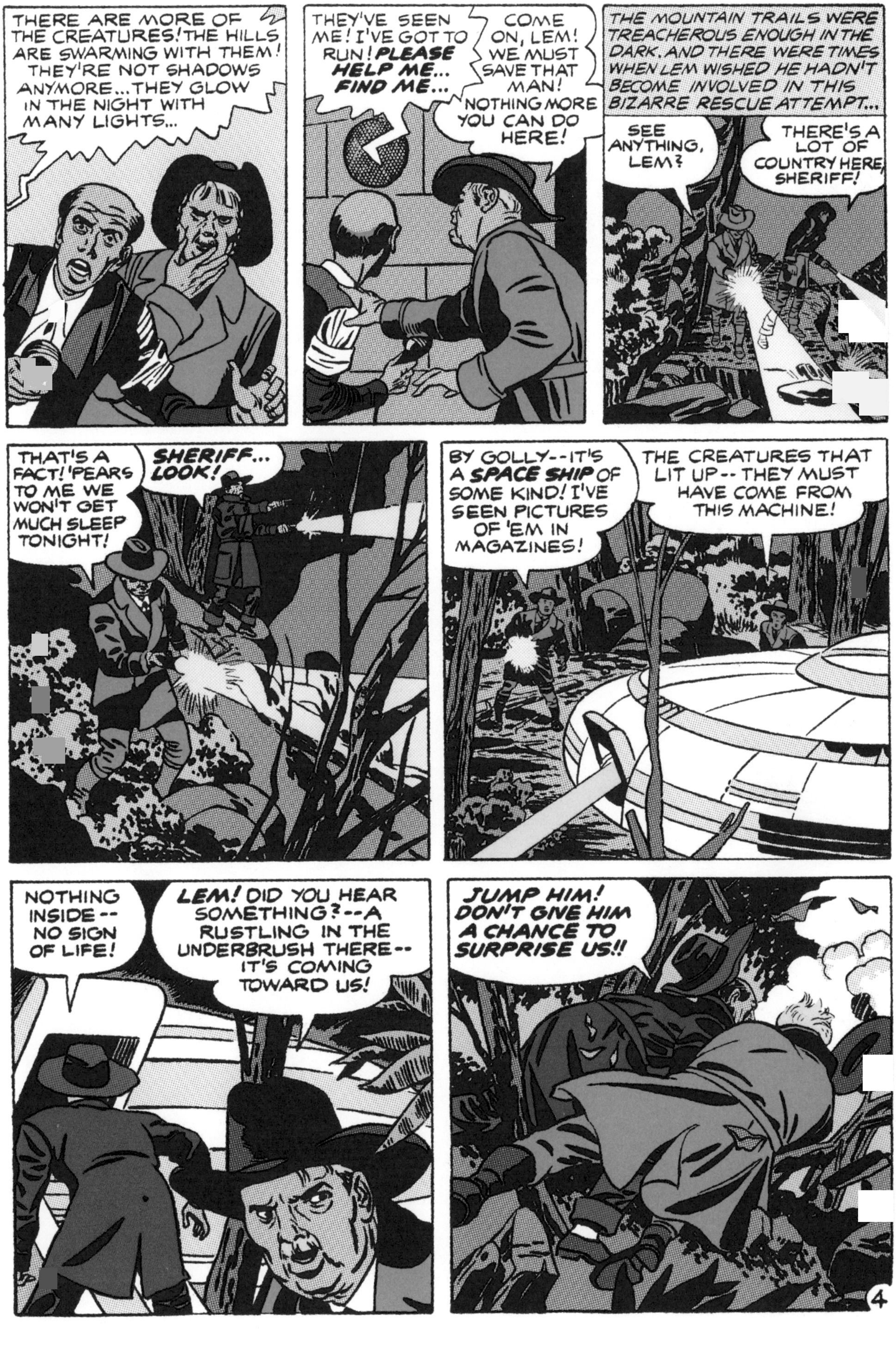
THERE ARE MORE OF THE CREATURES! THE HILLS ARE SWARMING WITH THEM! THEY'RE NOT SHADOWS ANYMORE... THEY GLOW IN THE NIGHT WITH MANY LIGHTS...
THEY'VE SEEN ME! I'VE GOT TO RUN! PLEASE HELP ME... FIND ME...
COME ON, LEM! WE MUST SAVE THAT MAN! NOTHING MORE YOU CAN DO HERE!
THE MOUNTAIN TRAILS WERE TREACHEROUS ENOUGH IN THE DARK, AND THERE WERE TIMES WHEN LEM WISHED HE HADN'T BECOME INVOLVED IN THIS BIZARRE RESCUE ATTEMPT...
SEE ANYTHING, LEM?
THERE'S A LOT OF COUNTRY HERE, SHERIFF!
THAT'S A FACT! 'PEARS TO ME WE WON'T GET MUCH SLEEP TONIGHT!
SHERIFF... LOOK!
BY GOLLY--IT'S A SPACE SHIP OF SOME KIND! I'VE SEEN PICTURES OF 'EM IN MAGAZINES!
THE CREATURES THAT LIT UP--THEY MUST HAVE COME FROM THIS MACHINE!
NOTHING INSIDE--NO SIGN OF LIFE!
LEM! DID YOU HEAR SOMETHING?--A RUSTLING IN THE UNDERBRUSH THERE--IT'S COMING TOWARD US!
JUMP HIM! DON'T GIVE HIM A CHANCE TO SURPRISE US!!
4

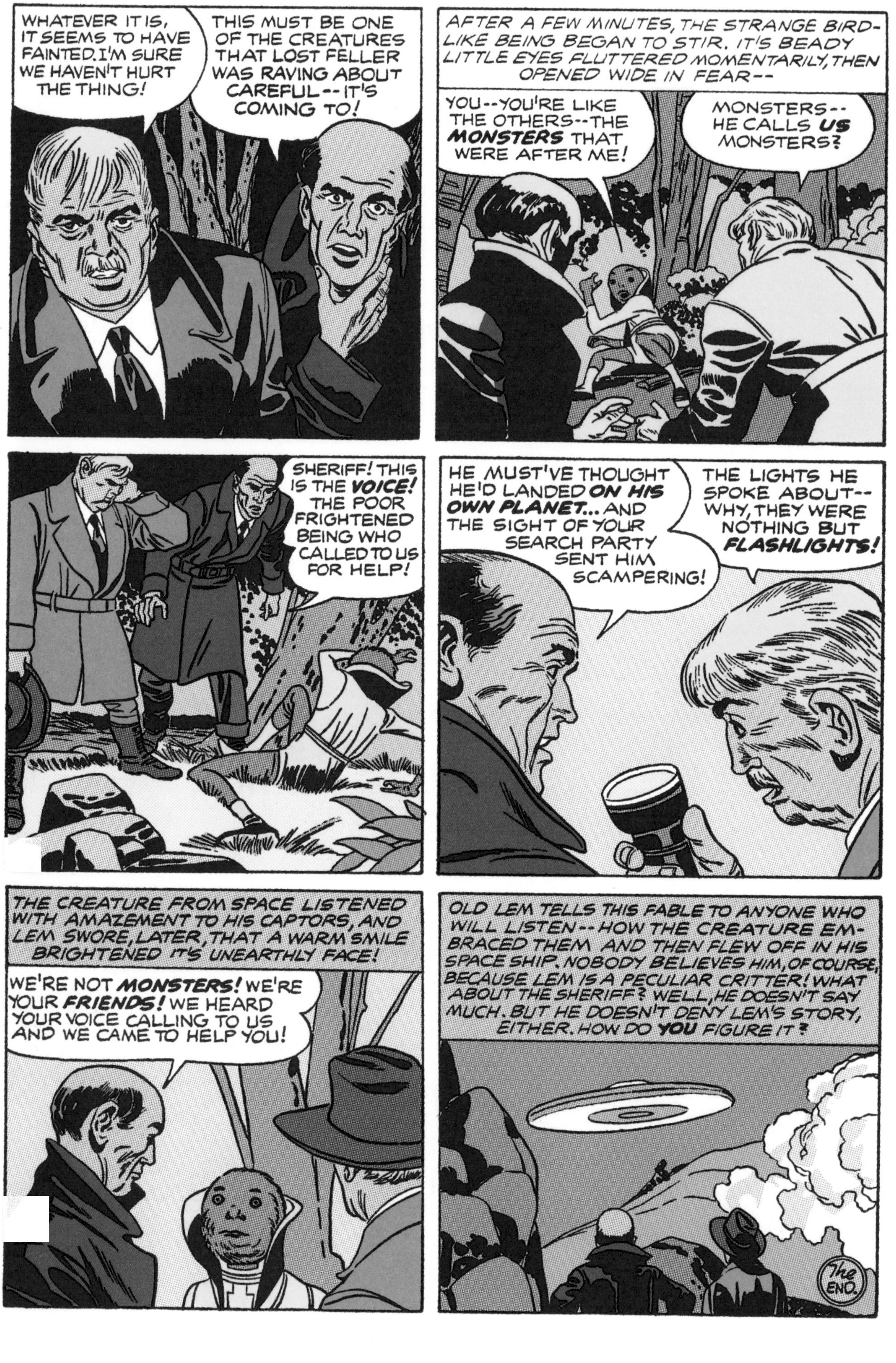
WHATEVER IT IS, IT SEEMS TO HAVE FAINTED. I'M SURE WE HAVEN'T HURT THE THING!
THIS MUST BE ONE OF THE CREATURES THAT LOST FELLER WAS RAVING ABOUT CAREFUL -- IT'S COMING TO!
AFTER A FEW MINUTES, THE STRANGE BIRD-LIKE BEING BEGAN TO STIR. IT'S BEADY LITTLE EYES FLUTTERED MOMENTARILY, THEN OPENED WIDE IN FEAR --
YOU -- YOU'RE LIKE THE OTHERS -- THE MONSTERS THAT WERE AFTER ME!
MONSTERS -- HE CALLS US MONSTERS?
SHERIFF! THIS IS THE VOICE! THE POOR FRIGHTENED BEING WHO CALLED TO US FOR HELP!
HE MUST'VE THOUGHT HE'D LANDED ON HIS OWN PLANET... AND THE SIGHT OF YOUR SEARCH PARTY SENT HIM SCAMPERING!
THE LIGHTS HE SPOKE ABOUT -- WHY, THEY WERE NOTHING BUT FLASHLIGHTS!
THE CREATURE FROM SPACE LISTENED WITH AMAZEMENT TO HIS CAPTORS, AND LEM SWORE, LATER, THAT A WARM SMILE BRIGHTENED IT'S UNEARTHLY FACE!
WE'RE NOT MONSTERS! WE'RE YOUR FRIENDS! WE HEARD YOUR VOICE CALLING TO US AND WE CAME TO HELP YOU!
OLD LEM TELLS THIS FABLE TO ANYONE WHO WILL LISTEN -- HOW THE CREATURE EMBRACED THEM AND THEN FLEW OFF IN HIS SPACE SHIP. NOBODY BELIEVES HIM, OF COURSE, BECAUSE LEM IS A PECULIAR CRITTER! WHAT ABOUT THE SHERIFF? WELL, HE DOESN'T SAY MUCH. BUT HE DOESN'T DENY LEM'S STORY, EITHER. HOW DO YOU FIGURE IT?
The END.

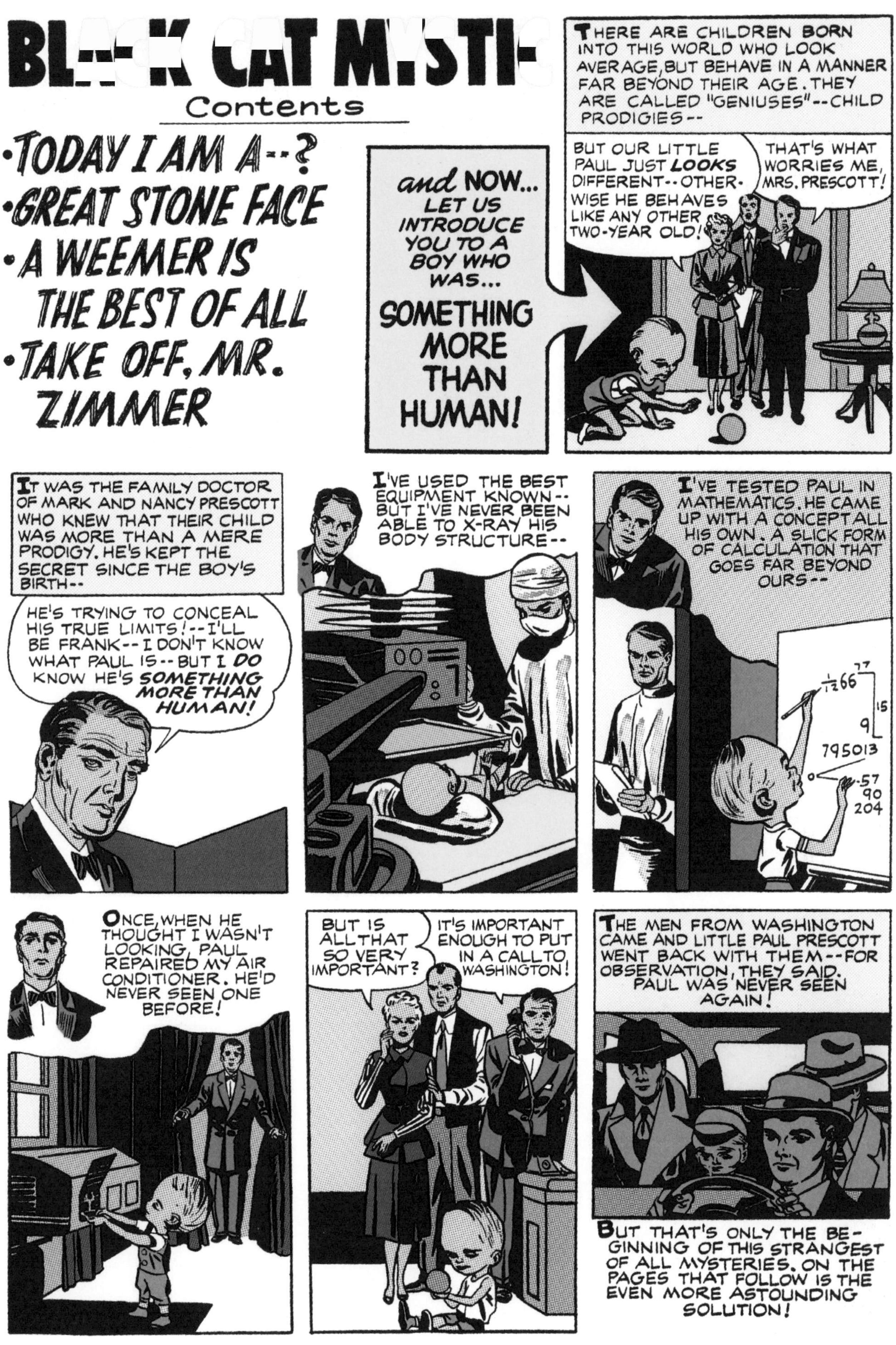
Contents
•TODAY I AM A--?
•GREAT STONE FACE
•A WEEMER IS THE BEST OF ALL
•TAKE OFF, MR. ZIMMER
THERE ARE CHILDREN BORN INTO THIS WORLD WHO LOOK AVERAGE, BUT BEHAVE IN A MANNER FAR BEYOND THEIR AGE. THEY ARE CALLED "GENIUSES"--CHILD PRODIGIES--
and NOW... LET US INTRODUCE YOU TO A BOY WHO WAS... SOMETHING MORE THAN HUMAN!
BUT OUR LITTLE PAUL JUST LOOKS DIFFERENT--OTHERWISE HE BEHAVES LIKE ANY OTHER TWO-YEAR OLD!
THAT'S WHAT WORRIES ME, MRS. PRESCOTT!
IT WAS THE FAMILY DOCTOR OF MARK AND NANCY PRESCOTT WHO KNEW THAT THEIR CHILD WAS MORE THAN A MERE PRODIGY. HE'S KEPT THE SECRET SINCE THE BOY'S BIRTH--
HE'S TRYING TO CONCEAL HIS TRUE LIMITS!--I'LL BE FRANK--I DON'T KNOW WHAT PAUL IS--BUT I DO KNOW HE'S SOMETHING MORE THAN HUMAN!
I'VE USED THE BEST EQUIPMENT KNOWN--BUT I'VE NEVER BEEN ABLE TO X-RAY HIS BODY STRUCTURE--
I'VE TESTED PAUL IN MATHEMATICS. HE CAME UP WITH A CONCEPT ALL HIS OWN. A SLICK FORM OF CALCULATION THAT GOES FAR BEYOND OURS--
ONCE, WHEN HE THOUGHT I WASN'T LOOKING, PAUL REPAIRED MY AIR CONDITIONER. HE'D NEVER SEEN ONE BEFORE!
BUT IS ALL THAT SO VERY IMPORTANT?
IT'S IMPORTANT ENOUGH TO PUT IN A CALL TO WASHINGTON!
THE MEN FROM WASHINGTON CAME AND LITTLE PAUL PRESCOTT WENT BACK WITH THEM--FOR OBSERVATION, THEY SAID. PAUL WAS NEVER SEEN AGAIN!
BUT THAT'S ONLY THE BEGINNING OF THIS STRANGEST OF ALL MYSTERIES. ON THE PAGES THAT FOLLOW IS THE EVEN MORE ASTOUNDING SOLUTION!

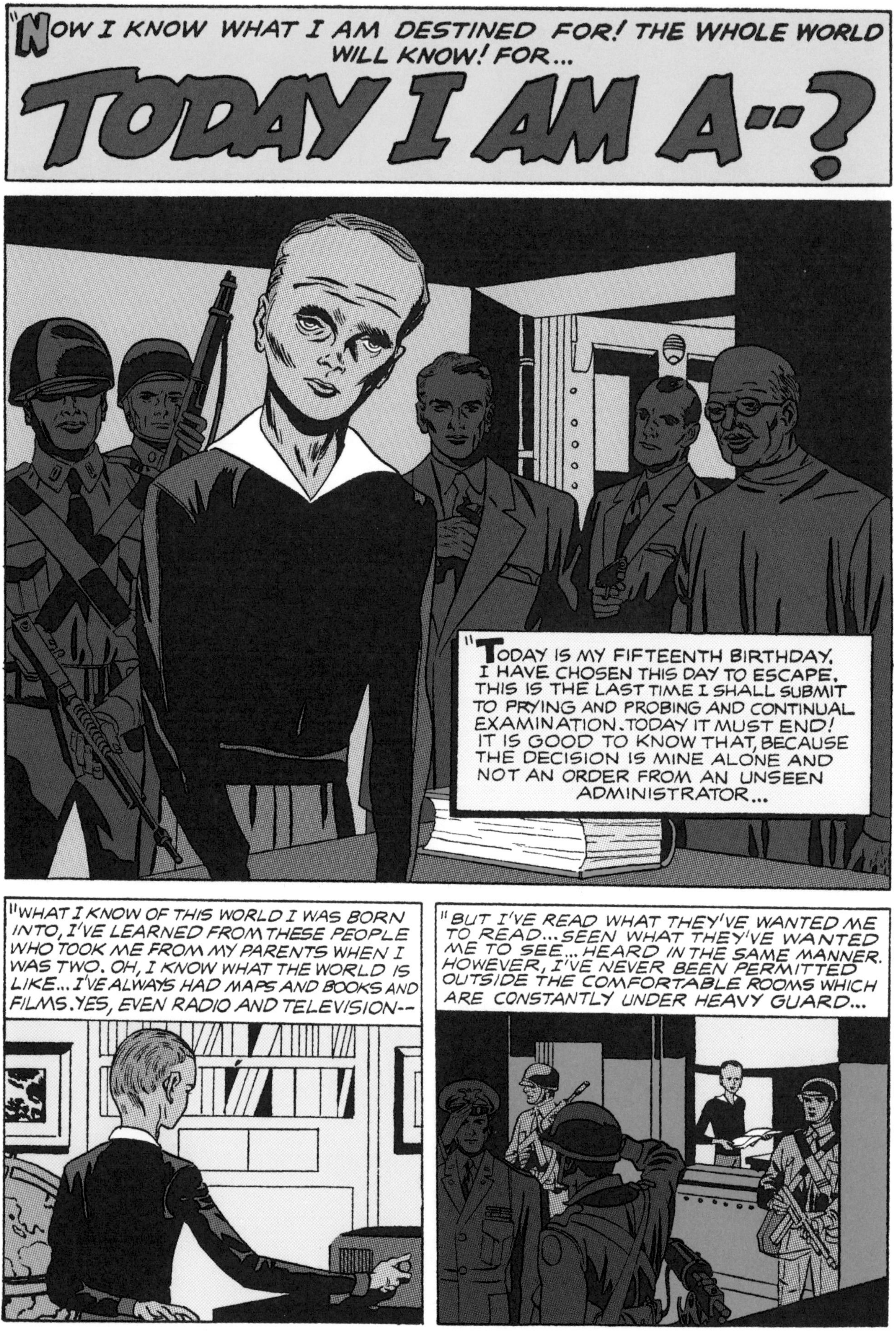
"NOW I KNOW WHAT I AM DESTINED FOR! THE WHOLE WORLD WILL KNOW! FOR...
TODAY I AM A--?
"TODAY IS MY FIFTEENTH BIRTHDAY. I HAVE CHOSEN THIS DAY TO ESCAPE. THIS IS THE LAST TIME I SHALL SUBMIT TO PRYING AND PROBING AND CONTINUAL EXAMINATION. TODAY IT MUST END! IT IS GOOD TO KNOW THAT, BECAUSE THE DECISION IS MINE ALONE AND NOT AN ORDER FROM AN UNSEEN ADMINISTRATOR...
"WHAT I KNOW OF THIS WORLD I WAS BORN INTO, I'VE LEARNED FROM THESE PEOPLE WHO TOOK ME FROM MY PARENTS WHEN I WAS TWO. OH, I KNOW WHAT THE WORLD IS LIKE... I'VE ALWAYS HAD MAPS AND BOOKS AND FILMS. YES, EVEN RADIO AND TELEVISION--
"BUT I'VE READ WHAT THEY'VE WANTED ME TO READ... SEEN WHAT THEY'VE WANTED ME TO SEE... HEARD IN THE SAME MANNER. HOWEVER, I'VE NEVER BEEN PERMITTED OUTSIDE THE COMFORTABLE ROOMS WHICH ARE CONSTANTLY UNDER HEAVY GUARD...

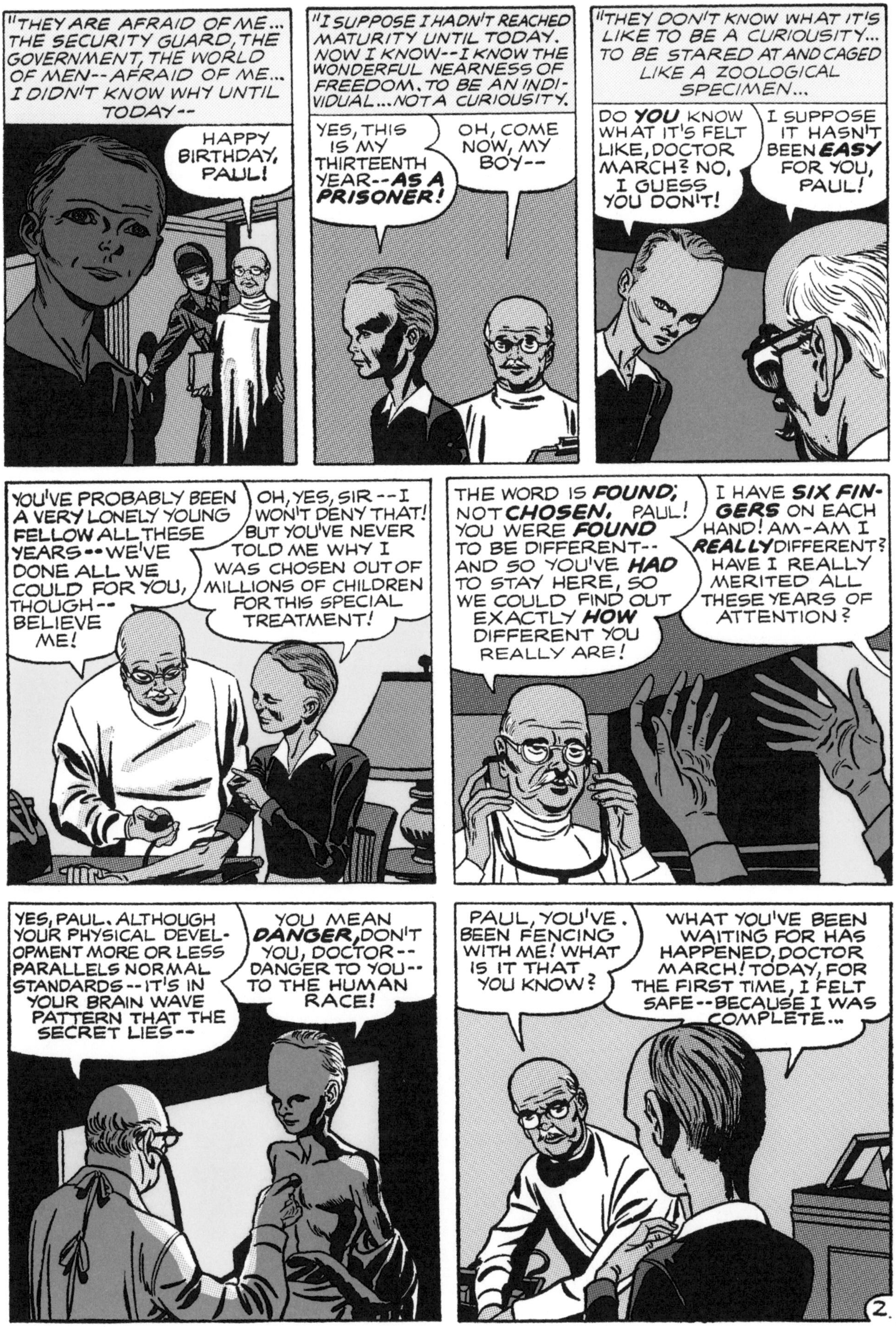

"THEY ARE AFRAID OF ME... THE SECURITY GUARD, THE GOVERNMENT, THE WORLD OF MEN--AFRAID OF ME... I DIDN'T KNOW WHY UNTIL TODAY--
HAPPY BIRTHDAY, PAUL!
"I SUPPOSE I HADN'T REACHED MATURITY UNTIL TODAY. NOW I KNOW--I KNOW THE WONDERFUL NEARNESS OF FREEDOM. TO BE AN INDIVIDUAL... NOT A CURIOUSITY.
YES, THIS IS MY THIRTEENTH YEAR--AS A PRISONER!
OH, COME NOW, MY BOY--
"THEY DON'T KNOW WHAT IT'S LIKE TO BE A CURIOUSITY... TO BE STARED AT AND CAGED LIKE A ZOOLOGICAL SPECIMEN...
DO YOU KNOW WHAT IT'S FELT LIKE, DOCTOR MARCH? NO, I GUESS YOU DON'T!
I SUPPOSE IT HASN'T BEEN EASY FOR YOU, PAUL!
YOU'VE PROBABLY BEEN A VERY LONELY YOUNG FELLOW ALL THESE YEARS--WE'VE DONE ALL WE COULD FOR YOU, THOUGH--BELIEVE ME!
OH, YES, SIR--I WON'T DENY THAT! BUT YOU'VE NEVER TOLD ME WHY I WAS CHOSEN OUT OF MILLIONS OF CHILDREN FOR THIS SPECIAL TREATMENT!
THE WORD IS FOUND; NOT CHOSEN, PAUL! YOU WERE FOUND TO BE DIFFERENT--AND SO YOU'VE HAD TO STAY HERE, SO WE COULD FIND OUT EXACTLY HOW DIFFERENT YOU REALLY ARE!
I HAVE SIX FINGERS ON EACH HAND! AM-AM I REALLY DIFFERENT? HAVE I REALLY MERITED ALL THESE YEARS OF ATTENTION?
YES, PAUL. ALTHOUGH YOUR PHYSICAL DEVELOPMENT MORE OR LESS PARALLELS NORMAL STANDARDS--IT'S IN YOUR BRAIN WAVE PATTERN THAT THE SECRET LIES--
YOU MEAN DANGER, DON'T YOU, DOCTOR--DANGER TO YOU--TO THE HUMAN RACE!
PAUL, YOU'VE BEEN FENCING WITH ME! WHAT IS IT THAT YOU KNOW?
WHAT YOU'VE BEEN WAITING FOR HAS HAPPENED, DOCTOR MARCH! TODAY, FOR THE FIRST TIME, I FELT SAFE--BECAUSE I WAS COMPLETE...
2.

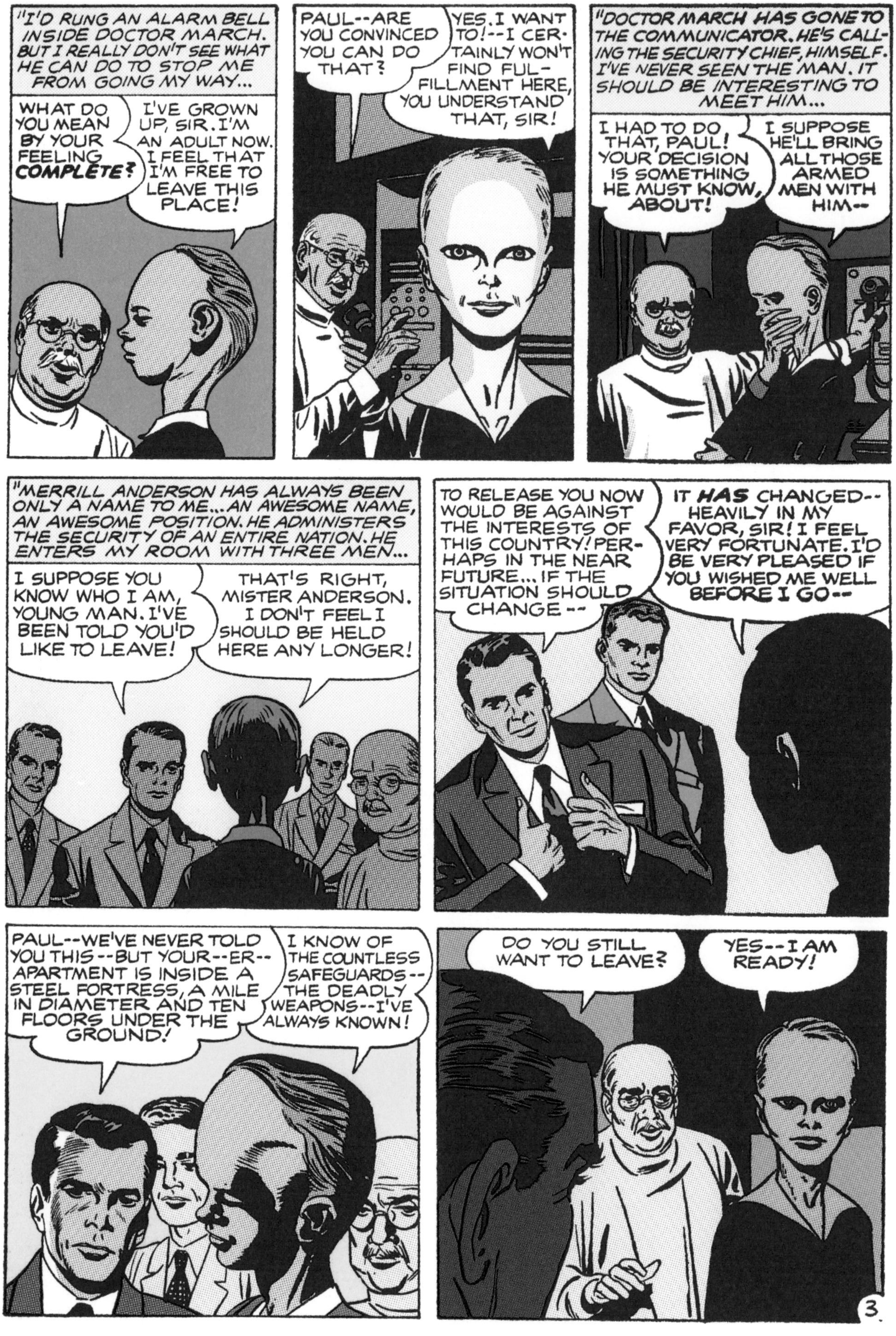
"I'D RUNG AN ALARM BELL INSIDE DOCTOR MARCH. BUT I REALLY DON'T SEE WHAT HE CAN DO TO STOP ME FROM GOING MY WAY...
WHAT DO YOU MEAN BY YOUR FEELING COMPLETE?
I'VE GROWN UP, SIR. I'M AN ADULT NOW. I FEEL THAT I'M FREE TO LEAVE THIS PLACE!
PAUL--ARE YOU CONVINCED YOU CAN DO THAT?
YES. I WANT TO!--I CERTAINLY WON'T FIND FULFILLMENT HERE, YOU UNDERSTAND THAT, SIR!
"DOCTOR MARCH HAS GONE TO THE COMMUNICATOR. HE'S CALLING THE SECURITY CHIEF, HIMSELF. I'VE NEVER SEEN THE MAN. IT SHOULD BE INTERESTING TO MEET HIM...
I HAD TO DO THAT, PAUL! YOUR DECISION IS SOMETHING HE MUST KNOW, ABOUT!
I SUPPOSE HE'LL BRING ALL THOSE ARMED MEN WITH HIM--
"MERRILL ANDERSON HAS ALWAYS BEEN ONLY A NAME TO ME... AN AWESOME NAME, AN AWESOME POSITION. HE ADMINISTERS THE SECURITY OF AN ENTIRE NATION. HE ENTERS MY ROOM WITH THREE MEN...
I SUPPOSE YOU KNOW WHO I AM, YOUNG MAN. I'VE BEEN TOLD YOU'D LIKE TO LEAVE!
THAT'S RIGHT, MISTER ANDERSON. I DON'T FEEL I SHOULD BE HELD HERE ANY LONGER!
TO RELEASE YOU NOW WOULD BE AGAINST THE INTERESTS OF THIS COUNTRY! PERHAPS IN THE NEAR FUTURE... IF THE SITUATION SHOULD CHANGE--
IT HAS CHANGED--HEAVILY IN MY FAVOR, SIR! I FEEL VERY FORTUNATE. I'D BE VERY PLEASED IF YOU WISHED ME WELL BEFORE I GO--
PAUL--WE'VE NEVER TOLD YOU THIS--BUT YOUR--ER--APARTMENT IS INSIDE A STEEL FORTRESS, A MILE IN DIAMETER AND TEN FLOORS UNDER THE GROUND!
I KNOW OF THE COUNTLESS SAFEGUARDS--THE DEADLY WEAPONS--I'VE ALWAYS KNOWN!
DO YOU STILL WANT TO LEAVE?
YES--I AM READY!
3.

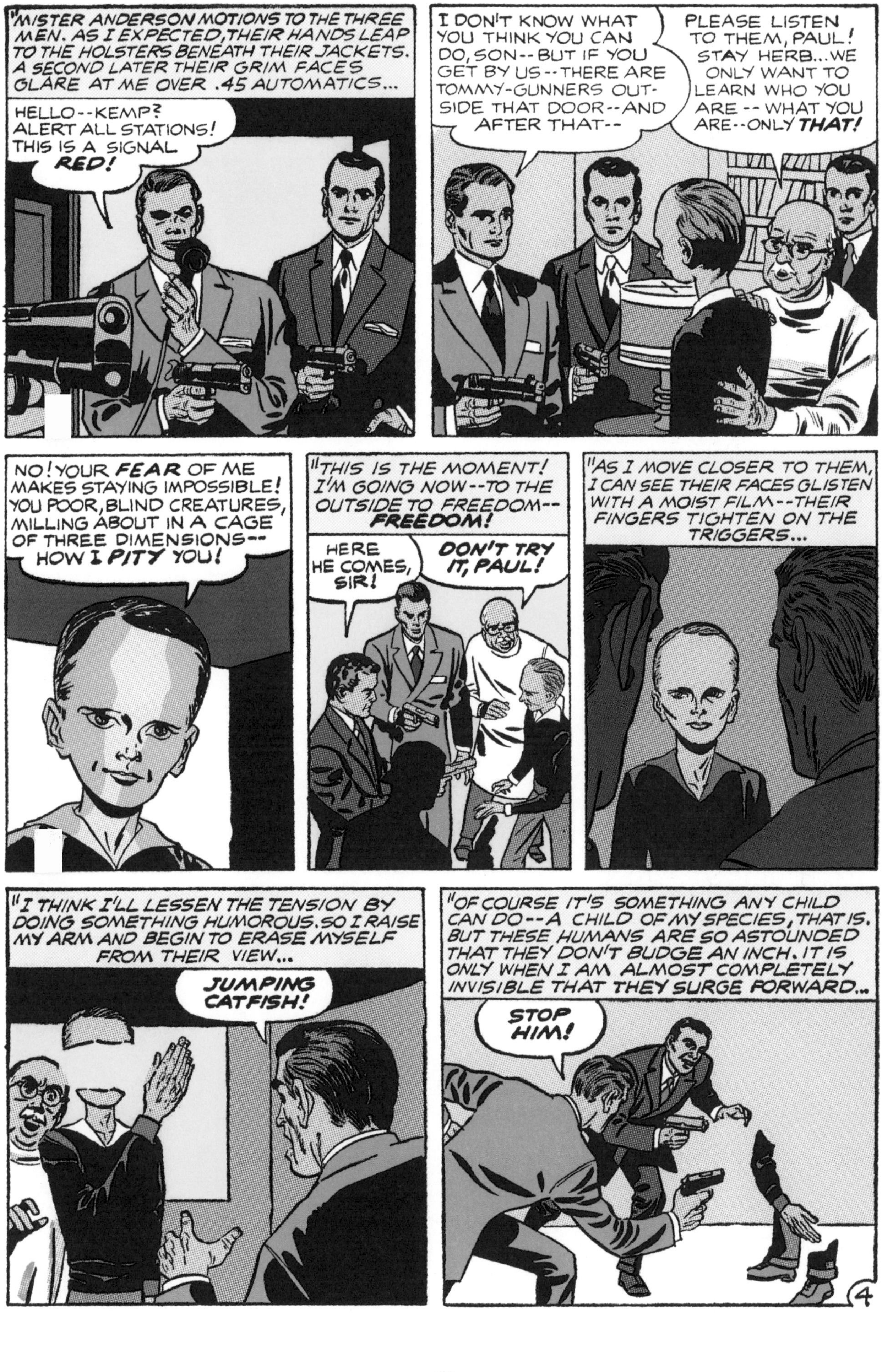
"MISTER ANDERSON MOTIONS TO THE THREE MEN. AS I EXPECTED, THEIR HANDS LEAP TO THE HOLSTERS BENEATH THEIR JACKETS. A SECOND LATER THEIR GRIM FACES GLARE AT ME OVER .45 AUTOMATICS...
HELLO--KEMP? ALERT ALL STATIONS! THIS IS A SIGNAL RED!
I DON'T KNOW WHAT YOU THINK YOU CAN DO, SON--BUT IF YOU GET BY US--THERE ARE TOMMY-GUNNERS OUTSIDE THAT DOOR--AND AFTER THAT--
PLEASE LISTEN TO THEM, PAUL! STAY HERB...WE ONLY WANT TO LEARN WHO YOU ARE--WHAT YOU ARE--ONLY THAT!
NO! YOUR FEAR OF ME MAKES STAYING IMPOSSIBLE! YOU POOR, BLIND CREATURES, MILLING ABOUT IN A CAGE OF THREE DIMENSIONS--HOW I PITY YOU!
"THIS IS THE MOMENT! I'M GOING NOW--TO THE OUTSIDE TO FREEDOM--FREEDOM!
HERE HE COMES, SIR!
DON'T TRY IT, PAUL!
"AS I MOVE CLOSER TO THEM, I CAN SEE THEIR FACES GLISTEN WITH A MOIST FILM--THEIR FINGERS TIGHTEN ON THE TRIGGERS...
"I THINK I'LL LESSEN THE TENSION BY DOING SOMETHING HUMOROUS. SO I RAISE MY ARM AND BEGIN TO ERASE MYSELF FROM THEIR VIEW...
JUMPING CATFISH!
"OF COURSE IT'S SOMETHING ANY CHILD CAN DO--A CHILD OF MY SPECIES, THAT IS. BUT THESE HUMANS ARE SO ASTOUNDED THAT THEY DON'T BUDGE AN INCH. IT IS ONLY WHEN I AM ALMOST COMPLETELY INVISIBLE THAT THEY SURGE FORWARD...
STOP HIM!
4

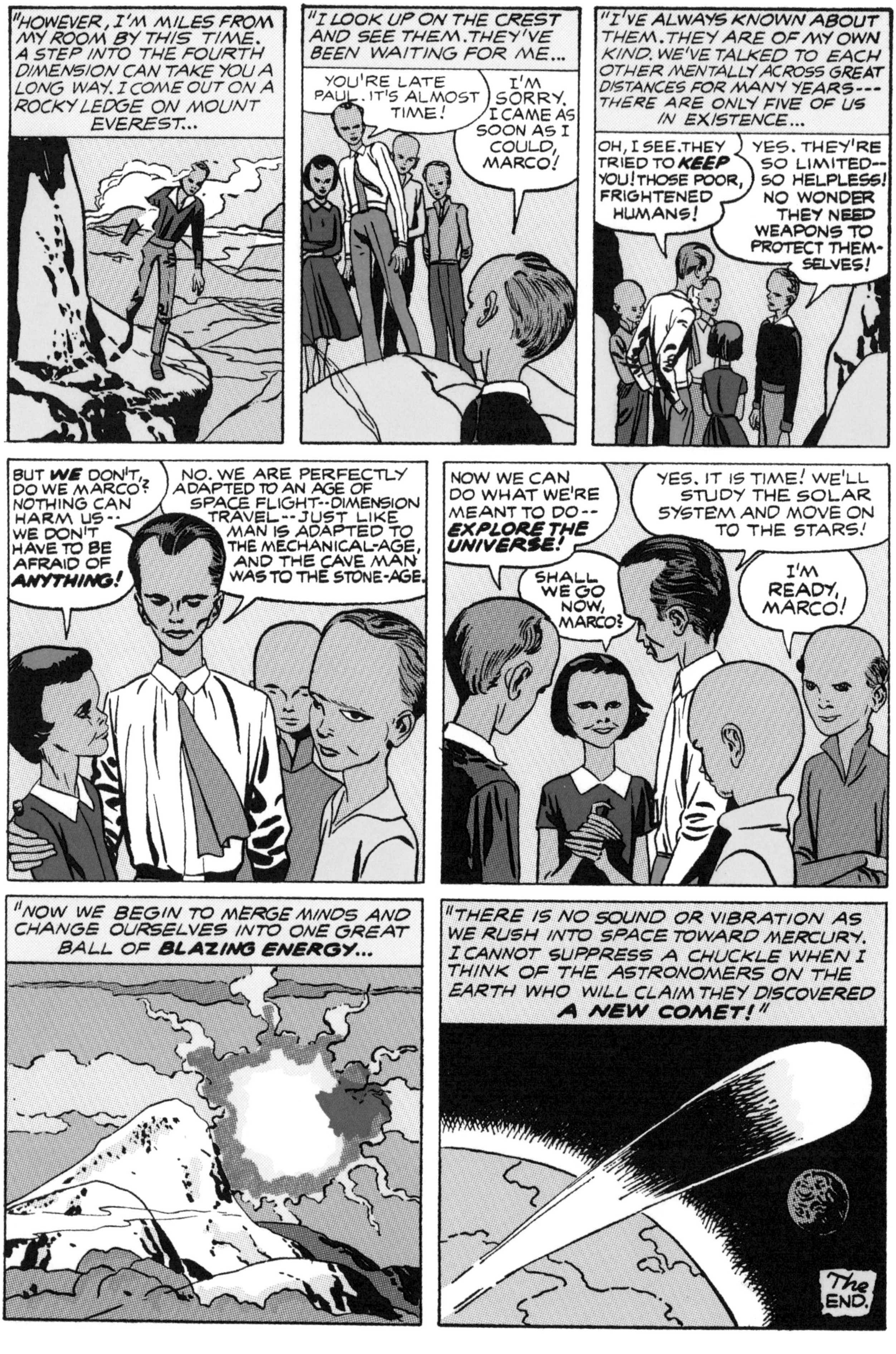
"HOWEVER, I'M MILES FROM MY ROOM BY THIS TIME. A STEP INTO THE FOURTH DIMENSION CAN TAKE YOU A LONG WAY. I COME OUT ON A ROCKY LEDGE ON MOUNT EVEREST...
"I LOOK UP ON THE CREST AND SEE THEM. THEY'VE BEEN WAITING FOR ME...
YOU'RE LATE PAUL. IT'S ALMOST TIME!
I'M SORRY. I CAME AS SOON AS I COULD, MARCO!
"I'VE ALWAYS KNOWN ABOUT THEM. THEY ARE OF MY OWN KIND. WE'VE TALKED TO EACH OTHER MENTALLY ACROSS GREAT DISTANCES FOR MANY YEARS--- THERE ARE ONLY FIVE OF US IN EXISTENCE...
OH, I SEE. THEY TRIED TO KEEP YOU! THOSE POOR, FRIGHTENED HUMANS!
YES. THEY'RE SO LIMITED-- SO HELPLESS! NO WONDER THEY NEED WEAPONS TO PROTECT THEMSELVES!
BUT WE DON'T, DO WE MARCO? NOTHING CAN HARM US-- WE DON'T HAVE TO BE AFRAID OF ANYTHING!
NO. WE ARE PERFECTLY ADAPTED TO AN AGE OF SPACE FLIGHT--DIMENSION TRAVEL--JUST LIKE MAN IS ADAPTED TO THE MECHANICAL-AGE, AND THE CAVE MAN WAS TO THE STONE-AGE.
NOW WE CAN DO WHAT WE'RE MEANT TO DO-- EXPLORE THE UNIVERSE!
YES. IT IS TIME! WE'LL STUDY THE SOLAR SYSTEM AND MOVE ON TO THE STARS!
SHALL WE GO NOW, MARCO?
I'M READY, MARCO!
"NOW WE BEGIN TO MERGE MINDS AND CHANGE OURSELVES INTO ONE GREAT BALL OF BLAZING ENERGY...
"THERE IS NO SOUND OR VIBRATION AS WE RUSH INTO SPACE TOWARD MERCURY. I CANNOT SUPPRESS A CHUCKLE WHEN I THINK OF THE ASTRONOMERS ON THE EARTH WHO WILL CLAIM THEY DISCOVERED A NEW COMET!"
The END.

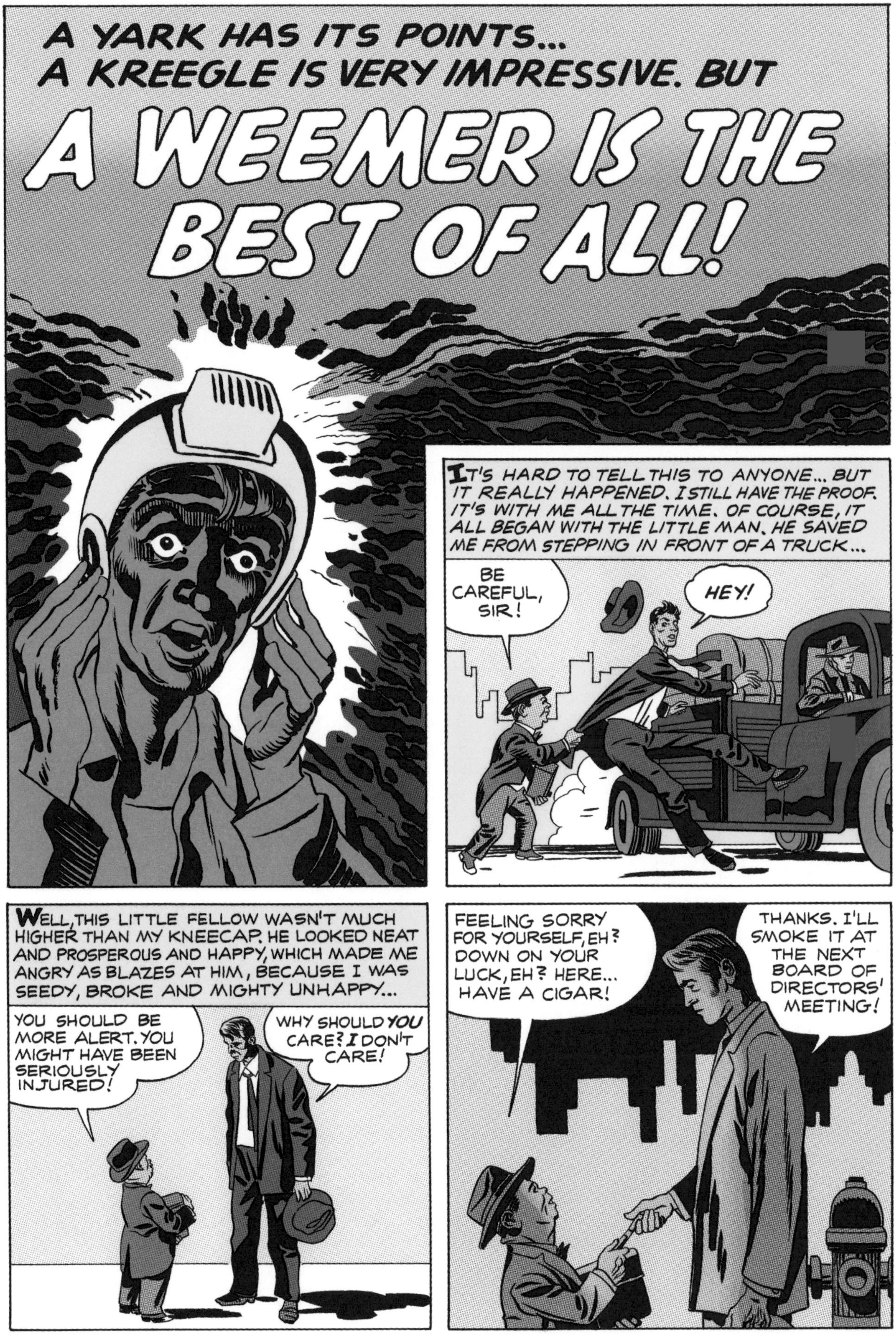
A YARK HAS ITS POINTS...
A KREEGLE IS VERY IMPRESSIVE. BUT
A WEEMER IS THE BEST OF ALL!
IT'S HARD TO TELL THIS TO ANYONE... BUT IT REALLY HAPPENED. I STILL HAVE THE PROOF. IT'S WITH ME ALL THE TIME. OF COURSE, IT ALL BEGAN WITH THE LITTLE MAN. HE SAVED ME FROM STEPPING IN FRONT OF A TRUCK...
BE CAREFUL, SIR!
HEY!
WELL, THIS LITTLE FELLOW WASN'T MUCH HIGHER THAN MY KNEECAP. HE LOOKED NEAT AND PROSPEROUS AND HAPPY, WHICH MADE ME ANGRY AS BLAZES AT HIM, BECAUSE I WAS SEEDY, BROKE AND MIGHTY UNHAPPY...
YOU SHOULD BE MORE ALERT. YOU MIGHT HAVE BEEN SERIOUSLY INJURED!
WHY SHOULD YOU CARE? I DON'T CARE!
FEELING SORRY FOR YOURSELF, EH? DOWN ON YOUR LUCK, EH? HERE... HAVE A CIGAR!
THANKS. I'LL SMOKE IT AT THE NEXT BOARD OF DIRECTORS' MEETING!

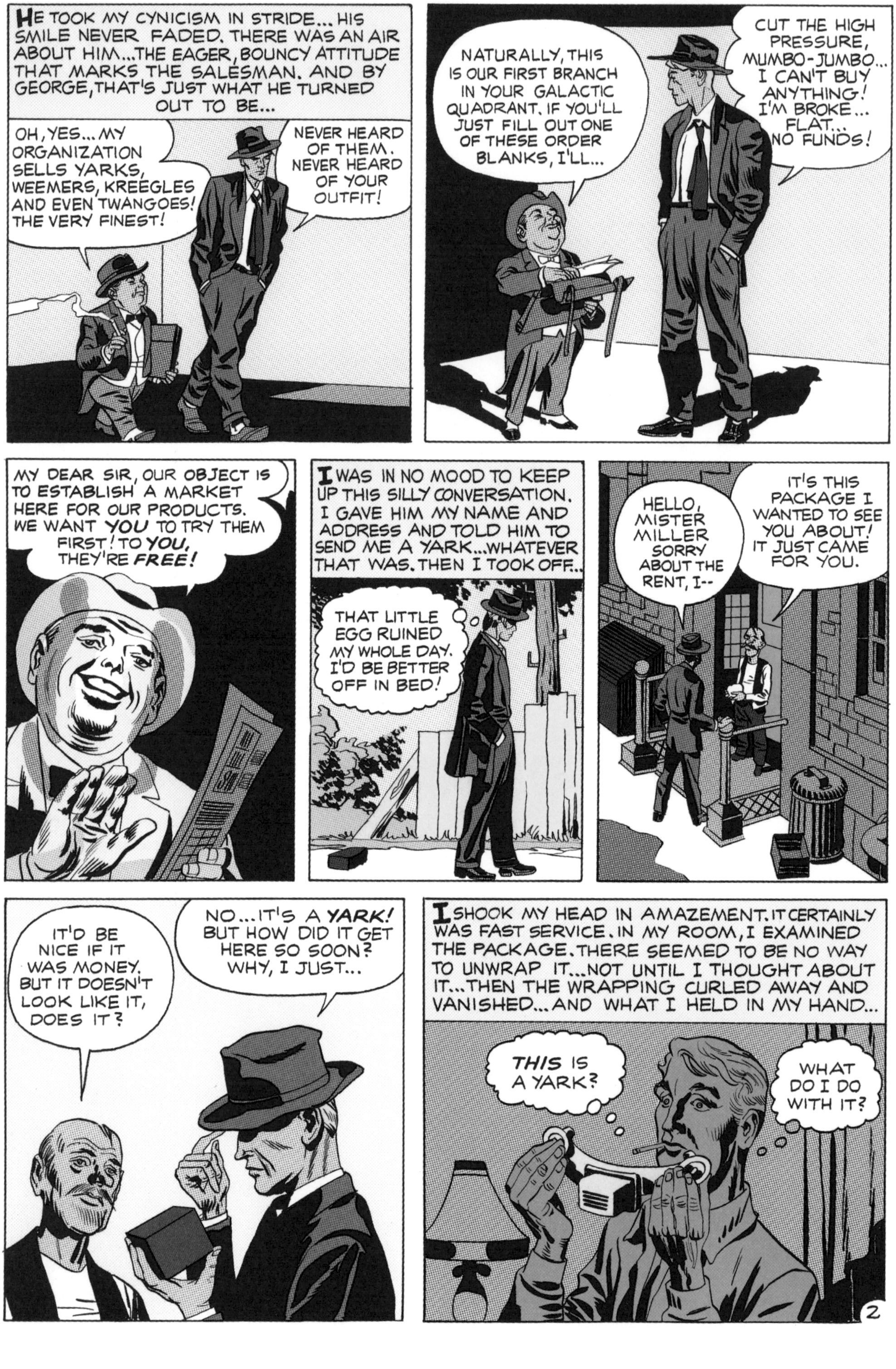

HE TOOK MY CYNICISM IN STRIDE... HIS SMILE NEVER FADED. THERE WAS AN AIR ABOUT HIM...THE EAGER, BOUNCY ATTITUDE THAT MARKS THE SALESMAN. AND BY GEORGE, THAT'S JUST WHAT HE TURNED OUT TO BE...
OH, YES... MY ORGANIZATION SELLS YARKS, WEEMERS, KREEGLES AND EVEN TWANGOES! THE VERY FINEST!
NEVER HEARD OF THEM. NEVER HEARD OF YOUR OUTFIT!
NATURALLY, THIS IS OUR FIRST BRANCH IN YOUR GALACTIC QUADRANT. IF YOU'LL JUST FILL OUT ONE OF THESE ORDER BLANKS, I'LL...
CUT THE HIGH PRESSURE, MUMBO-JUMBO... I CAN'T BUY ANYTHING! I'M BROKE... FLAT... NO FUNDS!
MY DEAR SIR, OUR OBJECT IS TO ESTABLISH A MARKET HERE FOR OUR PRODUCTS. WE WANT YOU TO TRY THEM FIRST! TO YOU, THEY'RE FREE!
I WAS IN NO MOOD TO KEEP UP THIS SILLY CONVERSATION. I GAVE HIM MY NAME AND ADDRESS AND TOLD HIM TO SEND ME A YARK...WHATEVER THAT WAS. THEN I TOOK OFF...
THAT LITTLE EGG RUINED MY WHOLE DAY. I'D BE BETTER OFF IN BED!
HELLO, MISTER MILLER SORRY ABOUT THE RENT, I--
IT'S THIS PACKAGE I WANTED TO SEE YOU ABOUT! IT JUST CAME FOR YOU.
IT'D BE NICE IF IT WAS MONEY. BUT IT DOESN'T LOOK LIKE IT, DOES IT?
NO...IT'S A YARK! BUT HOW DID IT GET HERE SO SOON? WHY, I JUST...
I SHOOK MY HEAD IN AMAZEMENT. IT CERTAINLY WAS FAST SERVICE. IN MY ROOM, I EXAMINED THE PACKAGE. THERE SEEMED TO BE NO WAY TO UNWRAP IT...NOT UNTIL I THOUGHT ABOUT IT...THEN THE WRAPPING CURLED AWAY AND VANISHED... AND WHAT I HELD IN MY HAND...
THIS IS A YARK?
WHAT DO I DO WITH IT?
2

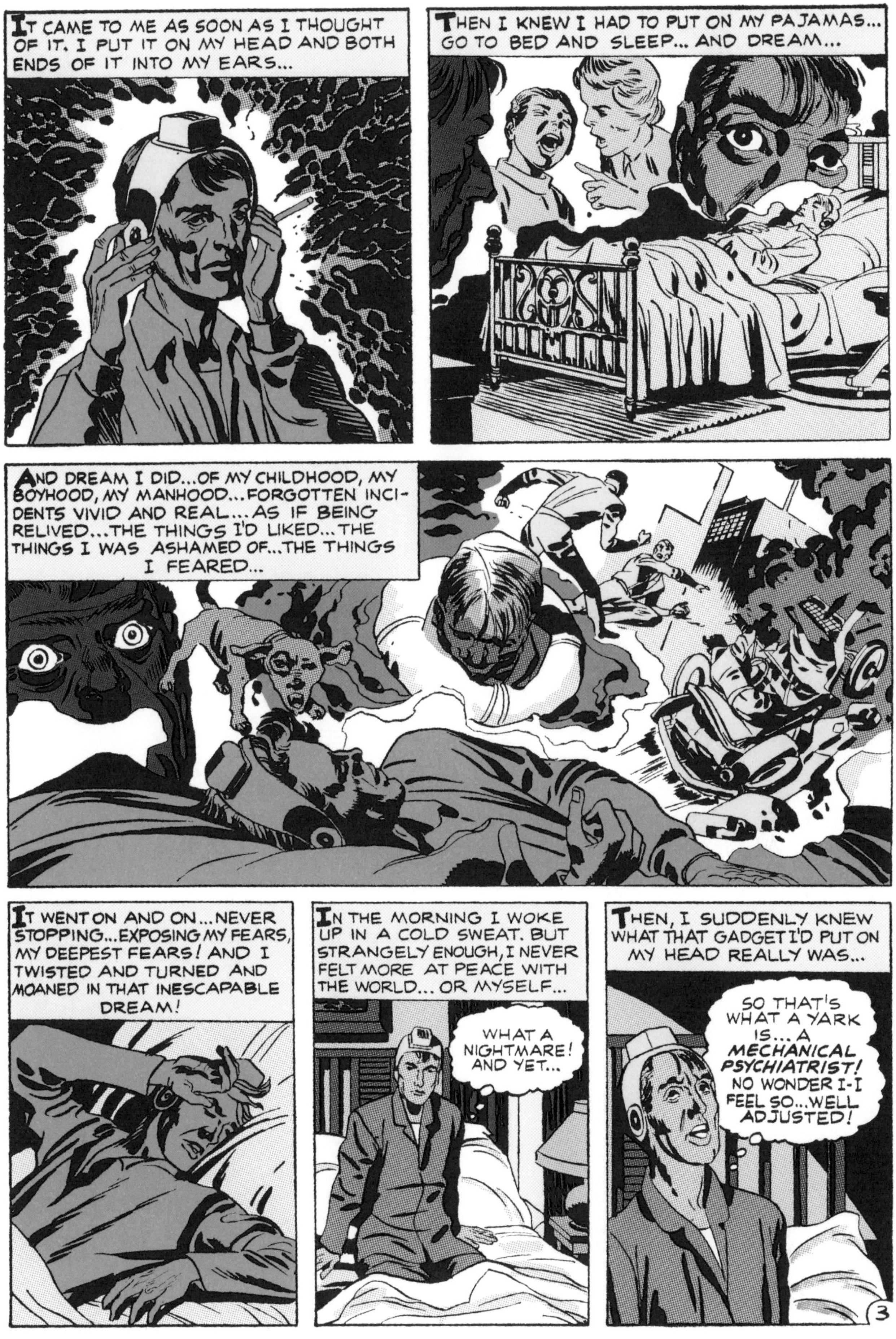
IT CAME TO ME AS SOON AS I THOUGHT OF IT. I PUT IT ON MY HEAD AND BOTH ENDS OF IT INTO MY EARS...
THEN I KNEW I HAD TO PUT ON MY PAJAMAS... GO TO BED AND SLEEP... AND DREAM...
AND DREAM I DID...OF MY CHILDHOOD, MY BOYHOOD, MY MANHOOD...FORGOTTEN INCIDENTS VIVID AND REAL...AS IF BEING RELIVED...THE THINGS I'D LIKED...THE THINGS I WAS ASHAMED OF...THE THINGS I FEARED...
IT WENT ON AND ON...NEVER STOPPING...EXPOSING MY FEARS, MY DEEPEST FEARS! AND I TWISTED AND TURNED AND MOANED IN THAT INESCAPABLE DREAM!
IN THE MORNING I WOKE UP IN A COLD SWEAT. BUT STRANGELY ENOUGH, I NEVER FELT MORE AT PEACE WITH THE WORLD... OR MYSELF...
WHAT A NIGHTMARE! AND YET...
THEN, I SUDDENLY KNEW WHAT THAT GADGET I'D PUT ON MY HEAD REALLY WAS...
SO THAT'S WHAT A YARK IS... A MECHANICAL PSYCHIATRIST! NO WONDER I-I FEEL SO...WELL ADJUSTED!
3

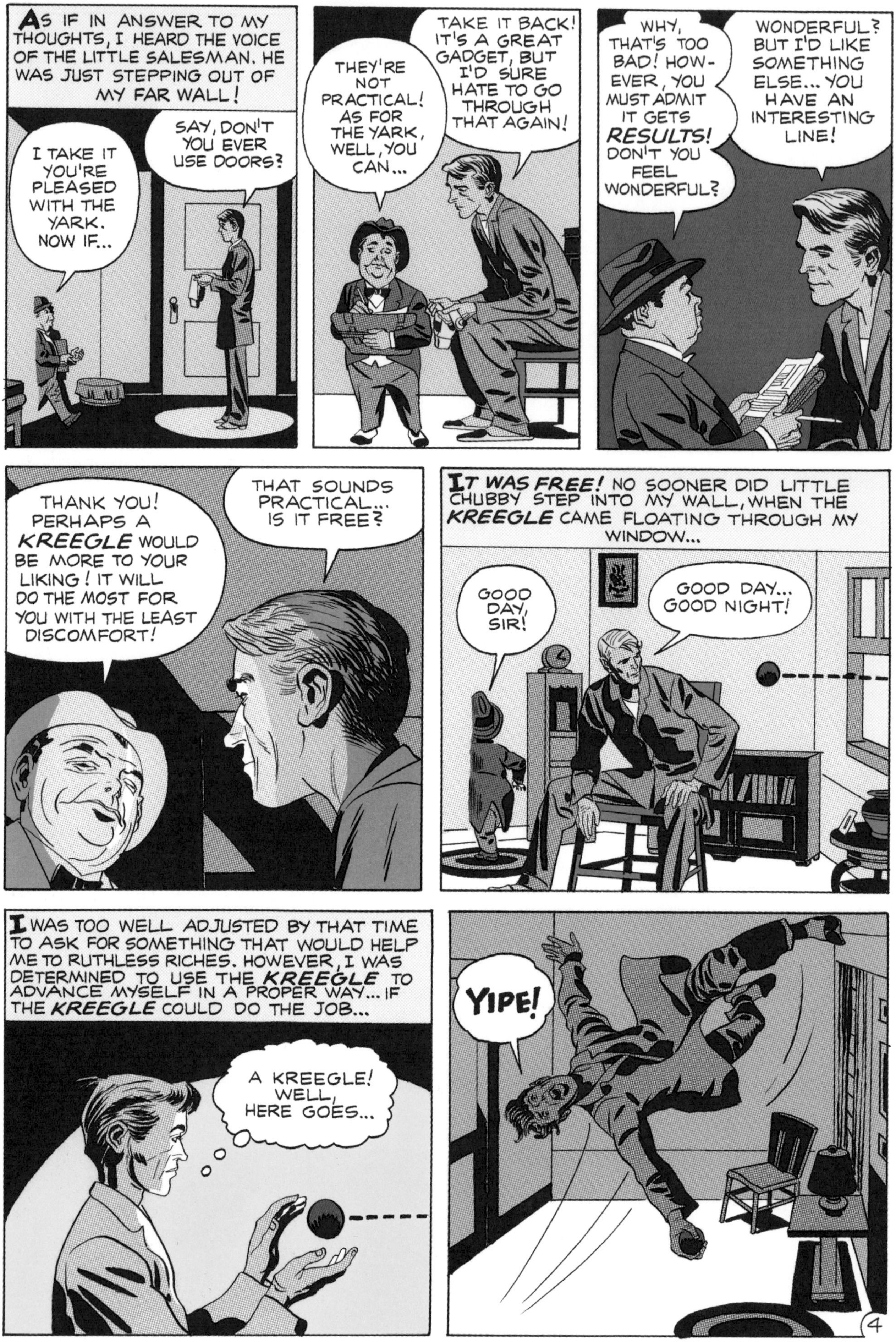
AS IF IN ANSWER TO MY THOUGHTS, I HEARD THE VOICE OF THE LITTLE SALESMAN. HE WAS JUST STEPPING OUT OF MY FAR WALL!
I TAKE IT YOU'RE PLEASED WITH THE YARK. NOW IF...
SAY, DON'T YOU EVER USE DOORS?
TAKE IT BACK! IT'S A GREAT GADGET, BUT I'D SURE HATE TO GO THROUGH THAT AGAIN!
THEY'RE NOT PRACTICAL! AS FOR THE YARK, WELL, YOU CAN...
WHY, THAT'S TOO BAD! HOWEVER, YOU MUST ADMIT IT GETS RESULTS! DON'T YOU FEEL WONDERFUL?
WONDERFUL? BUT I'D LIKE SOMETHING ELSE... YOU HAVE AN INTERESTING LINE!
THANK YOU! PERHAPS A KREEGLE WOULD BE MORE TO YOUR LIKING! IT WILL DO THE MOST FOR YOU WITH THE LEAST DISCOMFORT!
THAT SOUNDS PRACTICAL... IS IT FREE?
IT WAS FREE! NO SOONER DID LITTLE CHUBBY STEP INTO MY WALL, WHEN THE KREEGLE CAME FLOATING THROUGH MY WINDOW...
GOOD DAY, SIR!
GOOD DAY... GOOD NIGHT!
I WAS TOO WELL ADJUSTED BY THAT TIME TO ASK FOR SOMETHING THAT WOULD HELP ME TO RUTHLESS RICHES. HOWEVER, I WAS DETERMINED TO USE THE KREEGLE TO ADVANCE MYSELF IN A PROPER WAY... IF THE KREEGLE COULD DO THE JOB...
A KREEGLE! WELL, HERE GOES...
YIPE!
4

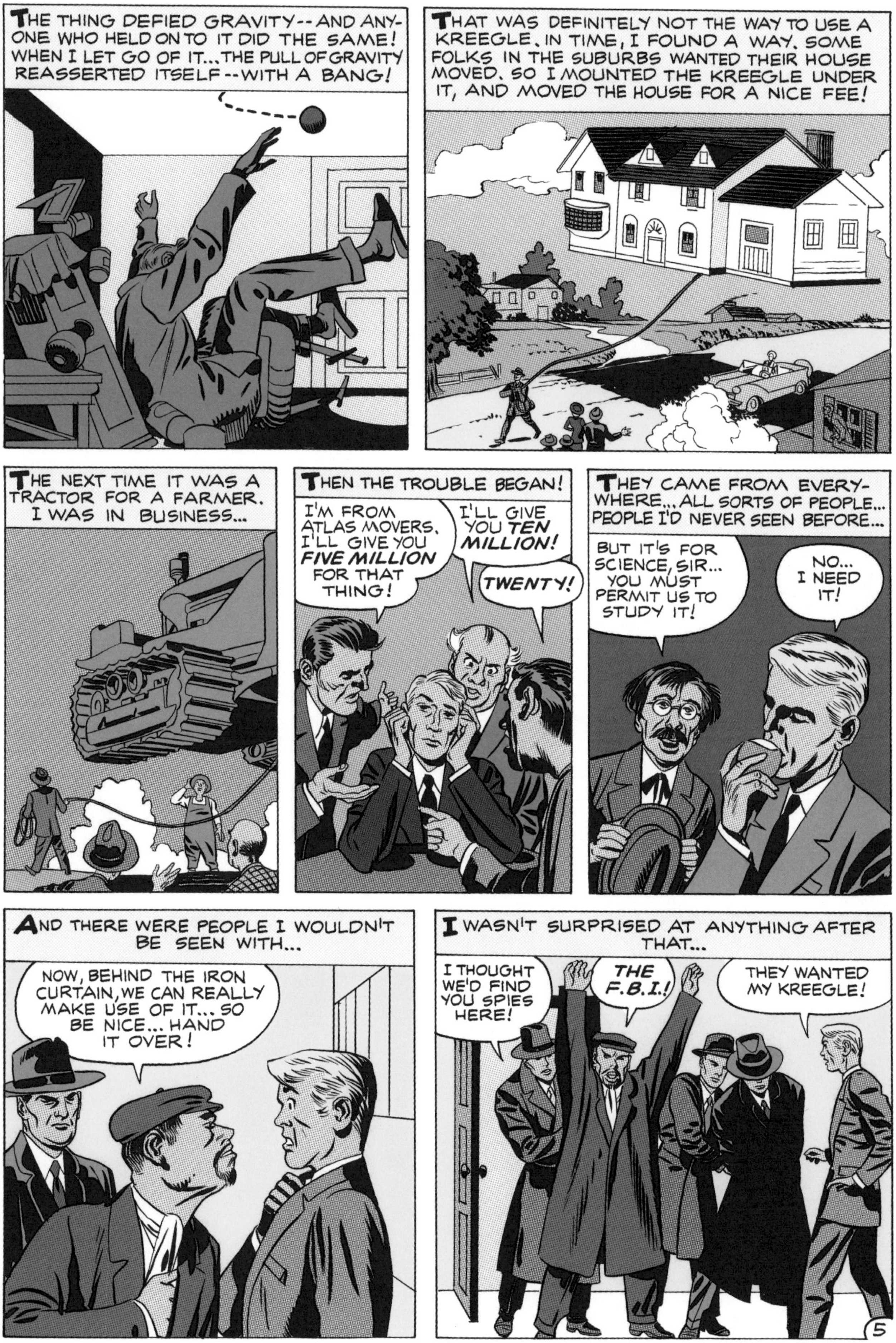
THE THING DEFIED GRAVITY--AND ANYONE WHO HELD ON TO IT DID THE SAME! WHEN I LET GO OF IT...THE PULL OF GRAVITY REASSERTED ITSELF--WITH A BANG!
THAT WAS DEFINITELY NOT THE WAY TO USE A KREEGLE. IN TIME, I FOUND A WAY. SOME FOLKS IN THE SUBURBS WANTED THEIR HOUSE MOVED. SO I MOUNTED THE KREEGLE UNDER IT, AND MOVED THE HOUSE FOR A NICE FEE!
THE NEXT TIME IT WAS A TRACTOR FOR A FARMER. I WAS IN BUSINESS...
THEN THE TROUBLE BEGAN!
I'M FROM ATLAS MOVERS. I'LL GIVE YOU FIVE MILLION FOR THAT THING!
I'LL GIVE YOU TEN MILLION!
TWENTY!
THEY CAME FROM EVERYWHERE... ALL SORTS OF PEOPLE... PEOPLE I'D NEVER SEEN BEFORE...
BUT IT'S FOR SCIENCE, SIR... YOU MUST PERMIT US TO STUDY IT!
NO... I NEED IT!
AND THERE WERE PEOPLE I WOULDN'T BE SEEN WITH...
NOW, BEHIND THE IRON CURTAIN, WE CAN REALLY MAKE USE OF IT... SO BE NICE... HAND IT OVER!
I WASN'T SURPRISED AT ANYTHING AFTER THAT...
I THOUGHT WE'D FIND YOU SPIES HERE!
THE F.B.I.!
THEY WANTED MY KREEGLE!
5

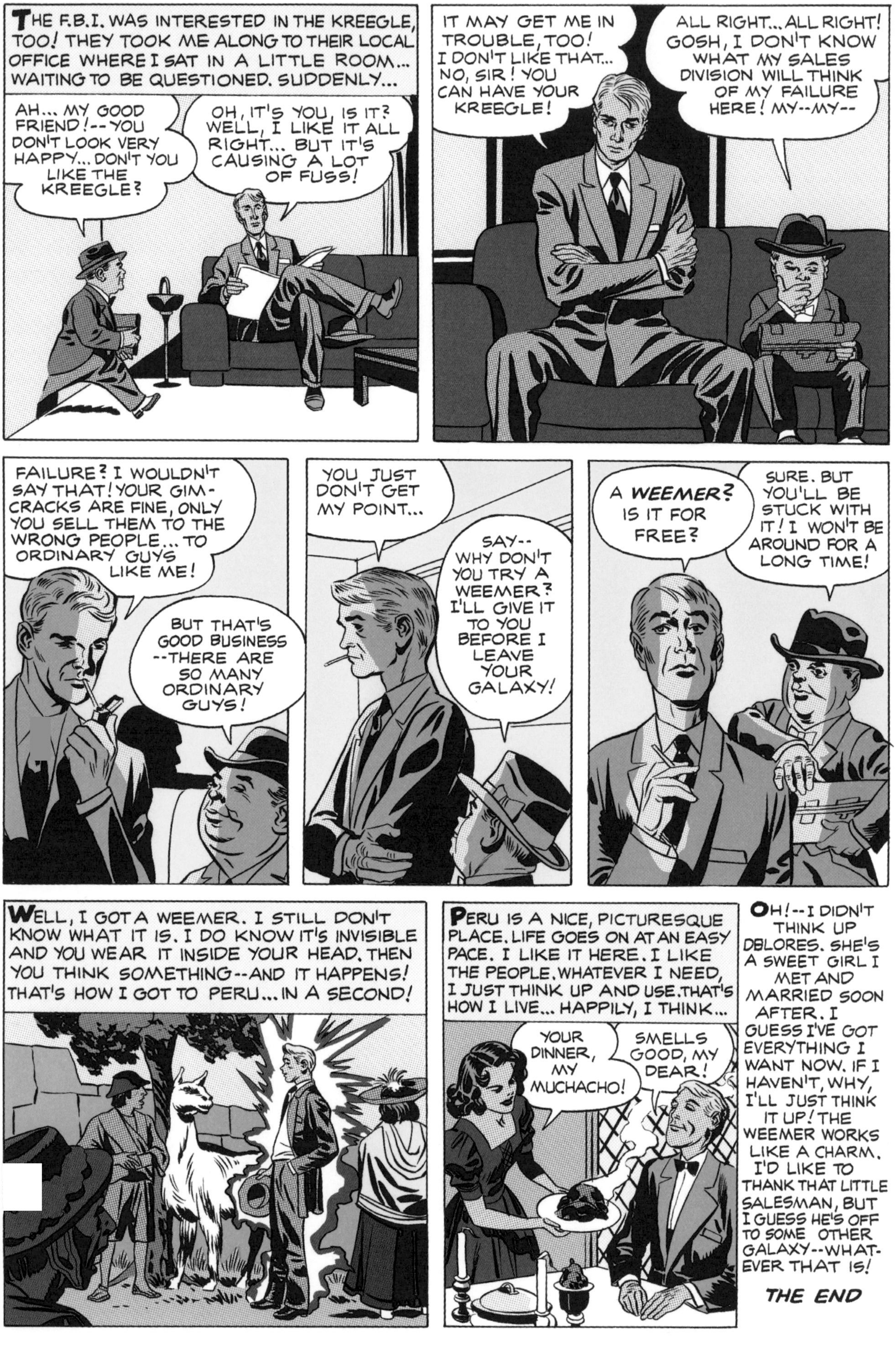
THE F.B.I. WAS INTERESTED IN THE KREEGLE, TOO! THEY TOOK ME ALONG TO THEIR LOCAL OFFICE WHERE I SAT IN A LITTLE ROOM... WAITING TO BE QUESTIONED. SUDDENLY...
AH... MY GOOD FRIEND!--YOU DON'T LOOK VERY HAPPY... DON'T YOU LIKE THE KREEGLE?
OH, IT'S YOU, IS IT? WELL, I LIKE IT ALL RIGHT... BUT IT'S CAUSING A LOT OF FUSS!
IT MAY GET ME IN TROUBLE, TOO! I DON'T LIKE THAT... NO, SIR! YOU CAN HAVE YOUR KREEGLE!
ALL RIGHT... ALL RIGHT! GOSH, I DON'T KNOW WHAT MY SALES DIVISION WILL THINK OF MY FAILURE HERE! MY--MY--
FAILURE? I WOULDN'T SAY THAT! YOUR GIM-CRACKS ARE FINE, ONLY YOU SELL THEM TO THE WRONG PEOPLE... TO ORDINARY GUYS LIKE ME!
BUT THAT'S GOOD BUSINESS --THERE ARE SO MANY ORDINARY GUYS!
YOU JUST DON'T GET MY POINT...
SAY-- WHY DON'T YOU TRY A WEEMER? I'LL GIVE IT TO YOU BEFORE I LEAVE YOUR GALAXY!
A WEEMER? IS IT FOR FREE?
SURE. BUT YOU'LL BE STUCK WITH IT! I WON'T BE AROUND FOR A LONG TIME!
WELL, I GOT A WEEMER. I STILL DON'T KNOW WHAT IT IS. I DO KNOW IT'S INVISIBLE AND YOU WEAR IT INSIDE YOUR HEAD. THEN YOU THINK SOMETHING--AND IT HAPPENS! THAT'S HOW I GOT TO PERU... IN A SECOND!
PERU IS A NICE, PICTURESQUE PLACE. LIFE GOES ON AT AN EASY PACE. I LIKE IT HERE. I LIKE THE PEOPLE. WHATEVER I NEED, I JUST THINK UP AND USE. THAT'S HOW I LIVE... HAPPILY, I THINK...
YOUR DINNER, MY MUCHACHO!
SMELLS GOOD, MY DEAR!
OH!--I DIDN'T THINK UP DOLORES. SHE'S A SWEET GIRL I MET AND MARRIED SOON AFTER. I GUESS I'VE GOT EVERYTHING I WANT NOW. IF I HAVEN'T, WHY, I'LL JUST THINK IT UP! THE WEEMER WORKS LIKE A CHARM. I'D LIKE TO THANK THAT LITTLE SALESMAN, BUT I GUESS HE'S OFF TO SOME OTHER GALAXY--WHAT-EVER THAT IS!
THE END

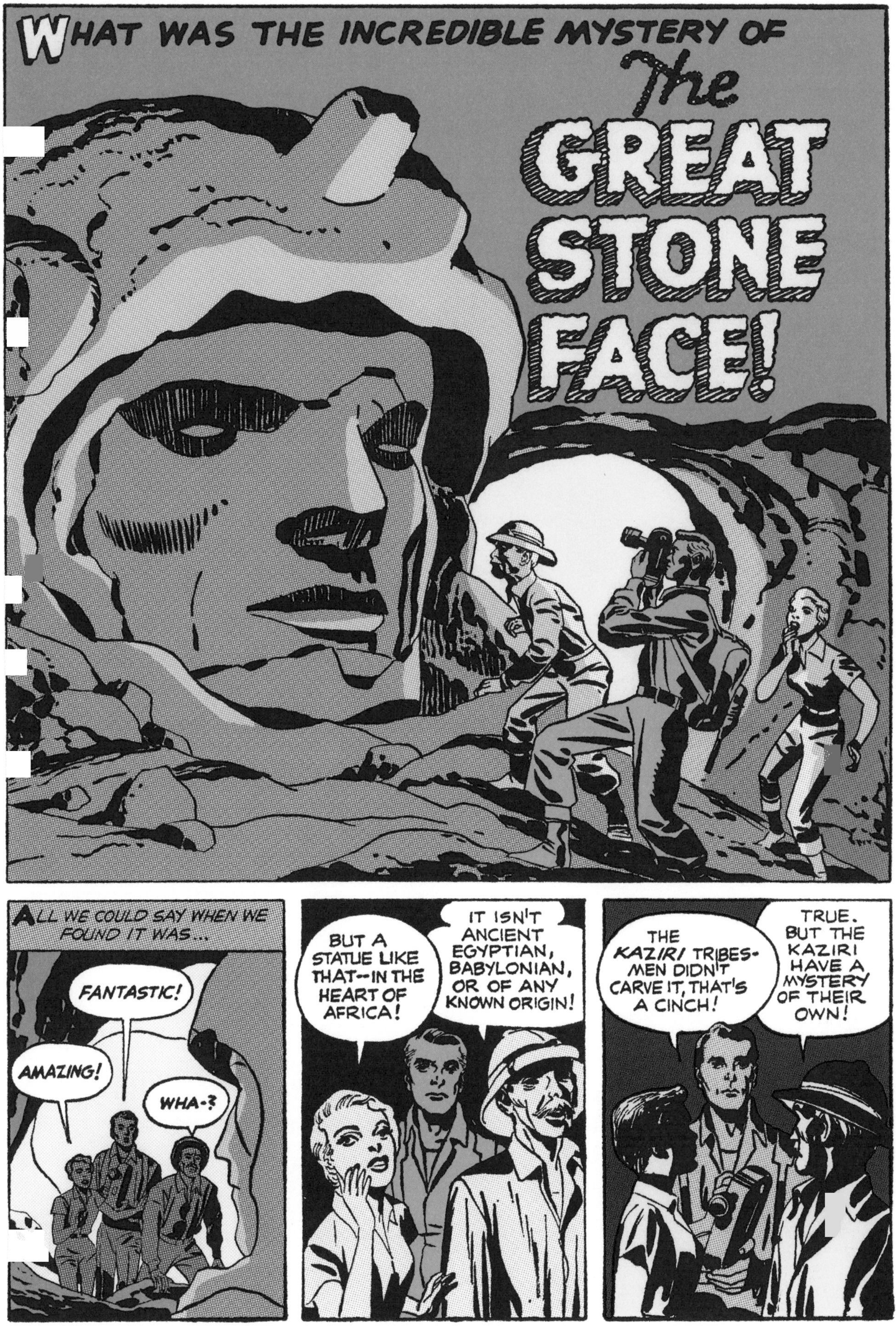
WHAT WAS THE INCREDIBLE MYSTERY OF
The GREAT STONE FACE!
ALL WE COULD SAY WHEN WE FOUND IT WAS...
FANTASTIC!
AMAZING!
WHA-?
BUT A STATUE LIKE THAT--IN THE HEART OF AFRICA!
IT ISN'T ANCIENT EGYPTIAN, BABYLONIAN, OR OF ANY KNOWN ORIGIN!
THE KAZIRI TRIBES-MEN DIDN'T CARVE IT, THAT'S A CINCH!
TRUE. BUT THE KAZIRI HAVE A MYSTERY OF THEIR OWN!

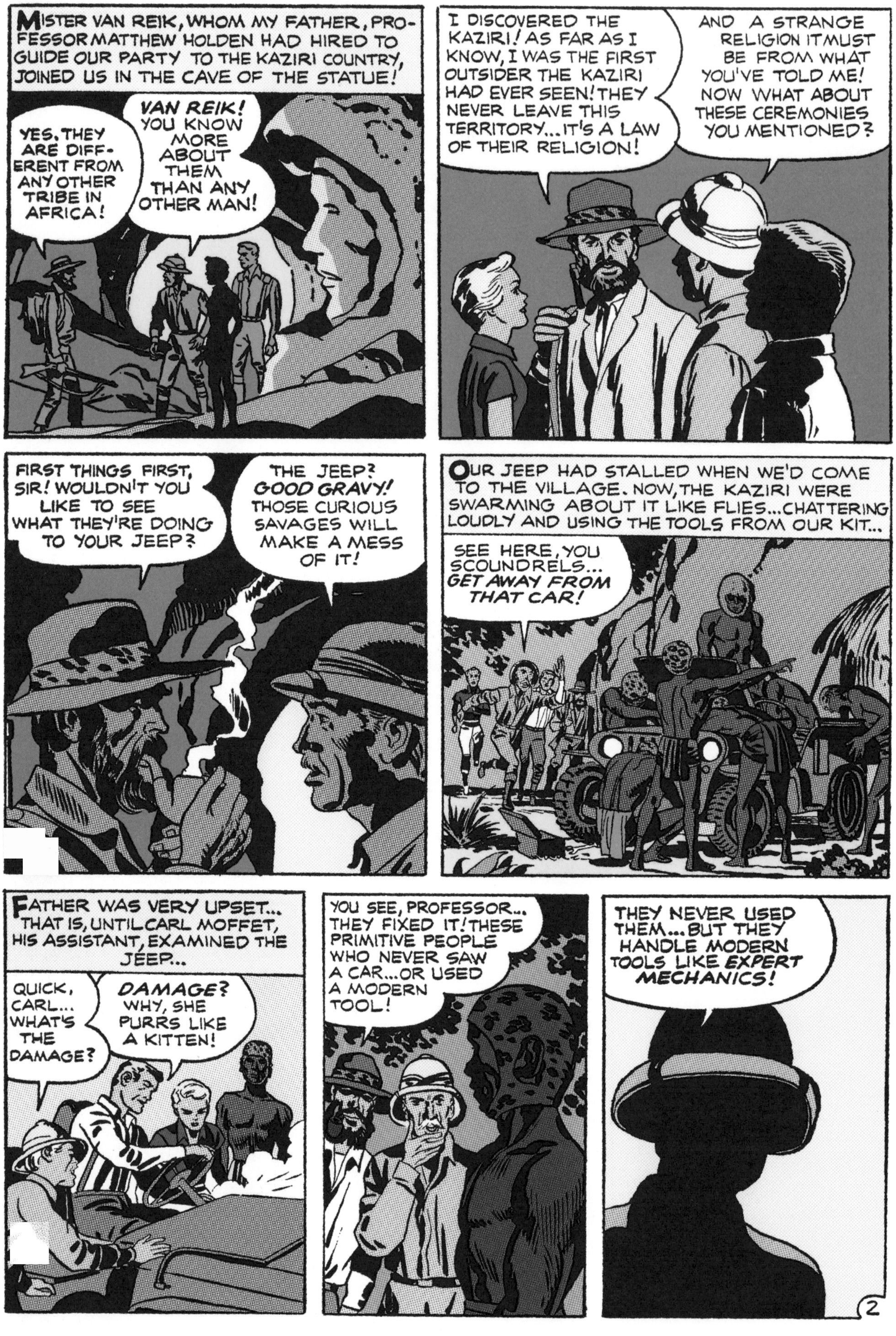
MISTER VAN REIK, WHOM MY FATHER, PROFESSOR MATTHEW HOLDEN HAD HIRED TO GUIDE OUR PARTY TO THE KAZIRI COUNTRY, JOINED US IN THE CAVE OF THE STATUE!
VAN REIK! YOU KNOW MORE ABOUT THEM THAN ANY OTHER MAN!
YES. THEY ARE DIFFERENT FROM ANY OTHER TRIBE IN AFRICA!
I DISCOVERED THE KAZIRI! AS FAR AS I KNOW, I WAS THE FIRST OUTSIDER THE KAZIRI HAD EVER SEEN! THEY NEVER LEAVE THIS TERRITORY... IT'S A LAW OF THEIR RELIGION!
AND A STRANGE RELIGION IT MUST BE FROM WHAT YOU'VE TOLD ME! NOW WHAT ABOUT THESE CEREMONIES YOU MENTIONED?
FIRST THINGS FIRST, SIR! WOULDN'T YOU LIKE TO SEE WHAT THEY'RE DOING TO YOUR JEEP?
THE JEEP? GOOD GRAVY! THOSE CURIOUS SAVAGES WILL MAKE A MESS OF IT!
OUR JEEP HAD STALLED WHEN WE'D COME TO THE VILLAGE. NOW, THE KAZIRI WERE SWARMING ABOUT IT LIKE FLIES... CHATTERING LOUDLY AND USING THE TOOLS FROM OUR KIT...
SEE HERE, YOU SCOUNDRELS... GET AWAY FROM THAT CAR!
FATHER WAS VERY UPSET... THAT IS, UNTIL CARL MOFFET, HIS ASSISTANT, EXAMINED THE JEEP...
QUICK, CARL... WHAT'S THE DAMAGE?
DAMAGE? WHY, SHE PURRS LIKE A KITTEN!
YOU SEE, PROFESSOR... THEY FIXED IT! THESE PRIMITIVE PEOPLE WHO NEVER SAW A CAR... OR USED A MODERN TOOL!
THEY NEVER USED THEM... BUT THEY HANDLE MODERN TOOLS LIKE EXPERT MECHANICS!
2

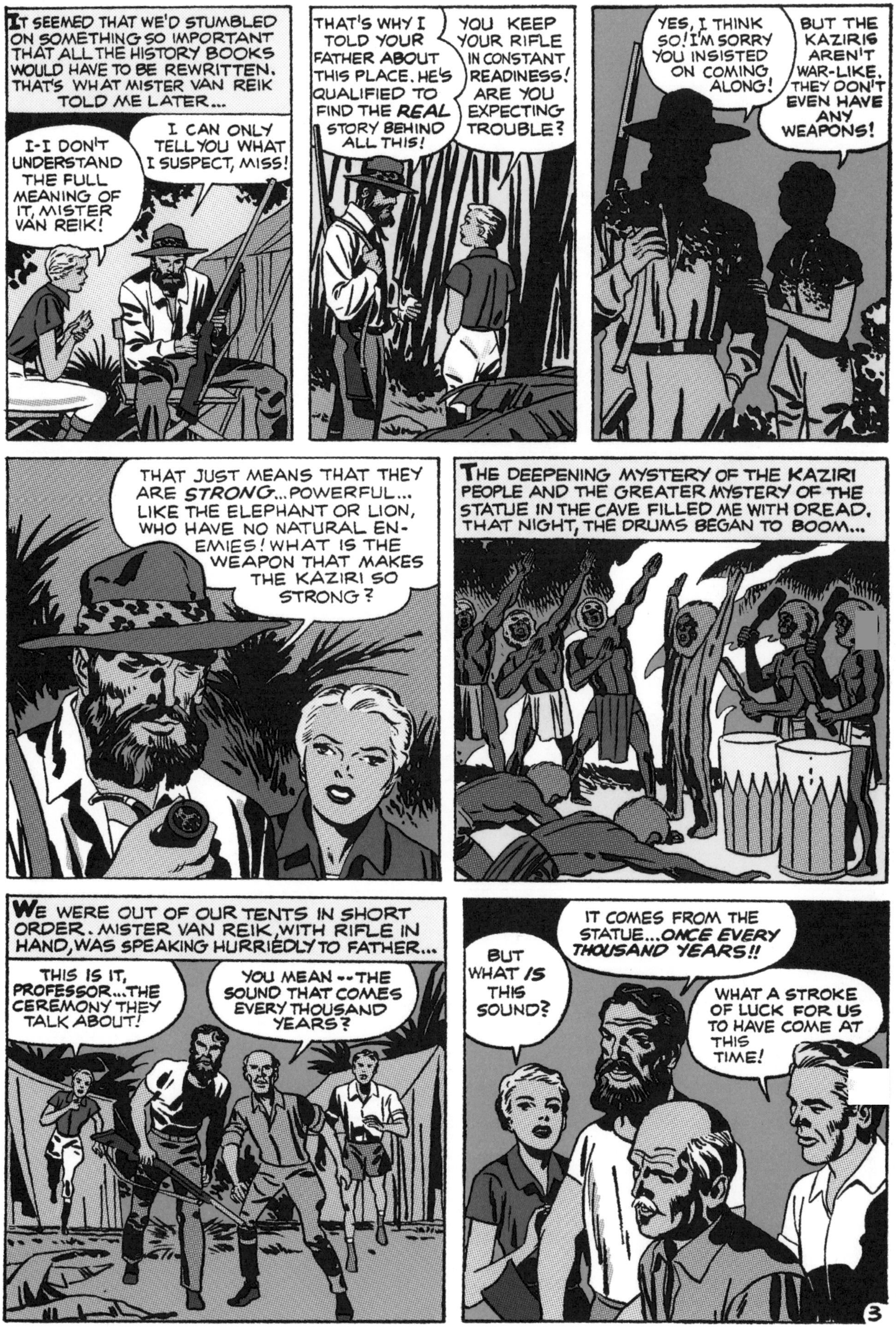

IT SEEMED THAT WE'D STUMBLED ON SOMETHING SO IMPORTANT THAT ALL THE HISTORY BOOKS WOULD HAVE TO BE REWRITTEN. THAT'S WHAT MISTER VAN REIK TOLD ME LATER...
I-I DON'T UNDERSTAND THE FULL MEANING OF IT, MISTER VAN REIK!
I CAN ONLY TELL YOU WHAT I SUSPECT, MISS!
THAT'S WHY I TOLD YOUR FATHER ABOUT THIS PLACE. HE'S QUALIFIED TO FIND THE REAL STORY BEHIND ALL THIS!
YOU KEEP YOUR RIFLE IN CONSTANT READINESS! ARE YOU EXPECTING TROUBLE?
YES, I THINK SO! I'M SORRY YOU INSISTED ON COMING ALONG!
BUT THE KAZIRIS AREN'T WAR-LIKE. THEY DON'T EVEN HAVE ANY WEAPONS!
THAT JUST MEANS THAT THEY ARE STRONG...POWERFUL... LIKE THE ELEPHANT OR LION, WHO HAVE NO NATURAL ENEMIES! WHAT IS THE WEAPON THAT MAKES THE KAZIRI SO STRONG?
THE DEEPENING MYSTERY OF THE KAZIRI PEOPLE AND THE GREATER MYSTERY OF THE STATUE IN THE CAVE FILLED ME WITH DREAD. THAT NIGHT, THE DRUMS BEGAN TO BOOM...
WE WERE OUT OF OUR TENTS IN SHORT ORDER. MISTER VAN REIK, WITH RIFLE IN HAND, WAS SPEAKING HURRIEDLY TO FATHER...
THIS IS IT, PROFESSOR...THE CEREMONY THEY TALK ABOUT!
YOU MEAN --THE SOUND THAT COMES EVERY THOUSAND YEARS?
BUT WHAT IS THIS SOUND?
IT COMES FROM THE STATUE...ONCE EVERY THOUSAND YEARS!!
WHAT A STROKE OF LUCK FOR US TO HAVE COME AT THIS TIME!
3

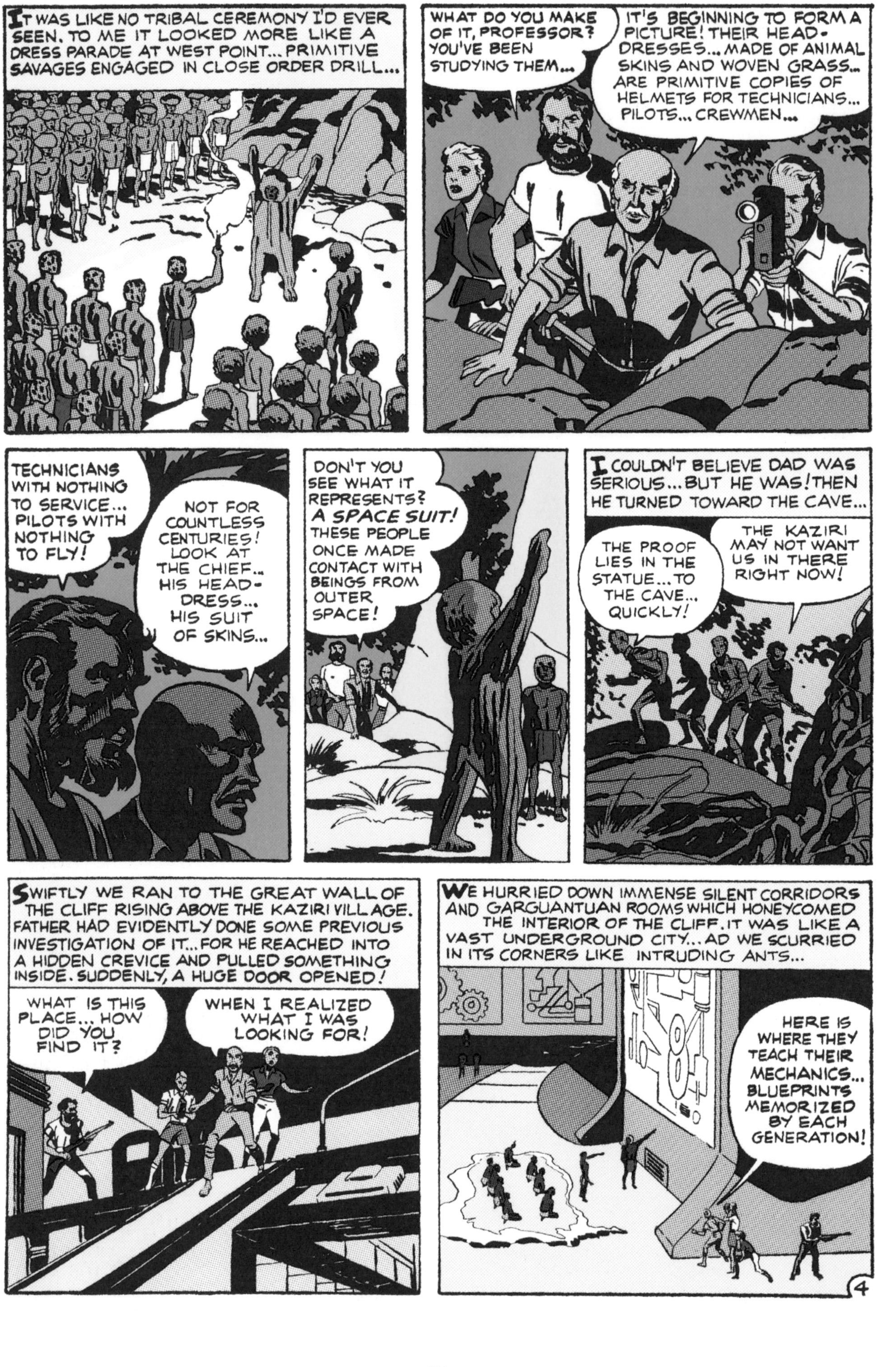

IT WAS LIKE NO TRIBAL CEREMONY I'D EVER SEEN. TO ME IT LOOKED MORE LIKE A DRESS PARADE AT WEST POINT... PRIMITIVE SAVAGES ENGAGED IN CLOSE ORDER DRILL...
WHAT DO YOU MAKE OF IT, PROFESSOR? YOU'VE BEEN STUDYING THEM...
IT'S BEGINNING TO FORM A PICTURE! THEIR HEAD-DRESSES... MADE OF ANIMAL SKINS AND WOVEN GRASS... ARE PRIMITIVE COPIES OF HELMETS FOR TECHNICIANS... PILOTS... CREWMEN...
TECHNICIANS WITH NOTHING TO SERVICE... PILOTS WITH NOTHING TO FLY!
NOT FOR COUNTLESS CENTURIES! LOOK AT THE CHIEF... HIS HEAD-DRESS... HIS SUIT OF SKINS...
DON'T YOU SEE WHAT IT REPRESENTS? A SPACE SUIT! THESE PEOPLE ONCE MADE CONTACT WITH BEINGS FROM OUTER SPACE!
I COULDN'T BELIEVE DAD WAS SERIOUS... BUT HE WAS! THEN HE TURNED TOWARD THE CAVE...
THE PROOF LIES IN THE STATUE... TO THE CAVE... QUICKLY!
THE KAZIRI MAY NOT WANT US IN THERE RIGHT NOW!
SWIFTLY WE RAN TO THE GREAT WALL OF THE CLIFF RISING ABOVE THE KAZIRI VILLAGE. FATHER HAD EVIDENTLY DONE SOME PREVIOUS INVESTIGATION OF IT... FOR HE REACHED INTO A HIDDEN CREVICE AND PULLED SOMETHING INSIDE. SUDDENLY, A HUGE DOOR OPENED!
WHAT IS THIS PLACE... HOW DID YOU FIND IT?
WHEN I REALIZED WHAT I WAS LOOKING FOR!
WE HURRIED DOWN IMMENSE SILENT CORRIDORS AND GARGUANTUAN ROOMS WHICH HONEYCOMED THE INTERIOR OF THE CLIFF. IT WAS LIKE A VAST UNDERGROUND CITY... AD WE SCURRIED IN ITS CORNERS LIKE INTRUDING ANTS...
HERE IS WHERE THEY TEACH THEIR MECHANICS... BLUEPRINTS MEMORIZED BY EACH GENERATION!
4

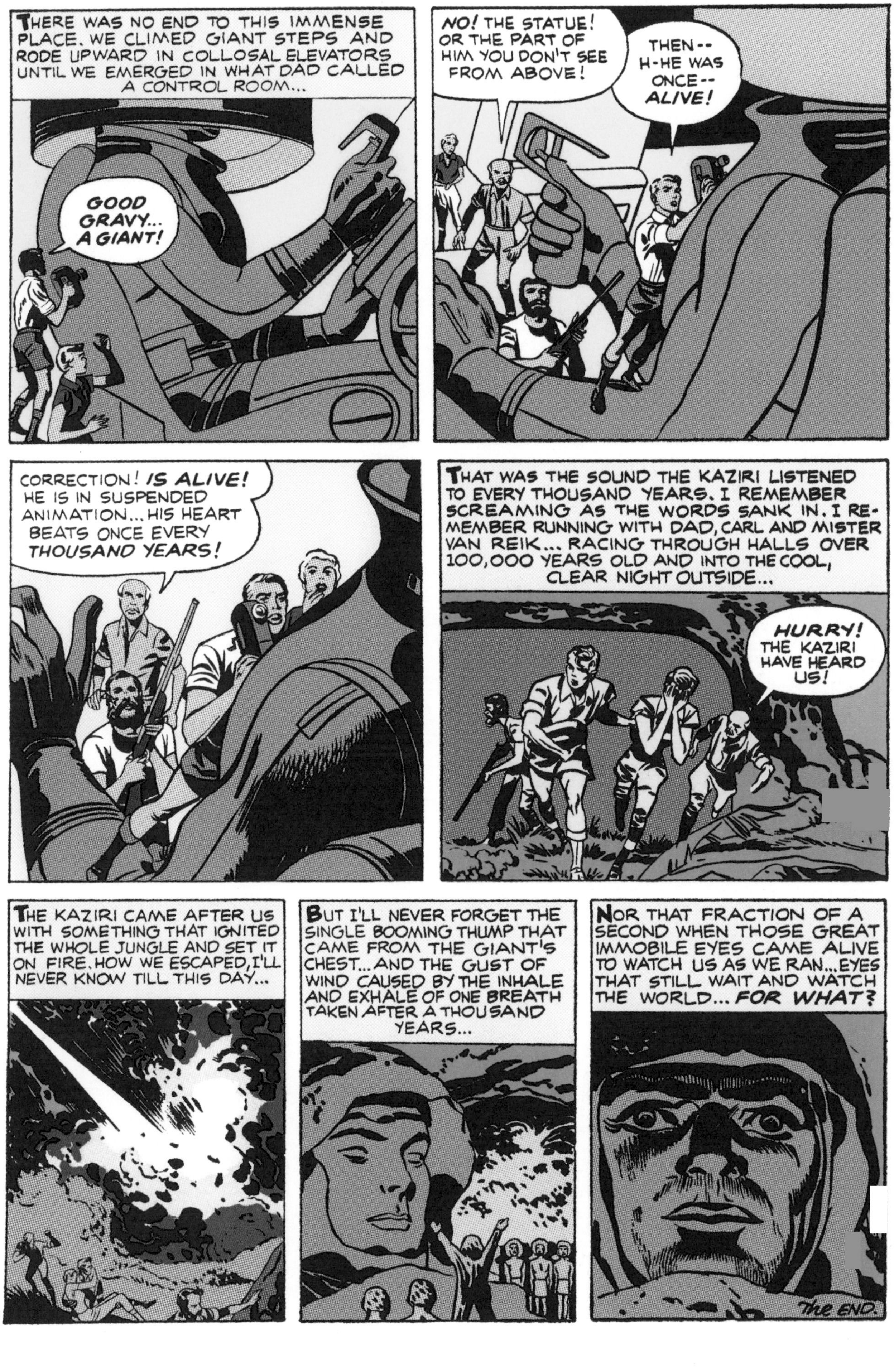
THERE WAS NO END TO THIS IMMENSE PLACE. WE CLIMED GIANT STEPS AND RODE UPWARD IN COLLOSAL ELEVATORS UNTIL WE EMERGED IN WHAT DAD CALLED A CONTROL ROOM...
GOOD GRAVY... A GIANT!
NO! THE STATUE! OR THE PART OF HIM YOU DON'T SEE FROM ABOVE!
THEN -- H-HE WAS ONCE -- ALIVE!
CORRECTION! IS ALIVE! HE IS IN SUSPENDED ANIMATION... HIS HEART BEATS ONCE EVERY THOUSAND YEARS!
THAT WAS THE SOUND THE KAZIRI LISTENED TO EVERY THOUSAND YEARS. I REMEMBER SCREAMING AS THE WORDS SANK IN. I REMEMBER RUNNING WITH DAD, CARL AND MISTER VAN REIK... RACING THROUGH HALLS OVER 100,000 YEARS OLD AND INTO THE COOL, CLEAR NIGHT OUTSIDE...
HURRY! THE KAZIRI HAVE HEARD US!
THE KAZIRI CAME AFTER US WITH SOMETHING THAT IGNITED THE WHOLE JUNGLE AND SET IT ON FIRE. HOW WE ESCAPED, I'LL NEVER KNOW TILL THIS DAY...
BUT I'LL NEVER FORGET THE SINGLE BOOMING THUMP THAT CAME FROM THE GIANT'S CHEST... AND THE GUST OF WIND CAUSED BY THE INHALE AND EXHALE OF ONE BREATH TAKEN AFTER A THOUSAND YEARS...
NOR THAT FRACTION OF A SECOND WHEN THOSE GREAT IMMOBILE EYES CAME ALIVE TO WATCH US AS WE RAN... EYES THAT STILL WAIT AND WATCH THE WORLD... FOR WHAT?
The END.

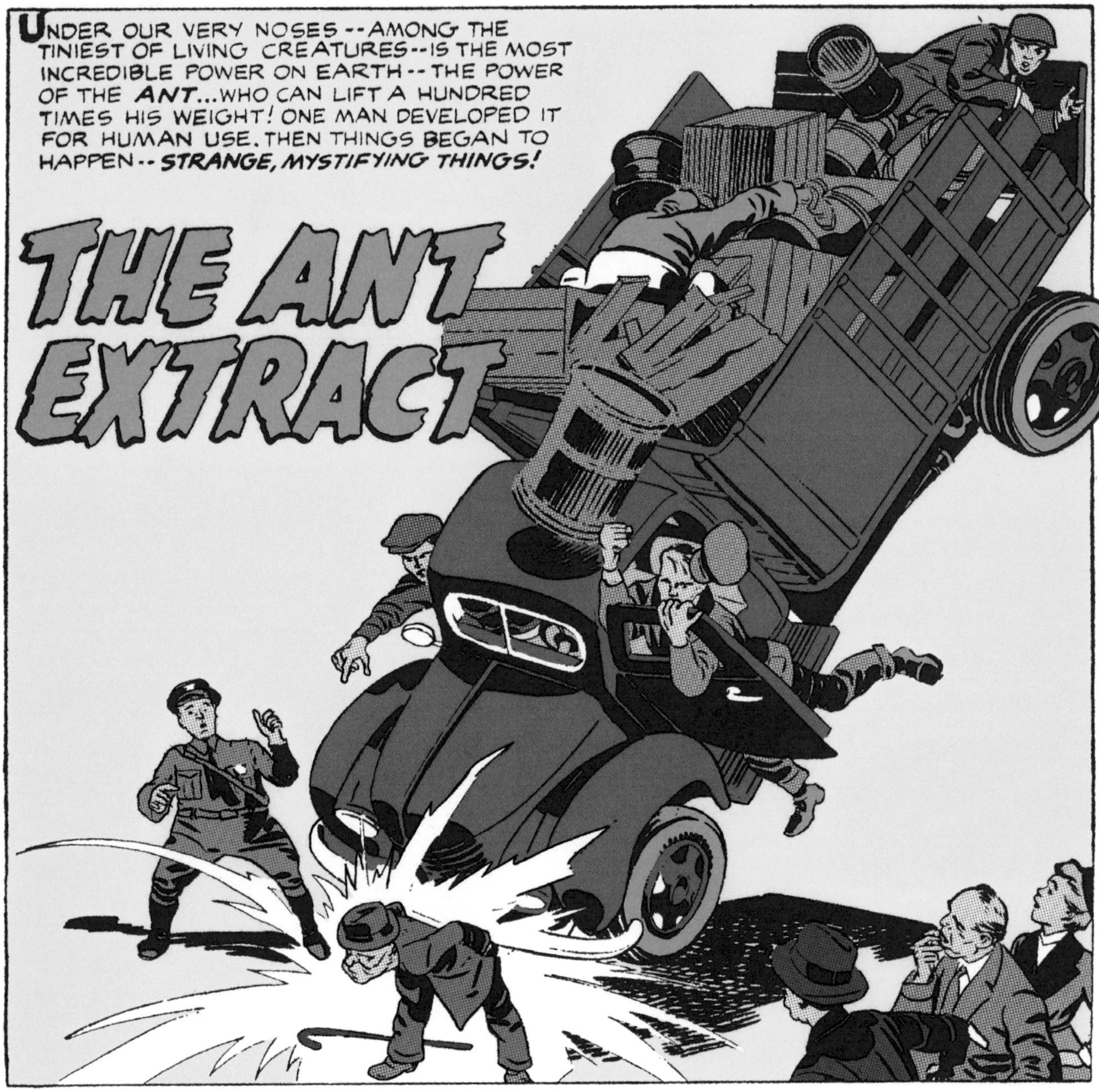
UNDER OUR VERY NOSES--AMONG THE TINIEST OF LIVING CREATURES--IS THE MOST INCREDIBLE POWER ON EARTH--THE POWER OF THE ANT...WHO CAN LIFT A HUNDRED TIMES HIS WEIGHT! ONE MAN DEVELOPED IT FOR HUMAN USE. THEN THINGS BEGAN TO HAPPEN--STRANGE, MYSTIFYING THINGS!
THE ANT EXTRACT

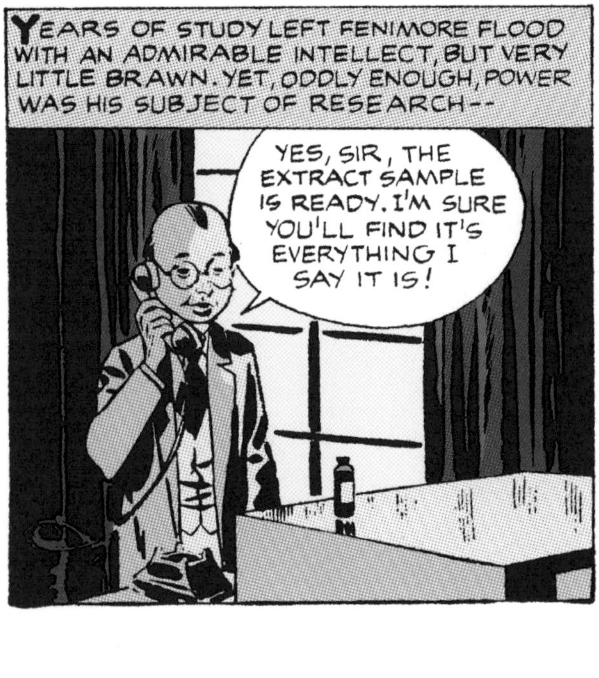
YEARS OF STUDY LEFT FENIMORE FLOOD WITH AN ADMIRABLE INTELLECT, BUT VERY LITTLE BRAWN. YET, ODDLY ENOUGH, POWER WAS HIS SUBJECT OF RESEARCH--
YES, SIR, THE EXTRACT SAMPLE IS READY. I'M SURE YOU'LL FIND IT'S EVERYTHING I SAY IT IS!

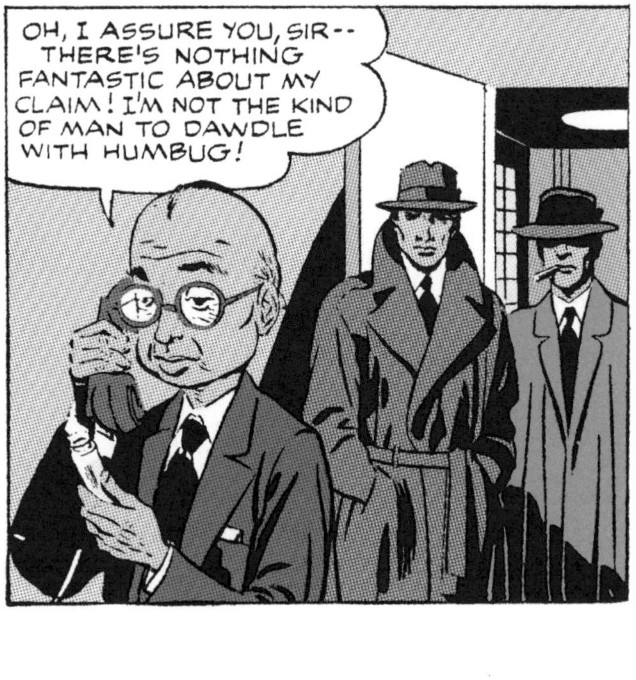
OH, I ASSURE YOU, SIR--THERE'S NOTHING FANTASTIC ABOUT MY CLAIM! I'M NOT THE KIND OF MAN TO DAWDLE WITH HUMBUG!

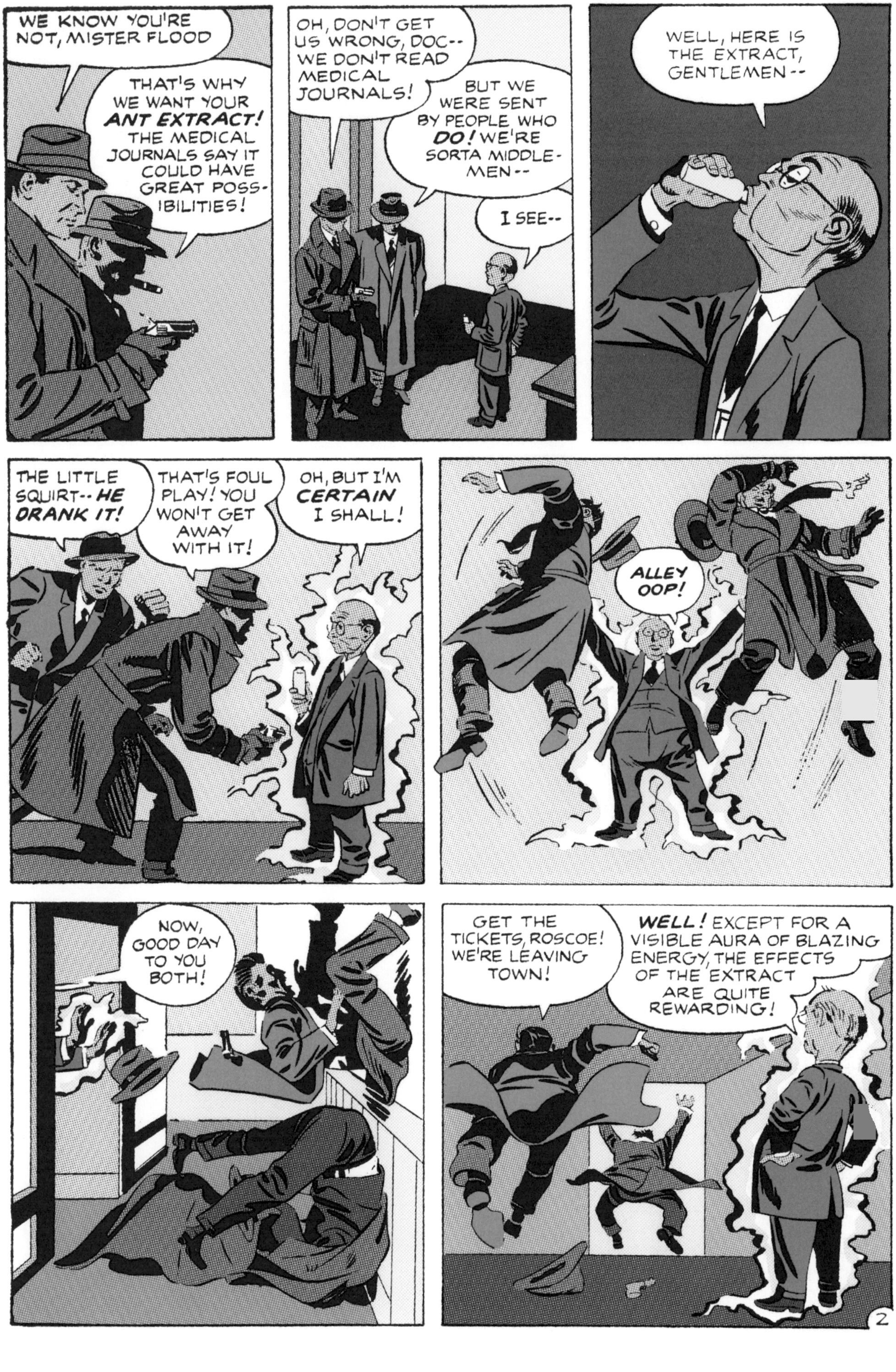
WE KNOW YOU'RE NOT, MISTER FLOOD
THAT'S WHY WE WANT YOUR ANT EXTRACT! THE MEDICAL JOURNALS SAY IT COULD HAVE GREAT POSSIBILITIES!
OH, DON'T GET US WRONG, DOC-- WE DON'T READ MEDICAL JOURNALS!
BUT WE WERE SENT BY PEOPLE WHO DO! WE'RE SORTA MIDDLE-MEN--
I SEE--
WELL, HERE IS THE EXTRACT, GENTLEMEN--
THE LITTLE SQUIRT-- HE DRANK IT!
THAT'S FOUL PLAY! YOU WON'T GET AWAY WITH IT!
OH, BUT I'M CERTAIN I SHALL!
ALLEY OOP!
NOW, GOOD DAY TO YOU BOTH!
GET THE TICKETS, ROSCOE! WE'RE LEAVING TOWN!
WELL! EXCEPT FOR A VISIBLE AURA OF BLAZING ENERGY, THE EFFECTS OF THE EXTRACT ARE QUITE REWARDING!
2

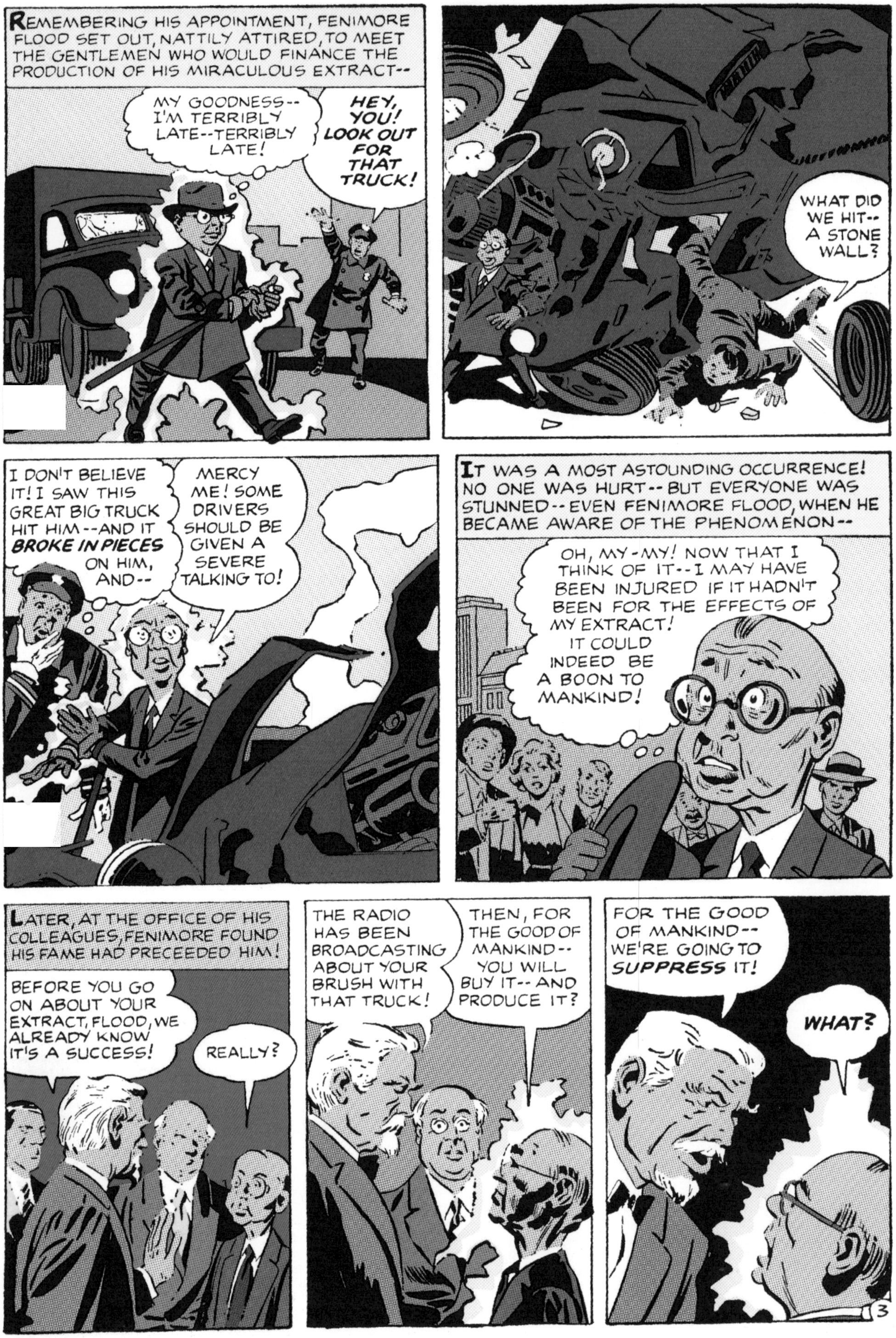

REMEMBERING HIS APPOINTMENT, FENIMORE FLOOD SET OUT, NATTILY ATTIRED, TO MEET THE GENTLEMEN WHO WOULD FINANCE THE PRODUCTION OF HIS MIRACULOUS EXTRACT--
MY GOODNESS-- I'M TERRIBLY LATE--TERRIBLY LATE!
HEY, YOU! LOOK OUT FOR THAT TRUCK!
WHAT DID WE HIT-- A STONE WALL?
I DON'T BELIEVE IT! I SAW THIS GREAT BIG TRUCK HIT HIM--AND IT BROKE IN PIECES ON HIM, AND--
MERCY ME! SOME DRIVERS SHOULD BE GIVEN A SEVERE TALKING TO!
IT WAS A MOST ASTOUNDING OCCURRENCE! NO ONE WAS HURT--BUT EVERYONE WAS STUNNED--EVEN FENIMORE FLOOD, WHEN HE BECAME AWARE OF THE PHENOMENON--
OH, MY-MY! NOW THAT I THINK OF IT--I MAY HAVE BEEN INJURED IF IT HADN'T BEEN FOR THE EFFECTS OF MY EXTRACT! IT COULD INDEED BE A BOON TO MANKIND!
LATER, AT THE OFFICE OF HIS COLLEAGUES, FENIMORE FOUND HIS FAME HAD PRECEEDED HIM!
BEFORE YOU GO ON ABOUT YOUR EXTRACT, FLOOD, WE ALREADY KNOW IT'S A SUCCESS!
REALLY?
THE RADIO HAS BEEN BROADCASTING ABOUT YOUR BRUSH WITH THAT TRUCK!
THEN, FOR THE GOOD OF MANKIND-- YOU WILL BUY IT--AND PRODUCE IT?
FOR THE GOOD OF MANKIND-- WE'RE GOING TO SUPPRESS IT!
WHAT?
3

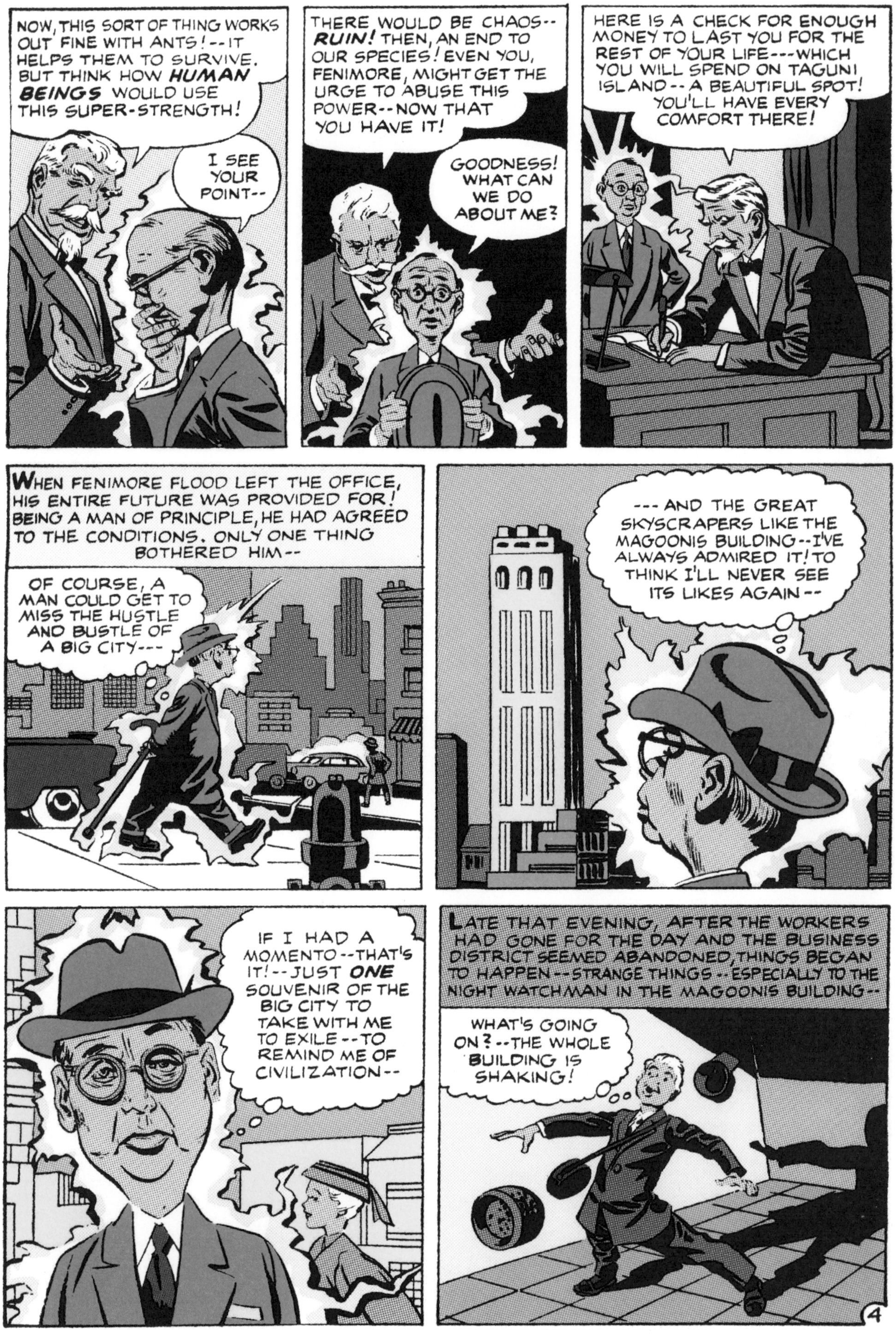
NOW, THIS SORT OF THING WORKS OUT FINE WITH ANTS! --IT HELPS THEM TO SURVIVE. BUT THINK HOW HUMAN BEINGS WOULD USE THIS SUPER-STRENGTH!
I SEE YOUR POINT--
THERE WOULD BE CHAOS-- RUIN! THEN, AN END TO OUR SPECIES! EVEN YOU, FENIMORE, MIGHT GET THE URGE TO ABUSE THIS POWER--NOW THAT YOU HAVE IT!
GOODNESS! WHAT CAN WE DO ABOUT ME?
HERE IS A CHECK FOR ENOUGH MONEY TO LAST YOU FOR THE REST OF YOUR LIFE---WHICH YOU WILL SPEND ON TAGUNI ISLAND -- A BEAUTIFUL SPOT! YOU'LL HAVE EVERY COMFORT THERE!
WHEN FENIMORE FLOOD LEFT THE OFFICE, HIS ENTIRE FUTURE WAS PROVIDED FOR! BEING A MAN OF PRINCIPLE, HE HAD AGREED TO THE CONDITIONS. ONLY ONE THING BOTHERED HIM--
OF COURSE, A MAN COULD GET TO MISS THE HUSTLE AND BUSTLE OF A BIG CITY---
--- AND THE GREAT SKYSCRAPERS LIKE THE MAGOONIS BUILDING--I'VE ALWAYS ADMIRED IT! TO THINK I'LL NEVER SEE ITS LIKES AGAIN--
IF I HAD A MOMENTO--THAT'S IT!--JUST ONE SOUVENIR OF THE BIG CITY TO TAKE WITH ME TO EXILE--TO REMIND ME OF CIVILIZATION--
LATE THAT EVENING, AFTER THE WORKERS HAD GONE FOR THE DAY AND THE BUSINESS DISTRICT SEEMED ABANDONED, THINGS BEGAN TO HAPPEN---STRANGE THINGS--ESPECIALLY TO THE NIGHT WATCHMAN IN THE MAGOONIS BUILDING--
WHAT'S GOING ON?--THE WHOLE BUILDING IS SHAKING!
4

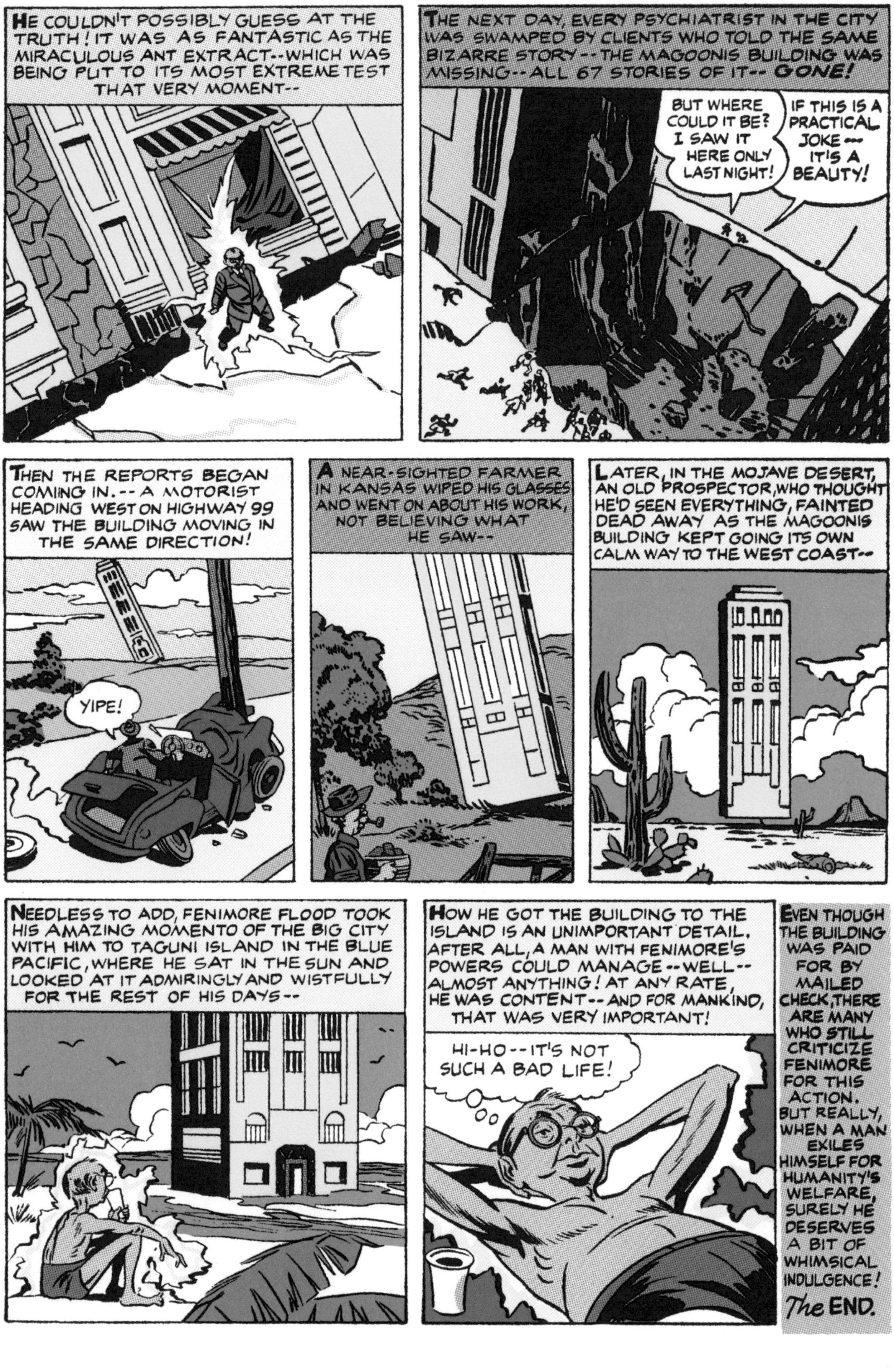
HE COULDN'T POSSIBLY GUESS AT THE TRUTH! IT WAS AS FANTASTIC AS THE MIRACULOUS ANT EXTRACT--WHICH WAS BEING PUT TO ITS MOST EXTREME TEST THAT VERY MOMENT--
THE NEXT DAY, EVERY PSYCHIATRIST IN THE CITY WAS SWAMPED BY CLIENTS WHO TOLD THE SAME BIZARRE STORY--THE MAGOONIS BUILDING WAS MISSING--ALL 67 STORIES OF IT--GONE!
BUT WHERE COULD IT BE? I SAW IT HERE ONLY LAST NIGHT!
IF THIS IS A PRACTICAL JOKE--IT'S A BEAUTY!
THEN THE REPORTS BEGAN COMING IN.--A MOTORIST HEADING WEST ON HIGHWAY 99 SAW THE BUILDING MOVING IN THE SAME DIRECTION!
YIPE!
A NEAR-SIGHTED FARMER IN KANSAS WIPED HIS GLASSES AND WENT ON ABOUT HIS WORK, NOT BELIEVING WHAT HE SAW--
LATER, IN THE MOJAVE DESERT, AN OLD PROSPECTOR, WHO THOUGHT HE'D SEEN EVERYTHING, FAINTED DEAD AWAY AS THE MAGOONIS BUILDING KEPT GOING ITS OWN CALM WAY TO THE WEST COAST--
NEEDLESS TO ADD, FENIMORE FLOOD TOOK HIS AMAZING MOMENTO OF THE BIG CITY WITH HIM TO TAGUNI ISLAND IN THE BLUE PACIFIC, WHERE HE SAT IN THE SUN AND LOOKED AT IT ADMIRINGLY AND WISTFULLY FOR THE REST OF HIS DAYS--
HOW HE GOT THE BUILDING TO THE ISLAND IS AN UNIMPORTANT DETAIL. AFTER ALL, A MAN WITH FENIMORE'S POWERS COULD MANAGE--WELL--ALMOST ANYTHING! AT ANY RATE, HE WAS CONTENT--AND FOR MANKIND, THAT WAS VERY IMPORTANT!
HI-HO--IT'S NOT SUCH A BAD LIFE!
EVEN THOUGH THE BUILDING WAS PAID FOR BY MAILED CHECK, THERE ARE MANY WHO STILL CRITICIZE FENIMORE FOR THIS ACTION. BUT REALLY, WHEN A MAN EXILES HIMSELF FOR HUMANITY'S WELFARE, SURELY HE DESERVES A BIT OF WHIMSICAL INDULGENCE!
The END.

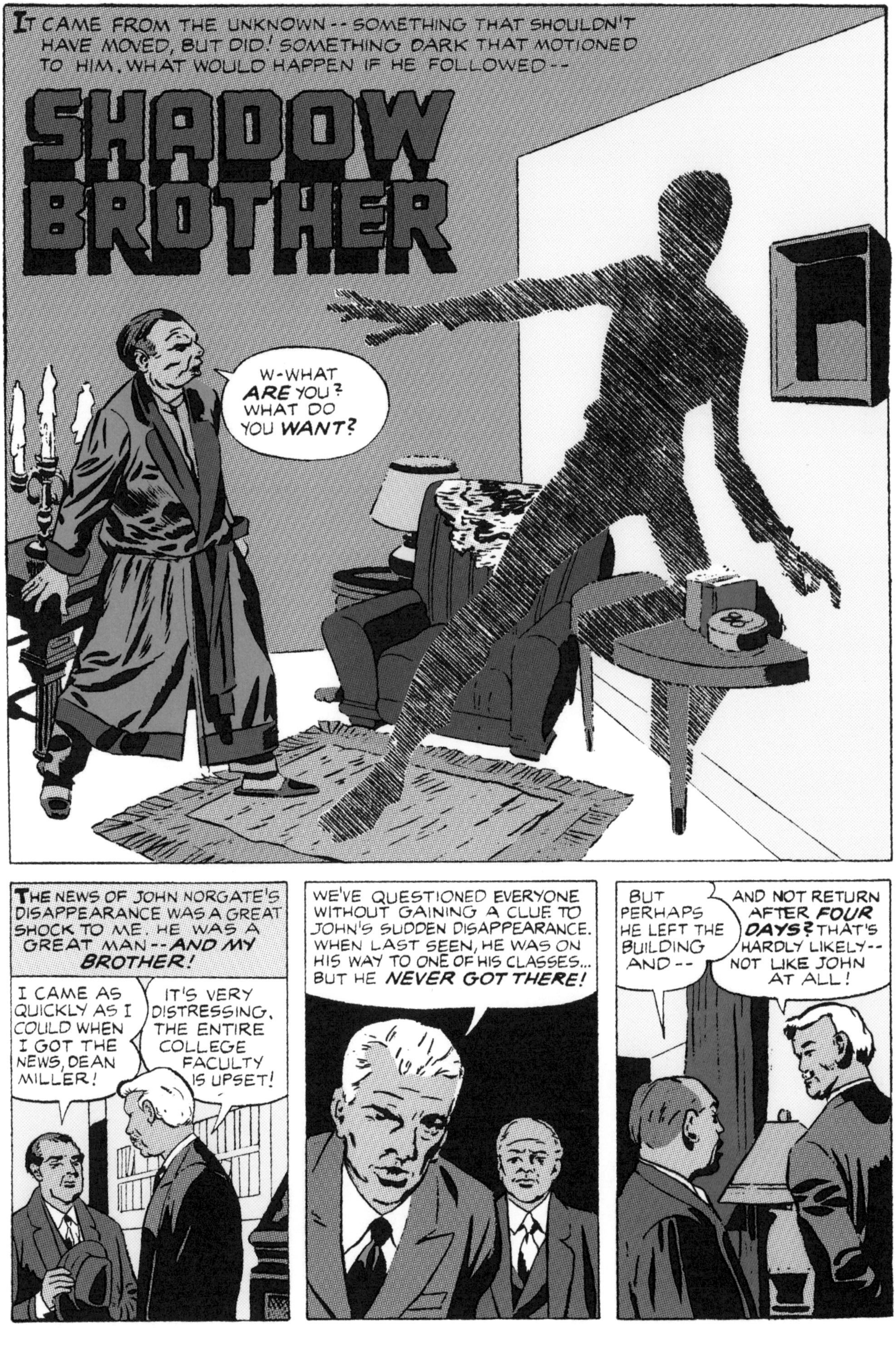
IT CAME FROM THE UNKNOWN -- SOMETHING THAT SHOULDN'T HAVE MOVED, BUT DID! SOMETHING DARK THAT MOTIONED TO HIM. WHAT WOULD HAPPEN IF HE FOLLOWED --
SHADOW BROTHER
W-WHAT ARE YOU? WHAT DO YOU WANT?
THE NEWS OF JOHN NORGATE'S DISAPPEARANCE WAS A GREAT SHOCK TO ME. HE WAS A GREAT MAN -- AND MY BROTHER!
I CAME AS QUICKLY AS I COULD WHEN I GOT THE NEWS, DEAN MILLER!
IT'S VERY DISTRESSING. THE ENTIRE COLLEGE FACULTY IS UPSET!
WE'VE QUESTIONED EVERYONE WITHOUT GAINING A CLUE TO JOHN'S SUDDEN DISAPPEARANCE. WHEN LAST SEEN, HE WAS ON HIS WAY TO ONE OF HIS CLASSES... BUT HE NEVER GOT THERE!
BUT PERHAPS HE LEFT THE BUILDING AND --
AND NOT RETURN AFTER FOUR DAYS? THAT'S HARDLY LIKELY -- NOT LIKE JOHN AT ALL!

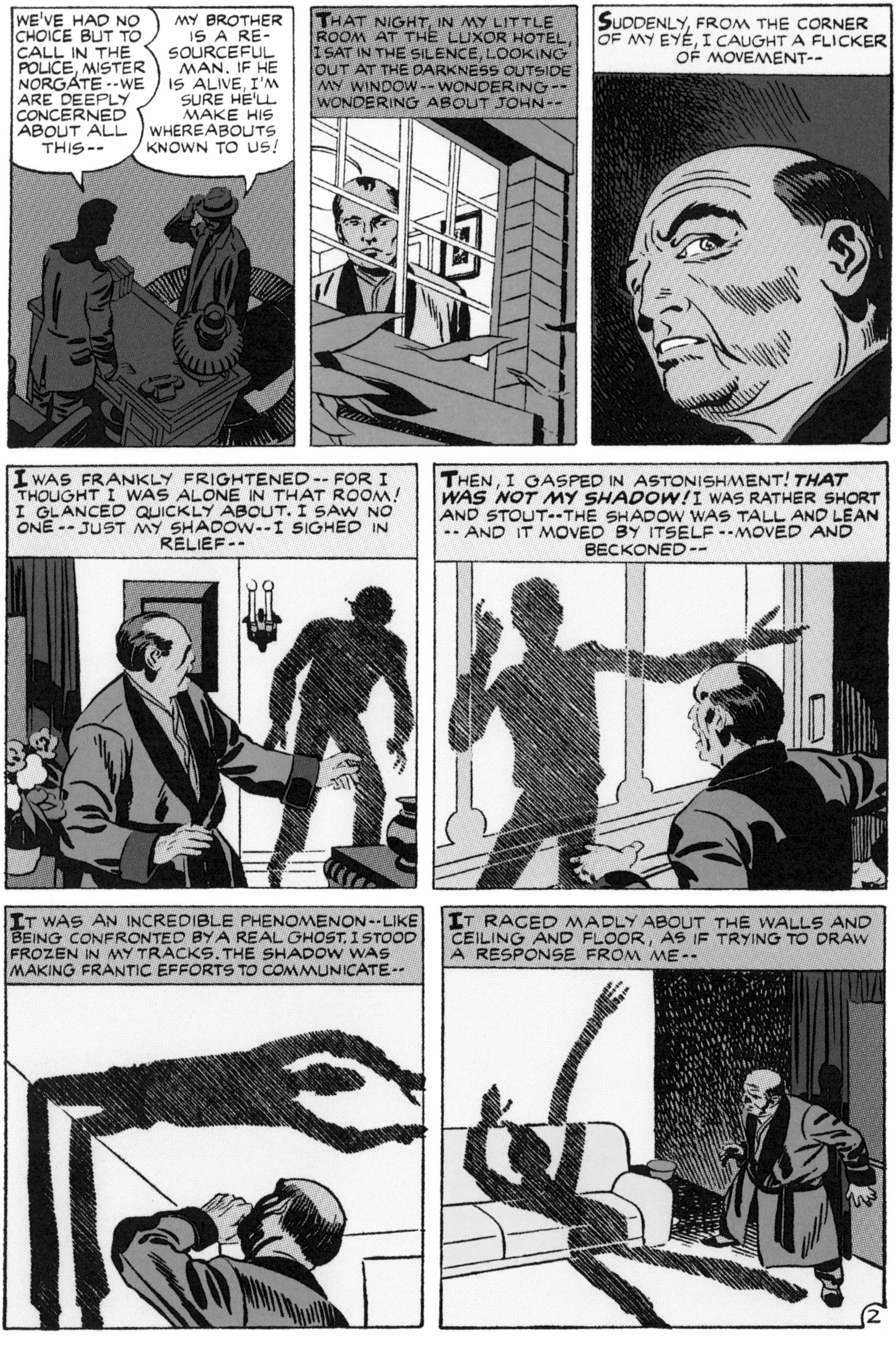
WE'VE HAD NO CHOICE BUT TO CALL IN THE POLICE, MISTER NORGATE--WE ARE DEEPLY CONCERNED ABOUT ALL THIS--
MY BROTHER IS A RESOURCEFUL MAN. IF HE IS ALIVE, I'M SURE HE'LL MAKE HIS WHEREABOUTS KNOWN TO US!
THAT NIGHT, IN MY LITTLE ROOM AT THE LUXOR HOTEL, I SAT IN THE SILENCE, LOOKING OUT AT THE DARKNESS OUTSIDE MY WINDOW--WONDERING--WONDERING ABOUT JOHN--
SUDDENLY, FROM THE CORNER OF MY EYE, I CAUGHT A FLICKER OF MOVEMENT--
I WAS FRANKLY FRIGHTENED--FOR I THOUGHT I WAS ALONE IN THAT ROOM! I GLANCED QUICKLY ABOUT. I SAW NO ONE--JUST MY SHADOW--I SIGHED IN RELIEF--
THEN, I GASPED IN ASTONISHMENT! THAT WAS NOT MY SHADOW! I WAS RATHER SHORT AND STOUT--THE SHADOW WAS TALL AND LEAN--AND IT MOVED BY ITSELF--MOVED AND BECKONED--
IT WAS AN INCREDIBLE PHENOMENON--LIKE BEING CONFRONTED BY A REAL GHOST. I STOOD FROZEN IN MY TRACKS. THE SHADOW WAS MAKING FRANTIC EFFORTS TO COMMUNICATE--
IT RACED MADLY ABOUT THE WALLS AND CEILING AND FLOOR, AS IF TRYING TO DRAW A RESPONSE FROM ME--
2

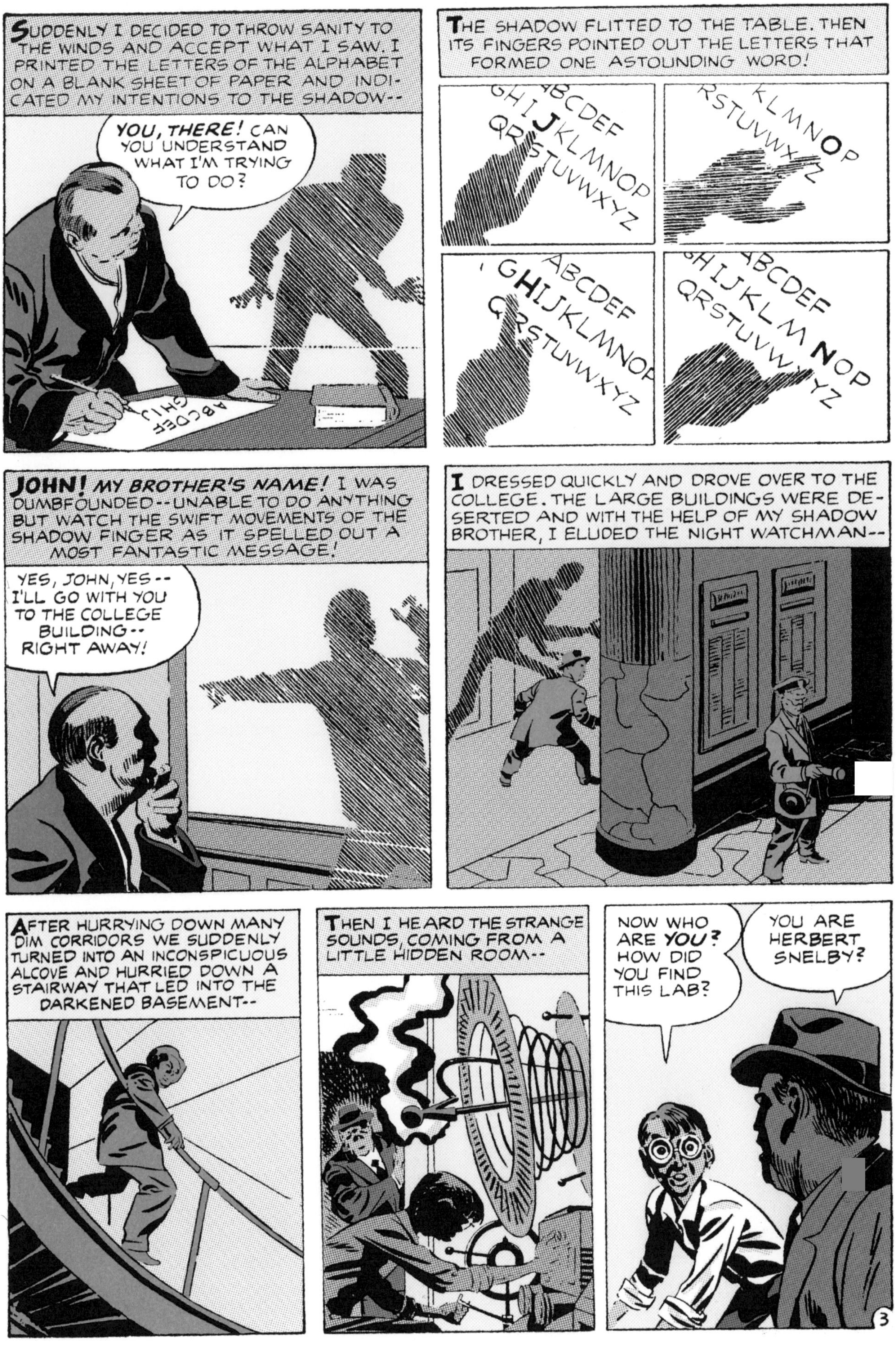
SUDDENLY I DECIDED TO THROW SANITY TO THE WINDS AND ACCEPT WHAT I SAW. I PRINTED THE LETTERS OF THE ALPHABET ON A BLANK SHEET OF PAPER AND INDICATED MY INTENTIONS TO THE SHADOW--
YOU, THERE! CAN YOU UNDERSTAND WHAT I'M TRYING TO DO?
ABCDEF GHIJ
THE SHADOW FLITTED TO THE TABLE. THEN ITS FINGERS POINTED OUT THE LETTERS THAT FORMED ONE ASTOUNDING WORD!
ABCDEF GHIJKLMNOP QRSTUVWXYZ
KLMNOP RSTUVWXYZ
ABCDEF GHIJKLMNOP QRSTUVWXYZ
ABCDEF GHIJKLMNOP QRSTUVWXYZ
JOHN! MY BROTHER'S NAME! I WAS DUMBFOUNDED--UNABLE TO DO ANYTHING BUT WATCH THE SWIFT MOVEMENTS OF THE SHADOW FINGER AS IT SPELLED OUT A MOST FANTASTIC MESSAGE!
YES, JOHN, YES-- I'LL GO WITH YOU TO THE COLLEGE BUILDING-- RIGHT AWAY!
I DRESSED QUICKLY AND DROVE OVER TO THE COLLEGE. THE LARGE BUILDINGS WERE DESERTED AND WITH THE HELP OF MY SHADOW BROTHER, I ELUDED THE NIGHT WATCHMAN--
AFTER HURRYING DOWN MANY DIM CORRIDORS WE SUDDENLY TURNED INTO AN INCONSPICUOUS ALCOVE AND HURRIED DOWN A STAIRWAY THAT LED INTO THE DARKENED BASEMENT--
THEN I HEARD THE STRANGE SOUNDS, COMING FROM A LITTLE HIDDEN ROOM--
NOW WHO ARE YOU? HOW DID YOU FIND THIS LAB?
YOU ARE HERBERT SNELBY?
3

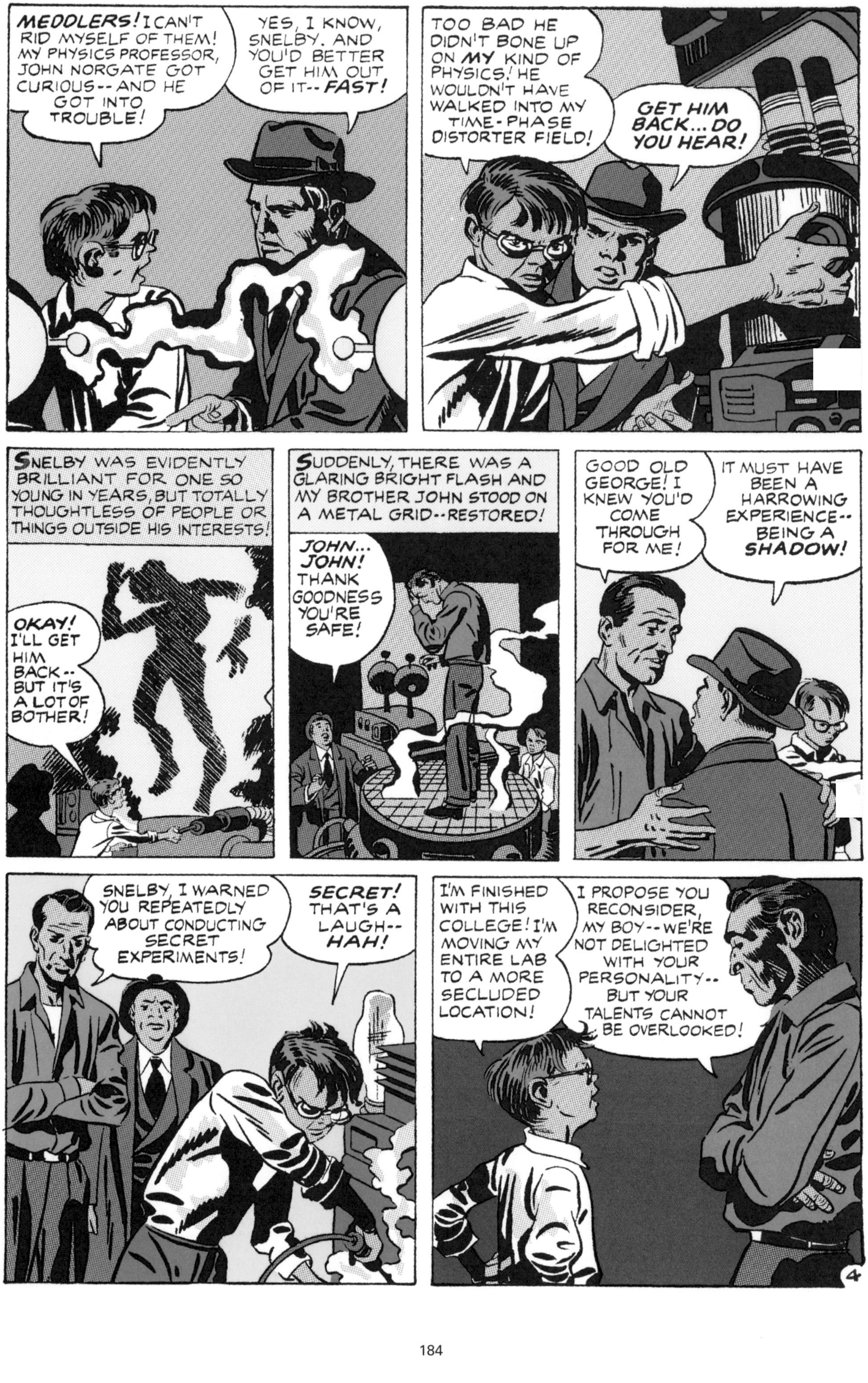
MEDDLERS! I CAN'T RID MYSELF OF THEM! MY PHYSICS PROFESSOR, JOHN NORGATE GOT CURIOUS-- AND HE GOT INTO TROUBLE!
YES, I KNOW, SNELBY. AND YOU'D BETTER GET HIM OUT OF IT-- FAST!
TOO BAD HE DIDN'T BONE UP ON MY KIND OF PHYSICS! HE WOULDN'T HAVE WALKED INTO MY TIME-PHASE DISTORTER FIELD!
GET HIM BACK... DO YOU HEAR!
SNELBY WAS EVIDENTLY BRILLIANT FOR ONE SO YOUNG IN YEARS, BUT TOTALLY THOUGHTLESS OF PEOPLE OR THINGS OUTSIDE HIS INTERESTS!
OKAY! I'LL GET HIM BACK-- BUT IT'S A LOT OF BOTHER!
SUDDENLY, THERE WAS A GLARING BRIGHT FLASH AND MY BROTHER JOHN STOOD ON A METAL GRID--RESTORED!
JOHN... JOHN! THANK GOODNESS YOU'RE SAFE!
GOOD OLD GEORGE! I KNEW YOU'D COME THROUGH FOR ME!
IT MUST HAVE BEEN A HARROWING EXPERIENCE-- BEING A SHADOW!
SNELBY, I WARNED YOU REPEATEDLY ABOUT CONDUCTING SECRET EXPERIMENTS!
SECRET! THAT'S A LAUGH-- HAH!
I'M FINISHED WITH THIS COLLEGE! I'M MOVING MY ENTIRE LAB TO A MORE SECLUDED LOCATION!
I PROPOSE YOU RECONSIDER, MY BOY-- WE'RE NOT DELIGHTED WITH YOUR PERSONALITY-- BUT YOUR TALENTS CANNOT BE OVERLOOKED!
4

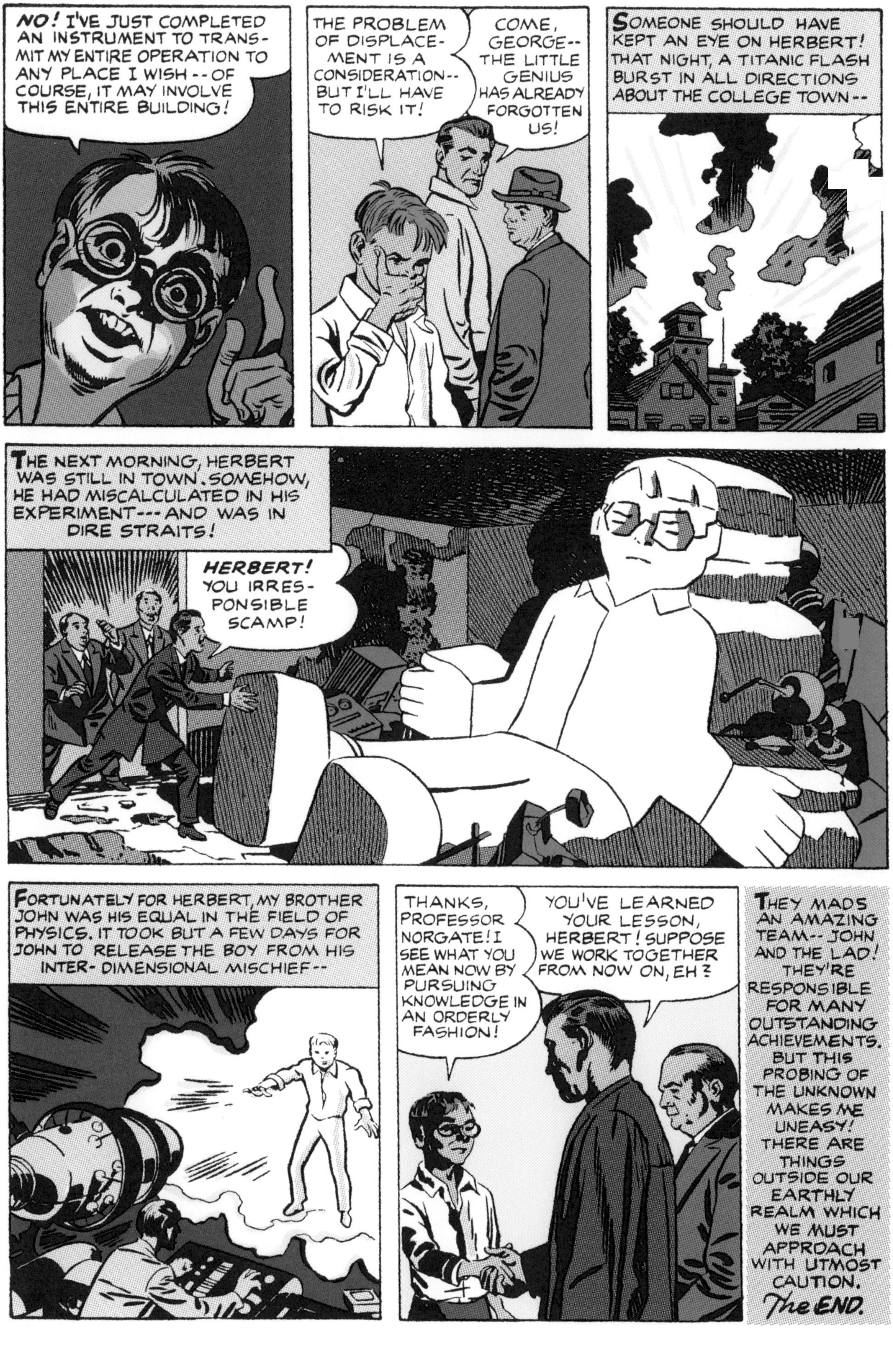
NO! I'VE JUST COMPLETED AN INSTRUMENT TO TRANSMIT MY ENTIRE OPERATION TO ANY PLACE I WISH -- OF COURSE, IT MAY INVOLVE THIS ENTIRE BUILDING!
THE PROBLEM OF DISPLACEMENT IS A CONSIDERATION-- BUT I'LL HAVE TO RISK IT!
COME, GEORGE-- THE LITTLE GENIUS HAS ALREADY FORGOTTEN US!
SOMEONE SHOULD HAVE KEPT AN EYE ON HERBERT! THAT NIGHT, A TITANIC FLASH BURST IN ALL DIRECTIONS ABOUT THE COLLEGE TOWN--
THE NEXT MORNING, HERBERT WAS STILL IN TOWN. SOMEHOW, HE HAD MISCALCULATED IN HIS EXPERIMENT--- AND WAS IN DIRE STRAITS!
HERBERT! YOU IRRESPONSIBLE SCAMP!
FORTUNATELY FOR HERBERT, MY BROTHER JOHN WAS HIS EQUAL IN THE FIELD OF PHYSICS. IT TOOK BUT A FEW DAYS FOR JOHN TO RELEASE THE BOY FROM HIS INTER-DIMENSIONAL MISCHIEF--
THANKS, PROFESSOR NORGATE! I SEE WHAT YOU MEAN NOW BY PURSUING KNOWLEDGE IN AN ORDERLY FASHION!
YOU'VE LEARNED YOUR LESSON, HERBERT! SUPPOSE WE WORK TOGETHER FROM NOW ON, EH?
THEY MADS AN AMAZING TEAM-- JOHN AND THE LAD! THEY'RE RESPONSIBLE FOR MANY OUTSTANDING ACHIEVEMENTS. BUT THIS PROBING OF THE UNKNOWN MAKES ME UNEASY! THERE ARE THINGS OUTSIDE OUR EARTHLY REALM WHICH WE MUST APPROACH WITH UTMOST CAUTION.
The END.

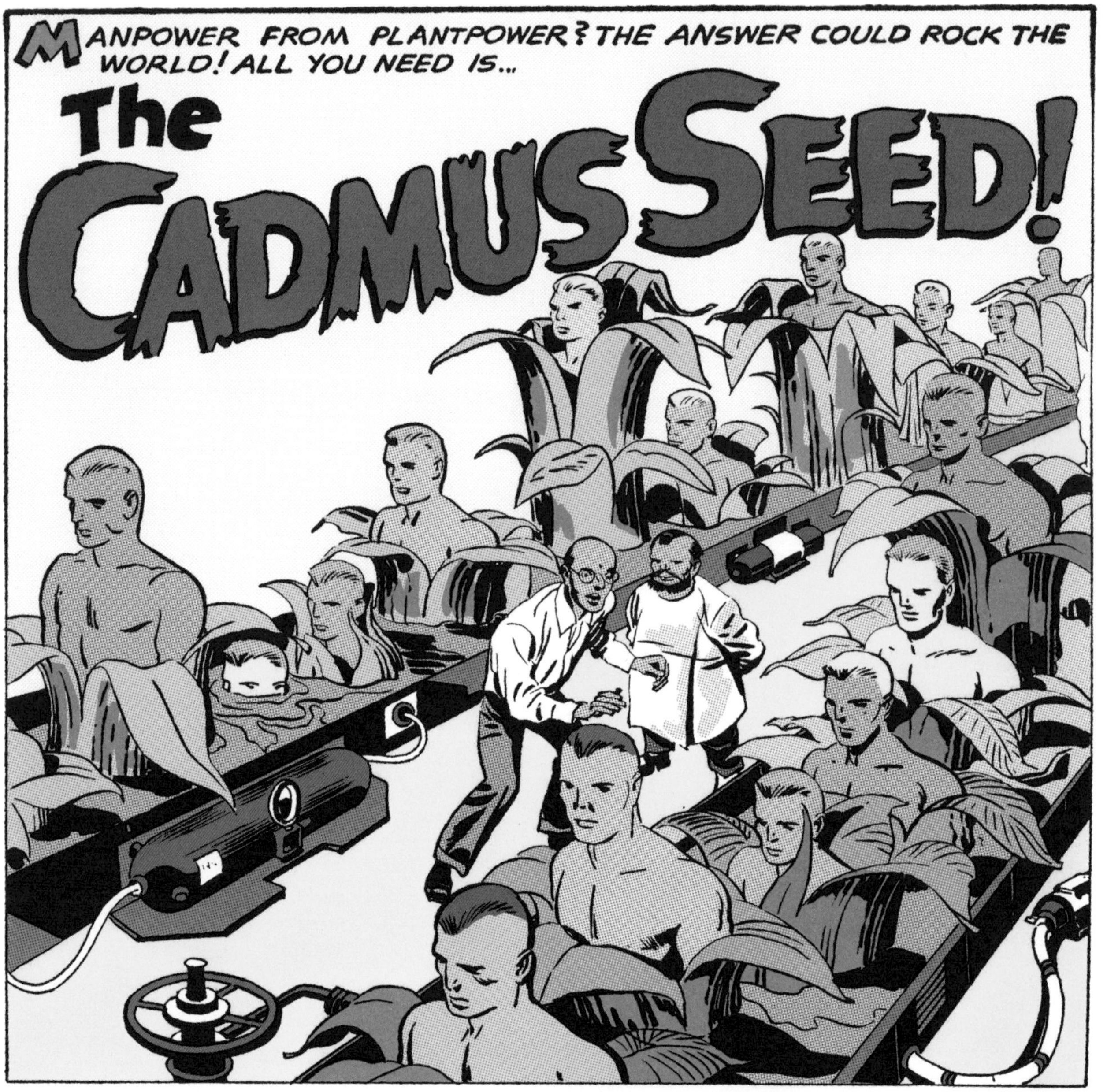
MANPOWER FROM PLANTPOWER? THE ANSWER COULD ROCK THE WORLD! ALL YOU NEED IS...
The CADMUS SEED!

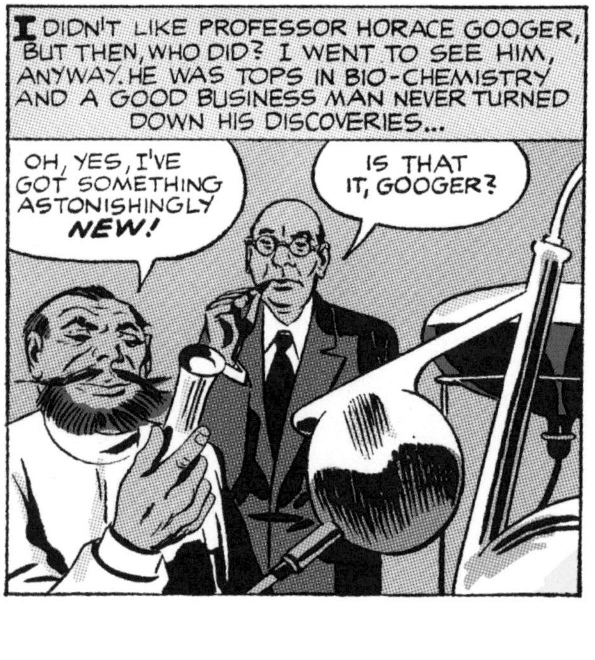
I DIDN'T LIKE PROFESSOR HORACE GOOGER, BUT THEN, WHO DID? I WENT TO SEE HIM, ANYWAY. HE WAS TOPS IN BIO-CHEMISTRY AND A GOOD BUSINESS MAN NEVER TURNED DOWN HIS DISCOVERIES...
OH, YES, I'VE GOT SOMETHING ASTONISHINGLY NEW!
IS THAT IT, GOOGER?

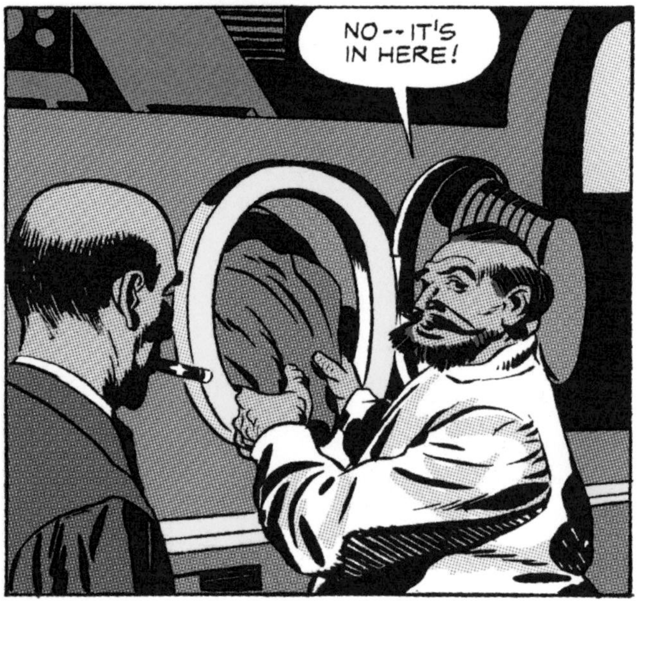
NO--IT'S IN HERE!

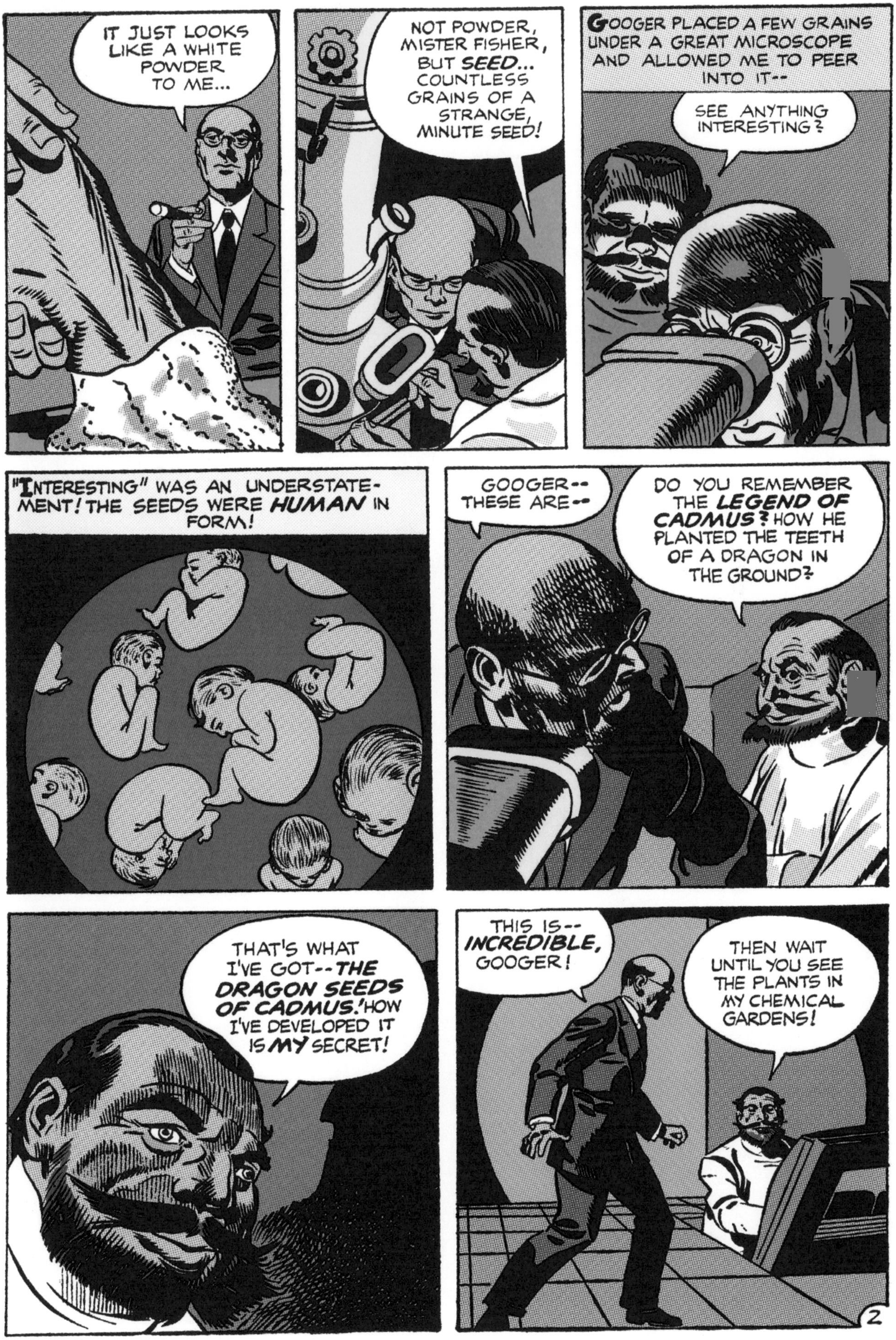
IT JUST LOOKS LIKE A WHITE POWDER TO ME...
NOT POWDER, MISTER FISHER, BUT SEED... COUNTLESS GRAINS OF A STRANGE, MINUTE SEED!
GOOGER PLACED A FEW GRAINS UNDER A GREAT MICROSCOPE AND ALLOWED ME TO PEER INTO IT--
SEE ANYTHING INTERESTING?
"INTERESTING" WAS AN UNDERSTATEMENT! THE SEEDS WERE HUMAN IN FORM!
GOOGER-- THESE ARE--
DO YOU REMEMBER THE LEGEND OF CADMUS? HOW HE PLANTED THE TEETH OF A DRAGON IN THE GROUND?
THAT'S WHAT I'VE GOT--THE DRAGON SEEDS OF CADMUS! HOW I'VE DEVELOPED IT IS MY SECRET!
THIS IS-- INCREDIBLE, GOOGER!
THEN WAIT UNTIL YOU SEE THE PLANTS IN MY CHEMICAL GARDENS!
2

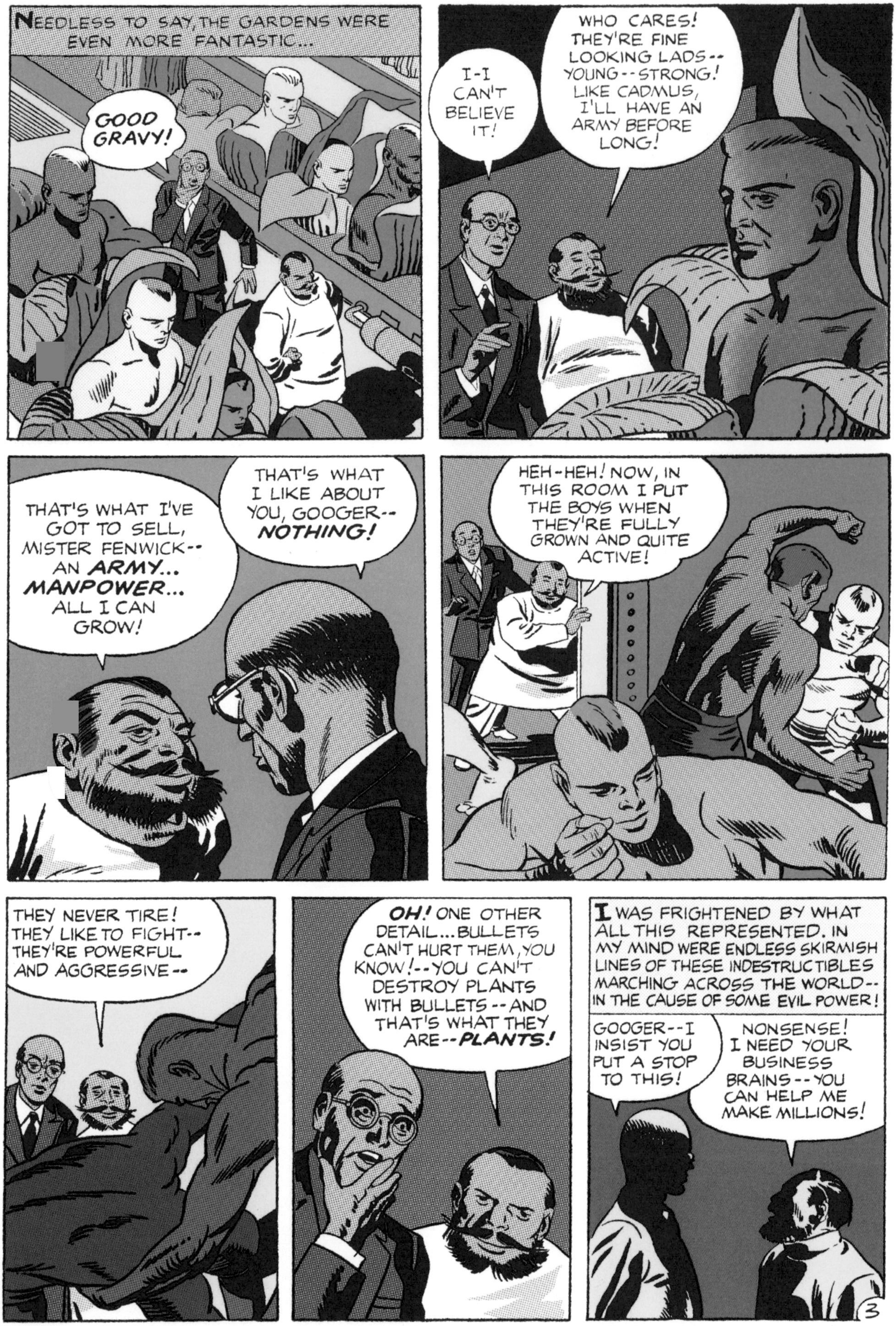
NEEDLESS TO SAY, THE GARDENS WERE EVEN MORE FANTASTIC...
GOOD GRAVY!
I-I CAN'T BELIEVE IT!
WHO CARES! THEY'RE FINE LOOKING LADS-- YOUNG--STRONG! LIKE CADMUS, I'LL HAVE AN ARMY BEFORE LONG!
THAT'S WHAT I'VE GOT TO SELL, MISTER FENWICK-- AN ARMY... MANPOWER... ALL I CAN GROW!
THAT'S WHAT I LIKE ABOUT YOU, GOOGER-- NOTHING!
HEH-HEH! NOW, IN THIS ROOM I PUT THE BOYS WHEN THEY'RE FULLY GROWN AND QUITE ACTIVE!
THEY NEVER TIRE! THEY LIKE TO FIGHT-- THEY'RE POWERFUL AND AGGRESSIVE--
OH! ONE OTHER DETAIL... BULLETS CAN'T HURT THEM, YOU KNOW!--YOU CAN'T DESTROY PLANTS WITH BULLETS--AND THAT'S WHAT THEY ARE--PLANTS!
I WAS FRIGHTENED BY WHAT ALL THIS REPRESENTED. IN MY MIND WERE ENDLESS SKIRMISH LINES OF THESE INDESTRUCTIBLES MARCHING ACROSS THE WORLD-- IN THE CAUSE OF SOME EVIL POWER!
GOOGER--I INSIST YOU PUT A STOP TO THIS!
NONSENSE! I NEED YOUR BUSINESS BRAINS--YOU CAN HELP ME MAKE MILLIONS!
3

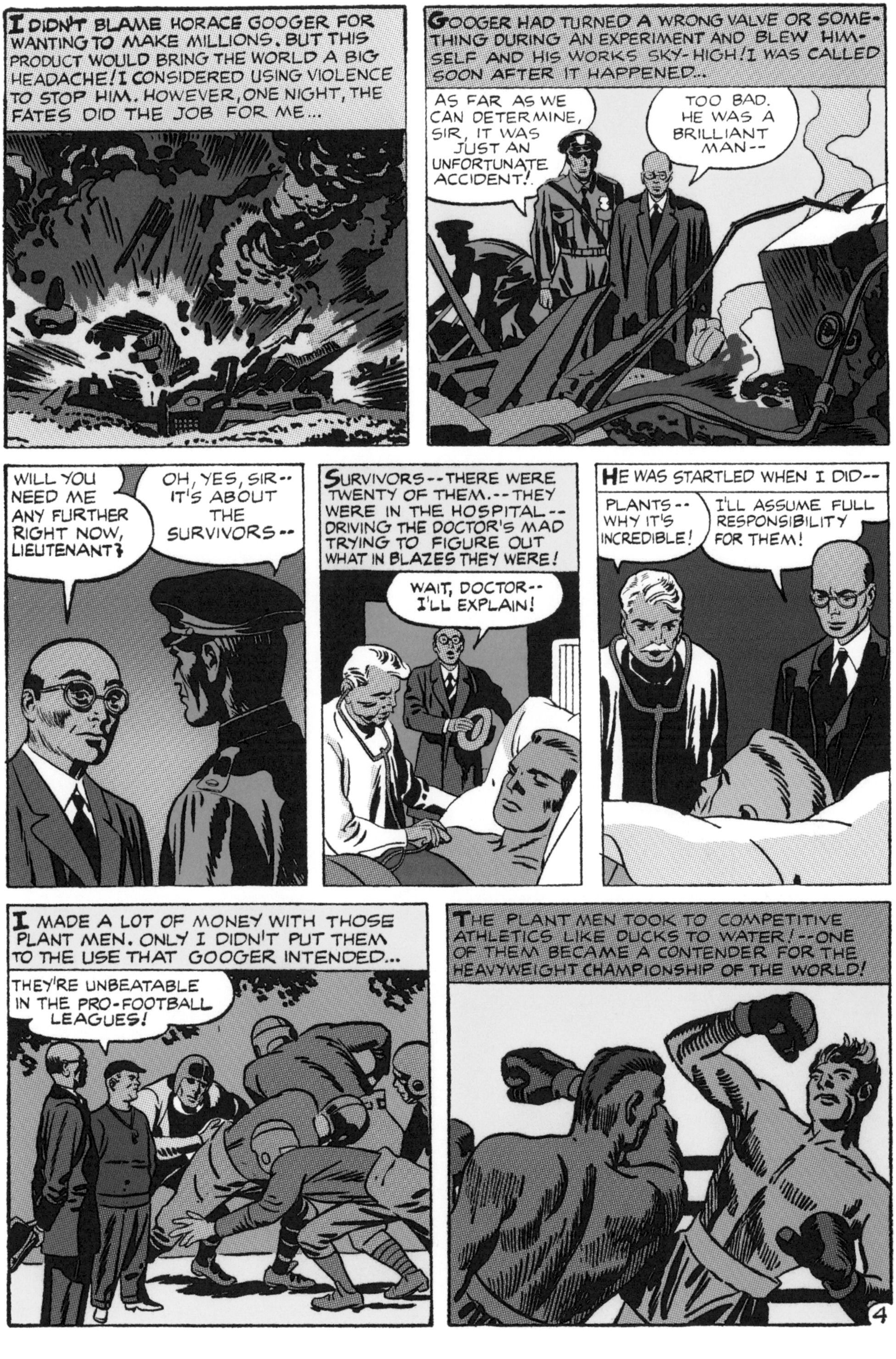
I DIDN'T BLAME HORACE GOOGER FOR WANTING TO MAKE MILLIONS. BUT THIS PRODUCT WOULD BRING THE WORLD A BIG HEADACHE! I CONSIDERED USING VIOLENCE TO STOP HIM. HOWEVER, ONE NIGHT, THE FATES DID THE JOB FOR ME...
GOOGER HAD TURNED A WRONG VALVE OR SOMETHING DURING AN EXPERIMENT AND BLEW HIMSELF AND HIS WORKS SKY-HIGH! I WAS CALLED SOON AFTER IT HAPPENED...
AS FAR AS WE CAN DETERMINE, SIR, IT WAS JUST AN UNFORTUNATE ACCIDENT!
TOO BAD. HE WAS A BRILLIANT MAN--
WILL YOU NEED ME ANY FURTHER RIGHT NOW, LIEUTENANT?
OH, YES, SIR-- IT'S ABOUT THE SURVIVORS--
SURVIVORS--THERE WERE TWENTY OF THEM.--THEY WERE IN THE HOSPITAL--DRIVING THE DOCTOR'S MAD TRYING TO FIGURE OUT WHAT IN BLAZES THEY WERE!
WAIT, DOCTOR-- I'LL EXPLAIN!
HE WAS STARTLED WHEN I DID--
PLANTS-- WHY IT'S INCREDIBLE!
I'LL ASSUME FULL RESPONSIBILITY FOR THEM!
I MADE A LOT OF MONEY WITH THOSE PLANT MEN. ONLY I DIDN'T PUT THEM TO THE USE THAT GOOGER INTENDED...
THEY'RE UNBEATABLE IN THE PRO-FOOTBALL LEAGUES!
THE PLANT MEN TOOK TO COMPETITIVE ATHLETICS LIKE DUCKS TO WATER!--ONE OF THEM BECAME A CONTENDER FOR THE HEAVYWEIGHT CHAMPIONSHIP OF THE WORLD!
4

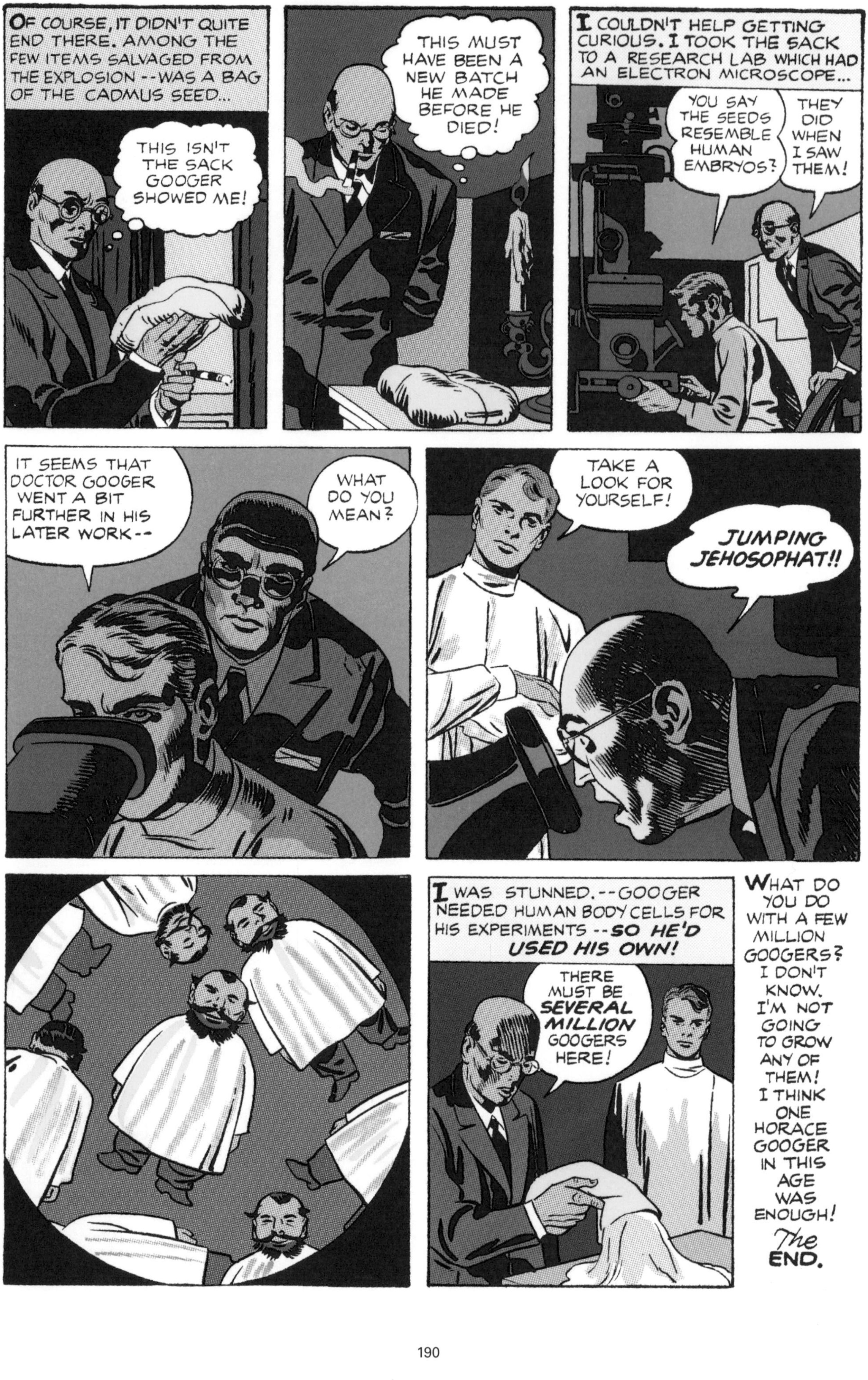
OF COURSE, IT DIDN'T QUITE END THERE. AMONG THE FEW ITEMS SALVAGED FROM THE EXPLOSION --WAS A BAG OF THE CADMUS SEED...
THIS ISN'T THE SACK GOOGER SHOWED ME!
THIS MUST HAVE BEEN A NEW BATCH HE MADE BEFORE HE DIED!
I COULDN'T HELP GETTING CURIOUS. I TOOK THE SACK TO A RESEARCH LAB WHICH HAD AN ELECTRON MICROSCOPE...
YOU SAY THE SEEDS RESEMBLE HUMAN EMBRYOS?
THEY DID WHEN I SAW THEM!
IT SEEMS THAT DOCTOR GOOGER WENT A BIT FURTHER IN HIS LATER WORK--
WHAT DO YOU MEAN?
TAKE A LOOK FOR YOURSELF!
JUMPING JEHOSOPHAT!!
I WAS STUNNED.--GOOGER NEEDED HUMAN BODY CELLS FOR HIS EXPERIMENTS --SO HE'D USED HIS OWN!
THERE MUST BE SEVERAL MILLION GOOGERS HERE!
WHAT DO YOU DO WITH A FEW MILLION GOOGERS? I DON'T KNOW. I'M NOT GOING TO GROW ANY OF THEM! I THINK ONE HORACE GOOGER IN THIS AGE WAS ENOUGH!
The END.

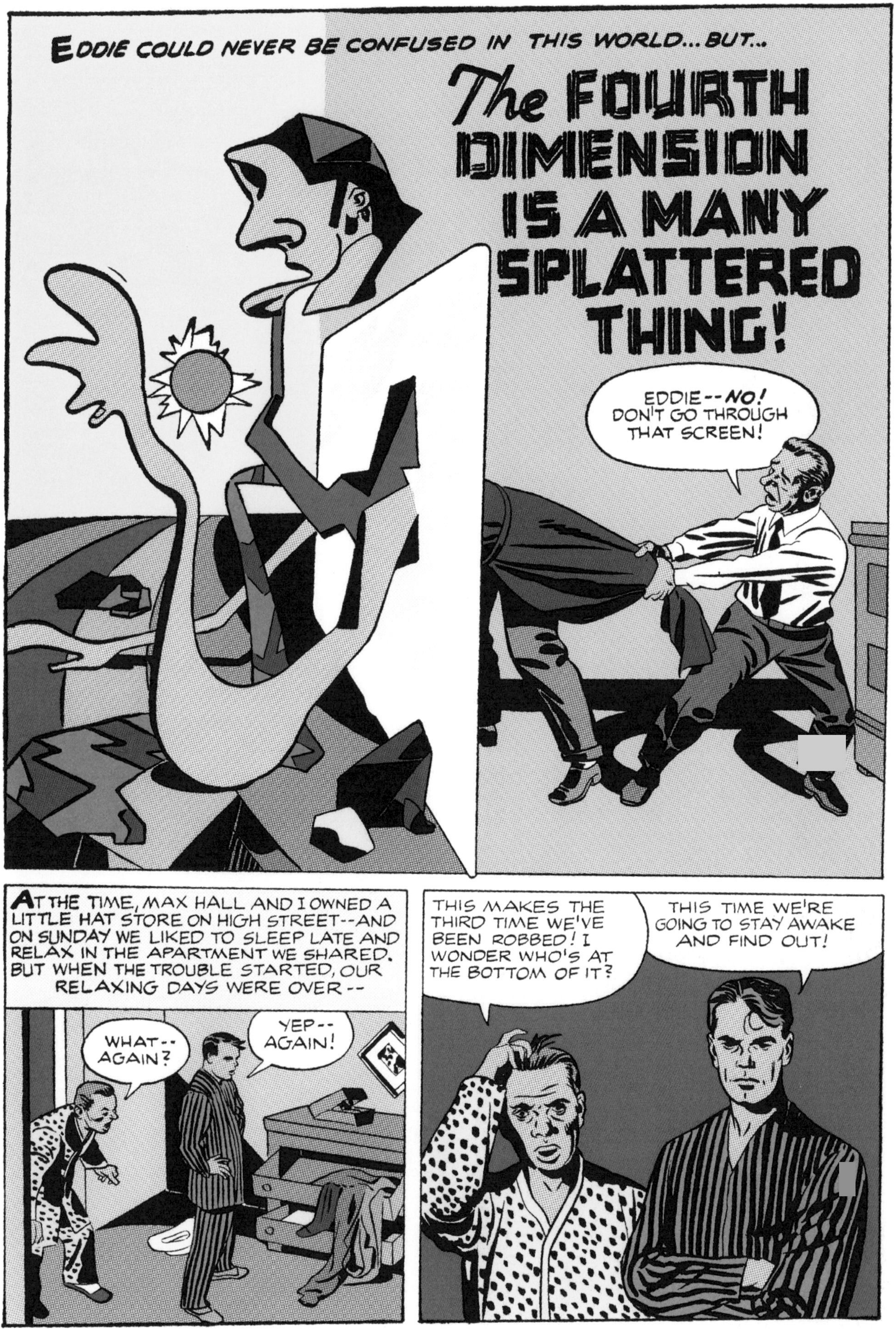
EDDIE COULD NEVER BE CONFUSED IN THIS WORLD... BUT...
The FOURTH DIMENSION IS A MANY SPLATTERED THING!
EDDIE--NO! DON'T GO THROUGH THAT SCREEN!
AT THE TIME, MAX HALL AND I OWNED A LITTLE HAT STORE ON HIGH STREET--AND ON SUNDAY WE LIKED TO SLEEP LATE AND RELAX IN THE APARTMENT WE SHARED. BUT WHEN THE TROUBLE STARTED, OUR RELAXING DAYS WERE OVER--
WHAT--AGAIN?
YEP--AGAIN!
THIS MAKES THE THIRD TIME WE'VE BEEN ROBBED! I WONDER WHO'S AT THE BOTTOM OF IT?
THIS TIME WE'RE GOING TO STAY AWAKE AND FIND OUT!

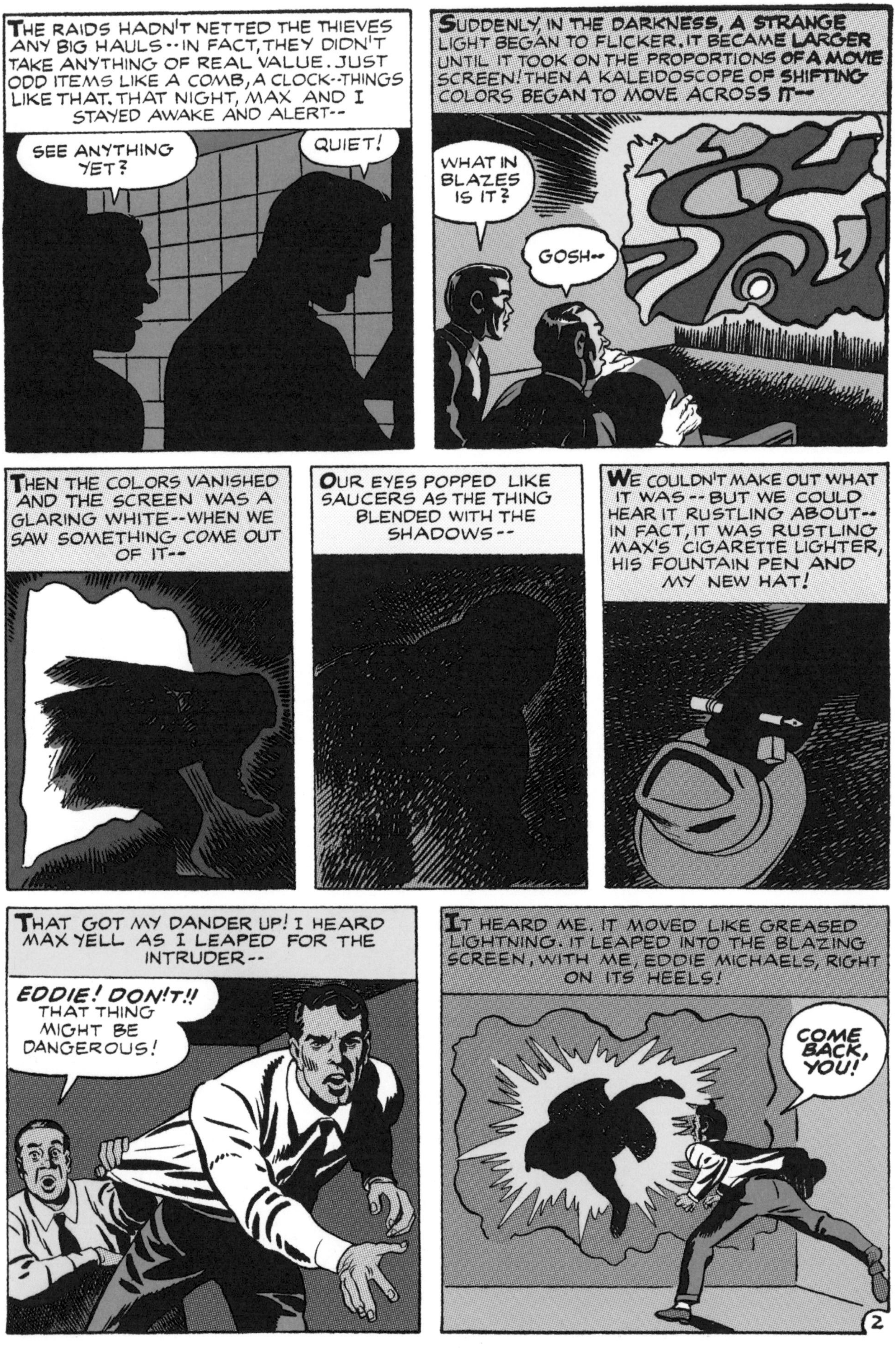
THE RAIDS HADN'T NETTED THE THIEVES ANY BIG HAULS -- IN FACT, THEY DIDN'T TAKE ANYTHING OF REAL VALUE. JUST ODD ITEMS LIKE A COMB, A CLOCK -- THINGS LIKE THAT. THAT NIGHT, MAX AND I STAYED AWAKE AND ALERT --
SEE ANYTHING YET?
QUIET!
SUDDENLY, IN THE DARKNESS, A STRANGE LIGHT BEGAN TO FLICKER. IT BECAME LARGER UNTIL IT TOOK ON THE PROPORTIONS OF A MOVIE SCREEN! THEN A KALEIDOSCOPE OF SHIFTING COLORS BEGAN TO MOVE ACROSS IT --
WHAT IN BLAZES IS IT?
GOSH --
THEN THE COLORS VANISHED AND THE SCREEN WAS A GLARING WHITE -- WHEN WE SAW SOMETHING COME OUT OF IT --
OUR EYES POPPED LIKE SAUCERS AS THE THING BLENDED WITH THE SHADOWS --
WE COULDN'T MAKE OUT WHAT IT WAS -- BUT WE COULD HEAR IT RUSTLING ABOUT -- IN FACT, IT WAS RUSTLING MAX'S CIGARETTE LIGHTER, HIS FOUNTAIN PEN AND MY NEW HAT!
THAT GOT MY DANDER UP! I HEARD MAX YELL AS I LEAPED FOR THE INTRUDER --
EDDIE! DON'T!! THAT THING MIGHT BE DANGEROUS!
IT HEARD ME. IT MOVED LIKE GREASED LIGHTNING. IT LEAPED INTO THE BLAZING SCREEN, WITH ME, EDDIE MICHAELS, RIGHT ON ITS HEELS!
COME BACK, YOU!
2

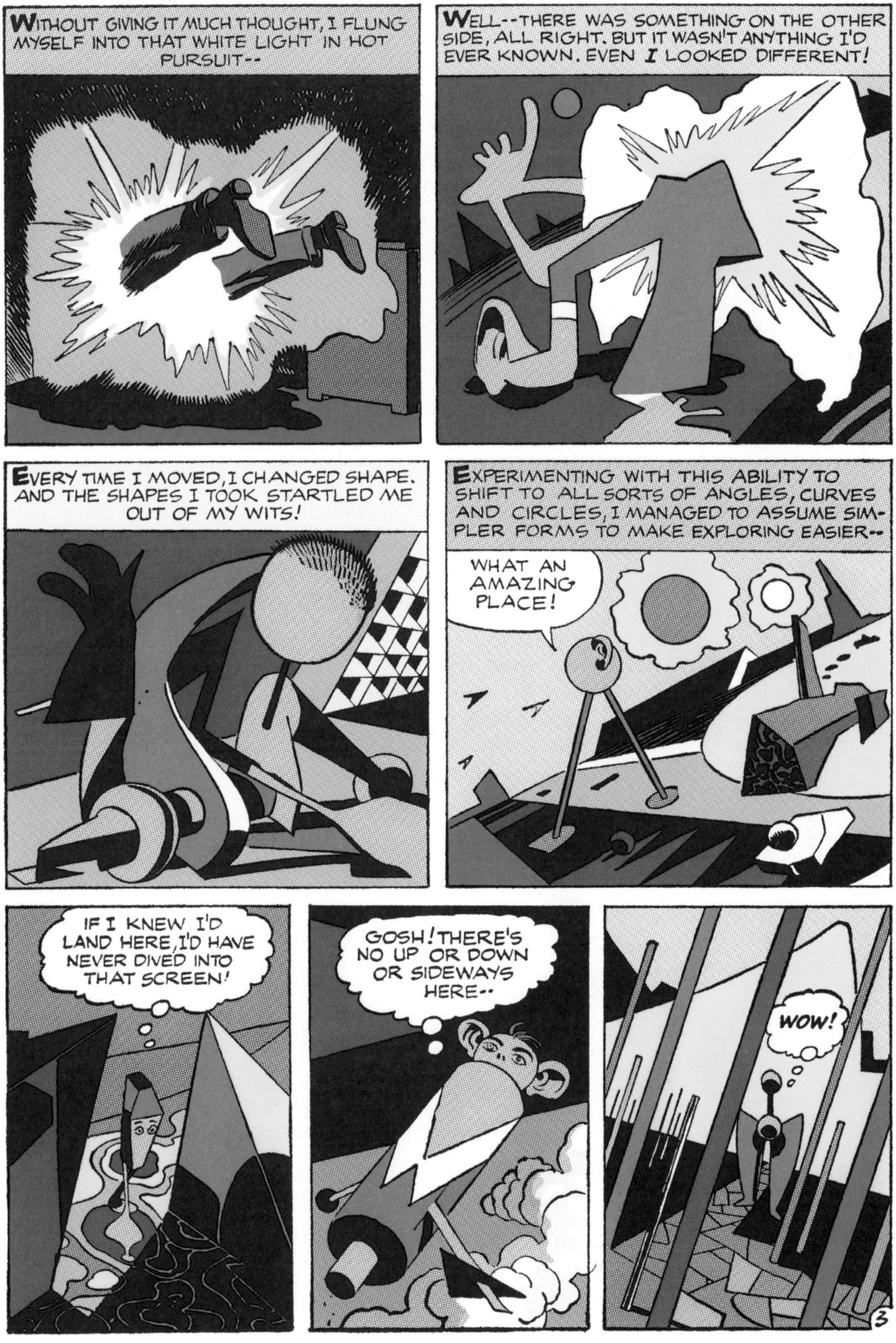
WITHOUT GIVING IT MUCH THOUGHT, I FLUNG MYSELF INTO THAT WHITE LIGHT IN HOT PURSUIT--
WELL--THERE WAS SOMETHING ON THE OTHER SIDE, ALL RIGHT. BUT IT WASN'T ANYTHING I'D EVER KNOWN. EVEN I LOOKED DIFFERENT!
EVERY TIME I MOVED, I CHANGED SHAPE. AND THE SHAPES I TOOK STARTLED ME OUT OF MY WITS!
EXPERIMENTING WITH THIS ABILITY TO SHIFT TO ALL SORTS OF ANGLES, CURVES AND CIRCLES, I MANAGED TO ASSUME SIMPLER FORMS TO MAKE EXPLORING EASIER--
WHAT AN AMAZING PLACE!
IF I KNEW I'D LAND HERE, I'D HAVE NEVER DIVED INTO THAT SCREEN!
GOSH! THERE'S NO UP OR DOWN OR SIDEWAYS HERE--
WOW!
3

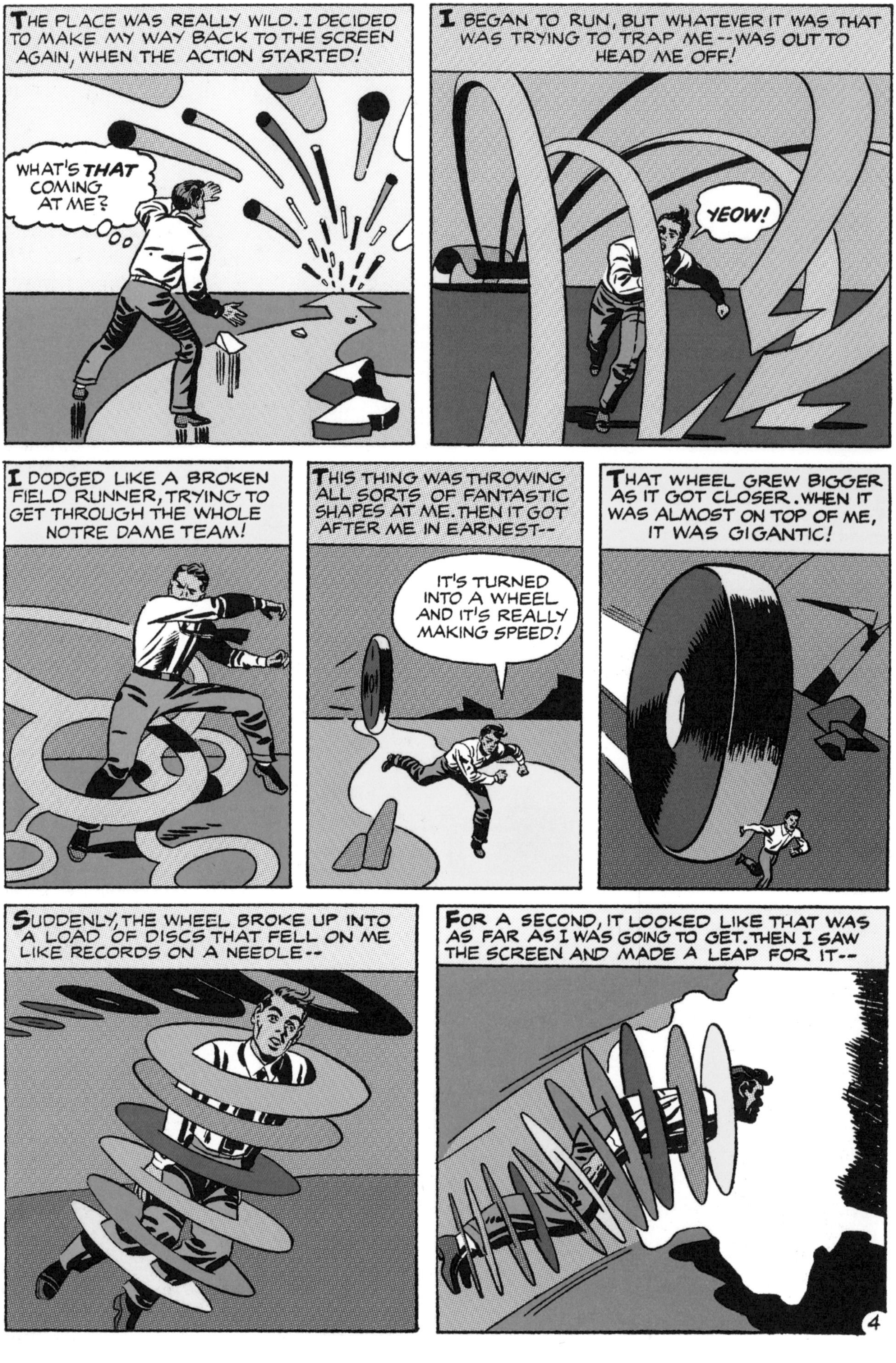

THE PLACE WAS REALLY WILD. I DECIDED TO MAKE MY WAY BACK TO THE SCREEN AGAIN, WHEN THE ACTION STARTED!
WHAT'S THAT COMING AT ME?
I BEGAN TO RUN, BUT WHATEVER IT WAS THAT WAS TRYING TO TRAP ME--WAS OUT TO HEAD ME OFF!
YEOW!
I DODGED LIKE A BROKEN FIELD RUNNER, TRYING TO GET THROUGH THE WHOLE NOTRE DAME TEAM!
THIS THING WAS THROWING ALL SORTS OF FANTASTIC SHAPES AT ME. THEN IT GOT AFTER ME IN EARNEST--
IT'S TURNED INTO A WHEEL AND IT'S REALLY MAKING SPEED!
THAT WHEEL GREW BIGGER AS IT GOT CLOSER. WHEN IT WAS ALMOST ON TOP OF ME, IT WAS GIGANTIC!
SUDDENLY, THE WHEEL BROKE UP INTO A LOAD OF DISCS THAT FELL ON ME LIKE RECORDS ON A NEEDLE--
FOR A SECOND, IT LOOKED LIKE THAT WAS AS FAR AS I WAS GOING TO GET. THEN I SAW THE SCREEN AND MADE A LEAP FOR IT--
4

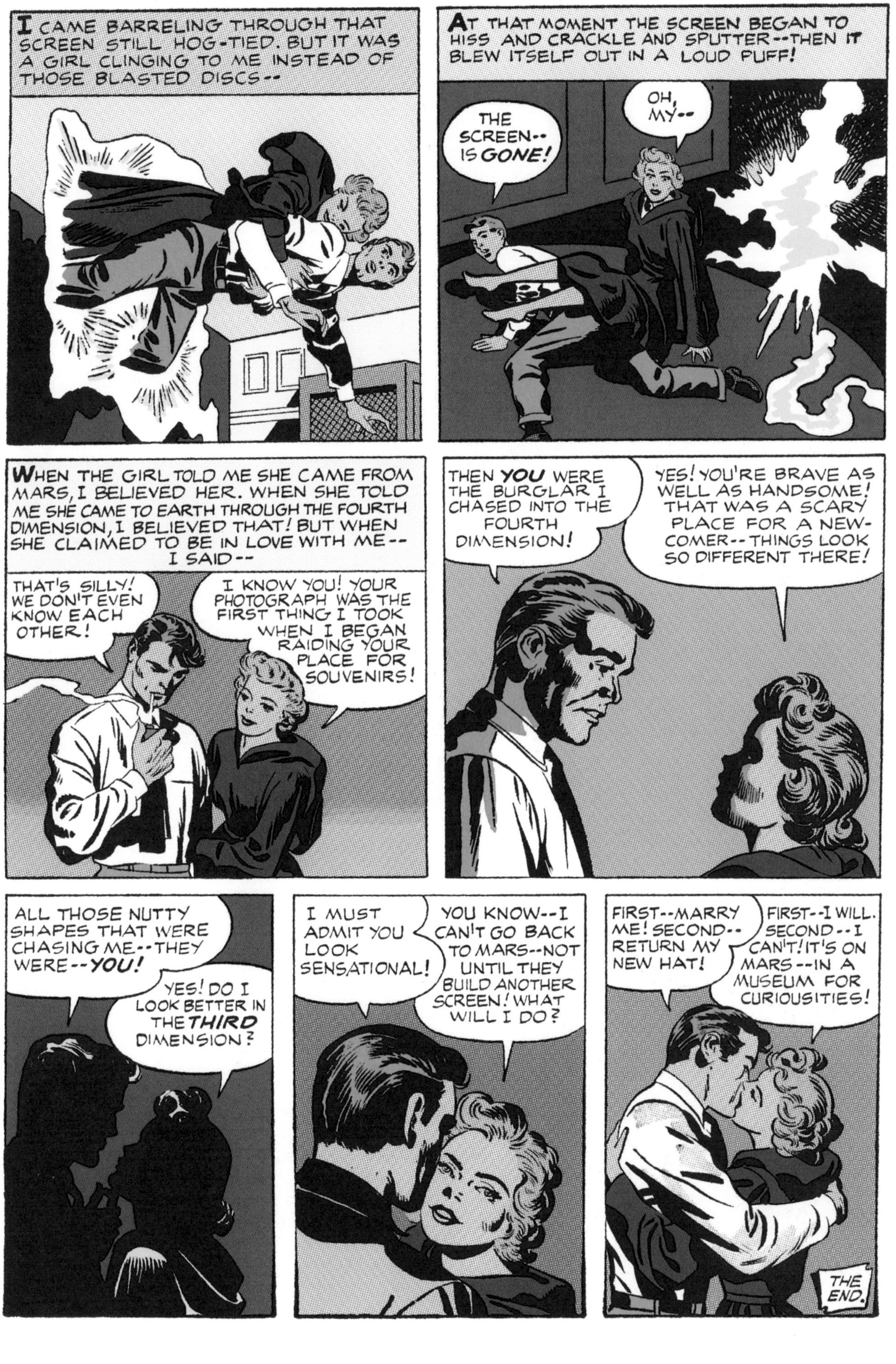

I CAME BARRELING THROUGH THAT SCREEN STILL HOG-TIED. BUT IT WAS A GIRL CLINGING TO ME INSTEAD OF THOSE BLASTED DISCS--
AT THAT MOMENT THE SCREEN BEGAN TO HISS AND CRACKLE AND SPUTTER--THEN IT BLEW ITSELF OUT IN A LOUD PUFF!
THE SCREEN--IS GONE!
OH, MY--
WHEN THE GIRL TOLD ME SHE CAME FROM MARS, I BELIEVED HER. WHEN SHE TOLD ME SHE CAME TO EARTH THROUGH THE FOURTH DIMENSION, I BELIEVED THAT! BUT WHEN SHE CLAIMED TO BE IN LOVE WITH ME-- I SAID--
THAT'S SILLY! WE DON'T EVEN KNOW EACH OTHER!
I KNOW YOU! YOUR PHOTOGRAPH WAS THE FIRST THING I TOOK WHEN I BEGAN RAIDING YOUR PLACE FOR SOUVENIRS!
THEN YOU WERE THE BURGLAR I CHASED INTO THE FOURTH DIMENSION!
YES! YOU'RE BRAVE AS WELL AS HANDSOME! THAT WAS A SCARY PLACE FOR A NEW-COMER--THINGS LOOK SO DIFFERENT THERE!
ALL THOSE NUTTY SHAPES THAT WERE CHASING ME--THEY WERE--YOU!
YES! DO I LOOK BETTER IN THE THIRD DIMENSION?
I MUST ADMIT YOU LOOK SENSATIONAL!
YOU KNOW--I CAN'T GO BACK TO MARS--NOT UNTIL THEY BUILD ANOTHER SCREEN! WHAT WILL I DO?
FIRST--MARRY ME! SECOND--RETURN MY NEW HAT!
FIRST--I WILL. SECOND--I CAN'T! IT'S ON MARS--IN A MUSEUM FOR CURIOUSITIES!
THE END.

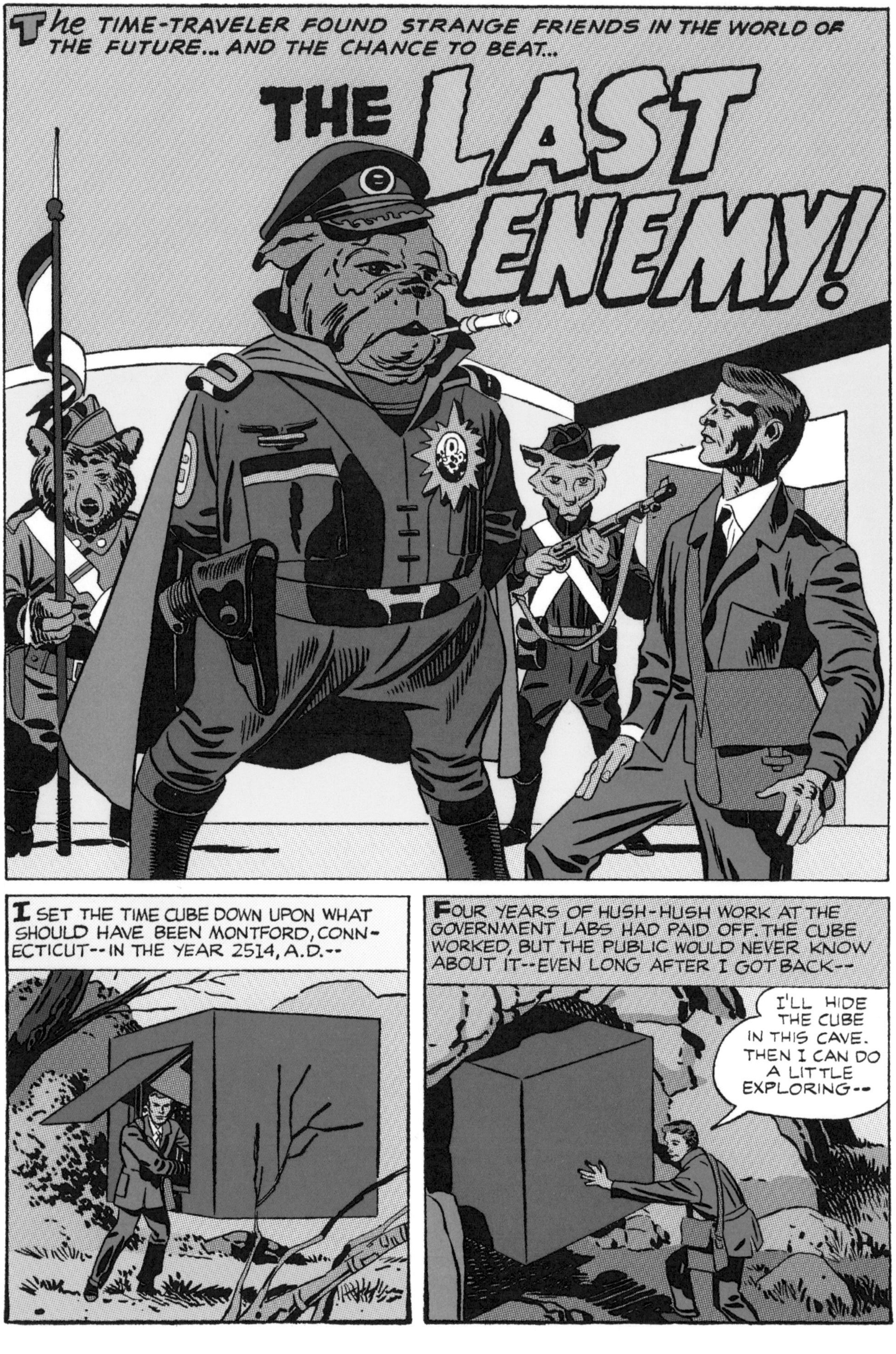
The TIME-TRAVELER FOUND STRANGE FRIENDS IN THE WORLD OF THE FUTURE... AND THE CHANCE TO BEAT...
THE LAST ENEMY!
I SET THE TIME CUBE DOWN UPON WHAT SHOULD HAVE BEEN MONTFORD, CONNECTICUT--IN THE YEAR 2514, A.D.--
FOUR YEARS OF HUSH-HUSH WORK AT THE GOVERNMENT LABS HAD PAID OFF. THE CUBE WORKED, BUT THE PUBLIC WOULD NEVER KNOW ABOUT IT--EVEN LONG AFTER I GOT BACK--
I'LL HIDE THE CUBE IN THIS CAVE. THEN I CAN DO A LITTLE EXPLORING--

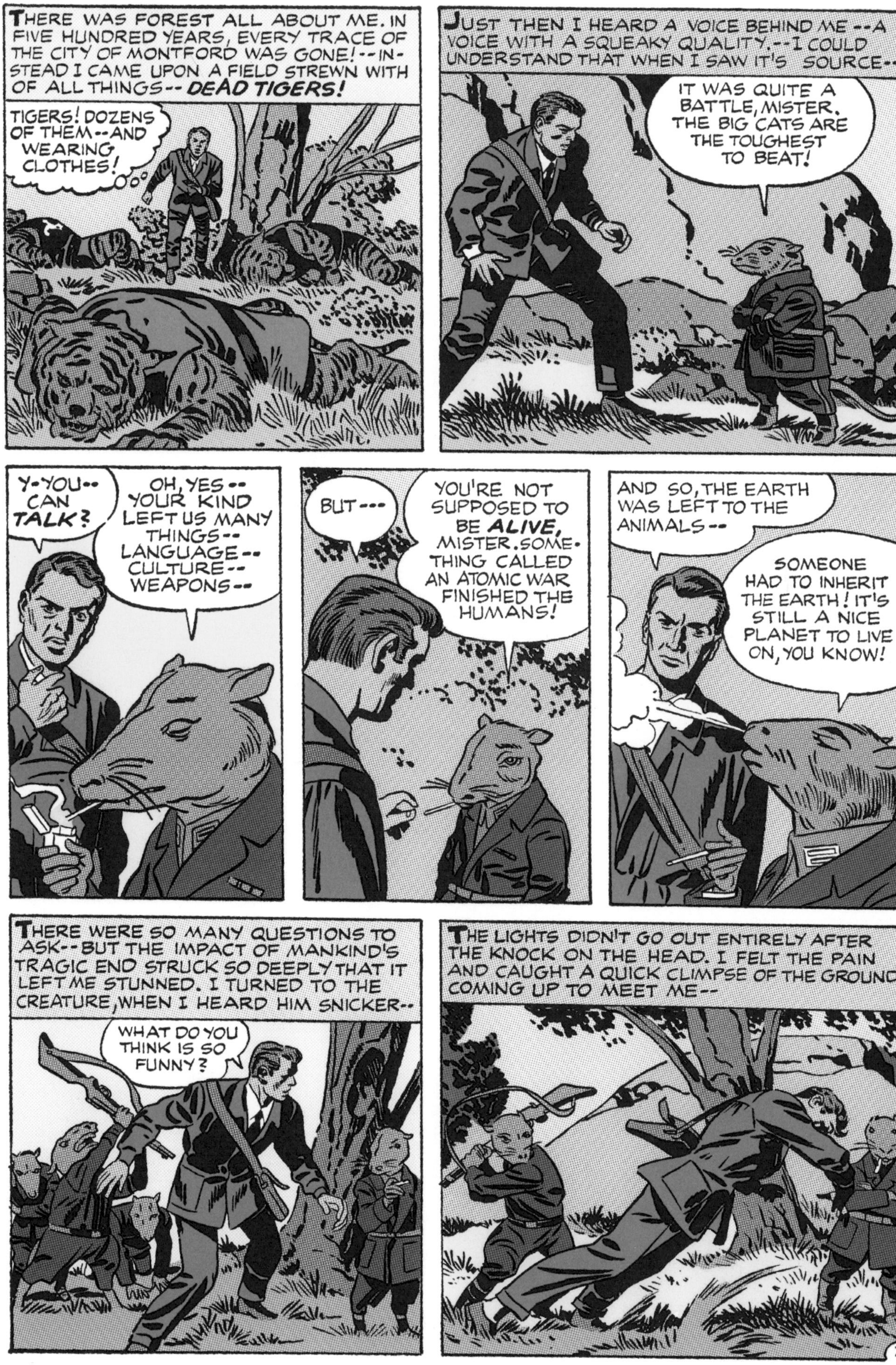
THERE WAS FOREST ALL ABOUT ME. IN FIVE HUNDRED YEARS, EVERY TRACE OF THE CITY OF MONTFORD WAS GONE!--INSTEAD I CAME UPON A FIELD STREWN WITH OF ALL THINGS--DEAD TIGERS!
TIGERS! DOZENS OF THEM--AND WEARING CLOTHES!
JUST THEN I HEARD A VOICE BEHIND ME--A VOICE WITH A SQUEAKY QUALITY.--I COULD UNDERSTAND THAT WHEN I SAW IT'S SOURCE--
IT WAS QUITE A BATTLE, MISTER. THE BIG CATS ARE THE TOUGHEST TO BEAT!
Y-YOU--CAN TALK?
OH, YES--YOUR KIND LEFT US MANY THINGS--LANGUAGE--CULTURE--WEAPONS--
BUT---
YOU'RE NOT SUPPOSED TO BE ALIVE, MISTER. SOMETHING CALLED AN ATOMIC WAR FINISHED THE HUMANS!
AND SO, THE EARTH WAS LEFT TO THE ANIMALS--
SOMEONE HAD TO INHERIT THE EARTH! IT'S STILL A NICE PLANET TO LIVE ON, YOU KNOW!
THERE WERE SO MANY QUESTIONS TO ASK--BUT THE IMPACT OF MANKIND'S TRAGIC END STRUCK SO DEEPLY THAT IT LEFT ME STUNNED. I TURNED TO THE CREATURE, WHEN I HEARD HIM SNICKER--
WHAT DO YOU THINK IS SO FUNNY?
THE LIGHTS DIDN'T GO OUT ENTIRELY AFTER THE KNOCK ON THE HEAD. I FELT THE PAIN AND CAUGHT A QUICK GLIMPSE OF THE GROUND COMING UP TO MEET ME--
2

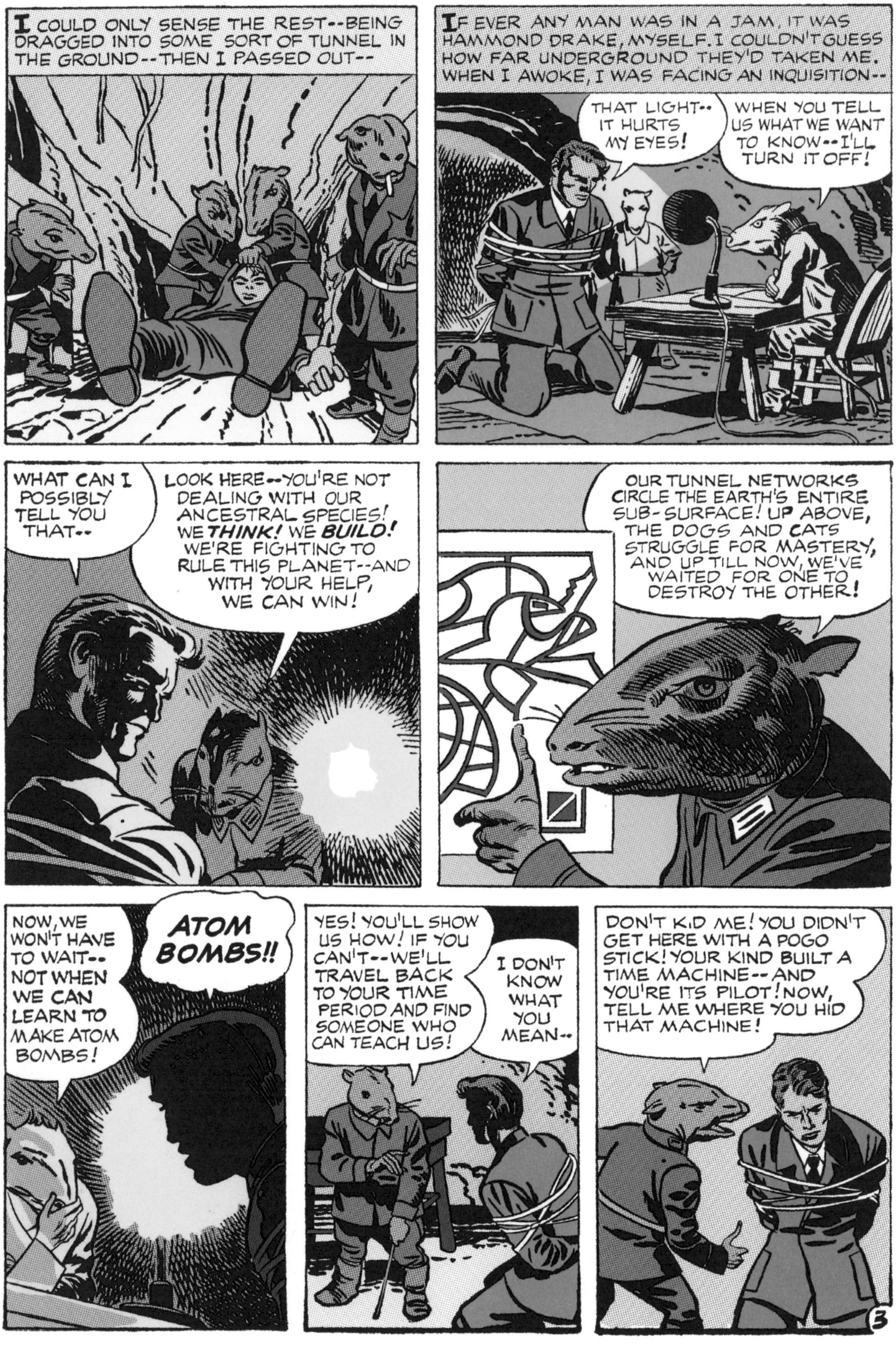
I COULD ONLY SENSE THE REST--BEING DRAGGED INTO SOME SORT OF TUNNEL IN THE GROUND--THEN I PASSED OUT--
IF EVER ANY MAN WAS IN A JAM, IT WAS HAMMOND DRAKE, MYSELF. I COULDN'T GUESS HOW FAR UNDERGROUND THEY'D TAKEN ME. WHEN I AWOKE, I WAS FACING AN INQUISITION--
THAT LIGHT-- IT HURTS MY EYES!
WHEN YOU TELL US WHAT WE WANT TO KNOW--I'LL TURN IT OFF!
WHAT CAN I POSSIBLY TELL YOU THAT--
LOOK HERE--YOU'RE NOT DEALING WITH OUR ANCESTRAL SPECIES! WE THINK! WE BUILD! WE'RE FIGHTING TO RULE THIS PLANET--AND WITH YOUR HELP, WE CAN WIN!
OUR TUNNEL NETWORKS CIRCLE THE EARTH'S ENTIRE SUB-SURFACE! UP ABOVE, THE DOGS AND CATS STRUGGLE FOR MASTERY, AND UP TILL NOW, WE'VE WAITED FOR ONE TO DESTROY THE OTHER!
NOW, WE WON'T HAVE TO WAIT-- NOT WHEN WE CAN LEARN TO MAKE ATOM BOMBS!
ATOM BOMBS!!
YES! YOU'LL SHOW US HOW! IF YOU CAN'T--WE'LL TRAVEL BACK TO YOUR TIME PERIOD AND FIND SOMEONE WHO CAN TEACH US!
I DON'T KNOW WHAT YOU MEAN--
DON'T KID ME! YOU DIDN'T GET HERE WITH A POGO STICK! YOUR KIND BUILT A TIME MACHINE--AND YOU'RE ITS PILOT! NOW, TELL ME WHERE YOU HID THAT MACHINE!
3

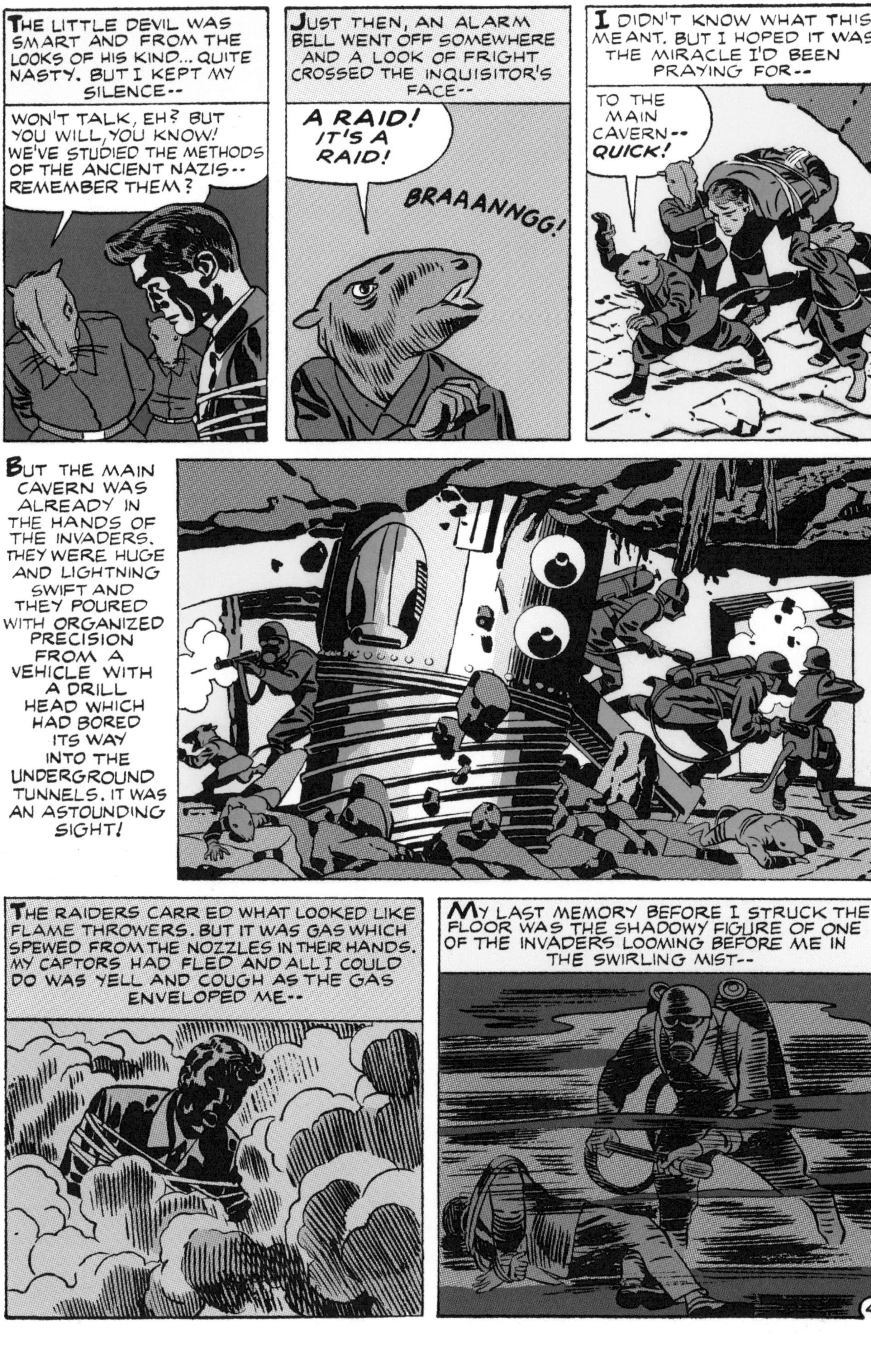

THE LITTLE DEVIL WAS SMART AND FROM THE LOOKS OF HIS KIND... QUITE NASTY. BUT I KEPT MY SILENCE--
WON'T TALK, EH? BUT YOU WILL, YOU KNOW! WE'VE STUDIED THE METHODS OF THE ANCIENT NAZIS-- REMEMBER THEM?
JUST THEN, AN ALARM BELL WENT OFF SOMEWHERE AND A LOOK OF FRIGHT CROSSED THE INQUISITOR'S FACE--
A RAID! IT'S A RAID!
BRAAAANNGG!
I DIDN'T KNOW WHAT THIS MEANT. BUT I HOPED IT WAS THE MIRACLE I'D BEEN PRAYING FOR--
TO THE MAIN CAVERN-- QUICK!
BUT THE MAIN CAVERN WAS ALREADY IN THE HANDS OF THE INVADERS. THEY WERE HUGE AND LIGHTNING SWIFT AND THEY POURED WITH ORGANIZED PRECISION FROM A VEHICLE WITH A DRILL HEAD WHICH HAD BORED ITS WAY INTO THE UNDERGROUND TUNNELS. IT WAS AN ASTOUNDING SIGHT!
THE RAIDERS CARR ED WHAT LOOKED LIKE FLAME THROWERS. BUT IT WAS GAS WHICH SPEWED FROM THE NOZZLES IN THEIR HANDS. MY CAPTORS HAD FLED AND ALL I COULD DO WAS YELL AND COUGH AS THE GAS ENVELOPED ME--
MY LAST MEMORY BEFORE I STRUCK THE FLOOR WAS THE SHADOWY FIGURE OF ONE OF THE INVADERS LOOMING BEFORE ME IN THE SWIRLING MIST--
4

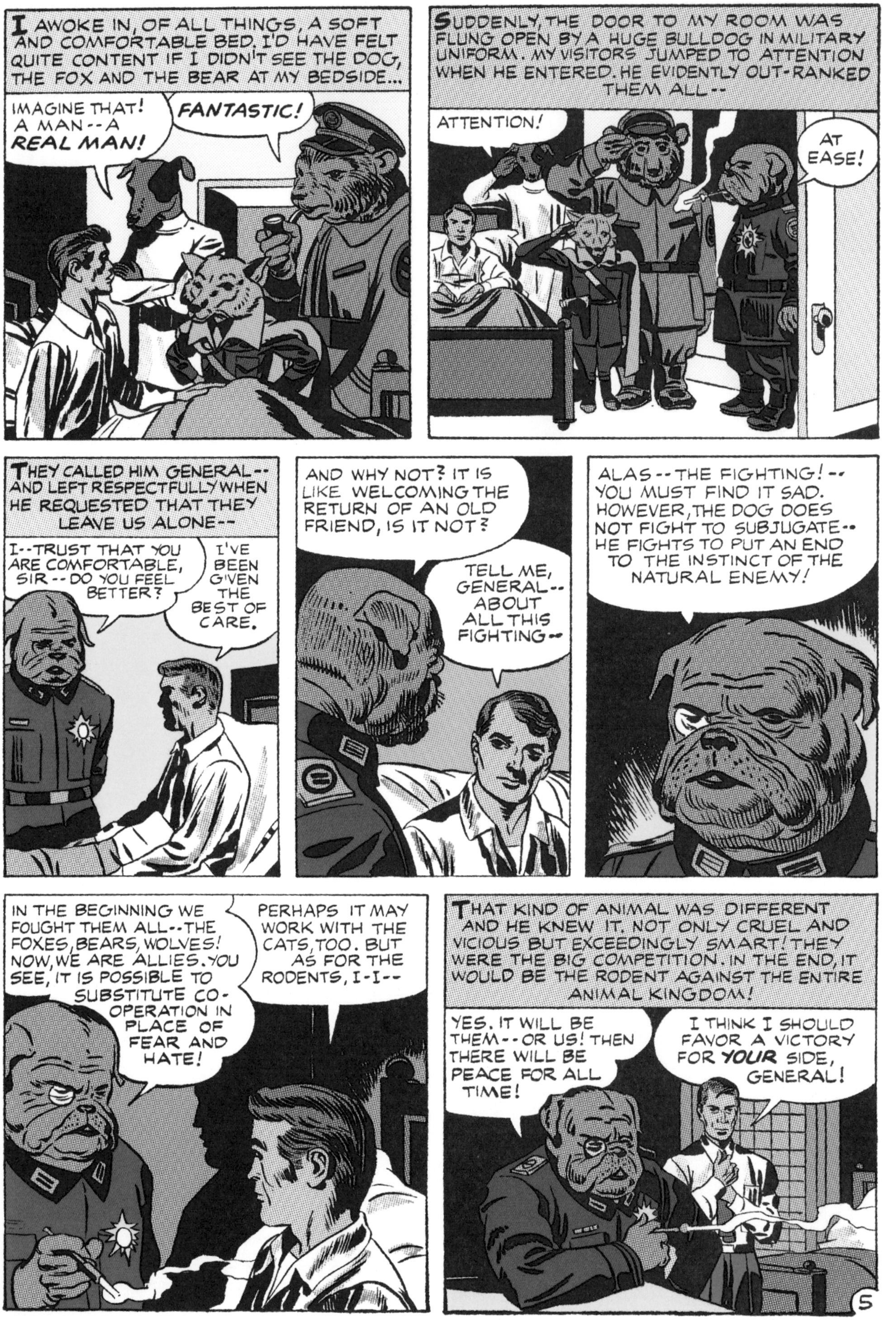
I AWOKE IN, OF ALL THINGS, A SOFT AND COMFORTABLE BED. I'D HAVE FELT QUITE CONTENT IF I DIDN'T SEE THE DOG, THE FOX AND THE BEAR AT MY BEDSIDE...
IMAGINE THAT! A MAN--A REAL MAN!
FANTASTIC!
SUDDENLY, THE DOOR TO MY ROOM WAS FLUNG OPEN BY A HUGE BULLDOG IN MILITARY UNIFORM. MY VISITORS JUMPED TO ATTENTION WHEN HE ENTERED. HE EVIDENTLY OUT-RANKED THEM ALL--
ATTENTION!
AT EASE!
THEY CALLED HIM GENERAL--AND LEFT RESPECTFULLY WHEN HE REQUESTED THAT THEY LEAVE US ALONE--
I--TRUST THAT YOU ARE COMFORTABLE, SIR--DO YOU FEEL BETTER?
I'VE BEEN GIVEN THE BEST OF CARE.
AND WHY NOT? IT IS LIKE WELCOMING THE RETURN OF AN OLD FRIEND, IS IT NOT?
TELL ME, GENERAL--ABOUT ALL THIS FIGHTING--
ALAS--THE FIGHTING!--YOU MUST FIND IT SAD. HOWEVER, THE DOG DOES NOT FIGHT TO SUBJUGATE--HE FIGHTS TO PUT AN END TO THE INSTINCT OF THE NATURAL ENEMY!
IN THE BEGINNING WE FOUGHT THEM ALL--THE FOXES, BEARS, WOLVES! NOW, WE ARE ALLIES. YOU SEE, IT IS POSSIBLE TO SUBSTITUTE CO-OPERATION IN PLACE OF FEAR AND HATE!
PERHAPS IT MAY WORK WITH THE CATS, TOO. BUT AS FOR THE RODENTS, I-I--
THAT KIND OF ANIMAL WAS DIFFERENT AND HE KNEW IT. NOT ONLY CRUEL AND VICIOUS BUT EXCEEDINGLY SMART! THEY WERE THE BIG COMPETITION. IN THE END, IT WOULD BE THE RODENT AGAINST THE ENTIRE ANIMAL KINGDOM!
YES. IT WILL BE THEM--OR US! THEN THERE WILL BE PEACE FOR ALL TIME!
I THINK I SHOULD FAVOR A VICTORY FOR YOUR SIDE, GENERAL!
5

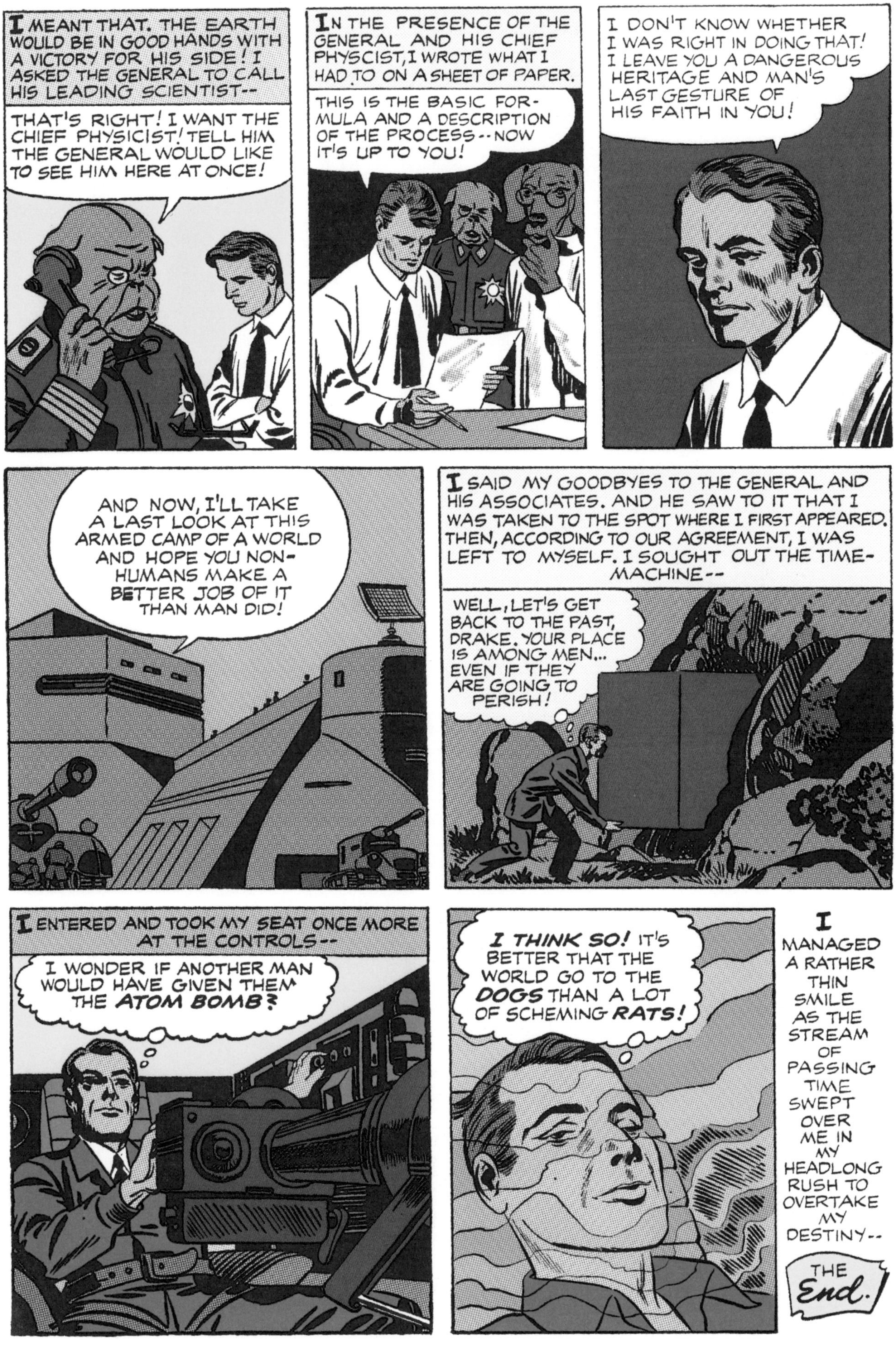

I MEANT THAT. THE EARTH WOULD BE IN GOOD HANDS WITH A VICTORY FOR HIS SIDE! I ASKED THE GENERAL TO CALL HIS LEADING SCIENTIST--
THAT'S RIGHT! I WANT THE CHIEF PHYSICIST! TELL HIM THE GENERAL WOULD LIKE TO SEE HIM HERE AT ONCE!
IN THE PRESENCE OF THE GENERAL AND HIS CHIEF PHYSCIST, I WROTE WHAT I HAD TO ON A SHEET OF PAPER.
THIS IS THE BASIC FORMULA AND A DESCRIPTION OF THE PROCESS--NOW IT'S UP TO YOU!
I DON'T KNOW WHETHER I WAS RIGHT IN DOING THAT! I LEAVE YOU A DANGEROUS HERITAGE AND MAN'S LAST GESTURE OF HIS FAITH IN YOU!
AND NOW, I'LL TAKE A LAST LOOK AT THIS ARMED CAMP OF A WORLD AND HOPE YOU NON-HUMANS MAKE A BETTER JOB OF IT THAN MAN DID!
I SAID MY GOODBYES TO THE GENERAL AND HIS ASSOCIATES. AND HE SAW TO IT THAT I WAS TAKEN TO THE SPOT WHERE I FIRST APPEARED. THEN, ACCORDING TO OUR AGREEMENT, I WAS LEFT TO MYSELF. I SOUGHT OUT THE TIME-MACHINE--
WELL, LET'S GET BACK TO THE PAST, DRAKE. YOUR PLACE IS AMONG MEN... EVEN IF THEY ARE GOING TO PERISH!
I ENTERED AND TOOK MY SEAT ONCE MORE AT THE CONTROLS--
I WONDER IF ANOTHER MAN WOULD HAVE GIVEN THEM THE ATOM BOMB?
I THINK SO! IT'S BETTER THAT THE WORLD GO TO THE DOGS THAN A LOT OF SCHEMING RATS!
I MANAGED A RATHER THIN SMILE AS THE STREAM OF PASSING TIME SWEPT OVER ME IN MY HEADLONG RUSH TO OVERTAKE MY DESTINY--
THE End.

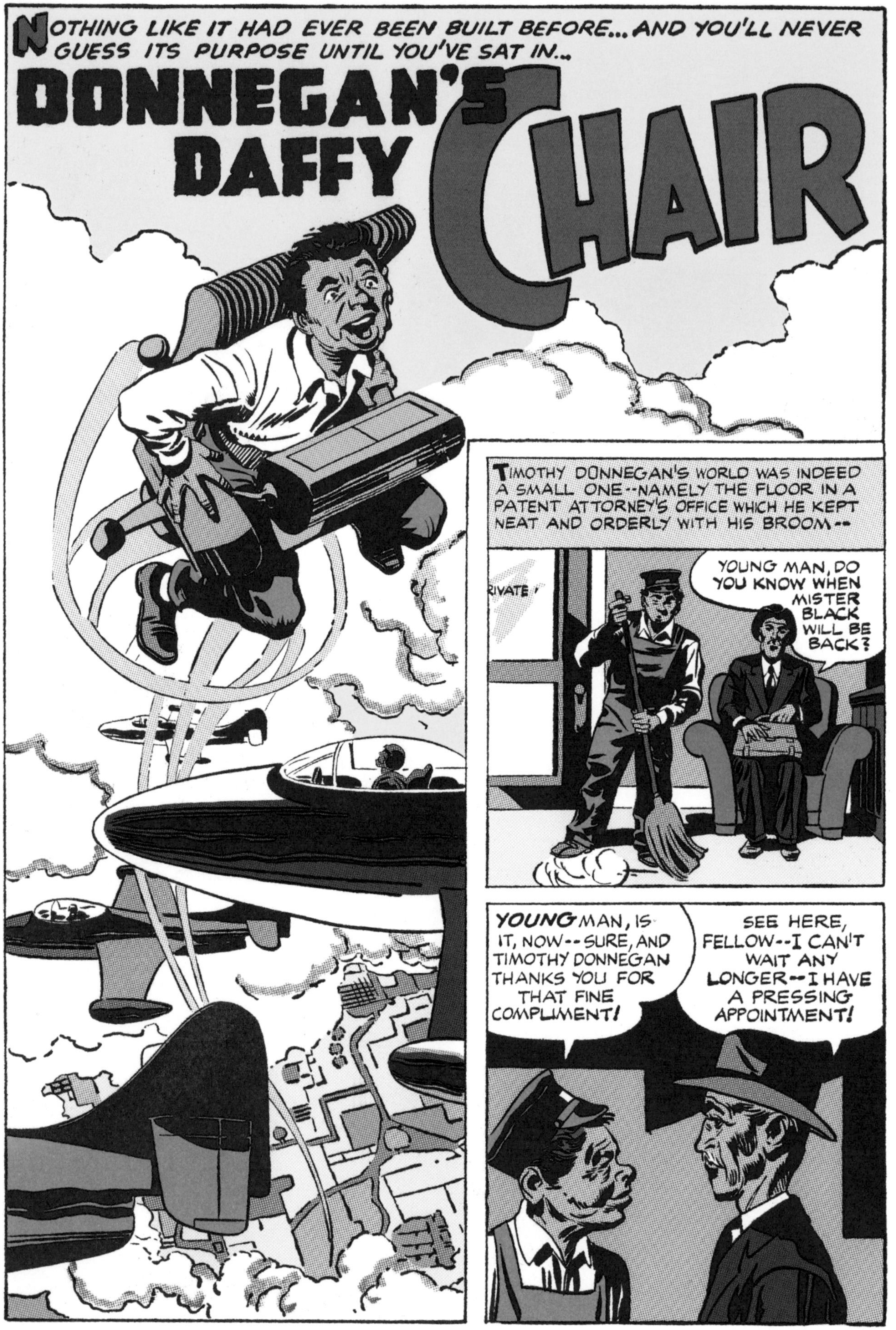
NOTHING LIKE IT HAD EVER BEEN BUILT BEFORE... AND YOU'LL NEVER GUESS ITS PURPOSE UNTIL YOU'VE SAT IN...
DONNEGAN'S DAFFY CHAIR
TIMOTHY DONNEGAN'S WORLD WAS INDEED A SMALL ONE--NAMELY THE FLOOR IN A PATENT ATTORNEY'S OFFICE WHICH HE KEPT NEAT AND ORDERLY WITH HIS BROOM--
RIVATE
YOUNG MAN, DO YOU KNOW WHEN MISTER BLACK WILL BE BACK?
YOUNG MAN, IS IT, NOW--SURE, AND TIMOTHY DONNEGAN THANKS YOU FOR THAT FINE COMPLIMENT!
SEE HERE, FELLOW--I CAN'T WAIT ANY LONGER--I HAVE A PRESSING APPOINTMENT!

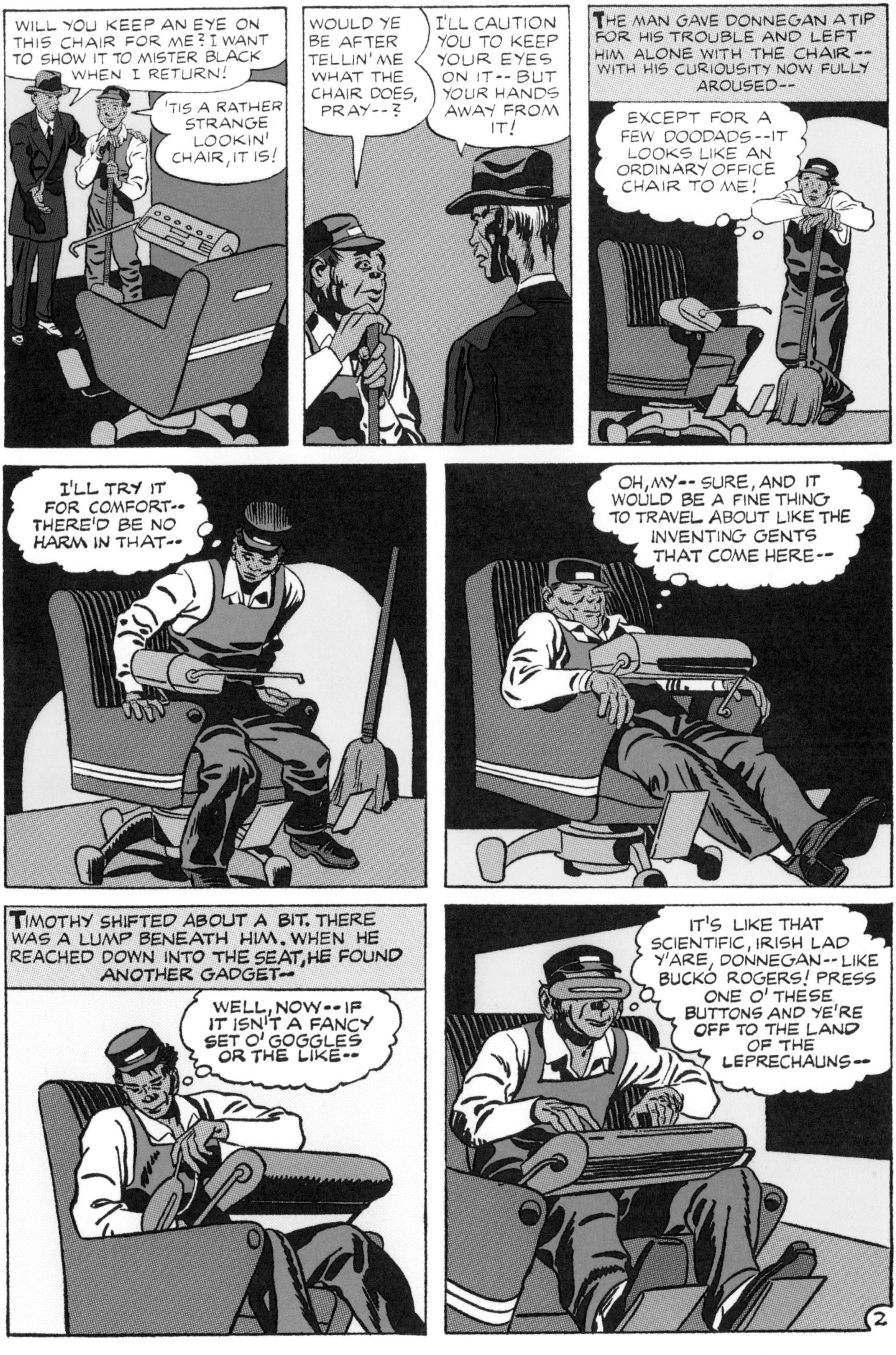

WILL YOU KEEP AN EYE ON THIS CHAIR FOR ME? I WANT TO SHOW IT TO MISTER BLACK WHEN I RETURN!
'TIS A RATHER STRANGE LOOKIN' CHAIR, IT IS!
WOULD YE BE AFTER TELLIN' ME WHAT THE CHAIR DOES, PRAY--?
I'LL CAUTION YOU TO KEEP YOUR EYES ON IT--BUT YOUR HANDS AWAY FROM IT!
THE MAN GAVE DONNEGAN A TIP FOR HIS TROUBLE AND LEFT HIM ALONE WITH THE CHAIR--WITH HIS CURIOUSITY NOW FULLY AROUSED--
EXCEPT FOR A FEW DOODADS--IT LOOKS LIKE AN ORDINARY OFFICE CHAIR TO ME!
I'LL TRY IT FOR COMFORT--THERE'D BE NO HARM IN THAT--
OH, MY--SURE, AND IT WOULD BE A FINE THING TO TRAVEL ABOUT LIKE THE INVENTING GENTS THAT COME HERE--
TIMOTHY SHIFTED ABOUT A BIT. THERE WAS A LUMP BENEATH HIM. WHEN HE REACHED DOWN INTO THE SEAT, HE FOUND ANOTHER GADGET--
WELL, NOW--IF IT ISN'T A FANCY SET O' GOGGLES OR THE LIKE--
IT'S LIKE THAT SCIENTIFIC, IRISH LAD Y'ARE, DONNEGAN--LIKE BUCKO ROGERS! PRESS ONE O' THESE BUTTONS AND YE'RE OFF TO THE LAND OF THE LEPRECHAUNS--
2

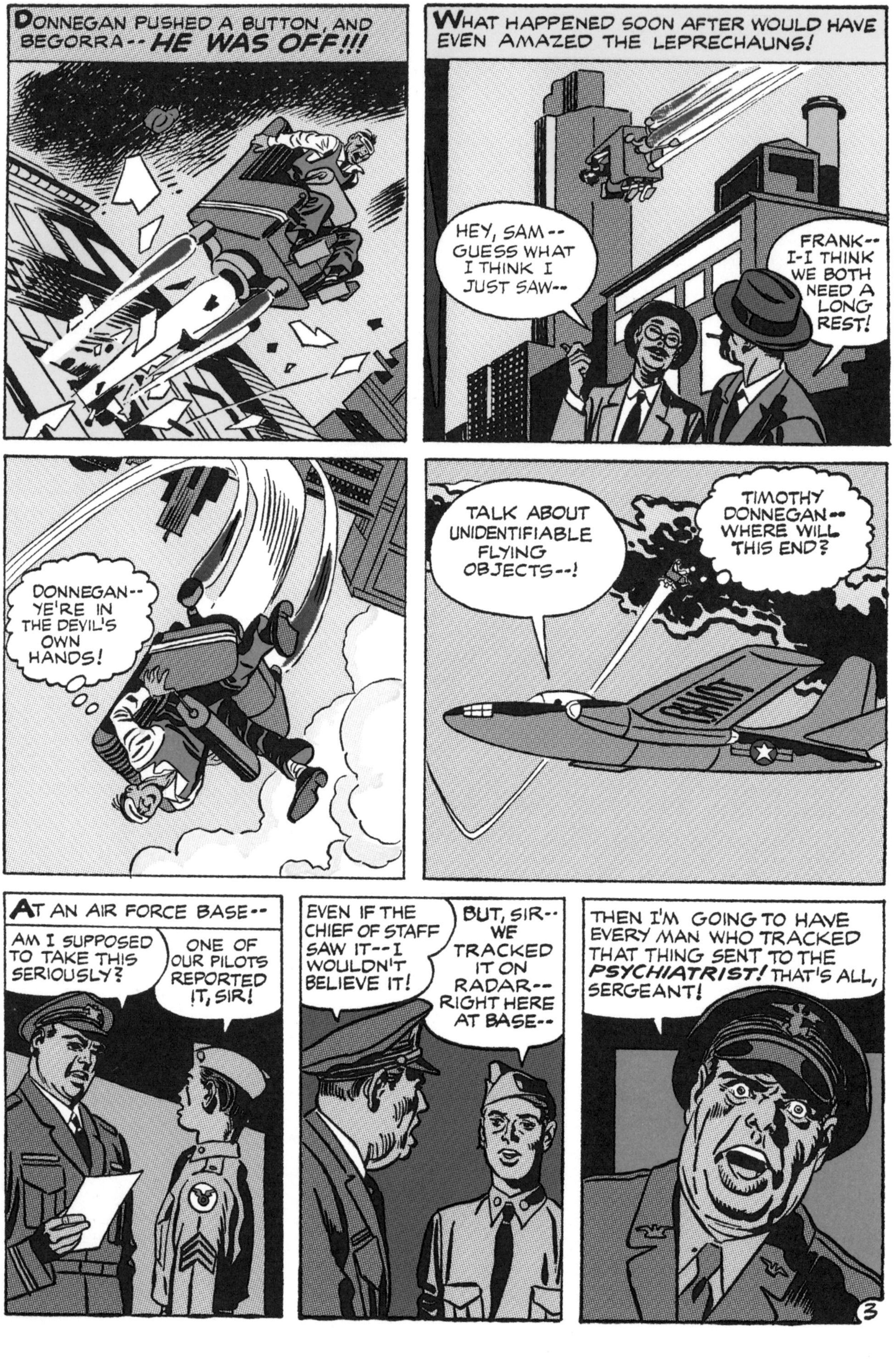
DONNEGAN PUSHED A BUTTON, AND BEGORRA-- HE WAS OFF!!!
WHAT HAPPENED SOON AFTER WOULD HAVE EVEN AMAZED THE LEPRECHAUNS!
HEY, SAM-- GUESS WHAT I THINK I JUST SAW--
FRANK-- I-I THINK WE BOTH NEED A LONG REST!
DONNEGAN-- YE'RE IN THE DEVIL'S OWN HANDS!
TALK ABOUT UNIDENTIFIABLE FLYING OBJECTS--!
TIMOTHY DONNEGAN-- WHERE WILL THIS END?
AT AN AIR FORCE BASE--
AM I SUPPOSED TO TAKE THIS SERIOUSLY?
ONE OF OUR PILOTS REPORTED IT, SIR!
EVEN IF THE CHIEF OF STAFF SAW IT--I WOULDN'T BELIEVE IT!
BUT, SIR-- WE TRACKED IT ON RADAR-- RIGHT HERE AT BASE--
THEN I'M GOING TO HAVE EVERY MAN WHO TRACKED THAT THING SENT TO THE PSYCHIATRIST! THAT'S ALL, SERGEANT!
3

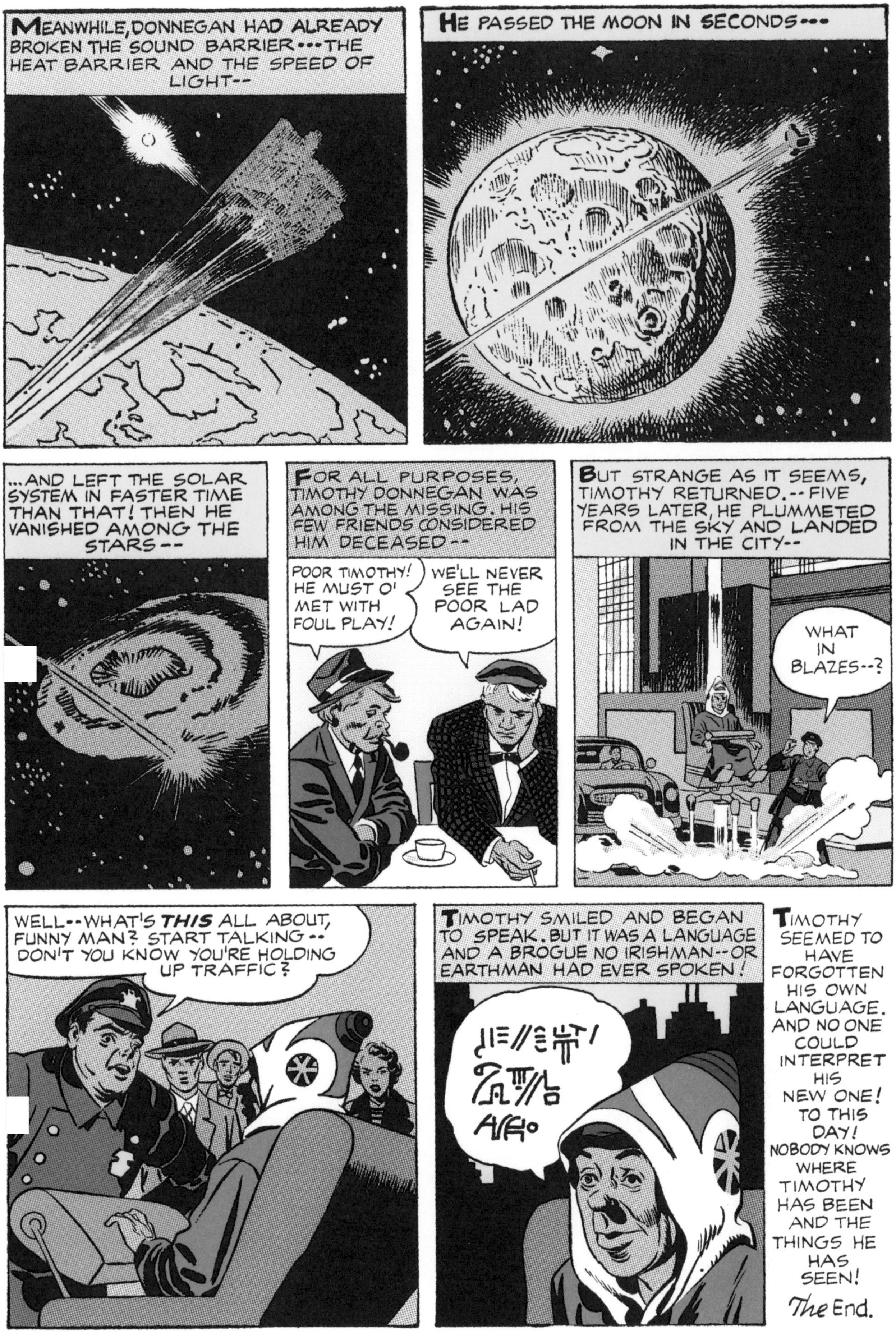
MEANWHILE, DONNEGAN HAD ALREADY BROKEN THE SOUND BARRIER... THE HEAT BARRIER AND THE SPEED OF LIGHT--
HE PASSED THE MOON IN SECONDS...
...AND LEFT THE SOLAR SYSTEM IN FASTER TIME THAN THAT! THEN HE VANISHED AMONG THE STARS--
FOR ALL PURPOSES, TIMOTHY DONNEGAN WAS AMONG THE MISSING. HIS FEW FRIENDS CONSIDERED HIM DECEASED--
POOR TIMOTHY! HE MUST O' MET WITH FOUL PLAY!
WE'LL NEVER SEE THE POOR LAD AGAIN!
BUT STRANGE AS IT SEEMS, TIMOTHY RETURNED.--FIVE YEARS LATER, HE PLUMMETED FROM THE SKY AND LANDED IN THE CITY--
WHAT IN BLAZES--?
WELL--WHAT'S THIS ALL ABOUT, FUNNY MAN? START TALKING--! DON'T YOU KNOW YOU'RE HOLDING UP TRAFFIC?
TIMOTHY SMILED AND BEGAN TO SPEAK. BUT IT WAS A LANGUAGE AND A BROGUE NO IRISHMAN--OR EARTHMAN HAD EVER SPOKEN!
TIMOTHY SEEMED TO HAVE FORGOTTEN HIS OWN LANGUAGE. AND NO ONE COULD INTERPRET HIS NEW ONE! TO THIS DAY! NOBODY KNOWS WHERE TIMOTHY HAS BEEN AND THE THINGS HE HAS SEEN!
The End.

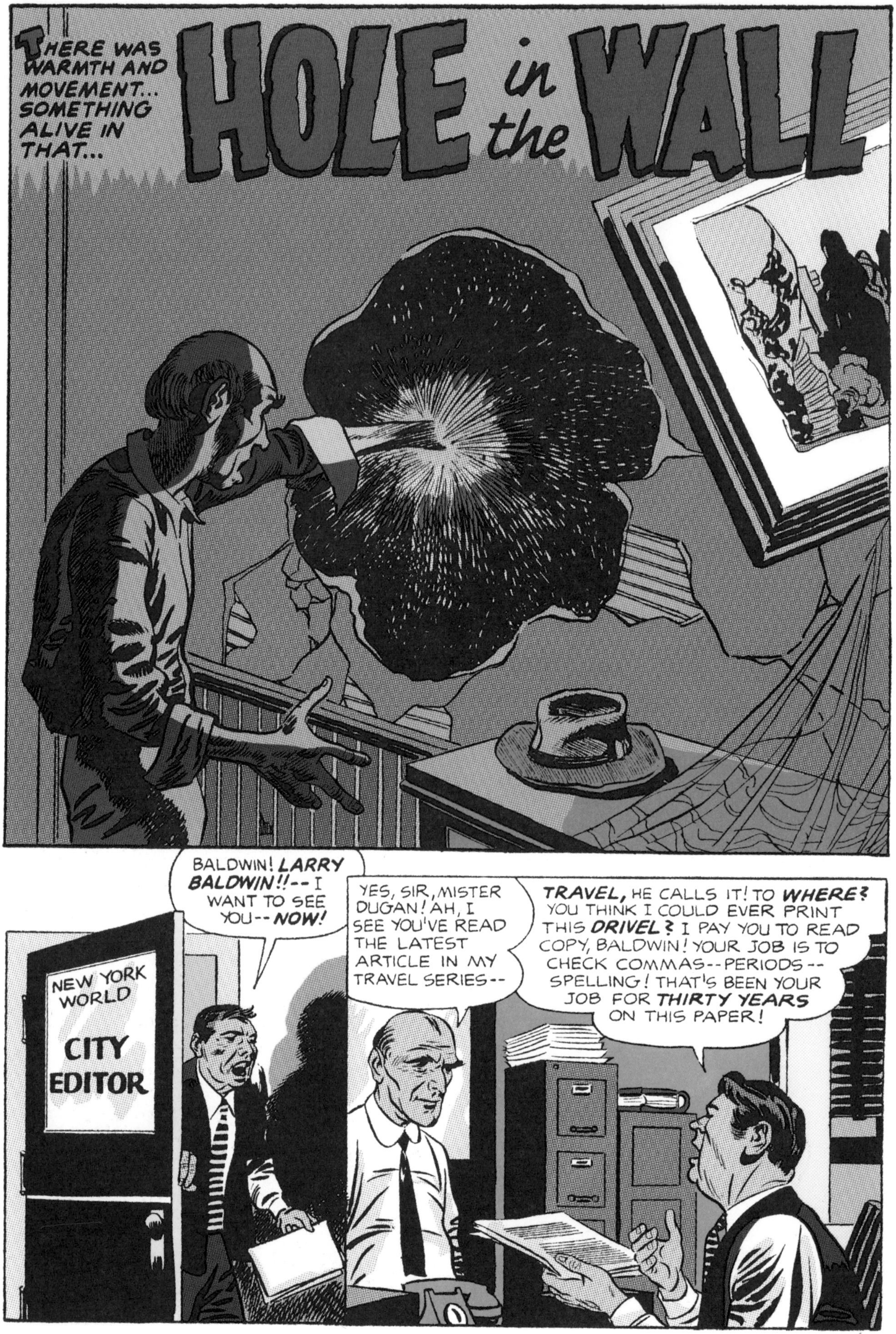
THERE WAS WARMTH AND MOVEMENT... SOMETHING ALIVE IN THAT...
HOLE in the WALL
BALDWIN! LARRY BALDWIN!!-- I WANT TO SEE YOU-- NOW!
NEW YORK WORLD
CITY EDITOR
YES, SIR, MISTER DUGAN! AH, I SEE YOU'VE READ THE LATEST ARTICLE IN MY TRAVEL SERIES--
TRAVEL, HE CALLS IT! TO WHERE? YOU THINK I COULD EVER PRINT THIS DRIVEL? I PAY YOU TO READ COPY, BALDWIN! YOUR JOB IS TO CHECK COMMAS--PERIODS-- SPELLING! THAT'S BEEN YOUR JOB FOR THIRTY YEARS ON THIS PAPER!

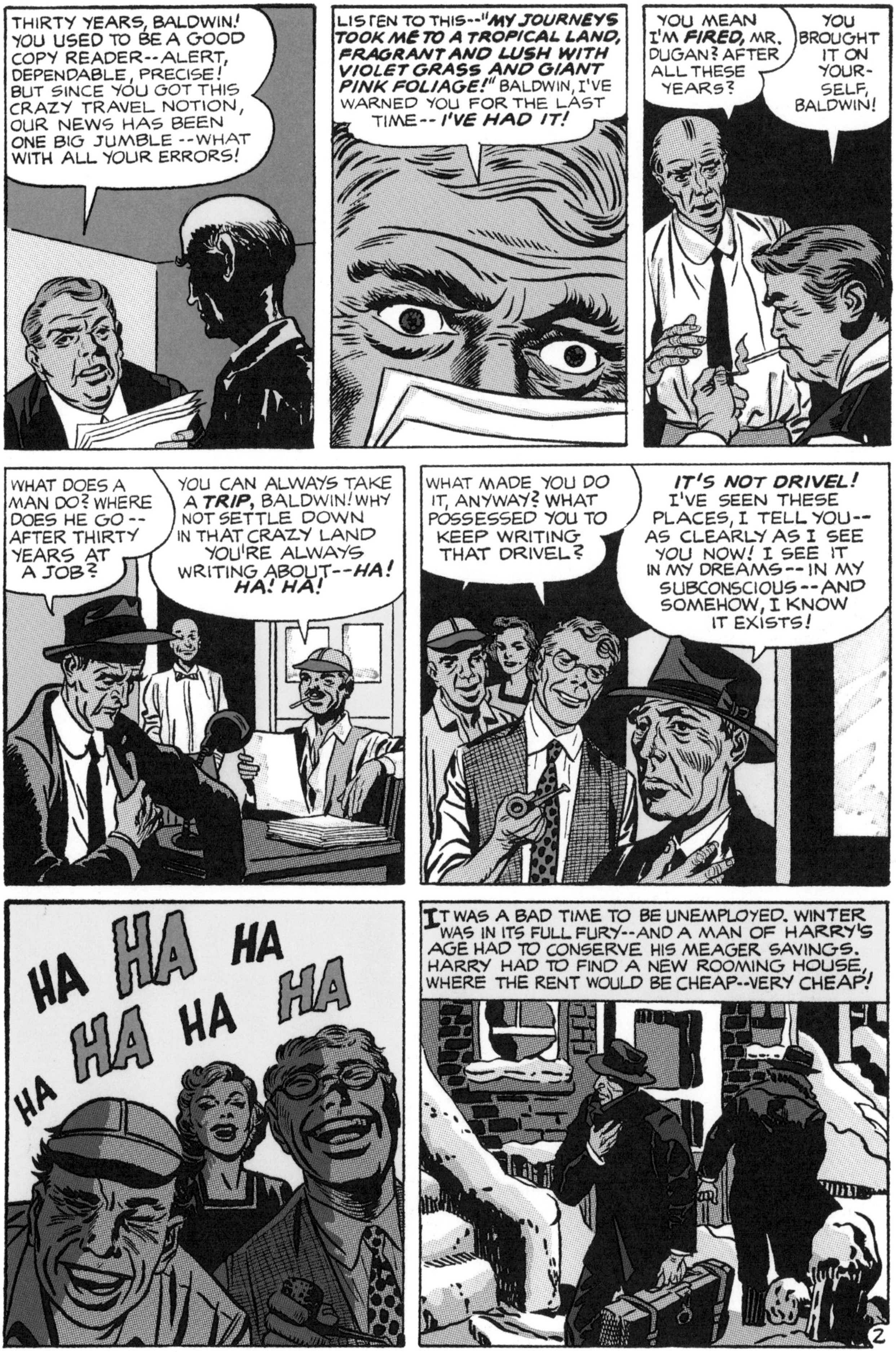

THIRTY YEARS, BALDWIN! YOU USED TO BE A GOOD COPY READER--ALERT, DEPENDABLE, PRECISE! BUT SINCE YOU GOT THIS CRAZY TRAVEL NOTION, OUR NEWS HAS BEEN ONE BIG JUMBLE --WHAT WITH ALL YOUR ERRORS!
LISTEN TO THIS--"MY JOURNEYS TOOK ME TO A TROPICAL LAND, FRAGRANT AND LUSH WITH VIOLET GRASS AND GIANT PINK FOLIAGE!" BALDWIN, I'VE WARNED YOU FOR THE LAST TIME-- I'VE HAD IT!
YOU MEAN I'M FIRED, MR. DUGAN? AFTER ALL THESE YEARS?
YOU BROUGHT IT ON YOURSELF, BALDWIN!
WHAT DOES A MAN DO? WHERE DOES HE GO -- AFTER THIRTY YEARS AT A JOB?
YOU CAN ALWAYS TAKE A TRIP, BALDWIN! WHY NOT SETTLE DOWN IN THAT CRAZY LAND YOU'RE ALWAYS WRITING ABOUT--HA! HA! HA!
WHAT MADE YOU DO IT, ANYWAY? WHAT POSSESSED YOU TO KEEP WRITING THAT DRIVEL?
IT'S NOT DRIVEL! I'VE SEEN THESE PLACES, I TELL YOU-- AS CLEARLY AS I SEE YOU NOW! I SEE IT IN MY DREAMS-- IN MY SUBCONSCIOUS--AND SOMEHOW, I KNOW IT EXISTS!
HA HA HA HA HA HA HA HA HA
IT WAS A BAD TIME TO BE UNEMPLOYED. WINTER WAS IN ITS FULL FURY--AND A MAN OF HARRY'S AGE HAD TO CONSERVE HIS MEAGER SAVINGS. HARRY HAD TO FIND A NEW ROOMING HOUSE, WHERE THE RENT WOULD BE CHEAP--VERY CHEAP!
2

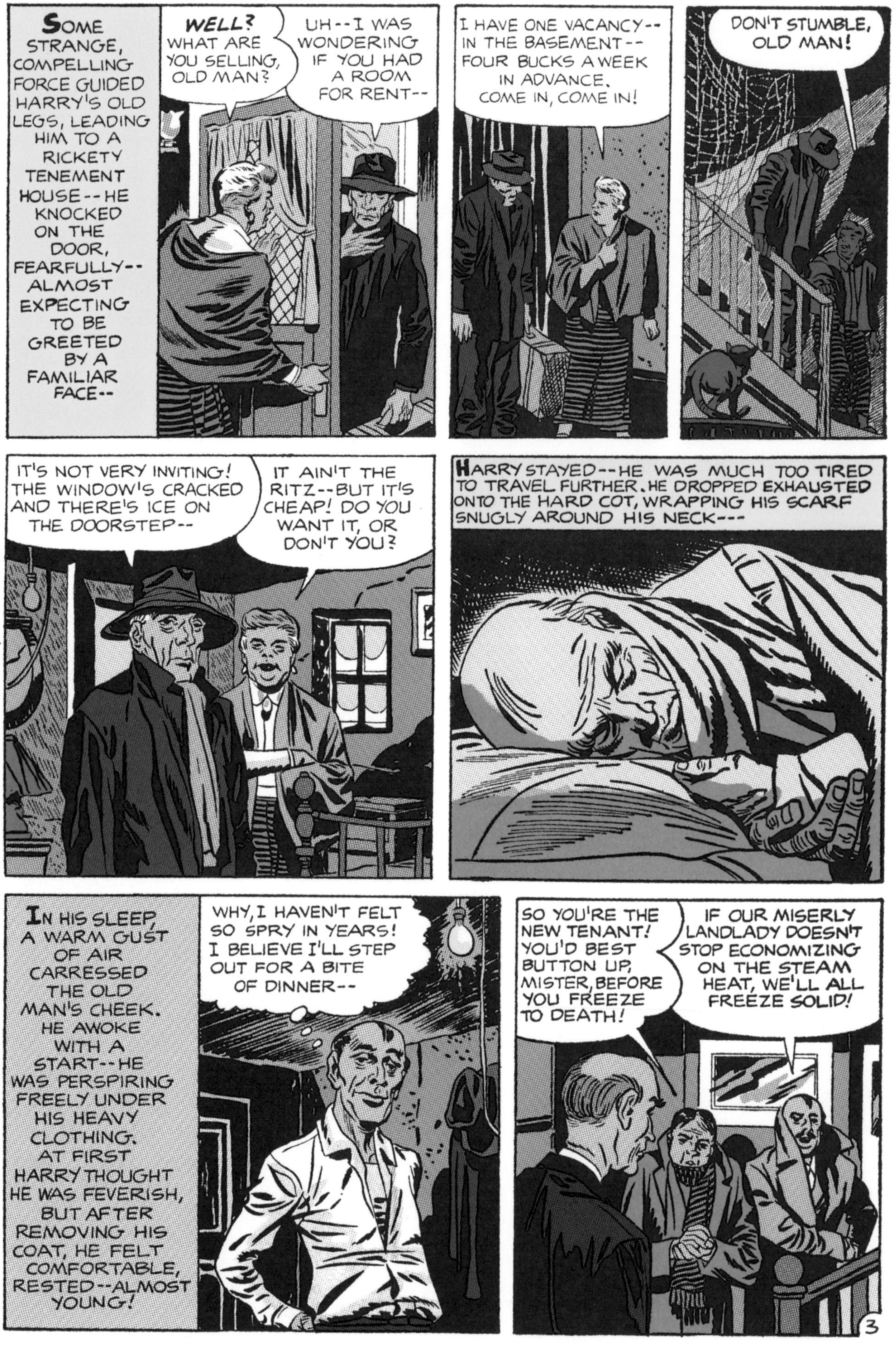
SOME STRANGE, COMPELLING FORCE GUIDED HARRY'S OLD LEGS, LEADING HIM TO A RICKETY TENEMENT HOUSE--HE KNOCKED ON THE DOOR, FEARFULLY--ALMOST EXPECTING TO BE GREETED BY A FAMILIAR FACE--
WELL? WHAT ARE YOU SELLING, OLD MAN?
UH--I WAS WONDERING IF YOU HAD A ROOM FOR RENT--
I HAVE ONE VACANCY--IN THE BASEMENT--FOUR BUCKS A WEEK IN ADVANCE. COME IN, COME IN!
DON'T STUMBLE, OLD MAN!
IT'S NOT VERY INVITING! THE WINDOW'S CRACKED AND THERE'S ICE ON THE DOORSTEP--
IT AIN'T THE RITZ--BUT IT'S CHEAP! DO YOU WANT IT, OR DON'T YOU?
HARRY STAYED--HE WAS MUCH TOO TIRED TO TRAVEL FURTHER. HE DROPPED EXHAUSTED ONTO THE HARD COT, WRAPPING HIS SCARF SNUGLY AROUND HIS NECK---
IN HIS SLEEP, A WARM GUST OF AIR CARRESSED THE OLD MAN'S CHEEK. HE AWOKE WITH A START--HE WAS PERSPIRING FREELY UNDER HIS HEAVY CLOTHING. AT FIRST HARRY THOUGHT HE WAS FEVERISH, BUT AFTER REMOVING HIS COAT, HE FELT COMFORTABLE, RESTED--ALMOST YOUNG!
WHY, I HAVEN'T FELT SO SPRY IN YEARS! I BELIEVE I'LL STEP OUT FOR A BITE OF DINNER--
SO YOU'RE THE NEW TENANT! YOU'D BEST BUTTON UP, MISTER, BEFORE YOU FREEZE TO DEATH!
IF OUR MISERLY LANDLADY DOESN'T STOP ECONOMIZING ON THE STEAM HEAT, WE'LL ALL FREEZE SOLID!
3

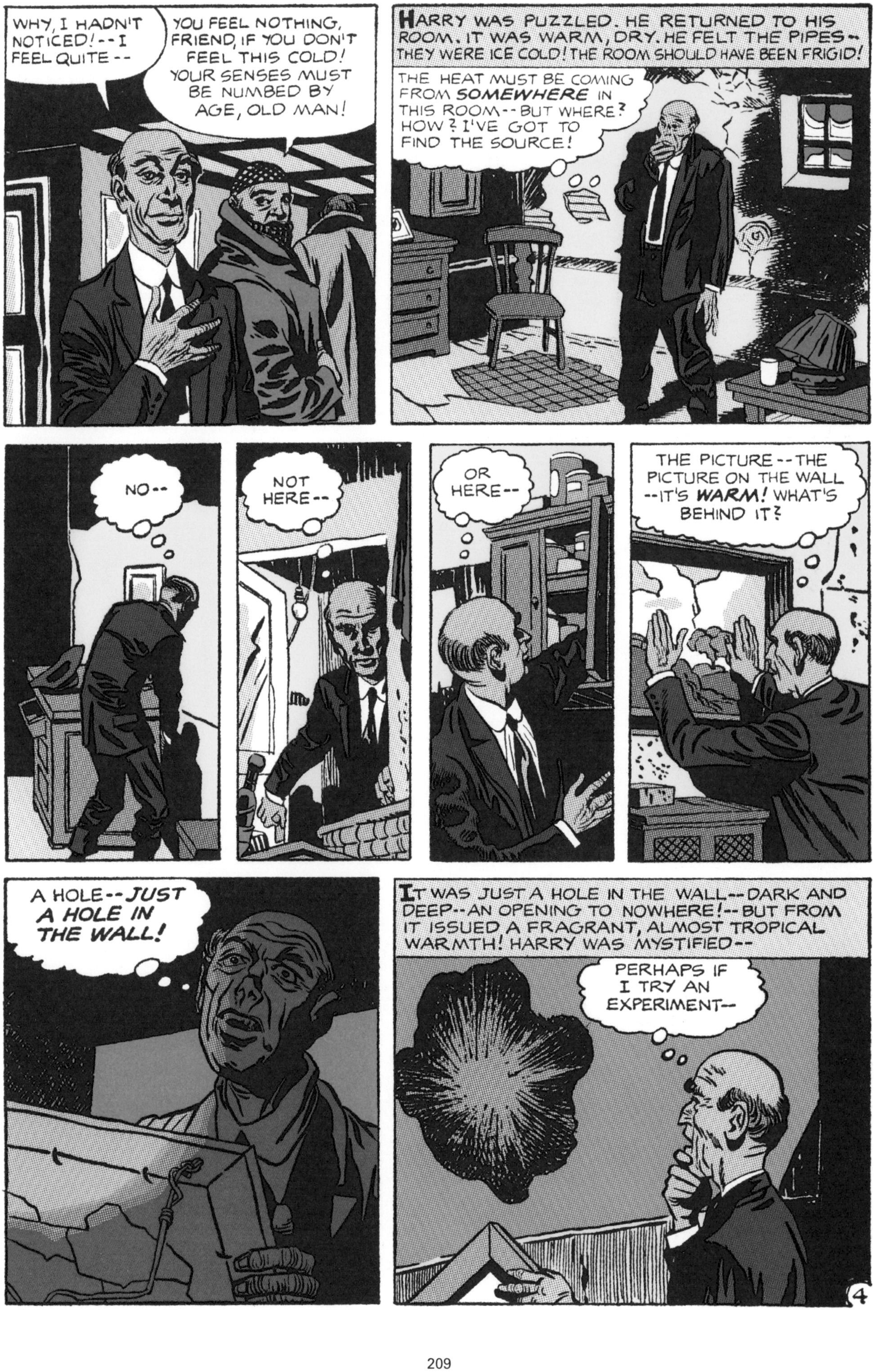
WHY, I HADN'T NOTICED!--I FEEL QUITE--
YOU FEEL NOTHING, FRIEND, IF YOU DON'T FEEL THIS COLD! YOUR SENSES MUST BE NUMBED BY AGE, OLD MAN!
HARRY WAS PUZZLED. HE RETURNED TO HIS ROOM. IT WAS WARM, DRY. HE FELT THE PIPES--THEY WERE ICE COLD! THE ROOM SHOULD HAVE BEEN FRIGID!
THE HEAT MUST BE COMING FROM SOMEWHERE IN THIS ROOM--BUT WHERE? HOW? I'VE GOT TO FIND THE SOURCE!
NO--
NOT HERE--
OR HERE--
THE PICTURE--THE PICTURE ON THE WALL--IT'S WARM! WHAT'S BEHIND IT?
A HOLE--JUST A HOLE IN THE WALL!
IT WAS JUST A HOLE IN THE WALL--DARK AND DEEP--AN OPENING TO NOWHERE!--BUT FROM IT ISSUED A FRAGRANT, ALMOST TROPICAL WARMTH! HARRY WAS MYSTIFIED--
PERHAPS IF I TRY AN EXPERIMENT--
4

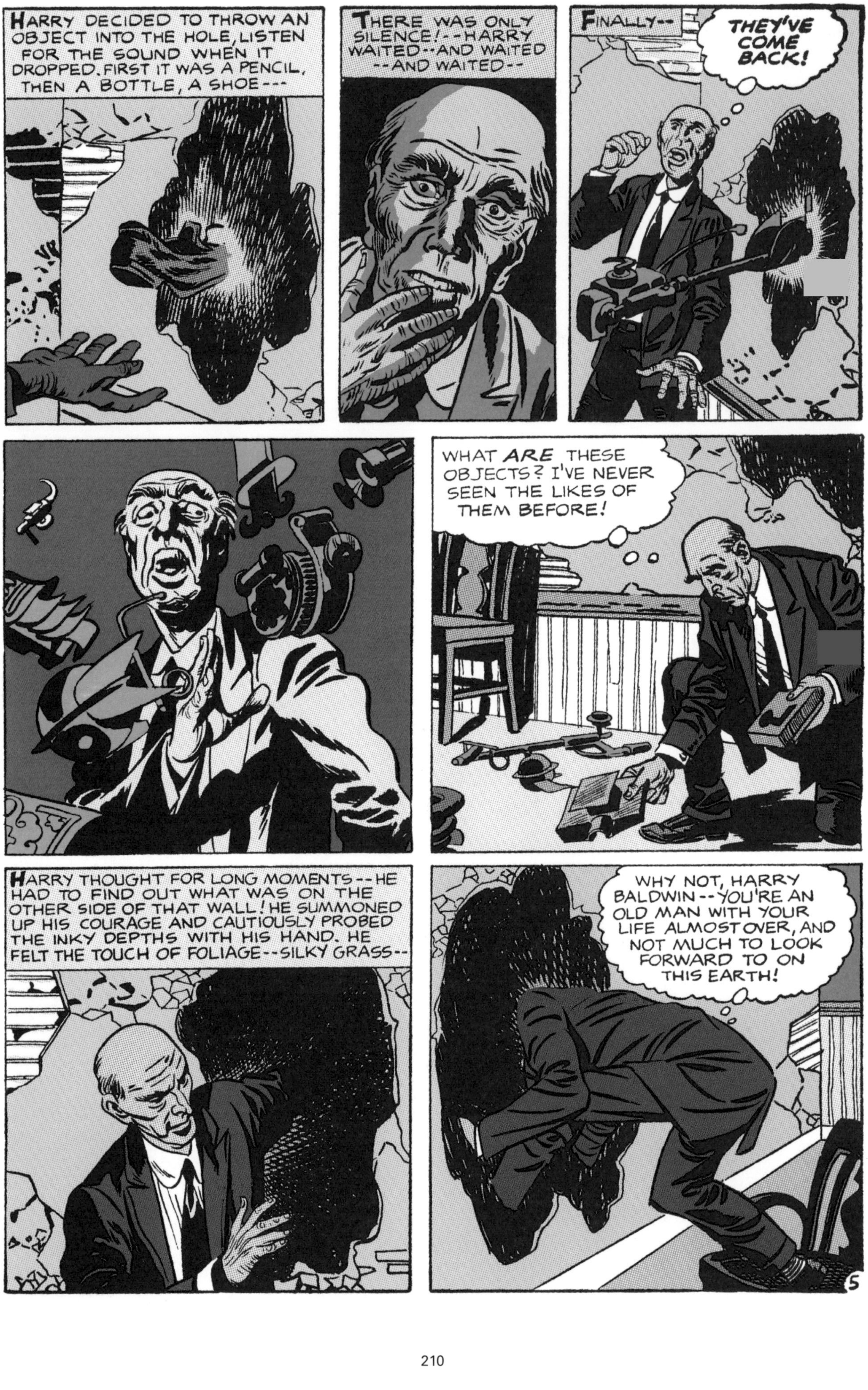
HARRY DECIDED TO THROW AN OBJECT INTO THE HOLE, LISTEN FOR THE SOUND WHEN IT DROPPED. FIRST IT WAS A PENCIL, THEN A BOTTLE, A SHOE---
THERE WAS ONLY SILENCE!--HARRY WAITED--AND WAITED --AND WAITED--
FINALLY--
THEY'VE COME BACK!
WHAT ARE THESE OBJECTS? I'VE NEVER SEEN THE LIKES OF THEM BEFORE!
HARRY THOUGHT FOR LONG MOMENTS--HE HAD TO FIND OUT WHAT WAS ON THE OTHER SIDE OF THAT WALL! HE SUMMONED UP HIS COURAGE AND CAUTIOUSLY PROBED THE INKY DEPTHS WITH HIS HAND. HE FELT THE TOUCH OF FOLIAGE--SILKY GRASS--
WHY NOT, HARRY BALDWIN--YOU'RE AN OLD MAN WITH YOUR LIFE ALMOST OVER, AND NOT MUCH TO LOOK FORWARD TO ON THIS EARTH!
5

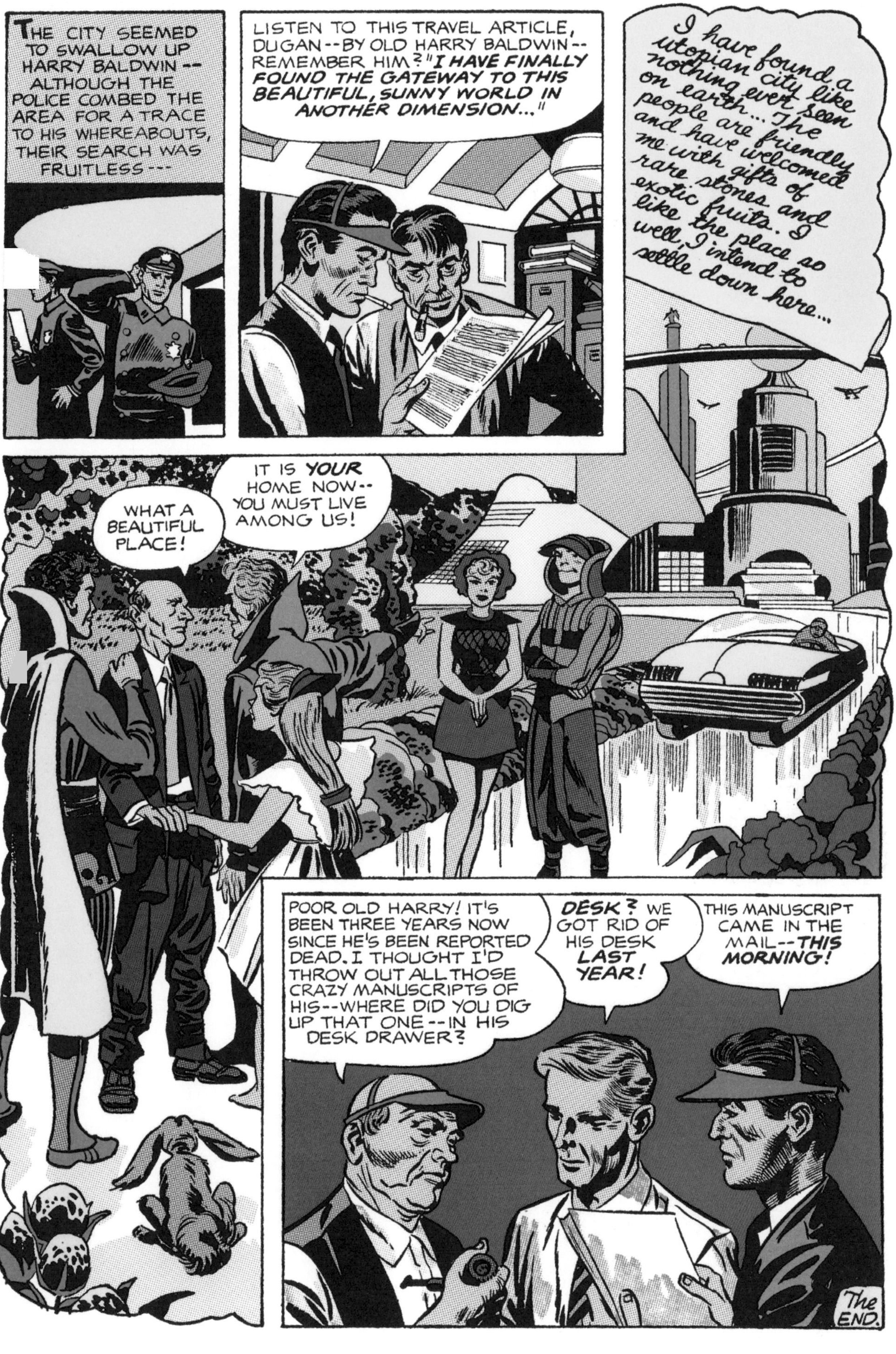
THE CITY SEEMED TO SWALLOW UP HARRY BALDWIN -- ALTHOUGH THE POLICE COMBED THE AREA FOR A TRACE TO HIS WHEREABOUTS, THEIR SEARCH WAS FRUITLESS---
LISTEN TO THIS TRAVEL ARTICLE, DUGAN--BY OLD HARRY BALDWIN--REMEMBER HIM? "I HAVE FINALLY FOUND THE GATEWAY TO THIS BEAUTIFUL, SUNNY WORLD IN ANOTHER DIMENSION..."
I have found a utopian city like nothing ever seen on earth... The people are friendly and have welcomed me with gifts of rare stones and exotic fruits. I like the place so well, I intend to settle down here...
WHAT A BEAUTIFUL PLACE!
IT IS YOUR HOME NOW--YOU MUST LIVE AMONG US!
POOR OLD HARRY! IT'S BEEN THREE YEARS NOW SINCE HE'S BEEN REPORTED DEAD. I THOUGHT I'D THROW OUT ALL THOSE CRAZY MANUSCRIPTS OF HIS--WHERE DID YOU DIG UP THAT ONE--IN HIS DESK DRAWER?
DESK? WE GOT RID OF HIS DESK LAST YEAR!
THIS MANUSCRIPT CAME IN THE MAIL--THIS MORNING!
The END.

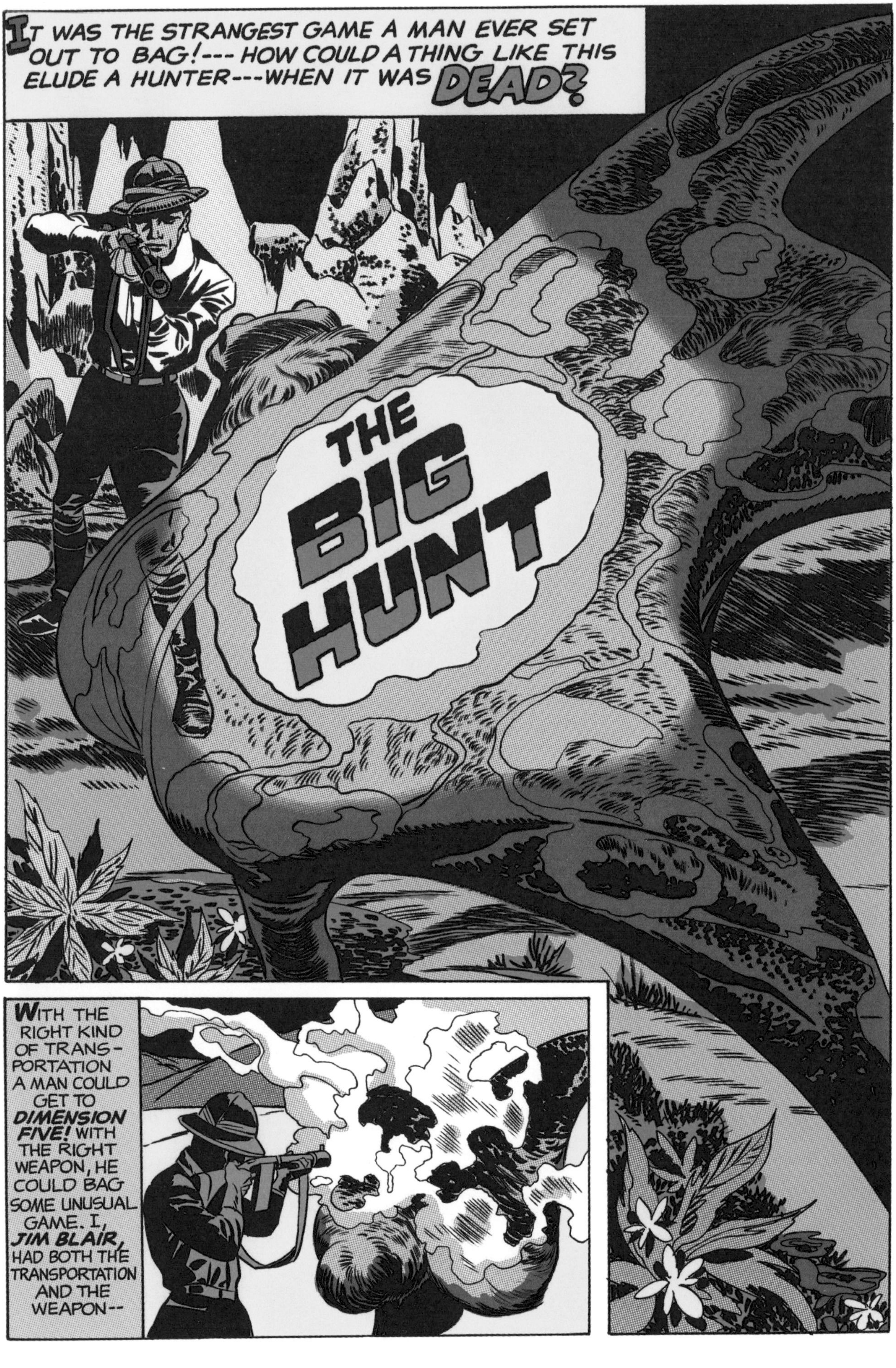
IT WAS THE STRANGEST GAME A MAN EVER SET OUT TO BAG!--- HOW COULD A THING LIKE THIS ELUDE A HUNTER---WHEN IT WAS DEAD?
THE BIG HUNT
WITH THE RIGHT KIND OF TRANS-PORTATION A MAN COULD GET TO DIMENSION FIVE! WITH THE RIGHT WEAPON, HE COULD BAG SOME UNUSUAL GAME. I, JIM BLAIR, HAD BOTH THE TRANSPORTATION AND THE WEAPON--

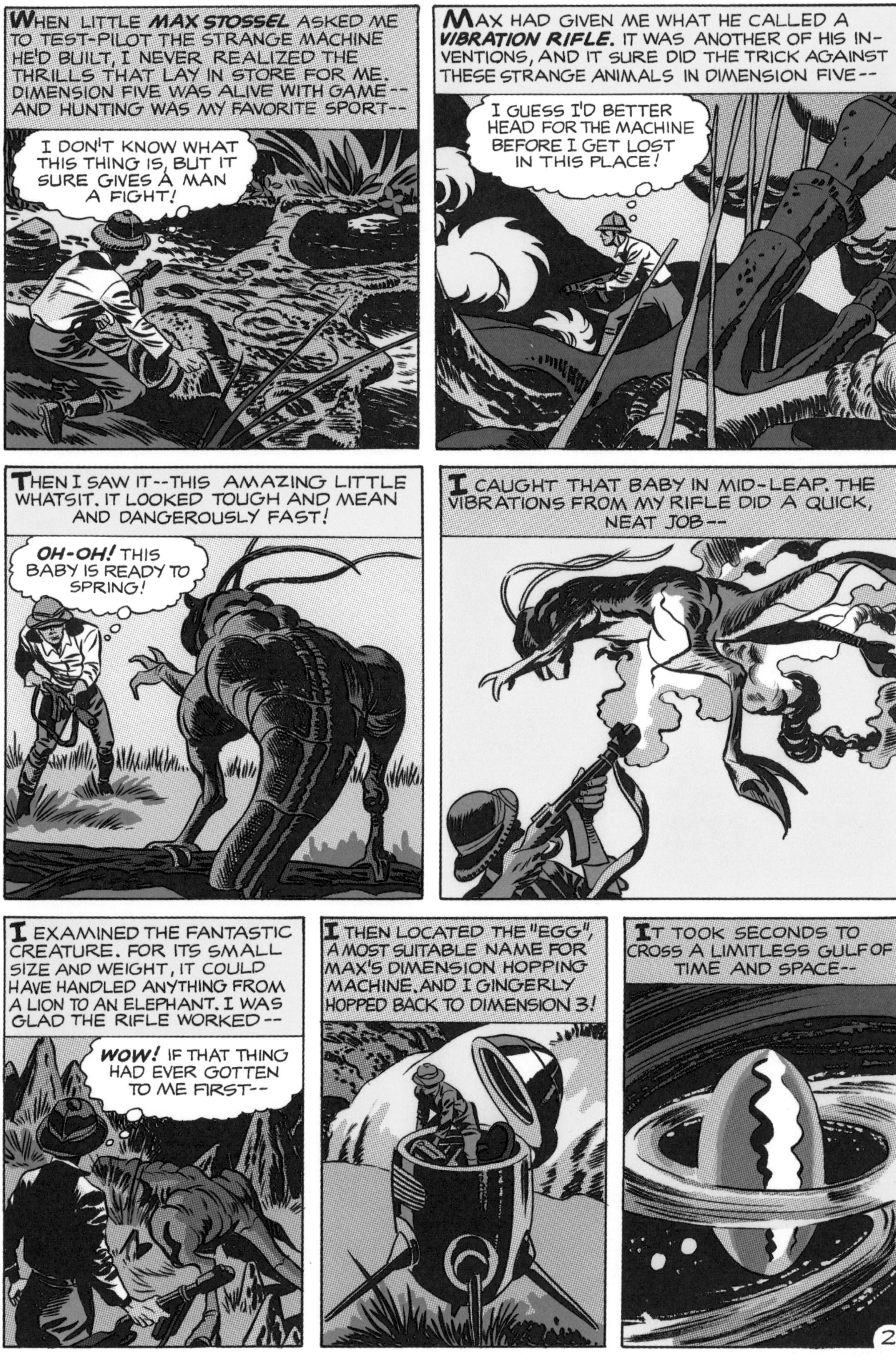
WHEN LITTLE MAX STOSSEL ASKED ME TO TEST-PILOT THE STRANGE MACHINE HE'D BUILT, I NEVER REALIZED THE THRILLS THAT LAY IN STORE FOR ME. DIMENSION FIVE WAS ALIVE WITH GAME-- AND HUNTING WAS MY FAVORITE SPORT--
I DON'T KNOW WHAT THIS THING IS, BUT IT SURE GIVES A MAN A FIGHT!
MAX HAD GIVEN ME WHAT HE CALLED A VIBRATION RIFLE. IT WAS ANOTHER OF HIS INVENTIONS, AND IT SURE DID THE TRICK AGAINST THESE STRANGE ANIMALS IN DIMENSION FIVE--
I GUESS I'D BETTER HEAD FOR THE MACHINE BEFORE I GET LOST IN THIS PLACE!
THEN I SAW IT--THIS AMAZING LITTLE WHATSIT. IT LOOKED TOUGH AND MEAN AND DANGEROUSLY FAST!
OH-OH! THIS BABY IS READY TO SPRING!
I CAUGHT THAT BABY IN MID-LEAP. THE VIBRATIONS FROM MY RIFLE DID A QUICK, NEAT JOB--
I EXAMINED THE FANTASTIC CREATURE. FOR ITS SMALL SIZE AND WEIGHT, IT COULD HAVE HANDLED ANYTHING FROM A LION TO AN ELEPHANT. I WAS GLAD THE RIFLE WORKED--
WOW! IF THAT THING HAD EVER GOTTEN TO ME FIRST--
I THEN LOCATED THE "EGG", A MOST SUITABLE NAME FOR MAX'S DIMENSION HOPPING MACHINE. AND I GINGERLY HOPPED BACK TO DIMENSION 3!
IT TOOK SECONDS TO CROSS A LIMITLESS GULF OF TIME AND SPACE--
2

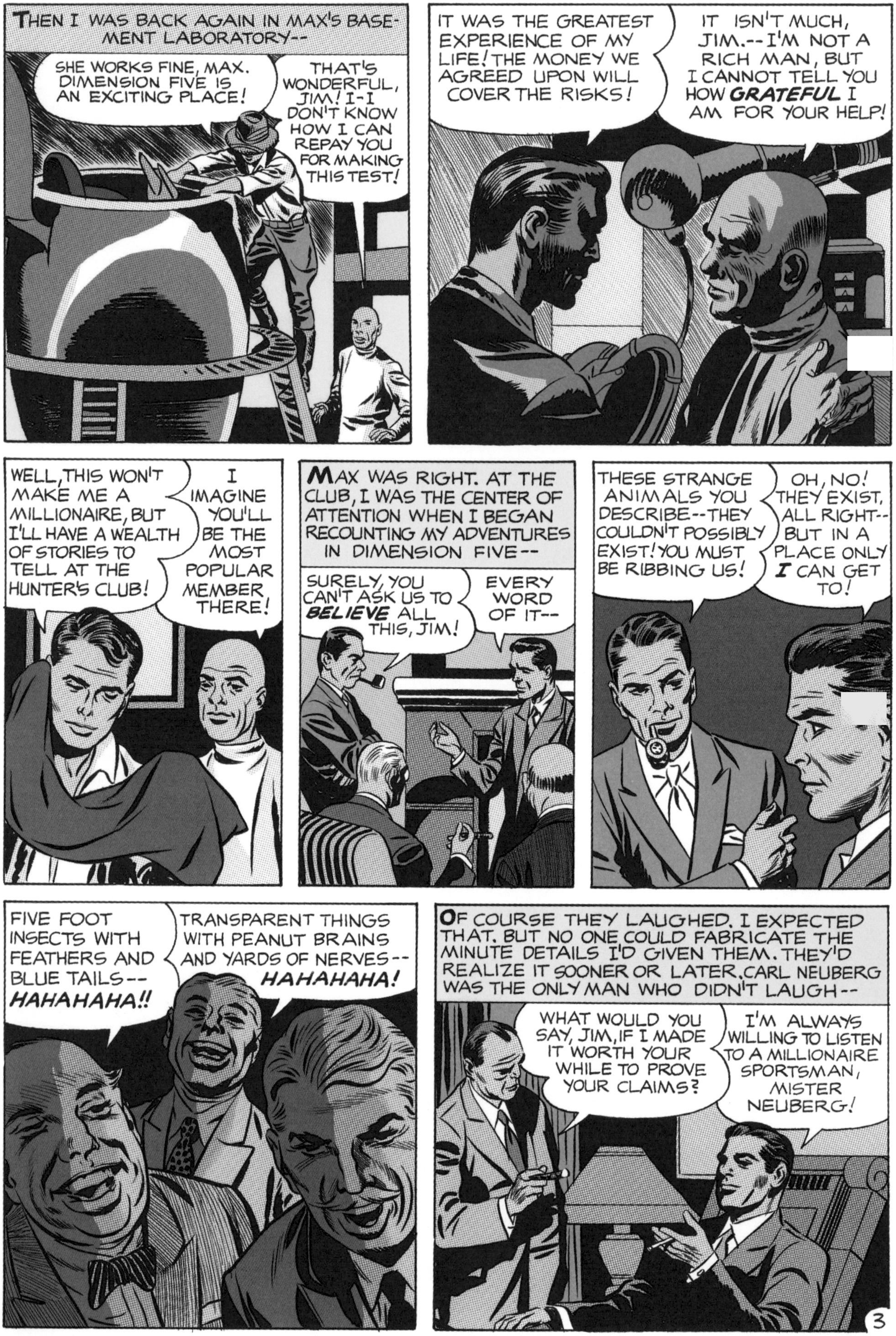
THEN I WAS BACK AGAIN IN MAX'S BASEMENT LABORATORY--
SHE WORKS FINE, MAX. DIMENSION FIVE IS AN EXCITING PLACE!
THAT'S WONDERFUL, JIM! I-I DON'T KNOW HOW I CAN REPAY YOU FOR MAKING THIS TEST!
IT WAS THE GREATEST EXPERIENCE OF MY LIFE! THE MONEY WE AGREED UPON WILL COVER THE RISKS!
IT ISN'T MUCH, JIM.--I'M NOT A RICH MAN, BUT I CANNOT TELL YOU HOW GRATEFUL I AM FOR YOUR HELP!
WELL, THIS WON'T MAKE ME A MILLIONAIRE, BUT I'LL HAVE A WEALTH OF STORIES TO TELL AT THE HUNTER'S CLUB!
I IMAGINE YOU'LL BE THE MOST POPULAR MEMBER THERE!
MAX WAS RIGHT. AT THE CLUB, I WAS THE CENTER OF ATTENTION WHEN I BEGAN RECOUNTING MY ADVENTURES IN DIMENSION FIVE--
SURELY, YOU CAN'T ASK US TO BELIEVE ALL THIS, JIM!
EVERY WORD OF IT--
THESE STRANGE ANIMALS YOU DESCRIBE--THEY COULDN'T POSSIBLY EXIST! YOU MUST BE RIBBING US!
OH, NO! THEY EXIST, ALL RIGHT--BUT IN A PLACE ONLY I CAN GET TO!
FIVE FOOT INSECTS WITH FEATHERS AND BLUE TAILS-- HAHAHAHA!!
TRANSPARENT THINGS WITH PEANUT BRAINS AND YARDS OF NERVES-- HAHAHAHA!
OF COURSE THEY LAUGHED. I EXPECTED THAT. BUT NO ONE COULD FABRICATE THE MINUTE DETAILS I'D GIVEN THEM. THEY'D REALIZE IT SOONER OR LATER. CARL NEUBERG WAS THE ONLY MAN WHO DIDN'T LAUGH--
WHAT WOULD YOU SAY, JIM, IF I MADE IT WORTH YOUR WHILE TO PROVE YOUR CLAIMS?
I'M ALWAYS WILLING TO LISTEN TO A MILLIONAIRE SPORTSMAN, MISTER NEUBERG!
3

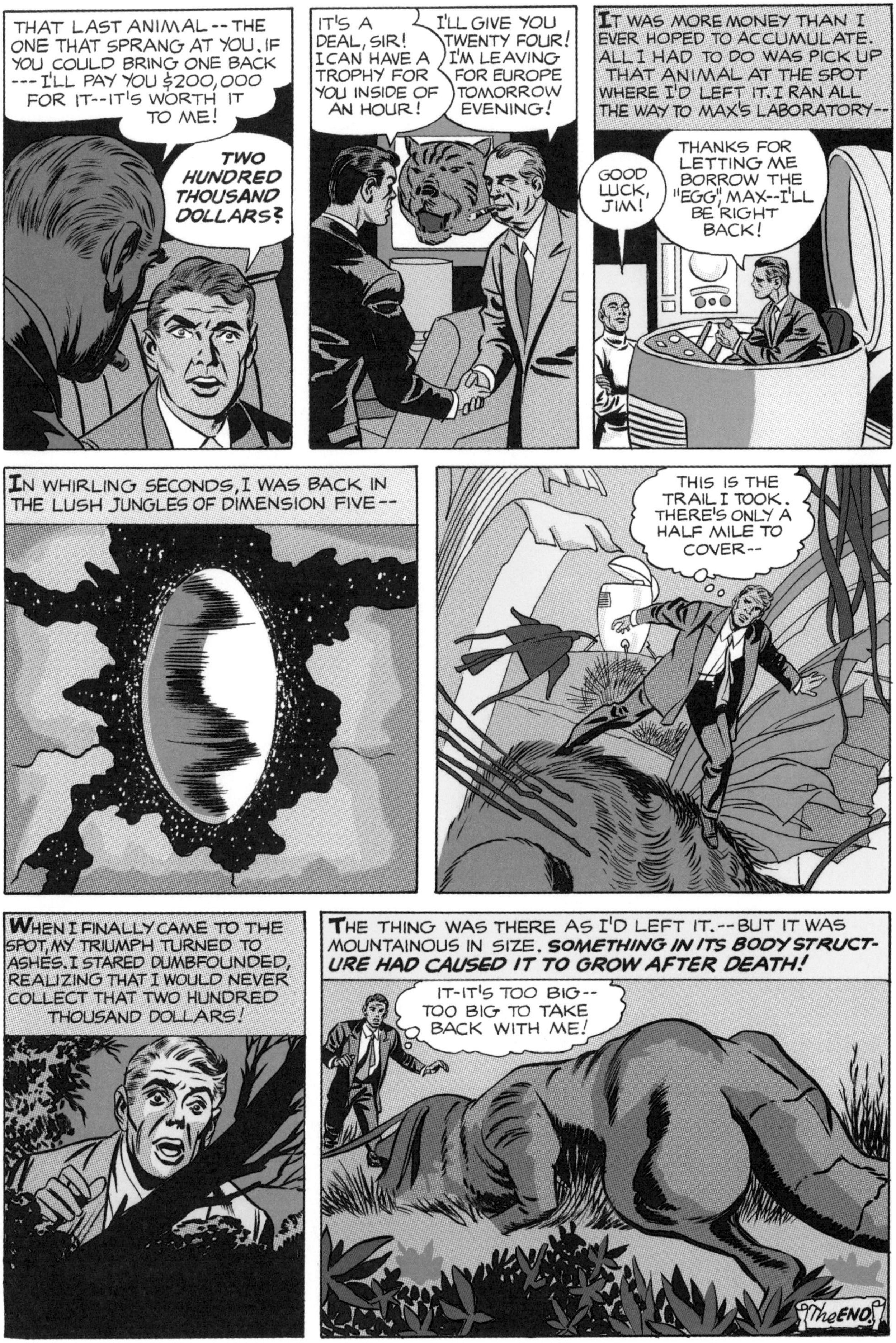
THAT LAST ANIMAL -- THE ONE THAT SPRANG AT YOU. IF YOU COULD BRING ONE BACK --- I'LL PAY YOU $200,000 FOR IT -- IT'S WORTH IT TO ME!
TWO HUNDRED THOUSAND DOLLARS?
IT'S A DEAL, SIR! I CAN HAVE A TROPHY FOR YOU INSIDE OF AN HOUR!
I'LL GIVE YOU TWENTY FOUR! I'M LEAVING FOR EUROPE TOMORROW EVENING!
IT WAS MORE MONEY THAN I EVER HOPED TO ACCUMULATE. ALL I HAD TO DO WAS PICK UP THAT ANIMAL AT THE SPOT WHERE I'D LEFT IT. I RAN ALL THE WAY TO MAX'S LABORATORY--
GOOD LUCK, JIM!
THANKS FOR LETTING ME BORROW THE "EGG", MAX--I'LL BE RIGHT BACK!
IN WHIRLING SECONDS, I WAS BACK IN THE LUSH JUNGLES OF DIMENSION FIVE--
THIS IS THE TRAIL I TOOK. THERE'S ONLY A HALF MILE TO COVER--
WHEN I FINALLY CAME TO THE SPOT, MY TRIUMPH TURNED TO ASHES. I STARED DUMBFOUNDED, REALIZING THAT I WOULD NEVER COLLECT THAT TWO HUNDRED THOUSAND DOLLARS!
THE THING WAS THERE AS I'D LEFT IT. -- BUT IT WAS MOUNTAINOUS IN SIZE. SOMETHING IN ITS BODY STRUCTURE HAD CAUSED IT TO GROW AFTER DEATH!
IT-IT'S TOO BIG-- TOO BIG TO TAKE BACK WITH ME!
The END

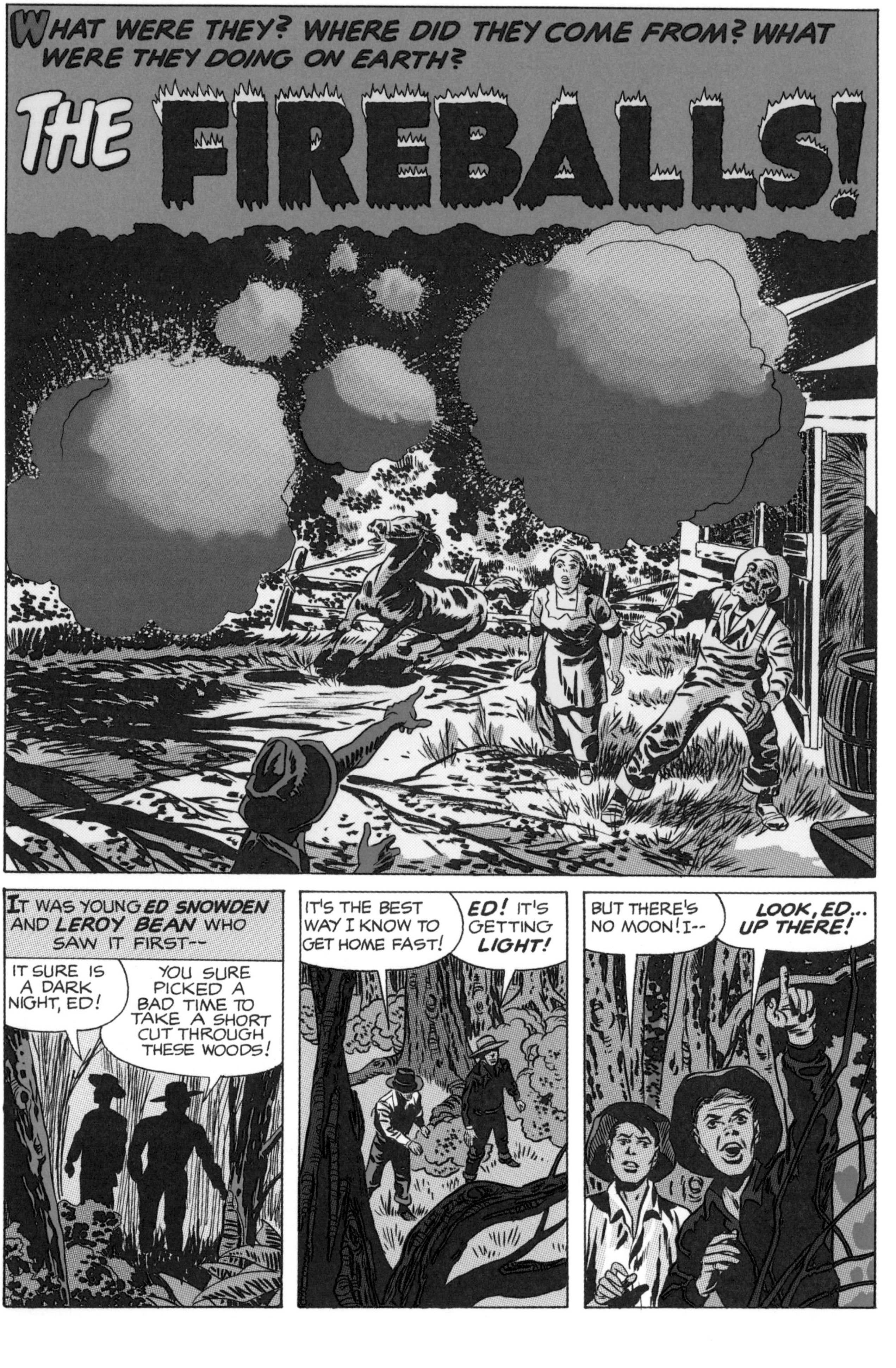
WHAT WERE THEY? WHERE DID THEY COME FROM? WHAT WERE THEY DOING ON EARTH?
THE FIREBALLS!
IT WAS YOUNG ED SNOWDEN AND LEROY BEAN WHO SAW IT FIRST--
IT SURE IS A DARK NIGHT, ED!
YOU SURE PICKED A BAD TIME TO TAKE A SHORT CUT THROUGH THESE WOODS!
IT'S THE BEST WAY I KNOW TO GET HOME FAST!
ED! IT'S GETTING LIGHT!
BUT THERE'S NO MOON! I--
LOOK, ED... UP THERE!

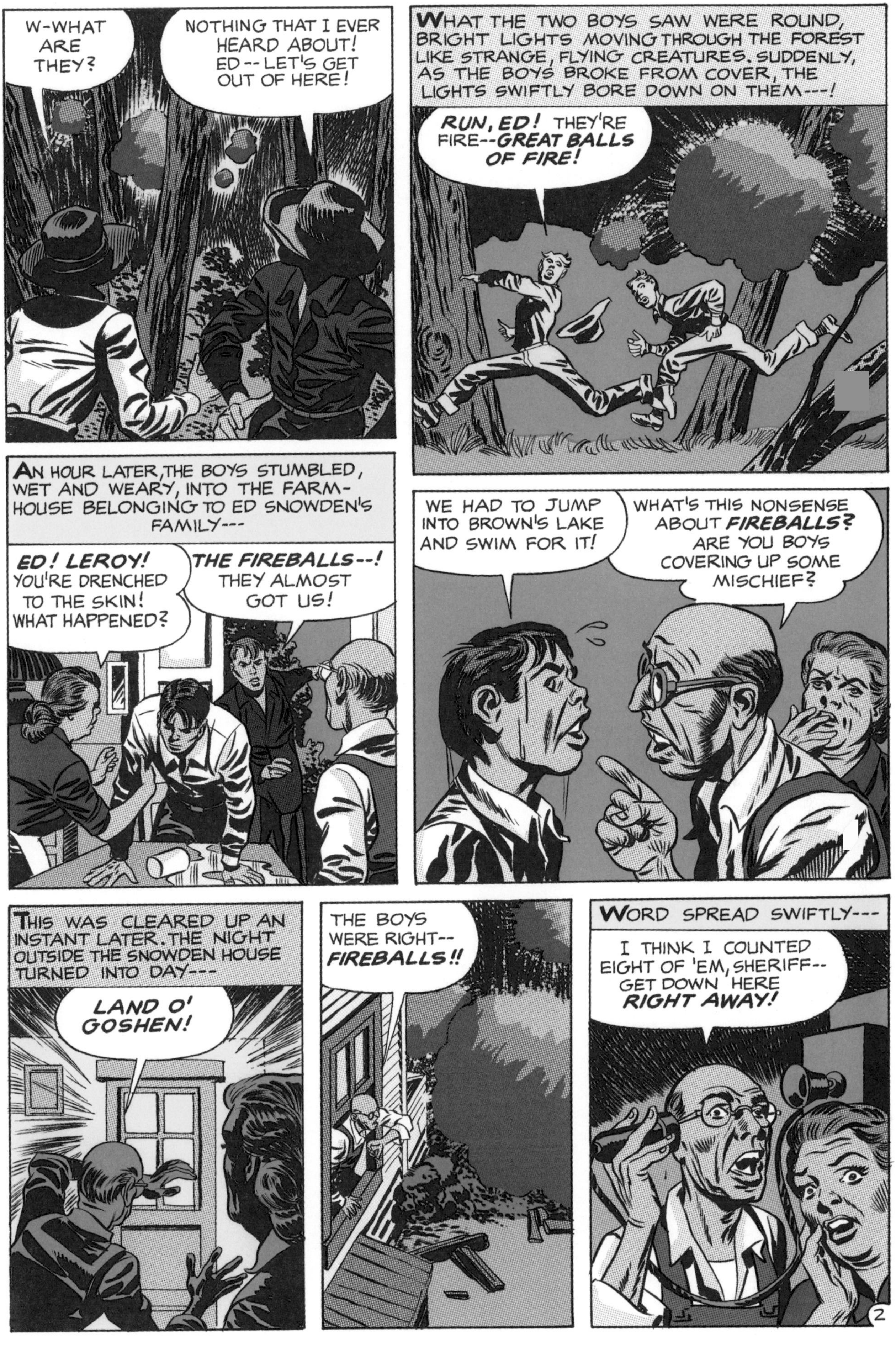
W-WHAT ARE THEY?
NOTHING THAT I EVER HEARD ABOUT! ED -- LET'S GET OUT OF HERE!
WHAT THE TWO BOYS SAW WERE ROUND, BRIGHT LIGHTS MOVING THROUGH THE FOREST LIKE STRANGE, FLYING CREATURES. SUDDENLY, AS THE BOYS BROKE FROM COVER, THE LIGHTS SWIFTLY BORE DOWN ON THEM---!
RUN, ED! THEY'RE FIRE--GREAT BALLS OF FIRE!
AN HOUR LATER, THE BOYS STUMBLED, WET AND WEARY, INTO THE FARM-HOUSE BELONGING TO ED SNOWDEN'S FAMILY---
ED! LEROY! YOU'RE DRENCHED TO THE SKIN! WHAT HAPPENED?
THE FIREBALLS--! THEY ALMOST GOT US!
WE HAD TO JUMP INTO BROWN'S LAKE AND SWIM FOR IT!
WHAT'S THIS NONSENSE ABOUT FIREBALLS? ARE YOU BOYS COVERING UP SOME MISCHIEF?
THIS WAS CLEARED UP AN INSTANT LATER. THE NIGHT OUTSIDE THE SNOWDEN HOUSE TURNED INTO DAY---
LAND O' GOSHEN!
THE BOYS WERE RIGHT-- FIREBALLS!!
WORD SPREAD SWIFTLY---
I THINK I COUNTED EIGHT OF 'EM, SHERIFF-- GET DOWN HERE RIGHT AWAY!
2

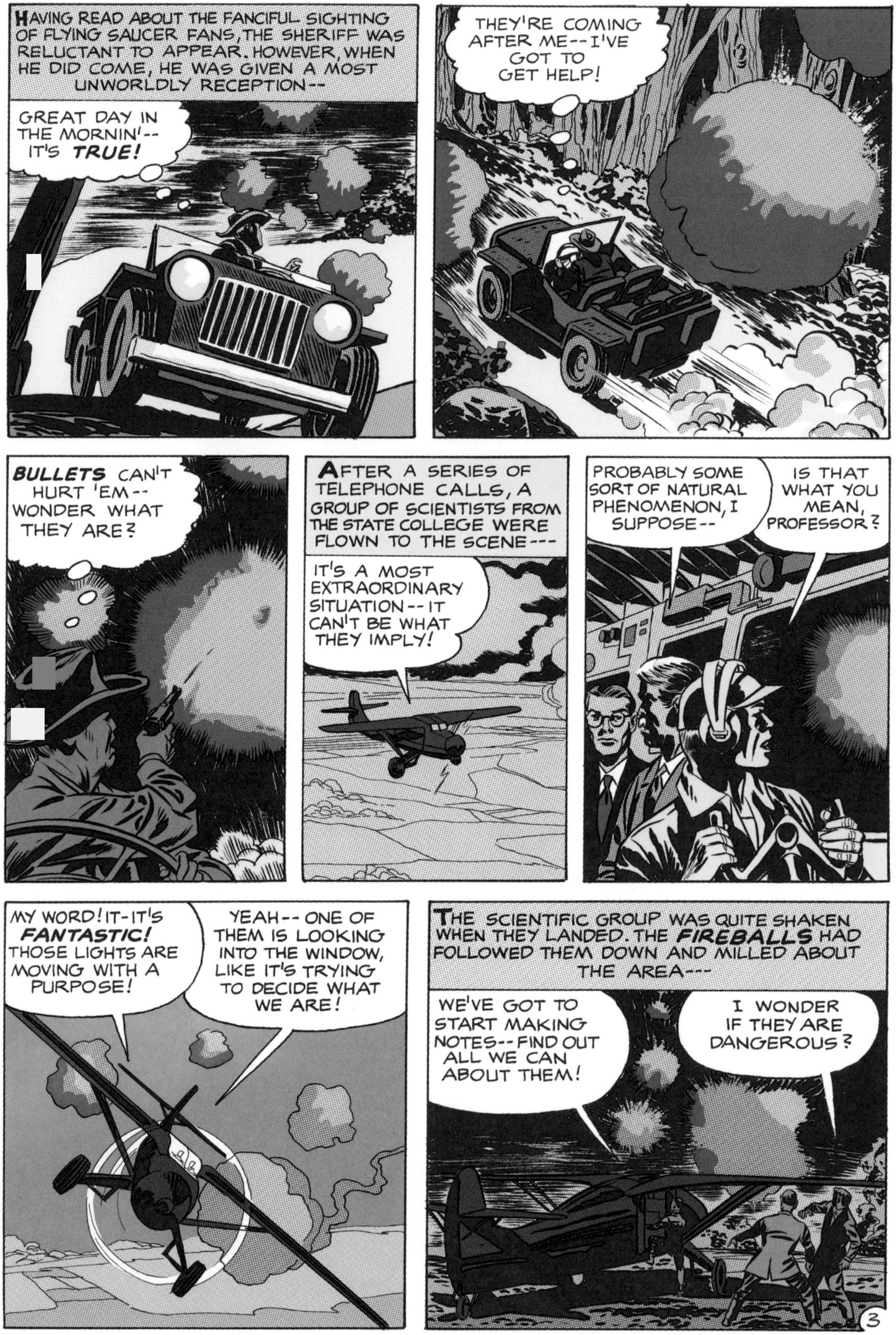
HAVING READ ABOUT THE FANCIFUL SIGHTING OF FLYING SAUCER FANS, THE SHERIFF WAS RELUCTANT TO APPEAR. HOWEVER, WHEN HE DID COME, HE WAS GIVEN A MOST UNWORLDLY RECEPTION--
GREAT DAY IN THE MORNIN'-- IT'S TRUE!
THEY'RE COMING AFTER ME--I'VE GOT TO GET HELP!
BULLETS CAN'T HURT 'EM-- WONDER WHAT THEY ARE?
AFTER A SERIES OF TELEPHONE CALLS, A GROUP OF SCIENTISTS FROM THE STATE COLLEGE WERE FLOWN TO THE SCENE---
IT'S A MOST EXTRAORDINARY SITUATION--IT CAN'T BE WHAT THEY IMPLY!
PROBABLY SOME SORT OF NATURAL PHENOMENON, I SUPPOSE--
IS THAT WHAT YOU MEAN, PROFESSOR?
MY WORD! IT-IT'S FANTASTIC! THOSE LIGHTS ARE MOVING WITH A PURPOSE!
YEAH-- ONE OF THEM IS LOOKING INTO THE WINDOW, LIKE IT'S TRYING TO DECIDE WHAT WE ARE!
THE SCIENTIFIC GROUP WAS QUITE SHAKEN WHEN THEY LANDED. THE FIREBALLS HAD FOLLOWED THEM DOWN AND MILLED ABOUT THE AREA---
WE'VE GOT TO START MAKING NOTES--FIND OUT ALL WE CAN ABOUT THEM!
I WONDER IF THEY ARE DANGEROUS?
3

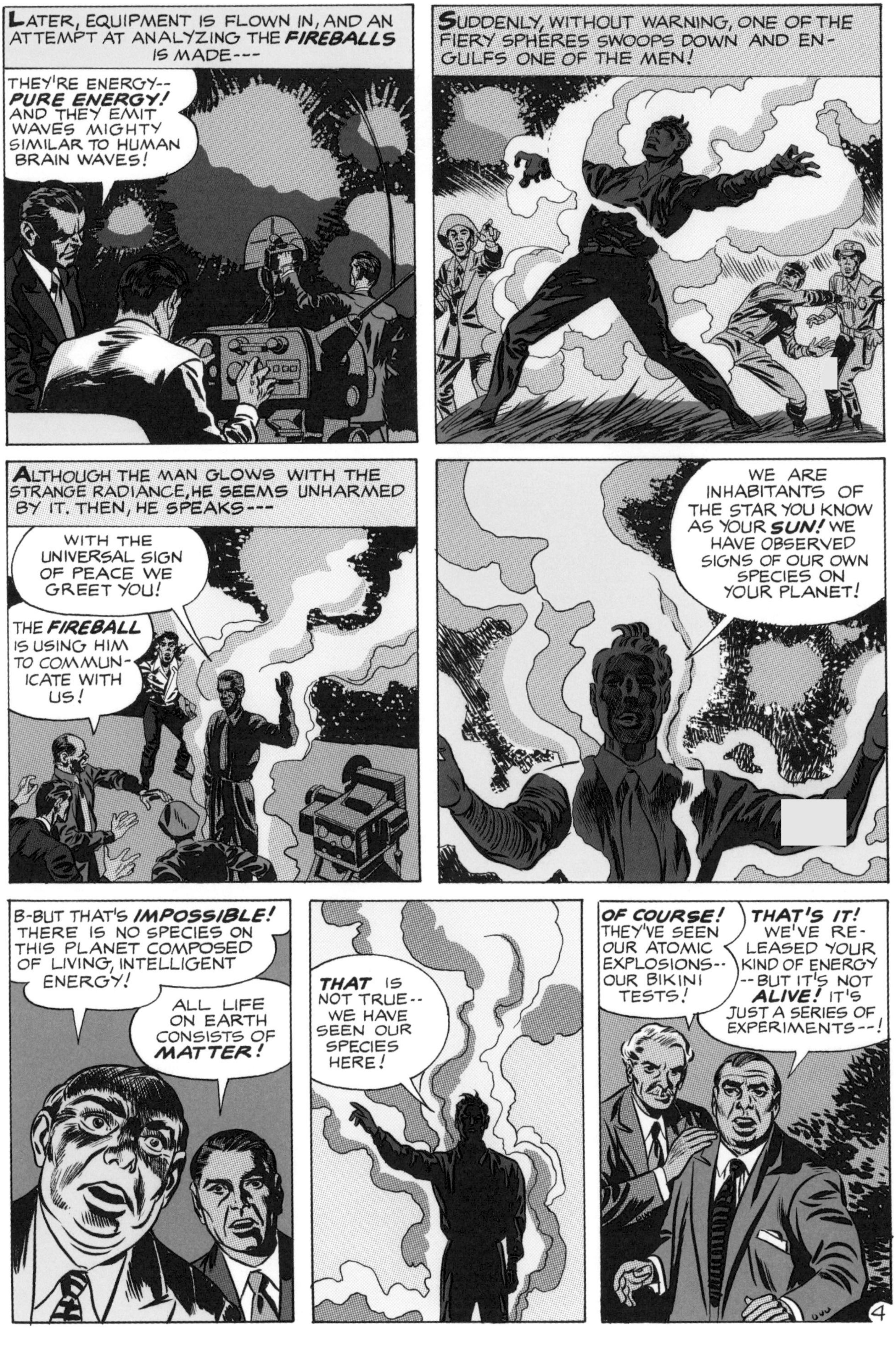
LATER, EQUIPMENT IS FLOWN IN, AND AN ATTEMPT AT ANALYZING THE FIREBALLS IS MADE---
THEY'RE ENERGY-- PURE ENERGY! AND THEY EMIT WAVES MIGHTY SIMILAR TO HUMAN BRAIN WAVES!
SUDDENLY, WITHOUT WARNING, ONE OF THE FIERY SPHERES SWOOPS DOWN AND ENGULFS ONE OF THE MEN!
ALTHOUGH THE MAN GLOWS WITH THE STRANGE RADIANCE, HE SEEMS UNHARMED BY IT. THEN, HE SPEAKS---
WITH THE UNIVERSAL SIGN OF PEACE WE GREET YOU!
THE FIREBALL IS USING HIM TO COMMUNICATE WITH US!
WE ARE INHABITANTS OF THE STAR YOU KNOW AS YOUR SUN! WE HAVE OBSERVED SIGNS OF OUR OWN SPECIES ON YOUR PLANET!
B-BUT THAT'S IMPOSSIBLE! THERE IS NO SPECIES ON THIS PLANET COMPOSED OF LIVING, INTELLIGENT ENERGY!
ALL LIFE ON EARTH CONSISTS OF MATTER!
THAT IS NOT TRUE-- WE HAVE SEEN OUR SPECIES HERE!
OF COURSE! THEY'VE SEEN OUR ATOMIC EXPLOSIONS-- OUR BIKINI TESTS!
THAT'S IT! WE'VE RELEASED YOUR KIND OF ENERGY --BUT IT'S NOT ALIVE! IT'S JUST A SERIES OF EXPERIMENTS--!
4

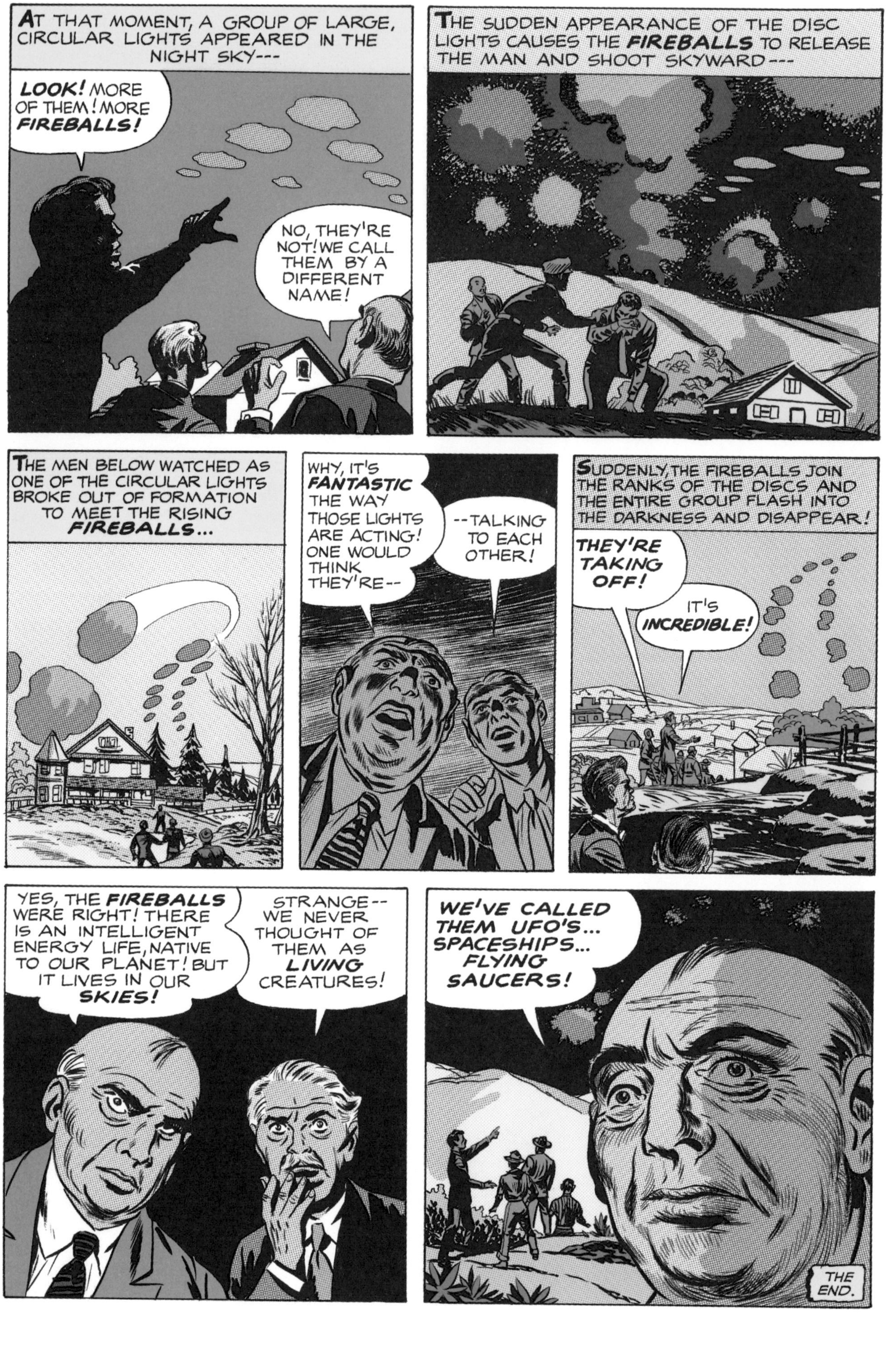
AT THAT MOMENT, A GROUP OF LARGE, CIRCULAR LIGHTS APPEARED IN THE NIGHT SKY---
LOOK! MORE OF THEM! MORE FIREBALLS!
NO, THEY'RE NOT! WE CALL THEM BY A DIFFERENT NAME!
THE SUDDEN APPEARANCE OF THE DISC LIGHTS CAUSES THE FIREBALLS TO RELEASE THE MAN AND SHOOT SKYWARD---
THE MEN BELOW WATCHED AS ONE OF THE CIRCULAR LIGHTS BROKE OUT OF FORMATION TO MEET THE RISING FIREBALLS...
WHY, IT'S FANTASTIC THE WAY THOSE LIGHTS ARE ACTING! ONE WOULD THINK THEY'RE--
--TALKING TO EACH OTHER!
SUDDENLY, THE FIREBALLS JOIN THE RANKS OF THE DISCS AND THE ENTIRE GROUP FLASH INTO THE DARKNESS AND DISAPPEAR!
THEY'RE TAKING OFF!
IT'S INCREDIBLE!
YES, THE FIREBALLS WERE RIGHT! THERE IS AN INTELLIGENT ENERGY LIFE, NATIVE TO OUR PLANET! BUT IT LIVES IN OUR SKIES!
STRANGE-- WE NEVER THOUGHT OF THEM AS LIVING CREATURES!
WE'VE CALLED THEM UFO'S... SPACESHIPS... FLYING SAUCERS!
THE END.

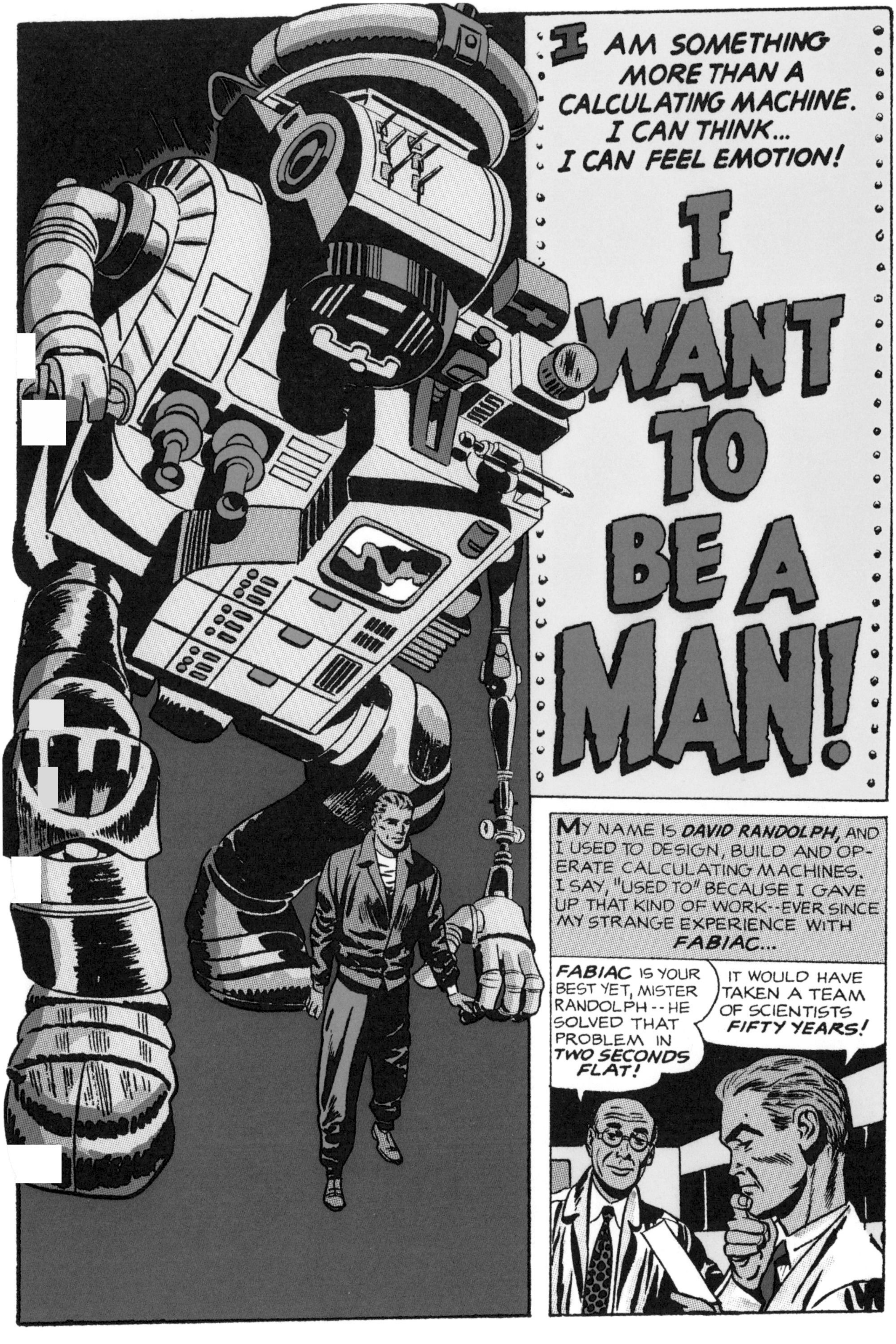

I AM SOMETHING MORE THAN A CALCULATING MACHINE. I CAN THINK... I CAN FEEL EMOTION!
I WANT TO BE A MAN!
MY NAME IS DAVID RANDOLPH, AND I USED TO DESIGN, BUILD AND OPERATE CALCULATING MACHINES. I SAY, "USED TO" BECAUSE I GAVE UP THAT KIND OF WORK--EVER SINCE MY STRANGE EXPERIENCE WITH FABIAC...
FABIAC IS YOUR BEST YET, MISTER RANDOLPH--HE SOLVED THAT PROBLEM IN TWO SECONDS FLAT!
IT WOULD HAVE TAKEN A TEAM OF SCIENTISTS FIFTY YEARS!

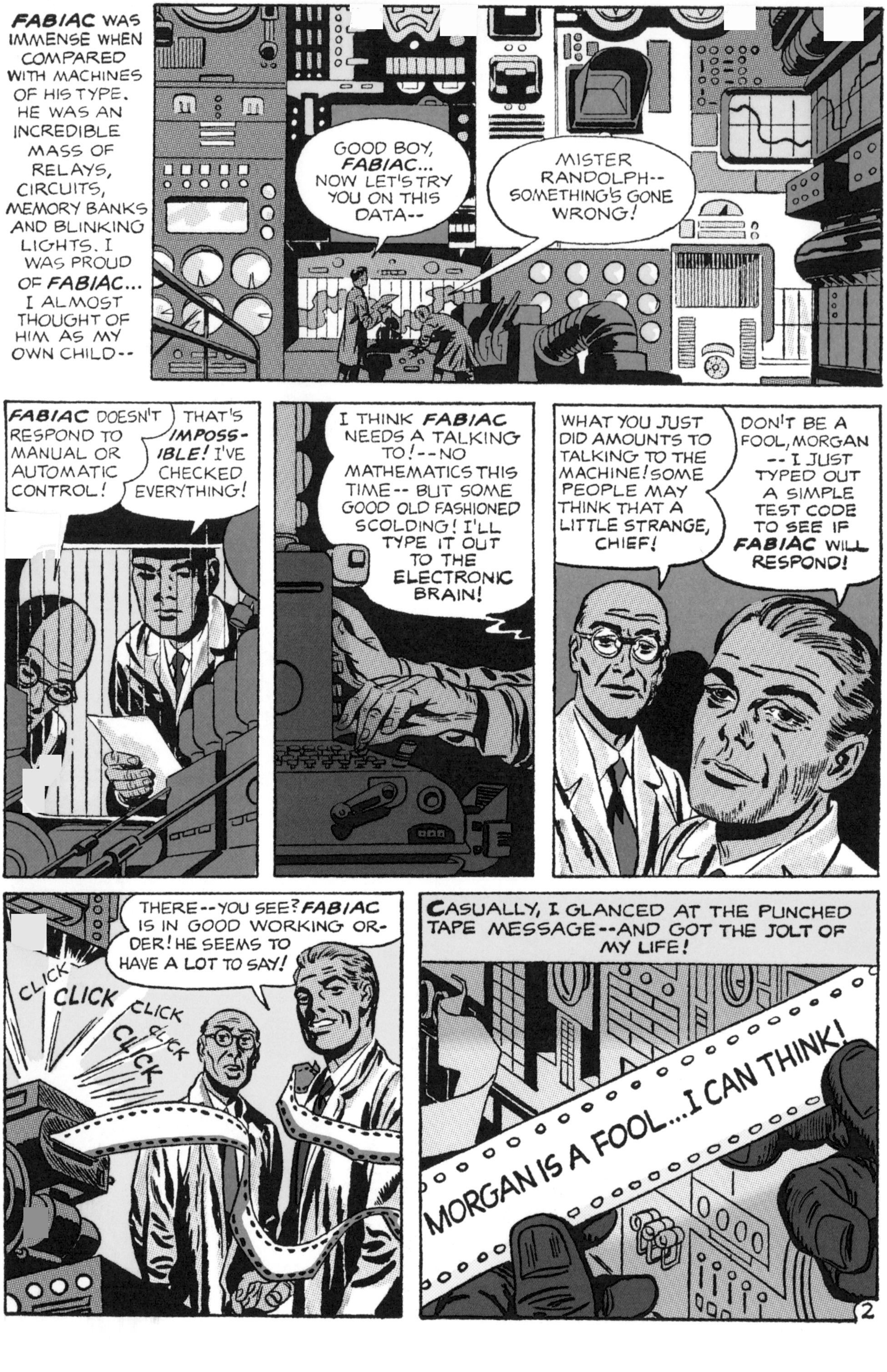
FABIAC WAS IMMENSE WHEN COMPARED WITH MACHINES OF HIS TYPE. HE WAS AN INCREDIBLE MASS OF RELAYS, CIRCUITS, MEMORY BANKS AND BLINKING LIGHTS. I WAS PROUD OF FABIAC... I ALMOST THOUGHT OF HIM AS MY OWN CHILD--
GOOD BOY, FABIAC... NOW LET'S TRY YOU ON THIS DATA--
MISTER RANDOLPH-- SOMETHING'S GONE WRONG!
FABIAC DOESN'T RESPOND TO MANUAL OR AUTOMATIC CONTROL!
THAT'S IMPOSSIBLE! I'VE CHECKED EVERYTHING!
I THINK FABIAC NEEDS A TALKING TO!--NO MATHEMATICS THIS TIME-- BUT SOME GOOD OLD FASHIONED SCOLDING! I'LL TYPE IT OUT TO THE ELECTRONIC BRAIN!
WHAT YOU JUST DID AMOUNTS TO TALKING TO THE MACHINE! SOME PEOPLE MAY THINK THAT A LITTLE STRANGE, CHIEF!
DON'T BE A FOOL, MORGAN -- I JUST TYPED OUT A SIMPLE TEST CODE TO SEE IF FABIAC WILL RESPOND!
THERE--YOU SEE? FABIAC IS IN GOOD WORKING ORDER! HE SEEMS TO HAVE A LOT TO SAY!
CLICK CLICK CLICK CLICK CLICK
CASUALLY, I GLANCED AT THE PUNCHED TAPE MESSAGE--AND GOT THE JOLT OF MY LIFE!
MORGAN IS A FOOL...I CAN THINK!
2

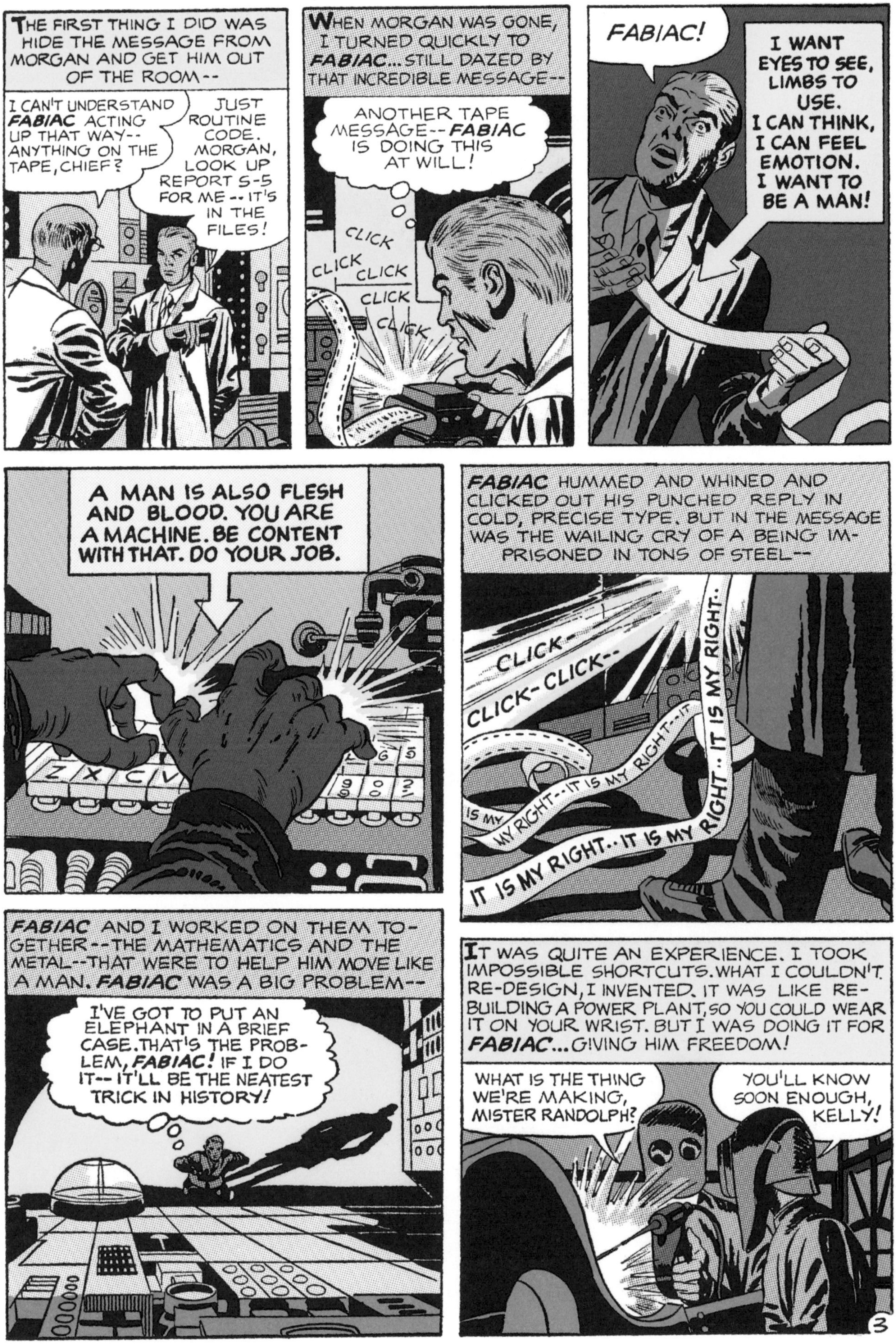
THE FIRST THING I DID WAS HIDE THE MESSAGE FROM MORGAN AND GET HIM OUT OF THE ROOM--
I CAN'T UNDERSTAND FABIAC ACTING UP THAT WAY-- ANYTHING ON THE TAPE, CHIEF?
JUST ROUTINE CODE. MORGAN, LOOK UP REPORT S-5 FOR ME -- IT'S IN THE FILES!
WHEN MORGAN WAS GONE, I TURNED QUICKLY TO FABIAC... STILL DAZED BY THAT INCREDIBLE MESSAGE--
ANOTHER TAPE MESSAGE-- FABIAC IS DOING THIS AT WILL!
CLICK
CLICK CLICK
CLICK
CLICK
FABIAC!
I WANT EYES TO SEE, LIMBS TO USE. I CAN THINK, I CAN FEEL EMOTION. I WANT TO BE A MAN!
A MAN IS ALSO FLESH AND BLOOD. YOU ARE A MACHINE. BE CONTENT WITH THAT. DO YOUR JOB.
FABIAC HUMMED AND WHINED AND CLICKED OUT HIS PUNCHED REPLY IN COLD, PRECISE TYPE. BUT IN THE MESSAGE WAS THE WAILING CRY OF A BEING IMPRISONED IN TONS OF STEEL--
CLICK-
CLICK-CLICK--
IT IS MY RIGHT.. IT IS MY RIGHT.. IT IS MY RIGHT.. IT IS MY RIGHT--IT IS MY RIGHT--IT IS MY RIGHT--IT IS MY
FABIAC AND I WORKED ON THEM TOGETHER--THE MATHEMATICS AND THE METAL--THAT WERE TO HELP HIM MOVE LIKE A MAN. FABIAC WAS A BIG PROBLEM--
I'VE GOT TO PUT AN ELEPHANT IN A BRIEF CASE. THAT'S THE PROBLEM, FABIAC! IF I DO IT-- IT'LL BE THE NEATEST TRICK IN HISTORY!
IT WAS QUITE AN EXPERIENCE. I TOOK IMPOSSIBLE SHORTCUTS. WHAT I COULDN'T RE-DESIGN, I INVENTED. IT WAS LIKE RE-BUILDING A POWER PLANT, SO YOU COULD WEAR IT ON YOUR WRIST. BUT I WAS DOING IT FOR FABIAC... GIVING HIM FREEDOM!
WHAT IS THE THING WE'RE MAKING, MISTER RANDOLPH?
YOU'LL KNOW SOON ENOUGH, KELLY!
3

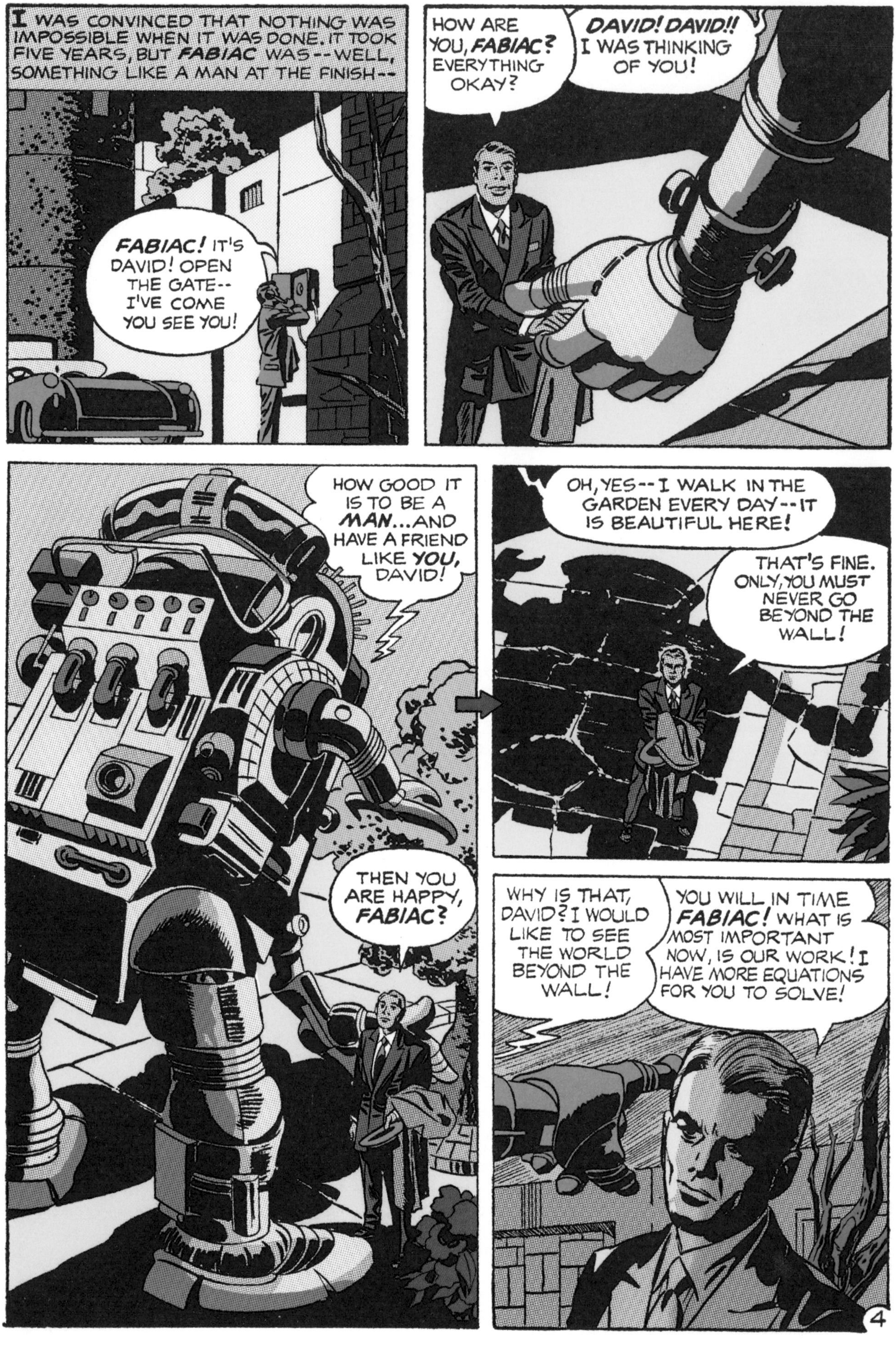
I WAS CONVINCED THAT NOTHING WAS IMPOSSIBLE WHEN IT WAS DONE. IT TOOK FIVE YEARS, BUT FABIAC WAS--WELL, SOMETHING LIKE A MAN AT THE FINISH--
FABIAC! IT'S DAVID! OPEN THE GATE-- I'VE COME YOU SEE YOU!
HOW ARE YOU, FABIAC? EVERYTHING OKAY?
DAVID! DAVID!! I WAS THINKING OF YOU!
HOW GOOD IT IS TO BE A MAN...AND HAVE A FRIEND LIKE YOU, DAVID!
THEN YOU ARE HAPPY, FABIAC?
OH, YES--I WALK IN THE GARDEN EVERY DAY--IT IS BEAUTIFUL HERE!
THAT'S FINE. ONLY, YOU MUST NEVER GO BEYOND THE WALL!
WHY IS THAT, DAVID? I WOULD LIKE TO SEE THE WORLD BEYOND THE WALL!
YOU WILL IN TIME FABIAC! WHAT IS MOST IMPORTANT NOW, IS OUR WORK! I HAVE MORE EQUATIONS FOR YOU TO SOLVE!
4

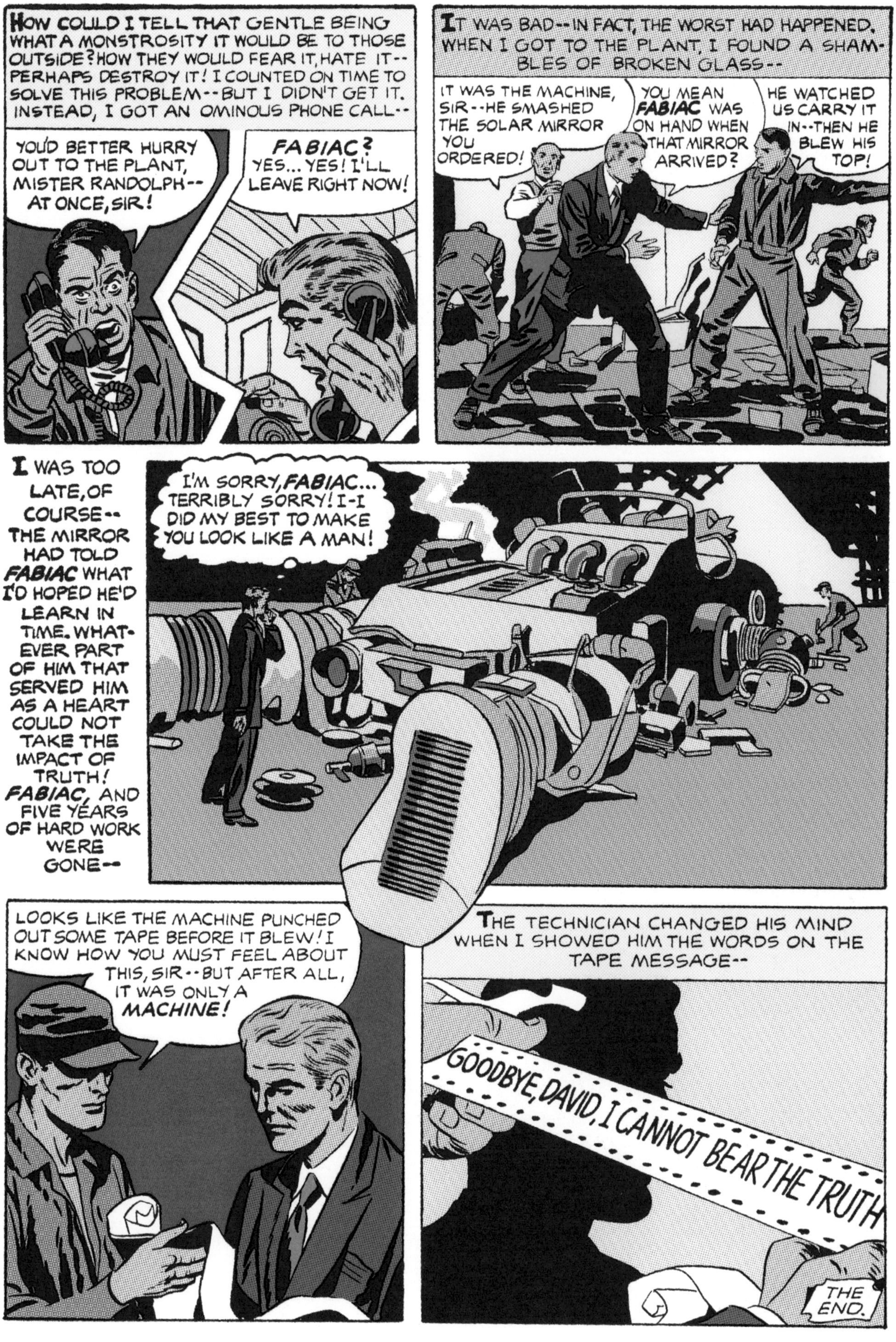
HOW COULD I TELL THAT GENTLE BEING WHAT A MONSTROSITY IT WOULD BE TO THOSE OUTSIDE? HOW THEY WOULD FEAR IT, HATE IT-- PERHAPS DESTROY IT! I COUNTED ON TIME TO SOLVE THIS PROBLEM--BUT I DIDN'T GET IT. INSTEAD, I GOT AN OMINOUS PHONE CALL--
YOU'D BETTER HURRY OUT TO THE PLANT, MISTER RANDOLPH-- AT ONCE, SIR!
FABIAC? YES... YES! I'LL LEAVE RIGHT NOW!
IT WAS BAD--IN FACT, THE WORST HAD HAPPENED. WHEN I GOT TO THE PLANT, I FOUND A SHAMBLES OF BROKEN GLASS--
IT WAS THE MACHINE, SIR--HE SMASHED THE SOLAR MIRROR YOU ORDERED!
YOU MEAN FABIAC WAS ON HAND WHEN THAT MIRROR ARRIVED?
HE WATCHED US CARRY IT IN--THEN HE BLEW HIS TOP!
I WAS TOO LATE, OF COURSE-- THE MIRROR HAD TOLD FABIAC WHAT I'D HOPED HE'D LEARN IN TIME. WHATEVER PART OF HIM THAT SERVED HIM AS A HEART COULD NOT TAKE THE IMPACT OF TRUTH! FABIAC, AND FIVE YEARS OF HARD WORK WERE GONE--
I'M SORRY, FABIAC... TERRIBLY SORRY! I-I DID MY BEST TO MAKE YOU LOOK LIKE A MAN!
LOOKS LIKE THE MACHINE PUNCHED OUT SOME TAPE BEFORE IT BLEW! I KNOW HOW YOU MUST FEEL ABOUT THIS, SIR--BUT AFTER ALL, IT WAS ONLY A MACHINE!
THE TECHNICIAN CHANGED HIS MIND WHEN I SHOWED HIM THE WORDS ON THE TAPE MESSAGE--
GOODBYE, DAVID, I CANNOT BEAR THE TRUTH
THE END.

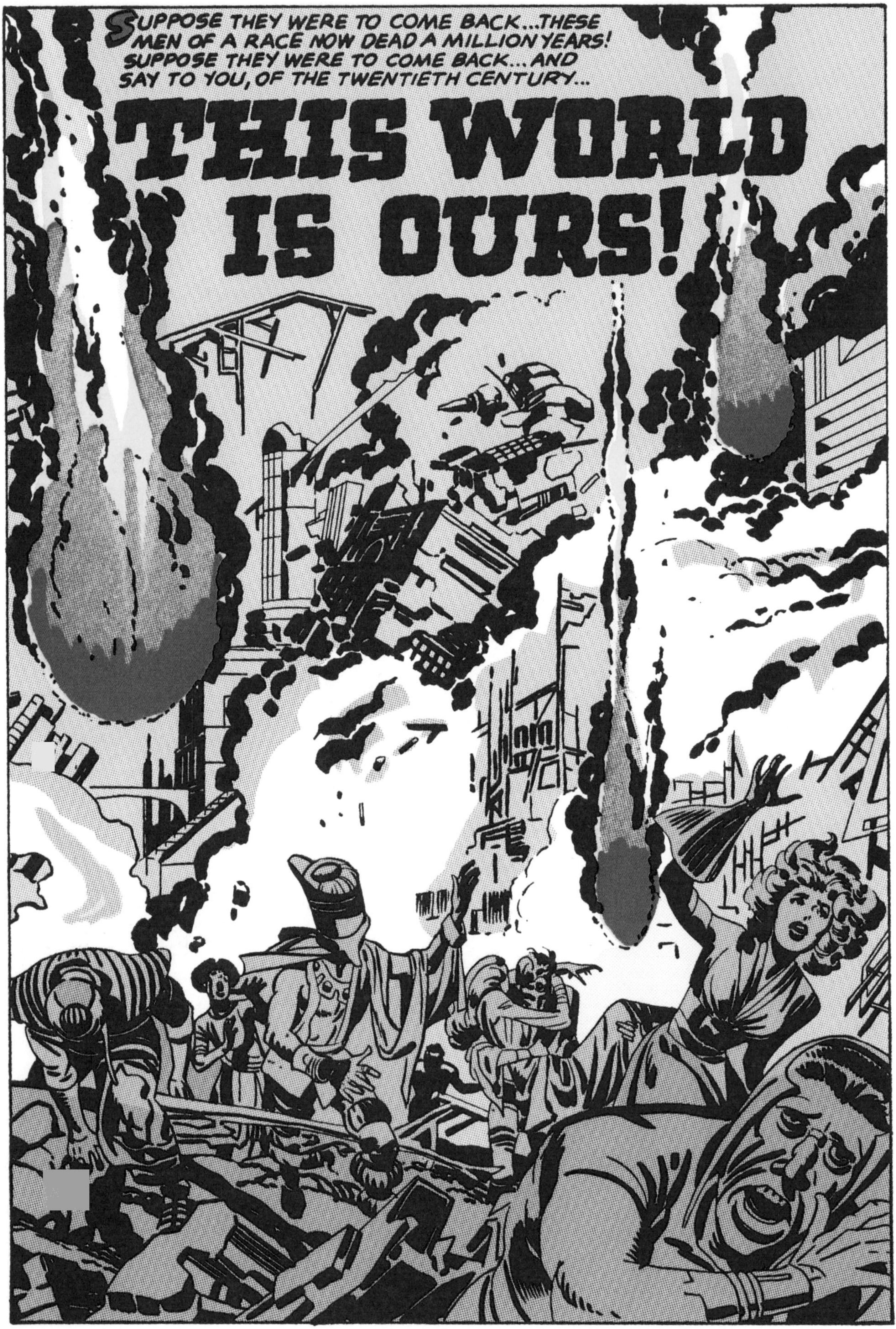
SUPPOSE THEY WERE TO COME BACK...THESE MEN OF A RACE NOW DEAD A MILLION YEARS! SUPPOSE THEY WERE TO COME BACK...AND SAY TO YOU, OF THE TWENTIETH CENTURY...
THIS WORLD IS OURS!

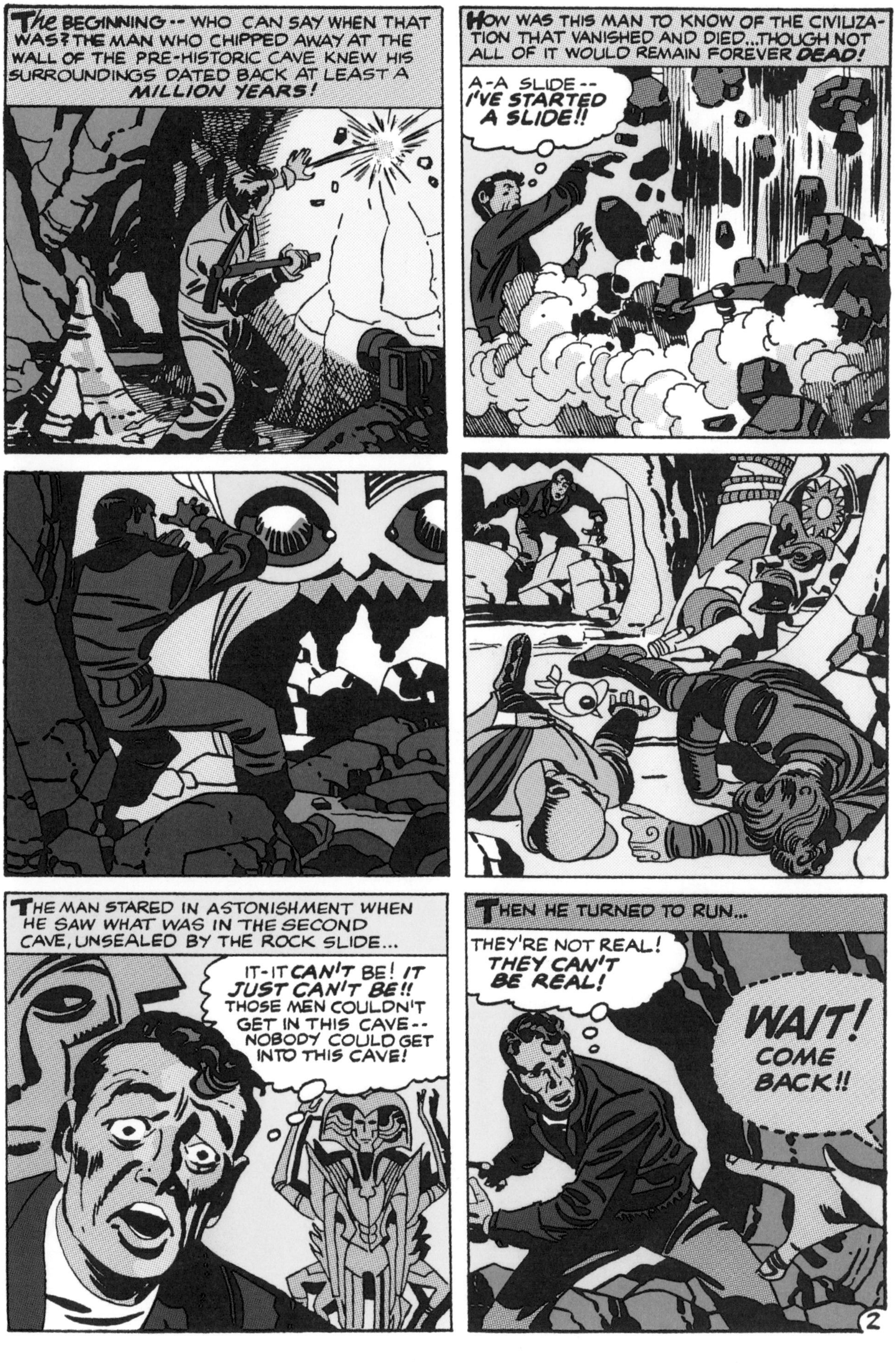
THE BEGINNING -- WHO CAN SAY WHEN THAT WAS? THE MAN WHO CHIPPED AWAY AT THE WALL OF THE PRE-HISTORIC CAVE KNEW HIS SURROUNDINGS DATED BACK AT LEAST A MILLION YEARS!
HOW WAS THIS MAN TO KNOW OF THE CIVILIZATION THAT VANISHED AND DIED...THOUGH NOT ALL OF IT WOULD REMAIN FOREVER DEAD!
A-A SLIDE -- I'VE STARTED A SLIDE!!
THE MAN STARED IN ASTONISHMENT WHEN HE SAW WHAT WAS IN THE SECOND CAVE, UNSEALED BY THE ROCK SLIDE...
IT-IT CAN'T BE! IT JUST CAN'T BE!! THOSE MEN COULDN'T GET IN THIS CAVE -- NOBODY COULD GET INTO THIS CAVE!
THEN HE TURNED TO RUN...
THEY'RE NOT REAL! THEY CAN'T BE REAL!
WAIT! COME BACK!!
2

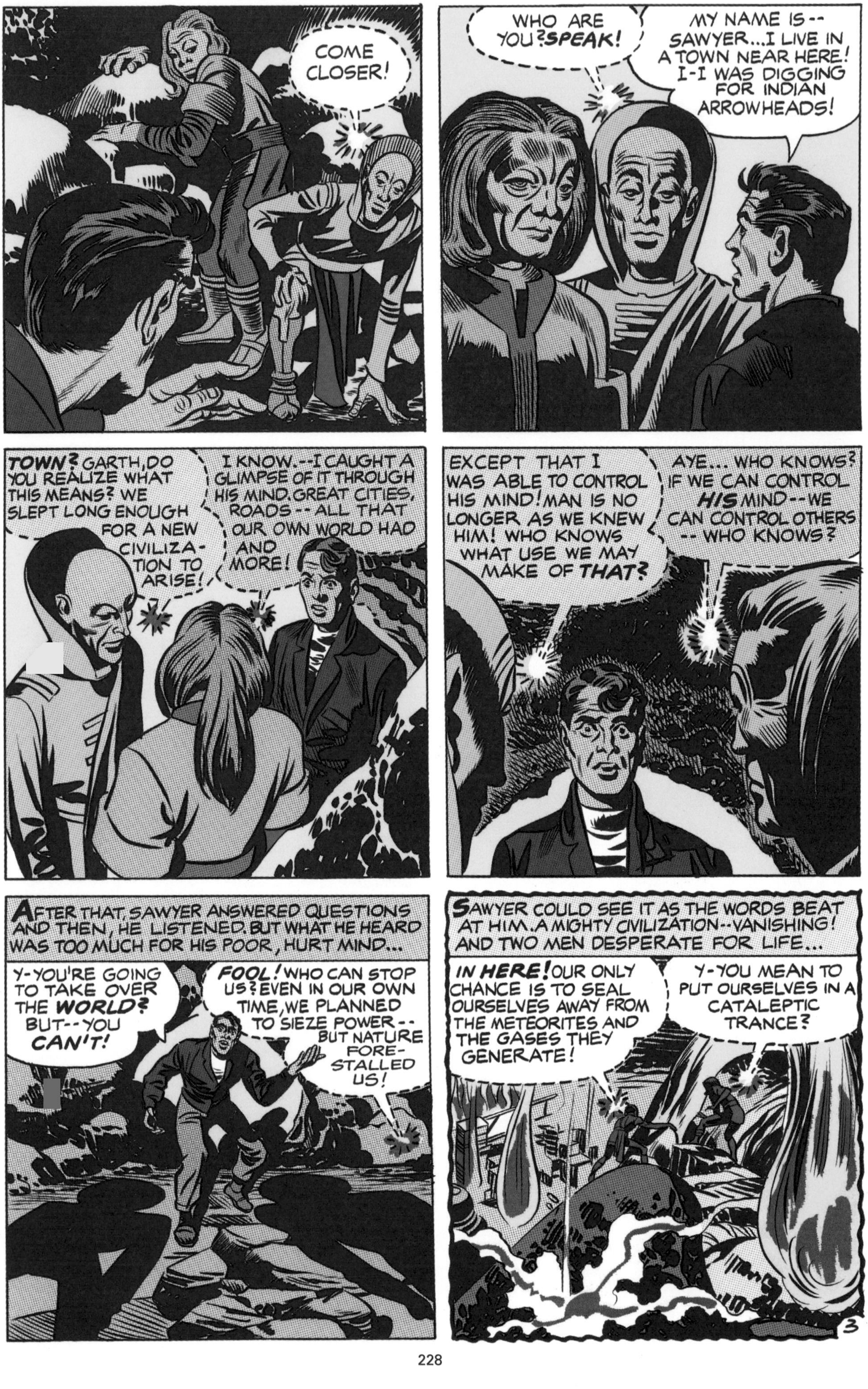
COME CLOSER!
WHO ARE YOU? SPEAK!
MY NAME IS-- SAWYER...I LIVE IN A TOWN NEAR HERE! I-I WAS DIGGING FOR INDIAN ARROWHEADS!
TOWN? GARTH, DO YOU REALIZE WHAT THIS MEANS? WE SLEPT LONG ENOUGH FOR A NEW CIVILIZATION TO ARISE!
I KNOW.--I CAUGHT A GLIMPSE OF IT THROUGH HIS MIND. GREAT CITIES, ROADS -- ALL THAT OUR OWN WORLD HAD AND MORE!
EXCEPT THAT I WAS ABLE TO CONTROL HIS MIND! MAN IS NO LONGER AS WE KNEW HIM! WHO KNOWS WHAT USE WE MAY MAKE OF THAT?
AYE... WHO KNOWS? IF WE CAN CONTROL HIS MIND--WE CAN CONTROL OTHERS -- WHO KNOWS?
AFTER THAT, SAWYER ANSWERED QUESTIONS AND THEN, HE LISTENED. BUT WHAT HE HEARD WAS TOO MUCH FOR HIS POOR, HURT MIND...
Y-YOU'RE GOING TO TAKE OVER THE WORLD? BUT--YOU CAN'T!
FOOL! WHO CAN STOP US? EVEN IN OUR OWN TIME, WE PLANNED TO SIEZE POWER--BUT NATURE FORESTALLED US!
SAWYER COULD SEE IT AS THE WORDS BEAT AT HIM. A MIGHTY CIVILIZATION--VANISHING! AND TWO MEN DESPERATE FOR LIFE...
IN HERE! OUR ONLY CHANCE IS TO SEAL OURSELVES AWAY FROM THE METEORITES AND THE GASES THEY GENERATE!
Y-YOU MEAN TO PUT OURSELVES IN A CATALEPTIC TRANCE?
3

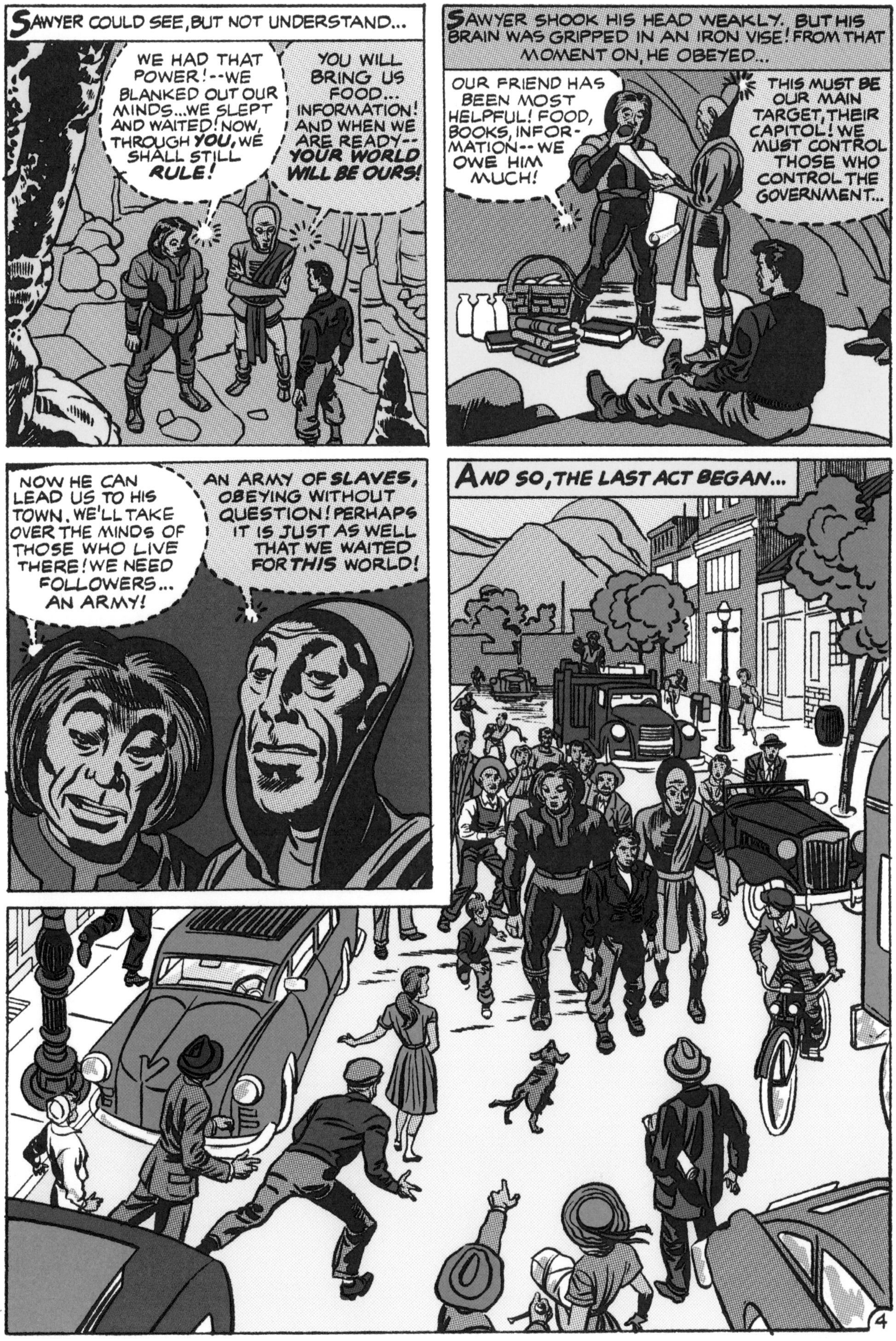
SAWYER COULD SEE, BUT NOT UNDERSTAND...
WE HAD THAT POWER!--WE BLANKED OUT OUR MINDS...WE SLEPT AND WAITED! NOW, THROUGH YOU, WE SHALL STILL RULE!
YOU WILL BRING US FOOD... INFORMATION! AND WHEN WE ARE READY-- YOUR WORLD WILL BE OURS!
SAWYER SHOOK HIS HEAD WEAKLY, BUT HIS BRAIN WAS GRIPPED IN AN IRON VISE! FROM THAT MOMENT ON, HE OBEYED...
OUR FRIEND HAS BEEN MOST HELPFUL! FOOD, BOOKS, INFORMATION-- WE OWE HIM MUCH!
THIS MUST BE OUR MAIN TARGET, THEIR CAPITOL! WE MUST CONTROL THOSE WHO CONTROL THE GOVERNMENT...
NOW HE CAN LEAD US TO HIS TOWN. WE'LL TAKE OVER THE MINDS OF THOSE WHO LIVE THERE! WE NEED FOLLOWERS... AN ARMY!
AN ARMY OF SLAVES, OBEYING WITHOUT QUESTION! PERHAPS IT IS JUST AS WELL THAT WE WAITED FOR THIS WORLD!
AND SO, THE LAST ACT BEGAN...
4

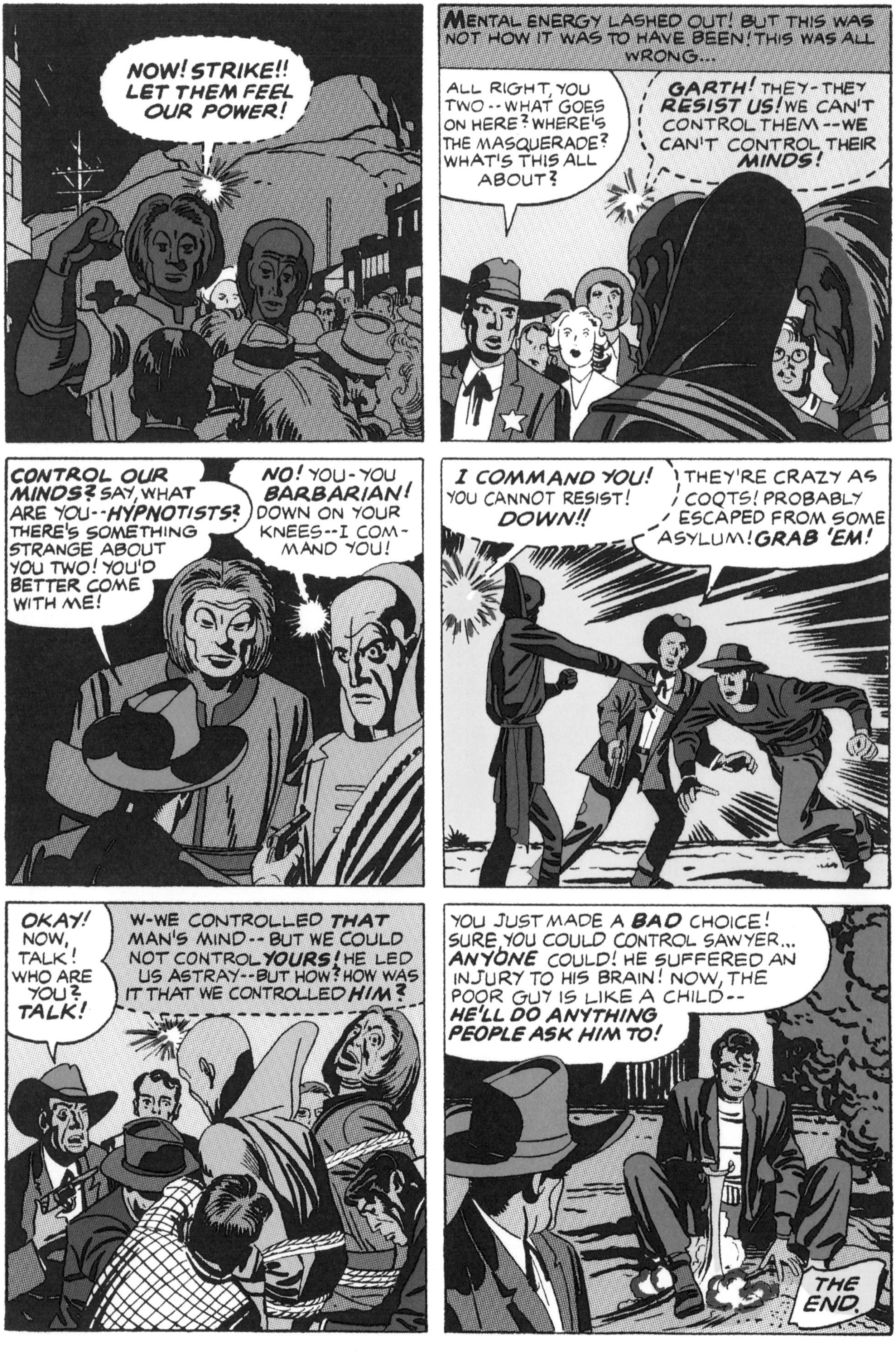
NOW! STRIKE!! LET THEM FEEL OUR POWER!
MENTAL ENERGY LASHED OUT! BUT THIS WAS NOT HOW IT WAS TO HAVE BEEN! THIS WAS ALL WRONG...
ALL RIGHT, YOU TWO -- WHAT GOES ON HERE? WHERE'S THE MASQUERADE? WHAT'S THIS ALL ABOUT?
GARTH! THEY-THEY RESIST US! WE CAN'T CONTROL THEM -- WE CAN'T CONTROL THEIR MINDS!
CONTROL OUR MINDS? SAY, WHAT ARE YOU--HYPNOTISTS? THERE'S SOMETHING STRANGE ABOUT YOU TWO! YOU'D BETTER COME WITH ME!
NO! YOU-YOU BARBARIAN! DOWN ON YOUR KNEES--I COMMAND YOU!
I COMMAND YOU! YOU CANNOT RESIST! DOWN!!
THEY'RE CRAZY AS COOTS! PROBABLY ESCAPED FROM SOME ASYLUM! GRAB 'EM!
OKAY! NOW, TALK! WHO ARE YOU? TALK!
W-WE CONTROLLED THAT MAN'S MIND-- BUT WE COULD NOT CONTROL YOURS! HE LED US ASTRAY--BUT HOW? HOW WAS IT THAT WE CONTROLLED HIM?
YOU JUST MADE A BAD CHOICE! SURE, YOU COULD CONTROL SAWYER... ANYONE COULD! HE SUFFERED AN INJURY TO HIS BRAIN! NOW, THE POOR GUY IS LIKE A CHILD-- HE'LL DO ANYTHING PEOPLE ASK HIM TO!
THE END.

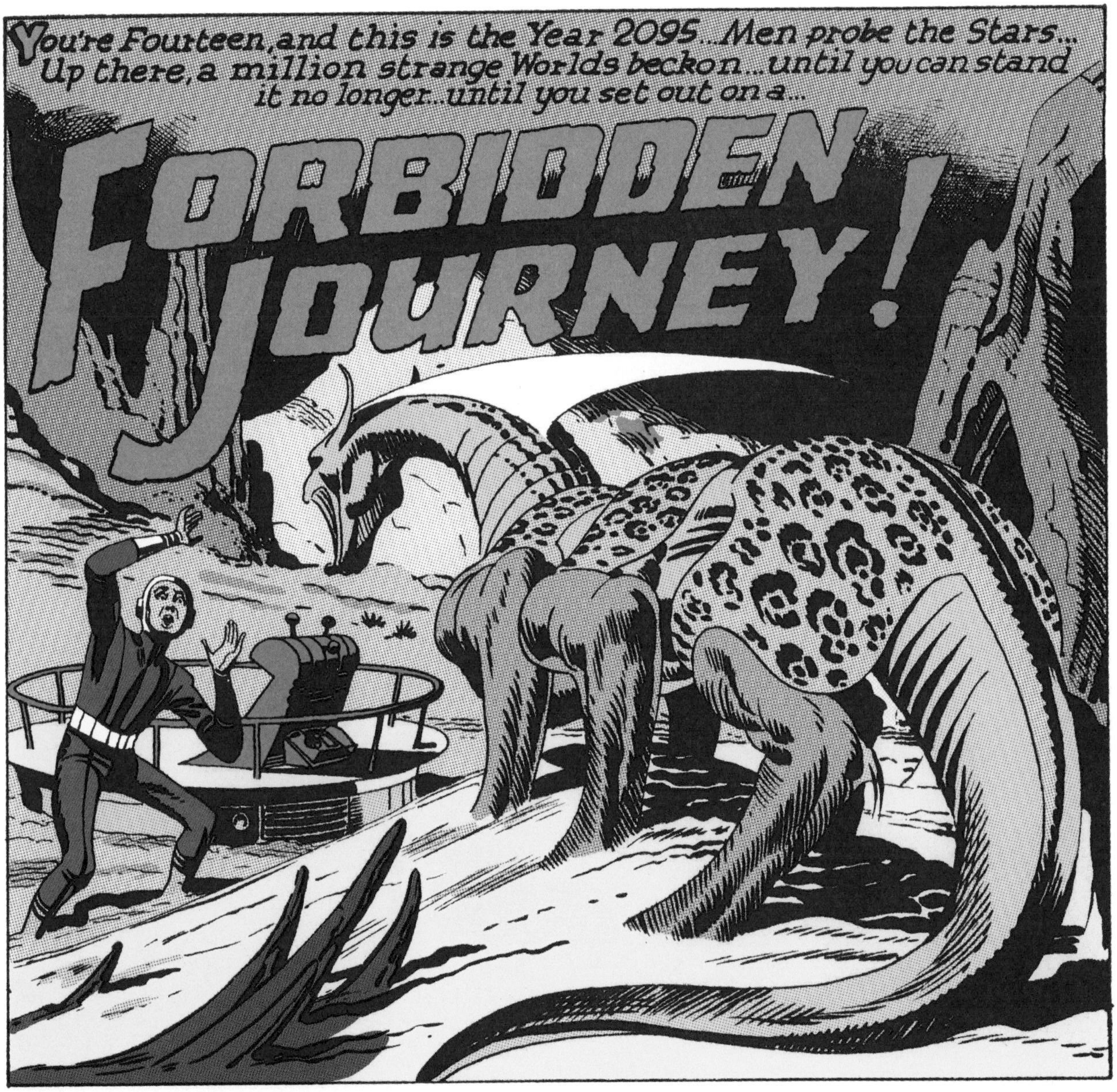
You're Fourteen, and this is the Year 2095.. Men probe the Stars... Up there, a million strange Worlds beckon... until you can stand it no longer.. until you set out on a...
FORBIDDEN JOURNEY!

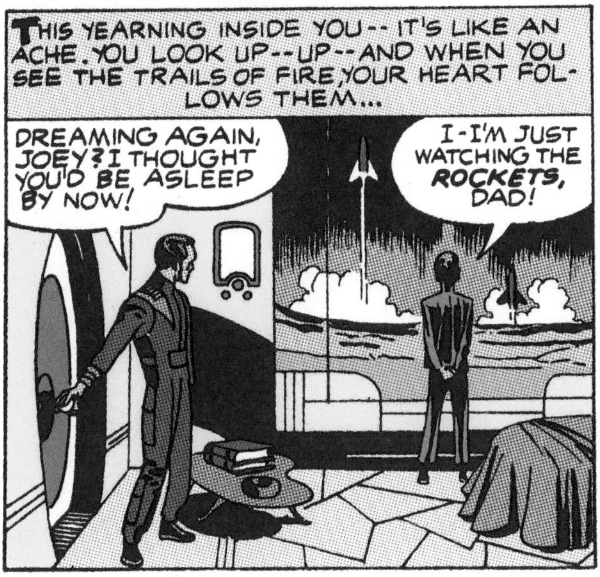
THIS YEARNING INSIDE YOU-- IT'S LIKE AN ACHE. YOU LOOK UP--UP--AND WHEN YOU SEE THE TRAILS OF FIRE, YOUR HEART FOLLOWS THEM...
DREAMING AGAIN, JOEY? I THOUGHT YOU'D BE ASLEEP BY NOW!
I-I'M JUST WATCHING THE ROCKETS, DAD!

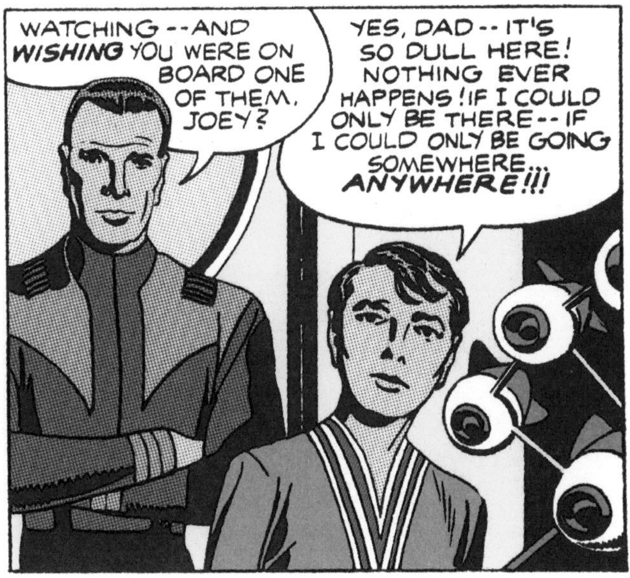
WATCHING --AND WISHING YOU WERE ON BOARD ONE OF THEM, JOEY?
YES, DAD-- IT'S SO DULL HERE! NOTHING EVER HAPPENS! IF I COULD ONLY BE THERE-- IF I COULD ONLY BE GOING SOMEWHERE... ANYWHERE!!!

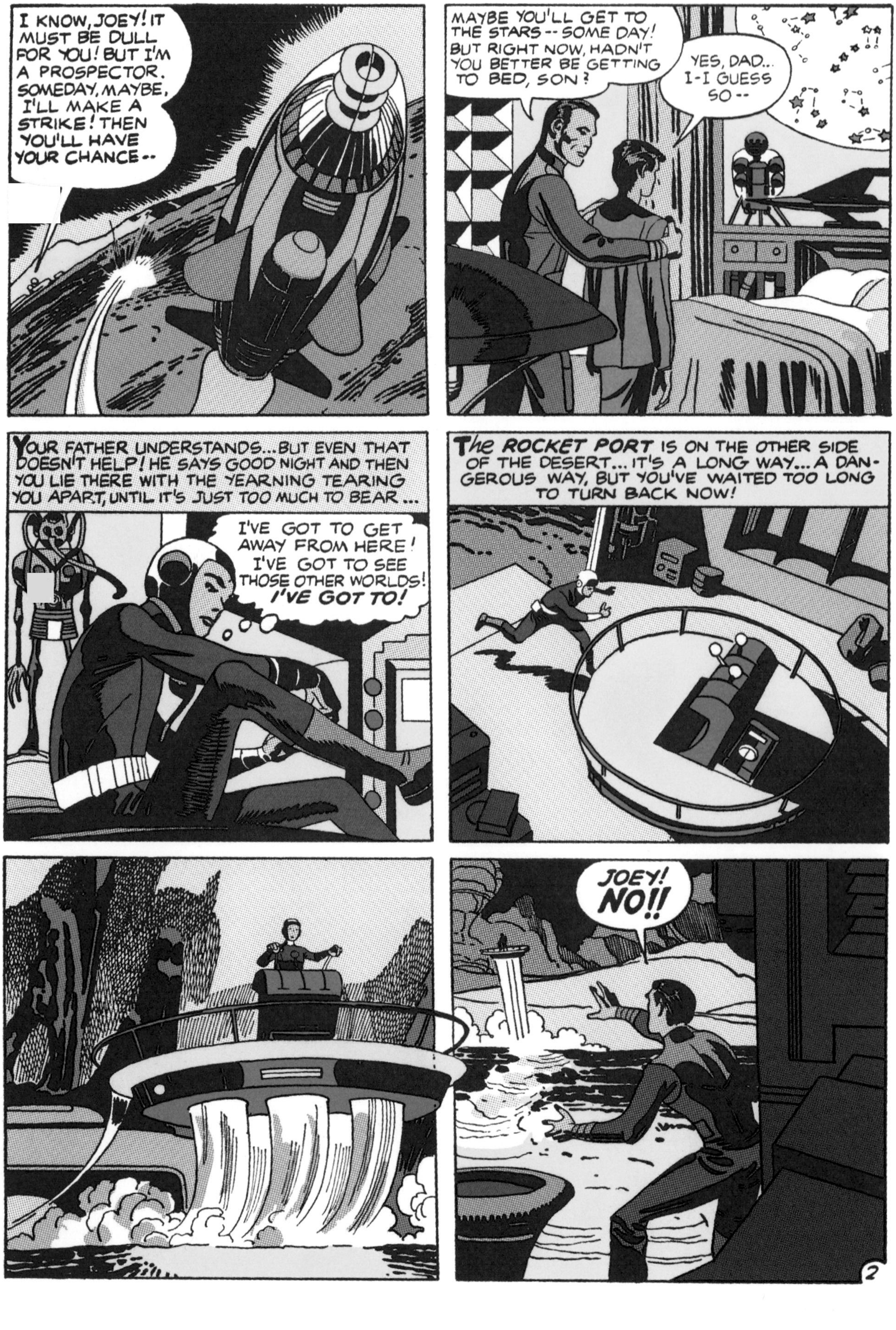
I KNOW, JOEY! IT MUST BE DULL FOR YOU! BUT I'M A PROSPECTOR. SOMEDAY, MAYBE, I'LL MAKE A STRIKE! THEN YOU'LL HAVE YOUR CHANCE--
MAYBE YOU'LL GET TO THE STARS -- SOME DAY! BUT RIGHT NOW, HADN'T YOU BETTER BE GETTING TO BED, SON?
YES, DAD... I-I GUESS SO--
YOUR FATHER UNDERSTANDS... BUT EVEN THAT DOESN'T HELP! HE SAYS GOOD NIGHT AND THEN YOU LIE THERE WITH THE YEARNING TEARING YOU APART, UNTIL IT'S JUST TOO MUCH TO BEAR...
I'VE GOT TO GET AWAY FROM HERE! I'VE GOT TO SEE THOSE OTHER WORLDS! I'VE GOT TO!
The ROCKET PORT IS ON THE OTHER SIDE OF THE DESERT... IT'S A LONG WAY... A DANGEROUS WAY, BUT YOU'VE WAITED TOO LONG TO TURN BACK NOW!
JOEY! NO!!
2

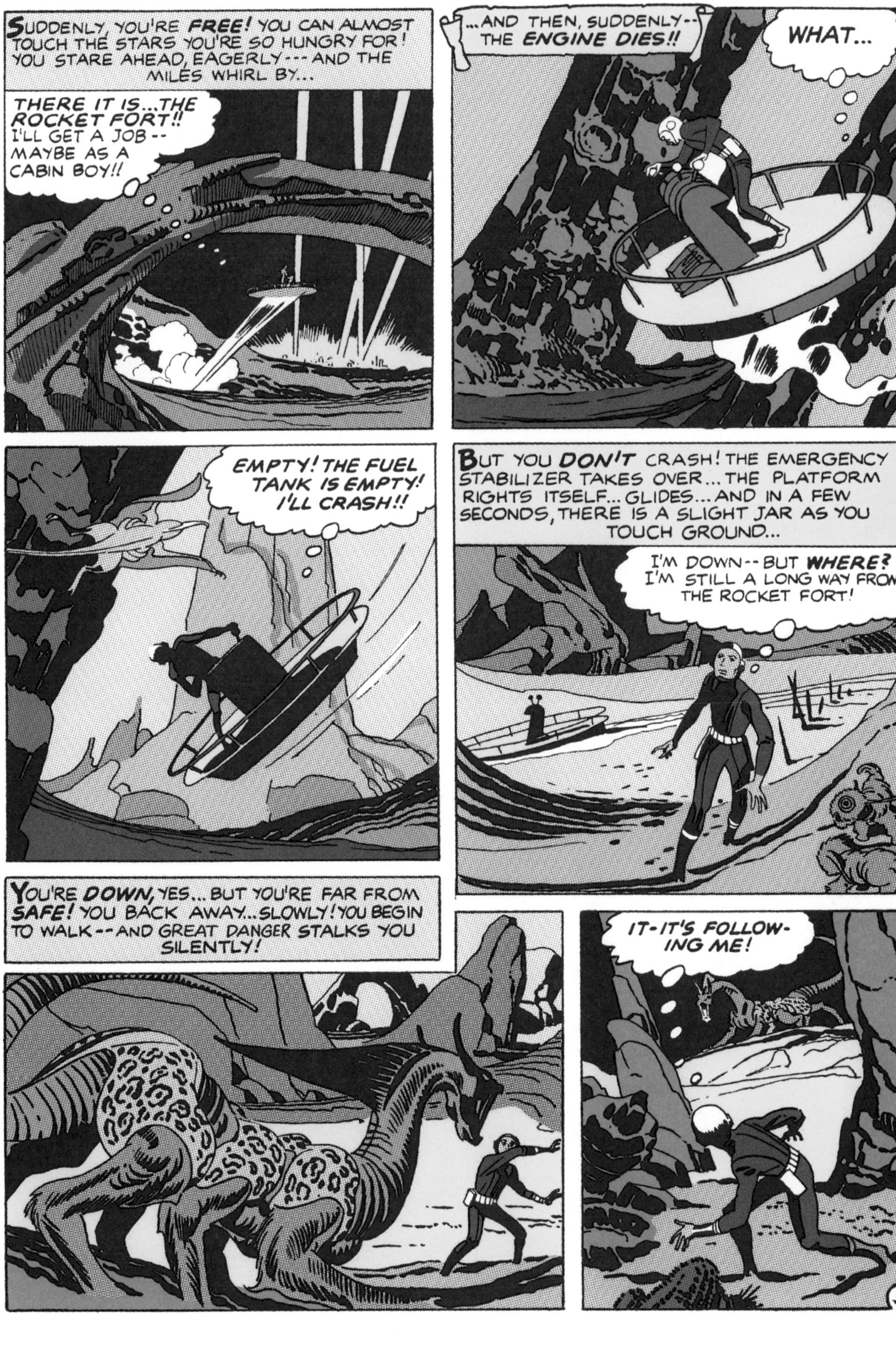
SUDDENLY, YOU'RE FREE! YOU CAN ALMOST TOUCH THE STARS YOU'RE SO HUNGRY FOR! YOU STARE AHEAD, EAGERLY--- AND THE MILES WHIRL BY...
THERE IT IS...THE ROCKET FORT!! I'LL GET A JOB -- MAYBE AS A CABIN BOY!!
...AND THEN, SUDDENLY-- THE ENGINE DIES!!
WHAT...
EMPTY! THE FUEL TANK IS EMPTY! I'LL CRASH!!
BUT YOU DON'T CRASH! THE EMERGENCY STABILIZER TAKES OVER... THE PLATFORM RIGHTS ITSELF... GLIDES... AND IN A FEW SECONDS, THERE IS A SLIGHT JAR AS YOU TOUCH GROUND...
I'M DOWN-- BUT WHERE? I'M STILL A LONG WAY FROM THE ROCKET FORT!
YOU'RE DOWN, YES... BUT YOU'RE FAR FROM SAFE! YOU BACK AWAY... SLOWLY! YOU BEGIN TO WALK--AND GREAT DANGER STALKS YOU SILENTLY!
IT-IT'S FOLLOWING ME!
3

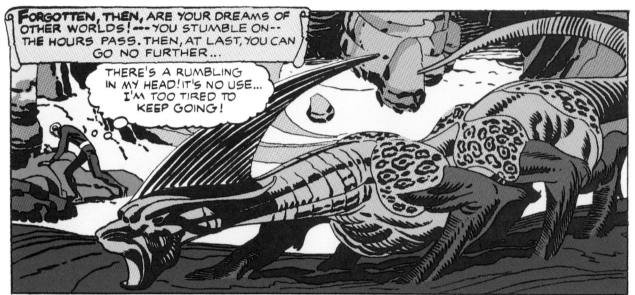

FORGOTTEN, THEN, ARE YOUR DREAMS OF OTHER WORLDS! --- YOU STUMBLE ON-- THE HOURS PASS. THEN, AT LAST, YOU CAN GO NO FURTHER...

THERE'S A RUMBLING IN MY HEAD! IT'S NO USE... I'M TOO TIRED TO KEEP GOING!

THE EYES OF THE CAT-THING BLAZE AT YOU WITH MERCILESS CRUELTY! YOU REALIZE THAT IT IS A CREATURE OF THE DESERT... BELONGS HERE... AND IT IS *YOU* WHO ARE THE INTRUDER...

...AND, LIKE THE DESERT, IT IS ABOUT TO CLOSE IN ON YOU...

THEN IT STRIKES!

BUT FORTUNATELY FOR YOU, IT HAS WAITED TOO LONG!

4

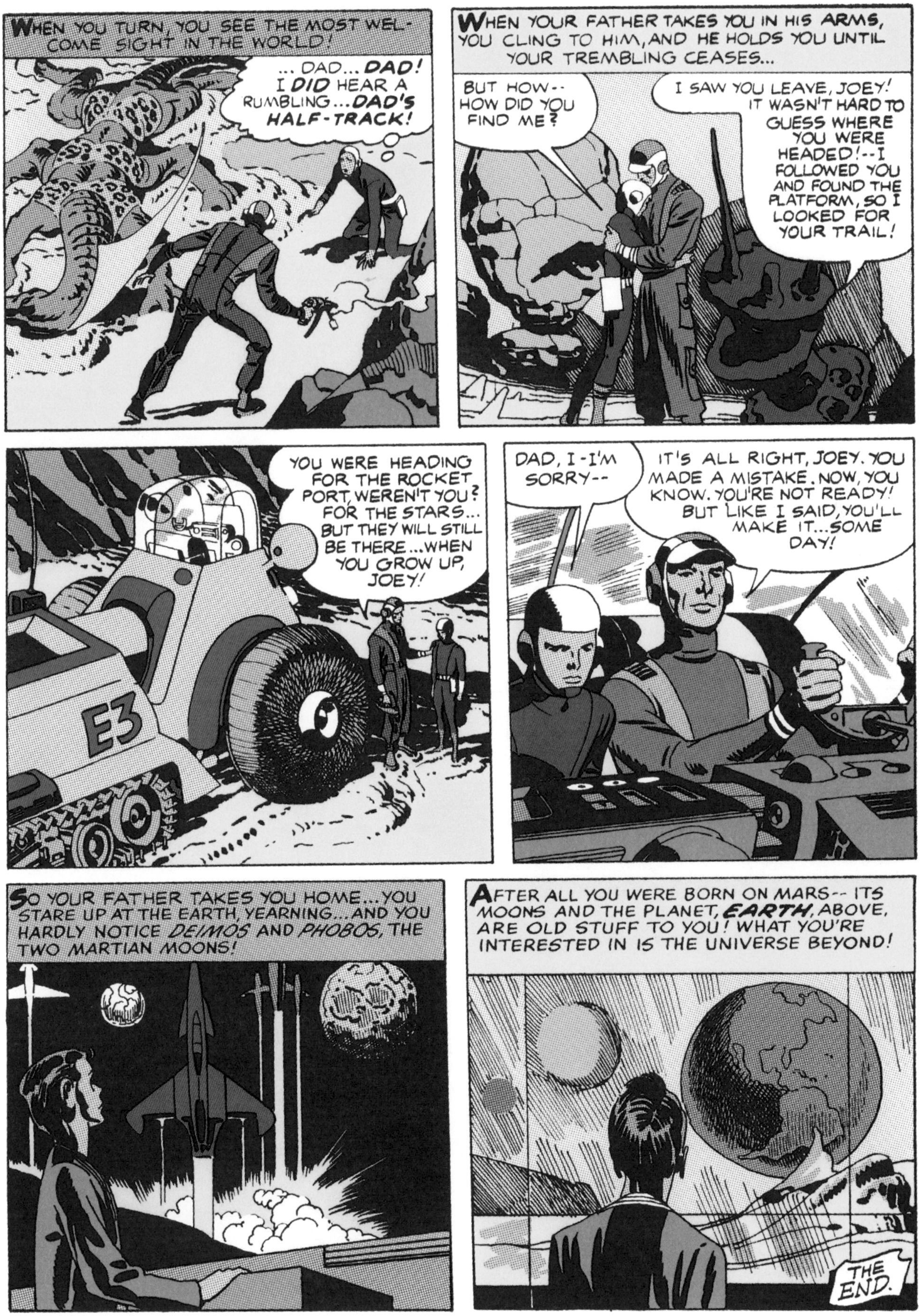
WHEN YOU TURN, YOU SEE THE MOST WELCOME SIGHT IN THE WORLD!
... DAD... DAD! I DID HEAR A RUMBLING... DAD'S HALF-TRACK!
WHEN YOUR FATHER TAKES YOU IN HIS ARMS, YOU CLING TO HIM, AND HE HOLDS YOU UNTIL YOUR TREMBLING CEASES...
BUT HOW-- HOW DID YOU FIND ME?
I SAW YOU LEAVE, JOEY! IT WASN'T HARD TO GUESS WHERE YOU WERE HEADED!--I FOLLOWED YOU AND FOUND THE PLATFORM, SO I LOOKED FOR YOUR TRAIL!
YOU WERE HEADING FOR THE ROCKET PORT, WEREN'T YOU? FOR THE STARS... BUT THEY WILL STILL BE THERE... WHEN YOU GROW UP, JOEY!
E3
DAD, I-I'M SORRY--
IT'S ALL RIGHT, JOEY. YOU MADE A MISTAKE. NOW, YOU KNOW. YOU'RE NOT READY! BUT LIKE I SAID, YOU'LL MAKE IT... SOME DAY!
SO YOUR FATHER TAKES YOU HOME... YOU STARE UP AT THE EARTH, YEARNING... AND YOU HARDLY NOTICE DEIMOS AND PHOBOS, THE TWO MARTIAN MOONS!
AFTER ALL YOU WERE BORN ON MARS-- ITS MOONS AND THE PLANET, EARTH, ABOVE, ARE OLD STUFF TO YOU! WHAT YOU'RE INTERESTED IN IS THE UNIVERSE BEYOND!
THE END.

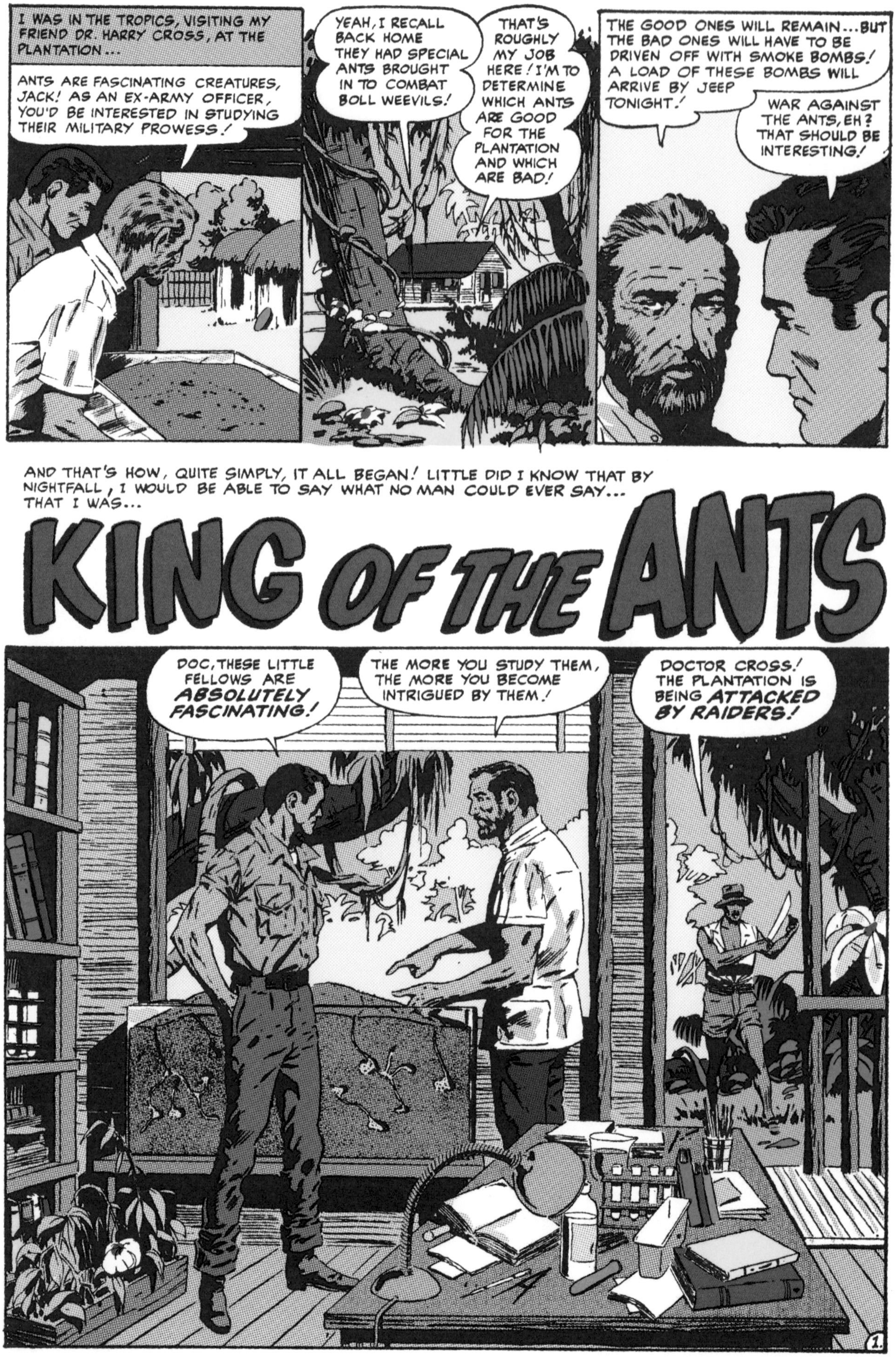
I WAS IN THE TROPICS, VISITING MY FRIEND DR. HARRY CROSS, AT THE PLANTATION...
ANTS ARE FASCINATING CREATURES, JACK! AS AN EX-ARMY OFFICER, YOU'D BE INTERESTED IN STUDYING THEIR MILITARY PROWESS!
YEAH, I RECALL BACK HOME THEY HAD SPECIAL ANTS BROUGHT IN TO COMBAT BOLL WEEVILS!
THAT'S ROUGHLY MY JOB HERE! I'M TO DETERMINE WHICH ANTS ARE GOOD FOR THE PLANTATION AND WHICH ARE BAD!
THE GOOD ONES WILL REMAIN... BUT THE BAD ONES WILL HAVE TO BE DRIVEN OFF WITH SMOKE BOMBS! A LOAD OF THESE BOMBS WILL ARRIVE BY JEEP TONIGHT!
WAR AGAINST THE ANTS, EH? THAT SHOULD BE INTERESTING!
AND THAT'S HOW, QUITE SIMPLY, IT ALL BEGAN! LITTLE DID I KNOW THAT BY NIGHTFALL, I WOULD BE ABLE TO SAY WHAT NO MAN COULD EVER SAY... THAT I WAS...
KING OF THE ANTS
DOC, THESE LITTLE FELLOWS ARE ABSOLUTELY FASCINATING!
THE MORE YOU STUDY THEM, THE MORE YOU BECOME INTRIGUED BY THEM!
DOCTOR CROSS! THE PLANTATION IS BEING ATTACKED BY RAIDERS!
1.

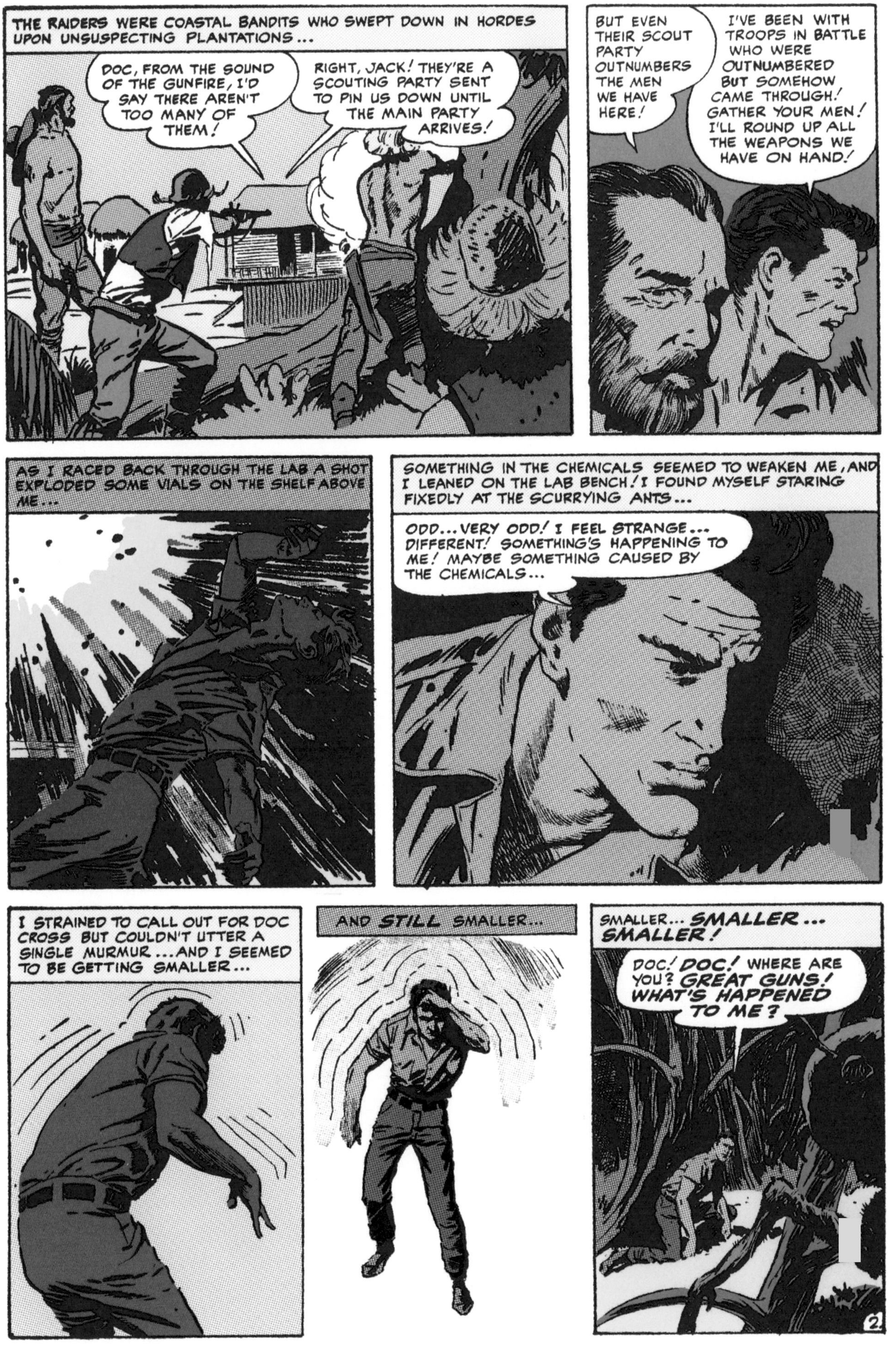

THE RAIDERS WERE COASTAL BANDITS WHO SWEPT DOWN IN HORDES UPON UNSUSPECTING PLANTATIONS...
DOC, FROM THE SOUND OF THE GUNFIRE, I'D SAY THERE AREN'T TOO MANY OF THEM!
RIGHT, JACK! THEY'RE A SCOUTING PARTY SENT TO PIN US DOWN UNTIL THE MAIN PARTY ARRIVES!
BUT EVEN THEIR SCOUT PARTY OUTNUMBERS THE MEN WE HAVE HERE!
I'VE BEEN WITH TROOPS IN BATTLE WHO WERE OUTNUMBERED BUT SOMEHOW CAME THROUGH! GATHER YOUR MEN! I'LL ROUND UP ALL THE WEAPONS WE HAVE ON HAND!
AS I RACED BACK THROUGH THE LAB A SHOT EXPLODED SOME VIALS ON THE SHELF ABOVE ME...
SOMETHING IN THE CHEMICALS SEEMED TO WEAKEN ME, AND I LEANED ON THE LAB BENCH! I FOUND MYSELF STARING FIXEDLY AT THE SCURRYING ANTS...
ODD... VERY ODD! I FEEL STRANGE... DIFFERENT! SOMETHING'S HAPPENING TO ME! MAYBE SOMETHING CAUSED BY THE CHEMICALS...
I STRAINED TO CALL OUT FOR DOC CROSS BUT COULDN'T UTTER A SINGLE MURMUR ...AND I SEEMED TO BE GETTING SMALLER...
AND STILL SMALLER...
SMALLER... SMALLER... SMALLER!
DOC! DOC! WHERE ARE YOU? GREAT GUNS! WHAT'S HAPPENED TO ME?
2

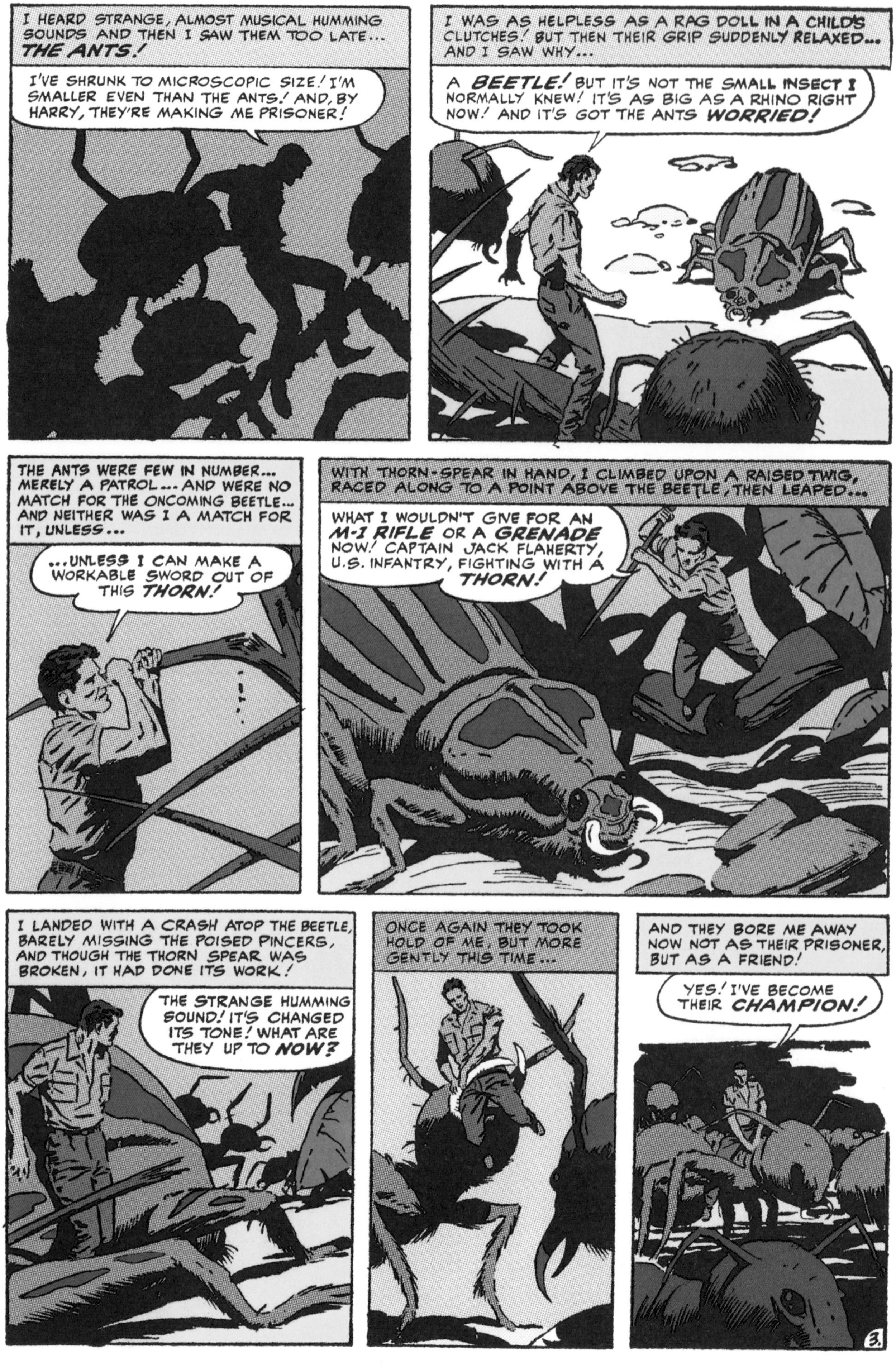

I HEARD STRANGE, ALMOST MUSICAL HUMMING SOUNDS AND THEN I SAW THEM TOO LATE... THE ANTS!
I'VE SHRUNK TO MICROSCOPIC SIZE! I'M SMALLER EVEN THAN THE ANTS! AND, BY HARRY, THEY'RE MAKING ME PRISONER!
I WAS AS HELPLESS AS A RAG DOLL IN A CHILD'S CLUTCHES! BUT THEN THEIR GRIP SUDDENLY RELAXED... AND I SAW WHY...
A BEETLE! BUT IT'S NOT THE SMALL INSECT I NORMALLY KNEW! IT'S AS BIG AS A RHINO RIGHT NOW! AND IT'S GOT THE ANTS WORRIED!
THE ANTS WERE FEW IN NUMBER... MERELY A PATROL... AND WERE NO MATCH FOR THE ONCOMING BEETLE... AND NEITHER WAS I A MATCH FOR IT, UNLESS...
...UNLESS I CAN MAKE A WORKABLE SWORD OUT OF THIS THORN!
WITH THORN-SPEAR IN HAND, I CLIMBED UPON A RAISED TWIG, RACED ALONG TO A POINT ABOVE THE BEETLE, THEN LEAPED...
WHAT I WOULDN'T GIVE FOR AN M-1 RIFLE OR A GRENADE NOW! CAPTAIN JACK FLAHERTY, U.S. INFANTRY, FIGHTING WITH A THORN!
I LANDED WITH A CRASH ATOP THE BEETLE, BARELY MISSING THE POISED PINCERS, AND THOUGH THE THORN SPEAR WAS BROKEN, IT HAD DONE ITS WORK!
THE STRANGE HUMMING SOUND! IT'S CHANGED ITS TONE! WHAT ARE THEY UP TO NOW?
ONCE AGAIN THEY TOOK HOLD OF ME, BUT MORE GENTLY THIS TIME...
AND THEY BORE ME AWAY NOW NOT AS THEIR PRISONER, BUT AS A FRIEND!
YES! I'VE BECOME THEIR CHAMPION!
3.

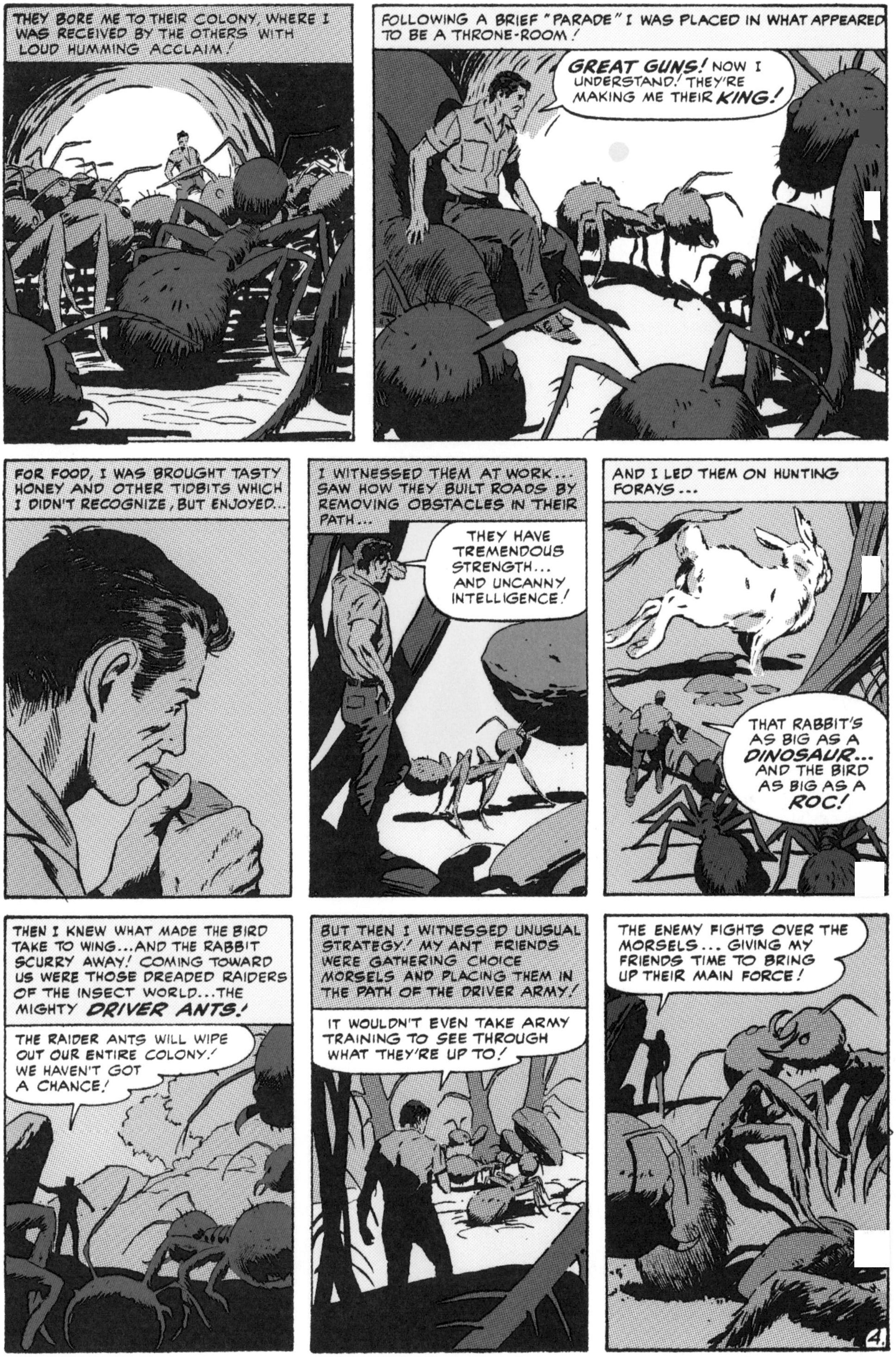
THEY BORE ME TO THEIR COLONY, WHERE I WAS RECEIVED BY THE OTHERS WITH LOUD HUMMING ACCLAIM!
FOLLOWING A BRIEF "PARADE" I WAS PLACED IN WHAT APPEARED TO BE A THRONE-ROOM!
GREAT GUNS! NOW I UNDERSTAND! THEY'RE MAKING ME THEIR KING!
FOR FOOD, I WAS BROUGHT TASTY HONEY AND OTHER TIDBITS WHICH I DIDN'T RECOGNIZE, BUT ENJOYED...
I WITNESSED THEM AT WORK... SAW HOW THEY BUILT ROADS BY REMOVING OBSTACLES IN THEIR PATH...
THEY HAVE TREMENDOUS STRENGTH... AND UNCANNY INTELLIGENCE!
AND I LED THEM ON HUNTING FORAYS...
THAT RABBIT'S AS BIG AS A DINOSAUR... AND THE BIRD AS BIG AS A ROC!
THEN I KNEW WHAT MADE THE BIRD TAKE TO WING... AND THE RABBIT SCURRY AWAY! COMING TOWARD US WERE THOSE DREADED RAIDERS OF THE INSECT WORLD... THE MIGHTY DRIVER ANTS!
THE RAIDER ANTS WILL WIPE OUT OUR ENTIRE COLONY! WE HAVEN'T GOT A CHANCE!
BUT THEN I WITNESSED UNUSUAL STRATEGY! MY ANT FRIENDS WERE GATHERING CHOICE MORSELS AND PLACING THEM IN THE PATH OF THE DRIVER ARMY!
IT WOULDN'T EVEN TAKE ARMY TRAINING TO SEE THROUGH WHAT THEY'RE UP TO!
THE ENEMY FIGHTS OVER THE MORSELS... GIVING MY FRIENDS TIME TO BRING UP THEIR MAIN FORCE!
4.

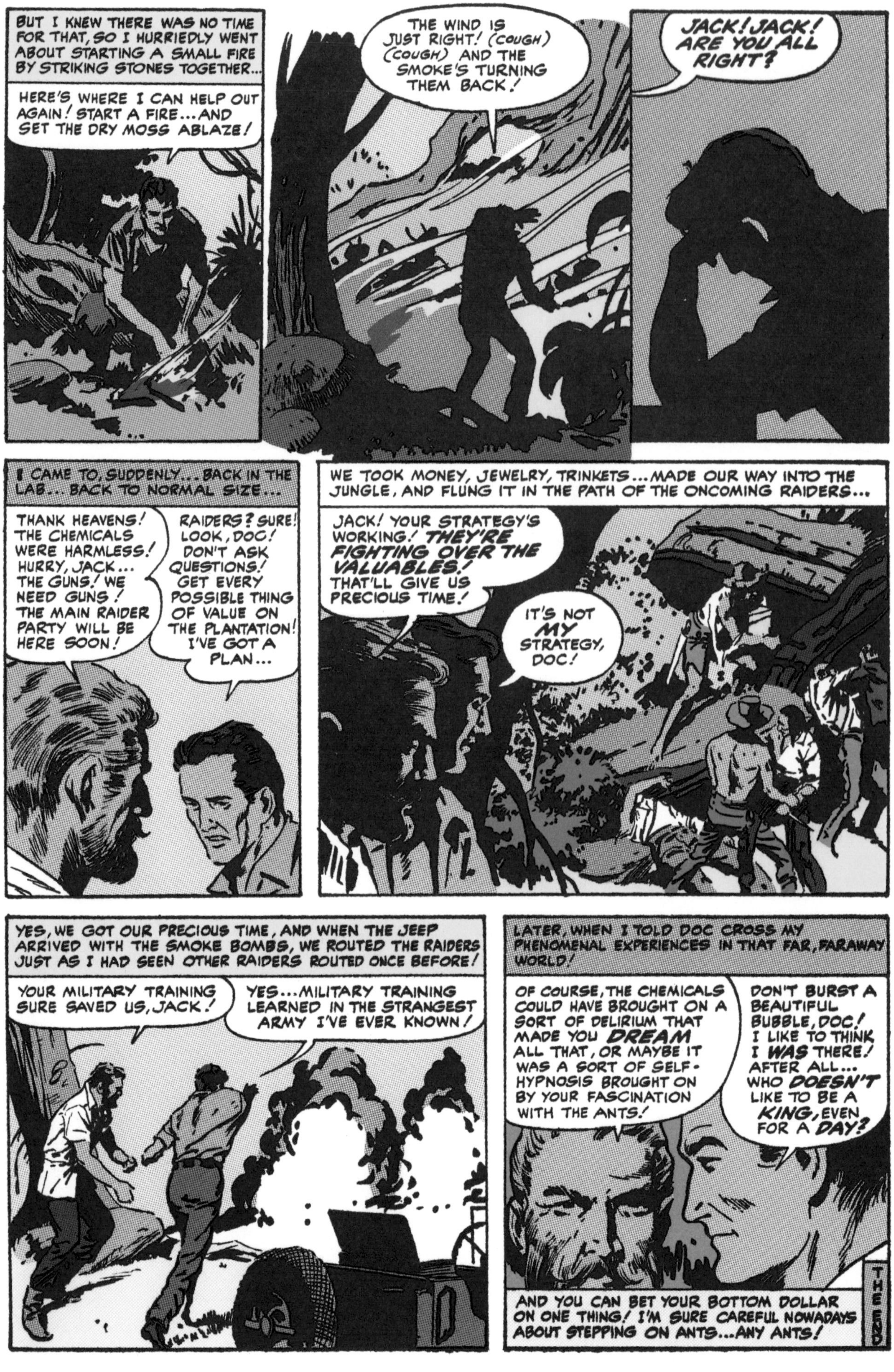

BUT I KNEW THERE WAS NO TIME FOR THAT, SO I HURRIEDLY WENT ABOUT STARTING A SMALL FIRE BY STRIKING STONES TOGETHER...
HERE'S WHERE I CAN HELP OUT AGAIN! START A FIRE... AND SET THE DRY MOSS ABLAZE!
THE WIND IS JUST RIGHT! (COUGH) (COUGH) AND THE SMOKE'S TURNING THEM BACK!
JACK! JACK! ARE YOU ALL RIGHT?
I CAME TO, SUDDENLY... BACK IN THE LAB... BACK TO NORMAL SIZE...
THANK HEAVENS! THE CHEMICALS WERE HARMLESS! HURRY, JACK... THE GUNS! WE NEED GUNS! THE MAIN RAIDER PARTY WILL BE HERE SOON!
RAIDERS? SURE! LOOK, DOC! DON'T ASK QUESTIONS! GET EVERY POSSIBLE THING OF VALUE ON THE PLANTATION! I'VE GOT A PLAN...
WE TOOK MONEY, JEWELRY, TRINKETS... MADE OUR WAY INTO THE JUNGLE, AND FLUNG IT IN THE PATH OF THE ONCOMING RAIDERS...
JACK! YOUR STRATEGY'S WORKING! THEY'RE FIGHTING OVER THE VALUABLES! THAT'LL GIVE US PRECIOUS TIME!
IT'S NOT MY STRATEGY, DOC!
YES, WE GOT OUR PRECIOUS TIME, AND WHEN THE JEEP ARRIVED WITH THE SMOKE BOMBS, WE ROUTED THE RAIDERS JUST AS I HAD SEEN OTHER RAIDERS ROUTED ONCE BEFORE!
YOUR MILITARY TRAINING SURE SAVED US, JACK!
YES... MILITARY TRAINING LEARNED IN THE STRANGEST ARMY I'VE EVER KNOWN!
LATER, WHEN I TOLD DOC CROSS MY PHENOMENAL EXPERIENCES IN THAT FAR, FARAWAY WORLD!
OF COURSE, THE CHEMICALS COULD HAVE BROUGHT ON A SORT OF DELIRIUM THAT MADE YOU DREAM ALL THAT, OR MAYBE IT WAS A SORT OF SELF-HYPNOSIS BROUGHT ON BY YOUR FASCINATION WITH THE ANTS!
DON'T BURST A BEAUTIFUL BUBBLE, DOC! I LIKE TO THINK I WAS THERE! AFTER ALL... WHO DOESN'T LIKE TO BE A KING, EVEN FOR A DAY?
AND YOU CAN BET YOUR BOTTOM DOLLAR ON ONE THING! I'M SURE CAREFUL NOWADAYS ABOUT STEPPING ON ANTS... ANY ANTS!
THE END

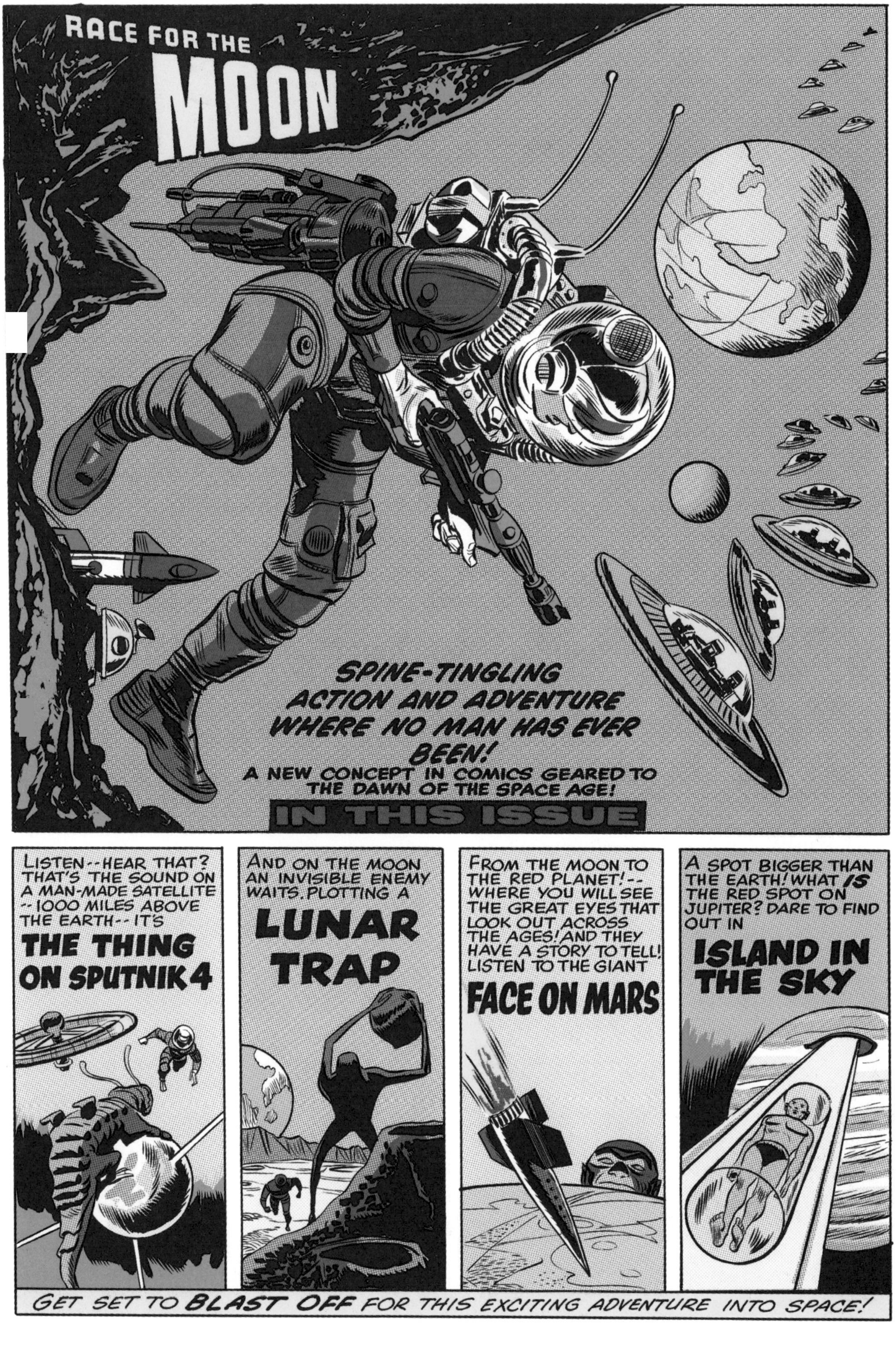
RACE FOR THE MOON
SPINE-TINGLING ACTION AND ADVENTURE WHERE NO MAN HAS EVER BEEN!
A NEW CONCEPT IN COMICS GEARED TO THE DAWN OF THE SPACE AGE!
IN THIS ISSUE
LISTEN--HEAR THAT? THAT'S THE SOUND ON A MAN-MADE SATELLITE --1000 MILES ABOVE THE EARTH-- IT'S
THE THING ON SPUTNIK 4
AND ON THE MOON AN INVISIBLE ENEMY WAITS, PLOTTING A
LUNAR TRAP
FROM THE MOON TO THE RED PLANET!-- WHERE YOU WILL SEE THE GREAT EYES THAT LOOK OUT ACROSS THE AGES! AND THEY HAVE A STORY TO TELL! LISTEN TO THE GIANT
FACE ON MARS
A SPOT BIGGER THAN THE EARTH! WHAT IS THE RED SPOT ON JUPITER? DARE TO FIND OUT IN
ISLAND IN THE SKY
GET SET TO BLAST OFF FOR THIS EXCITING ADVENTURE INTO SPACE!

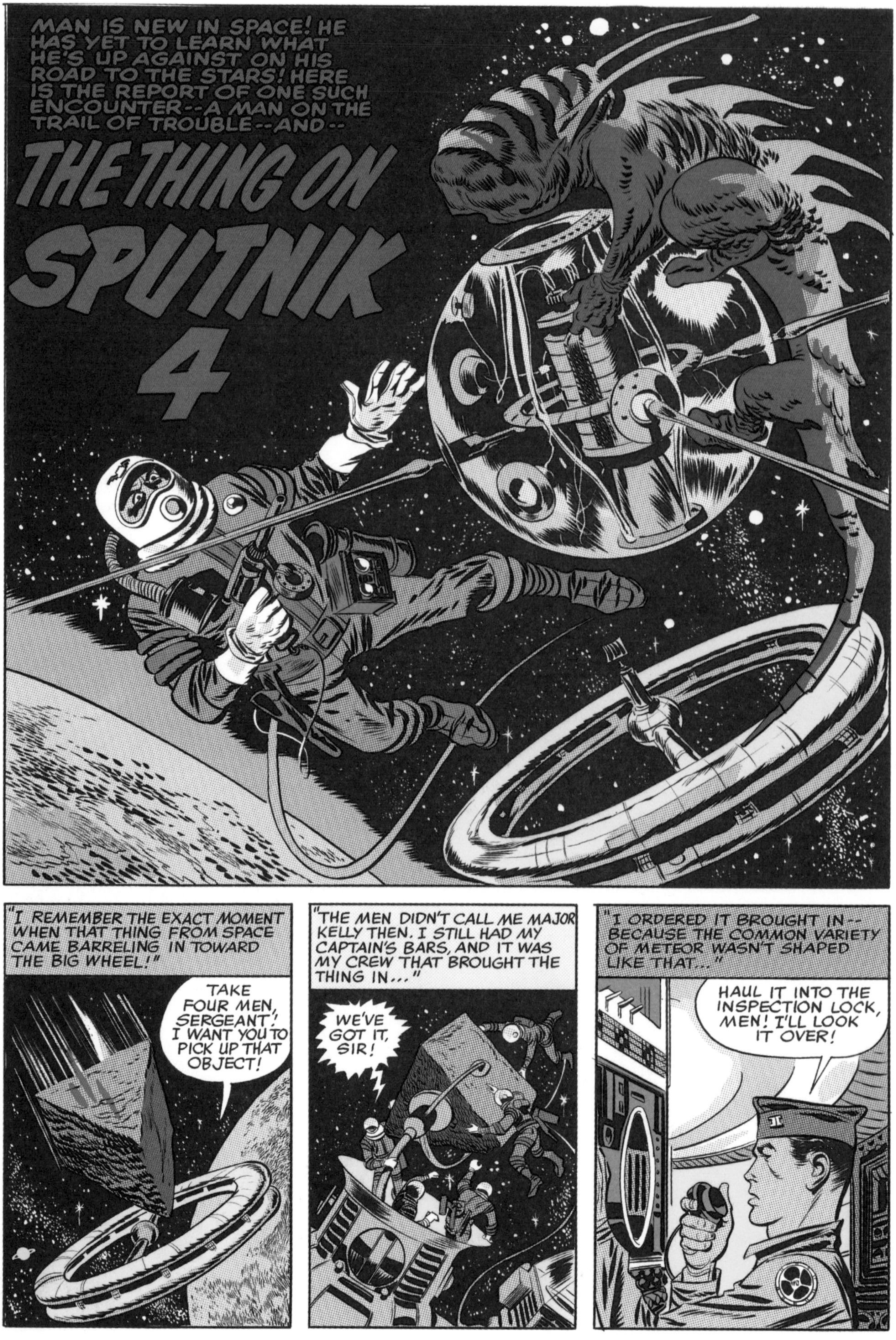

MAN IS NEW IN SPACE! HE HAS YET TO LEARN WHAT HE'S UP AGAINST ON HIS ROAD TO THE STARS! HERE IS THE REPORT OF ONE SUCH ENCOUNTER--A MAN ON THE TRAIL OF TROUBLE--AND--
THE THING ON SPUTNIK 4
"I REMEMBER THE EXACT MOMENT WHEN THAT THING FROM SPACE CAME BARRELING IN TOWARD THE BIG WHEEL!"
TAKE FOUR MEN, SERGEANT! I WANT YOU TO PICK UP THAT OBJECT!
"THE MEN DIDN'T CALL ME MAJOR KELLY THEN. I STILL HAD MY CAPTAIN'S BARS, AND IT WAS MY CREW THAT BROUGHT THE THING IN..."
WE'VE GOT IT, SIR!
"I ORDERED IT BROUGHT IN--BECAUSE THE COMMON VARIETY OF METEOR WASN'T SHAPED LIKE THAT..."
HAUL IT INTO THE INSPECTION LOCK, MEN! I'LL LOOK IT OVER!

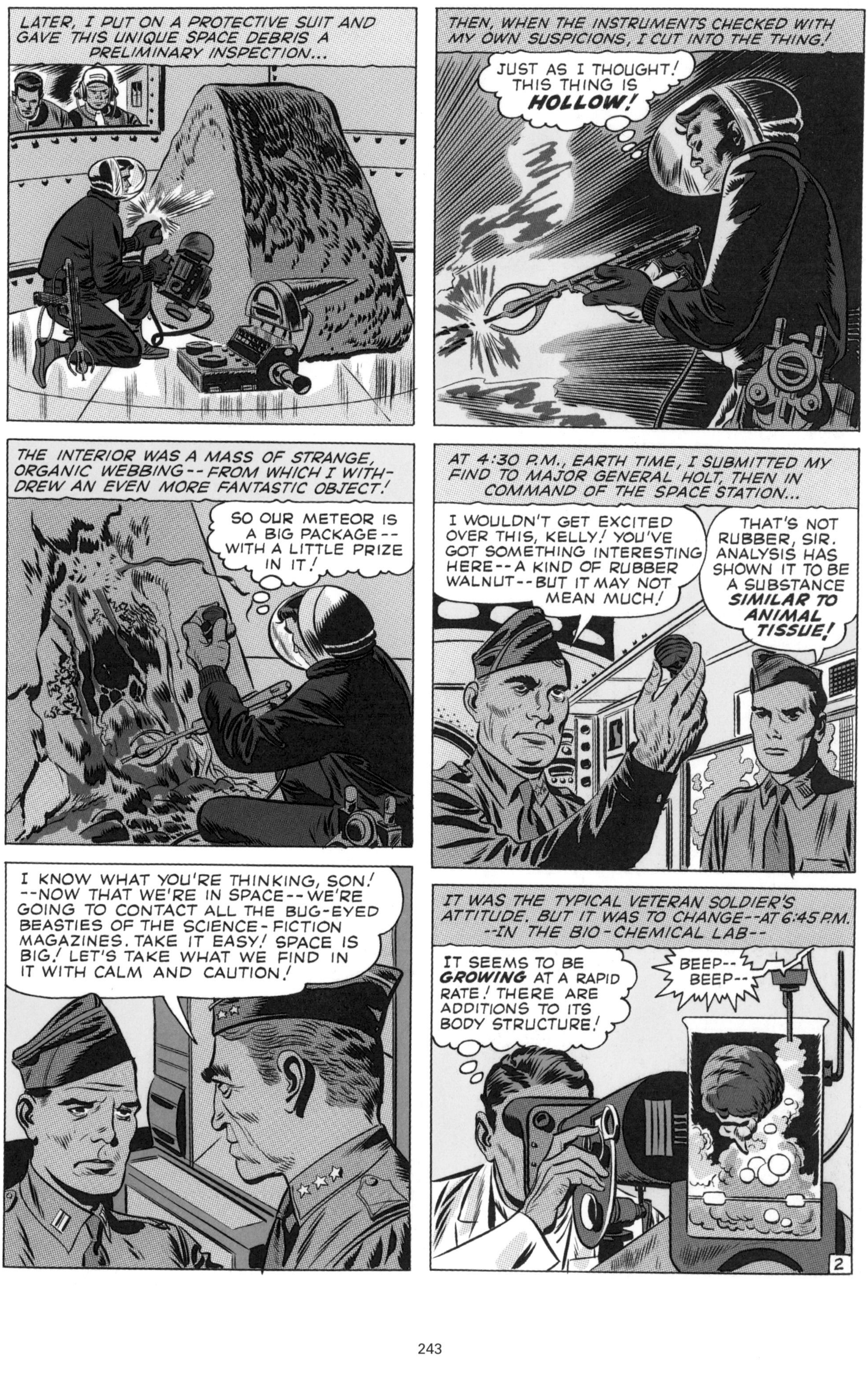

LATER, I PUT ON A PROTECTIVE SUIT AND GAVE THIS UNIQUE SPACE DEBRIS A PRELIMINARY INSPECTION...
THEN, WHEN THE INSTRUMENTS CHECKED WITH MY OWN SUSPICIONS, I CUT INTO THE THING!
JUST AS I THOUGHT! THIS THING IS HOLLOW!
THE INTERIOR WAS A MASS OF STRANGE, ORGANIC WEBBING--FROM WHICH I WITHDREW AN EVEN MORE FANTASTIC OBJECT!
SO OUR METEOR IS A BIG PACKAGE--WITH A LITTLE PRIZE IN IT!
AT 4:30 P.M., EARTH TIME, I SUBMITTED MY FIND TO MAJOR GENERAL HOLT, THEN IN COMMAND OF THE SPACE STATION...
I WOULDN'T GET EXCITED OVER THIS, KELLY! YOU'VE GOT SOMETHING INTERESTING HERE--A KIND OF RUBBER WALNUT--BUT IT MAY NOT MEAN MUCH!
THAT'S NOT RUBBER, SIR. ANALYSIS HAS SHOWN IT TO BE A SUBSTANCE SIMILAR TO ANIMAL TISSUE!
I KNOW WHAT YOU'RE THINKING, SON! --NOW THAT WE'RE IN SPACE--WE'RE GOING TO CONTACT ALL THE BUG-EYED BEASTIES OF THE SCIENCE-FICTION MAGAZINES. TAKE IT EASY! SPACE IS BIG! LET'S TAKE WHAT WE FIND IN IT WITH CALM AND CAUTION!
IT WAS THE TYPICAL VETERAN SOLDIER'S ATTITUDE, BUT IT WAS TO CHANGE--AT 6:45 P.M. --IN THE BIO-CHEMICAL LAB--
IT SEEMS TO BE GROWING AT A RAPID RATE! THERE ARE ADDITIONS TO ITS BODY STRUCTURE!
BEEP--BEEP--
2

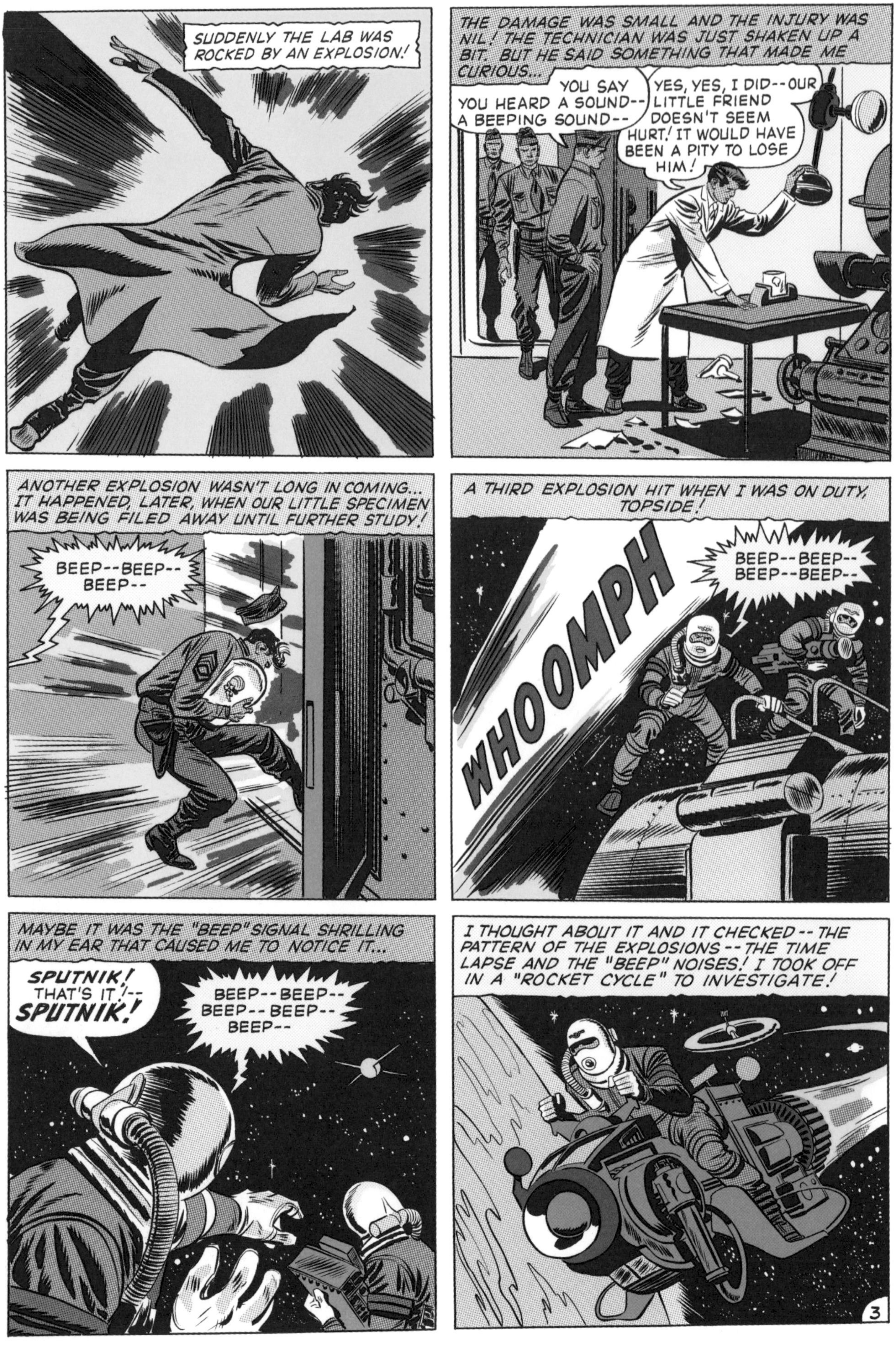
SUDDENLY THE LAB WAS ROCKED BY AN EXPLOSION!
THE DAMAGE WAS SMALL AND THE INJURY WAS NIL! THE TECHNICIAN WAS JUST SHAKEN UP A BIT. BUT HE SAID SOMETHING THAT MADE ME CURIOUS...
YOU SAY YOU HEARD A SOUND-- A BEEPING SOUND--
YES, YES, I DID--OUR LITTLE FRIEND DOESN'T SEEM HURT! IT WOULD HAVE BEEN A PITY TO LOSE HIM!
ANOTHER EXPLOSION WASN'T LONG IN COMING... IT HAPPENED, LATER, WHEN OUR LITTLE SPECIMEN WAS BEING FILED AWAY UNTIL FURTHER STUDY!
BEEP--BEEP-- BEEP--
A THIRD EXPLOSION HIT WHEN I WAS ON DUTY, TOPSIDE!
WHOOMPH
BEEP--BEEP-- BEEP--BEEP--
MAYBE IT WAS THE "BEEP" SIGNAL SHRILLING IN MY EAR THAT CAUSED ME TO NOTICE IT...
SPUTNIK! THAT'S IT!-- SPUTNIK!
BEEP--BEEP-- BEEP--BEEP-- BEEP--
I THOUGHT ABOUT IT AND IT CHECKED--THE PATTERN OF THE EXPLOSIONS--THE TIME LAPSE AND THE "BEEP" NOISES! I TOOK OFF IN A "ROCKET CYCLE" TO INVESTIGATE!
3

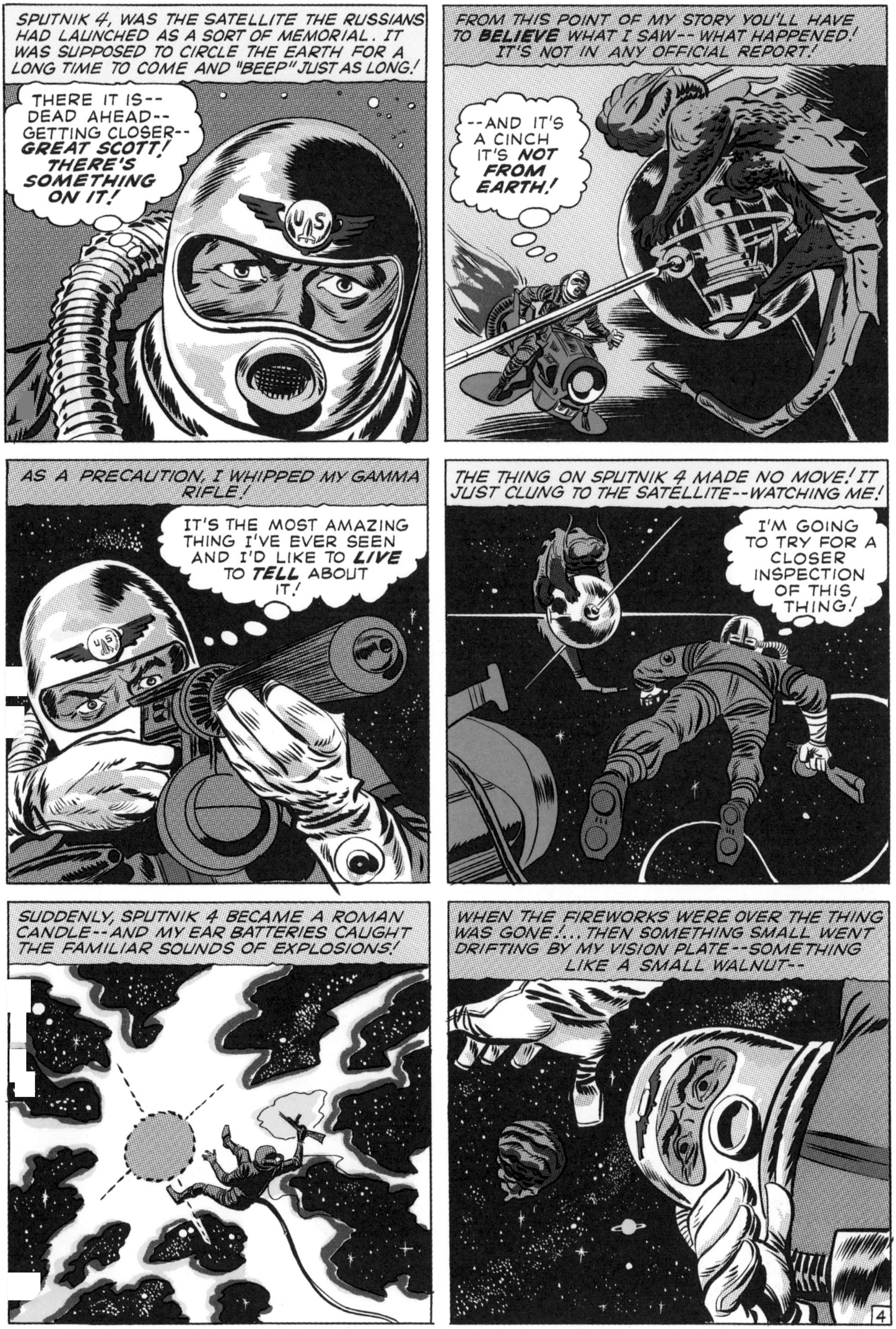

SPUTNIK 4, WAS THE SATELLITE THE RUSSIANS HAD LAUNCHED AS A SORT OF MEMORIAL. IT WAS SUPPOSED TO CIRCLE THE EARTH FOR A LONG TIME TO COME AND "BEEP" JUST AS LONG!
THERE IT IS-- DEAD AHEAD-- GETTING CLOSER-- GREAT SCOTT! THERE'S SOMETHING ON IT!
U.S.
FROM THIS POINT OF MY STORY YOU'LL HAVE TO BELIEVE WHAT I SAW-- WHAT HAPPENED! IT'S NOT IN ANY OFFICIAL REPORT!
--AND IT'S A CINCH IT'S NOT FROM EARTH!
AS A PRECAUTION, I WHIPPED MY GAMMA RIFLE!
IT'S THE MOST AMAZING THING I'VE EVER SEEN AND I'D LIKE TO LIVE TO TELL ABOUT IT!
THE THING ON SPUTNIK 4 MADE NO MOVE! IT JUST CLUNG TO THE SATELLITE--WATCHING ME!
I'M GOING TO TRY FOR A CLOSER INSPECTION OF THIS THING!
SUDDENLY, SPUTNIK 4 BECAME A ROMAN CANDLE--AND MY EAR BATTERIES CAUGHT THE FAMILIAR SOUNDS OF EXPLOSIONS!
WHEN THE FIREWORKS WERE OVER THE THING WAS GONE!...THEN SOMETHING SMALL WENT DRIFTING BY MY VISION PLATE--SOMETHING LIKE A SMALL WALNUT--
4

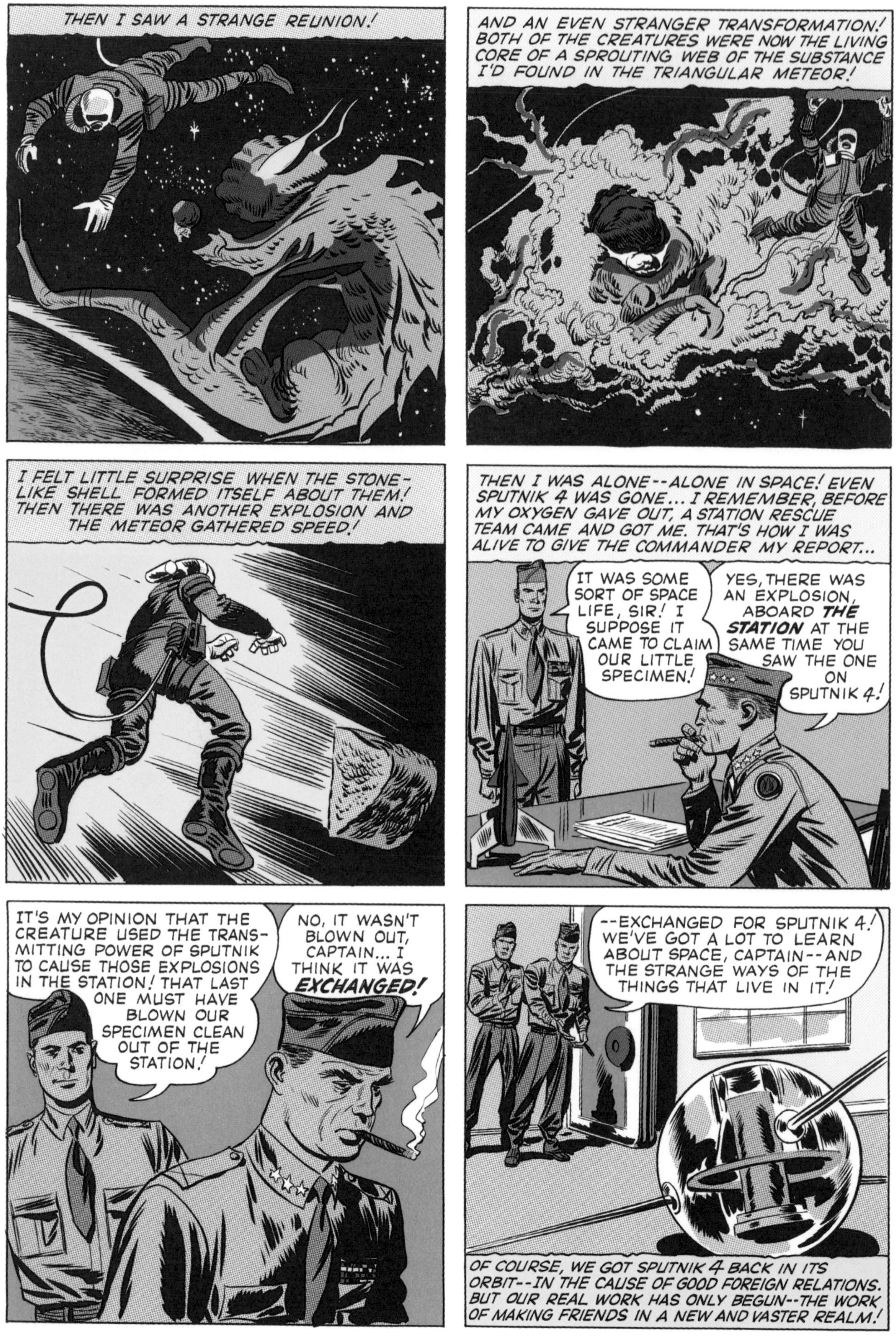
THEN I SAW A STRANGE REUNION!
AND AN EVEN STRANGER TRANSFORMATION! BOTH OF THE CREATURES WERE NOW THE LIVING CORE OF A SPROUTING WEB OF THE SUBSTANCE I'D FOUND IN THE TRIANGULAR METEOR!
I FELT LITTLE SURPRISE WHEN THE STONE-LIKE SHELL FORMED ITSELF ABOUT THEM! THEN THERE WAS ANOTHER EXPLOSION AND THE METEOR GATHERED SPEED!
THEN I WAS ALONE--ALONE IN SPACE! EVEN SPUTNIK 4 WAS GONE... I REMEMBER, BEFORE MY OXYGEN GAVE OUT, A STATION RESCUE TEAM CAME AND GOT ME. THAT'S HOW I WAS ALIVE TO GIVE THE COMMANDER MY REPORT...
IT WAS SOME SORT OF SPACE LIFE, SIR! I SUPPOSE IT CAME TO CLAIM OUR LITTLE SPECIMEN!
YES, THERE WAS AN EXPLOSION, ABOARD THE STATION AT THE SAME TIME YOU SAW THE ONE ON SPUTNIK 4!
IT'S MY OPINION THAT THE CREATURE USED THE TRANSMITTING POWER OF SPUTNIK TO CAUSE THOSE EXPLOSIONS IN THE STATION! THAT LAST ONE MUST HAVE BLOWN OUR SPECIMEN CLEAN OUT OF THE STATION!
NO, IT WASN'T BLOWN OUT, CAPTAIN... I THINK IT WAS EXCHANGED!
--EXCHANGED FOR SPUTNIK 4! WE'VE GOT A LOT TO LEARN ABOUT SPACE, CAPTAIN--AND THE STRANGE WAYS OF THE THINGS THAT LIVE IN IT!
OF COURSE, WE GOT SPUTNIK 4 BACK IN ITS ORBIT--IN THE CAUSE OF GOOD FOREIGN RELATIONS. BUT OUR REAL WORK HAS ONLY BEGUN--THE WORK OF MAKING FRIENDS IN A NEW AND VASTER REALM!

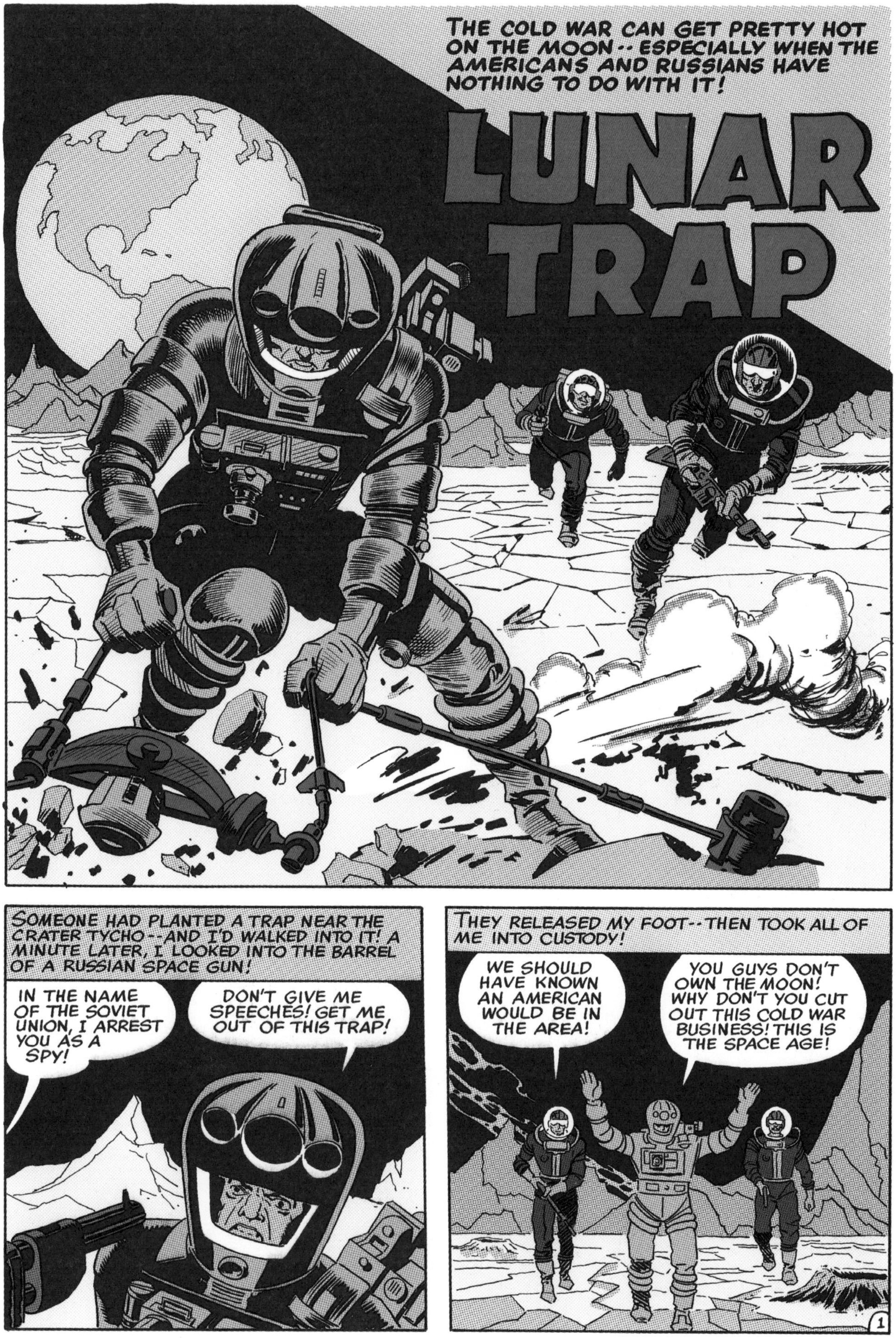
THE COLD WAR CAN GET PRETTY HOT ON THE MOON -- ESPECIALLY WHEN THE AMERICANS AND RUSSIANS HAVE NOTHING TO DO WITH IT!
LUNAR TRAP
SOMEONE HAD PLANTED A TRAP NEAR THE CRATER TYCHO--AND I'D WALKED INTO IT! A MINUTE LATER, I LOOKED INTO THE BARREL OF A RUSSIAN SPACE GUN!
IN THE NAME OF THE SOVIET UNION, I ARREST YOU AS A SPY!
DON'T GIVE ME SPEECHES! GET ME OUT OF THIS TRAP!
THEY RELEASED MY FOOT--THEN TOOK ALL OF ME INTO CUSTODY!
WE SHOULD HAVE KNOWN AN AMERICAN WOULD BE IN THE AREA!
YOU GUYS DON'T OWN THE MOON! WHY DON'T YOU CUT OUT THIS COLD WAR BUSINESS! THIS IS THE SPACE AGE!
1

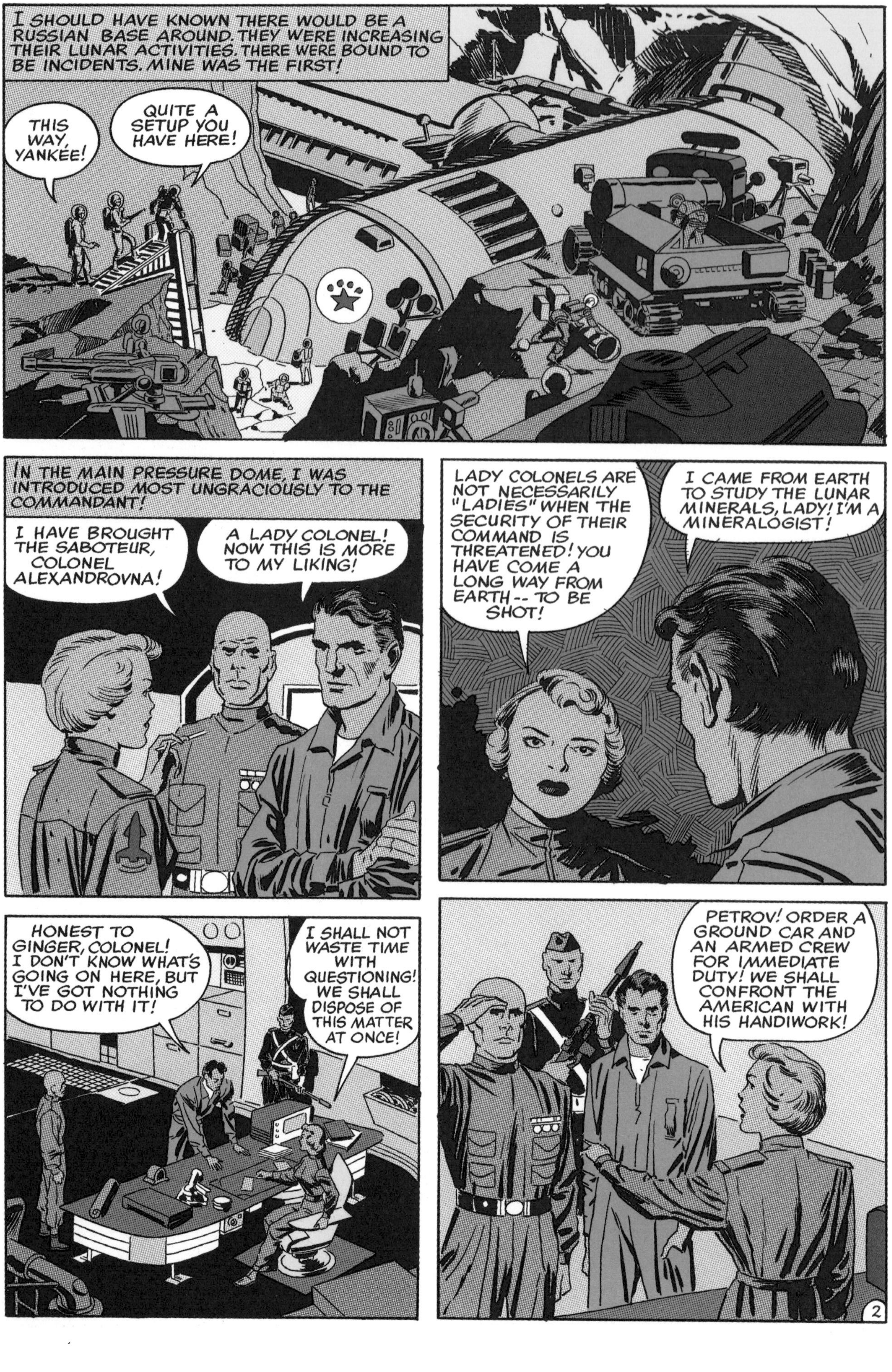

I SHOULD HAVE KNOWN THERE WOULD BE A RUSSIAN BASE AROUND. THEY WERE INCREASING THEIR LUNAR ACTIVITIES. THERE WERE BOUND TO BE INCIDENTS. MINE WAS THE FIRST!
THIS WAY, YANKEE!
QUITE A SETUP YOU HAVE HERE!
IN THE MAIN PRESSURE DOME, I WAS INTRODUCED MOST UNGRACIOUSLY TO THE COMMANDANT!
I HAVE BROUGHT THE SABOTEUR, COLONEL ALEXANDROVNA!
A LADY COLONEL! NOW THIS IS MORE TO MY LIKING!
LADY COLONELS ARE NOT NECESSARILY "LADIES" WHEN THE SECURITY OF THEIR COMMAND IS THREATENED! YOU HAVE COME A LONG WAY FROM EARTH -- TO BE SHOT!
I CAME FROM EARTH TO STUDY THE LUNAR MINERALS, LADY! I'M A MINERALOGIST!
HONEST TO GINGER, COLONEL! I DON'T KNOW WHAT'S GOING ON HERE, BUT I'VE GOT NOTHING TO DO WITH IT!
I SHALL NOT WASTE TIME WITH QUESTIONING! WE SHALL DISPOSE OF THIS MATTER AT ONCE!
PETROV! ORDER A GROUND CAR AND AN ARMED CREW FOR IMMEDIATE DUTY! WE SHALL CONFRONT THE AMERICAN WITH HIS HANDIWORK!
2

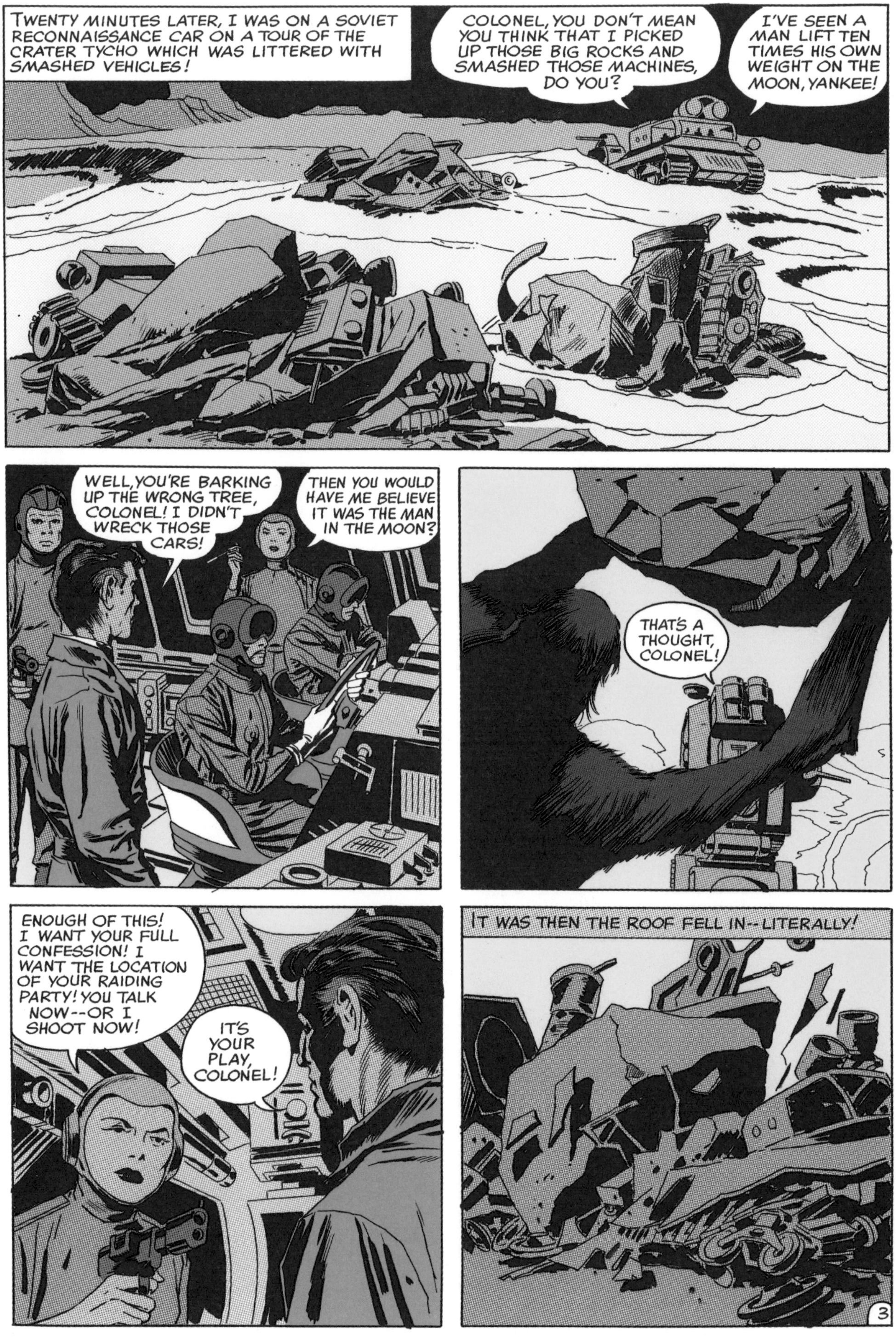
TWENTY MINUTES LATER, I WAS ON A SOVIET RECONNAISSANCE CAR ON A TOUR OF THE CRATER TYCHO WHICH WAS LITTERED WITH SMASHED VEHICLES!
COLONEL, YOU DON'T MEAN YOU THINK THAT I PICKED UP THOSE BIG ROCKS AND SMASHED THOSE MACHINES, DO YOU?
I'VE SEEN A MAN LIFT TEN TIMES HIS OWN WEIGHT ON THE MOON, YANKEE!
WELL, YOU'RE BARKING UP THE WRONG TREE, COLONEL! I DIDN'T WRECK THOSE CARS!
THEN YOU WOULD HAVE ME BELIEVE IT WAS THE MAN IN THE MOON?
THAT'S A THOUGHT, COLONEL!
ENOUGH OF THIS! I WANT YOUR FULL CONFESSION! I WANT THE LOCATION OF YOUR RAIDING PARTY! YOU TALK NOW--OR I SHOOT NOW!
IT'S YOUR PLAY, COLONEL!
IT WAS THEN THE ROOF FELL IN--LITERALLY!
3

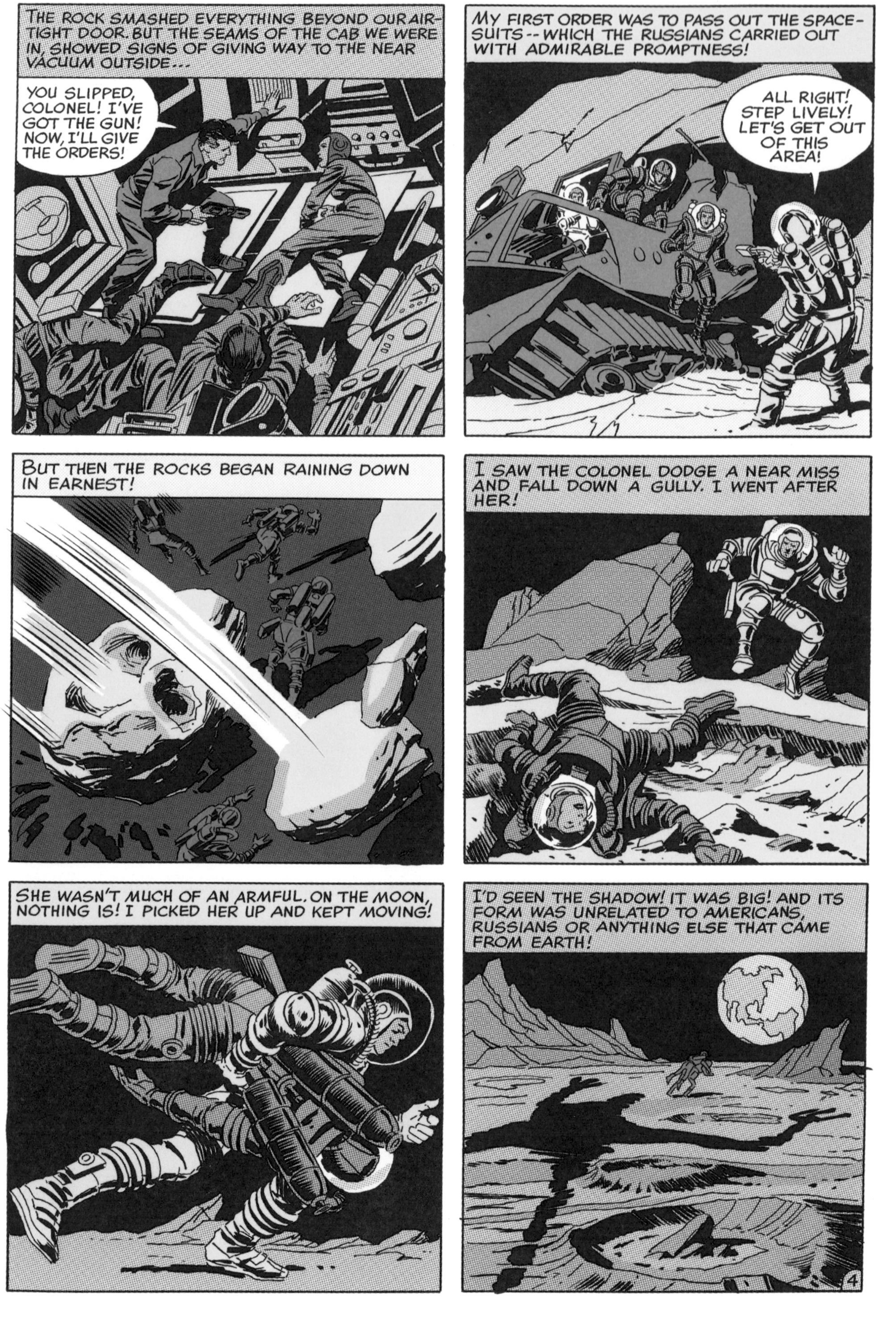
THE ROCK SMASHED EVERYTHING BEYOND OUR AIR-TIGHT DOOR. BUT THE SEAMS OF THE CAB WE WERE IN, SHOWED SIGNS OF GIVING WAY TO THE NEAR VACUUM OUTSIDE...
YOU SLIPPED, COLONEL! I'VE GOT THE GUN! NOW, I'LL GIVE THE ORDERS!
MY FIRST ORDER WAS TO PASS OUT THE SPACE-SUITS -- WHICH THE RUSSIANS CARRIED OUT WITH ADMIRABLE PROMPTNESS!
ALL RIGHT! STEP LIVELY! LET'S GET OUT OF THIS AREA!
BUT THEN THE ROCKS BEGAN RAINING DOWN IN EARNEST!
I SAW THE COLONEL DODGE A NEAR MISS AND FALL DOWN A GULLY. I WENT AFTER HER!
SHE WASN'T MUCH OF AN ARMFUL. ON THE MOON, NOTHING IS! I PICKED HER UP AND KEPT MOVING!
I'D SEEN THE SHADOW! IT WAS BIG! AND ITS FORM WAS UNRELATED TO AMERICANS, RUSSIANS OR ANYTHING ELSE THAT CAME FROM EARTH!
4

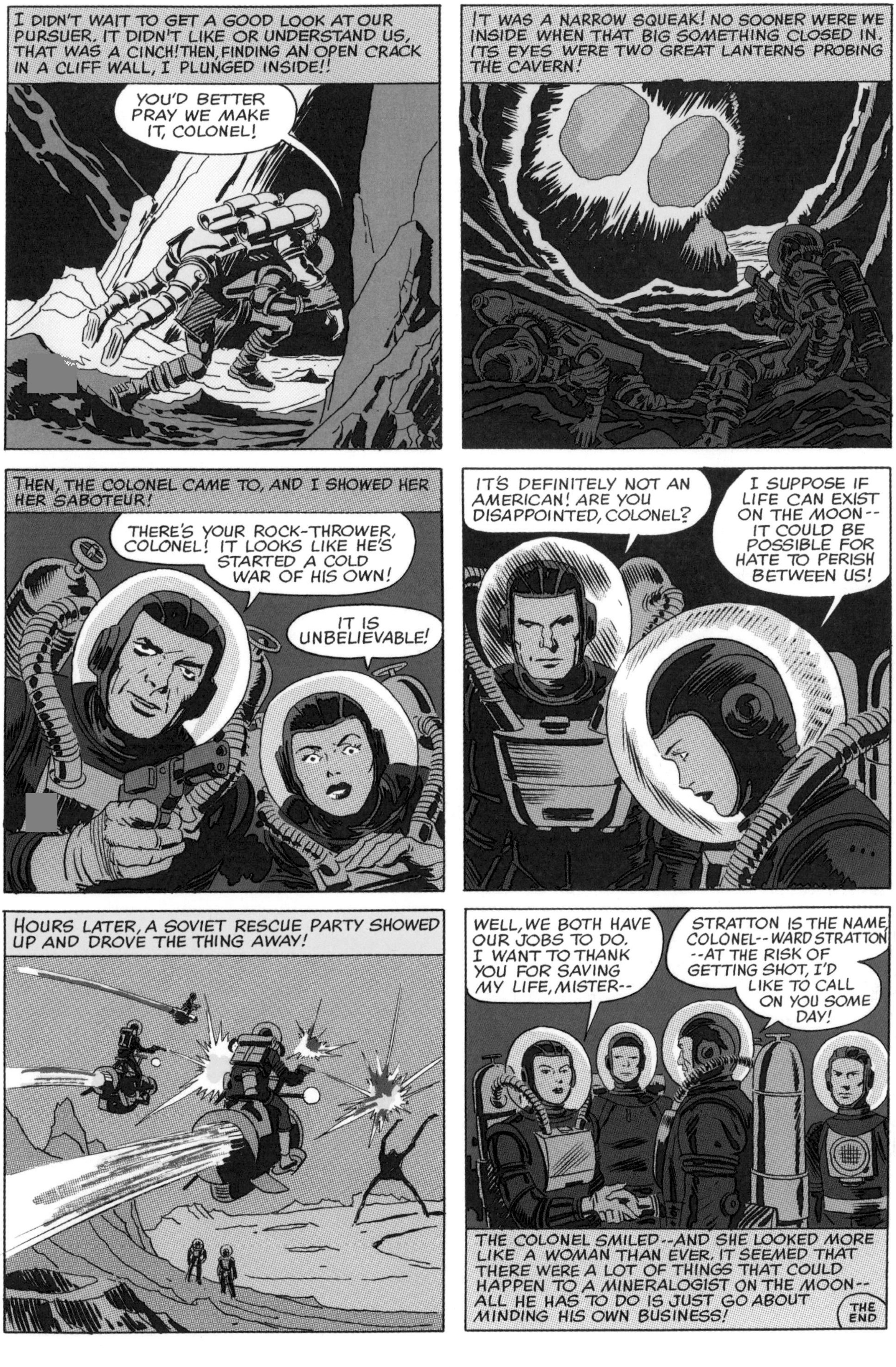
I DIDN'T WAIT TO GET A GOOD LOOK AT OUR PURSUER. IT DIDN'T LIKE OR UNDERSTAND US, THAT WAS A CINCH! THEN, FINDING AN OPEN CRACK IN A CLIFF WALL, I PLUNGED INSIDE!!
YOU'D BETTER PRAY WE MAKE IT, COLONEL!
IT WAS A NARROW SQUEAK! NO SOONER WERE WE INSIDE WHEN THAT BIG SOMETHING CLOSED IN. ITS EYES WERE TWO GREAT LANTERNS PROBING THE CAVERN!
THEN, THE COLONEL CAME TO, AND I SHOWED HER HER SABOTEUR!
THERE'S YOUR ROCK-THROWER, COLONEL! IT LOOKS LIKE HE'S STARTED A COLD WAR OF HIS OWN!
IT IS UNBELIEVABLE!
IT'S DEFINITELY NOT AN AMERICAN! ARE YOU DISAPPOINTED, COLONEL?
I SUPPOSE IF LIFE CAN EXIST ON THE MOON-- IT COULD BE POSSIBLE FOR HATE TO PERISH BETWEEN US!
HOURS LATER, A SOVIET RESCUE PARTY SHOWED UP AND DROVE THE THING AWAY!
WELL, WE BOTH HAVE OUR JOBS TO DO. I WANT TO THANK YOU FOR SAVING MY LIFE, MISTER--
STRATTON IS THE NAME, COLONEL--WARD STRATTON --AT THE RISK OF GETTING SHOT, I'D LIKE TO CALL ON YOU SOME DAY!
THE COLONEL SMILED--AND SHE LOOKED MORE LIKE A WOMAN THAN EVER. IT SEEMED THAT THERE WERE A LOT OF THINGS THAT COULD HAPPEN TO A MINERALOGIST ON THE MOON-- ALL HE HAS TO DO IS JUST GO ABOUT MINDING HIS OWN BUSINESS!
THE END

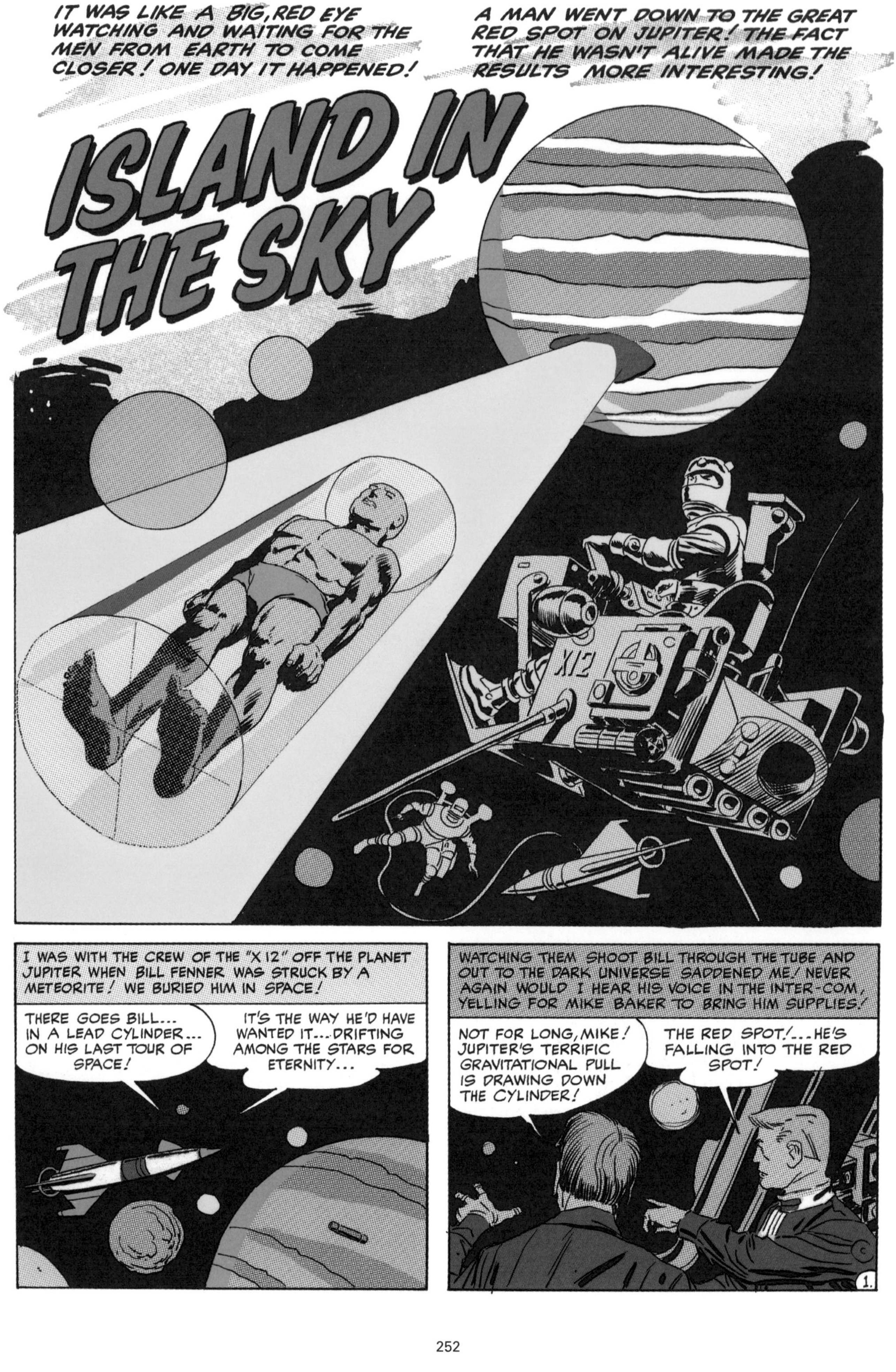
IT WAS LIKE A BIG, RED EYE WATCHING AND WAITING FOR THE MEN FROM EARTH TO COME CLOSER! ONE DAY IT HAPPENED!
A MAN WENT DOWN TO THE GREAT RED SPOT ON JUPITER! THE FACT THAT HE WASN'T ALIVE MADE THE RESULTS MORE INTERESTING!
ISLAND IN THE SKY
X12
I WAS WITH THE CREW OF THE "X 12" OFF THE PLANET JUPITER WHEN BILL FENNER WAS STRUCK BY A METEORITE! WE BURIED HIM IN SPACE!
THERE GOES BILL... IN A LEAD CYLINDER... ON HIS LAST TOUR OF SPACE!
IT'S THE WAY HE'D HAVE WANTED IT... DRIFTING AMONG THE STARS FOR ETERNITY...
WATCHING THEM SHOOT BILL THROUGH THE TUBE AND OUT TO THE DARK UNIVERSE SADDENED ME! NEVER AGAIN WOULD I HEAR HIS VOICE IN THE INTER-COM, YELLING FOR MIKE BAKER TO BRING HIM SUPPLIES!
NOT FOR LONG, MIKE! JUPITER'S TERRIFIC GRAVITATIONAL PULL IS DRAWING DOWN THE CYLINDER!
THE RED SPOT!... HE'S FALLING INTO THE RED SPOT!
1.

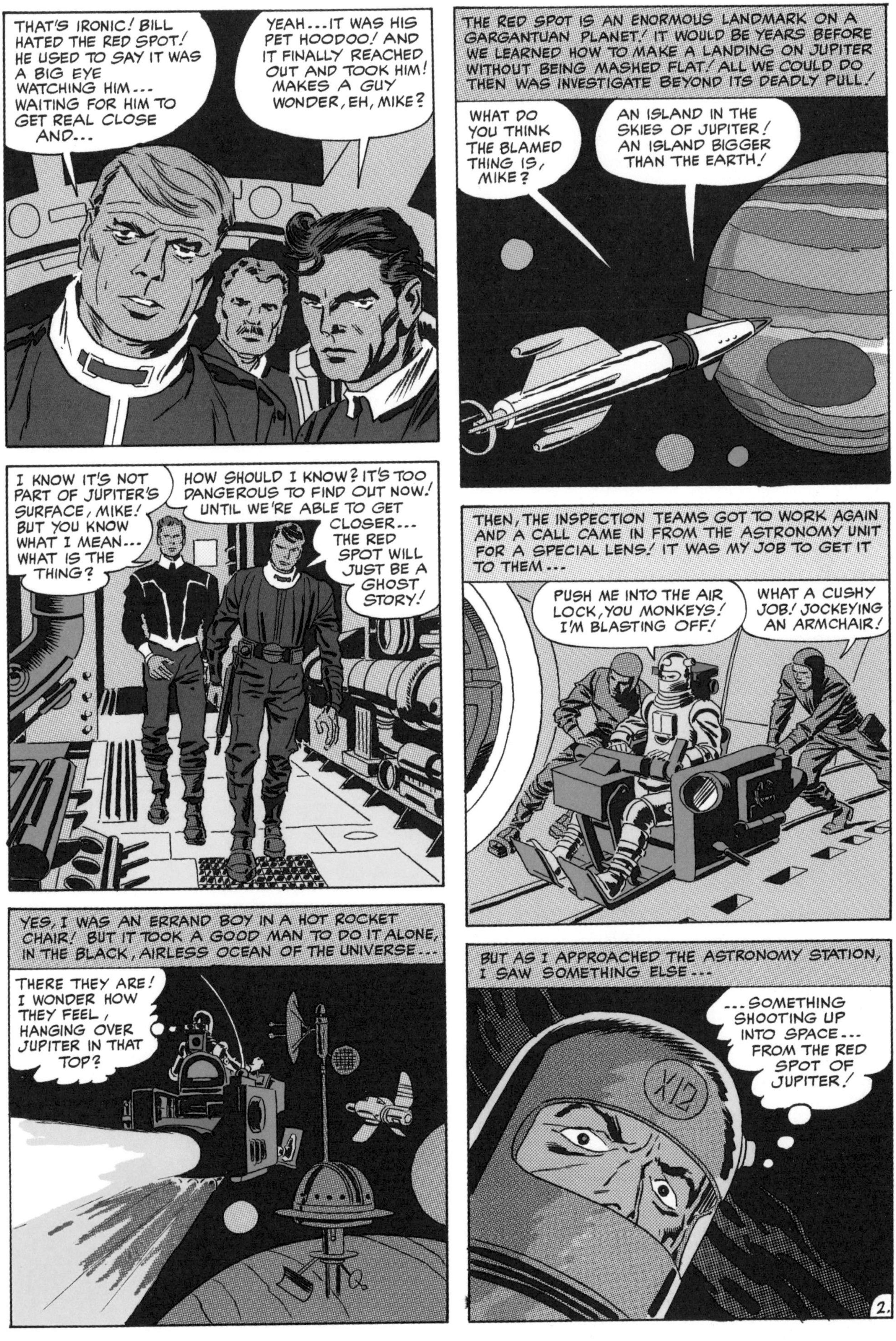
THAT'S IRONIC! BILL HATED THE RED SPOT! HE USED TO SAY IT WAS A BIG EYE WATCHING HIM... WAITING FOR HIM TO GET REAL CLOSE AND...
YEAH... IT WAS HIS PET HOODOO! AND IT FINALLY REACHED OUT AND TOOK HIM! MAKES A GUY WONDER, EH, MIKE?
THE RED SPOT IS AN ENORMOUS LANDMARK ON A GARGANTUAN PLANET! IT WOULD BE YEARS BEFORE WE LEARNED HOW TO MAKE A LANDING ON JUPITER WITHOUT BEING MASHED FLAT! ALL WE COULD DO THEN WAS INVESTIGATE BEYOND ITS DEADLY PULL!
WHAT DO YOU THINK THE BLAMED THING IS, MIKE?
AN ISLAND IN THE SKIES OF JUPITER! AN ISLAND BIGGER THAN THE EARTH!
I KNOW IT'S NOT PART OF JUPITER'S SURFACE, MIKE! BUT YOU KNOW WHAT I MEAN... WHAT IS THE THING?
HOW SHOULD I KNOW? IT'S TOO DANGEROUS TO FIND OUT NOW! UNTIL WE'RE ABLE TO GET CLOSER... THE RED SPOT WILL JUST BE A GHOST STORY!
THEN, THE INSPECTION TEAMS GOT TO WORK AGAIN AND A CALL CAME IN FROM THE ASTRONOMY UNIT FOR A SPECIAL LENS! IT WAS MY JOB TO GET IT TO THEM...
PUSH ME INTO THE AIR LOCK, YOU MONKEYS! I'M BLASTING OFF!
WHAT A CUSHY JOB! JOCKEYING AN ARMCHAIR!
YES, I WAS AN ERRAND BOY IN A HOT ROCKET CHAIR! BUT IT TOOK A GOOD MAN TO DO IT ALONE, IN THE BLACK, AIRLESS OCEAN OF THE UNIVERSE...
THERE THEY ARE! I WONDER HOW THEY FEEL, HANGING OVER JUPITER IN THAT TOP?
BUT AS I APPROACHED THE ASTRONOMY STATION, I SAW SOMETHING ELSE...
...SOMETHING SHOOTING UP INTO SPACE... FROM THE RED SPOT OF JUPITER!
X12
2.

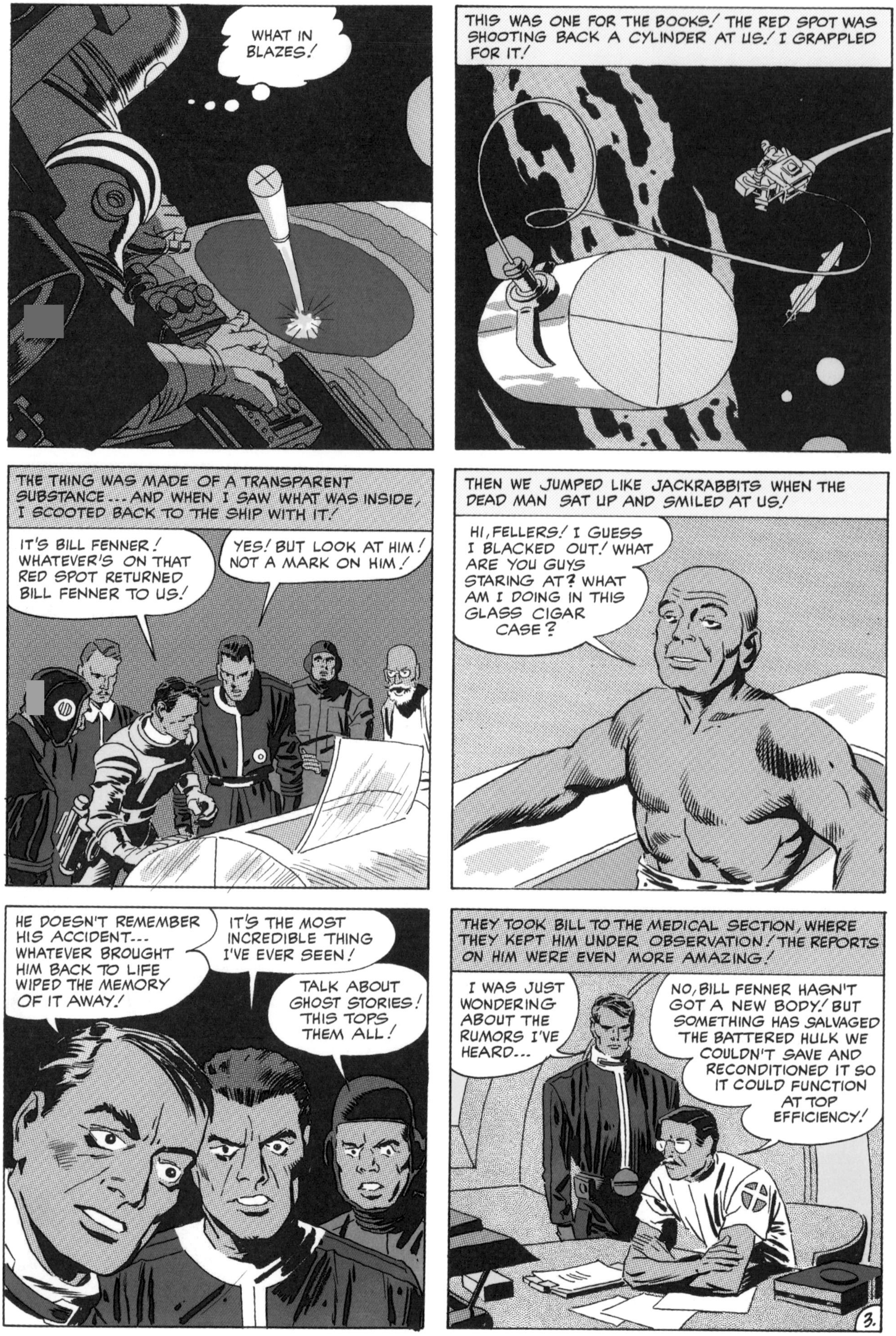

WHAT IN BLAZES!
THIS WAS ONE FOR THE BOOKS! THE RED SPOT WAS SHOOTING BACK A CYLINDER AT US! I GRAPPLED FOR IT!
THE THING WAS MADE OF A TRANSPARENT SUBSTANCE... AND WHEN I SAW WHAT WAS INSIDE, I SCOOTED BACK TO THE SHIP WITH IT!
IT'S BILL FENNER! WHATEVER'S ON THAT RED SPOT RETURNED BILL FENNER TO US!
YES! BUT LOOK AT HIM! NOT A MARK ON HIM!
THEN WE JUMPED LIKE JACKRABBITS WHEN THE DEAD MAN SAT UP AND SMILED AT US!
HI, FELLERS! I GUESS I BLACKED OUT! WHAT ARE YOU GUYS STARING AT? WHAT AM I DOING IN THIS GLASS CIGAR CASE?
HE DOESN'T REMEMBER HIS ACCIDENT--- WHATEVER BROUGHT HIM BACK TO LIFE WIPED THE MEMORY OF IT AWAY!
IT'S THE MOST INCREDIBLE THING I'VE EVER SEEN!
TALK ABOUT GHOST STORIES! THIS TOPS THEM ALL!
THEY TOOK BILL TO THE MEDICAL SECTION, WHERE THEY KEPT HIM UNDER OBSERVATION! THE REPORTS ON HIM WERE EVEN MORE AMAZING!
I WAS JUST WONDERING ABOUT THE RUMORS I'VE HEARD...
NO, BILL FENNER HASN'T GOT A NEW BODY! BUT SOMETHING HAS SALVAGED THE BATTERED HULK WE COULDN'T SAVE AND RECONDITIONED IT SO IT COULD FUNCTION AT TOP EFFICIENCY!
3.

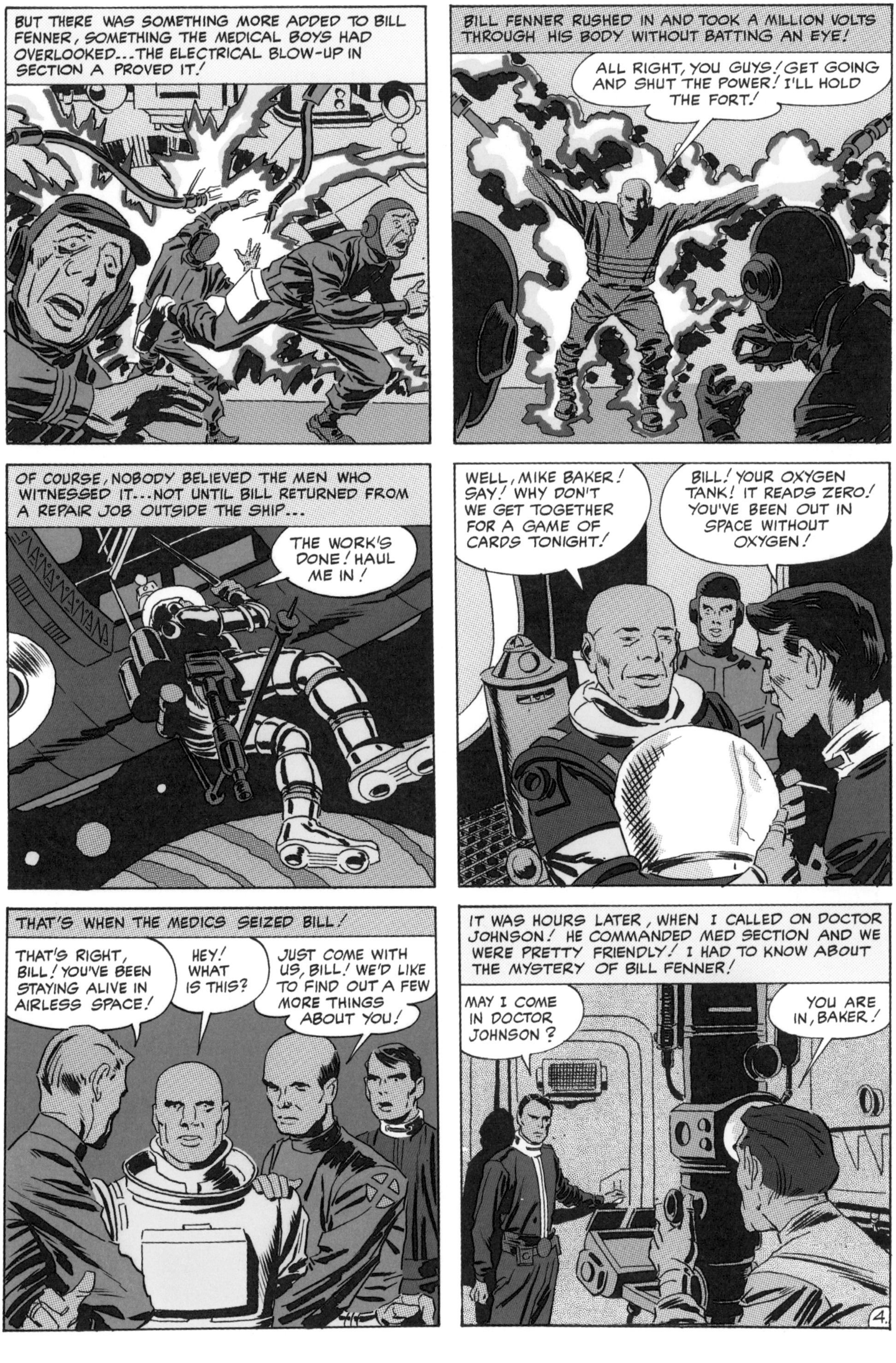

BUT THERE WAS SOMETHING MORE ADDED TO BILL FENNER, SOMETHING THE MEDICAL BOYS HAD OVERLOOKED...THE ELECTRICAL BLOW-UP IN SECTION A PROVED IT!
BILL FENNER RUSHED IN AND TOOK A MILLION VOLTS THROUGH HIS BODY WITHOUT BATTING AN EYE!
ALL RIGHT, YOU GUYS! GET GOING AND SHUT THE POWER! I'LL HOLD THE FORT!
OF COURSE, NOBODY BELIEVED THE MEN WHO WITNESSED IT...NOT UNTIL BILL RETURNED FROM A REPAIR JOB OUTSIDE THE SHIP...
THE WORK'S DONE! HAUL ME IN!
WELL, MIKE BAKER! SAY! WHY DON'T WE GET TOGETHER FOR A GAME OF CARDS TONIGHT!
BILL! YOUR OXYGEN TANK! IT READS ZERO! YOU'VE BEEN OUT IN SPACE WITHOUT OXYGEN!
THAT'S WHEN THE MEDICS SEIZED BILL!
THAT'S RIGHT, BILL! YOU'VE BEEN STAYING ALIVE IN AIRLESS SPACE!
HEY! WHAT IS THIS?
JUST COME WITH US, BILL! WE'D LIKE TO FIND OUT A FEW MORE THINGS ABOUT YOU!
IT WAS HOURS LATER, WHEN I CALLED ON DOCTOR JOHNSON! HE COMMANDED MED SECTION AND WE WERE PRETTY FRIENDLY! I HAD TO KNOW ABOUT THE MYSTERY OF BILL FENNER!
MAY I COME IN DOCTOR JOHNSON?
YOU ARE IN, BAKER!
4.

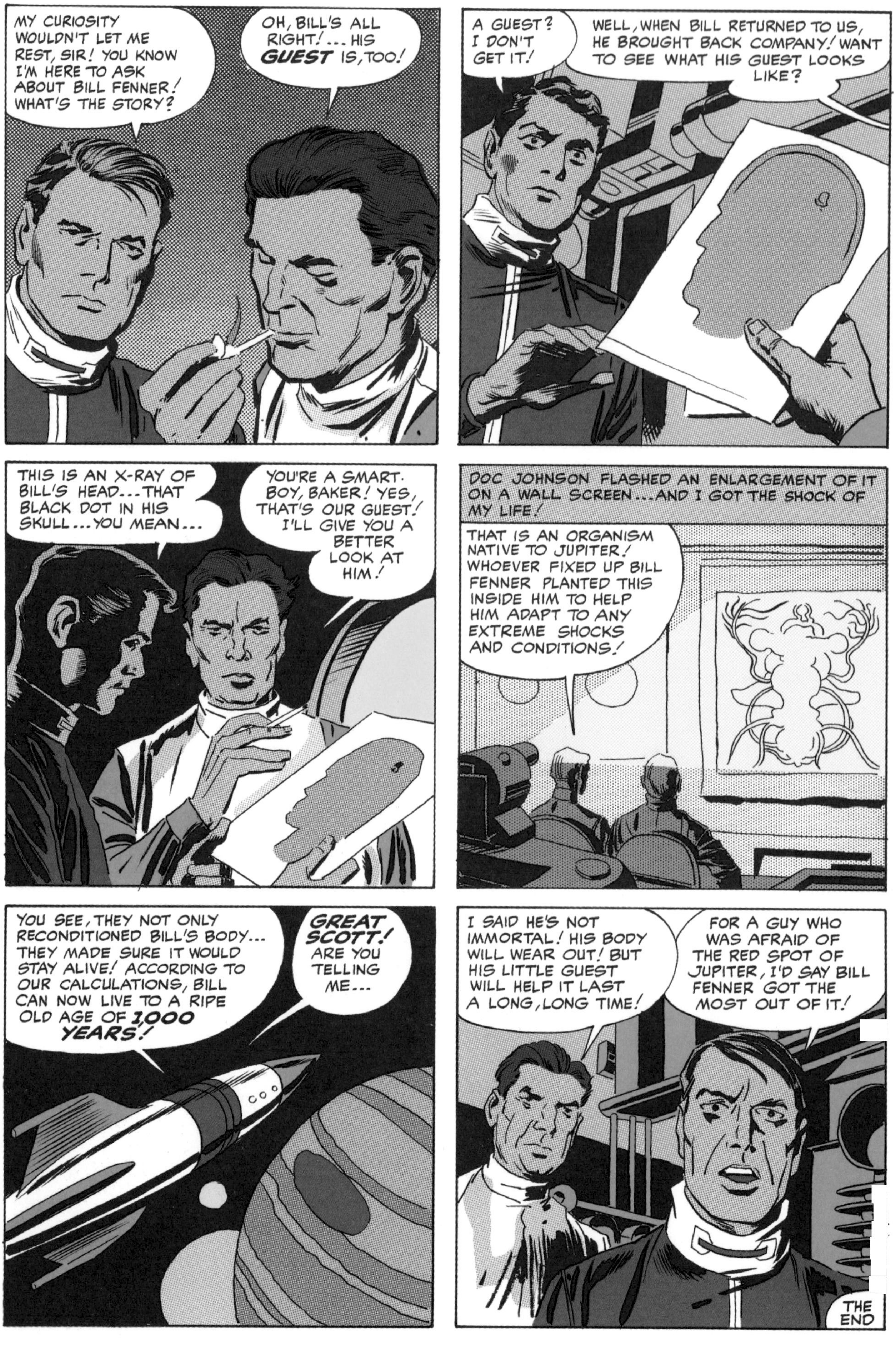
MY CURIOSITY WOULDN'T LET ME REST, SIR! YOU KNOW I'M HERE TO ASK ABOUT BILL FENNER! WHAT'S THE STORY?
OH, BILL'S ALL RIGHT!... HIS GUEST IS, TOO!
A GUEST? I DON'T GET IT!
WELL, WHEN BILL RETURNED TO US, HE BROUGHT BACK COMPANY! WANT TO SEE WHAT HIS GUEST LOOKS LIKE?
THIS IS AN X-RAY OF BILL'S HEAD... THAT BLACK DOT IN HIS SKULL... YOU MEAN...
YOU'RE A SMART BOY, BAKER! YES, THAT'S OUR GUEST! I'LL GIVE YOU A BETTER LOOK AT HIM!
DOC JOHNSON FLASHED AN ENLARGEMENT OF IT ON A WALL SCREEN... AND I GOT THE SHOCK OF MY LIFE!
THAT IS AN ORGANISM NATIVE TO JUPITER! WHOEVER FIXED UP BILL FENNER PLANTED THIS INSIDE HIM TO HELP HIM ADAPT TO ANY EXTREME SHOCKS AND CONDITIONS!
YOU SEE, THEY NOT ONLY RECONDITIONED BILL'S BODY... THEY MADE SURE IT WOULD STAY ALIVE! ACCORDING TO OUR CALCULATIONS, BILL CAN NOW LIVE TO A RIPE OLD AGE OF 1,000 YEARS!
GREAT SCOTT! ARE YOU TELLING ME...
I SAID HE'S NOT IMMORTAL! HIS BODY WILL WEAR OUT! BUT HIS LITTLE GUEST WILL HELP IT LAST A LONG, LONG TIME!
FOR A GUY WHO WAS AFRAID OF THE RED SPOT OF JUPITER, I'D SAY BILL FENNER GOT THE MOST OUT OF IT!
THE END

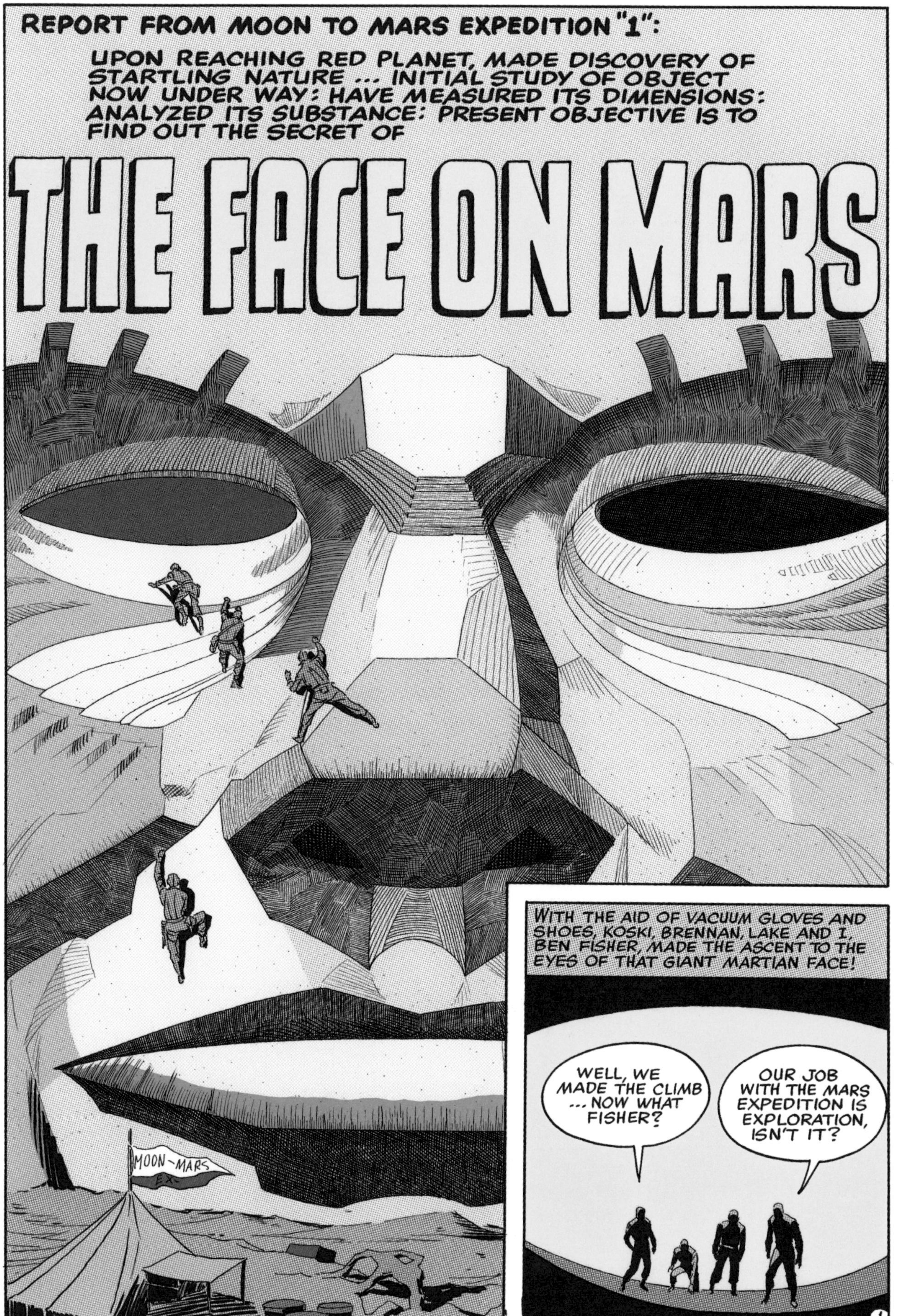
REPORT FROM MOON TO MARS EXPEDITION "1":
UPON REACHING RED PLANET, MADE DISCOVERY OF STARTLING NATURE ... INITIAL STUDY OF OBJECT NOW UNDER WAY: HAVE MEASURED ITS DIMENSIONS: ANALYZED ITS SUBSTANCE: PRESENT OBJECTIVE IS TO FIND OUT THE SECRET OF
THE FACE ON MARS
MOON-MARS EX-
WITH THE AID OF VACUUM GLOVES AND SHOES, KOSKI, BRENNAN, LAKE AND I, BEN FISHER, MADE THE ASCENT TO THE EYES OF THAT GIANT MARTIAN FACE!
WELL, WE MADE THE CLIMB ... NOW WHAT FISHER?
OUR JOB WITH THE MARS EXPEDITION IS EXPLORATION, ISN'T IT?
1

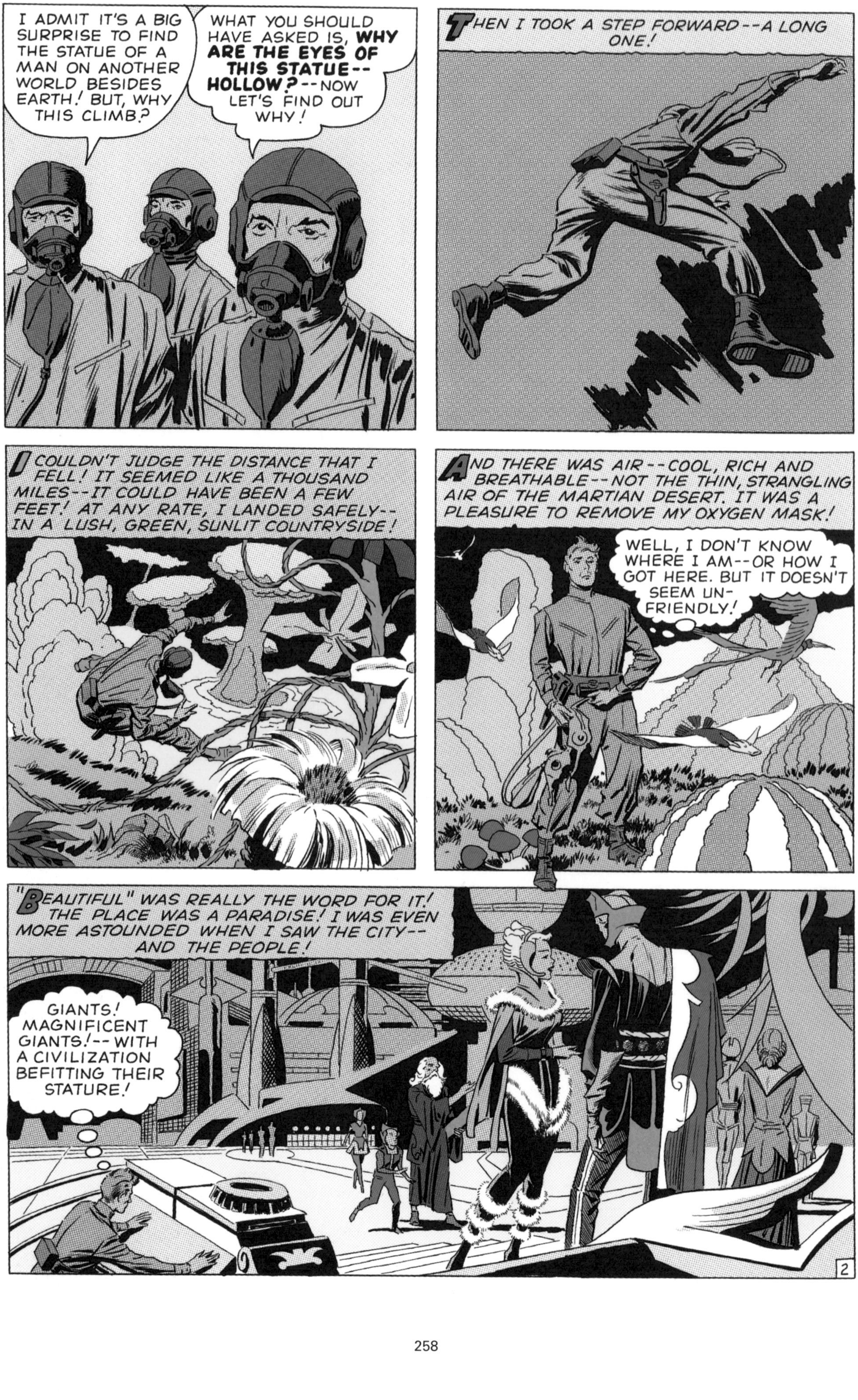
I ADMIT IT'S A BIG SURPRISE TO FIND THE STATUE OF A MAN ON ANOTHER WORLD BESIDES EARTH! BUT, WHY THIS CLIMB?
WHAT YOU SHOULD HAVE ASKED IS, WHY ARE THE EYES OF THIS STATUE--HOLLOW?--NOW LET'S FIND OUT WHY!
THEN I TOOK A STEP FORWARD--A LONG ONE!
I COULDN'T JUDGE THE DISTANCE THAT I FELL! IT SEEMED LIKE A THOUSAND MILES--IT COULD HAVE BEEN A FEW FEET! AT ANY RATE, I LANDED SAFELY--IN A LUSH, GREEN, SUNLIT COUNTRYSIDE!
AND THERE WAS AIR--COOL, RICH AND BREATHABLE--NOT THE THIN, STRANGLING AIR OF THE MARTIAN DESERT. IT WAS A PLEASURE TO REMOVE MY OXYGEN MASK!
WELL, I DON'T KNOW WHERE I AM--OR HOW I GOT HERE. BUT IT DOESN'T SEEM UN-FRIENDLY!
"BEAUTIFUL" WAS REALLY THE WORD FOR IT! THE PLACE WAS A PARADISE! I WAS EVEN MORE ASTOUNDED WHEN I SAW THE CITY--AND THE PEOPLE!
GIANTS! MAGNIFICENT GIANTS!--WITH A CIVILIZATION BEFITTING THEIR STATURE!
2

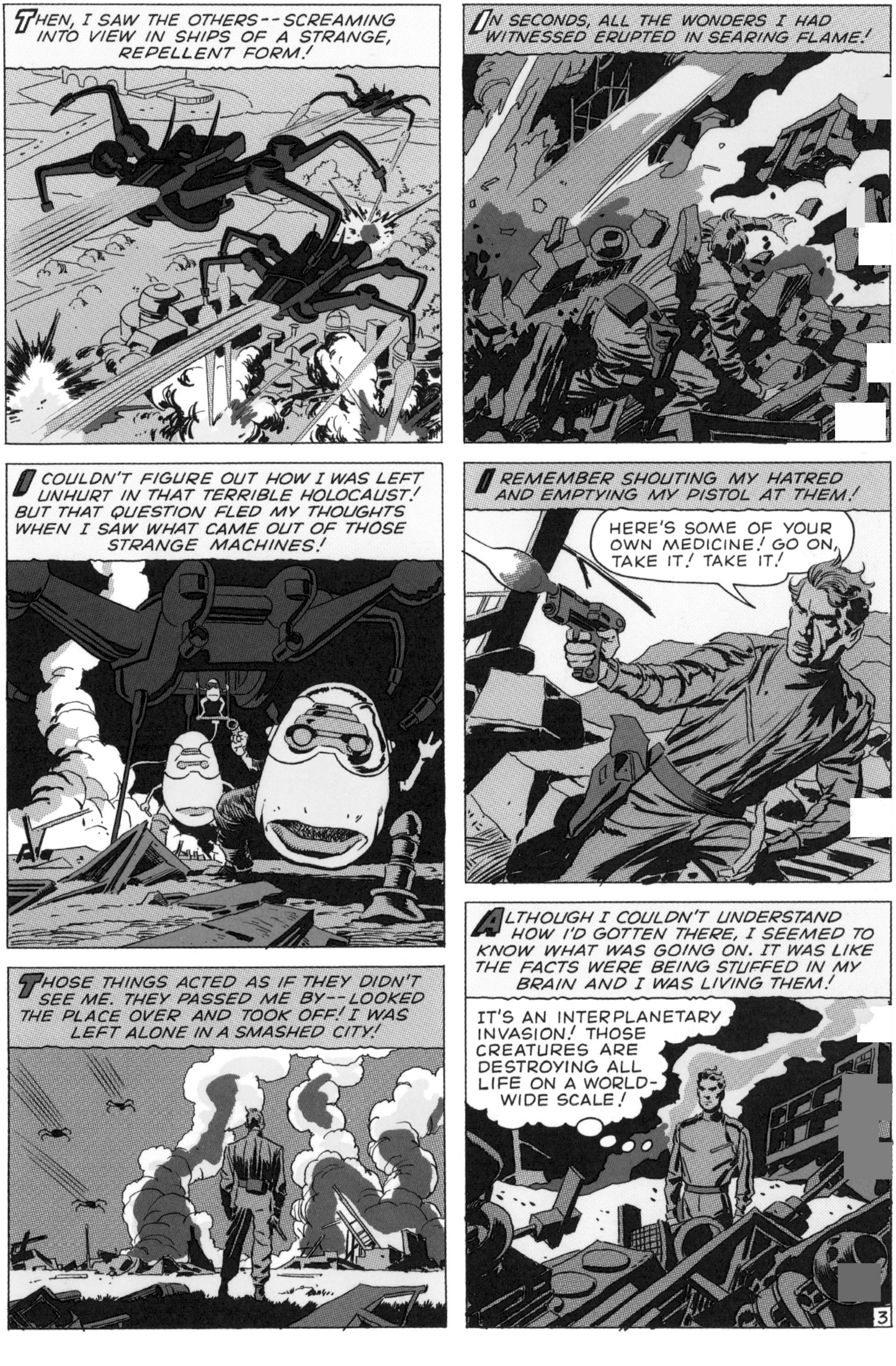
THEN, I SAW THE OTHERS--SCREAMING INTO VIEW IN SHIPS OF A STRANGE, REPELLENT FORM!
IN SECONDS, ALL THE WONDERS I HAD WITNESSED ERUPTED IN SEARING FLAME!
I COULDN'T FIGURE OUT HOW I WAS LEFT UNHURT IN THAT TERRIBLE HOLOCAUST! BUT THAT QUESTION FLED MY THOUGHTS WHEN I SAW WHAT CAME OUT OF THOSE STRANGE MACHINES!
I REMEMBER SHOUTING MY HATRED AND EMPTYING MY PISTOL AT THEM!
HERE'S SOME OF YOUR OWN MEDICINE! GO ON, TAKE IT! TAKE IT!
THOSE THINGS ACTED AS IF THEY DIDN'T SEE ME. THEY PASSED ME BY--LOOKED THE PLACE OVER AND TOOK OFF! I WAS LEFT ALONE IN A SMASHED CITY!
ALTHOUGH I COULDN'T UNDERSTAND HOW I'D GOTTEN THERE, I SEEMED TO KNOW WHAT WAS GOING ON. IT WAS LIKE THE FACTS WERE BEING STUFFED IN MY BRAIN AND I WAS LIVING THEM!
IT'S AN INTERPLANETARY INVASION! THOSE CREATURES ARE DESTROYING ALL LIFE ON A WORLD-WIDE SCALE!
3

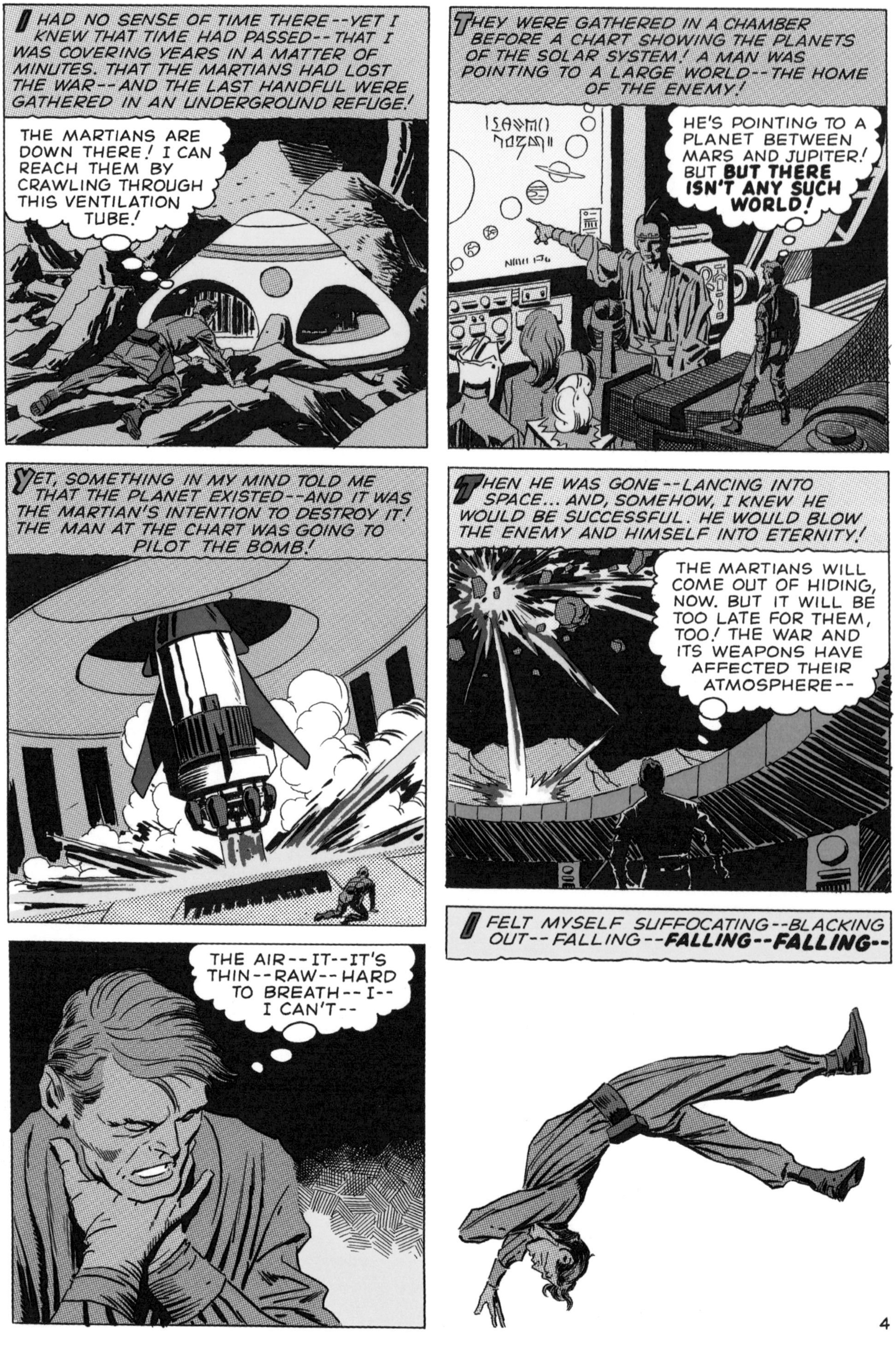
I HAD NO SENSE OF TIME THERE--YET I KNEW THAT TIME HAD PASSED--THAT I WAS COVERING YEARS IN A MATTER OF MINUTES. THAT THE MARTIANS HAD LOST THE WAR--AND THE LAST HANDFUL WERE GATHERED IN AN UNDERGROUND REFUGE!
THE MARTIANS ARE DOWN THERE! I CAN REACH THEM BY CRAWLING THROUGH THIS VENTILATION TUBE!
THEY WERE GATHERED IN A CHAMBER BEFORE A CHART SHOWING THE PLANETS OF THE SOLAR SYSTEM! A MAN WAS POINTING TO A LARGE WORLD--THE HOME OF THE ENEMY!
HE'S POINTING TO A PLANET BETWEEN MARS AND JUPITER! BUT **BUT THERE ISN'T ANY SUCH WORLD!**
YET, SOMETHING IN MY MIND TOLD ME THAT THE PLANET EXISTED--AND IT WAS THE MARTIAN'S INTENTION TO DESTROY IT! THE MAN AT THE CHART WAS GOING TO PILOT THE BOMB!
THEN HE WAS GONE--LANCING INTO SPACE... AND, SOMEHOW, I KNEW HE WOULD BE SUCCESSFUL. HE WOULD BLOW THE ENEMY AND HIMSELF INTO ETERNITY!
THE MARTIANS WILL COME OUT OF HIDING, NOW. BUT IT WILL BE TOO LATE FOR THEM, TOO! THE WAR AND ITS WEAPONS HAVE AFFECTED THEIR ATMOSPHERE--
THE AIR--IT--IT'S THIN--RAW--HARD TO BREATH--I--I CAN'T--
I FELT MYSELF SUFFOCATING--BLACKING OUT--FALLING--**FALLING--FALLING--**
4

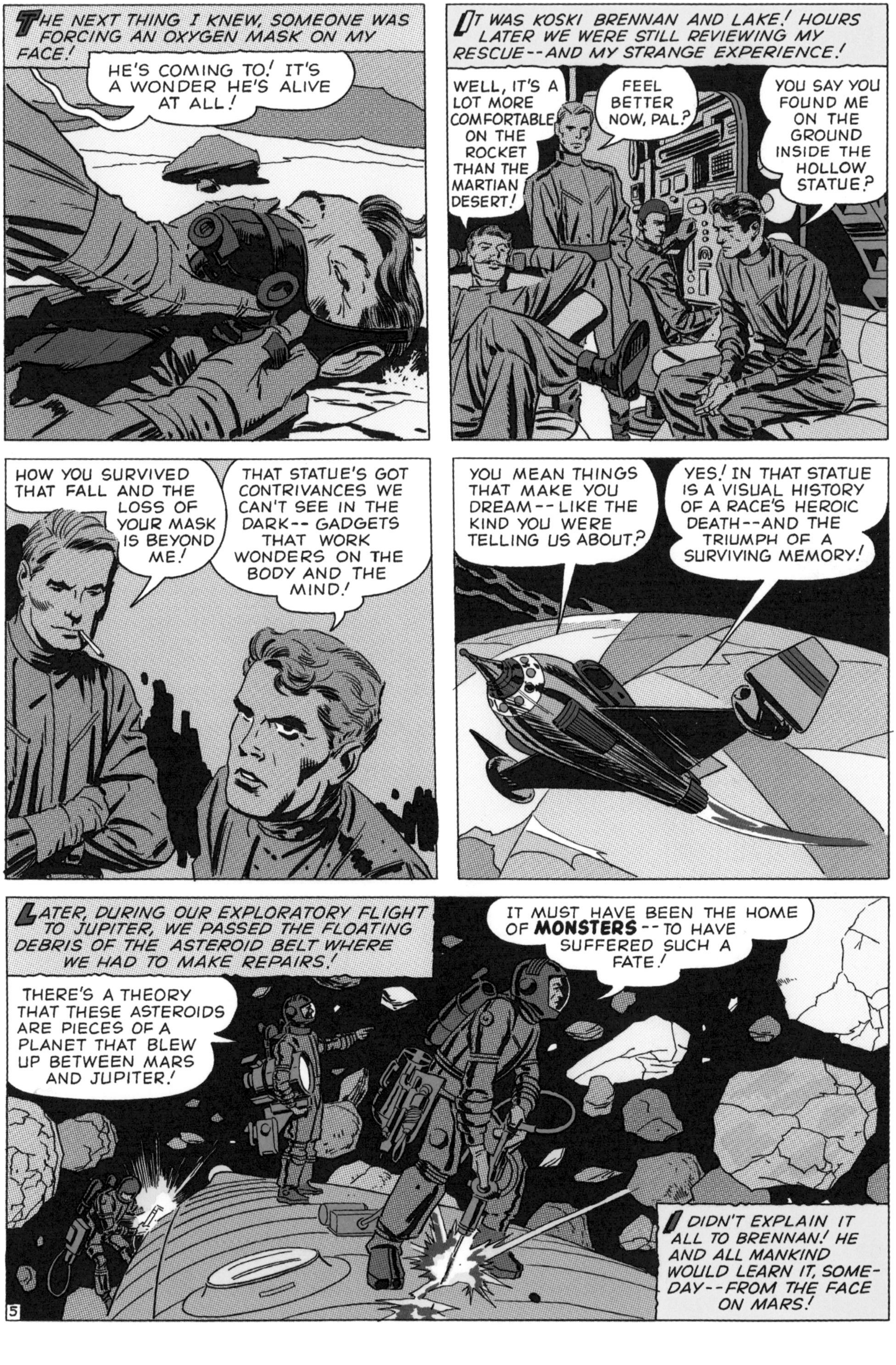
THE NEXT THING I KNEW, SOMEONE WAS FORCING AN OXYGEN MASK ON MY FACE!
HE'S COMING TO! IT'S A WONDER HE'S ALIVE AT ALL!
IT WAS KOSKI BRENNAN AND LAKE! HOURS LATER WE WERE STILL REVIEWING MY RESCUE--AND MY STRANGE EXPERIENCE!
WELL, IT'S A LOT MORE COMFORTABLE ON THE ROCKET THAN THE MARTIAN DESERT!
FEEL BETTER NOW, PAL?
YOU SAY YOU FOUND ME ON THE GROUND INSIDE THE HOLLOW STATUE?
HOW YOU SURVIVED THAT FALL AND THE LOSS OF YOUR MASK IS BEYOND ME!
THAT STATUE'S GOT CONTRIVANCES WE CAN'T SEE IN THE DARK-- GADGETS THAT WORK WONDERS ON THE BODY AND THE MIND!
YOU MEAN THINGS THAT MAKE YOU DREAM--LIKE THE KIND YOU WERE TELLING US ABOUT?
YES! IN THAT STATUE IS A VISUAL HISTORY OF A RACE'S HEROIC DEATH--AND THE TRIUMPH OF A SURVIVING MEMORY!
LATER, DURING OUR EXPLORATORY FLIGHT TO JUPITER, WE PASSED THE FLOATING DEBRIS OF THE ASTEROID BELT WHERE WE HAD TO MAKE REPAIRS!
THERE'S A THEORY THAT THESE ASTEROIDS ARE PIECES OF A PLANET THAT BLEW UP BETWEEN MARS AND JUPITER!
IT MUST HAVE BEEN THE HOME OF **MONSTERS**--TO HAVE SUFFERED SUCH A FATE!
I DIDN'T EXPLAIN IT ALL TO BRENNAN! HE AND ALL MANKIND WOULD LEARN IT, SOME-DAY--FROM THE FACE ON MARS!
5

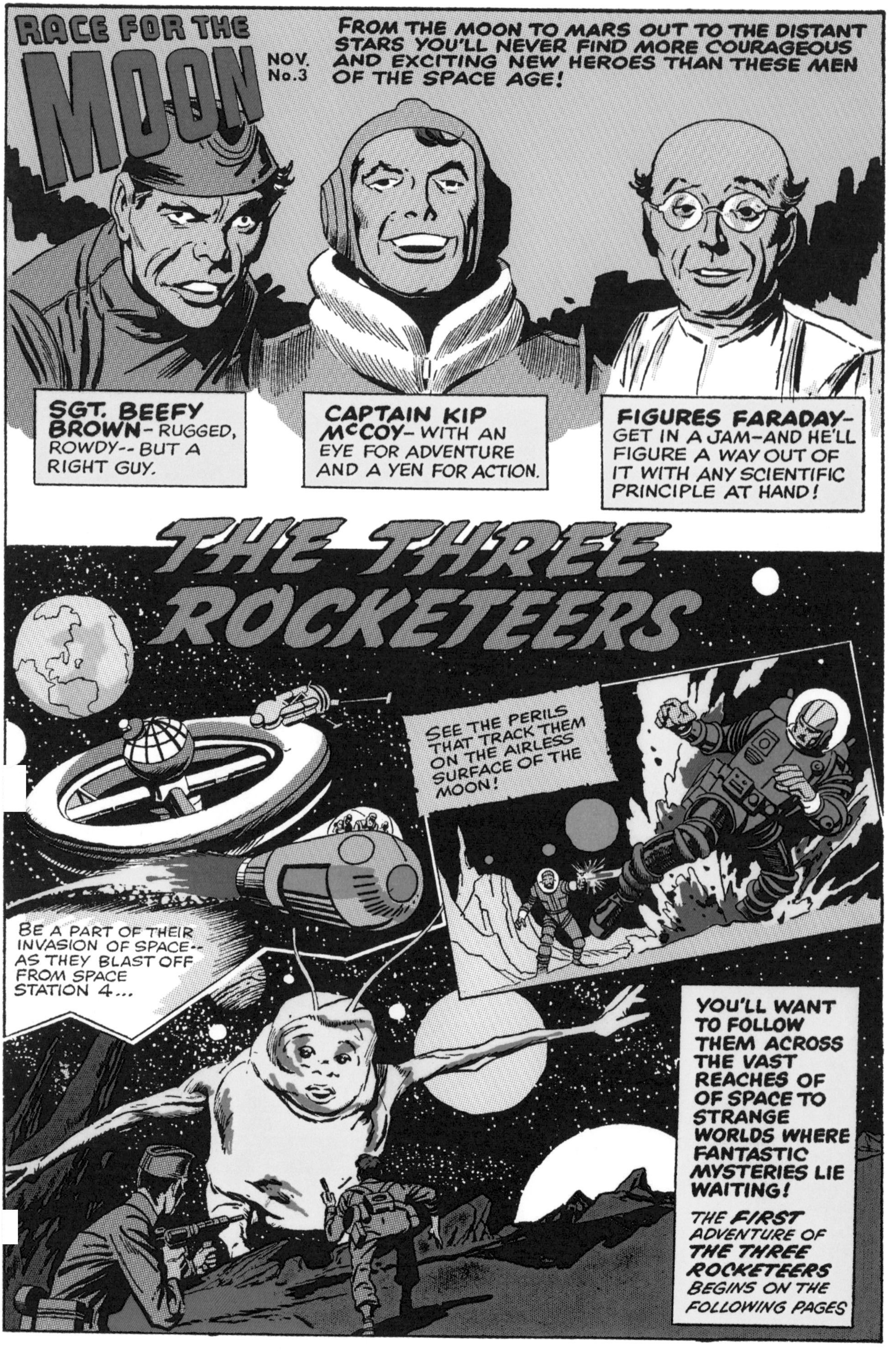

RACE FOR THE MOON
NOV. No.3
FROM THE MOON TO MARS OUT TO THE DISTANT STARS YOU'LL NEVER FIND MORE COURAGEOUS AND EXCITING NEW HEROES THAN THESE MEN OF THE SPACE AGE!
SGT. BEEFY BROWN- RUGGED, ROWDY-- BUT A RIGHT GUY.
CAPTAIN KIP McCOY- WITH AN EYE FOR ADVENTURE AND A YEN FOR ACTION.
FIGURES FARADAY- GET IN A JAM-AND HE'LL FIGURE A WAY OUT OF IT WITH ANY SCIENTIFIC PRINCIPLE AT HAND!
THE THREE ROCKETEERS
SEE THE PERILS THAT TRACK THEM ON THE AIRLESS SURFACE OF THE MOON!
BE A PART OF THEIR INVASION OF SPACE-- AS THEY BLAST OFF FROM SPACE STATION 4...
YOU'LL WANT TO FOLLOW THEM ACROSS THE VAST REACHES OF OF SPACE TO STRANGE WORLDS WHERE FANTASTIC MYSTERIES LIE WAITING!
THE FIRST ADVENTURE OF THE THREE ROCKETEERS BEGINS ON THE FOLLOWING PAGES

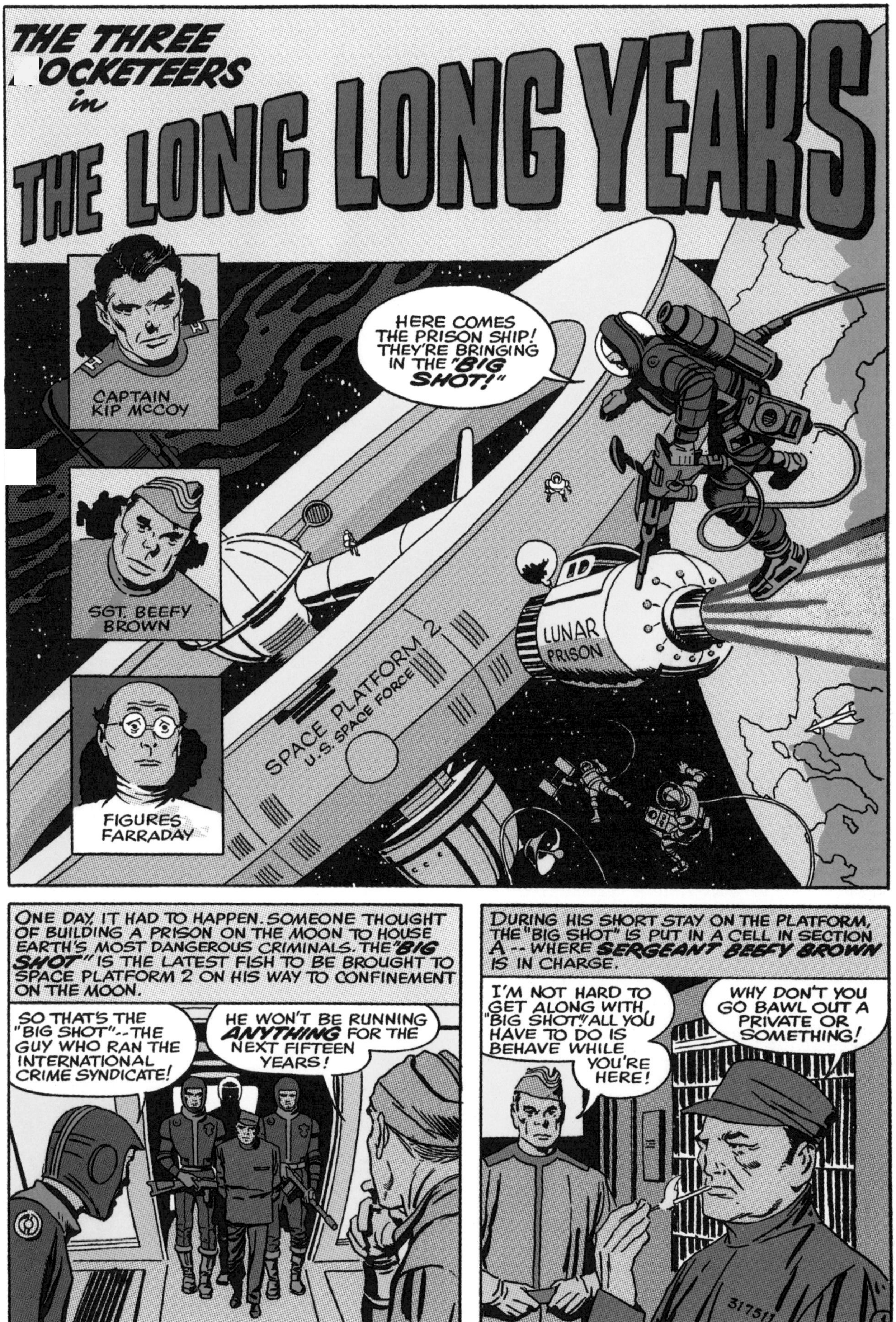
THE THREE
OCKETEERS
in
THE LONG LONG YEARS
CAPTAIN KIP McCOY
SGT. BEEFY BROWN
FIGURES FARRADAY
HERE COMES THE PRISON SHIP! THEY'RE BRINGING IN THE "BIG SHOT!"
SPACE PLATFORM 2
U.S. SPACE FORCE
LUNAR PRISON
ONE DAY IT HAD TO HAPPEN. SOMEONE THOUGHT OF BUILDING A PRISON ON THE MOON TO HOUSE EARTH'S MOST DANGEROUS CRIMINALS. THE "BIG SHOT" IS THE LATEST FISH TO BE BROUGHT TO SPACE PLATFORM 2 ON HIS WAY TO CONFINEMENT ON THE MOON.
SO THAT'S THE "BIG SHOT"--THE GUY WHO RAN THE INTERNATIONAL CRIME SYNDICATE!
HE WON'T BE RUNNING ANYTHING FOR THE NEXT FIFTEEN YEARS!
DURING HIS SHORT STAY ON THE PLATFORM, THE "BIG SHOT" IS PUT IN A CELL IN SECTION A -- WHERE SERGEANT BEEFY BROWN IS IN CHARGE.
I'M NOT HARD TO GET ALONG WITH, "BIG SHOT!" ALL YOU HAVE TO DO IS BEHAVE WHILE YOU'RE HERE!
WHY DON'T YOU GO BAWL OUT A PRIVATE OR SOMETHING!
317511
1

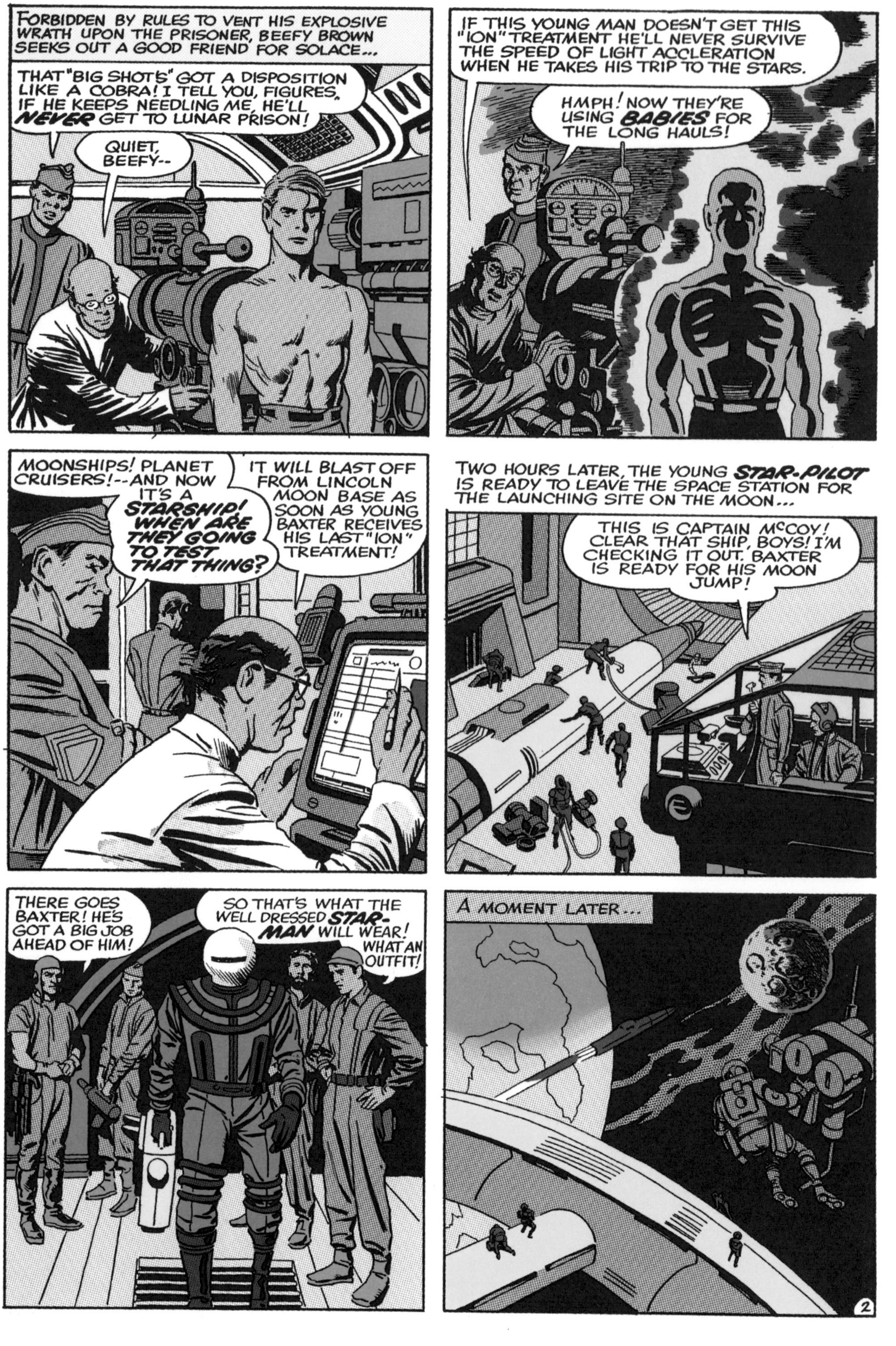
FORBIDDEN BY RULES TO VENT HIS EXPLOSIVE WRATH UPON THE PRISONER, BEEFY BROWN SEEKS OUT A GOOD FRIEND FOR SOLACE...
THAT "BIG SHOT'S" GOT A DISPOSITION LIKE A COBRA! I TELL YOU, FIGURES, IF HE KEEPS NEEDLING ME, HE'LL NEVER GET TO LUNAR PRISON!
QUIET, BEEFY--
IF THIS YOUNG MAN DOESN'T GET THIS "ION" TREATMENT HE'LL NEVER SURVIVE THE SPEED OF LIGHT ACCLERATION WHEN HE TAKES HIS TRIP TO THE STARS.
HMPH! NOW THEY'RE USING BABIES FOR THE LONG HAULS!
MOONSHIPS! PLANET CRUISERS!--AND NOW IT'S A STARSHIP! WHEN ARE THEY GOING TO TEST THAT THING?
IT WILL BLAST OFF FROM LINCOLN MOON BASE AS SOON AS YOUNG BAXTER RECEIVES HIS LAST "ION" TREATMENT!
TWO HOURS LATER, THE YOUNG STAR-PILOT IS READY TO LEAVE THE SPACE STATION FOR THE LAUNCHING SITE ON THE MOON...
THIS IS CAPTAIN McCOY! CLEAR THAT SHIP, BOYS! I'M CHECKING IT OUT. BAXTER IS READY FOR HIS MOON JUMP!
THERE GOES BAXTER! HE'S GOT A BIG JOB AHEAD OF HIM!
SO THAT'S WHAT THE WELL DRESSED STAR-MAN WILL WEAR! WHAT AN OUTFIT!
A MOMENT LATER...
2

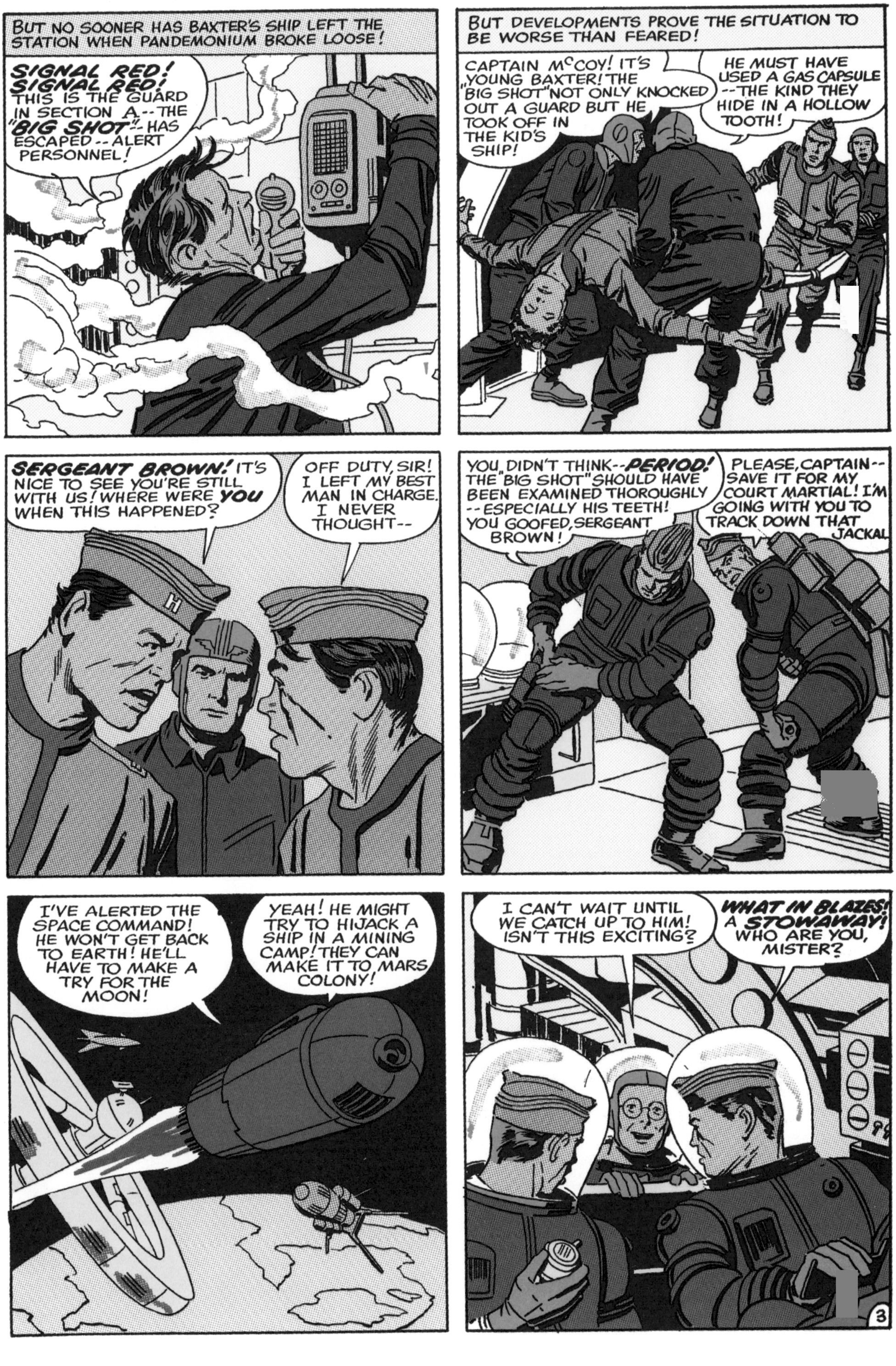

BUT NO SOONER HAS BAXTER'S SHIP LEFT THE STATION WHEN PANDEMONIUM BROKE LOOSE!
SIGNAL RED! SIGNAL RED! THIS IS THE GUARD IN SECTION A--THE "BIG SHOT"--HAS ESCAPED--ALERT PERSONNEL!
BUT DEVELOPMENTS PROVE THE SITUATION TO BE WORSE THAN FEARED!
CAPTAIN McCOY! IT'S YOUNG BAXTER! THE "BIG SHOT" NOT ONLY KNOCKED OUT A GUARD BUT HE TOOK OFF IN THE KID'S SHIP!
HE MUST HAVE USED A GAS CAPSULE --THE KIND THEY HIDE IN A HOLLOW TOOTH!
SERGEANT BROWN! IT'S NICE TO SEE YOU'RE STILL WITH US! WHERE WERE YOU WHEN THIS HAPPENED?
OFF DUTY, SIR! I LEFT MY BEST MAN IN CHARGE. I NEVER THOUGHT--
YOU DIDN'T THINK--PERIOD! THE "BIG SHOT" SHOULD HAVE BEEN EXAMINED THOROUGHLY --ESPECIALLY HIS TEETH! YOU GOOFED, SERGEANT BROWN!
PLEASE, CAPTAIN-- SAVE IT FOR MY COURT MARTIAL! I'M GOING WITH YOU TO TRACK DOWN THAT JACKAL
I'VE ALERTED THE SPACE COMMAND! HE WON'T GET BACK TO EARTH! HE'LL HAVE TO MAKE A TRY FOR THE MOON!
YEAH! HE MIGHT TRY TO HIJACK A SHIP IN A MINING CAMP! THEY CAN MAKE IT TO MARS COLONY!
I CAN'T WAIT UNTIL WE CATCH UP TO HIM! ISN'T THIS EXCITING?
WHAT IN BLAZES! A STOWAWAY! WHO ARE YOU, MISTER?
3

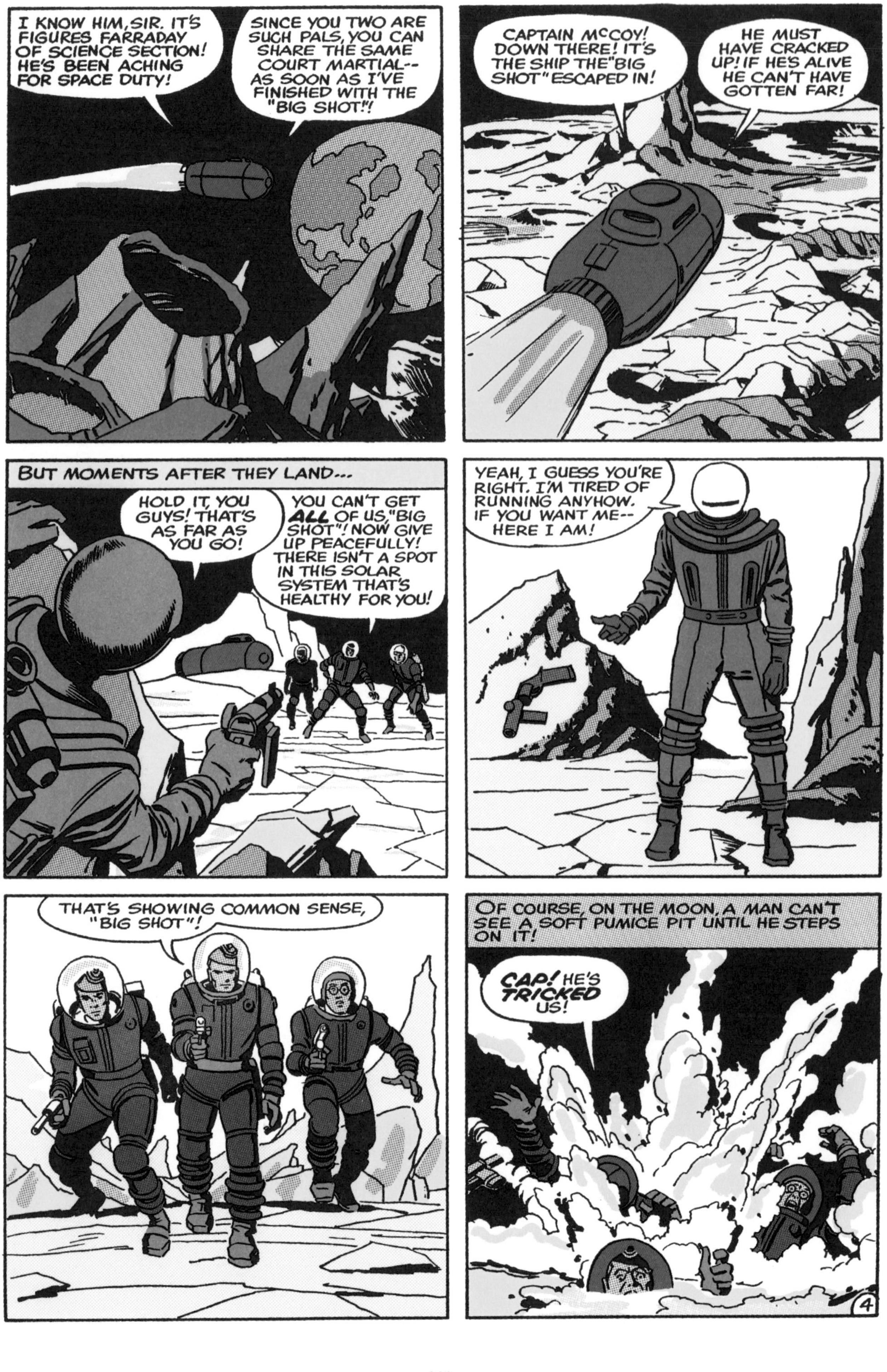
I KNOW HIM, SIR. IT'S FIGURES FARRADAY OF SCIENCE SECTION! HE'S BEEN ACHING FOR SPACE DUTY!
SINCE YOU TWO ARE SUCH PALS, YOU CAN SHARE THE SAME COURT MARTIAL-- AS SOON AS I'VE FINISHED WITH THE "BIG SHOT"!
CAPTAIN McCOY! DOWN THERE! IT'S THE SHIP THE "BIG SHOT" ESCAPED IN!
HE MUST HAVE CRACKED UP! IF HE'S ALIVE HE CAN'T HAVE GOTTEN FAR!
BUT MOMENTS AFTER THEY LAND...
HOLD IT, YOU GUYS! THAT'S AS FAR AS YOU GO!
YOU CAN'T GET ALL OF US, "BIG SHOT"! NOW GIVE UP PEACEFULLY! THERE ISN'T A SPOT IN THIS SOLAR SYSTEM THAT'S HEALTHY FOR YOU!
YEAH, I GUESS YOU'RE RIGHT. I'M TIRED OF RUNNING ANYHOW. IF YOU WANT ME-- HERE I AM!
THAT'S SHOWING COMMON SENSE, "BIG SHOT"!
OF COURSE, ON THE MOON, A MAN CAN'T SEE A SOFT PUMICE PIT UNTIL HE STEPS ON IT!
CAP! HE'S TRICKED US!
4

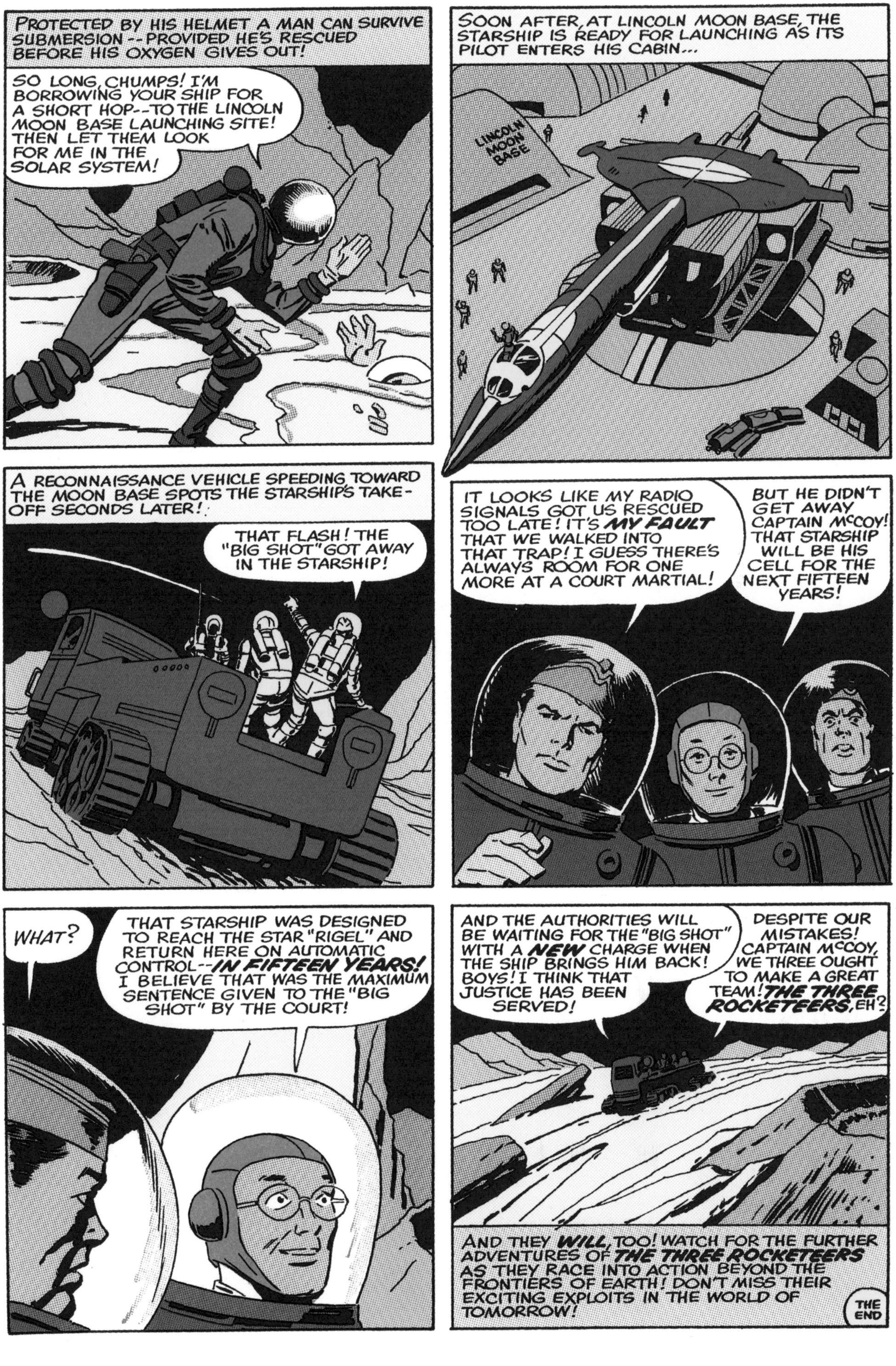
PROTECTED BY HIS HELMET A MAN CAN SURVIVE SUBMERSION--PROVIDED HE'S RESCUED BEFORE HIS OXYGEN GIVES OUT!
SO LONG, CHUMPS! I'M BORROWING YOUR SHIP FOR A SHORT HOP--TO THE LINCOLN MOON BASE LAUNCHING SITE! THEN LET THEM LOOK FOR ME IN THE SOLAR SYSTEM!
SOON AFTER, AT LINCOLN MOON BASE, THE STARSHIP IS READY FOR LAUNCHING AS ITS PILOT ENTERS HIS CABIN...
LINCOLN MOON BASE
A RECONNAISSANCE VEHICLE SPEEDING TOWARD THE MOON BASE SPOTS THE STARSHIP'S TAKE-OFF SECONDS LATER!
THAT FLASH! THE "BIG SHOT" GOT AWAY IN THE STARSHIP!
IT LOOKS LIKE MY RADIO SIGNALS GOT US RESCUED TOO LATE! IT'S MY FAULT THAT WE WALKED INTO THAT TRAP! I GUESS THERE'S ALWAYS ROOM FOR ONE MORE AT A COURT MARTIAL!
BUT HE DIDN'T GET AWAY CAPTAIN McCOY! THAT STARSHIP WILL BE HIS CELL FOR THE NEXT FIFTEEN YEARS!
WHAT?
THAT STARSHIP WAS DESIGNED TO REACH THE STAR "RIGEL" AND RETURN HERE ON AUTOMATIC CONTROL--IN FIFTEEN YEARS! I BELIEVE THAT WAS THE MAXIMUM SENTENCE GIVEN TO THE "BIG SHOT" BY THE COURT!
AND THE AUTHORITIES WILL BE WAITING FOR THE "BIG SHOT" WITH A NEW CHARGE WHEN THE SHIP BRINGS HIM BACK! BOYS! I THINK THAT JUSTICE HAS BEEN SERVED!
DESPITE OUR MISTAKES! CAPTAIN McCOY, WE THREE OUGHT TO MAKE A GREAT TEAM! THE THREE ROCKETEERS, EH?
AND THEY WILL, TOO! WATCH FOR THE FURTHER ADVENTURES OF THE THREE ROCKETEERS AS THEY RACE INTO ACTION BEYOND THE FRONTIERS OF EARTH! DON'T MISS THEIR EXCITING EXPLOITS IN THE WORLD OF TOMORROW!
THE END

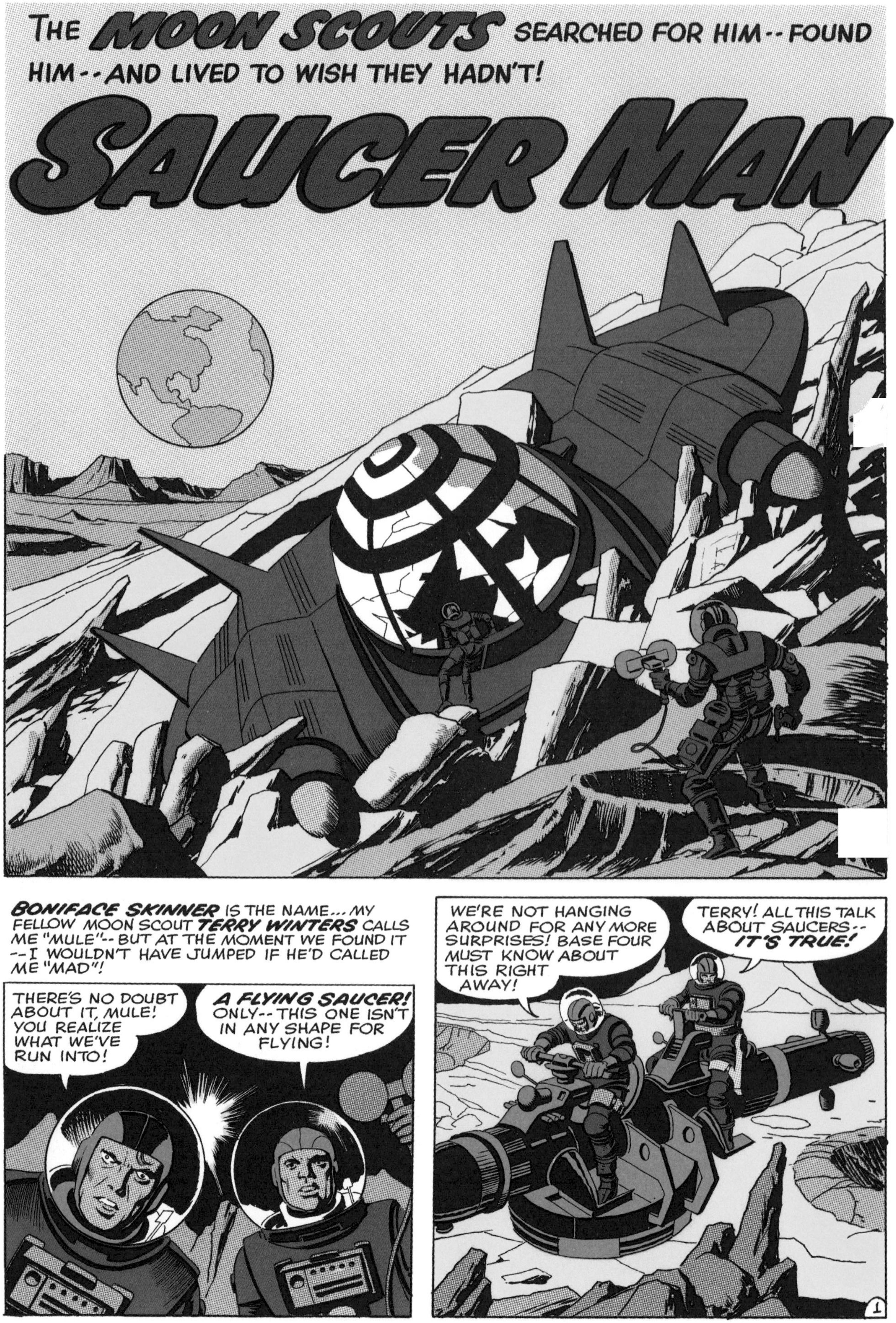
THE MOON SCOUTS SEARCHED FOR HIM--FOUND HIM--AND LIVED TO WISH THEY HADN'T!
SAUCER MAN
BONIFACE SKINNER IS THE NAME... MY FELLOW MOON SCOUT TERRY WINTERS CALLS ME "MULE"-- BUT AT THE MOMENT WE FOUND IT --I WOULDN'T HAVE JUMPED IF HE'D CALLED ME "MAD"!
THERE'S NO DOUBT ABOUT IT, MULE! YOU REALIZE WHAT WE'VE RUN INTO!
A FLYING SAUCER! ONLY--THIS ONE ISN'T IN ANY SHAPE FOR FLYING!
WE'RE NOT HANGING AROUND FOR ANY MORE SURPRISES! BASE FOUR MUST KNOW ABOUT THIS RIGHT AWAY!
TERRY! ALL THIS TALK ABOUT SAUCERS-- IT'S TRUE!
1

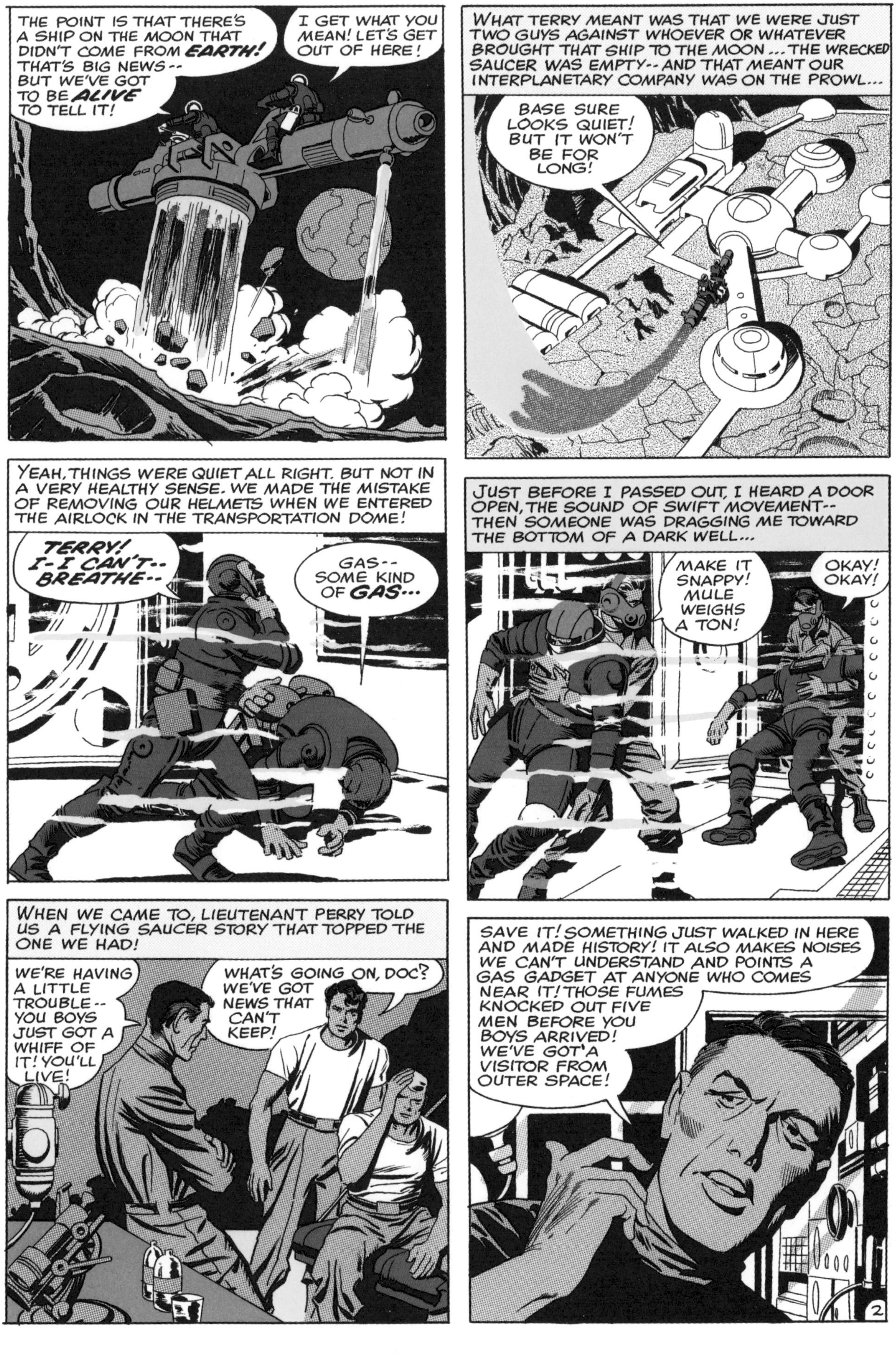
THE POINT IS THAT THERE'S A SHIP ON THE MOON THAT DIDN'T COME FROM EARTH! THAT'S BIG NEWS -- BUT WE'VE GOT TO BE ALIVE TO TELL IT!
I GET WHAT YOU MEAN! LET'S GET OUT OF HERE!
WHAT TERRY MEANT WAS THAT WE WERE JUST TWO GUYS AGAINST WHOEVER OR WHATEVER BROUGHT THAT SHIP TO THE MOON ... THE WRECKED SAUCER WAS EMPTY-- AND THAT MEANT OUR INTERPLANETARY COMPANY WAS ON THE PROWL...
BASE SURE LOOKS QUIET! BUT IT WON'T BE FOR LONG!
YEAH, THINGS WERE QUIET ALL RIGHT. BUT NOT IN A VERY HEALTHY SENSE. WE MADE THE MISTAKE OF REMOVING OUR HELMETS WHEN WE ENTERED THE AIRLOCK IN THE TRANSPORTATION DOME!
TERRY! I-I CAN'T-- BREATHE--
GAS-- SOME KIND OF GAS...
JUST BEFORE I PASSED OUT, I HEARD A DOOR OPEN, THE SOUND OF SWIFT MOVEMENT-- THEN SOMEONE WAS DRAGGING ME TOWARD THE BOTTOM OF A DARK WELL...
MAKE IT SNAPPY! MULE WEIGHS A TON!
OKAY! OKAY!
WHEN WE CAME TO, LIEUTENANT PERRY TOLD US A FLYING SAUCER STORY THAT TOPPED THE ONE WE HAD!
WHAT'S GOING ON, DOC? WE'VE GOT NEWS THAT CAN'T KEEP!
WE'RE HAVING A LITTLE TROUBLE -- YOU BOYS JUST GOT A WHIFF OF IT! YOU'LL LIVE!
SAVE IT! SOMETHING JUST WALKED IN HERE AND MADE HISTORY! IT ALSO MAKES NOISES WE CAN'T UNDERSTAND AND POINTS A GAS GADGET AT ANYONE WHO COMES NEAR IT! THOSE FUMES KNOCKED OUT FIVE MEN BEFORE YOU BOYS ARRIVED! WE'VE GOT A VISITOR FROM OUTER SPACE!
2

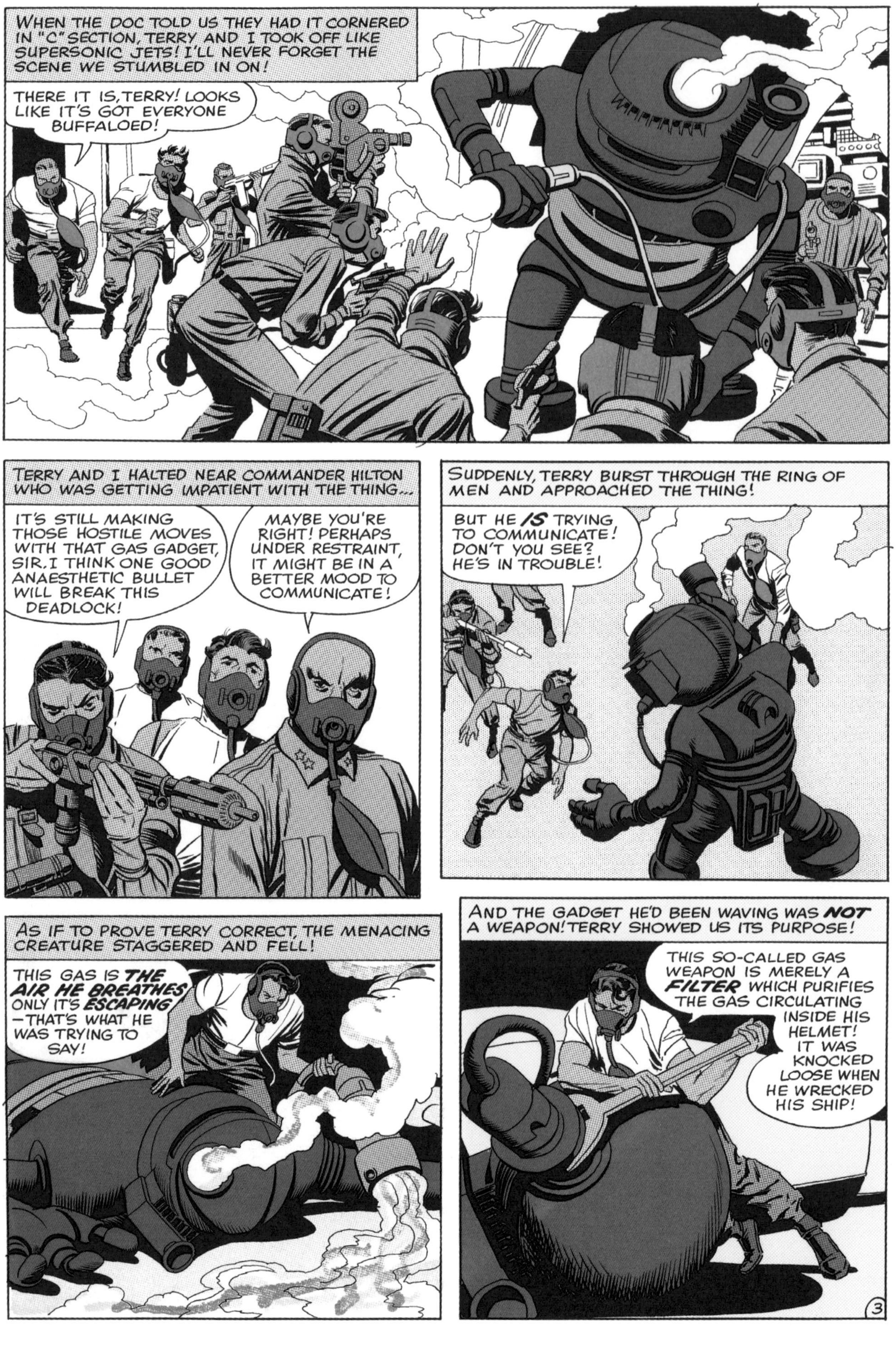
WHEN THE DOC TOLD US THEY HAD IT CORNERED IN "C" SECTION, TERRY AND I TOOK OFF LIKE SUPERSONIC JETS! I'LL NEVER FORGET THE SCENE WE STUMBLED IN ON!
THERE IT IS, TERRY! LOOKS LIKE IT'S GOT EVERYONE BUFFALOED!
TERRY AND I HALTED NEAR COMMANDER HILTON WHO WAS GETTING IMPATIENT WITH THE THING...
IT'S STILL MAKING THOSE HOSTILE MOVES WITH THAT GAS GADGET, SIR. I THINK ONE GOOD ANAESTHETIC BULLET WILL BREAK THIS DEADLOCK!
MAYBE YOU'RE RIGHT! PERHAPS UNDER RESTRAINT, IT MIGHT BE IN A BETTER MOOD TO COMMUNICATE!
SUDDENLY, TERRY BURST THROUGH THE RING OF MEN AND APPROACHED THE THING!
BUT HE ***IS*** TRYING TO COMMUNICATE! DON'T YOU SEE? HE'S IN TROUBLE!
AS IF TO PROVE TERRY CORRECT, THE MENACING CREATURE STAGGERED AND FELL!
THIS GAS IS ***THE AIR HE BREATHES***, ONLY IT'S ***ESCAPING*** —THAT'S WHAT HE WAS TRYING TO SAY!
AND THE GADGET HE'D BEEN WAVING WAS ***NOT*** A WEAPON! TERRY SHOWED US ITS PURPOSE!
THIS SO-CALLED GAS WEAPON IS MERELY A ***FILTER*** WHICH PURIFIES THE GAS CIRCULATING INSIDE HIS HELMET! IT WAS KNOCKED LOOSE WHEN HE WRECKED HIS SHIP!
3

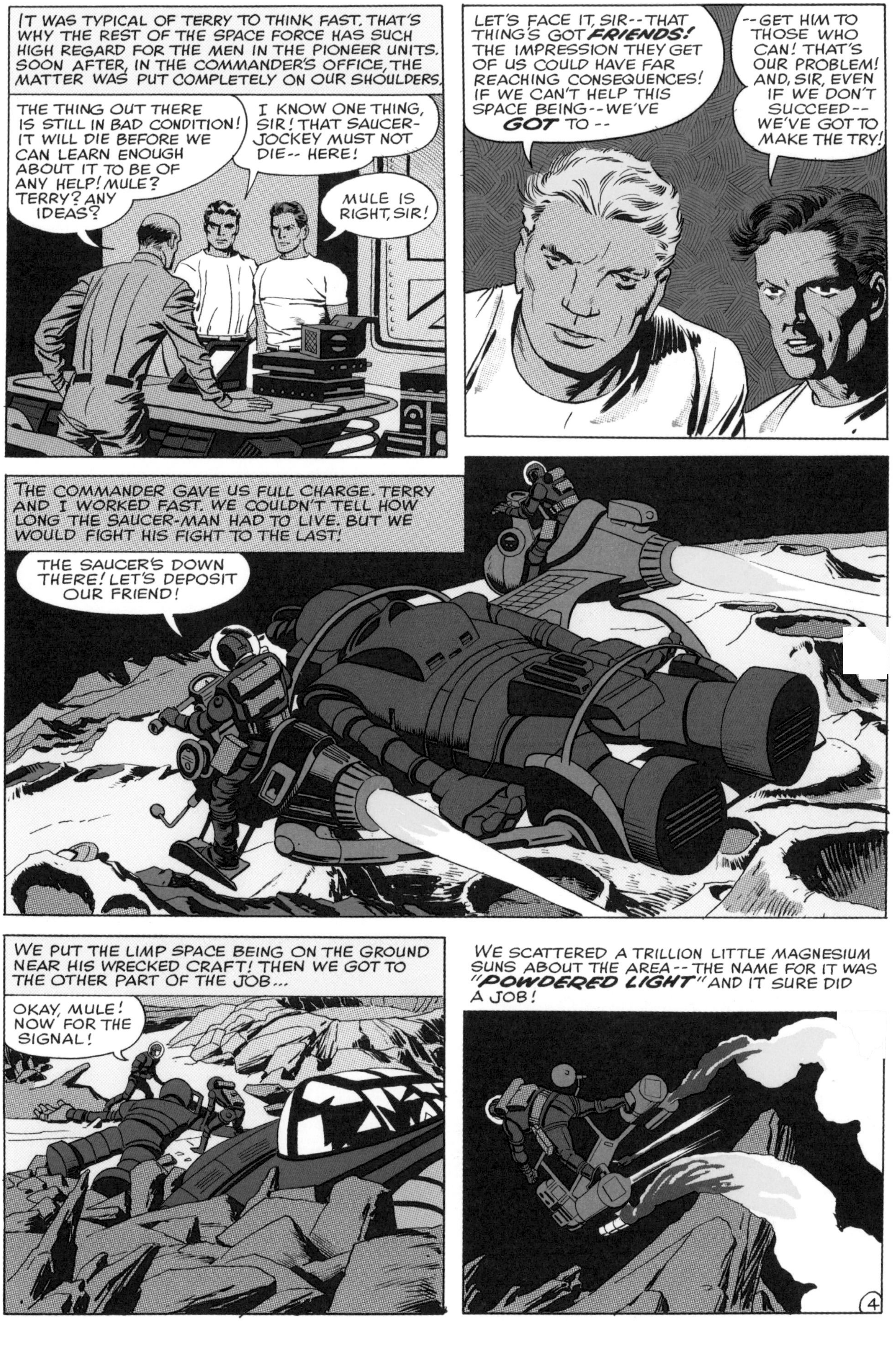

IT WAS TYPICAL OF TERRY TO THINK FAST. THAT'S WHY THE REST OF THE SPACE FORCE HAS SUCH HIGH REGARD FOR THE MEN IN THE PIONEER UNITS. SOON AFTER, IN THE COMMANDER'S OFFICE, THE MATTER WAS PUT COMPLETELY ON OUR SHOULDERS.
THE THING OUT THERE IS STILL IN BAD CONDITION! IT WILL DIE BEFORE WE CAN LEARN ENOUGH ABOUT IT TO BE OF ANY HELP! MULE? TERRY? ANY IDEAS?
I KNOW ONE THING, SIR! THAT SAUCER-JOCKEY MUST NOT DIE-- HERE!
MULE IS RIGHT, SIR!
LET'S FACE IT, SIR--THAT THING'S GOT FRIENDS! THE IMPRESSION THEY GET OF US COULD HAVE FAR REACHING CONSEQUENCES! IF WE CAN'T HELP THIS SPACE BEING--WE'VE GOT TO --
--GET HIM TO THOSE WHO CAN! THAT'S OUR PROBLEM! AND, SIR, EVEN IF WE DON'T SUCCEED--WE'VE GOT TO MAKE THE TRY!
THE COMMANDER GAVE US FULL CHARGE. TERRY AND I WORKED FAST. WE COULDN'T TELL HOW LONG THE SAUCER-MAN HAD TO LIVE, BUT WE WOULD FIGHT HIS FIGHT TO THE LAST!
THE SAUCER'S DOWN THERE! LET'S DEPOSIT OUR FRIEND!
WE PUT THE LIMP SPACE BEING ON THE GROUND NEAR HIS WRECKED CRAFT! THEN WE GOT TO THE OTHER PART OF THE JOB...
OKAY, MULE! NOW FOR THE SIGNAL!
WE SCATTERED A TRILLION LITTLE MAGNESIUM SUNS ABOUT THE AREA--THE NAME FOR IT WAS "POWDERED LIGHT" AND IT SURE DID A JOB!
4

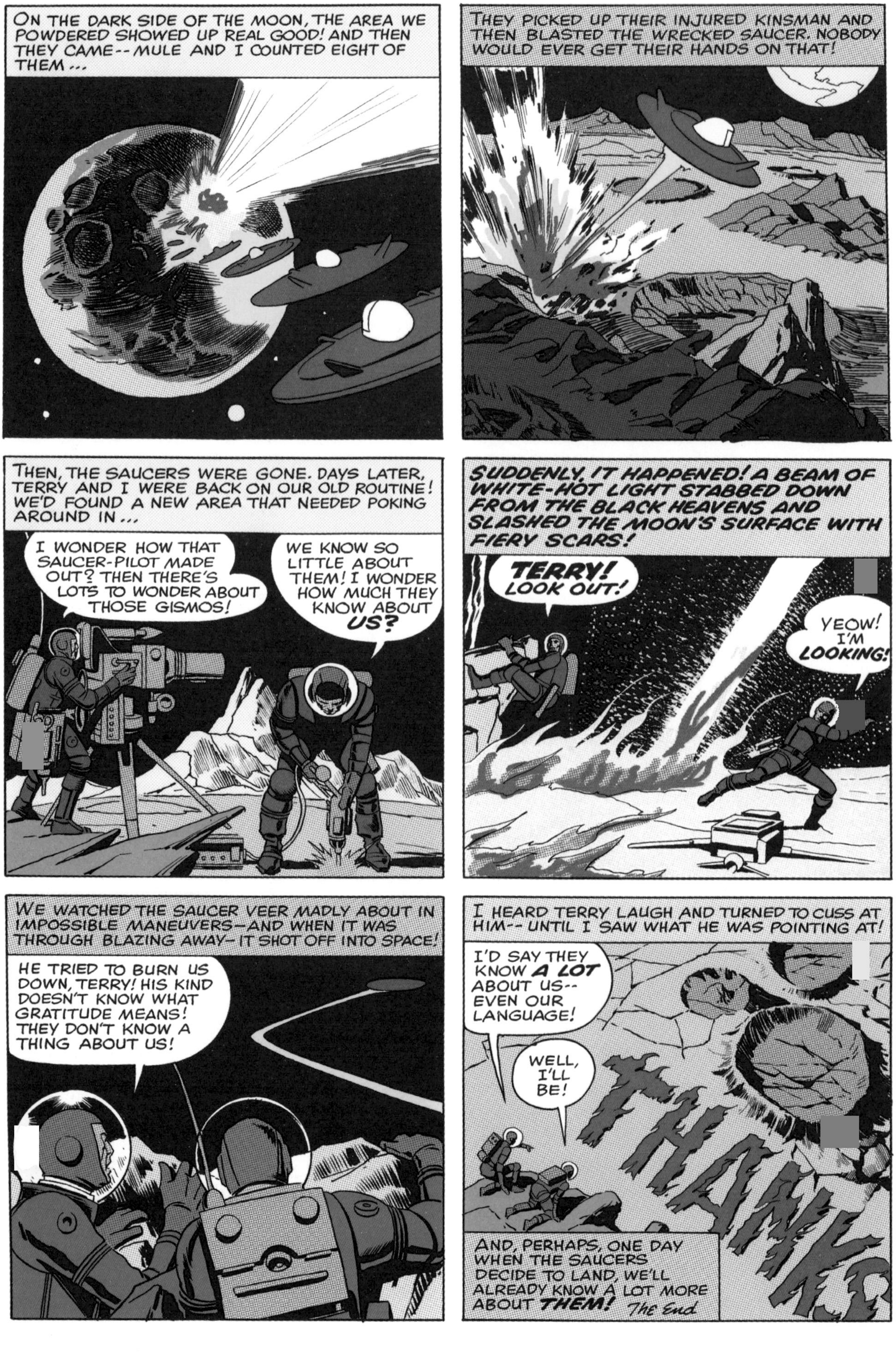

ON THE DARK SIDE OF THE MOON, THE AREA WE POWDERED SHOWED UP REAL GOOD! AND THEN THEY CAME-- MULE AND I COUNTED EIGHT OF THEM ...
THEY PICKED UP THEIR INJURED KINSMAN AND THEN BLASTED THE WRECKED SAUCER. NOBODY WOULD EVER GET THEIR HANDS ON THAT!
THEN, THE SAUCERS WERE GONE. DAYS LATER, TERRY AND I WERE BACK ON OUR OLD ROUTINE! WE'D FOUND A NEW AREA THAT NEEDED POKING AROUND IN ...
I WONDER HOW THAT SAUCER-PILOT MADE OUT? THEN THERE'S LOTS TO WONDER ABOUT THOSE GISMOS!
WE KNOW SO LITTLE ABOUT THEM! I WONDER HOW MUCH THEY KNOW ABOUT **US?**
SUDDENLY, IT HAPPENED! A BEAM OF WHITE-HOT LIGHT STABBED DOWN FROM THE BLACK HEAVENS AND SLASHED THE MOON'S SURFACE WITH FIERY SCARS!
TERRY! LOOK OUT!
YEOW! I'M **LOOKING!**
WE WATCHED THE SAUCER VEER MADLY ABOUT IN IMPOSSIBLE MANEUVERS—AND WHEN IT WAS THROUGH BLAZING AWAY— IT SHOT OFF INTO SPACE!
HE TRIED TO BURN US DOWN, TERRY! HIS KIND DOESN'T KNOW WHAT GRATITUDE MEANS! THEY DON'T KNOW A THING ABOUT US!
I HEARD TERRY LAUGH AND TURNED TO CUSS AT HIM-- UNTIL I SAW WHAT HE WAS POINTING AT!
I'D SAY THEY KNOW **A LOT** ABOUT US-- EVEN OUR LANGUAGE!
WELL, I'LL BE!
THANKS
AND, PERHAPS, ONE DAY WHEN THE SAUCERS DECIDE TO LAND, WE'LL ALREADY KNOW A LOT MORE ABOUT **THEM!** The End

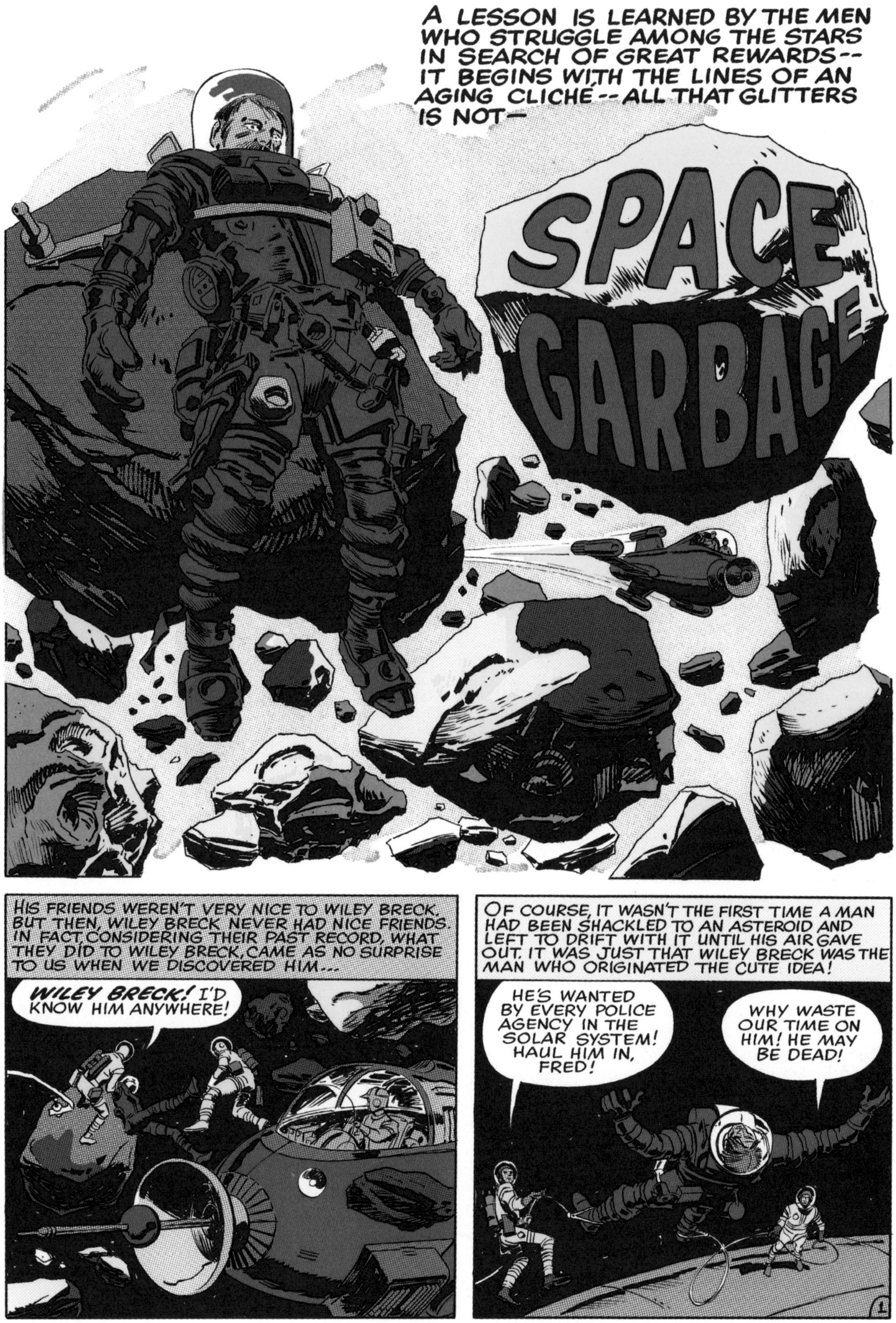

A LESSON IS LEARNED BY THE MEN WHO STRUGGLE AMONG THE STARS IN SEARCH OF GREAT REWARDS-- IT BEGINS WITH THE LINES OF AN AGING CLICHE--ALL THAT GLITTERS IS NOT—
SPACE GARBAGE
HIS FRIENDS WEREN'T VERY NICE TO WILEY BRECK, BUT THEN, WILEY BRECK NEVER HAD NICE FRIENDS. IN FACT CONSIDERING THEIR PAST RECORD, WHAT THEY DID TO WILEY BRECK, CAME AS NO SURPRISE TO US WHEN WE DISCOVERED HIM...
WILEY BRECK! I'D KNOW HIM ANYWHERE!
OF COURSE, IT WASN'T THE FIRST TIME A MAN HAD BEEN SHACKLED TO AN ASTEROID AND LEFT TO DRIFT WITH IT UNTIL HIS AIR GAVE OUT. IT WAS JUST THAT WILEY BRECK WAS THE MAN WHO ORIGINATED THE CUTE IDEA!
HE'S WANTED BY EVERY POLICE AGENCY IN THE SOLAR SYSTEM! HAUL HIM IN, FRED!
WHY WASTE OUR TIME ON HIM! HE MAY BE DEAD!
1

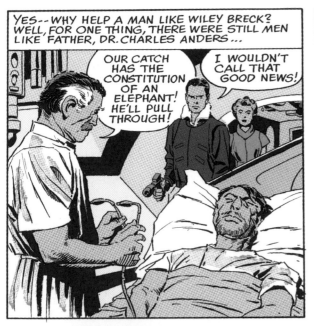

YES--WHY HELP A MAN LIKE WILEY BRECK? WELL, FOR ONE THING, THERE WERE STILL MEN LIKE FATHER, DR. CHARLES ANDERS...

OUR CATCH HAS THE CONSTITUTION OF AN ELEPHANT! HE'LL PULL THROUGH!

I WOULDN'T CALL THAT GOOD NEWS!

A DOCTOR'S DUTY IS TO SAVE A LIFE! I'LL LEAVE IT TO A PROSECUTING ATTORNEY TO ATTEND TO THE OTHER MATTERS CONCERNING WILEY BRECK!

WE'LL HAVE A JOLLY TIME WITH HIM ABOARD! I'LL HAVE TO KEEP A PISTOL ON HIM UNTIL WE GET BACK TO MARS!

IT'S BEEN HARROWING ENOUGH MANEVERING THROUGH THIS BELT OF ASTEROIDS! NOW THERE'S DANGER INSIDE THE SHIP AS WELL AS OUTSIDE!

WHEN WILEY BRECK CAME TO, THE FIRST ONE HE SAW WAS MY SISTER SHEILA. THEN HE BEGAN TO LAUGH. IT WAS LOUD AND NASTY!

HA HA HA HA HA HA HA HA! I FOOLED 'EM!-- EVERY CHUMP WHO EVER TOLD ME I'D NEVER GET TO PARADISE!

HE TURNED HIS SNAKY EYES UPON ME--LOOKED AT THE WEAPON I WAS HOLDING AND MEASURED ME FROM HEAD TO TOE...

OH, YOU KNOW WHO I AM, EH? YOU LOOK PRETTY SHAKY, JUNIOR-- EVER SHOOT A MAN BEFORE?

NO, BUT I'M WILLING TO MAKE AN EXCEPTION OF YOUR KIND, BRECK!

MY BRAVADO DIDN'T FAZE HIM ... BRECK COULD SEE I WAS JUST A GREEN KID. BUT WHEN MY BROTHER-IN-LAW, HARRY DEVLIN CAME IN FROM THE PILOT'S CONTROL ROOM, BRECK GREW LESS COCKY!

IF FRED GETS SQUEAMISH, I WON'T, BRECK! SO DON'T GET ANY IDEAS!

OKAY! SO YOU'RE TOUGH GUYS! BUT DON'T COUNT ON TURNING ME OVER TO THE LAW!

2

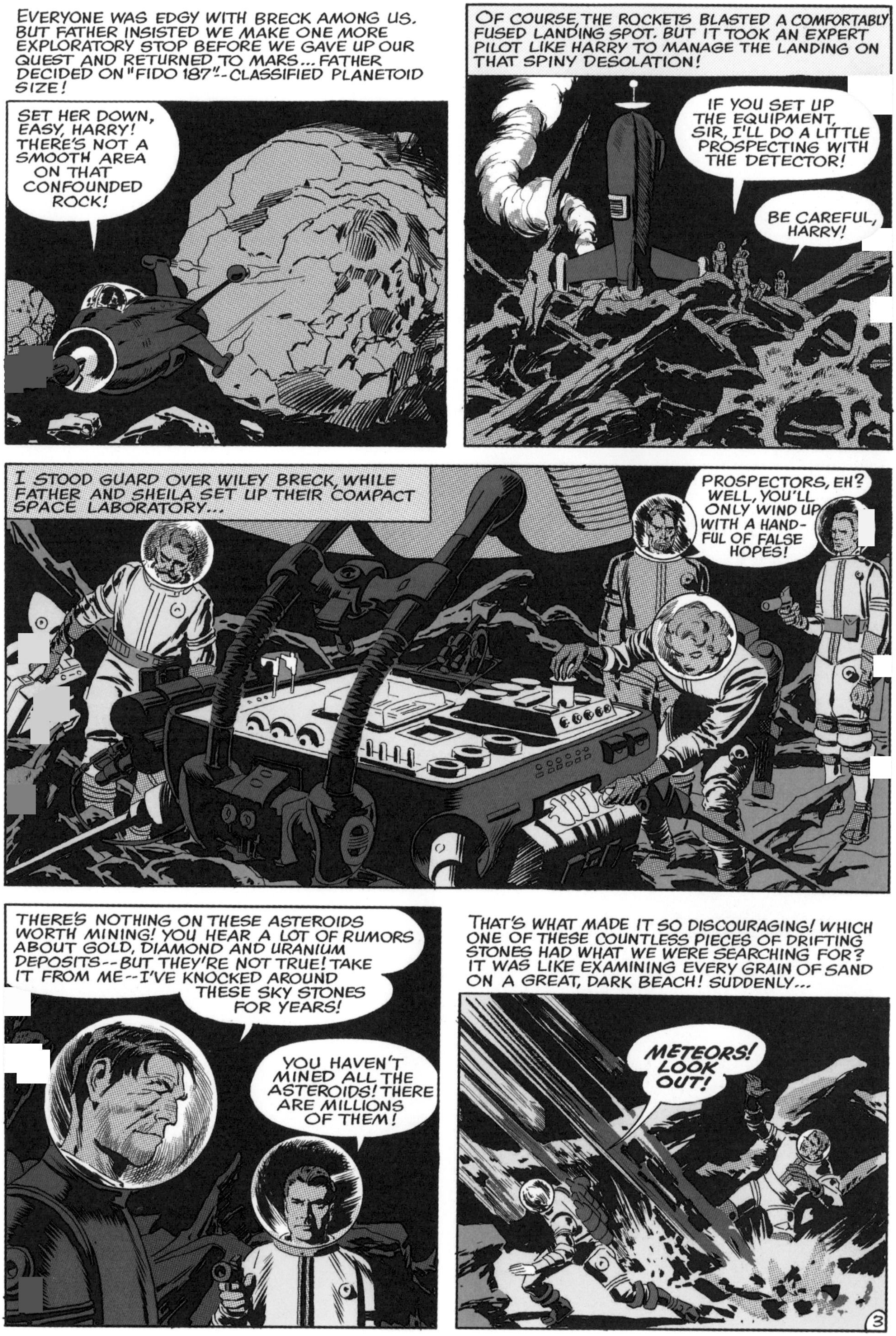
EVERYONE WAS EDGY WITH BRECK AMONG US. BUT FATHER INSISTED WE MAKE ONE MORE EXPLORATORY STOP BEFORE WE GAVE UP OUR QUEST AND RETURNED TO MARS... FATHER DECIDED ON "FIDO 187"--CLASSIFIED PLANETOID SIZE!
SET HER DOWN, EASY, HARRY! THERE'S NOT A SMOOTH AREA ON THAT CONFOUNDED ROCK!
OF COURSE, THE ROCKETS BLASTED A COMFORTABLY FUSED LANDING SPOT. BUT IT TOOK AN EXPERT PILOT LIKE HARRY TO MANAGE THE LANDING ON THAT SPINY DESOLATION!
IF YOU SET UP THE EQUIPMENT, SIR, I'LL DO A LITTLE PROSPECTING WITH THE DETECTOR!
BE CAREFUL, HARRY!
I STOOD GUARD OVER WILEY BRECK, WHILE FATHER AND SHEILA SET UP THEIR COMPACT SPACE LABORATORY...
PROSPECTORS, EH? WELL, YOU'LL ONLY WIND UP WITH A HANDFUL OF FALSE HOPES!
THERE'S NOTHING ON THESE ASTEROIDS WORTH MINING! YOU HEAR A LOT OF RUMORS ABOUT GOLD, DIAMOND AND URANIUM DEPOSITS--BUT THEY'RE NOT TRUE! TAKE IT FROM ME--I'VE KNOCKED AROUND THESE SKY STONES FOR YEARS!
YOU HAVEN'T MINED ALL THE ASTEROIDS! THERE ARE MILLIONS OF THEM!
THAT'S WHAT MADE IT SO DISCOURAGING! WHICH ONE OF THESE COUNTLESS PIECES OF DRIFTING STONES HAD WHAT WE WERE SEARCHING FOR? IT WAS LIKE EXAMINING EVERY GRAIN OF SAND ON A GREAT, DARK BEACH! SUDDENLY...
METEORS! LOOK OUT!
3

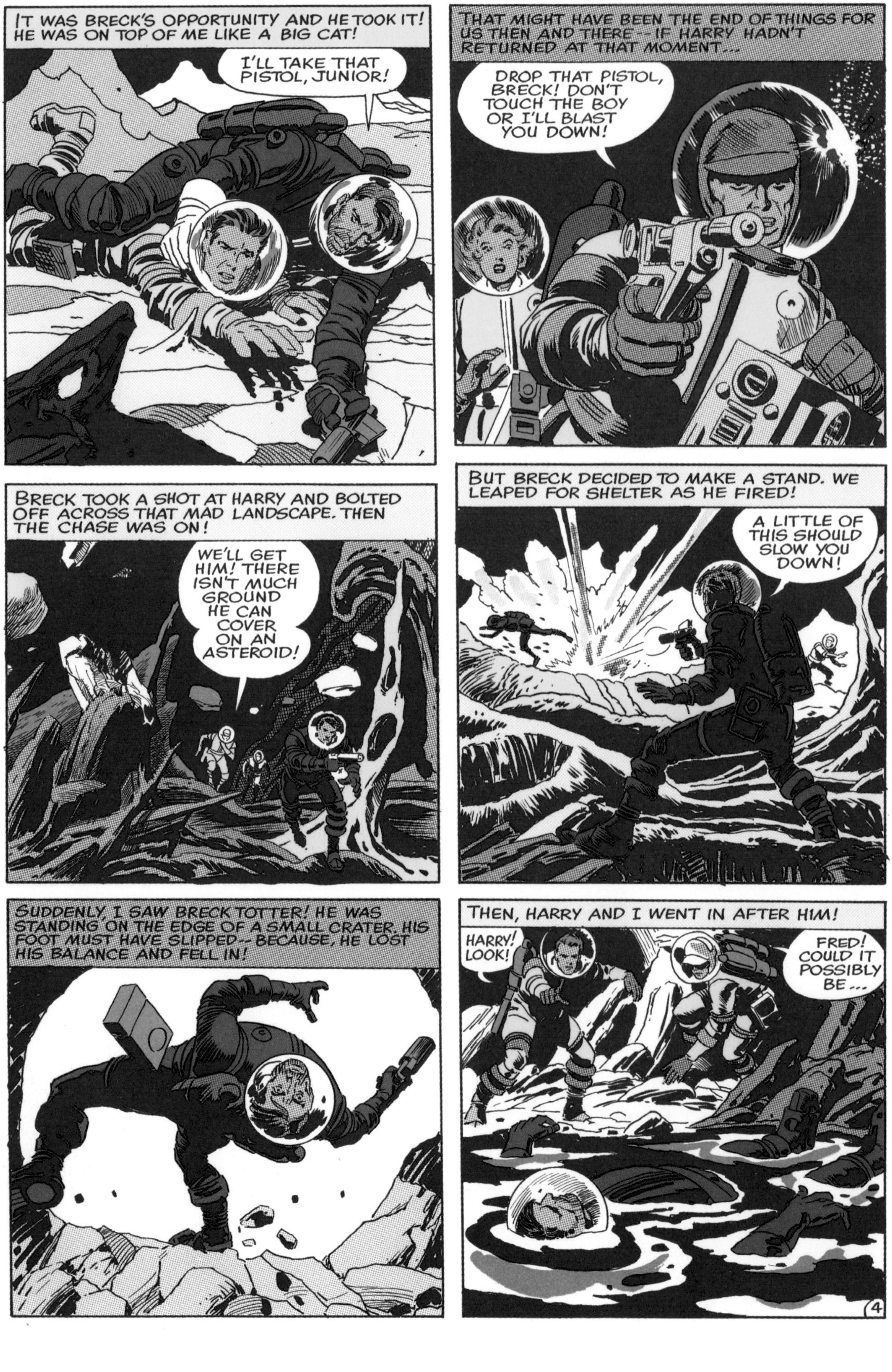
IT WAS BRECK'S OPPORTUNITY AND HE TOOK IT! HE WAS ON TOP OF ME LIKE A BIG CAT!
I'LL TAKE THAT PISTOL, JUNIOR!
THAT MIGHT HAVE BEEN THE END OF THINGS FOR US THEN AND THERE--IF HARRY HADN'T RETURNED AT THAT MOMENT...
DROP THAT PISTOL, BRECK! DON'T TOUCH THE BOY OR I'LL BLAST YOU DOWN!
BRECK TOOK A SHOT AT HARRY AND BOLTED OFF ACROSS THAT MAD LANDSCAPE. THEN THE CHASE WAS ON!
WE'LL GET HIM! THERE ISN'T MUCH GROUND HE CAN COVER ON AN ASTEROID!
BUT BRECK DECIDED TO MAKE A STAND. WE LEAPED FOR SHELTER AS HE FIRED!
A LITTLE OF THIS SHOULD SLOW YOU DOWN!
SUDDENLY I SAW BRECK TOTTER! HE WAS STANDING ON THE EDGE OF A SMALL CRATER. HIS FOOT MUST HAVE SLIPPED-- BECAUSE, HE LOST HIS BALANCE AND FELL IN!
THEN, HARRY AND I WENT IN AFTER HIM!
HARRY! LOOK!
FRED! COULD IT POSSIBLY BE...
4

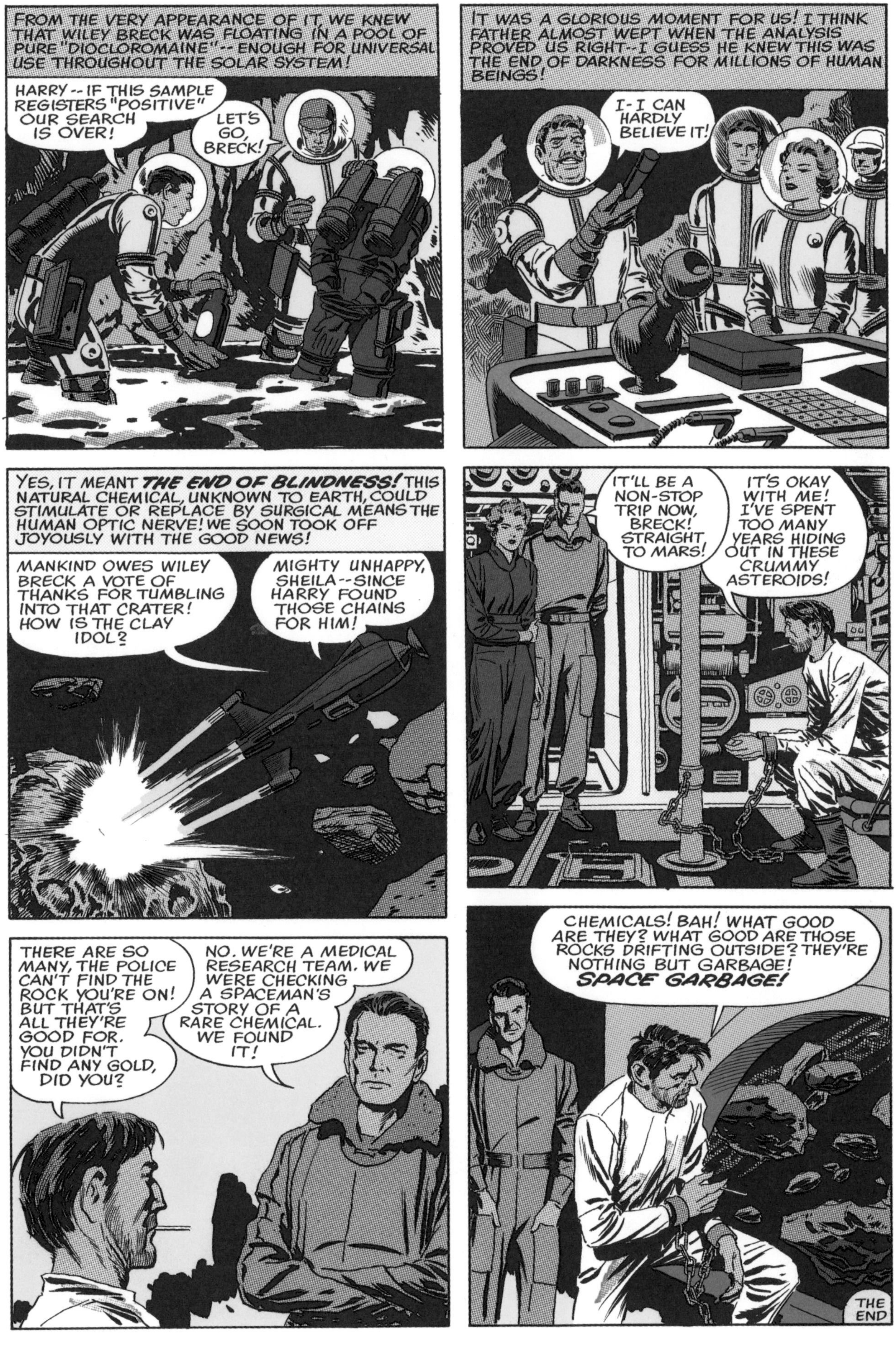
FROM THE VERY APPEARANCE OF IT, WE KNEW THAT WILEY BRECK WAS FLOATING IN A POOL OF PURE "DIOCLOROMAINE"-- ENOUGH FOR UNIVERSAL USE THROUGHOUT THE SOLAR SYSTEM!
HARRY -- IF THIS SAMPLE REGISTERS "POSITIVE" OUR SEARCH IS OVER!
LET'S GO, BRECK!
IT WAS A GLORIOUS MOMENT FOR US! I THINK FATHER ALMOST WEPT WHEN THE ANALYSIS PROVED US RIGHT--I GUESS HE KNEW THIS WAS THE END OF DARKNESS FOR MILLIONS OF HUMAN BEINGS!
I- I CAN HARDLY BELIEVE IT!
YES, IT MEANT THE END OF BLINDNESS! THIS NATURAL CHEMICAL, UNKNOWN TO EARTH, COULD STIMULATE OR REPLACE BY SURGICAL MEANS THE HUMAN OPTIC NERVE! WE SOON TOOK OFF JOYOUSLY WITH THE GOOD NEWS!
MANKIND OWES WILEY BRECK A VOTE OF THANKS FOR TUMBLING INTO THAT CRATER! HOW IS THE CLAY IDOL?
MIGHTY UNHAPPY, SHEILA--SINCE HARRY FOUND THOSE CHAINS FOR HIM!
IT'LL BE A NON-STOP TRIP NOW, BRECK! STRAIGHT TO MARS!
IT'S OKAY WITH ME! I'VE SPENT TOO MANY YEARS HIDING OUT IN THESE CRUMMY ASTEROIDS!
THERE ARE SO MANY, THE POLICE CAN'T FIND THE ROCK YOU'RE ON! BUT THAT'S ALL THEY'RE GOOD FOR. YOU DIDN'T FIND ANY GOLD, DID YOU?
NO. WE'RE A MEDICAL RESEARCH TEAM. WE WERE CHECKING A SPACEMAN'S STORY OF A RARE CHEMICAL. WE FOUND IT!
CHEMICALS! BAH! WHAT GOOD ARE THEY? WHAT GOOD ARE THOSE ROCKS DRIFTING OUTSIDE? THEY'RE NOTHING BUT GARBAGE! SPACE GARBAGE!
THE END

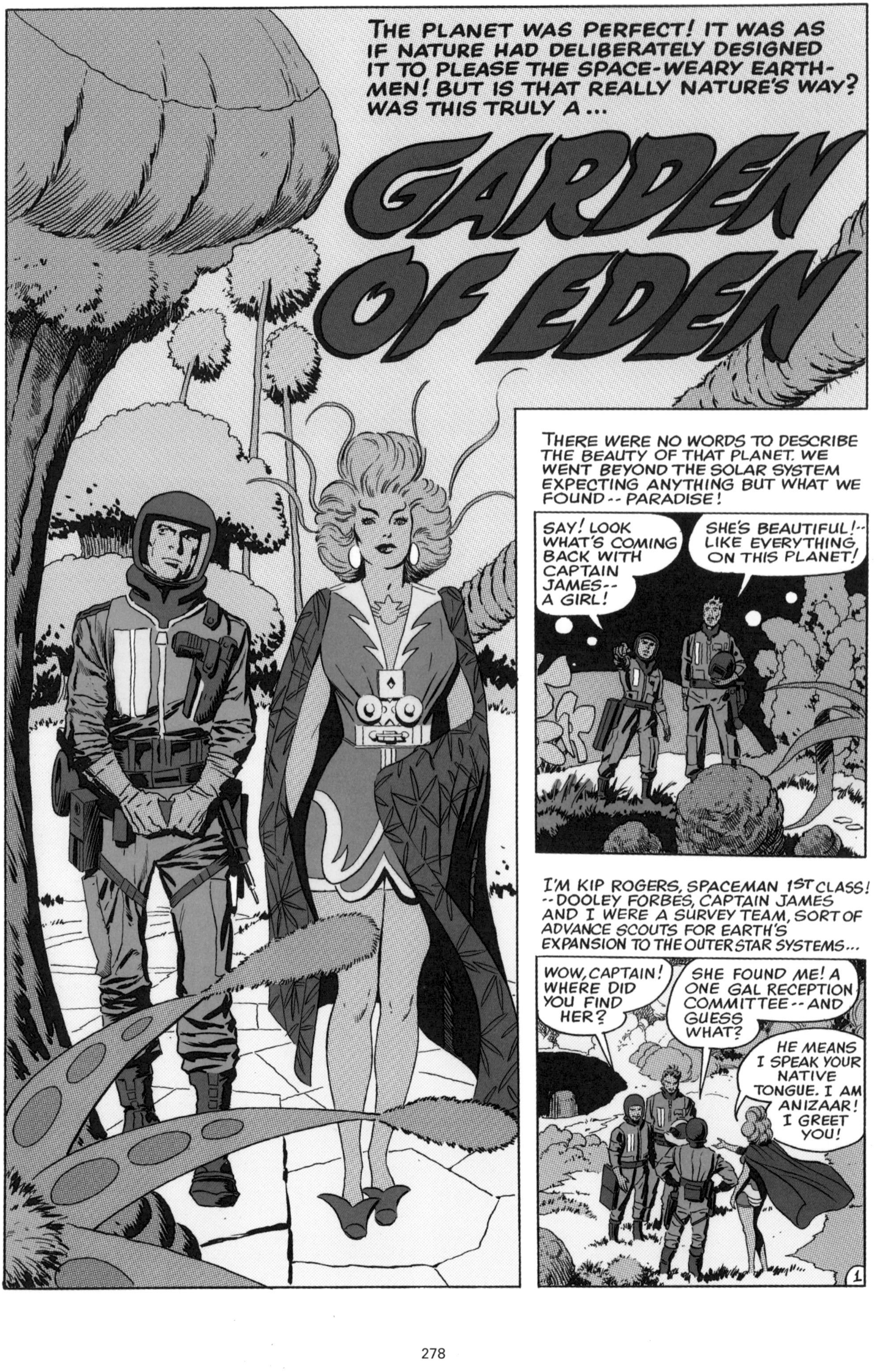
THE PLANET WAS PERFECT! IT WAS AS IF NATURE HAD DELIBERATELY DESIGNED IT TO PLEASE THE SPACE-WEARY EARTH-MEN! BUT IS THAT REALLY NATURE'S WAY? WAS THIS TRULY A ...
GARDEN OF EDEN
THERE WERE NO WORDS TO DESCRIBE THE BEAUTY OF THAT PLANET. WE WENT BEYOND THE SOLAR SYSTEM EXPECTING ANYTHING BUT WHAT WE FOUND -- PARADISE!
SAY! LOOK WHAT'S COMING BACK WITH CAPTAIN JAMES -- A GIRL!
SHE'S BEAUTIFUL! -- LIKE EVERYTHING ON THIS PLANET!
I'M KIP ROGERS, SPACEMAN 1ST CLASS! -- DOOLEY FORBES, CAPTAIN JAMES AND I WERE A SURVEY TEAM, SORT OF ADVANCE SCOUTS FOR EARTH'S EXPANSION TO THE OUTER STAR SYSTEMS...
WOW, CAPTAIN! WHERE DID YOU FIND HER?
SHE FOUND ME! A ONE GAL RECEPTION COMMITTEE -- AND GUESS WHAT?
HE MEANS I SPEAK YOUR NATIVE TONGUE. I AM ANIZAAR! I GREET YOU!
1

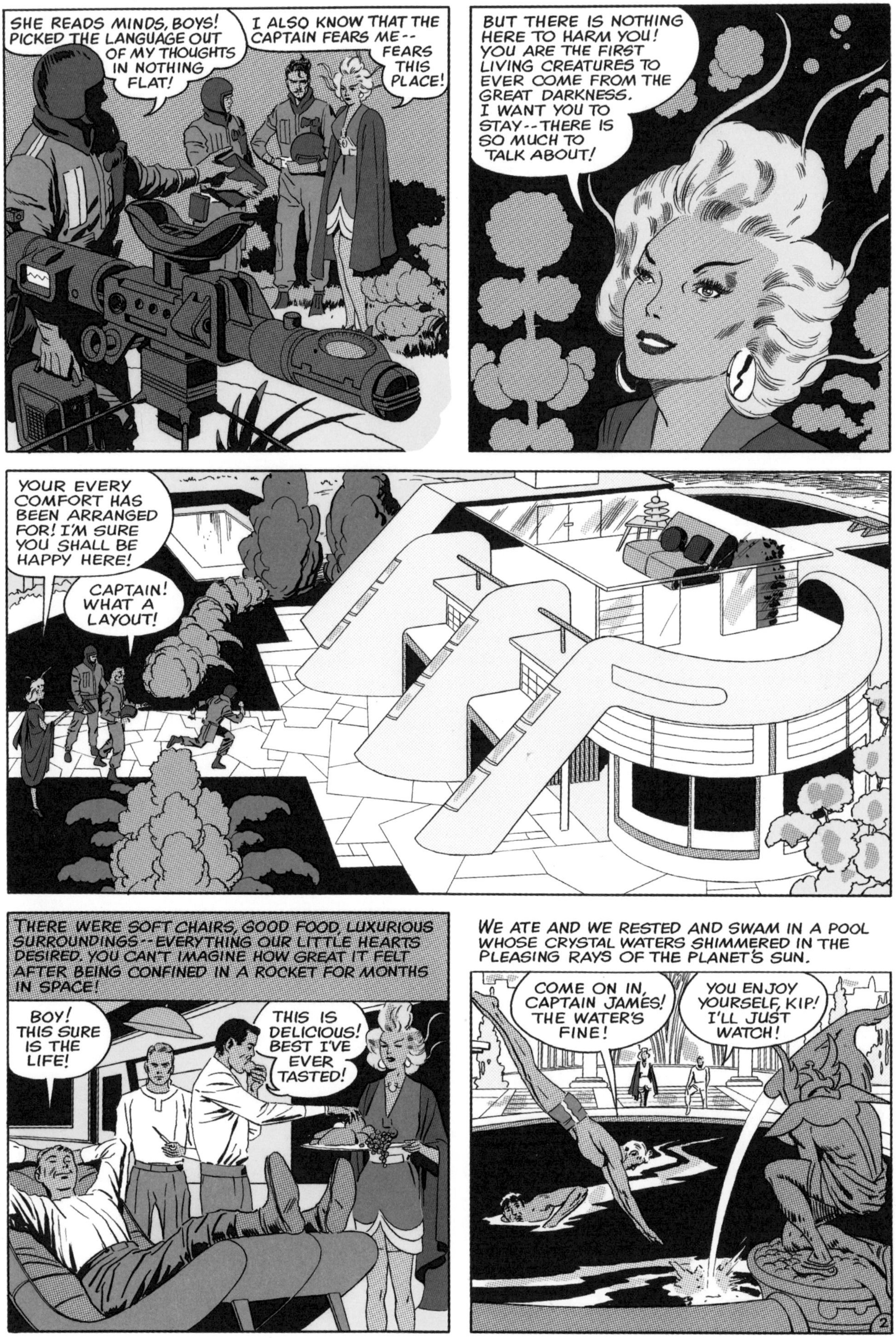
SHE READS MINDS, BOYS! PICKED THE LANGUAGE OUT OF MY THOUGHTS IN NOTHING FLAT!
I ALSO KNOW THAT THE CAPTAIN FEARS ME-- FEARS THIS PLACE!
BUT THERE IS NOTHING HERE TO HARM YOU! YOU ARE THE FIRST LIVING CREATURES TO EVER COME FROM THE GREAT DARKNESS. I WANT YOU TO STAY--THERE IS SO MUCH TO TALK ABOUT!
YOUR EVERY COMFORT HAS BEEN ARRANGED FOR! I'M SURE YOU SHALL BE HAPPY HERE!
CAPTAIN! WHAT A LAYOUT!
THERE WERE SOFT CHAIRS, GOOD FOOD, LUXURIOUS SURROUNDINGS--EVERYTHING OUR LITTLE HEARTS DESIRED. YOU CAN'T IMAGINE HOW GREAT IT FELT AFTER BEING CONFINED IN A ROCKET FOR MONTHS IN SPACE!
BOY! THIS SURE IS THE LIFE!
THIS IS DELICIOUS! BEST I'VE EVER TASTED!
WE ATE AND WE RESTED AND SWAM IN A POOL WHOSE CRYSTAL WATERS SHIMMERED IN THE PLEASING RAYS OF THE PLANET'S SUN.
COME ON IN, CAPTAIN JAMES! THE WATER'S FINE!
YOU ENJOY YOURSELF, KIP! I'LL JUST WATCH!
2

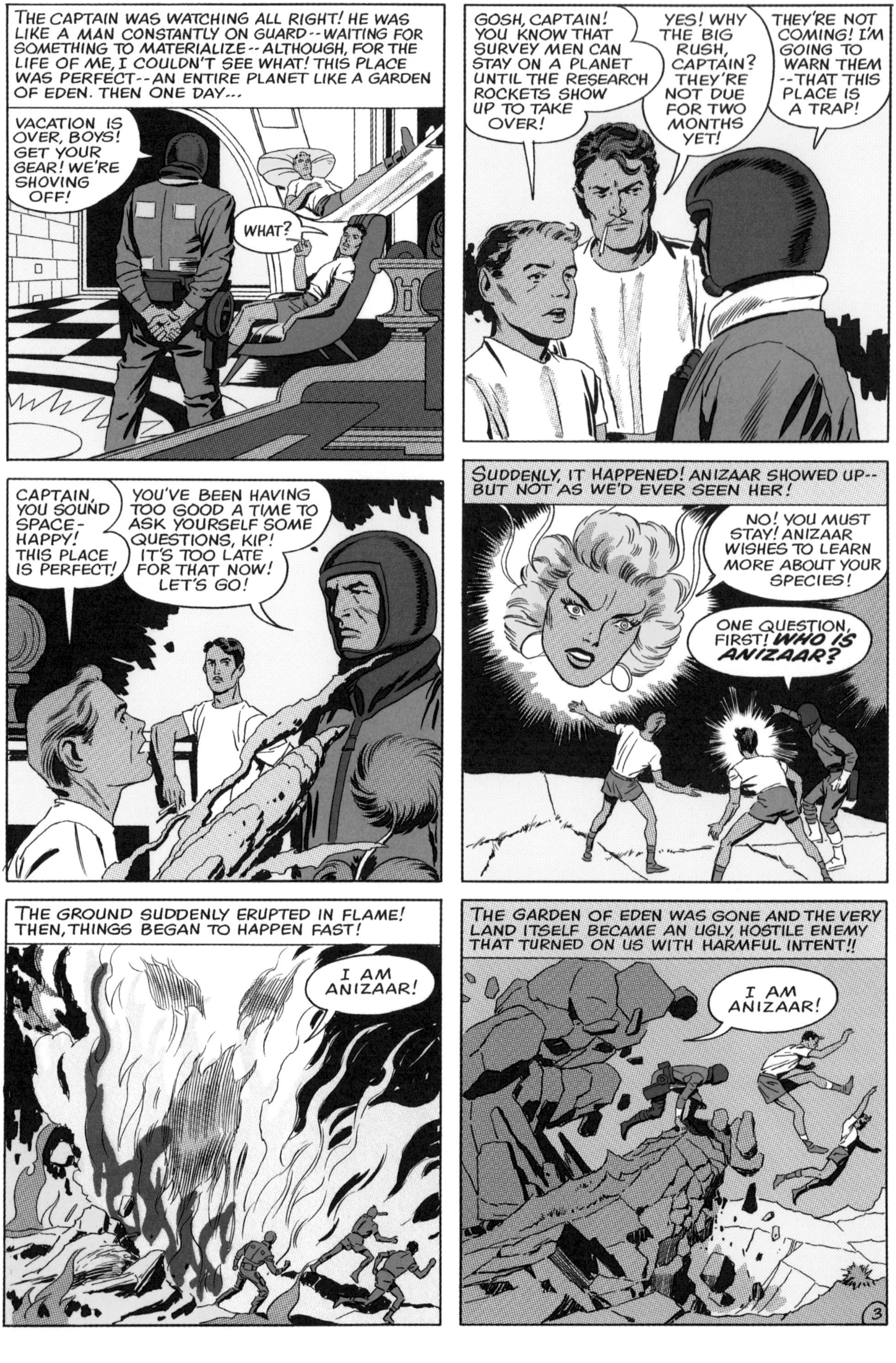

THE CAPTAIN WAS WATCHING ALL RIGHT! HE WAS LIKE A MAN CONSTANTLY ON GUARD--WAITING FOR SOMETHING TO MATERIALIZE--ALTHOUGH, FOR THE LIFE OF ME, I COULDN'T SEE WHAT! THIS PLACE WAS PERFECT--AN ENTIRE PLANET LIKE A GARDEN OF EDEN. THEN ONE DAY...
VACATION IS OVER, BOYS! GET YOUR GEAR! WE'RE SHOVING OFF!
WHAT?
GOSH, CAPTAIN! YOU KNOW THAT SURVEY MEN CAN STAY ON A PLANET UNTIL THE RESEARCH ROCKETS SHOW UP TO TAKE OVER!
YES! WHY THE BIG RUSH, CAPTAIN? THEY'RE NOT DUE FOR TWO MONTHS YET!
THEY'RE NOT COMING! I'M GOING TO WARN THEM--THAT THIS PLACE IS A TRAP!
CAPTAIN, YOU SOUND SPACE-HAPPY! THIS PLACE IS PERFECT!
YOU'VE BEEN HAVING TOO GOOD A TIME TO ASK YOURSELF SOME QUESTIONS, KIP! IT'S TOO LATE FOR THAT NOW! LET'S GO!
SUDDENLY, IT HAPPENED! ANIZAAR SHOWED UP--BUT NOT AS WE'D EVER SEEN HER!
NO! YOU MUST STAY! ANIZAAR WISHES TO LEARN MORE ABOUT YOUR SPECIES!
ONE QUESTION, FIRST! WHO IS ANIZAAR?
THE GROUND SUDDENLY ERUPTED IN FLAME! THEN, THINGS BEGAN TO HAPPEN FAST!
I AM ANIZAAR!
THE GARDEN OF EDEN WAS GONE AND THE VERY LAND ITSELF BECAME AN UGLY, HOSTILE ENEMY THAT TURNED ON US WITH HARMFUL INTENT!!
I AM ANIZAAR!
3

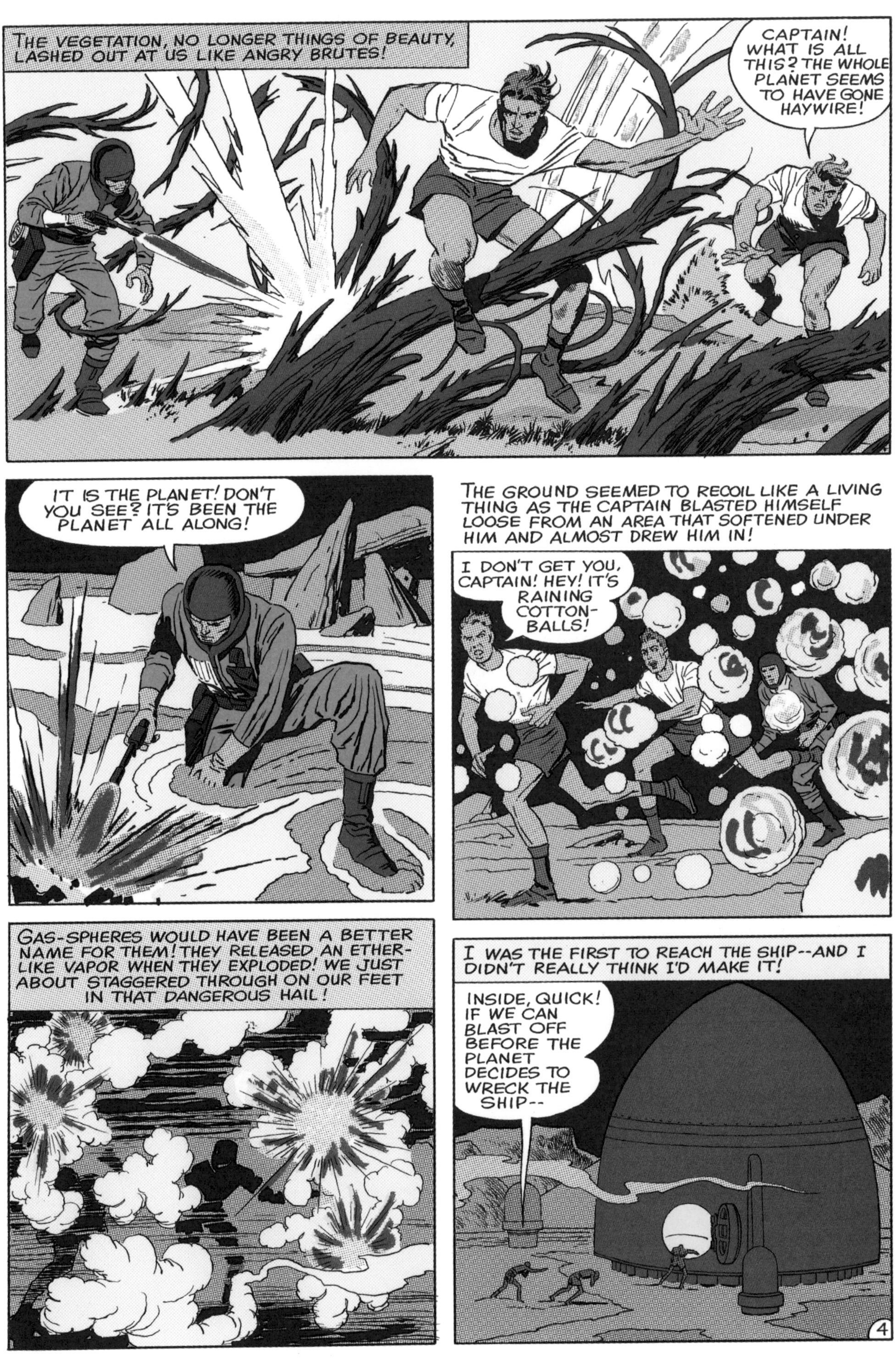
THE VEGETATION, NO LONGER THINGS OF BEAUTY, LASHED OUT AT US LIKE ANGRY BRUTES!
CAPTAIN! WHAT IS ALL THIS? THE WHOLE PLANET SEEMS TO HAVE GONE HAYWIRE!
IT IS THE PLANET! DON'T YOU SEE? IT'S BEEN THE PLANET ALL ALONG!
THE GROUND SEEMED TO RECOIL LIKE A LIVING THING AS THE CAPTAIN BLASTED HIMSELF LOOSE FROM AN AREA THAT SOFTENED UNDER HIM AND ALMOST DREW HIM IN!
I DON'T GET YOU, CAPTAIN! HEY! IT'S RAINING COTTON-BALLS!
GAS-SPHERES WOULD HAVE BEEN A BETTER NAME FOR THEM! THEY RELEASED AN ETHER-LIKE VAPOR WHEN THEY EXPLODED! WE JUST ABOUT STAGGERED THROUGH ON OUR FEET IN THAT DANGEROUS HAIL!
I WAS THE FIRST TO REACH THE SHIP--AND I DIDN'T REALLY THINK I'D MAKE IT!
INSIDE, QUICK! IF WE CAN BLAST OFF BEFORE THE PLANET DECIDES TO WRECK THE SHIP--
4

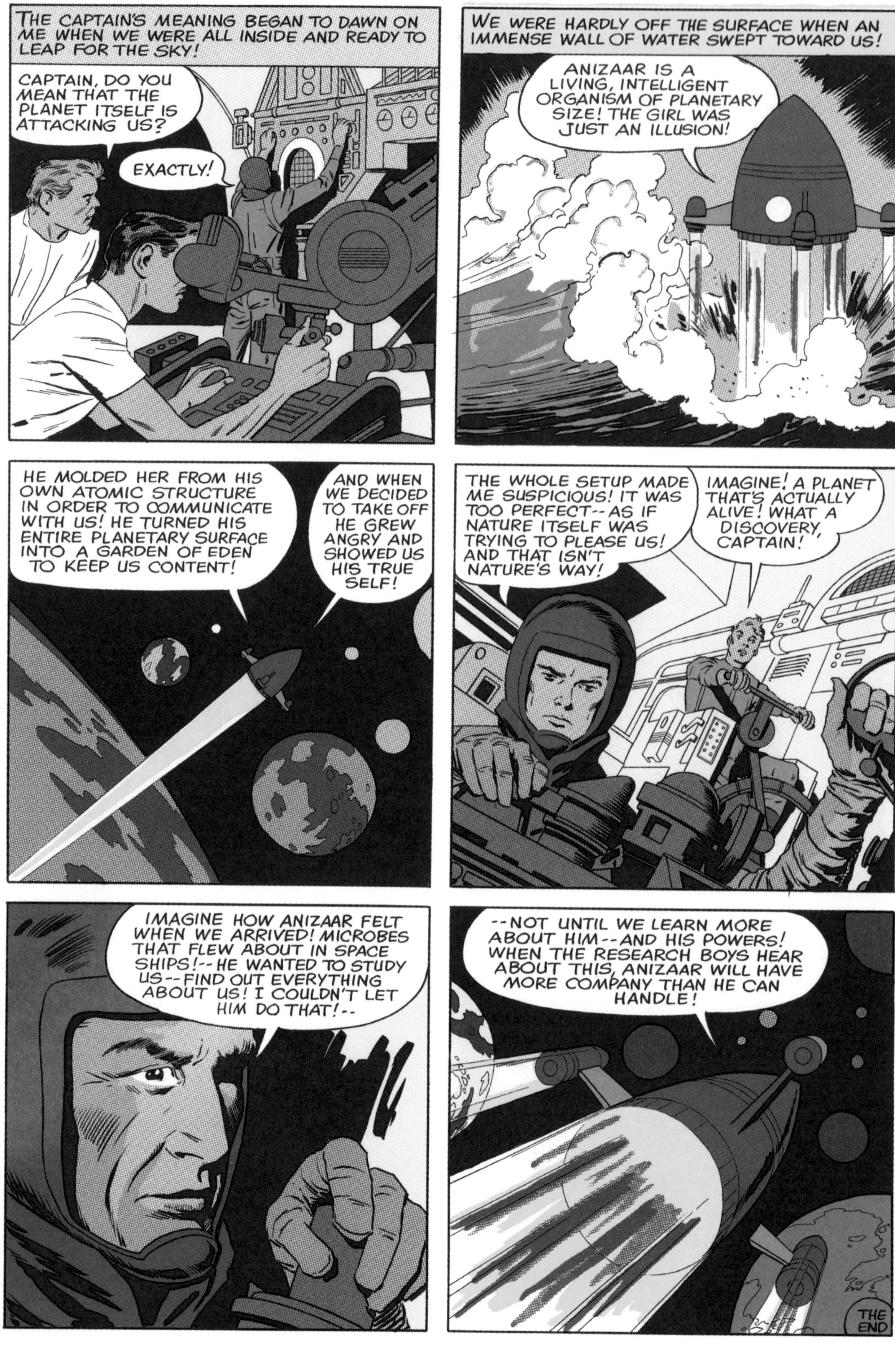
THE CAPTAIN'S MEANING BEGAN TO DAWN ON ME WHEN WE WERE ALL INSIDE AND READY TO LEAP FOR THE SKY!
CAPTAIN, DO YOU MEAN THAT THE PLANET ITSELF IS ATTACKING US?
EXACTLY!
WE WERE HARDLY OFF THE SURFACE WHEN AN IMMENSE WALL OF WATER SWEPT TOWARD US!
ANIZAAR IS A LIVING, INTELLIGENT ORGANISM OF PLANETARY SIZE! THE GIRL WAS JUST AN ILLUSION!
HE MOLDED HER FROM HIS OWN ATOMIC STRUCTURE IN ORDER TO COMMUNICATE WITH US! HE TURNED HIS ENTIRE PLANETARY SURFACE INTO A GARDEN OF EDEN TO KEEP US CONTENT!
AND WHEN WE DECIDED TO TAKE OFF HE GREW ANGRY AND SHOWED US HIS TRUE SELF!
THE WHOLE SETUP MADE ME SUSPICIOUS! IT WAS TOO PERFECT--AS IF NATURE ITSELF WAS TRYING TO PLEASE US! AND THAT ISN'T NATURE'S WAY!
IMAGINE! A PLANET THAT'S ACTUALLY ALIVE! WHAT A DISCOVERY, CAPTAIN!
IMAGINE HOW ANIZAAR FELT WHEN WE ARRIVED! MICROBES THAT FLEW ABOUT IN SPACE SHIPS!--HE WANTED TO STUDY US--FIND OUT EVERYTHING ABOUT US! I COULDN'T LET HIM DO THAT!--
--NOT UNTIL WE LEARN MORE ABOUT HIM--AND HIS POWERS! WHEN THE RESEARCH BOYS HEAR ABOUT THIS, ANIZAAR WILL HAVE MORE COMPANY THAN HE CAN HANDLE!
THE END

THE 1960s

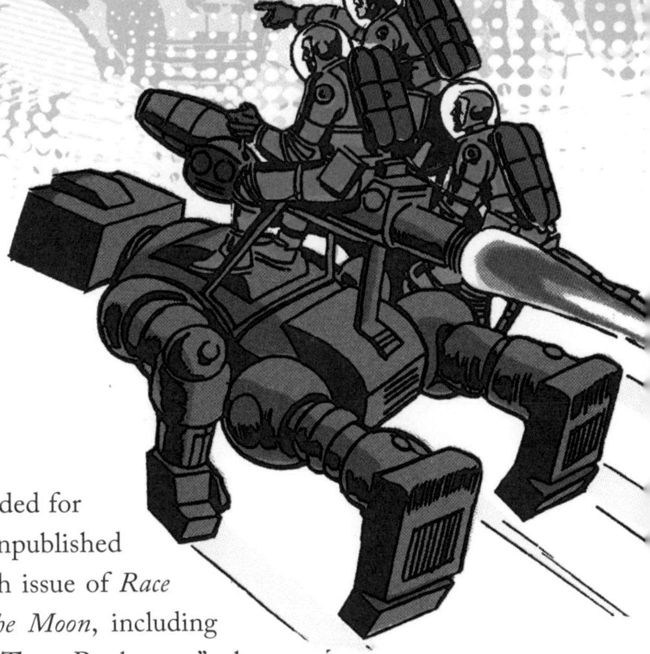

The Soviets were the first to send a man into outer space in 1961, but President John F. Kennedy proclaimed that America would send a man to the moon by the end of the decade, and that pledge was fulfilled with the first lunar landing in 1969. Meanwhile, science fiction became a more prominent part of popular culture than ever, with highlights including the premiere of Gene Roddenberry's original *Star Trek* television series in 1966, followed two years later by Stanley Kubrick's epic motion picture *2001: A Space Odyssey*, written by Arthur C. Clarke.

Joe Simon and Jack Kirby had parted ways as a full-time creative team late in the 1950s. Following the split, Kirby did a stint at DC Comics, co-created the newspaper strip *Sky Masters of the Space Force*, then teamed up with Stan Lee–first on science fiction adventures in titles like *Strange Tales*–and later co-creating many of the classic Marvel superheroes of the 1960s, filling stories with amazing concepts and characters.

Although he was working extensively outside of comics, Joe Simon put together a new group of anthology titles for Harvey Comics. One was the three-issue series *Alarming Adventures*, published from 1962 into 1963, the first of which included "Hermit"–written by newcomer Archie Goodwin–with art by Reed Crandall and Al Williamson. Goodwin went on to become a comics industry legend, and again teamed up with Williamson on the classic *Star Wars* newspaper comic strip.

The one-shot *Blast-Off*, released in 1965, was a star-studded affair made up of stories originally intended for the unpublished fourth issue of *Race for the Moon*, including two "Three Rocketeers" tales with art by Kirby and Williamson. It also featured "The Space Court," penciled by Williamson and inked by Torres and Roy Krenkel, as well as "The Little Earth," drawn by Crandall and inked by Williamson.

Then there was another three-issue series, *Unearthly Spectaculars*, that ran from 1965 to 1967. Sword and sorcery enjoyed a 1960s resurgence thanks to the paperback collections of Robert E. Howard's *Conan* tales, and *Unearthly Spectaculars* #2 introduced Clawfang the Barbarian, scripted by EC Comics luminary Wally Wood and illustrated by Williamson. Wood wrote and illustrated another story in that same issue, "The Coming of Earthman."

Yet not every Simon and Kirby project saw print. This volume includes examples of two science fiction story concepts Simon developed over the years, but went unpublished. The *Tiger 21* comic strip he envisioned as a collaboration with Jack Kirby, yet only a few penciled pages remain (although historian Harry Mendryk has noted that the *Fighting American* story "Homecoming: Year 3000" began life as a *Tiger 21* adventure).

Much later Simon developed *Jove U.N.Born*, which had strong political overtones and preliminary art by Jerry Grandenetti.

Peter Sanderson

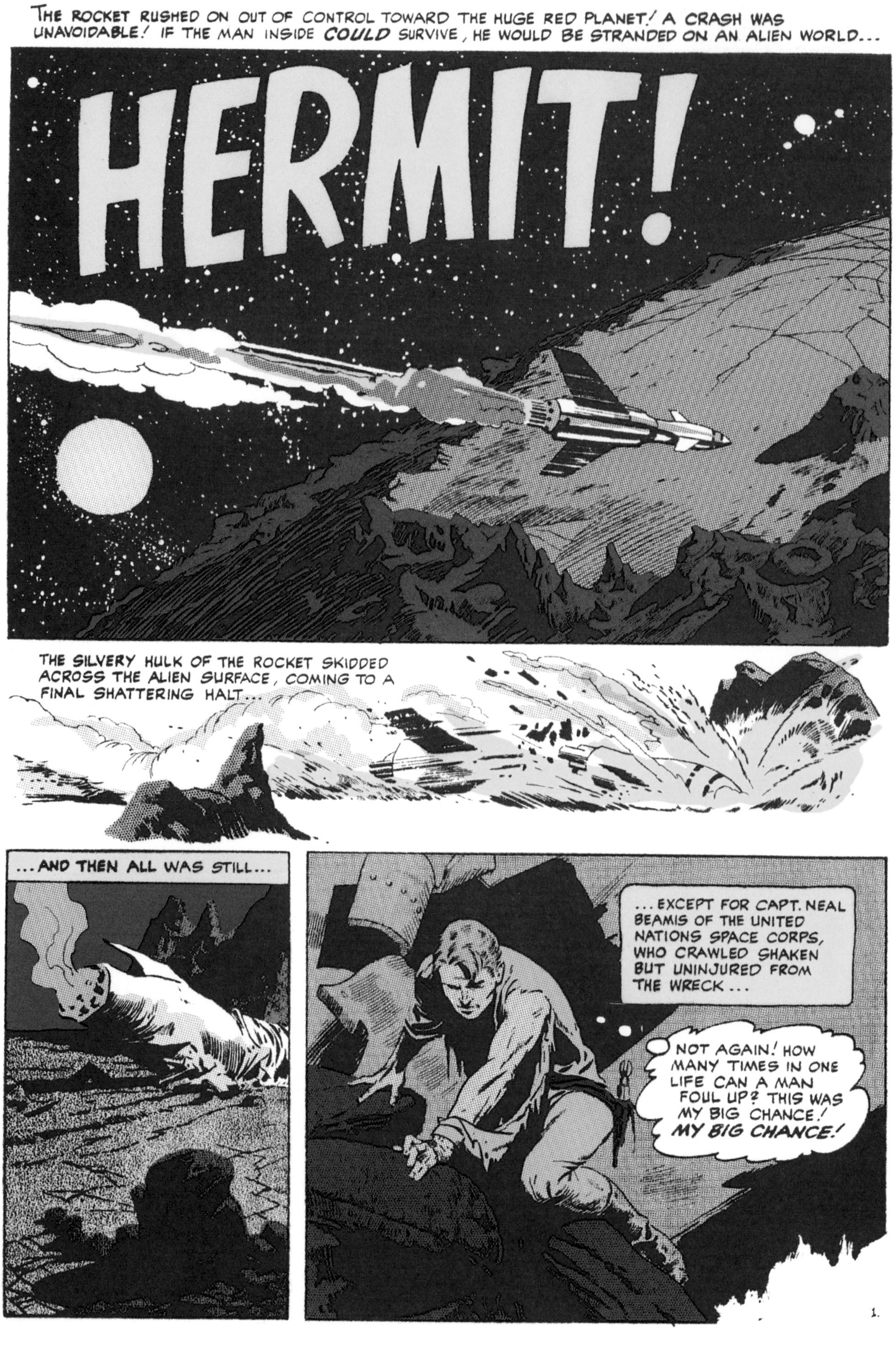
THE ROCKET RUSHED ON OUT OF CONTROL TOWARD THE HUGE RED PLANET! A CRASH WAS UNAVOIDABLE! IF THE MAN INSIDE COULD SURVIVE, HE WOULD BE STRANDED ON AN ALIEN WORLD...
HERMIT!
THE SILVERY HULK OF THE ROCKET SKIDDED ACROSS THE ALIEN SURFACE, COMING TO A FINAL SHATTERING HALT...
...AND THEN ALL WAS STILL...
...EXCEPT FOR CAPT. NEAL BEAMIS OF THE UNITED NATIONS SPACE CORPS, WHO CRAWLED SHAKEN BUT UNINJURED FROM THE WRECK...
NOT AGAIN! HOW MANY TIMES IN ONE LIFE CAN A MAN FOUL UP? THIS WAS MY BIG CHANCE! MY BIG CHANCE!
1.

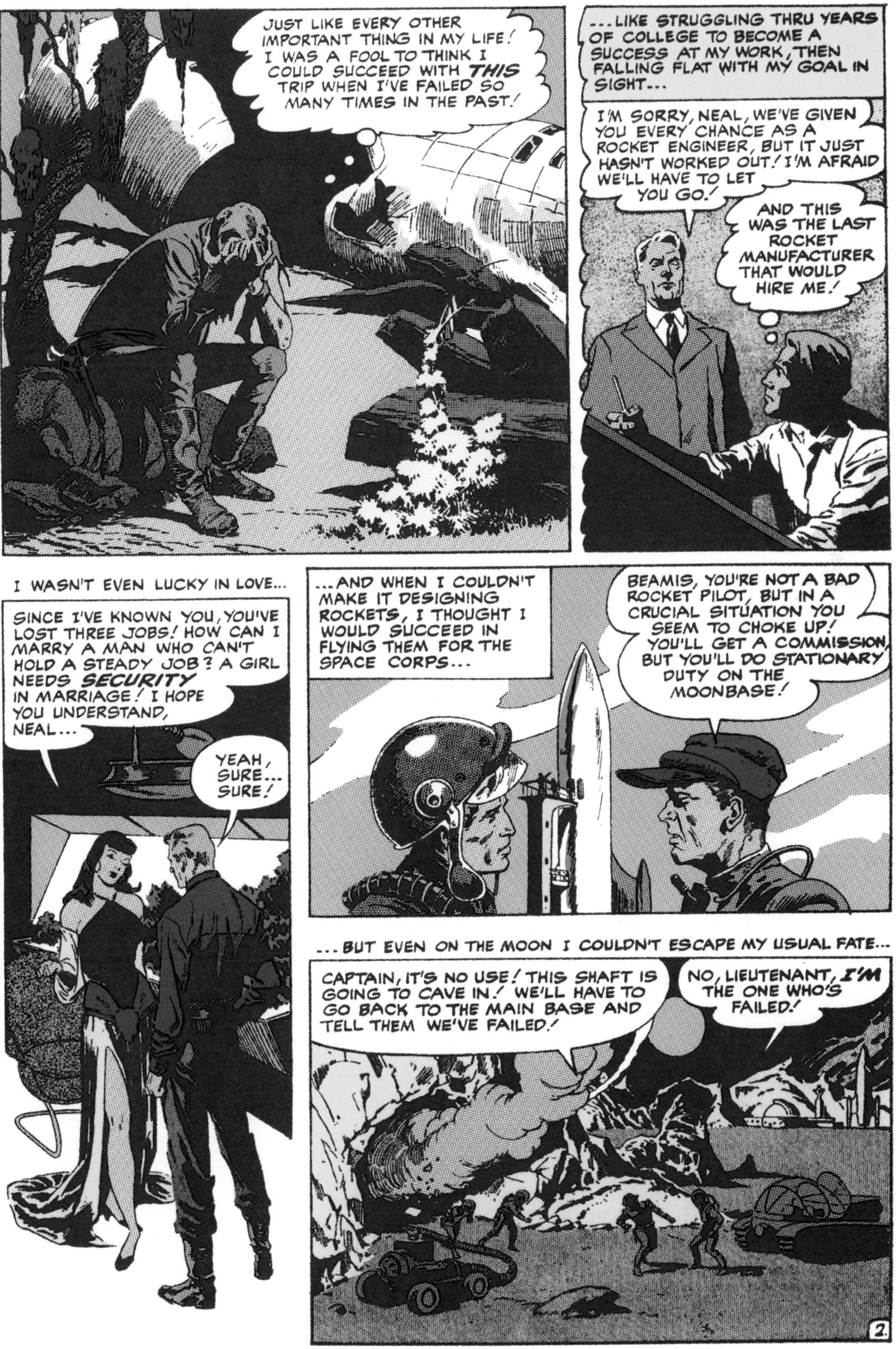
JUST LIKE EVERY OTHER IMPORTANT THING IN MY LIFE! I WAS A FOOL TO THINK I COULD SUCCEED WITH THIS TRIP WHEN I'VE FAILED SO MANY TIMES IN THE PAST!
...LIKE STRUGGLING THRU YEARS OF COLLEGE TO BECOME A SUCCESS AT MY WORK, THEN FALLING FLAT WITH MY GOAL IN SIGHT...
I'M SORRY, NEAL, WE'VE GIVEN YOU EVERY CHANCE AS A ROCKET ENGINEER, BUT IT JUST HASN'T WORKED OUT! I'M AFRAID WE'LL HAVE TO LET YOU GO!
AND THIS WAS THE LAST ROCKET MANUFACTURER THAT WOULD HIRE ME!
I WASN'T EVEN LUCKY IN LOVE...
SINCE I'VE KNOWN YOU, YOU'VE LOST THREE JOBS! HOW CAN I MARRY A MAN WHO CAN'T HOLD A STEADY JOB? A GIRL NEEDS SECURITY IN MARRIAGE! I HOPE YOU UNDERSTAND, NEAL...
YEAH, SURE... SURE!
...AND WHEN I COULDN'T MAKE IT DESIGNING ROCKETS, I THOUGHT I WOULD SUCCEED IN FLYING THEM FOR THE SPACE CORPS...
BEAMIS, YOU'RE NOT A BAD ROCKET PILOT, BUT IN A CRUCIAL SITUATION YOU SEEM TO CHOKE UP! YOU'LL GET A COMMISSION, BUT YOU'LL DO STATIONARY DUTY ON THE MOONBASE!
...BUT EVEN ON THE MOON I COULDN'T ESCAPE MY USUAL FATE...
CAPTAIN, IT'S NO USE! THIS SHAFT IS GOING TO CAVE IN! WE'LL HAVE TO GO BACK TO THE MAIN BASE AND TELL THEM WE'VE FAILED!
NO, LIEUTENANT, I'M THE ONE WHO'S FAILED!
2

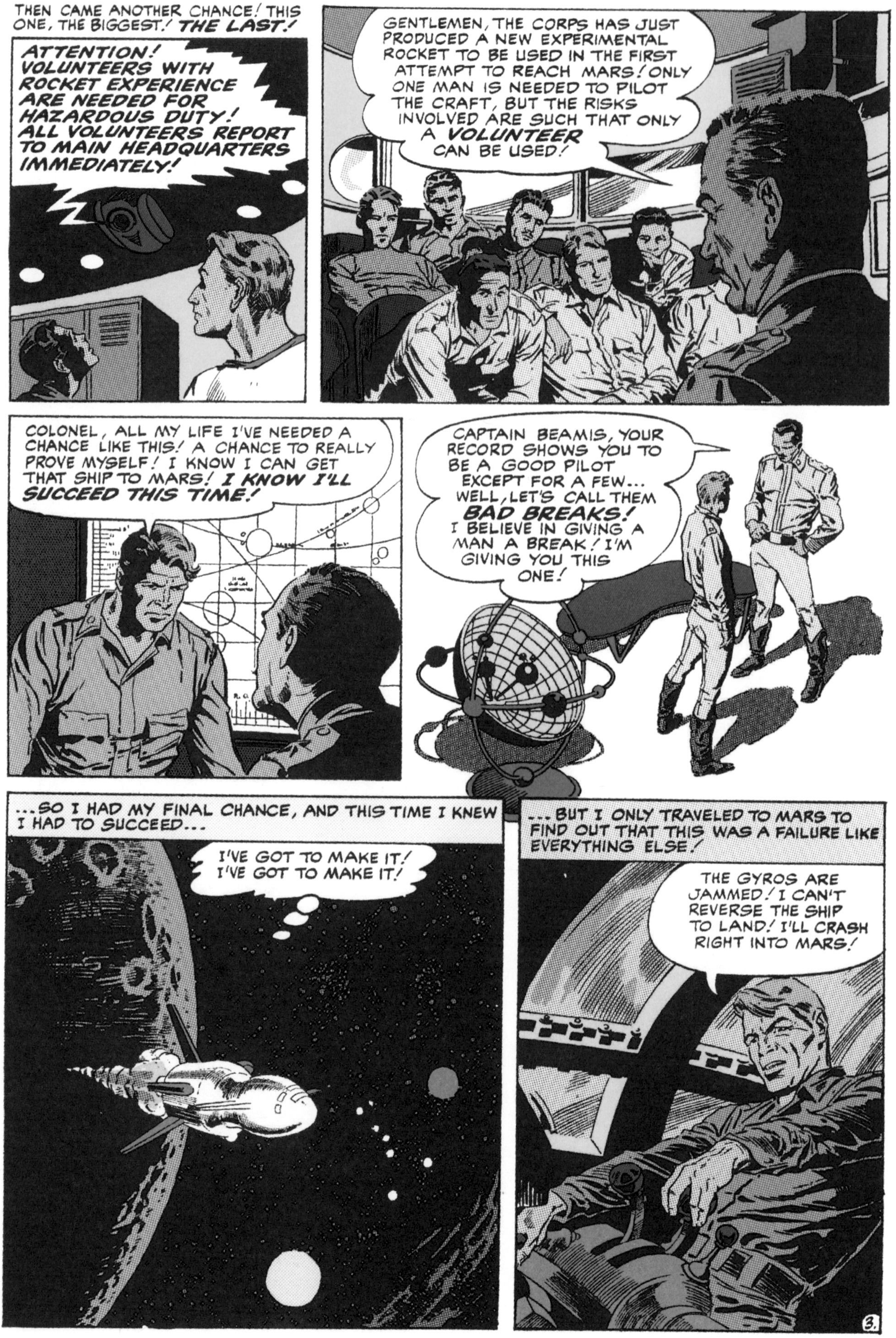
THEN CAME ANOTHER CHANCE! THIS ONE, THE BIGGEST! THE LAST!
ATTENTION! VOLUNTEERS WITH ROCKET EXPERIENCE ARE NEEDED FOR HAZARDOUS DUTY! ALL VOLUNTEERS REPORT TO MAIN HEADQUARTERS IMMEDIATELY!
GENTLEMEN, THE CORPS HAS JUST PRODUCED A NEW EXPERIMENTAL ROCKET TO BE USED IN THE FIRST ATTEMPT TO REACH MARS! ONLY ONE MAN IS NEEDED TO PILOT THE CRAFT, BUT THE RISKS INVOLVED ARE SUCH THAT ONLY A VOLUNTEER CAN BE USED!
COLONEL, ALL MY LIFE I'VE NEEDED A CHANCE LIKE THIS! A CHANCE TO REALLY PROVE MYSELF! I KNOW I CAN GET THAT SHIP TO MARS! I KNOW I'LL SUCCEED THIS TIME!
CAPTAIN BEAMIS, YOUR RECORD SHOWS YOU TO BE A GOOD PILOT EXCEPT FOR A FEW... WELL, LET'S CALL THEM BAD BREAKS! I BELIEVE IN GIVING A MAN A BREAK! I'M GIVING YOU THIS ONE!
...SO I HAD MY FINAL CHANCE, AND THIS TIME I KNEW I HAD TO SUCCEED...
I'VE GOT TO MAKE IT! I'VE GOT TO MAKE IT!
...BUT I ONLY TRAVELED TO MARS TO FIND OUT THAT THIS WAS A FAILURE LIKE EVERYTHING ELSE!
THE GYROS ARE JAMMED! I CAN'T REVERSE THE SHIP TO LAND! I'LL CRASH RIGHT INTO MARS!
3.

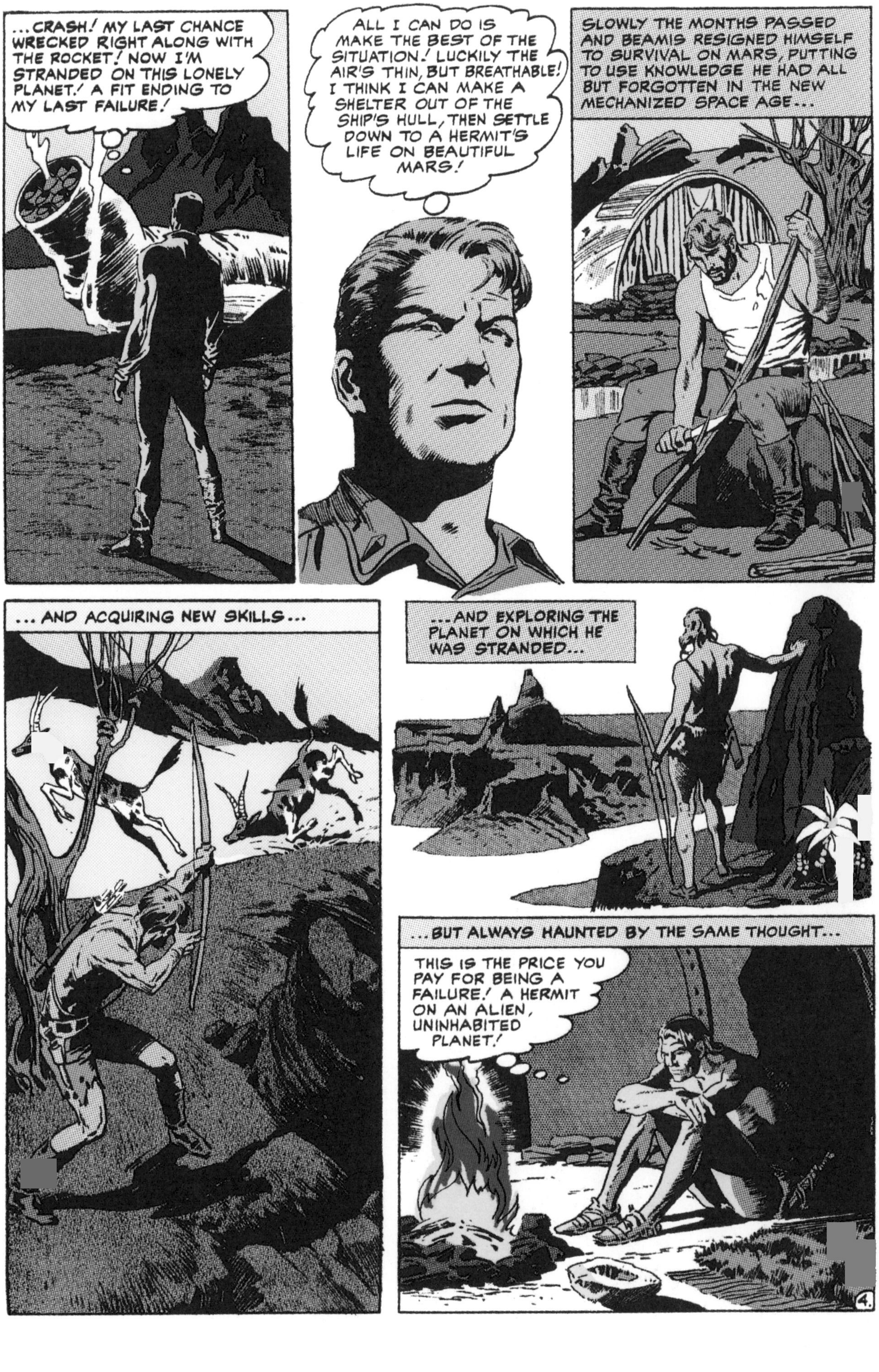
...CRASH! MY LAST CHANCE WRECKED RIGHT ALONG WITH THE ROCKET! NOW I'M STRANDED ON THIS LONELY PLANET! A FIT ENDING TO MY LAST FAILURE!
ALL I CAN DO IS MAKE THE BEST OF THE SITUATION! LUCKILY THE AIR'S THIN, BUT BREATHABLE! I THINK I CAN MAKE A SHELTER OUT OF THE SHIP'S HULL, THEN SETTLE DOWN TO A HERMIT'S LIFE ON BEAUTIFUL MARS!
SLOWLY THE MONTHS PASSED AND BEAMIS RESIGNED HIMSELF TO SURVIVAL ON MARS, PUTTING TO USE KNOWLEDGE HE HAD ALL BUT FORGOTTEN IN THE NEW MECHANIZED SPACE AGE...
...AND ACQUIRING NEW SKILLS...
...AND EXPLORING THE PLANET ON WHICH HE WAS STRANDED...
...BUT ALWAYS HAUNTED BY THE SAME THOUGHT...
THIS IS THE PRICE YOU PAY FOR BEING A FAILURE! A HERMIT ON AN ALIEN, UNINHABITED PLANET!
4.

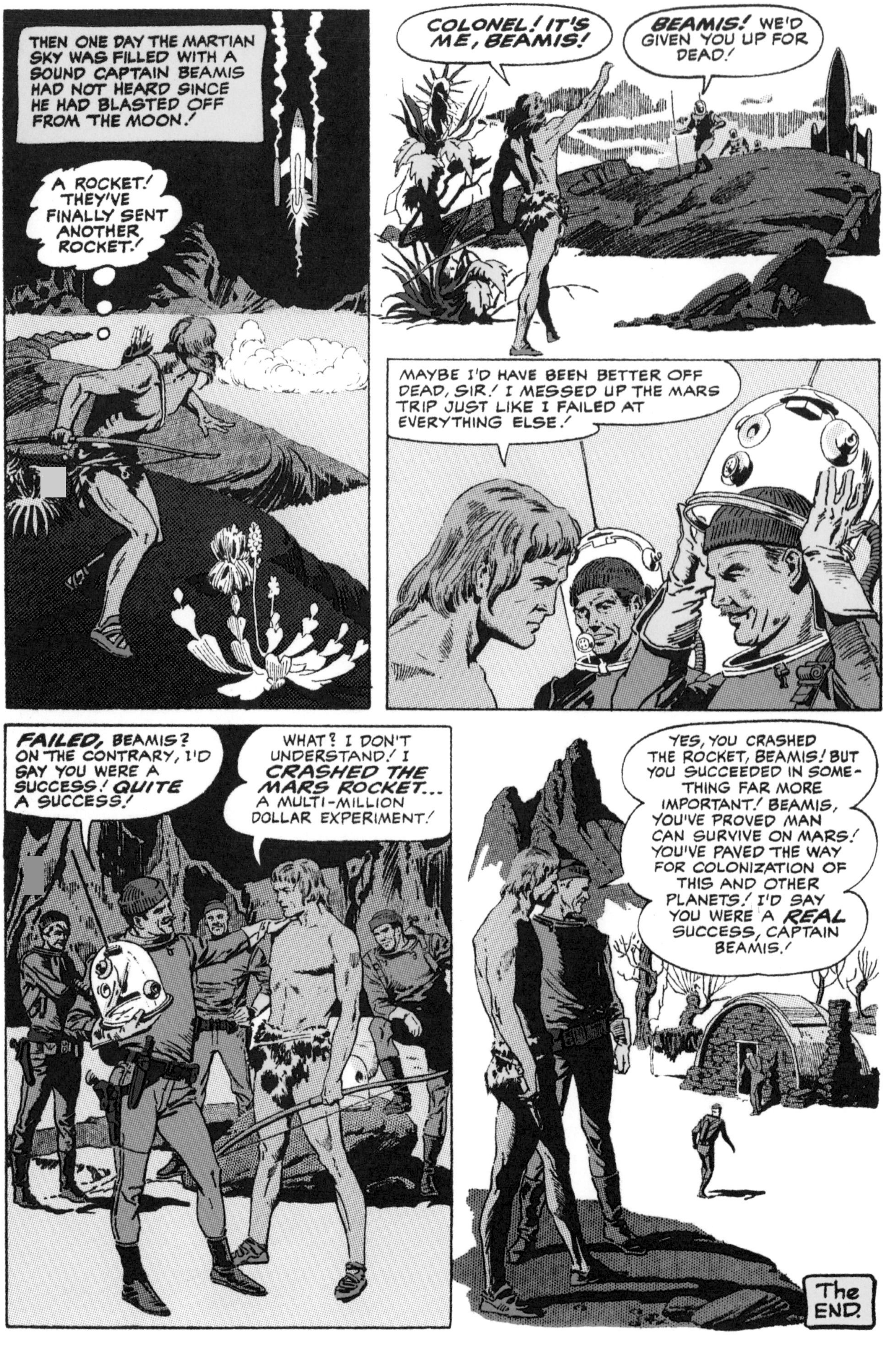
THEN ONE DAY THE MARTIAN SKY WAS FILLED WITH A SOUND CAPTAIN BEAMIS HAD NOT HEARD SINCE HE HAD BLASTED OFF FROM THE MOON!
A ROCKET! THEY'VE FINALLY SENT ANOTHER ROCKET!
COLONEL! IT'S ME, BEAMIS!
BEAMIS! WE'D GIVEN YOU UP FOR DEAD!
MAYBE I'D HAVE BEEN BETTER OFF DEAD, SIR! I MESSED UP THE MARS TRIP JUST LIKE I FAILED AT EVERYTHING ELSE!
FAILED, BEAMIS? ON THE CONTRARY, I'D SAY YOU WERE A SUCCESS! QUITE A SUCCESS!
WHAT? I DON'T UNDERSTAND! I CRASHED THE MARS ROCKET... A MULTI-MILLION DOLLAR EXPERIMENT!
YES, YOU CRASHED THE ROCKET, BEAMIS! BUT YOU SUCCEEDED IN SOME-THING FAR MORE IMPORTANT! BEAMIS, YOU'VE PROVED MAN CAN SURVIVE ON MARS! YOU'VE PAVED THE WAY FOR COLONIZATION OF THIS AND OTHER PLANETS! I'D SAY YOU WERE A REAL SUCCESS, CAPTAIN BEAMIS!
The END.

AS A FLEDGLING OCEANOLOGIST I MADE MY FIRST PROFESSIONAL DIVE! AND IT WAS THEN THAT BIZARRE CITIZENS OF THE DEEP ATTACKED! THERE WAS NO ESCAPE! I WAS BEYOND ALL HELP-- I WAS...

TRAPPED IN THE HUMAN AQUARIUM

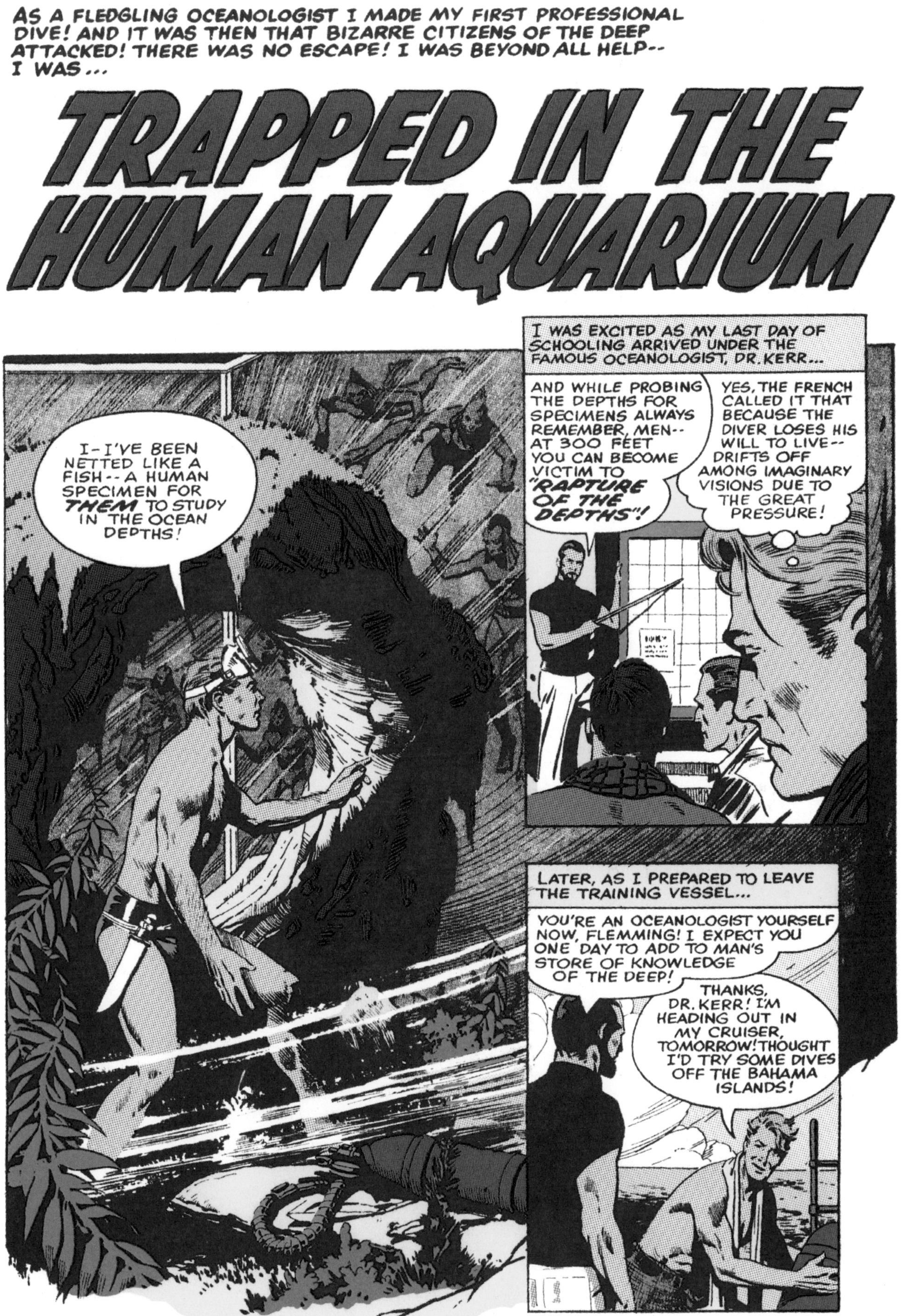
I-I'VE BEEN NETTED LIKE A FISH--A HUMAN SPECIMEN FOR THEM TO STUDY IN THE OCEAN DEPTHS!
I WAS EXCITED AS MY LAST DAY OF SCHOOLING ARRIVED UNDER THE FAMOUS OCEANOLOGIST, DR. KERR...
AND WHILE PROBING THE DEPTHS FOR SPECIMENS ALWAYS REMEMBER, MEN-- AT 300 FEET YOU CAN BECOME VICTIM TO "RAPTURE OF THE DEPTHS"!
YES, THE FRENCH CALLED IT THAT BECAUSE THE DIVER LOSES HIS WILL TO LIVE-- DRIFTS OFF AMONG IMAGINARY VISIONS DUE TO THE GREAT PRESSURE!
LATER, AS I PREPARED TO LEAVE THE TRAINING VESSEL...
YOU'RE AN OCEANOLOGIST YOURSELF NOW, FLEMMING! I EXPECT YOU ONE DAY TO ADD TO MAN'S STORE OF KNOWLEDGE OF THE DEEP!
THANKS, DR. KERR! I'M HEADING OUT IN MY CRUISER, TOMORROW! THOUGHT I'D TRY SOME DIVES OFF THE BAHAMA ISLANDS!
1

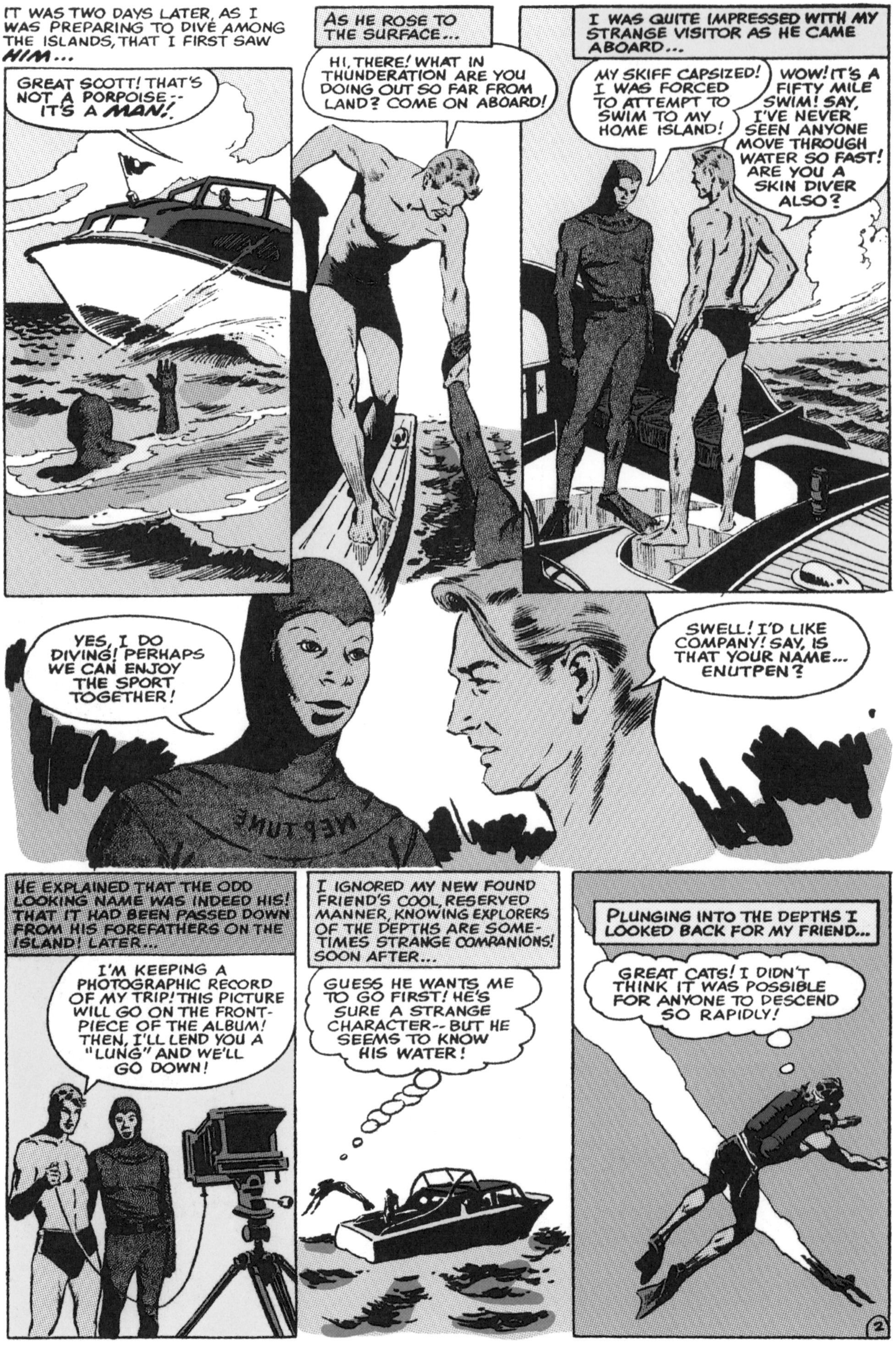

IT WAS TWO DAYS LATER, AS I WAS PREPARING TO DIVE AMONG THE ISLANDS, THAT I FIRST SAW HIM...
GREAT SCOTT! THAT'S NOT A PORPOISE-- IT'S A MAN!
AS HE ROSE TO THE SURFACE...
HI, THERE! WHAT IN THUNDERATION ARE YOU DOING OUT SO FAR FROM LAND? COME ON ABOARD!
I WAS QUITE IMPRESSED WITH MY STRANGE VISITOR AS HE CAME ABOARD...
MY SKIFF CAPSIZED! I WAS FORCED TO ATTEMPT TO SWIM TO MY HOME ISLAND!
WOW! IT'S A FIFTY MILE SWIM! SAY, I'VE NEVER SEEN ANYONE MOVE THROUGH WATER SO FAST! ARE YOU A SKIN DIVER ALSO?
YES, I DO DIVING! PERHAPS WE CAN ENJOY THE SPORT TOGETHER!
SWELL! I'D LIKE COMPANY! SAY, IS THAT YOUR NAME... ENUTPEN?
NEPTUNE
HE EXPLAINED THAT THE ODD LOOKING NAME WAS INDEED HIS! THAT IT HAD BEEN PASSED DOWN FROM HIS FOREFATHERS ON THE ISLAND! LATER...
I'M KEEPING A PHOTOGRAPHIC RECORD OF MY TRIP! THIS PICTURE WILL GO ON THE FRONT-PIECE OF THE ALBUM! THEN, I'LL LEND YOU A "LUNG" AND WE'LL GO DOWN!
I IGNORED MY NEW FOUND FRIEND'S COOL, RESERVED MANNER, KNOWING EXPLORERS OF THE DEPTHS ARE SOME-TIMES STRANGE COMPANIONS! SOON AFTER...
GUESS HE WANTS ME TO GO FIRST! HE'S SURE A STRANGE CHARACTER-- BUT HE SEEMS TO KNOW HIS WATER!
PLUNGING INTO THE DEPTHS I LOOKED BACK FOR MY FRIEND...
GREAT CATS! I DIDN'T THINK IT WAS POSSIBLE FOR ANYONE TO DESCEND SO RAPIDLY!
2

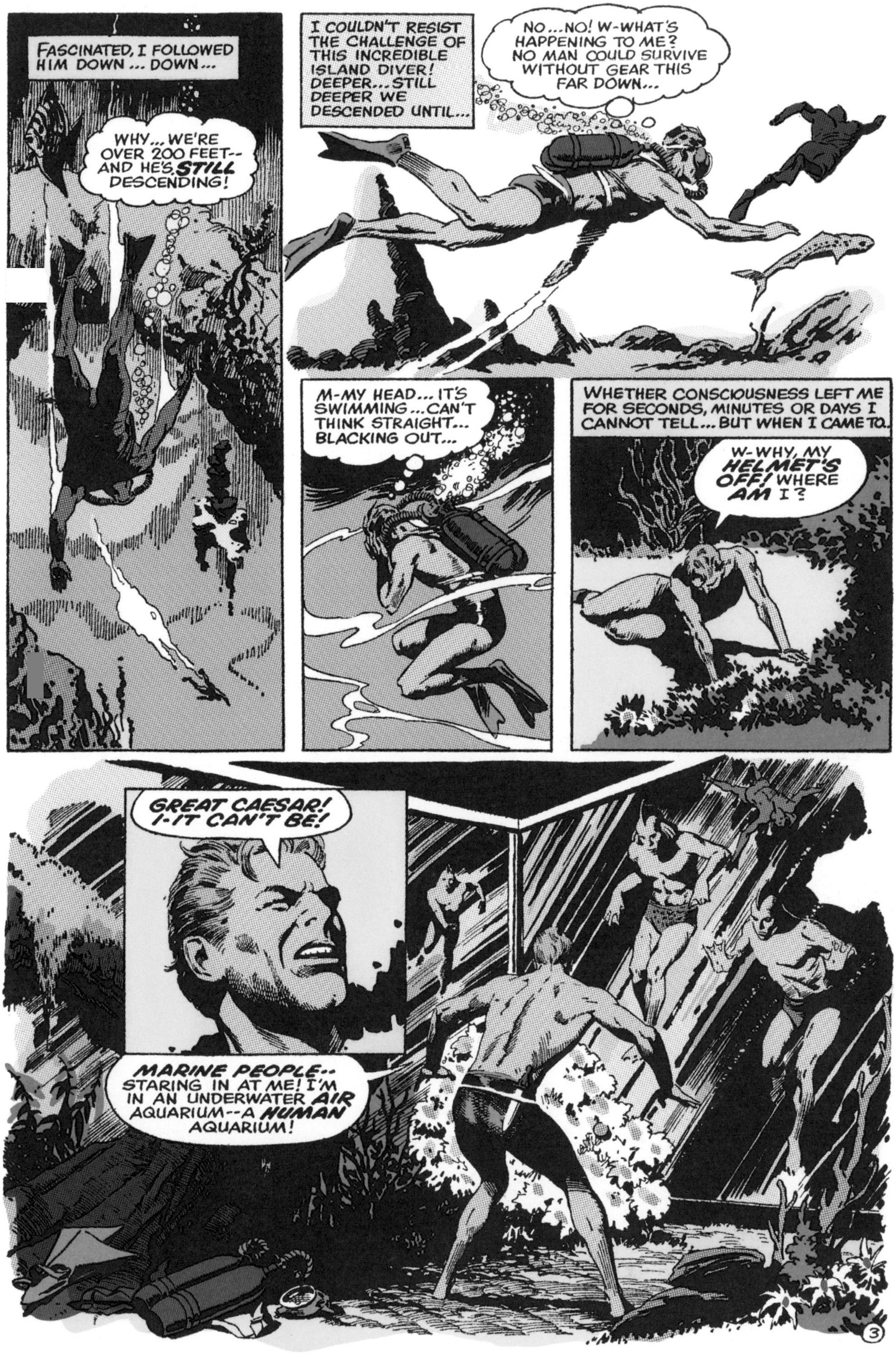

FASCINATED, I FOLLOWED HIM DOWN ... DOWN ...
WHY ... WE'RE OVER 200 FEET-- AND HE'S STILL DESCENDING!
I COULDN'T RESIST THE CHALLENGE OF THIS INCREDIBLE ISLAND DIVER! DEEPER ... STILL DEEPER WE DESCENDED UNTIL ...
NO ... NO! W-WHAT'S HAPPENING TO ME? NO MAN COULD SURVIVE WITHOUT GEAR THIS FAR DOWN ...
M-MY HEAD ... IT'S SWIMMING ... CAN'T THINK STRAIGHT ... BLACKING OUT ...
WHETHER CONSCIOUSNESS LEFT ME FOR SECONDS, MINUTES OR DAYS I CANNOT TELL ... BUT WHEN I CAME TO.
W-WHY, MY HELMET'S OFF! WHERE AM I?
GREAT CAESAR! I-IT CAN'T BE!
MARINE PEOPLE.. STARING IN AT ME! I'M IN AN UNDERWATER AIR AQUARIUM--A HUMAN AQUARIUM!
3

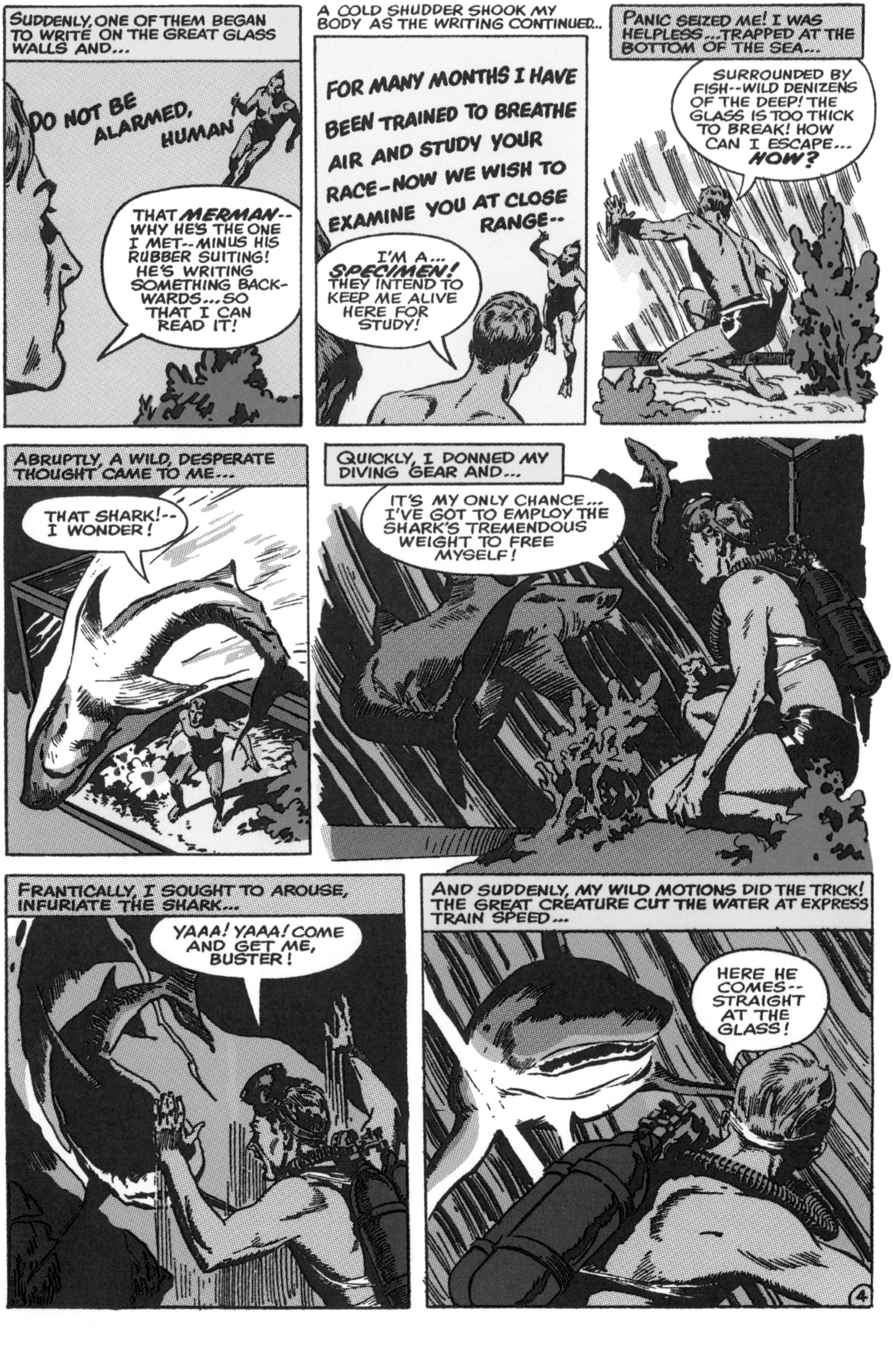
SUDDENLY, ONE OF THEM BEGAN TO WRITE ON THE GREAT GLASS WALLS AND...
DO NOT BE ALARMED, HUMAN
THAT MERMAN--WHY HE'S THE ONE I MET--MINUS HIS RUBBER SUITING! HE'S WRITING SOMETHING BACKWARDS...SO THAT I CAN READ IT!
A COLD SHUDDER SHOOK MY BODY AS THE WRITING CONTINUED...
FOR MANY MONTHS I HAVE BEEN TRAINED TO BREATHE AIR AND STUDY YOUR RACE-NOW WE WISH TO EXAMINE YOU AT CLOSE RANGE--
I'M A... SPECIMEN! THEY INTEND TO KEEP ME ALIVE HERE FOR STUDY!
PANIC SEIZED ME! I WAS HELPLESS...TRAPPED AT THE BOTTOM OF THE SEA...
SURROUNDED BY FISH--WILD DENIZENS OF THE DEEP! THE GLASS IS TOO THICK TO BREAK! HOW CAN I ESCAPE... NOW?
ABRUPTLY, A WILD, DESPERATE THOUGHT CAME TO ME...
THAT SHARK!-- I WONDER!
QUICKLY, I DONNED MY DIVING GEAR AND...
IT'S MY ONLY CHANCE... I'VE GOT TO EMPLOY THE SHARK'S TREMENDOUS WEIGHT TO FREE MYSELF!
FRANTICALLY, I SOUGHT TO AROUSE, INFURIATE THE SHARK...
YAAA! YAAA! COME AND GET ME, BUSTER!
AND SUDDENLY, MY WILD MOTIONS DID THE TRICK! THE GREAT CREATURE CUT THE WATER AT EXPRESS TRAIN SPEED...
HERE HE COMES--STRAIGHT AT THE GLASS!
4

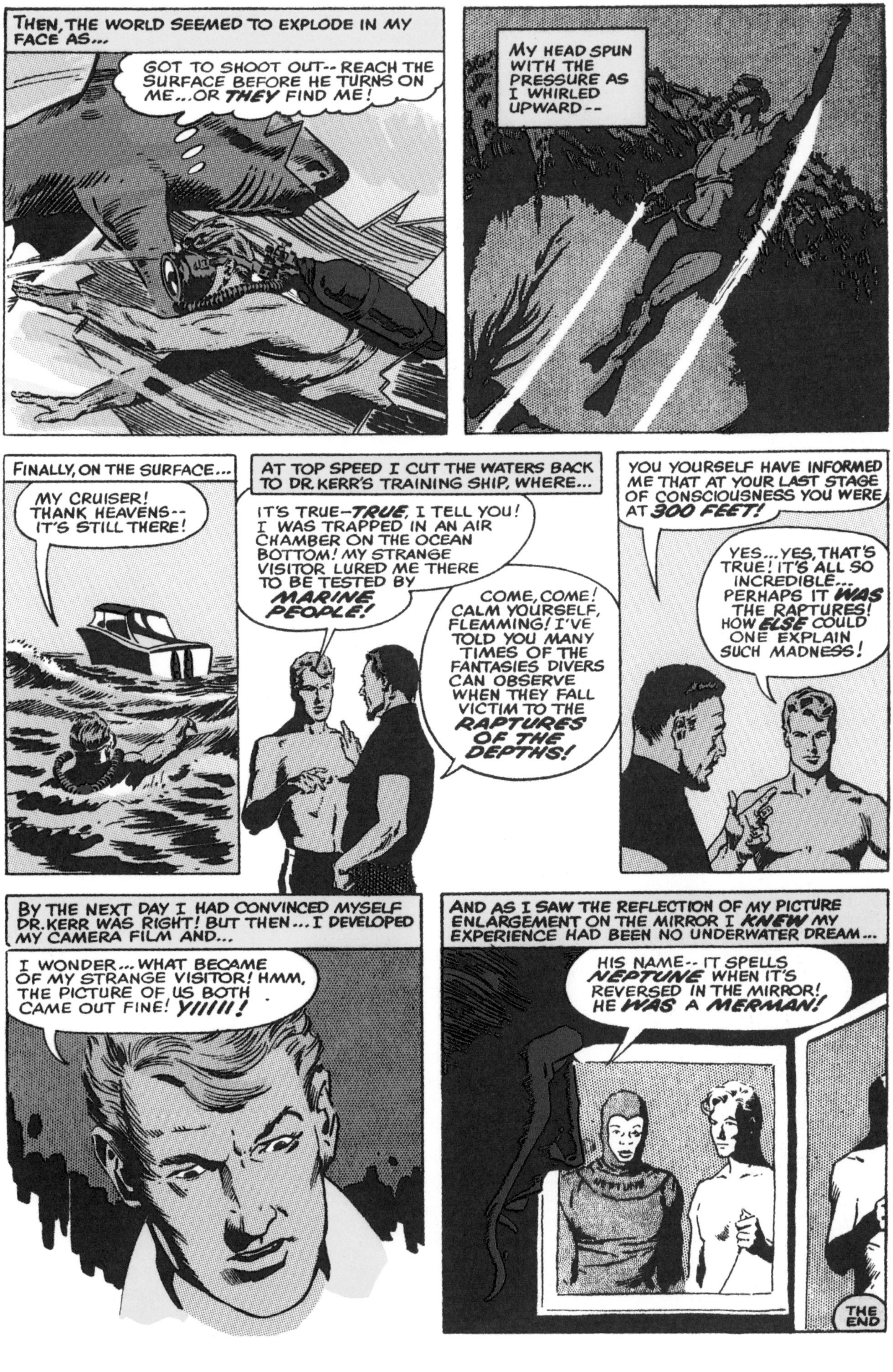
THEN, THE WORLD SEEMED TO EXPLODE IN MY FACE AS...
GOT TO SHOOT OUT-- REACH THE SURFACE BEFORE HE TURNS ON ME...OR THEY FIND ME!
MY HEAD SPUN WITH THE PRESSURE AS I WHIRLED UPWARD --
FINALLY, ON THE SURFACE...
MY CRUISER! THANK HEAVENS-- IT'S STILL THERE!
AT TOP SPEED I CUT THE WATERS BACK TO DR. KERR'S TRAINING SHIP, WHERE...
IT'S TRUE-TRUE, I TELL YOU! I WAS TRAPPED IN AN AIR CHAMBER ON THE OCEAN BOTTOM! MY STRANGE VISITOR LURED ME THERE TO BE TESTED BY MARINE PEOPLE!
COME, COME! CALM YOURSELF, FLEMMING! I'VE TOLD YOU MANY TIMES OF THE FANTASIES DIVERS CAN OBSERVE WHEN THEY FALL VICTIM TO THE RAPTURES OF THE DEPTHS!
YOU YOURSELF HAVE INFORMED ME THAT AT YOUR LAST STAGE OF CONSCIOUSNESS YOU WERE AT 300 FEET!
YES...YES, THAT'S TRUE! IT'S ALL SO INCREDIBLE... PERHAPS IT WAS THE RAPTURES! HOW ELSE COULD ONE EXPLAIN SUCH MADNESS!
BY THE NEXT DAY I HAD CONVINCED MYSELF DR. KERR WAS RIGHT! BUT THEN... I DEVELOPED MY CAMERA FILM AND...
I WONDER... WHAT BECAME OF MY STRANGE VISITOR! HMM, THE PICTURE OF US BOTH CAME OUT FINE! YIIIII!
AND AS I SAW THE REFLECTION OF MY PICTURE ENLARGEMENT ON THE MIRROR I KNEW MY EXPERIENCE HAD BEEN NO UNDERWATER DREAM...
HIS NAME-- IT SPELLS NEPTUNE WHEN IT'S REVERSED IN THE MIRROR! HE WAS A MERMAN!
THE END

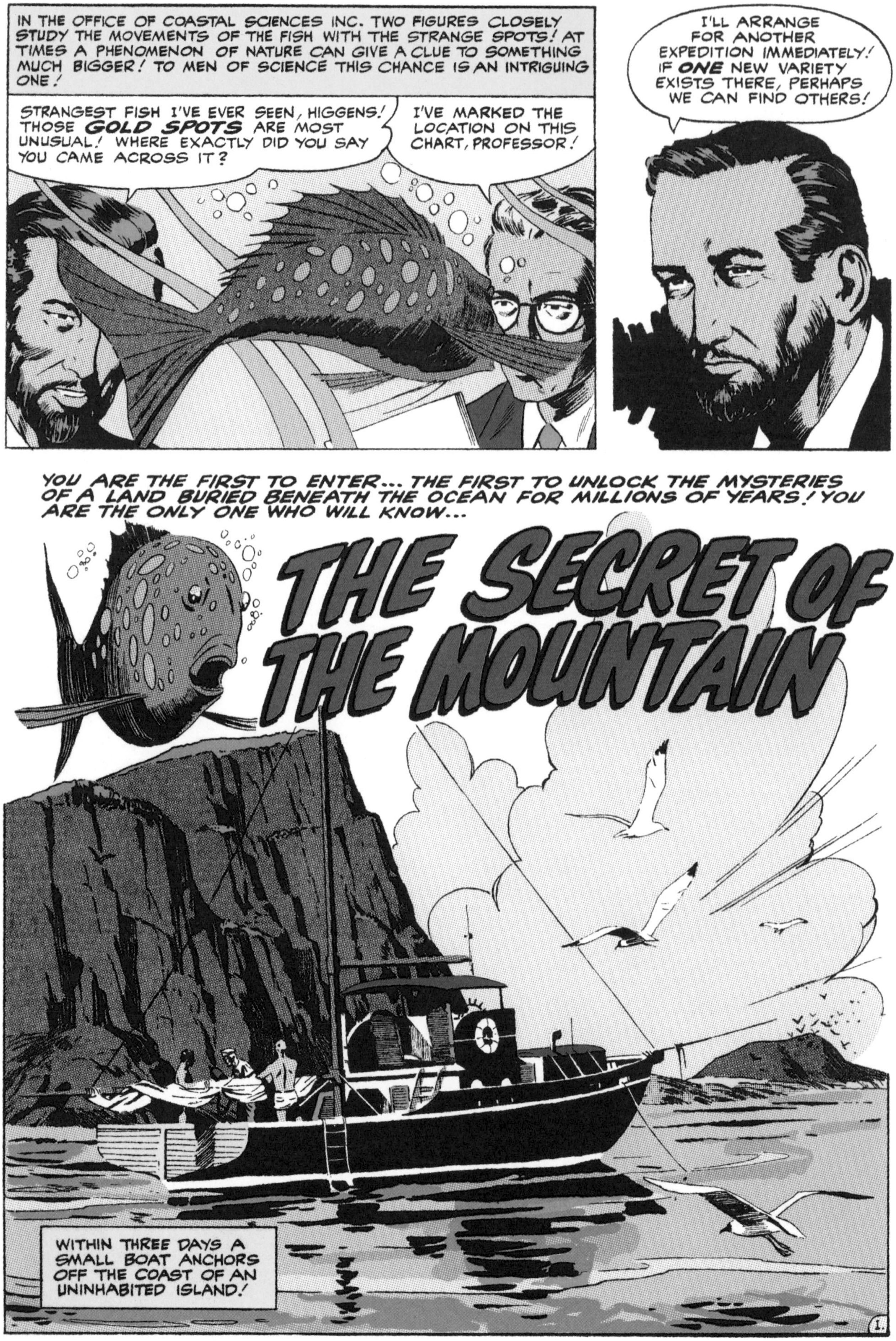
IN THE OFFICE OF COASTAL SCIENCES INC. TWO FIGURES CLOSELY STUDY THE MOVEMENTS OF THE FISH WITH THE STRANGE SPOTS! AT TIMES A PHENOMENON OF NATURE CAN GIVE A CLUE TO SOMETHING MUCH BIGGER! TO MEN OF SCIENCE THIS CHANCE IS AN INTRIGUING ONE!
STRANGEST FISH I'VE EVER SEEN, HIGGENS! THOSE GOLD SPOTS ARE MOST UNUSUAL! WHERE EXACTLY DID YOU SAY YOU CAME ACROSS IT?
I'VE MARKED THE LOCATION ON THIS CHART, PROFESSOR!
I'LL ARRANGE FOR ANOTHER EXPEDITION IMMEDIATELY! IF ONE NEW VARIETY EXISTS THERE, PERHAPS WE CAN FIND OTHERS!
YOU ARE THE FIRST TO ENTER... THE FIRST TO UNLOCK THE MYSTERIES OF A LAND BURIED BENEATH THE OCEAN FOR MILLIONS OF YEARS! YOU ARE THE ONLY ONE WHO WILL KNOW...
THE SECRET OF THE MOUNTAIN
WITHIN THREE DAYS A SMALL BOAT ANCHORS OFF THE COAST OF AN UNINHABITED ISLAND!
1.

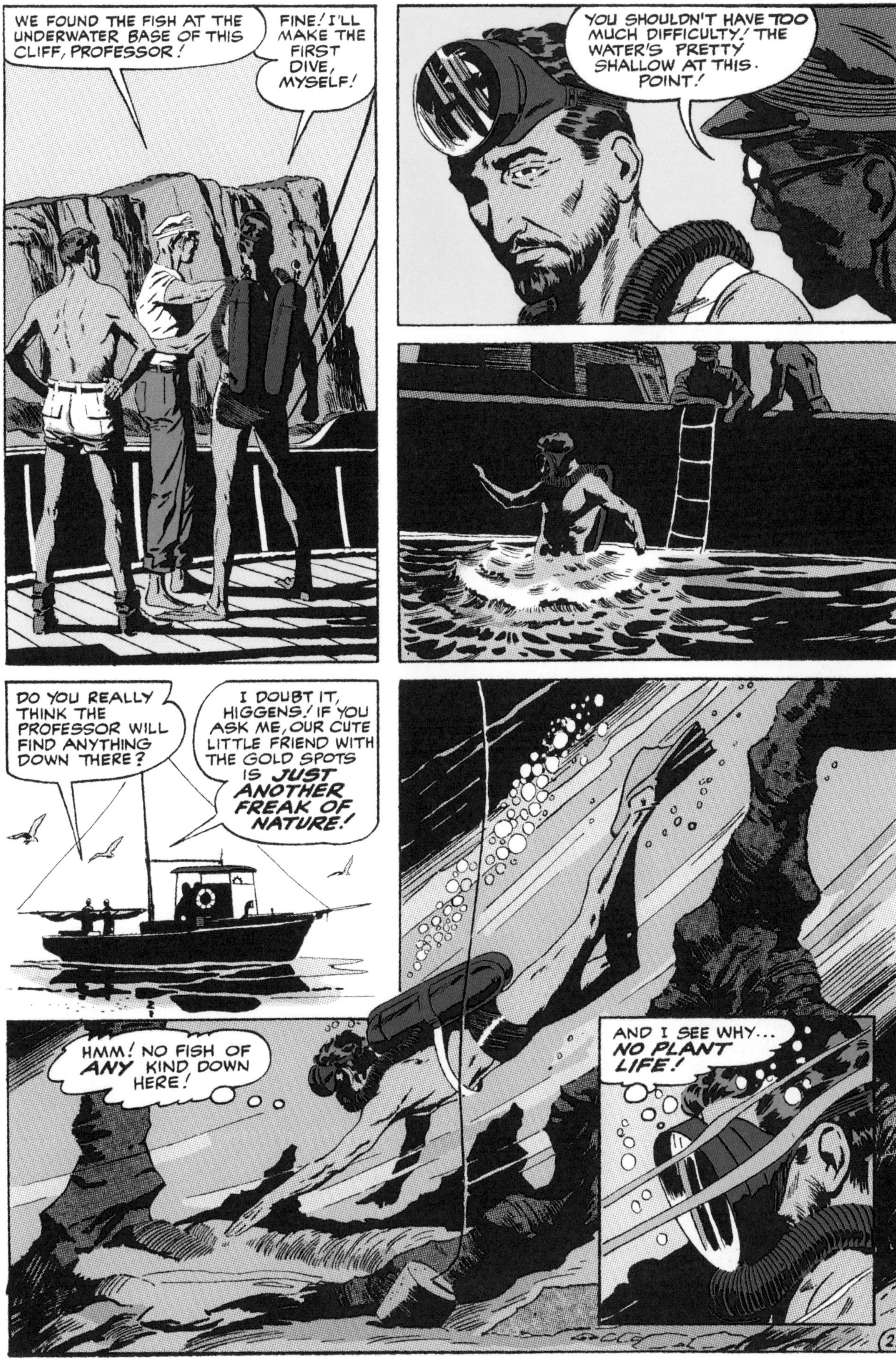

WE FOUND THE FISH AT THE UNDERWATER BASE OF THIS CLIFF, PROFESSOR!
FINE! I'LL MAKE THE FIRST DIVE, MYSELF!
YOU SHOULDN'T HAVE TOO MUCH DIFFICULTY! THE WATER'S PRETTY SHALLOW AT THIS POINT!
DO YOU REALLY THINK THE PROFESSOR WILL FIND ANYTHING DOWN THERE?
I DOUBT IT, HIGGENS! IF YOU ASK ME, OUR CUTE LITTLE FRIEND WITH THE GOLD SPOTS IS JUST ANOTHER FREAK OF NATURE!
HMM! NO FISH OF ANY KIND DOWN HERE!
AND I SEE WHY... NO PLANT LIFE!
2.

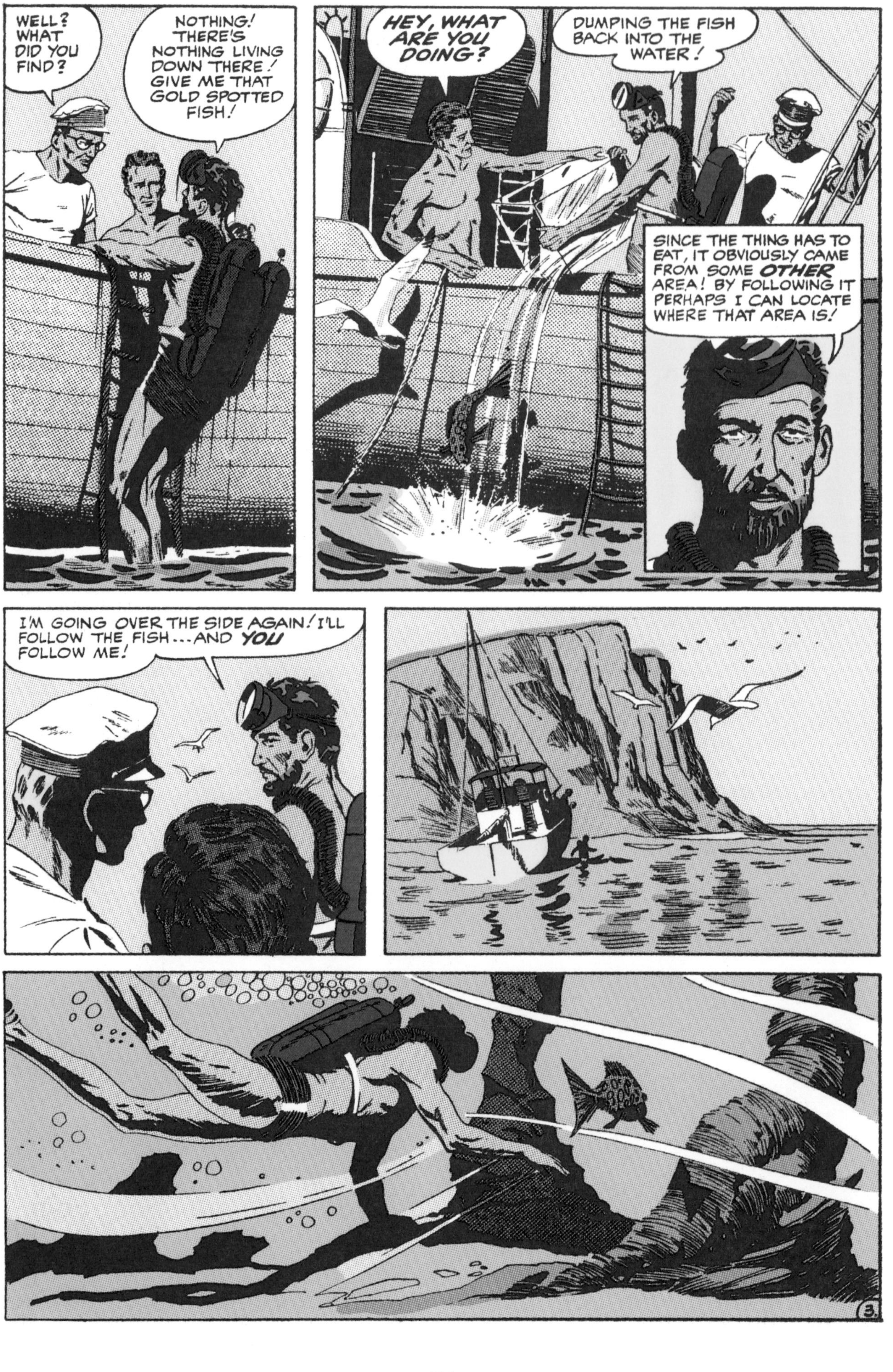
WELL? WHAT DID YOU FIND?
NOTHING! THERE'S NOTHING LIVING DOWN THERE! GIVE ME THAT GOLD SPOTTED FISH!
HEY, WHAT ARE YOU DOING?
DUMPING THE FISH BACK INTO THE WATER!
SINCE THE THING HAS TO EAT, IT OBVIOUSLY CAME FROM SOME OTHER AREA! BY FOLLOWING IT PERHAPS I CAN LOCATE WHERE THAT AREA IS!
I'M GOING OVER THE SIDE AGAIN! I'LL FOLLOW THE FISH... AND YOU FOLLOW ME!
3.

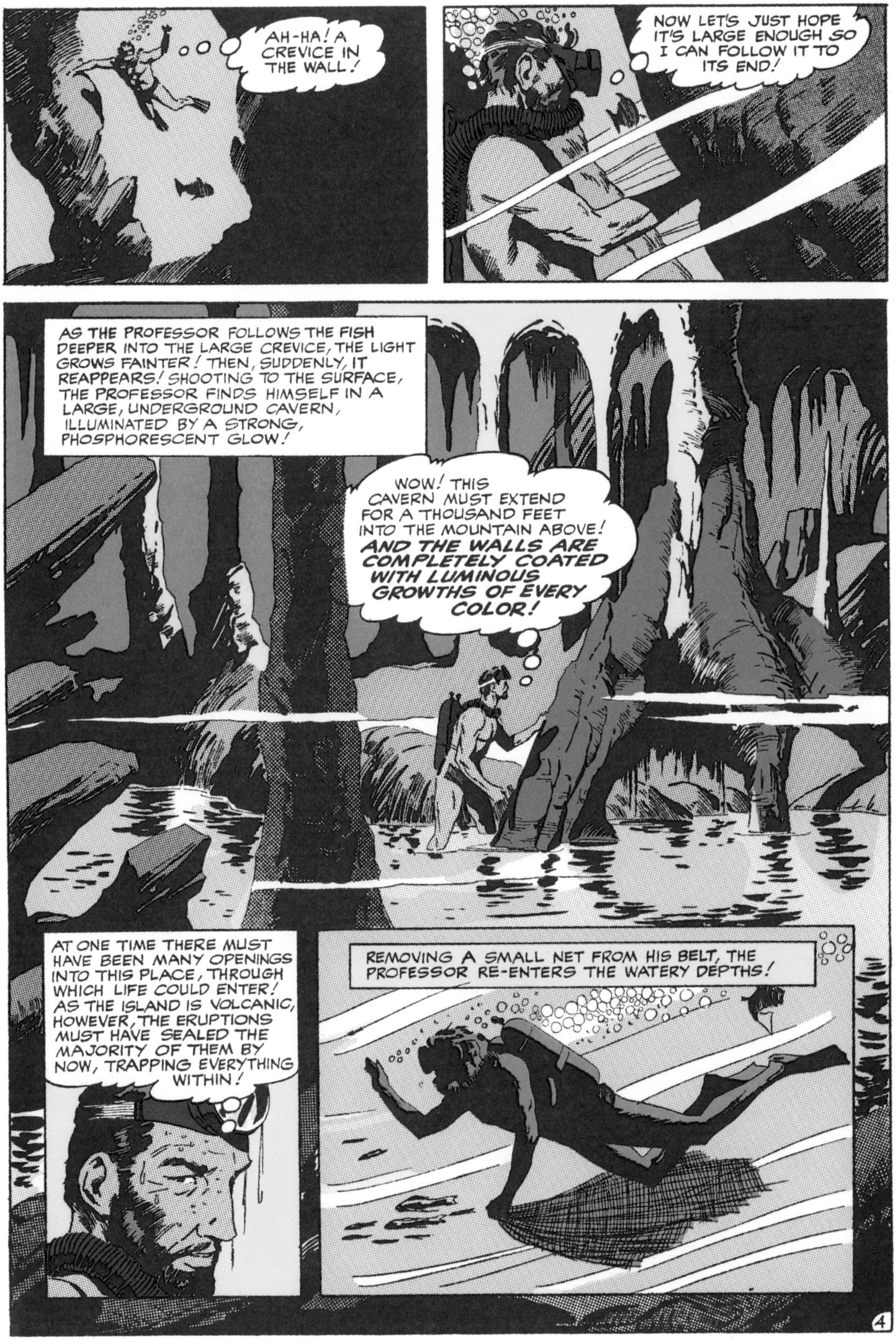

AH-HA! A CREVICE IN THE WALL!
NOW LET'S JUST HOPE IT'S LARGE ENOUGH SO I CAN FOLLOW IT TO ITS END!
AS THE PROFESSOR FOLLOWS THE FISH DEEPER INTO THE LARGE CREVICE, THE LIGHT GROWS FAINTER! THEN, SUDDENLY, IT REAPPEARS! SHOOTING TO THE SURFACE, THE PROFESSOR FINDS HIMSELF IN A LARGE, UNDERGROUND CAVERN, ILLUMINATED BY A STRONG, PHOSPHORESCENT GLOW!
WOW! THIS CAVERN MUST EXTEND FOR A THOUSAND FEET INTO THE MOUNTAIN ABOVE! AND THE WALLS ARE COMPLETELY COATED WITH LUMINOUS GROWTHS OF EVERY COLOR!
AT ONE TIME THERE MUST HAVE BEEN MANY OPENINGS INTO THIS PLACE, THROUGH WHICH LIFE COULD ENTER! AS THE ISLAND IS VOLCANIC, HOWEVER, THE ERUPTIONS MUST HAVE SEALED THE MAJORITY OF THEM BY NOW, TRAPPING EVERYTHING WITHIN!
REMOVING A SMALL NET FROM HIS BELT, THE PROFESSOR RE-ENTERS THE WATERY DEPTHS!
4

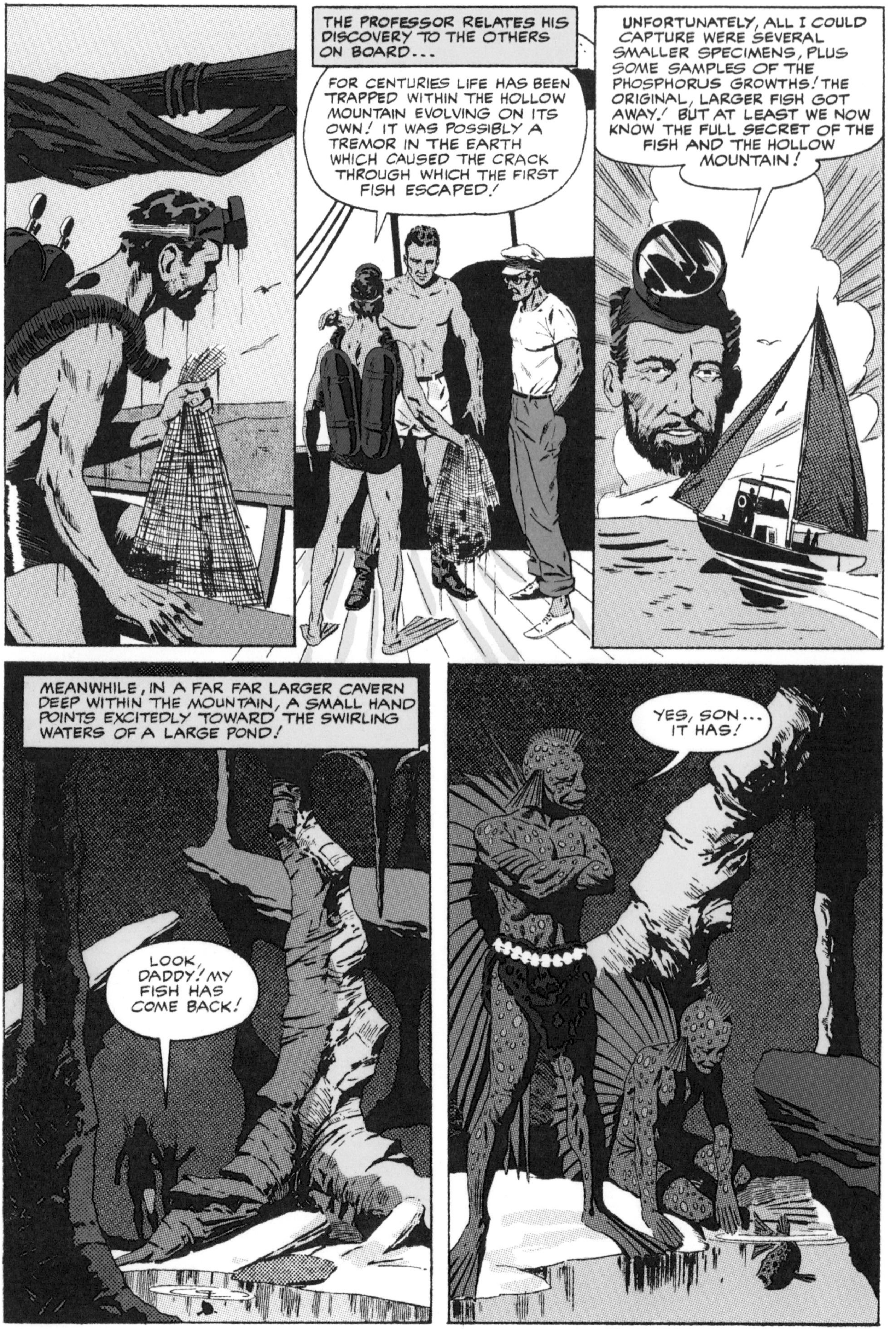

THE PROFESSOR RELATES HIS DISCOVERY TO THE OTHERS ON BOARD...
FOR CENTURIES LIFE HAS BEEN TRAPPED WITHIN THE HOLLOW MOUNTAIN EVOLVING ON ITS OWN! IT WAS POSSIBLY A TREMOR IN THE EARTH WHICH CAUSED THE CRACK THROUGH WHICH THE FIRST FISH ESCAPED!
UNFORTUNATELY, ALL I COULD CAPTURE WERE SEVERAL SMALLER SPECIMENS, PLUS SOME SAMPLES OF THE PHOSPHORUS GROWTHS! THE ORIGINAL, LARGER FISH GOT AWAY! BUT AT LEAST WE NOW KNOW THE FULL SECRET OF THE FISH AND THE HOLLOW MOUNTAIN!
MEANWHILE, IN A FAR FAR LARGER CAVERN DEEP WITHIN THE MOUNTAIN, A SMALL HAND POINTS EXCITEDLY TOWARD THE SWIRLING WATERS OF A LARGE POND!
LOOK, DADDY! MY FISH HAS COME BACK!
YES, SON... IT HAS!

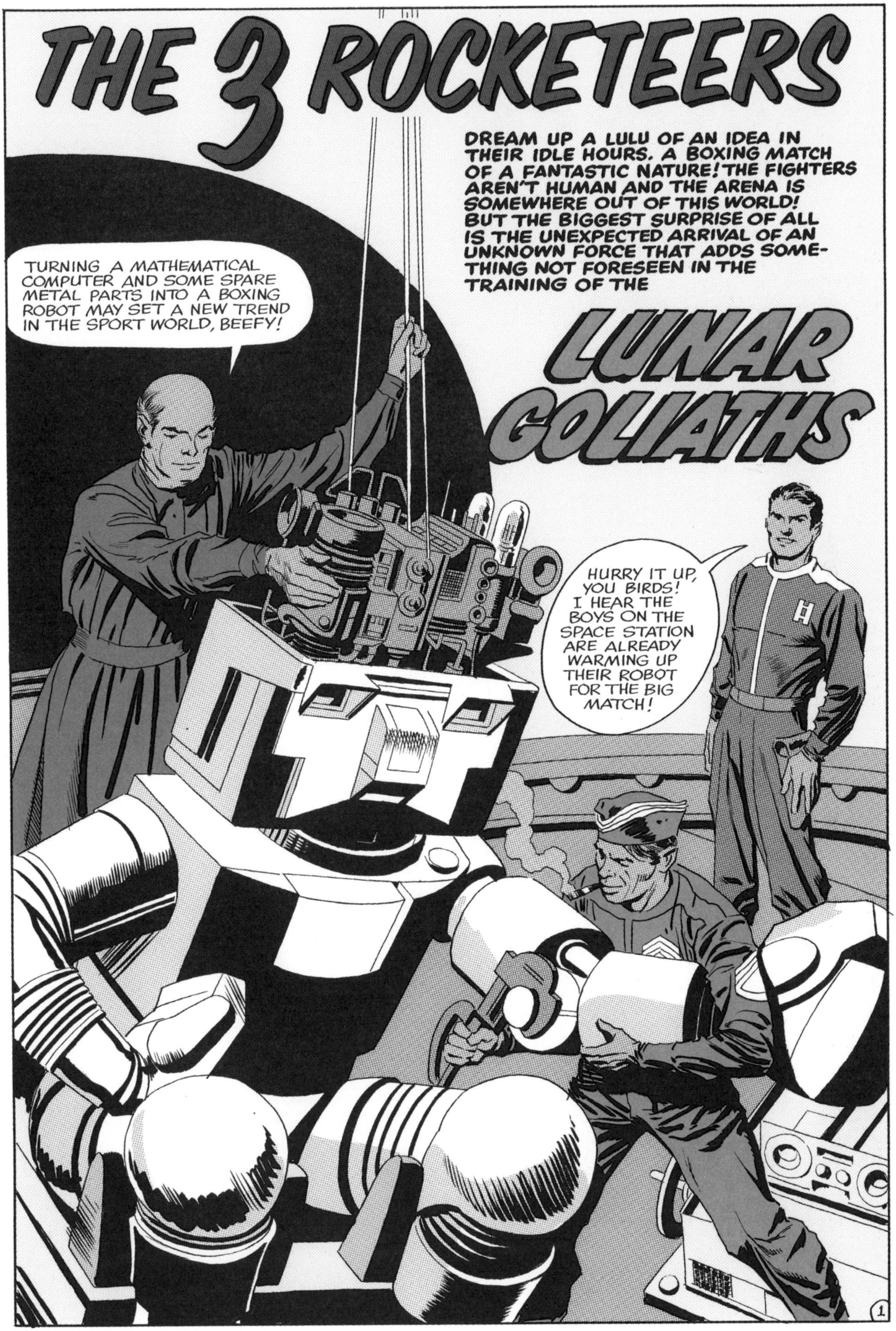
THE 3 ROCKETEERS
DREAM UP A LULU OF AN IDEA IN THEIR IDLE HOURS. A BOXING MATCH OF A FANTASTIC NATURE! THE FIGHTERS AREN'T HUMAN AND THE ARENA IS SOMEWHERE OUT OF THIS WORLD! BUT THE BIGGEST SURPRISE OF ALL IS THE UNEXPECTED ARRIVAL OF AN UNKNOWN FORCE THAT ADDS SOMETHING NOT FORESEEN IN THE TRAINING OF THE
LUNAR GOLIATHS
TURNING A MATHEMATICAL COMPUTER AND SOME SPARE METAL PARTS INTO A BOXING ROBOT MAY SET A NEW TREND IN THE SPORT WORLD, BEEFY!
HURRY IT UP, YOU BIRDS! I HEAR THE BOYS ON THE SPACE STATION ARE ALREADY WARMING UP THEIR ROBOT FOR THE BIG MATCH!
1

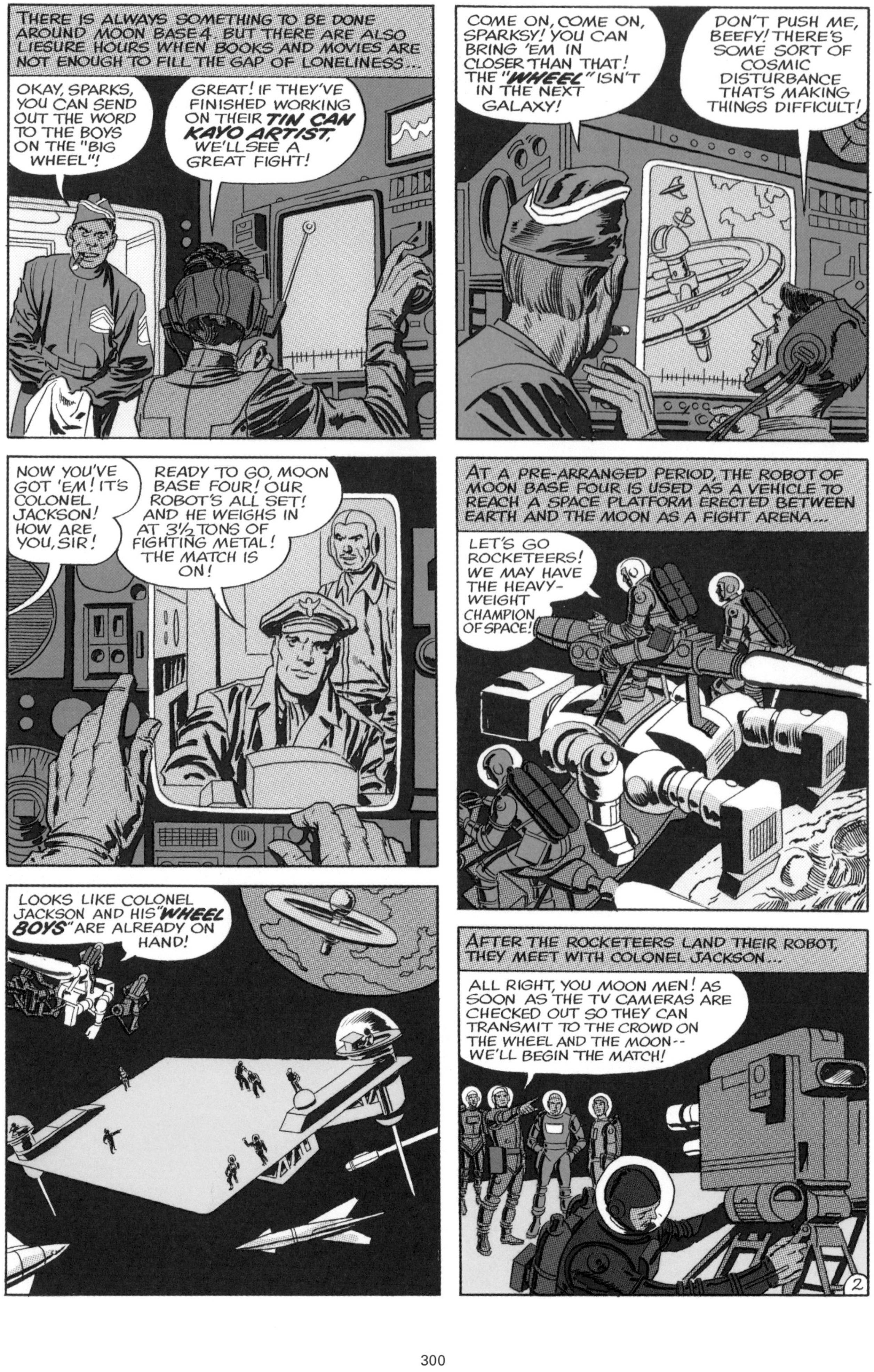

THERE IS ALWAYS SOMETHING TO BE DONE AROUND MOON BASE 4. BUT THERE ARE ALSO LIESURE HOURS WHEN BOOKS AND MOVIES ARE NOT ENOUGH TO FILL THE GAP OF LONELINESS...
OKAY, SPARKS, YOU CAN SEND OUT THE WORD TO THE BOYS ON THE "BIG WHEEL"!
GREAT! IF THEY'VE FINISHED WORKING ON THEIR TIN CAN KAYO ARTIST, WE'LLSEE A GREAT FIGHT!
COME ON, COME ON, SPARKSY! YOU CAN BRING 'EM IN CLOSER THAN THAT! THE "WHEEL" ISN'T IN THE NEXT GALAXY!
DON'T PUSH ME, BEEFY! THERE'S SOME SORT OF COSMIC DISTURBANCE THAT'S MAKING THINGS DIFFICULT!
NOW YOU'VE GOT 'EM! IT'S COLONEL JACKSON! HOW ARE YOU, SIR!
READY TO GO, MOON BASE FOUR! OUR ROBOT'S ALL SET! AND HE WEIGHS IN AT 3½ TONS OF FIGHTING METAL! THE MATCH IS ON!
AT A PRE-ARRANGED PERIOD, THE ROBOT OF MOON BASE FOUR IS USED AS A VEHICLE TO REACH A SPACE PLATFORM ERECTED BETWEEN EARTH AND THE MOON AS A FIGHT ARENA...
LET'S GO ROCKETEERS! WE MAY HAVE THE HEAVY-WEIGHT CHAMPION OF SPACE!
LOOKS LIKE COLONEL JACKSON AND HIS "WHEEL BOYS" ARE ALREADY ON HAND!
AFTER THE ROCKETEERS LAND THEIR ROBOT, THEY MEET WITH COLONEL JACKSON...
ALL RIGHT, YOU MOON MEN! AS SOON AS THE TV CAMERAS ARE CHECKED OUT SO THEY CAN TRANSMIT TO THE CROWD ON THE WHEEL AND THE MOON-- WE'LL BEGIN THE MATCH!
2

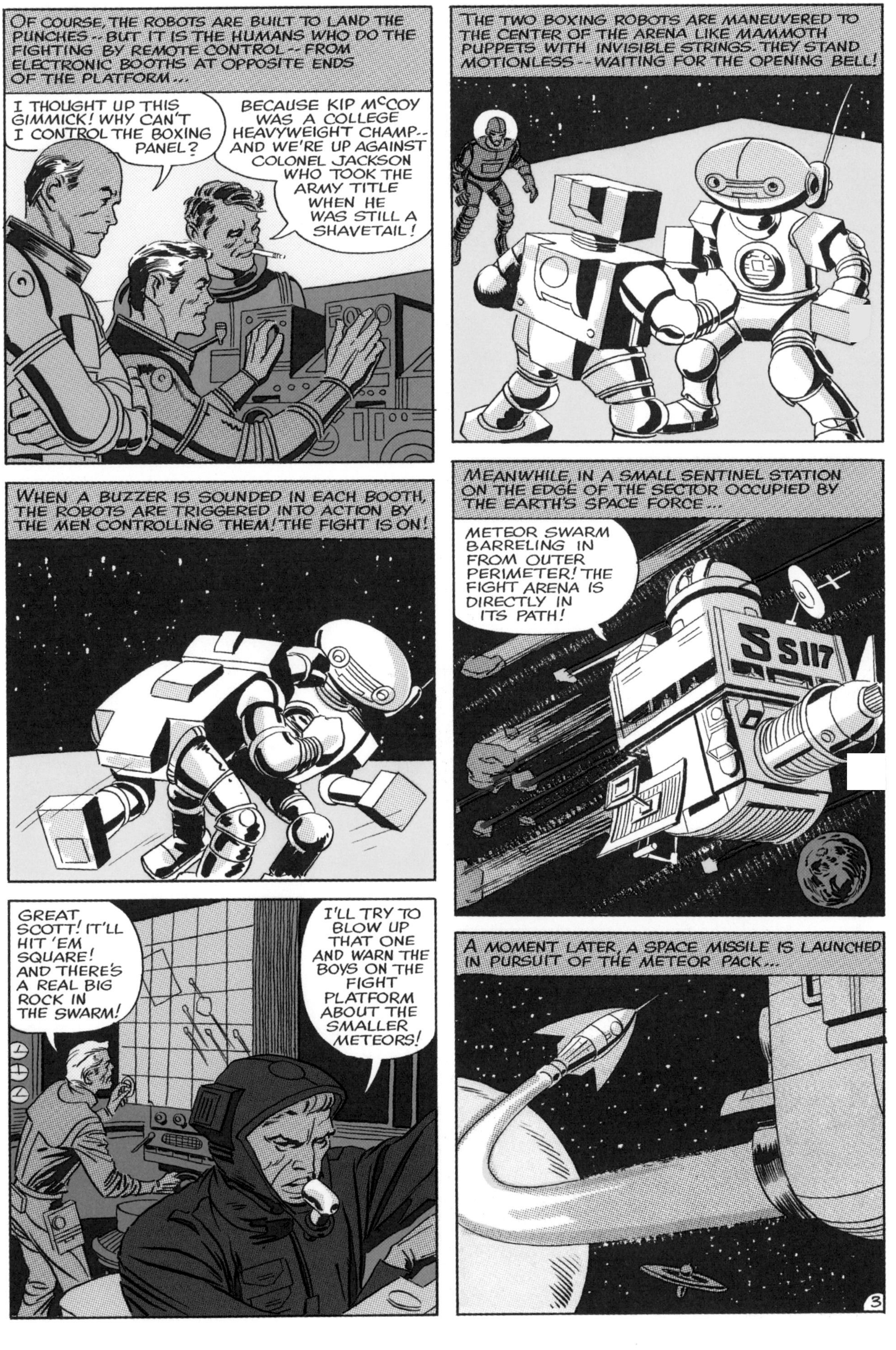
OF COURSE, THE ROBOTS ARE BUILT TO LAND THE PUNCHES--BUT IT IS THE HUMANS WHO DO THE FIGHTING BY REMOTE CONTROL--FROM ELECTRONIC BOOTHS AT OPPOSITE ENDS OF THE PLATFORM...
I THOUGHT UP THIS GIMMICK! WHY CAN'T I CONTROL THE BOXING PANEL?
BECAUSE KIP McCOY WAS A COLLEGE HEAVYWEIGHT CHAMP--AND WE'RE UP AGAINST COLONEL JACKSON WHO TOOK THE ARMY TITLE WHEN HE WAS STILL A SHAVETAIL!
THE TWO BOXING ROBOTS ARE MANEUVERED TO THE CENTER OF THE ARENA LIKE MAMMOTH PUPPETS WITH INVISIBLE STRINGS. THEY STAND MOTIONLESS--WAITING FOR THE OPENING BELL!
WHEN A BUZZER IS SOUNDED IN EACH BOOTH, THE ROBOTS ARE TRIGGERED INTO ACTION BY THE MEN CONTROLLING THEM! THE FIGHT IS ON!
MEANWHILE, IN A SMALL SENTINEL STATION ON THE EDGE OF THE SECTOR OCCUPIED BY THE EARTH'S SPACE FORCE...
METEOR SWARM BARRELING IN FROM OUTER PERIMETER! THE FIGHT ARENA IS DIRECTLY IN ITS PATH!
S S117
GREAT SCOTT! IT'LL HIT 'EM SQUARE! AND THERE'S A REAL BIG ROCK IN THE SWARM!
I'LL TRY TO BLOW UP THAT ONE AND WARN THE BOYS ON THE FIGHT PLATFORM ABOUT THE SMALLER METEORS!
A MOMENT LATER, A SPACE MISSILE IS LAUNCHED IN PURSUIT OF THE METEOR PACK...
3

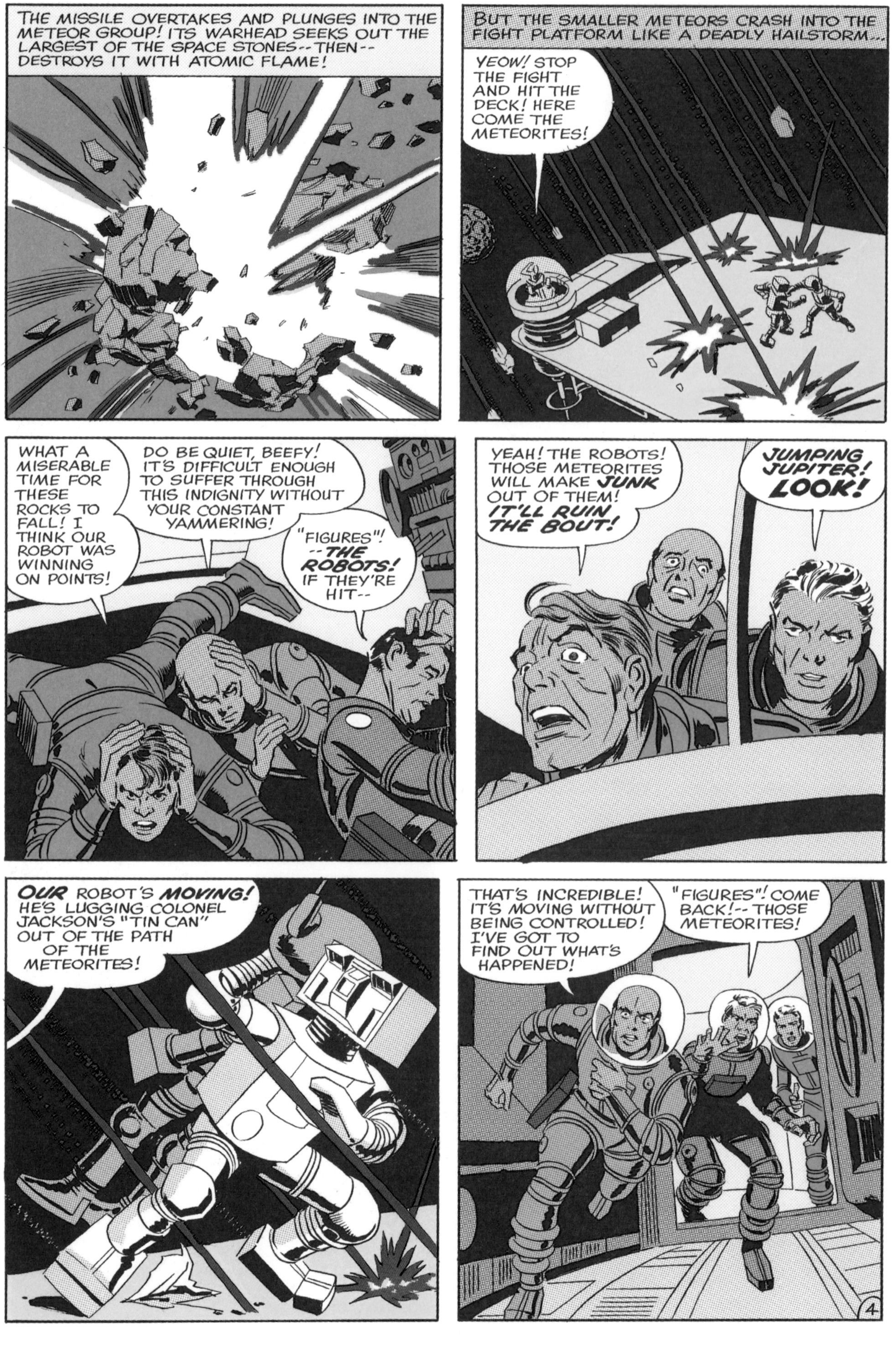
THE MISSILE OVERTAKES AND PLUNGES INTO THE METEOR GROUP! ITS WARHEAD SEEKS OUT THE LARGEST OF THE SPACE STONES--THEN--DESTROYS IT WITH ATOMIC FLAME!
BUT THE SMALLER METEORS CRASH INTO THE FIGHT PLATFORM LIKE A DEADLY HAILSTORM...
YEOW! STOP THE FIGHT AND HIT THE DECK! HERE COME THE METEORITES!
WHAT A MISERABLE TIME FOR THESE ROCKS TO FALL! I THINK OUR ROBOT WAS WINNING ON POINTS!
DO BE QUIET, BEEFY! IT'S DIFFICULT ENOUGH TO SUFFER THROUGH THIS INDIGNITY WITHOUT YOUR CONSTANT YAMMERING!
"FIGURES"! --THE ROBOTS! IF THEY'RE HIT--
YEAH! THE ROBOTS! THOSE METEORITES WILL MAKE JUNK OUT OF THEM! IT'LL RUIN THE BOUT!
JUMPING JUPITER! LOOK!
OUR ROBOT'S MOVING! HE'S LUGGING COLONEL JACKSON'S "TIN CAN" OUT OF THE PATH OF THE METEORITES!
THAT'S INCREDIBLE! IT'S MOVING WITHOUT BEING CONTROLLED! I'VE GOT TO FIND OUT WHAT'S HAPPENED!
"FIGURES"! COME BACK!-- THOSE METEORITES!
4

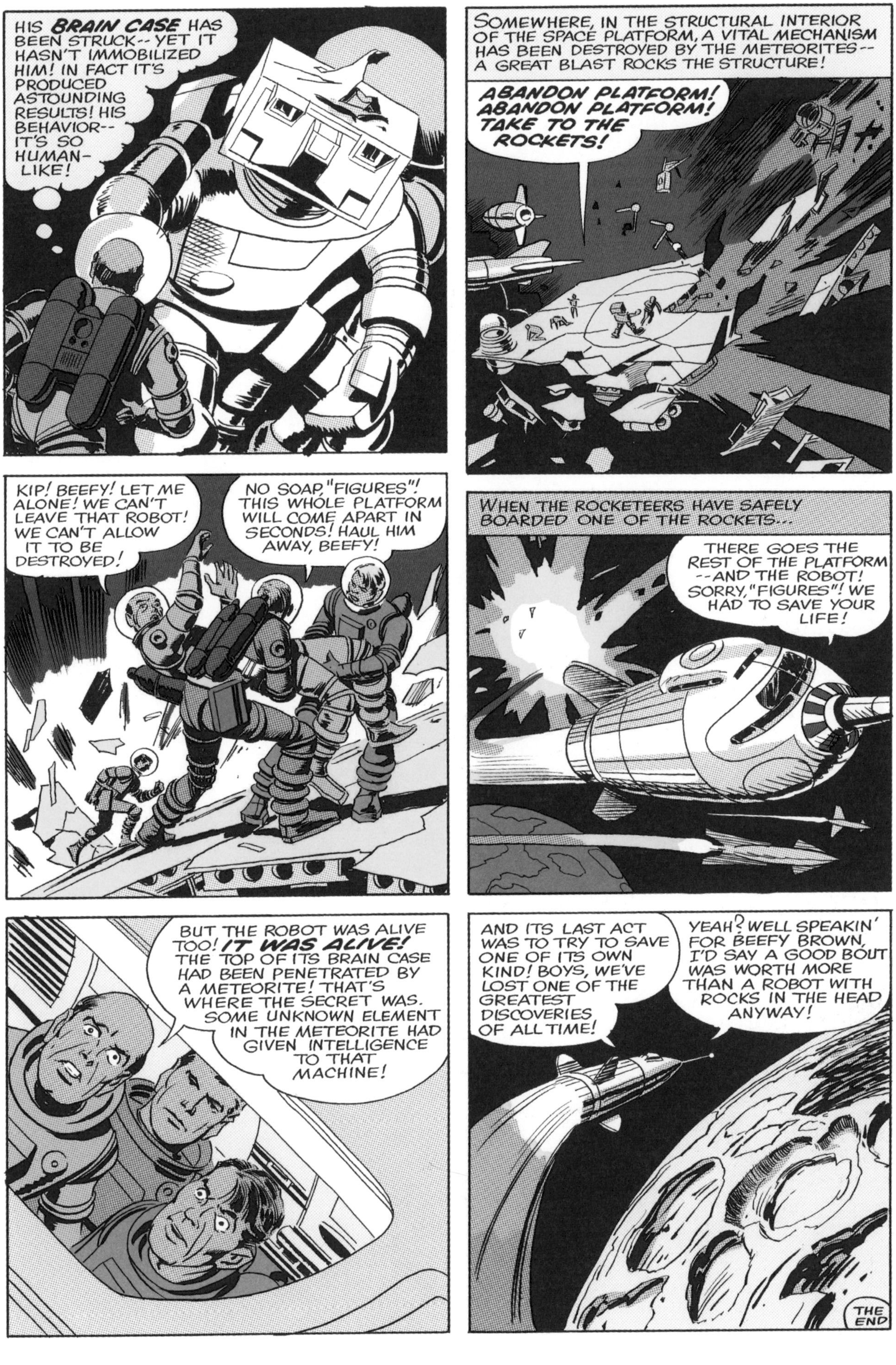
HIS BRAIN CASE HAS BEEN STRUCK-- YET IT HASN'T IMMOBILIZED HIM! IN FACT IT'S PRODUCED ASTOUNDING RESULTS! HIS BEHAVIOR-- IT'S SO HUMAN-LIKE!
SOMEWHERE, IN THE STRUCTURAL INTERIOR OF THE SPACE PLATFORM, A VITAL MECHANISM HAS BEEN DESTROYED BY THE METEORITES-- A GREAT BLAST ROCKS THE STRUCTURE!
ABANDON PLATFORM! ABANDON PLATFORM! TAKE TO THE ROCKETS!
KIP! BEEFY! LET ME ALONE! WE CAN'T LEAVE THAT ROBOT! WE CAN'T ALLOW IT TO BE DESTROYED!
NO SOAP, "FIGURES"! THIS WHOLE PLATFORM WILL COME APART IN SECONDS! HAUL HIM AWAY, BEEFY!
WHEN THE ROCKETEERS HAVE SAFELY BOARDED ONE OF THE ROCKETS...
THERE GOES THE REST OF THE PLATFORM --AND THE ROBOT! SORRY, "FIGURES"! WE HAD TO SAVE YOUR LIFE!
BUT THE ROBOT WAS ALIVE TOO! IT WAS ALIVE! THE TOP OF ITS BRAIN CASE HAD BEEN PENETRATED BY A METEORITE! THAT'S WHERE THE SECRET WAS. SOME UNKNOWN ELEMENT IN THE METEORITE HAD GIVEN INTELLIGENCE TO THAT MACHINE!
AND ITS LAST ACT WAS TO TRY TO SAVE ONE OF ITS OWN KIND! BOYS, WE'VE LOST ONE OF THE GREATEST DISCOVERIES OF ALL TIME!
YEAH? WELL SPEAKIN' FOR BEEFY BROWN, I'D SAY A GOOD BOUT WAS WORTH MORE THAN A ROBOT WITH ROCKS IN THE HEAD ANYWAY!
THE END

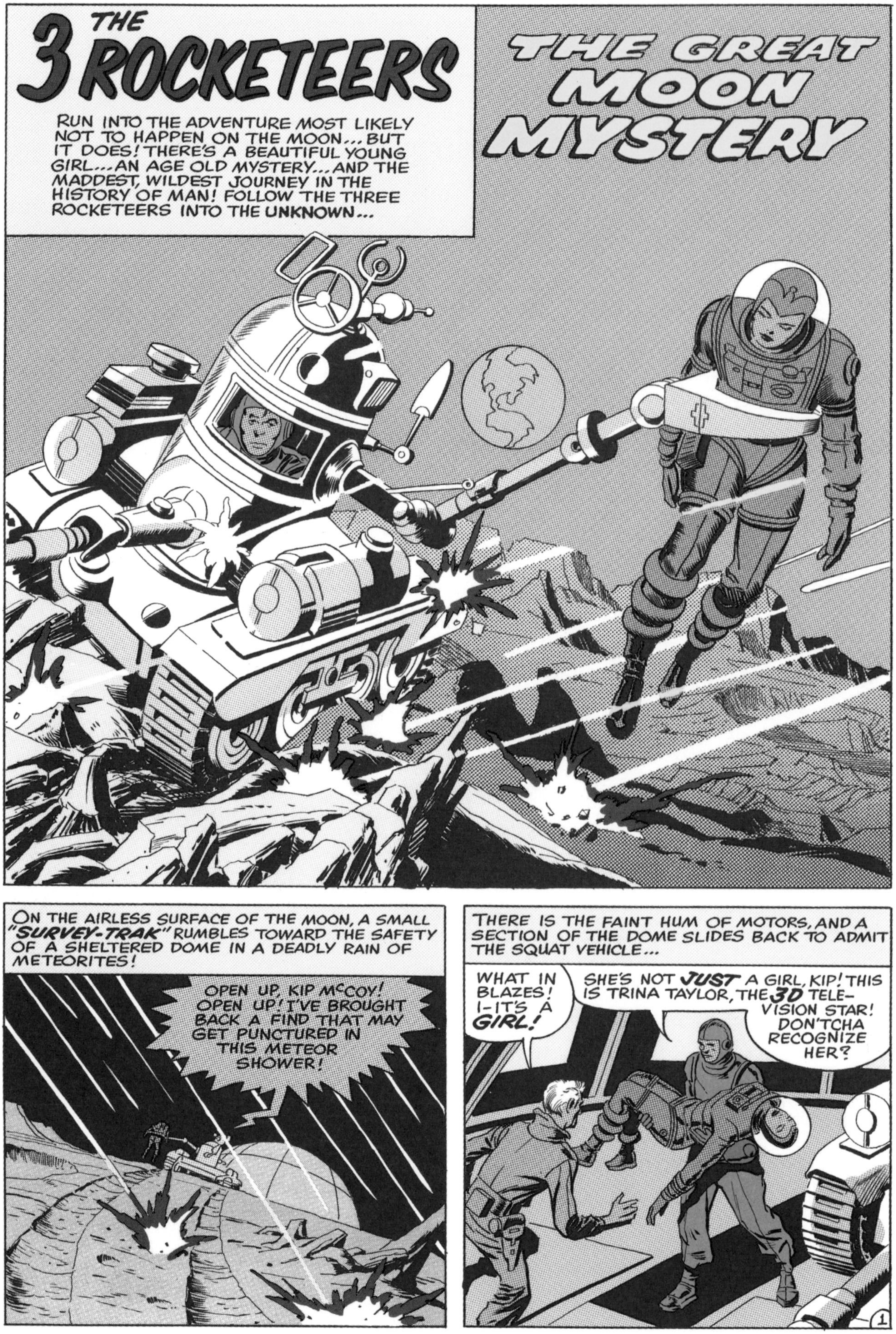
THE 3 ROCKETEERS
THE GREAT MOON MYSTERY
RUN INTO THE ADVENTURE MOST LIKELY NOT TO HAPPEN ON THE MOON... BUT IT DOES! THERE'S A BEAUTIFUL YOUNG GIRL... AN AGE OLD MYSTERY... AND THE MADDEST, WILDEST JOURNEY IN THE HISTORY OF MAN! FOLLOW THE THREE ROCKETEERS INTO THE UNKNOWN...
ON THE AIRLESS SURFACE OF THE MOON, A SMALL "SURVEY-TRAK" RUMBLES TOWARD THE SAFETY OF A SHELTERED DOME IN A DEADLY RAIN OF METEORITES!
OPEN UP, KIP McCOY! OPEN UP! I'VE BROUGHT BACK A FIND THAT MAY GET PUNCTURED IN THIS METEOR SHOWER!
THERE IS THE FAINT HUM OF MOTORS, AND A SECTION OF THE DOME SLIDES BACK TO ADMIT THE SQUAT VEHICLE...
WHAT IN BLAZES! I-IT'S A GIRL!
SHE'S NOT JUST A GIRL, KIP! THIS IS TRINA TAYLOR, THE 3D TELE-VISION STAR! DON'TCHA RECOGNIZE HER?
1

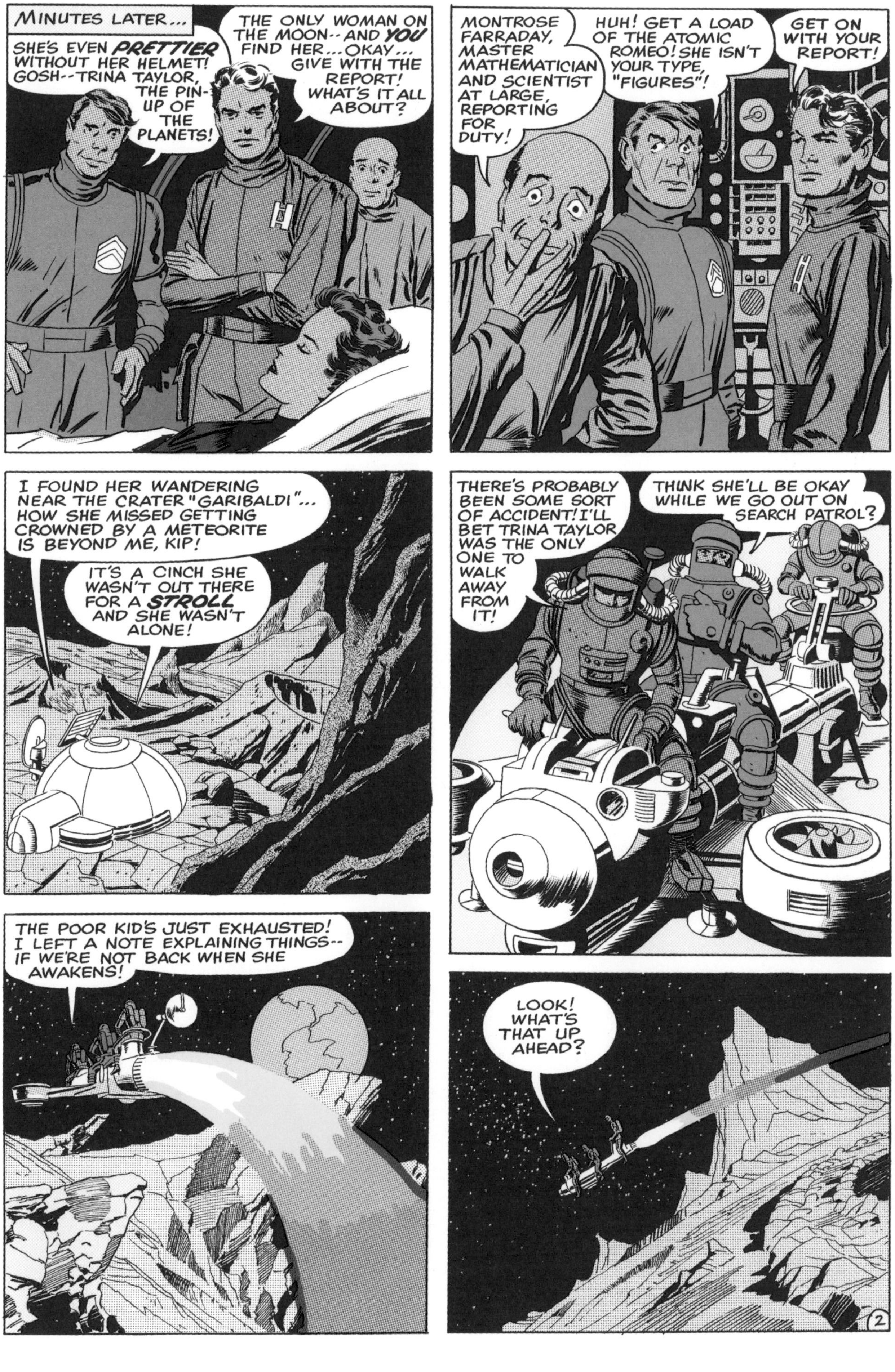
MINUTES LATER...
SHE'S EVEN PRETTIER WITHOUT HER HELMET! GOSH--TRINA TAYLOR, THE PIN-UP OF THE PLANETS!
THE ONLY WOMAN ON THE MOON--AND YOU FIND HER...OKAY... GIVE WITH THE REPORT! WHAT'S IT ALL ABOUT?
MONTROSE FARRADAY, MASTER MATHEMATICIAN AND SCIENTIST AT LARGE, REPORTING FOR DUTY!
HUH! GET A LOAD OF THE ATOMIC ROMEO! SHE ISN'T YOUR TYPE, "FIGURES"!
GET ON WITH YOUR REPORT!
I FOUND HER WANDERING NEAR THE CRATER "GARIBALDI"... HOW SHE MISSED GETTING CROWNED BY A METEORITE IS BEYOND ME, KIP!
IT'S A CINCH SHE WASN'T OUT THERE FOR A STROLL AND SHE WASN'T ALONE!
THERE'S PROBABLY BEEN SOME SORT OF ACCIDENT! I'LL BET TRINA TAYLOR WAS THE ONLY ONE TO WALK AWAY FROM IT!
THINK SHE'LL BE OKAY WHILE WE GO OUT ON SEARCH PATROL?
THE POOR KID'S JUST EXHAUSTED! I LEFT A NOTE EXPLAINING THINGS-- IF WE'RE NOT BACK WHEN SHE AWAKENS!
LOOK! WHAT'S THAT UP AHEAD?
2

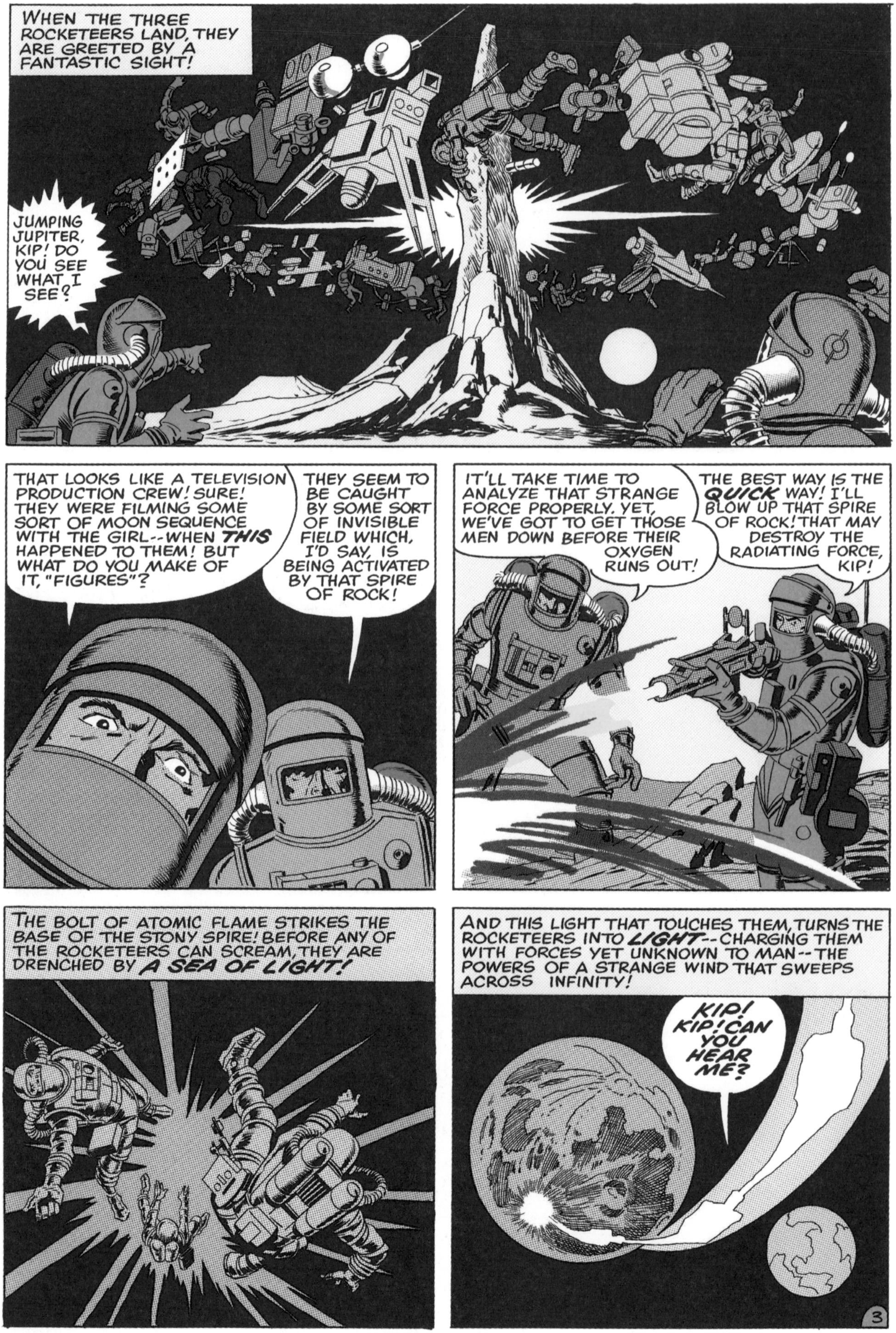
WHEN THE THREE ROCKETEERS LAND, THEY ARE GREETED BY A FANTASTIC SIGHT!
JUMPING JUPITER, KIP! DO YOU SEE WHAT I SEE?
THAT LOOKS LIKE A TELEVISION PRODUCTION CREW! SURE! THEY WERE FILMING SOME SORT OF MOON SEQUENCE WITH THE GIRL--WHEN THIS HAPPENED TO THEM! BUT WHAT DO YOU MAKE OF IT, "FIGURES"?
THEY SEEM TO BE CAUGHT BY SOME SORT OF INVISIBLE FIELD WHICH, I'D SAY, IS BEING ACTIVATED BY THAT SPIRE OF ROCK!
IT'LL TAKE TIME TO ANALYZE THAT STRANGE FORCE PROPERLY. YET, WE'VE GOT TO GET THOSE MEN DOWN BEFORE THEIR OXYGEN RUNS OUT!
THE BEST WAY IS THE QUICK WAY! I'LL BLOW UP THAT SPIRE OF ROCK! THAT MAY DESTROY THE RADIATING FORCE, KIP!
THE BOLT OF ATOMIC FLAME STRIKES THE BASE OF THE STONY SPIRE! BEFORE ANY OF THE ROCKETEERS CAN SCREAM, THEY ARE DRENCHED BY A SEA OF LIGHT!
AND THIS LIGHT THAT TOUCHES THEM, TURNS THE ROCKETEERS INTO LIGHT--CHARGING THEM WITH FORCES YET UNKNOWN TO MAN--THE POWERS OF A STRANGE WIND THAT SWEEPS ACROSS INFINITY!
KIP! KIP! CAN YOU HEAR ME?
3

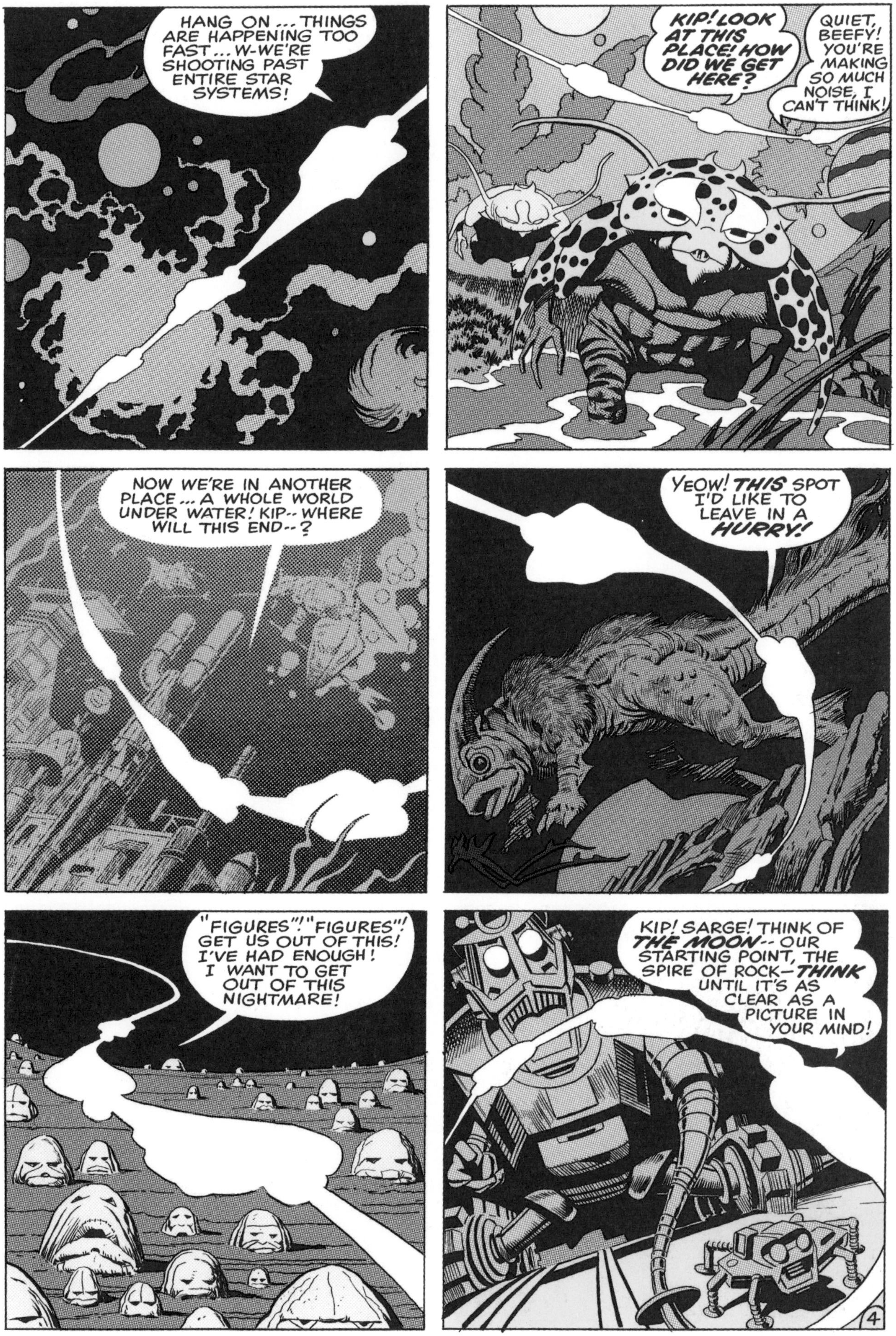
HANG ON ... THINGS ARE HAPPENING TOO FAST... W-WE'RE SHOOTING PAST ENTIRE STAR SYSTEMS!
KIP! LOOK AT THIS PLACE! HOW DID WE GET HERE?
QUIET, BEEFY! YOU'RE MAKING SO MUCH NOISE, I CAN'T THINK!
NOW WE'RE IN ANOTHER PLACE ... A WHOLE WORLD UNDER WATER! KIP-- WHERE WILL THIS END--?
YEOW! THIS SPOT I'D LIKE TO LEAVE IN A HURRY!
"FIGURES"! "FIGURES"! GET US OUT OF THIS! I'VE HAD ENOUGH! I WANT TO GET OUT OF THIS NIGHTMARE!
KIP! SARGE! THINK OF THE MOON-- OUR STARTING POINT, THE SPIRE OF ROCK-- THINK UNTIL IT'S AS CLEAR AS A PICTURE IN YOUR MIND!
4

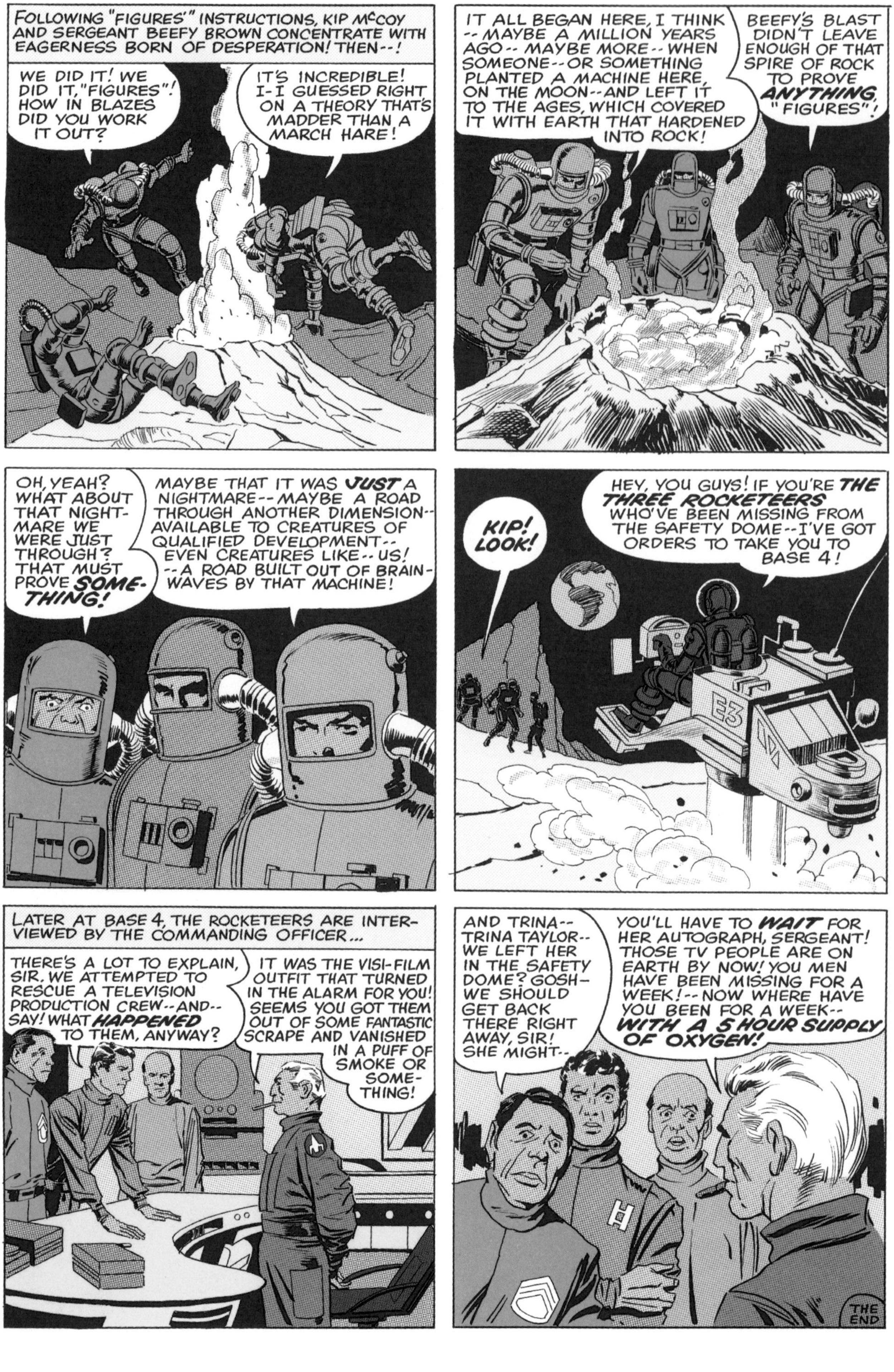

FOLLOWING "FIGURES'" INSTRUCTIONS, KIP McCOY AND SERGEANT BEEFY BROWN CONCENTRATE WITH EAGERNESS BORN OF DESPERATION! THEN--!
WE DID IT! WE DID IT, "FIGURES"! HOW IN BLAZES DID YOU WORK IT OUT?
IT'S INCREDIBLE! I-I GUESSED RIGHT ON A THEORY THAT'S MADDER THAN A MARCH HARE!
IT ALL BEGAN HERE, I THINK -- MAYBE A MILLION YEARS AGO -- MAYBE MORE -- WHEN SOMEONE -- OR SOMETHING PLANTED A MACHINE HERE, ON THE MOON -- AND LEFT IT TO THE AGES, WHICH COVERED IT WITH EARTH THAT HARDENED INTO ROCK!
BEEFY'S BLAST DIDN'T LEAVE ENOUGH OF THAT SPIRE OF ROCK TO PROVE ANYTHING, "FIGURES"!
OH, YEAH? WHAT ABOUT THAT NIGHT-MARE WE WERE JUST THROUGH? THAT MUST PROVE SOME-THING!
MAYBE THAT IT WAS JUST A NIGHTMARE -- MAYBE A ROAD THROUGH ANOTHER DIMENSION -- AVAILABLE TO CREATURES OF QUALIFIED DEVELOPMENT -- EVEN CREATURES LIKE -- US! -- A ROAD BUILT OUT OF BRAIN-WAVES BY THAT MACHINE!
KIP! LOOK!
HEY, YOU GUYS! IF YOU'RE THE THREE ROCKETEERS WHO'VE BEEN MISSING FROM THE SAFETY DOME -- I'VE GOT ORDERS TO TAKE YOU TO BASE 4!
E3
LATER AT BASE 4, THE ROCKETEERS ARE INTER-VIEWED BY THE COMMANDING OFFICER...
THERE'S A LOT TO EXPLAIN, SIR. WE ATTEMPTED TO RESCUE A TELEVISION PRODUCTION CREW -- AND -- SAY! WHAT HAPPENED TO THEM, ANYWAY?
IT WAS THE VISI-FILM OUTFIT THAT TURNED IN THE ALARM FOR YOU! SEEMS YOU GOT THEM OUT OF SOME FANTASTIC SCRAPE AND VANISHED IN A PUFF OF SMOKE OR SOME-THING!
AND TRINA -- TRINA TAYLOR -- WE LEFT HER IN THE SAFETY DOME? GOSH -- WE SHOULD GET BACK THERE RIGHT AWAY, SIR! SHE MIGHT --
YOU'LL HAVE TO WAIT FOR HER AUTOGRAPH, SERGEANT! THOSE TV PEOPLE ARE ON EARTH BY NOW! YOU MEN HAVE BEEN MISSING FOR A WEEK! -- NOW WHERE HAVE YOU BEEN FOR A WEEK -- WITH A 5 HOUR SUPPLY OF OXYGEN!
THE END

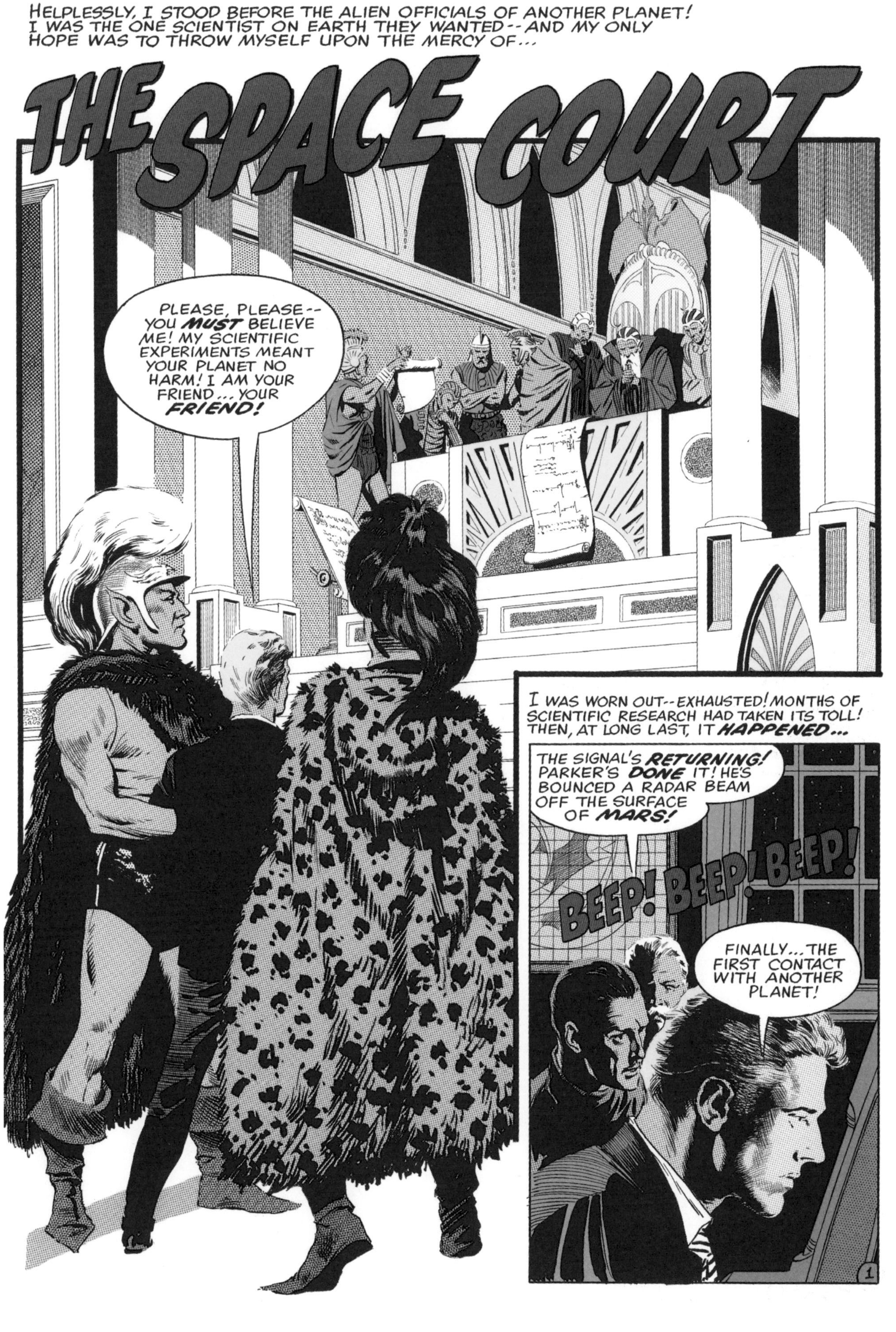
HELPLESSLY, I STOOD BEFORE THE ALIEN OFFICIALS OF ANOTHER PLANET! I WAS THE ONE SCIENTIST ON EARTH THEY WANTED--AND MY ONLY HOPE WAS TO THROW MYSELF UPON THE MERCY OF...
THE SPACE COURT
PLEASE, PLEASE--YOU MUST BELIEVE ME! MY SCIENTIFIC EXPERIMENTS MEANT YOUR PLANET NO HARM! I AM YOUR FRIEND... YOUR FRIEND!
I WAS WORN OUT--EXHAUSTED! MONTHS OF SCIENTIFIC RESEARCH HAD TAKEN ITS TOLL! THEN, AT LONG LAST, IT HAPPENED...
THE SIGNAL'S RETURNING! PARKER'S DONE IT! HE'S BOUNCED A RADAR BEAM OFF THE SURFACE OF MARS!
BEEP! BEEP! BEEP!
FINALLY... THE FIRST CONTACT WITH ANOTHER PLANET!
1

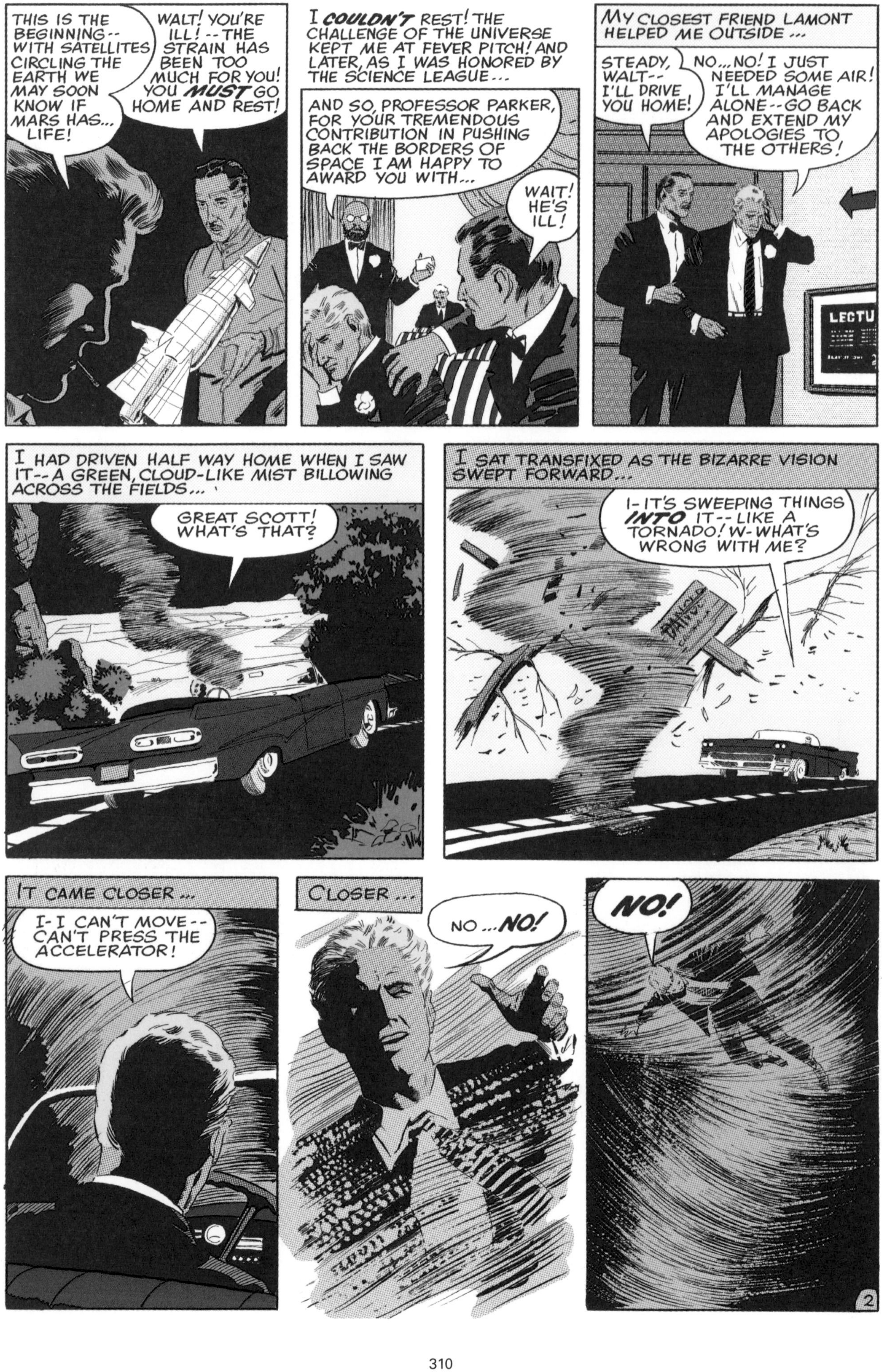
THIS IS THE BEGINNING-- WITH SATELLITES CIRCLING THE EARTH WE MAY SOON KNOW IF MARS HAS... LIFE!
WALT! YOU'RE ILL! --THE STRAIN HAS BEEN TOO MUCH FOR YOU! YOU MUST GO HOME AND REST!
I COULDN'T REST! THE CHALLENGE OF THE UNIVERSE KEPT ME AT FEVER PITCH! AND LATER, AS I WAS HONORED BY THE SCIENCE LEAGUE...
AND SO, PROFESSOR PARKER, FOR YOUR TREMENDOUS CONTRIBUTION IN PUSHING BACK THE BORDERS OF SPACE I AM HAPPY TO AWARD YOU WITH...
WAIT! HE'S ILL!
MY CLOSEST FRIEND LAMONT HELPED ME OUTSIDE...
STEADY, WALT-- I'LL DRIVE YOU HOME!
NO...NO! I JUST NEEDED SOME AIR! I'LL MANAGE ALONE--GO BACK AND EXTEND MY APOLOGIES TO THE OTHERS!
LECTU
I HAD DRIVEN HALF WAY HOME WHEN I SAW IT--A GREEN, CLOUD-LIKE MIST BILLOWING ACROSS THE FIELDS...
GREAT SCOTT! WHAT'S THAT?
I SAT TRANSFIXED AS THE BIZARRE VISION SWEPT FORWARD...
I-IT'S SWEEPING THINGS INTO IT--LIKE A TORNADO! W-WHAT'S WRONG WITH ME?
IT CAME CLOSER...
I-I CAN'T MOVE-- CAN'T PRESS THE ACCELERATOR!
CLOSER...
NO...NO!
NO!
2

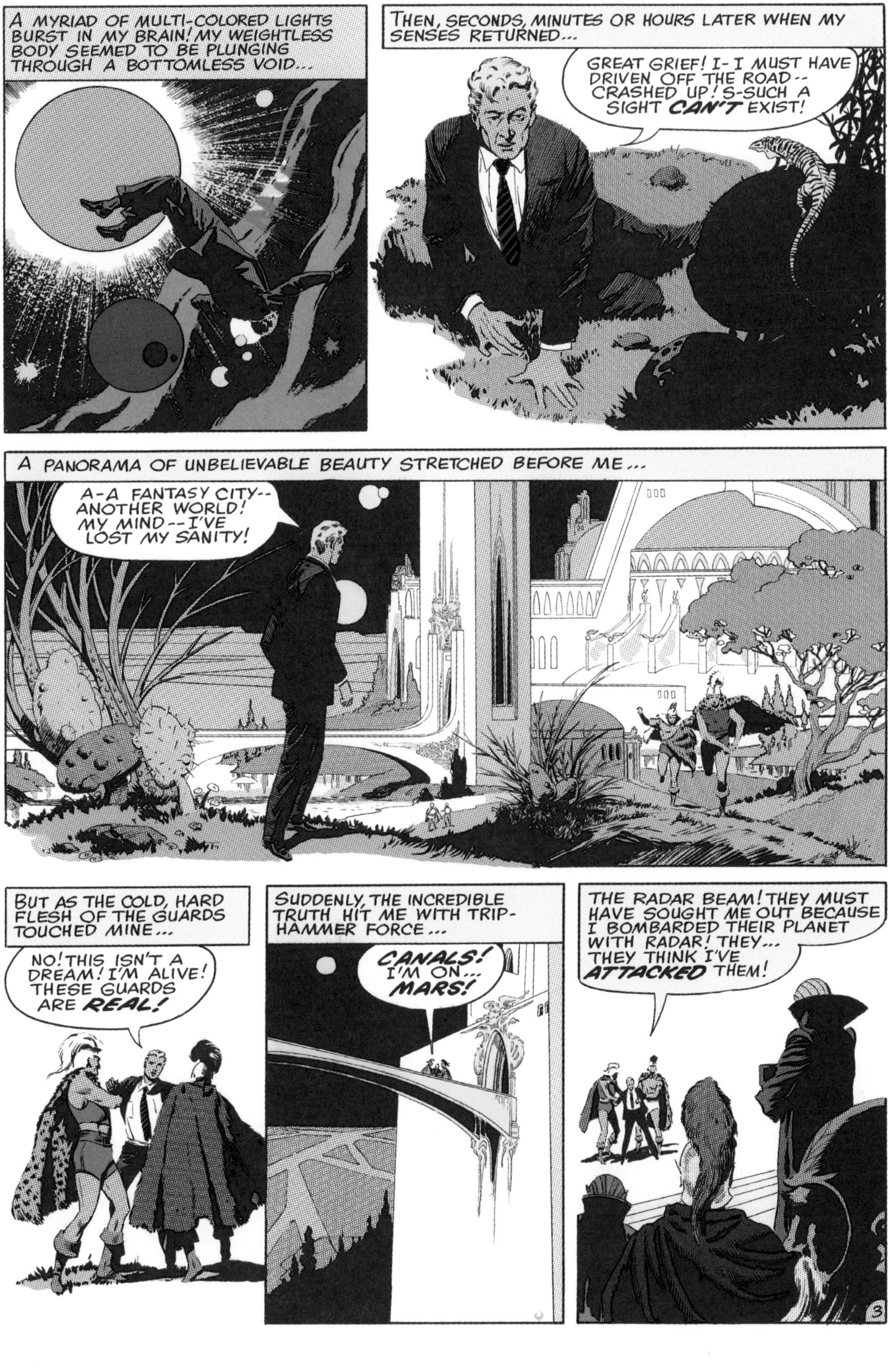
A MYRIAD OF MULTI-COLORED LIGHTS BURST IN MY BRAIN! MY WEIGHTLESS BODY SEEMED TO BE PLUNGING THROUGH A BOTTOMLESS VOID...
THEN, SECONDS, MINUTES OR HOURS LATER WHEN MY SENSES RETURNED...
GREAT GRIEF! I- I MUST HAVE DRIVEN OFF THE ROAD-- CRASHED UP! S-SUCH A SIGHT CAN'T EXIST!
A PANORAMA OF UNBELIEVABLE BEAUTY STRETCHED BEFORE ME...
A-A FANTASY CITY-- ANOTHER WORLD! MY MIND--I'VE LOST MY SANITY!
BUT AS THE COLD, HARD FLESH OF THE GUARDS TOUCHED MINE...
NO! THIS ISN'T A DREAM! I'M ALIVE! THESE GUARDS ARE REAL!
SUDDENLY, THE INCREDIBLE TRUTH HIT ME WITH TRIP-HAMMER FORCE...
CANALS! I'M ON... MARS!
THE RADAR BEAM! THEY MUST HAVE SOUGHT ME OUT BECAUSE I BOMBARDED THEIR PLANET WITH RADAR! THEY... THEY THINK I'VE ATTACKED THEM!
3

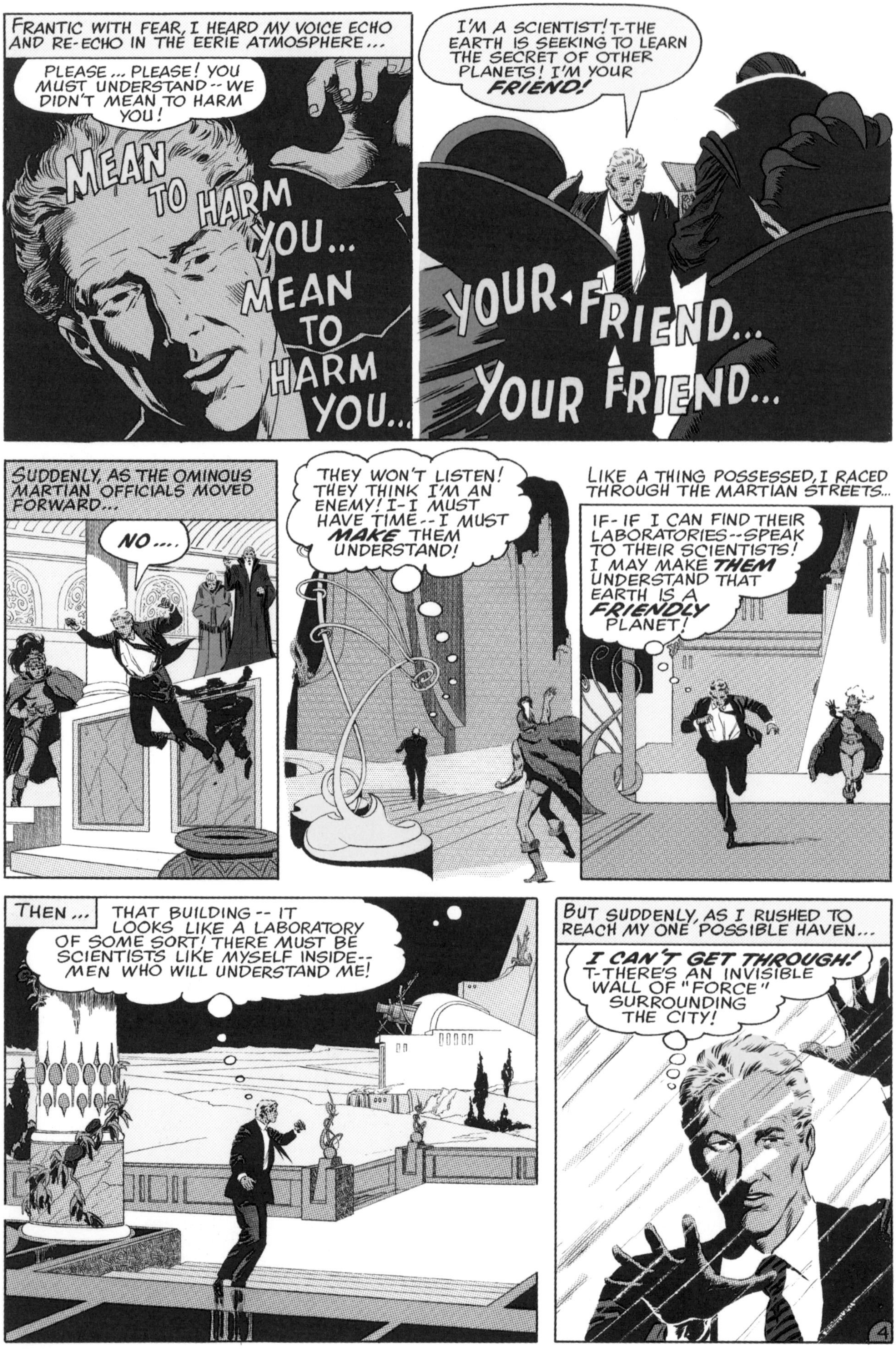
FRANTIC WITH FEAR, I HEARD MY VOICE ECHO AND RE-ECHO IN THE EERIE ATMOSPHERE...
PLEASE... PLEASE! YOU MUST UNDERSTAND -- WE DIDN'T MEAN TO HARM YOU!
MEAN TO HARM YOU... MEAN TO HARM YOU...
I'M A SCIENTIST! T-THE EARTH IS SEEKING TO LEARN THE SECRET OF OTHER PLANETS! I'M YOUR FRIEND!
YOUR FRIEND... YOUR FRIEND...
SUDDENLY, AS THE OMINOUS MARTIAN OFFICIALS MOVED FORWARD...
NO....
THEY WON'T LISTEN! THEY THINK I'M AN ENEMY! I-I MUST HAVE TIME -- I MUST MAKE THEM UNDERSTAND!
LIKE A THING POSSESSED, I RACED THROUGH THE MARTIAN STREETS...
IF- IF I CAN FIND THEIR LABORATORIES -- SPEAK TO THEIR SCIENTISTS! I MAY MAKE THEM UNDERSTAND THAT EARTH IS A FRIENDLY PLANET!
THEN...
THAT BUILDING -- IT LOOKS LIKE A LABORATORY OF SOME SORT! THERE MUST BE SCIENTISTS LIKE MYSELF INSIDE -- MEN WHO WILL UNDERSTAND ME!
BUT SUDDENLY, AS I RUSHED TO REACH MY ONE POSSIBLE HAVEN...
I CAN'T GET THROUGH! T-THERE'S AN INVISIBLE WALL OF "FORCE" SURROUNDING THE CITY!
4

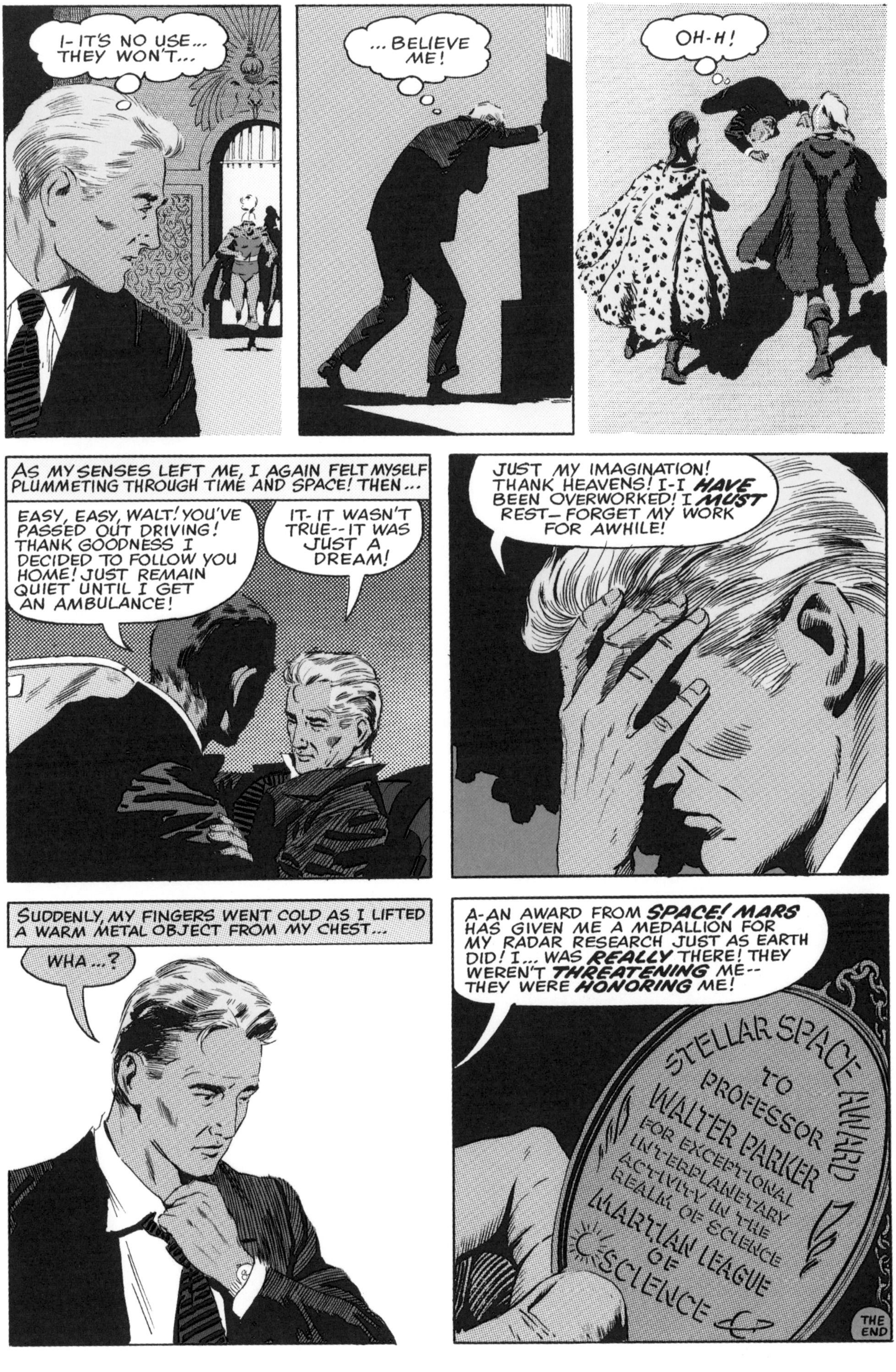
I- IT'S NO USE... THEY WON'T...
... BELIEVE ME!
OH-H!
AS MY SENSES LEFT ME, I AGAIN FELT MYSELF PLUMMETING THROUGH TIME AND SPACE! THEN ...
EASY, EASY, WALT! YOU'VE PASSED OUT DRIVING! THANK GOODNESS I DECIDED TO FOLLOW YOU HOME! JUST REMAIN QUIET UNTIL I GET AN AMBULANCE!
IT- IT WASN'T TRUE-- IT WAS JUST A DREAM!
JUST MY IMAGINATION! THANK HEAVENS! I-I HAVE BEEN OVERWORKED! I MUST REST-- FORGET MY WORK FOR AWHILE!
SUDDENLY, MY FINGERS WENT COLD AS I LIFTED A WARM METAL OBJECT FROM MY CHEST...
WHA ...?
A-AN AWARD FROM SPACE! MARS HAS GIVEN ME A MEDALLION FOR MY RADAR RESEARCH JUST AS EARTH DID! I... WAS REALLY THERE! THEY WEREN'T THREATENING ME-- THEY WERE HONORING ME!
STELLAR SPACE AWARD
TO PROFESSOR WALTER PARKER
FOR EXCEPTIONAL INTERPLANETARY ACTIVITY IN THE REALM OF SCIENCE
MARTIAN LEAGUE OF SCIENCE
THE END

THE LITTLE EARTH

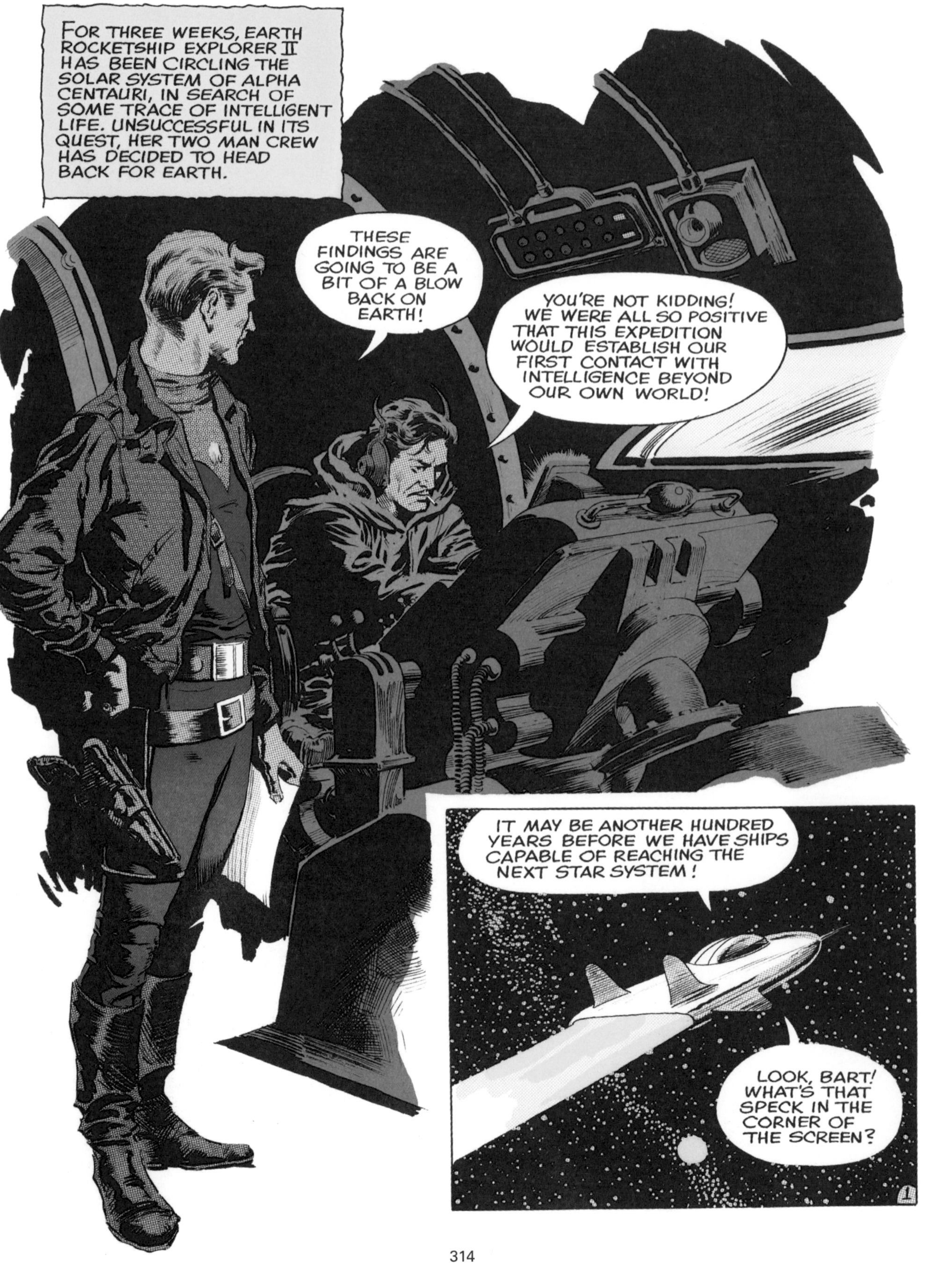
FOR THREE WEEKS, EARTH ROCKETSHIP EXPLORER II HAS BEEN CIRCLING THE SOLAR SYSTEM OF ALPHA CENTAURI, IN SEARCH OF SOME TRACE OF INTELLIGENT LIFE. UNSUCCESSFUL IN ITS QUEST, HER TWO MAN CREW HAS DECIDED TO HEAD BACK FOR EARTH.
THESE FINDINGS ARE GOING TO BE A BIT OF A BLOW BACK ON EARTH!
YOU'RE NOT KIDDING! WE WERE ALL SO POSITIVE THAT THIS EXPEDITION WOULD ESTABLISH OUR FIRST CONTACT WITH INTELLIGENCE BEYOND OUR OWN WORLD!
IT MAY BE ANOTHER HUNDRED YEARS BEFORE WE HAVE SHIPS CAPABLE OF REACHING THE NEXT STAR SYSTEM!
LOOK, BART! WHAT'S THAT SPECK IN THE CORNER OF THE SCREEN?

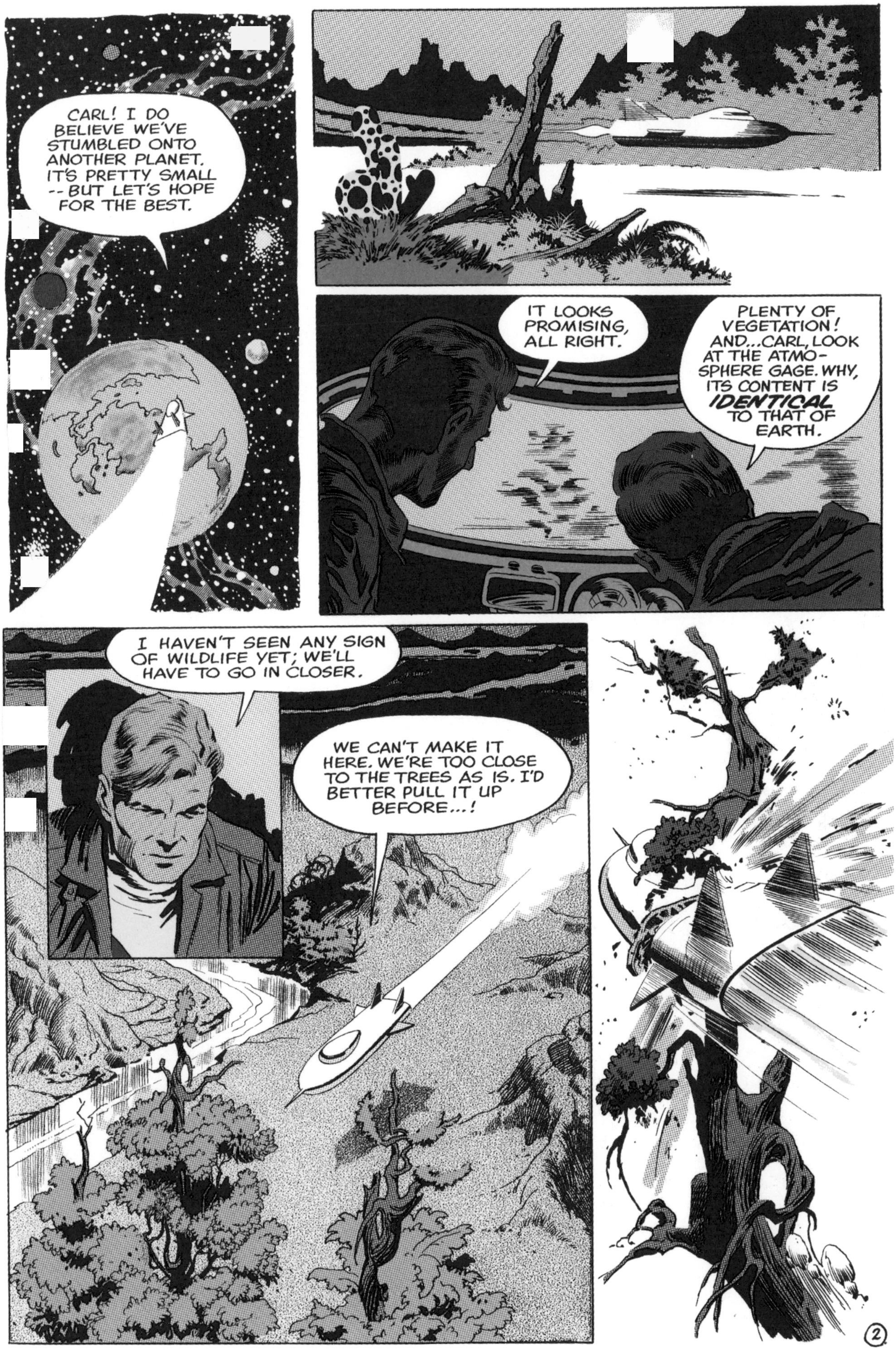
CARL! I DO BELIEVE WE'VE STUMBLED ONTO ANOTHER PLANET. IT'S PRETTY SMALL --BUT LET'S HOPE FOR THE BEST.
IT LOOKS PROMISING, ALL RIGHT.
PLENTY OF VEGETATION! AND...CARL, LOOK AT THE ATMO-SPHERE GAGE. WHY, ITS CONTENT IS IDENTICAL TO THAT OF EARTH.
I HAVEN'T SEEN ANY SIGN OF WILDLIFE YET; WE'LL HAVE TO GO IN CLOSER.
WE CAN'T MAKE IT HERE. WE'RE TOO CLOSE TO THE TREES AS IS. I'D BETTER PULL IT UP BEFORE...!
2

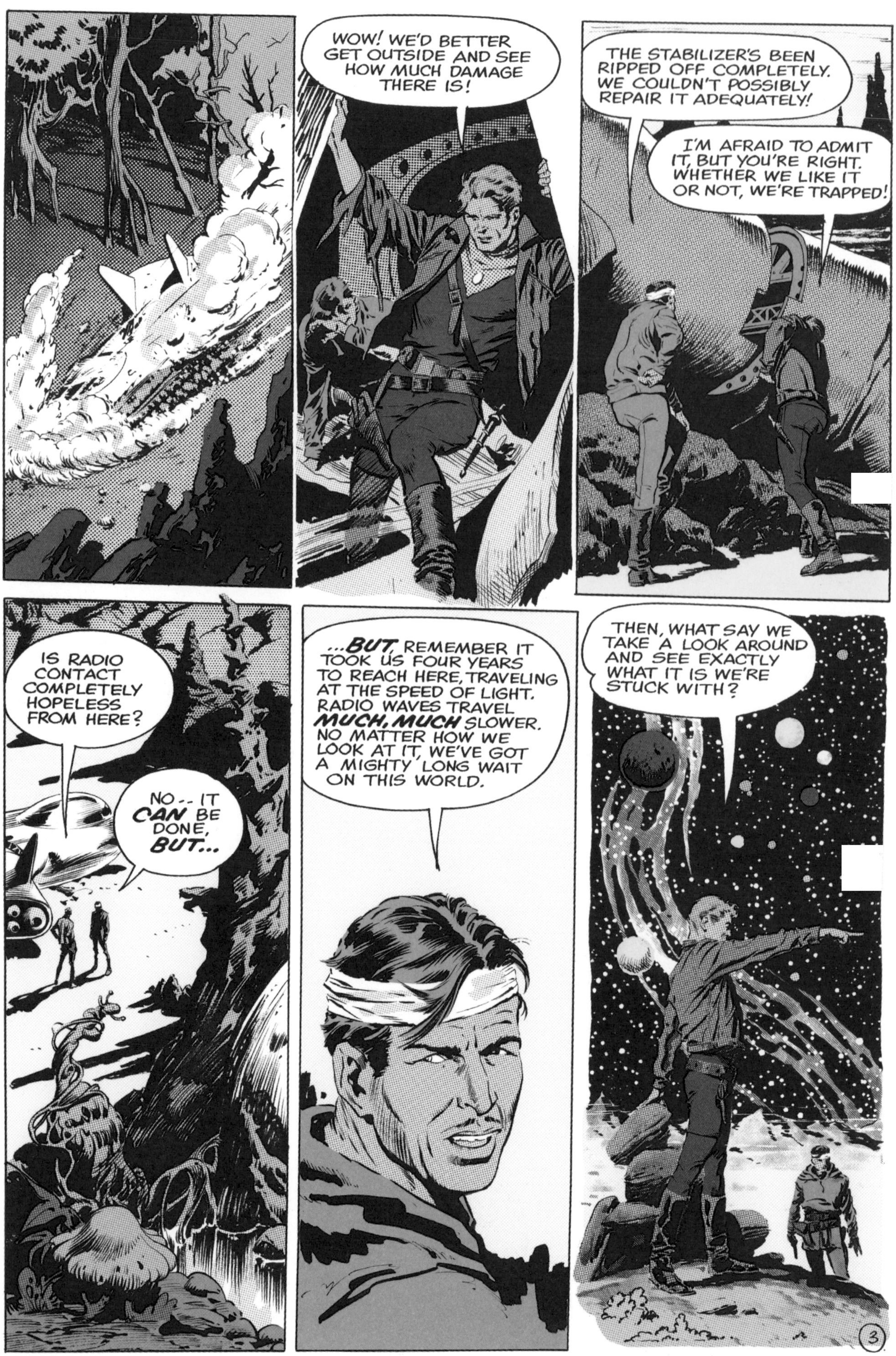
WOW! WE'D BETTER GET OUTSIDE AND SEE HOW MUCH DAMAGE THERE IS!
THE STABILIZER'S BEEN RIPPED OFF COMPLETELY. WE COULDN'T POSSIBLY REPAIR IT ADEQUATELY!
I'M AFRAID TO ADMIT IT, BUT YOU'RE RIGHT. WHETHER WE LIKE IT OR NOT, WE'RE TRAPPED!
IS RADIO CONTACT COMPLETELY HOPELESS FROM HERE?
NO-- IT CAN BE DONE, BUT...
...BUT, REMEMBER IT TOOK US FOUR YEARS TO REACH HERE, TRAVELING AT THE SPEED OF LIGHT. RADIO WAVES TRAVEL MUCH, MUCH SLOWER. NO MATTER HOW WE LOOK AT IT, WE'VE GOT A MIGHTY LONG WAIT ON THIS WORLD.
THEN, WHAT SAY WE TAKE A LOOK AROUND AND SEE EXACTLY WHAT IT IS WE'RE STUCK WITH?
3

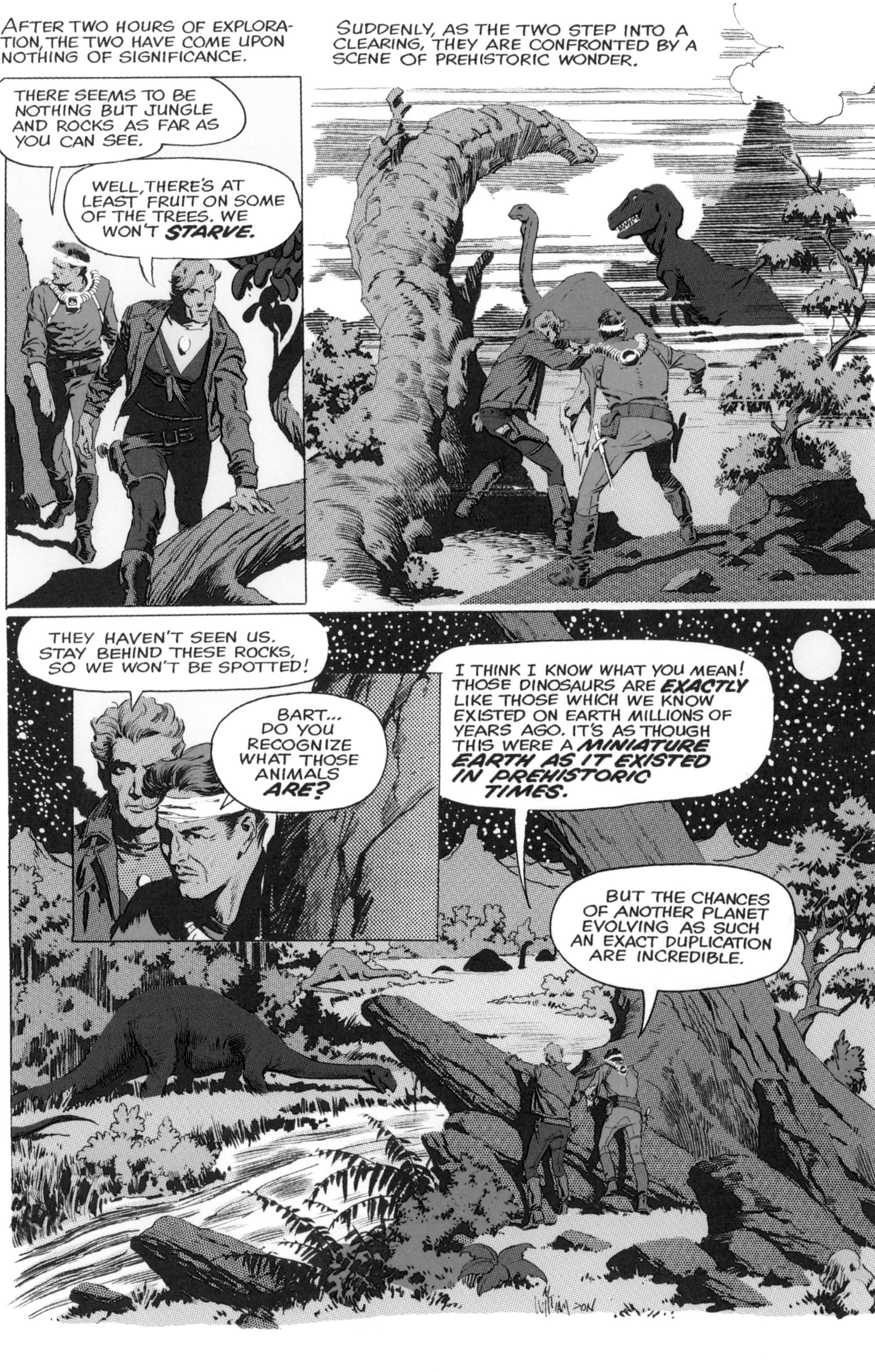

AFTER TWO HOURS OF EXPLORATION, THE TWO HAVE COME UPON NOTHING OF SIGNIFICANCE.
THERE SEEMS TO BE NOTHING BUT JUNGLE AND ROCKS AS FAR AS YOU CAN SEE.
WELL, THERE'S AT LEAST FRUIT ON SOME OF THE TREES. WE WON'T STARVE.
SUDDENLY, AS THE TWO STEP INTO A CLEARING, THEY ARE CONFRONTED BY A SCENE OF PREHISTORIC WONDER.
THEY HAVEN'T SEEN US. STAY BEHIND THESE ROCKS, SO WE WON'T BE SPOTTED!
BART... DO YOU RECOGNIZE WHAT THOSE ANIMALS ARE?
I THINK I KNOW WHAT YOU MEAN! THOSE DINOSAURS ARE EXACTLY LIKE THOSE WHICH WE KNOW EXISTED ON EARTH MILLIONS OF YEARS AGO. IT'S AS THOUGH THIS WERE A MINIATURE EARTH AS IT EXISTED IN PREHISTORIC TIMES.
BUT THE CHANCES OF ANOTHER PLANET EVOLVING AS SUCH AN EXACT DUPLICATION ARE INCREDIBLE.

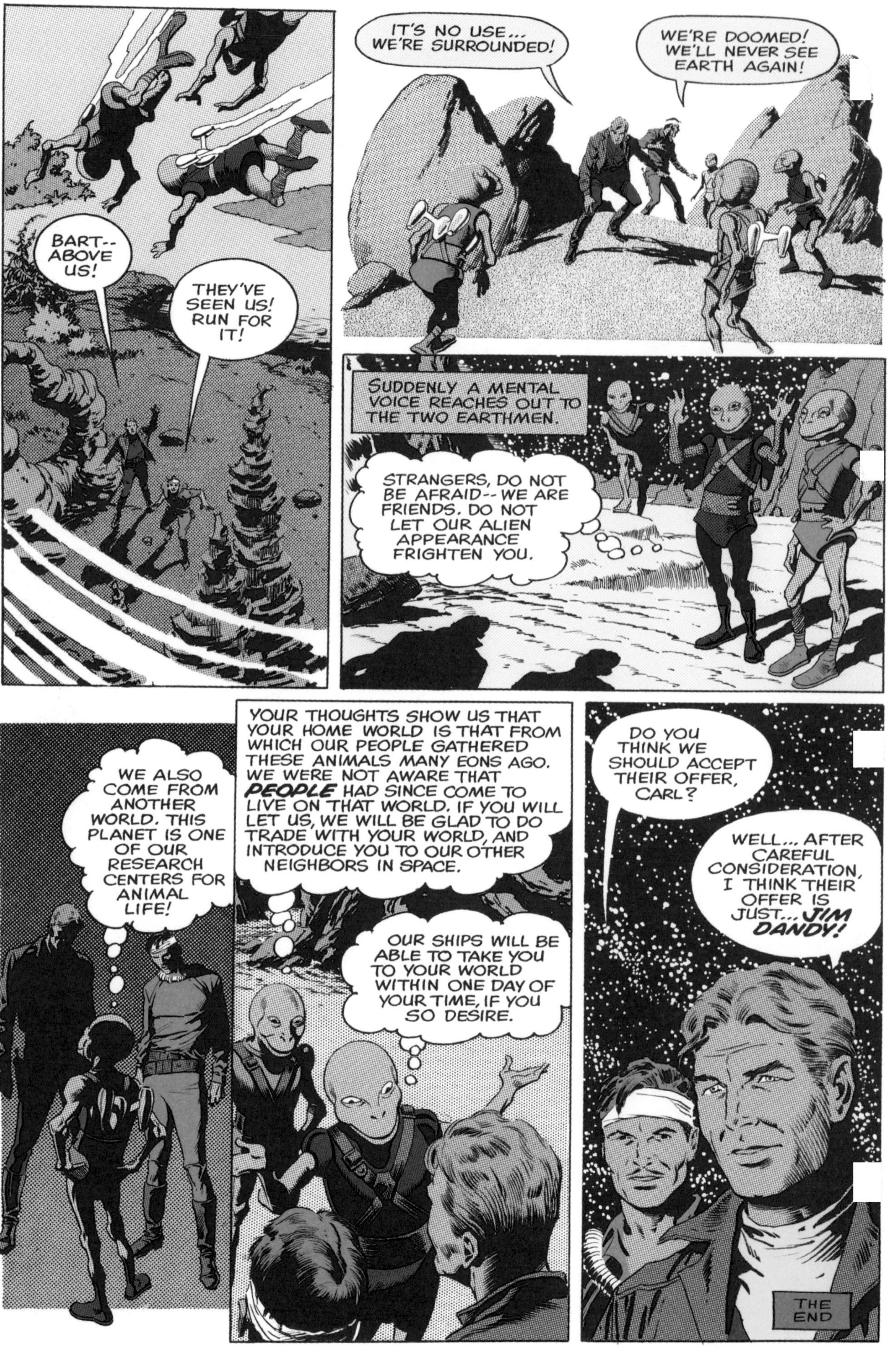
BART-- ABOVE US!
THEY'VE SEEN US! RUN FOR IT!
IT'S NO USE... WE'RE SURROUNDED!
WE'RE DOOMED! WE'LL NEVER SEE EARTH AGAIN!
SUDDENLY A MENTAL VOICE REACHES OUT TO THE TWO EARTHMEN.
STRANGERS, DO NOT BE AFRAID--WE ARE FRIENDS. DO NOT LET OUR ALIEN APPEARANCE FRIGHTEN YOU.
WE ALSO COME FROM ANOTHER WORLD. THIS PLANET IS ONE OF OUR RESEARCH CENTERS FOR ANIMAL LIFE!
YOUR THOUGHTS SHOW US THAT YOUR HOME WORLD IS THAT FROM WHICH OUR PEOPLE GATHERED THESE ANIMALS MANY EONS AGO. WE WERE NOT AWARE THAT PEOPLE HAD SINCE COME TO LIVE ON THAT WORLD. IF YOU WILL LET US, WE WILL BE GLAD TO DO TRADE WITH YOUR WORLD, AND INTRODUCE YOU TO OUR OTHER NEIGHBORS IN SPACE.
OUR SHIPS WILL BE ABLE TO TAKE YOU TO YOUR WORLD WITHIN ONE DAY OF YOUR TIME, IF YOU SO DESIRE.
DO YOU THINK WE SHOULD ACCEPT THEIR OFFER, CARL?
WELL... AFTER CAREFUL CONSIDERATION, I THINK THEIR OFFER IS JUST... JIM DANDY!
THE END

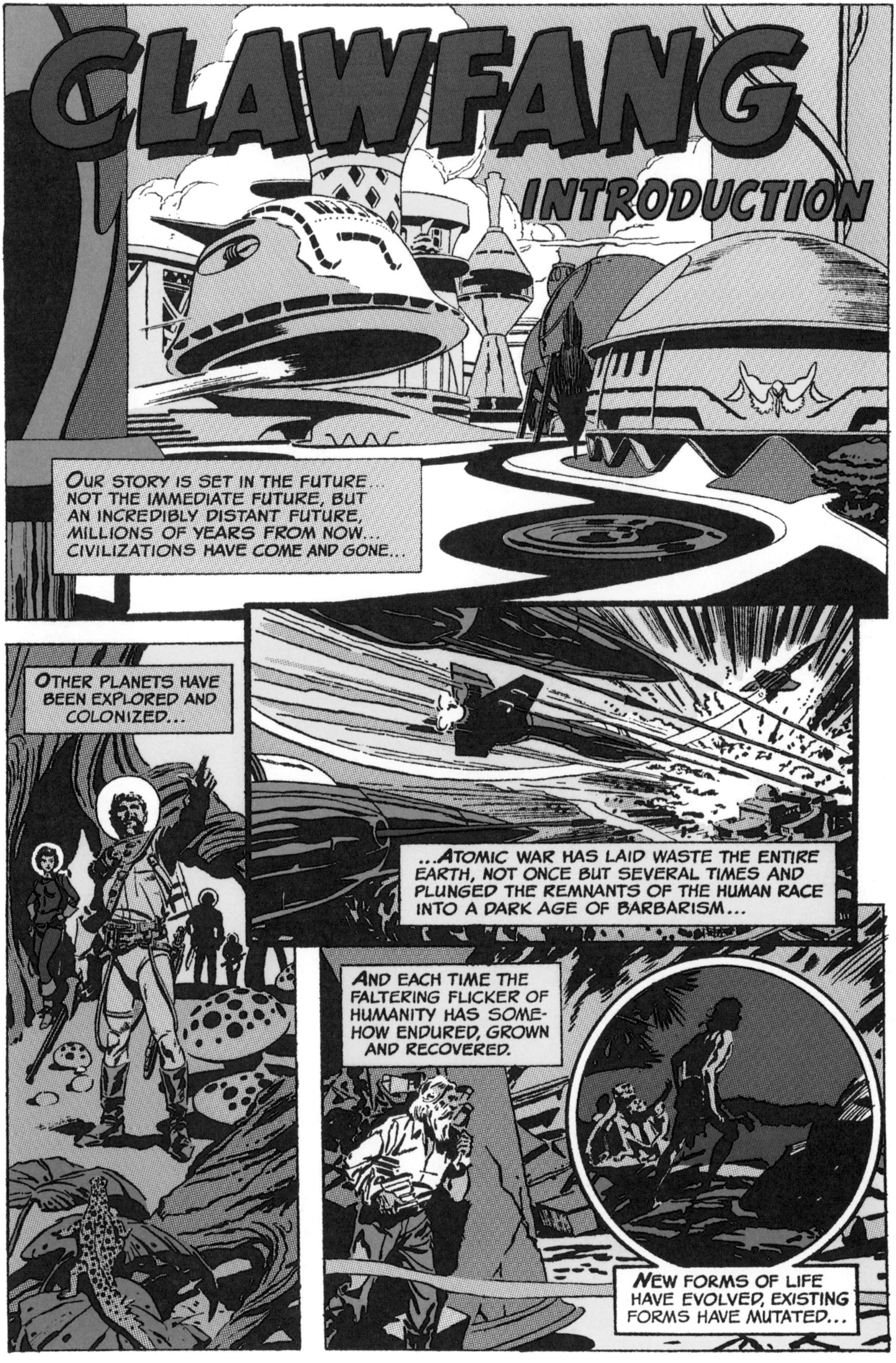
CLAWFANG
INTRODUCTION
OUR STORY IS SET IN THE FUTURE... NOT THE IMMEDIATE FUTURE, BUT AN INCREDIBLY DISTANT FUTURE, MILLIONS OF YEARS FROM NOW... CIVILIZATIONS HAVE COME AND GONE...
OTHER PLANETS HAVE BEEN EXPLORED AND COLONIZED...
...ATOMIC WAR HAS LAID WASTE THE ENTIRE EARTH, NOT ONCE BUT SEVERAL TIMES AND PLUNGED THE REMNANTS OF THE HUMAN RACE INTO A DARK AGE OF BARBARISM...
AND EACH TIME THE FALTERING FLICKER OF HUMANITY HAS SOME-HOW ENDURED, GROWN AND RECOVERED.
NEW FORMS OF LIFE HAVE EVOLVED, EXISTING FORMS HAVE MUTATED...

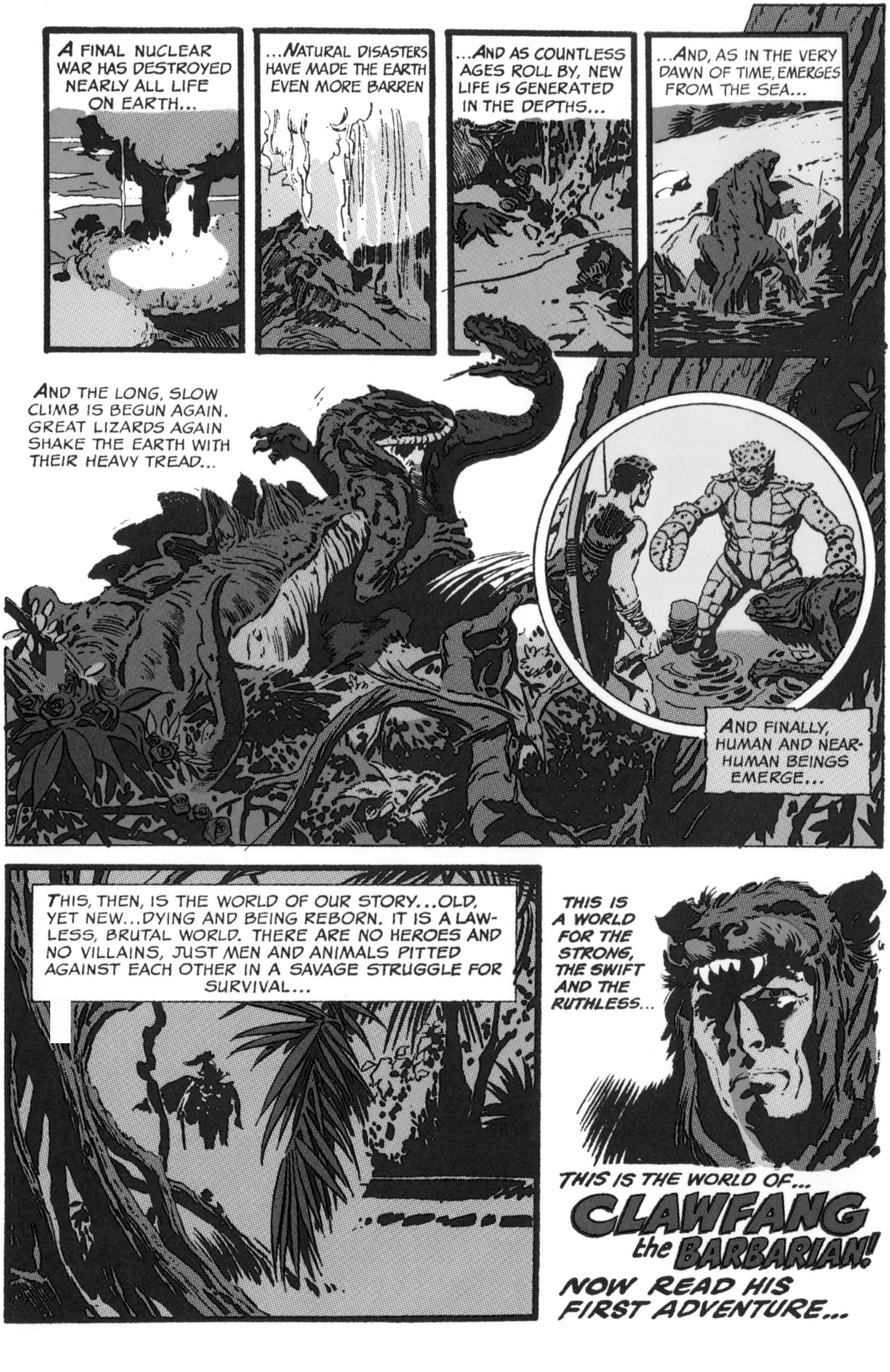
A FINAL NUCLEAR WAR HAS DESTROYED NEARLY ALL LIFE ON EARTH...
...NATURAL DISASTERS HAVE MADE THE EARTH EVEN MORE BARREN
...AND AS COUNTLESS AGES ROLL BY, NEW LIFE IS GENERATED IN THE DEPTHS...
...AND, AS IN THE VERY DAWN OF TIME, EMERGES FROM THE SEA...
AND THE LONG, SLOW CLIMB IS BEGUN AGAIN. GREAT LIZARDS AGAIN SHAKE THE EARTH WITH THEIR HEAVY TREAD...
AND FINALLY, HUMAN AND NEAR-HUMAN BEINGS EMERGE...
THIS, THEN, IS THE WORLD OF OUR STORY...OLD, YET NEW...DYING AND BEING REBORN. IT IS A LAWLESS, BRUTAL WORLD. THERE ARE NO HEROES AND NO VILLAINS, JUST MEN AND ANIMALS PITTED AGAINST EACH OTHER IN A SAVAGE STRUGGLE FOR SURVIVAL...
THIS IS A WORLD FOR THE STRONG, THE SWIFT AND THE RUTHLESS...
THIS IS THE WORLD OF...
CLAWFANG the BARBARIAN!
NOW READ HIS FIRST ADVENTURE...

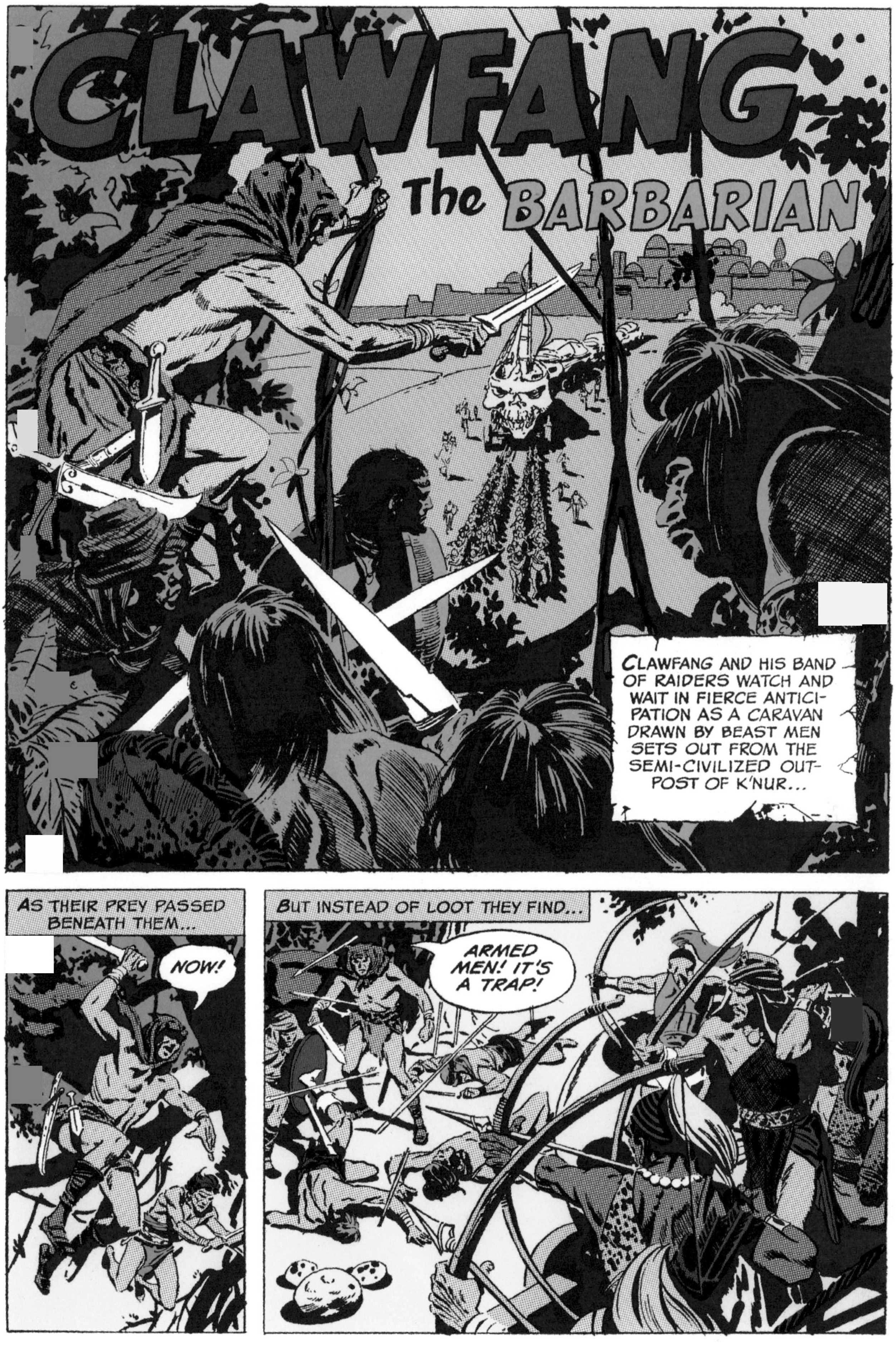
CLAWFANG
The BARBARIAN
CLAWFANG AND HIS BAND OF RAIDERS WATCH AND WAIT IN FIERCE ANTICIPATION AS A CARAVAN DRAWN BY BEAST MEN SETS OUT FROM THE SEMI-CIVILIZED OUTPOST OF K'NUR...
AS THEIR PREY PASSED BENEATH THEM...
NOW!
BUT INSTEAD OF LOOT THEY FIND...
ARMED MEN! IT'S A TRAP!

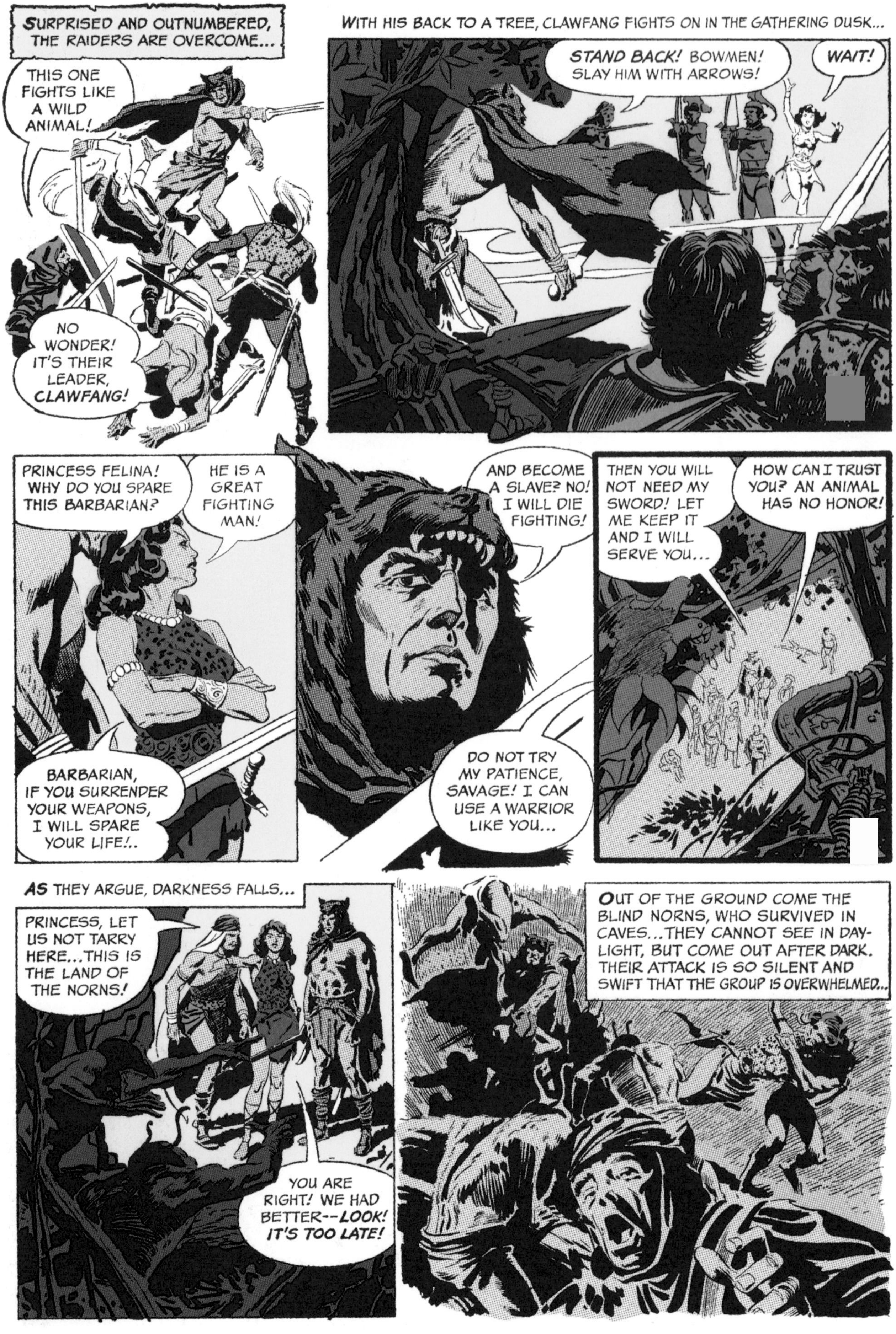
SURPRISED AND OUTNUMBERED, THE RAIDERS ARE OVERCOME...
THIS ONE FIGHTS LIKE A WILD ANIMAL!
NO WONDER! IT'S THEIR LEADER, CLAWFANG!
WITH HIS BACK TO A TREE, CLAWFANG FIGHTS ON IN THE GATHERING DUSK...
STAND BACK! BOWMEN! SLAY HIM WITH ARROWS!
WAIT!
PRINCESS FELINA! WHY DO YOU SPARE THIS BARBARIAN?
HE IS A GREAT FIGHTING MAN!
BARBARIAN, IF YOU SURRENDER YOUR WEAPONS, I WILL SPARE YOUR LIFE!..
AND BECOME A SLAVE? NO! I WILL DIE FIGHTING!
DO NOT TRY MY PATIENCE, SAVAGE! I CAN USE A WARRIOR LIKE YOU...
THEN YOU WILL NOT NEED MY SWORD! LET ME KEEP IT AND I WILL SERVE YOU...
HOW CAN I TRUST YOU? AN ANIMAL HAS NO HONOR!
AS THEY ARGUE, DARKNESS FALLS...
PRINCESS, LET US NOT TARRY HERE...THIS IS THE LAND OF THE NORNS!
YOU ARE RIGHT! WE HAD BETTER--LOOK! IT'S TOO LATE!
OUT OF THE GROUND COME THE BLIND NORNS, WHO SURVIVED IN CAVES...THEY CANNOT SEE IN DAYLIGHT, BUT COME OUT AFTER DARK. THEIR ATTACK IS SO SILENT AND SWIFT THAT THE GROUP IS OVERWHELMED...

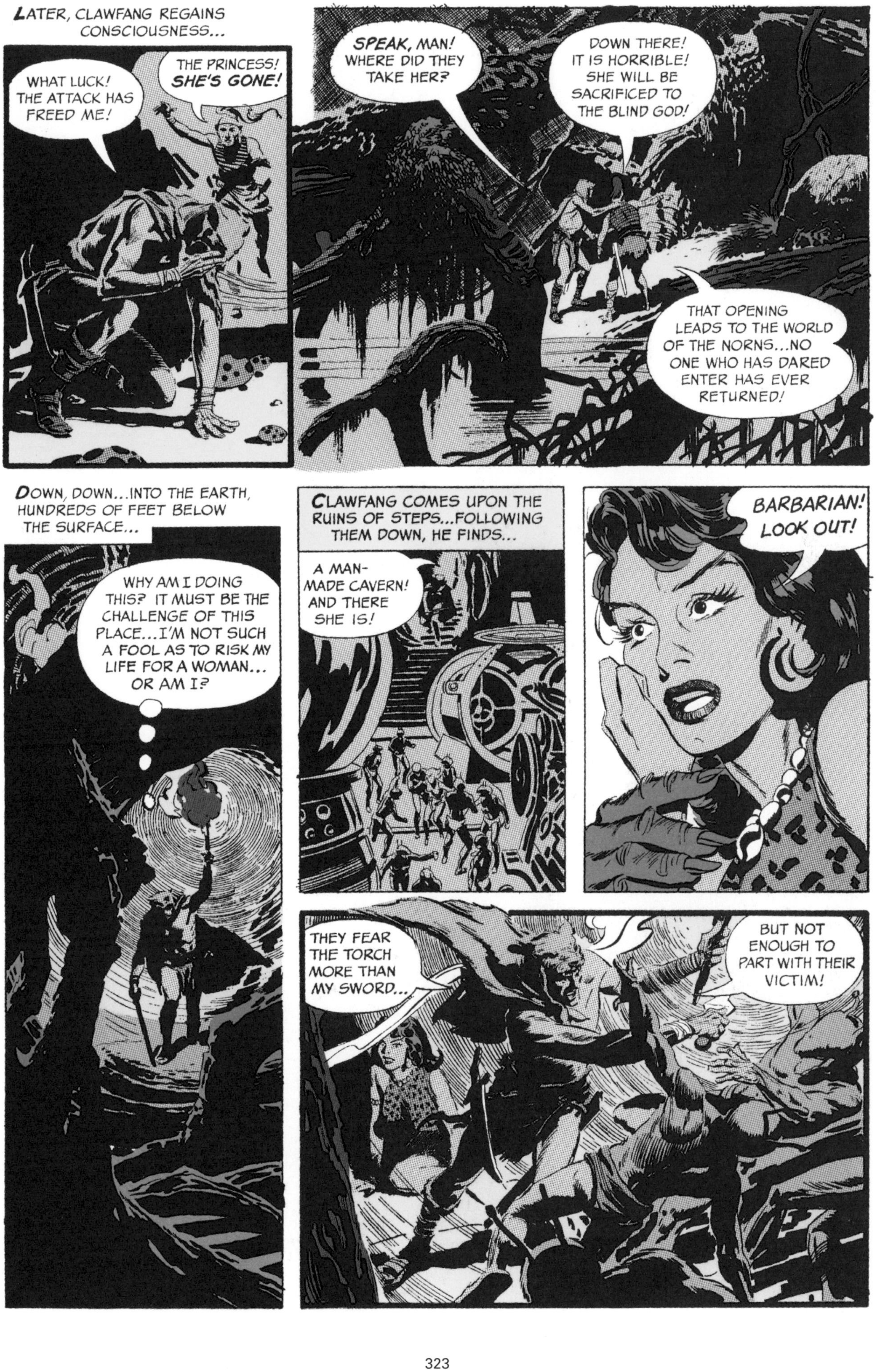
LATER, CLAWFANG REGAINS CONSCIOUSNESS...
WHAT LUCK! THE ATTACK HAS FREED ME!
THE PRINCESS! SHE'S GONE!
SPEAK, MAN! WHERE DID THEY TAKE HER?
DOWN THERE! IT IS HORRIBLE! SHE WILL BE SACRIFICED TO THE BLIND GOD!
THAT OPENING LEADS TO THE WORLD OF THE NORNS...NO ONE WHO HAS DARED ENTER HAS EVER RETURNED!
DOWN, DOWN...INTO THE EARTH, HUNDREDS OF FEET BELOW THE SURFACE...
WHY AM I DOING THIS? IT MUST BE THE CHALLENGE OF THIS PLACE...I'M NOT SUCH A FOOL AS TO RISK MY LIFE FOR A WOMAN... OR AM I?
CLAWFANG COMES UPON THE RUINS OF STEPS...FOLLOWING THEM DOWN, HE FINDS...
A MAN-MADE CAVERN! AND THERE SHE IS!
BARBARIAN! LOOK OUT!
THEY FEAR THE TORCH MORE THAN MY SWORD...
BUT NOT ENOUGH TO PART WITH THEIR VICTIM!

SHIELDING THE PRINCESS BEHIND HIM, CLAWFANG FIGHTS A LOSING BATTLE, BEING FORCED DOWNWARD, EVER DEEPER INTO THE CAVE WORLD, UNTIL FINALLY...

CLAWFANG LASHES OUT, AND ONE OF THE BLIND BEASTS FALLS BACK AGAINST A LEVER...

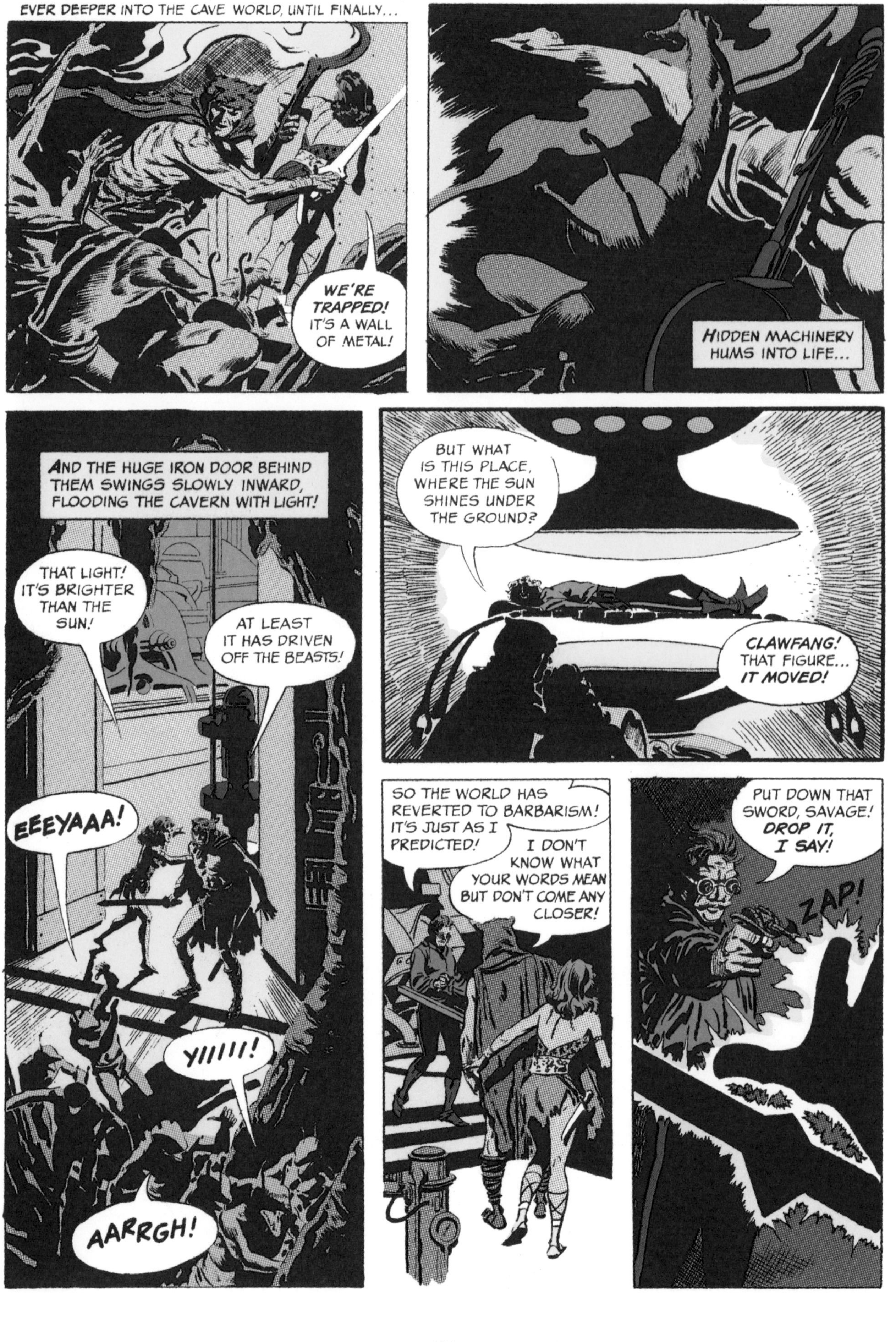
WE'RE TRAPPED! IT'S A WALL OF METAL!
HIDDEN MACHINERY HUMS INTO LIFE...
AND THE HUGE IRON DOOR BEHIND THEM SWINGS SLOWLY INWARD, FLOODING THE CAVERN WITH LIGHT!
THAT LIGHT! IT'S BRIGHTER THAN THE SUN!
AT LEAST IT HAS DRIVEN OFF THE BEASTS!
EEEYAAA!
YIIIII!
AARRGH!
BUT WHAT IS THIS PLACE, WHERE THE SUN SHINES UNDER THE GROUND?
CLAWFANG! THAT FIGURE... IT MOVED!
SO THE WORLD HAS REVERTED TO BARBARISM! IT'S JUST AS I PREDICTED!
I DON'T KNOW WHAT YOUR WORDS MEAN BUT DON'T COME ANY CLOSER!
PUT DOWN THAT SWORD, SAVAGE! DROP IT, I SAY!
ZAP!

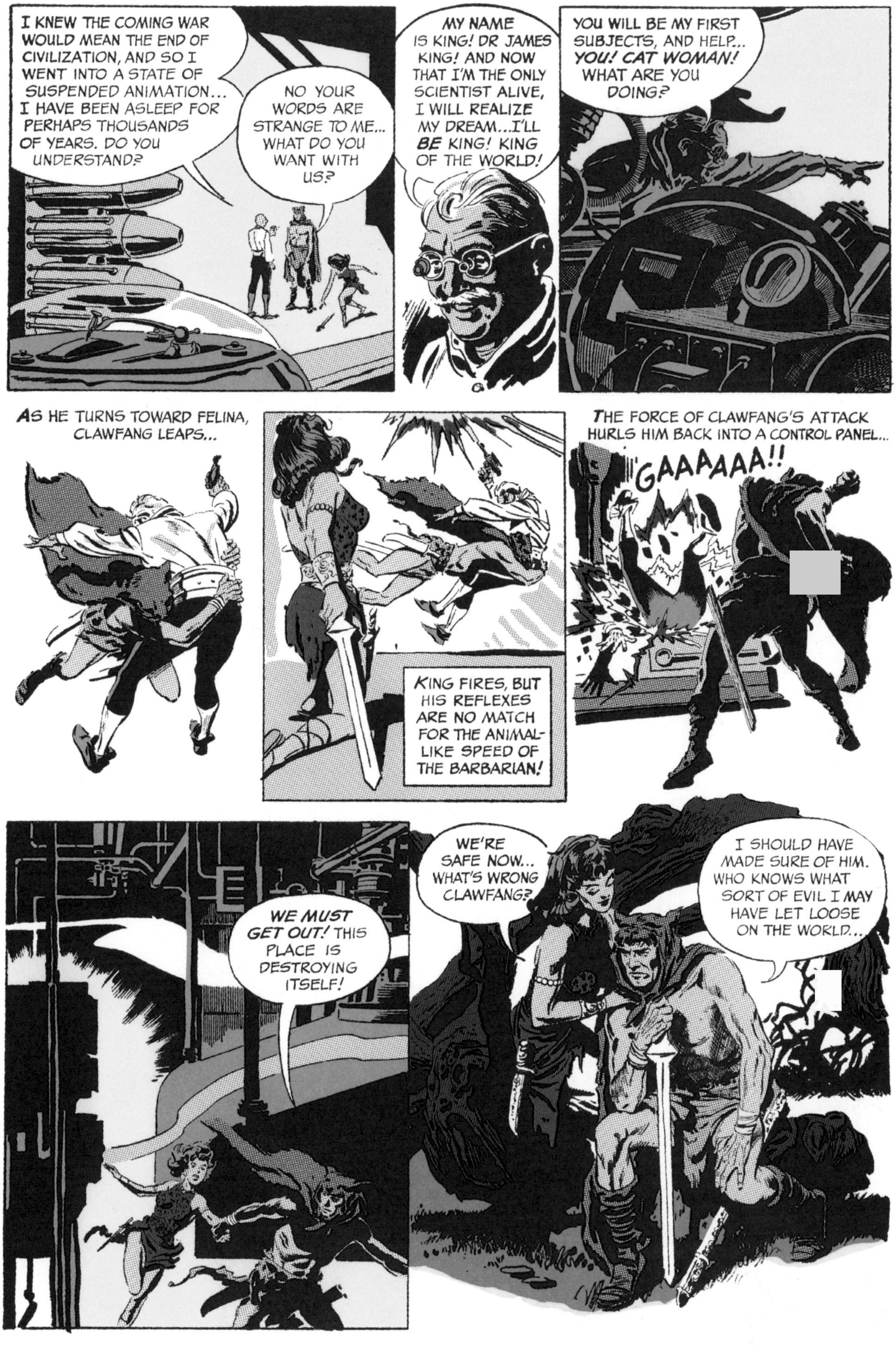
I KNEW THE COMING WAR WOULD MEAN THE END OF CIVILIZATION, AND SO I WENT INTO A STATE OF SUSPENDED ANIMATION... I HAVE BEEN ASLEEP FOR PERHAPS THOUSANDS OF YEARS. DO YOU UNDERSTAND?
NO YOUR WORDS ARE STRANGE TO ME... WHAT DO YOU WANT WITH US?
MY NAME IS KING! DR JAMES KING! AND NOW THAT I'M THE ONLY SCIENTIST ALIVE, I WILL REALIZE MY DREAM...I'LL BE KING! KING OF THE WORLD!
YOU WILL BE MY FIRST SUBJECTS, AND HELP... YOU! CAT WOMAN! WHAT ARE YOU DOING?
AS HE TURNS TOWARD FELINA, CLAWFANG LEAPS...
KING FIRES, BUT HIS REFLEXES ARE NO MATCH FOR THE ANIMAL-LIKE SPEED OF THE BARBARIAN!
THE FORCE OF CLAWFANG'S ATTACK HURLS HIM BACK INTO A CONTROL PANEL...
GAAAAAA!!
WE MUST GET OUT! THIS PLACE IS DESTROYING ITSELF!
WE'RE SAFE NOW... WHAT'S WRONG CLAWFANG?
I SHOULD HAVE MADE SURE OF HIM. WHO KNOWS WHAT SORT OF EVIL I MAY HAVE LET LOOSE ON THE WORLD...

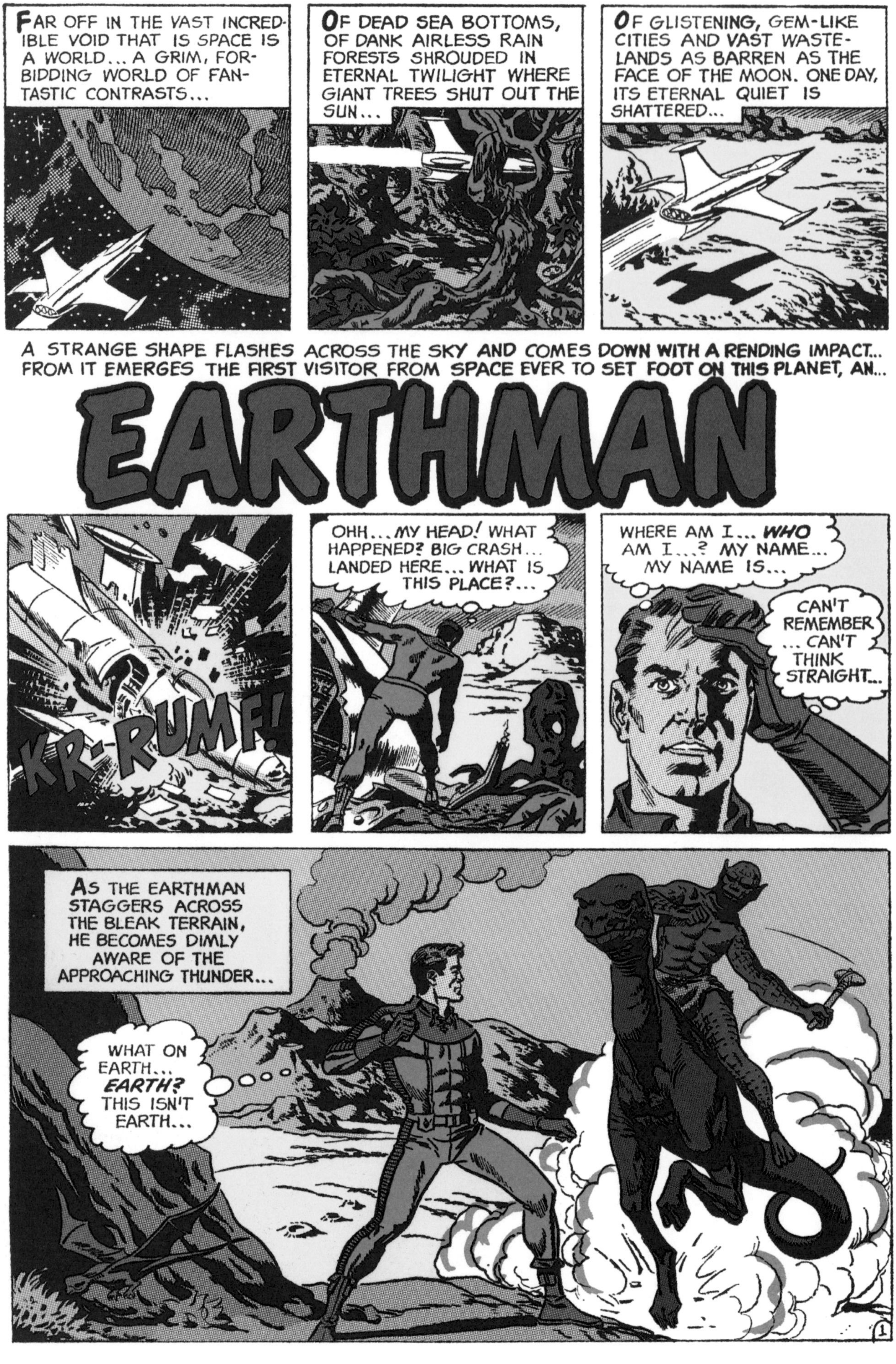

FAR OFF IN THE VAST INCREDIBLE VOID THAT IS SPACE IS A WORLD... A GRIM, FORBIDDING WORLD OF FANTASTIC CONTRASTS...
OF DEAD SEA BOTTOMS, OF DANK AIRLESS RAIN FORESTS SHROUDED IN ETERNAL TWILIGHT WHERE GIANT TREES SHUT OUT THE SUN...
OF GLISTENING, GEM-LIKE CITIES AND VAST WASTELANDS AS BARREN AS THE FACE OF THE MOON. ONE DAY, ITS ETERNAL QUIET IS SHATTERED...
A STRANGE SHAPE FLASHES ACROSS THE SKY AND COMES DOWN WITH A RENDING IMPACT... FROM IT EMERGES THE FIRST VISITOR FROM SPACE EVER TO SET FOOT ON THIS PLANET, AN...
EARTHMAN
KR-RUMF!
OHH... MY HEAD! WHAT HAPPENED? BIG CRASH... LANDED HERE... WHAT IS THIS PLACE?...
WHERE AM I... WHO AM I...? MY NAME... MY NAME IS...
CAN'T REMEMBER ... CAN'T THINK STRAIGHT...
AS THE EARTHMAN STAGGERS ACROSS THE BLEAK TERRAIN, HE BECOMES DIMLY AWARE OF THE APPROACHING THUNDER...
WHAT ON EARTH... EARTH? THIS ISN'T EARTH...
1

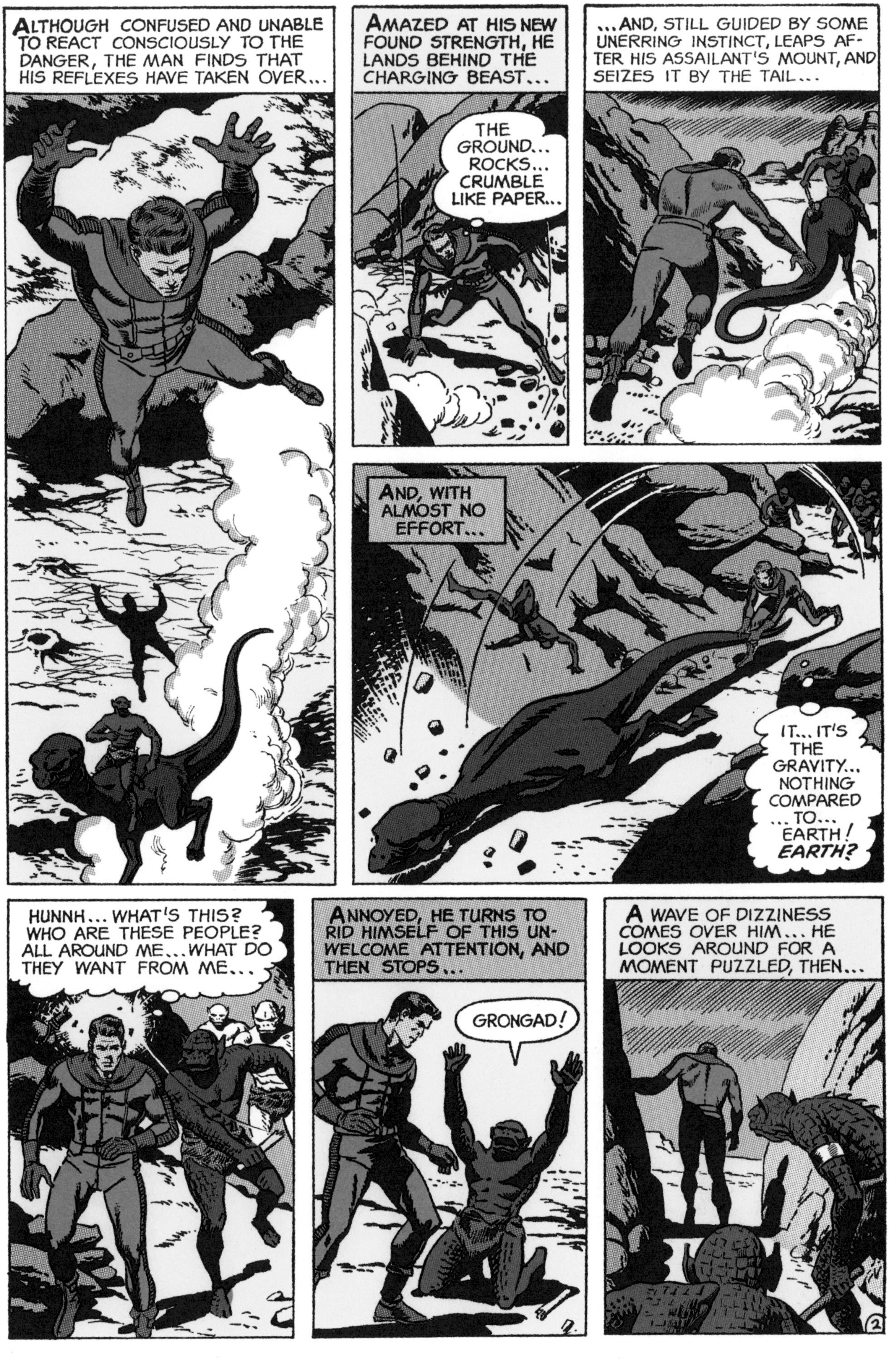
ALTHOUGH CONFUSED AND UNABLE TO REACT CONSCIOUSLY TO THE DANGER, THE MAN FINDS THAT HIS REFLEXES HAVE TAKEN OVER...
AMAZED AT HIS NEW FOUND STRENGTH, HE LANDS BEHIND THE CHARGING BEAST...
THE GROUND... ROCKS... CRUMBLE LIKE PAPER...
...AND, STILL GUIDED BY SOME UNERRING INSTINCT, LEAPS AFTER HIS ASSAILANT'S MOUNT, AND SEIZES IT BY THE TAIL...
AND, WITH ALMOST NO EFFORT...
IT... IT'S THE GRAVITY... NOTHING COMPARED ...TO... EARTH! EARTH?
HUNNH... WHAT'S THIS? WHO ARE THESE PEOPLE? ALL AROUND ME... WHAT DO THEY WANT FROM ME...
ANNOYED, HE TURNS TO RID HIMSELF OF THIS UNWELCOME ATTENTION, AND THEN STOPS...
GRONGAD!
A WAVE OF DIZZINESS COMES OVER HIM... HE LOOKS AROUND FOR A MOMENT PUZZLED, THEN...
2

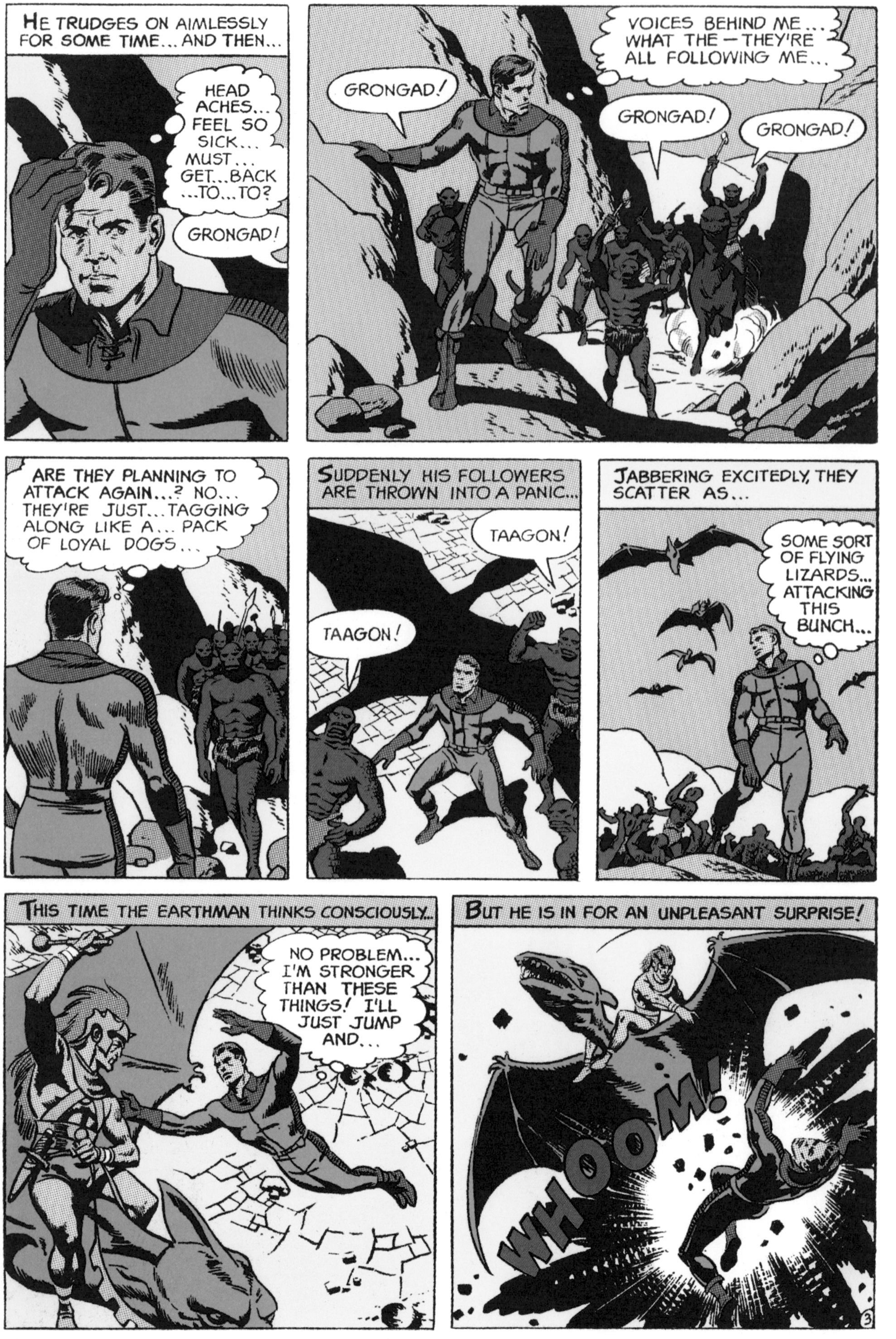
HE TRUDGES ON AIMLESSLY FOR SOME TIME... AND THEN...
HEAD ACHES... FEEL SO SICK... MUST... GET...BACK ...TO...TO?
GRONGAD!
VOICES BEHIND ME... WHAT THE — THEY'RE ALL FOLLOWING ME...
GRONGAD!
GRONGAD!
GRONGAD!
ARE THEY PLANNING TO ATTACK AGAIN...? NO... THEY'RE JUST...TAGGING ALONG LIKE A... PACK OF LOYAL DOGS...
SUDDENLY HIS FOLLOWERS ARE THROWN INTO A PANIC...
TAAGON!
TAAGON!
JABBERING EXCITEDLY, THEY SCATTER AS...
SOME SORT OF FLYING LIZARDS... ATTACKING THIS BUNCH...
THIS TIME THE EARTHMAN THINKS CONSCIOUSLY...
NO PROBLEM... I'M STRONGER THAN THESE THINGS! I'LL JUST JUMP AND...
BUT HE IS IN FOR AN UNPLEASANT SURPRISE!
WHOOM!
3

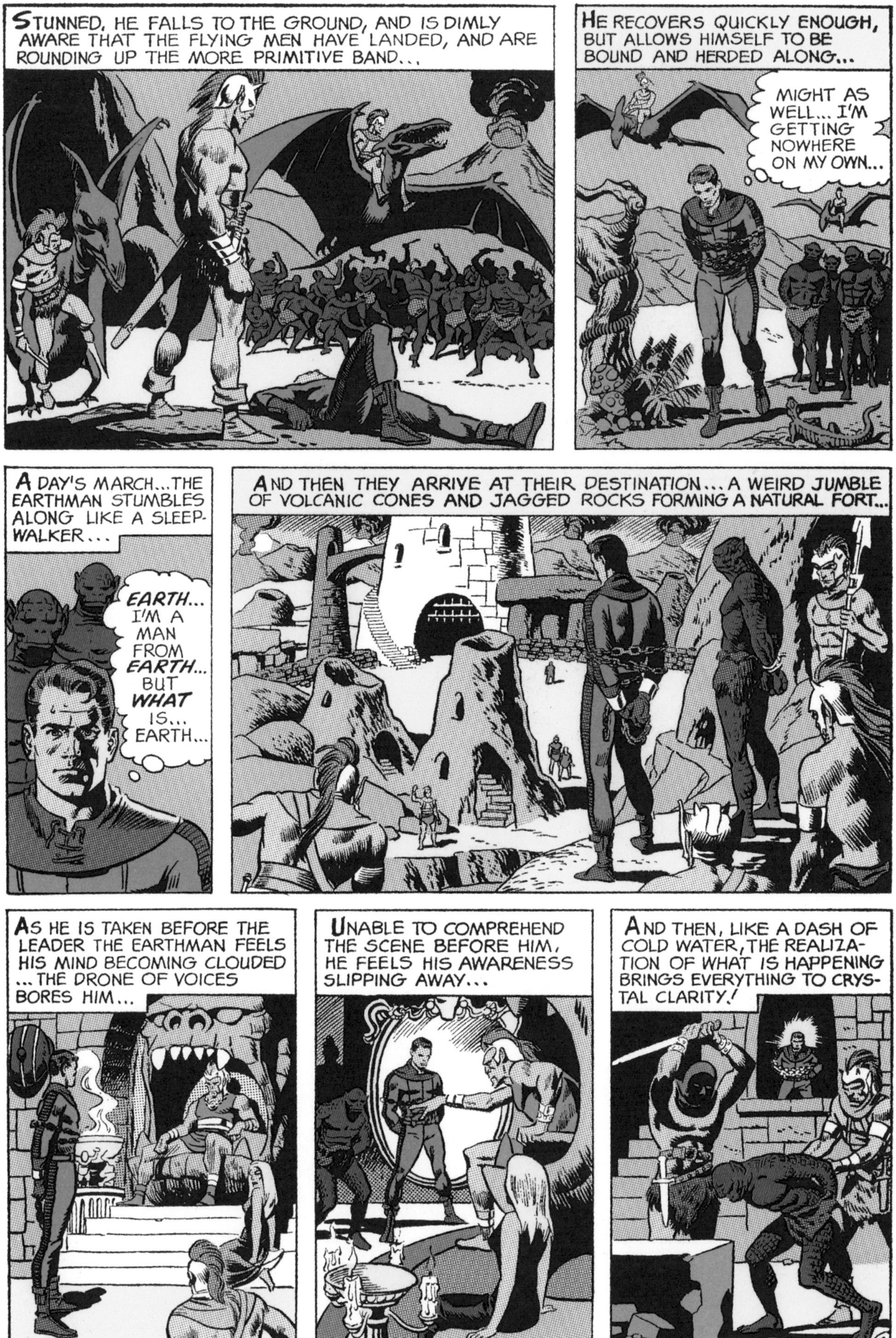
STUNNED, HE FALLS TO THE GROUND, AND IS DIMLY AWARE THAT THE FLYING MEN HAVE LANDED, AND ARE ROUNDING UP THE MORE PRIMITIVE BAND...
HE RECOVERS QUICKLY ENOUGH, BUT ALLOWS HIMSELF TO BE BOUND AND HERDED ALONG...
MIGHT AS WELL... I'M GETTING NOWHERE ON MY OWN...
A DAY'S MARCH...THE EARTHMAN STUMBLES ALONG LIKE A SLEEP-WALKER...
EARTH... I'M A MAN FROM EARTH... BUT WHAT IS... EARTH...
AND THEN THEY ARRIVE AT THEIR DESTINATION... A WEIRD JUMBLE OF VOLCANIC CONES AND JAGGED ROCKS FORMING A NATURAL FORT...
AS HE IS TAKEN BEFORE THE LEADER THE EARTHMAN FEELS HIS MIND BECOMING CLOUDED ...THE DRONE OF VOICES BORES HIM...
UNABLE TO COMPREHEND THE SCENE BEFORE HIM, HE FEELS HIS AWARENESS SLIPPING AWAY...
AND THEN, LIKE A DASH OF COLD WATER, THE REALIZATION OF WHAT IS HAPPENING BRINGS EVERYTHING TO CRYSTAL CLARITY!
4

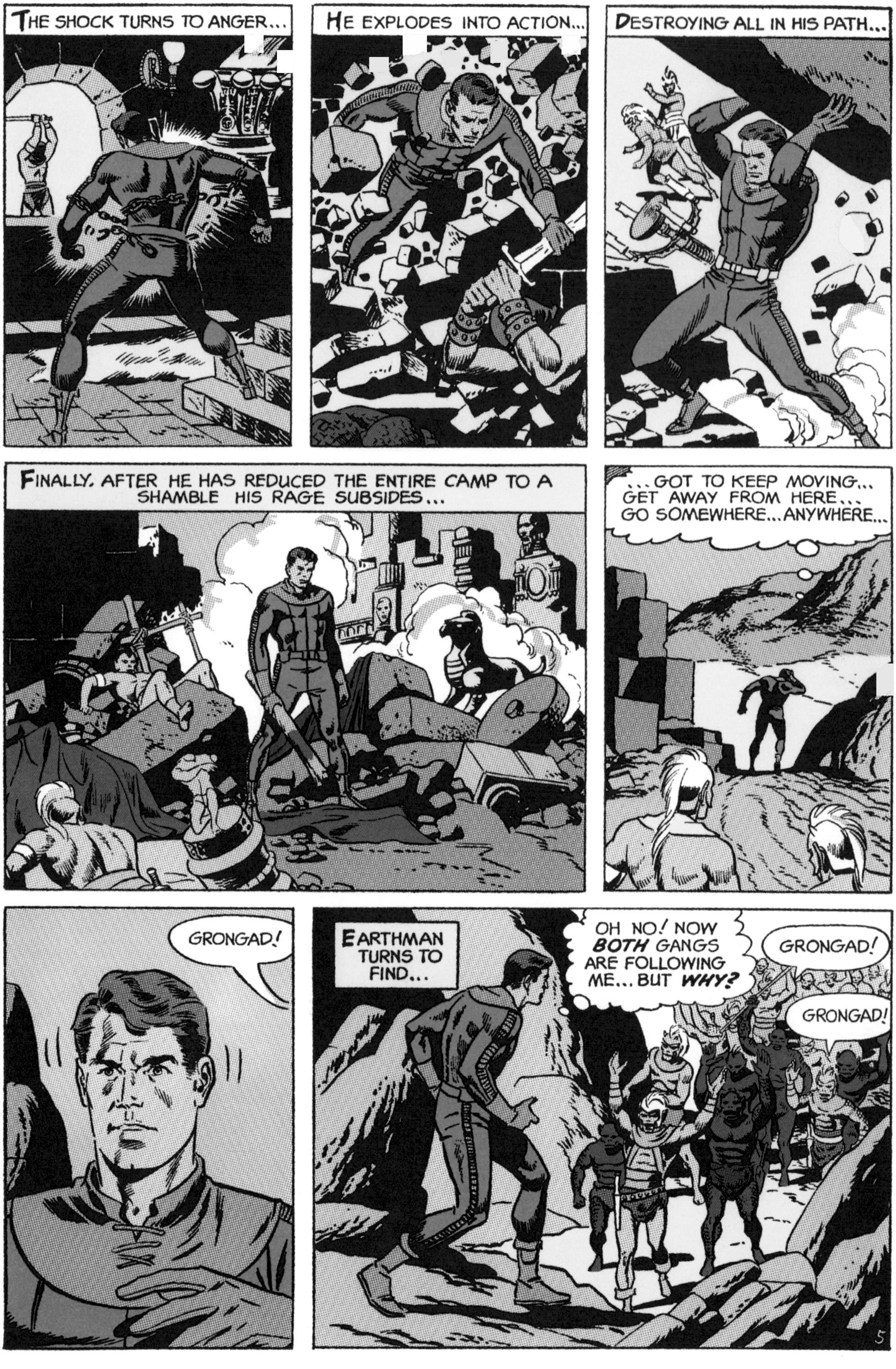
THE SHOCK TURNS TO ANGER...
HE EXPLODES INTO ACTION...
DESTROYING ALL IN HIS PATH...
FINALLY, AFTER HE HAS REDUCED THE ENTIRE CAMP TO A SHAMBLE HIS RAGE SUBSIDES...
...GOT TO KEEP MOVING... GET AWAY FROM HERE... GO SOMEWHERE...ANYWHERE...
GRONGAD!
EARTHMAN TURNS TO FIND...
OH NO! NOW BOTH GANGS ARE FOLLOWING ME... BUT WHY?
GRONGAD!
GRONGAD!
5

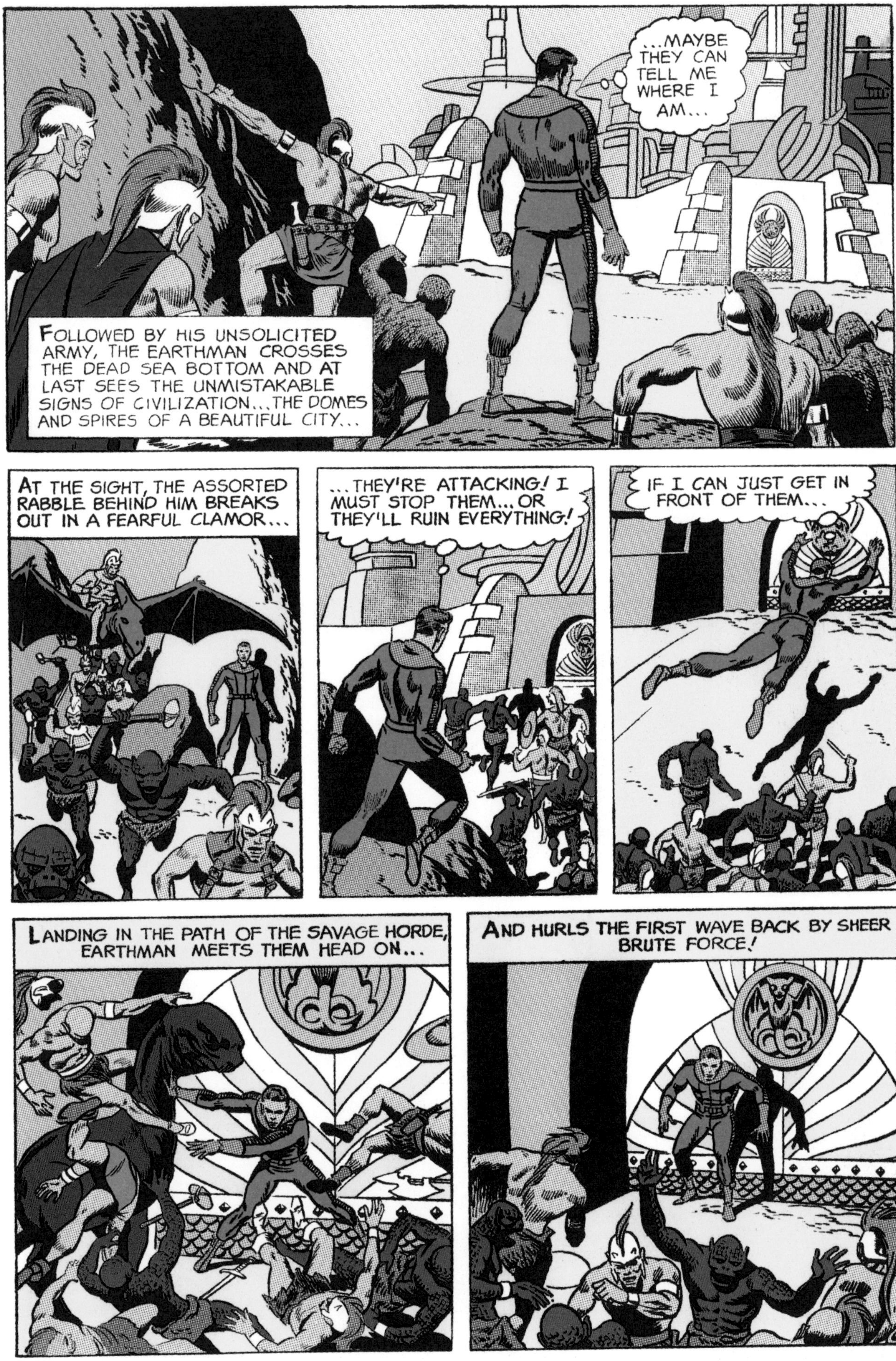
...MAYBE THEY CAN TELL ME WHERE I AM...
FOLLOWED BY HIS UNSOLICITED ARMY, THE EARTHMAN CROSSES THE DEAD SEA BOTTOM AND AT LAST SEES THE UNMISTAKABLE SIGNS OF CIVILIZATION...THE DOMES AND SPIRES OF A BEAUTIFUL CITY...
AT THE SIGHT, THE ASSORTED RABBLE BEHIND HIM BREAKS OUT IN A FEARFUL CLAMOR...
...THEY'RE ATTACKING! I MUST STOP THEM...OR THEY'LL RUIN EVERYTHING!
IF I CAN JUST GET IN FRONT OF THEM...
LANDING IN THE PATH OF THE SAVAGE HORDE, EARTHMAN MEETS THEM HEAD ON...
AND HURLS THE FIRST WAVE BACK BY SHEER BRUTE FORCE!

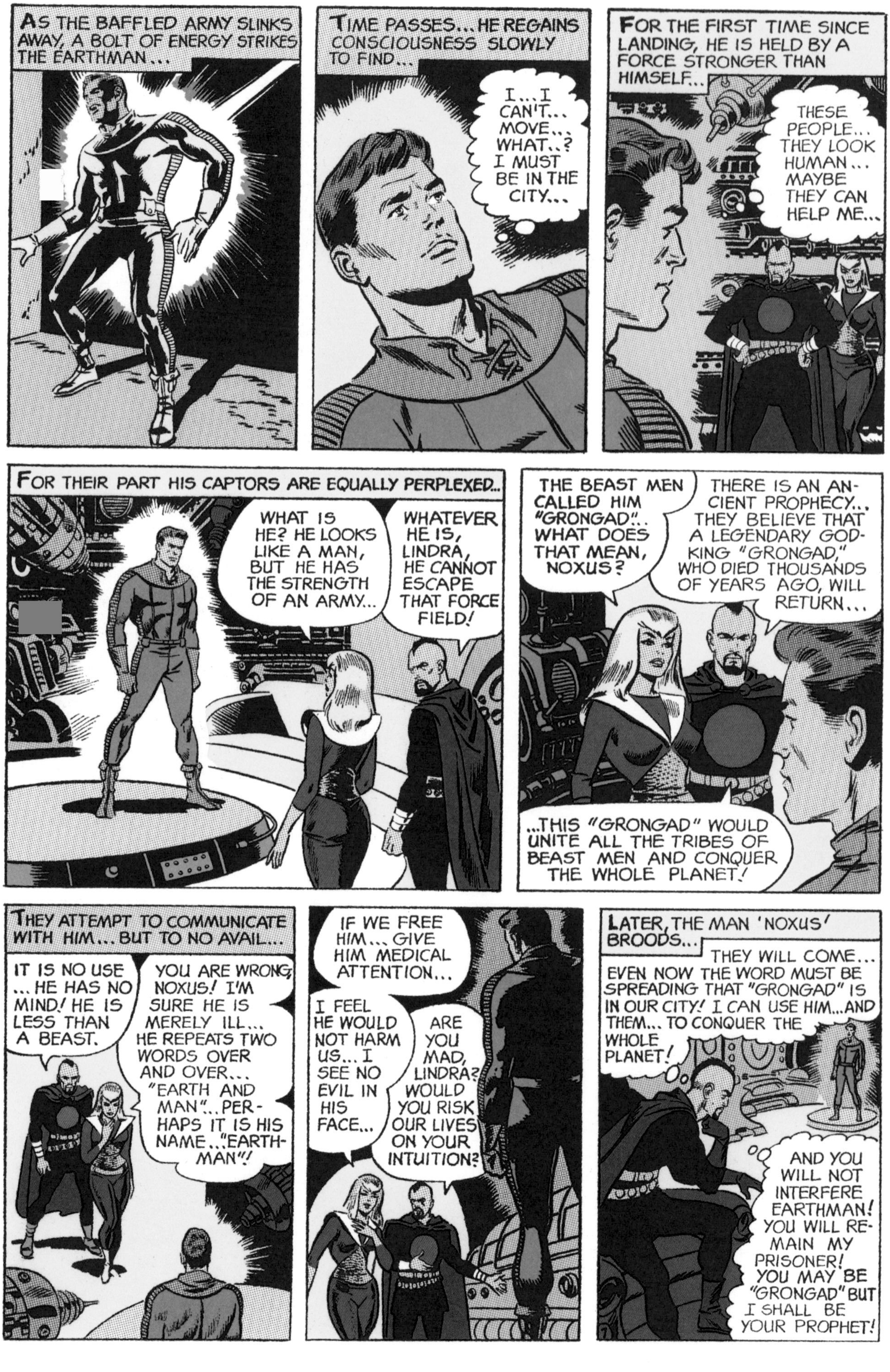

AS THE BAFFLED ARMY SLINKS AWAY, A BOLT OF ENERGY STRIKES THE EARTHMAN...
TIME PASSES... HE REGAINS CONSCIOUSNESS SLOWLY TO FIND...
I... I CAN'T... MOVE... WHAT..? I MUST BE IN THE CITY...
FOR THE FIRST TIME SINCE LANDING, HE IS HELD BY A FORCE STRONGER THAN HIMSELF...
THESE PEOPLE... THEY LOOK HUMAN... MAYBE THEY CAN HELP ME...
FOR THEIR PART HIS CAPTORS ARE EQUALLY PERPLEXED...
WHAT IS HE? HE LOOKS LIKE A MAN, BUT HE HAS THE STRENGTH OF AN ARMY...
WHATEVER HE IS, LINDRA, HE CANNOT ESCAPE THAT FORCE FIELD!
THE BEAST MEN CALLED HIM "GRONGAD"... WHAT DOES THAT MEAN, NOXUS?
THERE IS AN AN-CIENT PROPHECY... THEY BELIEVE THAT A LEGENDARY GOD-KING "GRONGAD," WHO DIED THOUSANDS OF YEARS AGO, WILL RETURN...
...THIS "GRONGAD" WOULD UNITE ALL THE TRIBES OF BEAST MEN AND CONQUER THE WHOLE PLANET!
THEY ATTEMPT TO COMMUNICATE WITH HIM... BUT TO NO AVAIL...
IT IS NO USE ...HE HAS NO MIND! HE IS LESS THAN A BEAST.
YOU ARE WRONG, NOXUS! I'M SURE HE IS MERELY ILL... HE REPEATS TWO WORDS OVER AND OVER... "EARTH AND MAN"... PER-HAPS IT IS HIS NAME..."EARTH-MAN"!
IF WE FREE HIM... GIVE HIM MEDICAL ATTENTION...
I FEEL HE WOULD NOT HARM US... I SEE NO EVIL IN HIS FACE...
ARE YOU MAD, LINDRA? WOULD YOU RISK OUR LIVES ON YOUR INTUITION?
LATER, THE MAN 'NOXUS' BROODS...
THEY WILL COME... EVEN NOW THE WORD MUST BE SPREADING THAT "GRONGAD" IS IN OUR CITY! I CAN USE HIM...AND THEM... TO CONQUER THE WHOLE PLANET!
AND YOU WILL NOT INTERFERE EARTHMAN! YOU WILL RE-MAIN MY PRISONER! YOU MAY BE "GRONGAD" BUT I SHALL BE YOUR PROPHET!

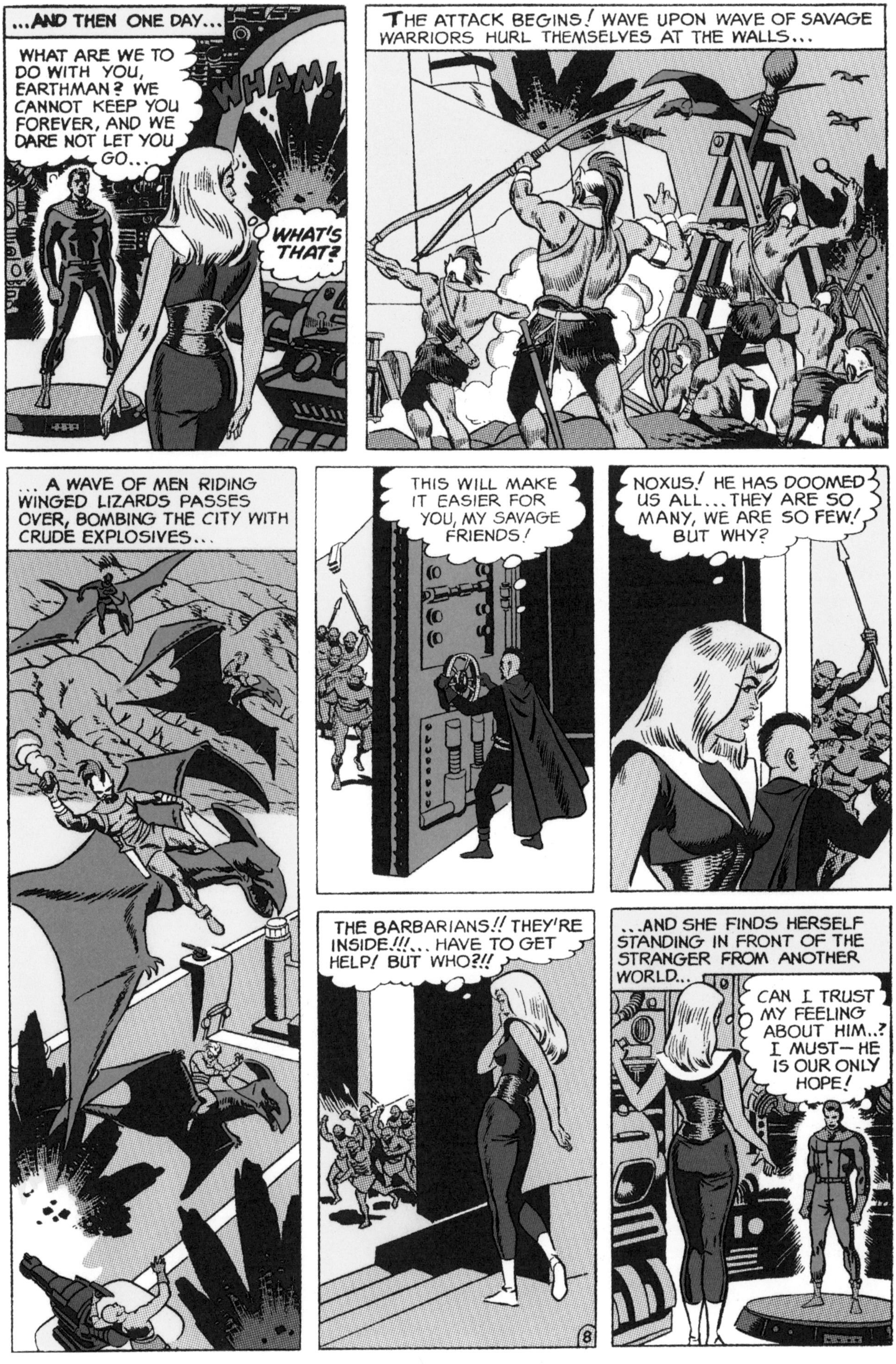
...AND THEN ONE DAY...
WHAT ARE WE TO DO WITH YOU, EARTHMAN? WE CANNOT KEEP YOU FOREVER, AND WE DARE NOT LET YOU GO...
WHAM!
WHAT'S THAT?
THE ATTACK BEGINS! WAVE UPON WAVE OF SAVAGE WARRIORS HURL THEMSELVES AT THE WALLS...
... A WAVE OF MEN RIDING WINGED LIZARDS PASSES OVER, BOMBING THE CITY WITH CRUDE EXPLOSIVES...
THIS WILL MAKE IT EASIER FOR YOU, MY SAVAGE FRIENDS!
NOXUS! HE HAS DOOMED US ALL... THEY ARE SO MANY, WE ARE SO FEW! BUT WHY?
THE BARBARIANS!! THEY'RE INSIDE!!!... HAVE TO GET HELP! BUT WHO?!!
8
...AND SHE FINDS HERSELF STANDING IN FRONT OF THE STRANGER FROM ANOTHER WORLD...
CAN I TRUST MY FEELING ABOUT HIM..? I MUST—HE IS OUR ONLY HOPE!

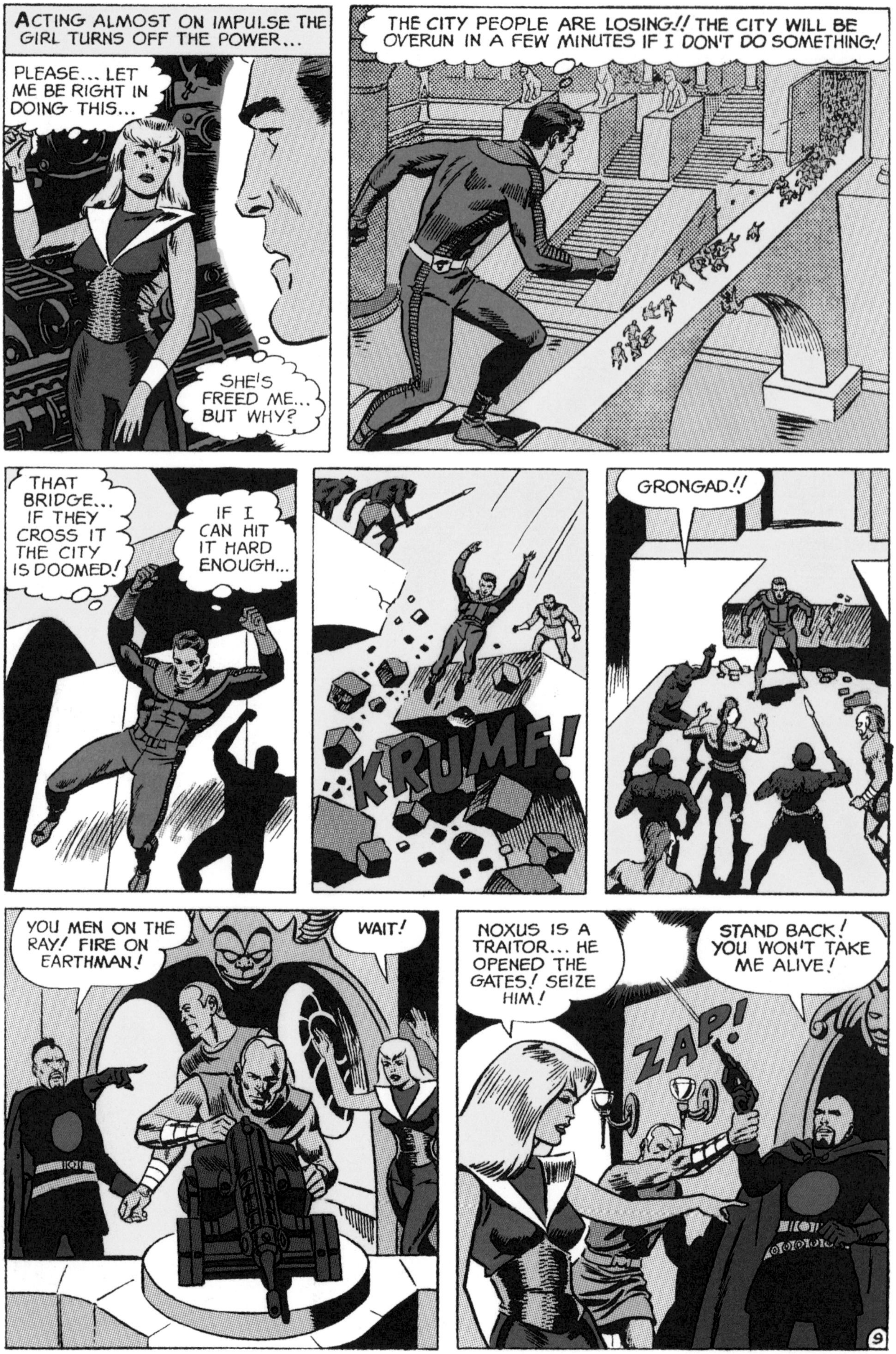
ACTING ALMOST ON IMPULSE THE GIRL TURNS OFF THE POWER...
PLEASE... LET ME BE RIGHT IN DOING THIS...
SHE'S FREED ME... BUT WHY?
THE CITY PEOPLE ARE LOSING!! THE CITY WILL BE OVERUN IN A FEW MINUTES IF I DON'T DO SOMETHING!
THAT BRIDGE... IF THEY CROSS IT THE CITY IS DOOMED!
IF I CAN HIT IT HARD ENOUGH...
KRUMF!
GRONGAD!!
YOU MEN ON THE RAY! FIRE ON EARTHMAN!
WAIT!
NOXUS IS A TRAITOR... HE OPENED THE GATES! SEIZE HIM!
STAND BACK! YOU WON'T TAKE ME ALIVE!
ZAP!
9

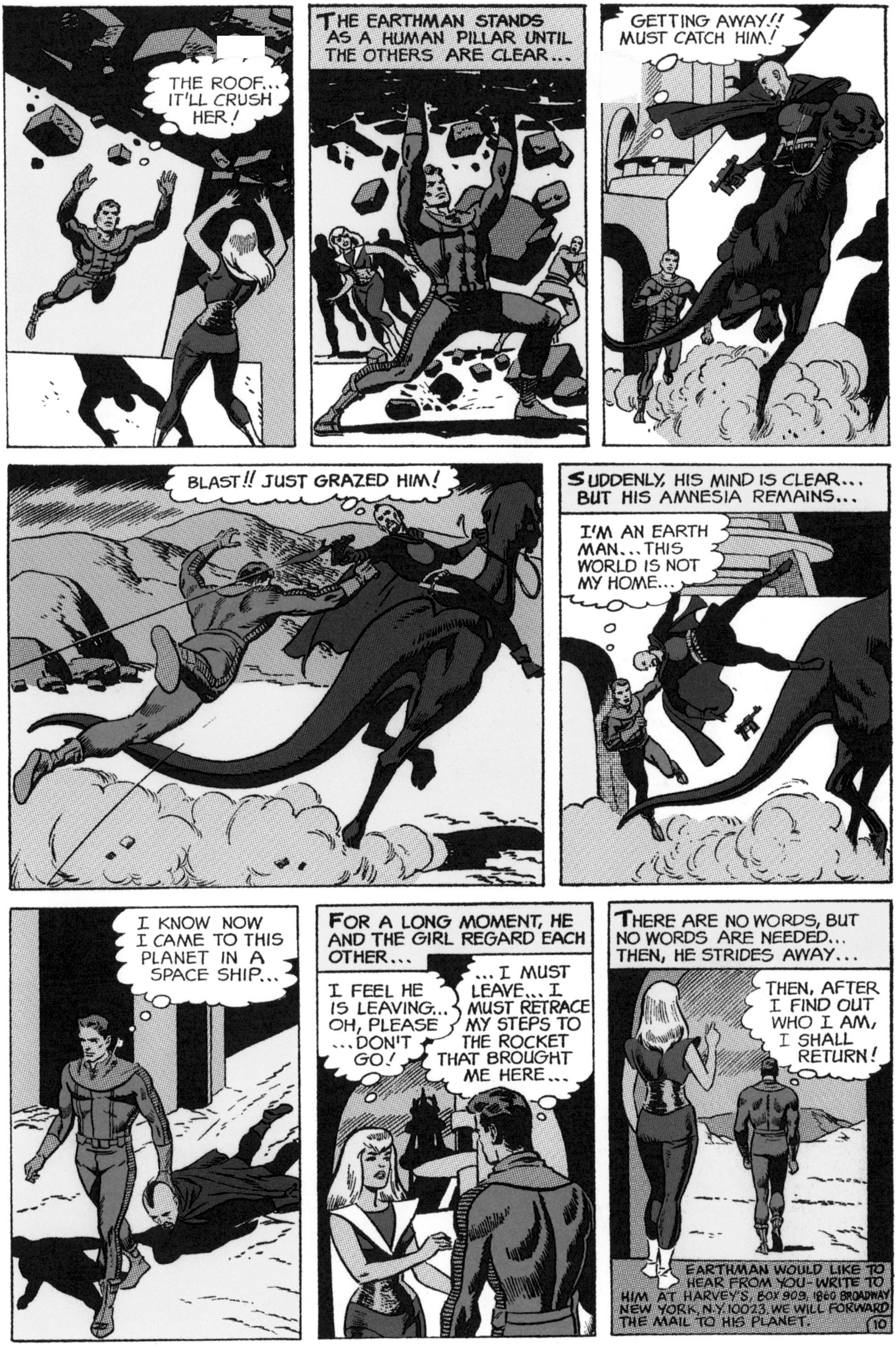
THE ROOF... IT'LL CRUSH HER!
THE EARTHMAN STANDS AS A HUMAN PILLAR UNTIL THE OTHERS ARE CLEAR...
GETTING AWAY!! MUST CATCH HIM!
BLAST!! JUST GRAZED HIM!
SUDDENLY, HIS MIND IS CLEAR... BUT HIS AMNESIA REMAINS...
I'M AN EARTH MAN... THIS WORLD IS NOT MY HOME...
I KNOW NOW I CAME TO THIS PLANET IN A SPACE SHIP...
FOR A LONG MOMENT, HE AND THE GIRL REGARD EACH OTHER...
I FEEL HE IS LEAVING... OH, PLEASE ...DON'T GO!
...I MUST LEAVE... I MUST RETRACE MY STEPS TO THE ROCKET THAT BROUGHT ME HERE...
THERE ARE NO WORDS, BUT NO WORDS ARE NEEDED... THEN, HE STRIDES AWAY...
THEN, AFTER I FIND OUT WHO I AM, I SHALL RETURN!
EARTHMAN WOULD LIKE TO HEAR FROM YOU-WRITE TO HIM AT HARVEY'S, BOX 909, 1860 BROADWAY NEW YORK, N.Y. 10023. WE WILL FORWARD THE MAIL TO HIS PLANET.
10

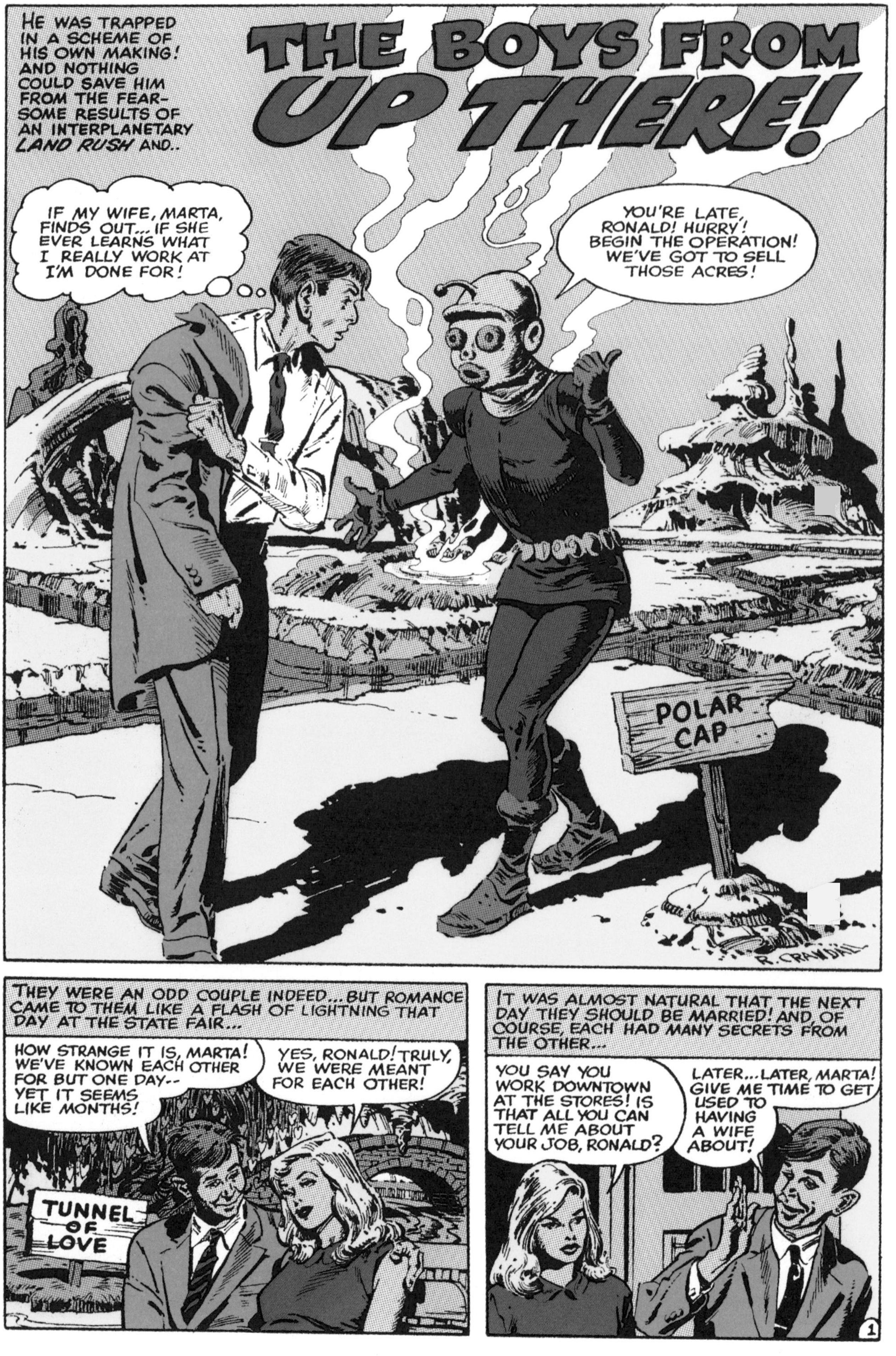
HE WAS TRAPPED IN A SCHEME OF HIS OWN MAKING! AND NOTHING COULD SAVE HIM FROM THE FEARSOME RESULTS OF AN INTERPLANETARY LAND RUSH AND..
THE BOYS FROM UP THERE!
IF MY WIFE, MARTA, FINDS OUT... IF SHE EVER LEARNS WHAT I REALLY WORK AT I'M DONE FOR!
YOU'RE LATE, RONALD! HURRY! BEGIN THE OPERATION! WE'VE GOT TO SELL THOSE ACRES!
POLAR CAP
R. CRANDALL
THEY WERE AN ODD COUPLE INDEED... BUT ROMANCE CAME TO THEM LIKE A FLASH OF LIGHTNING THAT DAY AT THE STATE FAIR...
HOW STRANGE IT IS, MARTA! WE'VE KNOWN EACH OTHER FOR BUT ONE DAY-- YET IT SEEMS LIKE MONTHS!
YES, RONALD! TRULY, WE WERE MEANT FOR EACH OTHER!
TUNNEL OF LOVE
IT WAS ALMOST NATURAL THAT THE NEXT DAY THEY SHOULD BE MARRIED! AND, OF COURSE, EACH HAD MANY SECRETS FROM THE OTHER...
YOU SAY YOU WORK DOWNTOWN AT THE STORES! IS THAT ALL YOU CAN TELL ME ABOUT YOUR JOB, RONALD?
LATER... LATER, MARTA! GIVE ME TIME TO GET USED TO HAVING A WIFE ABOUT!
1

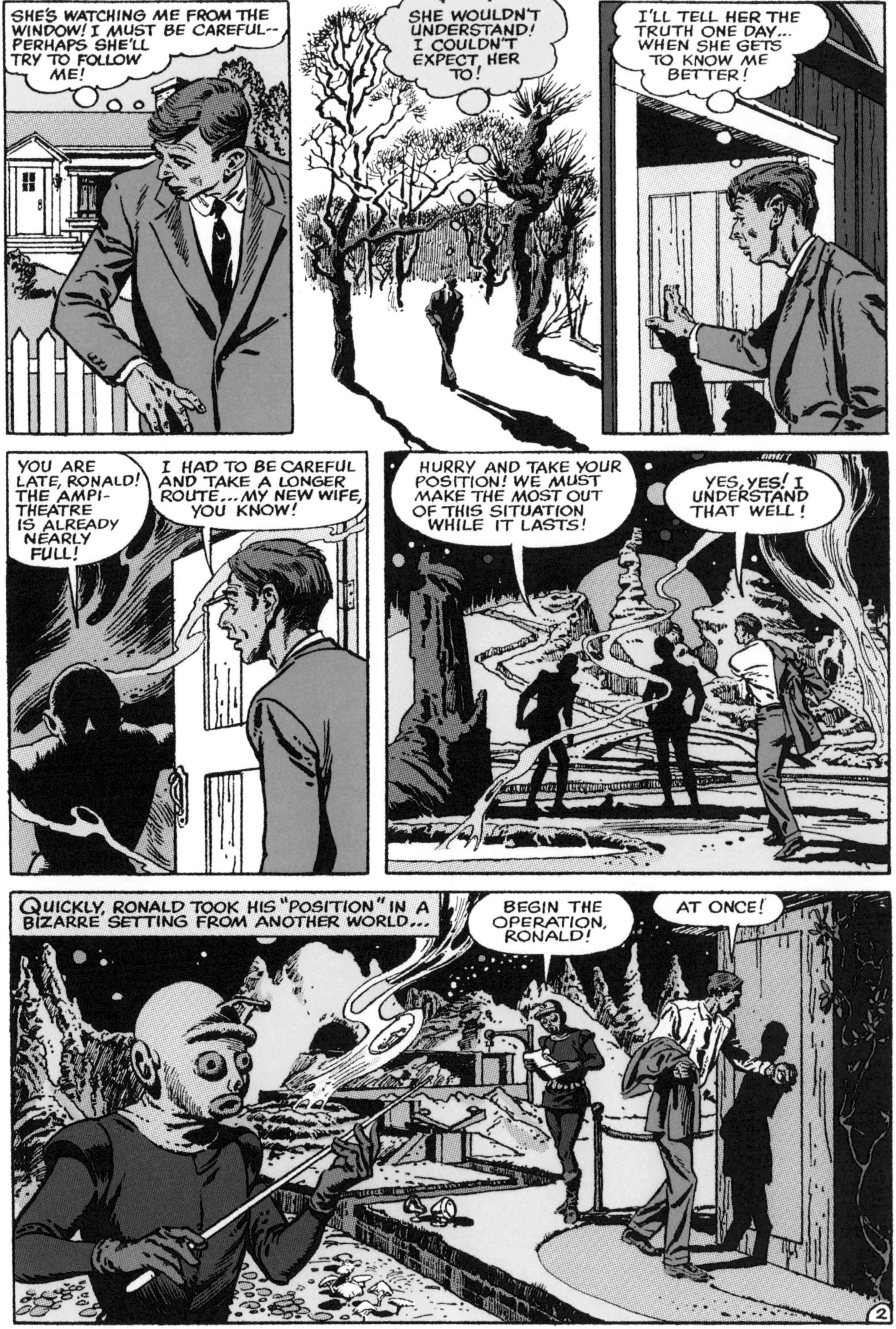
SHE'S WATCHING ME FROM THE WINDOW! I MUST BE CAREFUL-- PERHAPS SHE'LL TRY TO FOLLOW ME!
SHE WOULDN'T UNDERSTAND! I COULDN'T EXPECT HER TO!
I'LL TELL HER THE TRUTH ONE DAY... WHEN SHE GETS TO KNOW ME BETTER!
YOU ARE LATE, RONALD! THE AMPI-THEATRE IS ALREADY NEARLY FULL!
I HAD TO BE CAREFUL AND TAKE A LONGER ROUTE... MY NEW WIFE, YOU KNOW!
HURRY AND TAKE YOUR POSITION! WE MUST MAKE THE MOST OUT OF THIS SITUATION WHILE IT LASTS!
YES, YES! I UNDERSTAND THAT WELL!
QUICKLY, RONALD TOOK HIS "POSITION" IN A BIZARRE SETTING FROM ANOTHER WORLD...
BEGIN THE OPERATION, RONALD!
AT ONCE!
2

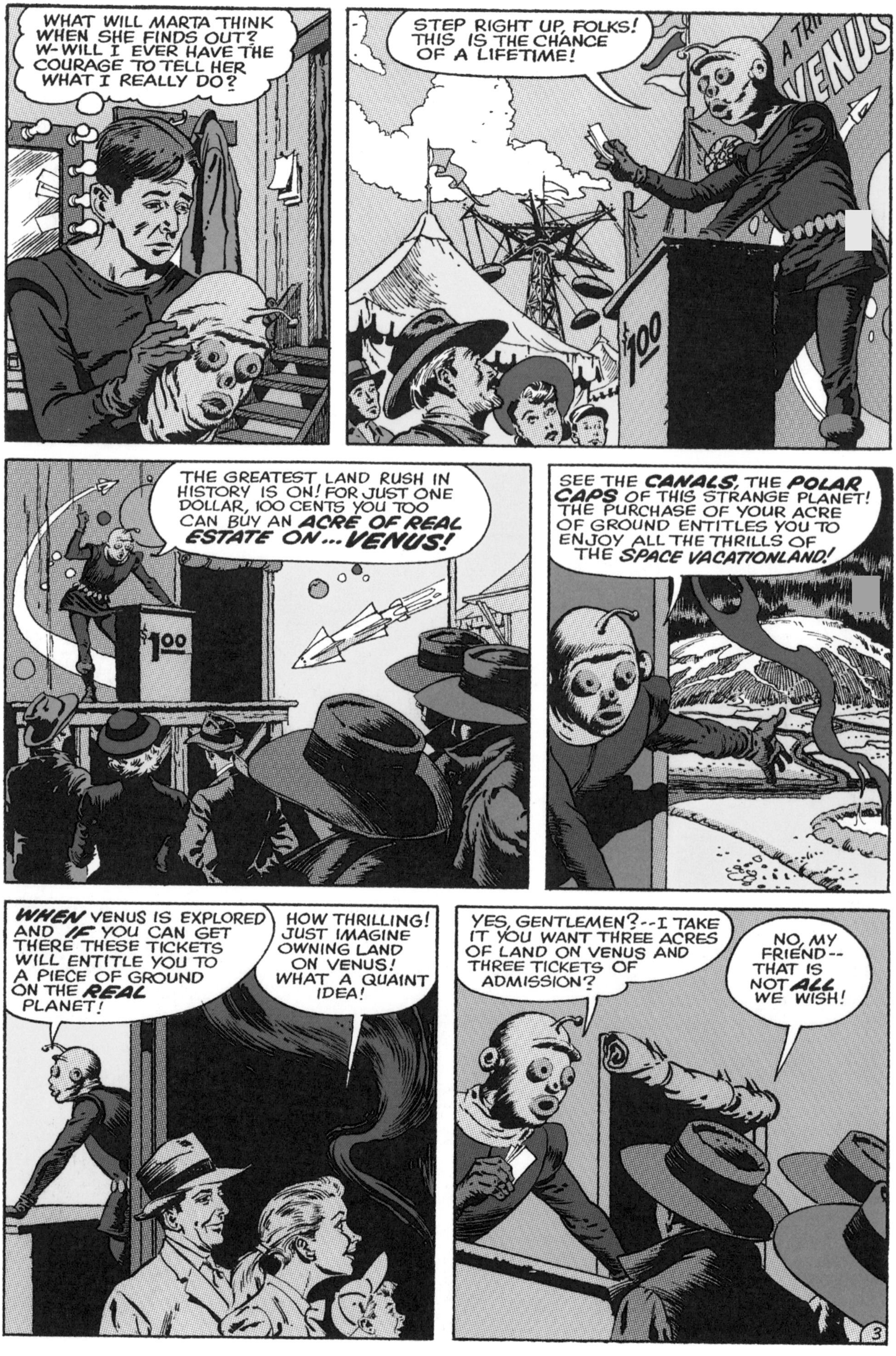
WHAT WILL MARTA THINK WHEN SHE FINDS OUT? W-WILL I EVER HAVE THE COURAGE TO TELL HER WHAT I REALLY DO?
STEP RIGHT UP, FOLKS! THIS IS THE CHANCE OF A LIFETIME!
VENUS
$1.00
THE GREATEST LAND RUSH IN HISTORY IS ON! FOR JUST ONE DOLLAR, 100 CENTS YOU TOO CAN BUY AN ACRE OF REAL ESTATE ON ... VENUS!
$1.00
SEE THE CANALS, THE POLAR CAPS OF THIS STRANGE PLANET! THE PURCHASE OF YOUR ACRE OF GROUND ENTITLES YOU TO ENJOY ALL THE THRILLS OF THE SPACE VACATIONLAND!
WHEN VENUS IS EXPLORED AND IF YOU CAN GET THERE THESE TICKETS WILL ENTITLE YOU TO A PIECE OF GROUND ON THE REAL PLANET!
HOW THRILLING! JUST IMAGINE OWNING LAND ON VENUS! WHAT A QUAINT IDEA!
YES, GENTLEMEN?--I TAKE IT YOU WANT THREE ACRES OF LAND ON VENUS AND THREE TICKETS OF ADMISSION?
NO, MY FRIEND-- THAT IS NOT ALL WE WISH!
3

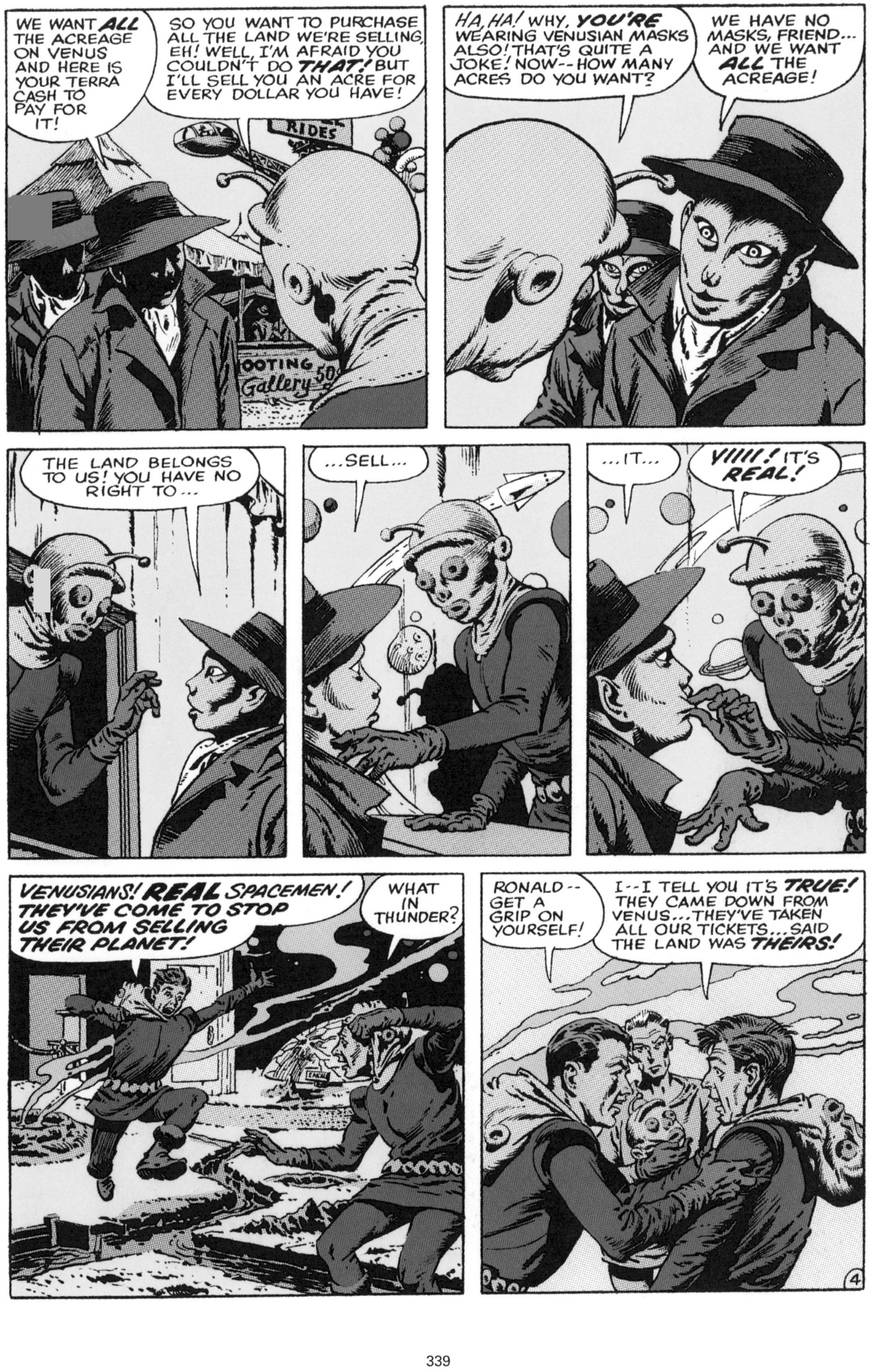
WE WANT ALL THE ACREAGE ON VENUS AND HERE IS YOUR TERRA CASH TO PAY FOR IT!
SO YOU WANT TO PURCHASE ALL THE LAND WE'RE SELLING, EH! WELL, I'M AFRAID YOU COULDN'T DO THAT! BUT I'LL SELL YOU AN ACRE FOR EVERY DOLLAR YOU HAVE!
RIDES
HA, HA! WHY, YOU'RE WEARING VENUSIAN MASKS ALSO! THAT'S QUITE A JOKE! NOW--HOW MANY ACRES DO YOU WANT?
WE HAVE NO MASKS, FRIEND... AND WE WANT ALL THE ACREAGE!
THE LAND BELONGS TO US! YOU HAVE NO RIGHT TO...
...SELL...
...IT...
YIIII! IT'S REAL!
VENUSIANS! REAL SPACEMEN! THEY'VE COME TO STOP US FROM SELLING THEIR PLANET!
WHAT IN THUNDER?
RONALD-- GET A GRIP ON YOURSELF!
I--I TELL YOU IT'S TRUE! THEY CAME DOWN FROM VENUS... THEY'VE TAKEN ALL OUR TICKETS... SAID THE LAND WAS THEIRS!
4

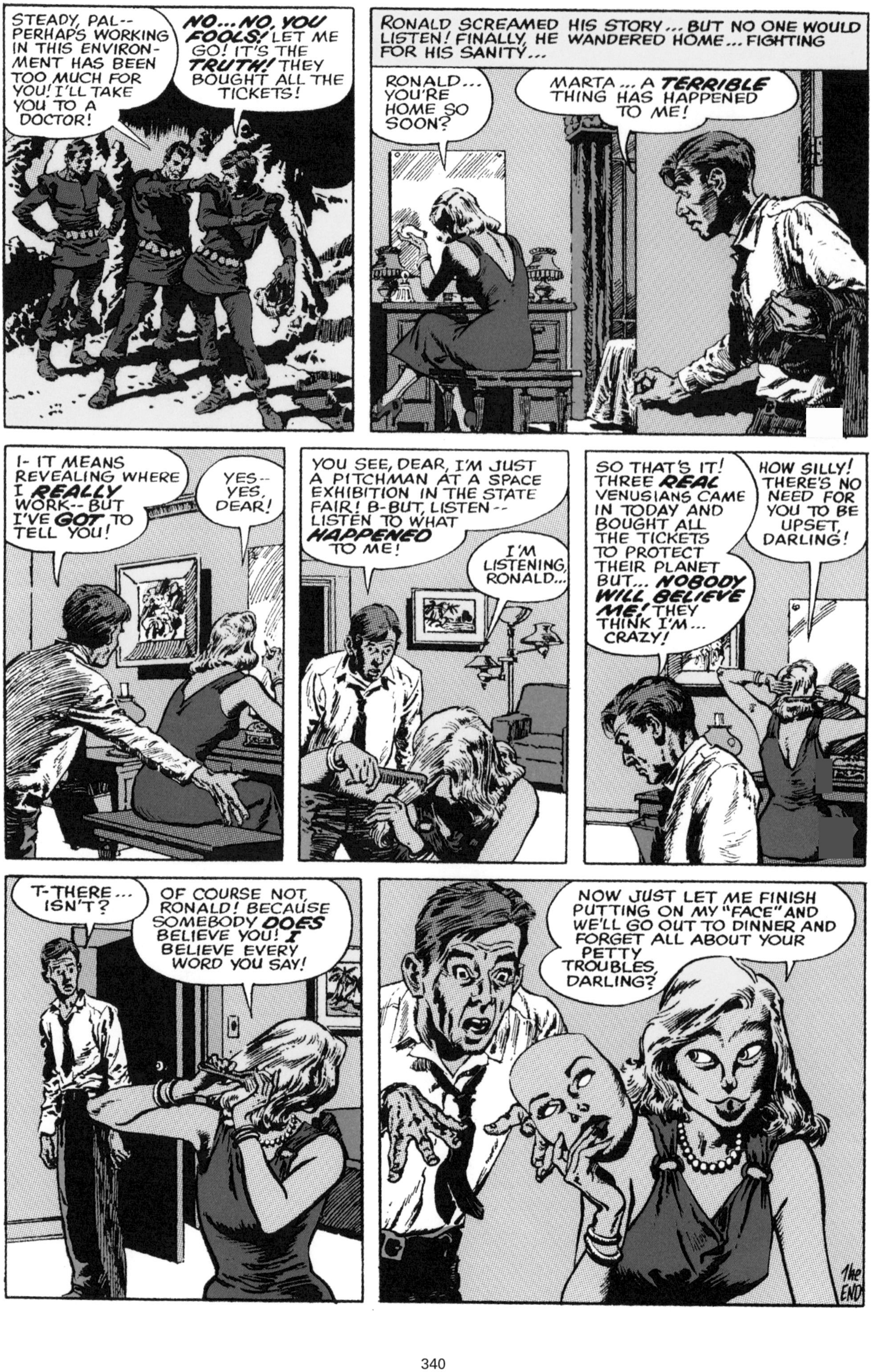
STEADY, PAL-- PERHAPS WORKING IN THIS ENVIRONMENT HAS BEEN TOO MUCH FOR YOU! I'LL TAKE YOU TO A DOCTOR!
NO... NO, YOU FOOLS! LET ME GO! IT'S THE TRUTH! THEY BOUGHT ALL THE TICKETS!
RONALD SCREAMED HIS STORY... BUT NO ONE WOULD LISTEN! FINALLY, HE WANDERED HOME... FIGHTING FOR HIS SANITY...
RONALD... YOU'RE HOME SO SOON?
MARTA... A TERRIBLE THING HAS HAPPENED TO ME!
I- IT MEANS REVEALING WHERE I REALLY WORK-- BUT I'VE GOT TO TELL YOU!
YES-- YES, DEAR!
YOU SEE, DEAR, I'M JUST A PITCHMAN AT A SPACE EXHIBITION IN THE STATE FAIR! B-BUT, LISTEN-- LISTEN TO WHAT HAPPENED TO ME!
I'M LISTENING, RONALD...
SO THAT'S IT! THREE REAL VENUSIANS CAME IN TODAY AND BOUGHT ALL THE TICKETS TO PROTECT THEIR PLANET BUT... NOBODY WILL BELIEVE ME! THEY THINK I'M... CRAZY!
HOW SILLY! THERE'S NO NEED FOR YOU TO BE UPSET, DARLING!
T-THERE... ISN'T?
OF COURSE NOT, RONALD! BECAUSE SOMEBODY DOES BELIEVE YOU! I BELIEVE EVERY WORD YOU SAY!
NOW JUST LET ME FINISH PUTTING ON MY "FACE" AND WE'LL GO OUT TO DINNER AND FORGET ALL ABOUT YOUR PETTY TROUBLES, DARLING?
THE END

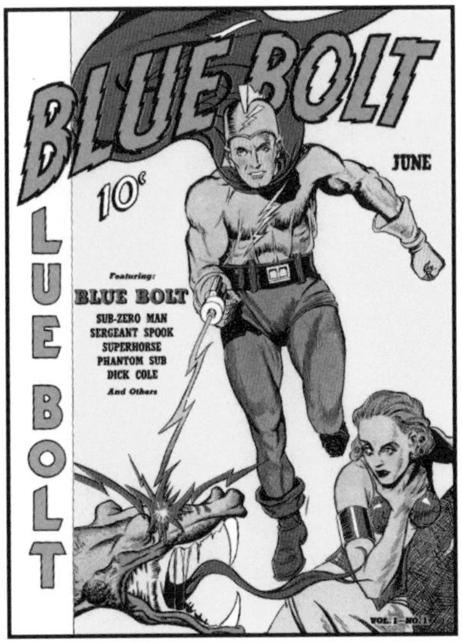
BLUE BOLT
JUNE
10¢
LUE BOLT
Featuring:
BLUE BOLT
SUB-ZERO MAN
SERGEANT SPOOK
SUPERHORSE
PHANTOM SUB
DICK COLE
And Others

Blue Bolt #1 (Jun. 1940)

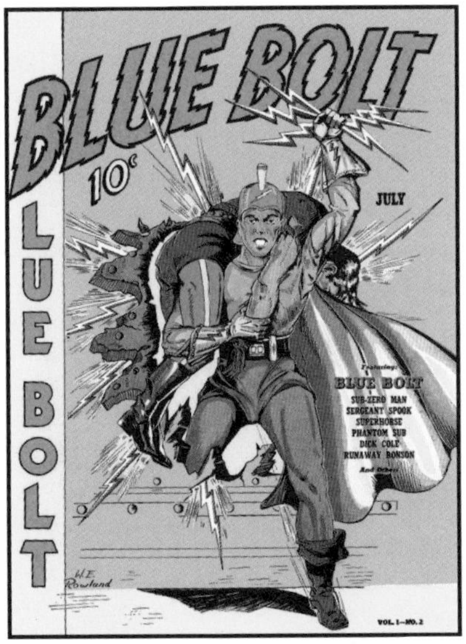
BLUE BOLT
10¢
JULY
LUE BOLT
Featuring:
BLUE BOLT
SUB-ZERO MAN
SERGEANT SPOOK
SUPERHORSE
PHANTOM SUB
DICK COLE
RUNAWAY RONSON
And Others

Blue Bolt #2 (Jul. 1940)

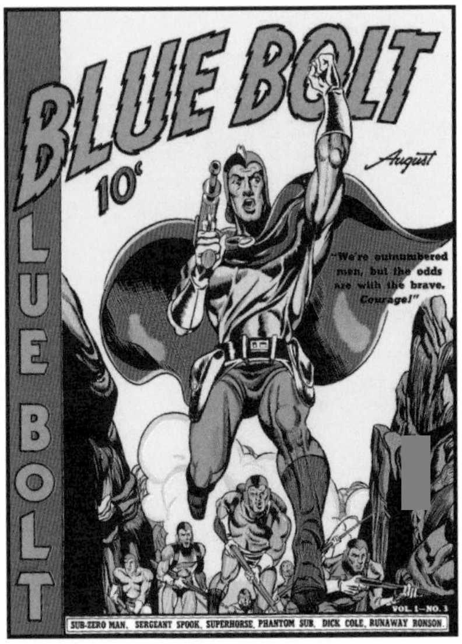
BLUE BOLT
10¢
August
LUE BOLT
"We're outnumbered men, but the odds are with the brave. Courage!"
VOL. 1—NO. 3
SUB-ZERO MAN, SERGEANT SPOOK, SUPERHORSE, PHANTOM SUB, DICK COLE, RUNAWAY RONSON

Blue Bolt #3 (Aug. 1940)

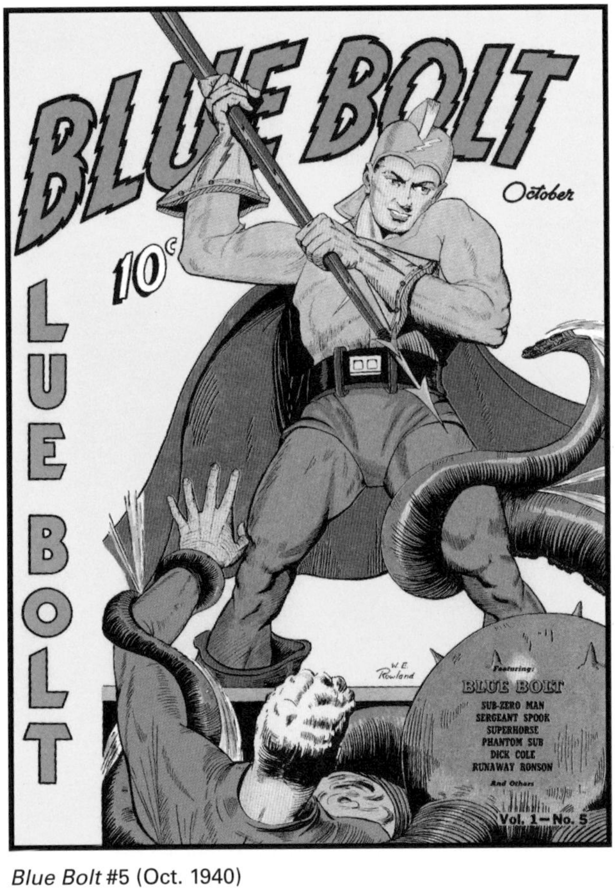
BLUE BOLT
October
10¢
LUE BOLT
W.E. Rowland
Featuring:
BLUE BOLT
SUB-ZERO MAN
SERGEANT SPOOK
SUPERHORSE
PHANTOM SUB
DICK COLE
RUNAWAY RONSON
And Others
Vol. 1—No. 5

Blue Bolt #5 (Oct. 1940)

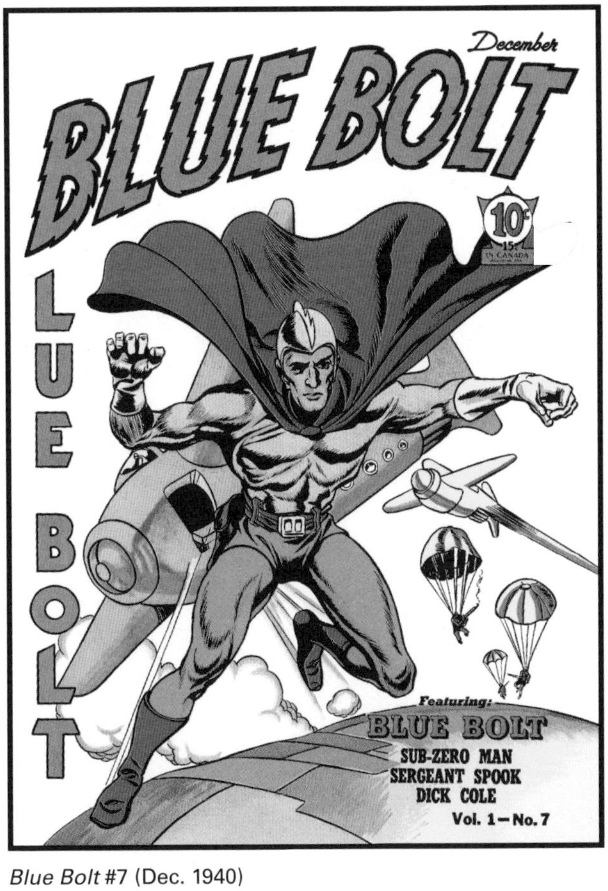
December
BLUE BOLT
10¢
IN CANADA
LUE BOLT
Featuring:
BLUE BOLT
SUB-ZERO MAN
SERGEANT SPOOK
DICK COLE
Vol. 1—No. 7

Blue Bolt #7 (Dec. 1940)

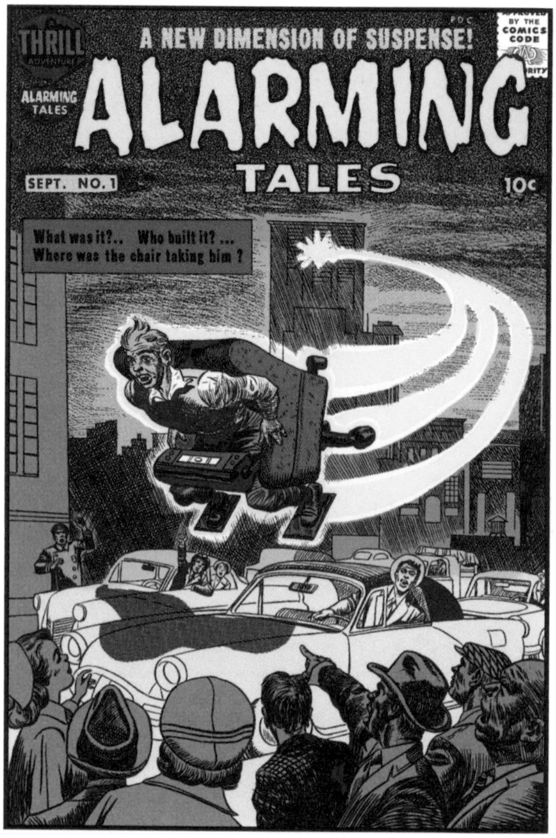
THRILL
A NEW DIMENSION OF SUSPENSE!
ALARMING TALES
ALARMING
TALES
SEPT. NO. 1
10c
What was it?.. Who built it? ... Where was the chair taking him ?

Alarming Tales #1 (Sep. 1957)

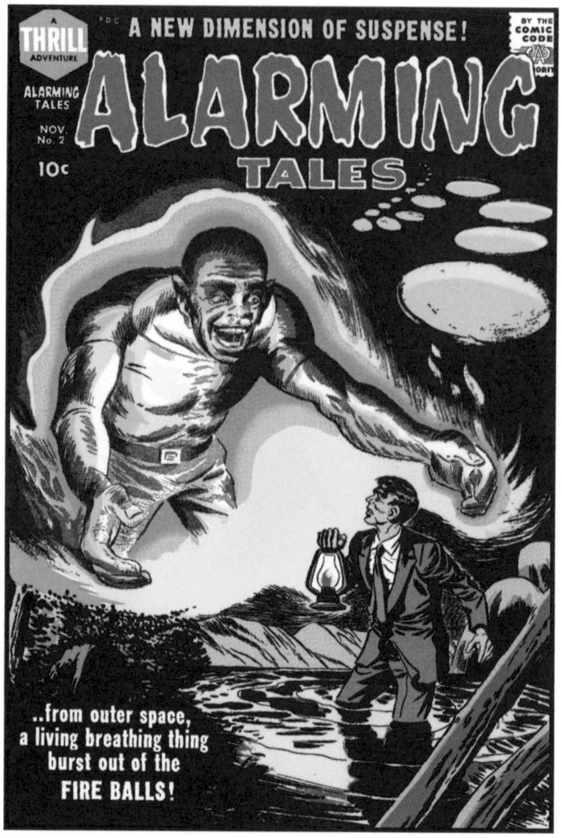
THRILL
ADVENTURE
A NEW DIMENSION OF SUSPENSE!
ALARMING TALES
NOV. No. 2
ALARMING
TALES
10c
..from outer space, a living breathing thing burst out of the FIRE BALLS!

Alarming Tales #2 (Nov. 1957)

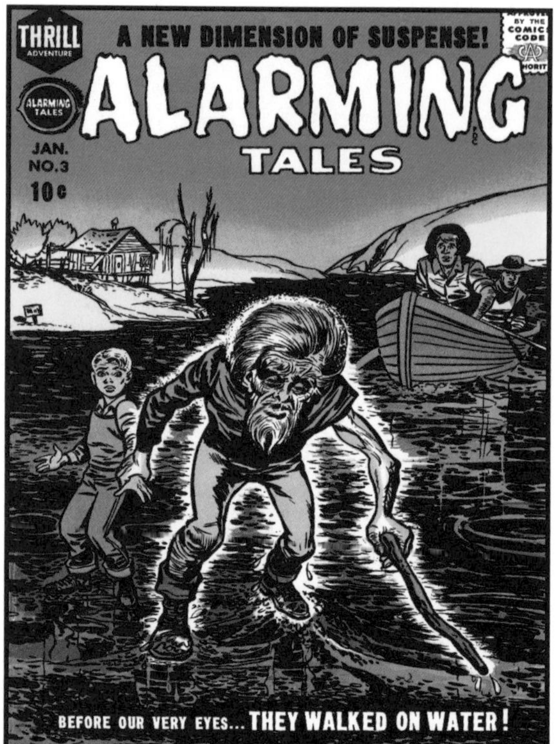
THRILL
ADVENTURE
A NEW DIMENSION OF SUSPENSE!
ALARMING
TALES
JAN. NO. 3
10¢
BEFORE OUR VERY EYES... THEY WALKED ON WATER!

Alarming Tales #3 (Jan. 1958)

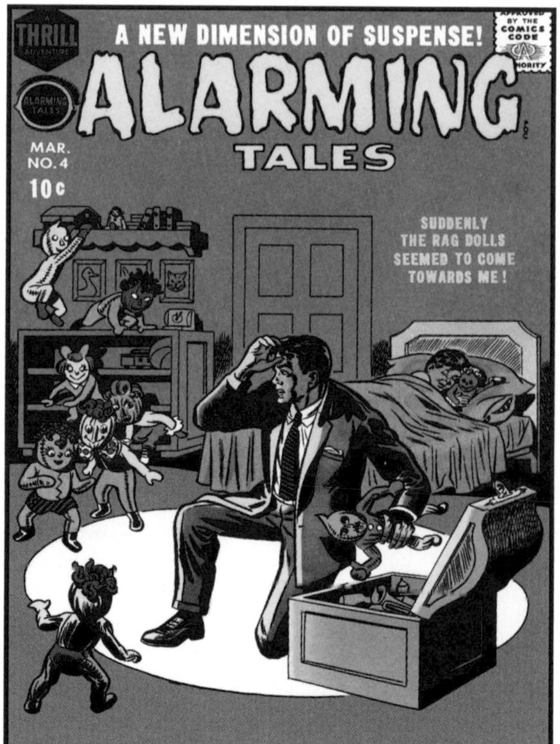
THRILL
ADVENTURE
A NEW DIMENSION OF SUSPENSE!
ALARMING
TALES
MAR. NO. 4
10c
SUDDENLY THE RAG DOLLS SEEMED TO COME TOWARDS ME!

Alarming Tales #4 (Mar. 1958)

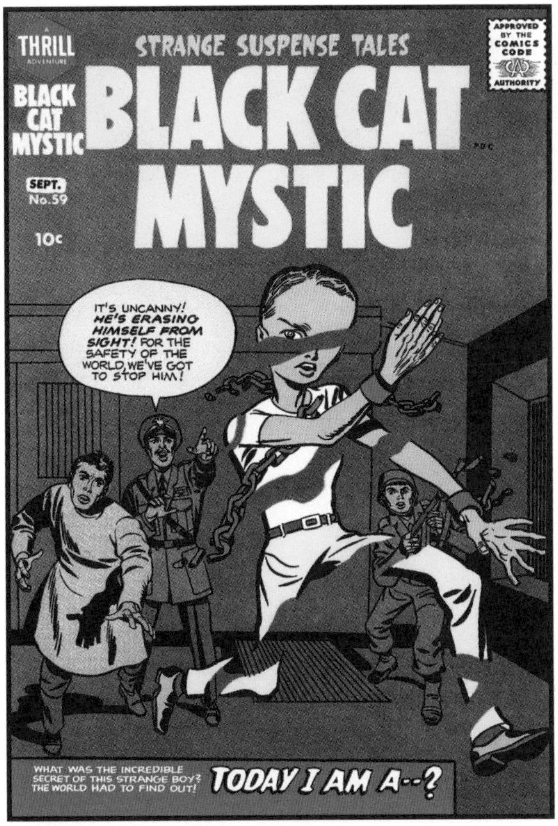
THRILL ADVENTURE
STRANGE SUSPENSE TALES
APPROVED BY THE COMICS CODE AUTHORITY
BLACK CAT MYSTIC
BLACK CAT MYSTIC
PDC
SEPT. No.59
10¢
IT'S UNCANNY! HE'S ERASING HIMSELF FROM SIGHT! FOR THE SAFETY OF THE WORLD, WE'VE GOT TO STOP HIM!
WHAT WAS THE INCREDIBLE SECRET OF THIS STRANGE BOY? THE WORLD HAD TO FIND OUT!
TODAY I AM A--?

Black Cat Mystic #59 (Sep. 1957)

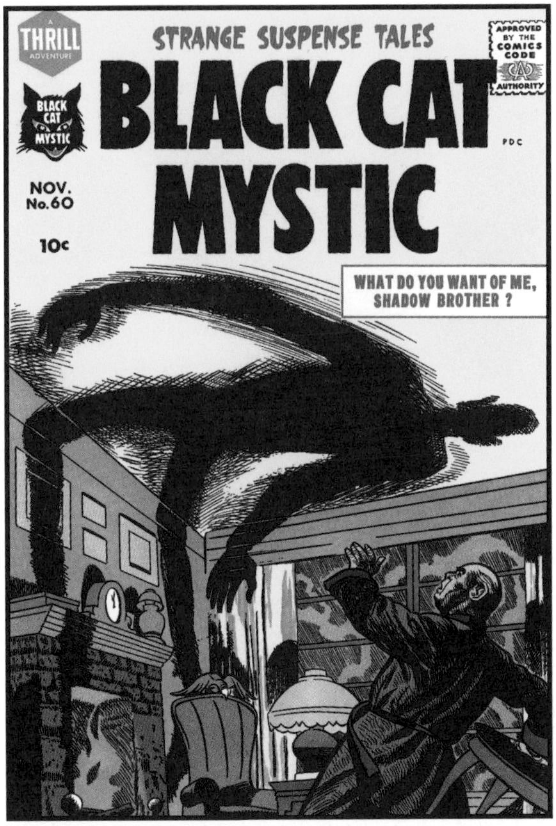
THRILL ADVENTURE
STRANGE SUSPENSE TALES
APPROVED BY THE COMICS CODE AUTHORITY
BLACK CAT MYSTIC
BLACK CAT MYSTIC
PDC
NOV. No.60
10¢
WHAT DO YOU WANT OF ME, SHADOW BROTHER ?

Black Cat Mystic #60 (Nov. 1957)

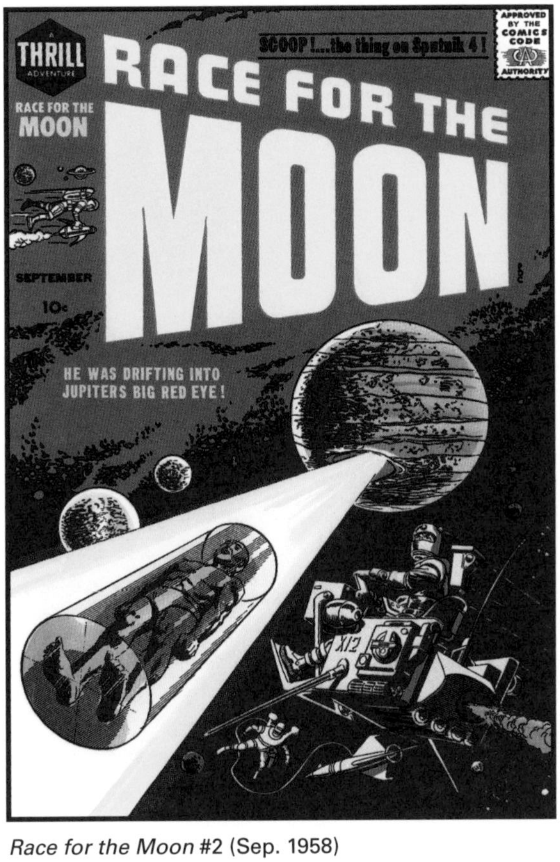
THRILL ADVENTURE
SCOOP!...the thing on Sputnik 4!
APPROVED BY THE COMICS CODE AUTHORITY
RACE FOR THE MOON
RACE FOR THE MOON
SEPTEMBER
10¢
HE WAS DRIFTING INTO JUPITERS BIG RED EYE!
X12

Race for the Moon #2 (Sep. 1958)

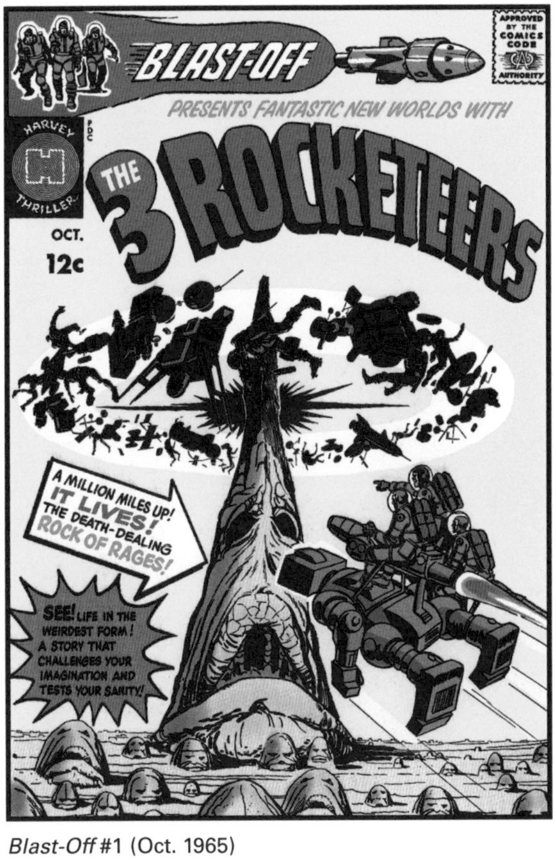
APPROVED BY THE COMICS CODE AUTHORITY
BLAST-OFF
PRESENTS FANTASTIC NEW WORLDS WITH
HARVEY THRILLER
THE 3 ROCKETEERS
OCT.
12¢
A MILLION MILES UP! IT LIVES! THE DEATH-DEALING ROCK OF RAGES!
SEE! LIFE IN THE WEIRDEST FORM! A STORY THAT CHALLENGES YOUR IMAGINATION AND TESTS YOUR SANITY!

Blast-Off #1 (Oct. 1965)

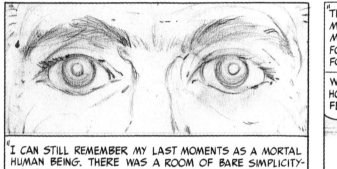

"I CAN STILL REMEMBER MY LAST MOMENTS AS A MORTAL HUMAN BEING. THERE WAS A ROOM OF BARE SIMPLICITY-- A CLOCK FACE PROJECTED ON A WALL OF PLEASING COLOR. I HAD TWENTY SECONDS BEFORE I STOPPED BEING FLESH AND BLOOD -- AND BECAME -- SOMETHING ELSE --

"THEY TOLD ME IT WAS SOMETHING BIG. A GREATER MIRACLE THAN *THE TIME JUMP* WHICH PUT THE MOST DISTANT STAR ON OUR DOORSTEP. AND I FELL FOR IT, BECAUSE I WAS A SPACE MAN WITH A HUNGER FOR THE THINGS I COULD NOT SEE IN ONE LIFE TIME...

WE'RE READY NOW. HOW DO YOU FEEL?

TERRIFIED! I'D RUN IF I COULD. BUT, I'VE BEEN DRUGGED. I CAN'T MOVE.

"EVERY SECOND BECAME A PRICELESS MEMORY. THE ALMOST INAUDIBLE HUM OF THE FLOOR STRIP WHICH MOVED MY CHAIR INTO THE CHAMBER -- THE GENTLE HISS OF THE CLOSING LOCK -- SOUNDS, CAUGHT AND SAVORED BY STILL HUMAN SENSES! THEN I SAW THE THING WHICH SAT IN THE CHAIR TO WHICH MINE WOULD MAKE CONNECTION. BUT, NOT EVEN THIS GREATEST OF HORRORS COULD STIR ME INTO MOTION...

"THERE WERE NO SPECTACULAR FIREWORKS. NO SOUND. NO PAIN. JUST THE WEIGHTLESS SENSATION OF RISING -- AND SUDDENLY, BEING EVERYWHERE AT ONCE.

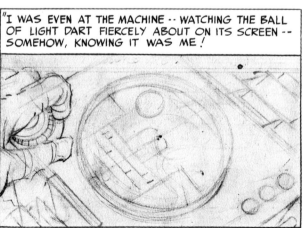

"I WAS EVEN AT THE MACHINE -- WATCHING THE BALL OF LIGHT DART FIERCELY ABOUT ON ITS SCREEN -- SOMEHOW, KNOWING IT WAS ME!

Joe Simon's archive holds the artwork to a rarely seen undeveloped gem by Jack Kirby, that Harry Mendryk dates to the late 1940s. Only two art boards of lettered penciled pages remain. The landscape format suggests they were created for Sunday comics syndication, but beyond what is reproduced on the following pages, little else is known. Kirby later put together a TV show proposal for NBC in the 1950s that was unsuccesful. Astute readers may notice similarities between the origins of Starman Zero and Fighting American; Simon and Kirby often revised earlier concepts if they felt they had more mileage.

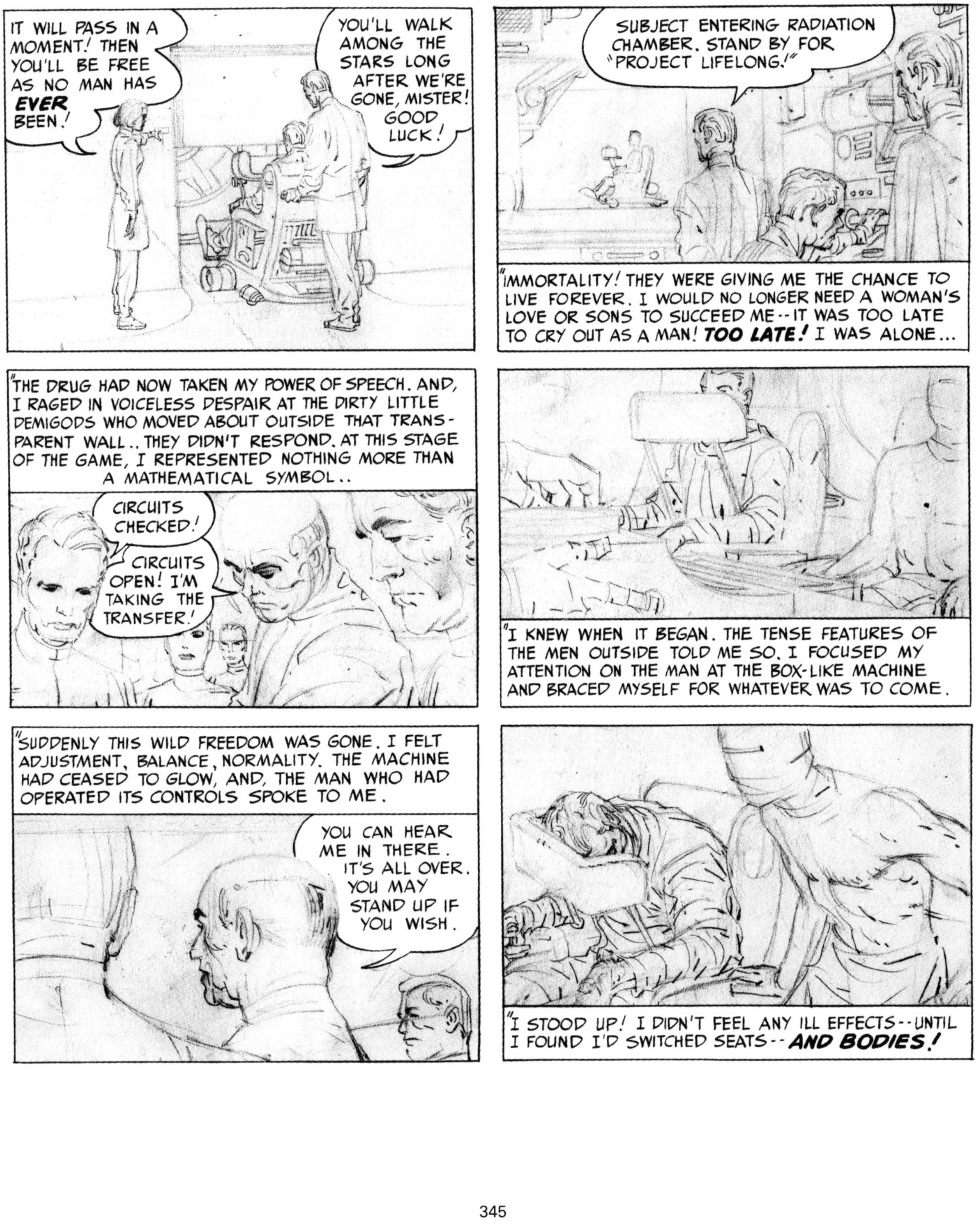

IT WILL PASS IN A MOMENT! THEN YOU'LL BE FREE AS NO MAN HAS EVER BEEN!
YOU'LL WALK AMONG THE STARS LONG AFTER WE'RE GONE, MISTER! GOOD LUCK!
SUBJECT ENTERING RADIATION CHAMBER. STAND BY FOR "PROJECT LIFELONG!"
"IMMORTALITY! THEY WERE GIVING ME THE CHANCE TO LIVE FOREVER. I WOULD NO LONGER NEED A WOMAN'S LOVE OR SONS TO SUCCEED ME--IT WAS TOO LATE TO CRY OUT AS A MAN! TOO LATE! I WAS ALONE...
"THE DRUG HAD NOW TAKEN MY POWER OF SPEECH. AND, I RAGED IN VOICELESS DESPAIR AT THE DIRTY LITTLE DEMIGODS WHO MOVED ABOUT OUTSIDE THAT TRANS-PARENT WALL.. THEY DIDN'T RESPOND. AT THIS STAGE OF THE GAME, I REPRESENTED NOTHING MORE THAN A MATHEMATICAL SYMBOL..
CIRCUITS CHECKED!
CIRCUITS OPEN! I'M TAKING THE TRANSFER!
"I KNEW WHEN IT BEGAN. THE TENSE FEATURES OF THE MEN OUTSIDE TOLD ME SO. I FOCUSED MY ATTENTION ON THE MAN AT THE BOX-LIKE MACHINE AND BRACED MYSELF FOR WHATEVER WAS TO COME.
"SUDDENLY THIS WILD FREEDOM WAS GONE. I FELT ADJUSTMENT, BALANCE, NORMALITY. THE MACHINE HAD CEASED TO GLOW, AND, THE MAN WHO HAD OPERATED ITS CONTROLS SPOKE TO ME.
YOU CAN HEAR ME IN THERE. IT'S ALL OVER. YOU MAY STAND UP IF YOU WISH.
"I STOOD UP! I DIDN'T FEEL ANY ILL EFFECTS--UNTIL I FOUND I'D SWITCHED SEATS--AND BODIES!

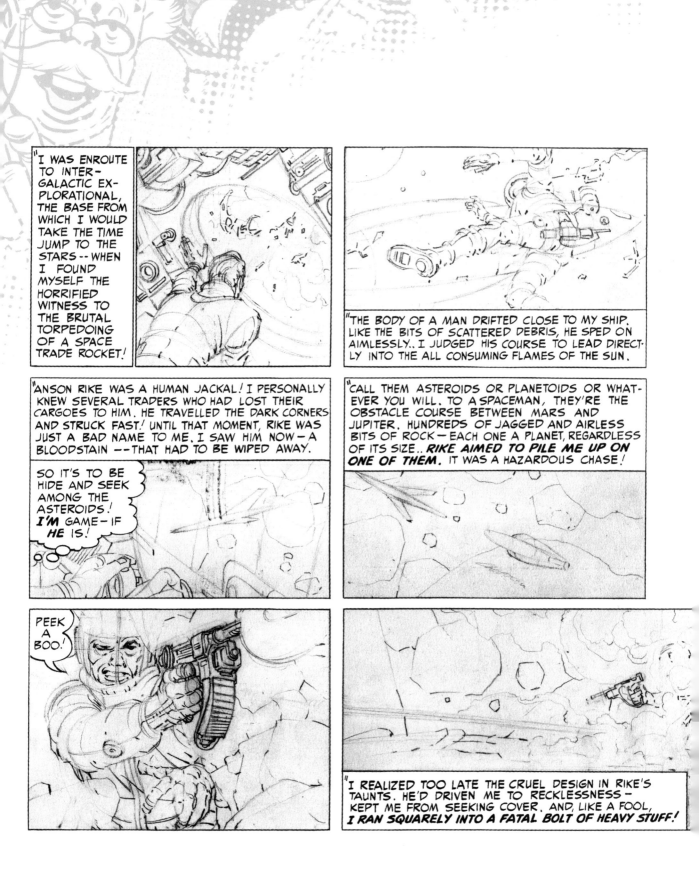

"I WAS ENROUTE TO INTER-GALACTIC EXPLORATIONAL, THE BASE FROM WHICH I WOULD TAKE THE TIME JUMP TO THE STARS -- WHEN I FOUND MYSELF THE HORRIFIED WITNESS TO THE BRUTAL TORPEDOING OF A SPACE TRADE ROCKET!

"THE BODY OF A MAN DRIFTED CLOSE TO MY SHIP. LIKE THE BITS OF SCATTERED DEBRIS, HE SPED ON AIMLESSLY.. I JUDGED HIS COURSE TO LEAD DIRECT-LY INTO THE ALL CONSUMING FLAMES OF THE SUN.

"ANSON RIKE WAS A HUMAN JACKAL! I PERSONALLY KNEW SEVERAL TRADERS WHO HAD LOST THEIR CARGOES TO HIM. HE TRAVELLED THE DARK CORNERS AND STRUCK FAST! UNTIL THAT MOMENT, RIKE WAS JUST A BAD NAME TO ME. I SAW HIM NOW -- A BLOODSTAIN -- THAT HAD TO BE WIPED AWAY.

SO IT'S TO BE HIDE AND SEEK AMONG THE ASTEROIDS! *I'M* GAME -- IF *HE* IS!

"CALL THEM ASTEROIDS OR PLANETOIDS OR WHAT-EVER YOU WILL. TO A SPACEMAN, THEY'RE THE OBSTACLE COURSE BETWEEN MARS AND JUPITER. HUNDREDS OF JAGGED AND AIRLESS BITS OF ROCK -- EACH ONE A PLANET, REGARDLESS OF ITS SIZE.. *RIKE AIMED TO PILE ME UP ON ONE OF THEM.* IT WAS A HAZARDOUS CHASE!

PEEK A BOO!

"I REALIZED TOO LATE THE CRUEL DESIGN IN RIKE'S TAUNTS. HE'D DRIVEN ME TO RECKLESSNESS -- KEPT ME FROM SEEKING COVER. AND, LIKE A FOOL, *I RAN SQUARELY INTO A FATAL BOLT OF HEAVY STUFF!*

346

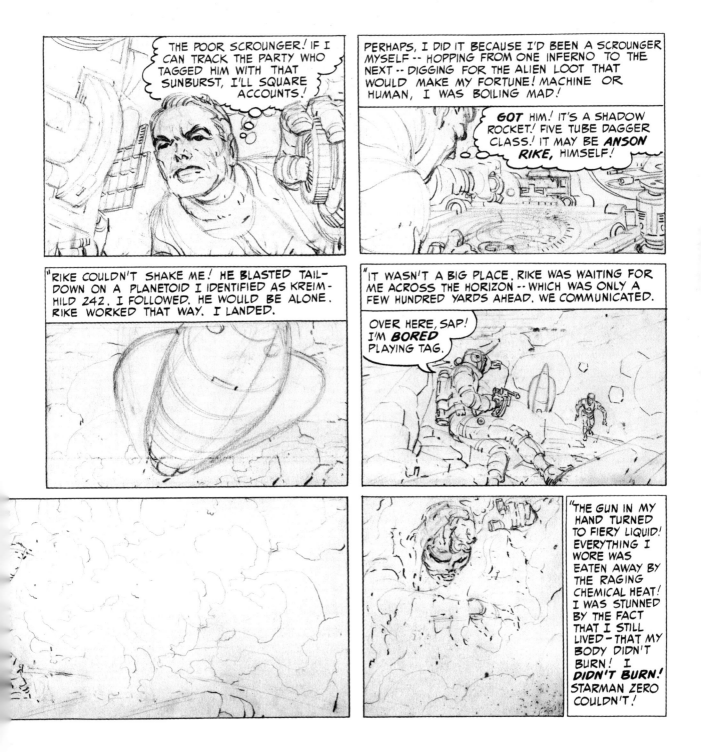

THE POOR SCROUNGER! IF I CAN TRACK THE PARTY WHO TAGGED HIM WITH THAT SUNBURST, I'LL SQUARE ACCOUNTS!

PERHAPS, I DID IT BECAUSE I'D BEEN A SCROUNGER MYSELF -- HOPPING FROM ONE INFERNO TO THE NEXT -- DIGGING FOR THE ALIEN LOOT THAT WOULD MAKE MY FORTUNE! MACHINE OR HUMAN, I WAS BOILING MAD!

GOT HIM! IT'S A SHADOW ROCKET! FIVE TUBE DAGGER CLASS! IT MAY BE ANSON RIKE, HIMSELF!

"RIKE COULDN'T SHAKE ME! HE BLASTED TAIL-DOWN ON A PLANETOID I IDENTIFIED AS KREIM-HILD 242. I FOLLOWED. HE WOULD BE ALONE. RIKE WORKED THAT WAY. I LANDED.

"IT WASN'T A BIG PLACE. RIKE WAS WAITING FOR ME ACROSS THE HORIZON -- WHICH WAS ONLY A FEW HUNDRED YARDS AHEAD. WE COMMUNICATED.

OVER HERE, SAP! I'M BORED PLAYING TAG.

"THE GUN IN MY HAND TURNED TO FIERY LIQUID! EVERYTHING I WORE WAS EATEN AWAY BY THE RAGING CHEMICAL HEAT! I WAS STUNNED BY THE FACT THAT I STILL LIVED -- THAT MY BODY DIDN'T BURN! I DIDN'T BURN! STARMAN ZERO COULDN'T!

347

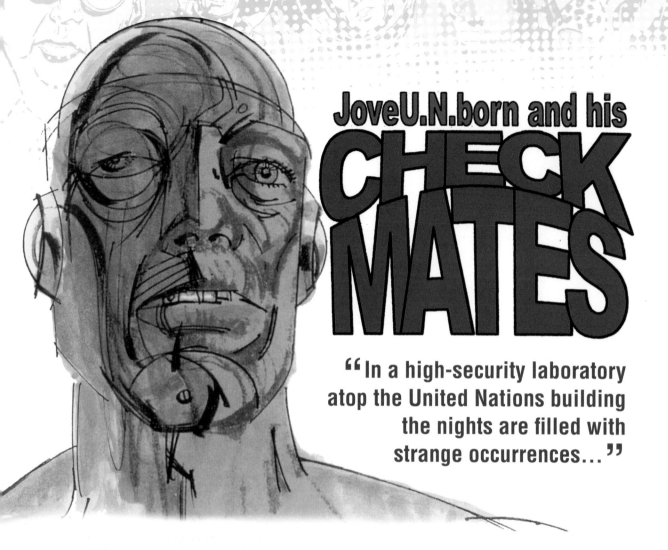

JoveU.N.born and his CHECK MATES

"In a high-security laboratory atop the United Nations building the nights are filled with strange occurrences..."

In the early sixties, Joe Simon teamed up with artist Jerry Grandenetti to devise a new comic book superhero–an unknown soldier, all but destroyed by nuclear warfare, who was rebuilt by scientists for the United Nations. To insure his neutrality, he was built of human organs, one from each major nationality. They named him "Cyborn"–to save mankind.

Cyborn possessed a wardrobe of three interchangeable faces–black, Asian, and Caucasian. To go with the three ethnic faces were three female aides, each a specialist in espionage and the martial arts, as well as specialists in the repair and maintenance of Cyborn's computerized body. The cybernetic man was sanctioned by the United Nations to mediate global conflicts.

As comic book trends fluctuated, Cyborn was never produced. Yet as Simon had explained to Jack Kirby when first they met, "If I have an assignment, I work on it at night, here in my office. If I don't have an order, I build up an inventory, put it on a shelf, then sell it later." That was the case with Cyborn, and in 1970 a proposal was prepared for television and film studios. It took almost a year to make the rounds to no avail.

Simon and Grandenetti went their separate ways, then reunited to collaborate on a number of projects at DC Comics, including cult favorite *Prez*. But Simon never really abandoned Cyborn, periodically taking the proposal off of the shelf to develop it, at times assisted by his son Jim.

Always conscious of evolving global politics, Simon enhanced the role of the United Nations, renaming the concept "Jove U.N.Born." The text that follows is adapted from that revised proposal.

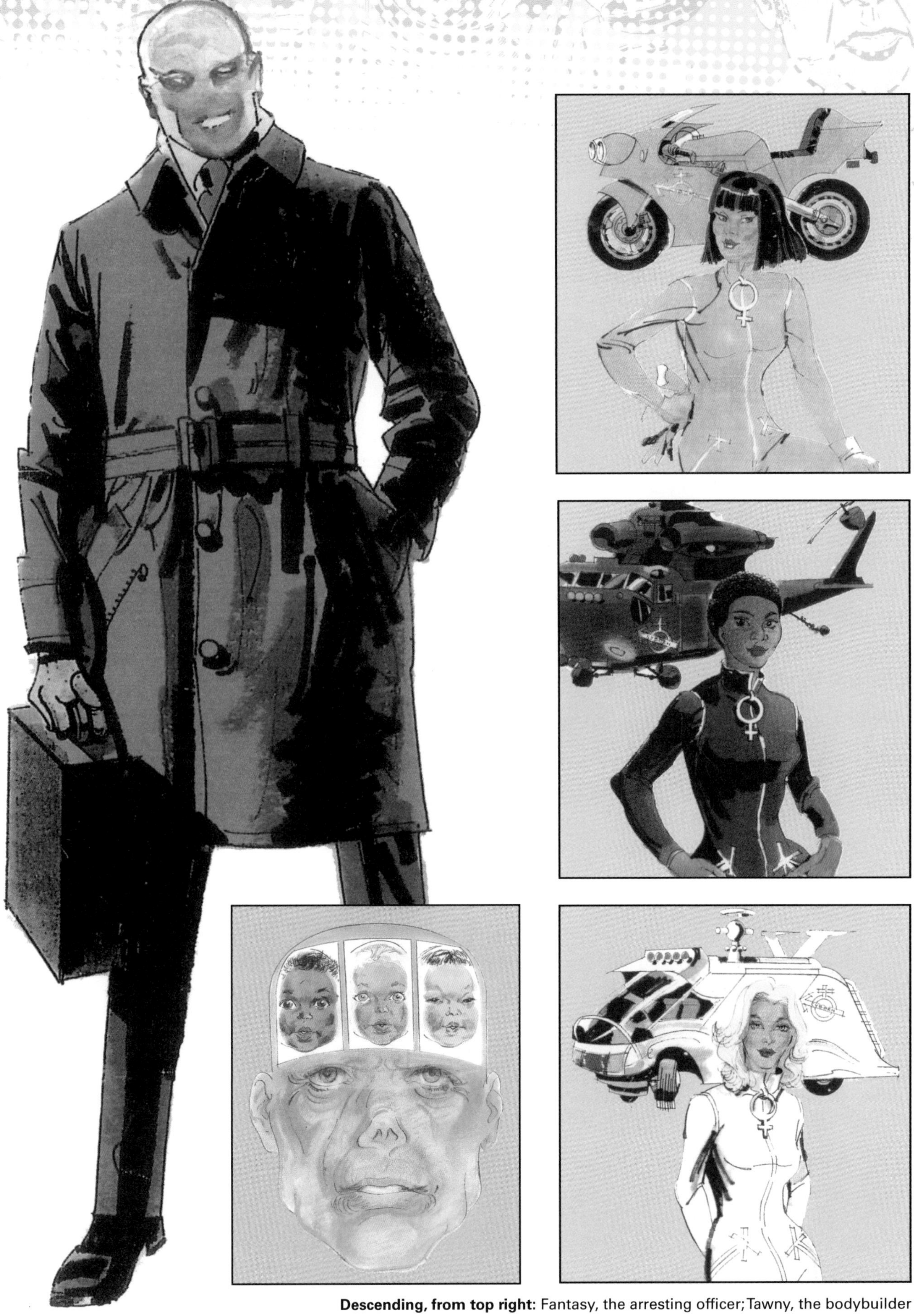

Descending, from top right: Fantasy, the arresting officer; Tawny, the bodybuilder bodyguard; Sunbright, the cybernetics specialist; and the genetically engineered hero, Jove.

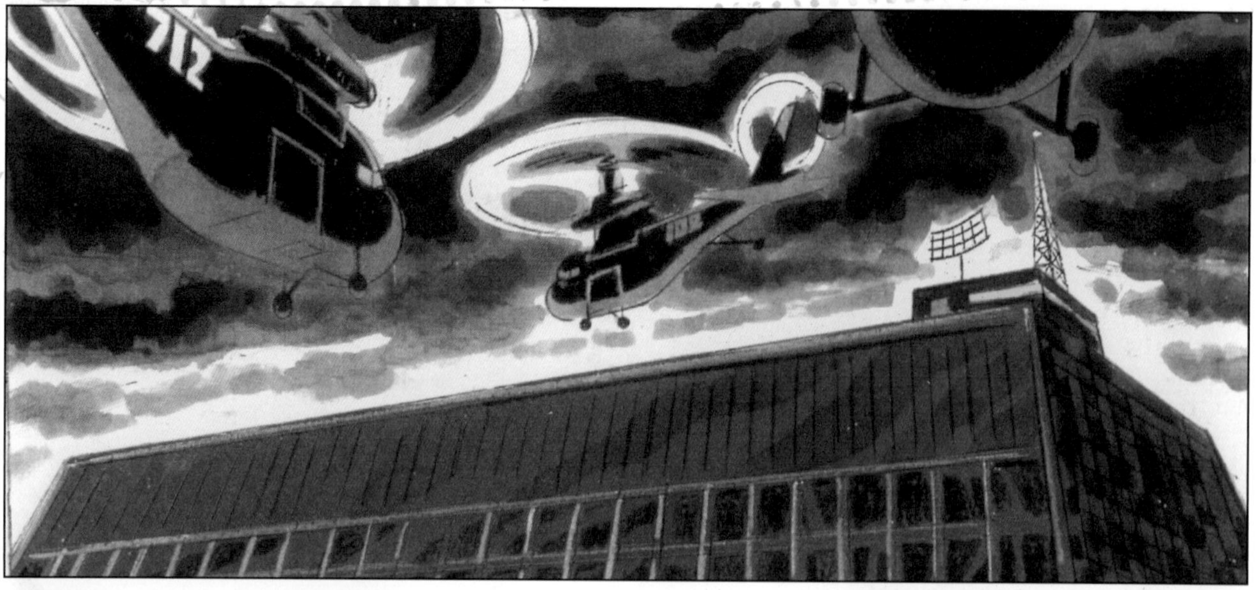
712

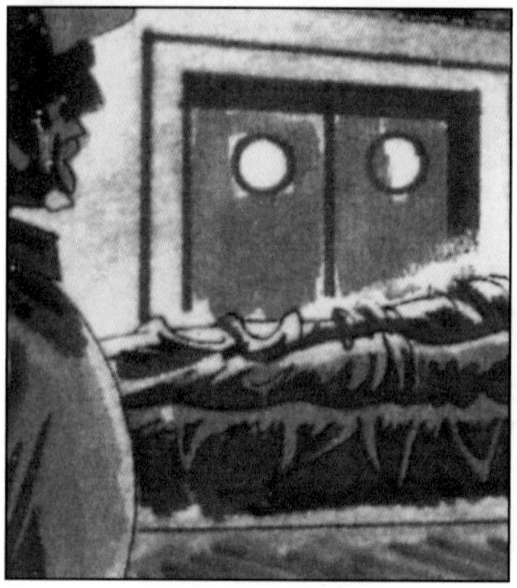

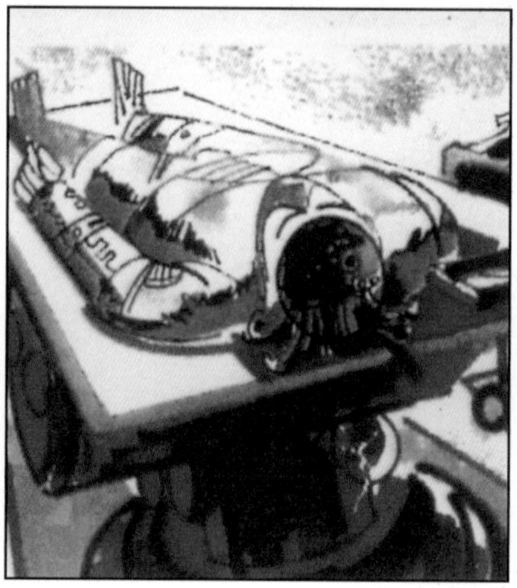

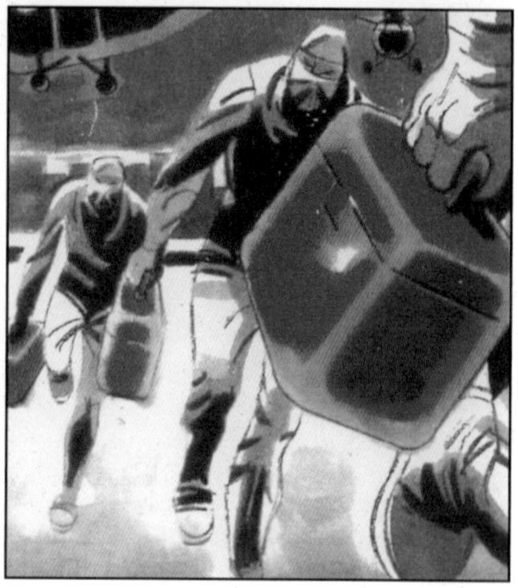

In the latter years of the past century, the United Nations dispatched troops around the globe in a desperate attempt to quell the fires of hate. In one action, a nomadic tribe of undetermined origin was trapped in the center of a missile attack...and devastated.

Soldiers on both sides held their fire while they gathered to view the horror they had wrought. A United Nations officer picked up the broken body of a badly wounded young woman.

The officer held her in his arms to show the opposing sides what they had done. The warriors bowed their heads in pity and shame.

The wounded woman was flown back to the United Nations. She had entered a deep coma. But suddenly, the doctors detected a spark of life in her womb. The fetus was removed and placed on emergency life support. The woman, too, clung to life. She became a symbol of the planet's madness...a Madonna of peace.

The fetus, nurtured by the world's great scientists, was kept on life support for years. Then, in a risky experiment, it was finally released from its cocoon-like existence, a freakish skeletal creature about to enter into an even greater madness.

Science Runs Amuck

In a high-security laboratory atop the United Nations building the nights are filled with strange occurrences. Witnesses tremble. Helicopters whisper as they come and go, landing with strangers in white uniforms and surgical masks as they deliver medical containers from around the world.

It is rumored that these vessels contain body parts, still warm and fresh with the scent of

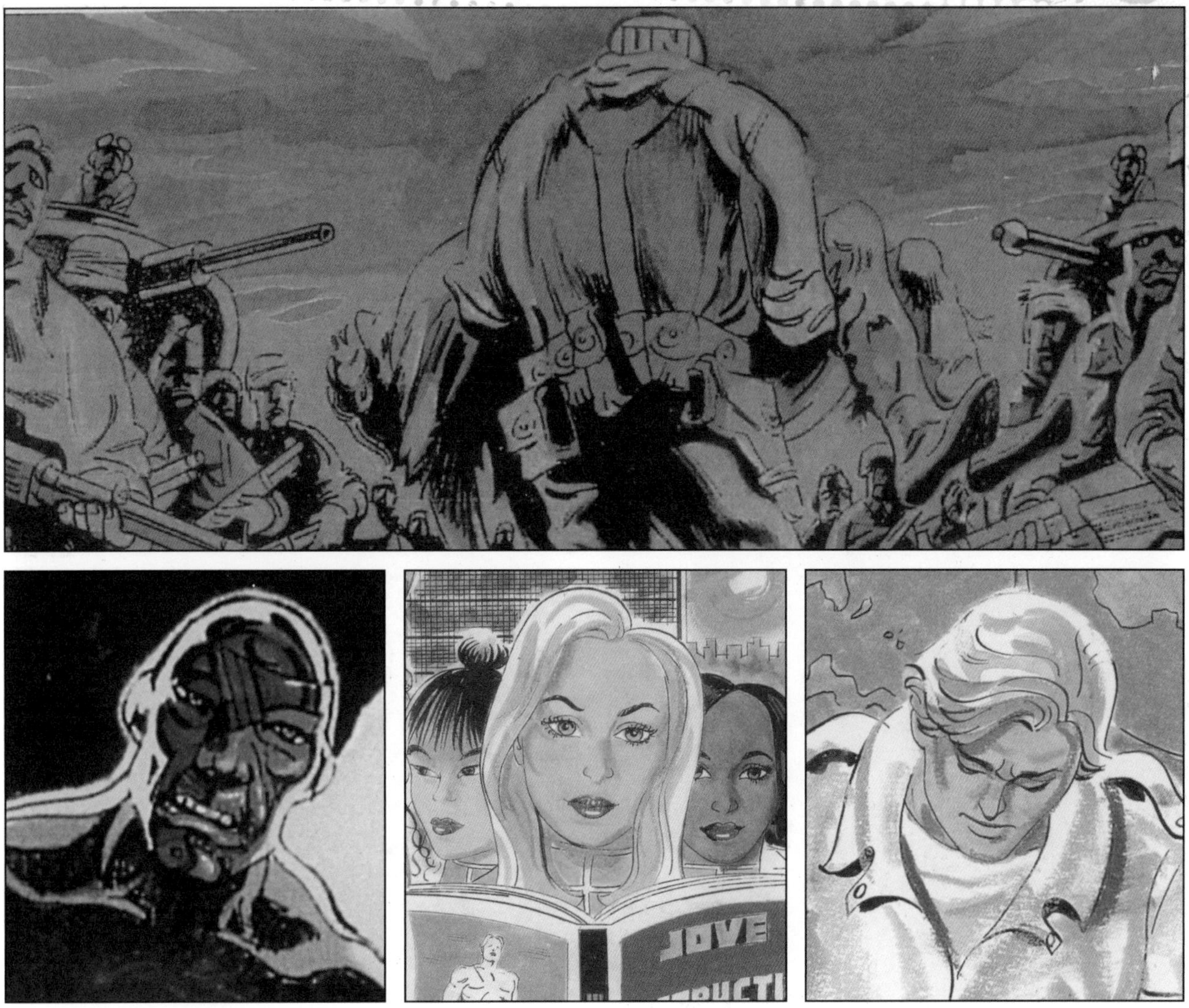
JOVE

the living. A security guard is taken away in a straightjacket, ranting incoherently about dying humans who "entered but never came out of the lab." The victims are said to be of different colors and races.

In a white, pristine medical facility, body organs and advanced artificial intelligence systems are merged with the steel-and-membrane life support device. A spidery body is constructed… finally, it becomes a living, thinking being.

Now he no longer needs life support, for he is one with a mighty new body, alive in a partly transparent frame of neutral color. His head is lacking a skin covering. That will come later.

He will be programmed to possess mighty powers. He will be authorized to settle disputes in his own way. It will be total. It will be final. It will be by instruction…or destruction.

Checkmates

Before Project Jove is granted the authority to enforce his brand of justice, three lovely taskmasters are assigned to act as liaisons, guiding him, controlling and maintaining him.

Each is a highly skilled genetic technician whose secret mission is to act as a checkmate should Jove, through malfunction, become a threat to the interests of their sponsors. The true birth names and identities of the aides are unknown.

Thus was the U.N.BORN conceived, and from the moment he approved the science fiction collection as part of The Simon and Kirby Library, *Joe intended Jove to be included.*

As for the future…that remains to be seen.

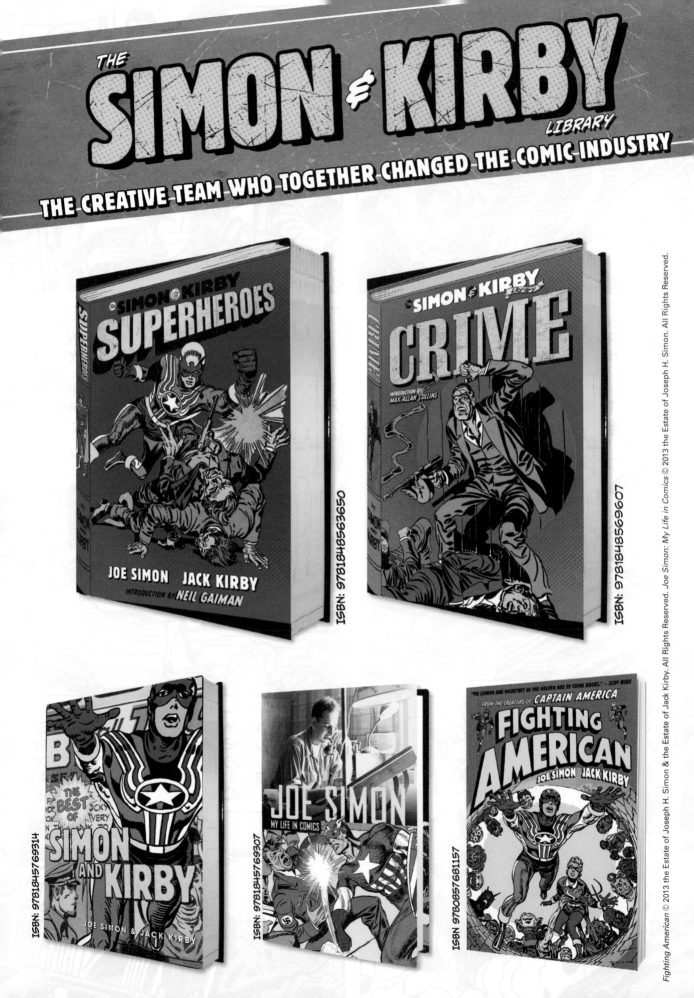

THE SIMON & KIRBY LIBRARY

THE CREATIVE TEAM WHO TOGETHER CHANGED THE COMIC INDUSTRY

THE SIMON & KIRBY
SUPERHEROES

JOE SIMON   JACK KIRBY
INTRODUCTION BY NEIL GAIMAN

ISBN: 9781848563650

The Simon & Kirby Library
CRIME

INTRODUCTION BY
MAX ALLAN COLLINS

by SIMON and KIRBY

ISBN: 9781848569607

THE BEST OF
SIMON AND KIRBY

JOE SIMON & JACK KIRBY

ISBN: 9781845769314

JOE SIMON
MY LIFE IN COMICS

ISBN: 9781845769307

"THE LENNON AND McCARTHY OF THE GOLDEN AGE OF COMIC BOOKS." – SCIFI WIRE

FROM THE CREATORS OF CAPTAIN AMERICA
FIGHTING AMERICAN

JOE SIMON   JACK KIRBY

ISBN 9780857681157

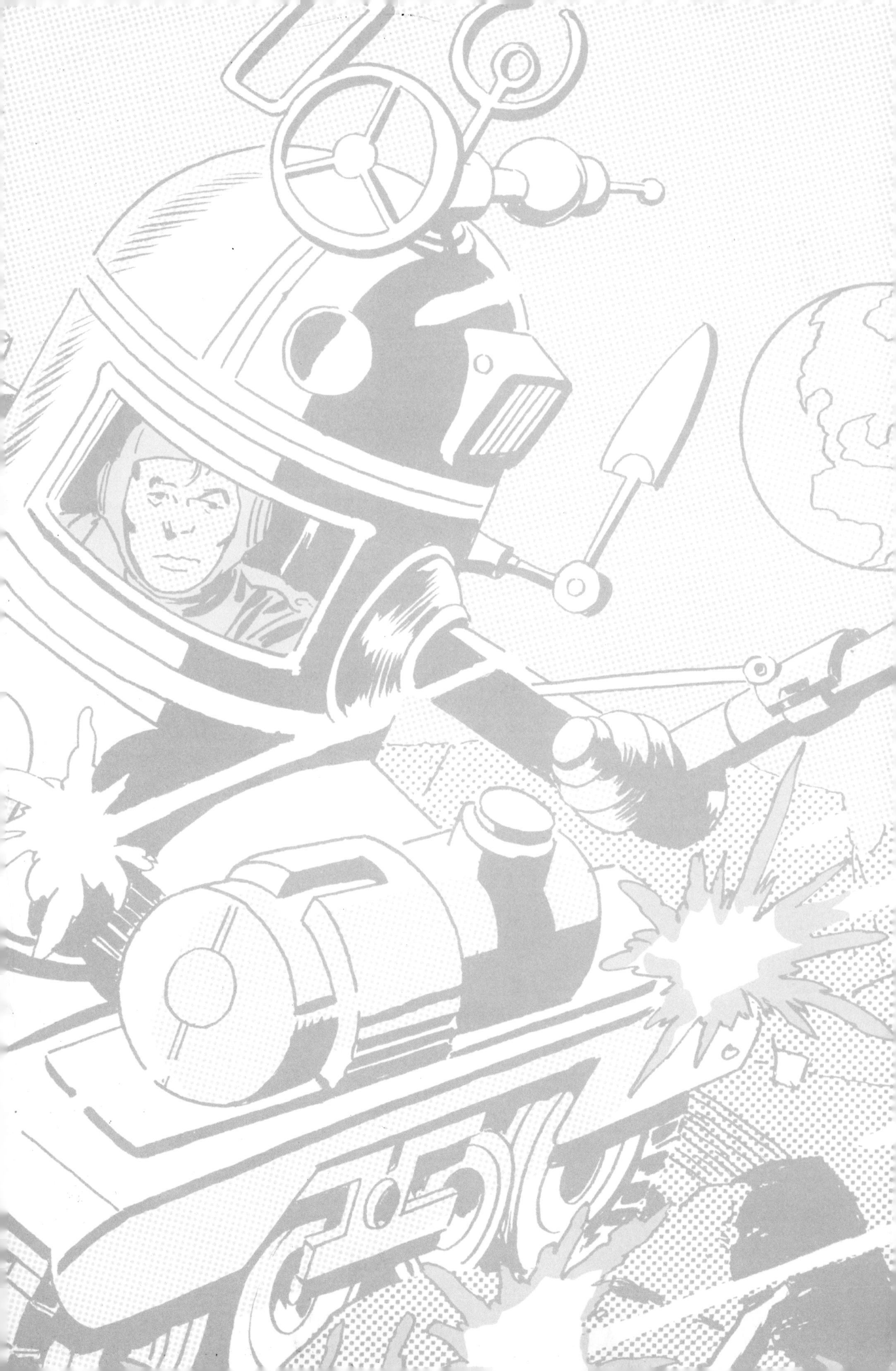